This invaluable inventory of published biographical items on 500 individuals from the era of slavery raises awareness of how much can be recovered from the anonymous institution of slavery. The professional metadata on each source provide a helpful tool for researchers and students, while the brief synopsis for each individual represents the initial interpretations of the primary sources underlying the presentation of Fogleman and his team. Undoubtedly many more accounts will surface in unpublished sources, which will supplement and extend the documentation in this excellent collection.

Paul E. Lovejoy FRSC
Distinguished Research Professor of History
York University

Aaron Fogleman and Robert Hanserd have assembled five hundred African voices that speak to us, sometimes in long and interesting narratives, but often in short snippets given in court or to a passing literate person. Their book is an amazing, digital-friendly compilation with full references and very often texts in the original language with English translations—a first-rate starting point for any research dealing with African perspectives on the Diaspora.

John K. Thornton
Professor of History and African American Studies
Boston University

Five Hundred African Voices is a remarkable achievement. Scholars of the Atlantic slave trade, the Atlantic world, Africa, slavery across the Americas, and abolition are among the those who will benefit, as the catalogue includes hundreds of accounts from around the Atlantic world in several languages. Also, the editors included useful guides for student researchers who can make very good use of the catalogue to locate primary and secondary sources, thus making it an indispensable resource for everyone.

Randy J. Sparks
Professor of History
Tulane University

D1560617

Five Hundred Voices showcases a diverse range of African narratives of the slave trade, including an unprecedented number of accounts by women. It also moves beyond the traditional but narrow confines of Anglo American sources to give a more accurate representation of the experiences of Africans enslaved by Portuguese, Spanish, French, Dutch, and other European powers.

Steven J. Niven
Executive Editor, Biographical Dictionaries, Hutchins Center for African
& African American Research
Harvard University and Enslaved.org/Stories

This is a magisterial scholarly undertaking that showcases the extraordinary corpus of voices of Africans enslaved by Europeans. By centering on Africa and the life stories of African-born individuals, the editors have created a truly astonishing research tool that expands our frame of reference for studying slave narratives, one that promises to shape the field for years to come.

Sophie White
Professor of American Studies
Notre Dame University
Author of *Voices of the Enslaved*

Five Hundred African Voices

Five Hundred African Voices

A Catalog of Published Accounts by Africans Enslaved in the Transatlantic Slave Trade, 1586–1936

Aaron Spencer Fogleman   **Robert Hanserd**

American Philosophical Society Press

Lightning Rod Press

American Philosophical Society

Held at Philadelphia

For Promoting Useful Knowledge

Volume 11

ISBN: 978-1-60618-926-9

Library of Congress Cataloging-in-Publication Data

Preface

This project began as a modest attempt to find what few, scattered publications we believed existed of African voices from survivors of the transatlantic slave trade. We began looking in familiar places and soon discovered there were many more African accounts than almost anyone realized and that there were many other places to look for still others. As the familiar turned into the unfamiliar and grew in number, it became clear that this material must be shared, so discovery turned into collection, followed by organization, assessment, and presentation. The number of African accounts now stands at nearly five hundred, including eighty-eight describing the Middle Passage, and it will continue to grow. Considering the breadth and depth of the transatlantic slave trade—12.5 million people taken throughout the Atlantic World over four centuries, we probably should not be surprised that there are so many, but we are. If one listens to the African voices in this now-large collection, then one hears much more than previously known about the tremendous diversity of experiences, lives lived, and struggles endured by so many millions over so many years. The stories they tell about life in Africa before enslavement, the Middle Passage, and life in slavery and freedom thereafter make it clear that there is no one simple way to understand slavery or "the African experience" in these matters. Everyone was unique and had a story to tell. Below are a few brief examples.

Many of us have contemplated the slave ship and its horrors one way or another, including what it took to survive this experience—it is something that has been well-known for centuries to anyone who bothered to pay attention, but consider that this awful experience happened to some individuals *twice*. One was a man from the Cameroons who came to be known as William Thomas. In about 1835, he was thrown onto a Spanish slave ship bound for the Caribbean that was intercepted at sea by a British warship whose crew liberated the enslaved passengers and took them to the colony of Sierra Leone. About seven years later while on a trading expedi-

tion, Thomas was captured again by Spanish traders and thrown onto a slave ship for a second time, but this time the ship crossed the Atlantic and took him to Havana, Cuba, where he was sold to a sugar plantation owner. Thomas provided his account after reaching England in 1843.

Rosa Egipcíaca was born in "Amina country" (modern Ghana or Togo) and was taken in 1725 at age six on a slave ship to Rio de Janeiro, Brazil, and eight years later to the province of Minas Gerais, where she was forced into sexual slavery. After a mystical religious conversion to Christianity, followed by manumission in 1749, she inspired a large religious following in Rio de Janeiro, but her visions and prophesying alarmed church authorities who had her imprisoned, beaten, and transported to Lisbon, Portugal. Here Egipcíaca appeared before the Inquisition, which sentenced her to prison, and there she died in 1771. Her account was recorded by the Inquisition in the 1760s, and those records were published by a modern scholar in 1987.

Phillis Wheatley, well-known to many for her literary contributions, was taken as a child from the Gambia River in West Africa to Boston in the British North American colony of Massachusetts and sold to a merchant. She quickly learned English and other subjects and, by age twelve, was writing poetry that eventually was published. Shortly thereafter during the imperial crisis leading to the American Revolution, she became the first African-born slave ship survivor anywhere in the Atlantic World to criticize transatlantic slavery because it violated Enlightenment and revolutionary principles of freedom and equality. Her collected poems were published in London in 1773, when Wheatley was only twenty years old.

Isaac Anderson was born in Angola and taken on a slave ship to the British North American colony of South Carolina, where in 1775 at the beginning of the American Revolutionary War, he ran away to join the British Army and reacquire his freedom. After the British defeat, he evacuated to Nova Scotia,

Canada, with others who had done the same, but in 1792, he sailed with a fleet carrying refugees to the new colony of Sierra Leone. There Anderson sought freedom as a land owner with representation in the colonial government, and he became a leader of the protest movement against British authorities denying them this—not unlike the protest movement he had witnessed in North America a few years prior. After serving illegally in the local parliament and commanding an armed rebellion to preserve theses rights, he was executed by British authorities in 1800.

Mohammedu Siseï, who provided his account in 1838, was a learned man born in a Mandinka village on the northern bank of the Gambia River (modern Gambia). He was married, taught Qur'anic school, traveled widely, and was captured during warfare and forced aboard a French slave ship. A British warship intercepted them at sea and took Siseï and the other enslaved passengers to Antigua in the Caribbean, where Siseï was liberated and served as a grenadier in the British Army for fourteen years. After his discharge on the island colony of Trinidad in 1825, Siseï received some land as a pension and helped establish a society of Muslims that purchased the freedom of fellow Muslims enslaved in the Caribbean.

After transport on a slave ship to Cuba, Sandi Quisi lived enslaved and worked on the Arcadia coffee plantation in the Mantanzas area, where he became involved in an insurrection in 1825. During the later official inquiry, Quisi testified that he and others had believed a rumor that a vessel was coming from his homeland loaded with warriors, who would fight on their behalf against the criollos and the whites. Thus Quisi and the others had made ready their weapons and rose up in order to fight in a war with Africans from both sides of the Atlantic against all others on Cuba.

These stories and hundreds of others in this volume provide a much broader understanding of the range of the possible among the millions who endured the transatlantic slave trade, and they highlight the importance and potential of using African voices to better understand these developments. Somehow the stories became lost, even though the print histories of many of them were always there, as this volume shows. Or rather, scholars lost track of them—the Africans and their descendants kept telling the stories among themselves. It is hoped that this volume will help scholars, teachers, and students rediscover these life stories and incorporate them into their understandings of Africans and African influences throughout the Atlantic World.

Why is it important to collect so many African voices? Readers will have to answer this question and discover its larger meaning for themselves. This volume offers vast potential for them to do that in multiple, perhaps conflicting ways. For me, it is about better understanding Africans in the Americas and elsewhere as immigrants—forced immigrants, but immigrants nevertheless—because they came from somewhere else, and that place mattered and influenced their lives and those of their descendants, as it does for almost all immigrants. I want to know, for example, how Africans responded to the contradictory environments of freedom and unfreedom as they were moved between worlds and how these drastic changes affected their identity while these free–unfree paradoxes crystalized during the Age of Revolutions (1770–1830) and continued to influence our lives in the Atlantic World until today. These African voices tell us what men and women actually wanted in their new worlds—what freedom acquired and denied meant to them and how closely related achieving freedom and opportunity was to unfreedom.

No one expressed this better than Boyrereau Brinch (Jeffrey Brace), the poor, blind veteran of the American Revolutionary War whose account was published in Vermont (USA) in 1810. Brinch described how he first longed to return to his home in West Africa, then fought in the war, yet still had to struggle to acquire liberty, equality, and opportunity for himself and all Black people in America thereafter. Years later, while reflecting on his military service to gain his own freedom and that of others, he wrote "I also entered the banners of freedom. Alas! Poor African Slave, to liberate freemen, my tyrants." Regardless of what approach readers might take with this volume or conclusions they might draw from it, they must recognize that connections throughout the Atlantic World to Africa ran deep, and transatlantic influences were long. When deciding anything of importance about that meaning, they must take African perspectives and voices into account, and we hope that providing so many of those voices in so many languages from so many places will help scholars, teachers, students, and others do just that.

Aaron Spencer Fogleman
September 2022

Contents

List of Indexes

List of Figures

Acknowledgments

This project has been special, if not unique. Among other things, I have never had the privilege to work with so many people from so many places on a topic of such importance. International scholars from throughout the Atlantic world have supported this work by listening patiently to explanations, offering criticism and encouragement, and taking direct action to make specific recommendations and contributions, some quite extensive. Keith Arbour and Paul Lovejoy worked at times formally on the project and made invaluable contributions—Keith by working on the print histories of individual catalog entries and Paul by providing guidance on African geography and other matters and by granting access to material in the vast *Freedom Narratives* project he directs. A number of scholars whom I met at conferences on the history of transatlantic slavery not only went out of their way to share and exchange information and ideas but also stayed in contact and generously shared their time and unpublished work, answering questions, reviewing maps and specific details of this project, and more. These include Randy Sparks, Steven Niven, Femi Kolopa, Henry Lovejoy, Robert Krueger, Sean Kelley, John Thornton, Bruno Veras, and Jane Landers. Hannah Durkin, Kathryn McKnight, Leo Garafalo, Laurent Dubois, Dominique Rogers, and Sophie White were instrumental in helping us get permission to use their published materials and also in providing encouragement and advice. Erika Delagado, Dr. Joseph Yannielli, and Fabio Silva helped with specific entries and more. Vera Lind and Spencer Fogleman (our art student) offered counsel on images, artwork, and many other aspects of the book.

A number of institutions and individuals connected to them provided permissions, advice, direct contributions, and financial support, sometimes going well beyond the norm to do so. These included Benjamin Asmussen of the Maritime Museum in Helsingør (Denmark), the staff of the National Portrait Gallery in London, Paul Peucker of the Moravian Archives in Bethlehem (Pennsylvania, USA), and Olaf Nippe of the Unity Archives in Herrnhut (Germany). Glen Pawelski and his staff at Mapping Specialists, Ltd. in Fitchburg (Wisconsin, USA) completed the maps, and Lori Martinsek was especially patient, flexible, and supportive during the process of proofing, typesetting, and assembling artwork and design for the volume, while other staff members at the American Philosophical Society have also been very helpful. Financial support came from a John Simon Guggenheim Memorial Foundation fellowship, Columbia College, and Northern Illinois University, the latter via a Research and Artistry Grant, a sabbatical fellowship, the Center for Latino and Latin American Studies, the College of Liberal Arts and Sciences, and the research fund of the United Faculty Alliance—our new faculty union at Northern Illinois University.

But assistance from Northern Illinois University has gone well beyond financial support, as a number of faculty, students, and staff have helped in sometimes small but important ways and at other times in essential ways that shaped this project. Among the Founders Library staff, Jamie Schumacher constructed the NIU Huskies Commons site, where a full text of a nearly half of the accounts in the catalog are now located. Also, first Jim Millhorn and then Dee Anna Phares, who followed Jim as humanities reference librarian after his retirement, helped us acquire rare images and publications with African accounts. Ron Barshinger and Keith Cochrane in Circulation managed the logistics of getting these obscure texts into our hands. Alecks Kosoric of the College of Liberal Arts and Sciences helped with the difficult task of setting up the URLs and QR codes used in each catalog entry. My colleague in the History Department, Ismael Montana, provided wise counsel on African history, geography, and people throughout this project, including when we team taught a new course on transatlantic slavery. A special thanks goes out to four NIU students who helped so much: Caleb Tomasewski, who did the initial digging as an undergraduate research assistant years ago; Nicole Dressler, a doctoral student who did a *lot* of trench work that helped the project take shape and then finished her

Acknowledgments

degree and went on to much grander things; Justin Iverson, a student who kept coming back summer after summer as a research assistant while writing his dissertation in order to complete a number of important components of this project (and who has also since then finished his PhD and moved on to grander things); and Alex Lundberg, Anne's doctoral student, who provided invaluable advice regarding slavery in Brazil in the latter phases of this project, while writing his dissertation on that subject that will surely also take him to grander places after its completion.

Aaron Spencer Fogleman

Additionally, I would like to thank my family and friends whose inspiration supported this endeavor, and thank you to everyone who assisted in identifying names, places, and historical events. They include Mark Dike DeLancey, Aly Drame, Emmanuel Kofi Bempong, Prince Marfo, One Africa, Samuel Twum Barimah, and Willie Adu Gyamfi. A special thank you to Haj Mademba Gueye, Sena Alinco, Nana Marfo, Rami Gabriel, and Columbia College Chicago for funding research trips to West Africa.

Robert Hanserd

Note on Translations and Transcriptions

In many cases editors of modern editions have provided English translations of African accounts originally recorded in other European languages that are reproduced in the individual entries at the institutional repository of Northern Illinois University associated with this project (see Huskie Commons at https://huskiecommons. lib.niu.edu/history-500africanvoices/). In these cases the text is first provided in the original recorded language, followed by the English translation. Two important exceptions are the German Moravian missionary Christian Georg Andreas Oldendorp's work on the Danish West Indies and Fritz Staehelin's documentary history of the Moravian mission in Suriname, for which no complete published English translations are available. Readers should be aware that the English translation of Oldendorp commonly used by Anglo-American scholars is an abridgment of a much larger work. Most of the accounts listed in the catalog for which full texts are provided on the Commons site were not included in the abridged edition. To read these accounts one must consult the recent edition of Oldendorp in the original German or the German texts with English translations provided at the Huskie Commons site. The original German from Staehelin's work and English translations are provided on this site as well.[11]

When working with Oldendorp and Staehelin I followed two principles in translation. The first was to translate as accurately as possible but as freely as necessary to clearly convey the meaning of the time period, and the second was to state in English whatever those who recorded the accounts appeared to be conveying in German. This included making minor changes to punctuation to provide clarity for English-language readers. It also included use of period terms no longer acceptable such as *Neger* (translated as Negro or Negroes) and *Negerin* (Negress) or the plural *Negerinnen* (Negresses). These European terms refer to people living in western Africa south of the Gambia River and their descendants in the Americas. Among other things, they connote developing European perceptions of a continental or racial identity similar to the term "African." Some people whose accounts are represented in this catalog began using this terminology and thought of themselves as "African," while others did not. For those who did, it almost always meant something different to them than it did to Europeans and their ancestors in the Americas.

– Aaron Spencer Fogleman

---

[1]For the English abridged version see C.G.A. Oldendorp, *A Caribbean Mission: History of the Mission of the Evangelical Brethren on the Caribbean Islands of St. Thomas, St. Croix, and St. John*, edited by Johann Jakob Bossard and translated by Arnold R. Highfield and Vladimir Barac (Ann Arbor, MI: Karoma Publishers, 1987). For the Suriname texts see Fritz Staehelin (ed.), *Die Mission der Brüdergemeine in Suriname und Berbice im achtzehnten Jahrhundert: Eine Missionsgeschichte hauptsächlich in Auszügen aus Briefen und Originalberichten* (Paramaribo: Verlag C. Kersten, 1913–1917).

List of Abbreviations

cf.   *confer* – compare

ESTC   English Short Title Catalog

et seq.   *et sequentes* – and the following

FN   Freedom Narratives

i.e.   *id est* – that is

n.b.   *nota bene* – note well

NUC   National Union Catalog

OCLC   Online Computer Library Center

8vo   *octavo* – a book size resulting from folding full sheets of paper on which sixteen pages of text were printed, which were then folded three times to produce eight leaves. Each leaf of an octavo book represents one eighth the size of the original sheet.

q.v.   *quod vide* – see

qqv.   *quae vide* – a cross-reference to more than one item

4to   *quarto* – a book size resulting from folding full sheets of paper on which eight pages of text were printed, which were then folded two times to produce four leaves. Each leaf of a quarto book represents one quarter the size of the original sheet.

tpv   title page variation

viz.   *videlicet* – that is to say

Glossary

Abassi: Moko deity, Ibibio people (Nigeria)

aquadore: door-to-door water deliverer (Cuba)

audiencia: tribunal (Spanish America, Peru)

Akuropon: eastern region of current Ghana

Andopi: West African deity, possibly Sasabonsam (Ghana)

barracoon: holding place for enslaved people before embarking on slave ships in Africa and after disembarking in the Americas

Barriadad: divinity, Bight of Benin (Benin)

berger: citizen (Bilad al Sudan, Africa)

beneficienza: charity institute (Spanish Caribbean, especially Cuba)

Bomba: black or enslaved supervisor (Danish West Indies and other regions)

Bornu: former empire, northeastern state (Nigeria)

bozales: Africans who did not speak Spanish (Spanish Caribbean, especially Cuba)

bussal: African man (Danish West Indies)

bussalin: African woman (Danish West Indies)

caboceiro, caboceer, or cabocero: political leader or chief, Gold Coast (Ghana)

calaboosh: slave-holding area (southeastern United States)

capataz: chief or leader of an association of fellow Africans (Spanish Caribbean, especially Cuba)

chacara: farmhouse (Spanish Caribbean, especially Cuba)

coartación: a system of self-emancipation (Cuba)

confraternity: social support society among primarily free Black persons, especially in Brazil and Spanish South America, which sometimes wielded political and financial influence on behalf of free and enslaved members of their ethnic-religious group

contramayoral: lower supervisor of enslaved workers (Spanish Caribbean, especially Cuba)

Creole: enslaved or free person not of mixed racial ancestry born in the Americas, or the language spoken by enslaved Blacks that contained elements of African and European languages

Criollo: enslaved or free person not of mixed racial ancestry born in the Americas (Spanish Americas)

curatada/curatado: (from coartación) an enslaved woman or man who worked off an agreed sum to achieve freedom (Cuba)

Didi: Kru deity (Liberia, Ivory Coast)

Djaubenje: Watje deity, Bight of Benin (Benin, Togo Nigeria)

dreisiman: curer, healer, Gold Coast (Ghana)

dunnukabam: kingdom, empire (Congo)

emancipado: emancipated captive (Spanish Caribbean, especially Cuba)

Gajiwodu: deity, Bight of Benin (Benin)

Gien: Kru speakers (Liberia and Ivory Coast)

Grebo: deity (Liberia and Ivory Coast)

Hausa: people from Hausaland kingdoms (Niger, Nigeria)

hungan: vodun priests, Dahomey (Benin)

imam: Muslim spiritual leader

Glossary

Jankombum: (Nyancopon) Akan divinity, Gold Coast (Ghana)

jihād: Religious reformism that included warfare, critiques of slavery, political reform, and socio-cultural transformation in West Africa, especially in Bilad Al Sudan

Kanuri: ethnic group of former Kanem and Bornu Empires (Niger, Nigeria, Sudan, Libya, and Cameroon)

Kinku: Kyenku deity and shrine, Gold Coast (Ghana)

kramukko: priestly practice, Gold Coast (northeast Ghana)

ladinos: Africans who spoke Spanish well (Spanish Caribbean, especially Cuba)

Lebenslauf: late-life memoir, Moravian

Liberated African: person rescued at sea from a slave ship, taken to Sierra Leone, and placed as an apprentice, normally working for years before acquiring full emancipation

lukuman: diviner, spiritualist, Gold Coast (Ghana)

mayordomo: servant of a household or confraternity member who administered funds and oversaw functions (Buenos Aires, Argentina)

mayoral: supervisor of enslaved workers (Spanish Caribbean, especially Cuba)

Maroons: African/indigenous settlements (Americas)

Ma-u: (Mawu) deity, Bight of Benin (Benin)

Mende: refers to people and language of people in present-day Sierra Leone

Moravians: mostly German Protestant Christian missionaries from Europe in the Americas and Africa

morena/moreno: free woman/man of color (Spanish Americas)

mulata/mulato: woman/man of mixed European and African heritage (English-speaking areas)

Nesua: Kanga deity (Liberia)

Niombo (Nyɔnmɔ): Ga deity, Gold Coast (Ghana)

obia: man spiritualist, ancestor communicator/healer (Dutch South America)

Orìsà: Yorùbá deity and spiritual practice (Togo, Benin, Nigeria)

palenque: Maroon settlement (Spanish Americas)

Saamaka (formerly Saramaka): Maroons in Suriname (Dutch South America)

Samibapungo: deity for people near Luanda (Congo)

sei: literally stool, a symbol of politico-religious authority for Ga people (Ghana)

So: Tchamba deity (northern Togo)

Tschabee: (also Nyame, Nyambe) Supreme being possibly of Kwahu (Akan) people, Gold Coast (Ghana)

Tjembotjauwi: Temba deity, Gold Coast (Ghana)

Urbarri, Da-uni, or Mansa: deity of peoples on the Gold Coast (northeast Ghana)

Vili: inhabitants near Loango (Congo)

Vodun: religion or spiritual practice of people in Dahomey (Bight of Benin)

List of Maps

Maps

The physical geography of African perspectives in transatlantic slavery was extremely important to the majority of the Africans who provided accounts for this volume, as well as to the abolitionists, scientists, missionaries, scholars, and others who recorded and published their accounts. For this reason, significant effort has been made to provide maps detailing important geographic features of the origins and destinations of the Africans. Following the book's theme of stressing African over European perspectives, the political boundaries for the maps of Africa reflect those of local and regional African powers relevant to the transatlantic slave trade, not those of imperial European powers. The borders depicted on both sides of the Atlantic are those of approximately 1800, with the exceptions of Map 2 Africa and Map 6 West Central Africa, for which better data was available for ca. 1750. Cities, towns, regions, and other locations denoted on the maps reflect places mentioned by Africans in their accounts. In a few cases, locations such as Selma, Alabama in the United States did not exist in 1800, but they are added to the map of southeastern North America because later someone who provided an account was there, in this case an African woman named Sylvia King, who provided her account from there in 1936. The biographical summary of each catalog entry references places mentioned on the appropriate maps to assist readers in learning the geography that was so important to the lives of the Africans highlighted in this catalog.

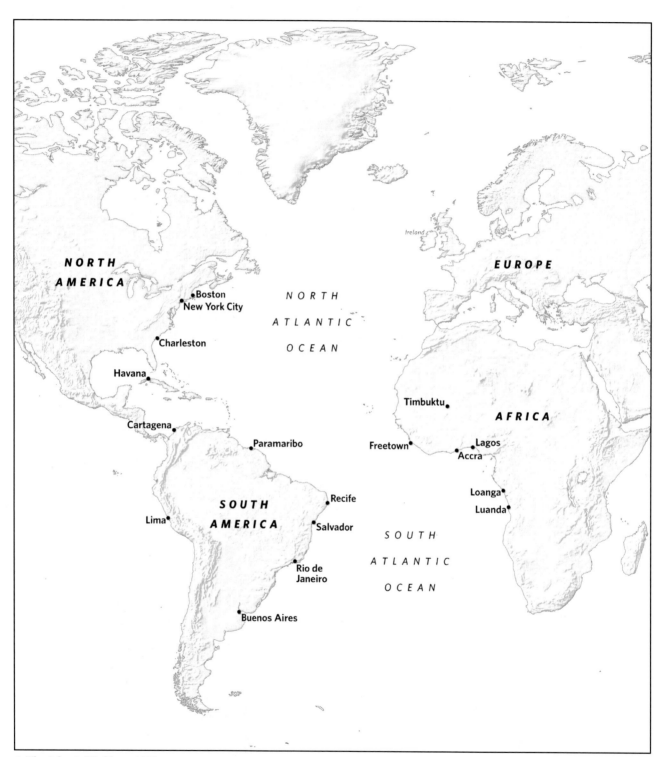

1. The Atlantic World, ca. 1800

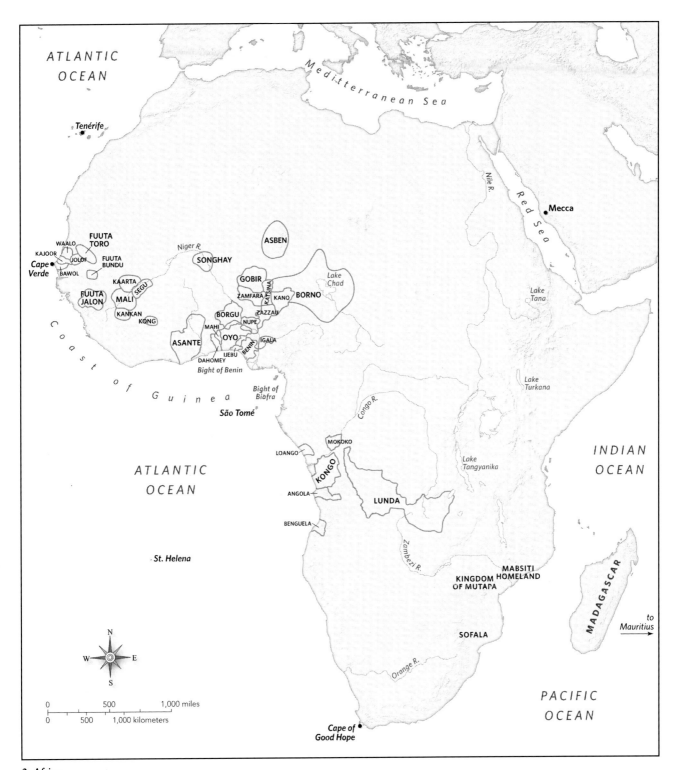

2. Africa

Select African states relevant to the transatlantic slave trade ca. 1800 (1750 for West Central Africa) are delineated.

Maps

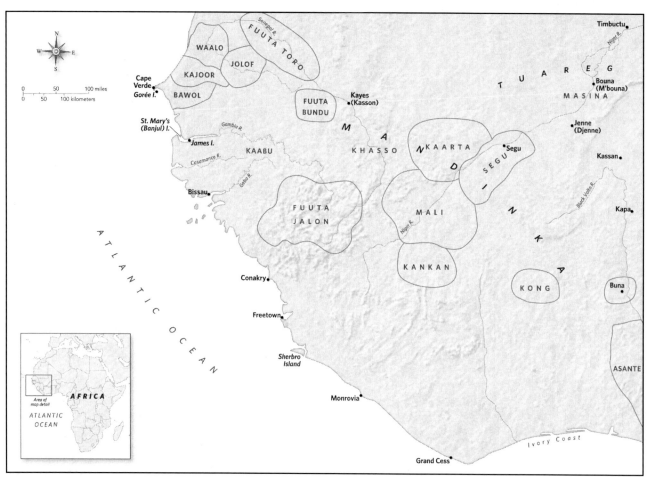

3. West Africa

Select African states relevant to the transatlantic slave trade ca. 1800 are delineated.

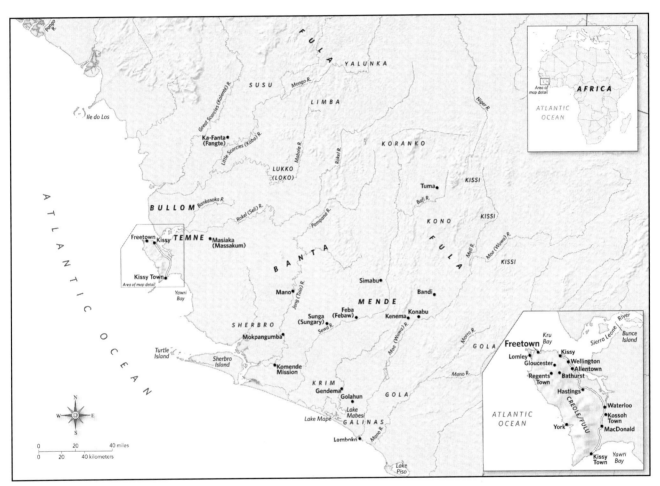

4. Sierra Leone

The map indicates indigenous settlements and various peoples of the region, as well as newer settlements that were part of the British colonial project. Africans providing accounts in this catalog came from both.

Maps

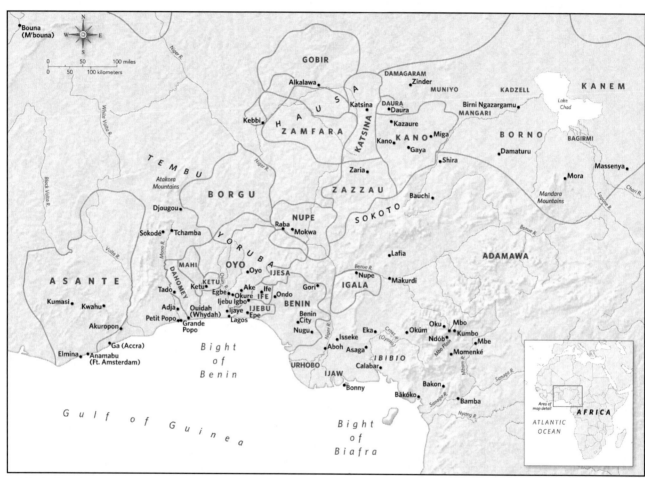

5. The Bights of Benin and Biafra

African states ca. 1800 and locations mentioned in the accounts listed in this catalog are provided.

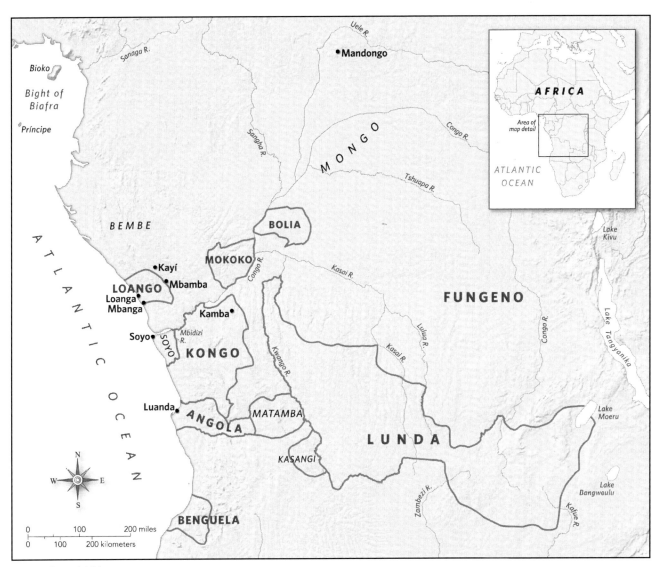

6. West Central Africa

Locations of peoples, select African states, and towns or cities mentioned this catalog are indicated. Select African states relevant to the transatlantic slave trade ca. 1750 are delineated.

7. Europe

Locations where Africans in this catalog were taken and select state boundaries ca. 1800 are delineated.

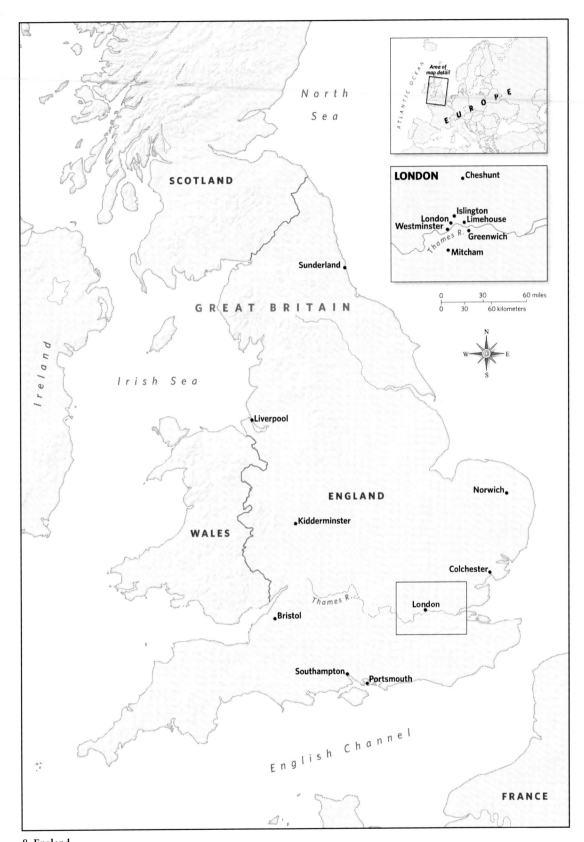

8. England

Locations where Africans in this catalog were taken are delineated.

9. South America

Locations where Africans in this catalog were taken and colonial boundaries ca. 1800 are delineated.

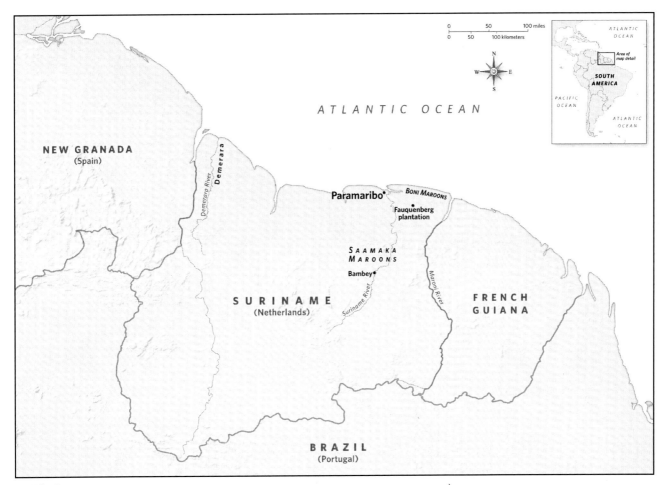

10. The Guyanas

Locations where Africans in this catalog were taken and peoples mentioned in this catalog are delineated.

Note that the region of Demerara was in the Dutch colony of Suriname in 1800, when these borders are depicted. It later became a separate British colony.

Maps

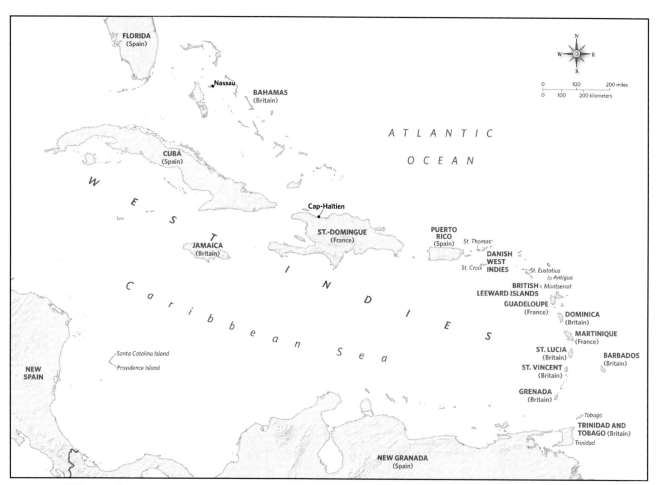

11. The Caribbean Region

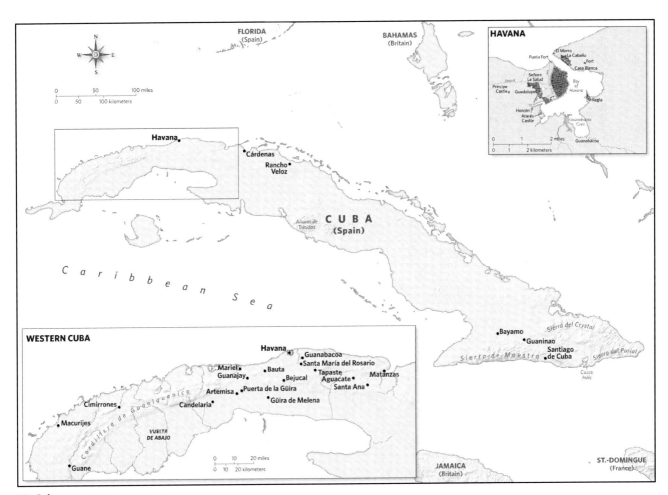

12. Cuba

Locations mentioned by Africans in this catalog are delineated.

Maps

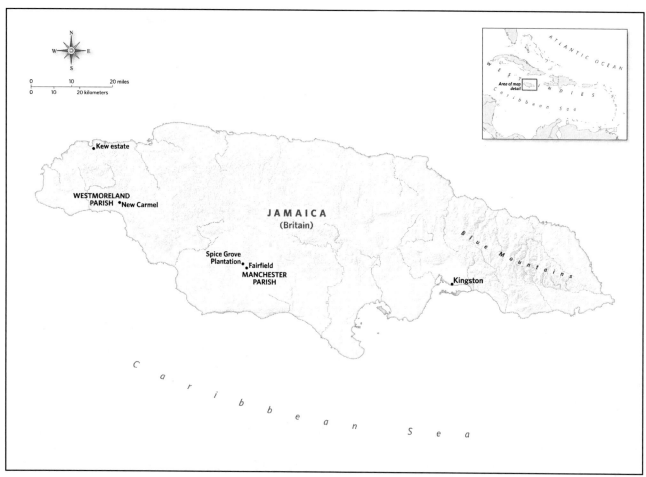

13. Jamaica

Locations mentioned by Africans in this catalog are delineated.

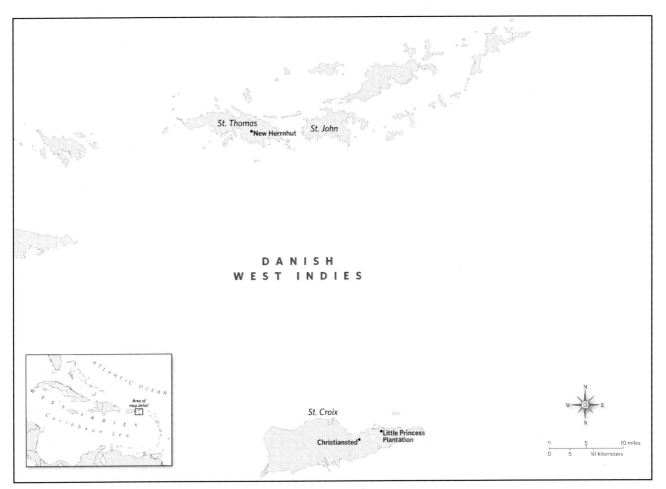

14. The Danish West Indies

The three islands of the Danish West Indies (St. Thomas, St. Croix, and St. John) and locations mentioned by Africans in this catalog are delineated.

Maps

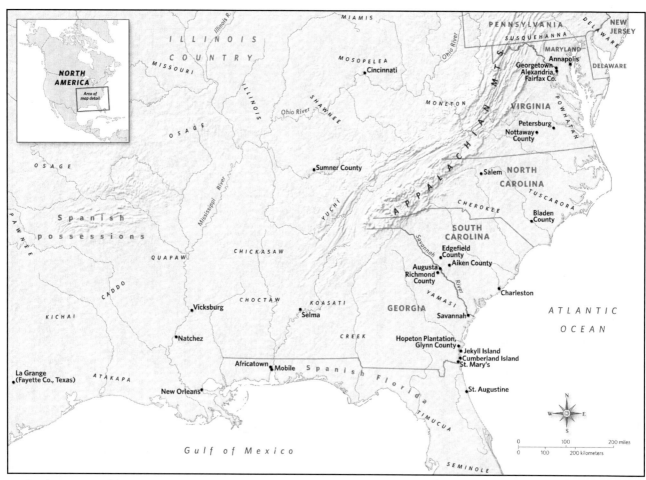

15. Southeastern North America

Locations mentioned by Africans in this catalog, as well as indigenous peoples and select state boundaries are delineated. Borders are ca. 1800, although in some instances specific towns or cities mentioned by Africans were from later periods.

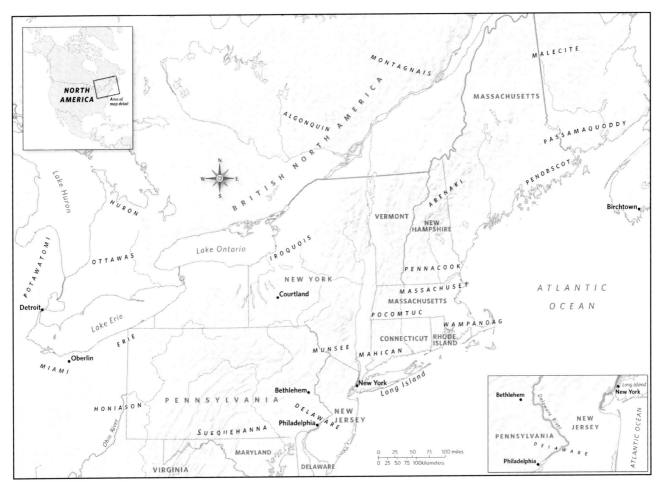

16. Northeastern North America

Locations mentioned by Africans in this catalog, as well as indigenous peoples and select state boundaries are delineated. Borders are ca. 1800, although in some instances specific towns or cities mentioned by Africans were from later periods.

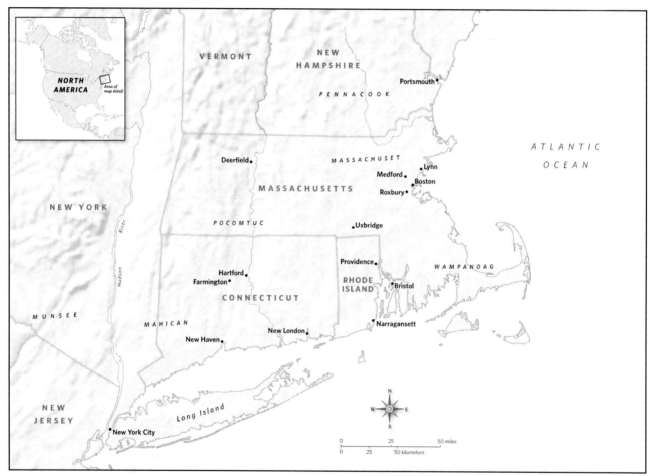

17. Southern New England and New York

Locations mentioned by Africans in this catalog, as well as indigenous peoples and state boundaries are delineated.

Five Hundred African Voices

Introduction

Overview

Historians, literary scholars, anthropologists, and others have studied "slave narratives" and the impact of the African slave trade on the Atlantic world for a long time, and most of them emphasize the importance of analyzing African voices to better understand their subjects. But finding African voices and distinguishing from them other voices, for example those born in the Americas as descendants of enslaved Africans or abolitionist editors and others who were never enslaved, can be difficult. This catalog of published *African* accounts of men and women taken into the transatlantic slave trade is intended to address this problem by providing the results of searches through catalogs, scholarship, contemporary publications, and other historical documents on slavery in the Atlantic world to find what is available and, by distinguishing those born in Africa and enslaved by Europeans from those born into slavery in the Americas, make African voices in all languages more easily available for research and pedagogy.[1] Further, this work allows readers to view the publication history of each account, so that they might assess the level of printed knowledge available that included African voices at any given time. With this catalog scholars, teachers, and students have a resource for investigating African perspectives on the transatlantic slave trade and the extraordinary life experiences before, during, and after the Middle Passage for hundreds of people throughout the Atlantic world over the course of four centuries. These incredible life stories depict a never-ending search to survive, resist, and just live. They provide rich detail of the physical and cultural geography of Africa, which was so important to the millions taken to the Americas. The collection dramatically expands our ability to understand and teach transatlantic slavery and related fields in classrooms, museums, and for researchers everywhere.

The project involves first the publication of this catalog of African accounts, followed by digitized online versions of them. The catalog provides detailed publication information of each account, along with a brief summary of its contents. In the coming years the online version will provide quick and easy access to this continually updated collection of texts, and it will interface with a large and growing number of online projects involving the lives of Africans, enslaved or not, in the Atlantic world. Further, although this volume is an important beginning, the online version will provide wide access to the full texts of all the printed African voices free of charge, as well as detailed maps of origins and destinations, portraits of Africans who provided accounts, original title pages, and more. While this volume includes QR codes that enable readers with appropriate electronic means to access the full text of at least one version of each published account, the online edition will also include links to maps, illustrations, and related online projects produced by other scholars.

The catalog is meant to be a research and pedagogical tool that will assist those writing everything from a class research paper or senior thesis to a dissertation and beyond. Students often find it a difficult if not overwhelming task to design an original

---

[1]There are important qualitative issues to consider about the term "African" concerning the development of an ethnic identity that occurred through the processes of enslavement, resistance, and in many cases emancipation. It includes attitudes toward the homelands and other people from there, as well as their descendants. These processes affected some more than others and did so in different ways. A great deal could be written about these issues based on the content of the published accounts in this catalog, but for the purposes of assembling the catalog, by "African" we refer to people who came from Africa, as distinguished from their descendants born in the Americas or Europe. For more on African identity in Atlantic context see, e.g., James Sidbury, *Becoming African in America: Race and Nation in the Early Black Atlantic* (Oxford: Oxford University Press, 2007).

project based on primary sources. Such projects tend to be most successful when students can identify an accessible body of primary sources from which they can gather evidence to present a new and original argument, and this catalog is intended to facilitate that search. Language is also a problem for many students wishing to study African perspectives in Atlantic slavery. Those who can tend to use a single language (often English) and find that a limited number of accounts by Africans are available, most of which have been heavily studied by scholars already. This catalog helps by providing hundreds of African accounts previously unknown to scholars (not to mention students) in English, English translation, or other languages, thus giving readers a wide range of primary sources to investigate. Moreover, the English-language material in the catalog includes African perspectives from all four continents, not just from the Anglo-American regions.

Some students and scholars assume that the slave narrative is an almost exclusively English-language genre relevant to Anglo-American regions and thus is hardly relevant to Latin America or elsewhere, yet the African voices in this catalog demonstrate that this simply is not true. Those with abilities in languages other than English will now be able to quickly locate texts they might study. Portuguese, Spanish, French, Dutch, German, and Arabic are the most numerous languages found in the catalog, but there are many others, including one text in the West African language of Kanuri (see Nr. 341Ali Eisami Gazirmabe or William Harding). In fact, there are 216 African accounts in the catalog originally published in non-English languages (44% of the total), and this does not include additional printings and translations in other languages. Also not included in this figure are many accounts by Africans enslaved in Cuba and other non-English-speaking areas that were first published in English. Presenting these works now in one place allows students and scholars of non-English-speaking areas of the Atlantic world relatively easy access to these African voices. It is also noteworthy that many of the English-language texts provide rich detail on the African homelands from the perspective of people enslaved in the Americas, which is relevant to Latin Americanists who wish to know more about the African backgrounds of the many millions of people they study who endured the Middle Passage. Further, some of the accounts were recorded or dictated initially in another language, such as Arabic, before an editor translated them into English for publication.[2] Thus from African perspectives, the voices revealed in these documents represent anything but a monolingual English experience. From the first entry dated 1586 by a Maroon leader in Ecuador to the last dated 1936 as a part of the US Federal Writers Project, the entire collection reflects experiences of Africans enslaved by Europeans on all Atlantic continents. The collection is diverse and complex, and the subsequent online edition will allow for the addition of newly discovered and/or published materials in all Atlantic languages.

This catalog will facilitate the study of African perspectives in slavery, emancipation, the African diaspora, transatlantic trade, Black studies, and more. With the catalog, those completing coursework or research in Latin American, African, European, North American, or maritime history (not to mention some combination of the above) can relatively easily find African voices with which they might develop projects focusing on African perspectives in the history of the Atlantic world. Students of literature and printing will find readily accessible material to investigate in a variety of formats and genres. The catalog will facilitate broader, primary source–based projects on exploratory topics such as "Children in the Middle Passage," "African Warriors in the Americas," "Enslaved Muslim Clerics on American Plantations," "Africans in the Middle Passage Who Made It Home," "Enslaved African Voices in New England," and much more.

There have, of course, been other collections of accounts by enslaved people, but they have had a different focus or scope. For many scholars and students,

---

[2]See, e.g., the catalog entry Nr. 11 for Ayuba Suleiman Diallo or Job ben Solomon, who wrote in Arabic, although his account appeared in English in 1734. Others in the catalog who wrote in Arabic include Umar ibn Sayyid or Uncle Moreau in 1831 (Nr.206), Abū Bakr Al-Ṣiddīq or Edward Doulan in 1834 (Nr.222), and Lamen Kebe or Old Paul in 1834 (Nr.226). For a thorough discussion of these and other examples see Allan D. Austin (ed.), *African Muslims in Antebellum America: A Source Book* (New York: Garland Publishing, 1984); Allen D. Austin, *African Muslims in Antebellum America: Transatlantic Stories and Spiritual Struggles* (New York: Routledge, 1997); and Muhammad A. Al-Ahari (ed.), *Five Classic Muslim Slave Narratives: Selim Aga, Job Ben Sulaiman, Nicholas Said, Omar ibn Said, Abu Bakr Sadiq* (Chicago: Magribine Press, 2006).

Philip Curtin's influential collection, first published in 1967, has been the starting point for studying transatlantic narratives. As an Africanist, Curtin was most interested in publishing African voices describing Africa, not experiences in the Americas. Thus, his collection includes many narratives by people who were never enslaved or never left the continent. He does present versions of eight narratives of Africans who experienced the Middle Passage and enslavement in the Americas but only reprints the portions of their accounts describing Africa.[3] John W. Blassingame's magisterial collection of documents by enslaved people in the United States includes both African- and American-born people but not Africans in the rest of the Atlantic world.[4] The largest collection, with over three hundred North American narratives, is that edited by William L. Andrews and published online in the *Documenting the American South* project. As important as it is, however, the Andrews collection does not distinguish accounts by enslaved people born in Africa from those born in the Americas, nor does it include all of the published accounts from people born in Africa.[5] Recently, historians have published collections of "African voices" that include scholarly analysis, and these have been very helpful in the compilation of this catalog, as many of them (not all) meet the criteria for inclusion in our project.[6]

The project piloted by Paul Lovejoy at the Harriet Tubman Institute in Toronto entitled "Freedom Narratives" represents by far the largest and most ambitious project to collect and disseminate testimonies and data on the lives of enslaved Africans. For years members of this project have collected information on many thousands of individual enslaved Africans and are now completing a website for their material, after which additions of new entries will continue. Freedom Narratives emphasizes the collection and online presentation of autobiographical testimony and data concerning the migration of Atlantic Africans within West Africa and in the Middle Passage. Because most of these individuals were born free and eventually reacquired freedom after enslavement, the project stresses these biographical accounts as "freedom" narratives. Whereas this project includes a large number of enslaved Africans who did not experience the Middle Passage and enslavement in the Americas (as well as those who did) and biographical data on many individuals, our catalog only includes individuals who were taken into the transatlantic slave trade and for whom there exists some published account of their lives as told by themselves. The focus on a more narrowly defined group and the presentation of the publication history of each African testimony is what distinguishes this catalog from Freedom Narratives and other collections. Exchanges between members of this project and those of Freedom Narratives have been fruitful, with the goal being to include all individuals from Freedom

---

[3]The eight are Ayuba Suleiman, Olaudah Equiano, Salih Bilali, Abū Bakr Al-Siddiq, Ali Eisami, Osifekunde, Samuel Crowther, and Joseph Wright. See Philip D. Curtin (ed.), *Africa Remembered: Narratives by West Africans from the Era of the Slave Trade* (Madison: University of Wisconsin Press, 1967).

[4]John W. Blassingame (ed.), *Slave Testimony: Two Centuries of Letters, Speeches, Interviews, and Autobiographies* (Baton Rouge: Louisiana State University, 1977).

[5]William L. Andrews (ed.), "North American Slave Narratives," *Documenting the American South* (University of North Carolina Library, 2004), http://docsouth.unc.edu/neh/. There are numerous other smaller published collections, such as Henry Louis Gates, Jr., (ed.), *The Classic Slave Narratives: The Life of Olaudah Equiano, The History of Mary Prince, Narrative of the Life of Frederick Douglass, Incidents in the Life of a Slave Girl* (New York: Mentor, 1987); Vincent Carretta (ed.), *Unchained Voices: An Anthology of Black Authors in the English-Speaking World of the 18th Century* (Lexington: University Press of Kentucky, 1996); Henry Louis Gates, Jr., and William L. Andrews, *Pioneers of the Black Atlantic: Five Slave Narratives from the Enlightenment, 1772–1815* (Washington, DC: Civitas Counterpoint, 1998); Anne C. Bailey also tends to blend African with African American voices in her assessment, but she also makes good use of oral history traditions. See Bailey, *African Voices of the Atlantic Slave Trade: Beyond the Silence and the Shame* (Boston: Beacon Press, 2005).

[6]See Gloria García Rodríguez (ed.), *Voices of the Enslaved in Nineteenth-Century Cuba: A Documentary History* (Chapel Hill: University of North Carolina Press, 2011); Kathryn Joy McKnight and Leo J. Garofalo (eds.), *Afro-Latino Voices: Narratives from the Early Modern Ibero-Atlantic World, 1550–1812* (Indianapolis: Hackett Publishing Co., 2009); Dominique Rogers (ed.), *Voix d'Esclaves: Antilles, Guyane et Louisiane Françaises, XVIIIe–XIXe Siècles* (Paris: Karthala, 2015); Sophie White, *Voices of the Enslaved: Love, Labor, and Longing in French Louisiana* (Chapel Hill: University of North Carolina Press, 2019).

Narratives who meet our criteria (see below) in this catalog and to ensure that all individual testimonies we have collected are incorporated into the Freedom Narratives project.[7]

As we move into the online phase of this project, we hope to continue the exchange with Freedom Narratives and Enslaved: Peoples of the Historical Slave Trade (see Enslaved.org) so that our catalog of published African accounts becomes linked electronically with numerous related projects concerning the history of Africa and the Black Atlantic during the era of transatlantic slavery (see the websites section of the bibliography for a list). The amount of information on Africans and transatlantic slavery becoming available online is tremendous, and we hope to participate in this development by sharing information and using controlled vocabulary so that students, teachers, scholars, and others might go to one website and access information on people, places, events, and the like that are available on many other websites.

In addition to benefitting from the work involved in the above online projects, we have been assisted by many individual scholars who have provided advice and critiques and have shared their work. We have recognized those individual contributions in specific entries where they have been particularly helpful, although there are many other examples where scholars assisted us in more general ways. Thus this collection joins an international community of scholars working to promote knowledge and share resources for better understanding Africa, Africans, slavery, and the Black Atlantic.

Few scholars and teachers are aware of the large number of published accounts of life in slavery provided by Africans, and many believe that almost all are in English, yet this catalog includes nearly *five hundred* discrete accounts in numerous Atlantic languages produced by people taken in the transatlantic slave trade to places throughout the Americas and in a few cases to Europe.[8] Many of these accounts are quite short—in some cases only a sentence or two and in other cases a paragraph or a page or two. Yet even these short accounts are revealing, because their context is known and they reflect an African perspective or voice. Many other accounts are quite extensive, ranging from several pages to book-length volumes.

While these five hundred voices represent only a tiny fraction of the millions of Africans caught in the transatlantic slave trade, when taken together they illuminate much more about the nature of the trade and how enslaved Africans perceived it and operated within it, as well as how they lived before, during, and after the Middle Passage. Having this many accounts in one place greatly enhances our ability to study and teach African perspectives in Atlantic slavery, and it allows us to better distinguish African from African American perspectives. In fact, African voices in the slave trade are critical to understanding the Atlantic world and slavery in the Americas. Their value should not be underestimated quantitatively, nor should African experiences and perspectives be subsumed into those of all enslaved people and slavery involving those of African descent born in the Americas.

This catalog provides a *much* more complete picture of published African accounts in the Atlantic world than previously available. It contains more than 2,500 printings of nearly five hundred discrete testimonies by people born in Africa who were captured or sold to Europeans or Euro-Americans in the transatlantic slave trade. Women produced ninety-four of them (19%), and at least seventy-one (14%) were produced by people captured in Africa

---

[7]See Paul E. Lovejoy, Freedom Narratives: Testimonies of West Africans from the Era of Slavery, www.freedomnarratives.org.

[8]For example, Jerome Handler published a list of fifteen autobiographical accounts by enslaved people who endured the Middle Passage, and while the accounts of these individuals (all included in this catalog) have been very helpful, it is now possible to go well beyond that number. See Jerome S. Handler, "Survivors of the Middle Passage: Life Histories of Enslaved Africans in British America," *Slavery & Abolition* 23(1) (2002): 23–56. Also, when making an important discovery of a new text by an African woman who experienced the Middle Passage, Hannah Durkin noted that the number of such accounts left by women was tiny, yet we have collected ninety-two accounts of women in this catalog, a number of which describe the Middle Passage. See Hannah Durkin, "Uncovering the Hidden Lives of Last *Clotilda* Survivor Matilda McCrear and Her Family," *Slavery & Abolition*, 41(3) (September 2020): 431–457.

as children who later produced accounts that were published. See Table 1 below.

Table 1: Quantitative Characteristics of Published African Voices in the Catalog

n	%	
94	19	produced by women
71	14	captured as children
216	44	non-English publications
490		total African voices

The publication histories of these works and how we have compiled and presented them are complex. Since many accounts were published together, there are fewer total publications than discrete accounts. For example, thirty-seven entries from Africans who survived the *Amistad* shipboard rebellion in 1839 and later told their stories (Nr. —265–301) appear in one publication edited by John Warner Barber and published in New Haven, Connecticut (USA) in 1840.[9] Also, it is important to note that there is a distinction between when the African's account was recorded and when it was published. (See the methodology section of this introduction.) Often the difference was only a matter of months, but in the case of manuscripts published by modern scholars, the difference was centuries. Thus, while the chronology

of when the original accounts were recorded ranges from 1586 to 1936, the publication dates range from 1734 to 2021.[10]

The languages and places of publication of the accounts changed significantly over time. For example, all entries before 1734 were recorded in Spanish or French and published in the 21st century, whereas most accounts recorded from 1734 to the 1830s were published in Britain, with the first being that of Ayuba Sulayman Diallo (Job ben Solomon, Nr. 11), appearing in London in 1734.[11] In 1739 the first of many African accounts was recorded by a woman named Damma (Magdalena, Nr. 12) on St. Thomas in her native Aja-Ayizo language and in Dutch Creole and published two years later in Leipzig (in the German state of Saxony).[12] In 1742 Jacobus Elisa Johannes Capitein (Nr. 13), after completing university studies at Leiden, in the Netherlands, published his degree-qualifying treatise in Latin.[13] The 1748 account of Chicaba (Mother Sor Teresa Juliana de Santo Domingo, Nr. 17) was published in Spanish in Salamanca, Spain in 1752.[14] From 1767 to 1769 a German Moravian missionary on St. Thomas in the Caribbean named Christian Georg Andreas Oldendorp recorded seventy-nine accounts (Nr. 30 to 110), a few of which were initially published in Barby and Leipzig in the German territories in 1777, while the majority did not appear until the early 21st century

[9]See John Warner Barber (ed.), *History of the* Amistad *Captives Being a Circumstantial Account of the Capture of the Spanish Schooner* Amistad, *by the Africans on Board* (New Haven, CT: Hitchcock and Stafford Printers, 1840). A few of the *Amistad* rebels also told their tales to others, which were published separately and are listed in the catalog.

[10]See, e.g., Abubakar or William Pascoe (Nr. 176 in the catalog), whose account was recorded in April 1823 and published in London later that year, and that of Alonso de Illescas (Nr. 1), recorded in what is now Ecuador in 1586 but not published until 2009 in Indianapolis, Indiana (USA).

[11]See Thomas Bluett, *Some Memoirs of the Life of Job, the Son of Solomon the High Priest of Boonda in Africa; Who was a Slave about two Years in Maryland; and afterwards being brought to England, was set free, and sent to his native Land in the Year 1734* (London: Richard Ford, 1734).

[12]See "Der Aeltestin der Gemeine der Negros in St. Thomas Schreiben an die Königin von Dännmarck. An. 1739," on pp. 485–487 in Part 4, *Büdingische Sammlung einiger in die Kirchen-historie einschlagender Sonderlich neuerer Schrifften* (Leipzig: David Korte, 1741).

[13]See Jacobus Elisa Johannes Capitein, *Dissertatio politico-theologica de servitute libertati Christianæ non contraria* (Leiden: Samuelem Luchtmans & filium, 1742).

[14]See *Compendio de la vida exemplar de la venerable madre Sor Teresa Juliana de Santo Domingo*, as told to and edited by Juan Carlos Miguel Pan y Agua (Salamanca, Spain: Eugenio García de Honorato y San Miguel, 1752).

in Berlin.[15] The first publication in what soon became the new United States was the collection of poems by Phillis Wheatley, which was published in London and Boston in 1773 (Nr. 113).[16] The first full-length (book form) African account (i.e., first edition) published in the United States was that of Broteer or Venture Smith (Nr. 155), which appeared in New London, Connecticut in 1798.[17] The listings after 1825 in the catalog reflect, among other things, the increased number of accounts recorded in Spanish in Cuba (published late in the 20th century), which reflect the later development of that slave society and recent scholarly interest. From the 1830s to the 1870s, both Britain and the United States dominated as the place of publication for the accounts.

It is important to note that in spite of the large number of Anglo-American publications in English, the accounts refer to African experiences throughout the Atlantic world. Unlike the well-known slave narratives predominantly produced by people born in the United States, accounts produced by people born in Africa that appear in this catalog have a much broader linguistic, geographic, and cultural scope. Thus the African accounts are by no means merely an American publication genre.[18]

Table 2 shows that 361 of the 490 accounts in the catalog (74%) were produced from 1770 to 1888—the Age of Revolutions and Emancipation in Atlantic history. Thus, the production and publication of African accounts during the era of transatlantic slavery were significantly associated with antislavery causes, although many were connected to scientific, religious, and other interests. Later publications produced on the era of transatlantic slavery have almost always promoted scholarship on and remembrance of the subject.

Table 3: Chronological Overview of African Account Publications in the Catalog

n	%	Dates
10	2	1586–1733
101	20	1734–1769
361	74	1770–1888 (Age of Revolution and Emancipation)
18	4	1889–1936
490	100%	*Total* (adjustment made for rounding error)

Methodology: How the Catalog Was Compiled

The catalog was compiled to assist students, teachers, and researchers in their search for African voices in the transatlantic slave trade. To that end, emphasis was placed on finding accounts in all languages in all areas of the Atlantic world—Africa, Latin America, North America, and Europe—produced by African victims of the trade and published at any time, from the era of slavery in the Americas to the present. To do this we established criteria for inclusion in the catalog, a method to search for accounts that met those criteria, and a method to organize and present our findings. Each of these subjects is discussed below.

Criteria for Inclusion in the Catalog

The criteria for inclusion in the catalog reflect its overall purpose—to provide an apparatus that will

---

[15]Christian Georg Andreas Oldendorp, *Geschichte der Mission der evangelischen Brueder auf den caraibischen Inseln S. Thomas, S. Croix, und S. Jan*, edited by Johann Jakob Bossart (Barby, Saxony-Anhalt: Christian Friedrich Laur, and Leipzig: Weidmanns Erben und Reich, 1777) and C. G. A. Oldendorp, *Historie der caribischen Inseln Sanct Thomas, Sanct Crux und Sanct Jan, insbesondere der dasigen Neger und der Mission der evangelischen Brüder unter denselben: kommentierte Ausgabe des vollständigen Manuskriptes aus dem Archiv der Evangelischen Brüder-Unität Herrnhut*, edited by Gudrun Meier et al., two volumes in four (Berlin: Verlag für Wissenschaft und Bildung, 2000–2002).

[16]Phillis Wheatley, *Poems on Various Subjects, Religious and Moral, by Phillis Wheatley, Negro Servant to Mr. John Wheatley, of Boston, in New England* (London: A. Bell, 1773).

[17]Venture Smith, *A Narrative of the Life and Adventures of Venture, a Native of Africa: but Resident above Sixty Years in the United States. Related by Himself* (New London, CT: C. Holt, 1798).

[18]Paul Lovejoy and others have written extensively on this subject. See, e.g., Lovejoy, "Biography as Source Material: Towards a Biographical Archive of Enslaved Africans," in Robin Law (ed.), *Source Material for Studying the Slave Trade and the African Diaspora* (Stirling, Scotland: Centre of Commonwealth Studies, University of Stirling, 1997), pp. 119–140, and Lovejoy, "'Freedom Narratives' of Transatlantic Slavery," *Slavery & Abolition*, 32(1) (2011): 91–107.

promote research and pedagogy on African voices in the transatlantic slave trade and their impact in the Atlantic world. To that end, only accounts produced by people born in Africa (particularly the areas of the African coast and interior directly involved in trade and in other ways with peoples in Europe and the Americas via the Atlantic Ocean) and purchased or captured by Europeans or Americans are included. The vast majority were taken to the Americas, but after the British banned the transatlantic trade in 1808, their warships freed thousands from the illegal trade and landed them in West Africa and in some cases the Caribbean, and accounts from this group are included in the catalog. A small number, for example those from Jacobus Elisa Johannes Capitein (Nr. 13) and Chicaba (Nr. 17), were produced by Africans enslaved and taken to Europe via the Atlantic Ocean, in these cases to the Netherlands and Spain, respectively.[19] In other words, those taken to Europe via the Atlantic trade are included, while those taken to Europe via the Mediterranean, through the Ottoman Empire or in other ways, are excluded. Accounts of any length are included, as long as they express life experiences before, during, and/or after enslavement in the transatlantic trade in a recognizable African voice—even if through mediation (which was almost always the case—see more on this subject in the next section on *genre*). Many of the accounts are quite short, such as the interviews of survivors of the *Amistad* ship-board revolt, whose tales were published collectively in 1839 and 1840, or the enslaved Hausa interviewed in Brazil in 1819 by the geographer, statesman, naturalist, and poet José Bonifácio de Andrada e Silva and published by the geographer Antônio de Menezes Vasconcellos Drummond.[20] In addition to works published during

the era of transatlantic slavery and abolition, those published later are also included, as scholars continue to find manuscripts from the period and publish them.[21] In these cases there was a long interval between when the account was recorded and when it was published—sometimes over three hundred years! The nature of editorial mediation is quite different in an account first published in a modern scholarly volume, as opposed to an abolitionist or scientific journal during the first half of the 19th century, and scholars, teachers, and students should keep this mind when working with these cases. The transatlantic slave trade ended in 1867, but many Africans who survived it lived long thereafter, and a few of them produced accounts that were recorded and published in the 20th century, so they, too, are included in the catalog.[22]

Developing criteria for inclusion and consistently applying them are difficult. Clearly, when an African like Phillis Wheatley published her poems about freedom based on her experiences in transatlantic slavery, hers is an African voice that should appear in the catalog. But what about a fictitious story purporting to be by an African, or a story told by an African American to a white traveler about a grandmother who experienced the Middle Passage, which then appeared years later in an abolitionist periodical? Is there an African voice present in such accounts? While clearly important to studying the history of slavery, should they appear in this catalog of *African* accounts? In fact, some form of non-African mediation is present in almost all these accounts, and the challenge is to recognize when that mediation becomes so great that an African voice is hardly present in the publication, if at all. The criterion we have applied is that if the publisher or editor spoke with

[19]For Africans in Europe in the era of the slave trade see David Northrup, *Africa's Discovery of Europe, 1450–1850* (New York: Oxford University Press, 2002).

[20]Barber, *History of the* Amistad *Captives*, and Antônio de Menezes Vasconcellos Drummond, "Lettres sur l'Afrique ancienne et moderne," *Journal des Voyages découvertes et navigations modernes, ou, Archives géographiques du XIXᵉ siècle*, 32(1826): 290–324, — 306–322 (note mispagination in printing). For more on Bonifácio see, e.g., Berenice Cavalcante, *José Bonifácio: Reason and Sensibility, a History in Three Times* (Rio de Janeiro: FGV, 2001).

[21]See, e.g., the narrative dictated by Sitiki or Jack Smith (Nr. 466), recorded in 1870–71 but first published in Patricia C. Griffin (ed.), *The Odyssey of an African Slave, By Sitiki* (Gainesville: University Press of Florida, 2009), pp. 11–38.

[22]See, e.g., the accounts of Abacky (Nr. 478) and Gossalow (Nr. 479) in Samuel Hawkins Marshall Byers, "The Last Slave Ship," *Harper's Monthly*, 113 (1906): 742–746, especially 742–43, and that of Kossula or Cudjoe Lewis (Nr. 482) in Zora Neale Hurston, *Barracoon: The Story of the Last "Black Cargo,"* edited by Deborah G. Plant (New York: Amistad of HarperCollins Publishers, 2018), which Hurston originally constructed in 1931.

the African and recorded some part of their life story that was ultimately published, then that account appears in the catalog. If that did not happen, no matter how revealing it might otherwise be, it is excluded. Ours are imperfect criteria that some might view as too exclusive, while others might view as too inclusive, but we chose them in the belief that scholars and others need to see more African voices when studying transatlantic slavery, yet those voices should one way or another be *African* and not those of African Americans or others interpreting them. Thus, otherwise valuable accounts—some quite familiar to researchers and teachers—are excluded from this catalog, foremost, published accounts by people born into slavery in the Americas, not Africa. Also excluded are accounts of slavery exclusively within Africa, Africans taken across the Sahara in the Mediterranean slave trade or elsewhere, and Africans who journeyed to Europe or the Americas voluntarily (not enslaved) who produced published accounts.

We have attempted to include all print editions of the accounts of African-born women and men who meet the above criteria, all printings of these editions from their earliest publications to the present, and all responsible treatments of these accounts, including complete and partial printings. With few exceptions, we have excluded on-demand single-copy and small-run printings because they do not constitute editions.

Many African accounts, some familiar to scholars, are excluded from this catalog because they do not meet our criteria. Some tell the story of an African ensnared by Europeans and taken into slavery in America and do so with an African voice, but they are abstracts and excerpts of accounts published elsewhere in full.

Some accounts are important to scholars of African and/or transatlantic slavery but fail to meet all of the criteria for inclusion in this catalog. Kwaku or Philip Quaque (1741–1816), for example, was born in West Africa and wrote quite a lot but did not endure capture by Europeans, the Middle Passage, or slavery in the Americas. Instead, he went voluntarily to Britain to live, converted to Christianity, and became an Anglican missionary in West Africa.[23] Some interesting and revealing cases, such as Maquama and Zangara, appear to be fiction, so they are excluded.[24] Another promising figure is Muhammad Kaba Saghanughu (or Dick or Robert Peart), who was born in West Africa, taken on a slave ship to Jamaica, and left a paper trail. Yet he must be excluded because nothing resembling an account of his life has yet been published.[25] Another example is Mohamed Ali Ben (Nicholas) Said (ca. 1836–1882), who was born in Africa, enslaved, and ultimately lived in the United States, where he produced a full-length published account familiar to many scholars. Said cannot be included in the catalog, however, because he was taken to the Ottoman Empire (first Tripoli and then Istanbul) and then Russia, and he had been emancipated by the time he crossed the Atlantic. Thus, he does not meet the criterion of having been a part of the transatlantic slave trade.[26] And there is also the interesting case of James Africanus Beale Horton (1835–1883), who wrote a scientific article and two books refuting the racist claims of European scholars about his homeland, but Horton was born free in Sierra Leone: it was his father who was captured, enslaved, and placed on a slave ship that was intercepted at sea by a British warship and taken to that colony.[27]

---

[23]Kwaku [Philip Quaque] (1741–1816), *The Life and Letters of Philip Quaque, the First African Anglican Missionary*, edited by Vincent Carretta and Ty M. Reese (Athens: University of Georgia Press, 2010).

[24]"The Discarded Negro Slave," pp. 64–79, and "Zangara, or The Negro Slave," pp. 1–52 in *The Negro's Friend, or, The Sheffield Anti-Slavery Album*, edited by James Montgomery and Samuel Roberts (Sheffield: J. Blackwell, Anne Gales and Hartshead [Yorkshire]: Longmen, Rees, Orme, Brown, and Green, 1826).

[25]See Lovejoy, "'Freedom Narratives' of Transatlantic Slavery."

[26]For Said's narrative see *The Autobiography of Nicholas Said; A Native of Bornou, Eastern Soudan, Central Africa* (Memphis, TN: Shotwell & Co., Publishers, 1873), and for commentary see Douglas R. Egerton, *Thunder at the Gates: The Black Civil War Regiments That Redeemed America* (New York: Basic Books, 2016), pp. 177–184 and 309–311.

[27]See Africanus Horton, "Geographical Constitution of Ahanta, Gold Coast," published in "Geographical Treatise by a Native African," *The African Repository*, 47 (January 1871): 18–22; James Africanus B. Horton, *West African Countries and Peoples, British and Native... and a Vindication of the African Race* (London: W. J. Johnson, 1968); and Horton, *The Political Economy of British West Africa: with the Requirements of Several Colonies and Settlements* (London, 1865).

There are other examples of enslaved Africans who have or may raise questions about their suitability for the catalog, some of whom have been included, while others have not. In recent years Vincent Carretta has found evidence that Olaudah Equiano (who preferred to be called Vassa) was born in South Carolina, not West Africa, as claimed in his book first published in 1789 (Nr. 130). The debate over this point among scholars has been fierce, yet almost all agree that regardless of where Vassa was born, his account provides invaluable perspective and evidence corroborated by other sources about life in West Africa, the Middle Passage, and slavery in the Americas. For this reason and because Vassa himself reported that he was from West Africa, his account is included in the catalog.[28] Maroon accounts are also in some ways questionable, not so much for what has been included in the catalog (e.g., Alsono de Illescas, Nr. 1) but because there are many more African Maroon voices that are absent. However, they will be included as they are discovered and published. This is also the case with wills and last testaments and Inquisition and police records. Currently, a small number of the former are included in the catalog (e.g., Nr. 226, Rosa Maria de Conceição, and Nr. 2, Juan Roque). There are likely many more documents of this nature that could be included after discovery and publication.[29] Also, documents associated with the Haitian Revolution and independence likely include many produced by Africans that contain accounts of their lives in transatlantic slavery, one way or another. The question is whether they have been published and how long it will take to discover them. To date, we only have two such examples (Nr. 148, Jean-Baptiste Belley, and Nr. 151, Aloon Kinson or Jean Jasmin Thoumazeau).[30]

Methods Employed to Search for African Accounts

To build a corpus of published African accounts, we searched a variety of sources to find both the discrete entries (nearly 500) and the subsequent imprints and editions, of which they are more than 2,500. During the search for the African voices that make up the discrete entries, at least two pairs of eyes assessed each entry. That is, at least two people read each entry in the catalog to verify that it met our criteria, was accurately transcribed, and that the biographical paragraph reflected the content of the account and its context. The subsequent imprints and editions of each discrete entry provide a print history of each published African account, including all editions and translations of each work from the time it first appeared until the present. This allows students and scholars not only to find and read various editions of any given account but also to study and assess the impact of these works individually or collectively at any given time.

To find the discrete entries, we searched collections, series, and individual works published during the era of transatlantic slavery and later scholarship up to the present. This included a thorough search of contemporary periodicals and series likely to produce accounts that meet our criteria, ranging from works that promoted scientific and cultural interest to abolitionist literature and British government records related to the suppression of the transatlantic slave trade as well as works related to developments in Sierra Leone, the British West African colony founded

---

[28]See, e.g., Vincent Carretta, "Olaudah Equiano or Gustavus Vassa? New Light on an Eighteenth-Century Question of Identity," *Slavery & Abolition*, 20(3) (1999): 96–105, and Paul E. Lovejoy, "Olaudah Equiano or Gustavus Vassa—What's in a Name?" *Atlantic Studies*, 9(2) (2012): 165–184. Lovejoy makes the point about Vassa's name preference.

[29]For the use of wills as autobiographical documents of Africans in 18th-century Brazil see Nielson Rosa Bezerra and Moisés Peixoto, "Biographies, Slavery, and Freedom: Wills as Autobiographical Documents of Africans in Diaspora," *African Economic History*, 48(1) (2020): 91–108.

[30]See Jean-Baptiste Belley, *Le Bout d'Oreille des Colons ou Le Système de l'Hôtel de Massiac, mis au jour par Gouli. Belley, Député noir de Saint-Domingue, à ses collegues* (Paris, n.d.), and the excerpt thereof published in English translation: "The True Colors of the Planters, or the System of the Hotel Massiac, Exposed by Gouli," in Laurent Dubois and John D. Garrigus (eds.), *Slave Revolution in the Caribbean, 1789–1804: A Brief History with Documents* (Boston: Bedford/St. Martin's, 2006), pp. 144–147; and Aloon Kinson (1714–c. 1798) in Médéric Louis Elie Moreau-Saint-Méry, *Description topographique, physique, Civile, Politique et Historique de la partie française de L'isle Saint-Domingue...*, 2 vols. (Philadelphia: Imprimé chez l'Auteur, 1797), here vol. 1, pp. 416–422.

Introduction

among other reasons as a refuge for liberated Africans. These included abolitionist works such as the newspapers *The Liberator* (Boston, 1831–1865), *The Anti-Slavery Reporter and Aborigines' Friend* or *British and Foreign Anti-Slavery Reporter* (London, 1825–1877),[31] and *Freedom's Journal* (New York, 1827–1829), as well as Christian periodicals that promoted missionary causes in the Americas or Africa (often, but not always, connected to the antislavery cause within Africa) such as *The Church Missionary Gleaner* (1846–1851), *Proceedings of the Church Missionary Society for Africa and the East* (London, 1801–1834 and beyond), and *The Church Missionary Intelligencer* (1850–1870 and beyond). Scientific periodicals investigated included *The Quarterly Journal of Science, Literature, and the Arts* (1816–1830), *The African Repository and Colonial Journal* (1825–1886), *Bulletin de la Société de Géographie* (1839–1849), and the *Journal of the Royal Geographical Society of London* (1830–1870). Periodicals of a more general nature investigated that included articles about Africans were *The Gentleman's Magazine* (1731–1860), the *Edinburgh Magazine and Review* (1773–1774), the *Edinburgh Review* (1802–1870), and the *Scots Magazine* (1774–1780 and 1800–1812). British government publications related to colonization in Africa, especially Sierra Leone, and the suppression of the illegal transatlantic slave trade, such as *Papers Relative to the Prevention of Slave Dealing at Sierra Leone* (London, 1853–1855), *British and Foreign State Papers* (London, numerous editions throughout the 19th century), and *British Parliamentary Papers* related to the slave trade (London, numerous editions

throughout the 19th century), yielded a number of entries for the catalog.

We also searched contemporary publications whose authors were known to engage with Africans meeting the criteria for inclusion in the catalog. The most fruitful of these was the work of the 18th-century German Moravian missionary Christian Georg Andreas Oldendorp in the Danish West Indies, which yielded eighty-one discrete entries for the catalog,[32] the diary of the Scottish-Dutch captain John Gabriel Stedman (who fought for Dutch colonial authorities in Suriname during the Boni Maroon war of the 1770s), which yielded five entries for the catalog,[33] and the 1840 publication by John Warner Barber describing and recording the accounts of the Africans who revolted on the Spanish slave ship *Amistad* in 1839 and were tried in Connecticut, which yielded thirty-seven entries.[34] In all of these publications, the author/editor published accounts by Africans with whom they spoke directly, thus meeting the criteria for inclusion in the catalog.

Another important source for finding African accounts was print and online collections compiled by scholars. We searched through a number of large collections with varying degrees of success in finding new accounts that meet the criteria for inclusion in this catalog. The *Documenting the American South* collection, edited by William L. Andrews, yielded significant results.[35] Also fruitful was a search of Peter Hogg's annotated bibliography of documents associated with the transatlantic slave trade and John Blassingame's *Slave Testimony: Two Centuries of Letters, Speeches, Interviews, and Autobiographies*.[36] Our search of the large collection by the US Federal Writ-

[31] Our search of *The Anti-Slavery Reporter* yielded seventeen catalog entries, all of Africans taken to Cuba, while that of *The British Emancipator* (the same periodical with a name change) yielded twelve.

[32] See Oldendorp, *Geschichte der Mission der evangelischen Brueder* (Barby: Christian Friedrich Laur, and Leipzig: Weidmanns Erben und Reich, 1777) and the modern unabridged edition, which yielded most of the catalog entries: Oldendorp, *Historie der caribischen Inseln Sanct Thomas, Sanct Crux und Sanct Jan* (Berlin: Verlag für Wissenschaft und Bildung, 2000–2002).

[33] For John Gabriel Stedman's work see Richard Price and Sally Price (eds.), *Narrative of a Five Years' Expedition against the Revolted Negroes of Surinam, in Guiana, on the Wild Coast of South America; from the year 1772, to 1777* (Baltimore: The Johns Hopkins University Press, 1988).

[34] Barber, *History of the* Amistad *Captives*.

[35] See Andrews, "North American Slave Narratives."

[36] Peter C. Hogg (ed.), *The African Slave Trade and Its Suppression: A Classified and Annotated Bibliography of Books, Pamphlets and Periodical Articles* (London: Routledge, 1973), and Blassingame, *Slave Testimony*.

ers Project of the 1930s yielded only one additional entry that met our criteria, as did Elizabeth Donnan's four-volume collection on the slave trade.[37] Much more fruitful was the search through the voluminous files of the Freedom Narratives project at the Harriet Tubman Center of York University in Toronto, which its directors, Paul Lovejoy and Érika Malek Delgado, generously made available to us. This search produced forty-six new entries, in addition to providing additional biographical information on other Africans whose accounts we had already collected.[38]

Another important source for finding accounts was modern scholarly editions of African voices. These editions were especially important for finding non-English language documents with African voices from Latin America. The collection on Cuba edited by Gloria García Rodríguez yielded sixty-three new entries, while that by Kathryn Joy McKnight and Leo J. Garafalo on colonial Latin America produced twelve. Recent work by Dominique Rogers and Sophie White produced a number of additional entries in French, and an early 20th-century work on missionaries in Suriname by Fritz Staehelin produced a few in German. Unlike in the past, the intentions of these scholars were not political, religious (with exception of Staehelin), or scientific, but rather academic (usually historical), which reflects a different kind of mediation than that of editors in previous centuries. This kind of work continues, assisted by digitization and

the internet, and allows us to have much broader and deeper access to African voices from the transatlantic slave trade throughout the Atlantic world.[39]

The final major source for finding African voices was in scholarly studies of Africans, which led to the discovery of new accounts in two ways. First, the footnotes of published works by Africanist scholars such as Paul Lovejoy led to books and articles by geographers, linguists, and others during the era of transatlantic slavery. Lovejoy's work, for example, led us to that of the German linguist Sigismund Wilhelm Koelle (which produced sixty entries), the French geographer Francis de Castelnau (which produced twenty-three entries), and the Portuguese or Brazilian geographer Antônio de Menezes Vasconcellos Drummond (five entries). Also the work of Erik Calonius and Hannah Durkin led to the discovery of nine accounts. In all of these cases and more, personal communication with the authors was invaluable and deeply appreciated. Second, scholarly works of specific Africans sometimes provided quotations of African voices that could be included in the catalog. That is, a modern scholar published a documented African voice verbatim.[40]

To compile these print histories, we searched a number of online catalogs and followed up by checking the items themselves, either the full text online or in print form. Catalogs searched included the National Union Catalog, the British Library catalog,

[37]*Slave Narratives: A Folk History of Slavery in the United States from Interviews with Former Slaves.* Federal Writers Project, Works Progress Administration (St. Clair Shores, MI: Scholarly Press, 1976), 17 vols.; George P. Rawick et al. (eds.); *The American Slave: A Composite Autobiography*, 41 vols., 1972–79 (Westport, CT: Greenwood Press); Elizabeth Donnan (ed.), *Documents Illustrative of the Slave Trade to America*, 4 vols., 1930–35 (Washington: Carnegie Institution).

[38]See Lovejoy, Freedom Narratives, freedomnarratives.org.

[39]See, e.g., García Rodríguez, *Voices of the Enslaved in Nineteenth-Century Cuba*; McKnight and Garofalo, *Afro-Latino Voices*; Rogers, *Voix d'Esclaves.* For a new collection of essays interpreting African voices see Sophie White and Trevor Burnard (eds.), *Hearing Enslaved Voices: African and Indian Slave Testimony in British and French America, 1700–1848* (New York: Routledge, 2020).

[40]Erik Calonius, *The Wanderer: The Last American Slave Ship and the Conspiracy That Set Its Sails* (New York: St. Martin's Press, 2006), which led to seven narratives (Nr. 476 and 479–484) in Charles J. Montgomery, "Survivors from the Cargo of the Negro Slave Yacht *Wanderer*," *American Anthropologist* n.s. 10(4) (1908): 611–623, and Hannah Durkin, "Finding Last Middle Passage Survivor Sally 'Redoshi' Smith on the Page and Screen," *Slavery & Abolition*, 40(4) (December 2019): 631–658, which led to the narrative of Redoshi (Nr. 488) in S. L. Flock, "Survivor of Last Slave Cargo Lives on Plantation near Selma," *The Montgomery Advertiser*, vol. 104, no. 31 (31 January 1932), p. 13, and Durkin, "Uncovering the Hidden Lives," which led to the discovery of Mathilda McCrear (Nr. 487) in "Woman Survivor of Last Slave Ship, Erect and Vigorous at Advanced Age, Walks Fifteen Miles for Gov't Help" *Selma Times-Journal*, 12(295) (20 December 1931): 11. For modern scholarship with useful quotations see, e.g., White, *Voices of the Enslaved* for entries Louis Congo (Nr. 10), Marguerite (Nr. 25), Jean (Nr. 26), Louis (Nr. 27), Essom (Nr. 28); and Démocrite (Nr. 29).

WorldCat, the English Short Title Catalog, and the Library of Congress catalog. In order to find translated editions, we searched the European Library and the Karlsruhe Virtual Catalog (*Karlsruhe Virtuel Katalog*), both of which are connected online to the catalogs of major research libraries in Europe, including those in Portugal, Spain, France, Germany, the Netherlands, and Britain.[41] In many cases we used Hathi Trust, the Internet Archive, Google Books, and other online platforms to view scanned versions of the originals. The number of printings in each discrete entry varies widely—for example, the entry for Phillis Wheatley (Nr. 113) contains sixty separate items, while other entries only have one. Compilation of these print histories, some of which are quite complex and contain additional important details and notes, reflect extensive, painstaking detective work.

Method to Organize and Present Findings

The catalog is organized and the material in it presented in a manner to allow scholars, teachers, and students to quickly find individual Africans and their accounts but also to assist them in searching for groups of Africans and their accounts in a variety of ways. To that end, each African receives a separate entry, even if their account was very short or published with others. The accounts are presented in chronological order and numbered accordingly, beginning with that of Alonso de Illescas in 1586, based on when they were recorded, not published. Each entry includes a heading with bibliographic information and URL and QR code for access to the full text of the recorded account, a one-paragraph biography of the African with reference material, a full publication history, and other publications by the African (if any). Geographic and linguistic designations, especially for Africa, are based on what the African provided, with added interpretation by modern scholars. Modern locations in Africa and the Americas are noted in parentheses. (Please see the

section entitled *How to Use this Catalog* for detailed explanations.)

Following the conclusion of the final catalog entry, that for Silvia King (Nr. 490), produced in 1936, is a series of indexes, which are intended to help scholars, teachers, and students quickly find individual accounts produced by people with characteristics for which there seems to be significant current interest. These include indexes for women, children (at the time of their Middle Passage), Muslims, publishers, places of publication, origins, destinations, and others.

As this project later moves into the online, digitized phase, more information will be added to each entry, and the entire catalog will interface with many other major online projects designed to enhance our understanding of and access to sources available for the study of Africa, Africans, and African Americans in or out of slavery in the Atlantic world. Each catalog entry will include links to manuscripts of published accounts, images of the Africans who provided them, and maps of places of origin and destination, only some of which could be presented in this volume. As new discoveries are made or new accounts published for the first time, they will be included in the online catalog. For this, the editors would be grateful if readers provided information for possible new entries that meet our criteria for inclusion, as they appear or are discovered. The online catalog will become part of a large and growing network of relational databases that allow scholars, teachers, and students to access a wealth of information about Africa and Africans in the era of transatlantic slavery. This includes the Freedom Narratives project at the Harriet Tubman Center in York University, Toronto and the Enslaved Project at Michigan State University.[42]

Genre

This catalog compiles and presents published African accounts, and the concepts involved require expla-

---

[41]Additionally, we have used portals of major research libraries in Germany, which have a long history of collecting works in other languages. The university library in Göttingen specializes in the period 1701–1800, the university library in Frankfurt specializes in the years 1801–1870, and the Staatsbibliothek Berlin for the years 1871–1912. I would like to thank Felix Kommnick, the research librarian at the Herzog-August Biblilothek in Wolfenbüttel, for his assistance in helping develop a strategy for searching European libraries for published translations of African accounts.

[42]See the pending essay collection explaining this project: Daryle Williams et al. (eds.), *The Enslaved Project* (East Lansing: Michigan State University Press, forthcoming).

nation. In many contexts the term "African" refers to a consciousness shared by people who came from anywhere on the continent or identified with the continent as their homeland or otherwise as a meaningful place to them. This consciousness often developed as people were taken out of the continent and faced oppressive circumstances among vastly different peoples. Until then, their identities or consciousness were usually local, regional, or associated with some group of people and their religion, such as Fon, Akan, and countless others. Thus, in a way, many people had to leave or be taken from Africa in order to become African. Further, in the Americas new group identities formed, such as the Lucumí and Mendi, that were influenced by slavery, heritage from their homelands, mixing with other groups, and other conditions. But many people, including a large number in this catalog—not all—developed an African consciousness that was reflected in their recorded accounts. For purposes of compiling this catalog we refer to "African" accounts as those of people born on the African continent, regardless of whether their recorded account or any other aspects of their lives reflect an African consciousness.

In compiling this catalog we employed an expanded view of the kinds of texts that qualify for inclusion. For too long, scholars focused their attention almost entirely on Anglo-American publications, often those associated with the abolitionist movement, which essentially ignored Latin America, where most enslaved Africans were actually taken. By expanding our view of what to look for and where, we found *many* more accounts by Africans in a much wider variety of languages and circumstances throughout the Atlantic world. Short accounts are included when they contain an important part of a life story before, during, or after the Middle Passage told in an African voice.

To be sure, a large number of African accounts in this catalog were published in English and were connected to the abolition movement, although in a larger variety of forms than most scholars, teachers, and students realize. Their political motivations were clear: The editors, publishers, and often the Africans who provided the accounts sought governmental legal action to end slavery immediately because they believed it was morally wrong. These publications emphasized in graphic detail the horrible impact of slavery on the enslaved, those who enslaved them, and society in general. They needed accounts from formerly enslaved people to show in detail just how widespread and deep the suffering was. Evangelical Christians heavily influenced the abolition movement, and they often fused their zeal to promote a Christian mission with the assault on slavery, especially in West Africa. Many abolitionists edited and published stand-alone works, such as the account of Boyrereau Brinch or Jeffrey Brace (Nr. 162, St. Albans, VT, 1810), but many others were parts of collections or anthologies, such as those edited by John Warner Barber (Nr. 265–301), Abigail Mott (Nr. 151.7, 158.8, 169.4, and 179.1), and Wilson Armistead (Nr. 151.13 and 222.7), which included many other kinds of materials intended to promote the abolitionist movement.[43] Many, not all, were dictated to the editor because the African could not write in English, could not write at all, or because it was the editor's project and they wanted to control its content. Thus African beliefs and traditions relative to enslavement and freedom could be distorted or ignored altogether. Readers should be aware of this mediation when studying these texts to find an African voice or perspective, yet most scholars agree that it is there. Contemporary works published by abolitionists also included poetry, such as that of Phillis Wheatley, in this case written in her own hand with almost no mediation.

Next to published works by abolitionists, the most prominent genre was scientific books and periodicals, which included African accounts in numerous languages throughout the Atlantic world. These geographers, linguists, and anthropologists met with Africans directly to learn more about their languages and the cultural and physical geography of their homelands in the hinterlands. Travel deep into the African interior was dangerous for most Europeans

---

[43]See Barber, *History of the* Amistad *Captives*; Abigail Mott, *Biographical Sketches and Interesting Anecdotes of a Person of Colour. To Which Is Added, a Selection of Pieces in Poetry* (New York: Mahlon Day, 1826); Wilson Armistead, *A Tribute for the Negro: Being a Vindication of the Moral, Intellectual, and Religious Capabilities of the Colored Portion of Mankind; with Particular Reference to the African Race* (Manchester & London: W. Irwin, 1848).

before the late 19th century, so these scholars circumvented this problem by meeting with enslaved Africans in Brazil or Cuba, where the transatlantic slave trade lasted the longest, and they recorded and published the substance of their conversations. Another relatively safe and effective alternative for European scientists was to travel to the British colony of Sierra Leone. While administered by British colonial authorities, this colony was originally settled by formerly enslaved refugees from the US American Revolutionary War, some of whom were born in Africa, and after 1808 it became the primary place to which British warships patrolling the Atlantic for ships transporting Africans illegally took their passengers to serve apprenticeships and live as "liberated Africans." Further, during the 19th century many enslaved Africans fled directly overland to Sierra Leone in order to regain their freedom, and some people enslaved in the Americas made their way to the colony after emancipation. In the 1850s the German linguist Sigismund Wilhelm Koelle spoke with hundreds of Africans (many formerly enslaved Africans and many not), recorded their responses, and published them. If they were born in Africa and were taken in the transatlantic slave trade, then they are included in this catalog, regardless of how they arrived in Sierra Leone. The remainder in Koelle's collection—that is, the majority—are excluded.[44]

As the British colonial project in Sierra Leone developed in the first half of the 19th century, so too did the Christian missionary movement, which provided yet another motive for publishing accounts by people who had been enslaved that meet the criteria for inclusion in this catalog. While their publications sometimes directly or indirectly criticized slavery within Africa, their primary motive was to bring news about the progress of spreading the Gos-

pel among the many non-Christian peoples in Africa. Among the missionaries writing these reports were Africans who had been taken in the Middle Passage themselves and later escaped slavery. Ajayi (or Samuel Crowther, Nr. 235) is the best known of these missionaries, but there were others, and their published work includes accounts of their own lives.[45]

African voices and partial or full-life accounts also exist in other documents, such as legal petitions, Inquisition records, and court testimonies. The goals of the people and institutions that produced these documents were shaped (and limited) by the circumstances of the situation: Francisco Carabalí (Nr. 303), for example, was questioned by authorities in Guaminao, Santiago de Cuba, in 1840 concerning his role in a violent uprising on a nearby plantation.[46] If he said anything else about his life, and some in his situation probably did, the authorities would not have recorded it because they were not interested. But in spite of the heavy mediation of interested authorities using language unfamiliar to most Africans struggling to be heard through these unequal power relationships, African voices are sometimes present. When that is the case, their account is included in the catalog. If, however, those voices are little more than scraps of information that reveal little, if anything, of the African life story, then they are not included.

Many entries in the catalog are the result of ongoing discovery and publication by recent scholars. Motivated by the desire to learn and understand more about African perspectives and to spread the word, these scholars present not only the accounts themselves, often discovered in libraries or archives throughout the Atlantic world, but also introductions, references, maps and other illustrations, and the like to assist readers. For example, *Harper's New Monthly Magazine* published an excerpt of the ac-

---

[44]See Carl Ritter, "Mittheilungen über einige westafricanische Stämme in Cuba, gesammelt von Hesse," *Monatsberichte über die Verhandlungen der Gesellschaft für Erdkunde zu Berlin*, n.s. 10 (1853): 12–16; Montgomery, "Survivors from the Cargo of the Negro Slave Yacht *Wanderer*"; Drummond, "Lettres sur l'Afrique ancienne et moderne"; Francis de Castelnau, *Renseignements sur l'Afrique Centrale et sur une Nation d'Hommes a Queue qui s'y Trouverait, d'après le Rapport de Nègres du Soudan, Esclaves a Bahia* (Paris: P. Bertrand, 1851); Sigismund Wilhelm Koelle, *Polyglotta Africana; or a Comparative Vocabulary of Nearly Three Hundred Words and Phrases, in More than One Hundred Distinct African Languages* (London, Church Missionary House, 1854).

[45]See Femi J. Kolapo, *Christian Missionary Engagement in Central Nigeria, 1857–1891: The Church Missionary Society's All-African Mission on the Upper Niger* (London: Palgrave Macmillan, 2019) and Kolapo (ed.), *The Journals of Church Missionary Society Agent, James Thomas, in Mid-Nineteenth Century Nigeria* (Lewiston, NY: Edwin Mellen Press, 2013).

[46]For Carabalí's testimony see García Rodríguez, *Voices of the Enslaved in Nineteenth-Century Cuba*, p. 116.

count of Sitiki or Jack Smith (Nr. 471) in 1875 that students of slavery and African American life hardly noticed, if at all. But Patricia Griffin's discovery of the full manuscript of 1871, which she published with a scholarly apparatus in 2009, provides us with a full account and analysis of Sitiki's life.[47] In fact, modern scholars are helping us to see and use more voices than ever—beyond the heavily Anglo-American abolitionist record—by scouring government, ecclesiastical, and court records. They then publish evidence produced by investigative committees, newspapers, and more throughout Latin America and print African voices in well-edited volumes.[48] Christian groups such as the mostly German Moravians had a tradition of recording and preserving the life stories or memoirs of members, including those by African converts, a few of which later scholars have published.[49] The result is that we now have published African voices in more languages and geographic areas than ever before.

Where do these published voices fit within an African *Weltanschauung*? The African voice invites the reader into a subjective Africa narrative, and this catalog promotes this endeavor and assists in answering this question by expanding and centering Africa in Atlantic and global histories. The African voices transformed by language and publication in this catalog reflect palpable tensions of authenticity, representation, otherness, and exploitation, as well as historical experience and cultural expression present in Western academia, Christian evangelism, and slave-based and postcolonial political economies. In addition to the African oracular voice, the collection of published voices in this catalog seeks to emphasize

life histories of African men, women, and children, which though mediated provide what Luise White, Stephan F. Miescher, and David William Cohen call a "usable tradition for the reconstruction of Africa's precolonial past." Thus, viable African perceptions on history, ethnicity, cosmology, political culture, slavery, and other topics can be elicited from the catalog, particularly in conjunction with innovative interdisciplinary analysis and resources.[50]

The published African voices in this catalog are distinct from the more familiar slave narratives because they were produced by people born in Africa and offer broader linguistic, geographic, and cultural insight, yet the former and the latter are inextricably bound by narrative and voice, most notably perhaps in published accounts by Africans themselves. Frequently, these early African writings emphasized ideations of self-validation: to prove the humanity of the African and to combat slavery and racism. Similarly, these voices reflect, as Henry Louis Gates Jr. puts it, African continuations and a rhetorical "chiasmus" of "repetition and reversal" notable in slave narratives and in this catalog of published African voices. Amid Afro-Atlantic literary inquiries of authenticity and tradition, slave texts or narrative voices evolved from a "testimony of defilement" to expressions of a "broad concord of sensibilities which the group expresses." That group certainly included African descendants born in the Americas and those born in Africa. This process of constructing identities as "speaking subjects" was essential to destroying taxonomies of Africans and their American descendants as commodities, objects, or liminal humans within Western culture generally. (For well-known examples

---

[47]See Griffin, *Odyssey of an African Slave*, pp. 11–38. The excerpt was published by Constance Fenimore Woolson in "The Ancient City," *Harper's New Monthly Magazine*, Part II (January 1875), L (296), pp. 165–185.

[48]See, e.g., McKnight and Garofalo, *Afro-Latino Voices* and García Rodríguez, *Voices of the Enslaved in Nineteenth-Century Cuba.*

[49]See, e.g., Magdalene Beulah Brockden (Nr. 19) in Katherine M. Faull (ed.), *Moravian Women's Memoirs: Their Related Lives, 1750–1820* (Syracuse, NY: Syracuse University Press, 1997), pp. 77–78, and Ibrahim (Nr. 153) in Jon F. Sensbach, *A Separate Canaan: The Making of an Afro-Moravian World in North Carolina, 1763–1840* (Chapel Hill: University of North Carolina Press, 1998), pp. 309–311.

[50]For African Weltanschauung see V.Y. Mudimbe, *The Invention of Africa: Gnosis, Philosophy, and the Order of Knowledge* (Bloomington: Indiana University Press, 1988). For oral voice see Luise White, Stephan F. Miescher, and David William Cohen (eds.), *African Words, African Voices: Critical Practices in Oral History* (Bloomington: Indiana University Press, 2001), pp. 10 and 13.

Introduction

in this catalog see Nr. 126, Cugoano, Nr. 235, Ajayi or Samuel Crowther, and Nr. 435, Baquaqua.)[51]

Publishing a catalog of African accounts invokes theoretical problems associated with defining narrative and voice, one of which is defining what a narrative is.[52] Literary scholars, historians, and others have spilled voluminous amounts of ink on this issue in ways that this volume cannot address. But here are some basics we employ: a narrative is a story or telling of related events to listeners or readers constructed by an individual. In the context used here, it is an autobiographical account of some portion of the individual's life. Narrative is a subjective form, meaning that it hardly if at all reflects some true experience of anyone beyond the narrator, and maybe not even that, because that person is not always aware of everything that is happening to or around them. Further, additional input from an editor or others who disseminate the narrative, or mediation, often shapes the final product in ways that they hope will have a desired impact on the audience. So editors produce (and often publish) narratives from other people that are shaped by their own views and target certain audiences, with little or no interest in what other audiences might think or want to see in a narrative.

Mediation of narratives through editors and the publication process was often heavy, yet the stories and perspectives of the Africans who told them are still apparent in the final texts listed in this catalog. An abolitionist editor, for example, might publish a so-called African slave narrative to awaken sympathy among people that might be ambivalent about slavery, hoping they will be moved to vote or oth-erwise take action to end the practice. Africans who provided such narratives were likely sympathetic to the cause and told their stories in ways that assisted the editors. In fact, beginning in the late 18th century African writers such as Ottobah Cugoano, John Jea, Ukawsaw Gronniosaw, and Vassa (all featured in this catalog) helped start a Black literary tradition that stressed telling their stories in ways that might evoke sympathy for abolition.[53] Further, editors of scientific periodicals published articles based on evidence from individuals who had experienced the Middle Passage in order to find out more and educate readers about the geography of the African interior, which before the mid to late 19th century was hardly known to most Europeans or people in the Americas. The Africans interviewed might have wanted to talk about, for example, how they raised crops in their homelands or how much they despised a new slave code in the Americas, but the editor either would not give them a chance to talk about such issues, or would not print it if they did. Yet when they did talk about their African homelands, they provided important details on their lives there and the place itself that are as valuable now to scholars and teachers trying to understand transatlantic slavery as they were to scientists at the time of publication trying to understand African geography.

It is important to realize that narrative construction and mediation occur in almost all (some would say all) historical documentation that scholars use in their work—not just in the accounts of Africans and other marginalized or oppressed people. A well-documented speech by Teddy Roosevelt or the complete, well-preserved diary of an articulate craftsman in

[51]Henry Louis Gates Jr., *The Signifying Monkey: A Theory of African-American Literary Criticism* (Oxford: Oxford University Press, 1988).

[52]On the challenges of producing biographies of enslaved people see, e.g., Lisa A. Lindsay and John Wood Sweet (eds.), *Biography and the Black Atlantic* (Philadelphia: University of Pennsylvania Press, 2014); Jeffrey A. Fortin and Mark Meuwese (eds.), *Atlantic Biographies: Individuals and Peoples in the Atlantic World* (Leiden, Netherlands, 2014), Part 2; Sue Peabody, "Microhistory, Biography, Fiction: The Politics of Narrating the Lives of People under Slavery," *Transatlantica*, no. 2 (2012), n.p.; and the papers presented at the symposium on "Voices in the Legal Archives in the French Atlantic," organized by Nancy Christie, Michael Gauvreau, and Clare Haru Crowston (North Hatley, Quebec, May 28–30, 2018). See also Nicole N. Aljoe, "'Going to Law': Legal Discourse and Testimony in Early West Indian Slave Narratives," *Early American Literature*, XLVI (2011): 351–381.

[53]See, e.g., Christine Levecq, *Slavery and Sentiment: The Politics of Feeling in Black Atlantic Antislavery Writing, 1770–1850* (Durham: University of New Hampshire Press, 2008); Gates and Andrews, *Pioneers of the Black Atlantic*, especially the preface (pp. vii–xi and 1–29); James Sidbury, "Early Slave Narratives and the Culture of the Atlantic Market," pp. 260–274 and 363–366 in *Empire and Nation: The American Revolution in the Atlantic World*, edited by Eliga H. Gould and Peter S. Onuf (Baltimore: The Johns Hopkins University Press, 2005).

18th-century France was shaped by expectations and questions for such narratives (What will move my audience? How am I supposed to write a diary?), and later scholars read and understand them in different ways, shaped by their changing times.

Finally, there is a problem with the concept of a "published" narrative, life story, or account. This catalog presents published accounts only because they are and have been accessible to many readers. It is not practical for more than a handful of scholars to access archival or other manuscripts in the Atlantic world. Continuing discovery and publication of such manuscripts in document collections significantly increases the number of accounts available, as do monographs and journal articles that reprint lengthy quotations from the original sources. But how much of an African manuscript testimony must be published by a modern scholar before we can consider it as an account of that person's life? We are not suggesting that two or three sentences from a court testimony in a documents collection or journal article or monograph are equivalent to a book publication such as that of Boyrereau Brinch (Nr. 162) or Sitiki (Nr. 471), even though each receives one entry in the catalog. But we are striving to increase knowledge of meaningful published material with African voices by showing readers where it exists and how they can obtain it. Some readers may object to the inclusion of very brief accounts. If so, they should not (and obviously will not) use them, but others may find them useful. One might also ask whether digitized material published online should be included in the catalog. We made an editorial decision that such material is now appearing so rapidly and is in such a state of flux that we will not try to address that issue until we reach the online phase of this project.

While generations of literary criticism and other scholarship have taught us that the narrative is a subjective construct often controlled by those wielding power over others and that it hardly reflects any

reality from long ago that one can begin to grasp, certainly not from those being exploited by those in power, there are workable solutions. This is why scholarship and increased understanding in humanities and related fields continues, much of it based on mediated narratives. For one, mediated documentation provides at least some historical information, and the mediation involved in producing it can tell us even more. For example, if we know how abolitionist, scientist, Christian, and other editors met individuals and published their narratives, then we learn more about the lives of Africans and others in slavery and the many obstacles they faced, including the obstacle of telling their stories. "What matters more," as Sean Kelly puts it in his study of 104 narratives in upper Guinea, "is how the document can be used."[54] In our view we are much better off trying to understand Africans and transatlantic slavery if we use the hundreds of accounts, such as they are, in this catalog than if we incorrectly assume there are practically no such voices available and rely instead on Euro-American documentation and voices. Perhaps this catalog makes this imperfect situation significantly less imperfect. Its purpose is to make African voices more available for teachers, students, and scholars. The latter will have to decide for themselves how to tackle the difficult problems of deconstructing narratives and interpreting their meaning.

This project contributes to the growing number of scholars who take an expanded view of what a narrative is and refer to them as "African voices." Instead of limiting their study to extended published narratives, which is overwhelmingly an Anglo-American genre, they are mining judicial, ecclesiastical, missionary, and other archives to publish these voices from throughout the Atlantic world.[55] By an African voice we mean not necessarily that of someone who identified as an African (although this was certainly the case in many instances) but rather the words and thoughts of someone born in Africa and enslaved or

---

[54]Sean Kelley, "Enslavement in Upper Guinea during the Era of the Transatlantic Slave Trade: Biographical Perspectives," *African Economic History*, 48(1) (2020): 46–73.

[55]The following edited volumes include texts of African voices: McKnight and Garfalo, *Afro-Latino Voices*; Rogers, *Voix d'Esclaves*; White, *Voices of Enslaved*; García Rodríguez, *Voices of the Enslaved*. For discussion of the concept see, in addition to the editorial apparatus of the above works, Lindsey and Sweet, *Biography and the Black Atlantic* (especially therein Jon Sensbach, "Black Pearls: Writing Black Atlantic Women's Biography," pp. 93–107, who argues for a more expansive approach to what constitutes a slave narrative), and White and Burnard, *Hearing Enslaved Voices*.

purchased for shipment to the Americas, as put into writing and ultimately published.

Many historians of Africa and slavery in the Americas are now collaborating to present and study African perspectives and voices in creative ways, ranging from data collection on slave ship voyages to illustrations of houses and body markings of Africans throughout the Atlantic world (see list in the bibliography). The publication of the African voices in this catalog is thus part of a larger project that allows scholars, teachers, and students to better understand Africa, the African diaspora, and the worlds in which Africans and African Americans moved and lived in many ways. The purpose of this collaborative work is to help us better understand those worlds, including the lives, thoughts, and activities of Euro-Americans, Native Americans, and others in them by giving people more access to African perspectives.

The problem of mediation can be a difficult one, but there are solutions. The historian of colonial Mexico Inga Clendinnen, when addressing the problem in the study of Mexica and other native groups resisting the Spanish conquest in the 16th century, wrote that "the challenge is to be at once responsive to the possibilities and yet respectful of the limitations of the material we happen to have."[56] Kathryn McKnight and Leo Garofalo, whose edited work is used in this volume, write that if read with care as rhetorical and symbolic texts, as well as straightforward historical documents, one can find the African voices through the layers of mediation and molding and note how the speakers exercised some control of the message. These African voices undo the inherent distortion of their representation by European and American authors. They reveal a double consciousness—their own worldview and the perspective of European colonizers in a slave society. Each voice was molded by its relative access to power and specific interests and aims. Each voice, for example, considered its audience. Thus, in spite of the layers of mediation, African voices are there.[57] In short, if the publications with African voices are read with empathy for African perspectives and with a careful eye for mediation, then they become invaluable resources for studying Africans and many other aspects of transatlantic slavery.

Working with a much larger number of African voices allows readers to explore more fully the variety of lived experiences of Africans in transatlantic slavery. For example, after a Mandinka man named Louis (Nr. 27) was taken on a slave ship to New Orleans in the French North American colony of Louisiana, he escaped and may have as gone as far north as the Illinois country on the upper Mississippi River. But he returned and, still avoiding capture, began visiting a plantation near New Orleans, where he developed an intimate relationship with an enslaved woman in ways that many enslaved people believed threatened their community on the plantation. He was finally captured in 1764. Louis's story emerged in trial records that included witnesses from the plantation community who testified against him. After his conviction for running away and other crimes, Louis was executed by breaking on the wheel.[58] Consider also the fascinating case of Nero Brewster (Nr. 120), who was taken on a slave ship to New England and was eventually chosen "king" of an African community in Portsmouth, New Hampshire. In 1779 he and others signed a petition to the state legislature that claimed their inherent right to freedom and equality and asked them to end slavery. Brewster's 1786 obituary stated that he was "a monarch held in reverential esteem by his subjects, whose death was greatly lamented."[59]

---

[56]Inga Clendinnen, "'Fierce and Unnatural Cruelty': Cortés and the Conquest of Mexico," *Representation*, 33: Special Issue: The New World (Winter, 1991): 65–100, especially 68.

[57]Most of my views on this subject were influenced by McKnight and Garofalo, *Afro-Latino Voices*, pp. xvii–xviii. On double consciousness see W. E. Burghardt Du Bois, *The Souls of Black Folk: Essays and Sketches* (Chicago: A. C. McClurg and Co., 1903), and Paul Gilroy, *The Black Atlantic: Modernity and Double Consciousness* (Cambridge, MA: Harvard University Press, 1993).

[58]See Cécile Vidal, "Comba, esclave noire de Louisiane. Marronage et sociabilité, 1764," in Rogers, *Voix d'Esclaves*, pp. 61–66.

[59]"The petition of [N. B.] Nero Brewster, and others, natives of Africa … Portsmouth, Nov. 12, 1779," in *The New-Hampshire Gazette*, vol. 24, no. 1233 (15 July 1780), p. 1; Obituary notice in the *New-Hampshire Mercury and General Advertiser*, vol. 30 (19 April 1786); Robert B. Dishman, "'Natives of Africa, Now Forcibly Detained': The Slave Petitioners of Revolutionary Portsmouth," *Historical New Hampshire* 61 (Concord, NH, 2007): 8–9.

There are many exceptions, but most accounts in the catalog came about when someone born in Africa told part of their life story to someone else who recorded it, which suggests that African oral traditions may have played an important role in the creation of these written published accounts. In other words, under certain circumstances it might not have seemed unusual to Africans to relate their life stories to others, and many of them may have been quite good at it. Or perhaps those who were good at it are those who produced the accounts we now find, or at least the more lengthy and articulate ones. In fact, judging from the entries in this catalog, they were. Thus, the final accounts we read now are, among other things, the product of African oral traditions and Euro-American written and publishing traditions, with all of the relevant mediation involved in both.[60] In any case, these stories defy common depictions and assumptions regarding slavery, and all of the nearly 500 voices in the catalog and their stories are unique.

How to Use this Catalog

The catalog is constructed so that users can follow the historical trajectory of the development of African voices in the entire Atlantic world—Africa, Europe, the Americas, and the ocean in between. To that end, all entries are arranged in chronological order according to when the account was produced, not when it was first published, which sometimes occurred centuries later. The numbering system refers to the original publication, with the digits following the decimal point numbering subsequent editions, imprints, and reprints. In most cases modern geographical references are used to help orient readers. The focus is on individual African voices, which means that if one publication included multiple voices, then there will be a separate entry for each discrete African account.[61]

The purpose in this respect is to stress individual African lives, not publications, and provide readers with valuable information and a link to the full text of an account for as many or as few as might interest them. Yet the publication or print history is important, and the bulk of material in the catalog is just that—a thorough representation of the print history of an account in all languages and places from the time it was produced until the present. Some readers might find this information valuable in their study of, for example, the abolition movement, the history of print technology and transatlantic slavery, or the history of publishing and printing in specific or all areas of the Atlantic world. Other readers might ignore most of this information and focus on finding the basic account and publication information—just enough to properly footnote their work. Be aware, however, in the latter case that sometimes alterations in the text occurred throughout its publication history.

The Structure of Each Catalog Entry

Under the date the account was produced, each catalog entry is divided into four parts, the first of which is the **heading**. This includes the name of the person whose account was recorded or a descriptor (e.g., Nr. 33.0, Unnamed African woman; Nr. 334.1, Second of two unnamed Nyungwe refugees) followed by years or approximations of their life spans, followed by variant names (cognomens). (Note: African names are listed first.[62]) Not all of this information is known in many cases, especially African names and birth and death dates, but we do provide what we have. On the second line begins a full bibliographic citation for the text, with brief explanations, as needed. If a manuscript with location or prepublication materials (such as printed prospectuses, e.g., Nr. 126.0) is known to exist, it is provided with a "0" suffix in the numbering scheme (Nr. 65.0, for example). Then follows the

---

[60]See Bailey, *African Voices of the Atlantic Slave Trade*, for an example that employs oral history, as well as written texts in its assessment.

[61]See, e.g., entries 427–443, all of which were taken from one magazine article: "Cuban Slaves in England," *The Anti-Slavery Reporter*, ser. 3, vol. 2 (2 October 1854), pp. 234–239.

[62]Paul E. Lovejoy, "Olaudah Equiano or Gustavus Vassa—What's in a Name?" *Atlantic Studies*, 9(2) (2012): 165–184, points out how problematic it can be to stress use of the African name, for example when the individual did not wish to. This catalog lists the African name first as part of its overall effort to distinguish life stories by those born in Africa and taken into the transatlantic slave trade. It will be up to readers of the texts to decide which names should be used in various contexts.

full title and the archives or library where it is stored. If there is no known manuscript, the heading begins with a "1" in the suffix (e.g., Nr. 232.1), followed by bibliographic information on where, by whom, and when the recorded account was published, as well other information on the size, format, and pagination of the volume. Our emphasis in this volume is to show for each entry when publication of a significant African voice began and not to provide comprehensive histories and locations of manuscripts.

Following the heading is one or more URLs linking readers to the full text of the account on the Internet. The URL judged to be the most comprehensive is co-located with the QR code (see below). Other URLs of additional printings and other relevant information are provided when available at the appropriate location in the entry. URLs are provided only when it is reasonably certain that they are at least relatively permanent, freely accessible links to digitized printed editions and digitized archival manuscripts and only if these materials are in the public domain or have been made available by, or with the explicit permission of, the copyright holder or (in the case of unique exemplars of materials in the public domain) material artifact owner. We have favored URLs over Hathitrust, Digital Public Library of America, Internet Archive, the University of North Carolina's *Documenting the American South's* pioneering digital transcriptions (which hold important places in the recent histories of these texts' transmission from their origins to the present), Google Books, and Project Gutenberg because we recommend the relative ease with which users can read these particular digitizations. Notable among the URLs we provide to exemplary individual library digitizations of rare items are links to African-born authors' works at Nr. 117.0, Nr. 165-A.1, Nr. 166-A.1, and Nr. 266.8. Our goal in the print edition is to provide readers with at least one URL per catalog entry, so that they might read the full text of any account listed in this volume. In many cases none of the above resources made it possible to do so. Thus, we created a storage bin at Northern Illinois University (called Huskie Commons) with free online access. When readers click on one of these URLs, they are taken to a page with information on the African in question and a full text of their account. It bears restating that none of the URL links we have provided is to be reproduced without the written permission of the copyright holder (if any) or material artifact owner.

Also listed in the head note is a QR code, which allows readers to access the full text with their cell phones. Finally, the heading includes reference numbers to other cataloging systems that contain the account, especially the English Short Title Catalog (ESTC) citation number, British Library catalog number, National Union Catalog number, World-Cat accession number and Online Computer Library Center (OCLC) identifier, Library of Congress catalog number, European Library reference number, Hogg catalog number, and the Freedom Narratives (FN) reference number, if available.

We have specified the wider contexts of place names (in head notes and elsewhere) in a manner some readers may consider redundant or excessive because the intended audience for this volume includes students throughout the Atlantic region. Not everyone is familiar with place names that people on another continent might find to be common or well-known. In fact, few people are thoroughly familiar with the local and regional geography of all four Atlantic continents. Moreover, cities named London, Waterloo, and many others may be found in more than one country or continent, so it is important to provide this extra detail in order that all readers may be accurately informed of the geography in question.

To facilitate the detailed study of the sale and geographical dispersal of specific editions beyond their place of publication, we include information in the heading and subsequent individual entries in the publication histories (see below) and on subscriber lists, addresses of where copies were sold, and the like, when available.

The second part of each catalog entry is the **biographical summary**, preceded by a pilcrow (¶). This brief overview of the African's life is intended to quickly inform readers on important features of that person's life, including their specific African origins, family circumstances, religion, ethnicity or language, how and when they were taken into the transatlantic slave trade, destinations, later family life, skills or occupations, circumstances of emancipation, further movements, death, and so forth. Modern place names are added to early African and other place names to help readers locate unfamiliar places in their own atlases and mapping apps—a process the map section of this catalog will facilitate. In some cases relatively little of this information is known. The summaries might help readers decide if the individual African is important to their particular project. (If so, they might click on a URL in the entry and read the entire text.) At the end of the paragraph we provide one or two secondary sources relevant to the African, if available, which will help readers find more about the man or woman of interest to them.

The third part of each catalog entry is the **publication history** of the account. Here each subsequent edition or other printing is provided in chronological order, with a suffix number (e.g., Nr. 258.2, Nr. 258.3). This includes reissues, reprintings, new editions, series volumes, translations, substantial excerpts, and quotations. Book titles and edition statements are included to indicate contents, textual changes, and differences between editions or printings. Some entries include many of these details and are quite extensive, such as that for Ukawsaw Gronniosaw in 1772 (Nr. 112) because his works have been reprinted many times since his lifetime. The entry for Chloe Spear in 1832 (Nr. 211), on the other hand, has only two entries.

The fourth and final part of each catalog entry is the list of **other publications** by the African who provided the account. A number of Africans, such as Ajayi or Samuel Ajayi Crowther (Nr. 235), produced additional nonautobiographical accounts that could have informed readers of the period. We have included this information in the entry because it assists current readers in understanding the complete life of the individual. Additional publications and their subsequent printings receive the number of the main entry, followed by a letter for each separate publication. Additional printings of these publications are numbered and listed in chronological order. Thus the second printing of Crowther's second publication, *A Vocabulary of the Yoruba Language*, receives the designation Nr. +235-B.2, where 235 refers to Crowther's place in the entire catalog, B refers to his second publication after his published life account, and 2 refers to the second printing of that publication. When especially significant largely nonautobiographical publications are the only published compositions by enslaved African-born authors who endured the Middle Passage, as with Lucy Bijah's poem "Bars Fight" (Nr. 15.1 et seq.) and Jean-Baptiste Belley's political speeches (Nr. 148.1 et seq.), they receive a discrete entry in the catalog.

Below is an outline of the construction of each account, including examples in some parts of the entry:

Date of Account

Heading:

1.1 African Last Name, First name [= Other Names] (birth and death dates)

Editor's name, *Title of the Publication.*

Place of Publication: Publisher, **date.** "Second edition." Actually reissue of 1734 edition with cancel title page, with reset index. Size, pagination et al. printing information, e.g. 8vo: [i–ii] iii–vi, [1]–200 [201–206].

URL link to full text of the account co-located with the QR code.
QR Code

Biographical summary:

¶ Brief description of the life of the African, with comments regarding the date and location of birth, the date of capture or purchase by Europeans, the destination, and certain biographical highlights provided thereafter, such as marriage, religious conversion, emancipation date, and occupation, as well as reference to select secondary works on the life of the African who provided the account. Brief reference to secondary sources on the narrator.

Publication history:

1.2——.

Editor's name, *Title of the Publication.*

London: J. Wilde, **1799.** "Second edition." Actually reissue of 1734 edition with cancel title page, with reset index. Size, pagination et al. printing information, e.g. 8vo: [i–ii] iii–vi, [1]–200 [201–204].

1.3——.

Editor's name, *Title of the Publication.*

London: J. Wilde, **1799.** "Third edition." Actually second edition.

Other publications:

+1-A.1

Editor's name, *Title of the Publication.* Further bibliographic information.

+1-A.2

Editor's name, *Title of the Publication.* Further bibliographic information.

+1-B.1

Editor's name, *Title of the Publication.* Further bibliographic information.

Further Research Potential of the Catalog

This collection of published African voices offers tremendous research potential for scholars as well as students, and this section describes some of that potential by addressing four questions: (1) What does this expanded corpus tell us about published accounts by enslaved African men and women? (2) What can this collection tell us about enslaved Africans in the Americas and the Atlantic world? (3) What can it tell us about transatlantic slavery? (4) What can it tell us about slavery altogether in this era? Obviously, volumes could be written about the subjects these questions address. What follows is intended to present ideas regarding the breadth and depth of the content of these African voices and how one might use them to study these questions.

1) What does this expanded corpus tell us about published accounts by enslaved African men and women?

When considering the corpus as a whole, one sees that the diversity in the makeup and experiences of the Africans was greater and more complex than many scholars and others have realized. Because of the availability and influence of accounts like that of Vassa, there tends to be an impression that the people providing the accounts were men when experiencing the Middle Passage (even though Vassa himself was only about eleven years old at the time), yet a significant minority were women and children, whose perspectives and experiences in the transatlantic slave trade were different and are not well studied. Age at capture and enslavement in Africa was an important factor influencing how these Africans later remembered their homelands and what, if anything, they told about them. A large majority of them came from West Africa, not West Central Africa, which reflects the geographic concentration of the British and US slave trade, the abolition movement, and the publication of African accounts. That is, the British slave trade focused on West Africa, the abolitionist movement was strongest in Britain and the United States, and most accounts were published in English with abolitionist editors, so most people who provided accounts for English publications during the slave era came from West Africa.[63]

While Anglo-American abolitionist perspectives in these texts are obviously extremely important, the collected accounts in the catalog allow us to look beyond these experiences to other African voices that express how people endured and acted within transatlantic slavery. The prevalence of alternative genres and other languages range from the poetry of Phillis Wheatley in English to the scientific inquiries of de Andrada and Drummond published in French (Nr. 184–188), to the legal records containing the voice of Ana de la Calle (Nr. 9) in Spanish to the spiritual accounts of Aneaso (Nr. 320, Moravian, in German), Chicaba (Nr. 17, Catholic, in Spanish), Jacobus Elisa Johannes Capitein (Nr. 13, Dutch Reformed Church member, in Latin), Ayuba Suleiman Diallo or Job ben Solomon (Nr. 11, Muslim, who wrote in Arabic, although his account was recorded in English), and the last will and testament of Rosa Maria de Conceição (Nr. 226, Catholic, in Portuguese) in Bahia, Brazil. And one should also consider the aged Silvia King's account of 1936 (Nr. 490) recorded by the Federal Writers Project long after US slavery had ended, which was motivated not by abolitionism but a desire to preserve the memory of enslaved people and their experiences. All of this and more supports the view that African voices were distinct from those of African Americans and that there are limits to the view that the published slave narrative was overwhelmingly an Anglo-American literary genre.

2) What can this collection tell us about enslaved Africans in the Americas and the Atlantic world?

The accounts focus primarily on African perspectives of transatlantic slavery through biography, and one might ask: What can the biographies of only about five hundred individuals tell us about the 12.5 million people who endured the Middle Passage? The work in this catalog follows and supports that of Freedom Narratives and others who have stressed the importance of individual biography to the study of transatlantic slavery. There was never a typical biography of people captured and sent on a slave ship

---

[63]Of the nearly three million Africans who disembarked in the Americas from US and British slave ships, 82 percent embarked in coastal regions of West Africa (including the Bight of Biafra), not West Central or Southeastern Africa, as calculated from the Estimates Section of *Slave Voyages 2.0*, accessed 8 April 2020.

to work on a tropical or subtropical plantation in the Americas: Each individual was unique. While many of the life stories in the catalog represent exceptional, relatively upwardly mobile people in the enslaved African population of the Americas, they illustrate that uniqueness and tremendous diversity of experiences among these millions. Following Lovejoy and others, a recent volume of essays on biography and the Black Atlantic edited by Lisa Lindsay and John Wood Sweet addresses this issue, and its authors collectively make a strong case for pursuing research into the biographies of individual enslaved Africans and African Americans in the Atlantic world, a case that the collected accounts in this catalog supports. James Campbell, for example, makes it clear that the biographical approach to the study of enslaved Africans in the Americas is important because such accounts reveal important details of the structures of the system that they escaped. They tell us a great deal about the realm of the possible and the connected lives of many people who made the Black Atlantic, and indeed the entire Atlantic world. Lindsay and Sweet argue that individual lives show that the creation of the Black Atlantic was not a unitary process of transformation from African to African American but rather a complex one that changed over time and place. Joseph Miller explains it well in a theoretical essay on the "biographical turn," in which scholars address the full humanity of enslaved people and their roles as humans acting in the system that oppressed them.[64]

The expanded corpus of African accounts with its more diverse voices can help scholars break new ground in the study of enslaved Africans in the Atlantic world and also explore familiar areas more thoroughly. If we ever want to better understand African life stories and experiences in Brazil and New Spain, for example, contemporary published accounts will hardly help, since there are virtually none. But, as Kathryn McKnight, Leo Garofalo, Gloria García Rodriguez, and others have already shown, we can investigate legal records, Maroon writings, and other sources to find African voices. Although Brazil is underrepresented in this catalog—that is, the portion of Africans taken there was higher than what is reflected in this catalog—it nevertheless provides many more accounts than most scholars have realized, and more will emerge in the future. This will likely lead to significantly altered views by scholars of Africans in Atlantic slavery. Further, an expanded collection of African voices allows for broader and deeper study of the impact of religion and spirituality on the cataclysmic events that shaped the individual lives of Africans caught in transatlantic slavery and the struggles for emancipation. The collection provides many more examples of how Islam and Christianity affected the lives of African slaves in the Atlantic world. If we read more accounts by, for example, Moravians such as Magdalene Beulah Brockden (Nr. 19) and Ofodobendo Wooma (Nr. 108), we gain the perspective of enslaved Africans in America who were never emancipated. In many ways the biggest change in Brockden's life after enduring the Middle Passage was not emancipation (because it never happened) but rather her conversion to Moravian Christianity.[65] At least on one level Ukawsaw Gronniosaw (Nr. 112) remained conscious of his elite African heritage, yet he accepted the plunge from a life of luxury to hard times enslaved in America and even as a freedman. His account does not express a desire to return to his former life in Africa but rather the desire to live in freedom as a Christian. When the opportunity arose, he first chose England over Africa, but when that did not work out, he decided to try life as a freed Christian in Holland. These biographies and perspectives, taken together, can tell us a lot more about the impact of Christianity on slavery, which has interested scholars for many years.

3) *What can this catalog tell us about transatlantic slavery?*

The expanded number and perspective of African voices in the Catalog provide more evidence for both sides of important, long-standing debates among

---

[64]All of these views are expressed in Lindsay and Sweet, *Biography and the Black Atlantic*, including that of James T. Campbell in the afterword (pp. 269–278). See also Adam Potkay and Sandra Burr (eds.), *Black Atlantic Writers of the Eighteenth Century: Living the New Exodus in England and the Americas* (New York: St. Martin's Press, 1995).

[65]For Wooma see Daniel Thorp (ed.), "Chattel with a Soul: The Autobiography of a Moravian Slave," *The Pennsylvania Magazine of History & Biography*, 112(3) (July 1988): 433–451.

scholars. For one, these accounts support the view that Africans maintained direct control of the transatlantic slave trade until the point when enslaved people embarked on the European slave ships, but there were important exceptions.[66] While a large majority of the familiar and less familiar accounts describe how individuals were captured in war or kidnapped, held, and transported often for long time periods and then sold to Europeans on the African coast, Boyrereau Brinch (Nr. 162), for example, describes how he was captured by white people and taken directly to their slave ship, which had ventured far upriver. And Ngeve or Catherine Mulgrave Zimmermann (Nr. 373), describes how she was taken on a beach in Luanda with two other girls by European sailors in 1833.

These African voices also provide more evidence on the long-standing debate about whether or to what degree African culture survived the Middle Passage and helped to shape the culture of enslaved people in the Americas. While offering no definitive answer to this complex, multifaceted question, the catalog entries make it clear that, among these Africans anyway, neither the slave ship experience nor anything else associated with the Middle Passage suppressed their memory or impressions of their homelands *if* they were not small children when the passage occurred. If enslaved or formerly enslaved people were born in Africa, were at least nine or ten years old when crossing the Atlantic, and later provided a recorded account of their experiences, then Africa remained an important part of their lives. This was even true for most freed Africans who declined a chance to return to Africa when it later came, and it was true for those who embraced freedom and Christianity in America after escaping slavery. This did not have to be the case—those providing their life accounts might have ignored Africa or their lives

there when telling their tales, but they did not. Clearly the horrors of the Middle Passage did not eradicate the memory of or willingness to talk about Africa, not for this group of enslaved people anyway.

Perhaps one of the most important contributions of this collection is that it provides a lot more evidence on the nature of the Middle Passage from those who experienced it while enslaved: Eighty-six accounts contain substantive descriptions of this event. Most scholars are familiar with individual descriptions of Vassa (Nr. 130), Baquaqua (Nr. 435), and a few others, as well as work on the slave ship experience altogether, but this catalog provides views of these and many other individuals. Children such as Aneaso (Nr. 320) described their preferential treatment as cabin boys to the ship captain, yet they also described how hundreds of men and women were kept below deck and how they heard their "heart-rending cries of anguish," as they longed for their homes and families while being denied proper food and drink.[67] Asa-Asa (Nr. 207) was captured as a boy in 1826 and five years later described how he was on a ship for five or six months, during which time he saw people chained together below deck, so that they could not move and were cruelly flogged, even though many of them were very ill.[68] A young man captured in war and taken to the coast believed the large ship with white people on board was the "most wonderful object in the world," until they purchased him and other men and women for liquor and cloth and confined them in irons in the dark hold of the ship. As they fastened the mothers in irons, the crew tore small children from their arms and threw them overboard. The women were allowed on deck after they were at sea, but the men remained chained in a sitting position in the hold through the entire voyage. This included the anonymous Muslim man (Nr. 164),

[66]See, e.g., John Thornton, *Africa and Africans in the Making of the Atlantic World, 1400–1800*, 2nd ed. (New York: Cambridge University Press, 1998).

[67]See the catalog entry Nr. 374 for Aneaso (or Archibald John Monteith) for 1853 and the text in Maureen Warner-Lewis, *Archibald Monteath: Igbo, Jamaican, Moravian* (Kingston: University of the West Indies Press, 2007), Appendix 2 "Archibald John Monteath: Native Helper and Assistant in the Jamaica Mission at New Carmel," pp. 286–304, especially p. 289.

[68]See catalog entry Nr. 207 for Asa-Asa for 1831 and the text in "A Negro Boy's Narrative," in *Mary Prince, The History of Mary Prince, A West Indian Slave, Related by Herself, with a Supplement by the Editor, to Which Is Added the Narrative of Asa-Asa, a Captured African* (London: F. Westley and A. H. Davis, 1831), pp. 42–44, especially 42.

who could not properly stand for many days after disembarking in Charleston, South Carolina.[69]

Some of the brief accounts confirm a great deal about the horrible conditions of the Middle Passage. Umar ibn Sayyid of Fut Tûr (Nr. 206) was captured in war, taken to the coast, and sold to Europeans "who bound me and sent me on board a great ship" for one and one-half months to Charleston, South Carolina.[70] In 1810 Boyrereau Brinch described how some people were drugged before being taken onto the slave ship, the sexual exploitation of women, tight packing, the sharks that followed their ship across the Atlantic and consumed the dead thrown overboard, a foiled plot among slaves to take over the ship and return home, and the "house of subjection" on Barbados, where hundreds of men, women, and children were abused after disembarking from the slave ships, before being sold to planters.[71] In 1787 Quobona Ottobah Cugoano (Nr. 126) wrote, "It would be needless to give a description of all the horrible scenes which we saw, and the base treatment which we met with in this dreadful captive situation, as the similar cases of thousands, which suffer by this infernal traffic, are well known," but then he did it anyway. As he and others were marched in chains to a fortress on the African coast, sold, and imprisoned, Cugoano did not think it could get any worse. "But when a vessel arrived to conduct us away to the ship, it was a most horrible scene; there was nothing to be heard but the rattling of chains, smacking of whips, and the groans and cries of our fellow-men." While waiting in the hold of the slave ship, death became more preferable to life. He and others plotted to "burn and blow up" the ship, but a woman in their group forced to sleep with the captain betrayed them. Like others, Cugoano went on to describe how the crews sexually abused enslaved women on the ship.[72]

The collected accounts also allow a kind of class analysis in the slave trade from African perspectives. A disproportionate number of those providing accounts were elites in their homelands, and their tales illuminate a great deal about both African and European attitudes toward these princes, princesses, kings, priests, scholars, and merchants. African status often mattered to Europeans, so sometimes elite enslaved people received preferential treatment when white people took an interest in them. This could even lead to their release and return to Africa, as was the case with two so-called princes from Calabar named Little Ephraim Robin John (Nr. 115) and Ancona Robin Robin John (Nr. 116), who told their tale in 1774. Europeans sometimes went to great lengths to accommodate African elites. Ayuba Suleiman Diallo (Nr. 11), whose account was published in 1734, was the son of a Muslim imam in Fuuta Bondu on the Senegal River. He was captured in 1730, sold to an English slave ship captain, and eventually ended up in Maryland. He wrote a letter to his father in Arabic asking for help to be "redeemed" and returned home. James Oglethorpe, who was organizing the settlement of the new British colony of Georgia, acquired the letter in London and arranged for Ayuba's purchase, release, and transportation to London. Thomas Bluett sailed with Ayuba from Maryland to London in 1733 and published his story after arriving. Oglethorpe's supporters paid for Ayuba's release and turned him over to the Royal Africa Company, which took him in during a subscription drive to pay for his release. Meanwhile, Ayuba became a celebrity, meeting the royal family (receiving a gold watch from the queen), the Duke of Montague, and other nota-

---

[69]Anonymous, in Charles Ball, *Slavery in the United States: A Narrative of the Life and Adventures of Charles Ball, a Black Man*, 3rd ed. (Pittsburgh: J. T. Shryock, 1853), pp. 703–704. For another description of "tight packing" on slave ships see that of Augustino in Robert Edgar Conrad, *Children of God's Fire: A Documentary History of Black Slavery in Brazil* (Princeton: Princeton University Press, 1983), pp. 37–39.

[70]Umar ibn Sayyid, "Autobiography of Omar Ibn Said, Slave in North Carolina, 1831," edited by John Franklin Jameson, *American Historical Review*, 30(4) (July 1925): 787–795, here 792–795.

[71]Boyrereau, Brinch, *The Blind African Slave, Or Memoirs of Boyrereau Brinch, Nicknamed Jeffrey Brace*, edited by Kari J. Winter (Madison: University of Wisconsin Press, 2004), pp. 120–129.

[72]Vincent Carretta (ed.), *Quobna Ottobah Cugoano: Thoughts and Sentiments on the Evil of Slavery and Other Writings* (New York: Penguin Books, 1999), pp. 123–125.

bles, and he received gifts worth £500. Among other things, Ayuba's story suggests that there were limits to the leveling process and elimination of African culture via the Middle Passage, as his status and worth as the son of an imam influenced his life after enslavement in America. It is difficult, if not impossible, for scholars to assess who was who and the nature of hierarchy, status, or class among African slaves without the voices of Africans themselves, because few Euro-Americans at the time were interested in or knowledgeable of these issues from African perspectives.[73]

In these cases and others, especially before the abolition movement began to gain momentum in the 1780s, Europeans worked hard to win the release of African elites, not because they found slavery itself offensive but because they found it offensive or wrong to enslave people of such high birth. When W. Reeves published Ansa Sasraku or William Ansah Sessarakoo's account (Nr. 16) in London in 1755, for example, it was not his intention to publish an abolitionist tract. Entitling the work *The Royal African: or, Memoirs of the Young Prince of Annamaboe*, Reeves wished instead to point out to readers that a man of such high station was being treated as a slave. He also wished to meet a demand for exotic information about Africa, using Sasraku as his vehicle. Reeves's use of Sasraku's account highlights the paucity of genuine antislavery discourse at this early date.[74]

An African account sixty years later in the midst of the abolition movement describes a much different European approach to African elites—one that deeply offended Boyrereau Brinch, who expressed his own views regarding class among enslaved Africans. Himself from a well-regarded family, as he put it, Brinch describes an assault on African class during the "seasoning" process in the house of subjection on Barbados. While in this torture chamber, he met the daughter of the king of Guingana and her little brother, who were decorated in a style equal to

their rank in their country. She and her brother had been sent there from Africa for an education, and she had married a rich English planter and slave owner. Her father, the king, had presented him with lavish gifts at the wedding. In Barbados, however, the English had taken everything from her and treated her maids of honor the same way, enslaving them all. They stripped them of their better clothes and jewelry, including a bracelet from her grandmother. The princess told Brinch that she feared she would have nothing in this "foreign land" to remember her grandmother by. After she gave an eloquent speech to her husband before the other Africans in the house of subjection, one of the drivers beat her to death and gave Brinch fifty stripes, presumably for trying to help her. Additionally, Brinch described sailors in the house of subjection raping African women. Those who ran the house treated the maids of honor the same as common African folk. In this manner the assault on African class in the house was part of an attempt to obliterate African culture and achieve the absolute subjection of everyone, regardless of their class, thus making African class meaningless among Africans. The extent to which they were successful is unknown and merits further investigation.[75]

4) What can the catalog tell us about slavery altogether in this era?

It may take time before a fuller understanding of what the expanded collection of African voices can tell us about slavery in the Americas altogether emerges, and whatever one concludes from this collection should be considered with the much larger Freedom Narratives project and other collections, but for now a few points come to mind. The transatlantic slave trade was a critical element that made the Atlantic world in the four centuries following Columbus and thus slavery itself in the Americas. Although there is only one account in the catalog for the first century and a quarter after Columbus, and that not until

---

[73]For Little Ephraim Robin John and Anacona Robin Robin John see Randy L. Sparks, *Two Princes of Calabar: An Eighteenth-Century Atlantic Odyssey* (Cambridge, MA: Harvard University Press, 2004). Sparks and Paul Lovejoy are currently preparing an edition with their writings. For Ayuba see Bluett, *Some Memoirs of the Life of Job.*

[74]*The Royal African: or, Memoirs of the Young Prince of Annamaboe. Comprehending a Distinct Account of his Country and Family ... the manner in which himself was confided by his father to the captain who sold him; his condition while a slave in Barbadoes ... his Voyage from thence; and Reception here in England...* (London: Printed for W. Reeves, 1749).

[75]Brinch, *Blind African Slave*, pp. 130–142.

1586, there are three and a half centuries of accounts thereafter, covering a much broader chronological range than most scholars are accustomed to discussing. Taken together and in conjunction with Freedom Narratives and other projects, the voices in the catalog allow for an improved understanding of Africans in Atlantic slavery, from developments in Africa itself to African influences in the Americas. Also, the catalog offers greater opportunities to assess the role of Africa, Africans, and African voices in the culture of enslaved people in the Americas. The African voice imbedded in Charles Ball's creole account (Nr. 164), for example, provides insight into the role of Africans in US slave communities at a time when the creole populations expanded dramatically. And the evidence in the expanded corpus of accounts in the catalog suggests that what limited African voices in the Americas was not the brutality of the Middle Passage or environmental factors in the Americas but rather access to power and publication, the slow ending of the transatlantic slave trade from the 1770s to the 1860s, and with the latter the declining relative importance in the enslaved populations of Africans, as opposed to African Americans.

* * *

The diversity alone and the small number out of millions (for nearly five hundred voices, while much higher than what we thought, is still small) testify to the terrible weight of silence and death in the slave system and to the immense variety within it. The pleas in these texts are proof of how native anger, ideologies, and situations combined in many to create informed fury at their situation. And they show how both Muslims and non-Muslims reacted to the terrible irony that those who held them captive were attached to various ideologies of "freedom." They are a great and terrible resource, and also a powerful rejection of the universal slave owner defense that they had saved these people from the horrors of Africa. They are also a powerful rejection of the modern notion that we cannot better study African voices due to the dearth of sources, for, in fact, the sources are there.

SPECIAL SECTION FOR STUDENTS

While this catalog should make it a lot easier to find and work with African voices in class assignments and research projects, it still will not be easy. This section is designed to help students in three important areas: interpreting and working with individual entries, dealing with the problem of mediation of African voices, and designing a research project.

For those unfamiliar with large bibliographies and catalogs, it may seem like a daunting task to wade through so much material and find something useful, but if you focus on the information you really need and ignore the rest, it will help. If you are interested in a chronological period, then go to that section of the catalog and begin reading. If you are interested in a geographic area (origins or destinations of the Africans, places of publication, etc.) or a cultural or other group (children, women, those describing the Middle Passage, etc.), then use the indexes to find the entries you need and only look at those (see below for more on the indexes). When working with an individual entry, begin by reading the head note and biographical paragraph to see if this individual will help with your project. If so, then begin looking through the following publication histories to find the text with the African voice you need. Normally, it will be best to find the most complete, easiest to read version. Often this will be the first listed (with a URL and QR code that will link you to the full text of the account), but in many cases modern editions published much later have a more complete version of the account, as well as useful footnotes and commentary to help you interpret the African voice. Be aware that in some cases the catalog lists incomplete or otherwise inferior versions of the original in order to provide a more complete publication history. Unless your project involves tracing that publication history in detail, you should avoid these entries. Translations are noted, but try to use the original language, if you can, because something usually goes lost, even in an expert translation. If this is not possible, use the English version or whatever works best, and you will be fine. (Just note in your paper, usually in a footnote, if you used a translation.) In most cases you can ignore the remaining entries, after finding the most suitable text with the African voices.

Earlier in this introduction we discussed mediation of African voices, and it is a problem for a number of reasons. For one, most readers are interested in discovering the thoughts or actions of the subject interviewed, not the editor or anyone else, so the mediation becomes an obstacle. Were it somehow neutral, mediation would be easier to address, but it is not. Instead, the difference in this case (and many others) between what the Africans wanted to tell about their lives and what was later printed resulted from unequal power relationships. The voices of people in government, military leaders, writers, owners of businesses and large plantations, and the heads of households dominate the historical record, even when they are writing about their subjects, troops, workers, slaves, and families. This means that the perspective of those with less power is often badly distorted, yet we know that they were important agents in history responsible for much historical change. It is important to know what workers in factories and on plantations thought and did because they made so much of our history, but to do so we must address the problem of mediation.

So our first word of advice on how to deal with the mediation shaping the published African voices in this catalog is to respond to the opportunity the catalog presents—read and write about African voices and perspectives from the transatlantic slave trade, which are presented here more than ever before. One cannot know the history of transatlantic slavery well enough without seriously incorporating African perspectives, and this is one good way to do it. Second, recognize and consider the nature of the mediation in each account. Watch for it—it is there—and ask yourself, Who or what caused this mediation and why? What were their interests in the project, and what did they want? How did these interests mediate or influence the final printed text that you are reading?

Third, develop and employ *empathy* for African perspectives, especially for the individual whose account you are reading. Empathy is the ability to understand and share the feelings of another. You may not know enough about Africans or African history to do this readily, so make an effort. In this case we are not interested, for example, in what Europeans did to Black people, as important as that is for other reasons. We are interested in the people who, with few exceptions, were born free in Africa, grew up and lived in villages and towns with their own family, religion, language, and other aspects of life, and then were suddenly and violently taken into the transatlantic slave trade and enslaved in the Americas. Most Africans listed in the catalog regained their freedom in an incredible variety of ways that can only be grasped by reading large numbers of their

accounts. They continued their lives in freedom or slavery in the Americas, or in some cases in Europe, Sierra Leone, or elsewhere in West Africa. Consider what it was *like* to have come from such backgrounds and to have had such experiences, and then read the text for evidence that will help you understand what happened in the part of this individual's life that the text addresses. For the moment, try to wear blinders to the interests of abolitionists, scientists, missionaries, and others, at least temporarily, to see what might have happened to the African from their point of view. Ask yourself what position they were in as an individual when these things happened—a small child, a Muslim cleric, a grieving mother, a warrior, the son or daughter of a powerful ruler or wealthy merchant? How might their background and lives in Africa have influenced their lives in America? Did it make a difference whether they were a man or a woman? (It almost always did; the question is, how?) We have discussed the interests of the mediators, but what might have been the interests of the African? Did they profess pious Christianity to elicit sympathy from readers who might contribute money so they could return to Africa as a missionary? If so, it does not necessarily mean that they were not true Christians, but it probably does mean that they *really* wanted to go home (or at least get back to their home continent), even after many years of living enslaved and free in the Americas. Not all Africans with published accounts in the catalog believed or wanted this, but in this case someone did, and now you know.

In short, by recognizing mediation when you see it and employing empathy for the perspective of the Africans whose accounts you are reading, you can develop your own interpretation of the documents, which might be different from what the editors intended, and it might be a perspective that is very useful to understanding more about Africa and Africans in transatlantic slavery.

Last, while preparing and conducting a research project based on primary sources listed in this catalog, it will be very important for you to make significant use of secondary sources—books and articles written by scholars of transatlantic slavery and the regions and events that might interest you. Secondary sources will be critical to help you understand the historical context you are researching and to inform you on what has already been done and still needs to be done in your area of interest. You will find important discussions, debates, and heated arguments among scholars in the secondary sources of which you ought to be aware so you can contribute to the discussion. The list of secondary sources in the bibliography and the references at the end of the biographical paragraphs in the catalog entries will help you get started with finding needed material, but you will probably need to go beyond these when choosing a focused topic. If you work hard with the secondary sources and complete an original project using material in this catalog, you will find that scholars throughout the world might be interested in what you have to say, if you say it well—even an undergraduate senior thesis!

How to Design a Research Project Using this Catalog

This catalog facilitates the creation and completion of original research projects involving African voices and perspectives from life in Africa through the Middle Passage to life in the Americas and elsewhere. Using this catalog, you can feel confident that you are working in a fairly comprehensive way with published accounts available in the Atlantic world (following the criteria explained earlier), and this will help with your assessment or analysis. (Be aware, however, that new discoveries might occur that will be added to the catalog later when it goes online.) The good news is that you will not have to spend a lot of time searching libraries, archives, and the footnotes of secondary sources to find documents for your study, nor will you have to travel or spend much time acquiring the documents—all of the texts are available online using the URLs and QR codes provided in each entry. Instead, to find and acquire your documents, you search this catalog, which has been organized and presented to help you do just that. In most cases, you should be able to find enough primary source material in this catalog to complete a research paper or senior thesis, and maybe even an MA thesis or dissertation. Of course, in the case of lengthier studies such as the latter two, you will likely need to work also with other documents not in this catalog, but the catalog might lead you toward those documents.

To make the most of this catalog when completing a research project, it is best to develop a plan or strategy, which involves things you should and will do and things you should not do. Normally, you should not develop a project based on a certain number of accounts and a certain number of pages to write, such as reading ten African accounts and writing a five-page paper about them. The problem with this approach is that the accounts vary widely in length and content, which means that you might not find enough material to write about anything important if you limit yourself to a certain number of accounts. Perhaps the accounts are so short you hardly know what to say about them. Or perhaps they are about a number of different issues, making it impossible for you to focus on one topic, which you must do when writing a paper.

A better strategy is to find a topic based on a group of some sort, that is, Africans with a common background, experience, or characteristic. You might use the indexes following the catalog entries to study publishers, women, children, or Muslims, for example. You might also use your imagination or pursue an interest developed from an earlier reading or class and create your own group and topic, such as people who came from one village or town in Africa, those who were taken to some particular colony or region in the Americas, or the like. Consider investigating accounts from people associated with a particular event, such as *jihād* in West Africa, those transported on one slave ship, participants in a single slave revolt, or a revolution and warfare in the Americas. Consider also accounts produced during a particular chronological era, such as before and after emancipation in a particular era, after the US and Britain banned the transatlantic slave trade in 1808 (or other countries at other times), or by those liberated at sea by British warships and taken to Sierra Leone during a certain period. You might also compare two or more groups, such as Africans interviewed by different European scientists (such as Koclle, de Andrada, Castelnau, and Montgomery), or those arriving on different slave ships, such as the *Wanderer* in 1858 or the *Clotilda* in 1860.

An alternative to a group study is a microhistory of an individual, a family, or the like, provided there is sufficient documentation. A study of one family over two or three generations could be invaluable, for example. You might also study a Muslim cleric who did (or did not?) convert to Christianity in the Americas, or a warrior in Africa who continued that pursuit enslaved, free, or as a Maroon in the Americas. The list of possibilities is nearly endless, but the key is to search the catalog to ensure sufficient documentation is available and to choose a topic that is significant, not trivial.

An important part of a successful research plan is to find and read secondary sources related to your topic. These sources are critical to informing you about the topic generally, providing the context needed to better understand the topic, and helping develop an original and significant project—not one that repeats the work of another or is trivial. The bibliography at the end of this volume on works addressing the transatlantic slave trade will help, but you will need more. The references to secondary works on the individual at the end of each biography should be very helpful but will not be enough. To finish the work of educating yourself about what we already know and do not know about a topic, you should carefully read the footnotes and bibliographies of the above works and also consult knowledgeable faculty members, who might make further suggestions. This is difficult work, but keep in mind that you do have an advantage when searching for an original, significant topic: few if any scholars have ever done a study of African voices in the transatlantic slave trade based on such a large collection of texts, and a *lot* of scholars, teachers, and others will welcome such work, if it is done well.

After familiarizing yourself with the accounts available for a chosen group (i.e., which ones and how many are available and how much detail they contain) and secondary sources directly and indirectly related to the topic, it is time to frame a research question. Developing a good research question and then answering it will help keep your work focused. Sometimes even professional historians become so infatuated with their subjects that they neglect to do this, and their writing becomes diffuse and difficult to follow. An original, significant research question clearly stated at the beginning of an essay helps readers understand what the author is trying to do, and it helps authors stay on track as they complete their research and write up the results. It is critical to present a research question that you can answer by finding evidence in the African voices you have decided to study. After you have finished the research (or most of it), the answer you present to your question will be your thesis or argument.

Here are some examples of projects you might complete using the catalog:

1. African perspectives on "first encounters" with Europeans. Many of the Africans in this catalog describe the first time they saw a white person, usually as they were transported enslaved from the African interior to the coast to be put on a slave ship. How did Africans in these circumstances characterize white people, and what does this tell us about African beliefs and mentalities of the day?

2. African shipboard bonding on the Atlantic in slavery and freedom. Investigate all of the accounts from those on the *Amistad*, who rebelled and took over their ship in 1839 and tried to return to Africa but ended up in a Connecticut prison, and compare them to another ship, such as the *Avon*, which carried self-emancipated Yorubá from Cuba returning to Africa via England in 1854. How, if at all, did the shipboard experience in freedom and slavery affect their relations with one another or as a group?

3. Investigate those few Africans in the catalog (such as Little Ephraim Robin John and Ancona Robin Robin [*sic*] John, Nrs. 115 and 116, respectively) who were taken to the Americas and enslaved but were able to return to Africa via Europe, thus experiencing life in slavery and freedom on three (sometimes all four) Atlantic continents. What can their perspectives tell us about the Atlantic world or the Black Atlantic and how it functioned at this time?

4. Investigate those few Africans who were enslaved in the Americas and returned not just to Africa but to their original homes. What were their reactions and what does this tell us about the creation of an African identity at this time (or not)?

5. Rescue at sea. British warships that intercepted slave ships operating in the Atlantic illegally usually took these liberated Africans to the British colony of Sierra Leone in West Africa but not always. What other experiences did liberated Africans have, and what does this tell us about their responses to British policy and practice at the time?

6. African descriptions of the Middle Passage experience. We know a lot about this subject, but the many voices of the people who directly experienced it as victims still have not been studied in a comprehensive way. What were the varieties of experiences, and what—if anything—does this tell us about one or more aspects of this awful, yet critical element in Atlantic history?

7. Enslaved Africans in the transatlantic passage to Europe. Distinguishing from studies of free Africans or those of enslaved Africans in Europe that do not rely on African voices, investigate the few cases in the catalog of accounts by people taken enslaved to Europe via the transatlantic trade, not the Americas. What were their experiences, and what do they tell us about Africans and Europeans at this time?

8. Abolition, science, literature, and printing. What was the printing or publication history of a single or series of African voices in the Atlantic world, comparing those with or without significant proliferation, and what does this tell us about printers, readers, Africans, and others at this time?

We wish you much luck and success in writing your research papers using African voices. If you make significant use of this catalog to frame your project and find African voices, we ask that you reference our work in the following ways: Early in your written work, normally in the introduction when explaining how you designed your project, mention either in the text or a footnote that you used this catalog to find and begin assessing your African voices, citing it like this:

Aaron Spencer Fogleman and Robert Hanserd (eds.), *Five Hundred African Voices: A Catalog of Published Accounts by Africans Enslaved in the Transatlantic Slave Trade, 1586–1936* (Philadelphia: American Philosophical Society, 2022).

Place this entry in your bibliography as well. Later in your work, as you cite individual published African voices, you should properly cite those specific accounts only in your footnotes. There is no need to keep citing the catalog in the footnotes. Good luck with your work, and if you complete a project for which the catalog played a significant role, please send us a copy!

Photographic Essay

Robert Hanserd

The photographs presented in this essay are of peoples, cultures, and histories of Benin, Togo, and especially Ghana today—the descendants and legacies of many of the nearly five hundred African voices presented in this catalog and the places where they lived. These images from West Africa are representative of the region, but one may perceive connections to Africa more broadly. An ant hill near Larabanga, the broad smile of an elder herbalist in Sunyani, father and son spirit practitioners near Akuropon, a vodun priestess recounting and foretelling, and a silent fontomfrom drum just prior to its powerful and communicative rhythmic vibrations are people and scenes one might find elsewhere on the continent. Other photos depict returnees amid discoveries of continuity and discontinuity: in castles and dungeons, monuments, sacred groves, or in dance and music tradition, all related to the people, places, and cultures connected to the transatlantic slave trade. These images represent several decades of inquiry, reflection, and participation related to the Africans in this catalog, the 12.5 million victims of the transatlantic slave trade they represent, and continued Atlantic reverberations of these long-ago events and peoples, reminding us that all of this happened not so long ago at all.

Note: All photographs were taken by Robert Hanserd.

Ahosi, Royal Palace, Porto Novo, Benin, 2006.

Anthill, Larabanga, Ghana, 2008.

Fishing village, Togo, 2006.

Kente loom and weaver, Kumasi, Ghana, 2015.

Okyeame[AF2] (linguist), Akyem, Eastern Region, Ghana, 2022.

Sacred Baobab Tree, Salaga, Ghana 2008.

Rubber Tree, Manhyia Palace, Kumasi, Ghana, 2022.

Okomfo[AF1] (priest) and son near Abiriw-Akuropon border, Eastern Region, Ghana, 2016.

Bosom (totem or shrine) Kintampo, Brong-Ahafo, Ghana, 2008.

Dancer, near Cape Coast, Ghana, 2022.

Dancer, Abomey, Benin, 2006.

Tano Boase sacred grove, Techiman, Brong-Ahafo, Ghana, 2008.   Kintampo Waterfalls, Brong-Ahafo, Ghana, 2008.

Cape Coast Castle, Ghana, 2008.

Fishing Boats, Cape Coast, Ghana, 2015.

Martine DeSousa-Vodun Priestess, Ouidah, Benin, 2008.

Opanyin Kwadwo Yeboah, Odunsuni (herbalist), Sunyani, Ghana, 2022.

Funeral attendees, Kumasi, Ghana, 2016.

Fontomfrom Drums, Akuropon, Ghana, 2015.

Ft. Amsterdam/Koromantee, Abandze, Ghana, 2022.

Youth attendee, Royal Palace, Porto Novo, Benin, 2006.

Aburi Gardens, Aburi, Eastern Region, Ghana, 2006.

"Diaspora Returnees and locals," Door of No Return, Ouidah, Benin, 2006.

Vodoun Shrine, Cotonou, Benin, 2006.

Catalog Entries

1586

1.0 Alonso de Illescas

Manuscript letter with autobiographical content from Alonso de Illescas in Province of Esmeraldas to King Don Felipe and the royal affiliate in Quito, 25 February **1586**, held in the Ministerio de Cultura, Archivo General de Indias, **Sevilla, Andalucía, España**, Sección Escribanía 922b, fols. 192v–193v.

¶ Illescas was raised on the island of Tenerife, a Spanish possession off the northwest coast of Africa (see Map 2). As a youth he was taken to Seville, Spain (Map 7), and then while in his early twenties to the Spanish West Indies as a personal servant. He later escaped and became a leader of a Maroon community in Esmeraldas, on the northern coast of the Audiencia of Quito (present-day Ecuador), which was then within the Viceroyalty of Peru in New Spain (Map 9). A Trinitarian friar probably penned Illescas's letter to Philip II for him. In it, Illescas proposed an alliance against the region's indigenous people, thereby hoping to negotiate control over his region.

Full text: https://huskiecommons.lib.niu.edu/history-500africanvoices/1/ [see 1.1].

1.1 ——.

"*Maroon* Chief Alonso de Illescas' Letter to the Crown, 1586," being 1.0 printed in Spanish with English translation, introduction, and annotations by Charles Beatty-Medina, on pp. 30–37 (especially 34–37) in *Afro-Latino Voices: Narratives from the Early Modern Ibero-Atlantic World, 1550–1812*, edited by Kathryn McKnight and Leo J. Garofalo.

Indianapolis [Indiana, U.S.A.]: Hackett Publishing Co., **2009**. 8vo (23 cm.): xxxvii, 377 p.

1.2 ——.

"*Maroon* Chief Alonso de Illescas' Letter to the Crown, 1586," being the English translation (only) of 1.0 first printed in 1.1, printed with introduction and annotations by Charles Beatty-Medina on pp. 20–25 in *Afro-Latino Voices, **Shorter Edition**: Translations of Early Modern Ibero-Atlantic Narratives*, edited by Kathryn McKnight and Leo J. Garofalo.

Indianapolis [Indiana, U.S.A.]: Hackett Publishing Co., **2015**. 8vo (23 cm.): xli, 263 p.

1623

2.0 Juan Roque (–ca. 1623)

Manuscript "Testamento de Juan Roque, *negro* libre," held in the Archivo General de la Nación, **México, Distrito Federal, Estados Unidos Mexicanos**, Bienes Nacionales, vol. 1175, exp. 11, fols. 6r–7r and 17r–29r.

¶ Roque, a native of the Zape "nation" (in the Sierra Leone River region—see Map 4), was most likely forcibly transported on a slave ship to New Spain, thereafter living primarily in Mexico City. There he obtained his freedom, accrued significant wealth, and married a woman also from the Zape nation. This was, we think, the only *cofradía* (confraternity)

Full text: https://huskiecommons.lib.niu.edu/history-500africanvoices/2/ [see 2.1].

in New Spain based on African ethnicity. He became a pious Catholic, was fluent in Castilian, obtained his daughter's freedom, and owned several houses. His life story comes from his last will and testament.

2.1 ——.

"Juan Roque's Donation of a House to the *Zape* Confraternity, Mexico City, 1623," being 2.0 and related documents printed in Spanish with English translation, introduction, and annotations by Nicole von Germeten on pp. 83–103 (especially 86–91) in *Afro-Latino Voices: Narratives from the Early Modern Ibero-Atlantic World, 1550–1812*, edited by Kathryn McKnight and Leo J. Garofalo.

Indianapolis [Indiana, U.S.A.]: Hackett Publishing Co., **2009**. 8vo (23 cm.): xxxvii, 377 p.

2.2 ———.

"Juan Roque's Donation of a House to the *Zape* Confraternity, Mexico City, 1623," being the English translation (only) of 2.0 and related documents first printed in 2.1, printed with introduction and annotations by Nicole von Germeten on pp. 56–67 in *Afro-Latino Voices,* **Shorter Edition:** *Translations of*

Early Modern Ibero-Atlantic Narratives, edited by Kathryn McKnight and Leo J. Garofalo.

Indianapolis [Indiana, U.S.A.]: Hackett Publishing Co., 2015. 8vo (23 cm.): xli, 263 p.

1634

3.0 Anchico (1612–) = Sebastián

Manuscript trial testimony held in the Ministerio de Cultura, Archivo General de Indias, **Sevilla, Andalucía, España,** Patronato 234, ramo 7, no. 2. (Digital images 283–84, 319–324, 533–42, 549–554, 556).

Full text: https://huskiecommons.lib.niu.edu/history-500africanvoices/3/ [see 3.1].

¶ Sebastián's African origins and the circumstances of his enslavement are not yet known, but he stated his birth name was Anchico. He was taken with Francisco Angola (q.v. 4.0) in the Middle Passage to Cartagena in New Spain (present-day Colombia—see Map 9), where he was sold to Doña María de Viloria. In 1632 Maroons captured the enslaved Anchico and took him to their *palenque* (Maroon settlement) called Polín in the María district. Still later, Maroons from the Limón *palenque* raided Polín and took Anchico and others to their settlement, where Anchico had to serve Juan Angola (a *criollo*). After colonial authorities captured him, he testified at an official inquiry into the violent disturbances involving Maroons.

3.1 ———.

"Elder, Slave, and Soldier: Maroon Voices from the Palenque del Limón, 1634," being 3.0 printed in Spanish with English translation, introduction, and annotations by Kathryn McKnight on pp. 64–81 (especially 68–71) in *Afro-Latino Voices: Narratives from the Early Modern Ibero-Atlantic World, 1550-–1812,* edited by Kathryn McKnight and Leo J. Garofalo.

Indianapolis [Indiana, U.S.A.]: Hackett Publishing Co., 2009. 8vo (23 cm.): xxxvii, 377 p.

3.2 ———.

"Soldier, Slave, and Elder [*sic*]: Maroon Voices from the Palenque del Limón, 1634," being the English translation (only) of 3.0 first printed in 3.1, printed with introduction and annotations by Kathryn McKnight on pp. 43–54 in *Afro-Latino Voices,* **Shorter Edition:** *Translations of Early Modern Ibero-Atlantic Narratives,* edited by Kathryn McKnight and Leo J. Garofalo.

Indianapolis [Indiana, U.S.A.]: Hackett Publishing Co., 2015. 8vo (23 cm.): xli, 263 p.

4.0 Francisco Angola (1574–)

Manuscript trial testimony held in the Ministerio de Cultura, Archivo General de Indias, **Sevilla, Andalucía, España,** Patronato 234, ramo 7, no. 2. (Digital images 283–84, 319–324, 533–42, 549–554, 556).

Full text: https://huskiecommons.lib.niu.edu/history-500africanvoices/4/ [see 4.1].

¶ Francisco Angola was captured as a small boy in Angola (see Map 6) and taken—along with Anchico (q.v. 3.0)—on a slave ship to Cartagena in New Spain (present-day Colombia, Map 9). He and a friend escaped and took refuge at the *palenque* (Maroon settlement) in Limón. He had been living there for at least three years when colonial authorities attacked the settlement and captured him and others. He testified in 1634 at an official inquiry into violent disturbances involving Maroons.

4.1 ———.

"Elder, Slave, and Soldier: Maroon Voices from the Palenque del Limón, 1634," being 4.0 printed in Spanish with English translation, introduction, and annotations by Kathryn McKnight on pp. 64–81 (especially 68–69) in *Afro-Latino Voices: Narratives from the Early Modern Ibero-Atlantic World, 1550–1812,* edited by Kathryn McKnight and Leo J. Garofalo.

Indianapolis [Indiana, U.S.A.]: Hackett Publishing Co., 2009. 8vo (23 cm.): xxxvii, 377 p.

4.2 ———.

"Soldier, Slave, and Elder [*sic*]: Maroon Voices from the Palenque del Limón, 1634," being the English translation (only) of 4.0 first printed in 4.1, printed with introduction and annotations by Kathryn McKnight on pp. 43–54 in *Afro-Latino Voices,* **Shorter Edition:** *Translations of Early Modern Ibero-Atlantic Narratives,* edited by Kathryn McKnight and Leo J. Garofalo.

Indianapolis [Indiana, U.S.A.]: Hackett Publishing Co., 2015. 8vo (23 cm.): xli, 263 p.

1635

5.0 Francisco Biáfara (1607–)

Manuscript containing his responses during an "Inquiry carried out by Captain Juan de Ribas, Alcalde Mayor, into the Population that [tore] the English Enemy on the Island of Santa Catalina," Portobelo, 9 May **1635**, held in the Ministerio de Cultura, Archivo General de Indias, **Sevilla, Andalucía, España**, Audiencia de Santa Fe 223, no. 34, fols. 5r–15v.

Full text: https://huskiecommons.lib.niu.edu/history-500africanvoices/5/ [see 5.1].

¶ Francisco Biáfara was identified as Beafada from Bissau on the Geba River (present-day Guinea-Bissau—see Map 3), where Spanish missionaries may have exposed him to Catholicism. He was enslaved and taken with Juan Biáfara (q.v. 6.0) to Cartagena in New Spain (present-day Colombia—see Map 9). There he became a sailor on his owner's boat operating on the Río Grande de la Magdalena, where he and the rest of the crew were captured by Dutch privateers and carried to Santa Catalina (Providence Island). After seven months of enslavement there, he and others escaped back to the Spanish-American mainland. They testified at a formal inquiry in Portobelo (in present-day Panama) in 1635. Francisco spoke Spanish but could not write. He presented himself as a devout Catholic.

5.1 ———.

"A Spanish Caribbean Captivity Narrative: African Sailors and Puritan Slavers, 1635," being 5.0 printed in Spanish with English translation, introduction, and annotations by David Wheat on pp. 195–213 (especially 200–205) in *Afro-Latino Voices: Narratives from the Early Modern Ibero-Atlantic World, 1550–1812*, edited by Kathryn McKnight and Leo J. Garofalo.

Indianapolis [Indiana, U.S.A.]: Hackett Publishing Co., 2009. 8vo (23 cm.): xxxvii, 377 p.

5.2 ———.

"A Spanish Caribbean Captivity Narrative: African Sailors and Puritan Slavers, 1635," being the English translation (only) of 5.0 first printed in 5.1, printed with introduction and annotations by David Wheat on pp. 126–136 in *Afro-Latino Voices, Shorter Edition: Translations of Early Modern Ibero-Atlantic Narratives*, edited by Kathryn McKnight and Leo J. Garofalo.

Indianapolis [Indiana, U.S.A.]: Hackett Publishing Co., 2015. 8vo (23 cm.): xli, 263 p.

6.0 Juan Biáfara (ca. 1598–)

Manuscript containing his responses during an "Inquiry carried out by Captain Juan de Ribas, Alcalde Mayor, into the Population that [tore] the English Enemy on the Island of Santa Catalina," Portobelo, 9 May **1635**, held in the Ministerio de Cultura, Archivo General de Indias, **Sevilla, Andalucía, España**, Audiencia de Santa Fe 223, no. 34, fols. 5r–15v.

Full text: https://huskiecommons.lib.niu.edu/history-500africanvoices/6/ [see 6.1].

¶ Juan Biáfara was identified as Beafada from Bissau on the Geba River (present-day Guinea Bissau—see Map 3), where Spanish missionaries may have exposed him to Catholicism. He was enslaved and taken with Francisco Biáfara (q.v. 5.0) to Cartagena in New Spain (present-day Colombia, Map 9). There he became a sailor on his owner's boat operating on the Río Grande de la Magdalena, where he and the rest of the crew were captured by Dutch privateers and carried to Santa Catalina (Providence Island). After seven months of enslavement there from 1634 to 1635, he and others escaped back to the mainland. He testified at a formal inquiry in Portobelo (in present-day Panama) in 1635.

6.1 ———.

"A Spanish Caribbean Captivity Narrative: African Sailors and Puritan Slavers, 1635," being 6.0 printed in Spanish with English translation, introduction, and annotations by David Wheat on pp. 195–213 (especially 206–213) in *Afro-Latino Voices: Narratives from the Early Modern Ibero-Atlantic World, 1550–1812*, edited by Kathryn McKnight and Leo J. Garofalo.

Indianapolis [Indiana, U.S.A.]: Hackett Publishing Co., 2009. 8vo (23 cm.): xxxvii, 377 p.

6.2 ———.

"A Spanish Caribbean Captivity Narrative: African Sailors and Puritan Slavers, 1635," being the English translation (only) of 6.0 first printed in 6.1, printed with introduction and annotations by David Wheat on pp. 126–136 in *Afro-Latino Voices, Shorter Edition: Translations of Early Modern Ibero-Atlantic Narratives*, edited by Kathryn McKnight and Leo J. Garofalo.

Indianapolis [Indiana, U.S.A.]: Hackett Publishing Co., 2015. 8vo (23 cm.): xli, 263 p.

1666

7.0 María de Huancavelica (–ca. 1666)

Manuscript "Testamento e inventario de bienes de María de Huancavelica, morena libre, de casta folupa, Albacea: Gracia de la Paz, *Negra folupa* libre," held in the Archivo Arzobispal de **Lima, Peru**, Tribunal de Bienes de Difuntos 69:6, 1666, 70 folios, Lima.

¶ Huancavelica's last will and testament reveals that she was a Floupes, that is, Diola/Jola, from the region of the Casamance River on the upper Guinea coast (present-day Senegal—see Map 3). She was taken to the Audiencia of Lima in the Viceroyalty of Peru (Map 9) as a slave, where she lived in Lima to an old age. After gaining her freedom she amassed a small fortune, loaned money to others, became a slave owner, and died espousing Catholicism.

Full text: https://huskiecommons.lib.niu.edu/history-500africanvoices/7/ [see 7.1].

7.1 ———.

Spanish text of 7.0 with English translation printed on pp. 118–125 of José R. Jouve-Martín, "Death, Gender, and Writing: Testaments of Women of African Origins in Seventeenth-Century Lima, 1651–1666," pp. 105–125 in *Afro-Latino Voices: Narratives from the Early Modern Ibero-Atlantic World, 1550–1812*, edited by Kathryn McKnight and Leo J. Garofalo.

Indianapolis [Indiana, U.S.A.]: Hackett Publishing Co., 2009. 8vo (23 cm.): xxxvii, 377 p.

7.2 ———.

English translation (only) of 7.0 first printed in 7.1 printed on pp. 77–80 of José R. Jouve-Martín, "Death, Gender, and Writing: Testaments of Women of African Origins in Seventeenth-Century Lima, 1651–1666," pp. 68–80 in *Afro-Latino Voices, Shorter Edition: Translations of Early Modern Ibero-Atlantic Narratives*, edited by Kathryn McKnight and Leo J. Garofalo.

Indianapolis [Indiana, U.S.A.]: Hackett Publishing Co., 2015. 8vo (23 cm.): xli, 263 p.

1711

8.0 Jeannot (ca. 1683–)

"Interrogatoire de Jeannot, esclave du Sieur Deloré, Octobre **1711**," in Collection Moreau de Saint-Méry, F3/26, pp. 418–420, held in the Archives Nationales d'Outre-Mer, Aix-en-Provence, France.

¶ Jeannot was born in West Africa and identified as Amina (a New World ethnic designation for Akan speakers near Elmina Castle, present-day Ghana—see Map 5). Before 1710 he was taken in the slave trade to Martinique, a French colony in the Caribbean, baptized into the Roman Catholic Church, and enslaved by militia officer Sieur Deloré. His ac-

Full text: https://huskiecommons.lib.niu.edu/history-500africanvoices/8/ [see 8.1].

count exists within his testimony in a police report regarding Maroon activity and a conspiracy in the previous year. It is not clear whether Jeannot himself was accused.

8.1 ———.

"Interrogatoire de Jeannot, esclave du Sieur Deloré, Octobre 1711," printed on pp. 48–51 within article by Myriam Cottias, "L'affaire dite du Gaoulet de 1710," on pp. 15–53 of *Voix d'Esclaves Antilles, Guyane et Louisane Françaises, XVIIIᵉ-XIXᵉ Siècles*, edited by Dominique Rogers.

Paris [France]: Karthala; CIRESC*; Fort-de-France [Martinique]: SAA, 2015. *Centre International de Recherches sur les Esclavages. **Society of American Archivists.** 8vo (22 cm.): 184 p., illus.

1719

9.0 Ana de la Calle (–ca. 1719)

Manuscript "Dossier filed by Don Ambrosio Girón de Estrada, public prosecutor of the bishopric of Trujillo, executor for the deceased Ana de la Calle, free *morena*, against Don Faus-

tino de Vidaurre, executor and trustee for the deceased Doña María de la Cruz Cavero, regarding payment of the rents owed on the lease imposed on the house that she had inherited from the said Ana de la Calle," held in the Archivo Departamental/Regional de La Libertad, Cabildo [**Trujillo, Libertad,**

Peru], Causas Ordinarias, legajo 41, exp. 753 (1727), fols. 8v–14v. *The present compilers thank Dr. Rachel Sarah O'Toole for assistance with this entry.*

¶ De la Calle called herself *Lucumí*—a New World ethnic identity attributed to the Yorùbá (present-day Nigeria, Benin, and Togo—see Map 5)—before being sold to Atlantic merchants. After enduring enslavement and the Middle Passage, she was freed (becoming a *morena*, i.e., free woman of color) and lived in Trujillo, in the Audiencia of Lima in the Spanish South American Viceroyalty of Peru (Map 9). She married twice—first, when pregnant, to a *moreno* (free man of color). She sold bread and other items in the streets and owned a house in Trujillo, where she also may have practiced as a ritual specialist. Her daughter, grandchildren, and their husbands, and an enslaved woman lived in the household. In her last will and testament, written in Trujillo in 1719, de la Calle declared her commitment to Catholic beliefs.

Full text: https://huskiecommons.lib.niu.edu/history-500africanvoices/9/ [see 9.1].

9.1 ——.

"The Making of a Free *Lucumí* Household: Ana de la Calle's Will and Goods, Northern Peruvian Coast, 1719," being 9.0 printed in Spanish with English translation, introduction, and annotations by Rachel Sarah O'Toole on pp. 142–153 (especially 146–151) in *Afro-Latino Voices: Narratives from the Early Modern Ibero-Atlantic World, 1550–1812,* edited by Kathryn McKnight and Leo J. Garofalo.

Indianapolis [Indiana, U.S.A.]: Hackett Publishing Co., 2009. 8vo (23 cm.): xxxvii, 377 p.

9.2 ——.

"The Making of a Free *Lucumí* Household: Ana de la Calle's Will and Goods, Northern Peruvian Coast, 1719," being the English translation (only) of 9.0 first printed in 9.1, printed with introduction and annotations by Rachel Sarah O'Toole on pp. 93–100 in *Afro-Latino Voices, Shorter Edition: Translations of Early Modern Ibero-Atlantic Narratives,* edited by Kathryn McKnight and Leo J. Garofalo.

Indianapolis [Indiana, U.S.A.]: Hackett Publishing Co., 2015. 8vo (23 cm.): xli, 263 p.

1725

10.0 Louis Congo

His account in Copy of Deliberations of Superior Council of Louisiana, 24 October 1725, New Orleans, Archives Nationales d'Outre-Mer (ANOM), **Aix-en-Provence, France,** C13A9, fol. 259, 21 Nov 1725, fol. 267v.

¶ Louis identified as Congo and was taken on the slave ship *La Néréide* from there to New Orleans (in the French colony of Louisiana in North America—see Map 15) in 1721 and sold to the Company of the Indies plantation. Because of his physical prowess and character he was offered the colony's public executioner position in 1725, which he accepted after negotiating for his own freedom and that of his wife, as well as other demands, including a plot of land sepa-

Full text: https://huskiecommons.lib.niu.edu/history-500africanvoices/10/ [see 10.1].

rate from the others'. He held this position until at least 1737, incurring resentment that led to his being physically assaulted on occasion by other Blacks and Native Americans in the colony. Eventually he became at least somewhat literate. For more on Louis Congo, see Shannon Lee Dawdy, *Building the Devil's Empire: French Colonial New Orleans* (Chicago: University of Chicago Press, 2008), pp. 189–91; and Gwendolyn Mildo Hall, *Africans in Colonial Louisiana* (Baton Rouge: Louisiana State University Press, 1992), pp. 132–133.

10.1 ——.

Quotation from 10.0 within account of his life printed on pp. 211–212 in Sophie White, *Voices of the Enslaved: Love, Labor, and Longing in French Louisiana.*

Chapel Hill [North Carolina, U.S.A.]: University of North Carolina Press, 2019. 8vo (24 cm.): viii, 344 p., illus.

1734

11.1 Ayuba Sulayman Diallo (1701–ca. 1772) = Dgiagola = Job ben Solomon = Sulaiman

Some Memoirs of the Life of Job, the Son of Solomon the High Priest of Boonda in Africa; Who was a Slave about two Years in Maryland; and afterwards being brought to England, was set free, and sent to his native Land in the Year 1734. By [i.e., as told to] *Thomas Bluett, Gent. who was intimately acquainted with him in America, and came over to England with him.*

11.1 Ayuba Sulayman Diallo

London [England]: Printed for Richard Ford, at the Angel in the Poultry, over against the Compter [sic], M.DCC.XXXIV [1734]. (Price one shilling.)
8vo: 63, [1] p.
Hogg 1457; ESTC t103023.

¶ Ayuba Sulayman Diallo was a well-educated Muslim from Fuuta Bondu or Bundu in the Senegal River valley of West Africa (see Map 3). Seized in 1730, he was sent to the British North American colony of Maryland (Map 15), where he remained enslaved until departing from Annapolis for England in 1733 with Thomas Bluett (ca. 1690–1749), an attorney interested in his case. Bluett secured Diallo's freedom and, aided by another enslaved African American serving as translator, prepared his memoirs (11.1) for publication. His fame increased when his engraved portrait appeared in *The Gentleman's Magazine* (London [England]: Printed by E. Cave) vol. 20 (1750), p. 272. He wrote a number of letters in Arabic, one of which is reprinted in Curtin's volume of narratives with an English translation (11.16); others (held in the British Library, London, England) have been translated by Paul Naylor and Marion Wallace and published in 2019 (+11-C.1). In 1734 Diallo sailed with Francis Moore, a Royal African Company agent, from London (Map 8) to the Gambia River in West Africa. For more on Ayuba Sulayman Diallo see: *Africa Remembered: Narratives by West Africans from the Era of the Slave Trade*, edited by Philip D. Curtin (Madison: Univ. of Wisconsin Press, 1967), pp. 17–34; Douglas Grant, *The Fortunate Slave: an Illustration of African Slavery in the Early Eighteenth Century* (London: Oxford University Press, 1968); and Allan D. Austin, *African Muslims in Antebellum America: Transatlantic Stories and Spiritual Struggles* (New York: Routledge, 1997), pp. 50–62.

http://docsouth.unc.edu/neh/bluett/bluett.html [see 11.1].

11.2 ——.

Substantive references to Ayuba Sulayman Diallo (as Job ben Solomon) published in Francis Moore, *Travels into the Inland Parts of Africa, containing a Description of the several Nations for the space of Six Hundred Miles up the River Gambia, their Trade, Habits, Customs, Language, Manners, Religions and Government; the Power, Disposition and Characters of some Negro Princes, **with a particular Account of Job Ben Solomon, a Pholey, who was in England in the Year 1733, and known by the Name of the African**. To which is added, Capt. Sibb's Voyage up the Gambia in the Year 1723, to make Discoveries. With an accurate Map of that River taken on the spot. And many other Copper Plates. Also extracts from the Nubian's Geography, Leo the African, and other authors antient [sic] and modern, concerning the Niger-Nile, or Gambia, and Observations thereon.*

London [England]: Printed by Edward Cave, at St. John's Gate, for the Author, and sold by J. Stagg in Westminster Hall and St. John's Gate aforesaid, M.DCC.XXXVIII [1738].
8vo: xi, xiii, 305, [1], 86; [4], 23, [1] p., plates, map. https://babel.hathitrust.org/cgi/pt?id=uc2.ark:/13960/t7zk5fs6r
https://archive.org/details/travelsintoinlan00moor/page/n6/mode/1up
ESTC t131766.

11.3 ——.

German translation of extracts from 11.1 printed as *Die merkwürdige Gefangenschaft und Befreyung Job ben Solomons ... nahe bey der Gambia, im Jahre 1732, welcher einige Anmerkungen von dem Königreiche Futa beygefüget sind* in vol. 3, pp. 127–139 of Johann Joachim Schwabe, *Allgemeine Historie der Reisen zu Wasser und Lande*.

Leipzig [Saxony, Germany]: bey Arkstee und Merkus, 1748.
4to (25 cm.): [10], 668, [26] p.
http://digitale.bibliothek.uni-halle.de/vd18/content/pageview/12363592

11.4 ——.

Substantive references to Ayuba Sulayman Diallo (as Job ben Solomon) published in Francis Moore, *Travels into the Inland Parts of Africa, containing a Description of the several Nations for the space of Six Hundred Miles up the River Gambia, their Trade, Habits, Customs, Language, Manners, Religions and Government; the Power, Disposition and Characters of some Negro Princes, with a particular Account of Job Ben Solomon, a Pholey, who was in England in the Year 1733, and known by the Name of the African. To which is added .... The Second Edition.*

London [England]: Printed by D. Henry and R. Cave, at St. John's Gate [1755?].
8vo: xi, xiii, 159, 168–229 [1], 84; [4], 25, [1] p., plates, map.
ESTC t147986.

11.5 ——.

Two-paragraph derivative biographical summary printed on p. 102 in *Biographical Sketches and Interesting Anecdotes of Persons of Color. To Which Is Added, a Selection of Pieces in Poetry*, compiled by A[bigail] Mott.

New York [New York, U.S.A.]: Printed and Sold by Mahlon Day, No. 376, Pearl-street, 1826.
12mo (18 cm.): iv, [5]-192 p. Preface dated on p. iv: *Hickory Grove* [N.Y.], 11*th* mo. 1825.
http://docsouth.unc.edu/neh/mott26/mott26.html
https://babel.hathitrust.org/cgi/pt?id=hvd.hn3m6e&view=1up&seq=106
Hogg 1467.

11.6 ———.

Two-paragraph derivative biographical summary printed on p. 147 in *Biographical Sketches and Interesting Anecdotes of Persons of Color*. Compiled by A[bigail] Mott.

York [England]: Printed and Sold by W. Alexander & Son, Castlegate; sold also by Harvey & Darton, W. Phillips, E. Fry, and W. Darton, **London**; R. Peart [*sic*], Birmingham; D. F. Gardiner, **Dublin** [Ireland], 1826.
12mo (20 cm.): xi, [2], 2–240 p.
https://babel.hathitrust.org/cgi/pt?id=nyp.33433081774204
&view=1up&seq=167

11.7 ———.

Two-paragraph derivative biographical summary printed on p. 147 in *Biographical Sketches and Interesting Anecdotes of Persons of Color. To Which Is Added, a Selection of Pieces in Poetry*, compiled by A[bigail] Mott. "Second Edition."

York [Yorkshire, England]: Printed and Sold by W. Alexander & Son; sold also by Harvey and Darton, W. Phillips, E. Fry, and W. Darton, **London** [England]; R. Peart [*sic*], **Birmingham** [England]; D. F. Gardiner, **Dublin** [Ireland], 1828.
8vo (19.8 cm.): xi, [1], 252 p.

11.8 ———.

Concise synopsis of his ordeal printed on pp. 165–166, within Chapter VI ("Intellect of Negroes") in Mrs. [Lydia Maria] Child, *An Appeal in Favor of that Class of Americans called Africans*.

Boston [Massachusetts, U.S.A.]: Allen and Ticknor, 1833. Tpv: Tuttle & Weeks, Printers, No. 8, School Street.
8vo (20 cm.): [vi], 323 p.
https://babel.hathitrust.org/cgi/pt?id=nyp.33433075994958
&view=1up&seq=179

11.9 ———.

Two-paragraph derivative biographical summary printed on p. 132 in *Biographical Sketches and Interesting Anecdotes of Persons of Color. To which is added, a Selection of Pieces in Poetry*, compiled by A[bigail] Mott. "Second Edition, much Enlarged."

New-York [New York, U.S.A.]: Mahlon Day, 374 Pearl-street, 1837. Tpv: "Note by the publisher. By consent of the Compiler, and at the recommendation of the Trustees of the African Free Schools in New York, (who have liberally patronized the work,) ..."
8vo (19 cm.): 260 p. (of which p. [256] is blank, and pp. 257–260 are table of contents).
https://babel.hathitrust.org/cgi/pt?id=hvd.32044004358602
&view=1up&seq=136

11.10 ———.

Two-paragraph derivative biographical summary printed on p. 212 in *Biographical Sketches and Interesting Anecdotes of Persons of Color. To which is added, a Selection of Pieces in Poetry*, compiled by A[bigail] Mott.

New York [New York, U.S.A.]: Stereotyped for and printed by order of the Trustees of the residuary estate of Lindley Murray, M. Day, Printer, 374 Pearl St., 1838.
8vo (18.7 cm.): iv, 408 p.

11.11 ———.

Two-paragraph derivative biographical summary printed on p. 212 in *Biographical Sketches and Interesting Anecdotes of Persons of Color. To Which Is Added, a Selection of Pieces in Poetry*, compiled by A[bigail] Mott.

New York [New York, U.S.A.]: Stereotyped for and printed by order of the Trustees of the residuary estate of Lindley Murray. M. Day, Printer, 271 Pearl St. [1839?]. Posited year of printing from p. [ii] "Advertisement" (could be slightly later).
12mo (19 cm.): vi, [7]–408 p.
https://archive.org/details/biographicalsket00mottrich/page/
n4 (incomplete 370-page exemplar).
https://babel.hathitrust.org/cgi/pt?id=loc.ark:/13960/t2q52p-
81p&view=1up&seq=3 (complete).

11.12 ———.

Derivative biographical sketch printed under heading "Job Ben Solliman" on pp. 239–241 in Wilson Armistead's compendium *A Tribute for the Negro: Being a Vindication of the Moral, Intellectual, and Religious Capabilities of the Colored Portion of Mankind; with Particular Reference to the African Race*.

Manchester [England]: William Irwin; **London**: Charles Gilpin; American Agent: Wm. Harned, Anti-Slavery Office, 61, John Street, **New York** [New York, U.S.A.]; and may be had of H. Longstreath and G.W. Taylor, **Philadelphia** [Pennsylvania, U.S.A.], 1848. Tpv: Manchester: Printed by William Irwin, 39, Oldham Street.
8vo (24 cm.): xxxv, 564 p.
https://babel.hathitrust.org/cgi/pt?id=nc01.ark:/13960/
t42r4z659;view=1up;seq=13
http://docsouth.unc.edu/neh/armistead/armistead.html

11.13 ———.

Two-paragraph derivative biographical summary printed on p. 212 in *Biographical Sketches and Interesting Anecdotes of Persons of Color. To which is added, a Selection of Pieces in Poetry*, compiled by A[bigail] Mott.

New York [New York, U.S.A.]: Stereotyped for and printed by order of the Trustees of the residuary estate of Lindley Murray, 1850.
12mo (20 cm.): iv, [7]–408 p.

11.14 ——.
Two-paragraph derivative biographical summary printed on p. 212 in *Biographical Sketches and Interesting Anecdotes of Persons of Color. To which is added, a Selection of Pieces in Poetry.* Compiled by A[bigail] Mott.

New York [New York, U.S.A.]: Stereotyped for and printed by order of the Trustees of the residuary estate of Lindley Murray. D. Fanshaw, Printer, 35 Ann, corner of Nassau-street, 1854.
12mo (19 cm.): iv, [7]–408 p.
https://digital.ncdcr.gov/digital/collection/p249901coll37/id/10410

11.15 ——.
Biographical summary comprising four long paragraphs printed on pp. 41–42 in Rev. S. R. B. Attoh Ahuma, *Memoirs of West African Celebrities Europe, &c. (1700–1850). With special reference to the Gold Coast.*

Liverpool [England]: D. Marples & Co., 508 Lord Street, 1905.
8vo (19 cm.): xix, 260 p., frontispiece portrait.
https://babel.hathitrust.org/cgi/pt?id=ien.35556038054839&view=1up&seq=71

11.16 ——.
Excerpt from 11.1 printed under heading "The Capture and Travels of Ayuba Suleiman Ibrahima" on pp. 34–59 of *Africa Remembered: Narratives by West Africans from the Era of the Slave Trade*, edited by Philip D. Curtin.

Madison [Wisconsin, U.S.A.]: University of Wisconsin Press, 1967.
8vo (24cm.): x, 363 p., illus., maps.

11.17 ——. [Second printing of 11.16]
Excerpt from 11.1 printed under heading "The Capture and Travels of Ayuba Suleiman Ibrahima" on pp. 34–59 of *Africa Remembered: Narratives by West Africans from the Era of the Slave Trade*, edited by Philip D. Curtin.

Madison [Wisconsin, U.S.A.]: University of Wisconsin Press, 1968.
8vo (22 cm.): x, 363 p., illus., maps.

11.18 ——.
Full account (11.1) with editorial apparatus and additional writings from Diallo printed on pp. 73–120 of *African Mus-

lims in Antebellum America: A Source Book*, edited by Allan D. Austin.

New York [New York, U.S.A.]: Garland Publishing, 1984.
8vo (23 cm.): xiv, 759 [*sic*] p., maps.

11.19 ——. [Another printing of 11.16]
"The Capture and Travels of Ayuba Suleiman Ibrahima" printed on pp. 34–59 of *Africa Remembered: Narratives by West Africans from the Era of the Slave Trade*, edited by Philip D. Curtin.

Prospect Heights [Illinois, U.S.A.]: Waveland Press, 1997.
8vo (23 cm.): x, 363 p., illus., maps.

11.20 ——. [Photomechanical reprint of 11.9]
Two-paragraph derivative biographical summary printed on p. 132 in 有色人に関する伝記的資料 / *Biographical Sketches and Interesting Anecdotes of Persons of Color. To which is added, a Selection of Pieces in Poetry*, compiled by A[bigail] Mott. "Second Edition, much Enlarged."

Tokyo, Japan: 日本図書センター, Nihon Tosho Senta, 2000.
8vo (27 cm.): 255 p.

11.21 ——.
"Some Memoirs of the Life of Job, the Son of Solomon," reprinted from 11.1 on pp. 37–96 in *Five Classic Muslim Slave Narratives: Selim Aga, Job Ben Sulaiman, Nicholas Said, Omar ibn Said, [and] Abu Bakr Sadiq*, edited by Muhammad A. Al-Ahari.

[Chicago, Illinois, U.S.A.]: Magribine Press, [2006]. "First edition." Examined exemplar colophon: Made in USA | Columbia, SC | 30 June 2018.
8vo (23 cm.): 210 p., illus. (portraits). Al-Ahari's introductory essay "Rescuing Arabic and English Islamic Slave Narratives from the Shifting Sands of Time: The Historicity of Muslim Narratives in the Americas," pp. 7–36.
Additional publications by Ayuba Suleiman Diallo

+11-A.1a ——.
Ayuba Suleiman Diallo's letter from London to his former owner in Maryland printed after prefatory explanation ("The following is a letter from the Negro Prince, sometime after he arrived in London, to his master in Maryland. Transcribed by Dr [*sic*] Desaguillier, of Cambridge, 1743" [typographical error for 1734]) in the June 1772 issue of *The Scots Magazine*, vol. 34, pp. 301–302, signed in type on p. 302: "*Dgiagola, Son of Dgiagola, Prince of Foat, Africa*" (Edinburgh [Scotland]: Printed by A. Murray and J. Cochran, 1772).

https://babel.hathitrust.org/cgi/pt?id=nyp.33433081660049; view=1up;seq=327. Hogg 1460.

Figure 1: Portrait of Ayuba Sulayman Diallo, also known as Dgiagola, Job ben Solomon, or Sulaiman (1701–ca. 1772), completed in 1733 while in London, after his release from enslavement in Maryland and before his return to his homeland on the Gambia River in West Africa.

Source: Oil on canvas by William Hoare, 1733, OM.762. Orientalist Museum, Doha. Qatar.

+11-A.1b ——.

Another issue of item +11-A.1a with *Scots Magazine* general title page for vol. 34 dated 1774. Hogg 1460.

+11-B.1 ——.

Ayuba Suleiman Diallo's (Job Ben Solomon's) letter from Yanimerow, Gambia River, to Mr. Smith, 27 January 1736, printed in vol. 2, pp. 455–456, of *Documents Illustrative of the History of the Slave Trade to America*, edited by Elizabeth Donnan (Washington [DC, U.S.A.]: Carnegie Institution of Washington, 1930–35). 4 vols., 4to. Donnan's editorial note: "From Shelburne MSS., XLIV. 869. 'In the archives of the Royal Society there are two letters, numbered r. 2. ax, and r. 2.22, Catalogue of Miscellaneous Manuscripts, p. 68, nos. 16:4, 1615."

+11-B.2 ——.

Photomechanical reprint of Elizabeth Donnan's *Documents Illustrative of the History of the Slave Trade to America* with imprint: New York [New York, U.S.A.]: Octagon Books, 1969.

+11-B.3-10 ——.

Ayuba Suleiman Diallo's (Job Ben Solomon's) letter from Yanimerow, Gambia River, to Mr. Smith, 27 January 1736, reprinted on pp. 5–7 in *Slave Testimony: Two Centuries of Letters, Speeches, Interviews, and Autobiographies,* edited by John W. Blassingame. Baton Rouge [Louisiana, U.S.A.]: Louisiana State University Press, *eight printings* 1977–2009.

+11-B.11 ——.

Photomechanical reprint of Elizabeth Donnan's *Documents Illustrative of the History of the Slave Trade to America* with imprint: Buffalo, New York [U.S.A.]: William S. Hein and Company, 2002. 4 vols., 4to.

+11-C.1 ——.

Additional letters written by Ayuba Suleiman Diallo published in Paul Naylor and Marion Wallace, "Author of his Own Fate? The Eighteenth-Century Writings of Ayuba Sulayman Diallo," *Journal of African History,* 60:3 (2019), pp. 343–77.

1739

12.0 Damma (ca. 1657–1745) = Marotta = Magdalena

Two manuscripts, both comprising Dutch Creole and Aja-Ayizo epistolary petitions to the Danish queen (i.e., Sophia Magdalene [1700–1770]) and king (Christian VI [1699–1746]) on behalf of Protestant Moravians of color residing on the island of St. Thomas, viz.:

https://archive.org/details/cgaoldendorpsges12olde/page/598/mode/2up [see 12.4].

12.0a: held in the Unity Archives, Herrnhut, Saxony, Germany (R.15.Ba.3.61); and
12.0b: held in the Moravian Archives, Bethlehem, Pennsylvania, U.S.A., among their collection of "Letters to the Danish King [*sic*]," St. Thomas Letters, 1734–1766.

¶ Damma, or Marotta, was from Grand Popo, the Popo (Hula) kingdom's political and trade center (port) in the Bight of Benin (present-day Benin, Togo, Nigeria—see Map 5). She and her family embraced Roman Catholicism, having probably converted after contact with Capuchin missionaries in the 1660s. Damma was baptized and grew up learning to read and write Aja-Ayizo (her first language) and perhaps Portuguese. In the 1690s she was sold during the civil wars and taken to

the Danish West Indies island of St. Thomas in the Caribbean. Her owner freed her in the early 1730s, probably because of her age. By then she was also literate in Dutch Creole. In 1736 she converted to the Protestant Moravians and became a leader in their new St. Thomas mission. Her petition to the Danish queen on their behalf includes elements of her life story. See Ray A. Kea, "From Catholicism to Moravian Pietism: The World of Marotta/ Magdalena, a Woman of Popo and St. Thomas," in *The Creation of the British Atlantic World,* edited by Elizabeth Mancke and Carole Shammas (Baltimore: The Johns Hopkins University Press, 2015), pp. 115–136.

12.1a ——.

Her Aja-Ayizo and Dutch Creole epistolary petitions printed under heading "Der Aeltestin der Gemeine der Negros in St. Thomas Schreiben an die Königin von Dännemarck. An. 1739" on pp. 485–487 in **Part 4** (the fourth of six sequentially published separate parts that would altogether eventually comprise vol. 1, *q.v.* 12.1b) of *Büdingische Sammlung einiger in die Kirchen-historie einschlagender Sonderlich neuerer Schrifften.*

Leipzig [Saxony, Germany]: in Commission bey D[avid] Korte, **1741.**

8vo (18 cm.): [4], 417–556 p.

12.1b ⸺.

Part 4 (carrying 12.1a, as specified immediately above) included whole within the completed first volume (comprising in all 6 parts initially separately published) of *Büdingische Sammlung einiger in die Kirchen-historie einschlagender Sonderlich neuerer Schrifften* with added general title page carrying imprint:

Leipzig [Saxony, Germany]: in Commission by D[avid] Korte, **1742.**
8vo (18 cm.): [34], 820, [22] p.
http://digital.bibliothek.uni-halle.de/hd/content/pageview/628783

12.2 ⸺.

"A Translation [into English, from 12.1] of Two Letters from some Negroes in the American Island of St. Thomas, belonging to the King of Denmark, which are brought to the Communion of the Gospel of our Blessed Lord and Saviour, and baptised by the Ministry of some Meravian [*i.e.* Moravian] Brethren" printed on pp. 58–60 in no. IV of *The Christian Monthly History: or An Account of the Revival and Progress of Religion, Abroad and at Home* [edited by James Robe].

Edinburgh [Scotland]: Printed by R. Fleming and A. Alison, and sold by the Booksellers in the Town and Country, M.DCC.XLIV [**1744**].
8vo (19 cm.).
ESTC P-176.

12.3a ⸺. [Reprinting of 12.2]

"A Translation of Two Letters from some Negroes in the American Island of St. Thomas, belonging to the King of Denmark, which are brought to the Communion of the Gospel of our Blessed Lord and Saviour, and baptised by the Ministry of some Meravian [*i.e.* Moravian] Brethren," on pp. 58–60 in monthly Part IV (1743) of [note altered title] *The Christian History, containing Account of the Revival and Propagation of Religion in Great-Britain & America* [edited by James Robe],

Boston [Massachusetts], N[ew] E[ngland]: Printed by S. Kneeland & T. Green, for T. Prince, Junr., **1743.**
8vo (21 cm.).
Evans 5360.

12.3b ⸺. [Reissue of 12.3a]

"A Translation of Two Letters from some Negroes in the American Island of St. Thomas, belonging to the King of Denmark, which are brought to the Communion of the Gospel of our Blessed Lord and Saviour, and baptised by the Ministry of some Meravian [*i.e.* Moravian] Brethren," on pp. 58–60 of vol. 1 of [note altered title] *The Christian History, contain-*

ing Account of the Revival and Propagation of Religion in Great-Britain & America [edited by James Robe].

Boston [Massachusetts], N[ew] E[ngland]: Printed by S. Kneeland & T. Green, for T. Prince, Junr., **1744–1745.**
2 vols., 8vo (21 cm.).
Evans 5360; ESTC w41560 ("First issued in 104 weekly parts, between March 5, 1743, and February 23, 1745, and reissued with indexes and general title pages").

12.4 ⸺.

German translation of epistolary petitions to the queen and king printed on pp. 598–600 in Christian Georg Andreas Oldendorp, *Geschichte der Mission der evangelischen Brueder auf den caraibischen Inseln S. Thomas, S. Croix, und S. Jan,* edited by Johann Jakob Bossart.

Barby [Saxony-Anhalt, Germany]: Christian Friedrich Laur; **Leipzig [Saxony, Germany]:** Weidmanns Erben und Reich, **1777.**
2 volumes in 1, 8vo (19 cm.).
https://archive.org/details/cgaoldendorpsges12olde/page/598/mode/2up

12.5 ⸺.

Photomechanical reprint of 12.1, "Der Aeltestin der Gemeine der Negros in St. Thomas Schreiben an die Königin von Dännmarck. An. 1739," on pp. 485–487 in *Büdingische Sammlung 4* (1741), in series *Ergänzungsbände zu den Hauptschriften,* vol. 4: Nikolaus Ludwig von Zinzendorf, *Theologische und dahin einschlagende Bedenken; Naturelle Reflexionen ueber allerhand Materien, nach der Art, wie er bei sich selbst zu denken gewohnt ist.*

Hildesheim [Lower Saxony, Germany]: Georg Olms Verlag, **1964.**
8vo (18 cm): XII, 820 p.

12.6 ⸺.

Epistolary petition to queen printed on p. 52 of Christian Degn, *Die Schimmelmanns im atlantischen Dreieckshandel: Gewinn und Gewissen.*

Neumünster [Germany]: Karl Wachholtz, **1974.**
8vo (26 cm.): 599 p., illus.

12.7 ⸺. [Second printing of 12.6]

Epistolary petition to queen printed on p. 52 of Christian Degn, *Die Schimmelmanns im atlantischen Dreieckshandel: Gewinn und Gewissen*

Neumünster [Germany]: Karl Wachholtz, **1984.**
8vo (26 cm.): 599 p., illus.

12.8 ———. [English translation of 12.4]

English translation of Damma's epistolary petition on p. 365 of Christian Georg Andreas Oldendorp, *History of the Mission of the Evangelical Brethren on the Caribbean Islands of St. Thomas, St. Croix, and St. John*, edited by Johann Jakob Bossard (i.e., Bossart), translated into English and further edited by Arnold R. Highfield and Vladimir Barac.

Ann Arbor [Michigan, U.S.A.]: Karoma Publishers, **1987**.
8vo (24 cm.): xxxv, 737 p., illus.

12.9 ———.

Another printing of 12.4 on pp. 598–600 of photomechanical reprint of the 1777 edition of Christian Georg Andreas Oldendorp, *Geschichte der Mission der evangelischen Brüder auf den caraibischen Inseln S. Thomas, S. Croix und S. Jan*, edited by Erich Beyreuther und Matthias Meyer (Volume 27.1 in Series 2 of Nikolaus Ludwig Graf von Zinzendorf, *Leben und Werk in Quellen und Darstellungen*).

Hildesheim [Saxony, Germany]: Georg Olms Verlag, **1995**.
8vo (20 cm.): 62, 444 p., illus.

12.10 ———.

Epistolary petition to queen printed in Creole and English on pp. 70–74 in *Die Creol Taal: 250 Years of Negerhollands Texts*, edited by Cefas van Rossem and Hein van der Voort.

Amsterdam [Netherlands]: Amsterdam University Press, **1996**.
8vo (24 cm.) 325 p., illus., map.

12.11 ———. [Third printing of 12.6]

Epistolary petition to queen printed on p. 52 in Christian Degn, *Die Schimmelmanns im atlantischen Dreieckshandel: Gewinn und Gewissen*.

Neumünster [Germany]: Karl Wachholtz, **2000**.
8vo (25 cm.): 599 p., illus.

12.12 ———.

Epistolary petition to queen and king printed on p. 357 of vol. 1 in Christian Georg Andreas Oldendorp, *Historie der caribischen Inseln Sanct Thomas, Sanct Crux und Sanct Jan, insbesondere der dasigen Neger und der Mission der evangelischen Brüder unter denselben: kommentierte Ausgabe des vollständigen Manuskriptes aus dem Archiv der Evangelischen Brüder-Unität Herrnhut*, edited by Gudrun Meier et al. (Band [Volume] 51 in the series *Abhandlungen und Berichte des Staatlichen Museums für Völkerkunde Dresden*,)

Berlin [Germany]: VWB, Verlag für Wissenschaft und Bildung, **2000–2002**.
2 vols. in 4, 8vo (24 cm.).
Vol. 1 (2000): 764 p.; xxxviii, illus.

12.13 ———.

English translation of Damma's epistolary petition printed on p. 145 and photomechanical reproduction of the Aja-Ayizo and Dutch Creole versions as printed in 1741 in *Büdingische Sammlung* 4 (12.1, above) printed on p. 146 of Jon F. Sensbach, *Rebecca's Revival: Creating Black Christianity in the Atlantic World*.

Cambridge [Massachusetts, U.S.A.]: Harvard University Press, **2005**.
8vo (22 cm.): 302 p., illus.

12.14 ———. [Paperback reprinting of 12.13]

English translation of Damma's epistolary petition printed on p. 145 and photomechanical reproduction of the Aja-Ayizo and Dutch Creole versions as printed in 1741 in *Büdingische Sammlung* 4 (12.1, above) printed on p. 146 of Jon F. Sensbach, *Rebecca's Revival: Creating Black Christianity in the Atlantic World*.

Cambridge [Massachusetts, U.S.A.]: Harvard University Press, **2006**.
8vo (22 cm.): 302 p., illus.

12.15 ———.

English translation of the Dutch Creole epistolary petition and reprinting of the German petition as printed in 1741 in *Büdingische Sammlung* 4 (12.1a-b) printed on pp. 112–113 and 111 (respectively) within the article "Damma/Marotta/Magdalena: Petition to Queen Sophia Magdalene of Denmark (1739)," pp. 110–113 in *Transatlantic Feminisms in the Age of Revolutions*, edited by Lisa L. Moore, Joanna Brooks, and Caroline Wigginton.

Oxford [England] [and] **New York** [New York, U.S.A.]: Oxford University Press, **2012**.
8vo (26 cm.): xii, 403 p, illus.

12.16 ———.

"Magdalena's Petition to the Danish-Norwegian Queen Sophia Magdalene" printed on p. 136 as an appendix to Ray A. Kea's article "From Catholicism to Moravian Pietism: The World of Marotta/Magdalena, a Woman of Popo and St. Thomas," pp. 115–136 in *The Creation of the British Atlantic World*, edited by Elizabeth Mancke and Carole Shammas.

Baltimore [Maryland, U.S.A.]: The Johns Hopkins University Press, **2015**.
8vo (25 cm.): 400 p., illus.

12.17 ———.

Photographic illustration of 12.0a, Damma/Marotta/Magdalena's Dutch Creole/Aja-Ayizo draft letter/petition (Unity

Archives, Herrnhut, Germany: R.15.Ba.3.61), printed on p. 166 of Katharine Gerbner, *Christian Slavery: Conversion and Race in the Protestant Atlantic World*.

Philadelphia [Pennsylvania, U.S.A.]: University of Pennsylvania Press, 2018.
8vo (24 cm.): 280 p., illus., maps.

1742

13.1 Jacobus Elisa Johannes Capitein (1717–1747)

Dissertatio politico-theologica de servitute libertati Christianæ non contraria, quam sub præside J. Van den Honert.

Lugduni Batavorum [i.e., **Leiden, Netherlands**]: Samuelem Luchtmans & filium, **1742**.
Small 4to (20 cm.): xiv [i.e., xvi], 17–44 p. Title-page vignette emblematically depicts the slave trade.
Hogg 1721a.

https://www.google.com/books/edition/Dissertatio_politico_theologica_de_servi/XhhZAAAAcAAJ?hl=en&gbpv=1&dq=Dissertatio+politico-theologica+de+-servitute&printsec=frontcover [see 13.1].

¶ As related by Grant Parker in 13.8, Capitein was born near but not on the Gold Coast (present-day Ghana—see Map 5), orphaned at age seven or eight, and then sold into slavery. A Dutch sea captain purchased him and sold him to a Dutch West Indies Company friend, who in 1728 took Capitein to the Netherlands (Map 7). Freed upon arrival (because slavery was illegal in the Netherlands), he received significant schooling there. He converted to Christianity and began theological studies at Leiden in 1737. Capitein wrote his *apologia* for slavery in Latin (13.1) as a degree requirement in 1742, and the same year was ordained and sent to West Africa as a missionary with the West Indies Company. The mission fared badly, and he died there five years later in debt and unhappy. For commentary, see Grant Parker's notes in his *The Agony of Asar: A Thesis on Slavery by the Former Slave Jacobus Eliza Johannes Capitein, 1717–1747* (Princeton: Markus Wiener, 2001); Kwesi Kwaa Prah, *Jacobus Eliza Johannes Capitein, 1717–1747: A Critical Study of an Eighteenth Century African* (Braamfontein: Skotaville, 1989); and David Nil Anum Kophi, *Saga of a Slave: Jacobus Capitein of Holland and Elmina* (Accra: SubSaharahn Publ., 2001). See also Grant Parker, "Capitein, Jacobus Elisa Johannes," in *Dictionary of African Biography*, ed. Emmanuel K. Akyeamnpong and Henry Louis Gates, Jr., (Oxford University Press, 2012), 2: 34–35.

13.2 ——. [Translation of 13.1 into Dutch by Hieronymus de Wilhelm]

Staatkundig-Godgeleerd Onderzoegschrift over De Slaverny, als niet Strydig tegen de Christelyke Vryheid, welk, onder het gehegngen van den Algenoegzamen God, En de Voorzittinge van den Hoog-Eerwaarden en Wyd-Beroemden Heere Joan van den Honert, T. H. Soon...

Leiden [Netherlands]: Philippus Bonk; **Amsterdam** [Netherlands]: Gerrit de Groot, **1742**.
Small 4to (20 cm.): 53, [19]p. Title-page vignette emblematically depicts the slave trade.
Hogg 1721b (reporting 72 p.).

13.3 ——. [Translation of 13.1 into Dutch by Hieronymus de Wilhelm]

Staatkundig-Godgeleerd Onderzoegschrift over De Slaverny, als niet Strydig tegen de Christelyke Vryheid, welk, onder het gehegngen van den Algenoegzamen God, En de Voorzittinge van den Hoog-Eerwaarden en Wyd-Beroemden Heere Joan van den Honert, T. H. Soon... De Derde Druk [= the third edition].

Leiden [Netherlands]: Philippus Bonk; **Amsterdam** [Netherlands]: Gerrit de Groot, **1742**.
Small 4to (21 cm.): 53, [19]p. Title-page vignette emblematically depicts the slave trade.
Cf. Hogg 1721b.

13.4 ——. [Translation of 13.1 into Dutch by Hieronymus de Wilhelm]

Staatkundig-Godgeleerd Onderzoegschrift over De Slaverny, als niet Strydig tegen de Christelyke Vryheid, welk, onder het gehegngen van den Algenoegzamen God, En de Voorzittinge van den Hoog-Eerwaarden en Wyd-Beroemden Heere Joan van den Honert, T. H. Soon...., De vierde Druk [= the fourth edition].

Leiden [Netherlands]: Philippus Bonk; **Amsterdam** [Netherlands]: Gerrit de Groot, **1742**.
Small 4to (20 cm.): 53, [19]p. Title-page vignette emblematically depicts the slave trade.
Cf. Hogg 1721b.

13.5 ——.

British Library reported to hold a "Xerocopy of a copy [of an English translation of 13.1?] in the library of the Rijksuniversiteit, Leyden. Made by the Rijksuniversiteit, Leyden [Netherlands], **1968**. Original copy apparently cropped."

OCLC 558746625

13.6 ——.

Photomechanical reprint of 13.1 in *Ad catholicum pariter et invictissimum Philippum dei gratia hispaniarum regem, de fo- elicissima per magistrum Ioannem Latinum. Tractatus de arte sobrie accurate philosophandi / Antonius Guilielmus Amo. Dissertatio politico-theologica, de servitute, libertati christianae non contraria / Jacobus Elisa Joannes Capitein.*

Nendeln, Lichtenstein: Kraus Reprint, **1971.**
8vo (26 cm.): 44 (*i.e.*, 88), 35 (i.e., 70), [11] p., illus.

13.7 ——.

English translation of 13.1 and other works by Capitein in David Nii Anum Kpobi, *Mission in Chains: The Life, Theology, and Ministry of the ex-slave Jacobus E. J. Capitein (1717– 1747) with a Translation of his Major Publications.*

Zoetermeer [Netherlands]: Uitgeverij Boekencentrum, **1993.**
8vo (24 cm.): 273 p. Editorial apparatus in Dutch.

13.8 ——.

Critical reprint of Latin original (13.1) with English translation and extensive editorial annotations by Grant Parker in *The Agony of Asar: A Thesis on Slavery by the Former Slave, Jacobus Eliza Johannes Capitein, 1717–1747.*

Princeton [New Jersey, U.S.A.]: Markus Wiener Publishers, **2001.**
8vo (23 cm.): x, 182 p., illus., maps.

Additional publications by Jacobus Elisa Johannes Capitein

+13-A.1 ——.

"Elegia" (elegy on the death of the Rev. Mr. Manger, written ca. 1741) printed in the original Latin on pp. 226–229 in Henri Grégoire, *De la Littérature des Nègres, ou Recherches sur leur Facultés Intellectuelles, leur Qualités Morales, et leur Littérature* (Paris [France]: Maradan, 1808).

https://archive.org/details/delalittraturede00grgo/page/226

+13-A.2 ——.

"Elegia" printed in the original Latin on pp. 226–229 in Henri Grégoire, *De la Littérature des Nègres, ou Recherches sur leur Facultés Intellectuelles, leur Qualités Morales, et leur Littérature* (Paris [France]: Perrin, 1808).

https://gallica.bnf.fr/ark:/12148/bpt6k844925/f239.item.texteImage

+13-A.3 ——.

"Elegia" printed in the original Latin from +12-A.2 on pp. 199–201 of D. B. Warden's English translation of Henri Grégoire's *An Enquiry Concerning the Intellectual and Moral Faculties, and Literature of Negroes* (Brooklyn [New York, U.S.A.]: Thomas Kirk, 1810).

https://archive.org/details/enquiryconcernin00gr/page/199/mode/1up?q

+13-A.4 ——.

"Elegia" printed in the original Latin on pp. 310–311 in *A Tribute for the Negro: Being a Vindication of the Moral, Intellectual, and Religious Capabilities of the Coloured Portion of Mankind; with Particular Reference to the African Race*, edited by Wilson Armistead (Manchester & London [England]: W. Irwin, 1848).

https://archive.org/details/tributefornegrob00armi/page/309/mode/1up

+13-A.5 ——.

"Elegia" printed in the original Latin on pp. 1074–1076 in William J. Simmons, *Men of Mark: Eminent, Progressive and Rising* (Cleveland, Ohio [U.S.A.]: Geo. M. Rewell & Co. [Press of W. W. Williams, Cleveland], 1887). "Sold exclusively by subscription"; yet we have not located exemplars of the related canvassing book or prospectus. Cf. Keith Arbour, *Canvassing Books* (1996), esp. xii n2.

https://babel.hathitrust.org/cgi/pt?id=hvd.32044010422384&view=1up&seq=15

+13-A.6 ——.

"Elegia" printed in the original Latin on p. 1074–1076 in William J. Simmons, *Men of Mark: Eminent, Progressive and Rising* (Cleveland, Ohio [U.S.A.]: Geo. M. Rewell & Co. [Press of W. W. Williams, Cleveland], 1890).

+13-A.7 ——.

"Elegia" printed in the original Latin on pp. 20–22 in S[amuel] R[ichard] B[rew] Attoh Ahuma, *Memoirs of West African Celebrities: Europe, &c (1700–1850) with special reference to the Gold Coast* (Liverpool [England]: Marples & Co., 1905).

https://babel.hathitrust.org/cgi/pt?id=ien.35556038054839

+13-A.8 ——.

"Elegia" printed in the original Latin on pp. 1074–1076 in photomechanical reprint of William J. Simmons, *Men of Mark: Eminent, Progressive and Rising* (Cleveland, Ohio [U.S.A.]: Geo. M. Rewell & Co., 1887), with new imprint: New York: Arno Press, 1968.

+13-A.9 ——.

"Elegia" printed in the original Latin on pp. 1074–1076 in photomechanical reprint of William J. Simmons, *Men of*

Mark: Eminent, Progressive and Rising (Cleveland, Ohio [U.S.A.]: Geo. M. Rewell & Co., 1887), with new imprint: Chicago [Illinois, U.S.A.]: Johnson Publishing Co., 1970. A volume in the series "Ebony Classics."

+13-A.10 ——.

"Elegia" printed in the original Latin on pp. 226–229 (first series) in photomechanical reprint of 1808 Paris edition of Henri Grégoire, *De la littérature des Nègres* [+13-A.2] and on pp. 199–201 (2nd series) in photomechanical reprint of 1810 Brooklyn, New York [+13-A.3], an English-language translation of the same work—the two printed together in one volume with imprint: Nendeln, Lichtenstein: Kraus Reprint, 1971.

+13-B.1 ——.

Uitgewrogte predikatien, zynde De trouwhertige vermaaninge van den Apostel der heydenen Paulus, aan zynen zoon Timotheus, uit 2 Timotheus II vers 8, te Muiderberg ... alsmede de voornaamste goederen van de opperste wysheit, uit Spreuken VIII. vers 18 in twee predikatien... (Amsterdam [Netherlands]: Bernardus Mourik en Jacobus Haffman, 1742). Collection of his sermons in the original Dutch.

https://dspace.library.uu.nl/handle/1874/363395

+13-C.1 ——.

Het groote genadeligt Gods in zyne dienaaren onder de bedienin der genade, ontdekt in een intree- predicatie over 2 Corinthen IV: 6 / door Jacobus Elisa Joannes Capitein ; en op zyn verzoek uitg. door Hieronymus de Wilhem. (Leiden [Netherlands]: Jacobus de Beunje; Amsterdam [Netherlands], De Janssoons van Waasberge, 1744).

+13-D.1 ——.

Vertaaling van het Onze Vader, de Twaalf geloofs-artykelen, en de Tien Geboden des Heeren (Leyden [Netherlands]: Jacobus de Beunje, 1744). 8vo: 19 p. Catalogued at BL.

+13-D.2 ——.

Vertaaling van het Onze Vader, de Twaalf geloofs-artykelen, en de Tien Geboden des Heeren (Leyden [Netherlands]: Jacobus de Beunje, 1745). 8vo: 15 p. Catalogued at Utrecht.

1743

14.0 Domingos Álvares (*ca.* 1710–)

His life story and responses to questioning were written out by the Inquisition at **Lisbon, Portugal**, where they are preserved in the Arquivo Nacional da Torre do Tombo, Inquisição de Évora, Processos, No. 7759, ff. 59–61, Genealogia (15 Mar 1743) and ff. 71–78, In Specie e mais confissão, 16 May **1743**.

¶ Álvares was born to parents who were *vodun* priests (hungan) in a Mahi village, north of Dahomey (present-day Benin—see Map 5). He became a healer and diviner. Around 1730, he was seized and shipped from the port of Jakin (Godomey) on Lake Nacoué (present-day Benin) to Goiana in Pernambuco, northeastern Brazil (Map 9), and there enslaved on a sugar plantation. Accused of being a fetisher or witch and sent to Lisbon, Portugal (Map 7), he stood trial before the Inquisition Court in 1743. After confessing under torture, Álvares was released and remained in Portugal, where he continued to practice spiritual healing.

Full text: https://huskiecommons.lib.niu.edu/history-500african-voices/11/ [see 14.1].

14.1 ——.

English translation of his life story and responses to the Inquisition at Lisbon printed on pp. 164–165 and 172–176 in James H. Sweet, *Domingos Álvares, African Healing, and the Intellectual History of the Atlantic World.*

Chapel Hill [North Carolina, U.S.A.]: The University of North Carolina Press, 2011. 8vo (24 cm.): xvii, 300 p.

14.2 ——. [Another printing of 14.1]

English translation of his life story and responses to the Inquisition at Lisbon printed on pp. 164–165 and 172–176 in James H. Sweet, *Domingos Álvares, African Healing, and the Intellectual History of the Atlantic World.*

[Chapel Hill, North Carolina, U.S.A.]: The University of North Carolina Press, 2013. 8vo (24 cm.): xvii, 300 p.

1746

15.0 Luce Bijah (ca. 1724–1821) = Lucy Terry = Lucy Terry Prince

"Bars Fight," a poem (currently the earliest known poem by an African American or African-born woman or man living in colonial British North America) describing a **1746** Indian attack on the largely Anglo-American community (in which Lucy Terry lived) of Deerfield, Massachusetts, subsequently passed down orally in the community, written out (for the first time?) on pp. 33–34 of Pliny Arms's (1778–1859) manuscript "History of Deerfield," which he probably wrote in **1819** for oral delivery at Conway, Massachusetts (15.49, p. 19). Preserved in the Arms Papers, Box 14, folder 1, Pocumtuck Valley Memorial Library Association (PVMA), **Deerfield, Massachusetts, U.S.A.** Fourth and third lines from end of poem read: Nor tommy-hawked her on her head, | And left her on the ground for dead.

¶ In about 1730 the child Bijah was taken from West Africa on a slaving ship to Bristol, a port town in the British North American colony of Rhode Island (see Map 17). By 1735 she was in Deerfield, a town in western Massachusetts (a province adjacent to Rhode Island), where she underwent Christian baptism in 1744, married Abijah Prince (a free black man) in 1756, and had seven children. She acquired her freedom shortly after marriage. By 1785 she resided with some of her family in Vermont (a newly organized state north of western Massachusetts), where she remained a forceful presence into extreme old age—witness her deeply respectful obituary notice (reprinted in 15.49, p. 6, and elsewhere). For more on her, see 15.49 and 15.57 and an earlier version of the former: David R. Proper, "Lucy Terry Prince: 'Singer of History,'" in *Contributions in Black Studies* 9 [1988–1992]: 187–214, which is available at https://scholarworks.umass.edu/cgi/viewcontent.cgi?article=1118&context=cibs.

15.1 ——.

"Bars Fight" printed on the first page of the November 20, 1854, issue of the *Springfield Daily Republican*, edited by Samuel Bowles (1826–1878).

Springfield, Massachusetts [U.S.A.]: Samuel Bowles & Co., 1854.

Broadsheet bifolia. Fourth and third lines from end of poem read: **Nor** tommy hawked **her** on her head, | And left her on the ground for dead.

https://babel.hathitrust.org/cgi/pt?id=nnc1.50216905&view=1up&seq=364 [see 15.2].

15.2 ——.

"Bars Fight" printed (with prefatory biographical sketch of the poem's author on pp. 359–360) on p. 360 in vol. 2 of Josiah Gilbert Holland, *History of Western Massachusetts: The Counties of Hampden, Hampshire, Franklin, and Berkshire. Embracing an Outline, or General History of the Section, an Account of Its Scientific Aspects and Leading Interests, and Separate Histories of Its One Hundred Towns.*

Springfield [Massachusetts, U.S.A.]: Published by Samuel Bowles and Company, 1855. Tpv: Samuel Bowles & Company, Printers and Stereotypers.

2 vols., 8vo (20 cm.). Fourth and third lines from end of poem read: **Nor** tommy hawked her on **her** head, | And left her on the ground for dead.

https://babel.hathitrust.org/cgi/pt?id=nnc1.50216905&view=1up&seq=364

15.3 ——.

"Bars Fight" reprinted on p. 80 of J. W. Phelps's history of Guilford, Vermont, which is printed in Part III of Volume V (*The Towns of Windham County, with histories of Sutton in Caledonia County, and Bennington in Bennington County*) of *Vermont Historical Gazetteer: A Local History of all the Towns in the State*, collated by Abby Maria Hemenway.

Brandon {Vermont, U.S.A.]: Published by Mrs. Carrie E. H. Page, 1891.

5 vols., 8vo (25 cm.). Final two lines of poem read: Nor tommy hawked her on **the** head | And left her on the ground for dead.

https://babel.hathitrust.org/cgi/pt?id=mdp.39015005194793&view=1up&seq=1142&q1

15.4 ——.

"Bars Fight" reprinted on p. 56 of George Sheldon (1818–1916), "Negro Slavery in Old Deerfield," pp. 49–60 in *New England Magazine*, New Series vol. 8 (O.S., vol. 14), no. 2.

Boston [Massachusetts, U.S.A.]: Warren F. Kellogg, Publishers, [March] 1893.

8vo (25 cm.). Fourth and third lines from end of poem read: **And** tommy hawked her on **the** head | And left her on the ground for dead.

https://babel.hathitrust.org/cgi/pt?id=njp.32101064987991&view=1up&seq=66

Note: David R. Proper prints on p. 206 of his article on Lucy Terry Prince (see lead note above) an account of Sheldon's circulation of "some hundred copies of" an off print of 15.4 to an extensive list of named recipients.

15.5 ———.

"Bars Fight" printed (with newly introduced stanza divisions) from 15.4 on pp. 68–69 of Emma Lewis Coleman, *A Historic and Present Day Guide to Old Deerfield.*

Boston [Massachusetts, U.S.A.]: [Emma Lewis Coleman], 1907. Tpv: *This book is sold for the benefit of the Deerfield Academy and Dickinson High School.* Price in paper, 50 cents; in cloth. $1.00 Copyright *1907*, by Emma Lewis Coleman | Boston *The Plimpton Press Norwood Mass U.S.A.*

8vo (19 cm.): [x], 116 p. Fourth and third lines from end of poem read: **Nor** tommy hawked her on **the** head, | And left her on the ground for dead.

https://babel.hathitrust.org/cgi/pt?id=loc.ark:/13960/t15m6cz1p&view=1up&seq=106

15.6 ———. [Second printing of 15.5]

"Bars Fight" printed (with newly introduced stanza divisions) from 15.4 on pp. 68–69 of Emma Lewis Coleman, *A Historic and Present Day Guide to Old Deerfield.*

Boston [Massachusetts, U.S.A.]: [Emma Lewis Coleman], 1912. Tpv: *This book is sold for the benefit of the Deerfield Academy and Dickinson High School.* Price in paper, 50 cents; in cloth. $1.00 Copyright *1907*, by Emma Lewis Coleman | Boston *The Plimpton Press Norwood Mass U.S.A.*

8vo (19 cm.): [x], 116 p. Fourth and third lines from end of poem read: **Nor** tommy hawked her on **the** head, | And left her on the ground for dead.

https://babel.hathitrust.org/cgi/pt?id=uiug.30112037942650&view=1up&seq=111

15.7 ———. [Third printing of 15.5]

"Bars Fight" printed (with newly introduced stanza divisions) from 15.4 on pp. 68–69 of Emma Lewis Coleman, *A Historic and Present Day Guide to Old Deerfield.*

Boston [Massachusetts, U.S.A.]: [Emma Lewis Coleman], 1926. Tpv: *This book is sold for the benefit of the Martha Goulding Pratt Memorial, "Our Village Room."* Price $1.00 Copyright *1907*, by Emma Lewis Coleman | Boston *The Plimpton Press, Norwood, Mass., U.S.A.*

8vo (19 cm.): [x], 116 p. Fourth and third lines from end of poem read: Nor tommy hawked her on **the** head, | And left her on the ground for dead.

15.8 ———. [Fourth printing of 15.5]

"Bars Fight" printed (with newly introduced stanza divisions) from 15.4 on pp. 68–69 of Emma Lewis Coleman, *A Historic and Present Day Guide to Old Deerfield.*

Boston [Massachusetts, U.S.A.]: [Emma Lewis Coleman], 1930. Tpv: *This book is sold for the benefit of the Martha Goulding Pratt Memorial, "Our Village Room."* Price

$1.00 Copyright *1907*, by Emma Lewis Coleman | Boston *The Plimpton Press, Norwood, Mass., U.S.A.*

8vo (19 cm.): [x], 116 p. Fourth and third lines from end of poem read: **Nor** tommy hawked her on **the** head, | And left her on the ground for dead.

https://babel.hathitrust.org/cgi/pt?id=bc.ark:/13960/t8z96x331&view=1up&seq=106

15.9 ———.

"Bars Fight" reprinted from 15.4 on pp. 242–243 in Lorenzo Johnston Greene, *The Negro in Colonial New England 1620–1776.*

New York [New York, U.S.A.]: Columbia University Press, [1942].

8vo (23 cm.): 404 p. Fourth and third lines from end of poem read: **And** tommyhawked her on **the** head | And left her on the ground for dead.

15.10 ———. [Second printing of 15.9]

"Bars Fight" reprinted from 15.4 on pp. 242–243 in Lorenzo Johnston Greene, *The Negro in Colonial New England 1620–1776.*

New York [New York, U.S.A.]: Columbia University Press, [1945].

8vo (23 cm.): 404 p. Fourth and third lines from end of poem read: **And** tommyhawked her on **the** head | And left her on the ground for dead.

https://babel.hathitrust.org/cgi/pt?id=mdp.49015000060286&view=1up&seq=246

15.11 ———.

"Bars Fight" reprinted from 15.4 on p. 3 (with editorial note on p. viii and biographical note on p. 406) in *The Poetry of the Negro, 1746–1949: An Anthology,* edited by Langston Hughes and Arna Bontemps.

Garden City, New York [U.S.A.]: Doubleday & Company, Inc., [1949].

8vo (21.5 cm.): xviii, 429 p. Fourth and third lines from end of poem read: And tommyhawked her on the head | And left her on the ground for dead.

15.12 ———. [Second printing of 15.11]

"Bars Fight" reprinted from 15.4 on p. 3 (with editorial note on p. viii and biographical note on p. 406) in *The Poetry of the Negro, 1746–1949,* edited by Langston Hughes and Arna Bontemps.

Garden City [New York, U.S.A.]: Doubleday and Co., 1951.

8vo (22 cm.): xviii, 429 p. Fourth and third lines from end of poem read: And tommyhawked her on the head | And left her on the ground for dead.

15.13 ——. [Japanese translation of 15.12]
"Bars Fight" translated into Japanese (from its printing in 15.12) in *The Poetry of the Negro, 1746–1949: [An Anthology*, edited by Langston Hughes and Arna Bontemps.]

Tokyo [Japan]: Mirai-Sha Press, [1952].
158 p., portraits.

15.14 ——. [Third printing of 15.11]
"Bars Fight" reprinted from 15.4 on p. 3 (with editorial note on p. viii and biographical note on p. 406) in *The Poetry of the Negro, 1746–1949: An Anthology*, edited by Langston Hughes and Arna Bontemps.

Garden City [New York, U.S.A.]: Doubleday and Co., **1953**.
8vo (22 cm.): xviii, 429 p. Fourth and third lines from end of poem read: And tommyhawked her on the head | And left her on the ground for dead.

15.15 ——. [Fourth printing of 15.11]
"Bars Fight" reprinted from 15.4 on p. 3 (with editorial note on p. viii and biographical note on p. 406) in *The Poetry of the Negro, 1746–1949: An Anthology*, edited by Langston Hughes and Arna Bontemps.

Garden City [New York, U.S.A.]: Doubleday & Company, Inc., **[1956]**.
8vo (22 cm.): xviii, 429 p. Fourth and third lines from end of poem read: And tommyhawked her on the head | And left her on the ground for dead.

15.16 ——.
"Bars Fight" reprinted from 15.4 (George Sheldon's article) on pp. 242–243 in photomechanical reprint of Lorenzo Johnston Greene, *The Negro in Colonial New England 1620–1776* with imprint:

Port Washington [New York, U.S.A.]: Kennikat Press, **[1966]**.
8vo (22 cm.): 404 p. Fourth and third lines from end of poem read: And tommyhawked her on the head | And left her on the ground for dead.

15.17 ——.
"Bars Fight" reprinted explicitly from 15.4 on p. 183, with variants drawn from other named sources, printed on pp. 183–184 in Bernard Katz's article "A Second Version of Lucy Terry's Early Ballad?" which is printed on pp. 183–184 in *The Negro History Bulletin*, vol. 29, no. 8.

Washington, D. C. [U.S.A.]: Association for the Study of Negro Life and History, [Fall] **1966**.
4to (28 cm.). Note the question mark closing the article's title.

15.18 ——.
"Bars Fight" reprinted from 15.4 on pp. 242–243 in photomechanical reprint of 15.5, Lorenzo Johnston Greene, *The Negro in Colonial New England 1620–1776*, with imprint:

New York [New York, U.S.A.]: Atheneum, **1968**.
8vo (21 cm.): 404 p. Fourth and third lines from end of poem read: And tommyhawked her on the head | And left her on the ground for dead.

15.19 ——.
"Bars Fight" printed from 15.2 with new historical introduction on pp. 3–4 in *Early Black American Poets: Selections with biographical and critical introductions* by William H. Robinson.

Dubuque [Iowa, U.S.A.]: Wm. C. Brown Company, Publishers, **[1969]**.
8vo (23 cm.): xviii, [2], 275 p. N.b.: "General Introduction," pp. xiii–xviii.
Fourth and third lines from end of poem read: And tommyhawked her on the head, | And left her on the ground for dead;

15.20 ——.
"Bars Fight" reprinted from 15.4 on pp. 242–243 in photomechanical reprint of 15.5, Lorenzo Johnston Greene, *The Negro in Colonial New England 1620–1776*, with imprint:

New York [New York, U.S.A.]: Atheneum, **1969**.
8vo (21 cm.): 404 p. Fourth and third lines from end of poem read: And tommyhawked her on the head | And left her on the ground for dead.

15.21 ——. [Second printing of 15.19]
"Bars Fight" printed from 15.2 with new historical introduction on pp. 3–4 in *Early Black American Poets: Selections with biographical and critical introductions* by William H. Robinson.

Dubuque {Iowa, U.S.A.]: Wm. C. Brown Company, Publishers, **[1970]**.
8vo (23 cm.): xviii, [2], 275 p. N.b.: "General Introduction," pp. xiii–xviii.
Fourth and third lines from end of poem read: And tommyhawked her on the head, | And left her on the ground for dead;

15.22 ——. [Revised and updated edition of 15.11]
"Bars Fight" reprinted from 15.4 on p. 3 (with editorial note on pp. xxi–xxii, and biographical note on p. 622) in *The Poetry of the Negro, 1746–1970: An Anthology*, edited by Langston Hughes and Arna Bontemps.

Garden City [New York, U.S.A.]: Doubleday & Company, Inc., [1970].

8vo (21 cm.): xxiv, 645 p.

15.23 ———. [Third printing of 15.19]

"Bars Fight" printed from 15.2 with new historical introduction on pp. 3–4 in *Early Black American Poets: Selections with biographical and critical introductions* by William H. Robinson.

Dubuque [Iowa, U.S.A.]: Wm. C. Brown Company, Publishers, [1971].

8vo (23 cm.): xviii, [2], 275 p. N.b.: "General Introduction," pp. xiii–xviii.

Fourth and third lines from end of poem read: And tommyhawked her on the head, | And left her on the ground for dead;

15.24 ———.

"Bars Fight" reprinted (from *Early Black American Poets*, edited by William H. Robinson) on p. 37 of *The Black Poets*, an anthology edited by Dudley Randall.

New York [New York, U.S.A.]: Bantam Books. [December 1971].

12mo (17.5 cm.): xxvi, 349 p. Fourth and third lines from end of poem read: And tommyhawked her on the head, | And left her on the ground for dead;

15.25 ———.

The Bars Fight. [Caption title.]

[Deerfield?, Massachusetts?, U.S.A.: s.n., ca. 1971]

Broadside (50 x 33 cm.), [1] p., illus., verso blank. The illustration, printed atop caption title and text, is an unsigned 10.2 x 8.2 cm. relief-cut silhouette of a young woman (in half-length profile) writing with a quill pen based directly or indirectly on the engraved 1773 portrait of Phillis Wheatley similarly posed (q.v. the frontispiece to 111.1). Fourth and third lines from end of poem read: **Nor** tommy-hawk'd her on **the** head, | And left her on the ground for dead. Signed in type at end of text: --Lucy Terry Prince (no punctuation). Examined exemplar (Historic Deerfield Library System/PVMA Flat file drawer 5) on thick paper, vertical chain-lines; poem not well inked.

15.26 ———.

Text of "Bars Fight" printed under caption title *Lucy Terry Describes Deerfield's Last Indian Raid.*

[Deerfield, Massachusetts, U.S.A.]: Hand printed at the Shop of John Wilson [by Jonathan Christman on the replica handpress], Deerfield, Massachusetts [ca. 1972].

Broadside (28 x 21.5 cm.), [1] p., verso blank. Single-paragraph editorial explanation of Terry's poem (asserting she composed it "when she was sixteen") printed between caption title and first line of poem. Fourth and third lines from end of poem read: **Nor** tommy hawked her on **the** head, | And left her on the ground for dead. Examined exemplar (Historic Deerfield [Massachusetts] Library System/PVMA call no. S 810.9896 P955L Manuscript [*sic*]) on machine-made (and machine-trimmed) paper with horizontal chain-lines. Present entry verified by Jonathan Christman, Wake Forest University, personal communication (e-mail) 4 June 2021.

15.27 ———. [Fourth printing of 15.19]

"Bars Fight" printed from 15.2 with new historical introduction on pp. 3–4 in *Early Black American Poets: Selections with biographical and critical introductions* by William H. Robinson.

Dubuque [Iowa, U.S.A.]: Wm. C. Brown Company, Publishers, [1973].

8vo (23 cm.): xviii, [2], 309 p. N.b.: "General Introduction," pp. xiii–xviii.

Fourth and third lines from end of poem read: And tommyhawked her on the head, | And left her on the ground for dead;

15.28 ———.

"Bars Fight" reprinted from 15.4 on pp. 242–243 in photomechanical reprint of 15.5, Lorenzo Johnston Greene, *The Negro in Colonial New England 1620–1776*, with imprint:

New York [New York, U.S.A.]: Atheneum, 1974.

8vo (21 cm.): 404 p. Fourth and third lines from end of poem read: And tommyhawked her on the head | And left her on the ground for dead.

15.29 ———.

"Bars Fight," printed or summarized with biographical sketch of author of magazine article by Angelo Costanzo, "Three Black Poets in Eighteenth Century America: Lucy Terry, Jupiter Hammon, and Phillis Wheatley," in *Shippensburg State College Review*.

Shippensburg [Pennsylvania, U.S.A.]: Shippensburg State College, 1977.

4to.

15.30 ———.

"Bars Fight," printed or summarized with biographical sketch of author on pp. 39–44 of William Loren Katz, *Black People Who Made the Old West*.

New York [New York, U.S.A.]: Crowell, **1977**.
8vo (24 cm.): x, 181, illus., portraits. For younger readers age 12 and up.

15.31–35 ——. [Second through sixth printings of 15.25]

"Bars Fight" reprinted (from *Early Black American Poets*, edited by William H. Robinson) on p. 37 of *The Black Poets*, an anthology edited by Dudley Randall.

New York [New York, U.S.A.]: Bantam Books. [ca. 1972–1977].
12mo (17.5 cm.): xxvi, 349 p. Entries posited from 15.23 and 15.36.

15.36 ——. [Seventh printing of 15.25]

"Bars Fight" reprinted (from *Early Black American Poets*, edited by William H. Robinson) on p. 37 of *The Black Poets*, an anthology edited by Dudley Randall.

New York [New York, U.S.A.]: Bantam Books. [1978].
12mo (17.5 cm.): xxvi, 349 p. Fourth and third lines from end of poem read: **And** tommyhawked her on **the** head, | And left her on the ground for dead;

15.37 ——.

"Bars Fight" reprinted in *Black Sister: Poetry by Black American Women, 1746–1980*, edited by Erlene Stetson.

Bloomington [Indiana, U.S.A.]: Indiana University Press, **1981**.
8vo (25 cm.): xxiv, 312 p.

15.38 ——.

"Bars Fight" reprinted on p. ca. 255–257 in *Women Poets in Pre-Revolutionary America: An Anthology*, edited by Pattie Cowell.

Troy [New York, U.S.A.]: Whiston Publishing Co., **1981**.
8vo (24 cm.): x, 407 p., illus., plates.

15.39 ——.

"Bars Fight," reprinted in Robert Merriam's article "The Liberation of Lucy Terry Prince: A Romance of Old Deerfield," which is printed in the May-June 1982 issue of the popular magazine *The Country Side*.

[Northampton? Massachusetts, U.S.A.]: 1982.
8vo (21 cm.).

15.40 ——.

"Bars Fight" printed, with new introductory note and references, on pp. 13–16 of *Afro-American Women Writers, 1746–*

1933: An Anthology and Critical Guide, edited by Ann Allen Shockley.

Boston [Massachusetts, U.S.A.]: G. K. Hall, **1988**.
8vo (24.2 cm.): xxviii, 465 p.

15.41–44 ——. [Eighth through eleventh printings of 15.25]

"Bars Fight" reprinted (from *Early Black American Poets*, edited by William H. Robinson) on p. 37 of *The Black Poets*, an anthology edited by Dudley Randall.

New York [New York, U.S.A.]: Bantam Books. [ca. 1979-1987].
12mo (17.5 cm.): xxvi, 349 p. Entries posited from 15.36 and 15.45.

15.45 ——. [Twelfth printing of 15.25]

"Bars Fight" reprinted (from *Early Black American Poets*, edited by William H. Robinson) on p. 37 of *The Black Poets*, an anthology edited by Dudley Randall.

New York [New York, U.S.A.]: Bantam Books. [May 1988].
12mo (17.5 cm.): xxvi, 349 p. Fourth and third lines from end of poem read: And tommyhawked her on the head, | And left her on the ground for dead;

15.46 ——. [Reprint of 15.30]

"Bars Fight," printed or summarized with biographical sketch of author in William Loren Katz, *Black People Who Made the Old West.*

Trenton [New Jersey, U.S.A.]: Africa World Press, **1992**.
8vo (24 cm.): x, 181, illus., portraits. For younger readers age twelve and up.

15.47 ——.

"Bars Fight" printed from 15.2 on pp. 137–138 of *The Norton Anthology of African American Literature*, edited by Henry Louis Gates, Jr., and Nellie Y. McKay.

New York [New York, U.S.A.]: W. W. Norton & Co., [1997].
8vo (24 cm.): xliv, [2], 2665 p.

15.48 ——. [Another printing of 15.30]

"Bars Fight," printed or summarized with biographical sketch of author in William Loren Katz, *Black People Who Made the Old West.*

Trenton [New Jersey, U.S.A.]: Africa World Press, **1997**.
8vo (24 cm.): x, 181, illus., portraits. For younger readers aged twelve and up.

15.49 ——.
"Bars Fight," printed on pp. 18–19 in David Proper, *Lucy Terry Prince, Singer of History: A Brief Biography*.

Deerfield [Massachusetts, U.S.A.]: Pocumtuck Memorial Association, **1997**.
8vo (23 cm.): 50 p., illus. Fourth and third lines from end of poem read: **Nor** tommyhawked her on **the** head, | And left her on the ground for dead.

15.50 ——.
"Bars Fight" reprinted from 15.4 on pp. 242–243 of photomechanical reprint of 15.5, Lorenzo Johnston Greene, *The Negro in Colonial New England 1620–1776*, with imprint:

Bowie [Maryland, U.S.A.]: Heritage Books, **1998**.
8vo (25 cm.): 404 p. Fourth and third lines from end of poem read: **And** tommyhawked her on **the** head | And left her on the ground for dead.

15.51 ——.
"Bars Fight," recited orally in audiobook *I, Too, Sing America* ("A collection of 36 poems by 25 African-American writers from Lucy Terry … to Rita Dove").

Northport [Maine, U.S.A.]: Audio Bookshelf, **2000**.

15.52 ——.
"Bars Fight" printed with editorial note on pp. 26–27 in *The Prentice Hall Anthology of African American Literature* [edited by] Rochelle Smith [and] Sharon L. Jones.

Upper Saddle River [New Jersey, U.S.A.]: Prentice Hall, **[2000]**.
8vo (23 cm.): xxii, 1130 p., plates + audio CD.

15.53 ——.
"Bars Fight," printed on pp. 199–200 in *Phillis Wheatley, Complete Writings*, edited by Vincent Carretta.

New York [New York, U.S.A.]: Penguin Books, **2001**.
8vo (20 cm.): xlvii, 224 p.

15.54 ——. [British printing of 15.53]
"Bars Fight," printed on pp. 199–200 in *Phillis Wheatley, Complete Writings*, edited by Vincent Carretta.

London [England]: Penguin Books, **2002**.
8vo (20 cm.): 272 p.

15.55 ——.
"Bars Fight," printed from 15.2 on p. 822 in the anthology *Early American Writings*, edited by Carla Mulford, Angela Vietto, and Amy E. Winans.

New York [New York, U.S.A.] [and] Oxford [England]: Oxford University Press, **2002**.
8vo (24 cm.): xxii, 1129 p.

15.56 ——.
"Bars Fight" printed from 15.2 on pp. 186–187 of *The Norton Anthology of African American Literature*, edited by Henry Louis Gates, Jr., and Nellie Y. McKay. **Second edition.**

New York [New York, U.S.A.]: W. W. Norton & Co., **[2004]**.
8vo (24 cm.): xlvii, 2776 p. + audio disc.

15.57 ——.
"Bars Fight" printed on p. 78 in Gretchen Holbrook Gerzina and Anthony Gerzina, *Mr. and Mrs. Prince: How an Extraordinary Eighteenth-Century Family Moved out of Slavery and into Legend*.

[New York, New York, U.S.A.]: Amistad, an imprint of HarperCollins Publishers, **[2008]**.
8vo (21 cm.): 256 p., illus., maps. Fourth and third lines from end of poem read: **Nor** tommy hawked her on **the** head, | And left her on the ground for dead.

15.58 ——. [Second printing of 15.57]
"Bars Fight" printed on p. 78 in Gretchen Holbrook Gerzina and Anthony Gerzina, *Mr. and Mrs. Prince: How an Extraordinary Eighteenth-Century Family Moved out of Slavery and into Legend*.

New York [New York, U.S.A.]: Amistad, an imprint of HarperCollins Publishers, **[2009]**.
8vo (21 cm.): 256 p., illus., maps.

15.59——.
"Bars Fight" printed in vol. 1 of *The Norton Anthology of African American Literature*, edited by Henry Louis Gates, Jr., and Valerie Smith. **Third edition.**

New York [New York, U.S.A.]: W. W. Norton & Co., **2014**.
2 vols., 8vo (24 cm.).

15.60 ——.
"Bars Fight" reprinted from 15.4 on pp. 242–243 of photomechanical reprint of 15.5, Lorenzo Johnston Greene, *The Negro in Colonial New England 1620–1776*, with imprint:

Eastford [Connecticut, U.S.A.]: Martino Fine Books, **2017**.
8vo (25 cm.): 404 p. Fourth and third lines from end of poem read: **And** tommyhawked her on **the** head | And left her on the ground for dead.

1749

16.1 Ansa Sasraku (1736–1770?) = William Ansah Sessarakoo = Prince of Anamabu

The Royal African: or, Memoirs of the Young Prince of Annamaboe. Comprehending a Distinct Account of his Country and Family ... the manner in which himself was confided by his father to the captain who sold him; his condition while a slave in Barbadoes ... his Voyage from thence; and Reception here in England. Interspers'd throughout with ... Remarks on the Commerce of the European Nations, whose subjects frequent the Coast of Guinea. To which is prefixed a letter ... in reference to some Natural Curiosities in Africa; as well as explaining the Motives which induced him to compose these Memoirs.

https://repository.library.northeastern.edu/downloads/neu:m0410804x-?datastream_id=-content [see 16.1].

London [England]: Printed for W. Reeve, at Shakespear's Head, Fleetstreet; G. Woodfall and J. Barnes, at Charing-Cross; and at the Court of Requests [1749].
8vo: [2], i–viii, 9–53 p.
https://repository.library.northeastern.edu/downloads/neu:m0410804x?datastream_id=content (lacks final page).
http://docsouth.unc.edu/neh/royal/royal.html
ESTC t78798 (noting review in the February 1749 issue of *The Gentleman's Magazine*).

¶ Sasraku was from Anamabu in the Fante (Akan people) country on the Gold Coast (present-day Ghana—see Map 5), where his father was the chief (*caboceiro*) of the region. His father sent him with an English captain to England to further his education, but the captain took him to the Caribbean instead. After treating him well during the voyage, the captain upon arrival in Barbados sold Sasraku into slavery. When Sasraku's father discovered this, he insisted through diplomatic negotiations in the war with Spain and France that his son be freed and sent to England for his education. This condition was agreed to, and Sasraku subsequently provided material for 16.1 while in London. Later he returned to the Gold Coast. Curtin (*Africa Remembered*, p. 5) considers this work to be based on Ayuba Sulaiman Diallo's story (q.v. 11.1) and the English experiences of a different African. Publicity derived from the account includes: brief notices in *The Gentleman's Magazine* (London [England]: Printed by E. Cave) vol. 19 (1749), p. 89 and 372, and vol. 20 (1750), p. 272 (the last with his engraved portrait); and a single-sheet mezzotint engraving of Gabriel Mathias's oil portrait of Sasraku, which was published in London, England, ca. 1749 and sold in shops for 1 shilling 6 pence (National Portrait Gallery, London, NPG D9199). See Robert

Hanserd, "Three Fingered Jack and King Shotaway: Impersonations in Atlantic Time and Space" (in progress).

16.2 ——.

The Royal African: or, Memoirs of the Young Prince of Annamaboe. Comprehending a Distinct Account of his Country and Family; his elder brother's Voyage to France, and Reception there; the Manner in which himself was confided by his Father to the Captain who sold him; his Condition while a Slave in Barbadoes; the true Cause of his being redeemed; his Voyage from thence; and Reception here in England. Interspers'd throughout With several Historical Remarks on the Commerce of the European Nations, whose Subjects frequent the Coast of Guinea. To which is prefixed A Letter from the Author to a Person of Distinction, in Reference to some natural Curiosities in Africa; as well as explaining the Motives which induced him to compose these Memoirs. **The Second Edition.**

London [England]: Printed for W. Reeve, at Shakespear's Head, Fleetstreet; G. Woodfall, and J. Barnes, at Charing-Cross; and at the Court of Requests, [1754?].
8vo: 55, [1] p.
ESTC t78797; Hogg 1458.

16.3 ——.

Anonymous reviewer's summary of Sasraku's Wednesday, 9 May 1759, autobiographical presentation at the Theatre Royal, Drury Lane, London, England, printed on p. 240, col. 1, in the May 1759 issue of *The Gentleman's Magazine and Historical Chronicle*, vol. 29, no. 5.

London [England]: Printed for D. Henry, and R. Cave, at St. Johns Gate, [May, 1759].
8vo (22 cm.).

16.4 ——.

Excerpts from 16.3 printed within quotation marks in Wylie Sypher, "The African Prince in London," pp. 237–247 in *Journal of the History of Ideas: a Quarterly devoted to Cultural and Intellectual History*, vol. 2, no. 2 (April 1941), edited by Arthur O. Lovejoy.

Baltimore [Maryland, U.S.A.]: Johns Hopkins University Press, April 1941. or
Lancaster [Pennsylvania, U.S.A.]: Journal of the History of Ideas, Inc., or University of Pennsylvania Press, April 1941.
8vo (26 cm.).

16.5 ——.

Excerpts from 16.1 printed on pp. 22–23 in *African Voices of the Global Past, 1500 to the Present*, edited by Trevor R. Getz.

Boulder [Colorado, U.S.A.]: Westview Press, [2014]. 8vo (22.7 cm.): xii, 223 p., illus., map. Note: Account 16.1's publication year as 1750 (p. 36, n14).

Additional work *presented to the public as written by* "*the African prince,*" i.e., Sessarakoo.

+16-A.1 [Dodd, William (1729–1777)]

"The African Prince, Now in England, to Zara at his Father's Court," *The Gentleman's Magazine* (London [England]: Printed by Edw. Cave) 19 (July 1749), pp. 323–325. In verse.

https://babel.hathitrust.org/cgi/pt?id=mdp.39015009221394
&view=1up&seq=353 Hogg 4163.

+16-A.2 ——.

The African Prince, now in England, to Zara at his Father's Court (London [England]: Printed for J. Payne and J. Bouquet, 1749). In verse. ESTC n42281.

+16-A.3 ——.

The African Prince, when in England, to Zara, at his Father's Court; and Zara's Answer. An Elegy on the Death of His Royal Highness Frederick Prince of Wales. And Diggon Davy's Resolution on the Death of his last Cow: a pastoral. **The second edition.** By William Dodd ... Late of Clare-Hall, Cambridge (London [England]: Printed for Mr. Waller in Fleet-Street; and Mr. Ward near the Royal Exchange, 1755). In verse. ESTC t134351.

+16-A.4 ——.

Abridgement in verse of +16-A.1 printed on pp. 201–203 of J. A. Carnes, *Journal of a Voyage from Boston to the West Coast of Africa; with a Full Description of the Manner of Trading with the Natives on the Coast* (Boston [Massachusetts, U.S.A.]: Published by John P. Jewett & Co.; Cleveland [Ohio, U.S.A.]: Jewett, Proctor & Worthington, 1852).

https://babel.hathitrust.org/cgi/pt?id=nyp.33433082441175
&view=1up&seq=211

1752

17.1 Chicaba (ca. 1676–1748) = Mother Sor Teresa Juliana de Santo Domingo

Compendio de la vida exemplar de la venerable madre Sor Teresa Juliana de Santo Domingo, [as told to, and edited by] Juan Carlos Miguel de Paniagua [i.e., Pan y Agua].

Salamanca [Spain]: por Eugenio Garcia de Honorato, J. S. Miguèl, Impressor de dicha Ciudad, y Universidad, [1752]. 4to (21 cm.): [24], 152, [4] p.

https://bibliotecadigital.jcyl.es/es/consulta/registro.cmd?id=4077

Full text in English translation: https://huskiecommons.lib.niu.edu/history-500africanvoices/12/ [see 17.1].

¶ Chicaba (meaning "golden child" or "divine gift") likely came from the coastal area east of Elmina Castle on the Gold Coast (present-day Ghana or Togo—see Map 5), possibly from an Ewe village or town. She was the daughter of a reigning prince and was known for her visions and spiritual healing powers as a child. After capture by Spanish traders she was baptized on São Tomé (the West African island in the Bight of Biafra) at age nine, named Teresa, taken to Madrid, Spain (Map 9), and there sold to Marchioness of Mancera, Juliana Teresa Portocarreto. After Mancera's death in 1703, the provisions of her will freed Chicaba, requested that she enter a convent, and left her an annuity. She entered the convent of

La Penitencia in Salamanca, Spain, in 1704, where she encountered significant racial and status prejudice but learned to write and lived a pious life. Shortly before she died, Father de Paniagua wrote out her story from her dictation. This was published four years later (17.1). For more on her, see Houchins and Fra-Molinero's commentary in 17.3.

17.2 ——. [Transcripción de 17.1 de María Eugenia Maeso, OP.]

Compendio de la vida ejemplar de la venerable madre Sor Teresa Juliana de Santo Domingo, tercera profesa en el Convento de Santa María Magdalena, vulgo de la Penitencia, Orden de Santo Domingo de la ciudad de Salamanca [as told to, and edited by] Juan Carlos Miguel de Paniagua [i.e., Pan y Agua].

Salamanca [Spain]: Dominicas Dueñas, 1999. 8vo (21 cm.): 205 p.

17.3 ——.

Extended excerpts printed in the original Spanish with English translation, introduction, and annotations by Sue E. Houchins and Baltasar Fra-Molinero printed in "The Saint's Life of Sister Chicaba, ca. 1676–1748: An As-Told-To Slave Narrative" on pp. 214–239 (especially 222–239) in *Afro-Latino Voices: Narratives from the Early Modern Ibero-Atlantic World, 1550–1812,* edited by Kathryn McKnight and Leo J. Garofalo.

Indianapolis [Indiana, U.S.A.]: Hackett Publishing Co., 2009. 8vo (23 cm.): xxxvii, 377 p.

Figure 2: First edition title page in original Spanish of Chicaba (Mother Sor Teresa Juliana de Santo Domingo), *Compendio de la vida exemplar de la venerable madre Sor Teresa Juliana de Santo Domingo,* edited by Juan Carlos Miguel de Paniagua [Pan y Agua] (Salamanca, Spain: Eugenio Garcia de Honorato and J. S. Miguèl, 1752). This book describes the life of Chicaba (ca. 1676–1748) from her origins in the coastal region of present-day Ghana to enslavement in Spain and residence in a convent in Salamanca, where she dictated her story to a priest in 1748.

17.4 ——.

Extended excerpts printed in English translation (only), with introduction and annotations by Sue E. Houchins and Baltasar Fra-Molinero printed in "The Saint's Life of Sister Chicaba, ca. 1676–1748: An As-Told-To Slave Narrative" on pp. 137–152 in *Afro-Latino Voices, Shorter Edition: Translations of Early Modern Ibero-Atlantic Narratives,* edited by Kathryn McKnight and Leo J. Garofalo.

Indianapolis [Indiana, U.S.A.]: Hackett Publishing Co., 2015.
8vo (23 cm.): xli, 263 p.

17.5 ——.

English translation of 17.1 with introduction and annotations by Sue E. Houchins and Baltasar Fra-Molinero published under title *Black Bride of Christ: Chicba, an African Nun in Eighteenth-Century Spain.*

Nashville [Tennessee, U.S.A.]: Vanderbilt University Press, 2018.
8vo (27 cm.); xvi, 307 p., illus.

1754

18.0 Kwasimukámba (ca. 1690–1787) = Kwasi/Quassi = Gramman/Graman Quacy

Two independent manuscript accounts exist, viz.:

18.0a: Manuscript account "Informatie over de neger Quassie," SS 294, October **1754**, Court of Policy, held in the Archives of the Sociëteit van Suriname, Algemeen Rijksarchief, **The Hague, Netherlands**; and

18.0b: John Gabriel Stedman's account of parts of Kwasimukámba's story included under date 28 January **1777** (when Stedman and Kwasi met) on pp. 759–762 (761 being blank) of Stedman's 1790 manuscript of his "Narrative, of a five years expedition against the Rebelled Negroes of Surinam..." This manuscript, which is preserved in the John Gabriel Stedman Collection at the University of Minnesota's James Ford Bell Library, **Minneapolis, Minnesota, U.S.A.,** was the heavily edited (see introduction to 18.16) basis of 18.1; it was first published *verbatim et literatim* in 1988, q.v. 18.16. Manuscript pages 759–762 have been digitized (as images 789–792) with the rest of the MS. by the James Ford Bell Library and are available at: https://umedia.lib.umn.edu/ item/p16022coll187:962/p16022coll187:862?child_index=788&query=&sidebar_page=263.

¶ **Born on the Guinea coast, possibly Akan from the Gold Coast (present-day Ghana—see Map 5), Kwasimukámba** was transported as an enslaved child to the Dutch South American colony of Suriname (Map 10). In 1712 he served there as a drummer in a military expedition and for the rest of his life assisted in colonial expeditions against Maroons, working variously as a scout, negotiator, and special forces commander. He was also a leading *dreisiman* (curer), *lukuman* (diviner), and *obiaman* (spirit/ancestor communicator/healer) in the colony. Ca. 1730 Kwasimukámba discovered medicinal properties in a tree that the Swedish botanist Carl Linnaeus consequently named in his honor. Suriname's governor purchased Kwasimukámba in 1744. In 1753 Kwasimukámba ran away. In 1754 he reemerged from the wilderness, having lived for a year with Saamaka [Saramaka] Maroons. His earlier account is found in the police report investigating the year he was missing (18.0a). In 1755 Kwasimukámba achieved manumission for his service against the Maroons. In the 1760s he became a planter, using Caribs for labor. In 1776 Willem V, Prince of Orange, welcomed Kwasimukámba at The Hague in the Netherlands (Map 7) and gave him gifts. About this time was painted the portrait

https://www.biodiversitylibrary.org/ item/163990# page/430/mode/1up [see 18.1a].

that William Blake (poet, artist, and engraver) later engraved for inclusion in Stedman's *Narrative* (18.1 et seq.). Leaving The Hague, Kwasimukámba returned in triumph to Suriname. Here John Gabriel Stedman met him in 1777, resulting in Stedman's written account of Graman Quacy's story (18.0b). After 1781 Kwasi retired to a good house (provided *gratis* by the government) in the colonial capital of Paramaribo and was given two slaves. In addition to his native African language and Dutch, Kwasimukámba spoke *Negerengels* (*Sranantongo*, the Creole language of coastal Suriname), Carib, and Arawak. For more on him, see Richard Price, *First-Time: The Historical Vision of an Afro-American People* (Baltimore: The Johns Hopkins University Press, 1983), especially pp. 153–159.

18.1a ———.

Heavily edited version of John Gabriel Stedman's understanding of Kwasimukámba's story (18.0b) printed on pp. 346–348 in chapter XXIX (with full-length portrait of Kwasi reproduced on engraved plate between pp. 348 and 349) in vol. 2 of John Gabriel Stedman, *Narrative, of a Five Years' Expedition, against the Revolted Negroes of Surinam, in Guiana, on the Wild Coast of South America; from the year 1772, to 1777...*

London [England]: Printed for J. Johnson, St. Paul's Church Yard, & J. Edwards, Pall Mall, **1796.** No colophon in vol. 2. **Regular paper issue** with un-colored plates.

2 vols., 4to. (28 cm.), folding map, plan, plates (some engraved by William Blake). **Includes list of subscribers.** https://www.biodiversitylibrary.org/item/163990#page/430/ mode/1up ESTC t146566; Price & Price 1.

18.1b ———.

Heavily edited version of John Gabriel Stedman's understanding of Kwasimukámba's story (18.0b) printed on pp. 346–348 in chapter XXIX (with full-length portrait of Kwasi reproduced on engraved plate between p. 348 and 349) in vol. 2 of John Gabriel Stedman, *Narrative, of a Five Years' Expedition, against the Revolted Negroes of Surinam, in Guiana, on the Wild Coast of South America; from the year 1772, to 1777...*

London [England]: Printed for J. Johnson, St. Paul's Church Yard, & J. Edwards, Pall Mall, **1796.** No colophon in vol. 2. **Large paper issue** with hand-colored title-page vignettes and plates.

2 vols., 4to. (28 cm.), folding map, plan, plates (some engraved by William Blake). **Includes list of subscribers.** https://archive.org/details/narrativeoffivey02sted_0/page/346/ mode/1up ESTC t146565; Price & Price 2.

18.0   Kwasimukámba

18.2 ———. [German translation of 18.1, abridged]

German translation of 18.1 printed on pp. 486–487 of John Gabriel Stedman, *Stedman's Nachrichten von Surinam und von seiner Expedition gegen die rebellischen Neger in dieser Kolonie in den Jahren 1772 bis 1777.*

Hamburg [Germany]: bei Benjamin Gotttlob [*sic*] Hoffmann, **1797**.
8vo: xiv, 522 p., illus., map.
https://www.e-rara.ch/zuz/nagezh/content/pageview/9727763
Price & Price 3.

18.3 ———. [Abridged French translation of 18.1]

French translation *of* 18.1 in vol. 3 of John Gabriel Stedman, *Voyage a Surinam et dans l'Intérieur de Guiane ...* translated from the English by P. F. Henry.

Paris [France]: chez F. Buisson, Imprimeur-Libraire, rue Hautefeuille, no. 20, an VII de la Republique [i.e., **1798**].
3 vols., 8vo.
Price & Price 6.

18.4 ———. [Unabridged? French translation of 18.1]

French translation of 18.1 in vol. 3 of John Gabriel Stedman, *Voyage à Surinam et dans l'intérieur de la Guiane. Contenant la relation de cinq années de courses et d'observations faites dans cette contrée intéressante et peu connue ; avec des détails sur les Indiens de la Guiane et les Nègres... traduit de l'anglais par P. F. Henry.*

Lausanne [Switzerland]: chez Hermann, **1799**.
3 vols., 8vo.

18.5 ———. [Dutch translation of 18.1]

Dutch translation of 18.1 in John Gabriel Stedman, *Reize in de Binnenlanden van Suriname.* Translated by J. D. Pasteur.

Leyden [Netherlands]: By A. en J. Hankoop, MDCCXC.IX, [**1799**].
8vo.

18.6 ———.

Dutch translation of 18.1 (supplemented with elements of the French in 18.4) printed on pp. 72 and 296–298 in vol. 3 of John Gabriel Stedman, *Reize naar Surinamen, en door der Binnenste Gedeelten van Guiana.*

Amsterdam [Netherlands]: by Johannes Allart, MDCCX-CIX-MDCCC [**1799–1800**].
4 vols., 8vo.
https://www.delpher.nl/nl/boeken/view?coll=boeken&identifier=dpo:8143:mpeg21:0325&cql%5B%5D=%28creator+exact+%22Stedman%2C+John+Gabrie%CC%88l%22%29&objectsearch=Quacy

18.7 ———.

Swedish translation of 18.1 printed on pp. 207 and 274–276 of *Capitain Johan Stedmans dagbok öfwer sina fälttåg i Surinam, jämte beskrifning om detta nybygges inwånare och öfriga märkwärdigheter*, translated by Samuel Ödmann.

Stockholm [Sweden]: Tryckt i Kongl. Ordens Boktryckeriet hos Assessoren Johan Pfeiffer, **1800**.
8vo (19 cm.): [6], 306, [14] p., plate, illus.
https://babel.hathitrust.org/cgi/pt?id=uc1.31175035187510&view=1up&seq=219&q1=Quacy

18.8 ———. [Second English edition of 18.1]

Heavily edited version of John Gabriel Stedman's understanding of Kwasimukámba's story (18.0b) printed on pp. 359–361 in chapter XXIX (with full-length portrait of Kwasi reproduced on engraved plate between pp. 360 and 361) in vol. 2 of John Gabriel Stedman, *Narrative, of a Five Years' Expedition, against the Revolted Negroes of Surinam, in Guiana, on the Wild Coast of South America; from the year 1772, to 1777... Second edition, corrected.*

London [England]: Printed for J. Johnson, St. Paul's Church Yard, and Th. Payne, Pall Mall, **1806**. Colophon: Luke Hansard, printer, near Lincoln's-Inn-Fields.
2 vols., 4to. (27 cm.), folding map, plan, plates (some engraved by William Blake).
https://babel.hathitrust.org/cgi/pt?id=gri.ark:/13960/t4jm38n7d&view=1up&seq=441
Price & Price 12.

18.9 ———. [Another printing of 18.8]

Heavily edited version of John Gabriel Stedman's understanding of Kwasimukámba's story (18.0b) printed on pp. 359–361 in chapter XXIX (with full-length portrait of Kwasi reproduced on engraved plate between pp. 360 and 361) in vol. 2 of John Gabriel Stedman, *Narrative, of a Five Years' Expedition, against the Revolted Negroes of Surinam, in Guiana, on the Wild Coast of South America; from the year 1772, to 1777... Second edition* [*sic*], *corrected.*

London [England]: Printed for J. Johnson, St. Paul's Church Yard, and Th. Payne, Pall Mall, **1813**. Colophon: Luke Hansard, printer, near Lincoln's-Inn-Fields.
2 vols., 4to. (27 cm.), folding map, plan, plates (some engraved by William Blake).
https://archive.org/details/narrativeoffivey02sted/page/359/mode/1up

18.10 ———. [Italian translation based on 18.4, the 1798 French translation]

Italian translation of 18.1 in *Viaggio al Surinam e nell'interno della Guiana ossia relazione di cinque anni di corse e di os-*

servazioni fatte in questo interessante e poco conosciuto paese .... Versione dal francese del Cav. [Bartolomeo] Borghi.

Milano [Italia]: dalla Tipografia di Giambattista Sonzogno, 1818.
4 vols., 12mo (18 cm.).

18.11 ———.

Heavily edited version of John Gabriel Stedman's understanding of Kwasimukámba's story (18.0b) printed from 18.1 on pp. 227–228 (with his full-length portrait facing p. 227) of John Gabriel Stedman, *Expedition to Surinam: being the Narrative of a Five Years' Expedition against the Revolted Negroes of Surinam in Guiana from the year 1772, to 1777 ... newly edited and abridged* [from 18.1] *by Christopher Bryant ...*

London [England]: The Folio Society, **1963**. Tpv: Printed in Great Britain. Printed and bound by Richard Clay & Co. Ltd, Bungay.
8vo (26 cm.): viii, [2], 239 p., plates.

18.12 ———. [Critical edition of 18.1]

Heavily edited version of John Gabriel Stedman's understanding of Kwasimukámba's story (18.0b) printed from 18.1 on pp. 409–411 (with reproduction of his portrait as engraved by William Blake between pages 412 and 413) in vol. 2 of John Gabriel Stedman, *Narrative, of a Five Years' Expedition, against the Revolted Negroes of Surinam, in Guiana, on the Wild Coast of South America; from the year 1772, to 1777...* [Introduction and notes by R. A. J. van Lier].

Barre, Massachusetts [U.S.A.]: Printed for the Imprint Society, **1971**. Colophon (vol. 2 only): ... printed ... by Joh. Enschede en Zonen, Haarlem, Holland....
2 vols. (continuously paged), 8vo (27.5 cm.): xviii, [10], 480, [1] p., plates, some folding.

18.13 ———. [Critical edition of 18.1]

Heavily edited version of John Gabriel Stedman's understanding of Kwasimukámba's story (18.0b) printed from 18.1 on pp. 409–411 (with reproduction of his portrait as engraved by William Blake between pages 412 and 413) of John Gabriel Stedman, *Narrative, of a Five Years' Expedition, against the Revolted Negroes of Surinam, in Guiana, on the Wild Coast of South America; from the year 1772, to 1777 ...* [Introduction and notes by R. A. J. van Lier].

Amherst [Massachusetts, U.S.A.]: University of Massachusetts Press, MCMLXXII [**1972**].
8vo (27.3 cm.): xviii, [10], 480 p., plates, some folding. Comprises sheets ("printed ... by Joh. Enschede en Zonen, Haarlem, Holland" as noted in 18.12) from 18.12 but here bound in one volume with distinct title-page.

18.14 ———.

Extended excerpts from 18.0a in Richard Price, "Kwasimukámba's Gambit," in the periodical *Bijdragen tot de Taal-, Land- en Volkenkunde* [anglicé *Journal of the humanities and social sciences of Southeast Asia and Oceania*], 135: 151–169, especially 157–158.

s'Gravenhage [Netherlands], Martinus Nijhoff, **1979**.
8vo (24 cm.).

18.15 ———.

Excerpts from 18.14 reprinted under heading "Kwasimukámba's Gambit, 1755" on pp. 153–159 in Richard Price, *First-Time: The Historical Vision of an Afro-American People.*

Baltimore [Maryland, U.S.A.]: The Johns Hopkins University Press, [**1983**].
8vo (26 cm.): 189 p., illus. (including portraits), maps.

18.16 ———.

First full *verbatim et literatim* transcription of 18.0b, John Gabriel Stedman's understanding of Kwasimukámba's story, printed under date 28 January 1777 on pp. 581–584 of Stedman's *Narrative of a Five Years' Expedition against the Revolted Negroes of Surinam, in Guiana, on the Wild Coast of South America; from the year 1772, to 1777 ... transcribed for the first time from the original 1790 manuscript; edited, and with an introduction and notes,* by Richard Price & Sally Price.

Baltimore [Maryland, U.S.A.]: The Johns Hopkins University Press, **1988**.
8vo (27 cm.): xcvii, 708 p., illus.

18.17 ———. [Second printing of 18.15]

Excerpts from 18.15 reprinted under heading "Kwasimukámba's Gambit, 1755" on pp. 153–159 in Richard Price, *First-Time: The Historical Vision of an Afro-American People.*

Baltimore [Maryland, U.S.A.]: The Johns Hopkins University Press, [**1989**].
8vo (26 cm.): 189 p., illus. (including portraits), maps.

18.18 ———. [Third printing of 18.15]

Excerpts from 18.15 reprinted under heading "Kwasimukámba's Gambit, 1755" on pp. 153–159 in Richard Price, *First-Time: The Historical Vision of an Afro-American People.*

Baltimore [Maryland, U.S.A.]: The Johns Hopkins University Press, [**1991**].
8vo (26 cm.): 189 p., illus. (including portraits), maps.

18.19 ———. [Abridged edition of 18.16]

John Gabriel Stedman's understanding of Kwasimukámba's story printed from 18.16 under date 28 January 1777 on pp. 300–301 (with full-length portrait of Kwasi reproduced on p. 302) of John Gabriel Stedman, *Stedman's Surinam Life in an Eighteenth-Century Slave Society An Abridged, Modernized Edition of Narrative of a Five Years* [sic] *Expedition against the Revolted Negroes of Surinam* by John Gabriel Stedman. Edited by Richard Price and Sally Price.

Baltimore [Maryland, U.S.A.]: The Johns Hopkins University Press, **[1992].**
8vo (23 cm.): lxxv, [3], [1-5] 6350 p., map, illus. Note: This abridgement "include[s] about 50 percent of the original text and 33 of the original 81 plates" (p. lxv).

18.20 ———. [French edition of 18.15]

Excerpts from 18.15 reprinted under heading "Les manoeuvres de Kwasimukamba, 1755" in Richard Price, *Les Premiers Temps: La Conception de l'histoire des Marrons Saramaka.* Traduit de l'anglais par Michèle Baj Strobel, avec la collaboration de l'auteur.

Paris [France]: Seuil, **1994.**
8vo (24 cm.): 279 p., illus. (including portraits), maps.

18.21 ———. [Second edition of 18.15]

Excerpts from 18.15 reprinted under heading "Kwasimukámba's Gambit, 1755" on pp. 153–159 in Richard Price, *First-Time: The Historical Vision of an African American People,* Second edition, with a new preface by the author.

Chicago [Illinois, U.S.A.]: University of Chicago Press, **[2002].**
8vo (26 cm.): xvi, 189 p., illus. (including portraits), maps.

18.22 ———. [Another (complete) printing of 18.16]

Full *verbatim et literatim* transcription of 18.0b, John Gabriel Stedman's understanding of Kwasimukámba's story, **reprinted** from 18.16 under date 28 January 1777 on pp. 581–584 of Stedman's *Narrative, of a Five Years' Expedition, against the Revolted Negroes of Surinam, in Guiana, on the Wild Coast of South America; from the year 1772, to 1777 … transcribed for the first time* [sic] *from the original 1790 manuscript;* edited, and with an introduction and notes, by Richard Price & Sally Price.

New York [New York, U.S.A.]: iUniverse.com, **[2010].**
8vo (27 cm.): xcvii, 708 p., illus.

18.23 ———. [Second French edition of 18.15]

Excerpts from 18.14 reprinted under heading "Les manoeuvres de Kwasimukamba, 1755" on pp. 252–263 in Richard Price, *Les Premiers Temps: La conception de l'histoire des Marrons saramaka.* Traduit de l'anglais (Etats-Unis) par Michèle Baj Strobel, avec la collaboration de l'auteur.

[La Roque-d'Anthéron, France]: Vents d'ailleurs **[2013].**
8vo (23 cm.): 299, [4] p., illus. (including portraits), maps. Traduction de l'Introduction a la seconde édition française par Catherine Bednarek.

18.24 ———. [Translation of 18.14 into Saamaka]

Excerpts from 18.14 translated into Saamaka in Richard Price, *Fesiten … Richard Price ku Sally Price puu di buku a Ingisitongo ko a Saamakatongo. Vinije Haabo heepi fu seeka di Saamaka Tongo ko moo gbelen gbelen.*

[La Roque-d'Anthéron, France]: Vents d'ailleurs **[2013].**
8vo (23 cm.): 251 p., illus. (including portraits), maps.

Ca. 1755

19.0   Magdalene Beulah Brockden (1731–1820)

Manuscript "Lebenslauf" (Memoir) written in German **ca. 1755** and preserved in the Moravian Archives, Bethlehem, Pennsylvania, U.S.A.

¶ Brockden was born in Petit Popo (present-day Togo—see Map 5) and captured by slavers as a small child. After forcible transportation to Philadelphia in the British North American colony of Pennsylvania, she was purchased by Charles Brockden, who sent her to the Moravian settlement in Bethlehem, Pennsylvania (Map 16), for religious conversion and

Full text: https://huskiecommons.lib.niu.edu/history-500africanvoices/13/ [see 19.1].

upbringing. Brockden manumitted her by degrees beginning in 1752. Baptized in 1748, she married in 1762 Ofodobendo Wooma/Andrew, an Igbo (present-day southeastern Nigeria) man (q.v. 106.0), who was also Moravian. Her husband died in 1779, but she remained in Bethlehem, working as a laundress. In 19.1 Katherine M. Faull estimates Brockden wrote her memoir in the mid-1750s.

19.1 ———.

First printing of 19.0, with English translation and editorial annotations on pp. 77–78 in Katherine M. Faull (ed.), *Moravian Women's Memoirs: Their Related Lives, 1750–1820.*

Syracuse [New York, U.S.A.]: Syracuse University Press, **1997.**
8vo (24 cm.): xl, 166 p., plates, illus., map.

19.2 ——.

Second printing of 19.0, with English translation and editorial annotations on pp. 77–78 in Katherine M. Faull (ed.), *Moravian Women's Memoirs: Their Related Lives, 1750–1820.*

Syracuse [New York, U.S.A.]: Syracuse University Press, 2009. 8vo (24 cm.): xl, 166 p., plates, illus., map.

1757

20.0 Médor (–1757)

20.0a: His life story written down in the manuscript headed "Déclaration du nègre Médor," le 26 mars [*sic*] 1757, aux A. M. C [Archives du Ministères des Colonies], CORR. gén., C⁹ [*Saint-Domingue*], vol. CII (*i.e.* 102),* held in the Archives Nationales, **Paris, France.**

*The present editors owe this reference to Pierre de Vaissières, *Saint-Domingue: la Société et la vie Créole sous l'Ancien Régime, 1629–1789* (Paris: Perrin, 1909), p. 247, n. 1; and Etienne Taillemite, "Les Archives des Colonies Françaises aux Archives Nationales," *Gazette des Archives* (1964), p. 101.

20.0b: His life story copied or partially copied from 20.0a into the manuscript headed "Extrait des déclarations de Médor," 26 Mai 1757, AC, série F3, vol. 88, folios 212–214, held in the Archives Nationales d'Outre-Mer (ANOM), **Aix-en-Provence, France.**

¶ **Médor was born in Africa and transported on a slave ship to Saint-Domingue (present-day Haiti), the French colony in the Caribbean (see Map 11), probably significantly before 1737. He lived with his owners in the mountainous northeastern district of Perches in Trou Parish. In 1757 he and Vénus (q.v. 21.0) confessed to poisoning (with herbs) their white owners as part of a larger years-long conspiracy by the colony's enslaved men and women to do the same to their owners. The day Médor confessed (apparently without torture) his own and many others' guilt, he, though guarded and in chains, was stabbed to death. His owner thought he committed suicide.**

20.1 ——.

Account printed from 20.0b with annotations in "La confession de Médor. Au commencement de l'affaire Macandal. Partie française de Saint-Domingue, 1757," edited by John Garrigus, on pp. 73–84 (including introductory material) in *Voix d'Esclaves Antilles, Guyane et Louisane Françaises, XVIIIᵉ-XIXᵉ Siècles,* edited by Dominique Rogers.

Paris [France]: Karthala; CIRESC*; **Fort-de-France [Martinique]:** SAA**, 2015.

Full text: https://huskiecommons.lib.niu.edu/history-500africanvoices/14/ [see 20.1].

*Centre Internationale de Recherches sur les Esclavages.
**Society of American Archivists.
8vo (22 cm.): 184 p., illus.

21.0 Vénus

21.0a: Account of her life written down within the manuscript headed "Déclaration du nègre Médor," le 26 mars [*sic*] 1757, aux A. M. C [Archives du Ministères des Colonies], CORR. gén., C⁹ [*Saint-Domingue*], vol. CII (*i.e.* 102),* held in the Archives Nationales, **Paris, France.** *The present editors owe this reference to Pierre de Vaissières, *Saint-Domingue: la Société et la vie Créole sous l'Ancien Régime, 1629–1789* (Paris: Perrin, 1909), p. 247, n. 1; and Etienne Taillemite, "Les Archives des Colonies Françaises aux Archives Nationales," *Gazette des Archives* (1964), p. 101.

21.0b: Account of her life copied or partially copied from 21.0a into the manuscript headed "Extrait des déclarations de Médor," 26 Mai 1757, AC, série F3, vol. 88, folios 212–214, held in the Archives Nationales d'Outre-Mer (ANOM), **Aix-en-Provence, France.**

¶ **Vénus spoke the same language as Médor (q.v. 20.0) and was also forcibly transported on a slave ship to Saint-Domingue (present-day Haiti), the French colony in the Caribbean. There she was purchased by Médor's owners and lived with them in the mountainous northeastern district of Perches in Trou Parish. In 1757 she confessed (as did Médor) to poisoning (with herbs) their white owners as part of a larger years-long conspiracy by the colony's enslaved men and women to do the same to their owners. Vénus declared she did this to avenge their owners' ill treatment of them all. While testifying she tried but failed to exonerate Médor, who was killed later that day. Her fate is not yet known.**

21.1 ——.

Account embedded within her comrade Médor's (q.v. 20.1) printed from 21.0b with annotations in "La confession de Médor. Au commencement de l'affaire Macandal. Partie française de Saint-Domingue, 1757," edited by John Garri-

Full text: https://huskiecommons.lib.niu.edu/history-500africanvoices/15/ [see 21.1].

gus, on pp. 73–84 (including introductory material) in *Voix d'Esclaves Antilles, Guyane et Louisane Françaises, XVIIIe-XIXe Siècles*, edited by Dominique Rogers.

Paris [France]: Karthala; CIRESC*; Fort-de-France [Martinique]: SAA**, 2015.
*Centre Internationale de Recherches sur les Esclavages.
**Society of American Archivists.
8vo (22 cm.): 184 p., illus.

1760

22.0   Apongo = Wager

His account incorporated in Thomas Thistlewood's diary entry for 4 December 1760, the original manuscript of which is among the Thomas Thistlewood Papers at the Beinecke Rare Books and Manuscripts Library, Yale University, New Haven, Connecticut, U.S.A.

¶ Apongo was identified as Fon, born in Dahomey (present-day Benin—see Map 5). There he was a prince who led a contingent of a hundred armed men to see the governor (John Cope Sr.) of Cape Coast Castle (present-day Ghana). He was kidnapped while hunting in the 1740s and sold to the captain of the HMS *Wager*, Arthur Forrest, RN, who took Apongo to his own plantation in Westmoreland Parish, Jamaica (Map 13), the British Caribbean colony. In Jamaica, Apongo again met Cope, who attempted to free him but died in 1756 before he could. In 1760 Apongo was tried, convicted, and executed for helping lead a large insurrection known as Tacky's Rebellion. For more on him, see indexed references in Vincent Brown, *Tacky's Revolt: The Story of an Atlantic Slave War* (Cambridge MA: Harvard University Press, 2020).

Full text: https://huskiecommons.lib.niu.edu/history-500africanvoices/16/ [see 22.3].

22.1 ———.

His account printed from 22.0 on pp. 105–106, with commentary through p. 107, in Douglas Hall, *In Miserable Slavery: Thomas Thistlewood in Jamaica, 1750–86*.

London [England]: Macmillan, 1989.
8vo (22 cm.): xxi, 322 p., illus. Series: Warwick University Caribbean Studies.
FN 000133.

22.2 ———.

His account printed from 22.0 on pp. 105–106, with commentary through p. 107, in Douglas Hall, *In Miserable Slavery: Thomas Thistlewood in Jamaica, 1750–86*. Revised edition.

Kingston [Jamaica]: University of West Indies Press, 1999.
8vo (22 cm.): xxiii, 321 p., illus.

22.3 ———.

His account printed from 22.0 on pp. 297–298*n*2 of Trevor Burnard, *Mastery, Tyranny, and Desire: Thomas Thistlewood and His Slaves in the Anglo-Jamaican World*.

Chapel Hill [North Carolina, U.S.A.]: University of North Carolina Press, [2004].
8vo (24 cm.): xii, 320 p., illus.

1763-65

23.0   Rosa Egipcíaca (1719–1771) = Rosa Maria Egipcíaca da Vera Cruz

Autobiographical information from Egipcíaca's trial testimony in Torre do Tombo, Lisbon, Portugal: Inquisition trial records; Rosa Egipcíaca's case *Processo 9,065* with 350 dictated pages (dating 1763–1765) and 26 of her letters and other addenda comprising her *Auto de Perguntas Feitas à Ré Rosa Maria Egipcíaca da Vera Cruz, Preta Forra*.

Full text: https://huskiecommons.lib.niu.edu/history-500africanvoices/17/ [see 23.3].

¶ Born in the country of the Amina people (coastal area of present-day Ghana or Togo—see Map 5), Egipcíaca was taken at age six (in 1725) on a slave ship to Rio de Janeiro, Brazil, where she was sold and baptized. In 1733 she was taken to the Brazilian province of Minas Gerais (Map 9) and forced into sexual slavery. In 1748 she underwent a mystical religious conversion and first saw visions, which continued sporadically for the rest of her life. Manumitted in 1749, she moved in 1751 to Rio de Janeiro and became a spiritual leader. She inspired a large and influential following in Rio, but her visions and prophesying kept her in trouble with church authorities, who had her imprisoned and beaten. In 1763 she was transported to Lisbon, Portugal ap 7), to appear before the Inquisition. There she languished in prison until she died in 1771. Her life story comes primarily from records of her six Inquisition hearings (held 1763–1765), with additions from letters she began writing in 1752. For extended biographical information, see Luiz Mott's 1993 biography (23.2) and Robert Krueger's 2002 article (23.3). Krueger has found twenty-five of her letters, as well as a book manuscript, tracts, and dictation, all totaling about two hundred pages, which await full publication. *The compilers thank Robert Krueger for information crucial to entries 23.0 to 23.4.*

23.1 ——.
Egipcíaca's autobiographical manuscripts mentioned in Luiz Mott, "Uma Santa Africana no Brasil Colonial," *D.O. Leitura* 6: 62: 4. Note: text in three columns, small type.

São Paulo, Brazil: Imprensa Oficial do Estado, July **1987**.

23.2 ——.
Extensive quotations from Egipcíaca's autobiographical manuscripts printed in Luiz Mott, *Rosa Egipcíaca. Uma Santa Africana no Brasil.*

Rio de Janeiro [Brazil]: Bertrand, **1993**. 8vo (21 cm.): 749 p.

23.3 ——.
Quotations from Egipcíaca's autobiographical manuscripts printed on pp. 175–177 in Robert Krueger, "Brazilian Slaves Represented in Their Own Words," in the academic journal *Slavery & Abolition*, 23(2): 169–186.

Abingdon, England: Routledge, **2002**.

23.4 ——.
Substantive quotations from Egipcíaca's autobiographical manuscripts printed in Luiz Mott, "Uma Santa Africana no Brasil Colonial," being number 38 (in the 3rd year) of series *Cadernos Idéias*.

São Leopoldo, Brazil: Instituto Humanitas Unisinos, Universidade do Vale do Rio dos Sinos (UNISINOS), **2005**. 8vo (23 cm.): [iv], 26 p.

1764

24.0 Comba (ca. 1714–) = Mama Comba = Julie

Manuscript: Interrogatoire de la négresse Comba, Registres du Counseil Supérieur de Louisiane, 1764/09/04/01 and other information in 1764/07/14/04, 7; 1764/07/14/04, 6–7; 1764/07/10/03, 2, held in the Louisiana State Museum, New Orleans, Louisiana, U.S.A.

Full text: https:// huskiecommons. lib.niu.edu/history-500africanvoices/18/ [see 24.2].

¶ Comba, a Mandinka (an ethnic group residing in southern Mali, Guinea, and Ivory Coast—see Map 3), was born ca. 1714. She was taken in the slave trade to New Orleans, the colonial French North American port near the mouth of the Mississippi River on the Gulf of Mexico (Map 15). She married and after losing her husband had a relationship with a Maroon. While living there in a hospital for the poor, she was arrested and questioned for assisting Maroons. Her account exists in the official report on this affair. Found guilty, she and another woman were condemned to watch the Maroon with whom she had the affair broken (executed) on the wheel.

24.1 ——.
Account edited by Cécile Vidal and printed under title "Comba, esclave noire de Louisane, Marronage et sociavilité" on

pp. 61–66 of *Voix d'Esclaves Antilles, Guyane et Louisane Françaises, XVIIIe–XIXe Siècle*, edited by Dominique Rogers.

Paris [France]: Karthala; CIRESC*; Fort-de-France [Martinique]: SAA**, **2015**. *Centre Internationale de Recherches sur les Esclavages. **Society of American Archivists. 8vo (22 cm.): 184 p., illus.

24.2 ——.
Additional aspects of this account with editor's commentary printed on pp. 160–162 in Sophie White, *Voices of the Enslaved: Love, Labor, and Longing in French Louisiana*

Chapel Hill [North Carolina, U.S.A.]: University of North Carolina Press, **2019**. 8vo (24 cm.): viii, 344 p., illus.

25.0 Marguerite (ca. 1739–)

Manuscript account recorded on 23 October 1764 (RSCL 1764/10/23/01, 1) preserved among Records of the [French] Superior Council of Louisiana, Louisiana State Museum, New Orleans, Louisiana, U.S.A.

Full text: https:// huskiecommons. lib.niu.edu/history-500africanvoices/19/ [see 25.1].

¶ Marguerite identified as Congo. She was taken on a slave ship directly or indirectly to the French North

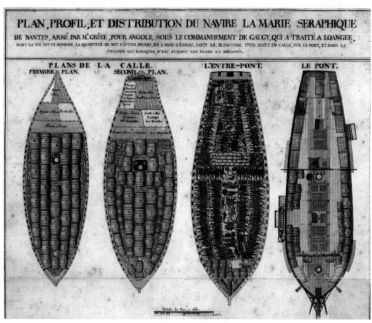

Figure 3: Slave sale on the French ship *La Marie Seraphique* of Nantes while anchored at Cap Français (Cap-Haïtien), Sainte-Domingue (Haiti) in 1773 after its third voyage from Angola.

Source: Watercolor and print possibly by Jean-Rene L'Hermite (second lieutenant) and Fautrel-Gaugy (captain). © Château des ducs de Bretagne-Musée d'Histoire de Nantes, France.

American colony of Louisiana, to its capital, New Orleans (see Map 15). She learned French and worked enslaved in a townhouse in the city, where her mistress mistreated her and had her whipped in the public square. She frequently visited a man (probably her lover) on a plantation many miles downriver but was eventually caught by the overseer and convicted by the court for running away. Her sentence included cutting off her ears, branding the *fleur-de-lis* on her right shoulder, and returning her to her New Orleans owners.

25.1 ——.

Quotations of account printed in original French with English translation and facsimile of French manuscript on pp. 1–3 and 191 in Sophie White, *Voices of the Enslaved: Love, Labor, and Longing in French Louisiana.*

Chapel Hill [North Carolina, U.S.A.]: University of North Carolina Press, 2019.
8vo (24 cm.): viii, 344 p., illus.

25.2 ——.

Brief quotation printed in English translation printed on p. 17 in Sophie White, "'Said Without Being Asked': Slavery, Testimony, and Autobiography," on pp. 17–39 in *Hearing Enslaved Voices African and Indian Slave Testimony in British and French America, 1700–1848*, edited by Sophie White and Trevor G. Burnard [*sic*].

New York [New York, U.S.A.]: Routledge, Taylor & Francis Group, 2020.
8vo (24 cm.): viii, 256 p., maps.

26.0 Jean

Manuscript account dated 31 July 1764 (RSCL 1764/07/31/01, 1; 1764/08/04/01, 2–3) preserved among Records of the [French] Superior Council of Louisiana, Louisiana State Museum, New Orleans, Louisiana, U.S.A.

¶ Jean identified as of the Nago nation (present-day Nigeria, Benin, and Togo—see Map 15). He was taken on a slave ship directly or indirectly to New Orleans (the port in the French North American colony of Louisiana, Map 15) and sold, eventually to a Mr. Mandeville. After previous punishment for offenses, including two hundred lashes, he was tried and convicted in 1764 for theft and running away. He was sentenced to a whipping, the

Full text: https://huskiecommons.lib.niu.edu/history-500africanvoices/20/ [see 26.1].

cutting of his hamstring, and branding of a "V" (for *voleur* = thief) on his cheek.

26.1 ——.

Extended quotations from the manuscript printed in French with English translation on pp. 41–42 (especially p. 41) in Sophie White, *Voices of the Enslaved: Love, Labor, and Longing in French Louisiana.*

Chapel Hill [North Carolina, U.S.A]: University of North Carolina Press, 2019.
8vo (24 cm.): viii, 344 p., illus.

27.0 Louis

Account in manuscripts dated 4 September 1764 (RSCL 1764/09/04/02, 14-15 and 1764/09/04 /04, 1) preserved among Records of the [French] Superior Council of Louisiana, held at the Louisiana State Museum, New Orleans, Louisiana, U.S.A.

¶ Louis identified as Mandinka (an ethnic group residing in southern Mali, Guinea, and Ivory Coast—see Map 3). He was taken on a slave ship directly or indirectly to New Orleans, the capital of the French North American colony of Louisiana (Map 15), and sold. At some point thereafter he and another man ran away, purportedly to Illinois Country, from up the Mississippi River. They returned, and Louis began visiting a plantation near New Orleans, where he developed an intimate relationship with an enslaved woman until captured. He described this situation at his 1764 trial (for running away and other crimes), at which witnesses contributed additional information about him. After his conviction Louis was executed by breaking on the wheel. For more on him see Cécile Vidal, "Comba, esclave noire de Louisiane: Marronage et sociabilité, 1764," in *Voix d'Esclaves Antilles, Guyane et Louisane Françaises, XVIIIe–XIXe Siècles*, edited by Dominique Rogers (Paris: Karthala, 2015), pp. 61–66.

Full text: https://huskiecommons.lib.niu.edu/history-500africanvoices/21/ [see 27.1].

27.1 ——.

Extended French-language quotations from 27.0 printed with English translations on pp. 39–40 and 160–162 in Sophie White, *Voices of the Enslaved: Love, Labor, and Longing in French Louisiana.*

Chapel Hill [North Carolina, U.S.A.]: University of North Carolina Press, 2019.
8vo (24 cm.): viii, 344 p., illus.

1765

28.0 Essom

Account in French manuscript dated 16 February **1765**, recorded by an interpreter who spoke Essom's Nago language (RCSL 1765/02/16/01, no. 1859), preserved among Records of the [French] Superior Council of Louisiana, held at the Louisiana State Museum, **New Orleans, Louisiana, U.S.A.**

¶ Essom identified as Nago (present-day Nigeria, Benin, and Togo—see Map 5). He was taken on a slave ship directly or indirectly to New Orleans, capital

Full text: https://huskiecommons.lib.niu.edu/history-500africanvoices/22/ [see 28.1].

of the French North American colony of Louisiana (Map 15), and sold. He ran away (as he explained in his brief account before the court after being caught) because his owner had taken away the woman or wife (*femme*) he had been given to prepare his food and drink.

28.1 ——.

Brief French-language quotation from 28.0 printed with English translation on p. 190 in Sophie White, *Voices of the Enslaved: Love, Labor, and Longing in French Louisiana.*

Chapel Hill [North Carolina, U.S.A.]: University of North Carolina Press, 2019.
8vo (24 cm.): viii, 344 p., illus.

1766

29.0 Démocrite (*ca.* 1726–)

Account in manuscript dated 29 July **1766** (RSCL 1766/07/29/04) preserved among Records of the [French] Superior Council of Louisiana, held at the Louisiana State Museum, **New Orleans, Louisiana, U.S.A.**

¶ Démocrite identified as Igbo (present-day southeastern Nigeria—see Map 5). He was taken on a slave ship directly or indirectly to New Orleans, the capital of the French North American colony of Louisiana (Map 15). Sieur Jacques Esmould de Livaudais, a former port captain, purchased him and put him to work on his outlying

Full text: https://huskiecommons.lib.niu.edu/history-500africanvoices/23/ [see 29.1].

plantation. In 1766 Démocrite was involved in a knife fight with an enslaved man who had run away many times and disturbed the lives of Démocrite and others on the plantation. For this Démocrite testified against the man at his 1766 trial. In 1773 Démocrite still lived on the same plantation.

29.1 ——.

English translation of brief quotation from 29.0 printed on pp. 132–134 and 140 with related discussion on pp. 132–179 in Sophie White, *Voices of the Enslaved: Love, Labor, and Longing in French Louisiana.*

Chapel Hill [North Carolina, U.S.A.]: University of North Carolina Press, 2019.
8vo (24 cm.): viii, 344 p., illus.

1767

¶ Note for entries 30 through 110: Moravian missionary Christian Georg Andreas Oldendorp recorded these accounts in German while touring his Protestant religious group's missions on the Danish Caribbean islands of St. Thomas, St. Croix, and St. John in 1767–1768 (see Map 14). He recorded the final three accounts (qq.v 108.0, 109.0, and 110.0) during a stopover in the British North American colony of Pennsylvania (Map 16) on his way home to Europe. An abridged version of Oldendorp's manuscript was published in 1777 (this is its *editio princeps*); yet this abridgement excluded many of the eighty-one accounts listed below. These eighty-one accounts were not all printed together until the first complete edition of Oldendorp's 3,000-page manuscript was published

in 2000–2002. As the following entries show, these accounts are printed in many different places in the 2000–2002 edition. Readers should note further that (1) during his Caribbean tour Oldendorp spoke with many more Africans and Creoles than we list here, (2) the responses of these *other* witnesses and information about them can be found in the complete 2000–2002 edition of Oldendorp's manuscript, but (3) only those women and men whose life experiences meet all the criteria of this catalog are presented here.

Note: See *"Note on Translations and Transcriptions"* in the introductory material of this volume for important information about the English translations of Oldendorp's work.

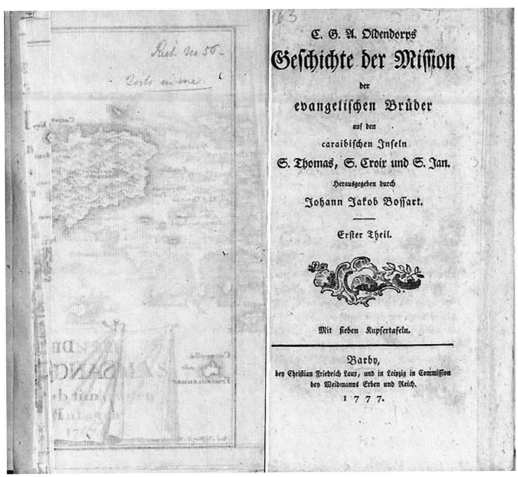

Figure 4: First edition title page in original German of Christian Georg Andreas Oldendorp, *Geschichte der Mission der evangelischen Brueder auf den caraibischen Inseln S. Thomas, S. Croix, und S. Jan,* edited by Johann Jakob Bossart (Barby, Germany: Christian Friedrich Laur and Leipzig, Germany: Weidmanns Erben and Reich, 1777).

30.0 Unnamed African woman

Aspects of this woman's life story summarized in Christian Georg Andreas Oldendorp's 3,000-page manuscript account of Oldendorp's 1767–1768 tour of Denmark's West Indian possessions, viz. "Manuskript für eine Geschichte der Mission auf den westindischen Inseln, verfasst von C. G. A. Oldendorp," R.28.63 and R.28.62, held in the Unity Archives, **Herrnhut,** Saxony, Germany.

Full text: https:// huskiecommons. lib.niu.edu/history-500africanvoices/24/ [see 30.1].

¶ This unnamed *Bussalin* (African woman) was taken in the slave trade to the Danish West Indies (see Map 14). She worked in the household of a woman who treated her badly but was able to spend a lot of time outside the household and earn money, most of which her owner appropriated. She was married to an enslaved man who had another wife, lived elsewhere, and rarely visited. She spoke neither European languages nor Dutch Creole well. Fed up with ill treatment by her owner, she ran away and tried to find her way back to Africa. After three weeks she returned and was punished. Thereafter, she began visiting the Moravian mission—one of the last of her slave ship companions to do so, she said. Hoping to be baptized, she told her story to Oldendorp in 1767.

30.1 ———.

Aspects of her life story transcribed from 30.0 and printed on p. 1697 in vol. 2, Part 3 of C. G. A. Oldendorp, *Historie der caribischen Inseln Sanct Thomas, Sanct Crux und Sanct Jan, insbesondere der dasigen Neger und der Mission der evangelischen Brüder unter denselben: kommentierte Ausgabe des vollständigen Manuskriptes aus dem Archiv der Evangelischen Brüder-Unität Herrnhut,* edited by Gudrun Meier et al. (Band [Volume] 51 in the series *Abhandlungen und Berichte des Staatlichen Museums für Völkerkunde Dresden*).

Berlin [Germany]: VWB, Verlag für Wissenschaft und Bildung, **2000–2002**.

2 vols. in 4, 8vo (24 cm.).

Vol. 2 (consecutively numbered), Part 3 (2002): vii; 1405–2171 p.

31.0 Unnamed African man

Aspects of this man's life story summarized in Christian Georg Andreas Oldendorp's 3,000-page manuscript account of Oldendorp's **1767–1768** tour of Denmark's West Indian possessions, viz. "Manuskript für eine Geschichte der Mission auf den westindischen Inseln, verfasst von C. G. A. Oldendorp," R.28.63 and R.28.62, held in the Unity Archives, **Herrnhut, Saxony, Germany.**

Full text: https://huskiecommons.lib.niu.edu/history-500africanvoices/25/ [see 31.1].

¶ This unnamed *Bussal* (African man) told Oldendorp that he had been taken in the slave trade through no fault of his own. His father was also enslaved but taken on a different ship, and father and son never saw each other again. After arrival on St. Thomas in the Danish West Indies (see Map 14), this unnamed *Bussal* began attending the Moravian mission and dedicated himself to living with them as a faithful member of the group. He told his story to Oldendorp in 1767.

31.1 ——.

Aspects of his life story transcribed from 31.0 and printed on p. 1698 in vol. 2, Part 3 of C. G. A. Oldendorp, *Historie der caribischen Inseln Sanct Thomas, Sanct Crux und Sanct Jan, insbesondere der dasigen Neger und der Mission der evangelischen Brüder unter denselben: kommentierte Ausgabe des vollständigen Manuskriptes aus dem Archiv der Evangelischen Brüder-Unität Herrnhut*, edited by Gudrun Meier et al. (Band [Volume] 51 in the series *Abhandlungen und Berichte des Staatlichen Museums für Völkerkunde Dresden*).

Berlin [Germany]: VWB, Verlag für Wissenschaft und Bildung, **2000–2002**.

2 vols. in 4, 8vo (24 cm.).

Vol. 2 (consecutively numbered), Part 3 (2002): vii; 1405–2171 p.

32.0 Unnamed African woman

Aspects of this woman's life story summarized in Christian Georg Andreas Oldendorp's 3,000-page manuscript account of Oldendorp's **1767–1768** tour of Denmark's West Indian possessions, viz. "Manuskript für eine Geschichte der Mission auf den westindischen Inseln, verfasst von C. G. A. Olden-

dorp," R.28.63 and R.28.62, held in the Unity Archives, **Herrnhut, Saxony, Germany.**

¶ After being taken in the transatlantic slave trade to St. Thomas in the Danish West Indies (see Map 14) and sold, this woman had two husbands (one after the other). The first treated her badly and left after they had a child, and the second was not much better. Thereafter, she lived alone and focused on saving her soul by joining the Moravian mission. She lived in a missionary house, attended meetings, confessed her sins committed in Africa and on St. Thomas, and devoted herself to Moravian piety and lifestyle. When she spoke to Oldendorp in 1767 she had not yet been baptized.

Full text: https://huskiecommons.lib.niu.edu/history-500africanvoices/26/ [see 32.1].

32.1 ——.

Aspects of her life story transcribed from 32.0 and printed on p. 1698 in vol. 2, Part 3 of C. G. A. Oldendorp, *Historie der caribischen Inseln Sanct Thomas, Sanct Crux und Sanct Jan, insbesondere der dasigen Neger und der Mission der evangelischen Brüder unter denselben: kommentierte Ausgabe des vollständigen Manuskriptes aus dem Archiv der Evangelischen Brüder-Unität Herrnhut*, edited by Gudrun Meier et al. (Band [Volume] 51 in the series *Abhandlungen und Berichte des Staatlichen Museums für Völkerkunde Dresden*).

Berlin [Germany]: VWB, Verlag für Wissenschaft und Bildung, **2000–2002**.

2 vols. in 4, 8vo (24 cm.).

Vol. 2 (consecutively numbered), Part 3 (2002): vii; 1405–2171 p.

33.0 Unnamed African woman

Aspects of this woman's life story summarized in Christian Georg Andreas Oldendorp's 3,000-page manuscript account of Oldendorp's **1767–1768** tour of Denmark's West Indian possessions, viz. "Manuskript für eine Geschichte der Mission auf den westindischen Inseln, verfasst von C. G. A. Oldendorp," R.28.63 and R.28.62, held in the Unity Archives, **Herrnhut, Saxony, Germany.**

Full text: https://huskiecommons.lib.niu.edu/history-500africanvoices/27/ [see 33.1].

¶ This African woman (*Bussalin*) was taken in the transatlantic slave trade to St. Thomas in the Danish West Indies and sold (see Map 14). She struggled to travel from a distant plantation to the Moravian mission at New Herrnhut; when she finally reached it, she embraced the Moravians' message and piety. She spoke with Oldendorp in 1767.

33.1 ——.

Aspects of her life story transcribed from 33.0 and printed on p. 1699 in vol. 2, Part 3 of C. G. A. Oldendorp, *Historie der caribischen Inseln Sanct Thomas, Sanct Crux und Sanct Jan, insbesondere der dasigen Neger und der Mission der evangelischen Brüder unter denselben: kommentierte Ausgabe des vollständigen Manuskriptes aus dem Archiv der Evangelischen Brüder-Unität Herrnhut,* edited by Gudrun Meier et al. (Band [Volume] 51 in the series *Abhandlungen und Berichte des Staatlichen Museums für Völkerkunde Dresden*).

Berlin [Germany]: VWB, Verlag für Wissenschaft und Bildung, 2000–2002.
2 vols. in 4, 8vo (24 cm.).
Vol. 2 (consecutively numbered), Part 3 (2002): vii; 1405–2171 p.

34.0 Bartholomäus (–1767)

Aspects of this man's life story summarized in Christian Georg Andreas Oldendorp's 3,000-page manuscript account of Oldendorp's **1767–1768** tour of Denmark's West Indian possessions, viz. "Manuskript für eine Geschichte der Mission auf den westindischen Inseln, verfasst von C. G. A. Oldendorp," R.28.63 and R.28.62, held in the Unity Archives, Herrnhut, Saxony, Germany.

Full text: https://huskiecommons.lib.niu.edu/history-500africanvoices/28/ [see 34.1].

¶ Bartholomäus identified as Amina (a New World ethnic designation for Akan speakers near Elmina Castle, present-day Ghana—see Map 5). Some point after being taken in the transatlantic slave trade to St. Croix in the Danish West Indies (Map 14) and sold there, he joined the Moravian mission. He was baptized in 1753, but for years thereafter continued to exhibit behavior unacceptable to the missionaries. After improvement he was allowed to receive communion. Although old and ill, he continued to work hard for his owner until the day before his own death. His wife also became a Moravian, and two of their many children were baptized. After Oldendorp spoke with Bartholomäus in 1767, he noted that many people attended his funeral.

34.1 ——.

Aspects of his life story transcribed from 34.0 and printed on pp. 1771–1772 in vol. 2, Part 3 of C. G. A. Oldendorp, *Historie der caribischen Inseln Sanct Thomas, Sanct Crux*

und Sanct Jan, insbesondere der dasigen Neger und der Mission der evangelischen Brüder unter denselben: kommentierte Ausgabe des vollständigen Manuskriptes aus dem Archiv der Evangelischen Brüder-Unität Herrnhut, edited by Gudrun Meier et al. (Band [Volume] 51 in the series *Abhandlungen und Berichte des Staatlichen Museums für Völkerkunde Dresden*).

Berlin [Germany]: VWB, Verlag für Wissenschaft und Bildung, 2000–2002.
2 vols. in 4, 8vo (24 cm.).
Vol. 2 (consecutively numbered), Part 3 (2002): vii; 1405–2171 p.

35.0 Jacob (–1767)

Aspects of this man's life story summarized in Christian Georg Andreas Oldendorp's 3,000-page manuscript account of Oldendorp's **1767–1768** tour of Denmark's West Indian possessions, viz. "Manuskript für eine Geschichte der Mission auf den westindischen Inseln, verfasst von C. G. A. Oldendorp," R.28.63 and R.28.62, held in the Unity Archives, Herrnhut, Saxony, Germany.

Full text: https://huskiecommons.lib.niu.edu/history-500africanvoices/29/ [see 35.1].

¶ Jacob identified as Sokko (possibly Nsoko, northeast Ghana—see Map 5). He was taken in the transatlantic slave trade to St. Croix in the Danish West Indies (Map 14) and sold. There he operated boiling vats in the sugar house of a plantation on the north side of the island. He joined the Moravian mission and was baptized in 1764, but because his work was hard he could not attend services often. He died a few hours after a terrible accident involving the boiling vats. He met Oldendorp during his last weeks of life in 1767.

35.1 ——.

Aspects of his life story transcribed from 35.0 and printed on p. 1772 in vol. 2, Part 3 of C. G. A. Oldendorp, *Historie der caribischen Inseln Sanct Thomas, Sanct Crux und Sanct Jan, insbesondere der dasigen Neger und der Mission der evangelischen Brüder unter denselben: kommentierte Ausgabe des vollständigen Manuskriptes aus dem Archiv der Evangelischen Brüder-Unität Herrnhut,* edited by Gudrun Meier et al. (Band [Volume] 51 in the series *Abhandlungen und Berichte des Staatlichen Museums für Völkerkunde Dresden*).

Berlin [Germany]: VWB, Verlag für Wissenschaft und Bildung, 2000–2002.
2 vols. in 4, 8vo (24 cm.).
Vol. 2 (consecutively numbered), Part 3 (2002): vii; 1405–2171 p.

36.0 Johannes (–1767)

Aspects of this man's life story summarized in Christian Georg Andreas Oldendorp's 3,000-page manuscript account of Oldendorp's **1767–1768** tour of Denmark's West Indian possessions, viz. "Manuskript für eine Geschichte der Mission auf den westindischen Inseln, verfasst von C. G. A. Oldendorp," R.28.63 and R.28.62, held in the Unity Archives, **Herrnhut, Saxony, Germany**.

¶ Johannes identified as Amina (a New World ethnic designation for Akan speakers near Elmina Castle, present-day Ghana—see Map 5). He was taken as a small child in the transatlantic slave trade to St. Thomas in the Caribbean (Map 14) and sold. He was taken to St. Croix in 1733 (when that island came under Danish control), and there he lived and worked enslaved on the Little Princess Plantation. After injuring his eyes, he became a cook. A well-known eye specialist

Full text: https://huskiecommons.lib.niu.edu/history-500africanvoices/30/ [see 36.1].

passing through treated him in 1735, and Johannes temporarily regained some eyesight but then went entirely blind. In 1766 he began attending the Moravian mission and met Oldendorp soon thereafter. He was baptized on his deathbed in 1767. Oldendorp noted that many people attended his burial.

36.1 ——.

Aspects of his life story transcribed from 36.0 and printed on p. 1773 in vol. 2, Part 3 of C. G. A. Oldendorp, *Historie der caribischen Inseln Sanct Thomas, Sanct Crux und Sanct Jan, insbesondere der dasigen Neger und der Mission der evangelischen Brüder unter denselben: kommentierte Ausgabe des vollständigen Manuskriptes aus dem Archiv der Evangelischen Brüder-Unität Herrnhut*, edited by Gudrun Meier et al. (Band [Volume] 51 in the series *Abhandlungen und Berichte des Staatlichen Museums für Völkerkunde Dresden*).

Berlin [Germany]: VWB, Verlag für Wissenschaft und Bildung, **2000–2002**.
2 vols. in 4, 8vo (24 cm.).
Vol. 2 (consecutively numbered), Part 3 (2002): vii; 1405–2171 p.

1767–1768

37.0 Unnamed Fula man

Aspects of this unnamed man's life story summarized in Christian Georg Andreas Oldendorp's 3,000-page manuscript account of Oldendorp's **1767–1768** tour of Denmark's West Indian possessions, viz. "Manuskript für eine Geschichte der Mission auf den westindischen Inseln, verfasst von C. G. A. Oldendorp," R.28.63 and R.28.62, held in the Unity Archives, **Herrnhut, Saxony, Germany**. Only an abbreviated version of this lengthy manuscript was published in 1777 (37.1). It was not published in its entirety until 2000–2002 (37.4).

¶ Identified as Fula (Fulani, Fulbi, or Peul peoples throughout West Africa), this unnamed man lived about two months travel up a river (probably the Gambia River—see Map 3) from the coast of West Africa, where nearby a people he called Naar lived (editors of the English edition, 37.2, think they might be Bendoin people). French people lived three miles away on Senegal Island. This Fula man was uncircumcised, thus not Muslim, although some Muslims lived there. The Fula king was named Samba, and Sorua people were their neighbors. There was much gold and many snakes, elephants, and cattle in the land. During a drought while he was young, his people migrat-

Full text: https://huskiecommons.lib.niu.edu/history-500africanvoices/31/ [see 37.6].

ed to Sorua lands and were there attacked at night by them. He was captured, traded to French people, and taken to their fort, but its personnel refused to accept him. He was later sold to a Danish slave ship captain and taken to the Portuguese colony on the island of São Tomé, west of present-day Gabon (Map 6). Unable to sell him there, the captain took him to the Danish island colony of St. Croix in the Caribbean (Map 14) and sold him. There he spoke with Oldendorp in 1767–1768.

37.1 ——.

Aspects of this unnamed man's life story printed on pp. 274–275 and 350 of Christian Georg Andreas Oldendorp, *Geschichte der Mission der evangelischen Brueder auf den caraibischen Inseln S. Thomas, S. Croix, und S. Jan*, edited by Johann Jakob Bossart.

Barby [Saxony-Anhalt, Germany]: bey Christian Friedrich Laur, und in Leipzig [Saxony, Germany]: in Commission bey Weidmanns Erben und Reich, **1777**.
2 volumes in 1, 8vo (19 cm.), folding plates and maps, [12], 1068, index [52], p.
https://archive.org/details/cgaoldendorpsges12olde/page/274

37.2 ——.

Danish translation of 37.1 (p. 350 only) printed on p. 178, Part 1, of Christian Georg Andreas Oldendorp, *Fuldstændigt Udtog af C.G.A. Oldendorps Missions-Historie om de evan-*

geliske Brødres Mission paa de caraibiske Øer St. Thomas, St. Crux og St. Jan, uitgivet paa Tydsk i to Dele.

Pt 1: *Kort Beskrivelse over Vestindien, især de Danske caraibiske Øer St. Crux, St. Thomas og St. Jan.*

Pt. 2: *Historisk Beretning om de hedenske Neger-Slavers Omvendelse paa de Danske Øer i Vestindien,* som et Udtog af C.G.A. Oldendorp's De Evangeliske Brødres Missions-Historie paa de Caraibiske Øer.

Copenhagen [Denmark]: Christ. L. Buchs Forlag, with J. Rud. Thiele, **1784.**
2 volumes in 1, with separate title pages and pagination, 8vo (18 cm): [4], 212 p. and 184, [4] p.

37.3 ——.
Swedish translation of 37.1, C. G. A. Oldendorp, *Historiska beskrifning öfwer ewangeliske brödernas miszions-arbete på caraibiske öarne St. Thomas St. Croix och St. Jan,* edited by Johann Jacob Bossart.

Stockholm [Sweden]: 1786–88.
[Vol. 1] *Första delen, som innehåller åtskilliga efterrättelser, hörande til öarnes geographie, natural-historia och politiska författningar.*
Stockholm [Sweden]: tryckt hos commiss. P.A. Brodin, **1786.**
8vo (18 cm): [4], 64, [2], 348 p., map, 1 folded table.

[Vol. 2] *Andra delen, som innehåller miszions-historien ifrån år 1732 til år 1768.* **Stockholm [Sweden]:** tryckt hos Johan Christopher Holmberg, **1788.**
8vo (18 cm): [2], 634, [4] p., folded leaves of plates: ill. (engravings).

37.4 ——.
English translation of 37.1 printed on pp. 161 and 208–209 of C. G. A. Oldendorp, *History of the Mission of the Evangelical Brethren on the Caribbean Islands of St. Thomas, St. Croix, and St. John,* edited by Johann Jakob Bossard (i.e., Bossart), translated into English and further edited by Arnold R. Highfield and Vladimir Barac.

Ann Arbor [Michigan, U.S.A.]: Karoma Publishers, **1987.**
8vo (24 cm.): xxxv, 737 p., illus.

37.5 ——.
37.1 printed on pp. 274–275 and 350 in photomechanical reprint of the 1777 edition of C. G. A. Oldendorp, *Geschichte der Mission der evangelischen Brüder auf den caraibischen Inseln S. Thomas, S. Croix und S. Jan,* edited by Erich Beyreuther and Matthias Meyer (Volume 27.1 in Series 2 of Nikolaus Ludwig Graf von Zinzendorf, *Leben und Werk in Quellen und Darstellungen*).

Hildesheim [Saxony, Germany]: Georg Olms Verlag, **1995.**
8vo (20 cm.): 62, 444 p., illus.

37.6 ——. **[Complete edition, with critical annotations, of 37.0]**
Aspects of his life story transcribed from 37.0 and printed on pp. 373–375 and 480 in vol. 1 of C. G. A. Oldendorp, *Historie der caribischen Inseln Sanct Thomas, Sanct Crux und Sanct Jan, insbesondere der dasigen Neger und der Mission der evangelischen Brüder unter denselben: kommentierte Ausgabe des vollständigen Manuskriptes aus dem Archiv der Evangelischen Brüder-Unität Herrnhut,* edited by Gudrun Meier et al. (Band [Volume] 51 in the series *Abhandlungen und Berichte des Staatlichen Museums für Völkerkunde Dresden*).

Berlin [Germany]: VWB, Verlag für Wissenschaft und Bildung, **2000–2002.**
2 vols. in 4, 8vo (24 cm.).
Vol. 1 (2000): 764 p.; xxxviii, illus.

38.0 Unnamed woman

Aspects of her life story included in C. G. A. Oldendorp's manuscript account of his **1767–1768** tour of Denmark's West Indian possessions, viz. "Manuskript für eine Geschichte der Mission auf den westindischen Inseln, verfasst von C. G. A. Oldendorp," R.28.63 and R.28.62, held in the Unity Archives, **Herrnhut, Saxony, Germany.**

Full text: https:// huskiecommons. lib.niu.edu/history-500africanvoices/32/ [see 38.1].

¶ After enslavement in an unknown area of West Africa and forcible transport on a slave ship to the Danish West Indies (see Map 14), this woman met Oldendorp in 1767–1768 and described the practice in her home village of cutting open the bodies of deceased people to see if death came from natural causes or via sorcery. If the latter, the body was burned.

38.1 ——. **[Complete edition, with critical annotations, of 38.0]**
Aspects of her life story (none included in any earlier printed editions of Oldendorp, q.v. 38.1 through 38.3) transcribed from 38.0 and printed on pp. 377–378 in vol. 1 of C. G. A. Oldendorp, *Historie der caribischen Inseln Sanct Thomas, Sanct Crux und Sanct Jan, insbesondere der dasigen Neger und der Mission der evangelischen Brüder unter denselben: kommentierte Ausgabe des vollständigen Manuskriptes aus dem Archiv der Evangelischen Brüder-Unität Herrnhut,* edited by Gudrun Meier et al. (Band [Volume] 51 in the series *Abhandlungen und Berichte des Staatlichen Museums für Völkerkunde Dresden*).

Berlin [Germany]: VWB, Verlag für Wissenschaft und Bildung, **2000–2002.**
2 vols. in 4, 8vo (24 cm.).
Vol. 1 (2000): 764 p.; xxxviii, illus.

39.0 Unnamed Mangree woman

Aspects of her life story summarized in Christian Georg Andreas Oldendorp's 3,000-page manuscript account of Oldendorp's **1767–1768** tour of Denmark's West Indian possessions, viz. "Manuskript für eine Geschichte der Mission auf den westindischen Inseln, verfasst von C. G. A. Oldendorp," R.28.63 and R.28.62, held in the Unity Archives, **Herrnhut, Saxony, Germany**. Only an abbreviated version of this lengthy manuscript was published in 1777 (39.1). It was not published in its entirety until 2000–2002 (39.4).

¶ **This woman identified as what Oldendorp called the "Mangree" nation (according to Gudrun Meier [q.v. 39.4], probably Kru language, perhaps Ngere [or Guéré] or Dan, in present-day northeastern Liberia and the west-central Ivory Coast—see Map 3) and said the Kanga were their neighbors and that they were not far from the Mandinka (an ethnic group residing in present-day southern Mali, Guinea, and Ivory Coast) and the Amina (a New World ethnic designation for Akan speakers near Elmina Castle, present-day Ghana, Map 4). Her land was far from the sea, and Oldendorp described body markings under her eyes. Gudrun Meier thought she spoke Kru. Her people often waged war against both the Asante (Akan people, present-day Ghana) and Mandinka and used muskets in fighting. She described her religion, noting her people's God was called Jankombum, and Didi was the figure representing evil. She was enslaved and forcibly taken aboard a slave ship to the Danish West Indies (Map 14), where she conversed with Oldendorp in 1767–1768.**

39.1 ———.

Aspects of her life story printed on p. 277 of Christian Georg Andreas Oldendorp, *Geschichte der Mission der evangelischen Brueder auf den caraibischen Inseln S. Thomas, S. Croix, und S. Jan*, edited by Johann Jakob Bossart.

Barby [Saxony-Anhalt, Germany]: bey Christian Friedrich Laur, und in **Leipzig [Saxony, Germany]:** in Commission bey Weidmanns Erben und Reich, **1777**.
2 volumes in 1, 8vo (19 cm.), folding plates and maps, [12], 1068, index [52], p.
https://archive.org/details/cgaoldendorpsges12olde/page/277

39.2 ———.

Swedish translation of 39.1, C. G. A. Oldendorp, *Historiska beskrifning öfwer ewangeliske brödernas miszions-arbete på*

Full text: https://huskiecommons.lib.niu.edu/history-500africanvoices/33/ [see 39.5].

caraibiske öarne St. Thomas St. Croix och St. Jan, edited by Johann Jacob Bossart.

Stockholm [Sweden]: 1786–1788.
[Vol. 1] *Första delen, som innehåller åtskilliga efterrättelser, hörande til öarnes geographie, natural-historia och politiska författningar.*
Stockholm [Sweden]: tryckt hos commiss. P.A. Brodin, **1786**.
8vo (18 cm): [4], 64, [2], 348 p., map, 1 folded table.

[Vol. 2] *Andra delen, som innehåller miszions-historien ifrån år 1732 til år 1768*. **Stockholm [Sweden]:** tryckt hos Johan Christopher Holmberg, **1788**.
8vo (18 cm): [2], 634, [4] p., folded leaves of plates: ill. (engravings).

39.3 ———.

English translation of 39.1 printed on p. 162 of C. G. A. Oldendorp, *History of the Mission of the Evangelical Brethren on the Caribbean Islands of St. Thomas, St. Croix, and St. John*, edited by Johann Jakob Bossard (i.e., Bossart), translated into English and further edited by Arnold R. Highfield and Vladimir Barac.

Ann Arbor [Michigan, U.S.A.]: Karoma Publishers, **1987**.
8vo (24 cm.): xxxv, 737 p., illus.

39.4 ———.

39.1 printed on p. 277 in photomechanical reprint of the 1777 edition of C. G. A. Oldendorp, *Geschichte der Mission der evangelischen Brüder auf den caraibischen Inseln S. Thomas, S. Croix und S. Jan*, edited by Erich Beyreuther and Matthias Meyer (Volume 27.1 in Series 2 of Nikolaus Ludwig Graf von Zinzendorf, *Leben und Werk in Quellen und Darstellungen*).

Hildesheim [Saxony, Germany]: Georg Olms Verlag, **1995**.
8vo (20 cm.): 62, 444 p., illus.

39.5 ———. **[Complete edition, with critical annotations, of 39.0]**

Aspects of her life story transcribed from 39.0 and printed on pp. 381–382 in vol. 1 of C. G. A. Oldendorp, *Historie der caribischen Inseln Sanct Thomas, Sanct Crux und Sanct Jan, insbesondere der dasigen Neger und der Mission der evangelischen Brüder unter denselben: kommentierte Ausgabe des vollständigen Manuskriptes aus dem Archiv der Evangelischen Brüder-Unität Herrnhut*, edited by Gudrun Meier et al. (Band [Volume] 51 in the series *Abhandlungen und Berichte des Staatlichen Museums für Völkerkunde Dresden*).

Berlin [Germany]: VWB, Verlag für Wissenschaft und Bildung, **2000–2002**.
2 vols. in 4, 8vo (24 cm.).
Vol. 1 (2000): 764 p.; xxxviii, illus.

40.0 Sanjam woman

Aspects of her life story summarized in Christian Georg Andreas Oldendorp's 3,000-page manuscript account of Oldendorp's 1767–1768 tour of Denmark's West Indian possessions, viz. "Manuskript für eine Geschichte der Mission auf den westindischen Inseln, verfasst von C. G. A. Oldendorp," R.28.63 and R.28.62, held in the Unity Archives, Herrnhut, Saxony, Germany.

Full text: https://huskiecommons.lib.niu.edu/history-500africanvoices/34/ [see 40.1].

¶ This woman came from Sanjam, near Kanga, Mandinka (an ethnic group residing in present-day southern Mali, Guinea, and Ivory Coast—see Map 3). She described how her people used iron rings as currency. Wealthy people had gold but did not use it for currency. She was taken on a slave ship to the Danish West Indies, where she conversed with Oldendorp in 1767–1768.

40.1 ——. [Complete edition, with critical annotations, of 40.0]

Aspects of her life story (none included in any earlier printed editions of Oldendorp, q.v. 39.1 through 39.3) transcribed from 40.0 and printed on pp. 378–379 in vol. 1 of C. G. A. Oldendorp, *Historie der caribischen Inseln Sanct Thomas, Sanct Crux und Sanct Jan, insbesondere der dasigen Neger und der Mission der evangelischen Brüder unter denselben: kommentierte Ausgabe des vollständigen Manuskriptes aus dem Archiv der Evangelischen Brüder-Unität Herrnhut,* edited by Gudrun Meier et al. (Band [Volume] 51 in the series *Abhandlungen und Berichte des Staatlichen Museums für Völkerkunde Dresden*).

Berlin [Germany]: VWB, Verlag für Wissenschaft und Bildung, 2000–2002.
2 vols. in 4, 8vo (24 cm.).
Vol. 1 (2000): 764 p.; xxxviii, illus.

41.0 Unnamed Gien man

Aspects of his life story summarized in Christian Georg Andreas Oldendorp's 3,000-page manuscript account of Oldendorp's 1767–1768 tour of Denmark's West Indian possessions, viz. "Manuskript für eine Geschichte der Mission auf den westindischen Inseln, verfasst von C. G. A. Oldendorp," R.28.63 and R.28.62, held in the Unity Archives, Herrnhut, Saxony, Germany.

¶ This man, who identified as Gien (Meier: spoke the Kru language, perhaps related to Kran) and came from an area that bordered on what Oldendorp called "Mangree" country, with a larger river running in between (possibly the Cavalla River, on the present-day Liberia and Ivory Coast border—see Map 3). He described their religion, including aspects of worship and their God, named Grebo. His people were cannibals, i.e., they cut up, cooked, and ate other peoples (not their own) they had killed in war—something he had himself done. After enslavement and transport to the Danish West Indies (Map 14) he met Oldendorp, who recorded his account in 1767–1768.

Full text: https://huskiecommons.lib.niu.edu/history-500africanvoices/35/ [see 41.1].

41.1 ——. [Complete edition, with critical annotations, of 41.0]

Aspects of his life story (none included in any earlier printed editions of Oldendorp, q.v. 39.1 through 39.3) transcribed from 41.0 and printed on p. 382 in vol. 1 of C. G. A. Oldendorp, *Historie der caribischen Inseln Sanct Thomas, Sanct Crux und Sanct Jan, insbesondere der dasigen Neger und der Mission der evangelischen Brüder unter denselben: kommentierte Ausgabe des vollständigen Manuskriptes aus dem Archiv der Evangelischen Brüder-Unität Herrnhut,* edited by Gudrun Meier et al. (Band [Volume] 51 in der Serie *Abhandlungen und Berichte des Staatlichen Museums für Völkerkunde Dresden*).

Berlin [Germany]: VWB, Verlag für Wissenschaft und Bildung, 2000–2002.
2 vols. in 4, 8vo (24 cm.).
Vol. 1 (2000): 764 p.; xxxviii, illus.

42.0 First unnamed Amina merchant [see Nr. 87 for second]

Aspects of this man's life story summarized in Christian Georg Andreas Oldendorp's 3,000-page manuscript account of Oldendorp's 1767–1768 tour of Denmark's West Indian possessions, viz. "Manuskript für eine Geschichte der Mission auf den westindischen Inseln, verfasst von C. G. A. Oldendorp," R.28.63 and R.28.62, held in the Unity Archives, Herrnhut, Saxony, Germany. Only an abbreviated version of this lengthy manuscript was published in 1777 (42.1). It was not published in its entirety until 2000–2002 (42.4).

Full text: https://huskiecommons.lib.niu.edu/history-500africanvoices/36/ [see 42.6].

¶ Formerly a rich West African merchant who identified as Amina (a New World ethnic designation for Akan speakers near Elmina Castle, present-day Ghana—see Map 5) and traded in slaves, iron, and ivory with English and Dutch factors using an aggressive credit system that supplied him with slaves, this Amina man was well-traveled, knew his home region, and described it well. After being taken in the slave trade himself, he was sent on a slave ship to the Danish West Indies (Map 14) and sold. There he met Oldendorp in 1767–1768.

42.1 ———.

Aspects of his life story printed on pp. 277 and 352–353 of Christian Georg Andreas Oldendorp, *Geschichte der Mission der evangelischen Brueder auf den caraibischen Inseln S. Thomas, S. Croix, und S. Jan*, edited by Johann Jakob Bossart.

Barby [Saxony-Anhalt, Germany]: bey Christian Friedrich Laur, und in **Leipzig** [Saxony, Germany]: in Commission bey Weidmanns Erben und Reich, **1777**.
2 volumes in 1, 8vo (19 cm.), folding plates and maps, [12], 1068, index [52], p.
https://archive.org/details/cgaoldendorpsges12olde/page/277

42.2 ———.

Danish translation of 42.1 (p. 350 only) printed on p. 178, Part 1, of Christian Georg Andreas Oldendorp, *Fuldstændigt Udtog af C.G.A. Oldendorps Missions-Historie om de evangeliske Brødres Mission paa de caraibiske Øer St. Thomas, St. Crux og St. Jan*, uitgivet paa Tydsk i to Dele.

Pt 1: *Kort Beskrivelse over Vestindien, især de Danske caraibiske Øer St. Crux, St. Thomas og St. Jan.*

Pt. 2: *Historisk Beretning om de hedenske Neger-Slavers Omvendelse paa de Danske Øer i Vestindien*, som et Udtog af C.G.A. Oldendorp's De Evangeliske Brødres Missions-Historie paa de Caraibiske Øer.

Copenhagen [Denmark]: Christ. L. Buchs Forlag, with J. Rud. Thiele, **1784**.
2 volumes in 1, with separate title pages and pagination, 8vo (18 cm): [4], 212 p. and 184, [4] p.

42.3 ———.

Swedish translation of 42.1, C. G. A. Oldendorp, *Historiska beskrifning öfwer ewangeliske brödernas miszions-arbete på caraibiske öarne St. Thomas St. Croix och St. Jan*, edited by Johann Jacob Bossart.

Stockholm [Sweden]: **1786–88**.
[Vol. 1] *Första delen, som innehåller åtskilliga efterrättelser, hörande til öarnes geographie, natural-historia och politiska författningar.*
Stockholm [Sweden]: tryckt hos commiss. P.A. Brodin, **1786**.
8vo (18 cm): [4], 64, [2], 348 p., map, 1 folded table.

[Vol. 2] *Andra delen, som innehåller miszions-historien ifrån år 1732 til år 1768.* **Stockholm** [Sweden]: tryckt hos Johan Christopher Holmberg, **1788**.
8vo (18 cm): [2], 634, [4] p., folded leaves of plates: ill. (engravings).

42.4 ———.

English translation of 42.1 printed on p. 162–163 of C. G. A. Oldendorp, *History of the Mission of the Evangelical Brethren on the Caribbean Islands of St. Thomas, St. Croix, and St. John*, edited by Johann Jakob Bossard (i.e., Bossart), translated into English and further edited by Arnold R. Highfield and Vladimir Barac.

Ann Arbor [Michigan, U.S.A.]: Karoma Publishers, **1987**.
8vo (24 cm.): xxxv, 737 p., illus.

42.5 ———.

42.1 printed on p. 277 in photomechanical reprint of the 1777 edition of C. G. A. Oldendorp, *Geschichte der Mission der evangelischen Brüder auf den caraibischen Inseln S. Thomas, S. Croix und S. Jan*, edited by Erich Beyreuther and Matthias Meyer (Volume 27.1 in Series 2 of Nikolaus Ludwig Graf von Zinzendorf, *Leben und Werk in Quellen und Darstellungen*).

Hildesheim [Saxony, Germany]: Georg Olms Verlag, **1995**.
8vo (20 cm.): 62, 444 p., illus.

42.6 ———. [Complete edition, with critical annotations, of 42.0]

Aspects of his life story transcribed from 42.0 and printed on pp. 382–385 in vol. 1 of C. G. A. Oldendorp, *Historie der caribischen Inseln Sanct Thomas, Sanct Crux und Sanct Jan, insbesondere der dasigen Neger und der Mission der evangelischen Brüder unter denselben: kommentierte Ausgabe des vollständigen Manuskriptes aus dem Archiv der Evangelischen Brüder-Unität Herrnhut*, edited by Gudrun Meier et al. (Band [Volume] 51 in the series *Abhandlungen und Berichte des Staatlichen Museums für Völkerkunde Dresden*).

Berlin [Germany]: VWB, Verlag für Wissenschaft und Bildung, **2000–2002**.
2 vols. in 4, 8vo (24 cm.).
Vol. 1 (2000): 764 p.; xxxviii, illus.

43.0   Unnamed brother of the Amina king

Aspects of this unnamed man's life story summarized in Christian Georg Andreas Oldendorp's 3,000-page manuscript account of Oldendorp's **1767–1768** tour of Denmark's West Indian possessions, viz. "Manuskript für eine Geschichte der Mission auf den westindischen Inseln, verfasst von C. G. A. Oldendorp," R.28.63 and R.28.62, held in the Unity Archives, **Herrnhut, Saxony, Germany.** Only an abbreviated version of this lengthy manuscript was published in 1777 (43.1). It was not published in its entirety until 2000–2002 (43.4).

Full text: https://huskiecommons.lib.niu.edu/history-500africanvoices/37/ [see 43.6].

¶ This man identified as the brother of the Amina king (referring to a New World ethnic designation for Akan speakers near Elmina Castle, present-day Ghana—see Map 3). During a local civil war his own people captured him, took him to a European fort, and sold him. He was then forcibly taken on a slave ship to the Danish West Indies (Map 14), where he conversed with Oldendorp in 1767–1768.

43.1 ———.

Aspects of this unnamed man's life story printed on pp. 277 and 351–352 of Christian Georg Andreas Oldendorp, *Geschichte der Mission der evangelischen Brueder auf den caraibischen Inseln S. Thomas, S. Croix, und S. Jan,* edited by Johann Jakob Bossart.

Barby [Saxony-Anhalt, Germany]: bey Christian Friedrich Laur, und in **Leipzig [Saxony, Germany]:** in Commission bey Weidmanns Erben und Reich, **1777.**
2 volumes in 1, 8vo (19 cm.), folding plates and maps, [12], 1068, index [52], p.
https://archive.org/details/cgaoldendorpsges12olde/page/277

43.2 ———.

Danish translation of 43.1 (p. 350 only) printed on pp. 178–179, Part 1, of Christian Georg Andreas Oldendorp, *Fuldstændigt Udtog af C.G.A. Oldendorps Missions-Historie om de evangeliske Brødres Mission paa de caraibiske Øer St. Thomas, St. Crux og St. Jan, uitgivet paa Tydsk i to Dele.*

Pt 1: *Kort Beskrivelse over Vestindien, især de Danske caraibiske Øer St. Crux, St. Thomas og St. Jan.*

Pt. 2: *Historisk Beretning om de hedenske Neger-Slavers Omvendelse paa de Danske Øer i Vestindien, som et Udtog af C.G.A. Oldendorp's De Evangeliske Brødres Missions-Historie paa de Caraibiske Øer.*

Copenhagen [Denmark]: Christ. L. Buchs Forlag, with J. Rud. Thiele, **1784.**
2 volumes in 1, with separate title pages and pagination, 8vo (18 cm): [4], 212 p. and 184, [4] p.

43.3 ———.

Swedish translation of 43.1, C. G. A. Oldendorp, *Historiska beskrifning öfwer ewangeliske brödernas miszions-arbete på caraibiske öarne St. Thomas St. Croix och St. Jan,* edited by Johann Jacob Bossart.

Stockholm [Sweden]: 1786–1788.
[Vol. 1] *Första delen, som innehåller åtskilliga efterrättelser, hörande til öarnes geographie, natural-historia och politiska författningar.*
Stockholm [Sweden]: tryckt hos commiss. P.A. Brodin, **1786.**

8vo (18 cm): [4], 64, [2], 348 p., map, 1 folded table.
[Vol. 2] *Andra delen, som innehåller miszions-historien ifrån år 1732 til år 1768.* **Stockholm [Sweden]:** tryckt hos Johan Christopher Holmberg, **1788.**
8vo (18 cm): [2], 634, [4] p., folded leaves of plates: ill. (engravings).

43.4 ———.

English translation of 43.1 printed on p. 163 of C. G. A. Oldendorp, *History of the Mission of the Evangelical Brethren on the Caribbean Islands of St. Thomas, St. Croix, and St. John,* edited by Johann Jakob Bossard (i.e., Bossart), translated into English and further edited by Arnold R. Highfield and Vladimir Barac.

Ann Arbor [Michigan, U.S.A.]: Karoma Publishers, **1987.**
8vo (24 cm.): xxxv, 737 p., illus.

43.5 ———.

43.1 reprinted on p. 277 of photomechanical reprint of the 1777 edition of C. G. A. Oldendorp, *Geschichte der Mission der evangelischen Brüder auf den caraibischen Inseln S. Thomas, S. Croix und S. Jan,* edited by Erich Beyreuther and Matthias Meyer (Volume 27.1 in Series 2 of Nikolaus Ludwig Graf von Zinzendorf, *Leben und Werk in Quellen und Darstellungen*).

Hildesheim [Saxony, Germany]: Georg Olms Verlag, **1995.**
8vo (20 cm.): 62, 444 p., illus.

43.6 ———. [Complete edition, with critical annotations, of 43.0]

Aspects of his life story transcribed from 43.0 and printed on pp. 383 and 482 in vol. 1 of C. G. A. Oldendorp, *Historie der caribischen Inseln Sanct Thomas, Sanct Crux und Sanct Jan, insbesondere der dasigen Neger und der Mission der evangelischen Brüder unter denselben: kommentierte Ausgabe des vollständigen Manuskriptes aus dem Archiv der Evangelischen Brüder-Unität Herrnhut,* edited by Gudrun Meier et al. (Band [Volume] 51 in the series *Abhandlungen und Berichte des Staatlichen Museums für Völkerkunde Dresden*).

Berlin [Germany]: VWB, Verlag für Wissenschaft und Bildung, **2000–2002.**
2 vols. in 4, 8vo (24 cm.).
Vol. 1 (2000): 764 p.; xxxviii, illus.

44.0   Unnamed Amina commander

Aspects of this unnamed Amina commander's life story summarized in Christian Georg Andreas Oldendorp's 3,000-page manuscript account of Oldendorp's **1767–1768** tour of Denmark's West Indian possessions, viz. "Manuskript für eine Geschichte der Mission auf den westindischen Inseln, verfasst von C. G. A. Oldendorp," R.28.63 and R.28.62, held in the Unity Archives, **Herrnhut, Saxony, Germany**. Only an abbreviated version of this lengthy manuscript was published in 1777 (44.1). It was not published in its entirety until 2000–2002 (44.4).

Full text: https://huskiecommons.lib.niu.edu/history-500africanvoices/38/ [see 44.5].

¶ This man, who identified as **Amina** (a New World ethnic designation for Akan speakers near Elmina Castle, present-day Ghana—see Map 5), was commander of more than three thousand warriors and a close relative of the vassal of the king. On a journey to Fante country (Akan people, present-day Ghana), with two young boys carrying his money and an older boy carrying his musket, he lost everything, including the servant, while gambling. The two small boys were enslaved and taken away, but the older boy escaped and told their family what happened. The commander was taken to a European fort for sale and arrived with gold bands on his arms and legs. When his brother arrived with slaves and goods to redeem him, the governor of the fort refused and sent the commander to another European fort. That governor decoyed his brother long enough to transport him to a slave ship, which sailed to the Danish West Indies (Map 14), where he was sold and later met Oldendorp in 1767–1768.

44.1 ———.

Aspects of his life story printed on pp. 277 and 351–352 of Christian Georg Andreas Oldendorp, *Geschichte der Mission der evangelischen Brueder auf den caraibischen Inseln S. Thomas, S. Croix, und S. Jan*, edited by Johann Jakob Bossart.

Barby [Saxony-Anhalt, Germany]: bey Christian Friedrich Laur, und in **Leipzig [Saxony, Germany]:** in Commission bey Weidmanns Erben und Reich, **1777**.
2 volumes in 1, 8vo (19 cm.), folding plates and maps, [12], 1068, index [52], p.
https://archive.org/details/cgaoldendorpsges12olde/page/277

44.2 ———.

Swedish translation of 44.1, C. G. A. Oldendorp, *Historiska beskrifning öfwer ewangeliske brödernas miszions-arbete på caraibiske öarne St. Thomas St. Croix och St. Jan*, edited by Johann Jacob Bossart.

Stockholm [Sweden]: 1786–1788.
[Vol. 1] *Första delen, som innehåller åtskilliga efterrättelser, hörande til öarnes geographie, natural-historia och politiska författningar.*
Stockholm [Sweden]: tryckt hos commiss. P.A. Brodin, **1786**.
8vo (18 cm): [4], 64, [2], 348 p., map, 1 folded table.
[Vol. 2] *Andra delen, som innehåller miszions-historien ifrån år 1732 til år 1768.* **Stockholm [Sweden]:** tryckt hos Johan Christopher Holmberg, **1788**.
8vo (18 cm): [2], 634, [4] p., folded leaves of plates: ill. (engravings).

44.3 ———.

English translation of 44.1 printed on pp. 163 and 209 of C. G. A. Oldendorp, *History of the Mission of the Evangelical Brethren on the Caribbean Islands of St. Thomas, St. Croix, and St. John*, edited by Johann Jakob Bossard (i.e., Bossart), translated into English and further edited by Arnold R. Highfield and Vladimir Barac.

Ann Arbor [Michigan, U.S.A.]: Karoma Publishers, **1987**.
8vo (24 cm.): xxxv, 737 p., illus.

44.4 ———.

44.1 printed on p. 277 and 351–352 in photomechanical reprint of the 1777 edition of C. G. A. Oldendorp, *Geschichte der Mission der evangelischen Brüder auf den caraibischen Inseln S. Thomas, S. Croix und S. Jan*, edited by Erich Beyreuther and Matthias Meyer (Volume 27.1 in Series 2 of Nikolaus Ludwig Graf von Zinzendorf, *Leben und Werk in Quellen und Darstellungen*).

Hildesheim [Saxony, Germany]: Georg Olms Verlag, **1995**.
8vo (20 cm.): 62, 444 p., illus.

44.5 ———. [Complete edition, with critical annotations, of 44.0]

Aspects of his life story transcribed from 44.0 and printed on pp. 383 and 482 in vol. 1 of C. G. A. Oldendorp, *Historie der caribischen Inseln Sanct Thomas, Sanct Crux und Sanct Jan, insbesondere der dasigen Neger und der Mission der evangelischen Brüder unter denselben: kommentierte Ausgabe des vollständigen Manuskriptes aus dem Archiv der Evangelischen Brüder-Unität Herrnhut*, edited by Gudrun Meier et al. (Band [Volume] 51 in the series *Abhandlungen und Berichte des Staatlichen Museums für Völkerkunde Dresden*).

Berlin [Germany]: VWB, Verlag für Wissenschaft und Bildung, **2000–2002**.
2 vols. in 4, 8vo (24 cm.).
Vol. 1 (2000): 764 p.; xxxviii, illus.

45.0 Unnamed Amina man

Aspects of this man's life story summarized in Christian Georg Andreas Oldendorp's 3,000-page manuscript account of Oldendorp's **1767–1768** tour of Denmark's West Indian possessions, viz. "Manuskript für eine Geschichte der Mission auf den westindischen Inseln, verfasst von C. G. A. Oldendorp," R.28.63 and R.28.62, held in the Unity Archives, Herrnhut, Saxony, Germany.

Full text: https://huskiecommons.lib.niu.edu/history-500africanvoices/39/ [see 45.1].

¶ This man identified as Amina (a New World ethnic designation for Akan speakers near Elmina Castle, present-day Ghana—see Map 5). After enslavement he was forced aboard a slave ship bound for the Danish West Indies (Map 14). Having been at sea for four months, the enslaved Africans rebelled, but the crew quickly overpowered them and put everyone in irons. After arrival and sale in the West Indies, he eventually became a *Bomba,* or enslaved supervisor, and was working in this capacity when he met Oldendorp and told his story in 1767–1768.

45.1 ——. [Complete edition, with critical annotations, of 45.0]

Aspects of his life story transcribed from 45.0 and printed on p. 504 in vol. 1 of C. G. A. Oldendorp, *Historie der caribischen Inseln Sanct Thomas, Sanct Crux und Sanct Jan, insbesondere der dasigen Neger und der Mission der evangelischen Brüder unter denselben: kommentierte Ausgabe des vollständigen Manuskriptes aus dem Archiv der Evangelischen Brüder-Unität Herrnhut,* edited by Gudrun Meier et al. (Band [Volume] 51 in the series *Abhandlungen und Berichte des Staatlichen Museums für Völkerkunde Dresden*).

Berlin [Germany]: VWB, Verlag für Wissenschaft und Bildung, **2000–2002.**
2 vols. in 1, 8vo (24 cm.).
Vol. 1 (2000): 764 p.; xxxviii, illus.

46.0 Unnamed Akyem man

Aspects of this unnamed man's life story summarized in Christian Georg Andreas Oldendorp's three thousand page manuscript account of Oldendorp's **1767–1768** tour of Denmark's West Indian possessions, viz. "Manuskript für eine Geschichte der Mission auf den westindischen Inseln, verfasst von C. G. A. Oldendorp," R.28.63 and R.28.62, held in the Unity

Full text: https://huskiecommons.lib.niu.edu/history-500africanvoices/40/ [see 46.5].

Archives, **Herrnhut, Saxony, Germany.** Only an abbreviated version of this lengthy manuscript was published in 1777 (46.1). It was not published in its entirety until 2000–2002 (46.4).

¶ **This man, identified as "Akkim"** (i.e., Akyem people, present-day Ghana—see Map 3) and lived two day's journey from the Danish Ft. Christiansborg, at the coastal town of Osu (present-day Accra, Ghana). He knew the Amina (a New World ethnic designation for Akan speakers near Elmina Castle, present-day Ghana) language and several others and described their large armies and religion at length, noting that their God was called Jankombum (Nyancopon) and that what Oldendorp described as the Devil was called Andopi (possibly Sasabonsam). He was taken in the slave trade to the Danish West Indies (Map 14), where he conversed with Oldendorp in 1767–1768.

46.1 ——.

Aspects of his life story printed on pp. 278–279 of Christian Georg Andreas Oldendorp, *Geschichte der Mission der evangelischen Brueder auf den caraibischen Inseln S. Thomas, S. Croix, und S. Jan,* edited by Johann Jakob Bossart.

Barby [Saxony-Anhalt, Germany]: bey Christian Friedrich Laur, und in Leipzig [Saxony, Germany]: in Commission bey Weidmanns Erben und Reich, **1777.**
2 volumes in 1, 8vo (19 cm.), folding plates and maps, [12], 1068, index [52], p.
https://archive.org/details/cgaoldendorpsges12olde/page/278

46.2 ——.

Swedish translation of 46.1, C. G. A. Oldendorp, *Historiska beskrifning öfwer ewangeliske brödernas miszions-arbete på caraibiske öarne St. Thomas St. Croix och St. Jan,* edited by Johann Jacob Bossart.

Stockholm [Sweden]: 1786–1788.
[Vol. 1] *Första delen, som innehåller åtskilliga efterrättelser, hörande til öarnes geographie, natural-historia och politiska författningar.*
Stockholm [Sweden]: tryckt hos commiss. P. A. Brodin, **1786.**
8vo (18 cm): [4], 64, [2], 348 p., map, 1 folded table.
[Vol. 2] *Andra delen, som innehåller miszions-historien ifrån år 1732 til år 1768.* Stockholm [Sweden]: tryckt hos Johan Christopher Holmberg, **1788.**
8vo (18 cm): [2], 634, [4] p., folded leaves of plates: ill. (engravings).

46.3 ——.

English translation of 46.1 printed on p. 163 of C. G. A. Oldendorp, *History of the Mission of the Evangelical Brethren on the Caribbean Islands of St. Thomas, St. Croix, and St. John,* edited by Johann Jakob Bossard (i.e., Bossart), translated into

English and further edited by Arnold R. Highfield and Vladimir Barac.

Ann Arbor [Michigan, U.S.A.]: Karoma Publishers, **1987.**
8vo (24 cm.): xxxv, 737 p., illus.

46.4 ———.
46.1 printed on pp. 278–279 in photomechanical reprint of the 1777 edition of C. G. A. Oldendorp, *Geschichte der Mission der evangelischen Brüder auf den caraibischen Inseln S. Thomas, S. Croix und S. Jan*, edited by Erich Beyreuther and Matthias Meyer (Volume 27.1 in Series 2 of Nikolaus Ludwig Graf von Zinzendorf, *Leben und Werk in Quellen und Darstellungen*).

Hildesheim [Saxony, Germany]: Georg Olms Verlag, **1995.**
8vo (20 cm.): 62, 444 p., illus.

46.5 ———. [Complete edition, with critical annotations, of 46.0]
Aspects of his life story transcribed from 46.0 and printed on pp. 392–395 in vol. 1 of C. G. A. Oldendorp, *Historie der caribischen Inseln Sanct Thomas, Sanct Crux und Sanct Jan, insbesondere der dasigen Neger und der Mission der evangelischen Brüder unter denselben: kommentierte Ausgabe des vollständigen Manuskriptes aus dem Archiv der Evangelischen Brüder-Unität Herrnhut*, edited by Gudrun Meier et al. (Band [Volume] 51 in the series *Abhandlungen und Berichte des Staatlichen Museums für Völkerkunde Dresden*).

Berlin [Germany]: VWB, Verlag für Wissenschaft und Bildung, **2000–2002.**
2 vols. in 4, 8vo (24 cm.).
Vol. 1 (2000): 764 p.; xxxviii, illus.

47.0   Unnamed Akropon man

Aspects of this man's life story summarized in Christian Georg Andreas Oldendorp's 3,000-page manuscript account of Oldendorp's **1767–1768** tour of Denmark's West Indian possessions, viz. "Manuskript für eine Geschichte der Mission auf den westindischen Inseln, verfasst von C. G. A. Oldendorp," R.28.63 and R.28.62, held in the Unity Archives, Herrnhut, Saxony, Germany.

Full text: https://huskiecommons.lib.niu.edu/history-500africanvoices/41/ [see 47.1].

¶ This man identified as Akropon (i.e., Akuropon, thirty miles north of Accra, present-day Ghana—see Map 5) and noted that his country bordered on that of the Amina (a New World ethnic designation for Akan speakers near Elmina Castle, present-day Ghana). After being taken on a slave ship to the Danish West Indies (Map 14), he met Oldendorp in 1767–1768 and provided his account, which included details on their religion, noting, for example, that they called God Kinku (Kyenku).

47.1 ———. [Complete edition, with critical annotations, of 47.0]
Aspects of his life story transcribed from 47.0 and printed on pp. 395–396 in vol. 1 of C. G. A. Oldendorp, *Historie der caribischen Inseln Sanct Thomas, Sanct Crux und Sanct Jan, insbesondere der dasigen Neger und der Mission der evangelischen Brüder unter denselben: kommentierte Ausgabe des vollständigen Manuskriptes aus dem Archiv der Evangelischen Brüder-Unität Herrnhut*, edited by Gudrun Meier et al. (Band [Volume] 51 in the series *Abhandlungen und Berichte des Staatlichen Museums für Völkerkunde Dresden*).

Berlin [Germany]: VWB, Verlag für Wissenschaft und Bildung, **2000–2002.**
2 vols. in 4, 8vo (24 cm.).
Vol. 1 (2000): 764 p.; xxxviii, illus.

48.0   Unnamed Okwa or Okoi man

Aspects of this man's life story summarized in Christian Georg Andreas Oldendorp's 3,000-page manuscript account of Oldendorp's **1767–1768** tour of Denmark's West Indian possessions, viz. "Manuskript für eine Geschichte der Mission auf den westindischen Inseln, verfasst von C. G. A. Oldendorp," R.28.63 and R.28.62, held in the Unity Archives, Herrnhut, Saxony, Germany.

Full text: https://huskiecommons.lib.niu.edu/history-500africanvoices/42/ [see 48.1].

¶ This man identified as Okwa or Okoi (Meier: perhaps = Kwahu, present-day Ghana—see Map 5). After being taken on a slave ship to the Danish West Indies (Map 14), he met Oldendorp in 1767–1768 and provided his account, which included cultural details about his people's religion (noting, for example, that they called God Tschabee (Nyame), but that he was aware of the deity called Kinku (Kyenku) and their use of cowries for currency.

48.1 ———. [Complete edition, with critical annotations, of 48.0]
Aspects of his life story transcribed from 48.0 and printed on p. 396 in vol. 1 of C. G. A. Oldendorp, *Historie der caribischen Inseln Sanct Thomas, Sanct Crux und Sanct Jan, insbesondere der dasigen Neger und der Mission der evangelischen Brüder unter denselben: kommentierte Ausgabe des vollständigen Manuskriptes aus dem Archiv der Evangelischen Brüder-Unität Herrnhut*, edited by Gudrun Meier et al. (Band

[Volume] 51 in the series *Abhandlungen und Berichte des Staatlichen Museums für Völkerkunde Dresden*).

Berlin [Germany]: VWB, Verlag für Wissenschaft und Bildung, 2000–2002.

2 vols. in 4, 8vo (24 cm.).

Vol. 1 (2000): 764 p.; xxxviii, illus.

49.0 Unnamed Accra man

Aspects of this man's life story summarized in Christian Georg Andreas Oldendorp's 3,000-page manuscript account of Oldendorp's 1767–1768 tour of Denmark's West Indian possessions, viz. "Manuskript für eine Geschichte der Mission auf den westindischen Inseln, verfasst von C. G. A. Oldendorp," R.28.63 and R.28.62, held in the Unity Archives, Herrnhut, Saxony, Germany.

Full text: https://huskiecommons.lib.niu.edu/history-500africanvoices/43/ [see 49.1].

¶ This man identified as Accra (Meier: = Gā today, in Accra, present-day Ghana—see Map 5). He described their body markings and noted that there was a Danish fort on the coast. They were at war with the Amina (a New World ethnic designation for Akan speakers near Elmina Castle, present-day Ghana) and were friendly with the Danes. Their God was called Niombo (Nyɔnmɔ). While traveling to Fante country (Akan people, present-day Ghana) to buy corn during a time of food shortages, he was captured on the road by highwaymen and taken to a European fort. His wealthy friends tried to exchange him for two enslaved people but arrived too late. The man was forced aboard a slave ship that sailed while his friends stood on the shore shouting to him. He was taken to the Danish West Indies (Map 14), where he conversed with Oldendorp in 1767–1768.

49.1 ——. [Complete edition, with critical annotations, of 49.0]

Aspects of his life story transcribed from 49.0 and printed on pp. 396–397 and 483–484 in vol. 1 of C. G. A. Oldendorp, *Historie der caribischen Inseln Sanct Thomas, Sanct Crux und Sanct Jan, insbesondere der dasigen Neger und der Mission der evangelischen Brüder unter denselben: kommentierte Ausgabe des vollständigen Manuskriptes aus dem Archiv der Evangelischen Brüder-Unität Herrnhut*, edited by Gudrun Meier et al. (Band [Volume] 51 in the series *Abhandlungen und Berichte des Staatlichen Museums für Völkerkunde Dresden*).

Berlin [Germany]: VWB, Verlag für Wissenschaft und Bildung, 2000–2002.

2 vols. in 4, 8vo (24 cm.).

Vol. 1 (2000): 764 p.; xxxviii, illus.

50.0 Unnamed Tambi man

Aspects of this man's life story summarized in Christian Georg Andreas Oldendorp's 3,000-page manuscript account of Oldendorp's 1767–1768 tour of Denmark's West Indian possessions, viz. "Manuskript für eine Geschichte der Mission auf den westindischen Inseln, verfasst von C. G. A. Oldendorp," R.28.63 and R.28.62, held in the Unity Archives, Herrnhut, Saxony, Germany.

Full text: https://huskiecommons.lib.niu.edu/history-500africanvoices/44/ [see 50.1].

¶ This man identified as Tambi (Adangbe, whose language is related to Gā according to Meier) and said that his country bordered on that of the Amina (a New World ethnic designation for Akan speakers near Elmina Castle, present-day Ghana—see Map 5), although their language was quite different. Their God was called Tjembotjauwi. After enslavement, he was taken to the Danish West Indies (Map 14), where he conversed with Oldendorp in 1767–1768.

50.1 ——. [Complete edition, with critical annotations, of 50.0]

Aspects of his life story transcribed from 50.0 and printed on p. 399 in vol. 1 of C. G. A. Oldendorp, *Historie der caribischen Inseln Sanct Thomas, Sanct Crux und Sanct Jan, insbesondere der dasigen Neger und der Mission der evangelischen Brüder unter denselben: kommentierte Ausgabe des vollständigen Manuskriptes aus dem Archiv der Evangelischen Brüder-Unität Herrnhut*, edited by Gudrun Meier et al. (Band [Volume] 51 in the series *Abhandlungen und Berichte des Staatlichen Museums für Völkerkunde Dresden*).

Berlin [Germany]: VWB, Verlag für Wissenschaft und Bildung, 2000–2002.

2 vols. in 4, 8vo (24 cm.).

Vol. 1 (2000): 764 p.; xxxviii, illus.

51.0 Unnamed Tembu (or Temba) man

Aspects of this unnamed Fulas man's life story summarized in Christian Georg Andreas Oldendorp's 3,000-page manuscript account of Oldendorp's 1767–1768 tour of Denmark's West Indian possessions, viz. "Manuskript für eine Geschichte der Mission auf den westindischen Inseln, verfasst von C. G. A. Oldendorp," R.28.63 and R.28.62, held in the Unity Archives, Herrnhut, Saxony, Germany. Only an abbreviated version of

Full text: https://huskiecommons.lib.niu.edu/history-500africanvoices/45/ [see 51.5].

this lengthy manuscript was published in 1777 (51.1). It was not published in its entirety until 2000–2002 (51.4).

¶ This man identified as Tembu (possibly Temba people in present-day northern Togo—see Map 5) and came from a large African town (said to be not much smaller than the West Indies island of St. Thomas) where every house was enclosed by a circular wall with a gate to guard them from attacks by the Amina (a New World ethnic designation for Akan speakers near Elmina Castle, present-day Ghana). Kassenti (Tchamba, Chamba, or Tjamba, hereafter Tchamba, possibly in present-day Togo) were also his neighbors (northern present-day Ghana). During an Asante (Akan people, present-day Ghana) attack, this man, his mother and sister, and other villagers were smoked out of their mountain cave hideout and taken to Asante country, thereafter to a European fort. Here he was sold and forcibly taken on a slave ship to the Danish West Indies (Map 14), where he conversed with Oldendorp in 1767–1768.

51.1 ——.

Aspects of his life story printed on p. 280 of Christian Georg Andreas Oldendorp, *Geschichte der Mission der evangelischen Brueder auf den caraibischen Inseln S. Thomas, S. Croix, und S. Jan*, edited by Johann Jakob Bossart.

Barby [Saxony-Anhalt, Germany]: bey Christian Friedrich Laur, und in **Leipzig [Saxony, Germany]:** in Commission bey Weidmanns Erben und Reich, **1777.**
2 volumes in 1, 8vo (19 cm.), folding plates and maps, [12], 1068, index [52], p.
https://archive.org/details/cgaoldendorpsges12olde/page/280

51.2 ——.

Swedish translation of 51.1, C. G. A. Oldendorp, *Historiska beskrifning öfwer ewangeliske brödernas miszions-arbete på caraibiske öarne St. Thomas St. Croix och St. Jan*, edited by Johann Jacob Bossart.

Stockholm [Sweden]: 1786–1788.
[Vol. 1] *Första delen, som innehåller åtskilliga efterrättelser, hörande til öarnes geographie, natural-historia och politiska författningar.*
Stockholm [Sweden]: tryckt hos commiss. P.A. Brodin, **1786.**
8vo (18 cm): [4], 64, [2], 348 p., map, 1 folded table.
[Vol. 2] *Andra delen, som innehåller miszions-historien ifrån år 1732 til år 1768.* **Stockholm [Sweden]:** tryckt hos Johan Christopher Holmberg, **1788.**
8vo (18 cm): [2], 634, [4] p., folded leaves of plates: ill. (engravings).

51.3 ——.

English translation of 51.1 printed on p. 164 of C. G. A. Oldendorp, *History of the Mission of the Evangelical Brethren on the Caribbean Islands of St. Thomas, St. Croix, and St. John*, edited by Johann Jakob Bossard (i.e., Bossart), translated into English and further edited by Arnold R. Highfield and Vladimir Barac.

Ann Arbor [Michigan, U.S.A.]: Karoma Publishers, **1987.**
8vo (24 cm.): xxxv, 737 p., illus.

51.4 ——.

51.1 printed on p. 280 in photomechanical reprint of the 1777 edition of C. G. A. Oldendorp, *Geschichte der Mission der evangelischen Brüder auf den caraibischen Inseln S. Thomas, S. Croix und S. Jan*, edited by Erich Beyreuther and Matthias Meyer (Volume 27.1 in Series 2 of Nikolaus Ludwig Graf von Zinzendorf, *Leben und Werk in Quellen und Darstellungen*).

Hildesheim [Saxony, Germany]: Georg Olms Verlag, **1995.**
8vo (20 cm.): 62, 444 p., illus.

51.5 ——. [Complete edition, with critical annotations, of 51.0]

Aspects of his life story transcribed from 51.0 and printed on pp. 399–400 and 484–485 in vol. 1 of C. G. A. Oldendorp, *Historie der caribischen Inseln Sanct Thomas, Sanct Crux und Sanct Jan, insbesondere der dasigen Neger und der Mission der evangelischen Brüder unter denselben: kommentierte Ausgabe des vollständigen Manuskriptes aus dem Archiv der Evangelischen Brüder-Unität Herrnhut*, edited by Gudrun Meier et al. (Band [Volume] 51 in the series *Abhandlungen und Berichte des Staatlichen Museums für Völkerkunde Dresden*).

Berlin [Germany]: VWB, Verlag für Wissenschaft und Bildung, **2000–2002.**
2 vols. in 4, 8vo (24 cm.).
Vol. 1 (2000): 764 p.; xxxviii, illus.

52.0 Unnamed Tembu (Temba) woman

Aspects of this unnamed woman's life story summarized in Christian Georg Andreas Oldendorp's 3,000-page manuscript account of Oldendorp's **1767–1768** tour of Denmark's West Indian possessions, viz. "Manuskript für eine Geschichte der Mission auf den westindischen Inseln, verfasst von C. G. A. Oldendorp," R.28.63 and R.28.62, held in the Unity Archives, **Herrnhut, Saxony, Germany.** Only an abbreviated version of this lengthy manuscript was published in 1777 (52.1). It was not published in its entirety until 2000–2002 (52.4).

Full text: https://huskiecommons.lib.niu.edu/history-500africanvoices/46/ [see 52.6].

¶ This woman identified as Tembu or Temba (possibly Temba people, northern Togo—see Map 5). In her homeland every village had a governor and worried at night about the threat of an attack and kidnapping by the Amina (a New World ethnic designation for Akan speakers near Elmina Castle, present-day Ghana). The Asante especially targeted Tembu children, whom they gagged and carried away in sacks. This particular witness was the daughter of a governor, and when he was away fighting the Asante (Akan people, present-day Ghana), her village was attacked by that group. They killed her brother and cut off her sister's hand to remove the gold bands from her arm. They would have cut off this woman's hand, had she not had a pox. Instead they carried her, her sister, and others away. Because they had already killed her brother, they refused her father's ransom payment of twelve slaves. Most of the prisoners were killed, but her life was spared because an Asante girl wanted her for a servant. Later she was taken to a fort, sold, and forcibly transported in the slave trade to the Danish West Indies (Map 14), where she conversed with Oldendorp in 1767–1768.

52.1 ———.

Aspects of her life story printed on p. 280 of Christian Georg Andreas Oldendorp, *Geschichte der Mission der evangelischen Brueder auf den caraibischen Inseln S. Thomas, S. Croix, und S. Jan*, edited by Johann Jakob Bossart.

Barby [Saxony-Anhalt, Germany]: bey Christian Friedrich Laur, und in Leipzig [Saxony, Germany]: in Commission bey Weidmanns Erben und Reich, **1777**.

2 volumes in 1, 8vo (19 cm.), folding plates and maps, [12], 1068, index [52], p.

https://archive.org/details/cgaoldendorpsges12olde/page/280

52.2 ———.

Danish translation of 52.1 (p. 350 only) printed on pp. 178–179, Part 1, of Christian Georg Andreas Oldendorp, *Fuldstændigt Udtog af C.G.A. Oldendorps Missions-Historie om de evangeliske Brødres Mission paa de caraibiske Øer St. Thomas, St. Crux og St. Jan*, uitgivet paa Tydsk i to Dele.

Pt 1: *Kort Beskrivelse over Vestindien, især de Danske caraibiske Øer St. Crux, St. Thomas og St. Jan.*

Pt. 2: *Historisk Beretning om de hedenske Neger-Slavers Omvendelse paa de Danske Øer i Vestindien*, som et Udtog af C.G.A. Oldendorp's De Evangeliske Brødres Missions-Historie paa de Caraibiske Øer.

Copenhagen [Denmark]: Christ. L. Buchs Forlag, with J. Rud. Thiele, **1784**.

2 volumes in 1, with separate title pages and pagination, 8vo (18 cm): [4], 212 p. and 184, [4] p.

52.3 ———.

Swedish translation of 52.1, C. G. A. Oldendorp, *Historiska beskrifning öfwer ewangeliske brödernas miszions-arbete på caraibiske öarne St. Thomas St. Croix och St. Jan*, edited by Johann Jacob Bossart.

Stockholm [Sweden]: 1786–1788.

[Vol. 1] *Första delen, som innehåller åtskilliga efterrättelser, hörande til öarnes geographie, natural-historia och politiska författningar.*

Stockholm [Sweden]: tryckt hos commiss. P.A. Brodin, **1786**.

8vo (18 cm): [4], 64, [2], 348 p., map, 1 folded table.

[Vol. 2] *Andra delen, som innehåller miszions-historien ifrån år 1732 til år 1768.* Stockholm [Sweden]: tryckt hos Johan Christopher Holmberg, **1788**.

8vo (18 cm): [2], 634, [4] p., folded leaves of plates: ill. (engravings).

52.4 ———.

English translation of 52.1 printed on p. 164 of C. G. A. Oldendorp, *History of the Mission of the Evangelical Brethren on the Caribbean Islands of St. Thomas, St. Croix, and St. John*, edited by Johann Jakob Bossard (i.e., Bossart), translated into English and further edited by Arnold R. Highfield and Vladimir Barac.

Ann Arbor [Michigan, U.S.A.]: Karoma Publishers, **1987**.

8vo (24 cm.): xxxv, 737 p., illus.

52.5 ———.

52.1 printed on p. 280 in photomechanical reprint of the 1777 edition of C. G. A. Oldendorp, *Geschichte der Mission der evangelischen Brüder auf den caraibischen Inseln S. Thomas, S. Croix und S. Jan*, edited by Erich Beyreuther and Matthias Meyer (Volume 27.1 in Series 2 of Nikolaus Ludwig Graf von Zinzendorf, *Leben und Werk in Quellen und Darstellungen*).

Hildesheim [Saxony, Germany]: Georg Olms Verlag, **1995**.

8vo (20 cm.): 62, 444 p., illus.

52.6 ———. [Complete edition, with critical annotations, of 52.0]

Aspects of her life story transcribed from 52.0 and printed on pp. 399–400 and 484 in vol. 1 of C. G. A. Oldendorp, *Historie der caribischen Inseln Sanct Thomas, Sanct Crux und Sanct Jan, insbesondere der dasigen Neger und der Mission der evangelischen Brüder unter denselben: kommentierte Ausgabe des vollständigen Manuskriptes aus dem Archiv der Evangelischen Brüder-Unität Herrnhut*, edited by Gudrun Meier et al. (Band [Volume] 51 in the series *Abhandlungen und Berichte des Staatlichen Museums für Völkerkunde Dresden*).

Berlin [Germany]: VWB, Verlag für Wissenschaft und Bildung, **2000–2002**.

2 vols. in 4, 8vo (24 cm.).

Vol. 1 (2000): 764 p.; xxxviii, illus.

53.0 Unnamed Tembu (Temba) merchant

This unnamed man's life story summarized in Christian Georg Andreas Oldendorp's 3,000-page manuscript account of Oldendorp's **1767–1768** tour of Denmark's West Indian possessions, viz. "Manuskript für eine Geschichte der Mission auf den westindischen Inseln, verfasst von C. G. A. Oldendorp," R.28.63 and R.28.62, held in the Unity Archives, **Herrnhut, Saxony, Germany**. Only an abbreviated version of this lengthy manuscript was published in 1777 (53.1). It was not published in its entirety until 2000–2002 (53.4).

Full text: https://huskiecommons.lib.niu.edu/history-500africanvoices/47/ [see 53.6].

¶ This merchant slave trader identified as Tembu or Temba. He traded with Kassenti (Tchamba, possibly northern Togo, se Map 5), Pari, and Adangme people and lived four days from the land of the Accra (present-day coastal Ghana). He described his people's religion (indicating their God was called So) and their use of poison arrows. While traveling in "Pari" country (which neither Meier nor the present compilers have identified) with another merchant to trade, they encountered a woman who pretended to be a beggar and approached them to give her food. When they assisted her, the woman's husband appeared, accused them of illicit intercourse with his wife, seized them, and sold them to Ko people in Amina country (a New World ethnic designation for Akan speakers near Elmina Castle, present-day Ghana). When these Ko people sent the present unnamed subject to the beach to buy gunpowder from European traders, he was seized on the way by Accra people, who sold him at a European fort. From there the Tembu merchant was forcibly transported on a slave ship to the Danish West Indies (Map 14), where he conversed with Oldendorp in 1767–1768.

53.1 ——.

Aspects of his life story printed on pp. 280 and 353 of Christian Georg Andreas Oldendorp, *Geschichte der Mission der evangelischen Brueder auf den caraibischen Inseln S. Thomas, S. Croix, und S. Jan*, edited by Johann Jakob Bossart.

Barby [Saxony-Anhalt, Germany]: bey Christian Friedrich Laur, und in **Leipzig [Saxony, Germany]:** in Commission bey Weidmanns Erben und Reich, **1777**.

2 volumes in 1, 8vo (19 cm.), folding plates and maps, [12], 1068, index [52], p.

https://archive.org/details/cgaoldendorpsges12olde/page/280

53.2 ——.

Danish translation of 53.1 (p. 350 only) printed on p. 179, Part 1, of Christian Georg Andreas Oldendorp, *Fuldstændigt*

Udtog af C.G.A. Oldendorps Missions-Historie om de evangeliske Brødres Mission paa de caraibiske Øer St. Thomas, St. Crux og St. Jan, uitgivet paa Tydsk i to Dele.

Pt 1: *Kort Beskrivelse over Vestindien, især de Danske caraibiske Øer St. Crux, St. Thomas og St. Jan.*

Pt. 2: *Historisk Beretning om de hedenske Neger-Slavers Omvendelse paa de Danske Øer i Vestindien,* som et Udtog af C.G.A. Oldendorp's De Evangeliske Brødres Missions-Historie paa de Caraibiske Øer.

Copenhagen [Denmark]: Christ. L. Buchs Forlag, with J. Rud. Thiele, **1784**.

2 volumes in 1, with separate title pages and pagination, 8vo (18 cm): [4], 212 p. and 184, [4] p.

53.3 ——.

Swedish translation of 53.1, C. G. A. Oldendorp, *Historiska beskrifning öfwer ewangeliske brödernas miszions-arbete på caraibiske öarne St. Thomas St. Croix och St. Jan*, edited by Johann Jacob Bossart.

Stockholm [Sweden]: 1786–1788.

[Vol. 1] *Första delen, som innehåller åtskilliga efterrättelser, hörande til öarnes geographie, natural-historia och politiska författningar.*
Stockholm [Sweden]: tryckt hos commiss. P.A. Brodin, **1786**.
8vo (18 cm): [4], 64, [2], 348 p., map, 1 folded table.

[Vol. 2] *Andra delen, som innehåller miszions-historien ifrån år 1732 til år 1768.* **Stockholm [Sweden]:** tryckt hos Johan Christopher Holmberg, **1788**.
8vo (18 cm): [2], 634, [4] p., folded leaves of plates: ill. (engravings).

53.4 ——.

English translation of 53.1 printed on pp. 164 and 210 of C. G. A. Oldendorp, *History of the Mission of the Evangelical Brethren on the Caribbean Islands of St. Thomas, St. Croix, and St. John*, edited by Johann Jakob Bossard (i.e., Bossart), translated into English and further edited by Arnold R. Highfield and Vladimir Barac.

Ann Arbor [Michigan, U.S.A.]: Karoma Publishers, **1987**.
8vo (24 cm.): xxxv, 737 p., illus.

53.5 ——.

53.1 printed on pp. 280 and 353 in photomechanical reprint of the 1777 edition of C. G. A. Oldendorp, *Geschichte der Mission der evangelischen Brüder auf den caraibischen Inseln S. Thomas, S. Croix und S. Jan*, edited by Erich Beyreuther and Matthias Meyer (Volume 27.1 in Series 2 of Nikolaus Ludwig Graf von Zinzendorf, *Leben und Werk in Quellen und Darstellungen*).

Hildesheim [Saxony, Germany]: Georg Olms Verlag, 1995.
8vo (20 cm.): 62, 444 p., illus.

53.6 ——. [Complete edition, with critical annotations, of 53.0]

Aspects of his life story transcribed from 53.0 and printed on pp. 400–404 and 485 in vol. 1 of C. G. A. Oldendorp, *Historie der caribischen Inseln Sanct Thomas, Sanct Crux und Sanct Jan, insbesondere der dasigen Neger und der Mission der evangelischen Brüder unter denselben: kommentierte Ausgabe des vollständigen Manuskriptes aus dem Archiv der Evangelischen Brüder-Unität Herrnhut*, edited by Gudrun Meier et al. (Band [Volume] 51 in the series *Abhandlungen und Berichte des Staatlichen Museums für Völkerkunde Dresden*).

Berlin [Germany]: VWB, Verlag für Wissenschaft und Bildung, 2000–2002.
2 vols. in 4, 8vo (24 cm.).
Vol. 1 (2000): 764 p.; xxxviii, illus.

54.0   Unnamed Tchamba woman

Aspects of this woman's life story summarized in Christian Georg Andreas Oldendorp's 3,000-page manuscript account of Oldendorp's 1767–1768 tour of Denmark's West Indian possessions, viz. "Manuskript für eine Geschichte der Mission auf den westindischen Inseln, verfasst von C. G. A. Oldendorp," R.28.63 and R.28.62, held in the Unity Archives, Herrnhut, Saxony, Germany.

Full text: https://huskiecommons.lib.niu.edu/history-500africanvoices/48/ [see 54.1].

¶ This older woman identified as Kassenti (Tchamba, possibly northern Togo) and came from a place called Natum (see Map 5). After she was enslaved she was forcibly transported on a slave ship to St. Thomas, the Caribbean island colonized by the Danish (Map 14). She was understood by few people there because she spoke half Creole, half "guinesch." On St. Thomas she continued to observe certain eating habits from her homeland, stating that the priests had demanded strict observance of such things. She also described her homeland priests' healing methods to Oldendorp, whom she met on St. Thomas in 1767–1768.

54.1 ——. [Complete edition, with critical annotations, of 54.0]

Aspects of her life story transcribed from 54.0 and printed on pp. 406–407 in vol. 1 of C. G. A. Oldendorp, *Historie der caribischen Inseln Sanct Thomas, Sanct Crux und Sanct Jan, insbesondere der dasigen Neger und der Mission der evangelischen Brüder unter denselben: kommentierte Ausgabe des*

vollständigen Manuskriptes aus dem Archiv der Evangelischen Brüder-Unität Herrnhut, edited by Gudrun Meier et al. (Band [Volume] 51 in the series *Abhandlungen und Berichte des Staatlichen Museums für Völkerkunde Dresden*).

Berlin [Germany]: VWB, Verlag für Wissenschaft und Bildung, 2000–2002.
2 vols. in 4, 8vo (24 cm.).
Vol. 1 (2000): 764 p.; xxxviii, illus.

55.0   First unnamed Sokko or Asokko man

Aspects of this man's life story summarized in Christian Georg Andreas Oldendorp's 3,000-page manuscript account of Oldendorp's 1767–1768 tour of Denmark's West Indian possessions, viz. "Manuskript für eine Geschichte der Mission auf den westindischen Inseln, verfasst von C. G. A. Oldendorp," R.28.63 and R.28.62, held in the Unity Archives, Herrnhut, Saxony, Germany.

Full text: https://huskiecommons.lib.niu.edu/history-500africanvoices/49/ [see 55.1].

¶ This man identified as Sokko, or Asokko (possibly Nsoko, northeast Ghana—see Map 5). His homeland bordered that of a group Oldendorp called the Uwang and Amina (a New World ethnic designation for Akan speakers near Elmina Castle, present-day Ghana)—about six or seven weeks' journey from the sea. Their king or governor was called Mansa. They made war with the Asante (Akan people, present-day Ghana) but only in self-defense, when the latter attacked to take their people. His own people sold those they captured from other lands. He and the second unnamed Sokko/Asokko man (q.v. 56.0) described their clothing, trade goods, currency, and metallurgy at length, as well as their various languages and religious beliefs and practices (including the name of their one God Urbarri, Da-uni, or Mansa; the evil spirit, Mussu; magic; priests called Kramukko; the calendar; marriage; burial, etc.). This man was taken as a small child by Amina and so had different body markings. He was taken in the slave trade to the Danish West Indies (Map 14), where he conversed with Oldendorp in 1767–1768.

55.1 ——. [Complete edition, with critical annotations, of 55.0]

Aspects of his life story transcribed from 55.0 and printed on pp. 407–410 and 485 in vol. 1 of C. G. A. Oldendorp, *Historie der caribischen Inseln Sanct Thomas, Sanct Crux und Sanct Jan, insbesondere der dasigen Neger und der Mission der evangelischen Brüder unter denselben: kommentierte Ausgabe des vollständigen Manuskriptes aus dem Archiv der*

Evangelischen Brüder-Unität Herrnhut, edited by Gudrun Meier et al. (Band [Volume] 51 in the series *Abhandlungen und Berichte des Staatlichen Museums für Völkerkunde Dresden*).

Berlin [Germany]: VWB, Verlag für Wissenschaft und Bildung, 2000–2002.
2 vols. in 4, 8vo (24 cm.).
Vol. 1 (2000): 764 p.; xxxviii, illus.

56.0   Second Sokko or Asokko man

Aspects of this man's life story summarized in Christian Georg Andreas Oldendorp's 3,000-page manuscript account of Oldendorp's **1767–1768** tour of Denmark's West Indian possessions, viz. "Manuskript für eine Geschichte der Mission auf den westindischen Inseln, verfasst von C. G. A. Oldendorp," R.28.63 and R.28.62, held in the Unity Archives, Herrnhut, Saxony, Germany.

Full text: https://huskiecommons.lib.niu.edu/history-500africanvoices/50/ [see 56.1].

¶ This man identified as Sokko, or Asokko (possibly Nsoko, northeast Ghana—see Map 5). His homeland bordered on that of a group Oldendorp called the Uwang and Amina (a New World ethnic designation for Akan speakers near Elmina Castle, modern Ghana)—about six or seven weeks' journey from the sea. Their king or governor was called Mansa. They made war with the Asante (Akan people, present-day Ghana) but only in self-defense, when the latter attacked to take their people. His own people sold those they captured from other lands. He and the first unnamed Sokko/Asokko man (q.v. 55.0) described their clothing, trade goods, currency, and metallurgy at length, as well as their various languages and religious beliefs and practices (including the name of their one God Urbarri, Da-uni, or Mansa; the evil spirit, Mussu; magic; priests called Kramukko; the calendar; marriage; burial, etc.). During his boyhood, this man was sent to work as a servant for his uncle, who beat him so much that he ran away. While on his way home he was captured by Amina, who held him enslaved for six or seven years and then sold him to Europeans at a coastal fort. From there he was taken forcibly on a slave ship to the Danish West Indies (Map 14), where he conversed with Oldendorp in 1767–1768.

56.1 ———. [Complete edition, with critical annotations, of 56.0]

Aspects of his life story transcribed from 56.0 and printed on pp. 407–410 and 485 in vol. 1 of C. G. A. Oldendorp, *Historie der caribischen Inseln Sanct Thomas, Sanct Crux und Sanct Jan, insbesondere der dasigen Neger und der Mis-*

sion der evangelischen Brüder unter denselben: kommentierte Ausgabe des vollständigen Manuskriptes aus dem Archiv der Evangelischen Brüder-Unität Herrnhut, edited by Gudrun Meier et al. (Band [Volume] 51 in the series *Abhandlungen und Berichte des Staatlichen Museums für Völkerkunde Dresden*).

Berlin [Germany]: VWB, Verlag für Wissenschaft und Bildung, 2000–2002.
2 vols. in 4, 8vo (24 cm.).
Vol. 1 (2000): 764 p.; xxxviii, illus.

57.0   Third unnamed Sokko or Asokko man

Aspects of this man's life story summarized in Christian Georg Andreas Oldendorp's 3,000-page manuscript account of Oldendorp's **1767–1768** tour of Denmark's West Indian possessions, viz. "Manuskript für eine Geschichte der Mission auf den westindischen Inseln, verfasst von C. G. A. Oldendorp," R.28.63 and R.28.62, held in the Unity Archives, Herrnhut, Saxony, Germany.

Full text: https://huskiecommons.lib.niu.edu/history-500africanvoices/51/ [see 57.1].

¶ This man identified as Sokko, or Asokko (possibly Nsoko, northeast Ghana—see Map 5) and was Muslim. His homeland was far away from the other two Sokko/Asokko men (qq.v. 55.0 and 56.0). He described some of their religious beliefs and practices: their God was Allah; they had services with a priest and a book in a mosque; they prayed on mats, had a form of baptism, and practiced circumcision. He told Oldendorp a story about a man who lived with his uncle, who taught him to weave and sew clothes. When traveling with his uncle to a nearby village they met a creditor who took them both for collateral until payment was made. The man who spoke with Oldendorp was the payment: he was exchanged for the uncle and nephew, then sold to Europeans, who forcibly transported him on a slave ship to the Danish West Indies (Map 14), where he conversed with Oldendorp in 1767–1768.

57.1 ———. [Complete edition, with critical annotations, of 57.0]

Aspects of his life story transcribed from 57.0 and printed on pp. 407–410 and 485 in vol. 1 of C. G. A. Oldendorp, *Historie der caribischen Inseln Sanct Thomas, Sanct Crux und Sanct Jan, insbesondere der dasigen Neger und der Mission der evangelischen Brüder unter denselben: kommentierte Ausgabe des vollständigen Manuskriptes aus dem Archiv der Evangelischen Brüder-Unität Herrnhut*, edited by Gudrun Meier et al. (Band [Volume] 51 in the series *Abhandlungen und Berichte des Staatlichen Museums für Völkerkunde Dresden).*

Berlin [Germany]: VWB, Verlag für Wissenschaft und Bildung, 2000–2002.

2 vols. in 4, 8vo (24 cm.).

Vol. 1 (2000): 764 p.; xxxviii, illus.

58.0   First unnamed Papaa (Popo) woman

Aspects of this woman's life story summarized in Christian Georg Andreas Oldendorp's 3,000-page manuscript account of Oldendorp's **1767–1768** tour of Denmark's West Indian possessions, viz. "Manuskript für eine Geschichte der Mission auf den westindischen Inseln, verfasst von C. G. A. Oldendorp," R.28.63 and R.28.62, held in the Unity Archives, **Herrnhut, Saxony, Germany.**

Full text: https:// huskiecommons. lib.niu.edu/history-500africanvoices/52/ [see 58.1].

¶ This woman, whose homeland bordered the sea, identified as Papaa (Popo, in the Bight of Benin, present-day Togo and Benin—see Map 5) and was the daughter of a *caboceer* or *cabocero* (i.e., local ruler or person of influence), and sometimes visited her sister, who lived with a group Oldendorp labeled the "Watje," an unknown people, likely from the Bight of Benin (Benin, Togo Nigeria). She and two other women who eventually spoke with Oldendorp (qq.v. 59.0 and 60.0) came from villages near one another and described their homeland and its people, including their people's body markings, the name of their king (Pagi), and their work mining gold. They also described their religion (including the name of their God in heaven, Ma-u, and others called Gajiwodu), magic, polygyny, justice, burial, and nonwork activities (such as dance and music). This particular woman was familiar with Danish and other European forts in the area. During wartime, the Amina (a New World ethnic designation for Akan speakers near Elmina Castle, present-day Ghana) attacked and took her and many others to one of the forts. There she was sold to Europeans, who forcibly took her on a slave ship to the Danish West Indies (Map 14), where she conversed with Oldendorp in 1767–1768.

58.1 ——. [Complete edition, with critical annotations, of 58.0]

Aspects of her life story transcribed from 58.0 and printed on pp. 410–412 and 485–486 in vol. 1 of C. G. A. Oldendorp, *Historie der caribischen Inseln Sanct Thomas, Sanct Crux und Sanct Jan, insbesondere der dasigen Neger und der Mission der evangelischen Brüder unter denselben: kommentierte Ausgabe des vollständigen Manuskriptes aus dem Archiv der*

Evangelischen Brüder-Unität Herrnhut, edited by Gudrun Meier et al. (Band [Volume] 51 in the series *Abhandlungen und Berichte des Staatlichen Museums für Völkerkunde Dresden*).

Berlin [Germany]: VWB, Verlag für Wissenschaft und Bildung, 2000–2002.

2 vols. in 4, 8vo (24 cm.).

Vol. 1 (2000): 764 p.; xxxviii, illus.

59.0   Second unnamed Papaa (Popo) woman

Aspects of this man's life story summarized in Christian Georg Andreas Oldendorp's 3,000-page manuscript account of Oldendorp's **1767–1768** tour of Denmark's West Indian possessions, viz. "Manuskript für eine Geschichte der Mission auf den westindischen Inseln, verfasst von C. G. A. Oldendorp," R.28.63 and R.28.62, held in the Unity Archives, **Herrnhut, Saxony, Germany.**

Full text: https:// huskiecommons. lib.niu.edu/history-500africanvoices/53/ [see 59.1].

¶ This woman identified as Papaa (Popo, in the Bight of Benin, present-day Togo and Benin—see Map 5). She and two other Papaa/Popo women who eventually spoke with Oldendorp (qq.v. 58.0 and 60.0) came from villages near one another and described their homeland and its people, including their body markings, the name of their king (Pagi), and their work mining gold. They also described their religion (including the name of their God in heaven, Ma-u, and another called Gajiwodu), magic, polygyny, justice, burial rituals, and nonwork activities (such as dance and music). She was familiar with Danish and other European forts in the area. During wartime, the Amina (a New World ethnic designation for Akan speakers near Elmina Castle, present-day Ghana) attacked her village to take slaves. She, her mother, her brother, and her baby sister ran into the bush to hide but were caught. The Asante (Akan people, present-day Ghana) sold her sister back to her father but sold the rest of them to a European fort. Here she was separated from her family (none of whom she ever saw again), forced aboard a slave ship, and taken to the Danish West Indies (Map 14), where she conversed with Oldendorp in 1767–1768.

59.1 ——. [Complete edition, with critical annotations, of 59.0]

Aspects of her life story transcribed from 59.0 and printed on pp. 410–412 and 486 in vol. 1 of C. G. A. Oldendorp, *Historie der caribischen Inseln Sanct Thomas, Sanct Crux und Sanct Jan, insbesondere der dasigen Neger und der Mission der evangelischen Brüder unter denselben: kommentierte Ausgabe des vollständigen Manuskriptes aus dem Archiv der Evangelischen Brüder-Unität Herrnhut*, edited by Gudrun Meier et al. (Band [Volume] 51 in the series *Abhandlungen und Berichte des Staatlichen Museums für Völkerkunde Dresden*).

Berlin [Germany]: VWB, Verlag für Wissenschaft und Bildung, 2000–2002.
2 vols. in 4, 8vo (24 cm.).
Vol. 1 (2000): 764 p.; xxxviii, illus.

60.0 Third unnamed Papaa (Popo) woman

Aspects of this woman's life story summarized in Christian Georg Andreas Oldendorp's 3,000-page manuscript account of Oldendorp's 1767–1768 tour of Denmark's West Indian possessions, viz. "Manuskript für eine Geschichte der Mission auf den westindischen Inseln, verfasst von C. G. A. Oldendorp," R.28.63 and R.28.62, held in the Unity Archives, **Herrnhut, Saxony, Germany.**

Full text: https://huskiecommons.lib.niu.edu/history-500africanvoices/54/ [see 60.1].

¶ This woman identified as Papaa (Popo, in the Bight of Benin, present-day Togo and Benin—see Map 5). She and two other Papaa/Popo women who eventually spoke with Oldendorp (qq.v. 58.0 and 59.0) came from villages near one another and described their homeland and people, including their body markings, the name of their king (Pagi), and work mining gold. They also described their religion, (including the name of their God in heaven, Ma-u, and another called Gajiwodu), magic, polygyny, justice, burial rituals, and leisure activities (such as dance and music). She was familiar with Danish and other European forts in the area. She was enslaved by her own people while gathering wood in the forest. She was bound and taken to a house, probably a barracoon, and kept for some time before being forced aboard a slave ship and taken to the Danish West Indies (Map 14), where she conversed with Oldendorp in 1767–1768.

60.1 ——. [Complete edition, with critical annotations, of 60.0]

Aspects of her life story transcribed from 60.0 and printed on pp. 410–412 and 486 in vol. 1 of C. G. A. Oldendorp, *Historie der caribischen Inseln Sanct Thomas, Sanct Crux und Sanct Jan, insbesondere der dasigen Neger und der Mission der evangelischen Brüder unter denselben: kommentierte Ausgabe des vollständigen Manuskriptes aus dem Archiv der Evangelischen Brüder-Unität Herrnhut*, edited by Gudrun Meier et al. (Band [Volume] 51 in the series *Abhandlungen und Berichte des Staatlichen Museums für Völkerkunde Dresden*).

Berlin [Germany]: VWB, Verlag für Wissenschaft und Bildung, **2000–2002.**
2 vols. in 4, 8vo (24 cm.).
Vol. 1 (2000): 764 p.; xxxviii, illus.

61.0 Unnamed Allada man (ca. 1667–)

Aspects of this Allada man's life story summarized in Christian Georg Andreas Oldendorp's 3,000-page manuscript account of Oldendorp's 1767–1768 tour of Denmark's West Indian possessions, viz. "Manuskript für eine Geschichte der Mission auf den westindischen Inseln, verfasst von C. G. A. Oldendorp," R.28.63 and R.28.62, held in the Unity Archives, **Herrnhut, Saxony, Germany.** Only an abbreviated version of this lengthy manuscript was published in 1777 (61.1). It was not published in its entirety until 2000–2002 (61.4).

Full text: https://huskiecommons.lib.niu.edu/history-500africanvoices/55/ [see 61.5].

¶ This man identified as coming from the Arrada (Allada, present-day Benin) nation of the Papaa (i.e., Popo, in the Bight of Benin, present-day Togo and Benin) kingdom (see Map 5). Their God was called Vodu (i.e., vodun). His king had a large army and fought a war with the Fida (of Ouidah, present-day Benin), from whom his own people appear to have originated. He was taken in the slave trade to St. Croix in the Danish West Indies (Map 14), where he conversed with Oldendorp in 1767–1768, when this man was supposed to be over a hundred years old.

61.1 ——.

Aspects of his life printed on p. 283 of Christian Georg Andreas Oldendorp, *Geschichte der Mission der evangelischen Brueder auf den caraibischen Inseln S. Thomas, S. Croix, und S. Jan*, edited by Johann Jakob Bossart.

Barby [Saxony-Anhalt, Germany]: bey Christian Friedrich Laur, und in **Leipzig [Saxony, Germany]:** in Commission bey Weidmanns Erben und Reich, **1777.**
2 volumes in 1, 8vo (19 cm.), folding plates and maps, [12], 1068, index [52], p.
https://archive.org/details/cgaoldendorpsges12olde/page/283

61.2 ——.

Swedish translation of 61.1, C. G. A. Oldendorp, *Historiska beskrifning öfwer ewangeliske brödernas miszions-arbete på caraibiske öarne St. Thomas St. Croix och St. Jan*, edited by Johann Jacob Bossart.

Stockholm [Sweden]: 1786–1788.

[Vol. 1] *Första delen, som innehåller åtskilliga efterrättelser, hörande til öarnes geographie, natural-historia och politiska författningar.*

Stockholm [Sweden]: tryckt hos commiss. P.A. Brodin, **1786.**

8vo (18 cm): [4], 64, [2], 348 p., map, 1 folded table.

[Vol. 2] *Andra delen, som innehåller miszions-historien ifrån år 1732 til år 1768.* **Stockholm [Sweden]:** tryckt hos Johan Christopher Holmberg, **1788.**

8vo (18 cm): [2], 634, [4] p., folded leaves of plates: ill. (engravings).

61.3 ——.

English translation of 61.1 printed on p. 165 of C. G. A. Oldendorp, *History of the Mission of the Evangelical Brethren on the Caribbean Islands of St. Thomas, St. Croix, and St. John,* edited by Johann Jakob Bossard (i.e., Bossart), translated into English and further edited by Arnold R. Highfield and Vladimir Barac.

Ann Arbor [Michigan, U.S.A.]: Karoma Publishers, **1987.**

8vo (24 cm.): xxxv, 737 p., illus.

61.4 ——.

61.1 reprinted on p. 283 of photomechanical reprint of the 1777 edition of C. G. A. Oldendorp, *Geschichte der Mission der evangelischen Brüder auf den caraibischen Inseln S. Thomas, S. Croix und S. Jan,* edited by Erich Beyreuther and Matthias Meyer (Volume 27.1 in Series 2 of Nikolaus Ludwig Graf von Zinzendorf, *Leben und Werk in Quellen und Darstellungen*).

Hildesheim [Saxony, Germany]: Georg Olms Verlag, **1995.**

8vo (20 cm.): 62, 444 p., illus.

61.5 ——. [Complete edition, with critical annotations, of 61.0]

Aspects of his life story transcribed from 61.0 and printed on pp. 412–413 in vol. 1 of C. G. A. Oldendorp, *Historie der caribischen Inseln Sanct Thomas, Sanct Crux und Sanct Jan, insbesondere der dasigen Neger und der Mission der evangelischen Brüder unter denselben: kommentierte Ausgabe des vollständigen Manuskriptes aus dem Archiv der Evangelischen Brüder-Unität Herrnhut,* edited by Gudrun Meier et al. (Band [Volume] 51 in the series *Abhandlungen und Berichte des Staatlichen Museums für Völkerkunde Dresden*).

Berlin [Germany]: VWB, Verlag für Wissenschaft und Bildung, **2000–2002.**

2 vols. in 4, 8vo (24 cm.).

Vol. 1 (2000): 764 p.; xxxviii, illus.

62.0   First unnamed Watje woman

Aspects of this woman's life story summarized in Christian Georg Andreas Oldendorp's 3,000-page manuscript account of Oldendorp's **1767–1768** tour of Denmark's West Indian possessions, viz. "Manuskript für eine Geschichte der Mission auf den westindischen Inseln, verfasst von C. G. A. Oldendorp," R.28.63 and R.28.62, held in the Unity Archives, **Herrnhut, Saxony, Germany.**

Full text: https:// huskiecommons. lib.niu.edu/history-500africanvoices/56/ [see 62.1].

¶ This woman identified as Watje, an unknown people likely from the Bight of Benin (Benin, Togo, Nigeria—see Map 5). Their king or governor was called Fegan. Neighboring peoples included Amina (a New World ethnic designation for Akan speakers near Elmina Castle, present-day Ghana), Kassenti (Tchamba, possibly northern Togo), and Sokko (possibly Nsoko, northeast Ghana). She (and other witnesses who spoke with Oldendorp) described their body markings, religion, and warfare with Asante using muskets (including execution and sale of prisoners). She described her own piety and a prayer to Djaubenje, her people's God in heaven and on earth. She was forced aboard a slave ship and taken to the Danish West Indies (Map 14), where she conversed with Oldendorp in 1767–1768.

62.1 ——. [Complete edition, with critical annotations, of 62.0]

Aspects of her life story transcribed from 62.0 and printed on pp. 413–418, and 486 in vol. 1 of C. G. A. Oldendorp, *Historie der caribischen Inseln Sanct Thomas, Sanct Crux und Sanct Jan, insbesondere der dasigen Neger und der Mission der evangelischen Brüder unter denselben: kommentierte Ausgabe des vollständigen Manuskriptes aus dem Archiv der Evangelischen Brüder-Unität Herrnhut,* edited by Gudrun Meier et al. (Band [Volume] 51 in the series *Abhandlungen und Berichte des Staatlichen Museums für Völkerkunde Dresden*).

Berlin [Germany]: VWB, Verlag für Wissenschaft und Bildung, **2000–2002.**

2 vols. in 4, 8vo (24 cm.).

Vol. 1 (2000): 764 p.; xxxviii, illus.

63.0   Second unnamed Watje woman

Aspects of this woman's life story summarized in Christian Georg Andreas Oldendorp's 3,000-page manuscript account of Oldendorp's **1767–1768** tour of Denmark's West Indian

Neighboring peoples included Amina (a New World ethnic designation for Akan speakers near Elmina Castle, present-day Ghana), Kassenti (Tchamba, possibly northern Togo) and Sokko (possibly Nsoko, northeast Ghana). He (and other witnesses who spoke with Oldendorp) described their body markings, religion, and warfare with Asante (Akan people, present-day Ghana) using muskets (including execution and sale of prisoners). After his wife left him, he sought another, and for this his own people seized him and sold him. Europeans subsequently forced him aboard a slave ship that took him to the Danish West Indies (Map 14), where he conversed with Oldendorp in 1767–1768. He and two other Watje men (qq.v. 64.0 and 66.0) spoke with Oldendorp, but it is unclear which of these three described an unsuccessful revolt by Africans enslaved aboard their ship.

65.1 ——. [Complete edition, with critical annotations, of 65.0]

Aspects of his life story transcribed from 65.0 and printed on pp. 413–418, 486, and 504 in vol. 1 of C. G. A. Oldendorp, *Historie der caribischen Inseln Sanct Thomas, Sanct Crux und Sanct Jan, insbesondere der dasigen Neger und der Mission der evangelischen Brüder unter denselben: kommentierte Ausgabe des vollständigen Manuskriptes aus dem Archiv der Evangelischen Brüder-Unität Herrnhut,* edited by Gudrun Meier et al. (Band [Volume] 51 in the series *Abhandlungen und Berichte des Staatlichen Museums für Völkerkunde Dresden*).

Berlin [Germany]: VWB, Verlag für Wissenschaft und Bildung, 2000–2002.

2 vols. in 4, 8vo (24 cm.).

Vol. 1 (2000): 764 p.; xxxviii, illus.

66.0 Third unnamed Watje man

Aspects of this man's life story summarized in Christian Georg Andreas Oldendorp's 3,000-page manuscript account of Oldendorp's **1767–1768** tour of Denmark's West Indian possessions, viz. "Manuskript für eine Geschichte der Mission auf den westindischen Inseln, verfasst von C. G. A. Oldendorp," R.28.63 and R.28.62, held in the Unity Archives, Herrnhut, Saxony, Germany.

Full text: https://huskiecommons.lib.niu.edu/history-500africanvoices/60/ [see 66.1].

¶ This man identified as Watje, an unknown people, likely from the Bight of Benin (modern Benin, Togo, and Nigeria—see Map 5). Their king or governor was called Fegan. Neighboring peoples included Amina (a New World ethnic designation for Akan speakers near Elmina Castle, present-day Ghana), Kassenti (Tchamba, possibly northern Togo),

and Sokko (possibly Nsoko, northeast Ghana). He (and other witnesses who spoke with Oldendorp) described their body markings, religion, and warfare with Asante (Akan people, present-day Ghana) using muskets (including execution and sale of prisoners). He was sold by his brother-in-law to pay a debt. Europeans subsequently forced him aboard a slave ship that took him to the Danish West Indies (Map 14), where he conversed with Oldendorp in 1767–1768. He and two other Watje men (qq.v. 64.0 and 65.0) spoke with Oldendorp, but it is unclear which of these three described an unsuccessful revolt by Africans enslaved aboard their ship.

66.1 ——. [Complete edition, with critical annotations, of 66.0]

Aspects of his life story transcribed from 66.0 and printed on pp. 413–418, 486, and 504 in vol. 1 of C. G. A. Oldendorp, *Historie der caribischen Inseln Sanct Thomas, Sanct Crux und Sanct Jan, insbesondere der dasigen Neger und der Mission der evangelischen Brüder unter denselben: kommentierte Ausgabe des vollständigen Manuskriptes aus dem Archiv der Evangelischen Brüder-Unität Herrnhut,* edited by Gudrun Meier et al. (Band [Volume] 51 in the series *Abhandlungen und Berichte des Staatlichen Museums für Völkerkunde Dresden*).

Berlin [Germany]: VWB, Verlag für Wissenschaft und Bildung, 2000–2002.

2 vols. in 4, 8vo (24 cm.).

Vol. 1 (2000): 764 p.; xxxviii, illus.

67.0 Unnamed Atja woman

Aspects of this woman's life story summarized in Christian Georg Andreas Oldendorp's 3,000-page manuscript account of Oldendorp's **1767–1768** tour of Denmark's West Indian possessions, viz. "Manuskript für eine Geschichte der Mission auf den westindischen Inseln, verfasst von C. G. A. Oldendorp," R.28.63 and R.28.62, held in the Unity Archives, Herrnhut, Saxony, Germany.

Full text: https://huskiecommons.lib.niu.edu/history-500africanvoices/61/ [see 67.1].

¶ This woman identified as Atja (present-day Aja, on the left bank of the Mono, in south Togo). She described their body markings and aspects of their religion. They called their God in heaven Gajiwodu. There were some people there called Lissa who were white (a possible reference to the Fon deity Lisa). In her country they practiced circumcision and magic. She also described marriage and the torture of prisoners of war. Her people were friendly with the Watje, an unknown people, likely from the Bight of Benin (modern Benin, Togo, and Nigeria—see Map 5). She was taken in the slave trade to the Danish

West Indies (Map 14), where she conversed with Oldendorp in 1767–1768.

67.1 ——. [Complete edition, with critical annotations, of 67.0]

Aspects of her life story transcribed from 67.0 and printed on pp. 419–420 in vol. 1 of C. G. A. Oldendorp, *Historie der caribischen Inseln Sanct Thomas, Sanct Crux und Sanct Jan, insbesondere der dasigen Neger und der Mission der evangelischen Brüder unter denselben: kommentierte Ausgabe des vollständigen Manuskriptes aus dem Archiv der Evangelischen Brüder-Unität Herrnhut*, edited by Gudrun Meier et al. (Band [Volume] 51 in the series *Abhandlungen und Berichte des Staatlichen Museums für Völkerkunde Dresden*).

Berlin [Germany]: VWB, Verlag für Wissenschaft und Bildung, **2000–2002.**

2 vols. in 4, 8vo (24 cm.).

Vol. 1 (2000): 764 p.; xxxviii, illus.

68.0 Unnamed Wawu woman

Aspects of this unnamed woman's life story summarized in Christian Georg Andreas Oldendorp's 3,000-page manuscript account of Oldendorp's **1767–1768** tour of Denmark's West Indian possessions, viz. "Manuskript für eine Geschichte der Mission auf den westindischen Inseln, verfasst von C. G. A. Oldendorp," R.28.63 and R.28.62, held in the Unity Archives, **Herrnhut, Saxony, Germany.** Only an abbreviated version of this lengthy manuscript was published in 1777 (68.1). It was not published in its entirety until 2000–2002 (68.4).

Full text: https://huskiecommons.lib.niu.edu/history-500africanvoices/62/ [see 68.5].

¶ This woman identified as Wawu and was from a populous nation deep within Africa's interior. Wawu might refer to the Borgu town of Wawa (present-day Nigeria), to the northeast of Dahomey (present-day Benin—see Map 5). Their king was called Atjuwi, and their neighbors included Tofa, Jani, Taku, Akisa, Fon, Dahomey, and others. They traded with Fida (Ouidah). She describes their religion at length. They called their God in heaven Gajiwodu. By a custom that she could not explain, boys were circumcised at age twelve. During a raid by Dahomey warriors she and others hid in the bush but were caught and sold. She was taken in the slave trade to the Danish West Indies (Map 14), where she conversed with Oldendorp in 1767–1768.

68.1 ——.

Aspects of her life story printed on p. 284 of Christian Georg Andreas Oldendorp, *Geschichte der Mission der evange-*

lischen Brueder auf den caraibischen Inseln S. Thomas, S. Croix, und S. Jan, edited by Johann Jakob Bossart.

Barby [Saxony-Anhalt, Germany]: bey Christian Friedrich Laur, und in **Leipzig [Saxony, Germany]:** in Commission bey Weidmanns Erben und Reich, **1777.**

2 volumes in 1, 8vo (19 cm.), folding plates and maps, [12], 1068, index [52], p.

https://archive.org/details/cgaoldendorpsges12olde/page/284

68.2 ——.

Swedish translation of 68.1, C. G. A. Oldendorp, *Historiska beskrifning öfwer ewangeliske brödernas miszions-arbete på caraibiske öarne St. Thomas St. Croix och St. Jan*, edited by Johann Jacob Bossart.

Stockholm [Sweden]: 1786–1788.

[Vol. 1] *Första delen, som innehåller åtskilliga efterrättelser, hörande til öarnes geographie, natural-historia och politiska författningar.*

Stockholm [Sweden]: tryckt hos commiss. P.A. Brodin, **1786.**

8vo (18 cm): [4], 64, [2], 348 p., map, 1 folded table.

[Vol. 2] *Andra delen, som innehåller miszions-historien ifrån år 1732 til år 1768.* **Stockholm [Sweden]:** tryckt hos Johan Christopher Holmberg, **1788.**

8vo (18 cm): [2], 634, [4] p., folded leaves of plates: ill. (engravings).

68.3 ——.

English translation of 68.1 printed on p. 166 of C. G. A. Oldendorp, *History of the Mission of the Evangelical Brethren on the Caribbean Islands of St. Thomas, St. Croix, and St. John*, edited by Johann Jakob Bossard (i.e., Bossart), translated into English and further edited by Arnold R. Highfield and Vladimir Barac.

Ann Arbor [Michigan, U.S.A.]: Karoma Publishers, **1987.**

8vo (24 cm.): xxxv, 737 p., illus.

68.4 ——.

68.1 printed on p. 284 in photomechanical reprint of the 1777 edition of C. G. A. Oldendorp, *Geschichte der Mission der evangelischen Brüder auf den caraibischen Inseln S. Thomas, S. Croix und S. Jan*, edited by Erich Beyreuther and Matthias Meyer (Volume 27.1 in Series 2 of Nikolaus Ludwig Graf von Zinzendorf, *Leben und Werk in Quellen und Darstellungen*).

Hildesheim [Saxony, Germany]: Georg Olms Verlag, **1995.**

8vo (20 cm.): 62, 444 p., illus.

68.5 ——. [Complete edition, with critical annotations, of 68.0]

Aspects of her life story transcribed from 68.0 and printed on pp. 423–425 and 486 in vol. 1 of C. G. A. Oldendorp,

Historie der caribischen Inseln Sanct Thomas, Sanct Crux und Sanct Jan, insbesondere der dasigen Neger und der Mission der evangelischen Brüder unter denselben: kommentierte Ausgabe des vollständigen Manuskriptes aus dem Archiv der Evangelischen Brüder-Unität Herrnhut, edited by Gudrun Meier et al. (Band [Volume] 51 in the series *Abhandlungen und Berichte des Staatlichen Museums für Völkerkunde Dresden*).

Berlin [Germany]: VWB, Verlag für Wissenschaft und Bildung, **2000–2002.**

2 vols. in 4, 8vo (24 cm.).

Vol. 1 (2000): 764 p.; xxxviii, illus.

69.0 Unnamed Wawu man

Aspects of this unnamed Wawu man's life story summarized in Christian Georg Andreas Oldendorp's 3,000-page manuscript account of Oldendorp's **1767–1768** tour of Denmark's West Indian possessions, viz. "Manuskript für eine Geschichte der Mission auf den westindischen Inseln, verfasst von C. G. A. Oldendorp," R.28.63 and R.28.62, held in the Unity Archives, **Herrnhut, Saxony, Germany.** Only an abbreviated version of this lengthy manuscript was published in 1777 (69.1). It was not published in its entirety until 2000–2002 (69.4).

Full text: https://huskiecommons.lib.niu.edu/history-500africanvoices/63/ [see 69.5].

¶ **This man identified as Wawu but was from a different area than the unnamed Wawu woman who spoke with Oldendorp (q.v. 68.0). Wawu might refer to the Borgu town of Wawa (present-day Nigeria), to the northeast of Dahomey (present-day day Benin—see Map 5). Their neighbors in Africa were Fra, Bente, Naena, Gui, Gurraa, Guaslee, and No. He briefly described his own people's religion, noting that their God was called Barriadad. Their king was called Atjuwi. This man was taken in the slave trade to the Danish West Indies (Map 14), where he conversed with Oldendorp in 1767–1768.**

69.1 ——.

Aspects of his life story printed on pp. 284–285 of Christian Georg Andreas Oldendorp, *Geschichte der Mission der evangelischen Brueder auf den caraibischen Inseln S. Thomas, S. Croix, und S. Jan,* edited by Johann Jakob Bossart.

Barby [Saxony-Anhalt, Germany]: bey Christian Friedrich Laur, und in **Leipzig [Saxony, Germany]:** in Commission bey Weidmanns Erben und Reich, **1777.**

2 volumes in 1, 8vo (19 cm.), folding plates and maps, [12], 1068, index [52], p.

https://archive.org/details/cgaoldendorpsges12olde/page/284

69.2 ——.

Swedish translation of 69.1, C. G. A. Oldendorp, *Historiska beskrifning öfwer ewangeliske brödernas miszions-arbete på caraibiske öarne St. Thomas St. Croix och St. Jan,* edited by Johann Jacob Bossart.

Stockholm [Sweden]: 1786–1788.

[Vol. 1] *Första delen, som innehåller åtskilliga efterrättelser, hörande til öarnes geographie, natural-historia och politiska författningar.*

Stockholm [Sweden]: tryckt hos commiss. P.A. Brodin, **1786.**

8vo (18 cm): [4], 64, [2], 348 p., map, 1 folded table.

[Vol. 2] *Andra delen, som innehåller miszions-historien ifrån år 1732 til år 1768.* **Stockholm [Sweden]:** tryckt hos Johan Christopher Holmberg, **1788.**

8vo (18 cm): [2], 634, [4] p., folded leaves of plates: ill. (engravings).

69.3 ——.

English translation of 69.1 printed on p. 166 of C. G. A. Oldendorp, *History of the Mission of the Evangelical Brethren on the Caribbean Islands of St. Thomas, St. Croix, and St. John,* edited by Johann Jakob Bossard (i.e., Bossart), translated into English and further edited by Arnold R. Highfield and Vladimir Barac.

Ann Arbor [Michigan, U.S.A.]: Karoma Publishers, **1987.**

8vo (24 cm.): xxxv, 737 p., illus.

69.4 ——.

69.1 printed on pp. 284–285 in photomechanical reprint of the 1777 edition of C. G. A. Oldendorp, *Geschichte der Mission der evangelischen Brüder auf den caraibischen Inseln S. Thomas, S. Croix und S. Jan,* edited by Erich Beyreuther and Matthias Meyer (Volume 27.1 in Series 2 of Nikolaus Ludwig Graf von Zinzendorf, *Leben und Werk in Quellen und Darstellungen*).

Hildesheim [Saxony, Germany]: Georg Olms Verlag, **1995.**

8vo (20 cm.): 62, 444 p., illus.

69.5 ——. [Complete edition, with critical annotations, of 69.0]

Aspects of his life story transcribed from 69.0 and printed on pp. 423–424 in vol. 1 of C. G. A. Oldendorp, *Historie der caribischen Inseln Sanct Thomas, Sanct Crux und Sanct Jan, insbesondere der dasigen Neger und der Mission der evangelischen Brüder unter denselben: kommentierte Ausgabe des vollständigen Manuskriptes aus dem Archiv der Evangelischen Brüder-Unität Herrnhut,* edited by Gudrun Meier et al. (Band [Volume] 51 in the series *Abhandlungen und Berichte des Staatlichen Museums für Völkerkunde Dresden*).

Berlin [Germany]: VWB, Verlag für Wissenschaft und Bildung, 2000–2002.

2 vols. in 4, 8vo (24 cm.).

Vol. 1 (2000): 764 p.; xxxviii, illus.

70.0   First unnamed Moko man

Aspects of this man's life story summarized in Christian Georg Andreas Oldendorp's 3,000-page manuscript account of Oldendorp's **1767–1768** tour of Denmark's West Indian possessions, viz. "Manuskript für eine Geschichte der Mission auf den westindischen Inseln, verfasst von C. G. A. Oldendorp," R.28.63 and R.28.62, held in the Unity Archives, Herrnhut, Saxony, Germany.

Full text: https://huskiecommons.lib.niu.edu/history-500africanvoices/64/ [see 70.5].

¶ This man identified as Moko (unknown, possibly Kamba people of northeastern Congo—see Map 6). He and the others from this area (qq.v. 71.0 and 72.0) described their body markings and noted that their neighbors were Bobumda (possibly Bamenda, present-day northwest Cameroon). They called their God in heaven, creator, and omnipotent ruler Abassi, and their evil spiritual figure Dausoa. This unnamed Moko man and the others provided more information on their religion, animal sacrifice, medical practice, justice, elite burial practice, marriage, and the circumcision of young boys. This man said that his father allowed him much freedom as he grew up, which made him arrogant and bold. When he took his father's slaves to a European ship, the captain bought them and seized the man himself. All were forcibly taken on a slave ship to the Danish West Indies (Map 14), where this man met Oldendorp in 1767–1768.

70.1 ——. [Complete edition, with critical annotations, of 70.0]

Aspects of his life story transcribed from 70.0 and printed on pp. 434–436 and 487 in vol. 1 of C. G. A. Oldendorp, *Historie der caribischen Inseln Sanct Thomas, Sanct Crux und Sanct Jan, insbesondere der dasigen Neger und der Mission der evangelischen Brüder unter denselben: kommentierte Ausgabe des vollständigen Manuskriptes aus dem Archiv der Evangelischen Brüder-Unität Herrnhut*, edited by Gudrun Meier et al. (Band [Volume] 51 in the series *Abhandlungen und Berichte des Staatlichen Museums für Völkerkunde Dresden*).

Berlin [Germany]: VWB, Verlag für Wissenschaft und Bildung, 2000–2002.

2 vols. in 4, 8vo (24 cm.).

Vol. 1 (2000): 764 p.; xxxviii, illus.

71.0 Second unnamed Moko man

Aspects of this man's life story summarized in Christian Georg Andreas Oldendorp's 3,000-page manuscript account of Oldendorp's **1767–1768** tour of Denmark's West Indian possessions, viz. "Manuskript für eine Geschichte der Mission auf den westindischen Inseln, verfasst von C. G. A. Oldendorp," R.28.63 and R.28.62, held in the Unity Archives, Herrnhut, Saxony, Germany.

Full text: https://huskiecommons.lib.niu.edu/history-500africanvoices/65/ [see 71.1].

¶ This man identified as Moko (unknown, possibly Kamba people of northeastern Congo—see Map 6). He and the others from this area (qq.v. 70.0 and 72.0) described their body markings and noted that their neighbors were Bobumda (possibly Bamenda, present-day northwest Cameroon). They called their God in heaven, creator, and omnipotent ruler Abassi, and their evil spiritual figure Dausoa. This second unnamed Moko man and the others provided more information on their religion, animal sacrifice, medical practice, justice, elite burial practice, marriage, and the circumcision of young boys. This man said that he worked as a factor for his ruler in the trade with Europeans, that is, he collected their payments for the slaves his ruler had delivered to the Europeans. During one trip to the coast a group of runaway slaves caught him and sold him to Europeans. He was then forcibly taken on a slave ship to the Danish West Indies (Map 14), where this man met Oldendorp in 1767–1768.

71.1 ——. [Complete edition, with critical annotations, of 71.0]

Aspects of his life story transcribed from 71.0 and printed on pp. 434–436 and 487 in vol. 1 of C. G. A. Oldendorp, *Historie der caribischen Inseln Sanct Thomas, Sanct Crux und Sanct Jan, insbesondere der dasigen Neger und der Mission der evangelischen Brüder unter denselben: kommentierte Ausgabe des vollständigen Manuskriptes aus dem Archiv der Evangelischen Brüder-Unität Herrnhut*, edited by Gudrun Meier et al. (Band [Volume] 51 in the series *Abhandlungen und Berichte des Staatlichen Museums für Völkerkunde Dresden*).

Berlin [Germany]: VWB, Verlag für Wissenschaft und Bildung, 2000–2002.

2 vols. in 4, 8vo (24 cm.).

Vol. 1 (2000): 764 p.; xxxviii, illus.

72.0 Unnamed Moko woman

Aspects of this woman's life story summarized in Christian Georg Andreas Oldendorp's 3,000-page manuscript account of Oldendorp's **1767–1768** tour of Denmark's West Indian possessions, viz. "Manuskript für eine Geschichte der Mission auf den westindischen Inseln, verfasst von C. G. A. Oldendorp," R.28.63 and R.28.62, held in the Unity Archives, Herrnhut, Saxony, Germany.

¶ This woman identified as Mokko (unknown, possibly Kamba people of northeastern Congo—see Map 6). She and two others from this area who spoke with Oldendorp (qq.v. 70.0 and 71.0) described their body markings, noted that their neighbors were Bobumda (possibly Bamenda, northwestern Cameroon), and spoke about their religion, animal sacrifice, medical practice, justice, elite burial practice, marriage, and circumcision of young boys. They called their God in heaven, creator, and omnipotent ruler Abassi, and their evil spiritual figure Dausoa. This woman said that she had been one of her husband's seven wives. After he died, she and one other wife were chosen to be killed and buried with him, following tradition. When she refused to comply, her husband's friends sold her into slavery. Eventually she was forcibly taken on a slave ship to the Danish West Indies (Map 14), where she conversed with Oldendorp in 1767–1768.

72.1 ——. [Complete edition, with critical annotations, of 72.0]

Aspects of her life story transcribed from 72.0 and printed on pp. 434–436 and 487 in vol. 1 of C. G. A. Oldendorp, *Historie der caribischen Inseln Sanct Thomas, Sanct Crux und Sanct Jan, insbesondere der dasigen Neger und der Mission der evangelischen Brüder unter denselben: kommentierte Ausgabe des vollständigen Manuskriptes aus dem Archiv der Evangelischen Brüder-Unität Herrnhut*, edited by Gudrun Meier et al. (Band [Volume] 51 in the series *Abhandlungen und Berichte des Staatlichen Museums für Völkerkunde Dresden*).

Berlin [Germany]: VWB, Verlag für Wissenschaft und Bildung, 2000–2002.
2 vols. in 4, 8vo (24 cm.).
Vol. 1 (2000): 764 p.; xxxviii, illus.

73.0 Unnamed Loango man

Aspects of this unnamed Loango man's life story summarized in Christian Georg Andreas Oldendorp's 3,000-page manuscript account of Oldendorp's 1767–1768 tour of Denmark's West Indian possessions, viz. "Manuskript für eine Geschichte der Mission auf den westindischen Inseln, verfasst von C. G. A. Oldendorp," R.28.63 and R.28.62, held in the Unity Archives, Herrnhut, Saxony, Germany. Only an abbreviated

Full text: https://huskiecommons.lib.niu.edu/history-500africanvoices/66/ [see 72.1].

version of this lengthy manuscript was published in 1777 (73.1). It was not published in its entirety until 2000–2002 (73.4).

¶ This man identified as Loango (present-day Congo, north of the Congo River—see Map 6). The inhabitants were called Vili, and their supreme ruler was Areffan Congo, a Christian. Loango was rich in gold and had two kings, Maluango and Macongo, who were Areffan's vassals. A war broke out between the two kings, which involved the use of firearms, bows, and arrows. English, French, and Dutch slave ships traded with them, and this unnamed Loango man told of an English captain who, with his hold already full of slaves, took more by force. A great number of Blacks encircled the ship with canoes, cut the anchor line, boarded the ship, freed the men and women enslaved on it, and punished the crew decisively. He also described Black Jews living in Loango who strictly observed the Sabbath, lived dispersed, engaged in trade, and maintained a separate burial ground. He elaborated at length on body markings, the filed teeth of some inhabitants, their religion (which was not that of the king), marriage, and other customs. When the king used this man as collateral for a debt that he failed to pay, the Loango man was sold into slavery. While being transported on a slave ship to the Danish West Indies (Map 14), some of the enslaved people planned to kill the crew but were betrayed. After arrival and sale, he met Oldendorp in 1767–1768.

73.1 ——.

Aspects of his life story printed on pp. 286–288 of Christian Georg Andreas Oldendorp, *Geschichte der Mission der evangelischen Brueder auf den caraibischen Inseln S. Thomas, S. Croix, und S. Jan*, edited by Johann Jakob Bossart.

Barby [Saxony-Anhalt, Germany]: bey Christian Friedrich Laur, und in Leipzig [Saxony, Germany]: in Commission bey Weidmanns Erben und Reich, 1777.
2 volumes in 1, 8vo (19 cm.), folding plates and maps, [12], 1068, index [52], p.
https://archive.org/details/cgaoldendorpsges12olde/page/286

73.2 ——.

Swedish translation of 73.1, C. G. A. Oldendorp, *Historiska beskrifning öfwer ewangeliske brödernas miszions-arbete på caraibiske öarne St. Thomas St. Croix och St. Jan*, edited by Johann Jacob Bossart.

Stockholm [Sweden]: 1786–1788.

Full text: https://huskiecommons.lib.niu.edu/history-500africanvoices/67/ [see 73.5].

73.0 Unnamed Loango man

Figure 5: Engraving of the city of Loango (present-day Republic of Congo and Gabon) on 1676, through which many enslaved Africans passed before transport to the Americas on slave ships, including *La Marie Seraphique* (pictured elsewhere).

Source: Olfert Dapper, *Naukeurige Beschrijvinge der Afrikaensche Gewesten* (Amsterdam: Jacob van Meurs, 1676), p. 144.

[Vol. 1] *Första delen, som innehåller åtskilliga efterrättelser, hörande til öarnes geographie, natural-historia och politiska författningar.*
Stockholm [Sweden]: tryckt hos commiss. P.A. Brodin, **1786**.
8vo (18 cm): [4], 64, [2], 348 p., map, 1 folded table.
[Vol. 2] *Andra delen, som innehåller miszions-historien ifrån år 1732 til år 1768.* **Stockholm [Sweden]:** tryckt hos Johan Christopher Holmberg, **1788**.
8vo (18 cm): [2], 634, [4] p., folded leaves of plates: ill. (engravings).

73.3 ——.
English translation of 73.1 printed on p. 167 of C. G. A. Oldendorp, *History of the Mission of the Evangelical Brethren on the* *Caribbean Islands of St. Thomas, St. Croix, and St. John*, edited by Johann Jakob Bossard (i.e., Bossart), translated into English and further edited by Arnold R. Highfield and Vladimir Barac.

Ann Arbor [Michigan, U.S.A.]: Karoma Publishers, **1987**.
8vo (24 cm.): xxxv, 737 p., illus.

73.4 ——.

73.1 printed on pp. 286–288 in photomechanical reprint of the 1777 edition of C. G. A. Oldendorp, *Geschichte der Mission der evangelischen Brüder auf den caraibischen Inseln S. Thomas, S. Croix und S. Jan*, edited by Erich Beyreuther and Matthias Meyer (Volume 27.1 in Series 2 of Nikolaus Ludwig Graf von Zinzendorf, *Leben und Werk in Quellen und Darstellungen*).

Hildesheim [Saxony, Germany]: Georg Olms Verlag, 1995.
8vo (20 cm.): 62, 444 p., illus.

73.5 ———. [Complete edition, with critical annotations, of 73.0]
Aspects of his life story transcribed from 73.0 and printed on pp. 436–441, 487–488, and 504 in vol. 1 of C. G. A. Oldendorp, *Historie der caribischen Inseln Sanct Thomas, Sanct Crux und Sanct Jan, insbesondere der dasigen Neger und der Mission der evangelischen Brüder unter denselben: kommentierte Ausgabe des vollständigen Manuskriptes aus dem Archiv der Evangelischen Brüder-Unität Herrnhut*, edited by Gudrun Meier et al. (Band [Volume] 51 in the series *Abhandlungen und Berichte des Staatlichen Museums für Völkerkunde Dresden*).

Berlin [Germany]: VWB, Verlag für Wissenschaft und Bildung, 2000–2002.
2 vols. in 4, 8vo (24 cm.).
Vol. 1 (2000): 764 p.; xxxviii, illus.

74.0   First unnamed Congo man

Aspects of this unnamed Congo man's life story summarized in Christian Georg Andreas Oldendorp's 3,000-page manuscript account of Oldendorp's **1767–1768** tour of Denmark's West Indian possessions, viz. "Manuskript für eine Geschichte der Mission auf den westindischen Inseln, verfasst von C. G. A. Oldendorp," R.28.63 and R.28.62, held in the Unity Archives, **Herrnhut, Saxony, Germany**. Only an abbreviated version of this lengthy manuscript was published in 1777 (74.1). It was not published in its entirety until 2000–2002 (74.4).

Full text: https://huskiecommons.lib.niu.edu/history-500africanvoices/68/ [see 74.5].

¶ This man identified as Congo, who came from the **Dunnukabam kingdom** (see **Map 6**), far from the areas of Portuguese control (yet the ruler was Christian and had learned Portuguese). He describes mixed Christian and non-Christian religious practice in his homeland, where they called God Sambiampungo. It is unclear how this man was enslaved, but he eventually met Oldendorp in the Danish West Indies (**Map 14**) in **1767–1768**. While talking with Oldendorp, he told how his Congo ruler had supplied an English ship with slaves and allowed his (the ruler's) son to embark on it for St. Thomas in the Caribbean, probably intending that the son would continue (after stopping there) on to England. But this ship was intercepted at sea by the French (suggesting that this might have occurred during the Seven Years' War, 1756–1763), so the *French* took the ship to St. Thomas and

sold the Africans who had been forcibly transported aboard it. On St. Thomas the prince was treated according to his station and eventually sent to Copenhagen, Denmark (**Map 7**), for passage home.

74.1 ———.
Aspects of his life story printed on p. 289 of Christian Georg Andreas Oldendorp, *Geschichte der Mission der evangelischen Brueder auf den caraibischen Inseln S. Thomas, S. Croix, und S. Jan*, edited by Johann Jakob Bossart.

Barby [Saxony-Anhalt, Germany]: bey Christian Friedrich Laur, und in **Leipzig** [Saxony, Germany]: in Commission bey Weidmanns Erben und Reich, **1777**.
2 volumes in 1, 8vo (19 cm.), folding plates and maps, [12], 1068, index [52], p.
https://archive.org/details/cgaoldendorpsges12olde/page/289

74.2 ———.
Swedish translation of 74.1, C. G. A. Oldendorp, *Historiska beskrifning öfwer ewangeliske brödernas miszions-arbete på caraibiske öarne St. Thomas St. Croix och St. Jan*, edited by Johann Jacob Bossart.

Stockholm [Sweden]: **1786–1788**.
[Vol. 1] *Första delen, som innehåller åtskilliga efterrättelser, hörande til öarnes geographie, natural-historia och politiska författningar.*
Stockholm [Sweden]: tryckt hos commiss. P.A. Brodin, **1786**.
8vo (18 cm): [4], 64, [2], 348 p., map, 1 folded table.
[Vol. 2] *Andra delen, som innehåller miszions-historien ifrån år 1732 til år 1768.* **Stockholm** [Sweden]: tryckt hos Johan Christopher Holmberg, **1788**.
8vo (18 cm): [2], 634, [4] p., folded leaves of plates: ill. (engravings).

74.3 ———.
English translation of 74.1 printed on p. 168 of C. G. A. Oldendorp, *History of the Mission of the Evangelical Brethren on the Caribbean Islands of St. Thomas, St. Croix, and St. John*, edited by Johann Jakob Bossard (i.e., Bossart), translated into English and further edited by Arnold R. Highfield and Vladimir Barac.

Ann Arbor [Michigan, U.S.A.]: Karoma Publishers, **1987**.
8vo (24 cm.): xxxv, 737 p., illus.

74.4 ———.
74.1 printed on p. 289 in photomechanical reprint of the 1777 edition of C. G. A. Oldendorp, *Geschichte der Mission der evangelischen Brüder auf den caraibischen Inseln S. Thomas, S. Croix und S. Jan*, edited by Erich Beyreuther and Matthias Meyer (Volume 27.1 in Series 2 of Nikolaus Ludwig Graf von Zinzendorf, *Leben und Werk in Quellen und Darstellungen*).

Hildesheim [Saxony, Germany]: Georg Olms Verlag, **1995**. 8vo (20 cm.): 62, 444 p., illus.

74.5 ——.[Complete edition, with critical annotations, of 74.0]

Aspects of his life story transcribed from 74.0 and printed on pp. 445–447 in vol. 1 of C. G. A. Oldendorp, *Historie der caribischen Inseln Sanct Thomas, Sanct Crux und Sanct Jan, insbesondere der dasigen Neger und der Mission der evangelischen Brüder unter denselben: kommentierte Ausgabe des vollständigen Manuskriptes aus dem Archiv der Evangelischen Brüder-Unität Herrnhut*, edited by Gudrun Meier et al. (Band [Volume] 51 in the series *Abhandlungen und Berichte des Staatlichen Museums für Völkerkunde Dresden*).

Berlin [Germany]: VWB, Verlag für Wissenschaft und Bildung, **2000–2002**.
2 vols. in 4, 8vo (24 cm.).
Vol. 1 (2000): 764 p.; xxxviii, illus.

75.0 Second unnamed Congo man

Aspects of this second unnamed Congo man's life story summarized in Christian Georg Andreas Oldendorp's 3,000-page manuscript account of Oldendorp's **1767–1768** tour of Denmark's West Indian possessions, viz. "Manuskript für eine Geschichte der Mission auf den westindischen Inseln, verfasst von C. G. A. Oldendorp," R.28.63 and R.28.62, held in the Unity Archives, **Herrnhut, Saxony, Germany**. Only an abbreviated version of this lengthy manuscript was published in 1777 (75.1). It was not published in its entirety until 2000–2002 (75.4).

Full text: https://huskiecommons.lib.niu.edu/history-500africanvoices/69/ [see 75.5].

¶ This man identified as Congo and lived near the Portuguese there (see Map 6). He knew the city of Luanda (in present-day Angola) well. His people had their own king, and he was a member of the king's family. He describes mixed Christian and Congo religion, including how priests examined and baptized those captured in war and enslaved. They called their god Sambiampungo; and priests considered him to be Christ. During a journey in his country this man was betrayed by his own people, who told slave hunters from a distant land where to find him. These slave hunters then sold him to Europeans at a barracoon on the coast, after which a Danish slave ship forcibly took him to the Danish West Indies (Map 14), where he conversed with Oldendorp in 1767–1768.

75.1 ——.

Aspects of his life story printed on p. 289 of Christian Georg Andreas Oldendorp, *Geschichte der Mission der evangelischen Brueder auf den caraibischen Inseln S. Thomas, S. Croix, und S. Jan*, edited by Johann Jakob Bossart.

Barby [Saxony-Anhalt, Germany]: bey Christian Friedrich Laur, und in **Leipzig [Saxony, Germany**]: in Commission bey Weidmanns Erben und Reich, **1777**.
2 volumes in 1, 8vo (19 cm.), folding plates and maps, [12], 1068, index [52], p.
https://archive.org/details/cgaoldendorpsges12olde/page/289

75.2 ——.

Swedish translation of 75.1, C. G. A. Oldendorp, *Historiska beskrifning öfwer ewangeliske brödernas miszions-arbete på caraibiske öarne St. Thomas St. Croix och St. Jan*, edited by Johann Jacob Bossart.

Stockholm [Sweden]: **1786–1788**.
[Vol. 1] *Första delen, som innehåller åtskilliga efterrättelser, hörande til öarnes geographie, natural-historia och politiska författningar.*
Stockholm [Sweden]: tryckt hos commiss. P.A. Brodin, **1786**.
8vo (18 cm): [4], 64, [2], 348 p., map, 1 folded table.
[Vol. 2] *Andra delen, som innehåller miszions-historien ifrån år 1732 til år 1768.* Stockholm [Sweden]: tryckt hos Johan Christopher Holmberg, **1788**.
8vo (18 cm): [2], 634, [4] p., folded leaves of plates: ill. (engravings).

75.3 ——.

English translation of 75.1 printed on p. 168 of C. G. A. Oldendorp, *History of the Mission of the Evangelical Brethren on the Caribbean Islands of St. Thomas, St. Croix, and St. John*, edited by Johann Jakob Bossard (i.e., Bossart), translated into English and further edited by Arnold R. Highfield and Vladimir Barac.

Ann Arbor [Michigan, U.S.A.]: Karoma Publishers, **1987**.
8vo (24 cm.): xxxv, 737 p., illus.

75.4 ——.

75.1 printed on p. 289 in photomechanical reprint of the 1777 edition of C. G. A. Oldendorp, *Geschichte der Mission der evangelischen Brüder auf den caraibischen Inseln S. Thomas, S. Croix und S. Jan*, edited by Erich Beyreuther and Matthias Meyer (Volume 27.1 in Series 2 of Nikolaus Ludwig Graf von Zinzendorf, *Leben und Werk in Quellen und Darstellungen*).

Hildesheim [Saxony, Germany]: Georg Olms Verlag, **1995**.
8vo (20 cm.): 62, 444 p., illus.

75.5 ——. [Complete edition, with critical annotations, of 75.0]

Aspects of his life story transcribed from 75.0 and printed on pp. 447–448 and 488 in vol. 1 of C. G. A. Oldendorp, *Historie der caribischen Inseln Sanct Thomas, Sanct Crux und Sanct Jan, insbesondere der dasigen Neger und der Mission der evangelischen Brüder unter denselben: kommentierte Ausgabe des vollständigen Manuskriptes aus dem Archiv der Evangelischen Brüder-Unität Herrnhut*, edited by Gudrun Meier et al. (Band [Volume] 51 in the series *Abhandlungen und Berichte des Staatlichen Museums für Völkerkunde Dresden*).

Berlin [Germany]: VWB, Verlag für Wissenschaft und Bildung, 2000–2002.
2 vols. in 4, 8vo (24 cm.).
Vol. 1 (2000): 764 p.; xxxviii, illus.

76.0   Third unnamed Congo man

Aspects of this second unnamed Congo man's life story summarized in Christian Georg Andreas Oldendorp's 3,000-page manuscript account of Oldendorp's **1767–1768** tour of Denmark's West Indian possessions, viz. "Manuskript für eine Geschichte der Mission auf den westindischen Inseln, verfasst von C. G. A. Oldendorp," R.28.63 and R.28.62, held in the Unity Archives, **Herrnhut, Saxony, Germany**. Only an abbreviated version of this lengthy manuscript was published in 1777 (76.1). It was not published in its entirety until 2000–2002 (76.4).

Full text: https://huskiecommons.lib.niu.edu/history-500africanvoices/70/ [see 76.5].

¶ This man identified as Congo and lived near the Portuguese there (see Map 6). He knew the city of Luanda (in present-day Angola) well. His people had their own king, and he was a member of the king's family. He describes mixed Christian and Congo religion, including how priests examined and baptized those captured in war and enslaved. They called their god Sambiampungo and priests considered him to be Christ. This man was betrayed by his own people, who told slave hunters from a distant land how to find him when he traveled to a certain place. These slave hunters then sold him to Europeans at a barracoon on the coast, after which a Danish slave ship forcibly took him to the Danish West Indies (Map 14), where he conversed with Oldendorp in 1767–1768.

76.1 ——.

Aspects of his life story printed on p. 289 of Christian Georg Andreas Oldendorp, *Geschichte der Mission der evangelischen Brueder auf den caraibischen Inseln S. Thomas, S. Croix, und S. Jan*, edited by Johann Jakob Bossart.

Barby [Saxony-Anhalt, Germany]: bey Christian Friedrich Laur, und in Leipzig [Saxony, Germany]: in Commission bey Weidmanns Erben und Reich, 1777.
2 volumes in 1, 8vo (19 cm.), folding plates and maps, [12], 1068, index [52], p.
https://archive.org/details/cgaoldendorpsges12olde/page/289

76.2 ——.

Swedish translation of 76.1, C. G. A. Oldendorp, *Historiska beskrifning öfwer ewangeliske brödernas miszions-arbete på caraibiske öarne St. Thomas St. Croix och St. Jan*, edited by Johann Jacob Bossart.

Stockholm [Sweden]: 1786–1788.
[Vol. 1] *Första delen, som innehåller åtskilliga efterrättelser, hörande til öarnes geographie, natural-historia och politiska författningar.*
Stockholm [Sweden]: tryckt hos commiss. P.A. Brodin, 1786.
8vo (18 cm): [4], 64, [2], 348 p., map, 1 folded table.
[Vol. 2] *Andra delen, som innehåller miszions-historien ifrån år 1732 til år 1768.* Stockholm [Sweden]: tryckt hos Johan Christopher Holmberg, 1788.
8vo (18 cm): [2], 634, [4] p., folded leaves of plates: ill. (engravings).

76.3 ——.

English translation of 76.1 printed on p. 168 of C. G. A. Oldendorp, *History of the Mission of the Evangelical Brethren on the Caribbean Islands of St. Thomas, St. Croix, and St. John*, edited by Johann Jakob Bossard (i.e., Bossart), translated into English and further edited by Arnold R. Highfield and Vladimir Barac.

Ann Arbor [Michigan, U.S.A.]: Karoma Publishers, 1987.
8vo (24 cm.): xxxv, 737 p., illus.

76.4 ——.

76.1 printed on p. 289 in photomechanical reprint of the 1777 edition of C. G. A. Oldendorp, *Geschichte der Mission der evangelischen Brüder auf den caraibischen Inseln S. Thomas, S. Croix und S. Jan*, edited by Erich Beyreuther and Matthias Meyer (Volume 27.1 in Series 2 of Nikolaus Ludwig Graf von Zinzendorf, *Leben und Werk in Quellen und Darstellungen*).

Hildesheim [Saxony, Germany]: Georg Olms Verlag, 1995.
8vo (20 cm.): 62, 444 p., illus.

76.5 ——. [Complete edition, with critical annotations, of 76.0]

Aspects of his life story transcribed from 76.0 and printed on pp. 447–448 and 488 in vol. 1 of C. G. A. Oldendorp, *Historie der caribischen Inseln Sanct Thomas, Sanct Crux und Sanct Jan, insbesondere der dasigen Neger und der Mission der evangelischen Brüder unter denselben: kommentierte Ausgabe des vollständigen Manuskriptes aus dem Archiv der Evangelischen Brüder-Unität Herrnhut*, edited by Gudrun Meier et al. (Band [Volume] 51 in the series *Abhandlungen und Berichte des Staatlichen Museums für Völkerkunde Dresden*).

Berlin [Germany]: VWB, Verlag für Wissenschaft und Bildung, 2000–2002.

2 vols. in 4, 8vo (24 cm.).

Vol. 1 (2000): 764 p.; xxxviii, illus.

77.0   Unnamed Coromantyn man

Aspects of this man's life story summarized in Christian Georg Andreas Oldendorp's 3,000-page manuscript account of Oldendorp's **1767–1768** tour of Denmark's West Indian possessions, viz. "Manuskript für eine Geschichte der Mission auf den westindischen Inseln, verfasst von C. G. A. Oldendorp," R.28.63 and R.28.62, held in the Unity Archives, Herrnhut, Saxony, Germany.

Full text: https://huskiecommons.lib.niu.edu/history-500africanvoices/71/ [see 77.1].

¶ This man identified as Coromantyn, an African and New World designator referring to people around Fort Amsterdam, near Etsi and Fante (i.e., Akan peoples, present-day Ghana—see Map 5). He described religious practice and social customs in his country at length. After enslavement and sale to Europeans, he was forcibly taken on a slave ship to the Danish West Indies (Map 14), where he spoke with Oldendorp in 1767–1768.

77.1 ———. [Complete edition, with critical annotations, of 77.0]

Aspects of his life story transcribed from 77.0 and printed on pp. 454–455 in vol. 1 of C. G. A. Oldendorp, *Historie der caribischen Inseln Sanct Thomas, Sanct Crux und Sanct Jan, insbesondere der dasigen Neger und der Mission der evangelischen Brüder unter denselben: kommentierte Ausgabe des vollständigen Manuskriptes aus dem Archiv der Evangelischen Brüder-Unität Herrnhut*, edited by Gudrun Meier et al. (Band [Volume] 51 in the series *Abhandlungen und Berichte des Staatlichen Museums für Völkerkunde Dresden*).

Berlin [Germany]: VWB, Verlag für Wissenschaft und Bildung, 2000–2002.

2 vols. in 4, 8vo (24 cm.).

Vol. 1 (2000): 764 p.; xxxviii, illus.

78.0   First unnamed Kanga man

Aspects of this man's life story summarized in Christian Georg Andreas Oldendorp's 3,000-page manuscript account of Oldendorp's **1767–1768** tour of Denmark's West Indian

possessions, viz. "Manuskript für eine Geschichte der Mission auf den westindischen Inseln, verfasst von C. G. A. Oldendorp," R.28.63 and R.28.62, held in the Unity Archives, Herrnhut, Saxony, Germany.

Full text: https://huskiecommons.lib.niu.edu/history-500africanvoices/72/ [see 78.1].

¶ This man identified as Kanga, a New World term referring to people from present-day southern Liberia (see Map 3) whose language was Kru (*pace* Meier). Their land stretched from far inland to the sea, where they traded enslaved people and goods with Europeans. Mandinka (an ethnic group residing in present-day southern Mali, Guinea, and Ivory Coast) and Fula (Fulani, Fulbi, or Peul peoples throughout West Africa) lived on their borders. (One woman in the group called their land Sanjam.) This man and the other Kanga with whom Oldendorp spoke described their body markings, use of iron rings for currency, religion (including the name of their God in heaven, Nesua, worship, magic, and soothsaying), justice system, polygyny, burial rituals, and war-making. This man was seized during a war waged to acquire slaves and sold. He was then forcibly taken aboard a slave ship to the Danish West Indies (Map 14), where he spoke with Oldendorp in 1767–1768.

78.1 ———. [Complete edition, with critical annotations, of 78.0]

Aspects of his life story transcribed from 78.0 and printed on pp. 378–381 and 481–482 in vol. 1 of C. G. A. Oldendorp, *Historie der caribischen Inseln Sanct Thomas, Sanct Crux und Sanct Jan, insbesondere der dasigen Neger und der Mission der evangelischen Brüder unter denselben: kommentierte Ausgabe des vollständigen Manuskriptes aus dem Archiv der Evangelischen Brüder-Unität Herrnhut*, edited by Gudrun Meier et al. (Band [Volume] 51 in the series *Abhandlungen und Berichte des Staatlichen Museums für Völkerkunde Dresden*).

Berlin [Germany]: VWB, Verlag für Wissenschaft und Bildung, 2000–2002.

2 vols. in 4, 8vo (24 cm.).

Vol. 1 (2000): 764 p.; xxxviii, illus.

79.0   Second unnamed Kanga man

Aspects of this man's life story summarized in Christian Georg Andreas Oldendorp's 3,000-page manuscript account of Oldendorp's **1767–1768** tour of Denmark's West Indian possessions, viz. "Manuskript für eine Geschichte der Mission auf den westindischen Inseln, verfasst von C. G. A. Oldendorp," R.28.63 and R.28.62, held in the Unity Archives, **Herrnhut, Saxony, Germany.**

¶ This man identified as Kanga, a New World term referring to people from present-day southern Liberia (see Map 3) whose language was Kru (*pace* Meier). Their land stretched from far inland to the sea, where they traded slaves and goods with the Europeans. Mandinka (an ethnic group residing in present-day southern Mali, Guinea, and Ivory Coast) and Fula (Fulani, Fulbi, or Peul peoples throughout West Africa) lived on their borders. (One woman in the group called their land Sanjam.) This man and the other Kangas with whom Oldendorp spoke described their body markings, use of iron rings for currency, religion (including their God in heaven Nesua, worship, magic, and soothsaying), justice, polygyny, burial, and war. This man was seized during war waged to acquire slaves and sold. He was then forcibly taken on a slave ship to the Danish West Indies (Map 14), where he spoke with Oldendorp in 1767–1768.

79.1 ——. [Complete edition, with critical annotations, of 79.0]

Aspects of his life story transcribed from 79.0 and printed on pp. 378–381 and 481–482 in vol. 1 of C. G. A. Oldendorp, *Historie der caribischen Inseln Sanct Thomas, Sanct Crux und Sanct Jan, insbesondere der dasigen Neger und der Mission der evangelischen Brüder unter denselben: kommentierte Ausgabe des vollständigen Manuskriptes aus dem Archiv der Evangelischen Brüder-Unität Herrnhut*, edited by Gudrun Meier et al. (Band [Volume] 51 in the series *Abhandlungen und Berichte des Staatlichen Museums für Völkerkunde Dresden*).

Berlin [Germany]: VWB, Verlag für Wissenschaft und Bildung, 2000–2002.
2 vols. in 4, 8vo (24 cm.).
Vol. 1 (2000): 764 p.; xxxviii, illus.

80.0 Third unnamed Kanga man

Aspects of this man's life story summarized in Christian Georg Andreas Oldendorp's 3,000-page manuscript account of Oldendorp's 1767–1768 tour of Denmark's West Indian possessions, viz. "Manuskript für eine Geschichte der Mission auf den westindischen Inseln, verfasst von C. G. A. Oldendorp," R.28.63 and R.28.62, held in the Unity Archives, Herrnhut, Saxony, Germany.

Full text: https://huskiecommons.lib.niu.edu/history-500africanvoices/73/ [see 79.1].

Full text: https://huskiecommons.lib.niu.edu/history-500africanvoices/74/ [see 80.1].

¶ This man identified as Kanga, a New World term referring to people from present-day southern Liberia (see Map 3) whose language was Kru (*pace* Meier). Their land stretched from far inland to the sea, where they traded slaves and goods with the Europeans. Mandinka (an ethnic group residing in present-day southern Mali, Guinea, and Ivory Coast) and Fula (Fulani, Fulbi, or Peul peoples throughout West Africa) lived on their borders. (One woman in the group called their land Sanjam.) This man and the other Kangas with whom Oldendorp spoke described their body markings, use of iron rings for currency, and their religion, including the name of their God in heaven (Nesua), worship, magic, and soothsaying, as well as justice, polygyny, burial, and war. This man was seized and sold in a war fought over the profits of the slave trade with Europeans. He was taken on a slave ship to the Danish West Indies (Map 14), where he spoke with Oldendorp in 1767–1768.

80.1 ——. [Complete edition, with critical annotations, of 80.0]

Aspects of his life story transcribed from 79.0 and printed on pp. 378–381 and 481–482 in vol. 1 of C. G. A. Oldendorp, *Historie der caribischen Inseln Sanct Thomas, Sanct Crux und Sanct Jan, insbesondere der dasigen Neger und der Mission der evangelischen Brüder unter denselben: kommentierte Ausgabe des vollständigen Manuskriptes aus dem Archiv der Evangelischen Brüder-Unität Herrnhut*, edited by Gudrun Meier et al. (Band [Volume] 51 in the series *Abhandlungen und Berichte des Staatlichen Museums für Völkerkunde Dresden*).

Berlin [Germany]: VWB, Verlag für Wissenschaft und Bildung, 2000–2002.
2 vols. in 4, 8vo (24 cm.).
Vol. 1 (2000): 764 p.; xxxviii, illus.

81.0 Fourth unnamed Kanga man

Aspects of this man's life story summarized in Christian Georg Andreas Oldendorp's 3,000-page manuscript account of Oldendorp's 1767–1768 tour of Denmark's West Indian possessions, viz. "Manuskript für eine Geschichte der Mission auf den westindischen Inseln, verfasst von C. G. A. Oldendorp," R.28.63 and R.28.62, held in the Unity Archives, Herrnhut, Saxony, Germany.

Full text: https://huskiecommons.lib.niu.edu/history-500africanvoices/75/ [see 81.4].

¶ This man identified as Kanga, a New World term referring to people from present-day southern Liberia (see Map 3) whose language was Kru (*pace* Meier). Their land stretched from far inland to the sea, where they traded slaves and goods with Europeans. Mandinka (an ethnic group residing in present-day southern Mali, Guinea, and Ivory Coast) and Fula (Fulani, Fulbi, or Peul peoples throughout West Africa) lived on their borders. (One woman in the group called their land Sanjam.) This man and the other Kangas with whom Oldendorp spoke described their body markings, use of iron rings for currency, and their religion, including the name of their God in heaven (Nesua), worship, magic, and soothsaying, as well as justice, polygyny, burial, and war. This man was enslaved after his sister took a husband in a distant place, decided she wanted him no longer, and returned. She asked another man to marry her and pay off her first husband. After it took him too long to raise the money, the first husband came for satisfaction. The sister had fled, so he took her brother and sold him. Eventually, he was taken on a slave ship to the Danish West Indies (Map 14), where he spoke with Oldendorp in 1767–1768.

81.1 ———.

Aspects of his life story printed on p. 351 of Christian Georg Andreas Oldendorp, *Geschichte der Mission der evangelischen Brueder auf den caraibischen Inseln S. Thomas, S. Croix, und S. Jan*, edited by Johann Jakob Bossart.

Barby [Saxony-Anhalt, Germany]: bey Christian Friedrich Laur, und in Leipzig [Saxony, Germany]: in Commission bey Weidmanns Erben und Reich, 1777.
2 volumes in 1, 8vo (19 cm.), folding plates and maps, [12], 1068, index [52], p.
https://archive.org/details/cgaoldendorpsges12olde/page/289

81.2 ———.

Danish translation of 81.1 (p. 350 only) printed on p. 178, Part 1, of Christian Georg Andreas Oldendorp, *Fuldstændigt Udtog af C.G.A. Oldendorps Missions-Historie om de evangeliske Brødres Mission paa de caraibiske Øer St. Thomas, St. Crux og St. Jan*, uitgivet paa Tydsk i to Dele.

Pt 1: *Kort Beskrivelse over Vestindien, især de Danske caraibiske Øer St. Crux, St. Thomas og St. Jan.*

Pt. 2: *Historisk Beretning om de hedenske Neger-Slavers Omvendelse paa de Danske Øer i Vestindien*, som et Udtog af C.G.A. Oldendorp's De Evangeliske Brødres Missions-Historie paa de Caraibiske Øer.

Copenhagen [Denmark]: Christ. L. Buchs Forlag, with J. Rud. Thiele, 1784.
2 volumes in 1, with separate title pages and pagination, 8vo (18 cm): [4], 212 p. and 184, [4] p.

81.3 ———.

Swedish translation of 81.1, C. G. A. Oldendorp, *Historiska beskrifning öfver ewangeliske brödernas miszions-arbete på caraibiske öarne St. Thomas St. Croix och St. Jan*, edited by Johann Jacob Bossart.

Stockholm [Sweden]: 1786–1788.
[Vol. 1] *Första delen, som innehåller åtskilliga efterrättelser, hörande til öarnes geographie, natural-historia och politiska författningar.*
Stockholm [Sweden]: tryckt hos commiss. P.A. Brodin, 1786.
8vo (18 cm): [4], 64, [2], 348 p., map, 1 folded table.
[Vol. 2] *Andra delen, som innehåller miszions-historien ifrån år 1732 til år 1768.* Stockholm [Sweden]: tryckt hos Johan Christopher Holmberg, 1788.
8vo (18 cm): [2], 634, [4] p., folded leaves of plates: ill. (engravings).

81.4 ———. [Complete edition, with critical annotations, of 81.0]

Aspects of his life story transcribed from 81.0 and printed on pp. 378–381 and 481–482 in vol. 1 of C. G. A. Oldendorp, *Historie der caribischen Inseln Sanct Thomas, Sanct Crux und Sanct Jan, insbesondere der dasigen Neger und der Mission der evangelischen Brüder unter denselben: kommentierte Ausgabe des vollständigen Manuskriptes aus dem Archiv der Evangelischen Brüder-Unität Herrnhut*, edited by Gudrun Meier et al. (Band [Volume] 51 in the series *Abhandlungen und Berichte des Staatlichen Museums für Völkerkunde Dresden*).

Berlin [Germany]: VWB, Verlag für Wissenschaft und Bildung, 2000–2002.
2 vols. in 4, 8vo (24 cm.).
Vol. 1 (2000): 764 p.; xxxviii, illus.

82.0 First unnamed Kanga woman

Aspects of this woman's life story summarized in Christian Georg Andreas Oldendorp's 3,000-page manuscript account of Oldendorp's 1767–1768 tour of Denmark's West Indian possessions, viz. "Manuskript für eine Geschichte der Mission auf den westindischen Inseln, verfasst von C. G. A. Oldendorp," R.28.63 and R.28.62, held in the Unity Archives, Herrnhut, Saxony, Germany.

Full text: https://huskiecommons.lib.niu.edu/history-500africanvoices/76/ [see 82.1].

¶ This woman identified as Kanga, a New World term referring to people from present-day southern Liberia (see Map 3) whose language was Kru (*pace* Meier). Their land stretched from far inland to the sea, where they traded slaves and goods with the Europeans. Mandinka (an ethnic group residing in present-day southern Mali, Guinea, and Ivory Coast) and Fula (Fulani, Fulbi, or Peul peoples throughout West Africa) lived on their borders. (One woman in the group called their land Sanjam.) This woman and the other Kangas with whom Oldendorp spoke described their body markings, use of iron rings for currency, and their religion, including the name of their God in heaven (Nesua), worship, magic, and soothsaying, as well as justice, polygyny, burial, and war. She was captured during a raid to gather slaves and eventually sold to Europeans, who took her on a slave ship to the Danish West Indies, where she spoke with Oldendorp in 1767–1768.

82.1 ———. [Complete edition, with critical annotations, of 82.0]

Aspects of her life story transcribed from 82.0 and printed on pp. 378–381 and 481–482 in vol. 1 of C. G. A. Oldendorp, *Historie der caribischen Inseln Sanct Thomas, Sanct Crux und Sanct Jan, insbesondere der dasigen Neger und der Mission der evangelischen Brüder unter denselben: kommentierte Ausgabe des vollständigen Manuskriptes aus dem Archiv der Evangelischen Brüder-Unität Herrnhut*, edited by Gudrun Meier et al. (Band [Volume] 51 in the series *Abhandlungen und Berichte des Staatlichen Museums für Völkerkunde Dresden*).

Berlin [Germany]: VWB, Verlag für Wissenschaft und Bildung, 2000–2002.

2 vols. in 4, 8vo (24 cm.).

Vol. 1 (2000): 764 p.; xxxviii, illus.

83.0 Second unnamed Kanga woman

Aspects of this woman's life story summarized in Christian Georg Andreas Oldendorp's 3,000-page manuscript account of Oldendorp's 1767–1768 tour of Denmark's West Indian possessions, viz. "Manuskript für eine Geschichte der Mission auf den westindischen Inseln, verfasst von C. G. A. Oldendorp," R.28.63 and R.28.62, held in the Unity Archives, **Herrnhut, Saxony, Germany.**

Full text: https://huskiecommons.lib.niu.edu/history-500africanvoices/77/ [see 83.1].

¶ This woman identified as Kanga, a New World term referring to people from present-day southern Liberia (see Map 3) whose language was Kru (*pace* Meier). Their land stretched from far inland to the sea, where they traded slaves and goods with the Europeans. Mandinka (an ethnic group residing in present-day southern Mali, Guinea, and Ivory Coast) and Fula (Fulani, Fulbi, or Peul peoples throughout

West Africa) lived on their borders. (One woman in the group called their land Sanjam.) This woman and the other Kangas with whom Oldendorp spoke described their body markings, use of iron rings for currency, and their religion, to include the name of their God in heaven (Nesua), worship, magic, and soothsaying, as well as justice, polygyny, burial, and war. She explained that during wartime the old people in her village buried their valuables. Their enemies knew this, and when they captured their village, they forced the wealthy people to show where they had hidden their goods. Even though relatives offered numerous slaves in exchange, they sold those wealthy people, including this woman, to Europeans. She was then taken on a slave ship to the Danish West Indies (Map 14), where she spoke with Oldendorp in 1767–1768.

83.1 ———. [Complete edition, with critical annotations, of 83.0]

Aspects of her life story transcribed from 83.0 and printed on pp. 378–381 and 481–482 in vol. 1 of C. G. A. Oldendorp, *Historie der caribischen Inseln Sanct Thomas, Sanct Crux und Sanct Jan, insbesondere der dasigen Neger und der Mission der evangelischen Brüder unter denselben: kommentierte Ausgabe des vollständigen Manuskriptes aus dem Archiv der Evangelischen Brüder-Unität Herrnhut*, edited by Gudrun Meier et al. (Band [Volume] 51 in the series *Abhandlungen und Berichte des Staatlichen Museums für Völkerkunde Dresden*).

Berlin [Germany]: VWB, Verlag für Wissenschaft und Bildung, 2000–2002.

2 vols. in 4, 8vo (24 cm.).

Vol. 1 (2000): 764 p.; xxxviii, illus.

84.0 First unnamed Tchamba man

Aspects of this man's life story summarized in Christian Georg Andreas Oldendorp's 3,000-page manuscript account of Oldendorp's 1767–1768 tour of Denmark's West Indian possessions, viz. "Manuskript für eine Geschichte der Mission auf den westindischen Inseln, verfasst von C. G. A. Oldendorp," R.28.63 and R.28.62, held in the Unity Archives, Herrnhut, Saxony, Germany.

Full text: https://huskiecommons.lib.niu.edu/history-500africanvoices/78/ [see 84.1].

¶ This man identified as Kassenti (Tchamba, possibly northern Togo—see Map 5). He was captured in war and sold to Europeans, who took him on a slave ship to the Danish West Indies (Map 14). There in 1767–1768 he met Oldendorp, who wrote down his brief account.

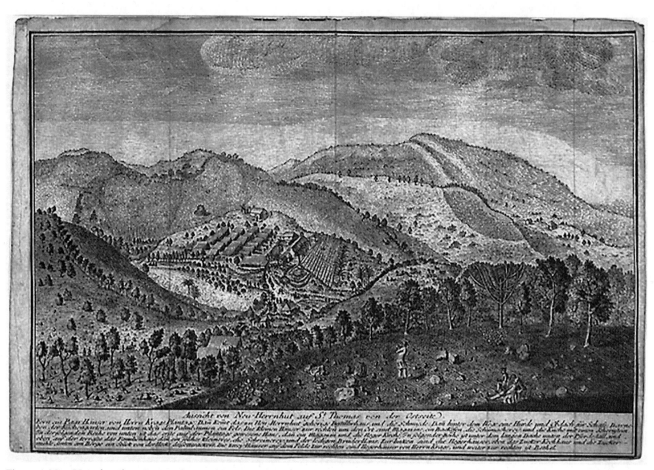

Figure 6: New Herrnhut (later Posauenberg), plantation of the German Moravian religious mission on St. Thomas in the Danish West Indies. The missionary Christian Georg Andreas Oldendorp recorded the accounts of eighty-one African-born slave ship survivors on St. Thomas and nearby St. Croix while visiting the islands in 1767–1768 to gather material to write his history of the mission.

Source: Engraving by Johann Georg Sturm, 1777. Moravian Archives, Bethlehem, Pennsylvania (U.S.A.).

84.1 ——. [Complete edition, with critical annotations, of 84.0]

Aspects of his life story transcribed from 84.0 and printed on p. 485 in vol. 1 of C. G. A. Oldendorp, *Historie der caribischen Inseln Sanct Thomas, Sanct Crux und Sanct Jan, insbesondere der dasigen Neger und der Mission der evangelischen Brüder unter denselben: kommentierte Ausgabe des vollständigen Manuskriptes aus dem Archiv der Evangelischen Brüder-Unität Herrnhut*, edited by Gudrun Meier et al. (Band [Volume] 51 in the series *Abhandlungen und Berichte des Staatlichen Museums für Völkerkunde Dresden*).

Berlin [Germany]: VWB, Verlag für Wissenschaft und Bildung, **2000–2002**.
2 vols. in 4, 8vo (24 cm.).
Vol. 1 (2000): 764 p.; xxxviii, illus.

85.0   Second unnamed Tchamba man

Aspects of this man's life story summarized in Christian Georg Andreas Oldendorp's 3,000-page manuscript account of Oldendorp's **1767–1768** tour of Denmark's West Indian possessions, viz. "Manuskript für eine Geschichte der Mission auf den westindischen Inseln, verfasst von C. G. A. Oldendorp," R.28.63 and R.28.62, held in the Unity Archives, **Herrnhut, Saxony, Germany.**

¶ This man identified as Kassenti (Tchamba, possibly northern Togo—see Map 5). He was captured while traveling and sold to Europeans, who took him on a slave ship to the Dan-

Full text: https://huskiecommons.lib.niu.edu/history-500africanvoices/79/ [see 85.1].

ish West Indies (Map 14). There in 1767–1768 he met Oldendorp, who wrote down his brief account.

85.1 ——. [Complete edition, with critical annotations, of 85.0]

Aspects of his life story transcribed from 85.0 and printed on p. 485 in vol. 1 of C. G. A. Oldendorp, *Historie der caribischen Inseln Sanct Thomas, Sanct Crux und Sanct Jan, insbesondere der dasigen Neger und der Mission der evangelischen Brüder unter denselben: kommentierte Ausgabe des vollständigen Manuskriptes aus dem Archiv der Evangelischen Brüder-Unität Herrnhut*, edited by Gudrun Meier et al. (Band [Volume] 51 in the series *Abhandlungen und Berichte des Staatlichen Museums für Völkerkunde Dresden*).

Berlin [Germany]: VWB, Verlag für Wissenschaft und Bildung, 2000–2002.

2 vols. in 4, 8vo (24 cm.).

Vol. 1 (2000): 764 p.; xxxviii, illus.

86.0   Third unnamed Tchamba man

Aspects of this woman's life story summarized in Christian Georg Andreas Oldendorp's 3,000-page manuscript account of Oldendorp's **1767–1768** tour of Denmark's West Indian possessions, viz. "Manuskript für eine Geschichte der Mission auf den westindischen Inseln, verfasst von C. G. A. Oldendorp," R.28.63 and R.28.62, held in the Unity Archives, **Herrnhut, Saxony, Germany**.

Full text: https://huskiecommons.lib.niu.edu/history-500africanvoices/80/ [see 86.1].

¶ This man identified as Kassenti (Tchamba, possibly Temba people in northern Togo—see Map 5). As he left his farm one day he was kidnapped by men hiding in the bush. Eventually, he was sold to Europeans, who took him on a slave ship to the Danish West Indies (Map 14). There in 1767–1768 he met Oldendorp, who wrote down his brief account.

86.1 ——. [Complete edition, with critical annotations, of 86.0]

Aspects of his life story transcribed from 86.0 and printed on p. 485 in vol. 1 of C. G. A. Oldendorp, *Historie der caribischen Inseln Sanct Thomas, Sanct Crux und Sanct Jan, insbesondere der dasigen Neger und der Mission der evangelischen Brüder unter denselben: kommentierte Ausgabe des vollständigen Manuskriptes aus dem Archiv der Evangelischen Brüder-Unität Herrnhut*, edited by Gudrun Meier et al. (Band [Volume] 51 in the series *Abhandlungen und Berichte des Staatlichen Museums für Völkerkunde Dresden*).

Berlin [Germany]: VWB, Verlag für Wissenschaft und Bildung, 2000–2002.

2 vols. in 4, 8vo (24 cm.).

Vol. 1 (2000): 764 p.; xxxviii, illus.

87.0   Second unnamed Amina merchant [See Nr. 42 for the first.]

Aspects of this unnamed man's life story summarized in Christian Georg Andreas Oldendorp's 3,000-page manuscript account of Oldendorp's **1767–1768** tour of Denmark's West Indian possessions, viz. "Manuskript für eine Geschichte der Mission auf den westindischen Inseln, verfasst von C. G. A. Oldendorp," R.28.63 and R.28.62, held in the Unity Archives, **Herrnhut, Saxony, Germany**. Only an abbreviated version of this lengthy manuscript was published in 1777 (86.1). It was not published in its entirety until 2000–2002 (86.4).

Full text: https://huskiecommons.lib.niu.edu/history-500africanvoices/81/ [see 87.6].

¶ Once a wealthy merchant who owned and sold slaves, this man identified as Amina (a New World ethnic designation for Akan speakers near Elmina Castle, present-day Ghana—see Map 5). His parents chose a small child as his bride, and while waiting for her to grow up, he consorted with other women, contrary to advice given him. When it was time to marry, he took many presents to a European fort to trade up for even more to give his bride. But at this fort a woman with whom he had been connected earlier betrayed him, after which he and all his servants and goods were seized and sold. The fort's governor arranged for him to receive relatively favorable treatment aboard the slave ship that took him to the Danish West Indies (Map 14). There he was sold separately from the others to a wealthy family. Later other enslaved people from his homeland honored him for his status there and helped him with his work. He had become a Christian by the time he met Oldendorp in 1767–1768.

87.1 ——.

Aspects of his life story printed on pp. 299 and 352–353 of Christian Georg Andreas Oldendorp, *Geschichte der Mission der evangelischen Brueder auf den caraibischen Inseln S. Thomas, S. Croix, und S. Jan*, edited by Johann Jakob Bossart.

Barby [Saxony-Anhalt, Germany]: bey Christian Friedrich Laur, und in **Leipzig [Saxony, Germany]**: in Commission bey Weidmanns Erben und Reich, **1777**.

2 volumes in 1, 8vo (19 cm.), folding plates and maps, [12], 1068, index [52], p.

https://archive.org/details/cgaoldendorpsges12olde/page/299

87.2 ———.

Danish translation of 87.1 (p. 350 only) printed on p. 178, Part 1, of Christian Georg Andreas Oldendorp, *Fuldstændigt Udtog af C.G.A. Oldendorps Missions-Historie om de evangeliske Brødres Mission paa de caraibiske Øer St. Thomas, St. Crux og St. Jan*, uitgivet paa Tydsk i to Dele.

Pt 1: *Kort Beskrivelse over Vestindien, især de Danske caraibiske Øer St. Crux, St. Thomas og St. Jan.*

Pt. 2: *Historisk Beretning om de hedenske Neger-Slavers Omvendelse paa de Danske Øer i Vestindien*, som et Udtog af C.G.A. Oldendorp's De Evangeliske Brødres Missions-Historie paa de Caraibiske Øer.

Copenhagen [Denmark]: Christ. L. Buchs Forlag, with J. Rud. Thiele, **1784.**

2 volumes in 1, with separate title pages and pagination, 8vo (18 cm): [4], 212 p. and 184, [4] p.

87.3 ———.

Swedish translation of 87.1, C. G. A. Oldendorp, *Historiska beskrifning öfwer ewangeliske brödernas miszions-arbete på caraibiske öarne St. Thomas St. Croix och St. Jan*, edited by Johann Jacob Bossart.

Stockholm [Sweden]: 1786–1788.

[Vol. 1] *Första delen, som innehåller åtskilliga efterrättelser, hörande til öarnes geographie, natural-historia och politiska författningar.*
Stockholm [Sweden]: tryckt hos commiss. P.A. Brodin, **1786.**
8vo (18 cm): [4], 64, [2], 348 p., map, 1 folded table.

[Vol. 2] *Andra delen, som innehåller miszions-historien ifrån år 1732 til år 1768.* **Stockholm [Sweden]:** tryckt hos Johan Christopher Holmberg, **1788.**
8vo (18 cm): [2], 634, [4] p., folded leaves of plates: ill. (engravings).

87.4 ———.

English translation of 87.1 printed on pp. 175 and 209–210 of C. G. A. Oldendorp, *History of the Mission of the Evangelical Brethren on the Caribbean Islands of St. Thomas, St. Croix, and St. John*, edited by Johann Jakob Bossard (i.e., Bossart), translated into English and further edited by Arnold R. Highfield and Vladimir Barac.

Ann Arbor [Michigan, U.S.A.]: Karoma Publishers, **1987.**
8vo (24 cm): xxxv, 737 p., illus.

87.5 ———.

87.1 printed on pp. 289 and 352–353 in photomechanical reprint of the 1777 edition of C. G. A. Oldendorp, *Geschichte der Mission der evangelischen Brüder auf den caraibischen Inseln S. Thomas, S. Croix und S. Jan*, edited by Erich Bey-

reuther and Matthias Meyer (Volume 27.1 in Series 2 of Nikolaus Ludwig Graf von Zinzendorf, *Leben und Werk in Quellen und Darstellungen*).

Hildesheim [Saxony, Germany]: Georg Olms Verlag, **1995.**
8vo (20 cm.): 62, 444 p., illus.

87.6 ———. [Complete edition, with critical annotations, of 87.0]

Aspects of his life story transcribed from 87.0 and printed on pp. 482–483 in vol. 1 of C. G. A. Oldendorp, *Historie der caribischen Inseln Sanct Thomas, Sanct Crux und Sanct Jan, insbesondere der dasigen Neger und der Mission der evangelischen Brüder unter denselben: kommentierte Ausgabe des vollständigen Manuskriptes aus dem Archiv der Evangelischen Brüder-Unität Herrnhut*, edited by Gudrun Meier et al. (Band [Volume] 51 in the series *Abhandlungen und Berichte des Staatlichen Museums für Völkerkunde Dresden*).

Berlin [Germany]: VWB, Verlag für Wissenschaft und Bildung, **2000–2002.**
2 vols. in 4, 8vo (24 cm.).
Vol. 1 (2000): 764 p.; xxxviii, illus.

88.0 First unnamed Mandinka man

Full text: https://huskiecommons.lib.niu.edu/history-500africanvoices/82/ [see 88.6].

Aspects of this unnamed man's life story summarized in Christian Georg Andreas Oldendorp's 3,000-page manuscript account of Oldendorp's 1767–1768 tour of Denmark's West Indian possessions, viz. "Manuskript für eine Geschichte der Mission auf den westindischen Inseln, verfasst von C. G. A. Oldendorp," R.28.63 and R.28.62, held in the Unity Archives, **Herrnhut, Saxony, Germany.** Only an abbreviated version of this lengthy manuscript was published in 1777 (88.1). It was not published in its entirety until 2000–2002 (88.6).

¶ **This man, who identified as Mandinka (an ethnic group residing in present-day southern Mali, Guinea, and Ivory Coast—see Map 3), was given into slavery as a boy to repay a debt. After his grandfather tried and failed to redeem him, he was sold to Europeans and forcibly placed aboard a slave ship. He jumped overboard and swam away, but was recaptured, chained, and taken to the Danish West Indies (Map 14), where he conversed with Oldendorp in 1767–1768.**

88.1 ———.

Aspects of this man's life story printed on pp. 350–351 of Christian Georg Andreas Oldendorp, *Geschichte der Mis-*

sion der evangelischen Brueder auf den caraibischen Inseln S. Thomas, S. Croix, und S. Jan, edited by Johann Jakob Bossart.

Barby [Saxony-Anhalt, Germany]: bey Christian Friedrich Laur, und in Leipzig [Saxony, Germany]: in Commission bey Weidmanns Erben und Reich, 1777.

2 volumes in 1, 8vo (19 cm.), folding plates and maps, [12], 1068, index [52], p.

https://archive.org/details/cgaoldendorpsges12olde/page/350

88.2 ———.

Danish translation of 88.1 (p. 350 only) printed on p. 178, Part 1, of Christian Georg Andreas Oldendorp, *Fuldstændigt Udtog af C.G.A. Oldendorps Missions-Historie om de evangeliske Brødres Mission paa de caraibiske Øer St. Thomas, St. Crux og St. Jan,* uitgivet paa Tydsk i to Dele.

Pt 1: *Kort Beskrivelse over Vestindien, især de Danske caraibiske Øer St. Crux, St. Thomas og St. Jan.*

Pt. 2: *Historisk Beretning om de hedenske Neger-Slavers Omvendelse paa de Danske Øer i Vestindien,* som et Udtog af C.G.A. Oldendorp's De Evangeliske Brødres Missions-Historie paa de Caraibiske Øer.

Copenhagen [Denmark]: Christ. L. Buchs Forlag, with J. Rud. Thiele, 1784.

2 volumes in 1, with separate title pages and pagination, 8vo (18 cm): [4], 212 p. and 184, [4] p.

88.3 ———.

Swedish translation of 88.1, C. G. A. Oldendorp, *Historiska beskrifning öfwer ewangeliske brödernas miszions-arbete på caraibiske öarne St. Thomas St. Croix och St. Jan,* edited by Johann Jacob Bossart.

Stockholm [Sweden]: 1786–1788.

[Vol. 1] *Första delen, som innehåller åtskilliga efterrättelser, hörande til öarnes geographie, natural-historia och politiska författningar.*
Stockholm [Sweden]: tryckt hos commiss. P.A. Brodin, 1786.
8vo (18 cm): [4], 64, [2], 348 p., map, 1 folded table.

[Vol. 2] *Andra delen, som innehåller miszions-historien ifrån år 1732 til år 1768.* Stockholm [Sweden]: tryckt hos Johan Christopher Holmberg, 1788.
8vo (18 cm): [2], 634, [4] p., folded leaves of plates: ill. (engravings).

88.4 ———.

English translation of 88.1 printed on p. 209 of C. G. A. Oldendorp, *History of the Mission of the Evangelical Brethren on the Caribbean Islands of St. Thomas, St. Croix, and St. John,* edited by Johann Jakob Bossard (i.e., Bossart), translated into English and further edited by Arnold R. Highfield and Vladimir Barac.

Ann Arbor [Michigan, U.S.A.]: Karoma Publishers, 1987.
8vo (24 cm.): xxxv, 737 p., illus.

88.5 ———.

88.1 reprinted on pp. 350–351 of photomechanical reprint of the 1777 edition of C. G. A. Oldendorp, *Geschichte der Mission der evangelischen Brüder auf den caraibischen Inseln S. Thomas, S. Croix und S. Jan,* edited by Erich Beyreuther and Matthias Meyer (Volume 27.1 in Series 2 of Nikolaus Ludwig Graf von Zinzendorf, *Leben und Werk in Quellen und Darstellungen*).

Hildesheim [Saxony, Germany]: Georg Olms Verlag, 1995.
8vo (20 cm.): 62, 444 p., illus.

88.6 ———. [Complete edition, with critical annotations, of 88.0]

Aspects of his life story transcribed from 88.0 and printed on p. 480–481 in vol. 1 of C. G. A. Oldendorp, *Historie der caribischen Inseln Sanct Thomas, Sanct Crux und Sanct Jan, insbesondere der dasigen Neger und der Mission der evangelischen Brüder unter denselben: kommentierte Ausgabe des vollständigen Manuskriptes aus dem Archiv der Evangelischen Brüder-Unität Herrnhut,* edited by Gudrun Meier et al. (Band [Volume] 51 in the series *Abhandlungen und Berichte des Staatlichen Museums für Völkerkunde Dresden*).

Berlin [Germany]: VWB, Verlag für Wissenschaft und Bildung, 2000–2002.
2 vols. in 4, 8vo (24 cm.).
Vol. 1 (2000): 764 p.; xxxviii, illus.

89.0 Second unnamed Mandinka man

Aspects of his life story summarized in Christian Georg Andreas Oldendorp's 3,000-page manuscript account of Oldendorp's 1767–1768 tour of Denmark's West Indian possessions, viz. "Manuskript für eine Geschichte der Mission auf den westindischen Inseln, verfasst von C. G. A. Oldendorp," R.28.63 and R.28.62, held in the Unity Archives, Herrnhut, Saxony, Germany.

Full text: https://huskiecommons.lib.niu.edu/history-500africanvoices/83/ [see 89.1].

¶ This man identified as Mandinka (an ethnic group residing in southern Mali, Guinea, and Ivory Coast—see Map 3). He, his mother, and brother were captured during an attack and enslaved. He was taken away from his family members (who he never saw again) to a European fort, sold, and forced aboard a slave ship that took him to the Danish West Indies (Map 14). There he met Oldendorp in 1767–1768.

89.1 ——.[Complete edition, with critical annotations, of 89.0]

Aspects of his life story (none included in any earlier printed editions of Oldendorp) transcribed from 89.0 and printed on p. 480 in vol. 1 of C. G. A. Oldendorp, *Historie der caribischen Inseln Sanct Thomas, Sanct Crux und Sanct Jan, insbesondere der dasigen Neger und der Mission der evangelischen Brüder unter denselben: kommentierte Ausgabe des vollständigen Manuskriptes aus dem Archiv der Evangelischen Brüder-Unität Herrnhut*, edited by Gudrun Meier et al. (Band [Volume] 51 in the series *Abhandlungen und Berichte des Staatlichen Museums für Völkerkunde Dresden*).

Berlin [Germany]: VWB, Verlag für Wissenschaft und Bildung, 2000–2002.

2 vols. in 4, 8vo (24 cm.).

Vol. 1 (2000): 764 p.; xxxviii, illus.

90.0 Third unnamed Mandinka man

Aspects of his life story summarized in Christian Georg Andreas Oldendorp's 3,000-page manuscript account of Oldendorp's **1767–1768** tour of Denmark's West Indian possessions, viz. "Manuskript für eine Geschichte der Mission auf den westindischen Inseln, verfasst von C. G. A. Oldendorp," R.28.63 and R.28.62, held in the Unity Archives, Herrnhut, Saxony, Germany.

Full text: https://huskiecommons.lib.niu.edu/history-500africanvoices/84/ [see 90.1].

¶ This man identified as Mandinka (an ethnic group residing in present-day southern Mali, Guinea, and Ivory Coast—see Map 3). With a large number of Amina (a New World ethnic designation for Akan speakers near Elmina Castle, present-day Ghana, Map 5) on the same slave ship, he was taken from West Africa to the Danish West Indies (Map 14). During the voyage four Asante (Akan peoples, present-day Ghana) loosened their leg irons and attempted to escape at night in a lifeboat, but the alarm was raised, and they were put back into irons and beaten so severely that three of them died. The Mandinka man told Oldendorp about this event when they conversed in the Danish West Indies (Map 14) in 1767–1768.

90.1 ——.[Complete edition, with critical annotations, of 90.0]

Aspects of his life story (none included in any earlier printed editions of Oldendorp) transcribed from 90.0 and printed on p. 504 in vol. 1 of C. G. A. Oldendorp, *Historie der caribischen Inseln Sanct Thomas, Sanct Crux und Sanct Jan, insbesondere der dasigen Neger und der Mission der evangelischen Brüder unter denselben: kommentierte Ausgabe des vollständigen Manuskriptes aus dem Archiv der Evangelischen Brüder-Unität Herrnhut*, edited by Gudrun Meier et al. (Band [Volume] 51 in the series *Abhandlungen und Berichte des Staatlichen Museums für Völkerkunde Dresden*).

Berlin [Germany]: VWB, Verlag für Wissenschaft und Bildung, 2000–2002.

2 vols. in 4, 8vo (24 cm.).

Vol. 1 (2000): 764 p.; xxxviii, illus.

91.0 Unnamed Mandinka woman

Aspects of her life story summarized in Christian Georg Andreas Oldendorp's 3,000-page manuscript account of Oldendorp's **1767–1768** tour of Denmark's West Indian possessions, viz. "Manuskript für eine Geschichte der Mission auf den westindischen Inseln, verfasst von C. G. A. Oldendorp," R.28.63 and R.28.62, held in the Unity Archives, Herrnhut, Saxony, Germany.

Full text: https://huskiecommons.lib.niu.edu/history-500africanvoices/85/ [see 91.1].

¶ This woman identified as Mandinka (an ethnic group residing in southern Mali, Guinea, and Ivory Coast—see Map 3). Along with her sister, she was taken by Europeans while her father was away in order to compensate for the father's unpaid debt. The father came later to redeem them, but they were already on the slave ship and were not released. Thereafter, the ship took them to the Danish West Indies (Map 14). The fate of this sister was not recorded when she met Oldendorp in 1767–1768.

91.1 ——.[Complete edition, with critical annotations, of 91.0]

Aspects of her life story (none included in any earlier printed editions of Oldendorp) transcribed from 91.0 and printed on p. 481 in vol. 1 of C. G. A. Oldendorp, *Historie der caribischen Inseln Sanct Thomas, Sanct Crux und Sanct Jan, insbesondere der dasigen Neger und der Mission der evangelischen Brüder unter denselben: kommentierte Ausgabe des vollständigen Manuskriptes aus dem Archiv der Evangelischen Brüder-Unität Herrnhut*, edited by Gudrun Meier et al. (Band [Volume] 51 in the series *Abhandlungen und Berichte des Staatlichen Museums für Völkerkunde Dresden*).

Berlin [Germany]: VWB, Verlag für Wissenschaft und Bildung, 2000–2002.

2 vols. in 4, 8vo (24 cm.).

Vol. 1 (2000): 764 p.; xxxviii, illus.

92.0 Unnamed Okwoi man

Aspects of this unnamed man's life story summarized in Christian Georg Andreas Oldendorp's 3,000-page manuscript account of Oldendorp's **1767–1768** tour of Denmark's West Indian possessions, viz. "Manuskript für eine Geschichte der Mission auf den westindischen Inseln, verfasst von C. G. A. Oldendorp," R.28.63 and R.28.62, held in the Unity Archives, **Herrnhut, Saxony, Germany**. Only an abbreviated version of this lengthy manuscript was published in 1777 (92.1). It was not published in its entirety until 2000–2002 (92.4).

¶ This son of a wealthy man identified as of the Okwoi nation. (This is a possible reference to the Ga peoples of the Gold Coast and their *sei* or stool, a symbol of politico-religious authority—see Map 5.) The father repeatedly paid this son's gambling debts and warned him to stop gambling. Yet the son continued to gamble. As punishment the father sold him to pay his final gambling debt. Thereafter, the son was taken in the slave trade to the Danish West Indies (Map 14), where he conversed with Oldendorp in 1767–1768.

92.1 ———.

Aspects of his life story printed on p. 353 of Christian Georg Andreas Oldendorp, *Geschichte der Mission der evangelischen Brueder auf den caraibischen Inseln S. Thomas, S. Croix, und S. Jan*, edited by Johann Jakob Bossart.

Barby [Saxony-Anhalt, Germany]: bey Christian Friedrich Laur, und in **Leipzig [Saxony, Germany]**: in Commission bey Weidmanns Erben und Reich, **1777**.
2 volumes in 1, 8vo (19 cm.), folding plates and maps, [12], 1068, index [52], p.
https://archive.org/details/cgaoldendorpsges12olde/page/353

92.2 ———.

Danish translation of 92.1 (p. 350 only) printed on p. 179, Part 1, of Christian Georg Andreas Oldendorp, *Fuldstændigt Udtog af C.G.A. Oldendorps Missions-Historie om de evangeliske Brødres Mission paa de caraibiske Øer St. Thomas, St. Crux og St. Jan*, uitgivet paa Tydsk i to Dele.

Pt 1: *Kort Beskrivelse over Vestindien, især de Danske caraibiske Øer St. Crux, St. Thomas og St. Jan.*

Pt. 2: *Historisk Beretning om de hedenske Neger-Slavers Omvendelse paa de Danske Øer i Vestindien*, som et Udtog af C.G.A. Oldendorp's De Evangeliske Brødres Missions-Historie paa de Caraibiske Øer.

Full text: https://huskiecommons.lib.niu.edu/history-500africanvoices/86/ [see 92.6].

Copenhagen [Denmark]: Christ. L. Buchs Forlag, with J. Rud. Thiele, **1784**.
2 volumes in 1, with separate title pages and pagination, 8vo (18 cm): [4], 212 p. and 184, [4] p.

92.3 ———.

Swedish translation of 92.1, C. G. A. Oldendorp, *Historiska beskrifning öfwer ewangeliske brödernas miszions-arbete på caraibiske öarne St. Thomas St. Croix och St. Jan*, edited by Johann Jacob Bossart.

Stockholm [Sweden]: 1786–1788.
[Vol. 1] *Första delen, som innehåller åtskilliga efterrättelser, hörande til öarnes geographie, natural-historia och politiska författningar.*
Stockholm [Sweden]: tryckt hos commiss. P.A. Brodin, **1786**.
8vo (18 cm): [4], 64, [2], 348 p., map, 1 folded table.
[Vol. 2] *Andra delen, som innehåller miszions-historien ifrån år 1732 til år 1768.* **Stockholm [Sweden]**: tryckt hos Johan Christopher Holmberg, **1788**.
8vo (18 cm): [2], 634, [4] p., folded leaves of plates: ill. (engravings).

92.4 ———.

English translation of 92.1 printed on p. 210 of C. G. A. Oldendorp, *History of the Mission of the Evangelical Brethren on the Caribbean Islands of St. Thomas, St. Croix, and St. John*, edited by Johann Jakob Bossard (i.e., Bossart), translated into English and further edited by Arnold R. Highfield and Vladimir Barac.

Ann Arbor [Michigan, U.S.A.]: Karoma Publishers, **1987**.
8vo (24 cm.): xxxv, 737 p., illus.

92.5 ———.

92.1 printed on p. 353 in photomechanical reprint of the 1777 edition of C. G. A. Oldendorp, *Geschichte der Mission der evangelischen Brüder auf den caraibischen Inseln S. Thomas, S. Croix und S. Jan*, edited by Erich Beyreuther and Matthias Meyer (Volume 27.1 in Series 2 of Nikolaus Ludwig Graf von Zinzendorf, *Leben und Werk in Quellen und Darstellungen*).

Hildesheim [Saxony, Germany]: Georg Olms Verlag, **1995**.
8vo (20 cm.): 62, 444 p., illus.

92.6 ———. [Complete edition, with critical annotations, of 92.0]

Aspects of his life story transcribed from 92.0 and printed on p. 484 in vol. 1 of C. G. A. Oldendorp, *Historie der caribischen Inseln Sanct Thomas, Sanct Crux und Sanct Jan, insbesondere der dasigen Neger und der Mission der evangelischen Brüder unter denselben: kommentierte Ausgabe des vollständigen Manuskriptes aus dem Archiv der Evangelischen*

Brüder-Unität Herrnhut, edited by Gudrun Meier et al. (Band [Volume] 51 in the series *Abhandlungen und Berichte des Staatlichen Museums für Völkerkunde Dresden*).

Berlin [Germany]: VWB, Verlag für Wissenschaft und Bildung, **2000–2002**.
2 vols. in 4, 8vo (24 cm.).
Vol. 1 (2000): 764 p.; xxxviii, illus.

93.0 Unnamed Carabali man

Aspects of this unnamed man's life story summarized in Christian Georg Andreas Oldendorp's 3,000-page manuscript account of Oldendorp's **1767–1768** tour of Denmark's West Indian possessions, viz. "Manuskript für eine Geschichte der Mission auf den westindischen Inseln, verfasst von C. G. A. Oldendorp," R.28.63 and R.28.62, held in the Unity Archives, **Herrnhut, Saxony, Germany**. Only an abbreviated version of this lengthy manuscript was published in 1777 (93.1). It was not published in its entirety until 2000–2002 (93.6).

Full text: https://huskiecommons.lib.niu.edu/history-500africanvoices/87/ [see 93.6].

¶ This man identified as Carabali, an Ijo subgroup (probably Ibibio, Cross River region, present-day Nigeria and northwestern Cameroon—see Map 5) living in mangrove swamps of the Niger River. They lived far from the sea, on a large river called Mini (meaning water). Their neighbors were Igbo (present-day southeastern Nigeria), with whom they were friendly and shared the same king, Apus, Bibi, and Biwi (frightening cannibals with filed teeth). He was a bad man, who often quarreled with men in his home village and beat them. When hunting birds in the bush one day, his opponents ambushed him, bound him, and took him to a sorcerer as a gift, so the latter could bring much needed rain. He was eventually sold to Europeans, who transported him enslaved to the Danish West Indies (Map 14), where he conversed with Oldendorp in 1767–1768.

93.1 ———.

Aspects of his life story printed on pp. 353–354 of Christian Georg Andreas Oldendorp, *Geschichte der Mission der evangelischen Brueder auf den caraibischen Inseln S. Thomas, S. Croix, und S. Jan*, edited by Johann Jakob Bossart.

Barby [Saxony-Anhalt, Germany]: bey Christian Friedrich Laur, und in **Leipzig [Saxony, Germany]**: in Commission bey Weidmanns Erben und Reich, **1777**.
2 volumes in 1, 8vo (19 cm.), folding plates and maps, [12], 1068, index [52], p.
https://archive.org/details/cgaoldendorpsges12olde/page/353

93.2 ———.

Danish translation of 93.1 (p. 350 only) printed on p. 179, Part 1, of Christian Georg Andreas Oldendorp, *Fuldstændigt Udtog af C.G.A. Oldendorps Missions-Historie om de evangeliske Brødres Mission paa de caraibiske Øer St. Thomas, St. Crux og St. Jan*, uitgivet paa Tydsk i to Dele.

Pt 1: *Kort Beskrivelse over Vestindien, især de Danske caraibiske Øer St. Crux, St. Thomas og St. Jan*.

Pt. 2: *Historisk Beretning om de hedenske Neger-Slavers Omvendelse paa de Danske Øer i Vestindien*, som et Udtog af C.G.A. Oldendorp's De Evangeliske Brødres Missions-Historie paa de Caraibiske Øer.

Copenhagen [Denmark]: Christ. L. Buchs Forlag, with J. Rud. Thiele, **1784**.
2 volumes in 1, with separate title pages and pagination, 8vo (18 cm): [4], 212 p. and 184, [4] p.

93.3 ———.

Swedish translation of 93.1, C. G. A. Oldendorp, *Historiska beskrifning öfwer ewangeliske brödernas miszions-arbete på caraibiske öarne St. Thomas St. Croix och St. Jan*, edited by Johann Jacob Bossart.

Stockholm [Sweden]: 1786–1788.
[Vol. 1] *Första delen, som innehåller åtskilliga efterrättelser, hörande til öarnes geographie, natural-historia och politiska författningar*.
Stockholm [Sweden]: tryckt hos commiss. P.A. Brodin, **1786**.
8vo (18 cm): [4], 64, [2], 348 p., map, 1 folded table.
[Vol. 2] *Andra delen, som innehåller miszions-historien ifrån år 1732 til år 1768*. **Stockholm [Sweden]**: tryckt hos Johan Christopher Holmberg, **1788**.
8vo (18 cm): [2], 634, [4] p., folded leaves of plates: ill. (engravings).

93.4 ———.

English translation of 93.1 printed on p. 210 of C. G. A. Oldendorp, *History of the Mission of the Evangelical Brethren on the Caribbean Islands of St. Thomas, St. Croix, and St. John*, edited by Johann Jakob Bossard (i.e., Bossart), translated into English and further edited by Arnold R. Highfield and Vladimir Barac.

Ann Arbor [Michigan, U.S.A.]: Karoma Publishers, **1987**.
8vo (24 cm.): xxxv, 737 p., illus.

93.5 ———.

93.1 printed on pp. 353–354 in photomechanical reprint of the 1777 edition of C. G. A. Oldendorp, *Geschichte der Mission der evangelischen Brüder auf den caraibischen Inseln S. Thomas, S. Croix und S. Jan*, edited by Erich Beyreuther and

Matthias Meyer (Volume 27.1 in Series 2 of Nikolaus Ludwig Graf von Zinzendorf, *Leben und Werk in Quellen und Darstellungen*).

Hildesheim [Saxony, Germany]: Georg Olms Verlag, 1995.
8vo (20 cm.): 62, 444 p., illus.

93.6 ——. [Complete edition, with critical annotations, of 93.0]

Aspects of his life story transcribed from 93.0 and printed on pp. 426–430 (general description of homeland by this and other Carabali) and 486–487 in vol. 1 of C. G. A. Oldendorp, *Historie der caribischen Inseln Sanct Thomas, Sanct Crux und Sanct Jan, insbesondere der dasigen Neger und der Mission der evangelischen Brüder unter denselben: kommentierte Ausgabe des vollständigen Manuskriptes aus dem Archiv der Evangelischen Brüder-Unität Herrnhut*, edited by Gudrun Meier et al. (Band [Volume] 51 in the series *Abhandlungen und Berichte des Staatlichen Museums für Völkerkunde Dresden*).

Berlin [Germany]: VWB, Verlag für Wissenschaft und Bildung, 2000–2002.
2 vols. in 4, 8vo (24 cm.).
Vol. 1 (2000): 764 p.; xxxviii, illus.

94.0 Unnamed Carabali Woman

This unnamed woman's life story summarized in Christian Georg Andreas Oldendorp's 3,000-page manuscript account of Oldendorp's 1767–1768 tour of Denmark's West Indian possessions, viz. "Manuskript für eine Geschichte der Mission auf den westindischen Inseln, verfasst von C. G. A. Oldendorp," R.28.63 and R.28.62, held in the Unity Archives, **Herrnhut, Saxony, Germany**. Only an abbreviated version of this lengthy manuscript was published in 1777 (94.1). It was not published in its entirety until 2000–2002 (94.4).

Full text: https://huskiecommons.lib.niu.edu/history-500africanvoices/88/ [see 94.6].

¶ This woman identified as Carabali, an Ijo subgroup who (probably Igbo, present-day southeastern Nigeria or Ibibio, Cross River region, Nigeria—see Map 5) lived far from the sea, on a large river called Mini (meaning water). Their neighbors were Igbo, with whom they were friendly and shared the same king, Apus, Bibi, and Biwi (frightening cannibals with filed teeth). She did not love her husband and left him, moving to another village. Her husband's brother, who lived in that village, then sold her as a slave. She was then transported to the Danish West Indies (Map 14), where she conversed with Oldendorp in 1767–1768.

94.1 ——.

Details of her life story printed on p. 354 of Christian Georg Andreas Oldendorp, *Geschichte der Mission der evangelischen Brueder auf den caraibischen Inseln S. Thomas, S. Croix, und S. Jan*, edited by Johann Jakob Bossart.

Barby [Saxony-Anhalt, Germany]: bey Christian Friedrich Laur, und in **Leipzig** [Saxony, Germany]: in Commission bey Weidmanns Erben und Reich, 1777.
2 volumes in 1, 8vo (19 cm.), folding plates and maps, [12], 1068, index [52], p.
https://archive.org/details/cgaoldendorpsges12olde/page/354

94.2 ——.

Danish translation of 94.1 (p. 350 only) printed on p. 179, Part 1, of Christian Georg Andreas Oldendorp, *Fuldstændigt Udtog af C.G.A. Oldendorps Missions-Historie om de evangeliske Brødres Mission paa de caraibiske Øer St. Thomas, St. Crux og St. Jan, uitgivet paa Tydsk i to Dele.*

Pt 1: *Kort Beskrivelse over Vestindien, især de Danske caraibiske Øer St. Crux, St. Thomas og St. Jan.*

Pt. 2: *Historisk Beretning om de hedenske Neger-Slavers Omvendelse paa de Danske Øer i Vestindien*, som et Udtog af C.G.A. Oldendorp's De Evangeliske Brødres Missions-Historie paa de Caraibiske Øer.

Copenhagen [Denmark]: Christ. L. Buchs Forlag, with J. Rud. Thiele, 1784.
2 volumes in 1, with separate title pages and pagination, 8vo (18 cm): [4], 212 p. and 184, [4] p.

94.3 ——.

Swedish translation of 94.1, C. G. A. Oldendorp, *Historiska beskrifning öfwer ewangeliske brödernas miszions-arbete på caraibiske öarne St. Thomas St. Croix och St. Jan*, edited by Johann Jacob Bossart.

Stockholm [Sweden]: 1786–1788.
[Vol. 1] *Första delen, som innehåller åtskilliga efterrättelser, hörande til öarnes geographie, natural-historia och politiska författningar.*
Stockholm [Sweden]: tryckt hos commiss. P.A. Brodin, 1786.
8vo (18 cm): [4], 64, [2], 348 p., map, 1 folded table.
[Vol. 2] *Andra delen, som innehåller miszions-historien ifrån år 1732 til år 1768.* Stockholm [Sweden]: tryckt hos Johan Christopher Holmberg, 1788.
8vo (18 cm): [2], 634, [4] p., folded leaves of plates: ill. (engravings).

94.4 ——.

English translation of 94.1 printed on p. 210 of C. G. A. Oldendorp, *History of the Mission of the Evangelical Brethren on the Caribbean Islands of St. Thomas, St. Croix, and St. John,* edited by Johann Jakob Bossard (i.e., Bossart), translated into English and further edited by Arnold R. Highfield and Vladimir Barac.

Ann Arbor [Michigan, U.S.A.]: Karoma Publishers, **1987.**
8vo (24 cm.): xxxv, 737 p., illus.

94.5 ———.
94.1 printed on p. 354 in photomechanical reprint of the 1777 edition of C. G. A. Oldendorp, *Geschichte der Mission der evangelischen Brüder auf den caraibischen Inseln S. Thomas, S. Croix und S. Jan,* edited by Erich Beyreuther and Matthias Meyer (Volume 27.1 in Series 2 of Nikolaus Ludwig Graf von Zinzendorf, *Leben und Werk in Quellen und Darstellungen*).

Hildesheim [Saxony, Germany]: Georg Olms Verlag, **1995.**
8vo (20 cm.): 62, 444 p., illus.

94.6 ———. [Complete edition, with critical annotations, of 94.0]
Aspects of his life story transcribed from 94.0 and printed on pp. 426–430 (general description of homeland by this and other Carabali) and 487 in vol. 1 of C. G. A. Oldendorp, *Historie der caribischen Inseln Sanct Thomas, Sanct Crux und Sanct Jan, insbesondere der dasigen Neger und der Mission der evangelischen Brüder unter denselben: kommentierte Ausgabe des vollständigen Manuskriptes aus dem Archiv der Evangelischen Brüder-Unität Herrnhut,* edited by Gudrun Meier et al. (Band [Volume] 51 in the series *Abhandlungen und Berichte des Staatlichen Museums für Völkerkunde Dresden*).

Berlin [Germany]: VWB, Verlag für Wissenschaft und Bildung, **2000–2002.**
2 vols. in 4, 8vo (24 cm.).
Vol. 1 (2000): 764 p.; xxxviii, illus.

95.0   Unnamed Igbo man

Aspects of this unnamed man's life story summarized in Christian Georg Andreas Oldendorp's 3,000-page manuscript account of Oldendorp's **1767–1768** tour of Denmark's West Indian possessions, viz. "Manuskript für eine Geschichte der Mission auf den westindischen Inseln, verfasst von C. G. A. Oldendorp," R.28.63 and R.28.62, held in the Unity Archives, **Herrnhut, Saxony, Germany.** Only an abbreviated version of this lengthy manuscript was published in 1777 (93.1). It was not published in its entirety until 2000–2002 (93.4).

Full text: https://huskiecommons.lib.niu.edu/history-500africanvoices/89/ [see 95.6].

¶ This man identified as Igbo (in present-day southeastern Nigeria—see Map 5). While traveling in another land he was seized by a man who had a claim for money against his nation. He was then forcibly transported to the Danish West Indies (Map 14), where he conversed with Oldendorp in 1767–1768.

95.1 ———.
Aspects of his life story printed on p. 354 of Christian Georg Andreas Oldendorp, *Geschichte der Mission der evangelischen Brueder auf den caraibischen Inseln S. Thomas, S. Croix, und S. Jan,* edited by Johann Jakob Bossart.

Barby [Saxony-Anhalt, Germany]: bey Christian Friedrich Laur, und in **Leipzig [Saxony, Germany]:** in Commission bey Weidmanns Erben und Reich, **1777.**
2 volumes in 1, 8vo (19 cm.), folding plates and maps, [12], 1068, index [52], p.
https://archive.org/details/cgaoldendorpsges12olde/page/354

95.2 ———.
Danish translation of 95.1 (p. 350 only) printed on p. 179, Part 1, of Christian Georg Andreas Oldendorp, *Fuldstændigt Udtog af C.G.A. Oldendorps Missions-Historie om de evangeliske Brødres Mission paa de caraibiske Øer St. Thomas, St. Crux og St. Jan, uitgivet paa Tydsk i to Dele.*

Pt 1: *Kort Beskrivelse over Vestindien, især de Danske caraibiske Øer St. Crux, St. Thomas og St. Jan.*

Pt. 2: *Historisk Beretning om de hedenske Neger-Slavers Omvendelse paa de Danske Øer i Vestindien,* som et Udtog af C.G.A. Oldendorp's De Evangeliske Brødres Missions-Historie paa de Caraibiske Øer.

Copenhagen [Denmark]: Christ. L. Buchs Forlag, with J. Rud. Thiele, **1784.**
2 volumes in 1, with separate title pages and pagination, 8vo (18 cm): [4], 212 p. and 184, [4] p.

95.3 ———.
Swedish translation of 95.1, C. G. A. Oldendorp, *Historiska beskrifning öfwer ewangeliske brödernas miszions-arbete på caraibiske öarne St. Thomas St. Croix och St. Jan,* edited by Johann Jacob Bossart.

Stockholm [Sweden]: 1786–1788.
[Vol. 1] *Första delen, som innehåller åtskilliga efterrättelser, hörande til öarnes geographie, natural-historia och politiska författningar.*
Stockholm [Sweden]: tryckt hos commiss. P.A. Brodin, **1786.**
8vo (18 cm): [4], 64, [2], 348 p., map, 1 folded table.
[Vol. 2] *Andra delen, som innehåller miszions-historien ifrån år 1732 til år 1768.* **Stockholm [Sweden]:** tryckt hos Johan Christopher Holmberg, **1788.**
8vo (18 cm): [2], 634, [4] p., folded leaves of plates: ill. (engravings).

Figure 7: Danish Fort Christiansborg, now Osu Castle near Accra (modern Ghana). This painting is possibly from the board room of the Westindian-Guinean Company in Copenhagen, which was responsible for the slave trade from around 1670 to 1754. Many West Africans who provided accounts for this catalog were traded here to Europeans and subsequently placed on slave ships.

Source: Color image, 18th century, unknown artist. The Danish Maritime Museum, Kronborg, Denmark.

95.4 ———.

English translation of 95.1 printed on p. 210 of C. G. A. Oldendorp, *History of the Mission of the Evangelical Brethren on the Caribbean Islands of St. Thomas, St. Croix, and St. John*, edited by Johann Jakob Bossard (i.e., Bossart), translated into English and further edited by Arnold R. Highfield and Vladimir Barac.

Ann Arbor [Michigan, U.S.A.]: Karoma Publishers, **1987**. 8vo (24 cm.): xxxv, 737 p., illus.

95.5 ———.

95.1 printed on p. 354 in photomechanical reprint of the 1777 edition of C. G. A. Oldendorp, *Geschichte der Mission der evangelischen Brüder auf den caraibischen Inseln S. Thomas, S. Croix und S. Jan*, edited by Erich Beyreuther and Matthias Meyer (Volume 27.1 in Series 2 of Nikolaus Ludwig Graf von Zinzendorf, *Leben und Werk in Quellen und Darstellungen*).

Hildesheim [Saxony, Germany]: Georg Olms Verlag, **1995**. 8vo (20 cm.): 62, 444 p., illus.

95.6 ———.[Complete edition, with critical annotations, of 95.0]

Aspects of his life story transcribed from 95.0 and printed on p. 487 in vol. 1 of C. G. A. Oldendorp, *Historie der caribischen Inseln Sanct Thomas, Sanct Crux und Sanct Jan, insbesondere der dasigen Neger und der Mission der evangelischen Brüder unter denselben: kommentierte Ausgabe des vollständigen Manuskriptes aus dem Archiv der Evangelischen Brüder-Unität Herrnhut*, edited by Gudrun Meier et al. (Band [Volume] 51 in the series *Abhandlungen und Berichte des Staatlichen Museums für Völkerkunde Dresden*).

Berlin [Germany]: VWB, Verlag für Wissenschaft und Bildung, **2000–2002.**
2 vols. in 4, 8vo (24 cm.).
Vol. 1 (2000): 764 p.; xxxviii, illus.

96.0 First unnamed Mandongo man

Aspects of this unnamed man's life story summarized in Christian Georg Andreas Oldendorp's 3,000-page manuscript account of Oldendorp's **1767–1768** tour of Denmark's West Indian possessions, viz. "Manuskript für eine Geschichte der Mission auf den westindischen Inseln, verfasst von C. G. A. Oldendorp," R.28.63 and R.28.62, held in the Unity Archives, **Herrnhut, Saxony, Germany**. Only an abbreviated version of this lengthy manuscript was published in 1777 (94.1). It was not published in its entirety until 2000–2002 (94.4).

Full text: https://huskiecommons.lib.niu.edu/history-500africanvoices/90/ [see 96.5].

¶ **This man identified as Mandongo (Bolia).** This was a large country far from the sea, with **Colombo, Cando,** and **Bogolo** subgroups who made war on each other (present-day Republic of Congo, west central Africa—see Map 6). After his mother sold his brother into slavery, he feared a similar fate, so he sought shelter with another family. After the death of that family's father, the others sold him to people of another country, who traded him to Loango (north of the Congo River, Congo) who in turn sold him to the captain of an English slave ship. In 1762, during wartime, this ship sailed to St. Thomas in the Danish West Indies (Map 14), where this man and the others were sold. He met Oldendorp there in 1767–1768.

96.1 ———.

Aspects of his life story printed on p. 354 of Christian Georg Andreas Oldendorp, *Geschichte der Mission der evangelischen Brueder auf den caraibischen Inseln S. Thomas, S. Croix, und S. Jan*, edited by Johann Jakob Bossart.

Barby [Saxony-Anhalt, Germany]: bey Christian Friedrich Laur, und in **Leipzig [Saxony, Germany]:** in Commission bey Weidmanns Erben und Reich, **1777.**
2 volumes in 1, 8vo (19 cm.), folding plates and maps, [12], 1068, index [52], p.
https://archive.org/details/cgaoldendorpsges12olde/page/354

96.2 ———.

Swedish translation of 96.1, C. G. A. Oldendorp, *Historiska beskrifning öfwer ewangeliske brödernas miszions-arbete på caraibiske öarne St. Thomas St. Croix och St. Jan*, edited by Johann Jacob Bossart.

Stockholm [Sweden]: 1786–1788.
[Vol. 1] *Första delen, som innehåller åtskilliga efterrättelser, hörande til öarnes geographie, natural-historia och politiska författningar.*
Stockholm [Sweden]: tryckt hos commiss. P.A. Brodin, **1786.**
8vo (18 cm): [4], 64, [2], 348 p., map, 1 folded table.
[Vol. 2] *Andra delen, som innehåller miszions-historien ifrån år 1732 til år 1768.* **Stockholm [Sweden]:** tryckt hos Johan Christopher Holmberg, **1788.**
8vo (18 cm): [2], 634, [4] p., folded leaves of plates: ill. (engravings).

96.3 ———.

English translation of 96.1 printed on p. 210 of C. G. A. Oldendorp, *History of the Mission of the Evangelical Brethren on the Caribbean Islands of St. Thomas, St. Croix, and St. John*, edited by Johann Jakob Bossard (i.e., Bossart), translated into English and further edited by Arnold R. Highfield and Vladimir Barac.

Ann Arbor [Michigan, U.S.A.]: Karoma Publishers, **1987.**
8vo (24 cm.): xxxv, 737 p., illus.

96.4 ———.

96.1 printed on p. 354 in photomechanical reprint of the 1777 edition of C. G. A. Oldendorp, *Geschichte der Mission der evangelischen Brüder auf den caraibischen Inseln S. Thomas, S. Croix und S. Jan*, edited by Erich Beyreuther and Matthias Meyer (Volume 27.1 in Series 2 of Nikolaus Ludwig Graf von Zinzendorf, *Leben und Werk in Quellen und Darstellungen*).

Hildesheim [Saxony, Germany]: Georg Olms Verlag, **1995.**
8vo (20 cm.): 62, 444 p., illus.

96.5 ———.[Complete edition, with critical annotations, of 96.0]

His and three others' contributions to a general description of their homeland transcribed from 96.0 and printed on pp. 441–444, and aspects of his own personal life story transcribed from 96.0 and printed on p. 488 in vol. 1 of C. G. A. Oldendorp, *Historie der caribischen Inseln Sanct Thomas, Sanct Crux und Sanct Jan, insbesondere der dasigen Neger und der Mission der evangelischen Brüder unter denselben: kommentierte Ausgabe des vollständigen Manuskriptes aus dem Archiv der Evangelischen Brüder-Unität Herrnhut*, edited by Gudrun Meier et al. (Band [Volume] 51 in the series *Abhandlungen und Berichte des Staatlichen Museums für Völkerkunde Dresden*).

Berlin [Germany]: VWB, Verlag für Wissenschaft und Bildung, 2000–2002.

2 vols. in 4, 8vo (24 cm.).

Vol. 1 (2000): 764 p.; xxxviii, illus.

97.0 Unnamed Mandongo woman

Aspects of this unnamed woman's life story summarized in Christian Georg Andreas Oldendorp's 3,000-page manuscript account of Oldendorp's **1767–1768** tour of Denmark's West Indian possessions, viz. "Manuskript für eine Geschichte der Mission auf den westindischen Inseln, verfasst von C. G. A. Oldendorp," R.28.63 and R.28.62, held in the Unity Archives, **Herrnhut, Saxony, Germany.**

Full text: https:// huskiecommons. lib.niu.edu/history-500africanvoices/91/ [see 97.1].

¶ This woman identified as Mandongo (Bolia). This was a large country far from the sea, with Colombo, Cando, and Bogolo subgroups who made war on each other (present-day Republic of Congo, west-central Africa—see Map 6). While traveling, she was taken by her own people to Loango (north of the Congo River, in present-day Congo) and sold to a Dutch slave ship, which took her to the Dutch island of St. Eustachius in the Caribbean (Map 11). Thereafter, she was taken to the Danish West Indies colony of St. Thomas (Map 14), where she conversed with Oldendorp in 1767–1768.

97.1 ———.

Her contribution to the general description of her homeland and aspects of her own life story transcribed and printed from 97.0 on p. 441–444 and 488 in vol. 1 of C. G. A. Oldendorp, *Historie der caribischen Inseln Sanct Thomas, Sanct Crux und Sanct Jan, insbesondere der dasigen Neger und der Mission der evangelischen Brüder unter denselben: kommentierte Ausgabe des vollständigen Manuskriptes aus dem Archiv der Evangelischen Brüder-Unität Herrnhut*, edited by Gudrun Meier et al. (Band [Volume] 51 in the series *Abhandlungen und Berichte des Staatlichen Museums für Völkerkunde Dresden*).

Berlin [Germany]: VWB, Verlag für Wissenschaft und Bildung, 2000–2002.

2 vols. in 4, 8vo (24 cm.).

Vol. 1 (2000): 764 p.; xxxviii, illus.

98.0 Second unnamed Mandongo man

Aspects of this unnamed man's life story summarized in Christian Georg Andreas Oldendorp's 3,000-page manuscript account of Oldendorp's **1767–1768** tour of Denmark's West Indian possessions, viz. "Manuskript für eine Geschichte der Mission auf den westindischen Inseln, verfasst von C. G. A. Oldendorp," R.28.63 and R.28.62, held in the Unity Archives, **Herrnhut, Saxony, Germany.**

Full text: https:// huskiecommons. lib.niu.edu/history-500africanvoices/92/ [see 98.1].

¶ This man identified as Mandongo (Bolia). This was a large country far from the sea, with Colombo, Cando, and Bogolo subgroups who made war on each other (present-day Republic of Congo, west central Africa—see Map 6). One day while near his home he was hunted by his own people until evening, captured, and enslaved. Thereafter, he was taken to Loango (north of the Congo River, in present-day Congo) and sold, eventually to a slave ship, which forcibly took him to the Danish West Indies (Map 14), where he conversed with Oldendorp in 1767–1768.

98.1 ———.

His contribution to the general description of his homeland and aspects of his own life story transcribed and printed from 98.0 on pp. 441–444 and 488 in vol. 1 of C. G. A. Oldendorp, *Historie der caribischen Inseln Sanct Thomas, Sanct Crux und Sanct Jan, insbesondere der dasigen Neger und der Mission der evangelischen Brüder unter denselben: kommentierte Ausgabe des vollständigen Manuskriptes aus dem Archiv der Evangelischen Brüder-Unität Herrnhut*, edited by Gudrun Meier et al. (Band [Volume] 51 in the series *Abhandlungen und Berichte des Staatlichen Museums für Völkerkunde Dresden*).

Berlin [Germany]: VWB, Verlag für Wissenschaft und Bildung, 2000–2002.

2 vols. in 4, 8vo (24 cm.).

Vol. 1 (2000): 764 p.; xxxviii, illus.

99.0 Unnamed father

This unnamed man's life story summarized in Christian Georg Andreas Oldendorp's 3,000-page manuscript account of Oldendorp's **1767–1768** tour of Denmark's West Indian possessions, viz. "Manuskript für eine Geschichte der Mission auf den westindischen Inseln, verfasst von C. G. A. Oldendorp," R.28.63 and R.28.62, held in the Unity Archives, **Herrnhut, Saxony, Germany**. Only an abbreviated version of this lengthy manuscript was published in 1777 (99.1). It was not published in its entirety until 2000–2002 (99.4).

Full text: https:// huskiecommons. lib.niu.edu/histo-ry-500africanvoic-es/93/ [see 99.5].

¶ Of unknown origins, this man traveled several days from his home to the sea upon hearing of the arrival of a ship. He went on board with his son to inquire into the possibility of acquiring goods for sale. Interested in exchanging goods, but having no means to do so, he left his son on board for security. While returning with payment he was captured by man hunters and sold to another ship. He was then transported to the Danish West Indies (see Map 14), where he conversed with Oldendorp in 1767–1768.

99.1 ——.

Account printed on p. 354 of Christian Georg Andreas Oldendorp, *Geschichte der Mission der evangelischen Brueder auf den caraibischen Inseln S. Thomas, S. Croix, und S. Jan*, edited by Johann Jakob Bossart.

Barby [Saxony-Anhalt, Germany]: bey Christian Friedrich Laur, und in **Leipzig [Saxony, Germany]:** in Commission bey Weidmanns Erben und Reich, **1777**.
2 volumes in 1, 8vo (19 cm.), folding plates and maps, [12], 1068, index [52], p.
https://archive.org/details/cgaoldendorpsges12olde/page/354

99.2 ——.

Swedish translation of 99.1, C. G. A. Oldendorp, *Historiska beskrifning öfwer ewangeliske brödernas miszions-arbete på caraibiske öarne St. Thomas St. Croix och St. Jan*, edited by Johann Jacob Bossart.

Stockholm [Sweden]: 1786–1788.
[Vol. 1] *Första delen, som innehåller åtskilliga efterrättelser, hörande til öarnes geographie, natural-historia och politiska författningar.*
Stockholm [Sweden]: tryckt hos commiss. P.A. Brodin, **1786**.
8vo (18 cm): [4], 64, [2], 348 p., map, 1 folded table.
[Vol. 2] *Andra delen, som innehåller miszions-historien ifrån år 1732 til år 1768.* **Stockholm [Sweden]:** tryckt hos Johan Christopher Holmberg, **1788**.
8vo (18 cm): [2], 634, [4] p., folded leaves of plates: ill. (engravings).

99.3 ——.

English translation of 99.1 printed on p. 211 of C. G. A. Oldendorp, *History of the Mission of the Evangelical Brethren on the Caribbean Islands of St. Thomas, St. Croix, and St. John*, edited by Johann Jakob Bossard (i.e., Bossart), translated into English and further edited by Arnold R. Highfield and Vladimir Barac.

Ann Arbor [Michigan, U.S.A.]: Karoma Publishers, **1987**.
8vo (24 cm.): xxxv, 737 p., illus.

99.4 ——.

99.1 printed on p. 354 in photomechanical reprint of the 1777 edition of C. G. A. Oldendorp, *Geschichte der Mission der evangelischen Brüder auf den caraibischen Inseln S. Thomas, S. Croix und S. Jan*, edited by Erich Beyreuther and Matthias Meyer (Volume 27.1 in Series 2 of Nikolaus Ludwig Graf von Zinzendorf, *Leben und Werk in Quellen und Darstellungen*).

Hildesheim [Saxony, Germany]: Georg Olms Verlag, **1995**.
8vo (20 cm.): 62, 444 p., illus.

99.5 ——.

His life story transcribed from 99.0 and printed on p. 488–489 in vol. 1 of C. G. A. Oldendorp, *Historie der caribischen Inseln Sanct Thomas, Sanct Crux und Sanct Jan, insbesondere der dasigen Neger und der Mission der evangelischen Brüder unter denselben: kommentierte Ausgabe des vollständigen Manuskriptes aus dem Archiv der Evangelischen Brüder-Unität Herrnhut*, edited by Gudrun Meier et al. (Band [Volume] 51 in the series *Abhandlungen und Berichte des Staatlichen Museums für Völkerkunde Dresden*).

Berlin [Germany]: VWB, Verlag für Wissenschaft und Bildung, **2000–2002**.
2 vols. in 4, 8vo (24 cm.).
Vol. 1 (2000): 764 p.; xxxviii, illus.

100.0 Unnamed man

A brief portion of this unnamed man's life story was recorded in Christian Georg Andreas Oldendorp's 3,000-page manuscript account of Oldendorp's **1767–1768** tour of Denmark's West Indian possessions, viz. "Manuskript für eine Geschichte der Mission auf den westindischen Inseln, verfasst von C. G. A. Oldendorp," R.28.63 and R.28.62, held in the Unity Archives, **Herrnhut, Saxony, Germany**.

Full text: https:// huskiecommons. lib.niu.edu/histo-ry-500africanvoic-es/94/ [see 100.1].

¶ This West African man was familiar with cannibals near his (unnamed) homeland. When forced aboard a slave ship bound for the Danish West Indies (see Map 14), he was terrified that the white people intended to eat him. He related this to Oldendorp when they met in 1767–1768.

100.1 ——.

Brief portion of his life story transcribed from 100.0 and printed on p. 495 in vol. 1 of C. G. A. Oldendorp, *Historie der caribischen Inseln Sanct Thomas, Sanct Crux und Sanct Jan, insbesondere der dasigen Neger und der Mission der evangelischen Brüder unter denselben: kommentierte Ausgabe des vollständigen Manuskriptes aus dem Archiv der Evangelischen Brüder-Unität Herrnhut*, edited by Gudrun Meier et al. (Band [Volume] 51 in the series *Abhandlungen und Berichte des Staatlichen Museums für Völkerkunde Dresden*).

Berlin [Germany]: VWB, Verlag für Wissenschaft und Bildung, 2000–2002.

2 vols. in 4, 8vo (24 cm.).
Vol. 1 (2000): 764 p.; xxxviii, illus.

101.0   First unnamed rebel

A brief portion of this unnamed man's life story was recorded in Christian Georg Andreas Oldendorp's 3,000-page manuscript account of Oldendorp's **1767–1768** tour of Denmark's West Indian possessions, viz. "Manuskript für eine Geschichte der Mission auf den westindischen Inseln, verfasst von C. G. A. Oldendorp," R.28.63 and R.28.62, held in the Unity Archives, **Herrnhut, Saxony, Germany.**

Full text: https://huskiecommons.lib.niu.edu/history-500africanvoices/95/ [see 101.1].

¶ This man was taken as a boy in the transatlantic slave trade. While he was on the slave ship, the captain made him a cabin boy, which gave him the opportunity to participate in a shipboard revolt with a man he remained close to in the West Indies (q.v. 102.0) and others. In the middle of the night he took the sleeping captain's gun, but just before the revolt was to begin at daybreak, a *Bomba* (Black supervisor) told the captain, who then had a cannon pointed at the place where the rebels emerged from below deck. The frightened rebels gave up, were placed in irons, and several of them were severely beaten. After arrival in the Danish West Indies (see Map 14), he was sold, and in 1767–1768 he and his friend (q.v. 102.0) spoke with Oldendorp about their experiences.

101.1 ——.

Brief portion of his life story transcribed from 101.0 and printed on pp. 504–505 in vol. 1 of C. G. A. Oldendorp, *Historie*

der caribischen Inseln Sanct Thomas, Sanct Crux und Sanct Jan, insbesondere der dasigen Neger und der Mission der evangelischen Brüder unter denselben: kommentierte Ausgabe des vollständigen Manuskriptes aus dem Archiv der Evangelischen Brüder-Unität Herrnhut, edited by Gudrun Meier et al. (Band [Volume] 51 in the series *Abhandlungen und Berichte des Staatlichen Museums für Völkerkunde Dresden*).

Berlin [Germany]: VWB, Verlag für Wissenschaft und Bildung, 2000–2002.

2 vols. in 4, 8vo (24 cm.).
Vol. 1 (2000): 764 p.; xxxviii, illus.

102.0   Second unnamed rebel

A brief portion of this unnamed man's life story was recorded in Christian Georg Andreas Oldendorp's 3,000-page manuscript account of Oldendorp's **1767–1768** tour of Denmark's West Indian possessions, viz. "Manuskript für eine Geschichte der Mission auf den westindischen Inseln, verfasst von C. G. A. Oldendorp," R.28.63 and R.28.62, held in the Unity Archives, **Herrnhut, Saxony, Germany.**

Full text: https://huskiecommons.lib.niu.edu/history-500africanvoices/96/ [see 102.1].

¶ This man from unspecified origins was taken in the transatlantic slave trade. While on the slave ship, he and others (including one who spoke with Oldendorp, q.v. 101.0) conspired to revolt. After a *Bomba* (Black supervisor) discovered the plan and informed the captain, the rebels found a cannon pointed at them as they began to emerge from below deck. He and the others then gave up and were placed in irons. Many of them, including this man, were severely flogged. After arrival in the Danish West Indies (see Map 14), he was sold, and in 1767–1768 he and his comrade (q.v. 101.0) told Oldendorp about their experiences.

102.1 ——. [Complete edition, with annotations, of 102.0]

Aspects of his life transcribed from 102.0 and printed on pp. 504–505 in vol. 1 of C. G. A. Oldendorp, *Historie der caribischen Inseln Sanct Thomas, Sanct Crux und Sanct Jan, insbesondere der dasigen Neger und der Mission der evangelischen Brüder unter denselben: kommentierte Ausgabe des vollständigen Manuskriptes aus dem Archiv der Evangelischen Brüder-Unität Herrnhut*, edited by Gudrun Meier et al. (Band [Volume] 51 in the series *Abhandlungen und Berichte des Staatlichen Museums für Völkerkunde Dresden*).

Berlin [Germany]: VWB, Verlag für Wissenschaft und Bildung, 2000–2002.

2 vols. in 4, 8vo (24 cm.).
Vol. 1 (2000): 764 p.; xxxviii, illus.

Figure 8: The frigate and slave ship *Fredensborg II*. The vessel is equipped with three large valves to supply air to the enslaved people below deck. It sailed from the Danish slave trading post Fort Christiansborg in Accra on the Gold Coast to the Danish West Indies.

Source: Colored drawing, late 18th century, artist unknown. The Danish Maritime Museum, Kronborg, Denmark.

1768

103.0 Joseph (ca. 1698–1768)

Aspects of this man's life story summarized in Christian Georg Andreas Oldendorp's 3,000-page manuscript account of Oldendorp's **1767–1768** tour of Denmark's West Indian possessions, viz. "Manuskript für eine Geschichte der Mission auf den westindischen Inseln, verfasst von C. G. A. Oldendorp," R.28.63 and R.28.62, held in the Unity Archives, **Herrnhut, Saxony, Germany.**

¶ Joseph identified as Kassenti (Tchamba, possibly Temba people in northern Togo—see Map 5). He was taken in the transatlantic slave trade to St. Croix in the Danish West Indies (Map 14). There he joined the Moravian mission and

Full text: https:// huskiecommons. lib.niu.edu/histo-ry-500africanvoic-es/97/ [see 103.1].

was baptized in 1752 at age fifty-four. Two years later he was admitted to communion. His overseer treated him badly and did not always allow him to attend services. He spoke with Oldendorp in 1767–1768 and died soon thereafter.

103.1 ——. [Complete edition, with annotations, of 103.0]

Aspects of his life story transcribed from 103.0 and printed on pp. 1820–1821 in vol. 2, Part 3 of C. G. A. Oldendorp, *Historie der caribischen Inseln Sanct Thomas, Sanct Crux und Sanct Jan, insbesondere der dasigen Neger und der Mission der evangelischen Brüder unter denselben: kommentierte Ausgabe des vollständigen Manuskriptes aus dem Archiv der Evangelischen Brüder-Unität Herrnhut*, edited by Gudrun Meier et al. (Band [Volume] 51 in the series *Abhandlungen und Berichte des Staatlichen Museums für Völkerkunde Dresden*).

Berlin [Germany]: VWB, Verlag für Wissenschaft und Bildung, 2000–2002.

2 vols. in 4, 8vo (24 cm.).

Vol. 2 (consecutively numbered), Part 3 (2002): vii; 1405–2171 p.

104.0 Aaron (1698–1768)

Aspects of this man's life story summarized in Christian Georg Andreas Oldendorp's 3,000-page manuscript account of Oldendorp's **1767–1768** tour of Denmark's West Indian possessions, viz. "Manuskript für eine Geschichte der Mission auf den westindischen Inseln, verfasst von C.G. A. Oldendorp," R.28.63 and R.28.62, held in the Unity Archives, Herrnhut, Saxony, Germany.

Full text: https://huskiecommons.lib.niu.edu/history-500africanvoices/98/ [see 104.1].

¶ Aaron identified as Amina (a New World ethnic designation for Akan speakers near Elmina Castle, present-day Ghana—see Map 5). He was taken in the transatlantic slave trade to St. Croix in the Danish West Indies (Map 14). In old age he joined the Moravian mission and was baptized in 1767. Thereafter, he embraced the Moravian faith and tried hard to attend services, even when ill and hindered by his Black supervisor (*Bomba*). In 1767–1768 he spoke with Oldendorp, who noted that when Aaron died in 1768 many people attended his funeral.

104.1 ——. [Complete edition, with annotations, of 104.0]

Aspects of his life story transcribed from 104.0 and printed on pp. 1821–1822 in vol. 2, Part 3 of C. G. A. Oldendorp, *Historie der caribischen Inseln Sanct Thomas, Sanct Crux und Sanct Jan, insbesondere der dasigen Neger und der Mission der evangelischen Brüder unter denselben: kommentierte Ausgabe des vollständigen Manuskriptes aus dem Archiv der Evangelischen Brüder-Unität Herrnhut*, edited by Gudrun Meier et al. (Band [Volume] 51 in the series *Abhandlungen und Berichte des Staatlichen Museums für Völkerkunde Dresden*).

Berlin [Germany]: VWB, Verlag für Wissenschaft und Bildung, 2000–2002.

2 vols. in 4, 8vo (24 cm.).

Vol. 2 (consecutively numbered), Part 3 (2002): vii; 1405–2171 p.

105.0 Anna Margaretha (–1768)

Aspects of this woman's life story summarized in Christian Georg Andreas Oldendorp's 3,000-page manuscript account of Oldendorp's **1767–1768** tour of Denmark's West Indian

possessions, viz. "Manuskript für eine Geschichte der Mission auf den westindischen Inseln, verfasst von C. G. A. Oldendorp," R.28.63 and R.28.62, held in the Unity Archives, Herrnhut, Saxony, Germany.

Full text: https://huskiecommons.lib.niu.edu/history-500africanvoices/99/ [see 105.1].

¶ Anna Margaretha identified as Carabali (Carabali—of Calabar, Cross River region, southeastern Nigeria and northwest Cameroon). She was taken in the transatlantic slave trade to St. Croix in the Danish West Indies and sold. Sometime thereafter she began attending the Moravian mission at Friedensthal and was baptized in 1761. Later she was admitted to communion, but weakness from old age prevented her from attending frequently. She died peacefully in 1768, not long after she and Oldendorp conversed.

105.1 ——. [Complete edition, with annotations, of 105.0]

Aspects of her life story transcribed from 105.0 and printed on p. 1822 in vol. 2, Part 3 of C. G. A. Oldendorp, *Historie der caribischen Inseln Sanct Thomas, Sanct Crux und Sanct Jan, insbesondere der dasigen Neger und der Mission der evangelischen Brüder unter denselben: kommentierte Ausgabe des vollständigen Manuskriptes aus dem Archiv der Evangelischen Brüder-Unität Herrnhut*, edited by Gudrun Meier et al. (Band [Volume] 51 in the series *Abhandlungen und Berichte des Staatlichen Museums für Völkerkunde Dresden*).

Berlin [Germany]: VWB, Verlag für Wissenschaft und Bildung, 2000–2002.

2 vols. in 4, 8vo (24 cm.).

Vol. 2 (consecutively numbered), Part 3 (2002): vii; 1405–2171 p.

106.0 Barbara (–1768)

Aspects of this woman's life story summarized in Christian Georg Andreas Oldendorp's 3,000-page manuscript account of Oldendorp's **1767–1768** tour of Denmark's West Indian possessions, viz. "Manuskript für eine Geschichte der Mission auf den westindischen Inseln, verfasst von C. G. A. Oldendorp," R.28.63 and R.28.62, held in the Unity Archives, Herrnhut, Saxony, Germany.

Full text: https://huskiecommons.lib.niu.edu/history-500africanvoices/100/ [see 106.1].

¶ Barbara said that she was from a place in West Africa called Tim (referring possibly to the Temne people in present-day

Sierra Leone—see Map 4). She was taken in the transatlantic slave trade to St. Croix in the Danish West Indies (Map 14). She joined the Moravian mission and was baptized in 1755 but did not immediately fully embrace the faith. She was ill for many years before she and Oldendorp conversed on St. Croix, where she died in 1768.

106.1 ——. [Complete edition, with annotations, of 106.0]

Aspects of her life story transcribed from 106.0 and printed on p. 1822 in vol. 2, Part 3 of C. G. A. Oldendorp, *Historie der caribischen Inseln Sanct Thomas, Sanct Crux und Sanct Jan, insbesondere der dasigen Neger und der Mission der evangelischen Brüder unter denselben: kommentierte Ausgabe des vollständigen Manuskriptes aus dem Archiv der Evangelischen Brüder-Unität Herrnhut*, edited by Gudrun Meier et al. (Band [Volume] 51 in the series *Abhandlungen und Berichte des Staatlichen Museums für Völkerkunde Dresden*).

Berlin [Germany]: VWB, Verlag für Wissenschaft und Bildung, 2000–2002.
2 vols. in 4, 8vo (24 cm.).
Vol. 2 (consecutively numbered), Part 3 (2002): vii; 1405–2171 p.

107.0 Jonathan (–1768)

Aspects of this man's life story summarized in Christian Georg Andreas Oldendorp's 3,000-page manuscript account of Oldendorp's 1767–1768 tour of Denmark's West Indian possessions, viz. "Manuskript für eine Geschichte der Mission auf den westindischen Inseln, verfasst von C. G. A. Oldendorp," R.28.63 and R.28.62, held in the Unity Archives, **Herrnhut, Saxony, Germany.**

¶ Jonathan, who identified as Carabali (Carabali—Calabar, Cross River region, southeastern Nigeria and northwest Cameroon), was taken in the transatlantic slave trade to St. Croix in the Danish West Indies (see Map 14) and sold. While enslaved he learned the wheelwright's trade. He joined the Moravian mission, was baptized in 1755, and was admitted to communion in 1761. Eventually, physical weakness and the distance to the mission made it difficult for him to attend services. He died peacefully on St. Croix in 1768, shortly after conversing with Oldendorp.

Full text: https:// huskiecommons. lib.niu.edu/history-500africanvoices/101/ [see 107.1].

107.1 ——. [Complete edition, with annotations, of 107.0]

Aspects of his life story transcribed from 107.0 and printed on pp. 1824–1825 in vol. 2, Part 3 of C. G. A. Oldendorp, *Historie der caribischen Inseln Sanct Thomas, Sanct Crux und Sanct Jan, insbesondere der dasigen Neger und der Mission der evangelischen Brüder unter denselben: kommentierte Ausgabe des vollständigen Manuskriptes aus dem Archiv der Evangelischen Brüder-Unität Herrnhut*, edited by Gudrun Meier et al. (Band [Volume] 51 in the series *Abhandlungen und Berichte des Staatlichen Museums für Völkerkunde Dresden*).

Berlin [Germany]: VWB, Verlag für Wissenschaft und Bildung, 2000–2002.
2 vols. in 4, 8vo (24 cm.).
Vol. 2 (consecutively numbered), Part 3 (2002): vii; 1405–2171 p.

1768–1769

108.0 Ofodobendo Wooma (ca. 1726–1779) = Andrew the Moor

Two manuscript sources of variant (complementary) accounts are extant, viz.:

108.0a: Christian Georg Andreas Oldendorp summarized Ofodobendo Wooma's life story (without naming him, but as heard directly from him) in his own 3,000-page manuscript account of his (Oldendorp's) 1767–1768 tour of Denmark's West Indian possessions, viz. "Manuskript für eine Geschichte der Mission auf den westindischen Inseln, verfasst von C. G. A. Oldendorp," R.28.63 and R.28.62, held in the Unity Archives,

Full text: https:// huskiecommons. lib.niu.edu/history-500africanvoices/102/ [see 108.6].

Herrnhut, Saxony, Germany. Only an abbreviated version of this lengthy manuscript was published in 1777 (108.1). It was not published in its entirety until 2000–2002 (108.6).

108.0b: Ofodobendo Wooma's own undated manuscript memoir (Lebenslauf) survives in German and English in the Moravian Archives, **Bethlehem, Pennsylvania, U.S.A.** This was first published in 1988 (108.4).

¶ Ofodobendo Wooma identified as Ibo (Igbo, present-day southeastern Nigeria). He came from a place called Alo (Meier: Edo? Or less probably, Aro?), in a large country deep in the interior, not far from Egypt (see Map 5). His people had no body markings and traded for Turkish goods. He described their religious practices, including healing, which he himself experienced after a severe illness or injury. When he was about eight years old his father died, after which his half-brother sent him to another man as a servant for two years. In the late 1730s he was about twelve when his half-brother sold him into slavery. His first owners took him on a long journey (during which he encountered many different peoples whose customs he details) to the seacoast, where European slave traders sold him to an English slave ship that took him to Antigua, the British colony in the Caribbean (Map 11). From there ca. 1741 he was taken to the colonial British North American port of New York (Map 17). There a Moravian came across Ofodobendo Wooma—who was then contemplating suicide—and purchased him. In 1745, after he had embraced Moravian Christianity, he was taken to that group's mostly German settlement of Bethlehem, in the nearby British colony of Pennsylvania (Map 16), where he lived enslaved for the rest of his life. In 1762 Ofodobendo Wooma married Magdelene Beulah Brocken (q.v. 19.0), a freed Moravian woman, and together they had three children. In 1768 or 1769 he met Oldendorp (who had stopped in Bethlehem on his journey back to Europe from his mission in the West Indies) and told him his life story up to that year (108.0a). Later, in the 1770s, Ofodobendo Wooma wrote a late-life memoir, or *Lebenslauf*, in German (108.0b), as was customary for Moravians.

108.1 ———.

Account printed from 108.0a on pp. 286 and 307 of Christian Georg Andreas Oldendorp, *Geschichte der Mission der evangelischen Brueder auf den caraibischen Inseln S. Thomas, S. Croix, und S. Jan*, edited by Johann Jakob Bossart.

Barby [Saxony-Anhalt, Germany]: bey Christian Friedrich Laur, und in **Leipzig [Saxony, Germany]:** in Commission bey Weidmanns Erben und Reich, **1777.**
2 volumes in 1, 8vo (19 cm.), folding plates and maps, [12], 1068, index [52], p.
https://archive.org/details/cgaoldendorpsges12olde/page/286

108.2 ———.

Swedish translation of 108.1, C. G. A. Oldendorp, *Historiska beskrifning öfwer evangeliske brödernas miszions-arbete på caraibiske öarne St. Thomas St. Croix och St. Jan*, edited by Johann Jacob Bossart.

Stockholm [Sweden]: 1786–1788.
[Vol. 1] *Första delen, som innehåller åtskilliga efterrättelser, hörande til öarnes geographie, natural-historia och politiska författningar.*
Stockholm [Sweden]: tryckt hos commiss. P.A. Brodin, **1786.**
8vo (18 cm): [4], 64, [2], 348 p., map, 1 folded table.
[Vol. 2] *Andra delen, som innehåller miszions-historien ifrån år 1732 til år 1768.* **Stockholm [Sweden]:** tryckt hos Johan Christopher Holmberg, **1788.**
8vo (18 cm): [2], 634, [4] p., folded leaves of plates: ill. (engravings).

108.3 ———.

English translation of 108.1 printed on p. 167 and 179 of C. G. A. Oldendorp, *History of the Mission of the Evangelical Brethren on the Caribbean Islands of St. Thomas, St. Croix, and St. John*, edited by Johann Jakob Bossard (i.e., Bossart), translated into English and further edited by Arnold R. Highfield and Vladimir Barac.

Ann Arbor [Michigan, U.S.A.]: Karoma Publishers, **1987.**
8vo (24 cm.): xxxv, 737 p., illus.

108.4 ———.

His memoir/*Lebenslauf* (108.0b) printed in German and English with commentary and editorial annotations by Daniel Thorp as "Chattel With a Soul: The Autobiography of a Moravian Slave," in the academic journal *The Pennsylvania Magazine of History & Biography* 112(3) (July 1988): 433–451.

Philadelphia, Pennsylvania [U.S.A.]: Historical Society of Pennsylvania, **1988.**
8vo (24.2 cm.).

108.5 ———.

108.1 printed on pp. 286 and 307 in photomechanical reprint of the 1777 edition of C. G. A. Oldendorp, *Geschichte der Mission der evangelischen Brüder auf den caraibischen Inseln S. Thomas, S. Croix und S. Jan*, edited by Erich Beyreuther and Matthias Meyer (Volume 27.1 in Series 2 of Nikolaus Ludwig Graf von Zinzendorf, *Leben und Werk in Quellen und Darstellungen*).

Hildesheim [Saxony, Germany]: Georg Olms Verlag, **1995.**
8vo (20 cm.): 62, 444 p., illus.

108.6 ———. [Complete edition, with annotations, of 108.0a]

Account transcribed from 108.0a and printed on pp. 431–434 and 487 in vol. 1 of C. G. A. Oldendorp, *Historie der caribischen Inseln Sanct Thomas, Sanct Crux und Sanct Jan, insbesondere der dasigen Neger und der Mission der evangelischen Brüder unter denselben: kommentierte Ausgabe des vollständigen Manuskriptes aus dem Archiv der Evangelischen Brüder-Unität Herrnhut*, edited by Gudrun Meier et al. (Band [Volume] 51 in the series *Abhandlungen und Berichte des Staatlichen Museums für Völkerkunde Dresden*).

Berlin [Germany]: VWB, Verlag für Wissenschaft und Bildung, **2000–2002.**
2 vols. in 4, 8vo (24 cm.).
Vol. 1 (2000): 764 p.; xxxviii, illus.

109.0   First unnamed African man in Pennsylvania

This unnamed man's life story summarized in Christian Georg Andreas Oldendorp's 3,000-page manuscript account of Oldendorp's **1767–1768** tour of Denmark's West Indian possessions, viz. "Manuskript für eine Geschichte der Mission auf den westindischen Inseln, verfasst von C. G. A. Oldendorp," R.28.63 and R.28.62, held in the Unity Archives, **Herrnhut, Saxony, Germany.**

Full text: https://huskiecommons.lib.niu.edu/history-500africanvoices/103/ [see 109.1].

¶ Married and with children, this West African man was kidnapped one night while getting water at a well for a sick child. He never saw his family again and was taken in the transatlantic slave trade by some unknown route to the British North American province of Pennsylvania (see Map 16). By the time he conversed with Oldendorp there in 1768 or 1769 he had learned English.

109.1———. [Complete edition, with annotations, of 109.0]

Account transcribed from 109.0 and printed on p. 568–569 in vol. 1 of C. G. A. Oldendorp, *Historie der caribischen Inseln Sanct Thomas, Sanct Crux und Sanct Jan, insbesondere der dasigen Neger und der Mission der evangelischen Brüder unter denselben: kommentierte Ausgabe des vollständigen Manuskriptes aus dem Archiv der Evangelischen Brüder-Unität Herrnhut,* edited by Gudrun Meier et al. (= Band [Volume] 51 in the series *Abhandlungen und Berichte des Staatlichen Museums für Völkerkunde Dresden*).

Berlin [Germany]: VWB, Verlag für Wissenschaft und Bildung, 2000–2002.
2 vols. in 4, 8vo (24 cm.).
Vol. 1 (2000): 764 p.; xxxviii, illus.

110.0   Second unnamed African man in Pennsylvania

This unnamed man's life story summarized in Christian Georg Andreas Oldendorp's 3,000-page manuscript account of Oldendorp's **1767–1768** tour of Denmark's West Indian possessions, *viz.* "Manuskript für eine Geschichte der Mission auf den westindischen Inseln, verfasst von C. G. A. Oldendorp," R.28.63 and R.28.62, held in the Unity Archives, **Herrnhut, Saxony, Germany.**

Full text: https://huskiecommons.lib.niu.edu/history-500africanvoices/104/ [see 110.1].

¶ This man was from some unknown place in West Africa (Guinea—see Map 3)), where he was married and had three children. After capture, separation from his family, and forcible transportation on a slave ship to Jamaica in the West Indies (Map 13), he married again and had two more children. After several years in Jamaica he was separated from this family, sold, and transported to the British North American colony of South Carolina (Map 15). There he married a third time and had one child before he was sold away from his wife and child and forcibly transported north to the province of Pennsylvania (Map 16), where he conversed with Oldendorp in 1768–69.

110.1———. [Complete edition, with annotations, of 110.0]

His life story transcribed from 110.0 and printed on p. 569 in vol. 1 of C. G. A. Oldendorp, *Historie der caribischen Inseln Sanct Thomas, Sanct Crux und Sanct Jan, insbesondere der dasigen Neger und der Mission der evangelischen Brüder unter denselben: kommentierte Ausgabe des vollständigen Manuskriptes aus dem Archiv der Evangelischen Brüder-Unität Herrnhut,* edited by Gudrun Meier et al. (Band [Volume] 51 in the series *Abhandlungen und Berichte des Staatlichen Museums für Völkerkunde Dresden*).

Berlin [Germany]: VWB, Verlag für Wissenschaft und Bildung, 2000–2002.
2 vols. in 4, 8vo (24 cm.).
Vol. 1 (2000): 764 p.; xxxviii, illus.

1769

111.1   Ignatius Sancho (1729–1780)

Letters of the late Ignatius Sancho, an African. In two volumes [edited by Miss Frances Crewe]. *To which are prefixed, Memoirs of his Life* [by Joseph Jekyll] …

London [England]: Printed by J. Nichols: and sold by J. Dodsley, in Pall Mall; J. Robson, in New Bond Street; J. Walter,

Charing Cross; R. Baldwin, Paternoster-Row; and J. Sewell, Cornhill, MDCCLXXXII [1782].
Note: According to Vincent Carretta (in 109.20, below), the earliest of Sancho's letters here published for the first time dates from 1769.

2 vols., 8vo (18 cm.), plates (including portrait of Sancho engraved by Francesco Bartelozzi after the oil portrait by

Thomas Gainsborough, now in Canada's National Gallery of Art, Ottawa, Ontario), and a **list of subscribers**.
ESTC t100345.

¶ Sancho was born *ca.* 1729 on a slave ship bound for the port of Cartegena in the Spanish South American province of New Grenada (modern Colombia—see Map 9). Sancho's mother died shortly after their arrival, and his father was said to have committed suicide. In 1731, aged two, Sancho was sent to Greenwich (a town on the Thames River east of London), England, as a gift to a family there (Map 8). Mistreated by the recipients, he was nonetheless educated through the efforts of the second Duke of Montagu (John Montagu, 1690–1749), who became his patron. In 1758 Sancho married a black woman. In 1773 he published some of his musical compositions. He began keeping a grocery store in nearby Westminster and doubling as a butler and valet in 1774, when he also became the first Afro-Briton to gain the right to vote. He died in 1780. Two years later one of his female correspondents, Frances Crewe, edited and published his letters (111.1). For more on Sancho see Vincent Carretta's introduction to *Ignatius Sancho: Letters of the Late Ignatius Sancho, an African* (New York: Penguin Books, 1998), ix–xxxii.

111.2 ——.

*Letters of the late Ignatius Sancho, an African. In two volumes. To which are prefixed, Memoirs of his life. ... **The second edition.***

London [England]: Printed for J. Nichols; and C. Dilly, in the Poultry, MDCCLXXXIII [1783].
2 vols., 8vo (18 cm.), plate.
ESTC t100276 ("Vol.2 is without an edition statement").

111.3 ——.

Letters of the late Ignatius Sancho, an African. To which are prefixed, Memoirs of his life. **The third edition.**

London [England]: Printed by J. Nichols; and sold by C. Dilly, in the Poultry, MDCCLXXXIV [1784].
12mo (18 cm.): xiv, 393, [1]p., engraved portrait.
https://archive.org/details/lettersoflateign00sanc_0
ESTC n2867.

111.4 ——.

Letters of the late Ignatius Sancho, an African. In two volumes. To which is prefixed, Memoirs of his life. The third edition.

Vol. 1: http://docsouth.unc.edu/neh/sancho1/sancho1.html
Vol. 2: http://docsouth.unc.edu/neh/sancho2/sancho2.html [see 111.1].

Dublin [Ireland]: Printed by Brett Smith, for Richard Moncrieffe, **1784**.
2 vols. (continuously paged) in one, 12mo (18 cm.): xiii, [1], 310 p., portrait.
ESTC t180688.

111.5 ——.

Letters of the late Ignatius Sancho, an African. In two volumes. To which is prefixed, Memoirs of his life.

Dublin [Ireland]: Printed by Pat. Byrne, No. 35, College-Green, MDCCLXXXIV [1784].
2 vols. In one, 12mo (18 cm.): (continuously paged) xiii, [1], 310 p., portrait.
https://babel.hathitrust.org/cgi/pt?id=chi.090385369&view=1up&seq=9
ESTC t119146 ("The title page to vol.1 is a cancel" and "Possibly another issue of the 1784 Dublin edition printed by Brett Smith for Richard Moncrieffe," *i.e.* 109.4 above).

111.6 ——.

*Letters of the late Ignatius Sancho, an African. To which are prefixed, Memoirs of his life, by Joseph Jekyll ... **The fifth edition.***

London [England]: Printed for William Sancho, Charles-Street, Westminster, 1803. (Wilks and Taylor, Printers, Chancery-lane.)
8vo (22 cm.): 2 p.1., xvi, 310 p., frontispiece portrait, folding facsimile.
https://babel.hathitrust.org/cgi/pt?id=hvd.hxger6&view=1up&seq=11

111.7——.

Condensed biographical sketch including quotations from his letters printed as nine numbered paragraphs on pp. 6–8 in *Biographical Sketches and Interesting Anecdotes of Persons of Color. To Which Is Added, a Selection of Pieces in Poetry*, compiled by A[bigail] Mott.

New York [New York, U.S.A.]: Printed and Sold by Mahlon Day, No. 376, Pearl-street, **1826**.
12mo (18 cm.): iv, [5]-192 p. Preface dated on p. iv: *Hickory Grove* [N.Y.], 11th mo. 1825.
http://docsouth.unc.edu/neh/mott26/mott26.html
https://babel.hathitrust.org/cgi/pt?id=hvd.hn3m6e&view=1up&seq=10
Hogg 1467.

111.8——.

Condensed biographical sketch including quotations from his letters printed under heading "Ignatius Sancho" on pp. 3–5 in *Biographical Sketches and Interesting Anecdotes of Persons of Colour*, compiled by A[bigail] Mott.

York [Yorkshire, England]: Printed and Sold by W. Alexander & Son, Castlegate; sold also by Harvey & Darton, W. Phillips, E. Fry, and W. Darton, **London [England]**; R. Peart [*sic*], **Birmingham [England]**; D. F. Gardiner, **Dublin [Ireland]**, 1826.
12mo (20 cm.): xi, [2], 2–240 p.
https://babel.hathitrust.org/cgi/pt?id=nyp.33433081774204&view=1up&seq=23

111.9——.

Condensed biographical sketch including quotations from his letters printed under heading "Ignatius Sancho" on pp. 3–5 in *Biographical Sketches and Interesting Anecdotes of Persons of Color. To Which Is Added, a Selection of Pieces in Poetry*, compiled by A[bigail] Mott. "Second Edition."

York [Yorkshire, England]: Printed and Sold by W. Alexander & Son; sold also by Harvey and Darton, W. Phillips, E. Fry, and W. Darton, **London [England]**; R. Peart, **Birmingham [England]**; D. F. Gardiner, **Dublin [Ireland]**, 1828.
8vo (19.8 cm.): xi, [1], 252 p.

111.10 ——.

Concise account of his life printed on pp. 169–170, within Chapter VI ("Intellect of Negroes") in Mrs. [Lydia Maria] Child, *An Appeal in Favor of that Class of Americans called Africans.*

Boston [Massachusetts, U.S.A.]: Allen and Ticknor, 1833. Tpv: Tuttle & Weeks, Printers, No. 8, School Street.
8vo (20 cm.): [vi], 323 p.
https://babel.hathitrust.org/cgi/pt?id=nyp.33433075994958&view=1up&seq=183

111.11——.

Condensed biographical sketch including quotations from his letters printed under heading "Ignatius Sancho" on pp. 6–8 in *Biographical Sketches and Interesting Anecdotes of Persons of Color. To Which Is Added, a Selection of Pieces in Poetry*, compiled by A[bigail] Mott. "Second Edition, much Enlarged."

New-York [New York, U.S.A.]: Mahlon Day, 374 Pearl-street, 1837. Tpv: "Note by the publisher. By consent of the Compiler, and at the recommendation of the Trustees of the African Free Schools in New York, (who have liberally patronized the work,) …"
8vo (19 cm.): 260 p. (of which p. [256] is blank, and pp. 257–260 are table of contents).
https://babel.hathitrust.org/cgi/pt?id=hvd.32044004358602;view=1up;seq=5

111.12——.

Condensed biographical sketch including quotations from his letters printed under heading "Ignatius Sancho" on pp. 9–11 in *Biographical Sketches and Interesting Anecdotes of Persons of Color. To Which Is Added, a Selection of Pieces in Poetry*, compiled by A[bigail] Mott.

New York [New York, U.S.A.]: Stereotyped for and printed by order of the Trustees of the residuary estate of Lindley Murray, M. Day, Printer, 374 Pearl St., 1838.
8vo (18.7 cm.): iv, 408 p.

111.13——.

Condensed biographical sketch including quotations from his letters printed under heading "Ignatius Sancho" on pp. 9–11 in *Biographical Sketches and Interesting Anecdotes of Persons of Color. To Which Is Added, a Selection of Pieces in Poetry*, compiled by A[bigail] Mott.

New York [New York, U.S.A.]: Stereotyped for and printed by order of the Trustees of the residuary estate of Lindley Murray. M. Day, Printer, 271 Pearl St. [1839]. Approximate year of printing (could be slightly later) from "Advertisement," p. [ii].
12mo (19 cm.): vi, [7]–408 p.
https://archive.org/details/biographicalsket00mottrich/page/n4 (incomplete 370-page exemplar).
https://babel.hathitrust.org/cgi/pt?id=loc.ark:/13960/t2q52p81p&view=1up&seq=3

111.14——.

Biographical sketch with letters printed under heading "Ignatius Sancho" on pp. 410–425 of Wilson Armistead's compendium *A Tribute for the Negro: Being a Vindication of the Moral Intellectual, and Religious Capabilities of the Colored Portion of Mankind; with Particular Reference to the African Race.*

Manchester [England]: William Irwin; **London [England]**: Charles Gilpin; American Agent: Wm. Harned, Anti-Slavery Office, 61, John Street, **New York [New York, U.S.A.]**; and may be had of H. Longstreath and G.W. Taylor, **Philadelphia [Pennsylvania, U.S.A.]**, 1848. Tpv: Manchester: Printed by William Irwin, 39, Oldham Street.
8vo (24 cm.): xxxv, 564 p.
https://babel.hathitrust.org/cgi/pt?id=nc01.ark:/13960/t42r4z659;view=1up;seq=13
http://docsouth.unc.edu/neh/armistead/armistead.html

111.15 ——.

Condensed biographical sketch including quotations from his letters printed under heading "Ignatius Sancho" on pp. 9–11 in *Biographical Sketches and Interesting Anecdotes of Persons* of Color. To Which Is Added, a Selection of Pieces in Poetry, compiled by A[bigail] Mott.

New York [New York, U.S.A.]: Stereotyped for and printed by order of the Trustees of the residuary estate of Lindley Murray, **1850.**
8vo (20 cm.): iv, [7]-408 p.

111.16——.
Condensed biographical sketch including quotations from his letters printed under heading "Ignatius Sancho" on pp. 9–11 in *Biographical Sketches and Interesting Anecdotes of Persons of Color. To Which Is Added, a Selection of Pieces in Poetry,* compiled by A[bigail] Mott.

New York [New York, U.S.A.]: Stereotyped for and printed by order of the Trustees of the residuary estate of Lindley Murray. D. Fanshaw, Printer, 35 Ann, corner of Nassau-street, **1854.**
12mo (19 cm.): iv, [7]-408 p.
https://digital.ncdcr.gov/digital/collection/p249901coll37/id/10207

111.17——. **[Photomechanical reprint of 109.6 (London, 1803), with new intro.]**
Letters of the late Ignatius Sancho, an African. To which are prefixed, Memoirs of his Life, by Joseph Jekyll, With [new] introduction by Paul Edwards.

London [England]: Dawson's, **1968.**
8vo (22 cm.): [4], xxvii, xvi, 310 p., illus., portrait.

111.18——. **[Photomechanical reprint of 109.6 (London, 1803)]**
Letters of the late Ignatius Sancho, an African. To which are prefixed, Memoirs of his Life, by Joseph Jekyll.

Freeport, New York [U.S.A.]: Books for Libraries Press, **1971.**
8vo (23 cm.): xvi, 310 p., illus., portrait. "First published 1802," an error for 1803.

111.19——.
Excerpts from his letters printed from 111.6 as reprinted in 111.17, with new introductory note, on pp. 24–38 in *Black Writers in Britain, 1760–1890: An Anthology,* edited by Paul Edwards and David Dabydeen.

Edinburgh [Scotland]: Edinburgh University Press, **1991.**
8vo (22 cm.): xv, 239 p.

111.20——.
The Letters of Ignatius Sancho, edited by Paul Edwards and Polly Rewt.

Edinburgh [Scotland]: Edinburgh University Press, **1994.**
8vo (23 cm.): xvi, 288 p.

111.21——. **[Second printing of 111.19]**
Excerpts from his letters printed from 111.6 as reprinted in 111.17, with new introductory note, on pp. 24–38 in *Black Writers in Britain, 1760–1890: An Anthology,* edited by Paul Edwards and David Dabydeen.

Edinburgh [Scotland]: Edinburgh University Press, **1995.**
8vo (22 cm.): xv, 239 p.

111.22——.
Letters of the Late Ignatius Sancho, An African, edited by Vincent Carretta.

New York [New York, U.S.A.]: Penguin Books, **1998.**
8vo (20 cm.): xlii, 336 p.

111.23——. **[Photomechanical reprint of 111.11]**
Condensed biographical sketch including quotations from his letters printed under heading "Ignatius Sancho" on pp. 6–8 in 有色人に関する伝記的資料 / *Biographical Sketches and Interesting Anecdotes of Persons of Color. To which is added, a Selection of Pieces in Poetry,* compiled by A[bigail] Mott. "Second Edition, much Enlarged."

Tokyo, Japan: 日本図書センター, Nihon Tosho Senta, **2000.**
8vo (27 cm.): 255 p.

111.24——.
Letters of the Late Ignatius Sancho, edited with introduction and notes by S. E. Ogude.

Lagos [Nigeria]: Centre for Black and African Arts and Civilization (CBAAC), **2002.**
8vo (22 cm.): x, 381 p.

111.25——. **[Third printing of 111.19]**
Excerpts from his letters printed from 111.6 as reprinted in 111.17, with new introductory note, on pp. 24–38 in *Black Writers in Britain, 1760–1890: An Anthology,* edited by Paul Edwards and David Dabydeen.

Edinburgh [Scotland]: Edinburgh University Press, **2003.**
8vo (22 cm.): xv, 239 p.

111.26——.
Extracts "From Letters of the Late Ignatius Sancho, an African" in *Early Black British Writing: Olaudah Equiano, Mary Prince, and others: Selected texts with introduction, critical essays,* edited by Alan Richardson and Debbie Lee.

Boston [Massachusetts, U.S.A.]: Houghton Mifflin; **London [England:]** Hi Marketing, 2003.
8vo (21 cm.): ix, 443 p.

111.27 ——.

Extracts "From Letters of the Late Ignatius Sancho, an African" in *Early Black British Writing: Olaudah Equiano, Mary Prince, and others: Selected texts with introduction, critical essays*, edited by Alan Richardson and Debbie Lee.

Boston [Massachusetts, U.S.A.]: Houghton Mifflin, **2004.**
8vo (21 cm.): ix, 443 p.

111.28 ——.

Account printed in vol. 1 of *The Norton Anthology of African American Literature*, edited by Henry Louis Gates Jr., Valerie Smith, and Robert G. O'Meally. **Second edition.**

New York [New York, U.S.A.]: W. W. Norton & Co., **2004.**
8vo (24 cm.): xlvii, 2776 p. + audio disc.

111.29 ——.

Account printed in vol. 1 of *The Norton Anthology of African American Literature*, edited by Henry Louis Gates Jr. and Valerie Smith. **Third edition.**

New York [New York, U.S.A.]: W. W. Norton & Co., **2014.**
2 vols., 8vo (24 cm.).

111.30 ——.

Letters of the Late Ignatius Sancho, An African, edited by Vincent Carretta.

Peterborough, Ontario [Canada]: Broadview Press, **2015**
8vo (22 cm.): xvi, 288 p.

Additional publications and unlocated works by Sancho

+111-A.1 ——.

Letter to Laurence Sterne, published in vol. 3, pp. 22–26 of *Letters of the late Rev. Mr. Laurence Sterne, to his most intimate friends. With a fragment in the manner of Rabelais. To which are prefix'd, Memoirs of his Life and Family. Writ-* ten by himself. And published by his daughter, Mrs. Medalle (London [England]: Printed for T. Becket, 1775). 3 vols., 8vo. Note: This letter subsequently included in the 1782 collection of Sancho's letters.

https://quod.lib.umich.edu/e/ecco/004792533.0001.003/1:2.6?rgn=div2;view=fulltext

+111-A.2 ——.

Letter to Laurence Sterne, being item +111-A.1 reprinted on p. 29 of *The Gentleman's Magazine* (London [England]: Printed for D. Henry) 46 (1776): 29.

https://babel.hathitrust.org/cgi/pt?id=pst.000068789299;view=1up;seq=41

+111-B.1 ——.

Twelve country dances for the year 1779. Set for the harpsichord. By permission humbly dedicated to the Right Honourable Miss North, by her most obedient servant Ignatius Sancho (London [England]: S. and A. Thompson [1779]). 13 leaves, including title leaf, engraved on one side only; the whole measuring 12 x 24 cm. https://imslp.org/wiki/12_Country_Dances_(Sancho%2C_Ignatius)

+111-C.1 ——.

Ignatius Sancho (1729–1780), An Early African Composer in England: The Collected Editions of his Music in Facsimile, edited by Josephine R. B. Wright (New York [New York, U.S.A.]: Garland Publishing, 1981).

+111-D.1 ——.

Two Minuets and a Rondo for the year 1767, for String Orchestra, edited by William Bauer (Louisville, Kentucky, [U.S.A.]: Africanus Editions, [1998]).

+111-E.1, etc. ——.

According to Carretta (*Ignatius Sancho*, xiii) Sancho also wrote and published a *Theory of Music* (of which no exemplars have yet been identified or located), two plays, and several newspaper essays.

1772

112.1 Ukawsaw Gronniosaw (1712–) = James Albert Ukawsaw Gronniosaw

A Narrative of the Most Remarkable Particulars in the Life of James Albert Ukawsaw Gronniosaw, an African Prince, as Related by Himself.

Bath [Somerset, England]: Printed by W. Gye in Westgate-Street: and sold by T. Mills, Bookseller, in King's-Mead Square. Price Six-Pence. [1772].
12mo (17.5 cm.): v, [1], 39 p. Preface signed in type: W. Shirley.

http://docsouth.unc.edu/neh/gronniosaw/gronnios.html

http://www.gutenberg.org/files/ 15042/15042-h/15042-h.htm
Porter 95 (positing date 1780?); ESTC t173626 (positing date 1775?, apparently discounting significance of "Republish'd" in ESTC n504730's imprint [our 112.3], and unaware of Vincent Carretta's 1996 publication [in our 112.34] of 21 and 27 December 1772 newspaper advertisements for the present edition). Some exemplars formerly catalogued with 1770 as supplied year of printing. Hogg 1459.

https://babel. hathitrust.org/cgi/ pt?id=mdp.690150 00002903&view= 1up&seq=9 (lacking the half-title) [see 112.9].

¶ Gronniosaw was born in Bournou (probably Borno, modern Nigeria—see Map 5), supposedly the grandson of the king. He was taken to the Gold Coast (modern Ghana) and sold to a Dutch captain. The captain took him to Barbados in the Caribbean (Map 11) and there sold him to a man from New York, who took him to that British North American port city and kept him enslaved as a house servant before reselling him (Map 17). Sent to school by his new owner, Gronniosaw converted to Christianity. Shortly before this owner died, he freed Gronniosaw. Later Gronniosaw sailed with a privateer, fought in the Caribbean during the Seven Years War (1756–1763), then traveled to England, living in Portsmouth and London (Map 8). After moving to Amsterdam, Holland (Map 7), he was examined by Calvinist ministers and worked for a year as a merchant's butler. He then returned to England, married a widow, and became associated with the Huntingdonian Methodists (q.v. "Huntingdon, Selina" in *The Oxford Dictionary of the Christian Church*, edited by F. L. Cross, 1957 et seq.). Thereafter he and his wife lived in poverty with their children in Essex, Colchester, Norwich (Norfolk), and Kidderminster [England]. For more on him see *Oxford Dictionary of National Biography* (online), 28 May 2015.

112.2 ——.
A Narrative of the Most Remarkable Particulars in the Life of James Albert Ukawsaw Gronniosaw, an African prince, as Related by Himself.

Bath [Somerset, England]: Printed and sold by S. Hazard, in King's-Mead-Square. - Sold also by T. Mills, Wine-Street, **Bristol** [England]; S. Chirm, near Aldersgate-Bars, **London** [England]; and by W. Walker, **Ashburn, Derbyshire** [England]. Price Six-Pence. [1774?].
12mo: 49, [1] p. Preface signed in type: W. Shirley.
Porter 91 (positing date 1770?); ESTC t66449 (positing date 1780, apparently unaware of Vincent Carretta's 1996 publication [in 112.34, on his p. 54] of evidence suggesting the date 1774).

112.3 ——.
A Narrative of the Most Remarkable Particulars in the Life of James Albert Ukawsaw Gronniosaw, an African prince, as Related by Himself.

[N.b.] Republish'd by H.G. **Canterbury** [Kent, England]: Printed and sold by T. Smith and Son (Price six-pence), **1774**.
12mo (18 cm.): vii, [1], 39, [1] p.
Not in Porter; ESTC n504730.

112.4 ——.
A Narrative of the Most Remarkable Particulars in the Life of James Albert Ukawsaw Gronnoisaw, an African Prince, [n.b.] *Written by Himself.*

Bath Printed: **Newport, Rhode-Island**: Reprinted [from 112.1 or 112.2?] and sold by S. Southwick, in Queen-Street, **1774**.
8vo (17.5 cm.): 48 p. Preface signed in type: W. Shirley.
Note: Printer-publisher Solomon Southwick (1731–1797) was father to the Solomon Southwick (1773–1839) who (with his own brother-in-law and business partner John Barber) published Phyllis Wheatley at Albany, NY, in 1793 (our 111.6 below).
Evans 13311 (under Grouniosaw [sic], James Albert Ukuwsau [sic]); Alden 541 (under author's name as spelled on title-page; and locating "just published" advertisement in a 22 August 1774 newspaper); Porter 93; ESTC w13758.

112.5 ——. [German version]
Merkwürdige Lebensbeschreibung Jacob Alberts oder Ukasow Gronniosaw, eines afrikanischen Prinzen: herausgegeben von W. Shirley; nebst den Gedanken über die Sklaverey von John Wesley. Aus dem Englischen übersetzt.

Leipzig [Saxony, Germany]: bey Christian Gottlob Hilschern, **1777**.
8vo: [8], 102 p. *Vorrede* signed in type: W. Shirley.
http://reader.digitale-sammlungen.de/de/fs1/object/display/ bsh10067469_00001.html.

112.6 ——. [Welsh version]
Berr hanes o'r pethau mwyaf hynod ym mywyd James Albert Ukawsaw Gronniosaw, Tywysog o Affrica - fel yr adroddwyd ganddo ef ei hun. Aberhonddu, Argraffwyd dros y Parch.

Aberhonddu (Brecon) [Wales]: Argraphwyd dros y Parch. Mr. W. Williams, gan E. Evans, **1779**.
12mo (16.5 cm.): 48 p. Preface signed in type: W. Shirley. Translated from English into Welsh by William Williams (1717–1791) of Pant-y-Celyn.
Porter 94; ESTC t89375.

112.7 ——. [Welsh version]

Berr hanes o'r pethau mwyaf hynod ym mywyd James Albert Ukawsaw Gronniosaw, Tywysog o Affrica - fel yr adroddwyd ganddo ef ei hun. Aberhonddu, Argraffwyd dros y Parch.

Aberhonddu (Brecon) [Wales]: Argraphwyd dros y Parch. Mr. W. Williams, gan E. Evans, **1780.**

12mo (17 cm.): 48 p. Preface signed in type: W. Shirley. Translated from English into Welsh by William Williams (1717–1791) of Pant-y-Celyn.

Not in Porter; not in ESTC as of 26 Nov. 2002 (as noted in OCLC 1118592231) nor as of 30 March 2021.

112.8 ——.

A Narrative of the Most Remarkable Particulars in the Life of James Albert Ukawsaw Gronnoisaw, an African Prince, Written by Himself.

Providence, Rhode-Island [U.S.A.]: Printed by Bennett Wheeler, **1781.**

No copy located.

Evans 17180 (under Grouniosaw [*sic*], James Albert Ukuwsaw [*sic*]); Alden 858 (citing Evans's entry, but like him locating no copy); Porter 96 (no copy located); Shipton-Mooney (vol. 1, p. 12, under "Albert, James, Ukawsaw Gronniosaw"), noting "Entry from an advt.," and asserting "probably for a remainder of the 1774 ed.," i.e., our item 112.4. *Nota bene*: The present compilers suggest that if printer-publisher Bennett Wheeler handled this supposititious seven-year-old remainder, he would very likely have printed a new title leaf, making it a reissue of our item 110.4 with cancellans title leaf (and thus a discrete book). Yet he might have printed an entirely new edition. Be this as it may, the supposition of a remainder sale for so old a book at this time *without* cancellans title leaf seems strained. Either a re-issue with cancellans title leaf or a new edition would qualify for this entry—and Wheeler's advertisement was, we think, probably for one or the other.

112.9 ——.

*A Narrative of the Most Remarkable Particulars in the Life of James Albert Ukawsaw Gronniosaw, an African Prince, as Related by Himself. ... **The Second Edition.***

[?Glasgow, Scotland?, 1785?].

12mo (16 cm.): 47, [1] p. Does not include W. Shirley's preface. Type size reduced after p. 44.

https://babel.hathitrust.org/cgi/pt?id=mdp.69015000002903 &view=1up&seq=9 (lacking the half-title).

Porter 92; ESTC t88121.

112.10 ——. [Same work, retitled]

The Life and Conversion of James Albert Ukawsaw Gronniosaw, an African Prince. Giving an Account of the Religion, Customs, Manners, &c. of the Natives of Zaara, in Africa. As Related by Himself.

Clonmel [Ireland]: Printed by Thomas Lord, In the year M,D-CC,LXXXVI. [**1786**].

16mo: 50 p.

Not in Porter; ESTC t169038. Exemplar at the National Library of Ireland, Dublin.

112.11 ——.

A Narrative of the Most Remarkable Particulars in the Life of James Albert Ukawsaw Gronniosaw, an African Prince, as Related by Himself.

Dublin [Ireland]: Printed by B. Dugdale, No. 150, Capel-Street, M,DCC,XC. [**1790**].

12mo (16 cm.): 45 p. + advertisements. Preface signed in type: W. Shirley.

https://babel.hathitrust.org/cgi/pt?id=emu.010002406384&v iew=1up&seq=1

Porter 97 (reporting 48 p.); ESTC t88120.

112.12a ——.

A Narrative of the Most Remarkable Particulars in the Life of James Albert Ukawsaw Gronniosaw, an African Prince, as Related by Himself. ... To which is added, An Authentic Account of the Conversion and Experience of a Negro.

Edinburgh [Scotland]: Printed and sold by Hugh Inglis; and sold by W. Laing, Bookseller, M.DCC.XC. [**1790**]. [Exemplar in Princeton Theological Seminary Library, Princeton, New Jersey, U.S.A..]

12mo (18 cm.): viii, [9]-48 p. Preface signed in type: W. Shirley (p. viii). **Additional text** printed after caption title on p. 45: "An Authentic Account of the Conversion and Experience of a Negro." Of this additional text (most of it recorded as direct speech by "an English gentleman" who, happening to be in North America, conversed with "a middle-aged Negro" in the province of New York, where his 'massah [i.e., master]' was a Quaker), this is the earliest *explicitly dated* edition (*cf.* ESTC t478773, etc.) yet located (it might have had an earlier periodical printing). It has its own history of subsequent printings.

https://archive.org/details/narrativeofmostr00gron_1/ mode/1up

Cf. ESTC t218600.

112.12b ——. [112.12a with variant title-page imprint]

A Narrative of the Most Remarkable Particulars in the Life of James Albert Ukawsaw Gronniosaw, an African Prince, as Related by Himself. ... To which is added, An Authentic Account of the Conversion and Experience of a Negro.

Edinburgh [Scotland]: Printed and sold by Hugh Inglis. Also sold by John Campbell, Merchant, **1790**. [Reported exemplar in the Aberdeen (Scotland) University Library.]

12mo (18 cm.): viii, [9]-48 p. Preface signed in type: W. Shirley (p. viii). Additional text printed after caption title on p. 45: "An Authentic Account of the Conversion and Experience of a Negro." Regarding this additional text, see our note under 112.12a.

Not in Porter; ESTC t218600.

112.13——. [Same work, retitled]

Wonderous Grace Display'd in the Life and Conversion of James Albert Ukawsaw Gronniosaw, an African Prince. Giving an Account of the Religion, Customs, Manners, &c. of the Natives of Zaara, in Africa. As Related by Himself. **The Third Edition.**

Leeds [Yorkshire, England]: Printed for W. Nicholson, at **Shore, in Yorkshire**; and sold by G. Nicholson, and J. Smith, **Bradford** [West Yorkshire]; T. Nicholson, **Kighley** [West Yorkshire]; W. Edwards and Son, and A. Smith, **Halifax** [West Yorkshire]; and J. Binns, **Leeds** [Yorkshire], [**1790**?].

12mo: 48 p.

Not in Porter; ESTC t88122.

112.14——.

A Narrative of the Most Remarkable Particulars in the Life of James Albert, a Black: with a preface by the Late Honourable and Reverend, Walter Shirly [sic?].

Cork [Ireland]: James Haly, printer, King's-Arms, Main-Street, **1791**. Price, Three-Pence.

12mo: 28 p.

Not in Porter; ESTC t173625.

112.15——.

His account printed serially in vol. 1 of the *American Moral and Sentimental Magazine, consisting of a collection of select pieces, in p[rose and verse, from the best authors, on religious, moral, and sentimental subjects, calculated to form the understanding, and improve the heart,* edited by Thomas Kirk.

New York [New York, U.S.A.]: Printed by the Editor [Thomas Kirk], 112, Chatham-Street, next door to the Tea-Water Pump, July 3–September 25, **1797**.

Evans 31724.

112.16——.

Wonderous Grace Displayed in the Life and Conversion, of James Albert Ukawsaw Gronniosaw, an African Prince. Giving an Account of the Religion, Customs, Manners, &c. of the Natives of Zaara, in Africa. As Related by Himself. **A New Edition.**

Leeds [Yorkshire, England]: Printed by Binns & Brown, for Walker and Nicholsons, printers and booksellers, **Halifax** [Yorkshire, England], **1800**.

12mo: 48 p.

Not in Porter; ESTC t201444.

112.17——.

Wholly derivative retelling of his life printed as section III of Philip Doddridge, *Interesting Memoirs: or: Lives of the following Eminent Persons, viz. I ... The Rt. Hon. Colonel James Gardiner, II ... Selina, Countess Dowager of Huntingdon, III ... James Albert Uwawsaw Gronniosaw: to which is added Cornelius Cayley's Tour through Holland, Flanders, and part of France; interspersed with many useful reflections, which may render it both of moral, civil, and religious utility: also the Death of Abel.*

Liverpool [England]: H. Foreshaw, **1801**.

8vo (22 m.): 576 p.

112.18——. and Hannah More.

The Black Prince: being a Narrative of the most remarkable Occurrences and strange Vicissitudes, exhibited in the Life and Experience of James Albert Ukawsaw Gronniosaw, an African prince, as was Related by Himself.

Salem [New York, U.S.A.]: Printed and sold by Dodd & Rumsey, **1809**.

12mo: 68 p.

Note: In 1995 Adam Potkay and Sandra Burr deemed this edition a "key text that has languished in obscurity" and "the only one we have seen that identifies Hannah More (1745–1833) ... as Gronniosaw's amanuensis, the 'young Lady of the town of Leominster [England]'" (112.32, pp. 25–26).

Welch, D.A. *Amer. Children's Books*, 880.

112.19——.

A Narrative of the Most Remarkable Particulars in the Life of James Albert Ukawsaw Gronniosaw, an African Prince, as Related by Himself.

Leeds [Yorkshire, England]: Printed by Davies and Co. at the Stanhope Press, Vicar Lane, **1810**.

12mo: 47 p.

Not in Porter.

112.20————.

A Narrative of the Most Remarkable Particulars in the Life of James Albert Ukawsaw Gronniosaw, an African Prince, as Related by Himself.

Leeds [Yorkshire, England]: Printed by Davies and Co. at the Stanhope Press, Vicar Lane, **1810**.

8vo: 32 p. Preface signed in type: W. Shirley. Note: Finis and colophon at foot of p. 32.

Not in Porter.

https://archive.org/details/59821725.4769.emory.edu/page/n3/mode/1up

112.21————.

A Narrative of the Most Remarkable Particulars in the Life of James Albert, Akawsaw, Granwasa [sic], *as Dictated by Himself.* **Second American edition.**

Catskill [New York, U.S.A.]: Printed at the Eagle office, **1810.**
12mo (13.5 cm.): 96 p., including "The Pious Negro Woman" on pp. 91–96.
Porter 98.

112.22————. [Welsh version]

Hanes y pethau hynotaf yn mywyd James Albert, Ukawsaw Groniosaw, tywysog o Affrica: fel yr adroddwyd ganddo ef ei hun.

Aberystwyth [Ceredigion, Wales]: Argraffwyd ac ar werth gan James a Williams, **1811.** Pris chwe'-cheiniog.
12mo (16 cm.): 63, [1] p. Rhagymadrodd gan W. Shirley.
Not in Porter.

112.23————.

A Narrative of the Most Remarkable Particulars in the Life of James Albert Ukawsaw Gronniosaw, an African Prince, as Related by Himself.

Leeds [Yorkshire, England]: Printed by Davies and Booth, at the Stanhope Press, Vicar Lane, **1811.**
8vo (20 cm.): 32 pages.
Porter 99.

112.24————.

A Narrative of the Most Remarkable Particulars in the Life of James Albert Ukawsaw Gronniosaw, an African Prince, as Related by Himself, etc.

Leeds [Yorkshire, England]: G. Wilson, Printer, **1814.**
12mo (17 cm.): 47 p.
Not in Porter.

112.25————.

A Narrative of the Most Remarkable Particulars in the Life of James Albert Ukawsaw Gronniosaw, an African Prince.

Leeds [Yorkshire, England]: Printed by Davies and Booth, at the Stanhope Press, **1814.**
8vo (20 cm.): 32, [2] p., [1] leaf of plates.
Porter 100.

112.26————.

Wonderous Grace Displayed in the Life and Conversion of James Albert Ukawsaw Gronniosaw, an African Prince, giving an Account of the Religion, Customs, Manners, &c. of the Natives of Zaara, in Africa.

Halifax [Yorkshire, England]: Printed by Nicholsons and Walker [**1820?**]
8vo: 48p.
NUC NG 0537600

112.27————. [Welsh version]

Hanes y pethau hynotaf yn mywyd James Albert, Ukawsaw Groniosaw, tywysog o Affrica: fel yr adroddwyd ganddo ef ei hun.

Merthyr [Merthyr Tydfil, Wales]: Argraffwyd gan T. Price, **1838.** Pris chwe' cheiniog.
12mo (17 cm.): 56 p.

112.28————.

A Narrative of the Most Remarkable Particulars in the Life of James Albert Ukawsaw Gronniosaw, an African Prince,

London [England]: R. Groombridge, Panyer-Alley, Paternoster-Row; **Manchester [England]:** J. Gadsby, Newall's-Buildings, Market-Street; **Glasgow [Scotland]:** David Robertson, Trongate, **1840.**
12mo (18 cm.): 24 p.

112.29————.

Photomechanical reprint of of 112.28, the London 1840 edition of *A Narrative of the Most Remarkable Particulars in the Life of James Albert Ukawsaw Gronniosaw, an African Prince*, with imprint:

[**Nendeln, Lichtenstien:** Kraus Reprint, **1972.**]
8vo (25 cm.): 24 p.

112.30————.

Excerpts from 112.28 as reprinted in 112.29 printed, with new introductory note, on pp. 7–23 in *Black Writers in Britain, 1760–1890: An Anthology*, edited by Paul Edwards and David Dabydeen.

Edinburgh [Scotland]: Edinburgh University Press, **1991.**
8vo (22 cm.): xv, 239 p.

112.31————. [Second printing of 112.30]

Excerpts from 112.28 as reprinted in 112.29 printed, with new introductory note, on pp. 7–23 in *Black Writers in Britain, 1760–1890: An Anthology*, edited by Paul Edwards and David Dabydeen.

Edinburgh [Scotland]: Edinburgh University Press, **1995**.
8vo (22 cm.): xv, 239 p.

112.32————.

Critical printing of excerpts of Gronniosaw's *Narrative* based on 112.4 (Newport, RI 1774), with new introduction, bibliographical note, and annotations, on pp. 23–63 in *Black Atlantic Writers of the Eighteenth Century: Living the New Exodus in England and the Americas*, edited by Adam Potkay and Sandra Burr.

New York [New York, U.S.A.]: St. Martin's Press, **[1995]**.
8vo (22 cm.): xii, 268 p.

112.33————. [English issue of previous item]

Critical printing of excerpts of Gronniosaw's *Narrative* based on 112.4 (Newport, RI 1774), with new introduction, bibliographical note, and annotations, on pp. 23–63 in *Black Atlantic Writers of the Eighteenth Century: Living the New Exodus in England and the Americas*, edited by Adam Potkay and Sandra Burr.

Basingstoke [and] **London** [England]: Macmillan, **1995**.
8vo (22 cm.): xii, 268 p.

112.34————.

A Narrative of the Most Remarkable Particulars in the Life of James Albert Ukawsaw Gronniosaw, an African Prince, as Related by Himself printed from 110.1 on pp. 32–53 (with explanatory notes on pp. 53–58) in *Unchained Voices: An Anthology of Black Authors in the English-Speaking World of the 18th Century*, edited by Vincent Carretta.

Lexington [Kentucky, U.S.A.]: University Press of Kentucky, **1996**.
8vo (24 cm.): xi, 387 p.

112.35 ————.

Included with commentary on pp. viii, 4–10, and 30–59 in *Pioneers of the Black Atlantic: Five Slave Narratives from the English Enlightenment, 1772–1815*, edited by Henry Louis Gates Jr., and William L. Andrews.

Washington, DC [U.S.A.]: Civitas Counterpoint, **1998**.
8vo (23 cm.): xiv, 439 p

112.36————.

Extract from his *Narrative* reprinted on pp. 17–21 in *Autobiography of a People: Three Centuries of African American History Told by Those who Lived It*, edited by Herb Boyd.

New York [New York, U.S.A.]: Doubleday, **[2000]**.
8vo (24.2 cm.): xviii, [2], 459, [3] p.

112.37————.

His *Narrative* reprinted from 112.1 on pp. 1–34 in *Slave Narratives*, edited by William L. Andrews and Henry Louis Gates Jr.

New York [New York, U.S.A.]: The Library of America, **[2000]**.
8vo (20.7 cm.): x, 1035, [11] p.

112.38————. [Third printing of 112.30]

Excerpts from 112.28 as reprinted in 112.29 printed, with new introductory note, on pp. 7–23 in *Black Writers in Britain, 1760–1890: An Anthology*, edited by Paul Edwards and David Dabydeen.

Edinburgh [Scotland]: Edinburgh University Press, **2003**.
8vo (22 cm.): xv, 239 p.

112.39————. [Second edition of 112.34]

A Narrative of the Most Remarkable Particulars in the Life of James Albert Ukawsaw Gronniosaw, an African Prince, as Related by Himself printed from 112.1 on pp. 32–53 (with explanatory notes on pp. 53–58) in *Unchained Voices: An Anthology of Black Authors in the English-Speaking World of the 18th Century*, **expanded edition**, edited by Vincent Carretta.

Lexington [Kentucky, U.S.A.]: University Press of Kentucky, **2004**.
8vo (24 cm.): xi, 400 p.

112.40————.

Abridgement of *A Narrative of the Most Remarkable Particulars in the Life of … An African Prince* (1770) printed in *Empire and Identity: An Eighteenth-Century Sourcebook*, edited by Stephen H. Gregg.

Basingstoke [England]: Palgrave Macmillan, **2005**.
8vo (23 cm.): xvii, 246 p.

112.41————Discrete printing of 112.40 for the United States market]

Abridgement of *A Narrative of the Most Remarkable Particulars in the Life of … An African Prince* (1770) printed in *Empire and Identity: An Eighteenth-Century Sourcebook*, edited by Stephen H. Gregg.

New York [New York, U.S.A.]: Palgrave Macmillan, **2005**.
8vo (23 cm.): xvii, 246 p.

112.42————.

Excerpts from 112.1 printed on pp. 20–21 in *African Voices of the Global Past, 1500 to the Present*, edited by Trevor R. Getz.

[Boulder, Colorado, U.S.A.]: Westview Press, **[2014]**.
8vo (22.7 cm.): xii, 223 p., illus., map. P. 35, note 12, accounts 112.1's printing date as "1770."

1773

113.0 Phillis Wheatley (ca. 1753–1784) = Phillis Peters

Printed advertisement in the 29 February, 14 March, and 11 April, 1772, issues of Ezekiel Russell's Boston, Massachusetts (the colonial British North American province) newspaper *The Censor* under heading "Proposals For Printing by Subscription, A Collection of Poems" (including "On being brought from Africa to America" written in 1768), reading in part: "poems wrote at several times, and upon various occasions, by Phillis, a Negro Girl, from the strength of her own Genius, it being but a few years since she first came to this town an uncultivated Barbarian from Africa.... It is supposed they [i.e., the poems] will make one small octavo volume, and will contain about 200 pages.... The work will be put to press as soon as three hundred copies are subscribed for.... Subscriptions are taken in by E. Russell, in Marlborough Street."

http://common-place.org/wp-content/uploads/2017/05/ 17.3-Monescalchi-2.jpg

Note: This proposed edition came to naught (that is, the venture failed for lack of sufficient interest to suggest it would be profitable to the proposers); and the contents detailed in this prospectus were first collected (and most, first printed; cf. +113-A.1 etc.) at London, England, in 1773, *q.v.* 113.1.

¶ Wheatley was born ca. 1753 in West Africa, probably along the Gambia River (see Map 3). In 1761 she was taken on the slave ship *Phillis* to the port city of Boston, in the British North American province of Massachusetts (Map 17), and there purchased by the Boston merchant John Wheatley. She quickly learned to read English, read what literature she could find (especially poetry), and learned geography, history, the Bible, and some Latin. Ca. 1765 she began composing poems, the first of which was published in 1770. In 1771 she underwent baptism in the Congregational Church. In 1773 Wheatley and her owners visited England (Map 8), where she strengthened contacts in literary circles. Her owner freed her five weeks after they returned to Boston that year. When anti-British activity increased in Boston in 1774, she and her Loyalist employers fled to the port city Providence in Rhode Island (another maritime province adjacent to Massachusetts). Wheatley returned to Boston in 1776 and wrote poetry promoting the patriot cause. After her benefactors died, she struggled financially. Her marriage to the free black man John Peters in 1778 brought no financial relief. She bore three children, who all died young. Wheatley died in Boston in 1784. Biographical and critical textual studies of Wheatley and her work are extensive.

https://babel.hathi-trust.org/cgi/pt?id= uiuc.5618715 [see first of 113.1].

For an introduction to later 20th-century critical studies, see John C. Shields's biographical sketch of Wheatley and his note on sources in *American National Biography*, edited by John A. Garraty and Mark C. Carnes (New York: Oxford University Press, 1999), 23: 121–122.

113.1 ———.

"On being brought from Africa to America," "To S.M. a young African painter, on seeing his works," and other poems printed in Phillis Wheatley, *Poems on Various Subjects, Religious and Moral, by Phillis Wheatley, Negro Servant to Mr. John Wheatley, of Boston, in New England.*

London [England]: Printed for A. Bell, Bookseller, Aldgate; and sold by Messrs. Cox and Berry, King-Street, **Boston** [Massachusetts], M DCC LXXIII [1773].

8vo (18 cm.): 124, [4] p., frontispiece portrait.

https://babel.hathitrust.org/cgi/pt?id=uiuc.5618715

https://archive.org/details/poemsonvariouss00whea/page/n7/ mode/1up

https://digital.tcl.sc.edu/digital/collection/pwp/id/6

Heartman (1915) 13; Porter 270; ESTC t153734.

No entry. ———.

"On being brought from Africa to America," "To S.M. a young African painter, on seeing his works," and other poems supposedly printed in Phillis Wheatley, *Poems on Various Subjects, Religious and Moral* (Albany [New York, U.S.A.]: s.n., 1779). Not in Evans, Heartman, Porter, or ESTC. Bristol B-4994 (no copy located). Douglas C. McMurtrie posited this edition, perhaps seriously, without locating any exemplar in his *Check List of Eighteenth Century Albany Imprints* (Albany: The University of the State of New York, 1939). In this enumerative bibliography McMurtrie's entry number 10 (p. 17) cites as evidence "N. R. Campbell & Co. catalogue, Summer 1929, p. 22," on which this supposed edition of Wheatley was allegedly described as "on vellum and possibly unique." This unverified Campbell catalog listing (if it ever existed) strikes the present compilers as either itself risible, or mendacious, or as a hoax erroneously credited by "N. R. Campbell & Co."

113.2 ———.

"On being brought from Africa to America," "To S.M. a young African painter, on seeing his works," and other poems printed in Phillis Wheatley, *Poems on Various Subjects, Religious and Moral* …

London, Printed. **Philadelphia [Pennsylvania, U.S.A.]**: Re-Printed, and sold by Joseph Crukshank in Market-street, Between Second and Third Streets, M,DCC,LXXXVI [1786].

12mo (16 cm.): 66, [2] p.

Evans 19913; Heartman (1915) 19; Porter 272; ESTC w24491.

113.3 ——. [Reissue of sheets of 113.1 with cancellans title leaf]

"On being brought from Africa to America," "To S.M. a young African painter, on seeing his works," and other poems printed in Phillis Wheatley, *Poems on* [n.b.] *Comic, Serious, and Moral Subjects, by Phillis Wheatley, Negro Servant to Mr. John Wheatley, of Boston, in New England. The Second edition. Corrected* [sic].

London [England]: printed for J. French, Bookseller, No. 164, Fenchurch-street, and may be had of the Booksellers in Town and Country. [1787] Price, One shilling and sixpence, sewed.

8vo (18 cm.): 124, [4] p., frontispiece portrait.

Heartman (1915) 14 (positing date 1773); Porter 269 (following Heartman but locating no copy); ESTC n473250.

113.4 ——.

"On being brought from Africa to America," "To S.M. a young African painter, on seeing his works," and other poems printed in Phillis Wheatley, *Poems on Various Subjects, Religious and Moral ...*

Philadelphia [Pennsylvania, U.S.A.]: Printed by Joseph James, in Chesnut-street, M.DCC.LXXXVII [1787].

12mo (16 cm.): 55, [5] p.

Not in Evans (1907); Heartman (1915) 20; Porter 273; Bristol (1970) B-6639; ESTC w24492.

113.5 ——.

"On being brought from Africa to America," "To S.M. a young African painter, on seeing his works," and other poems printed in Phillis Wheatley, *Poems on Various Subjects, Religious and Moral ...*

Philadelphia [Pennsylvania, U.S.A.]: Re-Printed, and sold by Joseph Crukshank in Market-Street, Between Second and Third-Streets, MDCCLXXXIX [1789].

12mo (16 cm.): 66, [2] p.

Not in Evans (1912); not in Heartman (1915); Porter 274; Bristol B-7221; ESTC w24493.

113.6 ——.

"On being brought from Africa to America," "To S.M. a young African painter, on seeing his works," and other poems printed in Phillis Wheatley, *Poems on Various Subjects, Religious and Moral ...*

Albany [New York, U.S.A.]: Re-Printed, from the London edition, by Barber & Southwick, for Thomas Spencer, Book-Seller, Market-street, 1793.

16mo (15 cm.): 89, [3] p.

Note: Printer-publisher Solomon Southwick (1773–1839), Albany, NY, business partner and brother-in-law of John Barber (1758–1808), was a son of the Solomon Southwick (1731–1797) who published Ukasaw Gronniosaw at Newport, RI, in 1774 (our 113.4 above).

Heartman (1915) 21; Evans (1925) 25983; Porter 275; ESTC w24494.

https://babel.hathitrust.org/cgi/pt?id=mdp.69015000003505 &view=1up&seq=7

113.7 ——.

"On being brought from Africa to America," "To S.M. a young African painter, on seeing his works," and other poems originally printed in Phillis Wheatley, *Poems on Various Subjects, Religious and Moral ... reprinted on pp. 167–238 (mispaged '248') in vol. 2 as an addition to Joseph Lavallée, The Negro Equalled by Few Europeans, translated from the French. To which are added, Poems on Various Subjects,* [n.b.] *Moral and Entertaining; by Phillis Wheatley, Negro Servant to Mr. John Wheatley, of Boston, in New-England.*

Philadelphia [Pennsylvania, U.S.A]: Printed by and for William W. Woodward, No. 17, Chesnut [sic] Street, 1801.

2 vols., 12mo (17 cm.). Cf. the 1790 London edition of J. Trapp's translation of Lavallée ("printed for the author"), which does not include any of Wheatley's poetry. **List of subscribers** printed on pp. 239–244 of vol. 2.

https://babel.hathitrust.org/cgi/pt?id=mdp.69015000003208 &view=1up&seq=173

Heartman (1915) 22; Porter 276.

113.8 ——.

"On being brought from Africa to America," "To S.M. a young African painter, on seeing his works," and other poems printed in Phillis Wheatley, *Poems on Various Subjects, Religious and Moral ...*

Walpole [New Hampshire, U.S.A.]: Printed for Thomas & Thomas, By David Newhall, 1802.

12mo (14.5 cm.): 86 p.

Heartman (1915) 23; Porter 277.

113.9 ——.

"On being brought from Africa to America," "To S.M. a young African painter, on seeing his works," and other poems printed in Phillis Wheatley, *Poems on Various Subjects, Religious and Moral ...*

Hartford [Connecticut, U.S.A.]: Printed by Oliver Steele, 1804.

12mo (17 cm.): 92, [2] p.

Heartman (1915) 24; Porter 278.

113.10 ——.

"On being brought from Africa to America," "To S.M. a young African painter, on seeing his works," and other poems printed in *The Interesting Narrative of the Life of Olaudah Equiano, or Gustavus Vassa, the African. Written by Himself ... To which are added, Poems on Various Subjects, by Phillis Wheatly* [sic], *Negro Servant to Mr. John Wheatly* [sic] *of Boston in new* [sic] *England.*

Halifax [Yorkshire, England]: Printed at the office of J. Nicholson & Co., **1813.**

12mo (18 cm.): 514, [2] p., frontispiece portrait. Exemplar at Library of Congress (rare books call no. HT869. E6/A3/1813); title-page reproduced in Sidney Kaplan and Emma Nogrady Kaplan, *The Black Presence in the Era of the American Revolution*, revised ed. (Amherst: Univ. of Massachusetts Press, 1989), p. 218, fig. 147.

Note: This edition is occasionally misidentified in catalogs as the "1st Canadian edition." It is not in Patricia Lockhart Fleming, *Atlantic Canadian Imprints 1801–1820* (Toronto: University of Toronto Press, 1991 and 2014), in which no Nicholson appears as printer or publisher.

Heartman (1915) 26; not in Porter.

113.11 ——.

"On being brought from Africa to America," "To S.M. a young African painter, on seeing his works," and other poems printed in Phillis Wheatley, *Poems on Various Subjects, Religious and Moral ...*

London ... Printed. Re-printed, in New-England [**Massachusetts? U.S.A.**], **1816.**

16mo (16.5 cm.): 120 p.

Heartman (1915) 27; Porter 279; Shaw-Shoemaker 39794.

113.12——.

Biographical sketch, including twelve lines of poetry from "one of her communications to the Earl of Dartmouth, on the subject of *Freedom*," printed as ten numbered paragraphs under heading "A Short Account of Phillis Wheatley" on pp. 10–12 in *Biographical Sketches and Interesting Anecdotes of Persons of Color. To Which Is Added, a Selection of Pieces in Poetry*, compiled by A[bigail] Mott.

New York [New York, U.S.A.]: Printed and Sold by Mahlon Day, No. 376, Pearl-street, **1826.**

12mo (18 cm.): iv, [5]–192 p. Preface dated on p. iv: *Hickory Grove* [NY], 11*th mo*. 1825.

http://docsouth.unc.edu/neh/mott26/mott26.html

https://babel.hathitrust.org/cgi/pt?id=hvd.hn3m6e&view=1up&seq=126

Hogg 1467.

113.13——.

Biographical sketch, including twelve lines of poetry from "one of her communications to the Earl of Dartmouth, on the subject of *Freedom*," printed on pp. 9–12 in *Biographical Sketches and Interesting Anecdotes of Persons of Colour.* Compiled by A[bigail] Mott.

York [Yorkshire, England]: Printed and Sold by W. Alexander & Son, Castlegate; sold also by Harvey & Darton, W. Phillips, E. Fry, and W. Darton, **London [England]**; R. Peart [sic], **Birmingham [England]**; D. F. Gardiner, **Dublin [Ireland]**, **1826.**

12mo (20 cm.): xi, [2], 2–240 p.

https://babel.hathitrust.org/cgi/pt?id=nyp.33433081774204&view=1up&seq=195

113.14——.

Biographical sketch, including twelve lines of poetry from "one of her communications to the Earl of Dartmouth, on the subject of *Freedom*," printed on pp. 9–12 in *Biographical Sketches and Interesting Anecdotes of Persons of Color. To Which Is Added, a Selection of Pieces in Poetry*, compiled by A[bigail] Mott. "Second Edition."

York [Yorkshire, England]: Printed and Sold by W. Alexander & Son; sold also by Harvey and Darton, W. Phillips, E. Fry, and W. Darton, **London [England]**; R. Peart, **Birmingham [England]**; D. F. Gardiner, **Dublin [Ireland]**, **1828.**

8vo (19.8 cm.): xi, [1], 252 p.

113.15——.

"On Being Brought from Africa to America" by Phillis Wheatley, printed on p. 44 of the antislavery newspaper *The Liberator*, vol. 2 no. 11. [Note: this is one of *many* Wheatley poems reprinted in issues of *The Liberator* from February through December 1832.]

Boston [Massachusetts, U.S.A.]: William Lloyd Garrison and Isaac Knapp, Publishers, March 17, **1832.**

Broadsheet bifolium (49 cm.): 4 p.

http://fair-use.org/the-liberator/1832/03/17/the-liberator-02-11.pdf

113.16——.

"To S.M. A Young African Painter, on Seeing His Works" by Phillis Wheatley printed on p. 116 of the antislavery newspaper *The Liberator*, vol. 2 no. 29. [Note: this is one of *many* Wheatley poems reprinted in issues of *The Liberator* from February through December 1832.]

Boston [Massachusetts, U.S.A.]: William Lloyd Garrison and Isaac Knapp, Publishers, July 21, **1832.**

Broadsheet bifolium (49 cm.): 4 p.

http://fair-use.org/the-liberator/1832/07/21/the-liberator-02-29.pdf

113.17——.

"On being brought from Africa to America," "To S.M. a young African painter, on seeing his works," and other poems printed in *Memoir and Poems of Phillis Wheatley, a Native African and a Slave. Dedicated to the Friends of the Africans.*

Boston [Massachusetts, U.S.A.]: Published by Geo. W. Light, Lyceum Depository, 3 Cornhill, **1834**. Tpv carries Geo. W. Light's 1834 copyright notice. [See publication notices in *The Liberator* (Boston: Garrison and Knapp), vol. 4, no 12 (March 22 1834), p. 47, col. 6., and vol. 3, no. 17 (April 26, 1834), p. 68, col. 6 (the *latter* specifying "This day published … **March 18**" (http://fair-use.org/the-liberator/1834/04/26/the-liberator-04-17.pdf)].

8vo (18 cm.): viii, [9]-103 p., frontispiece portrait.

Note: "Memoir" (p. [9]-29) by Margaretta Matilda Odell.

Heartman (1915) 28.

https://babel.hathitrust.org/cgi/pt?id=njp.32101041427301

https://docsouth.unc.edu/neh/wheatley/wheatley.html

113.18——.

"On being brought from Africa to America," "To S.M. a young African painter, on seeing his works," and other poems printed in *Memoir and Poems of Phillis Wheatley, a Native African and a Slave. Dedicated to the Friends of the Africans. Second edition.*

Boston [Massachusetts, U.S.A.]: Light & Horton, **1835**.

12mo (16 cm.): 114 p. Note: "Memoir" (p. [9]-37) by Margaretta Matilda Odell.

Heartman (1915) 32.

113.19——.

Biographical sketch, including twelve lines of poetry from "one of her communications to the Earl of Dartmouth, on the subject of *Freedom,*" printed on pp. 10–12 in *Biographical Sketches and Interesting Anecdotes of Persons of Color. To Which Is Added, a Selection of Pieces in Poetry,* compiled by A[bigail] Mott. "Second Edition, much Enlarged."

New-York [New York, U.S.A.]: Mahlon Day, 374 Pearl-street, **1837**. Tpv: "Note by the publisher. By consent of the Compiler, and at the recommendation of the Trustees of the African Free Schools in New York, (who have liberally patronized the work,) …"

8vo (19 cm.): 260 p. (of which p. [256] is blank, and pp. 257–260 are table of contents).

https://babel.hathitrust.org/cgi/pt?id=hvd.32044004358602;view=1up;seq=5

113.20——.

"On being brought from Africa to America" printed as numbered paragraph 5 in a ten-paragraph summary biography on pp. 15–18 in *Biographical Sketches and Interesting Anecdotes of Persons of Color. To Which Is Added, a Selection of Pieces in Poetry,* compiled by A[bigail] Mott.

New York [New York, U.S.A.]: Stereotyped for and printed by order of the Trustees of the residuary estate of Lindley Murray, M. Day, Printer, 374 Pearl St., **1838**.

8vo (18.7 cm.): iv, 408 p.

113.21——.

"On being brought from Africa to America" printed as numbered paragraph 5 in a ten-paragraph summary biography on pp. 15–18 in *Biographical Sketches and Interesting Anecdotes of Persons of Color. To Which Is Added, a Selection of Pieces in Poetry,* compiled by A[bigail] Mott.

New York [New York, U.S.A.]: Stereotyped for and printed by order of the Trustees of the residuary estate of Lindley Murray. M. Day, Printer, 271 Pearl St. **[1839]**. Approximate year of printing (could be slightly later) from "Advertisement," p. [ii].

12mo (19 cm.): vi, [7]-408 p.

https://archive.org/details/biographicalsket00mottrich/page/n4 (incomplete 370-page exemplar).

https://babel.hathitrust.org/cgi/pt?id=loc.ark:/13960/t2q52p-81p&view=1up&seq=3 (complete).

113.22——.

Biographical sketch with selection of poems (not including "On being brought from Africa to America," or "To S.M. a young African painter, on seeing his works") printed on pp. 332–348 in Wilson Armistead's compendium *A Tribute for the Negro: Being a Vindication of the Moral Intellectual, and Religious Capabilities of the Colored Portion of Mankind; with Particular Reference to the African Race.*

Manchester [England]: William Irwin; **London [England]:** Charles Gilpin; American Agent: Wm. Harned, Anti-Slavery Office, 61, John Street, **New York [New York, U.S.A.]**; and may be had of H. Longstreath and G.W. Taylor, **Philadelphia [Pennsylvania, U.S.A.], 1848**. Tpv: Manchester: Printed by William Irwin, 39, Oldham Street.

8vo (24 cm.): xxxv, 564 p.

https://babel.hathitrust.org/cgi/pt?id=nc01.ark:/13960/t42r4z659;view=1up;seq=13

http://docsouth.unc.edu/neh/armistead/armistead.html

113.23——.

"On being brought from Africa to America" printed as numbered paragraph 5 in a ten-paragraph summary biography on pp. 15–18 in *Biographical Sketches and Interesting Anecdotes of Persons of Color. To Which Is Added, a Selection of Pieces in Poetry,* compiled by A[bigail] Mott.

New York [New York, U.S.A.]: Stereotyped for and printed by order of the Trustees of the residuary estate of Lindley Murray, **1850.**
8vo (20 cm.): iv, [7]-408 p.

113.24———.
"On being brought from Africa to America" printed as numbered paragraph 5 in a ten-paragraph summary biography on pp. 15–18 in *Biographical Sketches and Interesting Anecdotes of Persons of Color. To Which Is Added, a Selection of Pieces in Poetry*, compiled by A[bigail] Mott.

New York [New York, U.S.A.]: Stereotyped for and printed by order of the Trustees of the residuary estate of Lindley Murray. D. Fanshaw, Printer, 35 Ann, corner of Nassau-street, **1854.**
12mo (19 cm.): iv, [7]-408 p.
https://digital.ncdcr.gov/digital/collection/p249901coll37/id/10213

113.25 ———.
"On being brought from Africa to America," "To S.M. a young African painter, on seeing his works," and other poems printed in Phillis Wheatley, *Poems on Various Subjects, Religious and Moral. By Phillis Wheatley, Negro Servant to Mr. John Wheatley, of Boston, in New England. With Memoirs, by W. A. Jackson.*

Denver, Colo[rado, U.S.A.]: W. H. Lawrence & Co., **1887.**
  Tpv: Copyright, 1886, By W. H. Lawrence & Co.
8vo (18 cm.): 149 p., portrait. The title page exists in two states: in the first, the author's name is misprinted as W. H. Jackson; in the second, it has been corrected to W. A. Jackson.
Heartman (1915) 39. Memoirs of Phillis Wheatley, Benjamin Banneker, Thomas Fuller, and James Durham (misprinted as "Dunham" in Table of Contents), pp. 117–149.
https://babel.hathitrust.org/cgi/pt?id=chi.24980701&view=1up&seq=9

113.26 ———.
"On being brought from Africa to America," "To S.M. a young African painter, on seeing his works," and other poems printed in Phillis Wheatley, *The Poems of Phillis Wheatley. As they were originally published in London 1773.*

Philadelphia [Pennsylvania, U.S.A.]: R. R. & C. C. Wright, **1909.** Tpv: A. M. C. Book Concern | Printers | Philadelphia.
12mo (18 cm.): 88 p., frontispiece portrait.
Note: This edition's publishers (and authors of its prefatory "Note") identify themselves on p. 4 as Richard R. Wright Jr. and Charlotte Crogman Wright.
Heartman (1915) 40.
https://babel.hathitrust.org/cgi/pt?id=uc2.ark:/13960/t05x-25j8h&view=1up&seq=7

113.27 ———.
"On being brought from Africa to America," "To S.M. a young African painter, on seeing his works," and other poems printed in Phillis Wheatley, *Poems and Letters. First Collected Edition. Edited by Chas. Fred. Heartman. With an Appreciation by Arthur A. Schomberg.*

New York City [New York, U.S.A.]: Four hundred copies printed for Chas. Fred. Heartman, **1915.**
Large 8vo (25 cm.): 111 p.
Heartman (1915) 42.

113.28———.
"On being brought from Africa to America," "To S.M. a young African painter, on seeing his works," and other poems printed in Herbert G. Renfro, *Life and Works of Phillis Wheatley, containing her Complete Poetical Works, Numerous Letters, and a Complete Biography of this Famous Poet of a Century and a half ago.*

Washington, D.C. [U.S.A.]: Robert L. Pendleton, **1916.**
8vo (20 cm.): 112 p., portrait.
https://babel.hathitrust.org/cgi/pt?id=emu.010001353748&view=1up&seq=1

113.29———.
"On being brought from Africa to America," "To S.M. a young African painter, on seeing his works," and other poems printed in Phillis Wheatley, *Poems on Various Subjects, Religious and Moral, by Phillis Wheatley,* edited with an introduction and notes by Theodore T. Fletcher. Columbia University, Department of English Literature, New York, Master's Essay.

New York [New York, U.S.A.], 1932.
4to. Columbia University Libraries, Special Collections call no. MA 1932 FLETT.
For biographical sketch of Theodore Thomas F. Fletcher, Sr. (1906–1988; A.B. Fisk Univ. 1928; M.A. Columbia Univ. 1932; Ph.D. New York Univ. 1945) see *Notable Kentucky African Americans Database* (NKAA) at http://nkaa.uky.edu/nkaa/items/show/2399

113.30———.
"On being brought from Africa to America," "To S.M. a young African painter, on seeing his works," and other poems printed in *The Poems of Phillis Wheatley.* Edited with an introduction by Julian D. Mason Jr.

Chapel Hill [North Carolina, U.S.A.]: University of North Carolina Press, **1966.**
8vo (22 cm.): lviii, 113 p., portrait, facsimiles.

113.31———.

"On being brought from Africa to America," "To S.M. a young African painter, on seeing his works," and other poems printed with critical introduction on pp. 97–112 in *Early Black American Poets: Selections with biographical and critical introductions* by William H. Robinson.

Dubuque, Iowa [U.S.A.]: Wm. C. Brown Company, Publishers, [1969].

8vo (23 cm.): xviii, [2], 275 p.

113.32———. [Second printing of 113.31]

"On being brought from Africa to America," "To S.M. a young African painter, on seeing his works," and other poems printed with critical introduction on pp. 97–112 in *Early Black American Poets: Selections with biographical and critical introductions* by William H. Robinson.

Dubuque, Iowa [U.S.A.]: Wm. C. Brown Company, Publishers, [1970].

8vo (23 cm.): xviii, [2], 275 p.

113.33———. [Photomechanical reprint of 113.28]

"On being brought from Africa to America," "To S.M. a young African painter, on seeing his works," and other poems printed in Herbert G. Renfro, *Life and Works of Phillis Wheatley, containing her Complete Poetical Works, Numerous Letters, and a Complete Biography of this Famous Poet of a Century and a half ago.*

Freeport, New York [U.S.A.]: Books for Libraries Press, 1970.

8vo (23 cm.): 112 p., portrait.

113.34———. [Third printing of 113.31]

"On being brought from Africa to America," "To S.M. a young African painter, on seeing his works," and other poems printed with critical introduction on pp. 97–112 in *Early Black American Poets: Selections with biographical and critical introductions* by William H. Robinson.

Dubuque, Iowa [U.S.A.]: Wm. C. Brown Company, Publishers, [1971].

8vo (23 cm.): xviii, [2], 275 p.

113.35———. [Photomechanical reprint of 113.28; second printing of 113.33]

"On being brought from Africa to America," "To S.M. a young African painter, on seeing his works," and other poems printed in Herbert G. Renfro, *Life and Works of Phillis Wheatley, containing her Complete Poetical Works, Numerous Letters, and a Complete Biography of this Famous Poet of a Century and a half ago.*

Freeport, New York [U.S.A.]: Books for Libraries Press, 1972.

8vo (23 cm.): 112 p., portrait.

113.36———.

"On being brought from Africa to America," and other poems with brief introduction in vol. 1, pp. 13–18 of *Afro-American Writing: An Anthology of Prose and Poetry*, edited by Richard A. Long and Eugenia W. Collier.

New York [New York, U.S.A.]: New York University Press, 1972.

2 vols., 8vo. (24 cm.): xlii, 794 p.

113.37———. [Fourth printing of 113.31]

"On being brought from Africa to America," "To S.M. a young African painter, on seeing his works," and other poems printed with critical introduction on pp. 97–112 in *Early Black American Poets: Selections with biographical and critical introductions* by William H. Robinson.

Dubuque, Iowa [U.S.A.]: Wm. C. Brown Company, Publishers, [1973].

8vo (23 cm.): xviii, [2], 309 p.

113.38 ———. [Photomechanical reprint of 113.2]

"On being brought from Africa to America," "To S.M. a young African painter, on seeing his works," and other poems printed in Phillis Wheatley, *Poems on Various Subjects, Religious and Moral ...* (Philadelphia ... Re-printed ... by Joseph Crukshank, [1786]) with imprint:

New York [New York, U.S.A.]: AMS Press, 1976.

8vo (23 cm.): 66 p.

113.39———. [Photomechanical reprint of 113.28]

"On being brought from Africa to America," "To S.M. a young African painter, on seeing his works," and other poems printed in Herbert G. Renfro, *Life and Works of Phillis Wheatley, containing her Complete Poetical Works, Numerous Letters, and a Complete Biography of this Famous Poet of a Century and a half ago.*

Salem, New Hampshire [U.S.A.]: Ayer Co., Publishers, 1984.

8vo (23 cm.): 112 p., portrait.

113.40———.

"On being brought from Africa to America," "To S.M. a young African painter, on seeing his works," and other poems printed with introductory material and annotations on pp. 246–249 in *The Norton Anthology of Literature by Women*, edited by Sandra M. Gilbert and Susan Gubar.

New York [New York, U.S.A.]: W. W. Norton & Company, [1985].
8vo (22 cm.): xxxiv, 2457 p.

113.41———.
"On being brought from Africa to America," "To S.M. a young African painter, on seeing his works," and other poems printed with introductory material and annotations printed on pp. 17–25 in *Afro-American Women Writers 1746–1933: An Anthology and Critical Guide*, edited by Ann Allen Shockley.

Boston, Mass[achusetts, U.S.A.]: G. K. Hall & Co., [1988].
8vo (24.2 cm.): xxviii, 465 p.

113.42———. [Photomechanical reprint of 113.28; second printing of 113.39]
"On being brought from Africa to America," "To S.M. a young African painter, on seeing his works," and other poems printed in Herbert G. Renfro, *Life and Works of Phillis Wheatley, containing her Complete Poetical Works, Numerous Letters, and a Complete Biography of this Famous Poet of a Century and a half ago.*

Salem, New Hampshire [U.S.A.]: Ayer Co., Publishers, 1988.
8vo (23 cm.): 112 p., portrait.

113.43———.
"On being brought from Africa to America," "To S.M. a young African painter, on seeing his works," and other poems printed in *The Poems of Phillis Wheatley*. Revised and enlarged edition (of 111.30). Edited with an introduction by Julian D. Mason Jr.

Chapel Hill [North Carolina, U.S.A.]: University of North Carolina Press, 1989.
8vo (23 cm.): xvi, [2], 235 p.

113.44———. [Photomechanical reprint of 113.28; third printing of 113.39]
"On being brought from Africa to America," "To S.M. a young African painter, on seeing his works," and other poems printed in Herbert G. Renfro, *Life and Works of Phillis Wheatley, containing her Complete Poetical Works, Numerous Letters, and a Complete Biography of this Famous Poet of a Century and a half ago.*

Salem, New Hampshire [U.S.A.]: Ayer Co., Publishers, 1993.
8vo (23 cm.): 112 p., portrait.

113.45———.
"On being brought from Africa to America," "To S.M. a young African painter, on seeing his works," and other poems printed with introductory material and annotations on pp.

246–249 in *The Norton Anthology of Literature by Women: The Traditions in English*, edited by Sandra M. Gilbert and Susan Gubar. **Second edition.**

New York [New York, U.S.A.]: W. W. Norton & Company, [1996].
8vo (24 cm.): xxxviii, 2452, p.

113.46———.
"On being brought from Africa to America," "To S.M. a young African painter, on seeing his works," and other poems printed with introductory material and annotations on pp. 164–177 of *The Norton Anthology of African American Literature*, edited by Henry Louis Gates Jr. and Nellie Y. McKay.

New York [New York, U.S.A.]: W. W. Norton & Co., 1997.
8vo (24 cm.): xliv, 2665 p.

113.47———.
"On being brought from Africa to America," and another poem reprinted on pp. 29–30 in *Autobiography of a People: Three Centuries of African American History Told by Those who Lived It*, edited by Herb Boyd.

New York [New York, U.S.A.]: Doubleday, [2000].
8vo (24.2 cm.): xviii, [2], 459, [3] p.

113.48———. [Photomechanical reprint of 113.19]
Biographical sketch, including twelve lines of poetry from "one of her communications to the Earl of Dartmouth, on the subject of *Freedom*," printed on pp. 10–12 in 有色人に関する伝記的資料 / *Biographical Sketches and Interesting Anecdotes of Persons of Color. To which is added, a Selection of Pieces in Poetry*, compiled by A[bigail] Mott. "Second Edition, much Enlarged."

Tokyo, Japan: 日本図書センター, Nihon Tosho Senta, 2000.
8vo (27 cm.): 255 p.

113.49———.
"On being brought from Africa to America," "To S.M. a young African painter, on seeing his works," and other poems printed on pp. 888–901 in the anthology *Early American Writings*, edited by Carla Mulford, Angela Vietto, and Amy E. Winans.

New York [New York, U.S.A.] [and] Oxford [England]: Oxford University Press, 2002.
8vo (24 cm.): xxii, 1129 p.

113.50———.
"On being brought from Africa to America," "To S.M. a young African painter, on seeing his works," and other poems printed with introductory material and annotations on

p. 213-224 of *The Norton Anthology of African American Literature*, edited by Henry Louis Gates, Jr., Valerie Smith, and Robert G. O'Meally. **Second edition.**

New York [New York, U.S.A.]: W. W. Norton & Co., 2004. 8vo (24 cm.): xlvii, 2776 p. + audio disc.

113.51——.

"On being brought from Africa to America," "To S.M. a young African painter, on seeing his works," and other poems printed with introductory material and annotations in vol. 1 of *The Norton Anthology of Literature by Women: The Traditions in English*, edited by Sandra M. Gilbert and Susan Gubar. **Third edition.**

New York [New York, U.S.A.]: W. W. Norton & Company, [2007].
2 vols., 8vo (24 cm.).

113.52——.

"On being brought from Africa to America," "To S.M. a young African painter, on seeing his works," and other poems printed with introductory material and annotations in vol. 1 of *The Norton Anthology of African American Literature*, edited by Henry Louis Gates Jr. and Valerie Smith. **Third edition.**

New York [New York, U.S.A.]: W. W. Norton & Co., 2014.
2 vols., 8vo (24 cm.), illustrations, maps, music.

Additional pre-1774 publications of Phillis Wheatley

+113-A.1 ——.

An Elegiac Poem, on … George Whitefield (Boston [Massachusetts]: Russell and Boyles, [1770]). 8 p.

+113-A.2 ——.

An Elegiac Poem, on … George Whitefield Boston [Massachusetts]: Russell and Boyles, [1770]. Broadside. [1] p., verso blank.

+113-A.3 ——.

An Elegiac Poem, on … George Whitefield (New York [New York]: Inslee and Car, [1770]). Advertised. No copy known.

+113-A.4 ——.

An Elegiac Poem, on … George Whitefield (Philadelphia [Pennsylvania]: Goddard, [1770]). Advertised. No copy known.

+113-A.5 ——.

An Elegiac Poem, on … George Whitefield (Newport, Rhode Island: Southwick, [1770]). Broadside.

+113-A.6 ——.

An Elegiac Poem, on … George Whitefield (Newport, Rhode Island: Southwick, [1770]). 8 p.

+113-A.7 ——.

An Elegiac Poem, on …George Whitefield (Boston [Massachusetts]: Fowle, [1770]). 8 p.

+113-B.1 ——.

An Elegy to Miss Mary Moorehead, on the Death of her Father, The Rev. Mr. John Moorhead … Decem. 15, 1773. ([Boston, Massachusetts]: M'Alpine, [1773]). Broadside. [1] p., verso blank.

1774

114.0 Joanna's Grandfather (–1776)

Very short account of his life written within Chapter XII under 5 March **1774** entry on p. 291 of John Gabriel Stedman's 1790 manuscript of his "Narrative, of a five years expedition against the Rebelled Negroes of Surinam …" This manuscript, which is preserved in the John Gabriel Stedman Collection at the University of Minnesota's James Ford Bell Library, **Minneapolis, Minnesota, U.S.A.,** was the heavily edited (see introduction to 114.16) ba-

https://archive.org/details/narrative-offivey_01sted/page/n409/mode/1up [see 114.1a].

sis of 114.1; it was first published verbatim et literatim in 1988, q.v. 114.16. Manuscript page 291 has been digitized (as image 321) with the rest of the manuscript by the James Ford Bell Library and is available at:

https://umedia.lib.umn.edu/item/p16022coll187:962/p16022coll187:394?child_index=320&facets%5Bcollection_name_s%5D%5B%5D=John%20Gabriel%20Stedman%20Archive%20and%20Book%20Manuscript&q=stedman&query=&sidebar_page=107

¶ **Born on the "Coast of Guinea" (in 114.0; "Africa" alone substituted for the whole phrase in 114.1 et seq. until 114.15), Joanna's grandfather was a man of significant stature in his community until he was taken on a slave ship to Suriname on the**

Caribbean coast of South America (see Map 10), where he lived enslaved the rest of his life. He had at least two children and lived on Fauquenberg Plantation. Gray-headed, blind, and supported by his large family, he briefly told his life story to John Gabriel Stedman (see above), who visited him with his (Stedman's) mistress, Joanna, who was the aged African's granddaughter.

114.1a——.

Very short account of his life as told to John Gabriel Stedman printed in Chapter XII under date 5 March **1774** on p. 306 in vol. 1 of Stedman's *Narrative, of a Five Years' Expedition, against the Revolted Negroes of Surinam, in Guiana, on the Wild Coast of South America; from the year 1772, to 1777...*

London [England]: Printed for J. Johnson, St. Paul's Church Yard, & J. Edwards, Pall Mall, **1796** (*sic*). No colophon in vol. 2. **Regular paper issue** with un-colored plates.

2 vols., 4to. (28 cm.), folding map, plan, plates (some engraved by William Blake). Includes list of subscribers.

https://archive.org/details/narrativeoffivey_01sted/page/n409/mode/1up

ESTC t146566; Price & Price 1.

114.1b——.

Very short account of his life as told to John Gabriel Stedman printed in Chapter XII under date 5 March **1774** on p. 306 in vol. 1 of Stedman's *Narrative, of a Five Years' Expedition, against the Revolted Negroes of Surinam, in Guiana, on the Wild Coast of South America; from the year 1772, to 1777...*

London [England]: Printed for J. Johnson, St. Paul's Church Yard, & J. Edwards, Pall Mall, **1796** (*sic*). No colophon in vol. 2. **Large paper issue** with hand-colored title-page vignettes and plates.

2 vols., 4to. (28 cm.), folding map, plan, plates (some engraved by William Blake). Includes list of subscribers.

ESTC t146565; Price & Price 2.

114.2 ——. [German translation of 114.1]

Very short account of his life as told to John Gabriel Stedman printed on p. 242 of Stedman's *Nachrichten von Surinam und von seiner Expedition gegen die rebellischen Neger in dieser Kolonie in den Jahren 1772 bis 1777.*

Hamburg [Germany]: bei Benjamin Gotttlob [*sic*] Hoffmann, **1797**.

8vo: xiv, 522 p., illus., map.

Price & Price 3.

https://www.e-rara.ch/zuz/nagezh/content/structure/9727324

114.3a ——. [Abridged German translation of 114.1]

Very short account of his life as told to John Gabriel Stedman printed on p. 183 of John Gabriel Stedman, *Stedman's Nach-*

richten von Suriname, dem letzten Aufruhr der dortigen Negersclaven umd ihrer Bezwingung in den Jahren 1772, bis 1777.

Halle [Saxony-Anhalt, Germany]: in der Rengerschen Buchhandlung, **1797**.

8vo.

Price & Price 4.

https://archive.org/details/bub_gb_fBhZAAAAcAAJ/page/n185/mode/2up?q=Joanna

114.3b ——. [Abridged German translation of 114.1]

112.3a issued as vols. 8 and 9 of M. C. Sprengel, *Auswahl der besten ausländischen geographischen und statistischen Nachrichten.*

Halle [Saxony-Anhalt, Germany]: in der Rengerschen Buchhandlung, **1797**.

2 vols., 8vo.

Price & Price 5.

114.4 ——. [Abridged French translation of 114.1]

Very short account of his life as told to John Gabriel Stedman printed in Chapter XII under date 5 March **1774** of Stedman's *Voyage a Surinam et dans l'Intérieur de Guiane ... traduit de l'Anglais par P. F. Henry.*

Paris [France]: chez F. Buisson, Imprimeur-Libraire, rue Hautefeuille, no. 20, an VII de la Republique [i.e., **1798**].

3 vols., 8vo.

Price & Price 6.

114.5——. [Unabridged? French translation of 114.1]

Very short account of his life printed in John Gabriel Stedman, *Voyage à Surinam et dans l'intérieur de la Guiane. Contenant la relation de cinq années de courses et d'observations faites dans cette contrée intéressante et peu connue; avec des détails sur les Indiens de la Guiane et les Nègres... traduit de l'anglais par P. F. Henry.*

Lausanne [Switzerland]: chez Hermann, **1799**.

3 vols., 8vo.

114.6 ——. [Dutch translation of 114.1]

Very short account of his life as told to John Gabriel Stedman translated into Dutch (supplemented with elements of the French in 107.4) printed on p. 66, vol. 2 of Stedman's *Reize naar Surinamen, en door der Binnenste Gedeelten van Guiana*

Amsterdam [Netherlands]: by Johannes Allart, MDCCXCIX–MDCCC [**1799–1800**].

4 vols.

https://www.delpher.nl/nl/boeken/view?coll=boeken&identifier=dpo:8142:mpeg21:0084&cql%5B%5D=%28creator+exact+%22Stedman%2C+John+Gabrie%CC%88l%22%29&objectsearch=Grootvader

114.7 ———. [Dutch translation]

Very short account of his life as told to John Gabriel Stedman printed in Chapter XII under date 5 March **1774** in Stedman's *Reize in de Binnenlanden van Suriname*. Translated by J. D. Pasteur.

Leyden [Netherlands]: By A. en J. Hankoop, MDCCXC.IX [1799].

114.8 ———. [Second English edition of 114.1]

Very short account of his life as told to John Gabriel Stedman printed in Chapter XII under date 5 March **1774** on p. 319 in vol. 1 of Stedman's *Narrative, of a Five Years' Expedition, against the Revolted Negroes of Surinam, in Guiana, on the Wild Coast of South America; from the year 1772, to 1777... Second edition, corrected.*

London [England]: Printed for J. Johnson, St. Paul's Church Yard, and Th. Payne, Pall Mall, **1806**. Colophon: Luke Hansard, printer, near Lincoln's-Inn-Fields.

2 vols., 4to. (27 cm.), folding map, plan, plates (some engraved by William Blake).

https://babel.hathitrust.org/cgi/pt?id=gri.ark:/13960/t5s76ct09&view=1up&seq=411

Price & Price 12.

114.9 ———. [Another printing of 114.8]

Very short account of his life as told to John Gabriel Stedman printed in Chapter XII under date 5 March **1774** on p. 319 in vol. 1 of Stedman's *Narrative, of a Five Years' Expedition, against the Revolted Negroes of Surinam, in Guiana, on the Wild Coast of South America; from the year 1772, to 1777... Second edition* [sic], *corrected.*

London [England]: Printed for J. Johnson, St. Paul's Church Yard, and Th. Payne, Pall Mall, **1813**. Colophon: Luke Hansard, printer, near Lincoln's-Inn-Fields.

2 vols., 4to. (27 cm.), folding map, plan, plates (some engraved by William Blake).

https://archive.org/details/narrativeoffivey01sted/page/319/mode/1up

114.10 ———. [Italian translation]

Very short account of his life as told to John Gabriel Stedman printed in Chapter XII under date 5 March **1774** in Stedman's *Viaggio al Surinam e nell'interno della Guiana ossia relazione di cinque anni di corse e di osservazioni fatte in questo interessante e poco conosciuto paese .... Versione dal francese del Cav. [Bartolomeo] Borghi.*

Milano [Italia]: dalla Tipografia di Giambattista Sonzogno, **1818**.

4 vols., 8vo.

114.11 ———.

Very short account of his life as told to John Gabriel Stedman printed on p. 76 within Stedman's account of Joanna's life printed on pp. 65–105 in the avowedly abolitionist gift book (or annual) *The Oasis*, edited by Mrs. [Lydia Maria] Child.

Boston [Massachusetts, U.S.A.]: Allen and Ticknor, **1834**. Tpv: Entered according to act of Congress, in the year 1834, by Allen & Ticknor ... Boston: Tuttle and Weeks, Printers, No. 8, School Street.

12mo (16 cm.): xiv, 276 p., plates (including engraved full-length depiction of Joanna). Includes introduction to this selection by Lydia Maria Child (signed in the "Editor") on p. 65.

https://babel.hathitrust.org/cgi/pt?id=osu.32435004550596&view=1up&seq=108

114.12 ———. [Distinct issue of 114.11 with variant title-page]

Very short account of his life as told to John Gabriel Stedman printed on p. 76 within Stedman's account of Joanna's life printed on pp. 65–105 in the avowedly abolitionist gift book (or annual) *The Oasis*, edited by Mrs. [Lydia Maria] Child.

Boston [Massachusetts, U.S.A.]: Benjamin C. Bacon, **1834**. Tpv: Entered according to act of Congress, in the year 1834, by Allen & Ticknor ... Boston: Tuttle and Weeks, Printers, No. 8, School Street.

12mo (16 cm.): xiv, 276 p., plates (including engraved full-length depiction of Joanna). Includes introduction to this selection by Lydia Maria Child (signed in the "Editor") on p. 65.

https://babel.hathitrust.org/cgi/pt?id=hvd.32044011434495&view=1up&seq=108

114.13 ———.

Very short account of his life as told to John Gabriel Stedman reprinted from *The Oasis* (114.11 or 114.12) on pp.19–20 of *Narrative of Joanna; an Emancipated Slave, of Surinam (From Stedman's Narrative of a Five Years' Expedition against the Revolted Negroes of Surinam.)*

Boston [Massachusetts, U.S.A.]: Published by Isaac Knapp, 25, Cornhill, **1838**.

12mo (16 cm.): 64 p., plates (including engraved full-length depiction of Joanna). Includes related editorial text by Lydia Maria Child reprinted from *The Oasis*. Parentheses ( ) replace square brackets [ ] in title-page transcription.

https://babel.hathitrust.org/cgi/pt?id=hvd.32044020349544&view=1up&seq=41

114.14 ———. [Critical edition of 114.1]

Very short account of his life as told to John Gabriel Stedman printed in Chapter 12 under date 5 March **1774** on pp. 166–167 in vol. 1 of Stedman's *Narrative, of a Five Years'*

Expedition, against the Revolted Negroes of Surinam, in Guiana, on the Wild Coast of South America; from the year 1772, to 1777 … [Introduction and notes by R. A. J. van Lier].

Barre, Massachusetts [U.S.A.]: Printed for the Imprint Society, **1971.** Colophon (vol. 2 only): … printed … by Joh. Enschede en Zonen, Haarlem, Holland….

2 vols. (continuously paged), 8vo (27.5 cm.): xviii, [10], 480, [1] p., plates, some folding.

114.15——. [Critical edition of 114.1]

Very short account of his life as told to John Gabriel Stedman printed in Chapter 12 under date 5 March **1774** on pp. 166–167 of Stedman's *Narrative, of a Five Years' Expedition, against the Revolted Negroes of Surinam, in Guiana, on the Wild Coast of South America; from the year 1772, to 1777 …* [Introduction and notes by R. A. J. van Lier].

Amherst, Massachusetts [U.S.A.]: University of Massachusetts Press, MCMLXXII **[1972].**

8vo (27.3 cm.): xviii, [10], 480 p., plates, some folding. Comprises sheets ("printed … by Joh. Enschede en Zonen, Haarlem, Holland" as noted in 116.11) from 116.11 but here bound in one volume with distinct title-page.

114.16——.

Very short account of his life as told to John Gabriel Stedman printed in Chapter XII under date 5 March **1774** on p. 249 in Stedman's *Narrative, of a Five Years' Expedition, against the Revolted Negroes of Surinam, in Guiana, on the Wild Coast of South America; from the year 1772, to 1777 … transcribed for the first time from the original 1790 manuscript; edited,* and with an introduction and notes, by Richard Price & Sally Price.

Baltimore [Maryland, U.S.A.]: The Johns Hopkins University Press, **1988.**

8vo (27 cm.): xcvii, 708 p., illus.

114.17——. [Abridged edition of 114.16]

Very short account of his life as told to John Gabriel Stedman printed in Chapter XIIth on p. 138 in *Stedman's Surinam Life in an Eighteenth-Century Slave Society An Abridged, Modernized Edition of Narrative of a Five Years* [sic] *Expedition against the Revolted Negroes of Surinam by John Gabriel Stedman. Edited by Richard Price and Sally Price.*

Baltimore [Maryland, U.S.A.]: The Johns Hopkins University Press, **[1992].**

8vo (23 cm.): lxxv, [3], [1–5] 6–350 p., map, illus. Note: This abridgement "include[s] about 50 percent of the original text and 33 of the original 81 plates" (p. lxv).

114.18——. [Another (complete) printing of 114.16]

Very short account of his life as told to John Gabriel Stedman printed in Chapter XII under date 5 March **1774** on p. 249 in Stedman's *Narrative, of a Five Years' Expedition, against the Revolted Negroes of Surinam, in Guiana, on the Wild Coast of South America; from the year 1772, to 1777 … transcribed for the first time from the original 1790 manuscript; edited, and with an introduction and notes, by Richard Price & Sally Price.*

New York [New York, U.S.A.]: iUniverse.com, **[2010].**
8vo (27 cm.): xcvii, 708 p., illus.

1774–1775

115.0 Ephraim Robin John

Eight letters written to Charles Wesley, Ambrose Lace, and Thomas Jones **1774–1775**, by Little Ephraim Robin John, some coauthored with Ancona Robin Robin John (q.v. 116.0). Original manuscripts in the Charles Wesley Papers, John Rylands Library, **Manchester, England.**

¶ Ephraim Robin John and Ancona Robin Robin John (q.v. 116.0) were members of a prominent merchant family in the Calabar ward of Old Town (Cross River region, southeastern Nigeria and northwest Cameroon—see Map 5) involved in slave trading. They were seized in 1767 when British ship captains and local rival Calabar merchants from the

https://babel.hathitrust.org/cgi/pt?id=iau.3185802205845 1&view=1up&seq=102 [see 115.1].

ward of Duke Town (also called New Town) staged a conspiracy and ambushed the Old Town merchants, killing many and selling the survivors into slavery. The Robin Johns were sold into slavery on Dominica in the Caribbean (Map 11), then escaped. They were reenslaved in the British North American colony of Virginia (Map 15), taken to Bristol, England (Map 8), released, and returned to Calabar, where they resumed trading slaves to Europeans for guns and other imports. They told their story in letters to each other, and to others who reproduced them in court depositions. For more on these two men see Randy Sparks, *The Two Princes of Calabar: An Eighteenth-Century Atlantic Odyssey* (Cambridge, MA: Harvard University Press, 2004).

115.1 ——.

"An Extract from the Depositions of William Floyd, of the City of Bristol, Mariner, and Little Ephraim Robin-John, and Ancona Robin Robin-John, of Old Town, Old Calabar, on the

Coast of Africa," printed in three parts in three issues (February, March, April) of the *Arminian Magazine, for the year 1783, consisting of Extracts and Original Treatises on Universal Redemption*, vol. 6, pp. 98–99, 152–153, and 211–212.

London [England]: Printed by J. Paramore, at the Foundery, Moorfields; And sold at the New Chapel, City-Road, and by all the Booksellers in Town and Country, **1783**.

https://babel.hathitrust.org/cgi/pt?id=iau.31858022058451& view=1up&seq=102

115.2———.

All letters, court depositions, and related materials printed in *The Notorious Massacre at Calabar in 1767*, edited by David L. Imbua, Paul E. Lovejoy, Nicholas Radburn, and Randy J. Sparks.

Trenton, New Jersey [U.S.A.]: Africa World Press, **2021**, reportedly pending in 2021.
8vo (23 cm.): 348 p.

116.0 Ancona Robin Robin John [sic]

Several letters written to Charles Wesley, Ambrose Lace, and Thomas Jones, 1774–1775, coauthored with Little Ephraim Robin-John (q.v. 114.0). Original manuscripts in the Charles Wesley Papers, John Rylands Library, Manchester, England.

https://babel.hathitrust.org/cgi/ pt?id=iau.31858 022058451&vie w=1up&seq=102 [see 116.1].

¶ Ancona Robin Robin John and Ephraim Robin John (q.v. 114.0) were members of a prominent merchant family in the Calabar ward of Old Town (Cross River region, southeastern Nigeria and northwest Cameroon—see Map 5) involved in slave trading. They were seized in 1767 when British ship captains and local rival Calabar mer-

chants from the ward of Duke Town (also called New Town) staged a conspiracy and ambushed the Old Town merchants, killing many and selling the survivors into slavery. The Robin Johns were sold into slavery on Dominica in the Caribbean (Map 11), then escaped. They were reenslaved in the British North American colony of Virginia (Map 15), taken to Bristol, England (Map 8), released, and returned to Calabar, where they resumed trading slaves to Europeans for guns and other imports. They told their story in letters to each other and to others who reproduced them in court depositions. For more on these two men see Randy Sparks, *The Two Princes of Calabar: An Eighteenth-Century Atlantic Odyssey* (Cambridge, MA: Harvard University Press, 2004).

116.1 ———.

"An Extract from the Depositions of William Floyd, of the City of Bristol, Mariner, and Little Ephraim Robin-John, and Ancona Robin Robin-John, of Old Town, Old Calabar, on the Coast of Africa," printed in three parts in three issues (February, March, April) of the *Arminian Magazine, for the year 1783, consisting of Extracts and Original Treatises on Universal Redemption*, vol. 6, pp. 98–99, 152–153, and 211–212.

London [England]: Printed by J. Paramore, at the Foundery, Moorfields; And sold at the New Chapel, City-Road, and by all the Booksellers in Town and Country, **1783**.

https://babel.hathitrust.org/cgi/pt?id=iau.31858022058451& view=1up&seq=102

116.2———.

All letters, court depositions, and related materials printed in *The Notorious Massacre at Calabar in 1767*, edited by David L. Imbua, Paul E. Lovejoy, Nicholas Radburn, and Randy J. Sparks.

Trenton, New Jersey [U.S.A.]: Africa World Press, **2021**.
8vo (23 cm.): 348 p.

1776

117.0 Unnamed heroic man (–1776)

Two autobiographical gallows speeches (with intervening remarks of his "master," who was also one of his judges) written within quotation marks in "Chapter 24th" (under "The day Following" 27 February 1776) on pp. 614–615 of Stedman's 1790 manuscript of his "Narrative, of a five years expedition against the Rebelled Negroes of Surinam ..." N.b.: One of the unnamed heroic man's

https://www.biodiversitylibrary.org/ item/163990#page/266/ mode/1up [see 117.1a].

owners, a chief, is here named **Bony** (p. 614). This manuscript, which is preserved in the John Gabriel Stedman Collection at the University of Minnesota's James Ford Bell Library, Minneapolis, Minnesota, U.S.A., was the heavily edited (see introduction to 117.39) basis of 117.1; it was first published *verbatim et literatim* in 1988, q.v. 117.39. Manuscript pages 614 and 615 have been digitized (as images 644 and 645) with the rest of the manuscript by the James Ford Bell Library and are available at:

https://umedia.lib.umn.edu/item/p16022coll187:962/ p16022coll187:717?child_index=643&facets%5Bcollection_ name_s%5D%5B%5D=John%20Gabriel%20Stedman%20 Archive%20and%20Book%20Manuscript&q=stedman &query=&sidebar_page=215

117.0   Unnamed heroic man (–1776)

¶ This warrior and hunter was born in Africa, taken captive in battle while defending his prince, and sold on the Guinea coast (see Map 3) by his own countrymen to Europeans who took him to the Dutch South American colony of Suriname (Map 10), probably ca. 1770. After suffering cruel treatment, he ran away and joined the Boni Maroons, who were fighting a guerilla war against the colonial government. After suffering even crueler treatment from the Maroons, he ran away from them ca. 1774 and lived alone in the wilderness in misery, until captured by colonial militia and taken before a tribunal. Upon hearing the tribunal's verdict, the warrior spoke briefly and bravely, as Stedman witnessed and recorded these autobiographical speeches. When the warrior finished speaking, he was tortured and executed, according to John Gabriel Stedman (see above) bearing this treatment in silence and with a smile.

117.1a ——.

Two autobiographical gallows speeches (with intervening remarks of his "master," who was also one of his judges) printed within quotation marks in chapter XXIV (under date 27 February 1776) on pp. 208–210 in vol. 2 of John Gabriel Stedman, *Narrative, of a Five Years' Expedition, against the Revolted Negroes of Surinam, in Guiana, on the Wild Coast of South America; from the year 1772, to 1777…*

London [England]: Printed for J. Johnson, St. Paul's Church Yard, & J. Edwards, Pall Mall, **1796** (*sic*). No colophon in vol. 2. **Regular paper issue** with uncolored plates.

2 vols., 4to. (28 cm.), folding map, plan, plates (some engraved by William Blake). Includes list of subscribers.

N.b.: One of the speaker's owners, a chief, is here named **Bonny** (2:209).

https://www.biodiversitylibrary.org/item/163990#page/266/mode/1up
ESTC t146566; Price & Price 1.

117.1b——.

Two autobiographical gallows speeches (with intervening remarks of his "master," who was also one of his judges) printed within quotation marks in chapter XXIV (under apparent date 27 February 1776) on pp. 208–210 in vol. 2 of John Gabriel Stedman, *Narrative, of a Five Years' Expedition, against the Revolted Negroes of Surinam, in Guiana, on the Wild Coast of South America; from the year 1772, to 1777…*

London [England]: Printed for J. Johnson, St. Paul's Church Yard, & J. Edwards, Pall Mall, **1796** (*sic*). No colophon in vol. 2. **Large paper issue** with hand-colored title-page vignettes and plates.

2 vols., 4to. (28 cm.), folding map, plan, plates (some engraved by William Blake). Includes list of subscribers.

N.b.: One of the speaker's owners, a chief, is here named Bonny (2:209).

https://archive.org/details/narrativeoffivey02sted_0/page/208
ESTC t146565; Price & Price 2.

117.2 ——. [German translation of 117.1]

Two autobiographical gallows speeches (with intervening remarks of his "master," who was also one of his judges) printed within quotation marks in chapter XXIV (under date 27 February **1776**) on pp. 414–416 of John Gabriel Stedman, *Stedman's Nachrichten von Surinam und von seiner Expedition gegen die rebellischen Neger in dieser Kolonie in den Jahren 1772 bis 1777.*

Hamburg [Germany]: bei Benjamin Gotttlob [*sic*] Hoffmann, **1797.**

8vo: xiv, 522 p., illus., map.

N.b.: One of the speaker's owners, a chief, is here named Bonny (414).

https://www.e-rara.ch/zuz/nagezh/content/pageview/9727763
Price & Price 3.

117.3a ——. [Abridged German translation of 117.1]

Two autobiographical gallows speeches (with intervening remarks of his "master," who was also one of his judges) printed within quotation marks in chapter XXIV (under date 27 February **1776**) on pp. 109–111 in vol. 2 of John Gabriel Stedman, *Stedman's Nachrichten von Suriname, dem letzten Aufruhr der dortigen Negersclaven umd ihrer Bezwingung in den Jahren 1772, bis 1777.*

Halle [Saxony-Anhalt, Germany]: in der Rengerschen Buchhandlung, **1797.**

2 vols., 8vo.

N.b.: One of the speaker's owners, a chief, is here named **Bonny** (2:110).

https://archive.org/details/bub_gb_iBhZAAAAcAAJ/page/n110/mode/1up
Price & Price 4.

117.3b ——. [Abridged German translation of 117.1]

115.3a issued as vols. 8 and 9 of M. C. Sprengel, *Auswahl der besten ausländischen geographischen und statistischen Nachrichten.*

Halle [Saxony-Anhalt, Germany]: in der Rengerschen Buchhandlung, **1797.**

2 vols., 8vo.

N.b.: One of the speaker's owners, a chief, is here named Bonny (9:110).

Price & Price 5.

117.4 ——. [Abridged French translation of 117.1]

Two autobiographical gallows speeches (with intervening remarks of his "master," who was also one of his judges) printed within quotation marks in chapter XXIV (under date 27

February **1776**) on pp. 426–428 in vol. 3 of John Gabriel Stedman, *Voyage a Surinam et dans l'Intérieur de Guiane …* traduit de l'Anglais par P. F. Henry.

Paris [France]: chez F. Buisson, Imprimeur-Libraire, rue Hautefeuille, no. 20, an VII de la Republique [*i.e.* 1798].

3 vols., 8vo.

N.b.: One of the speaker's owners, a chief, is here named Bonny (3:426).

Price & Price 6.

117.5 ———. [Unabridged? French translation of 117.1]

Two autobiographical gallows speeches (with intervening remarks of his "master," who was also one of his judges) printed within quotation marks in chapter XXIV (under date 27 February **1776**) in vol. 3 of John Gabriel Stedman, *Voyage à Surinam et dans l'intérieur de la Guiane. Contenant la relation de cinq années de courses et d'observations faites dans cette contrée intéressante et peu connue; avec des détails sur les Indiens de la Guiane et les Nègres… traduit de l'anglais par P. F. Henry.*

Lausanne [Switzerland]: chez Hermann, **1799**.

3 vols., 8vo.

117.6 ———. [Dutch translation of 117.1]

Two autobiographical gallows speeches (with intervening remarks of his "master," who was also one of his judges) translated from 115.1a (supplemented with elements of the French in 115.4) printed within quotation marks in chapter XXIV (under date 27 February **1776**) on pp. 174–176 in vol. 3 of John Gabriel Stedman, *Reize naar Surinamen, en door der Binnenste Gedeelten van Guiana.*

Amsterdam [Netherlands]: by Johannes Allart, MDCCXCIX–MDCCXXX [1799–1800].

4 vols.

https://www.delpher.nl/nl/boeken/view?coll=boeken&identifier=dpo:8143:mpeg21:0194&cql%5B%5D=%28creator+exact+%22Stedman%2C+John+Gabrie%CC%88l%22%29&objectsearch=1776

117.7 ———. [Dutch translation]

Two autobiographical gallows speeches (with intervening remarks of his "master," who was also one of his judges) printed within quotation marks in chapter XXIV (under date 27 February **1776**) in John Gabriel Stedman, *Reize in de Binnenlanden van Suriname.* Translated by J. D. Pasteur.

Leyden [Netherlands]: By A. en J. Hankoop, MDCCXC.IX, [1799].

117.8 ———. [Swedish translation]

Two autobiographical gallows speeches (with intervening remarks of his "master," who was also one of his judges) print-

ed within quotation marks in chapter XXIV (under date 27 February **1776**) on pp. 229–230 of *Capitain Johan Stedmans dagbok öfwer sina fälttåg i Surinam, jämte beskrifning om detta nybygges inwånare och öfriga märkwärdigheter,* translated by Samuel Ödmann.

Stockholm [Sweden]: Tryckt i Kongl. Ordens Boktryckeriet hos Assessoren Johan Pfeiffer, **1800**.

8vo (19 cm.): [6], 306, [14] p., plate, illus.

N.b.: One of the speaker's owners, a chief, is here named Bonny (229).

https://babel.hathitrust.org/cgi/pt?id=uc1.31175035187510&view=1up&seq=241

117.9 ———. [Second English edition of 117.1]

Two autobiographical gallows speeches (with intervening remarks of his "master," who was also one of his judges) printed within quotation marks in chapter XXIV (under date 27 February **1776**) on pp. 215–217 in vol. 2 of John Gabriel Stedman, *Narrative, of a Five Years' Expedition, against the Revolted Negroes of Surinam, in Guiana, on the Wild Coast of South America; from the year 1772, to 1777… **Second edition**, corrected.*

London [England]: Printed for J. Johnson, St. Paul's Church Yard, and Th. Payne, Pall Mall, **1806**. Colophon: Luke Hansard, printer, near Lincoln's-Inn-Fields.

2 vols., 4to. (27 cm.), folding map, plan, plates (some engraved by William Blake).

N.b.: One of the speaker's owners, a chief, is here named **Bonny** (2:216).

https://babel.hathitrust.org/cgi/pt?id=gri.ark:/13960/t4jm38n7d&view=1up&seq=273

Price & Price 12.

117.10 ———.

Two autobiographical gallows speeches (with intervening remarks of his 'master,' who was also one of his judges) translated into French from the first edition of Stedman (117.1) and printed on pp. 260–262 in vol. 1 of J. J. Dauxion Lavaysse, *Voyage aux îles de Trinidad, de Tabago, de la Marguerite, et dans diverse parties, de Vénézuéla, dans l'Amérique Méridionale*

Paris [France]: F. Schoell, Libraire, rue de Fosses-Montmartre, no. 14, **1813**.

2 vols., 8vo.

N.b.: One of the speaker's owners, a chief, is here named **Bonny** (1:260).

117.11 ———. [Another printing of 117.9]

Two autobiographical gallows speeches (with intervening remarks of his "master," who was also one of his judges) printed within quotation marks in chapter XXIV (under date 27 February **1776**) on pp. 215–217 in vol. 2 of John Gabriel

117.0   Unnamed heroic man (–1776)

Stedman, *Narrative, of a Five Years' Expedition, against the Revolted Negroes of Surinam, in Guiana, on the Wild Coast of South America; from the year 1772, to 1777... Second edition* [sic], *corrected*.

London [England]: Printed for J. Johnson, St. Paul's Church Yard, and Th. Payne, Pall Mall, **1813**. Colophon: Luke Hansard, printer, near Lincoln's-Inn-Fields.

2 vols., 4to. (27 cm.), folding map, plan, plates (some engraved by William Blake).

N.b.: One of the speaker's owners, a chief, is here named Bonny (2:216).

https://archive.org/details/narrativeoffivey02sted/page/215

117.12 ——. [Italian translation]

Two autobiographical gallows speeches (with intervening remarks of his "master," who was also one of his judges) printed within quotation marks in chapter XXIV (under date 27 February 1776) in *Viaggio al Surinam e nell'interno della Guiana ossia relazione di cinque anni di corse e di osservazioni fatte in questo interessante e poco conosciuto paese .... Versione dal francese del Cav.* [Bartolomeo] *Borghi*.

Milano [Italy]: dalla Tipografia di Giambattista Sonzogno, **1818**.

4 vols., 8vo.

117.13 ——. [English translation of 117.10]

Two autobiographical gallows speeches (with intervening remarks of his "master," who was also one of his judges) originating in the first edition of Stedman (117.1) translated back into English from 117.10 and printed on pp. 378–380 in J. J. Dauxion Lavaysse, *A Statistical, Commercial, and Political Description of Venezuela, Trinidad, Margarita, and Tobago: containing Various Anecdotes and Observations, illustrative of the past and present state of these interesting countries; from the French of M. Lavaysse; with an introduction and explanatory notes by the editor* [Edward Blaquiere].

London [England]: Printed for G. and W. B. Whittaker, 13, Ave-Maria Lane, **1820**. Tpv: W. Shackell, Printer, Johnson's-court, Fleet-street, London.

8vo (23 cm.): [2], [v]-xxxix, 479 p., folding map.

N.b.: One of the speaker's owners, a chief, is here named Bonnay (378).

https://babel.hathitrust.org/cgi/pt?id=nyp.33433081701090&view=1up&seq=420&q1

117.14 ——.

Two autobiographical gallows speeches (with intervening remarks of his "master," who was also one of his judges) reprinted (less omissions) from Stedman (i.e., 117.1, 117.9, or 117.11), within quotation marks under heading "Heroic

Negro" on pp.159–161 in vol. 7 (volume for "Anecdotes of Eloquence") of *The Percy Anecdotes. Original and select. By Sholto and Reuben Percy* [pseudonyms of Joseph Clinton Robertson and Thomas Byerley]; *Brothers of the Benedictine Monastery, Mount Benger*.

London [England]: Printed for T. Boys, Ludgate Hill, **1820**. Colophon: London: Printed by D. Cartwright, 91, Bartholomew Close.

20 vols., 12mo.

N.b.: One of the speaker's owners, a chief, is here named Bonnas (7:160).

https://babel.hathitrust.org/cgi/pt?id=uc1.b0000163428&view=1up&seq=171

117.15 ——.

Two autobiographical gallows speeches (with intervening remarks of his 'master,' who was also one of his judges) reprinted as in 117.13, within quotation marks under heading "Heroic Negro" in *The Percy Anecdotes...*

New York [New York, U.S.A.]: Richard Scott, **1822**.

12mo (16 cm.): 143 p.

117.16 ——.

Two autobiographical gallows speeches (with intervening remarks of his 'master,' who was also one of his judges) reprinted (less omissions), within quotation marks under heading "Heroic Negro" on pp. 62–63 of *The Genius of Universal Emancipation. A Monthly Paper, containing Original Essays and Selections, on the subject of African Slavery*, vol. 2, no. 4 (whole no. 16).

Greenville, Tennessee [U.S.A.]: Edited and published by Benjamin Lundy, Tenth Month [*i.e.* October], **1822**.

N.b.: One of the speaker's owners, a chief, is here named **Bonas** (62).

https://archive.org/details/ASPC0002419402/page/n65

117.17 ——.

Two autobiographical gallows speeches (with intervening remarks of his 'master,' who was also one of his judges) reprinted as in 117.4, within quotation marks under heading "Heroic Negro" in *The Percy Anecdotes....*

Philadelphia [Pennsylvania, U.S.A.]: Published by George Bewley, **1823**.

12mo (15 cm.): [2], 214 p.

117.18 ——.

Two autobiographical gallows speeches (with intervening remarks of his "master," who was also one of his judges) reprinted (less omissions), within quotation marks under heading "Heroic Negro" on pp. 159–161 in vol. 2 (subtitled *Eloquence & Patriotism*) of *The Percy Anecdotes. Original and select. By Sholto and Reuben Percy* [pseudonyms of Joseph Clinton Robertson and Thomas Byerley], *Brothers of the Benedictine Monastery, Mount Benger.*

London [England]: Printed for J. Cumberland, 19, Ludgate Hill, 1826.

20 vols., 12mo.

N.b.: One of the speaker's owners, a chief, is here named Bonas (2:160).

https://babel.hathitrust.org/cgi/pt?id=uc1.$b325328&view=1up&seq=169

117.19 ———.

Two autobiographical gallows speeches (with intervening remarks of his "master," who was also one of his judges) reprinted (less omissions), within quotation marks under heading "Heroic Negro" on p. 23 in vol. 1 of *The Percy Anecdotes, Revised Edition. To which is added A Valuable Collection of American Anecdotes original & select.*

New York [New York, U.S.A.]: J. & J. Harper, 82 Cliff Street, 1832.

2 vols., 8vo (24 cm.).

N.b.: One of the speaker's owners, a chief, is here named Bonas (1:23).

https://babel.hathitrust.org/cgi/pt?id=uva.x001191690&view=1up&seq=25

117.20 ———.

Two autobiographical gallows speeches (with intervening remarks of his "master," who was also one of his judges) reprinted (less omissions), within quotation marks under heading "Heroic Negro" on pp. 202–203 in *The Scrap Book; A Selection of Humorous Stories, Interesting Fables, and Authentic Anecdotes.*

New York [New York, U.S.A.]: Published by Jesse Smith, 1834.

12mo (15 cm.): 288 p., plates.

N.b.: One of the speaker's owners, a chief, is here named Bonas (202).

https://babel.hathitrust.org/cgi/pt?id=njp.32101071986994&view=1up&seq=238

117.21 ———. [Another printing of previous item]

Two autobiographical gallows speeches (with intervening remarks of his 'master,' who was also one of his judges) reprinted (less omissions), within quotation marks under heading "Heroic Negro" on pp. 202–203 in *The Scrap Book; A Selection of Humorous Stories, Interesting Fables, and Authentic Anecdotes.*

New York [New York, U.S.A.]: Published for the Booksellers, [n.d., *ca.* 1834?].

12mo (15 cm.): 288 p., plates.

N.b.: One of the speaker's owners, a chief, is here named Bonas (202).

https://babel.hathitrust.org/cgi/pt?id=hvd.32044020547568&view=1up&seq=232

117.22 ———.

Two autobiographical gallows speeches (with intervening remarks of his 'master,' who was also one of his judges) reprinted (less omissions), within quotation marks under heading "Heroic Negro" on pp. 159–161 in vol. 2 (subtitled *Eloquence & Patriotism*) of *The Percy Anecdotes. Original and select. By Sholto and Reuben Percy* [pseudonyms of Joseph Clinton Robertson and Thomas Byerley], *Brothers of the Benedictine Monastery, Mount Benger.*

London [England]: George Berger, Holywell Street, Strand, [n.d., *ca.* 1835 +/- 3 yrs. (KA)]. Colophon: J. Cumberland, Cumberland Terrace, Camden New Town.

20 vols., 12mo (15 cm.).

N.b.: One of the speaker's owners, a chief, is here named Bonas (2:160).

https://babel.hathitrust.org/cgi/pt?id=nyp.33433067305395&view=1up&seq=169

117.23 ———.

Two autobiographical gallows speeches (with intervening remarks of his "master," who was also one of his judges) reprinted (less omissions), within quotation marks under heading "Heroic Negro" on pp. 399–400 of *Anecdotal Olio: being a collection of Literary, Moral, Religious, and Miscellaneous Anecdotes.* Selected and arranged by the Rev. Messrs. Hoes and Way [perhaps the upstate New York Methodist ministers Schuyler Hoes and P. M. Way].

New York [New York, U.S.A.]: Harper & Brothers. Cliff-Street, 1838.

8vo (22 cm.): xiv, [21]-408 p. Introduction dated "Utica, 1838."

N.b.: One of the speaker's owners, a chief, is here named Bonas (399).

https://babel.hathitrust.org/cgi/pt?id=chi.087560023&view=1up&seq=405

117.24———.

Two autobiographical gallows speeches (with intervening remarks of his "master," who was also one of his judges) reprinted (less omissions), within quotation marks under heading "Heroic Negro" on p. 23 in vol. 1 of *The Percy Anecdotes, Revised Edition. To which is added, A Valuable Collection of American Anecdotes. Original and select.*

New York [New York, U.S.A.]: Harper & Brothers. 82 Cliff-Street, **1839**.

2 vols., 8vo (24 cm.).

N.b.: One of the speaker's owners, a chief, is here named Bonas (1:23).

https://babel.hathitrust.org/cgi/pt?id=hvd.hn2vbg&view=1up&seq=35

117.25 ———.

Two autobiographical gallows speeches (with intervening remarks of his "master," who was also one of his judges) reprinted (less omissions), within quotation marks under heading "Heroic Negro" on p. 23 in vol. 1 of *The Percy Anecdotes, Revised Edition. To which is added, A Valuable Collection of American Anecdotes. Original and select.*

New York [New York, U.S.A.]: Published by Harper & Brothers, **1843**.

2 vols., 8vo (24 cm.).

N.b.: One of the speaker's owners, a chief, is here named Bonas (1:23).

https://babel.hathitrust.org/cgi/pt?id=njp.32101041622513&view=1up&seq=31

117.26———.

Two autobiographical gallows speeches (with intervening remarks of his "master," who was also one of his judges) reprinted (less omissions), within quotation marks under heading "Heroic Negro" on pp. 202–203 in *Tales of Humour: A Scrap-Book of Choice Stories of Wit, Interesting Fables, and Authentic Anecdotes.* [Note: Contents same as 115.20 and 115.21, *The Scrap Book.*]

Philadelphia [Pennsylvania, U.S.A.]: Published by Leary & Getz, No. 138 North Second Street, [n.d., ca. 1845?].

12mo (16 cm.): 288 p., plates.

N.b.: One of the speaker's owners, a chief, is here named Bonas (202).

https://babel.hathitrust.org/cgi/pt?id=nyp.33433082526744&view=1up&seq=210

117.27———.

Two autobiographical gallows speeches (with intervening remarks of his "master,"who was also one of his judges) reprinted (less omissions), within quotation marks under heading "Heroic Negro" on p. 23 in vol. 1 of *The Percy Anecdotes, Revised Edition. To which is added, A Valuable Collection of American Anecdotes. Original and select.*

New York [New York, U.S.A.]: Published by Harper & Brothers No. 82 Cliff-Street, **1847**.

2 vols., 8vo (24 cm.).

N.b.: One of the speaker's owners, a chief, is here named Bonas (1:23).

https://babel.hathitrust.org/cgi/pt?id=nyp.33433074921788&view=1up&seq=35

117.28 ———. [Another printing of 117.23]

Two autobiographical gallows speeches (with intervening remarks of his 'master,' who was also one of his judges) reprinted (less omissions), within quotation marks under heading "Heroic Negro" on pp. 399–400 of *Anecdotal Olio: being a collection of Literary, Moral, Religious, and Miscellaneous Anecdotes.* Selected and arranged by the Rev. Messrs. Hoes and Way [perhaps the upstate New York Methodist ministers Schuyler Hoes and P. M. Way].

New York [New York, U.S.A.]: Harper & Brother, Publishers, Franklin Square, **1856**.

8vo (24 cm.): xiv, [2], [21]-408 p. Introduction dated "Utica, 1838."

N.b.: One of the speaker's owners, a chief, is here named Bonas (399).

https://babel.hathitrust.org/cgi/pt?id=loc.ark:/13960/t7sn1gm0n&view=1up&seq=403

117.29 ———.

Two autobiographical gallows speeches (with intervening remarks of his "master," who was also one of his judges) reprinted (less omissions), within quotation marks under heading "Heroic Negro" on pp. 202–203 in vol. 2 of *New Book of A Thousand Anecdotes, wit, humor, odd scraps, tales, legends, bon mots, off-hand hits, sketches, &c., &c., &c.* Selected and arranged by A. Wag [pseud.], Esq. [Note: Contents same as 117.20 and 117.21, *The Scrap Book,* and 115.26, *Tales of Humor.*]

New York [New York, U.S.A.]: Richard Marsh, 138 William Street, **1856**.

2 vols in one, 12mo (19 cm.).

N.b.: One of the speaker's owners, a chief, is here named Bonas (202).

https://babel.hathitrust.org/cgi/pt?id=nyp.33433082291505&view=1up&seq=496&q1

117.30 ———. [Another printing of 117.23]

Two autobiographical gallows speeches (with intervening remarks of his "master," who was also one of his judges) reprinted (less omissions), within quotation marks under heading "Heroic Negro" on pp. 399–400 of *Anecdotal Olio: being a collection of Literary, Moral, Religious, and Miscellaneous Anecdotes.* Selected and arranged by the Rev. Messrs. Hoes and Way [*perhaps* the upstate New York Methodist ministers Schuyler Hoes and P. M. Way].

New York [New York, U.S.A.]: Harper & Brother, Publishers, Franklin Square, **1858.**

8vo (24 cm.): xiv, [2], [21]-408 p. Introduction dated "Utica, 1838."

N.b.: One of the speaker's owners, a chief, is here named Bonas (399).

https://babel.hathitrust.org/cgi/pt?id=loc.ark:/13960/t9378n-j2n&view=1up&seq=401

117.31 ——.

Two autobiographical gallows speeches (with intervening remarks of his "master," who was also one of his judges) reprinted (less omissions), within quotation marks under heading "Heroic Negro" on p. 23 in vol. 1 of *The Percy Anecdotes, Revised Edition. To which is added, A Valuable Collection of American Anecdotes. Original and select.*

New York [New York, U.S.A.]: Harper & Brother, Publishers, Franklin Square, **1859.**

2 vols., 8vo (24 cm.).

N.b.: One of the speaker's owners, a chief, is here named Bonas (1:23).

https://babel.hathitrust.org/cgi/pt?id=uva.x030803948&view=1up&seq=35

117.32 ——.

Two autobiographical gallows speeches (with intervening remarks of his "master," who was also one of his judges) reprinted (less omissions), within quotation marks under heading "Heroic Negro" (*sub* "Anecdotes of Eloquence") on p. 141 in vol. 1 of *The Percy Anecdotes collected and edited by Reuben and Sholto Percy A Verbatim Reprint of the Original Edition with a Preface by John Timbs, F.S.A.* At head of title: *Chandos Library.*

London [England]: Frederick Warne and Co. Bedford Street, Convent Garden. New York [New York, U.S.A.]: Scribner, Welford and Co. [n.d., ca. 1868?]. Tpv: London: Savill, Edwards and Co., Printers, Chandos Street, Convent Garden.

4 vols., 8vo (20 cm.). Timbs's Preface dated in type: London, *September* 1868 (1: vi).

N.b.: One of the speaker's owners, a chief, is here named Bonas (1:141).

Note: The title-page claim that this (double column) edition was "A Verbatim Reprint of the Original Edition" is incorrect.

https://babel.hathitrust.org/cgi/pt?id=umn.319510020405988a&view=1up&seq=157

117.33 ——.

Two autobiographical gallows speeches (with intervening remarks of his 'master,' who was also one of his judges) reprint-

ed (less omissions), within quotation marks under heading "Heroic Negro" (*sub* "Anecdotes of Eloquence") on p. 141 in vol. 1 of *The Percy Anecdotes collected and edited by Reuben and Sholto Percy A Verbatim Reprint of the Original Edition with a Preface by John Timbs, F.S.A.*

New York [New York, U.S.A.]: Scribner, Welford & Co. [*ca.* 1885?].

Format: pagination.

117.34 ——.

Two autobiographical gallows speeches (with intervening remarks of his 'master,' who was also one of his judges) reprinted (less omissions), within quotation marks under heading "Heroic Negro" (*sub* "Anecdotes of Eloquence") on p. 141 in *The Percy Anecdotes collected and edited by Reuben and Sholto Percy A Verbatim Reprint of the Original Edition with a Preface by John Timbs, F.S.A.*

London [England] and New York [New York, U.S.A.]: F. Warne and Co., [n.d., ca. 1885?].

8vo (18 cm.): 988 p.

117.35 ——.

Two autobiographical gallows speeches (with intervening remarks of his "master," who was also one of his judges) reprinted (less omissions), within quotation marks under heading "Heroic Negro" (*sub* "Anecdotes of Eloquence") on p. 141 in vol. 1 of *The Percy Anecdotes collected and edited by Reuben and Sholto Percy A Verbatim Reprint of the Original Edition with a Preface by John Timbs, F.S.A.* At head of title: *The "Chandos Classics".*

London [England] and New York [New York, U.S.A.]: Frederick Warne and Co., [ca. 1887].

4 vols., 8vo (19.7 cm.).

N.b.: One of the speaker's owners, a chief, is here named Bonas (1:141).

Note: The title-page claim that this (double column) edition was "A Verbatim Reprint of the Original Edition" is incorrect; this edition appears to have been printed from the stereotype plates used to print 115.28, though after effacement of the preface date, alteration of page number placement, etc.

https://babel.hathitrust.org/cgi/pt?id=mdp.39015047658102&view=1up&seq=157

117.36 ——.

Two autobiographical gallows speeches (with intervening remarks of his "master," who was also one of his judges) printed within quotation marks in chapter 20 (under date 27 February 1776) on pp. 199–200 of John Gabriel Stedman, *Expedition to Surinam: being the Narrative of a Five Years' Expedition against the Revolted Negroes of Surinam in Gui-*

ana from the year 1772, to 1777 … newly edited and abridged [from 117.1] *by Christopher Bryant …*

London [England]: The Folio Society, **1963**. Tpv: Printed in Great Britain Printed and bound by Richard Clay & Co, Ltd, Bungay [Suffolk, England].

8vo (26 cm.): viii, 239 p., plates.

N.b.: One of the speaker's owners, a chief, is here named Bonny (199).

117.37 ——. [Photomechanical reprint of 117.13]

Two autobiographical gallows speeches (with intervening remarks of his "master," who was also one of his judges) originating in the first edition of Stedman (117.1) translated back into English from 117.10 and printed on pp. 378–380 in J. J. Dauxion Lavaysse, *A Statistical, Commercial, and Political Description of Venezuela, Trinidad, Margarita, and Tobago … from the French of M. Lavaysse; with an introduction and explanatory notes by the editor* (London: G. and W. B. Whittaker, 1820) with imprint:

Westport, Connecticut [U.S.A.]: Negro Universities Press, [1969].

8vo (23 cm.): [2], [v]-xxxix, 479 p., folding map.

N.b.: One of the speaker's owners, a chief, is here named Bonnay (378).

https://babel.hathitrust.org/cgi/pt?id=txu.059173011685834&view=1up&seq=428

117.38 ——. [Critical edition of 117.1]

Two autobiographical gallows speeches (with intervening remarks of his 'master,' who was also one of his judges) printed (the first indented, the second within quotation marks) in chapter 24 (under date 27 February 1776) on pp. 334–335 in vol. 2 of John Gabriel Stedman, *Narrative, of a Five Years' Expedition, against the Revolted Negroes of Surinam, in Guiana, on the Wild Coast of South America; from the year 1772, to 1777 … [Introduction and notes by R. A. J. van Lier].*

Barre, Massachusetts [U.S.A.]: Printed for the Imprint Society, MCMLXXI [1971]. Colophon (vol. 2 only): … printed … by Joh. Enschede en Zonen, Haarlem, Holland….

2 vols. (continuously paged), 8vo (27.5 cm.): xviii, [10], 480, [1] p., plates, some folding.

N.b.: One of the speaker's owners, a chief, is here named **Bonny** (2:334).

117.39 ——. [Critical edition of 117.1]

Two autobiographical gallows speeches (with intervening remarks of his "master," who was also one of his judges) printed (the first indented, the second within quotation marks) in chapter 24 (under date 27 February 1776) on pp. 334–335 of John Gabriel Stedman, *Narrative, of a Five Years' Expedition,* *against the Revolted Negroes of Surinam, in Guiana, on the Wild Coast of South America; from the year 1772, to 1777 …* [Introduction and notes by R. A. J. van Lier].

Amherst, Massachusetts [U.S.A.]: University of Massachusetts Press, MCMLXXII [1972].

8vo (27.3 cm.): xviii, [10], 480 p., plates, some folding. Comprises sheets ("printed … by Joh. Enschede en Zonen, Haarlem, Holland" as noted in 117.33) from 117.33 but here bound in one volume with distinct title page.

N.b.: One of the speaker's owners, a chief, is here named Bonny (334).

117.40 ——.

Two autobiographical gallows speeches (with intervening remarks of his "master," who was also one of his judges) printed (the first indented, the second within quotation marks) in "Chapter 24th" (under "The day Following" 27 February 1776) on pp. 480–482 (with full-page illustration occupying p. 481) of John Gabriel Stedman, *Narrative, of a Five Years' Expedition, against the Revolted Negroes of Surinam, in Guiana, on the Wild Coast of South America; from the year 1772, to 1777 … transcribed for the first time from the original 1790 manuscript; edited, and with an introduction and notes,* by Richard Price & Sally Price.

Baltimore [Maryland, U.S.A.]: The Johns Hopkins University Press, **1988**.

8vo (27 cm.): xcvii, 708 p., illus.

N.b.: One of the speaker's owners, a chief, is here named Bony (482).

117.41 ——. [Abridged edition of 117.39]

Two autobiographical gallows speeches (with intervening remarks of his "master," who was also one of his judges) printed (the first indented, the second within quotation marks) in "Chapter 24th" on pp. 246–247 of John Gabriel Stedman, *Stedman's Surinam Life in an Eighteenth-Century Slave Society An Abridged, Modernized Edition of Narrative of a Five Years* [sic] *Expedition against the Revolted Negroes of Surinam by John Gabriel Stedman. Edited by Richard Price and Sally Price.*

Baltimore [Maryland, U.S.A.]: The Johns Hopkins University Press, [1992].

8vo (23 cm.): lxxv, [3], [1–5] 6–350 p., map, illus. Note: This abridgement "include[s] about 50 percent of the original text and 33 of the original 81 plates" (p. lxv).

N.b.: One of the speaker's owners, a chief, is here named Boni (246).

117.42 ——. [Another (complete) printing of 117.39]

Two autobiographical gallows speeches (with intervening remarks of his "master," who was also one of his judges) printed (the first indented, the second within quotation marks) in "Chapter 24th" (under "The day Following" 27 February 1776) on pp. 480–482 (with full-page illustration occupying p. 481) of John Gabriel Stedman, *Narrative, of a Five Years' Expedition, against the Revolted Negroes of Surinam, in Guiana, on the Wild Coast of South America; from the year 1772, to 1777 …* transcribed for the first time from the original 1790 manuscript [cf. 115.37]; edited, and with an introduction and notes, by Richard Price & Sally Price.

New York [New York, U.S.A.]: iUniverse.com, [2010].
8vo (27 cm.): xcvii, 708 p., illus.
N.b.: One of the speaker's owners, a chief, is here named Bony (482).

118.0   William

Very short account written as direct speech in quotation marks under date 10 August **1776** within "Chapter 26th" on p. 679 of John Gabriel Stedman's 1790 manuscript of his "Narrative, of a five years expedition against the Rebelled Negroes of Surinam …" This manuscript, which is preserved in the John Gabriel Stedman Collection at the University of Minnesota's James Ford Bell Library, **Minneapolis, Minnesota, U.S.A.,** was the heavily edited (see introduction to 116.11) basis of 116.1; it was first published *verbatim et literatim* in 1988, q.v. 116.11. Manuscript page 679 has been digitized (as image 709) with the rest of the manuscript by the James Ford Bell Library and are available at:

https://umedia.lib.umn.edu/item/p16022coll187:962/
    p16022coll187:782?child_index=708&query=&sidebar_
    page=237

¶ William was the son of a king, somewhere in the interior of West Africa. While hunting for the men who had assassinated his father, he was ambushed and taken to the Guinea coast, where he was sold to Europeans, who took him on a slave ship to Suriname (see Map 10). There he became an enslaved attendant of the English captain John Gabriel Stedman, who fought with Dutch colonial forces in the Boni Maroon war of the 1770s, when he recorded William's account.

118.1a ———.

Very short account printed within quotation marks in chapter XXVI on pp. 271–272 in vol. 2 of John Gabriel Stedman, *Narrative, of a Five Years' Expedition, against the Revolted Negroes of Surinam, in Guiana, on the Wild Coast of South America; from the year 1772, to 1777…*

https://www.biodi-versitylibrary.org/item/163990#page/339/mode/1up [see 118.1a].

London [England]: Printed for J. Johnson, St. Paul's Church Yard, & J. Edwards, Pall Mall, **1796** (*sic*). No colophon in vol. 2. **Regular paper issue** with un-colored plates.
2 vols., 4to. (28 cm.), folding map, plan, plates (some engraved by William Blake). Includes list of subscribers.
https://www.biodiversitylibrary.org/item/163990#page/339/mode/1up
ESTC t146566; Price & Price 1.

118.1b ———.

Very short account printed within quotation marks in chapter XXVI on pp. 271–272 in vol. 2 of John Gabriel Stedman, *Narrative, of a Five Years' Expedition, against the Revolted Negroes of Surinam, in Guiana, on the Wild Coast of South America; from the year 1772, to 1777…*

London [England]: Printed for J. Johnson, St. Paul's Church Yard, & J. Edwards, Pall Mall, **1796** (*sic*). No colophon in vol. 2. Large paper issue with hand-colored title page vignettes and plates.
2 vols., 4to. (28 cm.), folding map, plan, plates (some engraved by William Blake). Includes list of subscribers.
https://archive.org/details/narrativeoffivey02sted_0/page/271/mode/1up
ESTC t146565; Price & Price 2.

118.2 ———. [Abridged French translation of 118.1]

Very short account printed within quotation marks in chapter XXVI in vol. 3 of John Gabriel Stedman, *Voyage a Surinam et dans l'Intérieur de Guiane … traduit de l'Anglais par P. F. Henry.*

Paris [France]: chez F. Buisson, Imprimeur-Libraire, rue Hautefeuille, no. 20, an VII de la Republique [i.e., **1798**].
3 vols., 8vo.
Price & Price 6.

118.3 ———. [Unabridged? French translation of 118.1]

Very short account printed within quotation marks in chapter XXVI in vol. 3 of John Gabriel Stedman, *Voyage à Surinam et dans l'intérieur de la Guiane. Contenant la relation de cinq années de courses et d'observations faites dans cette contrée intéressante et peu connue; avec des détails sur les Indiens de la Guiane et les Nègres… traduit de l'anglais par P. F. Henry.*

Lausanne [Switzerland]: chez Hermann, **1799**.
3 vols., 8vo.

118.4 ———. [Dutch translation of 118.1]

Very short account printed in Dutch translation (supplemented by French in 118.2) within quotation marks in chapter XXVI on p. 257 in vol. 3 of John Gabriel Stedman, *Reize naar Surinamen, en door der Binnenste Gedeelten van Guiana*

Amsterdam [Netherlands]: by Johannes Allart, MDCCXCIX–
MDCCC [1799–1800].

4 vols.

https://www.delpher.nl/nl/boeken/view?objectsearch=kon
ing&coll=boeken&identifier=dpo:8143:mpeg21:0281&c
ql%5B%5D=%28creator+exact+%22Stedman%2C+
John+Gabrie%CC%88l%22%29

118.5 ——. [Dutch translation]

Very short account printed within quotation marks in chapter
XXVI of John Gabriel Stedman, *Reize in de Binnenlanden van
Suriname*. Translated by J. D. Pasteur.

Leyden [Netherlands]: By A. en J. Hankoop, MDCCXC.IX,
[1799].

118.6 ——. [Second English edition of 118.1]

Very short account printed within quotation marks in chapter
XXVI on p. 282 in vol. 2 of John Gabriel Stedman, *Narrative,
of a Five Years' Expedition, against the Revolted Negroes of
Surinam, in Guiana, on the Wild Coast of South America;
from the year 1772, to 1777... Second edition, corrected.*

London [England]: Printed for J. Johnson, St. Paul's Church
Yard, and Th. Payne, Pall Mall, 1806. Colophon: Luke Hansard, printer, near Lincoln's-Inn-Fields.

2 vols., 4to. (27 cm.), folding map, plan, plates (some engraved by William Blake).

https://babel.hathitrust.org/cgi/pt?id=gri.ark:/13960/
t4jm38n7d&view=1up&seq=348

Price & Price 12.

118.7 ——. [Another printing of 118.6]

Very short account printed within quotation marks in chapter
XXVI on p. 282 in vol. 2 of John Gabriel Stedman, *Narrative,
of a Five Years' Expedition, against the Revolted Negroes of
Surinam, in Guiana, on the Wild Coast of South America;
from the year 1772, to 1777... Second edition [sic], corrected.*

London [England]: Printed for J. Johnson, St. Paul's Church
Yard, and Th. Payne, Pall Mall, 1813. Colophon: Luke Hansard, printer, near Lincoln's-Inn-Fields.

2 vols., 4to. (27 cm.), folding map, plan, plates (some engraved by William Blake).

https://archive.org/details/narrativeoffivey02sted/page/282/
mode/1up

118.8 ——. [Italian translation]

Very short account printed within quotation marks in chapter
XXVI in *Viaggio al Surinam e nell'interno della Guiana ossia relazione di cinque anni di corse e di osservazioni fatte in
questo interessante e poco conosciuto paese .... Versione dal
francese del Cav. [Bartolomeo] Borghi.*

Milano [Italia]: dalla Tipografia di Giambattista Sonzogno,
1818.

4 vols., 8vo.

118.9 ——. [Critical edition of 118.1]

Very short account printed within quotation marks in chapter
26 on p. 369 in vol. 2 of John Gabriel Stedman, *Narrative,
of a Five Years' Expedition, against the Revolted Negroes of
Surinam, in Guiana, on the Wild Coast of South America;
from the year 1772, to 1777 ... [Introduction and notes by R.
A. J. van Lier].*

Barre, Massachusetts [U.S.A.]: Printed for the Imprint Society, MCMLXXI [1971]. Colophon (vol. 2 only): ... printed
... by Joh. Enschede en Zonen, Haarlem, Holland....

2 vols. (continuously paged), 8vo (27.5 cm.): xviii, [10], 480,
[1] p., plates, some folding.

118.10 ——. [Critical edition of 118.1]

Very short account printed within quotation marks in chapter
26 on p. 369 of John Gabriel Stedman, *Narrative, of a Five
Years' Expedition, against the Revolted Negroes of Surinam,
in Guiana, on the Wild Coast of South America; from the year
1772, to 1777 ... [Introduction and notes by R. A. J. van Lier].*

Amherst, Massachusetts [U.S.A.]: University of Massachusetts Press, MCMLXXII [1972].

8vo (27.3 cm.): xviii, [10], 480 p., plates, some folding. Comprises sheets ("printed ... by Joh. Enschede en Zonen, Haarlem, Holland" as noted in 118.11) from 118.11 but here
bound in one volume with distinct title-page.

118.11 ——.

Very short account printed (under date 10 August 1776) on
p. 528 of John Gabriel Stedman, *Narrative, of a Five Years'
Expedition, against the Revolted Negroes of Surinam, in Guiana, on the Wild Coast of South America; from the year 1772,
to 1777 ... transcribed for the first time from the original
1790 manuscript; edited, and with an introduction and notes,
by Richard Price & Sally Price.*

Baltimore [Maryland, U.S.A.]: The Johns Hopkins University
Press, 1988.

8vo (27 cm.): xcvii, 708 p., illus.

118.12 ——. [Abridged edition of 118.11]

Very short account printed (under date 10 August 1776) as
direct speech (indented but without quotation marks) on p.
269 of John Gabriel Stedman, *Stedman's Surinam Life in an
Eighteenth-Century Slave Society An Abridged, Modernized
Edition of Narrative of a Five Years [sic] Expedition against
the Revolted Negroes of Surinam by John Gabriel Stedman.
Edited by Richard Price and Sally Price.*

Baltimore [Maryland, U.S.A.]: The Johns Hopkins University Press, [1992].

8vo (23 cm.): lxxv, [3], [1–5] 6–350 p., map, illus. Note: This abridgement "include[s] about 50 percent of the original text and 33 of the original 81 plates" (p. lxv).

118.13 ——. [Another (complete) printing of 118.11]

Very short account printed (under date 10 August 1776) on p. 528 of John Gabriel Stedman, *Narrative, of a Five Years' Expedition, against the Revolted Negroes of Surinam, in Guiana, on the Wild Coast of South America; from the year 1772, to 1777 … transcribed for the first time from the original 1790 manuscript* [cf. 116.13]; *edited, and with an introduction and notes, by Richard Price & Sally Price.*

New York [New York, U.S.A.]: iUniverse.com, [2010].
8vo (27 cm.): xcvii, 708 p., illus.

119.0 Gwacoo = Quaco = Quacoo

Short account written as direct speech in quotation marks under date 10 August **1776** within "Chapter 26th" on p. 679 of John Gabriel Stedman's 1790 manuscript of his "Narrative, of a five years expedition against the Rebelled Negroes of Surinam …" This manuscript, which is preserved in the John Gabriel Stedman Collection at the University of Minnesota's James Ford Bell Library, Minneapolis, Minnesota, U.S.A., was the heavily edited (see introduction to 119.11) basis of 119.1; it was first published *verbatim et literatim* in 1988, q.v. 119.11. Manuscript page 679 has been digitized (as image 709) with the rest of the manuscript by the James Ford Bell Library and are available at:

https://umedia.lib.umn.edu/item/p16022coll187:962/p16022coll187:782?child_index=708&query=&sidebar_page=237

https://www.biodiversitylibrary.org/item/163990#page/340/mode/1up [see 119.1a].

¶ Gwacoo's parents lived by hunting and fishing somewhere in West Africa. Kweku, Kuuku, or Kwaku is an Akan day name for a male born on Wednesday, suggesting Gwacoo may have come from the Gold Coast (modern Ghana—see Map 5). While very young and playing with his two little brothers "in the Sands," he was kidnapped and carried alone for many miles in a bag. He and many hundreds of others became enslaved to a king on the Guinea coast. After the king died, all prisoners except children were massacred. Gwacoo was given as a present to an army captain, who sold him to a Dutch slave ship captain for some powder and a musket. After transport to the Dutch South American colony of Suriname (Map 10) on a slave ship, Gwacoo became the valet of the English Captain John Gabriel Stedman, who kept him for years while fighting with Dutch colonial forces in the Boni Maroon war of the 1770s.

119.1a ——.

Short account printed as direct speech within quotation marks in chapter XXVI on p. 272 in vol. 2 of John Gabriel Stedman, *Narrative, of a Five Years' Expedition, against the Revolted Negroes of Surinam, in Guiana, on the Wild Coast of South America; from the year 1772, to 1777…*

London [England]: Printed for J. Johnson, St. Paul's Church Yard, & J. Edwards, Pall Mall, 1796 (*sic*). No colophon in vol. 2. Regular paper issue with un-colored plates.
2 vols., 4to. (28 cm.), folding map, plan, plates (some engraved by William Blake). Includes list of subscribers.
https://www.biodiversitylibrary.org/item/163990#page/340/mode/1up
ESTC t146566; Price & Price 1.

119.1b ——.

Short account printed as direct speech within quotation marks in chapter XXVI on p. 272 in vol. 2 of John Gabriel Stedman, *Narrative, of a Five Years' Expedition, against the Revolted Negroes of Surinam, in Guiana, on the Wild Coast of South America; from the year 1772, to 1777…*

London [England]: Printed for J. Johnson, St. Paul's Church Yard, & J. Edwards, Pall Mall, 1796 (*sic*). No colophon in vol. 2. Large paper issue with hand-colored title-page vignettes and plates.
2 vols., 4to. (28 cm.), folding map, plan, plates (some engraved by William Blake). Includes list of subscribers.
https://archive.org/details/narrativeoffivey02sted_0/page/272/mode/1up
ESTC t146565; Price & Price 2.

119.2 ——. [Abridged French translation of 119.1]

Short account printed as direct speech within quotation marks in chapter XXVI in vol. 3 of John Gabriel Stedman, *Voyage a Surinam et dans l'Intérieur de Guiane … traduit de l'Anglais par P. F. Henry.*

Paris [France]: chez F. Buisson, Imprimeur-Libraire, rue Hautefeuille, no. 20, an VII de la Republique [i.e., **1798**].
3 vols., 8vo.
Price & Price 6.

119.3 ——. [Unabridged? French translation of 119.1]

Short account printed as direct speech within quotation marks in chapter XXVI in vol. 3 of John Gabriel Stedman, *Voyage à Surinam et dans l'intérieur de la Guiane. Contenant la re-*

lation de cinq années de courses et d'observations faites dans cette contrée intéressante et peu connue; avec des détails sur les Indiens de la Guiane et les Nègres... traduit de l'anglais par P. F. Henry.

Lausanne [Switzerland]: chez Hermann, **1799.**
3 vols., 8vo.

119.4 ——. [Dutch translation of 119.1]

Short account printed as direct speech within quotation marks in chapter XXVI on pp. 257–258 in vol. 3 of f John Gabriel Stedman, *Reize naar Surinamen, en door der Binnenste Gedeelten van Guiana*

Amsterdam [Netherlands]: by Johannes Allart, MDCCXCIX–MDCCC [1799–1800].
4 vols.
https://www.delpher.nl/nl/boeken/view?objectsearch=koning&coll=boeken&identifier=dpo:8143:mpeg21:0281&cql%5B%5D=%28creator+exact+%22Stedman%2C+John+Gabrie%CC%88l%22%29

119.5 ——. [Dutch translation]

Short account printed as direct speech within quotation marks in chapter XXVI in John Gabriel Stedman, *Reize in de Binnenlanden van Suriname.* Translated by J. D. Pasteur.

Leyden [Netherlands]: By A. en J. Hankoop, MDCCXC.IX, [1799].

119.6 ——. [Second English edition of 119.1]

Short account printed as direct speech within quotation marks in chapter XXVI on pp. 282–283 in vol. 2 of John Gabriel Stedman, *Narrative, of a Five Years' Expedition, against the Revolted Negroes of Surinam, in Guiana, on the Wild Coast of South America; from the year 1772, to 1777... Second edition, corrected.*

London [England]: Printed for J. Johnson, St. Paul's Church Yard, and Th. Payne, Pall Mall, **1806.** Colophon: Luke Hansard, printer, near Lincoln's-Inn-Fields.
2 vols., 4to. (27 cm.), folding map, plan, plates (some engraved by William Blake).
https://babel.hathitrust.org/cgi/pt?id=gri.ark:/13960/t4jm38n7d&view=1up&seq=348
Price & Price 12.

119.7 ——. [Another printing of 119.6]

Short account printed as direct speech within quotation marks in chapter XXVI on pp. 282–283 in vol. 2 of John Gabriel Stedman, *Narrative, of a Five Years' Expedition, against the Revolted Negroes of Surinam, in Guiana, on the Wild Coast of South America; from the year 1772, to 1777... Second edition* [sic], *corrected.*

London [England]: Printed for J. Johnson, St. Paul's Church Yard, and Th. Payne, Pall Mall, **1813.** Colophon: Luke Hansard, printer, near Lincoln's-Inn-Fields.
2 vols., 4to. (27 cm.), folding map, plan, plates (some engraved by William Blake).
https://archive.org/details/narrativeoffivey02sted/page/282/mode/1up

119.8 ——. [Italian translation]

Short account printed as direct speech within quotation marks in chapter XXVI in *Viaggio al Surinam e nell'interno della Guiana ossia relazione di cinque anni di corse e di osservazioni fatte in questo interessante e poco conosciuto paese .... Versione dal francese del Cav. [Bartolomeo] Borghi.*

Milano [Italia]: dalla Tipografia di Giambattista Sonzogno, **1818.**
4 vols., 8vo.

119.9 ——. [Critical edition of 119.1]

Short account printed as direct speech within quotation marks in chapter 26 on p. 369 in vol. 2 of John Gabriel Stedman, *Narrative, of a Five Years' Expedition, against the Revolted Negroes of Surinam, in Guiana, on the Wild Coast of South America; from the year 1772, to 1777 ...* [Introduction and notes by R. A. J. van Lier].

Barre, Massachusetts [U.S.A.]: Printed for the Imprint Society, MCMLXXI [1971]. Colophon (vol. 2 only): ... printed ... by Joh. Enschede en Zonen, Haarlem, Holland....
2 vols. (continuously paged), 8vo (27.5 cm.): xviii, [10], 480, [1] p., plates, some folding.

119.10 ——. [Critical edition of 119.1]

Short account printed as direct speech within quotation marks in chapter 26 on p. 369 of John Gabriel Stedman, *Narrative, of a Five Years' Expedition, against the Revolted Negroes of Surinam, in Guiana, on the Wild Coast of South America; from the year 1772, to 1777 ...* [Introduction and notes by R. A. J. van Lier].

Amherst, Massachusetts [U.S.A.]: University of Massachusetts Press, MCMLXXII [1972].
8vo (27.3 cm.): xviii, [10], 480 p., plates, some folding. Comprises sheets ("printed ... by Joh. Enschede en Zonen, Haarlem, Holland" as noted in 119.11) from 119.11 but here bound in one volume with distinct title-page.

119.11 ——.

Short account printed (under date 10 August 1776) on pp. 528–529 of John Gabriel Stedman, *Narrative, of a Five Years' Expedition, against the Revolted Negroes of Surinam, in Guiana, on the Wild Coast of South America; from the year 1772,* to 1777 ... *transcribed for the first time from the original 1790 manuscript; edited, and with an introduction and notes, by Richard Price & Sally Price.*

Baltimore [Maryland, U.S.A.]: The Johns Hopkins University Press, 1988.
8vo (27 cm.): xcvii, 708 p., illus.

119.12 ——. [Abridged edition of 119.11]

Short account printed (under date 10 August 1776) as direct speech (indented but without quotation marks) on p. 269 of John Gabriel Stedman, *Stedman's Surinam Life in an Eighteenth-Century Slave Society An Abridged, Modernized Edition of Narrative of a Five Years* [sic] *Expedition against the Revolted Negroes of Surinam by John Gabriel Stedman. Edited by Richard Price and Sally Price.*

Baltimore [Maryland, U.S.A.]: The Johns Hopkins University Press, [1992].
8vo (23 cm.): lxxv, [3], [1–5] 6–350 p., map, illus. Note: This abridgement "include[s] about 50 percent of the original text and 33 of the original 81 plates" (p. lxv).

119.13 ——. [Another (complete) printing of 119.11]

Short account printed (under date 10 August 1776) on pp. 528–529 of John Gabriel Stedman, *Narrative, of a Five Years' Expedition, against the Revolted Negroes of Surinam, in Guiana, on the Wild Coast of South America; from the year 1772, to 1777 ... transcribed for the first time from the original 1790 manuscript* [cf. 116.13]; *edited and with an introduction and notes, by Richard Price & Sally Price.*

New York [New York, U.S.A.]: iUniverse.com, [2010].
8vo (27 cm.): xcvii, 708 p., illus.

1779

120.0 Nero Brewster (ca. 1711–1786)

Manuscript petition to end slavery in New Hampshire: "State of New Hampshire. To The Hon[ora]ble, The Council and House of Representatives of said State now sitting at Exeter in and for Said State: The Petition of Nero Brewster, Pharaoh Rogers, Romeo Rindge, Cato Newmarch, Cesar Gerrish, Zebulon Gardner, Quam Sherburne, Samuel Wentworth, Will Clarkson, Jack Odiorne, Cipio Hubbard, Seneca Hall, Peter Warner, Cato Warner, Pharaoh Shores, Windsor Moffatt, Garrott Colton, Kittindge Tuckerman, Peter Frost, and Prince Whipple, natives of Africa, now forcibly detained in slavery, in said State, most humbly Sheweth, that the God of Nature gave them, Life, and Freedom, upon [n.b.] the Terms of the most perfect Equality with other men ... Portsmouth **Nov. 12, 1779.**" Manuscript petition fully signed by Nero Brewster and all nineteen of his named African-born colleagues held at New Hampshire Division of Archives and Records Management, Concord, New Hampshire, U.S.A.

¶ Nero Brewster's African origins, circumstances of capture, and experience of the Middle Passage are not yet known. He may have been purchased in the West Indies in 1726. He long presided over formal meetings of the African community in Portsmouth, the leading port city in the colonial British North American province of New Hampshire (see Map 17), where he annually led inaugural processions of black elected officers. He acquired his freedom and died in 1786. An obituary notice in the *New-Hampshire Mercury and General Advertiser* (19

https://archive.org/details/granitemonthlyne04dove/page/108 [see 120.2].

April 1786) called him "King of the Africans in Portsmouth, a monarch held in reverential esteem by his subjects, whose death was greatly lamented." Brewster's important position in Portsmouth's African and African American community, the primacy of his name among the list of petitioners in the MS text proper, and the credit given him (and him alone) by name in 118.1, suggest that he probably composed the Portsmouth Africans' petition himself (in other words, that he was the petition's Thomas Jefferson and Benjamin Franklin rolled into one)--and that his fellow petitioners' contributions may have been limited to their advice, consent, and signatures. See Robert B. Dishman, "'Natives of Africa, Now Forcibly Detained': The Slave Petitioners of Revolutionary Portsmouth," *Historical New Hampshire* 61 (Concord, NH, 2007): 8–9.

120.1 ——.

First printing of 120.0: "THE petition of [n.b.] *Nero Brewster*, and others, natives of Africa, now forcibly detained in slavery, in said state, most humbly sheweth, That the God of Nature gave them life and freedom, upon [n.b.] terms of the most perfect equality with other men ... *Portsmouth, Nov.* 12, 1779." Petition printed *in extenso* except for omissions of other petitioner's names and any signatures in type in newspaper *The New-Hampshire Gazette*, vol. 24, no. 1233, p. [1].

Portsmouth, New Hampshire [U.S.A.]: [Daniel Fowle], 15 July 1780.
Broadsheet bifolium.

120.2 ——.

Petition printed from 120.0 (but with petitioners' names replaced by phrase "the subscribers" after the phrase "The petition of", arbitrary alteration of capitalization, and petitioners' signatures printed in type--with "Garrett Colton" misprinted as "Garrett Cotton" among type-set signatures after concluding date "Nov. 12, 1779") with introductory paragraphs in Isaac W. Hammond, "Slavery in New Hampshire in the Olden Time," *The Granite Monthly: A Magazine of History, Biography, Literature, and State Progress* 4: 108–110.

Concord, New Hampshire [U.S.A.]: John N. McClintock, Editor and Publisher, Evans & Sleeper, Printers, **1880.**
https://archive.org/details/granitemonthlyne04dove/page/108

120.3 ——.

Petition printed from 120.2 (including misprinting "Cotton" for "Colton" originated in 120.2) with new introductory paragraphs in Isaac W. Hammond, "Slavery in New Hampshire," *Magazine of American History with Notes and Queries,* edited by Mrs. Martha J. Lamb, 21: 62–65.

New York, New York [U.S.A.]: J.J. Little & Co., **1889.**
https://archive.org/details/magazineamerica00stevgoog/page/n88

120.4 ——.

Petition printed from 120.0 *verbatim et literatim* (with Garrett Colton's surname twice printed correctly) in *New Hampshire Miscellaneous Provincial and State Papers, 1725–1800,* compiled and edited by Isaac W. Hammond, 18: 705–707.

Manchester, New Hampshire [U.S.A.]: John B. Clarke, Public Printer, **1890.**
Large 8vo (25 cm.): xxix, 982, maps, illus.
https://babel.hathitrust.org/cgi/pt?id=uva.x000675942&view=1up&seq=743

120.5 ——.

Petition transcribed from 120.2 or 120.3 (including error "Cotton" for "Colton") by hand-typewriting on pp. 168–170 in Arthur Clinton Boggess, "Negro Slavery in the Northern Colonies," Thesis for the degree of Bachelor of Arts in Political Science in the College of Literature and Arts of the University of Illinois.

[Urbana-Champaign, Illinois, U.S.A.], May **1902.**
4to (28 cm.): 187 numbered leaves (versos blank).
https://babel.hathitrust.org/cgi/pt?id=uiuo.ark:/13960/t2x-36wm39&view=1up&seq=343&q1

120.6 ——.

Petition printed (with Garrett Colton's surname misprinted as Cotton), perhaps from 120.3, on pp. 200–202 within Isaac W. Hammond's article "Slavery in New Hampshire," which is printed on pp. 199–203 in *Granite State Magazine: An Illustrated Monthly Devoted to the History, Story, Scenery, Industry and Interest of New Hampshire* (edited by George Waldo Browne), vol. 4, no. 5.

Manchester, N[ew] H[ampshire, U.S.A.]: Granite State Publishing Company, November **1907.** Complete volume tpv: The Ruemely Press, Manchester, NH.
8vo (24 cm.)
https://babel.hathitrust.org/cgi/pt?id=mdp.39015070241370&view=1up&seq=248

120.7 ——.

Short excerpt of petition printed in article by Edie Clark on Valerie Cunningham and Mark J. Sammons's preparatory research for 120.8: "African Slaves in Portsmouth," in popular magazine promoting tourism in the New England region, *Yankee Magazine.*

Dublin, New Hampshire(?, February **1999.**

120.8 ——.

Petition printed *verbatim* but not *literatim* from 120.4 on pp. 66–67 in Mark J. Sammons and Valerie Cunningham, *Black Portsmouth: Three Centuries of African-American Heritage,* with partial photographic illustration of 62.1 on p. 68.

Durham, New Hampshire [U.S.A.]: University of New Hampshire Press, **2004.**
8vo (26 cm.): xi, 265 p.

120.9 ——.

Complete photographic reproduction of 120.1 printed (reduce) as full-page illustration on p. [6] of Robert B. Dishman, "'Natives of Africa, Now Forcibly Detained': The Slave Petitioners of Revolutionary Portsmouth," in academic journal *Historical New Hampshire* 61: 6–27.

Concord, New Hampshire [U.S.A.], **2007.**
4to.

120.10 ——.

Petition text and signatures printed from 120.3 in vol. 1, pp. 36–38 of *From Timbuktu to Katrina: Readings in African American History,* edited by Quintard Taylor.

Boston [Massachusetts, U.S.A.]: Thomson Wadsworth, **2008.**
8vo (24 cm.): xii, 177 p.

120.11 ——.

Petition text and signatures (Colton spelled correctly) printed from 120.0 in Michelle Arnosky Sherburne, *Slavery and the Underground Railroad in New Hampshire.*

Charleston, South Carolina [U.S.A.]: The History Press, **2016.**
8vo (23 cm.): 192 p., illus., map.

121.1 Unnamed young man in Paramaribo (ca. 1761–)

Account printed on pp. 83–85 in Johann Andreas Riemer, *Missions-Reise nach Suriname und Barbice zu einer am Surinamflusse im dritten Grad der Linie wohnenden Freynegernation.*

Zittau und **Leipzig** [**Saxony, Germany**]: beym Verfasser und in Kommission der Schöpfischen Buchhandlung, **1801**.
Small 8vo (17 cm.): 512 p., plates.
Sabin 71305; Price, *The Guiana Maroons*, 1060.

Full text: https://huskiecommons.lib.niu.edu/history-500africanvoices/105/ [see 121.3].

¶ This young man from some unknown location in West Africa was the son of a respected and well-off man who had many wives. After his mother died, his father lost interest in him and his brothers, took the young man to a port, and traded him to sailors, who bound and gagged him and took him to a slave ship, where the young man found one of his brothers. The ship transported him to Paramaribo, the capital of the Dutch South American colony of Suriname (see Map 10), where they arrived in 1779, his brother having died of despair during the voyage. After the ship's enslaved passengers were marched through the streets and displayed before a planter who inspected them, German Moravian missionaries who witnessed the scene were shocked and purchased the young man to work in their Paramaribo mission (perhaps in its tailor's shop), where they promptly recorded his account.

121.2 ——.

Account printed on pp. 83–85 in Johann Andreas Riemer, *Missions-Reise nach Suriname und Barbice zu einer am Surinamflusse im dritten Grad der Linie wohnenden Freynegernation. Zweite Auflage.*

Zittau [**Saxony, Germany**]: bei Riemers Erben, **1833**.
8vo: 512 p., plates.

121.3——.

Account printed (from 121.1) on pp. 295–296 (especially 296) under the date 15 August 1779 within excerpt (headed "Br. Riemer erzählt von seiner Ankunft und ersten Eindrücken folgendes") from J. A. Riemer, *Missions-Reise nach Suriname* (Zittau and Leipzig, 1801), this excerpt being vol. 2, part 3.1, pp. 295–303 of *Die Mission der Brüdergemeine in Suriname und Berbice im achtzehnten Jahrhundert. Eine Missionsgeschichte hauptsächlich in Auszügen aus Briefen und Originalberichten*, edited by Fritz Staehelin.

Herrnhut [**Saxony, Germany**]: Verlag C. Kersten in **Paramaribo** [**Suriname**] im Kommission bei der Missionsbuchhandlung in Herrnhut und für den Buchhandel bei der Unitätsbuchhandlung in **Gnadau** [**Saxony, Germany**], [**1913–1917**].
3 vols., 8vo (21.5 cm.), 422 p.

121. 4 ——.

Account printed on pp. 295–296—especially 296 (from 121.1) in photomechanical reprint of 121.3 with imprint:

Hildesheim [**Saxony, Germany**], **Zurich** [**Switzerland**]: Georg Olms Verlag, **1997**.
2 vols., 8vo (22 cm.).

1780

122.1 Unnamed African Man

Brief account included on pp. 9–10 under the date 2 April **1780** within "Paramaribo Diarium, February-December 1780" printed on pp. 8–12 of vol. 3, Part 3.2 of *Die Mission der Brüdergemeine in Suriname und Berbice im achtzehnten Jahrhundert. Eine Missionsgeschichte hauptsächlich in Auszügen aus Briefen und Originalberichten*, edited by Fritz Staehelin.

Full text: https://huskiecommons.lib.niu.edu/history-500africanvoices/106/ [see 122.1].

Herrnhut [**Saxony, Germany**]: Verlag C. Kersten in **Paramaribo** [**Suriname**] im Kommission bei der Missionsbuchhandlung in Herrnhut und für den Buchhandel bei der Unitätsbuchhandlung in **Gnadau** [**Saxony, Germany**], [**1913–1917**].

3 vols., 8vo (21.5 cm.).

¶ This man came from an unknown part of Africa and was taken on a slave ship to the Dutch South American colony of Suriname (see Map 10). Still enslaved as a young man, he joined the Moravian community in the colonial capital of Paramaribo. While applying for baptism he professed to a missionary his devotion to Christian ideals and expressed no resentment at being taken from his homeland.

122.2 ——.

Account included on pp. 9–10 within "Paramaribo Diarium, February-December 1780" printed on pp. 8–12 of vol. 3, Part 3.2 in photomechanical reprint of 120.1 with imprint:

Hildesheim [**Saxony, Germany**], **Zurich** [**Switzerland**]: Georg Olms Verlag, **1997**.
2 vols., 8vo (22 cm.).

1781

123.1 Simeon (–1781)

Account included on p. 52 under the date 11 September 1781 within "Bericht des Br. Wietz von seinem mit dem Br. Johannes Arrabini gemachten Besuch auf den oberen Dörfern im Freynegerlande" printed on pp. 47–53 in vol. 3, Part 3.2 of *Die Mission der Brüdergemeine in Suriname und Berbice im achtzehnten Jahrhundert. Eine Missionsgeschichte hauptsächlich in Auszügen aus Briefen und Originalberichten*, edited by Fritz Staehelin.

Herrnhut [Saxony, Germany]: Verlag C. Kersten in **Paramaribo [Suriname]** im Kommission bei der Missionsbuchhandlung in Herrnhut und für den Buchhandel bei der Unitätsbuchhandlung in **Gnadau [Saxony, Germany]**, [1913–1917]. 3 vols., 8vo (21.5 cm.).

¶ Simeon was born in West Africa and was forcibly transported on a slave ship to the Dutch South American

Full text: https://huskiecommons.lib.niu.edu/history-500african-voices/107/

colony of Suriname (see Map 10). After enslavement there for many years, he ran away and joined a Saamaka Maroon community at Bambey, on the upper Suriname River, where after losing his wife, he tended to small children in the community. After the Saamakas made peace with the colonial authorities in Paramaribo and invited Moravian missionaries into their territory, Simeon slowly began accepting Moravian ways. He was spiritually "awakened" in 1779, baptized in 1780, and fully accepted into the missionary community, where he delivered his account shortly before dying.

123.2 ———.

Account included on p. 52 within "Bericht des Br. Wietz von seinem mit dem Br. Johannes Arrabini gemachten Besuch auf den oberen Dörfern im Freynegerlande" printed on pp. 47–53 in vol. 3, Part 3.2 in photomechanical reprint of 121.1 with imprint:

Hildesheim [Saxony, Germany], Zurich [Switzerland]: Georg Olms Verlag, 1997. 2 vols., 8vo (22 cm.).

1783

124.0 Belinda (*ca.* 1712–*ca.* 1799) = Belinda Royall = Belinda Sutton

First of four petitions by her: "The Petition of Belinda an Affrican [*sic*]" headed "Commonwealth of Massachusetts | To the Honourable the Senate and the House of Representatives in General Court Assembled" and dated at end "Boston 14th February **1783**." Original manuscript held in the Massachusetts State Archives, **Boston, Massachusetts, U.S.A.**: Massachusetts Archives Collection. V. 239—Revolution Resolves, 1783. SC1/series 45X, Petition of Belinda. https://iiif.lib.harvard.edu/manifests/view/drs:50257769$1i

http://www.royallhouse.org/wp-content/uploads/2013/11/Belindas_Petition.pdf

See also her Second, Third, and Fourth Petitions (of 1785, 1787, and 1793, all also held in the Massachusetts Archives), of which we have yet found no printings, at:

https://dataverse.harvard.edu/dataverse/antislaverypetitionsma

https://babel.hathitrust.org/cgi/pt?id=uc1.b5219233&view=1up&seq=449&skin=2021 [see 124.11].

¶ Belinda was born *ca.* 1712 on the banks of the Volta River on the Gold Coast (modern Ghana and Togo border). While praying to an Orisa (maybe a reference to Òrìṣà deities, modern Nigeria, Benin and Togo—see Map 5) she was kidnapped from her family. Taken on a slave ship to the Americas (perhaps the Caribbean) ca. 1724, she lived most of her life in the colonial British North American province of Massachusetts (beginning in 1776, one of the United States of America's original member states and commonwealths) in the town of Medford (Map 17). In 1783 she petitioned the Massachusetts General Court (i.e., the commonwealth's legislature) to grant her a pension to be drawn from the confiscated estate of her last owner, the late Isaac Royall Jr. (1719–1781), a Tory who had fled the commonwealth. The petition was approved, but because payments were not made on schedule, she petitioned again and again (in 1785, 1788, and 1793) to obtain them. She signed her 1788 petition "Belinda Sutton of Boston … widow." The compilers owe entries 122.2 through 122.8 to Catherine Adams and Elizabeth H. Pleck, *Love of Freedom: Black Women in Colonial and Revolutionary New England* (New York: Oxford University Press, 2010), p. 254. See more information on all Belinda's petitions (prepared by the Royall House and Slave Quarters staff) at: http://www.royallhouse.org/slavery/belinda-sutton-and-her-petitions/

124.1 ——.

First petition printed in newspaper *The Massachusetts Spy*, vol. 13, no. 631, p. 2, col. 4 to p. 3, col. 1, "The Petition of Belinda an African" signed in type at end "*Boston, February, 1783.*"

Worcester, Massachusetts [U.S.A.]: Isaiah Thomas, May 29, **1783.**

124.2 ——.

First petition printed in newspaper *Salem Gazette*, 29 May **1783.**

Salem, Massachusetts [U.S.A.]: Samuel Hall, May 29, **1783.**

124.3——.

First petition printed in newspaper *Newport Mercury*, issue no. 1131, p. 2, col. 3 to p. 3, col. 1, "The Petition of Belinda an Affrican [*sic*]" signed in type at end "*Boston, Feb. 1783.*"

Newport, Rhode Island [U.S.A.]: Henry Barber, May 31, **1783.** Note: Seen exemplar damaged, with loss of large portions of petition's text.

124.4 ——.

First petition printed in newspaper *The Pennsylvania Evening Post, and Daily Advertiser*, vol. 9, no. 917, p. 66 (i.e., this issue's first page), col. 2 to p. 67, col. 1, "The Petition of Belinda an African" signed in type at end "Boston, February 1783."

Philadelphia, Pennsylvania [U.S.A.]: Benjamin Towne, June 11, **1783.**

124.5——.

First petition printed in newspaper *New Jersey Gazette*, 18 June 1783.

Trenton, New Jersey [U.S.A.]: Isaac Collins, June 18, **1783.**

124.6 ——.

First petition printed under heading "The Complaint of Belinda, an African," in *The Weekly Miscellany*, vol. 2, no. 35, pp. 207–208.

Sherborne, Dorset, England: September 1, **1783.**

124.7 ——.

First petition printed in the newspaper *Impartial Herald*, 12 July **1784** (perhaps the Newburyport ESSEX HERALD).

Newburyport, Massachusetts, U.S.A.

124.8 ——.

First petition printed in the weekly newspaper *The Western Star*, 5 August **1784.**

Stockbridge, Massachusetts [U.S.A.]: Loring Andrews, August 5, **1784.**

124.9 ——.

"Petition of an African [*sic*] slave, to the Legislature of Massachusetts," printed on pp. 538–540 (signed in type on p. 540: "BELINDA. Boston, February, 1782 [*sic*]") in the magazine *The American Museum, or Repository of Ancient and Modern Fugitive Pieces, Prose and Poetical*, 1: 6.

Philadelphia [Pennsylvania, U.S.A.]: Matthew Carey, June **1787.**
Hogg 1462.

124.10——.

"Petition of an African slave, to the Legislature of Massachusetts," (signed in type on p. 465: "BELINDA. Boston, February, 1782 [*sic*]") printed in the magazine *The American Museum, or Repository of Ancient and Modern Fugitive Pieces, Prose and Poetical*, 1: 6 (June 1787). **The Second Edition.**

Philadelphia [Pennsylvania, U.S.A.]: Matthew Carey, **date uncertain.**

124.11——.

"Petition of an African slave, to the Legislature of Massachusetts," printed on pp. 463–465 (signed in type on p. 465: "BELINDA. Boston, February, 1782 [*sic*]") in the magazine *The American Museum, or Repository of Ancient and Modern Fugitive Pieces, Prose and Poetical*, vol. 1, no. 6. **The Third Edition.**

Philadelphia [Pennsylvania, U.S.A.]: Carey, Stewart, and Co., June, **1790.**
https://babel.hathitrust.org/cgi/pt?id=uc1.b5219233&view=1up&seq=449&skin=2021

124.12——.

Three short numbered biographical paragraphs including quotation from her 1783 petition **as incorrectly dated 1782 in the *American Museum*** (i.e., 124.9) printed on p. 121 in *Biographical Sketches and Interesting Anecdotes of Persons of Color. To Which Is Added, a Selection of Pieces in Poetry*, compiled by A[bigail] Mott.

New York [New York, U.S.A.]: Printed and Sold by Mahlon Day, No. 376, Pearl-street, **1826.**
12mo (18 cm.): iv, [5]–192 p. Preface dated on p. iv: *Hickory Grove* [NY], 11*th mo.* 1825.
http://docsouth.unc.edu/neh/mott26/mott26.html
https://babel.hathitrust.org/cgi/pt?id=hvd.hn3m6e&view=1up&seq=125
Hogg 1467.

124.13———.

Three short biographical paragraphs including quotation from her 1783 petition **as incorrectly dated 1782 in the *American Museum*** (i.e., 124.9) printed under heading "Belinda" on p. 173 in *Biographical Sketches and Interesting Anecdotes of Persons of Colour,* compiled by A[bigail] Mott.

York [England]: Printed and Sold by W. Alexander & Son, Castlegate; sold also by Harvey & Darton, W. Phillips, E. Fry, and W. Darton, **London [England]**; R. Peart [*sic*], **Birmingham [England]**; D. F. Gardiner, **Dublin [Ireland]**, 1826.
12mo (20 cm.): xi, [2], 2–240 p.
https://babel.hathitrust.org/cgi/pt?id=nyp.33433081774204
&view=1up&seq=193

124.14———.

Three short biographical paragraphs including quotation from her 1783 petition **as incorrectly dated 1782 in the *American Museum*** (i.e., 124.9) printed under heading "Belinda" on p. 173 in *Biographical Sketches and Interesting Anecdotes of Persons of Color. To Which Is Added, a Selection of Pieces in Poetry,* compiled by A[bigail] Mott. "Second Edition."

York [Yorkshire, England]: Printed and Sold by W. Alexander & Son; sold also by Harvey and Darton, W. Phillips, E. Fry, and W. Darton, **London [England]**; R. Peart, **Birmingham [England]**; D. F. Gardiner, **Dublin [Ireland]**, 1828.
8vo (19.8 cm.): xi, [1], 252 p.

124.15 ———.

Substantive quotation from her "**1782**" (*sic*) petition (as "preserved" by "the authors of the American Museum") in the second of three numbered paragraphs about her headed "Belinda" on p. 169 in *Biographical Sketches and Interesting Anecdotes of Persons of Color. To Which Is Added, a Selection of Pieces in Poetry,* compiled by A[bigail] Mott. "Second Edition, much Enlarged."

New-York [New York, U.S.A.]: Mahlon Day, 374 Pearl-street, 1837. Tpv: "Note by the publisher. By consent of the Compiler, and at the recommendation of the Trustees of the African Free Schools in New York, (who have liberally patronized the work,) ..."
8vo (19 cm.): 260 p. (of which p. [256] is blank, and pp. 257–260 are table of contents).
https://babel.hathitrust.org/cgi/pt?id=hvd.32044004358602
&view=1up&seq=173

124.16———.

Substantive quotation from her "**1782**" (*sic*) petition (as "preserved" by "the authors of the American Museum") in the

second of three numbered paragraphs about her headed "Belinda" on p. 268 in *Biographical Sketches and Interesting Anecdotes of Persons of Color. To Which Is Added, a Selection of Pieces in Poetry,* compiled by A[bigail] Mott.

New York [New York, U.S.A.]: Stereotyped for and printed by order of the Trustees of the residuary estate of Lindley Murray. M. Day, Printer, 271 Pearl St. [1839]. Approximate year of printing (could be slightly later) from "Advertisement," p. [ii].
12mo (19 cm.): vi, [7]-408 p.
https://archive.org/details/biographicalsket00mottrich/page/n4 (incomplete 370-page exemplar).
https://babel.hathitrust.org/cgi/pt?id=loc.ark:/13960/t2q52p-81p&view=1up&seq=3 (complete).
Sabin 51111.

124.17———.

First petition (correctly dated at end) printed under heading "The Petition of Belinda, Servant of Isaac Royall, Esq. (Read before Sarah Bradley Fulton Chapter, D.A.R. [i.e., Daughters of the American Revolution], June 6, 2004)" on pp. 68–70 in *The Medford Historical Register,* vol. 7, no. 3.

Medford, Mass[achusetts, U.S.A.]: Published by the Medford Historical Society, July **1904**. Complete volume tpv: Medford[:] J. C. Miller Jr., Printer.
8vo (24 cm.).
https://babel.hathitrust.org/cgi/pt?id=njp.32101061423628&view=1up&seq=90

124.18———.

"Petition of an African slave, to the Legislature of Massachusetts," printed on pp. 463–465 (signed in type on p. 465: "BELINDA. Boston, February, **1782** [*sic*]") in the magazine *The American Museum, or Repository of Ancient and Modern Fugitive Pieces, Prose and Poetical,* 1: 6 (June 1787). Photomechanical reprint of 124.11 with imprint:

New York [New York, U.S.A.]: AMS Press, [**1965**].
https://babel.hathitrust.org/cgi/pt?id=uc1.b5219233;view=1up;seq=7

124.19———.

Petition printed from 124.9 under title "Belinda" on pp. 142–143 in *Unchained Voices: An Anthology of Black Authors in the English-Speaking World of the 18th Century,* edited by Vincent Carretta,

Lexington [Kentucky, U.S.A.]: The University Press of Kentucky, **1996**.
8vo (24 cm.): xi, 387 p.

Figure 9: House in Medford, Massachusetts where Belinda, also known as Belinda Royall and Belinda Sutton (ca. 1712–ca. 1799) lived most of her life. The house was owned by Isaac Royall, one of the wealthiest men in New England who owned a number of enslaved people. Belinda lived not in the slave quarters on the right, but in the large house in the background, where her owners dwelled, so that she could wait on them during the night. Here she did not have her own room or private space. The site is currently a museum entitled "The Royall House and Slave Quarters."

Source: Photographed by Aaron Spencer Fogleman, 2019.

124.20————.

Petition printed under heading "Belinda" from *Unchained Voices* (124.19) on pp. 50–51 in *Autobiography of a People: Three Centuries of African American History Told by Those who Lived It*, edited by Herb Boyd.

New York [New York, U.S.A.]: Doubleday, [2000].
8vo (24.2 cm.): xviii, [2], 459, [3] p.

124.21————. [Photomechanical reprint of 124.15]

Substantive quotation from her **"1782"** (*sic*) petition (as "preserved" by "the authors of the American Museum") in the second of three numbered paragraphs about her headed "Belinda" on p. 169 in 有色人に関する伝記的資料 / *Biographical Sketches and Interesting Anecdotes of Persons of Color. To which is added, a Selection of Pieces in Poetry*, compiled by A[bigail] Mott. "Second Edition, much Enlarged."

Tokyo, Japan: 日本図書センター, Nihon Tosho Senta, 2000.
8vo (27 cm.): 255 p.

124.22————, [Second edition of 124.19]

Petition printed from 124.9 under title "Belinda" on pp. 142–143 in *Unchained Voices: An Anthology of Black Authors in the English-Speaking World of the 18th Century*, **expanded edition**, edited by Vincent Carretta.

Lexington [Kentucky, U.S.A.]: University Press of Kentucky, 2004.
8vo (24 cm.): xi, 400 p.

124.23————.

Petition printed from 124.9 (repeating mistakenly dated type signature) as "Web Supplement for" Roy E. Finkenbine, "Belinda's Petition: Reparations for Slavery in Revolutionary

Massachusetts" in *William and Mary Quarterly*, 3rd series, vol. 64: 1: 95–104.

Williamsburg, Virginia [U.S.A.]: Omohundro Institute, 2007. 8vo (24 cm.).

https://oieahc-cf.wm.edu/wmq/Jan07/Finkbine.pdf

124.24 ——.

Excerpts of petition printed as from 122.6 on pp. 18–19 in *African Voices of the Global Past, 1500 to the Present*, edited by Trevor R. Getz.

[Boulder, Colorado, U.S.A.]: Westview Press, [2014]. 8vo (22.7 cm.): xii, 223 p., illus., map.

1784–1786

125.0   Francisco Alves de Souza

Rules, or statutes, in the form of a dialogue recorded from 1784 to 1786 in which the charity and almsgiving of souls is discussed, practiced by the Amina (a New World ethnic designation for Akan-speakers near Elmina Castle, modern Ghana) and their kinsmen in the state of Brazil, especially in Rio de Janeiro, where they must rule and govern themselves far from any heathen and superstitious abuses, composed by Francisco Alves de Souza, blacks and from the Kingdom of *Maki*, one of the best and most powerful of the region of the Amina, preserved in the Fundação Biblioteca Nacional, **Rio de Janeiro, Brazil**, Seção Manuscritos 9, 3, 11, fols. 1, 12–14, 16–26, 29–36, 38, 41–44.

¶ **Souza was taken from Mahi country north of Dahomey in the Bight of Benin (modern Benin—see Map 5) and endured the Middle Passage to Bahia in Brazil (Map 9). Attaining his freedom in 1748, he moved to Rio de Janeiro, Brazil and there joined the congregation of Amina (a New World ethnic designation for Akan-speakers near Elmina Castle, modern Ghana) and other "nations," and served as its regent. He became involved in disputes over the leadership of a black confraternity. The di-**

Full text: https://huskiecommons.lib.niu.edu/history-500africanvoices/108/ [see 125.1].

alogues (123.0), in which Souza's is the dominant African voice, resulted from a government investigation into this dispute.

125.1 ——.

125.0 published in the original Spanish with English translation, introduction, and annotations by Elizabeth W. Kiddy in "The *Regent*, the Secretary, and the Widow: Power, Ethnicity, and Gender in the Confraternity of Saints Elesbão and Iphigenia, Rio de Janeiro, 1784–1786," pp. 240–267 (especially 244-267) in *Afro-Latino Voices: Narratives from the Early Modern Ibero-Atlantic World, 1550–1812*, edited by Kathryn McKnight and Leo J. Garofalo.

Indianapolis [Indiana, U.S.A.]: Hackett Publishing Co., 2009. 8vo (23 cm.): xxxvii, 377 p.

125.2 ——.

123.0 published in English translation (only) with introduction and annotations by Elizabeth W. Kiddy in "The *Regent*, the Secretary, and the Widow: Power, Ethnicity, and Gender in the Confraternity of Saints Elesbão and Iphigenia, Rio de Janeiro, 1784–1786," pp. 153–168 in *Afro-Latino Voices, Shorter Edition: Translations of Early Modern Ibero-Atlantic Narratives*, edited by Kathryn McKnight and Leo J. Garofalo.

Indianapolis [Indiana, U.S.A.]: Hackett Publishing Co., 2015. 8vo (23 cm.): xli, 263 p.

1787

126.0   Quobna Ottabah Cugoano (ca. 1757–ca. 1791) = John Stuart = Ottobah Cugoano Steward

126.0a: *Thoughts and Sentiments on the Evil and Wicked Traffic of the Slavery and Commerce of the Human Species. Humbly submitted to the Inhabitants of Great-Britain by Ottabah Cugoano, a Native of Africa. London, July 1787.*

https://archive.org/details/ASPC0001997200/page/n124/mode/1up [see second of 126.6].

London [England]: Sold by T. Becket, Pall-Mall; also by Mr. Hall, at No. 25, Princes-Street, Soho; Mr. Phillips, George-Yard, Lombard-Street; and by the Author, at Mr. Cosway's, No. 88, Pall-Mall, 1787.
8vo: iv p. **Leaflet prospectus** for 124.1.
ESTC t6194. Eighteenth Century Collections Online (Gale) Unit 420 (The Eighteenth Century, reel 14685, no. 04).

126.0b: *Thoughts and Sentiments on the Evil and Wicked Traffic of the Slavery and Commerce of the Human Species. Humbly submitted to the Inhabitants of Great-Britain by Ottabah Cugoano, a Native of Africa. London, July 1787.*

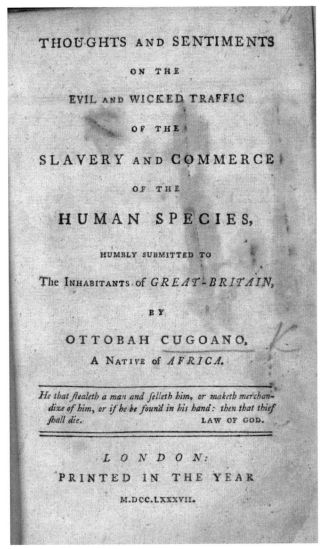

Figure 10: First edition title page of Ottabah Cugoano, *Thoughts and Sentiments on the Evil and Wicked Traffic of the Slavery and Commerce of the Human Species. Humbly submitted to the inhabitants of Great-Britain by Ottabah Cugoano, a Native of Africa* (London: multiple publishers, 1787). Cugoano came from a Fante town called Ajumako on the Gold Coast (modern Ghana) and was taken on a slave ship to Grenada in the Caribbean in 1772 and year later to London, where his book became an important early publication in the abolitionist movement.

London [England]: To be had of Mr. Hall, at No. 25, Princes-Street, Soho; Mr. Phillips, George-Yard, Lombard-Street; or of the Author, at Mr. Cosway's, No. 88, Pall-Mall. [1787.] 8vo: iv p. **Variant leaflet prospectus for 124.1.**
https://digitalcollections.nypl.org/items/0f82ba90-1615-0134-0bc9-00505686a51c#/?uuid=0f82ba90-1615-0134-0bc9-00505686a51c

¶ Cugoano was born in the Fante town of Ajumako ("Agimaque") on the Gold Coast (Akan peoples, modern Ghana—see Map 5). His father was a companion to the chief. In 1770 Cugoano, aged thirteen, was taken on a slave ship to the Caribbean island of Grenada (Map 11). He was sold there in 1772, then taken to London, England (Map 8) by his purchaser, who sponsored his education and freed him shortly thereafter. Cugoano underwent baptism in 1773 and took the name John Stuart. As an abolitionist, he published 124.1 to promote that cause. For more on him, see especially the introduction to 126.20, and Vincent Carretta, "Cugoano, Ottobah [John Stuart] (b. 1757?), Slavery Abolitionist and Writer," *Oxford Dictionary of National Biography* (Oxford: Oxford University Press, 2020 online).

126.1 ———.

Thoughts and Sentiments on the Evil and Wicked Traffic of the Slavery and Commerce of the Human Species. Humbly submitted to the inhabitants of Great-Britain by Ottabah Cugoano, a Native of Africa.

London [England]: Printed in the year M.DCC.LXXXVII
[1787].

8vo: [4], iv, 148 p.

https://babel.hathitrust.org/cgi/pt?id=uc1.$c32820;view=1up;
seq=7 (= 126.15, *q.v.*).

ESTC t50177; Hogg 1852.

126.2 ——. [French translation]

*Reflexions sur la Traite et l'Esclavage des Negres, Traduites
de l'Anglais, d'Ottobah Cugoano, afriquain* [sic], *esclave à La
Grénade et libre en Angleterre.*

A Londres [England]; Et se trouve a **Paris** [**France**], Chez
Royez, Libraire, Quai des Augustins, près le Pont-Neuf.
M.DCC.LXXXVIII [1788].

12mo: xii, 194 p.

https://digitalcollections.nypl.org/items/4aefc080-ae5d-0133-
c0b2-00505686a51c#/?uuid=4b4c2af0-ae5d-0133-303e-
00505686a51c

126.3 ——. [Abridgement of 126.1]

*Thoughts and Sentiments on the Evil of Slavery; or The nature
of Servitude as admitted by the law of God, compared to the
Modern Slavery of the Africans in the West Indies, in an answer to the advocate for Slavery and Oppression, addressed to
the sons of Africa, by a Native.*

London [England]: Printed for, and sold by, the Author ...
MDCCXCI [1791].

8vo: 46, [10]p.

ESTC t50178.

126.4 ——.

French-language memoir of Cugoano, with French translations of quotations from Cugoano's own writings, printed on
pp. 215–223 in Henri Grégoire, *De la littérature des Nègres,
ou, Recherches sur leurs facultés intellectuelles, leurs qualités
morales et leur littérature: suivies de notices sur la vie et les
ouvrages des Nègres qui se sont distingués dans les sciences,
les lettres et les arts.*

Paris [France]: Chez Maradan, Libraire, Rue des Grands-Augustins, No. 9, MD.CCC.VIII [1808].

8vo (20 cm.): xvi, 287, [1].

https://gallica.bnf.fr/ark:/12148/bpt6k844925/f228.item.tex-
teImage

126.5 ——. [English translation of 126.4]

English translation of Grégoire's memoir of Cugoano, with
quotations from Cugoano's own writings, printed on pp. 188–
196 in Henri Grégoire, *An Enquiry concerning the Intellectual
and Moral Faculties, and Literature of Negroes: followed
with an Account of the Life and Works of fifteen Negroes &*
Mulattoes, distinguished in Science, Literature, and the Arts
... translated by D. B. Warden.

Brooklyn [New York, U.S.A.]: Printed by Thomas Kirke,
Main-Street, 1810.

8vo (22 cm.): [4], vii (*i.e.*, viii), [1], 10–253, [3] p.

https://archive.org/details/enquiryconcernin00gr/page/188/
mode/1up?q=cugoano

126.6 ——. [Extract from 126.1 printed under heading:]

"Narrative of the Enslavement of Ottobah Cugoano, a Native
of Africa; published by Himself in the Year 1787" on pp. 120–
127 of *The Negro's Memorial; or, Abolitionist's Catechism; by
an Abolitionist* [i.e., Thomas Fisher].

London [England]: Printed for the Author, and sold by Hatchard
and Co., Piccadilly; and J. and A. Arch, Cornhill, 1825.
Colophon: Printed by James Bullock, Whitefriars, Fleet-Street.

8vo (22 cm.): iv, 127 p.

https://docsouth.unc.edu/neh/cugoano/cugoano.html

https://archive.org/details/ASPC0001997200/page/n124/
mode/1up

126.7 ——.

Derivative biographical sketch including quotations from his
work printed as ten numbered paragraphs on pp. 8–10 in *Biographical Sketches and Interesting Anecdotes of Persons of
Color. To Which Is Added, a Selection of Pieces in Poetry,*
compiled by A[bigail] Mott.

New York [New York, U.S.A.]: Printed and Sold by Mahlon
Day, No. 376, Pearl-street, 1826.

12mo (18 cm.): iv, [5]-192 p. Preface dated on p. iv: *Hickory
Grove* [N.Y.], 11*th mo.* 1825.

http://docsouth.unc.edu/neh/mott26/mott26.html

https://babel.hathitrust.org/cgi/pt?id=hvd.hn3m6e&view=
1up&seq=126

Hogg 1467.

126.8 ——.

Derivative biographical sketch including quotations from his
work printed under heading "Attobah Cugoano" on pp. 6–8
in *Biographical Sketches and Interesting Anecdotes of Persons
of Colour.* Compiled by A[bigail] Mott.

York [Yorkshire, England]: Printed and Sold by W. Alexander & Son, Castlegate; sold also by Harvey & Darton, W.
Phillips, E. Fry, and W. Darton, **London** [**England**]; R. Peart
[*sic*], **Birmingham** [**England**]; D. F. Gardiner, **Dublin** [**Ireland**], 1826.

12mo (20 cm.): xi, [2], 2–240 p.

https://babel.hathitrust.org/cgi/pt?id=nyp.33433081774204
&view=1up&seq=26

126.9——.

Derivative biographical sketch including quotations from his work printed on pp. 6–8 in *Biographical Sketches and Interesting Anecdotes of Persons of Color. To Which Is Added, a Selection of Pieces in Poetry*, compiled by A[bigail] Mott. "Second Edition."

York [Yorkshire, England]: Printed and Sold by W. Alexander & Son; sold also by Harvey and Darton, W. Phillips, E. Fry, and W. Darton, **London** [England]; R. Peart, **Birmingham** [England]; D. F. Gardiner, **Dublin** [Ireland]. 1828.
12mo (19.8 cm.): xi, [1], 252 p.

126.10——.

Part of his account printed (without naming him, but identifying him as a Fante man from Agimaque, i.e., the modern Fante town of Ajumako) within quotation marks under the heading "Juvenile Department" within "A short history of the poor slaves who are employed in cultivating Sugar, cotton, coffee, &c; intended to make little children pity them, and use their endeavours to relieve them from bondage. No III," on third page (i.e., 195), cols. 1–2, of the antislavery newspaper *The Liberator*, vol. 1, no. 49.

Boston [Massachusetts, U.S.A.]: William Lloyd Garrison and Isaac Knapp, Publishers, December 3, **1831**.
Broadsheet bifolium (49 cm.): 4 p.
http://fair-use.org/the-liberator/1831/12/03/the-liberator-01-49.pdf

126.11 ——.

Derivative biographical sketch including quotations from his work printed under heading "Attobah Cugoano" on pp. 8–10 in *Biographical Sketches and Interesting Anecdotes of Persons of Color. To Which Is Added, a Selection of Pieces in Poetry*, compiled by A[bigail] Mott. "Second Edition, much Enlarged."

New York [New York, U.S.A.]: Mahlon Day, 374 Pearl-street, 1837. Tpv: "Note by the publisher. By consent of the Compiler, and at the recommendation of the Trustees of the African Free Schools in New York, (who have liberally patronized the work,) ..."
8vo (19 cm.): 260 p. (of which p. [256] is blank, and pp. 257–260 are table of contents).
https://babel.hathitrust.org/cgi/pt?id=hvd.32044004358602;view=1up;seq=5

126.12 ——.

Derivative biographical sketch including quotations from his work printed under heading "Attobah Cugoano" on pp. 12–14 in *Biographical Sketches and Interesting Anecdotes of Persons of Color. To Which Is Added, a Selection of Pieces in Poetry*, compiled by A[bigail] Mott.

New York [New York, U.S.A.]: Stereotyped for and printed by order of the Trustees of the residuary estate of Lindley Murray, M. Day, Printer **1838**.
12mo (19 cm.): iv, 408 p.

126.13 ——.

Derivative biographical sketch including quotations from his work printed under heading "Attobah Cugoano" on pp. 12–14 in *Biographical Sketches and Interesting Anecdotes of Persons of Color. To Which Is Added, a Selection of Pieces in Poetry*, compiled by A[bigail] Mott.

New York [New York, U.S.A.]: Stereotyped for and printed by order of the Trustees of the residuary estate of Lindley Murray. M. Day, Printer, 271 Pearl St. [1839]. Approximate year of printing (could be slightly later) from "Advertisement," p. [ii].
12mo (19 cm.): vi, [7]-408 p.
https://archive.org/details/biographicalsket00mottrich/page/n4 (incomplete 370-page exemplar).
https://babel.hathitrust.org/cgi/pt?id=loc.ark:/13960/t2q52p-81p&view=1up&seq=3 (complete).

126.14 ——. [Very short summary printed under heading:]

"Attobah Cugoano' on pp. 329–331 of Wilson Armistead's compendium *A Tribute for the Negro: Being a Vindication of the Moral Intellectual, and Religious Capabilities of the Colored Portion of Mankind; with Particular Reference to the African Race.*

Manchester [England]: William Irwin; **London** [England]: Charles Gilpin; American Agent: Wm. Harned, Anti-Slavery Office, 61, John Street, **New York** [New York, U.S.A.]; and may be had of H. Longstreath and G.W. Taylor, **Philadelphia** [Pennsylvania, U.S.A.], 1848. Tpv: Manchester: Printed by William Irwin, 39, Oldham Street.
8vo (24 cm.): xxxv, 564 p.
https://babel.hathitrust.org/cgi/pt?id=nc01.ark:/13960/t42r4z659;view=1up;seq=13
http://docsouth.unc.edu/neh/armistead/armistead.html

126.15 ——.

Derivative biographical sketch including quotations from his work printed under heading "Attobah Cugoano" on pp. 12–14 in *Biographical Sketches and Interesting Anecdotes of Persons of Color. To Which Is Added, a Selection of Pieces in Poetry*, compiled by A[bigail] Mott.

New York [New York, U.S.A.]: Stereotyped for and printed by order of the Trustees of the residuary estate of Lindley Murray, **1850**.
8vo (20 cm.): iv, [7]-408 p.

126.16 ——.

Derivative biographical sketch including quotations from his work printed under heading "Attobah Cugoano" on pp. 12–14 in *Biographical Sketches and Interesting Anecdotes of Persons of Color. To Which Is Added, a Selection of Pieces in Poetry*, compiled by A[bigail] Mott.

New York [New York, U.S.A.]: Stereotyped for and printed by order of the Trustees of the residuary estate of Lindley Murray. D. Fanshaw, Printer, 35 Ann, corner of Nassau-street, **1854.** 12mo (19 cm.): iv, [7]-408 p. https://digital.ncdcr.gov/digital/collection/p249901coll37/id/10210

126.17 ——.

English translation of the Abbé Grégoire's biographical sketch of Cugoano (q.v. 126.4), including quotations of Cugoano's own statements, printed on pp. 61–63 in Rev. S. R. B. Attoh Ahuma, *Memoirs of West African Celebrities Europe, &c. (1700–1850). With special reference to the Gold Coast.*

Liverpool [England]: D. Marples & Co., 508 Lord Street, **1905.** 8vo (19 cm.): xix, 260 p., frontispiece portrait. https://babel.hathitrust.org/cgi/pt?id=ien.35556038054839&view=1up&seq=91

126.18 ——. [Mimeographed typescript transcription of 126.1]

Thoughts and Sentiments on the Evil and Wicked Traffic of the Slavery and Commerce of the Human Species. Humbly submitted to the inhabitants of Great-Britain by Ottabah Cugoano, a Native of Africa. [Sources and Documents Series, no. 5, of the Institute of African Studies, University of Ghana.]

[**Legon, Ghana:** Institute of African Studien, University of Ghana, 1965.] Exemplars found cataloged with a relatively wide range of posited late 20th-century years of publication. Tall 8vo (25 cm.): iv, 148 (*i.e.* leaves). Published in blue stiff paper covers. https://babel.hathitrust.org/cgi/pt?id=uc1.$c32820;view=1up;seq=7

126.19 ——.

Réflexions sur la traite et l'esclavage des nègres. Translated by Antoine Diannyère.

[**Paris, France:** Éditions d'Histoire Sociale, **1968.**] 8vo (21 cm.): xii, 194 p. Series: La Révolution française et l'abolition de l'esclavage, Tome 10.

126.20 ——.

Thoughts and Sentiments on the Evil and Wicked Traffic. Photomechanical reprint of 126.1, with new introduction by Paul Edwards, with imprint:

London [England]: Dawsons of Pall Mall, **1969.** 8vo (21 cm.): xxiii, lv, 148 p. Series: The Colonial History Series.

126.21 ——.

Excerpts from 126.1 printed, with an additional source text, and new introductory note, on pp. 39–53 in *Black Writers in Britain, 1760–1890: An Anthology,* edited by Paul Edwards and David Dabydeen.

Edinburgh [Scotland]: Edinburgh University Press, **1991.** 8vo (22 cm.): xv, 239 p.

126.22 ——. [Second printing of 126.21]

Excerpts from 126.1 printed, with an additional source text, and new introductory note, on pp. 39–53 in *Black Writers in Britain, 1760–1890: An Anthology,* edited by Paul Edwards and David Dabydeen.

Edinburgh [Scotland]: Edinburgh University Press, **1995.** 8vo (22 cm.): xv, 239 p.

126.23 ——.

Critical printing of excerpts of Cugoano's *Thoughts,* with new introduction, bibliographical note, and annotations, on pp. 125–156 in *Black Atlantic Writers of the Eighteenth Century: Living the New Exodus in England and the Americas,* edited by Adam Potkay and Sandra Burr.

New York [New York, U.S.A.]: St Martin's Press, [**1995**]. 8vo (22 cm.): xii, 268 p.

126.24 ——. [English issue of previous item]

Critical printing of excerpts of Cugoano's *Thoughts,* with new introduction, bibliographical note, and annotations, on pp. 23–63 in *Black Atlantic Writers of the Eighteenth Century: Living the New Exodus in England and the Americas,* edited by Adam Potkay and Sandra Burr.

Basingstoke [and] **London [England]:** Macmillan, **1995.** 8vo (22 cm.): xii, 268 p.

126.25 ——.

Quobna Ottobah Cugoano: Thoughts and Sentiments on the Evil of Slavery and Other Writings, edited by Vincent Carretta.

New York [New York, U.S.A.]: Penguin Books, **1999.** 8vo: xxxvi, 198 p.

126.26 ——. [Photomechanical reprint of 126.11]

Derivative biographical sketch including quotations from his work printed under heading "Attobah Cugoano" on pp. 8–10 in 有色人に関する伝記的資料 / *Biographical Sketches and*

Interesting Anecdotes of Persons of Color. To which is added, a Selection of Pieces in Poetry, compiled by A[bigail] Mott. "Second Edition, much Enlarged."

Tokyo, Japan: 日本図書センター, Nihon Tosho Senta, **2000.**
8vo (27 cm.): 255 p.

126.27——. [Third printing of 126.21]
Excerpts from 126.1 printed, with an additional source text, and new introductory note, on pp. 39–53 in *Black Writers in Britain, 1760–1890: An Anthology*, edited by Paul Edwards and David Dabydeen.

Edinburgh [Scotland]: Edinburgh University Press, **1995.**
8vo (22 cm.): xv, 239 p.

126.28 ——.
Extracts "From Thoughts and sentiments on the evil and wicked traffic of the slavery and commerce of the human species, humbly submitted to the inhabitants of Great Britain by Ottobah Cugoano, a native of Africa" printed in *Early Black British Writing: Olaudah Equiano, Mary Prince, and others: Selected texts with introduction, critical essays*, edited by Alan Richardson and Debbie Lee.

Boston [Massachusetts, U.S.A.]: Houghton Mifflin, **2004.**
8vo (21 cm.): ix, 443 p.

126.29——.
Réflexions sur la Traite et l'esclavage des Nègres. [With introduction by Jean Alix René.]

[Port-au-Prince, Haïti: Editions Presses Nationales d'Haïti, 2004.]
8vo (20 cm.): 151 p., illus.

126.30——.
Réflexions sur la Traite et l'esclavage des Nègres. Avant-propos de Elsa Dorlin.

Paris [France]: Zones, **2009.**
8vo (21 cm.): 116 p.

126.31 ——.
Réflexions sur la Traite et l'esclavage des nègres.

Paris [France]: La Découverte, **2009.**
117 p.

126.32 ——.
Excerpts from 126.6 printed on pp. 23–24 in *African Voices of the Global Past, 1500 to the Present*, edited by Trevor R. Getz.

[Boulder, Colorado, U.S.A.]: Westview Press, [2014].
8vo (22.7 cm.): xii, 223 p., illus., map.

Other publications by Ottobah Cugoano

+126-A.1-C.1 ——.
Three letters to Sir William Dolben, Bart., William Pitt, and Charles James Fox (one letter to each man), signed in type by Gustavus Vassa, Ottobah Cugoano Steward, and four others ("For ourselves and Brethren"), printed in the London, England, newspaper *The Morning Chronicle and London Advertiser*, 15 July 1788.

+126-A.2-C.2 ——.
+126-A.1, +126-B.1, and +126-C.1 printed on pp. 269–270 in Folarin Shyllon, *Black People in Britain 1555–1833* (Published for The Institute for Race Relations, London [England], by Oxford University Press, London, 1977).

+126-D.1 ——.
Letter to "Mr. William Dickson, formerly Private Secretary to the Hon. Edward Hay, Governor of the Island of Barbadoes," signed in type by Gustavus Vassa, Ottobah Cugoano Steward, and five others, printed in the London, England, newspaper *The Diary; or Woodfall's Register*, 25 April 1789.

+126-D.2 ——.
+126-D.1 printed on pp. 271–272 in Folarin Shyllon, *Black People in Britain 1555-1833* (Published for The Institute for Race Relations, London [England], by Oxford University Press, London, 1977).

+126-E.1 ——.
Letter of thanks to Granville Sharp signed by John Stuart (= Ottobah Coguano) and 11 others printed on pp. 333–334 in Prince Hoare, *Memoirs of Granville Sharp* (London [England], 1820).

https://babel.hathitrust.org/cgi/pt?id=uc2.ark:/13960/t2988hk17&view=1up&seq=371

+126-E.2 ——.
+126-E.1 printed on pp. 114–115 in vol. 2 of Prince Hoare, *Memoirs of Granville Sharp* (London [England], 1828), 2nd edition. https://babel.hathitrust.org/cgi/pt?id=nyp.33433082389879&view=1up&seq=132

+126-E.3 ——.
+126-E.2 printed on p. 267 in Folarin Shyllon, *Black People in Britain 1555–1833* (Published for The Institute for Race Relations, London [England], by Oxford University Press, London, 1977).

+126-E.4 ——.

+126-E.1 reprinted on pp. 333–334 in facsimile reprint of 1820 London edition of Prince Hoare, *Memoirs of Granville Sharp* (Oxford University Press, 2015).

+126-F.1 ——.

"Address of Thanks of the Sons of Africa to the Honourable Granville Sharp, Esq." dated December 15, 1787, signed by Ottobah Cugoano, Gustavus Vassa, and ten others, printed on pp. 374–375 in Prince Hoare, *Memoirs of Granville Sharp* (London [England], 1820).

https://babel.hathitrust.org/cgi/pt?id=uc2.ark:/13960/t2988hk17&view=1up&seq=412

+126-F.2 ——.

+126-F.1 printed on pp. 175–177 in vol. 2 of Prince Hoare, *Memoirs of Granville Sharp* (London [England], 1828), 2nd edition.

https://babel.hathitrust.org/cgi/pt?id=nyp.33433082389879&view=1up&seq=193

+126-F.3 ——.

+126-F.2 printed on pp. 268–269 in Folarin Shyllon, *Black People in Britain 1555–1833* (Published for The Institute for Race Relations, London [England], by Oxford University Press, London, 1977).

+126-F.4 ——.

+126-F.1 reprinted on pp. 374–375 in facsimile reprint of 1820 London edition of Prince Hoare, *Memoirs of Granville Sharp* (Oxford University Press, 2015).

127.0 Pablo Agüero

Manuscript "Testimony of Pablo Agüero, Native of *Guinea*" in "Information taken to clarify what [Manuel] Farías presents in his *memorial* against Pablo Agüero, both black men, officiated in **Buenos Aires [Argentina], 23 January 1787**," recorded in Chief Government Notary Office, Sala IX, 36:4:3, legajo 75, exp. 10.

Full text: https://huskiecommons.lib.niu.edu/history-500africanvoices/109/ [see 127.1].

¶ From an unknown location in West Africa, Agüero was captured, endured the Middle Passage, and was sold in Buenos Aires in the Spanish Viceroyalty of Río de la Plata (modern Argentina—see Map 9), where he lived in the Monserrat neighborhood. He was commissioned to arrest black men and women who fled from their masters. His and Duarte's (q.v. **128.0**) 1787 testimony were part of an investigation regarding the tensions and activities of Black confraternities.

127.1 ——.

"'El rey de los *congos*': The Clandestine Coronation of Pedro Duarte in Buenos Aires, 1787," being 127.0 printed in Spanish with English translations by Joseph P. Sánchez, Angelica Sánchez-Clark, and Larry D. Miller, and introduction and annotations by Patricia Fogelman and Marta Goldberg, on pp. 162–164 and 166–168 within their article on pp. 155–173 in *Afro-Latino Voices: Narratives from the Early Modern Ibero-Atlantic World, 1550–1812*, edited by Kathryn McKnight and Leo J. Garofalo.

Indianapolis [Indiana, U.S.A.]: Hackett Publishing Co., **2009**. 8vo (23 cm.): xxxvii, 377 p.

127.2 ——.

"'El rey de los *congos*': The Clandestine Coronation of Pedro Duarte in Buenos Aires, 1787," being 127.0 in English translation (only) by Joseph P. Sánchez, Angelica Sánchez-Clark, and Larry D. Miller, and introduction and annotations by Patricia Fogelman and Marta Goldberg, on pp. 101–113 in *Afro-Latino Voices, **Shorter Edition**: Translations of Early Modern Ibero-Atlantic Narratives*, edited by Kathryn McKnight and Leo J. Garofalo.

Indianapolis [Indiana, U.S.A.]: Hackett Publishing Co., **2015**. 8vo (23 cm.): xli, 263 p.

128.0 Pedro Duarte

Manuscript "Testimony of Pedro Duarte, Native of the *Congo Nation*," in "Information taken to clarify what [Manuel] Farías presents in his *memorial* against Pablo Agüero, both black men, officiated in **Buenos Aires [Argentina], 23 January 1787**," recorded in Chief Government Notary Office, Sala IX, 36:4:3, legajo 75, exp. 10.

Full text: https://huskiecommons.lib.niu.edu/history-500africanvoices/110/ [see 128.1].

¶ Duarte, of the Kongo nation (modern Congo—see Map 6), was captured, endured the Middle Passage, and was sold in Buenos Aires, in the Spanish Viceroyalty of Río de la Plata (in modern Argentina—Map 9). His and Agüero's (q.v. 127.0) 1787 testimony were part of an investigation regarding the tensions and activities of Black confraternities. The Black *majordomo* of the confraternity of Saint Balthasar selected Duarte to be king (or mayor, as he put it) of the Congos.

128.1 ——.

"'El rey de los *congos*': The Clandestine Coronation of Pedro Duarte in Buenos Aires, 1787," being 128.0 printed in Spanish with English translations by Joseph P. Sánchez, Angelica Sánchez-Clark, and Larry D. Miller, and introduction and annotations by Patricia Fogelman and Marta Goldberg, on pp. 166–167 within their article on pp. 155–173 in *Afro-Latino Voices: Narratives from the Early Modern Ibero-Atlantic World, 1550–1812*, edited by Kathryn McKnight and Leo J. Garofalo.

Indianapolis [Indiana, U.S.A.]: Hackett Publishing Co., 2009. 8vo (23 cm.): xxxvii, 377 p.

128.2 ——.

"'El rey de los *congos*': The Clandestine Coronation of Pedro Duarte in Buenos Aires, 1787," being 128.0 in English translation (only) by Joseph P. Sánchez, Angelica Sánchez-Clark, and Larry D. Miller, and introduction and annotations by Patricia Fogelman and Marta Goldberg, on pp. 101–113 in *Afro-Latino Voices, **Shorter Edition:** Translations of Early Modern Ibero-Atlantic Narratives,* edited by Kathryn McKnight and Leo J. Garofalo.

Indianapolis [Indiana, U.S.A.]: Hackett Publishing Co., 2015. 8vo (23 cm.): xli, 263 p.

1788

129.1-2 Thomas Fuller (ca. 1718–1790) = Tom = Negro Tom = African Calculator = The Virginia Calculator

Two nearly simultaneous, incomplete original printings whose chronological order is unclear, one likely being a reprint of the other, and one likely misprinting the date:

129.1

Account of Thomas Fuller's life and skills included in a letter by Dr. Benjamin Rush, of which part (only) is printed under heading "An Account of the extraordinary Powers of Calculation, by Memory, possessed by a Negro Slave, **in Maryland**, communicated in a Letter from Dr. Rush, of Philadelphia, to a Gentleman in Manchester [i.e., Dr. Thomas Percival (1740–1804)]" with dateline "Philadelphia, **Sept. 15** [*sic*], **1788**" on p. 306 of the December 1788 issue (vol. 83, no. 581) of *The Universal Magazine of Knowledge and Pleasure*.**London [England]:** Published under his Majesty's Royal License, By W. Bent, at the King's Arms, Pater-Noster Row, [December 1788].

8vo (25 cm.).

https://babel.hathitrust.org/cgi/pt?id=nyp.33433095197103 &view=1up&seq=752

129.2

Account of Thomas Fuller's life and skills included in a letter by Dr. Benjamin Rush, of which part (only) is printed under heading "An Account of the extraordinary Powers of Calculation by Memory, possessed by a Negro Slave **in Maryland**, communicated by Dr. Rush of Philadelphia, to a Gentleman in Manchester [i.e., Dr. Thomas Percival (1740–1804)]" with dateline "Philadelphia, **Sept. 25** [*sic*]. **1788**" on p. 580 of the December 1788 issue (vol. 50, no. 12) of *The Scots Magazine.*

https://archive.org/details/lettersonslavery-00dick/page/184/mode/1up [see 129.8].

Edinburgh [Scotland]: Printed by Murray and Cochrane, [December] 1788.

8vo (20 cm.).

https://babel.hathitrust.org/cgi/pt?id=hvd.32044092547330 &view=1up&seq=586

Note that the first complete printing of the account is in 129.8.

¶ Fuller was born ca. 1710 and grew up possibly in Ouidah (the port city in modern Benin—see Map 5). When aged ca. fourteen, he was sold and forcibly transported on a slave ship to the British North American colony of Virginia in 1724 (Map 15). There he was sold to Presley Cox and his wife Elizabeth Cox, who owned a plantation about four miles west of the city of Alexandria, in Fairfax County, Virginia, where he lived and worked for the rest of his life. At some point, very likely as a youth in Africa, Fuller developed an extraordinary ability to make large, complex mathematical calculations very quickly without writing. His renown spread to Philadelphia (nearly 150 miles away in the state of Pennsylvania), from where in 1788 several men visited Fuller in Virginia, asked him a series of complex mathematical questions, timed the intervals preceding his responses, manually checked the correctness of these responses, and recorded the results, including direct quotations of Fuller's speech. They then presented this material to their colleague in Philadelphia, Dr. Benjamin Rush, who copied it into his letter of 14 November 1788 (see above) and formally attested to its accuracy. For more on Fuller see John Fauvel and Paulus Gerdes, "African Slave and Calculating Prodigy: Bicentenary of the Death of Thomas Fuller," *Historia Mathematica*, 17:2 (May 1990): 141–151, which includes a reprinting of Fuller's obituary printed in the *Columbian Centinel*, Nr. 707, col. 2, p. 123 (29 December 1790), Boston, Massachusetts [U.S.A.].

129.3 ——. [Condensed account from 129.1 or 129.2]

Essence of Dr. Rush's 15 or 25 September 1788 account (not here dated) of Thomas Fuller's skills printed (**without naming him, but locating him in Maryland**) with additional concluding statement (viz. "The publication of these *facts* seems to have an *end* in view, which, however, will by no means lessen their credit, when recorded by Dr. Rush on his *own knowledge*" [emphasis in original]) on p. 1112, col. 2, of the December 1788 issue (vol. 58, part 2, no. 6) of *The Gentleman's Magazine: and Historical Chronicle*.

London [England]: Printed by John Nichols, for David Henry, late of St. John's Gate; and sold by Eliz. Newbery [*sic*], the corner of St. Paul's Church yard, Ludgate Street, [**December**] **1788**.
8vo (22 cm.). Auditors' perception of Fuller's accent reproduced in their spellings of *only one* of his words; his owner not named.
https://babel.hathitrust.org/cgi/pt?id=mdp.39015013472827&view=1up&seq=592

129.4 ——. [Reprinted from 129.1]
Account of Thomas Fuller's life and skills included in a letter by Dr. Benjamin Rush, of which part (only) is printed under heading "An Account of the extraordinary powers of calculation by memory, possessed by a Negro Slave **in Maryland** [*sic*], communicated in a letter from Dr. Rush, to a Gentleman in Manchester [i.e., Dr. Thomas Percival (1740–1804)]" with dateline "Philadelphia, **September 15, 1788**" on p. 14 of the *The British Mercury, or, Annals of History, Politics, Manners, Literature, Arts, etc. of the British Empire* (edited by I. W. von Archenholtz), vol. 8, no. 1.

Hamburg [Germany]: Printed for the Editor [i.e., Johann Wilhelm von Archenholtz (1743–1812)], and sold in [*sic*] Commission by B. C. Hoffman, **January 3, 1789**.
8vo (19 cm.).

129.5 ——. [First or second printing of 129.0c, slightly abbreviated]
Detailed account, written by Dr. Benjamin Rush, of Thomas Fuller's life and mathematical skills as the latter shared both William Hartshorne and Samuel Coates during conversations with them (some of these skills also witnessed by Thomas Wistar and Benjamin W. Morris) printed under heading "Account of a wonderful talent for arithmetical calculation, in an African slave living in [n.b.] Virginia," which follows the statement "At a meeting of the Pennsylvania Society for promoting the Abolition of Slavery and the relief of Free Negroes unlawfully held in Bondage---Order that the following certificate be published" in the weekly newspaper *The New Jersey Journal and Political Intelligencer*, no. 275.

Elizabeth-Town [New Jersey, U.S.A.]: Printed and published by Shepard Kollock, every Wednesday ... two dollars per annum ... **January 21, 1789**.
Broadsheet bifolium.

129.6 ——. [First or second printing of 129.0c, slightly abbreviated]
Detailed account, written by Dr. Benjamin Rush, of Thomas Fuller's life and mathematical skills as the latter shared both William Hartshorne and Samuel Coates during conversations with them (some of these skills also witnessed by Thomas Wistar and Benjamin W. Morris) printed under heading "Account of a wonderful talent for arithmetical calculation, in an African slave living in [n.b.] Virginia" and dateline "Philadelphia, **November 14, 1788**" on pp. 62–63 of the *American Museum: or Repository of Ancient and Modern Fugitive Pieces, &c. Prose and Poetical*, vol. 5, no. 1.

Philadelphia [Pennsylvania, U.S.A.]: Printed by Mathew Carey, **January 1789**.
8vo (21.5 cm.). Complete volume includes extensive **list of subscribers**. Note: Dr. Rush drew up this account on behalf of the Pennsylvania Society for Promoting the Abolition of Slavery, which at its January 5, 1789, meeting authorized that this account be sent to the Society for Abolishing the African Trade at London, England. Auditors' perception of Fuller's accent reproduced in their spellings of *several* of his words; owner's surname spelled **Coxe**.
https://babel.hathitrust.org/cgi/pt?id=osu.32435073185605&view=1up&seq=70

129.7 ——. [Reprinting of 129.1]
Account of Thomas Fuller's life and skills included in a letter by Dr. Benjamin Rush, of which part (only) is printed under heading "An account of the extraordinary powers of calculation by memory, possessed by a Negro Slave, **in Maryland** [*sic*]; communicated in a letter from Dr. Rush, of Philadelphia, to a gentleman in Manchester [i.e., Dr. Thomas Percival (1740–1804)]" with dateline "Philadelphia, **Sept. 15, 1788**" on p. 87 of the *The New Lady's Magazine; or, Polite, Entertaining, and Fashionable Companion for the Fair Sex*, vol. 83, no. 581.

London [England]: Printed, by Royal Authority, by Alex. Hogg, at the King's Arms, No. 16, Pater-Noster Row, (by whom the Communications, post-paid, of ingenious persons—Post Paid—will be received, and immediately transmitted to the Editor); and sold by all Booksellers, Stationers, and News-Carriers in Town and Country, (To be continued Monthly--Price only Six-pence) [**February 1789**].
8vo (22 cm.). Auditors' perception of Fuller's accent reproduced in their spellings of several of his words; owner's surname spelled **Coxe**.

129.8 ——.
First complete printing of Fuller's account in Dr. Benjamin Rush's 14 November 1788 letter under the heading "Accounts

of a Negro Practitioner of Physic, and a self-taught Negro Calculator, by Benjamin Rush, M.D. Prof. of Chem. in the Univ. of Pennsylvania, Mem. of the American Phil. Soc.---of the Med. Soc. of London---of the Liter. and Phil. Soc. of Manchester---Hon. Mem. of the Roy. Med. Soc. of Edinburgh, & &c." on pp. 184–187 in *Letters on Slavery, by William Dickson, Formerly private secretary to the late Hon. Edward Hay, Governor of Barbadoes. To which are added, Addresses to the Whites, and to the Free Negroes of Barbadoes; and Accounts of some Negroes eminent for their virtues and abilities.*

London [England]: Printed and sold by J. Phillips, George-Yard, Lombard-Street, and sold by J. Johnson, St. Paul's Church-yard, and Elliot and Kay, opposite Somerset Place, Strand--- M.DCC.LXXXIX [before **May 1789**].

8vo (23 cm.): [2], x, 190, [2] p. Auditors' perception of Fuller's accent reproduced in their spellings of *several* of his words; his owner's surname spelled **Cox**. Reviewed: within "Monthly Catalogue, for April, 1789," in *Monthly Review* (London [England]: R. Griffiths), vol. 80, no. 4 (April 1789): 351; among "New Publications" in *The Gentleman's Magazine* (London), vol. 59, part 1, no. 5 (May 1789): 433.

https://archive.org/details/lettersonslavery00dick/page/184/mode/1up

129.9 ——.

Account of Thomas Fuller's life and skills included in a letter by Dr. Benjamin Rush to Dr. Thomas Percival (named herein), of which part (only) is printed---with the added introduction "... I [i.e., Thomas Burgess] shall supply some particulars of the **Maryland** [sic] Negro, which I owe to the friendly communication of Dr. Thomas Percival, who received them from Dr. Rush. 'Of their authenticity,' says Dr. Percival, 'I have no doubt, as I know Dr. Rush to be a man of observation and probity; **and we have now a gentleman in Manchester, who has seen and conversed with the Slave, and who confirms the account, which has been given of him...'**"[*]—on pp. 149–150 of Thomas Burgess, *Considerations on the Abolition of Slavery and the Slave Trade, upon Grounds of Natural, Religious, and Political Duty.*

Oxford [England]: Sold by D. Prince and J. Cooke; J. and J. Fletcher: and by Elmsly, White, Payne, Cadell, London [England], MDCCLXXXIX [after February and before **July 1789**].

8vo (21 cm.): [4], 166, [2] p. *Note: According to its printing in Thomas Percival, *Works ... A New Edition* (London: Printed for J. Johnson, 1807), vol. 1, p. clvi, Dr. Perrcival dated this letter to Thomas Burgess "Manchester, March 5, 1789." Reviewed within the "Monthly Catalogue, for June, 1789," in *Monthly Review* (London [England]: R. Griffiths), vol. 80, no. 6 (June 1789): 561.

129.10 ——.

Account of Thomas Fuller's life and mathematical skills (including his interlocutors' leap-year error) printed under heading "Account of a wonderful talent for arithmetical calculation, in an African slave, living in Virginia" in *The Columbian Almanack; or the North American Calendar, for the year of our Lord 1791.*

Wilmington, Delaware [U.S.A.]: Printed and Sold by Andrews, Craig, and Brynberg, at the Post-Office, in Market-Street, [before or during December 1790].12mo: [48] p. The compilers owe this reference to Robert K. Dodge, *q.v.* 129.81. Evans 22411.

129.11 ——.

Obituary notice of Fuller printed in the newspaper *Virginia Gazette and Alexandria Advertiser.*

Alexandria [Virginia, U.S.A.]: Published by [Samuel] Hanson and [Thomas] Bond,
December 9, 1790.
Broadsheet bifolium: 4 p. Note: Apparently first brought to historians' attention by Dr. A. Glenn Crothers in his doctoral dissertation, *"The Projecting Spirit": Social, Economic, and Cultural Change in Post-Revolutionary Northern Virginia, 1780–1805* (Gainesville: University of Florida, 1997), p. 37 and 55, n. 47.

129.12 ——.

Variant obituary notice of Fuller printed on the first page of the December 16, 1790 issue of the newspaper *Pennsylvania Mercury and Universal Advertiser.*

Philadelphia [Pennsylvania, U.S.A.]: Daniel Humphreys, December 16, 1790.
4to quadrifolium.

129.13 ——.

Obituary notice of Fuller reprinted the last page of the December 21, 1790, issue of the newspaper *Pennsylvania Mercury and Universal Advertiser.*

Philadelphia [Pennsylvania, U.S.A.]: Daniel Humphreys, December 21, 1790.
4to quadrifolium.

129.14 ——.

Obituary notice of Fuller reprinted in the December 22, 1790 issue of the newspaper *New-York Daily Gazette.*

New York [New York, U.S.A.]: Archibald M'Lean, **December 22, 1790.**
Broadsheet bifolium .

129.15 ———.

Obituary notice of Fuller reprinted on the second and third pages of the December 22, 1790, issue of the newspaper *Freeman's Journal; or, The North-American Intelligencer*.

Philadelphia [Pennsylvania, U.S.A.]: Francis Bailey, **December 22, 1790.**
Broadsheet bifolium.

129.16 ———.

Obituary notice of Fuller reprinted on the third page of the December 25, 1790, issue of the newspaper *Independent Gazetteer, and Agricultural Repository*.

Philadelphia [Pennsylvania, U.S.A.]: Eleazer Oswald, **December 25, 1790.**
Broadsheet bifolium.

129.17 ———.

Obituary notice of Fuller reprinted (at first or second hand) from 129.11 on page 123, col. 2 of the newspaper *Columbian Centinel*, vol. 14, no. 31.

Boston [Massachusetts, U.S.A.]: Published by Benjamin Russell, **December 29, 1790.**
Broadsheet bifolium: 4 https://www.encyclopediavirginia.org/media_player?mets_filename=evr12581mets.xml

129.18 ———.

Obituary notice of Fuller reprinted on the third page of the January 4, 1791 issue of the newspaper *Salem Gazette*.

Salem [Massachusetts, U.S.A.]: **January 4, 1791.**
Broadsheet bifolium.

129.19 ———.

Obituary notice reprinted on the second page of the January 6, 1791, issue of the newspaper *Thomas's Massachusetts Spy; or, the Worcester Gazette*.

Worcester [Massachusetts, U.S.A.]: Isaiah Thoma, **January 6, 1791.**
Broadsheet bifolium.

129.20 ———.

Obituary notice of Fuller reprinted on the fourth page of the January 12, 1791 issue of the newspaper *Connecticut Journal*.

New Haven [Connecticut, U.S.A.]: Thomas and Samuel Green, **January 12, 1791.**
Broadsheet bifolium.

129.21 ———.

Obituary notice of Fuller reprinted on the third page of the January 12, 1791 issue of the weekly newspaper *Hampshire Gazette*.

Northampton [Massachusetts, U.S.A.]: William Butler, **January 12, 1791.**
Broadsheet bifolium.

129.22 ———.

Obituary notice of Fuller reprinted on the fourth page of the January 17, 1791 issue of the newspaper *Vermont Gazette*.

Bennington [Vermont, U.S.A.]: Anthony Haswell, **January 17, 1791.**
Broadsheet bifolium.

129.23 ———.

Obituary notice of Fuller reprinted on the first page of the January 18, 1791 issue of the newspaper *The Western Star*.

Stockbridge [Massachusetts, U.S.A.]: Loring Andrews, **January 18, 1791.**
Broadsheet bifolium.

129.24 ———.

Obituary notice of Fuller reprinted on the third page of the March 17, 1791 issue of the weekly newspaper *United States Chronicle: Political, Historical, and Commercial*.

Providence [Rhode Island, U.S.A.]: Bennett Wheeler, **March 17, 1791.**
Broadsheet bifolium.

129.25 ———.

Detailed notice* (derived from Dr. Rush, and probably from 127.6 [*American Museum*]; locating Fuller near Alexandria) of Thomas Fuller's calculating prowess (including account of his interlocutors' leap-year error) printed (within letter XXIV) on pp. 39–41 in vol. 2 of Jacques-Pierre Brissot de Warville, *Nouveau Voyage dans les Etats-Unis de l'Amerique Septentrionale, fait en 1788*.

Paris [France]: Chez Buisson, Imprimeur & Libraire, rue Haute-Feuille, no. 20, **Avril 1791.**
2 vols., 8vo (21 cm.): [ii], lii, 396; [iv], xxiv, 460 [*sic*] p., folding tables. A third volume is a distinct work.
*Note: In this notice Cox, Hartshorn[e], and Coates are named.
https://gallica.bnf.fr/ark:/12148/bpt6k824188/f42.item.texteImage

129.26 ——.

Detailed notice (derived from Dr. Rush; and probably from 129.6 [*American Museum*] locating Fuller near Alexandria) of Thomas Fuller's calculating prowess (including account of his interlocutors' leap-year error) printed (within letter XXIV) in Jacques-Pierre Brissot de Warville, *Nouveau Voyage dans les Etats-Unis de l'Amerique Septentrionale, fait en 1788.*

Paris [France]: Chez Buisson, Imprimeur & Libraire, rue Haute-Feuille, no. 20, **Avril 1791.**

2 vols., 8vo: xl, 275; [4], 317p. Text proper complete as in previous item, but in smaller type throughout.

129.27 ——.

German translation of detailed notice (derived from Dr. Rush) of Thomas Fuller's calculating prowess printed (within letter XXIV) in Jacques-Pierre Brissot de Warville, *Neue Reise durch die Vereinigten Staaten von Nord-Amerika im Jahr 1788.*

Bayreuth [Bavaria, Germany]: im Verlag der dasigen Zeitungsdruckerey, **1792.**

2 vols., 8vo (19 cm.).

129.28 ——.

German translation of detailed notice (derived from Dr. Rush) of Thomas Fuller's calculating prowess printed (within letter XXIV) in Jacques-Pierre Brissot de Warville, *Neue Reise durch die Nord-Amerikanisch Freistaaten im Jahr 1788, mit Anmerkungen von J. R. Foster, aus dem Französischen.*

Berlin [Prussia, Germany]: Vossischen Buchhandlung, **1792.**
8vo: xvi, [2], 292.

129.29 ——.

German translation of detailed notice (derived from Dr. Rush) of Thomas Fuller's calculating prowess printed (within letter XXIV) in Jacques-Pierre Brissot de Warville, *Neue Reise durch die Vereinigten Staaten von Nord-America, im Jahr 1788.... Aus dem Französischen von T. F. Ehrmann.*

Durkheim an der Haard [Germany]: F. L. Pfahler, **1792.**
8vo: lxvii, 628 p., folding table.

129.30 ——.

German translation of detailed notice (derived from Dr. Rush) of Thomas Fuller's calculating prowess printed (within letter XXIV) in Jacques-Pierre Brissot de Warville, *Reise durch die Vereinigten Staaten von Nord-America, im Jahr 1788.... Aus dem Französischen von T. F. Ehrmann.*

Heidelberg [Baden-Wurttemberg, Germany]: F. L. Pfahler, **1792.**

8vo: lxvii, 628 p., folding table. Sabin suggests this is 129.29 with cancellans title leaf.

129.31 ——. **[First English translation of 129.25/26]**

Terse (one-paragraph) English-language summary (derived from Dr. Rush; locating Fuller near Alexandria) of Fuller's calculating prowess printed (within letter XXIV) on p. 287 in Jacques-Pierre Brissot de Warville, *New Travels in the United States of America. Performed in 1788.... Translated from the French* [by Joel Barlow].

London [England]: Printed for J. S. Jordan, no. 166, Fleet-Street, MDCCXCII [1792].

8vo (21 cm.): [4], 483, [5], folding table. "Preface of the Translator" dated "London, Feb. 1, 1792" (p. viii). Note: First *complete* English translation of 127.25/26 is 127.58 below.

129.32 ——.

Terse (one-paragraph) English-language summary (derived from Dr. Rush; locating Fuller near Alexandria) of Thomas Fuller's calculating prowess printed (within letter XXII) on p. 287 in Jacques-Pierre Brissot de Warville, *New Travels in the United States of America. Performed in 1788.... Translated from the French* [by Joel Barlow].

Dublin [Ireland]: Printed by W. Corbet, for P. Byrne, A. Grueber, W. M'kenzie, J. Moore, W. Jones, R. M'Allister, and J. Rice, MDCCXCII [1792].

8vo: [4], 483, [5], folding table.
https://www.loc.gov/resource/lhbtn.12303/?sp=295

129.33 ——.

Terse (one paragraph) English-language summary (derived from Dr. Rush; locating Fuller near Alexandria) of Thomas Fuller's calculating prowess printed (in letter XXII) in Jacques-Pierre Brissot de Warville, *New Travels in the United States of America. Performed in 1788.... Translated from the French* [by Joel Barlow]. *Second edition, corrected.*

London [England]: Printed for J. S. Jordan, MDCCXCII [1792].

2 vols., 8vo (21 cm.). The second volume is, in fact, additional text.

129.34 ——.

Dutch translation of detailed notice (derived from Dr. Rush) of Thomas Fuller's calculating prowess printed (in letter XXII) in Jacques-Pierre Brissot de Warville, *Nieuwe reize in de Vereenigde Staaten van Noord-Amerika.*

Amsterdam [The Netherlands]: Bij Martinus de Bruijn ..., [1794?].

8vo (23 cm.): xlvii, 370 p.

129.35a ———.

Significant parts of 129.1 or 129.2 (including Fuller's interlocutors' leap year error, and locating Fuller in "Maryland, North America") printed within quotation marks on pp. 260–261 in vol. 2 of John Gabriel Stedman, *Narrative, of a Five Years' Expedition, against the Revolted Negroes of Surinam, in Guiana, on the Wild Coast of South America; from the year 1772, to 1777…*

London [England]: Printed for J. Johnson, St. Paul's Church Yard, & J. Edwards, Pall Mall, **1796** (*sic*). No colophon in vol. 2. **Regular paper issue** with un-colored plates.

2 vols., 4to. (28 cm.), folding map, plan, plates (some engraved by William Blake). **Includes list of subscribers.** Auditors' perception of Fuller's accent reproduced in their spellings of *two* of his words; his owner's surname spelled **Cox**.

https://www.biodiversitylibrary.org/item/163990#page/328/mode/1up

ESTC t146566; Price & Price 1.

129.35b ———.

Significant parts of 129.1 or 129.2 (including Fuller's interlocutors' leap year error, and locating Fuller in "Maryland, North America") printed within quotation marks on pp. 260–261 in vol. 2 of John Gabriel Stedman, *Narrative, of a Five Years' Expedition, against the Revolted Negroes of Surinam, in Guiana, on the Wild Coast of South America; from the year 1772, to 1777…*

London [England]: Printed for J. Johnson, St. Paul's Church Yard, & J. Edwards, Pall Mall, **1796** (*sic*). No colophon in vol. 2. **Large paper issue** with hand-colored title-page vignettes and plates.

2 vols., 4to. (28 cm.), folding map, plan, plates (some engraved by William Blake). **Includes list of subscribers.** Auditors' perception of Fuller's accent reproduced in their spellings of two of his words; his owner's surname spelled **Cox**.

https://archive.org/details/narrativeoffivey02sted_0/page/260/mode/1up

ESTC t146565; Price & Price 2.

129.36 ———.

English-language single-paragraph notice* (derived from Dr. Rush; locating Fuller near Alexandria) of Thomas Fuller's calculating prowess printed on p. 158 in Jacques-Pierre Brissot de Warville, *New Travels in the United States of America. Performed in 1788…. Translated from the French.*

Boston [Massachusetts, U.S.A.]: From the Press of Joseph Bumstead, Union-Street, **1797**.

8vo (18 cm.): 276, [3] p., folding table.

*Note: In this notice neither Cox, nor Hartshorne, nor Coates is named.

https://babel.hathitrust.org/cgi/pt?id=dul1.ark:/13960/t7qn-73v0w&view=1up&seq=164&q1

129.37 ———. [Abridged French translation of 129.35]

French translation of 129.35 printed on pp. 61–63 in vol. 3 of John Gabriel Stedman, *Voyage a Surinam et dans l'Intérieur de Guiane … traduit de l'Anglais par P. F. Henry.*

Paris [France]: chez F. Buisson, Imprimeur-Libraire, rue Hautefeuille, no. 20, an VII de la Republique [*i.e.* **1798**].

3 vols., 8vo (21 cm) + 4to atlas (30 cm.). As noted in 1808 by Henri Grégoire (129.41, p. 210), "dans la question adressée a *Fuller* a oublié le mot *secondes*, ce qui rend la question absurde." Price & Price 6.

129.38 ———. [Unabridged French translation of 129.35]

French translation of 127.35 printed in vol. 3 of John Gabriel Stedman, *Voyage à Surinam et dans l'intérieur de la Guiane. Contenant la relation de cinq années de courses et d'observations faites dans cette contrée intéressante et peu connue; avec des détails sur les Indiens de la Guiane et les Nègres … traduit de l'anglais par P. F. Henry.*

Lausanne [Switzerland]: chez Hermann, **1799**.

3 vols., 8vo.

129.39 ———. [Dutch translation of 129.35]

Dutch translation of 129.35 printed on pp. 243–244 in vol. 3 of John Gabriel Stedman, *Reize naar Surinamen, en door der Binnenste Gedeelten van Guiana.*

Amsterdam [Netherlands]: by Johannes Allart, MDCCXCIX [1799–1800].

4 vols. Vols. 1 and 2 dated 1799; vols. 3 and 4 dated 1800.

https://www.delpher.nl/nl/boeken/view?coll=boeken&identifier=dpo:8143:mpeg21:0267&cql%5B%5D=%28creator+exact+%22Stedman%2C+John+Gabrie%CC%88l%22%29&objectsearch=fuller

Price & Price 9.

129.40 ———. [Second English edition of 129.35]

Significant parts of 129.1 or 129.2 (including Fuller's interlocutors' leap year error, and locating Fuller in "Maryland, North America") printed within quotation marks on pp. 270–271 in vol. 2 of John Gabriel Stedman, *Narrative, of a Five Years' Expedition, against the Revolted Negroes of Surinam, in Guiana, on the Wild Coast of South America; from the year 1772, to 1777 … Second edition, corrected.*

London [England]: Printed for J. Johnson, St. Paul's Church Yard, and Th. Payne, Pall Mall, **1806**. Colophon: Luke Hansard, printer, near Lincoln's-Inn-Fields.

2 vols., 4to. (27 cm.), folding map, plan, plates (some engraved by William Blake). Auditors' perception of Fuller's accent reproduced in their spellings of two of his words; his owner's surname spelled **Cox**.

https://babel.hathitrust.org/cgi/pt?id=gri.ark:/13960/t4jm38n7d-&view=1up&seq=336
Price & Price 12.

129.41 ——.

French-language memoir composed from 129.6 (*American Museum*) and 129.35 (Stedman, 1796) printed on pp. 209–211 in Henri Grégoire, *De la littérature des Nègres, ou, Recherches sur leurs facultés intellectuelles, leurs qualités morales et leur littérature: suivies de notices sur la vie et les ouvrages des Nègres qui se sont distingués dans les sciences, les lettres et les arts.*

Paris [France]: Chez Maradan, Libraire, Rue des Grands-Augustins, No. 9, MD.CCC.VIII [1808].
8vo (20 cm.): xvi, 287, [1].
https://gallica.bnf.fr/ark:/12148/bpt6k844925/f222.item.texteImage

129.42 ——.

Detailed account of his life and mathematical skills printed from "a Virginia paper" (therein from 129.6)—with added introduction "Mr. Editor, Seeing in a Virginia paper the other day, the following account of extraordinary genius in an unlettered African, I take the liberty of transcribing it for your miscellany. G."—under heading "Account of a wonderful talent for arithmetical calculation, in an African slave" on pp. 348–350 in *The Lady's Weekly Miscellany*, vol. 8, no. 22.

New-York [New York, U.S.A.]: Printed and published by Edward Whitely [*sic*], No. 46 Fair Street, March 25, **1809**.
12mo (21 cm.). Owner's surname spelled **Cox.**

129.43 ——. [Reprinted from 129.2?]

Account of Thomas Fuller's life and skills included in a letter by Dr. Benjamin Rush, of which part (only) is printed with introduction "The following is an account of the extraordinary powers of calculation, by memory, possessed by a Negro Slave, **in Maryland** [*sic*], communicated in a letter from Dr. Rush, of Philadelphia, to a Gentleman in Manchester [i.e., Dr. Thomas Percival (1740–1804)]" with dateline "Philadelphia, **Sept. 25, 1788**" on pp. 348–349 of the *The Tradesman; or, Commercial Magazine: including subjects relative to Commerce, Foreign and Domestic; together with ... ,* vol. 2, no. 10.

London [England]: [Printed for the Proprietors, By J. G. Barnard, Skinner-Street, Snow-Hill. Published by Sherwood, Neely, & Jones, 21, Paternoster-Row; and may be had of every Bookseller in the United Kingdom]*, April 1, **1809**. Price: 1s. 6d.
*From the general title-page for the complete volume.
8vo.: p. 289–384. Auditors' perception of Fuller's accent reproduced in their spellings of *two* of his words; owner's surname spelled **Coxe.**

https://babel.hathitrust.org/cgi/pt?id=umn.31951002799089f&view=1up&seq=356

129.44 ——. [English translation of 129.41]

English translation of Grégoire's memoir of Fuller composed in French from 129.6 (*American Museum*) and 129.35 (Stedman, 1796) printed on pp. 183–185 in Henri Grégoire, *An Enquiry concerning the Intellectual and Moral Faculties, and Literature of Negroes: followed with an Account of the Life and Works of fifteen Negroes & Mulattoes, distinguished in Science, Literature, and the Arts ...* translated by D. B. Warden.

Brooklyn [New York, U.S.A.]: Printed by Thomas Kirke, Main-Street, **1810**.
8vo (22 cm.): [4], vii (*i.e.*, viii), [1], 10–253, [3] p.
https://archive.org/details/enquiryconcernin00gr/page/183/mode/1up

129.45 ——. [Another printing of 129.40]

Significant parts of 129.1 or 129.2 (including Fuller's interlocutors' leap year error, and locating Fuller in "Maryland, North America") printed within quotation marks on pp. 270–271 in vol. 2 of John Gabriel Stedman, *Narrative, of a Five Years' Expedition, against the Revolted Negroes of Surinam, in Guiana, on the Wild Coast of South America; from the year 1772, to 1777 ... Second edition* [sic], *corrected.*

London [England]: Printed for J. Johnson, St. Paul's Church Yard, and Th. Payne, Pall Mall, **1813**. Colophon: Luke Hansard, printer, near Lincoln's-Inn-Fields.
2 vols., 4to. (27 cm.), folding map, plan, plates (some engraved by William Blake).
https://archive.org/details/narrativeoffivey02sted/page/270/mode/1up

129.46 ——.

One-paragraph epitome of his life and mathematical skills (referencing Dr. Rush's account without giving its date) printed (with credit to "*Greg.* pp. 183–185 [*i.e.* 129.44]. *Rees under Man* [i.e., Abraham Rees, *The Cyclopaedia* (London, 1802 et seq.]") on p. 47 of Edward D. Griffin, D.D., *A Plea for Africa. A Sermon preached October 26, 1817, before the Synod of New-York and New-Jersey, at the request of the Board of Directors of the African School established by the Synod.*

New-York [New York, U.S.A.]: Gould, Printer, Chatham-St., **1817**.
8vo (22 cm.): 76 p. Epitome's first phrases: "*Thomas Fuller*, a native of Africa, and a resident near Alexandria in the district of Columbia ..." Owner's surname not recorded.
https://babel.hathitrust.org/cgi/pt?id=nnc2.ark:/13960/t5jb0rh4b&view=1up&seq=47

129.47 ——. [Italian translation of 129.37 or 129.38]
Italian translation of 127.37 or 127.38 printed in J. G. Stedman, *Viaggio al Surinam e nell'interno della Guiana ossia relazione di cinque anni di corse e di osservazioni fatte in questo interessante e poco conosciuto paese .... Versione dal francese del Cav. [Bartolomeo] Borghi.*

Milano [Italia]: dalla Tipografia di Giambattista Sonzogno, 1818.
4 vols., 8vo (18 cm.).

129.48 ——.
129.8 (?) reprinted under the headline "The Negro Calculator" on the fifth and sixth pages (i.e., 353–354) of the weekly magazine *The Kaleidoscope: or, Literary and Scientific Mirror*, vol. 8, no. 408.

Liverpool [England]: Printed, published, and sold every Tuesday, by E. Smith and Co., at their General Printing Office, Lord Street, Liverpool, and to be had of all Booksellers, April 22, 1828. Price, 3 and one-half pence.
4to (28 cm.): 8 pages per issue. Owner's surname spelled **Cox.**

129.49 ——.
Synopsis of part of 129.6 (*American Museum*), including Fuller's interlocutors' leap year error, printed on p. 168, within Chapter VI ("Intellect of Negroes") in Mrs. [Lydia Maria] Child, *An Appeal in Favor of that Class of Americans called Africans.*

Boston [Massachusetts, U.S.A.]: Allen and Ticknor, 1833. Tpv: Tuttle & Weeks, Printers, No. 8, School Street.
8vo (20 cm.): [vi], 323 p.
https://babel.hathitrust.org/cgi/pt?id=nyp.33433075994958&view=1up&seq=182

129.50 ——.
One-paragraph epitome of his life and mathematical skills (referencing Dr. Rush's account without giving its date) printed within quotation marks (explicitly from Dr. Griffin's *Plea for Africa*, i.e., 129.46) on p. 344 of William Cogswell, *The Harbinger of the Millennium; with An Appendix.*

Boston [Massachusetts, U.S.A.]: Published by Peirce and Parker, No. 9 Cornhill, MDCCCXXXIII [1833].
8vo (21 cm.): x, [13]-362 p. Epitome's first phrases: "Thomas Fuller, a native of Africa, and a resident near Alexandria in the District of Columbia …" Owner's surname not recorded.

129.51 ——.
129.6 reprinted—with added introduction "The following account of the surprising arithmetical powers of an African Slave, is extracted from a communication, which appeared in Carey's American Museum in the year 1789"—on the second page (i.e., 74), col.2–3, of *The Literary Journal, and Weekly Register of Science and the Arts*, vol. l, no. 10.

Providence [Rhode Island, U.S.A.]: Published by Joseph Knowles and Co., at Number Nine Market-Square, August 10, 1833.
4to (35 cm.): 8 pages per issue. Owner's surname spelled **Coxe.**

129.52 ——.
One-paragraph epitome of his life and mathematical skills (referencing Dr. Rush's account without giving its date) printed within quotation marks (explicitly from "the *Abbe Grégoire on the Literature of the Negroes*," i.e., 129.44) on p. 3 (of the issue, p. 135 of the volume) of the issue's lead article "Intellect of Colored Men" in *The Anti-Slavery Record*, vol. 3, no. 12 (whole no. 36).

New-York [New York, U.S.A.]: Published by the American Anti-Slavery Society, R. G. Williams, Publishing Agent, 143 Nassau Street, December 1833.
8vo (19 cm.). Epitome's first phrases: "Thomas Fuller, a native of Africa, and residing at the distance of four miles from Alexandria, in Virginia …" Owner's surname not recorded.
https://babel.hathitrust.org/cgi/pt?id=hvd.ah3ivd&view=1up&seq=149

129.53 ——. [Second edition of 129.50]
One-paragraph epitome of his life and mathematical skills (referencing Dr. Rush's account without giving its date) printed within quotation marks (explicitly from Rev. Dr. Griffin's *Plea for Africa*, i.e., 129.46) on p. 210 of William Cogswell, *The Christian Philanthropist; or Harbinger of the Millennium; with An Appendix … With an introductory essay by James Matheson, D.D. Wolverhampton, Eng. Second edition.*

Boston [Massachusetts, U.S.A.]: Published by Perkins and Marvin. **Philadelphia [Pennsylvania, U.S.A.]:** Henry Perkins, 1839.
8vo (20 cm.): 394 p. Epitome's first phrases: "Thomas Fuller, a native of Africa, and a resident near Alexandria in the District of Columbia …" Owner's surname not recorded.

129.54 ——.
Concise account of his life and skills (derived from a document or documents underlying 129.6) written by Edward Needles and printed on pp. 32–33 of his *An Historical Memoir of the Pennsylvania Society, for Promoting the Abolition of Slavery; the Relief of Free Negros Unlawfully held in Bondage, and for Improving the Condition of the African Race. Compiled from the Minutes of the Society, and other Official Documents. And published by authority of the Society.*

Philadelphia [Pennsylvania, U.S.A.]: Merrihew & Thompson, Printers, No. 7 Carter's Alley, 1848.

8vo (22 cm.): 116 p. Thomas Fuller misprinted as "Thomas Tuller" on p. 32.
https://babel.hathitrust.org/cgi/pt?id=wu.89062309380&view=1up&seq=36

129.55 ——.
Moderately detailed account of his life (locating him "on a poor Virginia farm near Alexandria") and mathematical skills printed under the heading "A Calculating Negro" on the second page, col. 2, of the newspaper *The Daily Constitutionalist and Republic* (edited by James Gardner Jr.), vol. 33 (new series vol. 8), no. 29.

Augusta [Georgia, U.S.A.]: James Gardner Jr., August 4, **1853.** Broadsheet bifolium: 4 p. None of the few words of Fuller's quoted statements are spelled in a way that attempts to suggest any accent. Owner's surname not recorded.
https://gahistoricnewspapers.galileo.usg.edu/lccn/sn85034437/1853-08-04/ed-1/seq-2/

129.56 ——.
Account of his life and mathematical skills (including his interlocutors' leap year error) attributed to Dr. Rush printed on p. 104 in Rev. O[liver] Prescott Hiller, *A Chapter on Slavery: A Sketch of its Origin and History, with the Reasons for its Permission, and of the Probable Manner of its Removal.*

London [England]: Hodson and Son, 22, Portugal Street. **New York [New York, U.S.A.]:** Mason, Brothers, [*sic*] 587, Mercer Street. **Boston [Massachusetts, U.S.A.]:** Otis Clapp. 3, Beacon Street, **1860.** Tpv carries the author's 1860 United States copyright notice.
8vo (18 cm.): v, 175 p.

129.57 ——.
Obituary notice reprinted from 129.17 (*Columbian Centinel*) on pp. 21–22 in William Frederick Poole, *Anti-Slavery Opinions before the year 1800. Read before the Cincinnati Literary Club, November 16, 1872…. To which is appended a Fac simile Reprint of Dr. George Buchanan's Oration on the Moral and Political Evil of Slavery, delivered at a public meeting of the of the Maryland Society for Promoting the Abolition of Slavery, Baltimore, July 4, 1791.*

Cincinnati [Ohio, U.S.A.]: Robert Clarke & Co., **1873.**
8vo (24 cm.): 82, [2], 20 p.
https://www.gutenberg.org/files/23956/23956-h/23956-h.htm

129.58 ——.
Account of his life and skills (including elaboration of Samuel Coates and William Hartshorne's visit to Fuller, and ending with complete quotation of 129.17, which is introduced with

the phrase "The following appeared in several newspapers at the time of his death") printed on pp. 399–400 in vol. 1 of George W[ashington] Williams, *History of the Negro Race in America from 1690 to 1880: Negroes as Slaves, as Soldiers, as Citizens. Together with a Preliminary Consideration of the Unity of the Human Family, an Historical Sketch of Africa, and an Account of the Negro Governments of Sierra Leone and Liberia.*

New York [New York, U.S.A.]: G. P. Putnam's Sons, 27 and 29 West 23rd Street, **1883.** Tpv: Press of G. P. Putnam's Sons New York.
2 vols., 8vo (24 cm.).
https://www.gutenberg.org/files/15735/15735-h/15735-h.htm

129.59 ——.
Memoir (including recapitulation of Samuel Coates and William Hartshorne's visit to Fuller but mistakenly adding Dr. Rush to that company, using Needles's account [127.54], and ending with complete quotation of 129.17) printed on pp. 144–147 under headline "Thomas Fuller" printed in Phillis Wheatley, *Poems on Various Subjects, Religious and Moral. By Phillis Wheatley, Negro Servant to Mr. John Wheatley, of Boston, in New England. With Memoirs, by W. A. Jackson.*

Denver, Colo[rado, U.S.A.]: W. H. Lawrence & Co., **1887.** Tpv: Copyright, 1886, By W. H. Lawrence & Co.
8vo (18 cm.): 149 p., portrait. The title page exists in two states: in the first, the author's name is misprinted as W. H. Jackson; in the second, it has been corrected to W. A. Jackson.
Heartman (1915) 39. Memoirs of Phillis Wheatley, Benjamin Banneker, Thomas Fuller, and James Durhaam, pp. 117–149, informed by primary works, one of the previous items, and other secondary works.
https://babel.hathitrust.org/cgi/pt?id=chi.24980701&view=1up&seq=152

129.60 ——.
Account of Fuller's life and mathematical skills derived from 129.6 (*American Museum*) and elsewhere, with detailed bibliographical notes on sources, printed on pp. 2–3 within E. W. Scripture's article "Arithmetical Prodigies," printed on pp. 1–59 in *The American Journal of Psychology* (edited by G. Stanley Hall), vol. 4, no. 1.

Worcester [Massachusetts, U.S.A.]: J. H. Orpha, Publisher, **April 1891.** Title page for collected volume dated 1892; tpv: Press of S. F. Blanchard and Company, Worcerster.
https://babel.hathitrust.org/cgi/pt?id=mdp.39015060441287&view=1up&seq=14

129.61 ——.
Account of Fuller's life and mathematical skills derived from 127.58 (Williams, 1883) and concluding with complete print-

ing of 129.17 printed on pp. 21–22 in Edward A. Johnson, *School History of the Negro Race in America from 1619 to 1890, with a short introdduction as to the Origin of the Race; also A short sketch of Liberia. First edition.*

Raleigh [North Carolina, U.S.A.]: Edwards and Broughton, **1890.** Tpv:

8vo: 194 p. Note: also sold by subscription ca. 1901, q.v. salesman's sample at UNC.

129.62 ——. **[Revised edition of 129.61]**

Account of Fuller's life and mathematical skills derived from 127.58 (Williams, 1883) and concluding with complete printing of 127.17 printed on pp. 20–22 in Edward A. Johnson, *School History of the Negro Race in America from 1619 to 1890, with a short introdduction as to the Origin of the Race; also A short sketch of Liberia … Revised edition.*

Chicago [Illinois, U.S.A.]: W. B. Conkey Company, Printers and Binders, **1895.** Tpv carries 1891 copyright notice of Edward A. Johnson, LL. B. Raleigh, N.C.

8vo (20 cm.): viii, 200 p.

https://babel.hathitrust.org/cgi/pt?id=hvd.hxdeew&view=1up&seq=24

129.63 ——. **[Another printing of 129.62]**

Account of Fuller's life and mathematical skills derived from 129.58 (Williams, 1883) and concluding with complete printing of 129.17 printed on pp. 20–22 in Edward A. Johnson, *School History of the Negro Race in America from 1619 to 1890, with a short introduction as to the Origin of the Race; also A short sketch of Liberia … Revised edition.*

Chicago [Illinois, U.S.A.]: W. B. Conkey Company, Printers and Binders, **1897.** Tpv carries 1891 copyright notice of Edward A. Johnson, LL.B. Raleigh, N.C.

8vo (20 cm.): viii, 200 p.

129.64 ——.

Most of his *Columbian Centinel* obituary notice (129.17) reprinted (drawing on information gleaned from Poole, 1873, 129.57) on p. 35 in Appleton P. C. Griffin, *A Catalogue of the Washington Collection in the Boston Athenaeum.*

Boston [Massachusetts, U.S.A.]: The Boston Athenaeum, **1897.** Tpv: University Press: John Wilson and Son, Cambridge, U.S.A.

8vo, (24 cm.): xi, 566 p.

https://babel.hathitrust.org/cgi/pt?id=coo1.ark:/13960/t4hm6ff07&view=1up&seq=69

129.65 ——.

Summary paragraph on his life and mathematical skills printed on pp. 62–63 in Frank D. Mitchell's article "Mathematical

Prodigies," which is printed on pp. 61–143 in *American Journal of Psychology* (edited by G. Stanley Hall), vol. 18, no.1.

Worcester, Mass[achusetts, U.S.A.]: Clark University, Florence Chandler, Publisher, January **1907.**

8vo (24 cm.).

https://babel.hathitrust.org/cgi/pt?id=uc1.b4270821&view=1up&seq=74

129.66 ——.

Two-paragraph account of his life and mathematical skills (referencing Dr. Rush's account without giving its date and concluding with echo of 129.17's conclusion) printed on pp. 523–524 of Rev. D. D. Buck, *The Progression of the Race In the United States and Canada, Treating of the Great Advancement of the Colored Race. Illustrated.* Price $3.50.

[Chicago, Illinois, U.S.A.]: [Atwell Printing and Binding Co.], [**1907**]. Tpv: Copyrighted, 1907, by Rev. D. D. Buck.

8vo (23 cm.): 540 p., illus., portraits. Note: Probably sold door-to-door by subscription.

129.67 ——. **[Another edition of 129.61]**

Account of Fuller's life and mathematical skills derived from 129.58 (Williams, 1883) and concluding with complete printing of 129.17 printed on pp. 20–22 in Edward A. Johnson, *School History of the Negro Race in America from 1619 to 1890, with a short introdduction as to the Origin of the Race; also A short sketch of Liberia … Revised edition.*

New York [New York, U.S.A.]: Isaac Goldmann, **1911.** Tpv carries 1891 copyright notice of Edward A. Johnson, LL.B. Raleigh, N.C.

8vo (21 cm.): 400 p., illus.

129.68 ——.

Summary paragraph on his life and mathematical skills (drawn explicitly from Scripture and Mitchell) printed on pp. 488–489 in Henry B. Howell's article "A Review of Representative Genetic Studies of Number: IV, Prodigies" which is printed on pp. 487–495 in *Educational Foundations*, vol. 25, no. 8.

New York City [New York, U.S.A.]: Educational Magazine Publishing Co, 31-33 East 27th Street, April **1914.**

129.69 ——.

Summary paragraph on his life and mathematical skills printed on p. 252 within the essay "Calculating Prodigies" (not included in editions previous to the 7th) in W. W. Rouse Ball, *Mathematical Recreations and Essays … Seventh Edition.*

London: [England]: Macmilland and Company, Limited, St. Martin's Street, **1917.**

8vo (21 cm.): xvi, 492 p. + advertisements.

https://babel.hathitrust.org/cgi/pt?id=uc2.ark:/13960/t24b-32k8g&view=1up&seq=272

129.70 ——.

Transcription by William A. Slade of "Account of a wonderful talent for arithmetical calculation, in an African slave living in Virginia" as it was printed in the weekly newspaper *The New Jersey Journal and Political Intelligencer*, no. 275 on January 21, 1789 (q.v. 129.5) printed on pp. 447–449 within article "An Old Case of Mathematical Prodigy," which is printed on pp. 446–450 in *Journal of the American Society for Psychical Research* (Section "B" of the American Institute for Scientific Research), vol. 12, no. 7.

York [Pennsylvania, U.S.A.]: American Society for Psychical Research, 12-26 South Water Street, July **1918**.
8vo.

129.71 ——. [Reprinting of 129.31 (1792 London edition)]

Terse (one-paragraph) English-language summary (derived from Dr. Rush, here misprinted as "Doctor Ruth"; locating Fuller near Alexandria) of Fuller's calculating prowess printed on p. 172 in Jacques-Pierre Brissot de Warville, *New Travels in the United States of America.*

Bowling Green, Ohio [U.S.A.]: Historical Publications Company, C. S. Van Tassel, Manager, [**1919**]. Tpv: Copyright, 1919, by C. S. Van Tassel.
8vo (24 cm.): 544 p. Series: Great American Historical Classics Series.
https://babel.hathitrust.org/cgi/pt?id=loc.ark:/13960/t5q81p35v
  &view=1up&seq=178&q1

129.72 ——.

In vol. 1 of Benjamin Rush, *Letters*, edited by Lyman H. Butterfield.

Princeton [New Jersey, U.S.A]: Princeton University Press for the American Philosophical Society [**Philadelphia, Pennsylvania, U.S.A.**], 1951.
2 vols., 8vo (25 cm.), continuously paged lxxxlii, 1295, illus., folding map. Series: Memoirs of the American Philosophical Society, vol. 30.

129.73 ——.

Life and skills summarized on pp. 17–18 in Fred Barlow, *Mental Prodigies: An Enquiry into the Faculties of Arithmetical, Chess and Musical Prodigies, Precocious Children and the Like, with Numerous examples of "Lighning" Calculations and Mental Magic.*

London [England]: Hutchinson's Scientific and Technical Publications, [**1951**].
8vo (20 cm.): 256 p.

129.74 ——. [United States edition of 129.73]

Life and skills summarized on pp. 17–18 in Fred Barlow, *Mental Prodigies: An Enquiry into the Faculties of Arithmetical, Chess and Musical Prodigies, Precocious Children and the Like, with Numerous examples of "Lighting" Calculations and Mental Magic.*

New York [New York, U.S.A]: Philosophical Library, [copyright **1952**].
8vo (20 cm.): 256 p.
https://babel.hathitrust.org/cgi/pt?id=mdp.39015035324022
  &view=1up&seq=17

129.75 ——. [First complete English translation of 129.25/26 (1791 Paris editions)]

English translation of detailed notice (derived from Dr. Rush) of Fuller's calculating prowess printed on pp. 235–236 in Jacques-Pierre Brissot de Warville, *New Travels in the United States of America. Performed in 1788.* Translated by Mara Soceanu Vamos and Durand Echeverria; edited by Durand Echeverria.

Cambridge [Massachusetts, U.S.A.]: The Belknap Press of Harvard University Press, **1964**.
8vo (24 cm.): xxviii, 447 p. Series: The John Harvard Library.

129.76 ——. [Photomechanical reprint of 129.67]

Account of Fuller's life and mathematical skills distantly derived from 129.6 and concluding with complete printing of 129.17 printed on pp. 20–22 in photomechanical reprint of Edward A. Johnson, *School History of the Negro Race in America from 1619 to 1890, with a short introduction as to the Origin of the Race; also A short sketch of Liberia … Revised edition* (1911) with new imprint:

New York [New York, U.S.A.]: AMS Press, **1969**.
8vo (21 cm.): viii, 400 p., illus.

129.77 ——. [Photomechanical reprint of 129.74]

Life and skills summarized on pp. 17–18 in Fred Barlow, *Mental Prodigies: An Enquiry into the Faculties of Arithmetical, Chess and Musical Prodigies, Precocious Children and the Like, with Numerous examples of "Lightning" Calculations and Mental Magic.*

New York [New York, U.S.A]: Greenwood Press, [**1959**].
8vo (23 cm.): 256 p.

129.78 ——. [Photomechanical reprint of 129.31 (1792 London edition)]

Terse (one-paragraph) English-language summary (derived from Dr. Rush; locating Fuller near Alexandria) of Fuller's calculating prowess printed (within letter XXIV) on p. 287 in Jacques-

Pierre Brissot de Warville, *New Travels in the United States of America. Performed in 1788.... Translated from the French.*

New York [New York, U.S.A.]: A. M. Kelley, [**1970**].
8vo (22 cm.): 483 p.

129.79 ——.

Summary of Fuller's life and mathematical skills printed on p. 31 within Henry Allen Bullock's article "A Hidden Passage in the Slave Regime," which is printed in *The Black Experience in America* [*Selected Essays*], edited by James C. Curtis and Lewis L. Gould.

Austin [Texas, U.S.A.]: University of Texas Press, [**1970**].
8vo (23 cm.): x, 199 p.

129.80 ——. [Photomechanical reprint of 129.8]

Dr. Benjamin Rush's 14 November 1788 account printed *in toto* **under the heading** "Accounts of a Negro Practitioner of Physic, and a self-taught Negro Calculator, by Benjamin Rush., M.D. ..." on pp. 184–187 in *Letters on Slavery, by William Dickson* (London 1789), with imprint:

Westport, Connecticut [U.S.A.]: Negro Universities Press, [**1970**].
8vo (23 cm.): x, 190, [1] p.

129.81 ——. [Critical edition of 129.35]

Significant parts of 129.1 or 129.2 (including Fuller's interlocutors' leap year error, and locating Fuller in "Maryland, North America") printed within quotation marks on p. 363 in vol. 2 of John Gabriel Stedman, *Narrative, of a Five Years' Expedition, against the Revolted Negroes of Surinam, in Guiana, on the Wild Coast of South America; from the year 1772, to 1777 ...* [Introduction and notes by R. A. J. van Lier].

Barre, Massachusetts [U.S.A.]: Printed for the Imprint Society, MCMLXXI [**1971**]. Colophon (vol. 2 only): ... printed ... by Joh. Enschede en Zonen, Haarlem, Holland....
2 vols. (continuously paged), 8vo (27.5 cm.): xviii, [10], 480, [1] p., plates, some folding.

129.82 ——. [Critical edition of 129.35]

Significant parts of 129.1 or 129.2 (including Fuller's interlocutors' leap year error, and locating Fuller in "Maryland, North America") printed within quotation marks on p. 363 of John Gabriel Stedman, *Narrative, of a Five Years' Expedition, against the Revolted Negroes of Surinam, in Guiana, on the Wild Coast of South America; from the year 1772, to 1777 ...* [Introduction and notes by R. A. J. van Lier].

Amherst, Massachusetts [U.S.A.]: University of Massachusetts Press, MCMLXXII [**1972**].

8vo (27.3 cm.): xviii, [10], 480 p., plates, some folding. Comprises sheets ("printed ... by Joh. Enschede en Zonen, Haarlem, Holland" as noted in 127.46) from 127.46 but here bound in one volume with distinct title-page.

129.83 ——. [Second printing of 129.79]

Summary of Fuller's life and mathematical skills printed on p. 31 within Henry Allen Bullock's article "A Hidden Passage in the Slave Regime," which is in *The Black Experience in America* [*Selected Essays*], edited by James C. Curtis and Lewis L. Gould.

Austin [Texas, U.S.A.]: University of Texas Press, [**1973**]. **Second printing.**
8vo (23 cm.): x, 199 p.

129.84 ——.

His arithmetical answers to detailed questions, and the facts of his life related (from readings of previous publications and new census research) included in article by Jane H. Pejsa headlined "A wizard in any age" (and concluding with final paragraph of 129.17) printed in the daily newspaper *The Christian Science Monitor*, no. 56.

Boston [Massachusetts, U.S.A.], February 12, **1980.** Broadsheet gatherings.

129.85 ——.

Account of Thomas Fuller's life and mathematical skills (including his interlocutors' leap-year error) printed from 129.10 under heading "Account of a wonderful talent for arithmetical calculation, in an African slave, living in Virginia" on pp. 71–72 in Robert K. Dodge, *Early American Almanac Humor.*

Bowling Green, Ohio [U.S.A.]: Bowling Green State University Popular Press, [**1987**].
8vo (24 cm.): 163 p.

129.86 ——.

Significant parts of 129.1 or 129.2 (including Fuller's interlocutors' leap year error, and locating Fuller in "Maryland, North America") printed within quotation marks on pp. 517–518 of John Gabriel Stedman, *Narrative, of a Five Years' Expedition, against the Revolted Negroes of Surinam, in Guiana, on the Wild Coast of South America; from the year 1772, to 1777 ... **transcribed for the first time from the original 1790 manuscript; edited, and with an introduction and notes, by Richard Price & Sally Price.***

Baltimore [Maryland, U.S.A.]: The Johns Hopkins University Press, **1988.**
8vo (27 cm.): xcvii, 708 p., illus.

129.87 ——.

129.6 (*American Museum* article) reprinted on p. 148 and 127.17 (*Columbian Centinel* obituary notice) printed on p. 149 as appendices to John Fauvel and Paulus Gerdes's article "African Slave and Calculating Prodigy: Bicentenary of the Death of Thomas Fuller," which is printed on pp. 141–151 in *Historia Mathematica*, vol. 17, issue 2.

Academic Press, Inc., May **1990**.
https://reader.elsevier.com/reader/sd/pii/031508609090050N?token=4564A1CD6420908B0A163B46D120BA6BB384BF-934CF5D1BC1A265710BC28E5EF98E90EEB4196C3A-1473F03550685159E

129.88——. [Abridged edition of 129.86]

Significant parts of 129.1 or 129.2 (including Fuller's interlocutors' leap year error, and locating Fuller in "Maryland, North America") printed within quotation marks on p. 262 of John Gabriel Stedman, *Stedman's Surinam Life in an Eighteenth-Century Slave Society An Abridged, Modernized Edition of Narrative of a Five Years* [sic] *Expedition against the Revolted Negroes of Surinam by John Gabriel Stedman.* Edited by Richard Price and Sally Price.

Baltimore [Maryland, U.S.A.]: The Johns Hopkins University Press, [1992].
8vo (23 cm.): lxxv, [3], [1–5] 6–350 p., map, illus. Note: This abridgement "include[s] about 50 percent of the original text and 33 of the original 81 plates" (p. lxv).

129.89 ——. [Photomechanical reprint of 129.31 (1792 London edition)]

Terse (one-paragraph) English-language summary (derived from Dr. Rush; locating Fuller near Alexandria) of Fuller's calculating prowess printed (within letter XXII) on p. 287 in Jacques-Pierre Brissot de Warville, *New Travels in the United States of America. Performed in 1788…. Translated from the French* [by Joel Barlow].

Otley, West Yorkshire, England: [and] Washington, D.C. [U.S.A.]: Woodstock Books, 2000.
8vo (21 cm.): [4], 483, [5] p. Series: Revolution and Romanticism, 1789–1834.

129.90 ——. [Another (complete) printing of 129.86]

Significant parts of 129.1 or 129.2 (including Fuller's *interlocutors'* leap year error, and locating Fuller in "Maryland, North America") printed within quotation marks on pp. 517–518 of John Gabriel Stedman, *Narrative, of a Five Years' Expedition, against the Revolted Negroes of Surinam, in Guiana, on the Wild Coast of South America; from the year 1772, to 1777 … transcribed for the first time from the original 1790 manuscript* [cf. 127.85]; edited, and with an introduction and notes, by Richard Price & Sally Price.

New York [New York, U.S.A.]: iUniverse.com, [2010].
8vo (27 cm.): xcvii, 708 p., illus.

1789

130.1 Olaudah Equiano (ca. 1742–1797) = Gustavus Vassa

The Interesting Narrative of the Life of Olaudah Equiano, or Gustavus Vassa, the African. Written by Himself.

London [England]: Printed for and Sold by the Author, No. 10, Union-Street, Middlesex-Hospital, Sold also by Mr. Johnson, St. Paul's Church-Yard; Mr. Murray, Fleet-Street; Messrs. Robson and Clark, Bond-Street; Mr. Davis, opposite Gray's-Inn, Holborn; Messrs. Shepperson [sic] and Reynolds, and Mr. Jackson, Oxford-Street; Mr. Lackington, Chiswell-Street; Mr. Matthews, Strand; Mr. Murray, Prince's-Street, Soho; Mess. Taylor & Co. South Arch; Royal Exchange; Mr. Button, Newington-Causeway; Mr. Parsons, Paternoster-Row; and may be had of all the Booksellers in Town and Country, [1789].

https://babel.hathitrust.org/cgi/pt?id=mdp.69015000002721&view=1up&seq=13 [see 130.2].

2 vols., 12mo. **Includes list of subscribers.** Prefatory letter signed and dated in type in vol. 1, p. v: Olaudah Equiano, or Gustavus Vassa. No. 10, Union-Street, Mary-le-bone, **March 24, 1789.**
Porter 65; ESTC t140573; Hogg 1463.
Vol. 1: http://docsouth.unc.edu/neh/equiano1/equiano1.html
Vol. 2: http://docsouth.unc.edu/neh/equiano2/equiano2.html
http://www.gutenberg.org/files/15399/15399-h/15399-h.htm

¶ According to his published account, Olaudah Equiano (= Gustavus Vassa) was born ca. 1742 in Essaka, in Igboland (modern southern Nigeria—see Map 5). When still a boy, he was kidnapped, enslaved, and forcibly taken aboard a slave ship to the island of Barbados in the Caribbean (see Map 11). Shortly thereafter he was taken to the British North American colony of Virginia (Map 15), and thence to London, England (Map 8). Thereafter he was always known as Gustavus Vassa, never as Olaudah Equiano (even though the latter name was perpetuated among readers who did not personally know him by its repetition on his book's many title pages from 1789 to the present). During the Seven Years War (1756–1763) he served aboard a British Navy vessel in Europe, North America, and the Mediterranean. In 1759 he embraced Christianity and was baptized. At war's end he was sold to a merchant working on the Caribbean island of Montserrat. (This merchant was a Quaker who came from Philadelphia, Pennsylvania—see Map 16.) Vassa purchased his freedom in 1766 and returned to England, where he became a prominent abolitionist. He published his autobiography (130.1) in 1789 as the British Parliament began to hold hearings on the transtlantic slave trade. He married Susanna Cullen of Soham, Cambridgeshire, in 1792, and they had two children. His wife died in 1796; Vassa died in London a year later. Scholarly work on Vassa is extensive. See Paul E. Lovejoy, "Olaudah Equiano or Gustavus Vassa—What's in a Name?" *Atlantic Studies*, 9:2 (June 2012): 165–184.

130.2 ——.

The Interesting Narrative of the Life of Olaudah Equiano, or Gustavus Vassa, the African. Written by Himself .... Second edition.

London [England]: Printed and Sold for the Author, by T. Wilkins, No. 23, Aldermanbury; Sold also by Mr. Johnson, St. Paul's Church-Yard; Mr. Buckland, Paternoster-Row; Messrs. Robson and Clark, Bond-Street; Mr. Davis, opposite Gray's-Inn, Holborn; Mr. Matthews, Strand; Mr [*sic*] Stockdale, Piccadilly; Mr. Richardson, Royal Exchange; Mr. Kearsley, Fleet-Street; and the Booksellers in **Oxford** and **Cambridge** [England], [1790].

2 vols., 12mo (18 cm.). **Includes a list of subscribers.** Prefatory letter signed and dated in type in vol. 1, p. v: Olaudah Equiano, or Gustavus Vassa. No. 10, Union-Street, Mary-le-bone, **Dec. 24, 1789** (*cf.* 130.1).

Porter 66 (without supplying date).

Note: Although ESTC and other cataloguers date this edition 1789, it seems unlikely (given London working men's customary Yuletide drinking) that this edition's sheets were perfected in time to be sewn together in boards (let alone bound) in time for copies to reach retail shelves before 1 January 1790—hence the year of publication posited in this entry.

https://babel.hathitrust.org/cgi/pt?id=mdp.69015000002721&view=1up&seq=13

ESTC t61470.

130.3 ——. [Dutch translation]

Merkwaardige levensgevallen van Olaudah Equiano of Gustavus Vassa, den Afrikaan, door hem zelven beschreeven en... verslag, van de zeden en gebruiken zijnes lands...van zijne schaaking, slaavernij...zonderlinge lotgevallen, zoo ter zee als te land, en van zijne bekeering tot het geloof in Christus...ook van de onmenschlijke wreedheden, welken omtrent de Negerslaaven doorgaands in de West-Indien worden gepleegd. Uit het Engelsch vertaald.

Rotterdam [Netherlands]: bij Pieter Holsteyn, Boekverkooper bezijden de Beurs. MDCCXC [1790].

8vo (22 cm.): [16], 365 p., frontispiece portrait.

https://www.delpher.nl/nl/boeken/view?coll=boeken&identifier=dpo:8413:mpeg21:0006

130.4 ——.

The Interesting Narrative of the Life of Olaudah Equiano. **Third edition.**

London [England]: Printed for, and sold by, the Author. Sold also by Mr. Johnson, St. Paul's Church-Yard; Messrs. Robinsons, Paternoster-Row; Mr. Robson and Mr. Clark, Bond-Street; Mr. Davis, Holborn; Mr. Matthews, Strand; Mr. Richardson, Royal Exchange; Mr. Chalmers, No. 81, Old-Street [London]; Mr. J. Thomson, **Manchester [England]**; and the Booksellers in **Oxford** and **Cambridge [England]**, [1790].

12mo: viii, [14], 359, [1]p. **Includes a list of subscribers.**

Not in Porter; ESTC t140574.

130.5 ——.

The Interesting Narrative of the Life of Olaudah Equiano. **Third edition, enlarged.**

London [England]: Printed for, and sold by, the Author. Sold also by Mr. Johnson; Messrs. Robinsons; Mr. Robson and Mr. Clark; Mr. Davis; Mr. Matthews; Mr. Richardson; Mr. Chalmers; Mr. J. Thomson, **Manchester [England]**; and the Booksellers in **Oxford** and **Cambridge [England]**, 1790. Price Four Shillings.

12mo (17 cm.): viii, [14], 359, [1]p. **Includes a list of subscribers.**

Porter 67; ESTC n28777.

130.6 ——.

The Interesting Narrative of the Life of Olaudah Equiano. **Fourth edition, enlarged.**

Dublin [Ireland]: Printed for, and sold by, the Author, Sold also at the Dublin Chronicle Office, by W. Sleater, No. 28, Dame-Street, and the other Booksellers in Dublin, [1791]. Price four British Shillings.

8vo (18 cm.): xxiv, 359 p. **Includes a list of Irish subscribers and a list of English subscribers.**

Porter 69; ESTC n17160.

130.7 ——.

The Interesting Narrative of the Life of Olaudah Equiano. **First American edition.**

New-York [New York, U.S.A.]: Printed and sold by W. Durell, at his book-store and printing-office, no. 19, Q Street, MD.CC.XCI [1791].

2 vols., 12mo (16 cm.), illus., portrait. **Includes a list of subscribers.**
Evans 23353; Porter 68; ESTC w20545.

130.8 ——. **[German translation by G. F. Benecke of 130.1]**

Olaudah Equiano's oder Gustav Wasa's, des Afrikaners merkwüridge Lebensgeschichte von ihm selbst geschrieben.

Göttingen [Lower Saxony, Germany]: bey Johann Christian Dieterich, **1792.**
8vo (17 cm.): x, 468 p., portrait.
https://gdz.sub.uni-goettingen.de/id/PPN627417922

130.9 ——.

The Interesting Narrative of the Life of Olaudah Equiano. **Fifth edition, enlarged.**

Edinburgh [Scotland]: Printed for, and sold by the Author, and C. C. J. and J. Robinson, Paternoster-Row, **London [England]**, 1792. Price four shillings.
12mo (16 cm.): xxvi, [2], 360 p.
Porter 70; ESTC n17046.

130.10 ——.

The Interesting Narrative of the Life of Olaudah Equiano. **Sixth edition, enlarged.**

London [England]: Printed for, and sold by the Author, [1793]. Price four shillings.
12mo (16 cm.): xxxiv, [2], 360 p.
Porter 71; ESTC t136631.

130.11 ——.

The Interesting Narrative of the Life of Olaudah Equiano. **Seventh edition, enlarged.**

London [England]: Printed for, and sold by the Author, [1793].
12mo (16 cm.): xxvi (i.e., xxxvi), 11, 360 p.
Porter 72; ESTC t136632.

130.12 ——.

The Interesting Narrative of the Life of Olaudah Equiano. **Eighth edition, enlarged.**

Norwich [Norfolk, England]: Printed for, and sold by the Author, **1794.**
12mo: xxxiv, 2–360 p.
Not in Porter; ESTC t136630.

130.13 ——.

The Interesting Narrative of the Life of Olaudah Equiano. **Ninth edition, enlarged.**

London [England]: Printed for, and sold by the Author, **1794.** Price five shillings, formerly sold for 7s.
12mo (16.5 cm.): xxxiv, 2–360 p.
Porter 74; ESTC n 28776.

130.14 ——. **[Russian translation]**

Žizn' Olaudacha Èkiano, ili Gustava Vazy Afrikanskago, rodivšegosja v 1745 godu, im samim pisannaja: soderžaščaja istoriju jego vospitanija meždu Afrikanskimi narodami ... so mnogimi trogatel'nymi i ljubopytnymi anekdotami i s prisovokuplenijem gravirovannago jego portreta.

Mockba [Russia]: s.n., **1794.**
2 vols. č. 1. [10], 311, [1] s. -- č. 2. [8], 246 p.

130.15 ——. **[Russian translation]**

Žizn' Olaudacha Èkiano, ili Gustava Vazy Afrikanskago, rodivšegosja v 1745 godu, im samim pisannaja: soderžaščaja istoriju jego vospitanija meždu Afrikanskimi narodami ... so mnogimi trogatel'nymi i ljubopytnymi anekdotami i s prisovokuplenijem gravirovannago jego portreta.

St. Petersburg [Russia]: s.n., **1794.**
2 vols., č. 1. [10], 311, [1] s.— č. 2. [8], 246 p.

130.16 ——.

French-language memoir of Vassa (claiming on p. 247 [mispaged "427"] to derive from the 9th ed., London, 1794, of Vassa's *Interesting Narrative*, i.e., 130.13) printed on pp. 245–252 in Henri Grégoire, *De la littérature des Nègres, ou, Recherches sur leurs facultés intellectuelles, leurs qualités morales et leur littérature: suivies de notices sur la vie et les ouvrages des Nègres qui se sont distingués dans les sciences, les lettres et les arts.*

Paris [France]: Chez Maradan, Libraire, Rue des Grands-Augustins, No. 9, MD.CCC.VIII [1808].
8vo (20 cm.): xvi, 287, [1].
https://gallica.bnf.fr/ark:/12148/bpt6k844925/f258.image.r=vassa

130.17 ——.

The Interesting Narrative of the Life of Olaudah Equiano; or, Gustavus Vassa, the African. Written by himself. "A new edition."

Belper [Derbyshire, England]: Printed and published by S[amuel] Mason; and sold by Tipper and Crosby, **London [England]**; Wilkins, **Derby [Derbyshire, England]**; and Dunn, **Nottingham [Nottinghamshire, England]**, 1809.
8vo (22 cm.): viii, 310 p., frontispiece portrait.
Not in Porter. Exemplar at Boston College Library.

130.18 ——. [English translation of 130.16]
English translation of Grégoire's memoir of Vassa (claiming on p. 222 to derive from "the 9th ed. 8vo. London, 1791" [*sic*] of Vassa's *Interesting Narrative* [cf. 130.16]) printed on pp. 219–227 in Henri Grégoire, *An Enquiry concerning the Intellectual and Moral Faculties, and Literature of Negroes: followed with an Account of the Life and Works of fifteen Negroes & Mulattoes, distinguished in Science, Literature, and the Arts ...* translated by D. B. Warden.

Brooklyn [New York, U.S.A.]: Printed by Thomas Kirke, Main-Street, **1810**.
8vo (22 cm.): [4], vii (*i.e.*, viii), [1], 10–253, [3] p.
https://archive.org/details/enquiryconcernin00gr/page/219/mode/1up?q=cugoano

130.19 ——.
The Interesting Narrative of the Life of Olaudah Equiano, or Gustavus Vassa, the African. Written by Himself ... To which are added, Poems on Various Subjects, by Phillis Wheatly [*sic*], *Negro Servant to Mr. John Wheatly* [*sic*] *of Boston in new* [*sic*] *England.*

Halifax [Yorkshire, England]: Printed at the office of J. Nicholson & Co., **1813**.
12mo (17.5 cm.): 514, [2] p., frontispiece portrait.
Porter 75.
Exemplar at Library of Congress (rare books call no. HT869. E6/A3/1813); title-page reproduced in Sidney Kaplan and Emma Nogrady Kaplan, *The Black Presence in the Era of the American Revolution*, revised ed. (Amherst: Univ. of Mass. Press, 1989), p. 218, fig. 147.
Note: This edition is occasionally misidentified in catalogs as the "1st Canadian edition." It is not in Patricia Lockhart Fleming, *Atlantic Canadian Imprints 1801–1820* (Toronto: University of Toronto Press, 1991 and 2014), in which *no-one* named Nicholson appears as printer *or* publisher.

130.20 ——.
The Interesting Narrative of the Life of Olaudah Equiano, or Gustavus Vassa, the African. Written by Himself... To which are added, Poems on Various Subjects, by Phillis Wheatly [*sic*], *Negro Servant to Mr. John Wheatly* [*sic*] *of Boston in new* [*sic*] *England.*

Halifax [Yorkshire, England]: Printed at the office of J. Nicholson & Co., **1814**.
12mo (17.5 cm.): 514, [2] p., frontispiece portrait.
Porter 77.

130.21 ——.
The interesting narrative of the life of Olaudah Equiano, or Gustavus Vassa, the African. Written by himself. **A new edition, corrected.**

Leeds [Yorkshire, England]: Printed for James Nichols; Cradock and Joy, **London [England]**; and W. H. Blackburn, **Darlington [Durham, England]**; and sold by all booksellers, **1814**.
12mo (17.5 cm.): x, 22, 236 p., frontispiece portrait.
Porter 76.

130.22 ——.
The Interesting Narrative of the Life of Olaudah Equiano, or Gustavus Vassa, the African. Written by himself.

Penryn [Cornwall, England]: Printed by and for W. Cock; and sold by his agents throughout the kingdom, **1815**. Colophon: Penaluna, Trathan, & Co. Printers, Falmouth [Cornwall].
8vo in fours (22 cm.): viii, [9]–192, 185–328 p., frontispiece. Preface dated on p. vi: April, 20th, 1815.
Note: signature lines on p. 97, 129, 161, etc., suggest that at least some of this edition's sheets were initially printed as parts of an edition to be issued in parts (or *were* issued as parts of an edition that *was* issued in parts), each of which comprised 4 sheets (= 32 p.). The *first* p. 192 is part No. 6's final page; the *second* p. 185 is part No. 7's first page.
https://babel.hathitrust.org/cgi/pt?id=mdp.69015000003034&view=1up&seq=7
Porter 78.

130.23 ——.
Excerpts printed as quotations in 35 numbered paragraphs (followed by two paragraphs numbered 36–37 summarizing part of Gregoire's biographical sketch of Vassa, from 130.18) under the heading "A Sketch of the Life of Gustavus Vassa, taken from his account, written about the year 1787" on pp. 55–64 in *Biographical Sketches and Interesting Anecdotes of Persons of Color. To Which Is Added, a Selection of Pieces in Poetry*, compiled by A[bigail] Mott.

New York [New York, U.S.A.]: Printed and Sold by Mahlon Day, No. 376, Pearl-street, **1826**.
12mo (18 cm.): iv, [5]–192 p. Preface dated on p. iv: *Hickory Grove [NY}*, 11*th mo*. 1825.
http://docsouth.unc.edu/neh/mott26/mott26.html
https://babel.hathitrust.org/cgi/pt?id=hvd.hn3m6e&view=1up&seq=59
Hogg 1467.

130.24 ——.
Excerpts printed within quotation marks (followed by two paragraphs summarizing part of Gregoire's biographical sketch of Vassa, from 130.18) under the heading "A Sketch of the Life of Gustavus Vassa. Taken from his Narrative, written about the year 1787" on pp. 80–94 in *Biographical Sketches and Interesting Anecdotes of Persons of Colour. Compiled by A[bigail] Mott.*

York [Yorkshire, England]: Printed and Sold by W. Alexander & Son, Castlegate; sold also by Harvey & Darton, W.

Phillips, E. Fry, and W. Darton, **London [England]**; R. Peart [*sic*], Birmingham; D. F. Gardiner, **Dublin [Ireland]**, **1826**.
12mo (20 cm.): xi, [2], 2–240 p.
https://babel.hathitrust.org/cgi/pt?id=nyp.33433081774204
&view=1up&seq=100

130.25———.

Excerpts printed within quotation marks (followed by two paragraphs summarizing part of Gregoire's biographical sketch of Vassa, from 130.18) under the heading "A Sketch of the Life of Gustavus Vassa. Taken from his Narrative, written about the year 1787" on pp. 80–94 *Biographical Sketches and Interesting Anecdotes of Persons of Color. To Which Is Added, a Selection of Pieces in Poetry*, compiled by A[bigail] Mott. "Second Edition."

York [Yorkshire, England]: Printed and Sold by W. Alexander & Son; sold also by Harvey and Darton, W. Phillips, E. Fry, and W. Darton, **London [England]**; R. Peart, **Birmingham [England]**; D. F. Gardiner, **Dublin [Ireland]**, **1828**.
12mo (19.8 cm.): xi, [1], 252 p.

130.26———.

*The interesting narrative of the life of Olaudah Equiano, or Gustavus Vassa, the African. Written by himself. **Abridged by A. Mott**. To which are added some remarks on the slave trade.*

New York [New York, U.S.A.]: Published by Samuel Wood & Sons, No. 261 Pearl-street B. & G. S. Wood, Printers, **1829**.
8vo (17.5 cm.): 36 p., frontispiece portrait.
https://babel.hathitrust.org/cgi/pt?id=mdp.69015000002853
&view=1up&seq=5
Porter 79; Hogg 1471.

130.27———. **[Abridgement]**

[Caption title:] *The Negro's Friend; containing the Entertaining and Affecting History of Gustavus Vassa, from a Narrative written by Himself.* [At head of title:] *No. 3.*

London [England]: Sold by Harvey and Darton; Westley and Davis; Houlston and Son; and other booksellers, **[1829?]**. [Bagster and Thoms, Printers.]
12mo (17.5 cm.): **12 p.** Exemplars: Library Company of Philadelphia; University of Wisconsin.

130.28———. **[Abridgement]**

[Caption title:] *The Negro's Friend; containing the Entertaining and Affecting History of Gustavus Vassa, from a Narrative written by Himself. **Second edition**.* [At head of title:] *No. 3.*

London [England]: Sold by Harvey and Darton; Westley and Davis; Houlston and Son; and other booksellers, **[1830?]**.
8vo (18 cm.): **16 p.**, illus. Exemplar: University of Wisconsin.

130.29 ———.

Concise account of his life (naming him Olandad [*sic*] Equiano and Gustavus Vasa) printed on pp. 168–169, within Chapter VI ("Intellect of Negroes") in Mrs. [Lydia Maria] Child, *An Appeal in Favor of that Class of Americans called Africans.*

Boston [Massachusetts, U.S.A.]: Allen and Ticknor, **1833**. Tpv: Tuttle & Weeks, Printers, No. 8, School Street.
8vo (20 cm.): [vi], 323 p.
https://babel.hathitrust.org/cgi/pt?id=nyp.33433075994958
&view=1up&seq=182

130.30———.

The Life of Olaudah Equiano, or Gustavus Vassa, the African. Written by himself... Two volumes in one.

Boston [Massachusetts, U.S.A.]: Published by Isaac Knapp, 25 Cornhill, **1837**.
12mo (17 cm.): 294 p., frontispiece portrait, folding plate.
https://babel.hathitrust.org/cgi/pt?id=wu.89094737376&view=1up&seq=11

130.31———.

"A Sketch of the Life of Gustavus Vassa, taken from his account, written about the year 1787" (followed by two paragraphs summarizing part of Gregoire's biographical sketch of Vassa, from 128.18) under the heading printed on pp. 74–83 in *Biographical Sketches and Interesting Anecdotes of Persons of Color. To Which Is Added, a Selection of Pieces in Poetry*, compiled by Abigail Mott. "Second Edition, much Enlarged."

New-York [New York, U.S.A.]: Mahlon Day, 374 Pearl-street, **1837**. Tpv: "Note by the publisher. By consent of the Compiler, and at the recommendation of the Trustees of the African Free Schools in New York, (who have liberally patronized the work,) ..."
8vo (19 cm.): 260 p. (of which p. [256] is blank, and pp. 257–260 are table of contents).
https://babel.hathitrust.org/cgi/pt?id=hvd.32044004358602
&view=1up&seq=78

130.32———.

"Gustavus Vasa. Taken from his Narrative, written about the year 1787," printed as 41 numbered paragraphs (followed by two paragraphs numbered 42–43 summarizing part of Gregoire's biographical sketch of Vassa, from 130.18) on pp. 119–132 in *Biographical Sketches and Interesting Anecdotes of Persons of Color. To Which Is Added, a Selection of Pieces in Poetry*, compiled by Abigail Mott.

New York [New York, U.S.A.]: Stereotyped for and printed by order of the Trustees of the residuary estate of Lindley Murray. M. Day, Printer, 271 Pearl St. **[1839]**. Approximate year of printing (could be slightly later) from "Advertisement," p. [ii].

12mo (19 cm.): vi, [7]-408 p.

https://archive.org/details/biographicalsket00mottrich/page/n4 (incomplete 370-page exemplar).

https://babel.hathitrust.org/cgi/pt?id=loc.ark:/13960/t2q52p-81p&view=1up&seq=3 (complete).

130.33———. [Abridgement]

Version "condensed from various editions of his 'Narrative'" (p. 193) printed on pp. 193–239 in Wilson Armistead's compendium *A Tribute for the Negro: Being a Vindication of the Moral, Intellectual, and Religious Capabilities of the Colored Portion of Mankind; with Particular Reference to the African Race.*

Manchester [England]: William Irwin; **London [England]:** Charles Gilpin; American Agent: Wm. Harned, Anti-Slavery Office, 61, John Street, **New York [New York, U.S.A.];** and may be had of H. Longstreath and G. W. Taylor, **Philadelphia [Pennsylvania, U.S.A.],** 1848. Tpv: Manchester: Printed by William Irwin, 39, Oldham Street.

8vo (24 cm.): xxxv, 564 p.

https://babel.hathitrust.org/cgi/pt?id=nc01.ark:/13960/t42r4z659;view=1up;seq=13

http://docsouth.unc.edu/neh/armistead/armistead.html

130.34———.

"Gustavus Vasa. Taken from his Narrative, written about the year 1787," printed as 41 numbered paragraphs (followed by two paragraphs numbered 42–43 summarizing part of Gregoire's biographical sketch of Vassa, from 130.18) on pp. 119–132 in *Biographical Sketches and Interesting Anecdotes of Persons of Color. To Which Is Added, a Selection of Pieces in Poetry,* compiled by A[bigail] Mott.

New York [New York, U.S.A.]: Stereotyped for and printed by order of the Trustees of the residuary estate of Lindley Murray, 1850.

8vo (20 cm.): iv, [7]-408 p.

130.35———.

"Gustavus Vasa. Taken from his Narrative, written about the year 1787," printed as 41 numbered paragraphs (followed by two paragraphs numbered 42–43 summarizing part of Gregoire's biographical sketch of Vassa, from 128.18) on pp. 119–132 in *Biographical Sketches and Interesting Anecdotes of Persons of Color. To Which Is Added, a Selection of Pieces in Poetry,* compiled by A[bigail] Mott.

New York [New York, U.S.A.]: Stereotyped for and printed by order of the Trustees of the residuary estate of Lindley Murray. D. Fanshaw, Printer, 35 Ann, corner of Nassau-street, 1854.

12mo (19 cm.): iv, [7]-408 p.

https://digital.ncdcr.gov/digital/collection/p249901coll37/id/10317

130.36———.

"[B]rief sketch of the life of Gustavus Vassa ... condensed from various editions of his *Narrative* ... written by himself about the year 1787" printed on pp. 117–174 (mostly long extracts printed within quotation marks) in Rev. S. R. B. Attoh Ahuma, *Memoirs of West African Celebrities Europe, &c. (1700–1850). With special reference to the Gold Coast.*

Liverpool [England]: D. Marples & Co., 508 Lord Street, 1905.

8vo (19 cm.): xix, 260 p., frontispiece portrait.

https://babel.hathitrust.org/cgi/pt?id=ien.35556038054839&view=1up&seq=147

130.37———. [Swedish translation]

Berättelsen om Olaudah Equiano eller Gustavus Vasa Afrikanen.

Stockholm [Sweden]: Tidens Forlag, 1964.

8vo, 219 p. "Oversättning av Kjell Ekström från den nionde engelska upplagan av år 1794 [*i.e.*, 128.13]."

130.38———. [Annotated abridgement]

Equiano's Travels: His Autobiography; The Interesting Narrative of the Life of Olaudah Equiano or Gustavus Vassa the African, abridged and edited by Paul Edwards.

London [England]: Heinemann, 1967.

8vo (19 cm.): xviii, 196 p., plates, maps.

Hogg 1594.

130.39———. [Photomechanical reprint of 130.1]

The Life of Olaudah Equiano, or Gustavus Vassa, the African. Written by himself. With a new introduction and notes by Paul Edwards.

London [England]: Dawsons of Pall Mall, [1969].

2 vols., 8vo (18 cm).

130.40———.

Equiano's Travels. His Autobiography. Interesting Narrative of the Life of Olaudah Equiano, or Gustavus Vassa, the African. Abridged and edited by Paul Edwards.

London [England]: Heinemann Educational Books, 1969.

8vo (18 cm): xix, 198 p.

130.41———. [Photomechanical reprint of the 1837 edition, 130.30]

The Life of Olaudah Equiano, or Gustavus Vassa, the African. Written by himself... Two volumes in one.

New York [New York, U.S.A.]: Negro Universities Press, [1969].
8vo (23 cm.): vi, 294 p., frontispiece portrait, folding plate.

130.42——. [Spanish translation]
Los viajes de Equiano. Translated by Carlos López Cruz. Epílogo Maria Teresa Ortega.

La Habana [Cuba]: Editorial Arte y Literatura, **1980.**
8vo (18 cm.): 164 p.

130.43——. [French translation]
La veridique histoire par lui meme d'Olaudah Equiano, Africain, esclave aux Caraïbes, homme libre. Introduction abregée de Paul Edwards; avant-propos de Elika M'Bokolo; traduit de l'anglais par Claire-Lise Charbonnier.

Paris [France]: Editions Caribéennes, **1983.**
8vo (23 cm.): xiv, 166 p., plates.

130.44–50——.
Photomechanical reprinting of 130.21 (Leeds, 1814) on pp. 1–182 in *The Classic Slave Narratives,* edited with an introduction by Henry Louis Gates Jr.

New York [New York, U.S.A.]: Mentor, **1987.** At least seven printings catalogued under this date.
8vo (18 cm.): xviii, 518 p.

130.51——. [Second printing of 130.43]
La veridique histoire par lui meme d'Olaudah Equiano, Africain, esclave aux Caraïbes, homme libre. Introduction abregée de Paul Edwards; avant-propos de Elika M'Bokolo; traduit de l'anglais par Claire-Lise Charbonnier.

Paris [France]: Editions Caribéennes, **1987.**
8vo (23 cm.): xiv, 166 p., plates.

130.52——. [Photomechanical reprint of 130.1]
The interesting narrative of the life of Olaudah Equiano, or Gustavus Vassa, the African written by himself.

Coral Gables [Florida, U.S.A.]: Mnemosyne Pub. Co., **1989.**
2 vols., 12mo (18 cm.): 294 p., frontispiece portrait, folding plate.

130.53——.
The interesting narrative of the life of Olaudah Equiano, or Gustavus Vassa, the African written by himself, edited with an introduction by Paul Edwards.

Harlow [Essex, England] and **White Plains [New York, U.S.A.]:** Longmans, **1989.**
8vo (20 cm.): xxxviii, 186 p.

130.54——. [German translation]
Merkwürdige Lebensgeschichte des Sklaven Olaudah Equiano: von ihm selbst veröffentlicht im Jahre 1789. Hrsg. von Paul Edwards. Aus dem Engl. übers. von Brigitte Wünnenberg.

Frankfurt am Main [Germany]: Insel-Verlag, **1990.**
8vo (18cm.): 281 p., illus.

130.55 ——.
Excerpts from 130.1 reprinted from 130.39, with new introductory note, on pp. 54–80 in *Black Writers in Britain, 1760–1890: An Anthology,* edited by Paul Edwards and David Dabydeen.

Edinburgh [Scotland]: Edinburgh University Press, **1991.**
8vo (22 cm.): xv, 239 p.

130.56——. [Spanish translation]
La interesante narración de Olaudah Equiano, o Gustavus Vassa, El Africano, escrita por si mismo: (capítulo II): (texto bilingüe).

León [Spain]: Universidad de León, Secretariado de Publicaciones, **1994.**
8vo (21 cm.): 95 p.

130.57——. [Reprint of 130.7 (New York, 1791)]
The interesting narrative of the life of Olaudah Equiano, or Gustavus Vassa, the African written by himself, edited with an introduction by Robert J. Allison.

Boston [Massachusetts, U.S.A.]: Bedford Books of St. Martin's Press, **1995.**
8vo (21 cm.): viii. 222, illus.

130.58 ——. [Second printing of 130.55]
Excerpts from 130.1 reprinted from 130.39, with new introductory note, on pp. 54–80 in *Black Writers in Britain, 1760–1890: An Anthology,* edited by Paul Edwards and David Dabydeen.

Edinburgh [Scotland]: Edinburgh University Press, **1995.**
8vo (22 cm.): xv, 239 p.

130.59——.
The Interesting Narrative and Other Writings, edited with an introduction and notes by Vincent Carretta.

London [England] and **New York [New York, U.S.A.]:** Penguin, **1995.**
8vo (20 cm.): xxxvii, 355 p.

130.60——.
Diplomatic reprint of *The Interesting Narrative* based on 130.21 (Leeds, London, and Darlington, 1814), with new introduction, bibliographical note, and annotations, on pp.

159–268 in *Black Atlantic Writers of the Eighteenth Century: Living the New Exodus in England and the Americas*, edited by Adam Potkay and Sandra Burr.

New York [New York, U.S.A.]: St Martin's Press, **1995**.
8vo (22 cm.): xii, 268 p.

130.61——.[British printing of previous item]
Diplomatic reprint of *The Interesting Narrative* based on 130.21 (Leeds, London, and Darlington, 1814), with new introduction, bibliographical note, and annotations, on pp. 159–268 in *Black Atlantic Writers of the Eighteenth Century: Living the New Exodus in England and the Americas*, edited by Adam Potkay and Sandra Burr.

Basingstoke [and] London [England]: Macmillan, **1995**.
8vo (22 cm.): xii, 268 p.

130.62——.
Extracts "From The Interesting Narrative of the Life of Olaudah Equiano, or Gustavus Vassa, the African, Written by Himself" printed from 130.1 with introduction and annotations on pp. 138–164 of *The Norton Anthology of African American Literature*, edited by Henry Louis Gates Jr. and Nellie Y. McKay.

New York [New York, U.S.A.]: W. W. Norton & Co., **[1997]**.
8vo (24 cm.): xliv, [2], 2665 p.

130.63——.
The African: The interesting narrative of the life of Olaudah Equiano.

London [England]: Black Classics, **1998**.
8vo (20 cm.): 217 p.

130.64——.[Swedish translation]
Gustavus Vassa, afrikanen: en slavs berättelse. Oversättning: Jan Anders Olsson; förord: Ola Larsmo.

Stockholm [Sweden]: Ordfront, **1998**.
8vo (22 cm.): 204 p.

130.65——.
130.12 (Norwich, 1794) reprinted on pp. 182–365 in *Pioneers of the Black Atlantic: Five Slave Narratives from the Enlightenment, 1772–1815*, edited by Henry Louis Gates Jr., and William L. Andrews.

Washington, D.C. [U.S.A.]: Civitas, **1998**.
8vo (23 cm): xiv, 439 p.

130.66——.[Spanish translation]
Narración de la vida de Olaudah Equiano, El Africano, escrita por él mismo: autobiografía de un esclavo liberto del s. XVIII. Edición y traducción de Celia Montolío.

Madrid [Spain]: Miraguano, **1999**.
8vo (24 cm.): 233 p.

130.67——.[Another printing of 130.21 (1814)]
The life of Olaudah Equiano, or Gustavus Vassa, the African.

Mineola, New York [U.S.A.]: Dover Publications, **1999**.
8vo (20 cm.): v, 184 p.

130.68——.
Excerpt "From *The Interesting Narrative of the Life of Olaudah Equiano, or Gustavus Vassa. Written by Himself*" printed on pp. 22–28 in *Autobiography of a People: Three Centuries of African American History Told by Those who Lived It*, edited by Herb Boyd.

New York [New York, U.S.A.]: Doubleday, **[2000]**.
8vo (24.2 cm.): xviii, [2], 459, [3] p.

130.69——.
His *Interesting Narrative* reprinted from 130.1 on pp. 35–242 (with original **1789 list of subscribers** reprinted on pp. 39–46) in *Slave Narratives*, edited by William L. Andrews and Henry Louis Gates Jr.

New York [New York, U.S.A.]: The Library of America, **[2000]**.
8vo (20.7 cm.): x, 1035, [11] p.

130.70——.[Photomechanical reprint of 130.31]
"A Sketch of the Life of Gustavus Vassa, taken from his account, written about the year 1787" (followed by two paragraphs summarizing part of Gregoire's biographical sketch of Vassa, from 128.18) under the heading printed on pp. 74–83 in 有色人に関する伝記的資料 / *Biographical Sketches and Interesting Anecdotes of Persons of Color. To which is added, a Selection of Pieces in Poetry*, compiled by A[bigail] Mott. "Second Edition, much Enlarged."

Tokyo, Japan: 日本図書センター, Nihon Tosho Senta, **2000**.
8vo (27 cm.): 255 p.

130.71——.
Extracts "From The Life of Olaudah Equiano, or Gustavus Vassa the African, Written by Himself" in *Anthology of American Literature, Seventh Edition, Volume I: Colonial through Romantic*, edited by George McMichael and others.

Upper Saddle River, New Jersey [U.S.A.]: Prentice Hall, **[2000]**.
8vo.

130.72——.
Chapter 2 "From The Interesting Narrative of the Life of Olaudah Equiano, or Gustavus Vassa, the African, Written

by Himself (1789)" printed with editorial note on pp. 9–19 in *The Prentice Hall Anthology of African American Literature* [edited by] Rochelle Smith [and] Sharon L. Jones.

Upper Saddle River, New Jersey [U.S.A.]: Prentice Hall, [2000].
8vo (23 cm.): xxii, 1130 p., plates, + audio CD.

130.73——. [Critical edition of 130.1]

The interesting narrative of the life of Olaudah Equiano, or Gustavus Vassa, the African, written by himself, edited by Werner Sollors.

New York [New York, U.S.A.]: Norton Critical Editions, 2001.
8vo (21 cm.): xxxiii, 403 p.

130.74——.

130.21 (Leeds, 1814) printed in *The Classic Slave Narratives,* edited with an introduction by Henry Louis Gates Jr.

New York [New York, U.S.A.]: Signet Classics, 2002.
8vo (18 cm.): 672 p.

130.75——.

Extracts "From The Interesting Narrative of the Life of Olaudah Equiano, or Gustavus Vassa, the African" printed, with new introduction and annotations, on pp. 912–927 in the anthology *Early American Writings,* edited by Carla Mulford, Angela Vietto, and Amy E. Winans.

New York [New York, U.S.A., and] Oxford [England]: Oxford University Press, 2002.
8vo (24 cm.): xxii, 1129 p.

130.76——.

The interesting narrative of the life of Olaudah Equiano, or, Gustavus Vassa, the African, written by himself, edited by Angelo Costanzo.

Peterborough, Ontario [Canada]: Broadview Press; **Letchworth [Hertfordshire, England]:** Turpin [Distribution Co.], 2002.
8vo (22 cm.): 331 p.

130.77——. [French translation of the first American edition, 130.7]

Olaudah Equiano ou Gustavus Vassa l'Africain: le passionnant récit de ma vie. Traduit et édité par Régine Mfoumou-Arthur. Préface par Serge Soupel.

Paris [France]: Harmattan, 2002.
8vo (22 cm.): 320 p.

130.78——. [French adaptation for younger readers]

Le prince esclave: une histoire vraie. Adaptée par Ann Cameron.

Paris [France]: Rageot, 2002.
8vo (19 cm.): 189 p., illus.

130.79——. [Third printing of 130.55]

Excerpts from 130.1 reprinted from 130.39, with new introductory note, on pp. 54–80 in *Black Writers in Britain, 1760–1890: An Anthology,* edited by Paul Edwards and David Dabydeen.

Edinburgh [Scotland]: Edinburgh University Press, 2003.
8vo (22 cm.): xv, 239 p.

130.80——.

The Interesting Narrative of the Life of Olaudah Equiano, edited by Shelly Eversley. Introduction by Robert Reid-Pharr.

[New York, New York, U.S.A.]: Modern Library Classics, 2004.
12mo, 336 p.

130.81——. [Second printing of 130.76]

The interesting narrative of the life of Olaudah Equiano, or, Gustavus Vassa, the African, written by himself, edited by Angelo Costanzo.

Peterborough, Ontario [Canada]: Broadview Press, 2004.
8vo (22 cm.): 331 p.

130.82——.

Extracts "From The interesting narrative of the life of Olaudah Equiano, or Gustavus Vassa, the African: written by himself" printed in *Early Black British Writing: Olaudah Equiano, Mary Prince, and others: Selected texts with introduction, critical essays,* edited by Alan Richardson and Debbie Lee.

Boston [Massachusetts, U.S.A.]: Houghton Mifflin, 2004.
8vo, ix, 443 p.

130.83——.

Extracts "From The Interesting Narrative of the Life of Olaudah Equiano, or Gustavus Vassa, the African, Written by Himself" printed from 128.1 with introduction and annotations on pp. 187–213 of *The Norton Anthology of African American Literature,* edited by Henry Louis Gates Jr. and Nellie Y. McKay. **Second edition.**

New York [New York, U.S.A.]: W. W. Norton & Co., [2004].
8vo (24 cm.): xlvii, 2776 p. + audio disc.

130.84——. [Abridged French translation]

Olaudah Equiano ou Gustavus Vassa l'Africain: la passionnante Autobiographie d'un Esclave Affranchi. Traduit et édité par Régine Mfoumou-Arthur.

Paris [France]: Harmattan, 2005.
8vo (22 cm.): 199 p., illus. (including portrait).

130.85———. [Reprint of 130.1 (London, 1789)]

The interesting narrative of the life of Olaudah Equiano, or Gustavus Vassa, the African written by himself, edited with an introduction by Robert J. Allison.

Boston [Massachusetts, U.S.A.]: Bedford Books of St. Martin's Press (second edition), **2007.**
8vo (21 cm.): viii. 244, illus.

130.86———. [French translation]

Ma véridique histoire: Africain, esclave en Amérique, homme libre. Traduit de l'anglais, présenté et annoté par Régine Mfounmou-Arthur.

Paris [France]: Mercure de France, **2008.**
8vo (18 cm.): 374 p., illus.

130.87———. [French adaptation for younger readers]

Le prince esclave: une histoire vraie. Adaptée par Ann Cameron.

Paris [France]: Rageot, **2008.**
8vo (19 cm.): 189 p., illus.

130.88———. [Italian translation]

L'incredibile storia di Olaudah Equiano, o Gustavus Vassa, detto l'Africano.

Milano [Italia]: Epoché, **2008.**
282 p.

130.89———. [Greek translation]

Το ενδιαφέρον αφήγημα της ζωής του Ολόντα Εκουιάνο, αφρικανού σκλάβου στην Αμερική, ελεύθερου ανθρώπου.

Αθήνα [Athens, Greece]: Ασβός, **2009.**

130.90———.

Photomechanical reprinting of 130.21 (Leeds, 1814) on pp. 1–182 in *The Classic Slave Narratives,* edited with an introduction by Henry Louis Gates Jr.

New York [New York, U.S.A.]: Signet Classics, **2012.**
8vo (18 cm.): xxx, 648 p.

130.91———.

Extracts "From The Interesting Narrative of the Life of Olaudah Equiano, or Gustavus Vassa, the African, Written by Himself" printed from 130.1 with introduction and annotations in vol. 1 of *The Norton Anthology of African Ameri-* *can Literature,* edited by Henry Louis Gates Jr. and Nellie Y. McKay. **Third edition.**

New York [New York, U.S.A.]: W. W. Norton & Co., [2014].
2 vols. 8vo (24 cm.): xiv, 1574 p.

130.92———.

Photomechanical reprinting of 130.21 (Leeds, 1814) on pp. 1–182 in *The Classic Slave Narratives,* edited and with an updated introduction by Henry Louis Gates, Jr.

New York [New York, U.S.A.]: Signet Classics, **2016.**
8vo, 480 p.

130.93———. [French adaptation for younger readers]

Le prince esclave: une histoire vraie. Adaptée par Ann Cameron.

Paris [France]: Rageot, **2017.**
8vo (19 cm.): 154 p., illus.

130.94———. [French translation]

Ma véridique histoire: Africain, esclave en Amérique, homme libre. Traduit de l'anglais, présenté et annoté par Régine Mfounmou-Arthur.

Paris [France]: Mercure de France, **2017.**
8vo (18 cm.): 374 p., illus.

130.95 ———. [Hebrew translation]

סובטסוג וא ונאיווקא הדולוא ייח לש ןיינעמה רופיסה ,ונאיקא הדולוא
ינקירפאה ,הסוו

Ra'anana [Israel]: The Open University of Israel, **2018.**

130.96 ———. [Online version]

The Interesting Narratives of the Life Olaudah Equiano, or Gustavus Vassa, the African, Written by Himself. Vol. 1 and Vol. 2. Editors described as a version, not an edition.

London [Britain]: The Equiano Society, **2020.**
255 p.
https://equiano.uk/the-2020-version-of-olaudah-equianos-interesting-narrative-1789-vol-i-ii/

Additional publications by Vassa

+130-A-S.1 ———.

Eighteen distinct letters and petitions written by Vassa to various people, some quoted in his *Narrative,* some published in the London, England, newspaper *The Public Advertiser,* some in *The Morning Chronicle and London Advertiser,* etc., 1779–1792. For texts and bibliographical details see following entry. The present editors have not searched for reprintings of these letters in 18th-century newspapers additional to those cited by Folarin Shyllon in the following entry.

+130-A-S.2 ———.

These 18 letters reprinted as Appendix I on pp. 245–266 in Folarin Shyllon, *Black People in Britain 1555–1833* (London [England]: Published for the Institute of Race Relations by Oxford University Press, 1977).

+130-T.1 ———.

Letter written by Vassa in 1792 in Paul Edwards, "'…Written by Himself'": a Manuscript Letter of Olaudah Equiano,"

in *Notes and Queries* (London, England), n.s., vol. 15, no. (1968), pp. 222–225. Hogg 1596.

+130-U.1 ———.

The Letters and Other Writings of Gustavus Vassa (Olaudah Equiano, the African) documenting Abolition of the Slave Trade, edited by Karlee Anne Sapoznik, foreword by Paul E. Lovejoy (Princeton [New Jersey, U.S.A.]: Markus Wiener Publishers, 2013).

1791

131.1 Molly

Account included on pp. 8–9 under the date 16 July 1791 within "Paramaribo Diarium, July-December 1791," printed on pp. 8–11 in section 3 of vol. 3, Part 3.3 of *Die Mission der Brüdergemeine in Suriname und Berbice im achtzehnten Jahrhundert. Eine Missionsgeschichte hauptsächlich in Auszügen aus Briefen und Originalberichten*, edited by Fritz Staehelin.

Full text: https://huskiecommons.lib.niu.edu/history-500africanvoices/111/ [see 131.1].

Herrnhut [Saxony, Germany]: Verlag C. Kersten in **Paramaribo [Suriname]** im Kommission bei der Missionsbuchhandlung in Herrnhut und für den Buchhandel bei der Unitätsbuchhandlung in **Gnadau [Saxony, Germany]**, [**1913–1917**].
3 vols., 8vo (21.5 cm.).

¶ As a small child, Molly was taken from an unknown place in West Africa on a slave ship to Antigua, the British colony in the West Indies (see Map 11), where she grew up enslaved. Later she was either sold or taken by her owner to the island of St. Johns in the Danish West Indies (see Map 14), where she became interested in the Moravians and was baptized. Still later, in 1788 (after she had a son and was probably married), she was either sold again or taken by her owner to the island of St. Eustachius. Thereafter, she and her family were taken back to Antigua, and in 1791 Molly and her son were taken (without her husband) on a slave ship to Paramaribo in the Dutch South American colony of Suriname (see Map 10). Here she joined the Moravian community and participated in their formal missionary planning meetings. She never learned the "Negro language" (*Negersprache*) well.

131.2———.

Narrative included on pp. 8–9 within "Paramaribo Diarium, July-December 1791," printed on pp. 8–11 of vol. 2, Part 3.3 in photomechanical reprint of 131.1 with imprint:

Hildesheim [Saxony, Germany], Zurich [Switzerland]: Georg Olms Verlag, **1997**.
2 vols., 8vo (22 cm.).

1792

132.0 Antson Zizer = Ansel

Life details in two different manuscripts, viz.:

132.0a, his manuscript letter to John Clarkson dated Freetown 26 November **1792,** held in The Sierra Leone Collection, Special Collections Department, The University Library, University of Illinois at Chicago, **Chicago, Illinois, U.S.A.**

http://collections.carli.illinois.edu/cdm/compoundobject/collection/uic_sierra/id/137/rec/31

Full text: https://huskiecommons.lib.niu.edu/history-500africanvoices/283/ [see 132.1].

132.0b, "Paper of Laws stuck up at Abram Smith's house by the Hundredors and Tythingmen, Sept 3rd **1800**" signed by Ansel Zizer, Isaac Anderson, and others, held in the [United Kingdom] National Archives (formerly the Public Records Office), **Kew, London, England**, CO270/5 Narrative of the Rebellion pp. 98–99.

¶ Zizer was born in Africa (132.1, p. 72) and taken to British North America on a slave ship before 1775. During the Revolutionary War he fled to British lines to escape slavery and was evacuated with thousands of others to Nova Scotia, Canada (see Map 16), after the British defeat in 1783. In 1792 he sailed from Canada with the fleet carrying African refugees to the new colony in Sierra Leone, West Africa (see Map 4).

There he became a leader of the settlers' protest movement against abusive British policy and served (illegally) in the local parliament until the British crushed the rebellion in 1800.

132.1 ——.

Life details in his letter to John Clarkson dated Freetown 26 November **1792** (132.0a) printed on p. 30; see also "Paper of Laws stuck up at Abram Smith's house by the Hundredors and Tythingmen Sept 3rd 1800" (130.0b) cosigned by Zizer

and printed on pp. 63–64 in *'Our Children Free and Happy': Letters from Black Settlers in Africa in the 1790s*, edited by Christopher Fyfe with a contribution by Charles Jones [viz. Appendix: Some grammatical characteristics of the Sierra Leone letters].

[Edinburgh, Scotland]: Edinburgh University Press, [1991]. Tpv: Typeset … by Nene Phototypesetters, Northampton, and printed in Great Britain by Hartnolls Limited, Bodmin, Cornwall. 8vo (23 cm.): x, 105 p.

1792 +/− 2 years

133.1 Tammata = Pierre

Account of his life (as told to Captain John Adams when Adams was trading in the Bight of Benin in the **early 1790s**) printed on pp. 82–87 in Captain John Adams, *Remarks on the Country extending from Cape Palmas to The River Congo, including Observations on the Manners and Customs of the Inhabitants. With an appendix containing An Account of the European Trade with the West Coast of Africa.*

https://babel.hathi-trust.org/cgi/pt?id=n-yp.33433082451026 [see 133.1].

London [England]: Printed for G. and W. B. Whitaker, 1823. 8vo (23 cm.): [4], ix, [1], 265 p., maps.

Note: This account of Tammata's life does not appear in what is sometimes catalogued as the first edition of Captain Adams's *Remarks* (viz., his 119-page *Sketches taken during Ten Voyages to Africa, between the Years 1786 and 1800* [London: Hurst, Robinson, and Co., 1822]) but dates from the years when Adams was trading in the Bight of Benin in the early 1790s, hence the present compilers' chronological placement of Tammata's account.

¶ Tammata was Hausa from the interior of the Bight of Benin (modern Benin, Togo, Nigeria—see Map 5). When young (in the 1770s or earlier) he was taken enslaved to France on a French vessel. Educated there (probably at La Rochelle—see Map 7), he subsequently assisted his owner on trading voyages to Africa. Because of his helpfulness, his owner freed him, then established him as a merchant in Porto Novo, the major port of the Oyo Empire on the lagoon at the coast of the Bight of Benin (modern Benin) in 1780s and 1790s, where he acquired wealth and influence. Tammata spoke Yorùbá and French as well as Hausa. As a leading merchant, he had extensive farmland and a large compound. He was the head of the Muslim community in Porto Novo, although the predominant religion in the town was the Orìṣà worship of the Yorùbá. For more on him see: Pierre Verger, *Trade Relations between the Bight of Benin and Bahia from the 17th to 19th Century*, translated by Evelyn Crawford (Ibadan, Nigeria: Ibadan University Press, 1976), pp. 186–87; and Pierre Verger, *Flux et reflux de la traite des nègres entre le Golfe de Bénin et Bahia de Todos os Santos du dix-septième au dix-neuvième siècle* (Paris: Mouton, 1968).

133.2——.

Photomechanical reprint of 133.1 with imprint:

London [England]: Cass, 1966. 8vo (23 cm.): [6], x, 265 p., map.

1793

134.1 Isaac Anderson (1753–1800)

Multiple documents written, signed by, or concerning Isaac Anderson in 1793 and subsequent years printed on pp. 35–43, 56–58, and 63–65 in *'Our Children Free and Happy': Letters from Black Settlers in Africa in the 1790s*, edited by Christopher Fyfe with a contribution by Charles Jones [viz. Appendix: Some grammatical characteristics of the Sierra Leone letters].

[Edinburgh, Scotland]: Edinburgh University Press, [1991]. Tpv: Typeset … by Nene Phototypesetters, Northampton, and printed in Great Britain by Hartnolls Limited, Bodmin, Cornwall. 8vo (23 cm.): x, 105 p. FN000936.

¶ Anderson was born in Angola (see Map 6) and taken on a slave ship to the British North American colony of South Carolina (Map 15). In 1775, at the beginning of the American Revolutionary War, he ran away from his owner to the British-controlled port city of Charleston, South Carolina, and evacuated with British forces first to North Carolina, then further north to New York City (Map 17). In the latter city he worked as a carpenter, married, and commenced raising children. At some point he became a Methodist. After the British defeat in 1783 he and his family evacuated with the fleet to Nova Scotia, Canada (Map 16), where he received land in Birchtown. In 1792 he sailed with the fleet carrying refugees from Canada to the new colony in Sierra Leone, West Africa (Map 4). There he became a leader of the settlers' protest movement against abusive British policy, which included taking a petition to London, serving illegally in the local parliament, and commanding what the British viewed as an armed rebellion. For the last, he was executed in 1800. For the larger context of his North American years, see Cassandra Pybus, *Epic Journeys of Freedom: Runaway Slaves of the American Revolution and Their Global Quest for Liberty* (Boston: Beacon Press, 2006), which includes a concise biographical sketch of Anderson on p. 209.

https://archive.org/details/ourchildrenfreeh0000unse/page/34/mode/2up [see 134.1].

134.2 ——.

Selection of the letters edited by Christopher Fyfe for 134.1 printed, with new introductory note, as chapter 7, "The Sierra Leone Settlers' Letters 1791–1800" on pp. 83–98 in *Black Writers in Britain 1760–1890: An Anthology*, edited by Paul Edwards and David Dabydeen.

Edinburgh [Scotland]: Edinburgh University Press, [1991]. 8vo (22 cm.): xv, 239 p.

134.3 ——.[Second printing 134.1]

Selection of the letters edited by Christopher Fyfe for 134.1 printed, with new introductory note, as chapter 7, "The Sierra Leone Settlers' Letters 1791–1800" on pp. 83–98 in *Black Writers in Britain 1760–1890: An Anthology*, edited by Paul Edwards and David Dabydeen.

Edinburgh [Scotland]: Edinburgh University Press, [1995]. 8vo (22 cm.): xv, 239 p.

134.4 ——. [Third printing of 134.1]

Selection of the letters edited by Christopher Fyfe for 134.1 printed, with new introductory note, as chapter 7, "The Sierra Leone Settlers' Letters 1791–1800" on pp. 83–98 in *Black Writers in Britain 1760–1890: An Anthology*, edited by Paul Edwards and David Dabydeen.

Edinburgh [Scotland]: Edinburgh University Press, [2003]. 8vo (22 cm.): xv, 239 p.

135.1 Unnamed Mandinka man

Life details of an "old and faithful Mandingo servant" printed on p. 61 in vol. II of Bryan Edwards, *The History, Civil and Commercial, of the British Colonies in the West Indies.*

London [England]: Printed for John Stockdale, MDCCXCIII [1793].
2 vols., 4to (28 cm.):
ESTC t137074. (Note that ESTC t194531 is the publisher's ephemeral four-page 8vo post-publication advertisement of this work's availability for 2 pounds, 12 shillings, and 6 pence per set.)

https://babel.hathitrust.org/cgi/pt?id=mdp.39015021776888&view=1up&seq=70&skin=2021 [see 135.2].

¶ This unnamed man was Muslim and identified as Mandinka (an ethnic group residing in modern southern Mali, Guinea, and Ivory Coast—see Map 3)). Captured at a very young age during a deadly skirmish while visiting a distant village where a relative resided near a Portuguese settlement, he was then taken with other captives down river, sold to a slave ship captain, and carried to Jamaica in the Caribbean (Map 13).

135.2——.

Life details of an "old and faithful Mandingo servant" printed on pp. 56–57 in vol. II of Bryan Edwards, *The History, Civil and Commercial, of the British Colonies in the West Indies.*

Dublin [Ireland]: Luke White, M.DCC.XCIII [1793].
2 vols., 8vo (21.5 cm.).
https://babel.hathitrust.org/cgi/pt?id=mdp.39015021776888&view=1up&seq=70&skin=2021
ESTC t136755.

135.3 ——.

Life details of an "old and faithful Mandingo servant" printed on p. 61 in vol. II of Bryan Edwards, *The History, Civil and Commercial, of the British Colonies in the West Indies. The Second Edition.*

London [England]: Printed for John Stockdale, Piccadilly, M.DCC.XCIV [1794].
2 vols., 4to (28 cm.).
ESTC t136756.

135.4 ——.

Life details of an "old and faithful Mandingo servant" printed on pp. 151–152 of *The History, Civil and Commercial, of the British Colonies in the West Indies. To which is added, an historical survey of the French colony in the island of St.*

Domingo. **Abridged from** *The History written by Bryan Edwards, Esq.*

London [England]: Printed for B. Crosby, Stationer's Court; for Mundell & Son, **Edinburgh [Scotland]**; and for J. Mundell, College, **Glasgow [Scotland]**, 1798.

8vo (22 cm.): xvi, 373 p. + map and advertisements. ESTC t137075.

135.5 ——.

Life details of an "old and faithful Mandingo servant" printed on pp. 151–152 of *The History, Civil and Commercial, of the British Colonies in the West Indies. To which is added, an historical survey of the French colony in the island of St. Domingo.* **Abridged from** *The History written by Bryan Edwards, Esq.*

London [England]: Printed for Crosby and Letterman, Stationer's Court, near Paternoster Row; for Mundell & Son, **Edinburgh [Scotland]**; and for J. Mundell, College, **Glasgow [Scotland]**, 1799.

8vo (22 cm.): xvi, 373 p. + map and advertisements. ESTC n17460.

135.6 ——.

Life details of an "old and faithful Mandingo servant" printed on pp. 71–72 in vol. II of Bryan Edwards, *The History, Civil and Commercial, of the British Colonies in the West Indies.* **Third Edition**, *with considerable additions.*

London [England]: Printed for John Stockdale, Piccadilly, 1801. Tpv: Printed by Luke Hansard, Great Turnstile, Lincoln's-Inn Fields.

3 vols., 4to (28 cm.).

https://babel.hathitrust.org/cgi/pt?id=aeu.ark:/13960/t5t73771p;view=1up;seq=88

https://archive.org/details/historycivilcomm04edwa/page/70/mode/1up

135.7 ——. [French translation by François Soulès of 135.6]

Loose translation from 135.6 on p. 207ff. in Bryan Edwards, *Histoire civile et commerciale des Colonies Anglaises dans les Indes Occidentales.*

Paris [France]: Dentu, Imprimere-Libraire, Palais de Tribunat, galeries de bois, no. 240, An IX (**1801**).

8vo (20 cm.): viii, 490 p., folding map.

https://babel.hathitrust.org/cgi/pt?id=aeu.ark:/13960/t1qf9b-m34&view=1up&seq=230

135.8 ——.

Life details of an "old and faithful Mandingo servant" printed on pp. 264–265 in vol. II of Bryan Edwards, *The History, Civil and Commercial, of the British Colonies in the West In-*

dies.... To which is added a general description of the Bahama Islands, by Daniel M'Kinnon, Esq.

Philadelphia [Pennsylvania, U.S.A.]: Printed and sold by James Humphreys, At the Corner of Second and Walnut-Streets, **1806**.

4 vols. (printed 1805–1806), 8vo (22 cm.).

https://babel.hathitrust.org/cgi/pt?id=nyp.33433081700688;view=1up;seq=272

https://www.biodiversitylibrary.org/item/271526#page/270/mode/1up

135.9——.

Life details of an "old and faithful Mandingo servant" printed on pp. 71–72 in vol. II of Bryan Edwards, *The History, Civil and Commercial, of the British Colonies in the West Indies.* **Fourth Edition**, *with considerable additions.*

London [England]: Printed for John Stockdale, Piccadilly, 1807. Tpv: T. Gillet, Printer, Wild-Court, Lincoln's-Inn-Fields.

3 vols., 8vo (22 cm.).

https://babel.hathitrust.org/cgi/pt?id=aeu.ark:/13960/t5v70g-z34;view=1up;seq=88

135.10 ——.

Life details of an "old and faithful Mandingo servant" printed on pp. 264–265 in vol. II of Bryan Edwards, *The History, Civil and Commercial, of the British Colonies in the West Indies.... To which is added a general description of the Bahama Islands, by Daniel M'Kinnon, Esq.*

Philadelphia [Pennsylvania, U.S.A.]: Levis & Weaver, 1810.

4 vols., 8vo (22 cm.).

Shaw & Shoemaker 20035.

135.11——.

Life details of an "old and faithful Mandingo servant" printed on pp. 71–72 in vol. II of Bryan Edwards, *The History, Civil and Commercial, of the British Colonies in the West Indies... With a continuation to the present time.* **Fifth Edition.**

London [England]: Printed by T. Miller, Noble Street, Cheapside; for G. and W. B. Whittaker; W. H. Reid; J. Nunn; J. M. Richardson; J. Cuthell; T. Boone; T. MacLean; T. and J. Allman; C. Brown; W. Mason; Lackington and Co.; Rodwell and Martin; Oliver and Boyd, **Edinburgh [Scotland]**; and Johnston and Deas, **Dublin [Ireland]**, 1818–1819.

5 vols., 8vo (21 cm.), and atlas.

https://babel.hathitrust.org/cgi/pt?id=mdp.39015011562678;view=1up;seq=85

135.12 ——. [Photomechanical reprint of 135.11]

Life details of an "old and faithful Mandingo servant" printed on pp. 71–72 in vol. II of Bryan Edwards, *The History, Civil and Commercial, of the British Colonies in the West Indies...* *With a continuation to the present time.* **Fifth Edition** (1818-1819) with imprint:

New York [New York, U.S.A.]: AMS Press, **1966.**
5 vols., 8vo (23 cm.).

135.13———. [Photomechanical reprint of 135.2 (Dublin, 1793)]

Life details of an "old and faithful Mandingo servant" printed on pp. 56–57 in vol. II of Bryan Edwards, *The History, Civil and Commercial, of the British Colonies in the West Indies.*

New York [New York, U.S.A.]: Arno Press, **1972.**
2 vols., 8vo (23 cm.).

136.1 Sarri = Adam

Account of his origins and enslavement printed on pp. 104–105 in vol. II of Bryan Edwards, *The History, Civil and Commercial, of the British Colonies in the West Indies.*

London [England]: Printed for John Stockdale, MDCCXCIII [1793].
2 vols., 4to (28 cm.).
ESTC t137074. (Note that ESTC t194531 is the publisher's ephemeral four-page 8vo post-publication advertisement of this work's availability for 2 pounds, 12 shillings, and 6 pence per set.)

https://babel.hathitrust.org/cgi/pt?id=mdp.39015021776888;view=1up;seq=111 [see 136.2].

¶ Sarri said that his father was a chief captain under the king and a great warrior and seller of slaves. Sarri was about fourteen years old when captured in the interior of the Kingdom of Kongo (modern Kongo—see Map 6) and sold initially for powder, shot, and salt, and later for a keg of brandy by a man who took him and others to the coast for sale to a slave ship, which took them to Jamaica in the Caribbean (Map 13).

136.2———.

Account of his origins and enslavement printed on p. 97 in vol. II of Bryan Edwards, *The History, Civil and Commercial, of the British Colonies in the West Indies.*

Dublin [Ireland]: Luke White, M.DCC.XCIII [1793].
2 vols., 8vo (21.5 cm.).
https://babel.hathitrust.org/cgi/pt?id=mdp.39015021776888;view=1up;seq=111
ESTC t136755.

136.3 ———.

Account of his origins and enslavement printed on pp. 104–105 in vol. II of Bryan Edwards, *The History, Civil and Commercial, of the British Colonies in the West Indies.* **The Second Edition.**

London [England]: Printed for John Stockdale, Piccadilly, M.DCC.XCIV [1794].
2 vols., 4to (28 cm.).
ESTC t136756.

136.4———.

Account of his origins and enslavement printed on p. 177 of *The History, Civil and Commercial, of the British Colonies in the West Indies. To which is added, an historical survey of the French colony in the island of St. Domingo.* **Abridged from** *The History written by Bryan Edwards, Esq.*

London [England]: Printed for B. Crosby, Stationer's Court; for Mundell & Son, Edinburgh [Scotland]; and for J. Mundell, College, Glasgow [Scotland], 1798.
8vo (22 cm.): xvi, 373 p. + map and advertisements.
STC t137075.

136.5———.

Account of his origins and enslavement printed on p. 177 of *The History, Civil and Commercial, of the British Colonies in the West Indies. To which is added, an historical survey of the French colony in the island of St. Domingo.* **Abridged from** *The History written by Bryan Edwards, Esq.*

London [England]: Printed for Crosby and Letterman, Stationer's Court, near Paternoster Row; for Mundell & Son, Edinburgh [Scotland]; and for J. Mundell, College, Glasgow [Scotland], 1799.
8vo (22 cm.): xvi, 373 p. + map and advertisements.
ESTC n17460.

136.6 ———.

Account of his origins and enslavement printed on p. 126 in vol. II of Bryan Edwards, *The History, Civil and Commercial, of the British Colonies in the West Indies.* **Third Edition,** *with considerable additions.*

London [England]: Printed for John Stockdale, Piccadilly, **1801.**
Tpv: Printed by Luke Hansard, Great Turnstile, Lincoln's-Inn Fields.
3 vols., 4to (28 cm.).
https://babel.hathitrust.org/cgi/pt?id=aeu.ark:/13960/t5t73771p&view=1up&seq=146
https://archive.org/details/historycivilcomm04edwa/page/126/mode/1up

136.7 ———. [French translation by François Soulès of 136.6]

Loose translation from 136.6 on p. 243 in Bryan Edwards, *Histoire civile et commerciale des Colonies Anglaises dans les Indes Occidentales.*

Paris [France]: Dentu, Imprimere-Libraire, Palais de Tribunat, galeries de bois, no. 240, An IX [1801].
8vo (20 cm.): viii, 490 p., folding map.
https://babel.hathitrust.org/cgi/pt?id=aeu.ark:/13960/t1qf9b-m34&view=1up&seq=266
Cf. Sabin 21902.

136.8 ——.

Account of his origins and enslavement printed on pp. 314–315 in vol. II of Bryan Edwards, *The History, Civil and Commercial, of the British Colonies in the West Indies…. To which is added a general description of the Bahama Islands, by Daniel M'Kinnon, Esq.*

Philadelphia [Pennsylvania, U.S.A.]: Printed and sold by James Humphreys, At the Corner of Second and Walnut-Streets, 1806.
4 vols. (printed 1805–1806), 8vo (22 cm.).
https://babel.hathitrust.org/cgi/pt?id=nyp.33433081700688&view=1up&seq=322
https://www.biodiversitylibrary.org/item/271526#page/320/mode/1up

136.9 ——.

Account of his origins and enslavement printed on p. 126 in vol. II of Bryan Edwards, *The History, Civil and Commercial, of the British Colonies in the West Indies. **Fourth Edition**, with considerable additions.*

London [England]: Printed for John Stockdale, Piccadilly, 1807. Tpv: T. Gillet, Printer, Wild-Court, Lincoln's-Inn-Fields.
3 vols., 8vo (22 cm.).
https://babel.hathitrust.org/cgi/pt?id=aeu.ark:/13960/t5v70g-z34&view=1up&seq=146

136.10 ——.

Account of his origins and enslavement printed on pp. 314–315 in vol. II of Bryan Edwards, *The History, Civil and Commercial, of the British Colonies in the West Indies…. To which is added a general description of the Bahama Islands, by Daniel M'Kinnon, Esq.*

Philadelphia [Pennsylvania, U.S.A.]: Levis & Weaver, 1810.
4 vols., 8vo (22 cm.).
Shaw & Shoemaker 20035.

136.11 ——.

Account of his origins and enslavement printed on p. 126 in vol. II of Bryan Edwards, *The History, Civil and Commercial, of the British Colonies in the West Indies… With a continuation to the present time. **Fifth Edition**.*

London [England]: Printed by T. Miller, Noble Street, Cheapside; for G. and W. B. Whittaker; W. H. Reid; J. Nunn; J. M. Richardson; J. Cuthell; T. Boone; T. MacLean; T. and J. Allman; C. Brown; W. Mason; Lackington and Co.; Rodwell and Martin; Oliver and Boyd, **Edinburgh [Scotland]**; and Johnston and Deas, **Dublin [Ireland]**, 1818–1819.
5 vols., 8vo (21 cm.), and atlas.
https://babel.hathitrust.org/cgi/pt?id=mdp.39015011562678&view=1up&seq=140

136.12 ——. [Photomechanical reprint of 136.11]

Account of his origins and enslavement printed on p. 126 in vol. II of Bryan Edwards, *The History, Civil and Commercial, of the British Colonies in the West Indies… With a continuation to the present time. **Fifth Edition*** (1818–1819) with imprint:

New York [New York, U.S.A.]: AMS Press, **1966**.
5 vols., 8vo (23 cm.).

136.13 ——. [Photomechanical reprint of 136.2 (Dublin, 1793)]

Account of his origins and enslavement printed on p. 97 in vol. II of Bryan Edwards, *The History, Civil and Commercial, of the British Colonies in the West Indies.*

New York [New York, U.S.A.]: Arno Press, **1972**.
2 vols., 8vo (23 cm.).

137.1   Afia = Afiba (ca. 1778–)

Terse account of her origins and enslavement printed on p. 105 in vol. II of Bryan Edwards, *The History, Civil and Commercial, of the British Colonies in the West Indies.*

London [England]: Printed for John Stockdale, MDCCXCIII [1793].
2 vols., 4to (28 cm.).
ESTC t137074. (Note that ESTC t194531 is the publisher's ephemeral four-page 8vo post-publication advertisement of this work's availability for 2 pounds, 12 shillings, and 6 pence per set.)

https://babel.hathitrust.org/cgi/pt?id=mdp.39015021776888;view=1up;seq=112 [see 137.2].

¶ Afiba or Afia, an Akan name for a female born on a Friday, was about fifteen years old when enslaved to Quamina (Kwamena) Yati on the Gold Coast (modern Ghana—see Map 5). Her first owner sold her and two others to a slave ship captain for a quantity of linen and other goods. They were then transported to Jamaica in the Caribbean (Map 13).

137.2 ——.

Terse account of her origins and enslavement printed on p. 98 in vol. II of Bryan Edwards, *The History, Civil and Commercial, of the British Colonies in the West Indies.*

Dublin [Ireland]: Luke White [*sic*], M.DCC.XCIII [1793].
2 vols., 8vo (21.5 cm.)
https://babel.hathitrust.org/cgi/pt?id=mdp.39015021776888;
  view=1up;seq=112
ESTC t136755.

137.3 ——.

Terse account of her origins and enslavement printed on p. 105 in vol. II of Bryan Edwards, *The History, Civil and Commercial, of the British Colonies in the West Indies*. **The Second Edition.**

London [England]: Printed for John Stockdale, Piccadilly, M.DCC.XCIV [1794].
2 vols., 4to (28 cm.).
ESTC t136756.

137.4 ——.

Terse account of her origins and enslavement printed on p. 177 of *The History, Civil and Commercial, of the British Colonies in the West Indies. To which is added, an historical survey of the French colony in the island of St. Domingo. Abridged from The History written by Bryan Edwards, Esq.*

London [England]: Printed for B. Crosby, Stationer's Court; for Mundell & Son, **Edinburgh [Scotland]**; and for J. Mundell, College, **Glasgow [Scotland]**, 1798.
8vo (22 cm.): xvi, 373 p. + map and advertisements.
ESTC t137075.

137.5 ——.

Terse account of her origins and enslavement printed on p. 177 of *The History, Civil and Commercial, of the British Colonies in the West Indies. To which is added, an historical survey of the French colony in the island of St. Domingo. Abridged from The History written by Bryan Edwards, Esq.*

London [England]: Printed for Crosby and Letterman, Stationer's Court, near Paternoster Row; for Mundell & Son, **Edinburgh [Scotland]**; and for J. Mundell, College, **Glasgow [Scotland]**, 1799.
8vo (22 cm.): xvi, 373 p. + map and advertisements.
ESTC n17460.

137.6 ——.

Terse account of her origins and enslavement printed on p. 126 in vol. II of Bryan Edwards, *The History, Civil and Commercial, of the British Colonies in the West Indies*. **Third Edition,** *with considerable additions.*

London [England]: Printed for John Stockdale, Piccadilly, 1801. Tpv: Printed by Luke Hansard, Great Turnstile, Lincoln's-Inn Fields.

3 vols., 4to (28 cm.).
https://babel.hathitrust.org/cgi/pt?id=aeu.ark:/13960/
  t5t73771p&view=1up&seq=146
https://archive.org/details/historycivilcomm04edwa/page/126/
  mode/1up

137.7 ——. [French translation by François Soulès of 137.6]

Loose translation (spelling her name Asiba) from 137.6 on p. 243 in Bryan Edwards, *Histoire civile et commerciale des Colonies Anglaises dans les Indes Occidentales.*

Paris [France]: Dentu, Imprimere-Libraire, Palais de Tribunat, galeries de bois, no. 240, An IX (**1801**).
8vo (20 cm.): viii, 490 p., folding map.
https://babel.hathitrust.org/cgi/pt?id=aeu.ark:/13960/t1qf9b-
  m34&view=1up&seq=266
Cf. Sabin 21902.

137.8 ——.

Terse account of her origins and enslavement printed on p. 315 in vol. II of Bryan Edwards, *The History, Civil and Commercial, of the British Colonies in the West Indies.... To which is added a general description of the Bahama Islands, by Daniel M'Kinnon, Esq.*

Philadelphia [Pennsylvania, U.S.A.]: Printed and sold by James Humphreys, At the Corner of Second and Walnut-Streets, **1806.**
4 vols. (printed 1805–1806), 8vo (22 cm.).
https://babel.hathitrust.org/cgi/pt?id=nyp.33433081700688;
  view=1up;seq=323
https://www.biodiversitylibrary.org/item/271526#page/321/
  mode/1up

137.9 ——.

Terse account of her origins and enslavement printed on p. 126 in vol. II of Bryan Edwards, *The History, Civil and Commercial, of the British Colonies in the West Indies*. **Fourth Edition,** *with considerable additions.*

London [England]: Printed for John Stockdale, Piccadilly, **1807.** Tpv: T. Gillet, Printer, Wild-Court, Lincoln's-Inn-Fields.
3 vols., 8vo (22 cm.).
https://babel.hathitrust.org/cgi/pt?id=aeu.ark:/13960/t5v70g-
  z34&view=1up&seq=146

137.10 ——.

Terse account of her origins and enslavement printed on p. 315 in vol. II of Bryan Edwards, *The History, Civil and Commercial, of the British Colonies in the West Indies.... To which is added a general description of the Bahama Islands, by Daniel M'Kinnon, Esq.*

Philadelphia [Pennsylvania, U.S.A.]: Levis & Weaver, **1810.**
4 vols., 8vo (22 cm.).
Shaw & Shoemaker 20035.

137.11 ⸻.

Terse account of her origins and enslavement printed on p. 126 in vol. II of Bryan Edwards, *The History, Civil and Commercial, of the British Colonies in the West Indies... With a continuation to the present time.* **Fifth Edition.**

London [England]: Printed by T. Miller, Noble Street, Cheapside; for G. and W. B. Whittaker; W. H. Reid; J. Nunn; J. M. Richardson; J. Cuthell; T. Boone; T. MacLean; T. and J. Allman; C. Brown; W. Mason; Lackington and Co.; Rodwell and Martin; Oliver and Boyd, **Edinburgh [Scotland]**; and Johnston and Deas, **Dublin [Ireland]**, **1818–1819.**
5 vols., 8vo (21 cm.), and atlas.
https://babel.hathitrust.org/cgi/pt?id=mdp.39015011562678&view=1up&seq=140

137.12 ⸻. [Photomechanical reprint of 137.10]

Terse account of her origins and enslavement printed on p. 126 in vol. II of Bryan Edwards, *The History, Civil and Commercial, of the British Colonies in the West Indies... With a continuation to the present time.* **Fifth Edition** (1818–1819) with imprint:

New York [New York, U.S.A.]: AMS Press, **1966.**
5 vols., 8vo (23 cm.).

137.13 ⸻. [Photomechanical reprint of 137.2 (Dublin, 1793)]

Terse account of her origins and enslavement printed on p. 98 in vol. II of Bryan Edwards, *The History, Civil and Commercial, of the British Colonies in the West Indies.*

New York [New York, U.S.A.]: Arno Press, **1972.**
2 vols., 8vo (23 cm.).

138.1 Clara

Report of her origins and enslavement, with direct speech, printed on p. 67 in vol. II of Bryan Edwards, *The History, Civil and Commercial, of the British Colonies in the West Indies.*

London [England]: Printed for John Stockdale, MDCCXCIII [1793].
2 vols., 4to (28 cm.).

https://babel.hathitrust.org/cgi/pt?id=mdp.39015021776888;view=1up;seq=76 [see 138.2].

ESTC t137074. (Note that ESTC t194531 is the publisher's ephemeral four-page 8vo post-publication advertisement of this work's availability for 2 pounds, 12 shillings, and 6 pence per set.)

¶ **Clara was born in a village near Anomabu on the Fante coast (Akan people, modern Ghana—see Map 5). Her parents and siblings were enslaved to Anamoa, a "great man," after whose death they were sold to pay his debts. She was captured and taken from the Gold Coast (modern Ghana) on a slave ship to Jamaica in 1784 (Map 13).**

138.2 ⸻.

Report of her origins and enslavement, with direct speech, printed on pp. 62–63 in vol. II of Bryan Edwards, *The History, Civil and Commercial, of the British Colonies in the West Indies.*

Dublin [Ireland]: Luke White, M.DCC.XCIII [1793].
2 vols., 8vo (21.5 cm.).
https://babel.hathitrust.org/cgi/pt?id=mdp.39015021776888; view=1up;seq=76
ESTC t136755.

138.3 ⸻.

Report of her origins and enslavement, with direct speech, printed on p. 67 in vol. II of Bryan Edwards, *The History, Civil and Commercial, of the British Colonies in the West Indies.* **The Second Edition.**

London [England]: Printed for John Stockdale, Piccadilly, M.DCC.XCIV [1794].
2 vols., 4to (28 cm.).
ESTC 136756.

138.4 ⸻.

Report of her origins and enslavement, with direct speech, printed on pp. 80–81 in vol. II of Bryan Edwards, *The History, Civil and Commercial, of the British Colonies in the West Indies.* **Third Edition, with considerable additions.**

London [England]: Printed for John Stockdale, Piccadilly, **1801.** Tpv: Printed by Luke Hansard, Great Turnstile, Lincoln's-Inn Fields.
3 vols., 4to (28 cm.).
https://babel.hathitrust.org/cgi/pt?id=aeu.ark:/13960/t5t73771p&view=1up&seq=100
https://archive.org/details/historycivilcomm04edwa/page/80/mode/1up

138.5 ⸻.

Report of her origins and enslavement, with direct speech, printed on p. 273 in vol. II of Bryan Edwards, *The History, Civil and Commercial, of the British Colonies in the West In-*

dies.... *To which is added a general description of the Bahama Islands, by Daniel M'Kinnon, Esq.*

Philadelphia [Pennsylvania, U.S.A.]: Printed and sold by James Humphreys, At the Corner of Second and Walnut-Streets, 1806.
4 vols. (printed 1805–1806), 8vo (22 cm.).
https://babel.hathitrust.org/cgi/pt?id=nyp.33433081700688&view=1up&seq=281
https://www.biodiversitylibrary.org/item/271526#page/279/mode/1up

138.6 ——.
Report of her origins and enslavement, with direct speech, printed on pp. 80–81 in vol. II of Bryan Edwards, *The History, Civil and Commercial, of the British Colonies in the West Indies.* **Fourth Edition,** *with considerable additions.*

London [England]: Printed for John Stockdale, Piccadilly, 1807. Tpv: T. Gillet, Printer, Wild-Court, Lincoln's-Inn-Fields.
3 vols., 8vo (22 cm.).
https://babel.hathitrust.org/cgi/pt?id=aeu.ark:/13960/t5v70gz34&view=1up&seq=100

138.7 ——.
Report of her origins and enslavement, with direct speech, printed on p. 273 in vol. II of Bryan Edwards, *The History, Civil and Commercial, of the British Colonies in the West Indies.... To which is added a general description of the Bahama Islands, by Daniel M'Kinnon, Esq.*

Philadelphia [Pennsylvania, U.S.A.]: Levis & Weaver, 1810.
4 vols., 8vo (22 cm.).
Shaw & Shoemaker 20035.

138.8 ——.
Report of her origins and enslavement, with direct speech, printed on pp. 80–81 in vol. II of Bryan Edwards, *The History, Civil and Commercial, of the British Colonies in the West Indies... With a continuation to the present time.* **Fifth Edition.**

London [England]: Printed by T. Miller, Noble Street, Cheapside; for G. and W. B. Whittaker; W. H. Reid; J. Nunn; J. M. Richardson; J. Cuthell; T. Boone; T. MacLean; T. and J. Allman; C. Brown; W. Mason; Lackington and Co.; Rodwell and Martin; Oliver and Boyd, **Edinburgh [Scotland];** and Johnston and Deas, **Dublin [Ireland],** 1818–1819.
5 vols., 8vo (21 cm.), and atlas.
https://babel.hathitrust.org/cgi/pt?id=mdp.39015011562678;view=1up;seq=94

138.9 ——. [Photomechanical reprint of 138.8]
Report of her origins and enslavement, with direct speech, printed on pp. 80–81 in vol. II of Bryan Edwards, *The Histo-*

ry, Civil and Commercial, of the British Colonies in the West Indies... With a continuation to the present time. **Fifth Edition** (1818-1819) with imprint:

New York [New York, U.S.A.]: AMS Press, 1966.
5 vols., 8vo (23 cm.).

138.10 ——. [Photomechanical reprint of 138.2 (Dublin, 1793)]
Report of her origins and enslavement, with direct speech, printed on pp. 62–63 in vol. II of Bryan Edwards, *The History, Civil and Commercial, of the British Colonies in the West Indies.*

New York [New York, U.S.A.]: Arno Press, 1972.
2 vols., 8vo (23 cm.).

139.1   Kojo = Cudjoe (ca. 1733–)

His account, including direct speech, printed on pp. 67–68 in vol. II of Bryan Edwards, *The History, Civil and Commercial, of the British Colonies in the West Indies.*

London [England]: Printed for John Stockdale, MDCCXCIII [1793].
2 vols., 4to (27 cm.).
ESTC t137074. (Note that ESTC t194531 is the publisher's ephemeral four-page 8vo post-publication advertisement of this work's availability for 2 pounds, 12 shillings, and 6 pence per set.)

https://babel.hathitrust.org/cgi/pt?id=mdp.39015021776888;view=1up;seq=77 [see first of 139.2].

¶ Kojo was born ca. 1733 in the kingdom of Asante (Akan people, modern Ghana—see Map 5). When Kojo was about sixteen, his older brother gave him as payment for a debt to a man who then sold him to a slave merchant. This merchant then carried Kojo and others to the sea coast (a two-month journey) and sold them to a slave ship captain, who took them to Jamaica in the Caribbean (Map 13).

139.2 ——.
His account, including direct speech, printed on pp. 63–64 in vol. II of Bryan Edwards, *The History, Civil and Commercial, of the British Colonies in the West Indies.*

Dublin [Ireland]: Luke White, M.DCC.XCIII [1793].
2 vols., 8vo (21.5 cm.).
https://babel.hathitrust.org/cgi/pt?id=mdp.39015021776888;view=1up;seq=77
https://ecda.northeastern.edu/item/neu:m0415069z/
ESTC t136755.

139.3 ——.

His account, including direct speech, printed on pp. 67–68 in vol. II of Bryan Edwards, *The History, Civil and Commercial, of the British Colonies in the West Indies*. **The Second Edition.**

London [England]: Printed for John Stockdale, Piccadilly, M.DCC.XCIV [**1794**].
2 vols., 4to (28 cm.).
ESTC t136756.

139.4 ——.

His account, including direct speech, printed on pp. 81–82 in vol. II of Bryan Edwards, *The History, Civil and Commercial, of the British Colonies in the West Indies*. **Third Edition**, *with considerable additions*.

London [England]: Printed for John Stockdale, Piccadilly, **1801**. Tpv: Printed by Luke Hansard, Great Turnstile, Lincoln's-Inn Fields.
3 vols., 8vo (28 cm.).
https://babel.hathitrust.org/cgi/pt?id=aeu.ark:/13960/t5t73771p;view=1up;seq=101
https://archive.org/details/historycivilcomm04edwa/page/81/mode/1up

139.5 ——.

His account, including direct speech, printed on pp. 273–274 in vol. II of Bryan Edwards, *The History, Civil and Commercial, of the British Colonies in the West Indies…. To which is added a general description of the Bahama Islands, by Daniel M'Kinnon, Esq.*

Philadelphia [Pennsylvania, U.S.A.]: Printed and sold by James Humphreys, At the Corner of Second and Walnut-Streets, **1806**.
4 vols. (printed 1805–1806), 8vo (22 cm.).
https://babel.hathitrust.org/cgi/pt?id=nyp.33433081700688;view=1up;seq=281
https://www.biodiversitylibrary.org/item/271526#page/279/mode/1up

139.6 ——.

His account, including direct speech, printed on pp. 81–82 in vol. II of Bryan Edwards, *The History, Civil and Commercial, of the British Colonies in the West Indies*. **Fourth Edition**, *with considerable additions*.

London [England]: Printed for John Stockdale, Piccadilly, **1807**. Tpv: T. Gillet, Printer, Wild-Court, Lincoln's-Inn-Fields.
3 vols., 8vo (22 cm.).
https://babel.hathitrust.org/cgi/pt?id=aeu.ark:/13960/t5v70gz34;view=1up;seq=101

139.7 ——.

His account, including direct speech, printed on pp. 273–274 in vol. II of Bryan Edwards, *The History, Civil and Commercial, of the British Colonies in the West Indies…. To which is added a general description of the Bahama Islands, by Daniel M'Kinnon, Esq.*

Philadelphia [Pennsylvania, U.S.A.]: Levis & Weaver, **1810**.
4 vols., 8vo (22 cm.).
Shaw & Shoemaker 20035.

139.8 ——.

His account, including direct speech, printed on pp. 81–82 in vol. II of Bryan Edwards, *The History, Civil and Commercial, of the British Colonies in the West Indies… With a continuation to the present time*. **Fifth Edition.**

London [England]: Printed by T. Miller, Noble Street, Cheapside; for G. and W. B. Whittaker; W. H. Reid; J. Nunn; J. M. Richardson; J. Cuthell; T. Boone; T. MacLean; T. and J. Allman; C. Brown; W. Mason; Lackington and Co.; Rodwell and Martin; Oliver and Boyd, **Edinburgh [Scotland]**; and Johnston and Deas, **Dublin [Ireland]**, **1818–1819**.
5 vols., 8vo (21 cm.), and atlas.
https://babel.hathitrust.org/cgi/pt?id=mdp.39015011562678;view=1up;seq=95

139.9 ——. [**Photomechanical reprint of 139.8**]

His account, including direct speech, printed on pp. 81–82 in vol. II of Bryan Edwards, *The History, Civil and Commercial, of the British Colonies in the West Indies… With a continuation to the present time*. **Fifth Edition** (1818–1819) with imprint:

New York [New York, U.S.A.]: AMS Press, **1966**.
5 vols., 8vo (23 cm.).

139.10 ——. [**Photomechanical reprint of 139.2 (Dublin, 1793)**]

His account, including direct speech, printed on pp. 63–64 in vol. II of Bryan Edwards, *The History, Civil and Commercial, of the British Colonies in the West Indies*.

New York [New York, U.S.A.]: Arno Press, **1972**.
2 vols., 8vo (23 cm.).

140.1 Esther

Her account printed on pp. 105–106 in vol. II of Bryan Edwards, *The History, Civil and Commercial, of the British Colonies in the West Indies*.

London [England]: Printed for John Stockdale, MDCCXCIII [**1793**].

2 vols., 4to (28 cm.).
ESTC t137074. (Note that ESTC t194531 is the publisher's ephemeral four-page 8vo post-publication advertisement of this work's availability for 2 pounds, 12 shillings, and 6 pence per set.)

¶ Esther was born in Igbo country (modern southeastern Nigeria), a day's journey from the sea coast (Bight of Biafra—see Map 5). Her father had a plantation of corn, yams, and tobacco, and held many enslaved people. She was captured during a raid while visiting her grandmother's village. Those able to be transported were taken to the coast and sold to Europeans; the others were killed. She was taken on a slave ship to Jamaica in the Caribbean (Map 13).

https://babel.hathitrust.org/cgi/pt?id=mdp.39015021776888;view=1up;seq=112 [see 140.2].

140.2 ——.
Her account printed on pp. 98–99 in vol. II of Bryan Edwards, *The History, Civil and Commercial, of the British Colonies in the West Indies.*

Dublin [Ireland]: Luke White, M.DCC.XCIII [1793].
2 vols., 8vo (21.5 cm.).
https://babel.hathitrust.org/cgi/pt?id=mdp.39015021776888;view=1up;seq=112
ESTC t136755.

140.3 ——.
Her account printed on pp. 105–106 in vol. II of Bryan Edwards, *The History, Civil and Commercial, of the British Colonies in the West Indies.* **The Second Edition.**

London [England]: Printed for John Stockdale, Piccadilly, M.DCC.XCIV [1794].
2 vols., 4to (28 cm.).
ESTC t136756.

140.4 ——.
Her account printed on p. 178 of *The History, Civil and Commercial, of the British Colonies in the West Indies. To which is added, an historical survey of the French colony in the island of St. Domingo.* **Abridged from** *The History written by Bryan Edwards, Esq.*

London [England]: Printed for B. Crosby, Stationer's Court; for Mundell & Son, **Edinburgh [Scotland]**; and for J. Mundell, College, **Glasgow [Scotland]**, 1798.
8vo (22 cm.): xvi, 373 p. + map and advertisements.
ESTC t137075.

140.5 ——.
Her account printed on p. 178 of *The History, Civil and Commercial, of the British Colonies in the West Indies. To which is added, an historical survey of the French colony in the island of St. Domingo.* **Abridged from** *The History written by Bryan Edwards, Esq.*

London [England]: Printed for Crosby and Letterman, Stationer's Court, near Paternoster Row; for Mundell & Son, Edinburgh [Scotland]; and for J. Mundell, College, **Glasgow** [Scotland], 1799.
8vo (22 cm.): xvi, 373 p. + map and advertisements.
ESTC n17460.

140.6 ——.
Her account printed on p. 127 in vol. II of Bryan Edwards, *The History, Civil and Commercial, of the British Colonies in the West Indies.* **Third Edition, with considerable additions.**

London [England]: Printed for John Stockdale, Piccadilly, 1801. Tpv: Printed by Luke Hansard, Great Turnstile, Lincoln's-Inn Fields.
3 vols., 4to (28 cm.).
https://babel.hathitrust.org/cgi/pt?id=aeu.ark:/13960/t5t73771p&view=1up&seq=147
https://archive.org/details/historycivilcomm04edwa/page/127/mode/1up

140.7 ——. [French translation by François Soulès of 140.6]
Loose translation from 140.6 on p. 244 in Bryan Edwards, *Histoire civile et commerciale des Colonies Anglaises dans les Indes Occidentales.*

Paris [France]: Dentu, Imprimere-Libraire, Palais de Tribunat, galeries de bois, no. 240, An IX (1801).
8vo (20 cm.): viii, 490 p., folding map.
https://babel.hathitrust.org/cgi/pt?id=aeu.ark:/13960/t1qf9bm34&view=1up&seq=267
Cf. Sabin 21902.

140.8 ——.
Her account printed on p. 316 in vol. II of Bryan Edwards, *The History, Civil and Commercial, of the British Colonies in the West Indies.... To which is added a general description of the Bahama Islands, by Daniel M'Kinnon, Esq.*

Philadelphia [Pennsylvania, U.S.A.]: Printed and sold by James Humphreys, At the Corner of Second and Walnut-Streets, 1806.
4 vols. (printed 1805–1806), 8vo (22 cm.).
https://babel.hathitrust.org/cgi/pt?id=nyp.33433081700688&view=1up&seq=324
https://www.biodiversitylibrary.org/item/271526#page/322/mode/1up

140.9 ——.

Her account printed on p. 127 in vol. II of Bryan Edwards, *The History, Civil and Commercial, of the British Colonies in the West Indies.* **Fourth Edition**, *with considerable additions.*

London [England]: Printed for John Stockdale, Piccadilly, **1807.** Tpv: T. Gillet, Printer, Wild-Court, Lincoln's-Inn-Fields.
3 vols., 8vo (22 cm.).
https://babel.hathitrust.org/cgi/pt?id=aeu.ark:/13960/t5v70g-z34;view=1up;seq=147

140.10 ——.

Her account printed on p. 316 in vol. II of Bryan Edwards, *The History, Civil and Commercial, of the British Colonies in the West Indies…. To which is added a general description of the Bahama Islands, by Daniel M'Kinnon, Esq.*

Philadelphia [Pennsylvania, U.S.A.]: Levis & Weaver, 1810.
4 vols., 8vo (22 cm.).
Shaw & Shoemaker 20035.

140.11 ——.

Her account printed on p. 127 in vol. II of Bryan Edwards, *The History, Civil and Commercial, of the British Colonies in the West Indies… With a continuation to the present time.* **Fifth Edition.**

London [England]: Printed by T. Miller, Noble Street, Cheapside; for G. and W. B. Whittaker; W. H. Reid; J. Nunn; J. M. Richardson; J. Cuthell; T. Boone; T. MacLean; T. and J. Allman; C. Brown; W. Mason; Lackington and Co.; Rodwell and Martin; Oliver and Boyd, **Edinburgh [Scotland]**; and Johnston and Deas, **Dublin [Ireland]**, **1818–1819.**
5 vols., 8vo (21 cm.), and atlas.
https://babel.hathitrust.org/cgi/pt?id=mdp.39015011562678&view=1up&seq=141

140.12 ——. [Photomechanical reprint of 140.11]

Her account printed on p. 127 in vol. II of Bryan Edwards, *The History, Civil and Commercial, of the British Colonies in the West Indies… With a continuation to the present time.* **Fifth Edition** (1818–1819) with imprint:

New York [New York, U.S.A.]: AMS Press, **1966.**
5 vols., 8vo (23 cm.).

140.13 ——. [Photomechanical reprint of 140.2 (Dublin, 1793)]

Her account printed on pp. 98–99 in vol. II of Bryan Edwards, *The History, Civil and Commercial, of the British Colonies in the West Indies.*

New York [New York, U.S.A.]: Arno Press, **1972.**
2 vols., 8vo (23 cm.).

141.1 Sang (ca. 1770–) = Oliver

Account of his origins and enslavement printed on p. 105 in vol. II of Bryan Edwards, *The History, Civil and Commercial, of the British Colonies in the West Indies.*

London [England]: Printed for John Stockdale, MDCCXCIII [1793].
2 vols., 4to (28 cm.).
ESTC t137074. (Note that ESTC t194531 is the publisher's ephemeral four-page 8vo post-publication advertisement of this work's availability for 2 pounds, 12 shillings, and 6 pence per set.)

https://babel.hathitrust.org/cgi/pt?id=mdp.39015021776888;view=1up;seq=112 [see 141.2].

¶ **Sang was from Asante (Akan people, modern Ghana—see Map 5), and his father, a carpenter, was a free man who lived in a village far from the sea. The village was attacked by Fante (Akan people, modern Ghana) from the coast, who killed most of the older people and took the young people as prisoners. They sold Sang and two others for gold to a merchant who took them to Fante country. Sang was sold or transferred at least six times, then sold to a slave ship captain who took him to Jamaica in the Caribbean (Map 13).**

141.2 ——.

Account of his origins and enslavement printed on p. 98 in vol. II of Bryan Edwards, *The History, Civil and Commercial, of the British Colonies in the West Indies.*

Dublin [Ireland]: Luke White, M.DCC.XCIII [1793].
2 vols., 8vo (21.5 cm.).
https://babel.hathitrust.org/cgi/pt?id=mdp.39015021776888;view=1up;seq=112
ESTC t136755.

141.3 ——.

Account of his origins and enslavement printedon p. 105 in vol. II of Bryan Edwards, *The History, Civil and Commercial, of the British Colonies in the West Indies.* **The Second Edition.**

London [England]: Printed for John Stockdale, Piccadilly, M.DCC.XCIV [1794].
2 vols., 4to (28 cm.).
ESTC t136756.

141.4 ——.

Account of his origins and enslavement printed on p. 178 of *The History, Civil and Commercial, of the British Colonies in the West Indies. To which is added, an historical survey of the French colony in the island of St. Domingo.* **Abridged from** *The History written by Bryan Edwards, Esq.*

London [England]: Printed for B. Crosby, Stationer's Court; for Mundell & Son, **Edinburgh [Scotland]**; and for J. Mundell, College, **Glasgow [Scotland]**, 1798.

8vo (22 cm.): xvi, 373 p. + map and advertisements.
ESTC t137075.

141.5 ———.

Account of his origins and enslavement printed on p. 178 of *The History, Civil and Commercial, of the British Colonies in the West Indies. To which is added, an historical survey of the French colony in the island of St. Domingo. **Abridged from** The History written by Bryan Edwards, Esq.*

London [England]: Printed for Crosby and Letterman, Stationer's Court, near Paternoster Row; for Mundell & Son, **Edinburgh [Scotland]**; and for J. Mundell, College, **Glasgow [Scotland]**, 1799.

8vo (22 cm.): xvi, 373 p. + map and advertisements.
ESTC n17460.

141.6 ———.

Account of his origins and enslavement printed on p. 127 in vol. II of Bryan Edwards, *The History, Civil and Commercial, of the British Colonies in the West Indies. **Third Edition**, with considerable additions.*

London [England]: Printed for John Stockdale, Piccadilly, 1801. Tpv: Printed by Luke Hansard, Great Turnstile, Lincoln's-Inn Fields.

3 vols., 4to (28 cm.).
https://babel.hathitrust.org/cgi/pt?id=aeu.ark:/13960/t5t73771p;view=1up;seq=147
https://archive.org/details/historycivilcomm04edwa/page/127/mode/1up

141.7 ———. [French translation by François Soulès of 141.6]

Loose translation (naming him Olivier) from 141.6 on p. 244 in Bryan Edwards, *Histoire civile et commerciale des Colonies Anglaises dans les Indes Occidentales.*

Paris [France]: Dentu, Imprimere-Libraire, Palais de Tribunat, galeries de bois, no. 240, An IX (**1801**).

8vo (20 cm.): viii, 490 p., folding map.
https://babel.hathitrust.org/cgi/pt?id=aeu.ark:/13960/t1qf9bm34&view=1up&seq=267
Cf. Sabin 21902.

141.8 ———.

Account of his origins and enslavement printed on pp. 315–316 in vol. II of Bryan Edwards, *The History, Civil and Commercial, of the British Colonies in the West Indies…. To which*

is added a general description of the Bahama Islands, by Daniel M'Kinnon, Esq.

Philadelphia [Pennsylvania, U.S.A.]: Printed and sold by James Humphreys, At the Corner of Second and Walnut-Streets, 1806.

4 vols. (printed 1805–1806), 8vo (22 cm.).
https://babel.hathitrust.org/cgi/pt?id=nyp.33433081700688&view=1up&seq=323
https://www.biodiversitylibrary.org/item/271526#page/321/mode/1up

141.9 ———.

Account of his origins and enslavement printed on p. 127 in vol. II of Bryan Edwards, *The History, Civil and Commercial, of the British Colonies in the West Indies. **Fourth Edition**, with considerable additions.*

London [England]: Printed for John Stockdale, Piccadilly, 1807. Tpv: T. Gillet, Printer, Wild-Court, Lincoln's-Inn-Fields.

3 vols., 8vo (22 cm.).
https://babel.hathitrust.org/cgi/pt?id=aeu.ark:/13960/t5v70gz34;view=1up;seq=147

141.10 ———.

Account of his origins and enslavement printed on pp. 315–316 in vol. II of Bryan Edwards, *The History, Civil and Commercial, of the British Colonies in the West Indies…. To which is added a general description of the Bahama Islands, by Daniel M'Kinnon, Esq.*

Philadelphia [Pennsylvania, U.S.A.]: Levis & Weaver, 1810.

4 vols., 8vo (22 cm.).
Shaw & Shoemaker 20035.

141.11 ———.

Account of his origins and enslavement printed on p. 127 in vol. II of Bryan Edwards, *The History, Civil and Commercial, of the British Colonies in the West Indies… With a continuation to the present time. **Fifth Edition**.*

London [England]: Printed by T. Miller, Noble Street, Cheapside; for G. and W. B. Whittaker; W. H. Reid; J. Nunn; J. M. Richardson; J. Cuthell; T. Boone; T. MacLean; T. and J. Allman; C. Brown; W. Mason; Lackington and Co.; Rodwell and Martin; Oliver and Boyd, **Edinburgh [Scotland]**; and Johnston and Deas, **Dublin [Ireland]**, 1818–1819.

5 vols., 8vo (21 cm.), and atlas.
https://babel.hathitrust.org/cgi/pt?q1=Oliver;id=mdp.39015011562678;view=1up;seq=141;start=1;sz=10;page=search;num=127

141.12 ——. [Photomechanical reprint of 141.11]

Account of his origins and enslavement printed on p. 127 in vol. II of Bryan Edwards, *The History, Civil and Commercial, of the British Colonies in the West Indies... With a continuation to the present time. Fifth Edition* (1818–1819) with imprint:

New York [New York, U.S.A.]: AMS Press, **1966**.
5 vols., 8vo (23 cm.).

141.13 ——. [Photomechanical reprint of 141.2 (Dublin, 1793)]

Account of his origins and enslavement printed on p. 98 in vol. II of Bryan Edwards, *The History, Civil and Commercial, of the British Colonies in the West Indies.*

New York [New York, U.S.A.]: Arno Press, **1972**.
2 vols., 8vo (23 cm.).

142.1 Yao (ca. 1773–) = Yaw = Quaw

His account printed on p. 105 in vol. II of Bryan Edwards, *The History, Civil and Commercial, of the British Colonies in the West Indies.*

London [England]: Printed for John Stockdale, MDCCXCIII [1793].
2 vols., 4to (28 cm.).
ESTC t137074. (Note that ESTC t194531 is the publisher's ephemeral four-page 8vo post-publication advertisement of this work's availability for 2 pounds, 12 shillings, and 6 pence per set.)

https://babel.hathitrust.org/cgi/pt?id=mdp.39015021776888;view=1up;seq=112 [see 142.2].

¶ Born into slavery, Yao and his brother Kwabena (q.v. 143.1) came from the Gold Coast (modern Ghana—see Map 5) and were Akan, which is reflected in their day names (Yao meaning Thursday, and Kwabena meaning Tuesday) according to Akan cosmology. To pay a debt, their owner sold both brothers to a slave ship captain, who took them to Jamaica in the Caribbean (Map 13).

142.2 ——.

His account printed on p. 98 in vol. II of Bryan Edwards, *The History, Civil and Commercial, of the British Colonies in the West Indies.*

Dublin [Ireland]: Luke White, M.DCC.XCIII [1793].
2 vols., 8vo (21.5 cm.).
https://babel.hathitrust.org/cgi/pt?id=mdp.39015021776888;view=1up;seq=112
ESTC t136755.

142.3 ——.

His account, including direct speech, printed on p. 105 in vol. II of Bryan Edwards, *The History, Civil and Commercial, of the British Colonies in the West Indies. The Second Edition.*

London [England]: Printed for John Stockdale, Piccadilly, M.DCC.XCIV [1794].
2 vols., 4to (28 cm.).
ESTC t136756.

142.4 ——.

His account printed on p. 177 of *The History, Civil and Commercial, of the British Colonies in the West Indies. To which is added, an historical survey of the French colony in the island of St. Domingo. Abridged from The History written by Bryan Edwards, Esq.*

London [England]: Printed for B. Crosby, Stationer's Court; for Mundell & Son, **Edinburgh [Scotland]**; and for J. Mundell, College, **Glasgow [Scotland]**, 1798.
8vo (22 cm.): xvi, 373 p. + map and advertisements.
ESTC t137075.

142.5 ——.

His account printed on p. 177 of *The History, Civil and Commercial, of the British Colonies in the West Indies. To which is added, an historical survey of the French colony in the island of St. Domingo. Abridged from The History written by Bryan Edwards, Esq.*

London [England]: Printed for Crosby and Letterman, Stationer's Court; near Paternoster Row; for Mundell & Son, **Edinburgh [Scotland]**; and for J. Mundell, College, **Glasgow [Scotland]**, 1799.
8vo (22 cm.): xvi, 373 p. + map and advertisements.
ESTC n17460.

142.6 ——.

His account, including direct speech, printed on p. 126 in vol. II of Bryan Edwards, *The History, Civil and Commercial, of the British Colonies in the West Indies. Third Edition, with considerable additions.*

London [England]: Printed for John Stockdale, Piccadilly, 1801. Tpv: Printed by Luke Hansard, Great Turnstile, Lincoln's-Inn Fields.
3 vols., 4to (28 cm.).
https://babel.hathitrust.org/cgi/pt?id=aeu.ark:/13960/t5t73771p;view=1up;seq=146
https://archive.org/details/historycivilcomm04edwa/page/126/mode/1up

142.7 ——. [French translation by François Soulès of 142.6]

Loose translation from 142.6 on p. 243 in Bryan Edwards, *Histoire civile et commerciale des Colonies Anglaises dans les Indes Occidentales.*

Paris [France]: Dentu, Imprimere-Libraire, Palais de Tribunat, galeries de bois, no. 240, An IX (**1801**).
8vo (20 cm.): viii, 490 p., folding map.
https://babel.hathitrust.org/cgi/pt?id=aeu.ark:/13960/t1qf9b-m34&view=1up&seq=266
Cf. Sabin 21902.

142.8 ——.

His account, including direct speech, printed on p. 315 in vol. II of Bryan Edwards, *The History, Civil and Commercial, of the British Colonies in the West Indies…. To which is added a general description of the Bahama Islands, by Daniel M'Kinnon, Esq.*

Philadelphia [Pennsylvania, U.S.A.]: Printed and sold by James Humphreys, At the Corner of Second and Walnut-Streets, **1806.**
4 vols. (printed 1805–1806), 8vo (22 cm.).
https://babel.hathitrust.org/cgi/pt?id=nyp.33433081700688&view=1up&seq=323
https://www.biodiversitylibrary.org/item/271526#page/321/mode/1up

142.9 ——.

His account, including direct speech, printed on p. 126 in vol. II of Bryan Edwards, *The History, Civil and Commercial, of the British Colonies in the West Indies. Fourth Edition, with considerable additions.*

London [England]: Printed for John Stockdale, Piccadilly, **1807.** Tpv: T. Gillet, Printer, Wild-Court, Lincoln's-Inn-Fields.
3 vols., 8vo (22 cm.).
https://babel.hathitrust.org/cgi/pt?id=aeu.ark:/13960/t5v70g-z34&view=1up&seq=146

142.10 ——.

His account, including direct speech, printed on p. 315 in vol. II of Bryan Edwards, *The History, Civil and Commercial, of the British Colonies in the West Indies…. To which is added a general description of the Bahama Islands, by Daniel M'Kinnon, Esq.*

Philadelphia [Pennsylvania, U.S.A.]: Levis & Weaver, **1810.**
4 vols., 8vo (22 cm.).
Shaw & Shoemaker 20035.

142.11 ——.

His account, including direct speech, printed on p. 126 in vol. II of Bryan Edwards, *The History, Civil and Commercial, of the British Colonies in the West Indies… With a continuation to the present time. Fifth Edition.*

London [England]: Printed by T. Miller, Noble Street, Cheapside; for G. and W. B. Whittaker; W. H. Reid; J. Nunn; J. M. Richardson; J. Cuthell; T. Boone; T. MacLean; T. and J. Allman; C. Brown; W. Mason; Lackington and Co.; Rodwell and Martin; Oliver and Boyd, **Edinburgh [Scotland];** and Johnston and Deas, **Dublin [Ireland],** 1818–1819.
5 vols., 8vo (21 cm.), and atlas.
https://babel.hathitrust.org/cgi/pt?id=mdp.39015011562678&view=1up&seq=140

142.12 ——. [Photomechanical reprint of 142.11]

His account, including direct speech, printed on p. 126 in vol. II of Bryan Edwards, *The History, Civil and Commercial, of the British Colonies in the West Indies… With a continuation to the present time. Fifth Edition* (1818–1819) with imprint:

New York [New York, U.S.A.]: AMS Press, **1966.**
5 vols., 8vo (23 cm.).

142.13 ——. [Photomechanical reprint of 142.2 (Dublin, 1793)]

His account, including direct speech, printed on p. 98 in vol. II of Bryan Edwards, *The History, Civil and Commercial, of the British Colonies in the West Indies.*

New York [New York, U.S.A.]: Arno Press, **1972.**
2 vols., 8vo (23 cm.).

143.1 Kwamena = Quamina (ca. 1775–)

His account printed on p. 105 in vol. II of Bryan Edwards, *The History, Civil and Commercial, of the British Colonies in the West Indies.*

London [England]: Printed for John Stockdale, MDCCXCIII [**1793**].
2 vols., 4to (28 cm.).
ESTC t137074. (Note that ESTC t194531 is the publisher's ephemeral four-page 8vo post-publication advertisement of this work's availability for 2 pounds, 12 shillings, and 6 pence per set.)

https://babel.hathitrust.org/cgi/pt?id=mdp.39015021776888;view=1up;seq=112 [see first 143.2].

¶ **Born into slavery, Kwamena and his brother Yao (Akan day names for Saturday and Thursday) (q.v. 142.1) came from the**

143.1 Kwamena

Gold Coast (modern Ghana – see Map 5). To pay a debt, their owner sold both brothers to a slave ship's captain, who took them to Jamaica in the Caribbean (Map 13).

143.2 ——.

His account printed on p. 98 in vol. II of Bryan Edwards, *The History, Civil and Commercial, of the British Colonies in the West Indies.*

Dublin [Ireland]: Luke White, M.DCC.XCIII [1793].
2 vols., 8vo (21.5 cm.).
https://babel.hathitrust.org/cgi/pt?id=mdp.39015021776888;
    view=1up;seq=112
https://ecda.northeastern.edu/item/neu:m042hj99v/
ESTC t136755.

143.3 ——.

His account printed on p. 105 in vol. II of Bryan Edwards, *The History, Civil and Commercial, of the British Colonies in the West Indies.* **The Second Edition.**

London [England]: Printed for John Stockdale, Piccadilly, M.DCC.XCIV [1794].
2 vols., 4to (28 cm.).
ESTC t136756.

143.4 ——.

His account printed on p. 177 of *The History, Civil and Commercial, of the British Colonies in the West Indies. To which is added, an historical survey of the French colony in the island of St. Domingo. Abridged from The History written by Bryan Edwards, Esq.*

London [England]: Printed for B. Crosby, Stationer's Court; for Mundell & Son, Edinburgh [Scotland]; and for J. Mundell, College, Glasgow [Scotland], 1798.
8vo (22 cm.): xvi, 373 p. + map and advertisements.
ESTC t137075.

143.5 ——.

His account printed on p. 177 of *The History, Civil and Commercial, of the British Colonies in the West Indies. To which is added, an historical survey of the French colony in the island of St. Domingo. Abridged from The History written by Bryan Edwards, Esq.*

London [England]: Printed for Crosby and Letterman, Stationer's Court;, near Paternoster Row; for Mundell & Son, Edinburgh [Scotland]; and for J. Mundell, College, Glasgow [Scotland], 1799.
8vo (22 cm.): xvi, 373 p. + map and advertisements.
ESTC n17460.

143.6 ——.

His account printed on p. 126 in vol. II of Bryan Edwards, *The History, Civil and Commercial, of the British Colonies in the West Indies.* **Third Edition,** *with considerable additions.*

London [England]: Printed for John Stockdale, Piccadilly, 1801. Tpv: Printed by Luke Hansard, Great Turnstile, Lincoln's-Inn Fields.
3 vols., 4to (28 cm.).
https://babel.hathitrust.org/cgi/pt?id=aeu.ark:/13960/
    t5t73771p;view=1up;seq=146
https://archive.org/details/historycivilcomm04edwa/page/
    126/mode/1up

143.7 ——. **[French translation by François Soulès of 143.6]**

Loose translation from 141.6 on p. 243 in Bryan Edwards, *Histoire civile et commerciale des Colonies Anglaises dans les Indes Occidentales.*

Paris [France]: Dentu, Imprimere-Libraire, Palais de Tribunat, galeries de bois, no. 240, An IX (**1801**).
8vo (20 cm.): viii, 490 p., folding map.
https://babel.hathitrust.org/cgi/pt?id=aeu.ark:/13960/t1qf9b-
    m34&view=1up&seq=266
Cf. Sabin 21902.

143.8 ——.

His account printed on p. 315 in vol. II of Bryan Edwards, *The History, Civil and Commercial, of the British Colonies in the West Indies.... To which is added a general description of the Bahama Islands, by Daniel M'Kinnon, Esq.*

Philadelphia [Pennsylvania, U.S.A.]: Printed and sold by James Humphreys, At the Corner of Second and Walnut-Streets, **1806.**
4 vols. (printed 1805–1806), 8vo (22 cm.).
https://babel.hathitrust.org/cgi/pt?id=nyp.33433081700688
    &view=1up&seq=323
https://www.biodiversitylibrary.org/item/271526#page/321/
    mode/1up

143.9 ——.

His account printed on p. 126 in vol. II of Bryan Edwards, *The History, Civil and Commercial, of the British Colonies in the West Indies.* **Fourth Edition,** *with considerable additions.*

London [England]: Printed for John Stockdale, Piccadilly, **1807.** Tpv: T. Gillet, Printer, Wild-Court, Lincoln's-Inn-Fields.
3 vols., 8vo (22 cm.).
https://babel.hathitrust.org/cgi/pt?id=aeu.ark:/13960/t5v70g-
    z34&view=1up&seq=146

143.10 ——.

His account printed on p. 315 in vol. II of Bryan Edwards, *The History, Civil and Commercial, of the British Colonies in the West Indies…. To which is added a general description of the Bahama Islands, by Daniel M'Kinnon, Esq.*

Philadelphia [Pennsylvania, U.S.A.]: Levis & Weaver, **1810**.
4 vols., 8vo (22 cm.).
Shaw & Shoemaker 20035.

143.11 ——.

His account printed on p. 126 in vol. II of Bryan Edwards, *The History, Civil and Commercial, of the British Colonies in the West Indies… With a continuation to the present time.* **Fifth Edition.**

London [England]: Printed by T. Miller, Noble Street, Cheapside; for G. and W. B. Whittaker; W. H. Reid; J. Nunn; J. M. Richardson; J. Cuthell; T. Boone; T. MacLean; T. and J. Allman; C. Brown; W. Mason; Lackington and Co.; Rodwell and Martin; Oliver and Boyd, **Edinburgh [Scotland]**; and Johnston and Deas, **Dublin [Ireland]**, **1818–1819**.
5 vols., 8vo (21 cm.), and atlas.
https://babel.hathitrust.org/cgi/pt?id=mdp.39015011562678&view=1up&seq=140

143.12 ——. [Photomechanical reprint of 143.11]

His account printed on p. 126 in vol. II of Bryan Edwards, *The History, Civil and Commercial, of the British Colonies in the West Indies… With a continuation to the present time.* **Fifth Edition** (1818–1819) with imprint:

New York [New York, U.S.A.]: AMS Press, **1966**.
5 vols., 8vo (23 cm.).

143.13 ——. [Photomechanical reprint of 143.2 (Dublin, 1793)]

His account printed on p. 98 in vol. II of Bryan Edwards, *The History, Civil and Commercial, of the British Colonies in the West Indies.*

New York [New York, U.S.A.]: Arno Press, **1972**.
2 vols., 8vo (23 cm.).

144.1 Yamousa (ca. 1777–)

His account, including direct speech, printed on p. 105 in vol. II of Bryan Edwards, *The History, Civil and Commercial, of the British Colonies in the West Indies.*

London [England]: Printed for John Stockdale, MDCCXCIII [1793].
2 vols., 4to (28 cm.).

ESTC t137074. (Note that ESTC t194531 is the publisher's ephemeral four-page 8vo post-publication advertisement of this work's availability for 2 pounds, 12 shillings, and 6 pence per set.)

¶ When interviewed by Bryan Edwards, Yamousa was identified as a Chamba (Kassenti Tchamba, Chamba, or Tjamba, hereafter Tchamba, possibly in modern Togo—see Map 5) youth of about sixteen, which probably meant he was Konkomba or from another Gur ethnic group north of Asante (Akan people, modern Ghana), inland from the Gold Coast. He was enslaved to a person named Soubadou, who sold him and a cow for a gun, a quantity of other goods, and some brandy. Thereafter, Yamousa was taken on a slave ship to Jamaica in the Caribbean (Map 13).

144.2 ——.

His account, including direct speech, printed on p. 98 in vol. II of Bryan Edwards, *The History, Civil and Commercial, of the British Colonies in the West Indies.*

Dublin [Ireland]: Luke White, M.DCC.XCIII [1793].
2 vols., 8vo (21.5 cm.).
https://babel.hathitrust.org/cgi/pt?id=mdp.39015021776888;view=1up;seq=112
https://ecda.northeastern.edu/item/neu/m042hk01p/
ESTC t136755.

144.3 ——.

His account, including direct speech, printed on p. 105 in vol. II of Bryan Edwards, *The History, Civil and Commercial, of the British Colonies in the West Indies.* **The Second Edition.**

London [England]: Printed for John Stockdale, Piccadilly, M.DCC.XCIV [1794].
2 vols., 4to (28 cm.).
ESTC t136756.

144.4 ——.

His account printed on p. 177 of *The History, Civil and Commercial, of the British Colonies in the West Indies. To which is added, an historical survey of the French colony in the island of St. Domingo. Abridged from The History written by Bryan Edwards, Esq.*

London [England]: Printed for B. Crosby, Stationer's Court; for Mundell & Son, **Edinburgh [Scotland]**; and for J. Mundell, College, **Glasgow [Scotland]**, **1798**.
8vo (22 cm.): xvi, 373 p. + map and advertisements.
ESTC t137075.

https://babel.hathitrust.org/cgi/pt?id=mdp.39015021776888;view=1up;seq=112 [see first of 144.2].

144.5 ———.

His account printed on p. 177 of *The History, Civil and Commercial, of the British Colonies in the West Indies. To which is added, an historical survey of the French colony in the island of St. Domingo. **Abridged from** The History written by Bryan Edwards, Esq.*

London [England]: Printed for Crosby and Letterman, Stationer's Court; near Paternoster Row; for Mundell & Son, **Edinburgh [Scotland]**; and for J. Mundell, College, **Glasgow [Scotland]**, **1799**.
8vo (22 cm.): xvi, 373 p. + map and advertisements.
ESTC n17460.

144.6 ———.

His account, including direct speech, printed on p. 127 in vol. II of Bryan Edwards, *The History, Civil and Commercial, of the British Colonies in the West Indies. **Third Edition**, with considerable additions.*

London [England]: Printed for John Stockdale, Piccadilly, **1801**. Tpv: Printed by Luke Hansard, Great Turnstile, Lincoln's-Inn Fields.
3 vols., 4to (28 cm.).
https://babel.hathitrust.org/cgi/pt?id=aeu.ark:/13960/t5t73771p&view=1up&seq=147
https://archive.org/details/historycivilcomm04edwa/page/127/mode/1up

144.7 ———. [French translation by François Soulès of 144.6]

Loose translation from 144.6 on p. 243 in Bryan Edwards, *Histoire civile et commerciale des Colonies Anglaises dans les Indes Occidentales.*

Paris [France]: Dentu, Imprimere-Libraire, Palais de Tribunat, galeries de bois, no. 240, An IX (**1801**).
8vo (20 cm.): viii, 490 p., folding map.
https://babel.hathitrust.org/cgi/pt?id=aeu.ark:/13960/t1qf9bm34&view=1up&seq=266
Cf. Sabin 21902.

144.8 ———.

His account, including direct speech, printed on p. 315 in vol. II of Bryan Edwards, *The History, Civil and Commercial, of the British Colonies in the West Indies…. To which is added a general description of the Bahama Islands, by Daniel M'Kinnon, Esq.*

Philadelphia [Pennsylvania, U.S.A.]: Printed and sold by James Humphreys, At the Corner of Second and Walnut-Streets, **1806**.
4 vols. (printed 1805–1806), 8vo (22 cm.).
https://babel.hathitrust.org/cgi/pt?id=nyp.33433081700688&view=1up&seq=323
https://www.biodiversitylibrary.org/item/271526#page/321/mode/1up

144.9 ———.

His account, including direct speech, printed on p. 126 in vol. II of Bryan Edwards, *The History, Civil and Commercial, of the British Colonies in the West Indies. **Fourth Edition**, with considerable additions.*

London [England]: Printed for John Stockdale, Piccadilly, **1807**. Tpv: T. Gillet, Printer, Wild-Court, Lincoln's-Inn-Fields.
3 vols., 8vo (22 cm.).
https://babel.hathitrust.org/cgi/pt?id=aeu.ark:/13960/t5v70gz34&view=1up&seq=146

144.10 ———.

His account, including direct speech, printed on p. 315 in vol. II of Bryan Edwards, *The History, Civil and Commercial, of the British Colonies in the West Indies…. To which is added a general description of the Bahama Islands, by Daniel M'Kinnon, Esq.*

Philadelphia [Pennsylvania, U.S.A.]: Levis & Weaver, **1810**.
4 vols., 8vo (22 cm.).
Shaw & Shoemaker 20035.

144.11 ———.

His account, including direct speech, printed on p. 126 in vol. II of Bryan Edwards, *The History, Civil and Commercial, of the British Colonies in the West Indies… With a continuation to the present time. **Fifth Edition**.*

London [England]: Printed by T. Miller, Noble Street, Cheapside; for G. and W. B. Whittaker; W. H. Reid; J. Nunn; J. M. Richardson; J. Cuthell; T. Boone; T. MacLean; T. and J. Allman; C. Brown; W. Mason; Lackington and Co.; Rodwell and Martin; Oliver and Boyd, **Edinburgh [Scotland]**; and Johnston and Deas, **Dublin [Ireland]**, **1818–1819**.
5 vols., 8vo (21 cm.), and atlas.
https://babel.hathitrust.org/cgi/pt?id=mdp.39015011562678&view=1up&seq=140

144.12 ———. [Photomechanical reprint of 144.11]

His account, including direct speech, printed on p. 126 in vol. II of Bryan Edwards, *The History, Civil and Commercial, of the British Colonies in the West Indies… With a continuation to the present time. **Fifth Edition** (1818–1819) with imprint:*

New York [New York, U.S.A.]: AMS Press, **1966**.
5 vols., 8vo (23 cm.).

144.13 ———. [Photomechanical reprint of 144.2 (Dublin, 1793)]

His account, including direct speech, printed on p. 98 in vol. II of Bryan Edwards, *The History, Civil and Commercial, of the British Colonies in the West Indies.*

New York [New York, U.S.A.]: Arno Press, **1972**.
2 vols., 8vo (23 cm.).

1794

145.1 Unnamed man from the Sierra Leone River (ca. 1767–)

Story of an African-born man told to British official and printed on pp. 79–80 in *Substance of the Report Delivered by the Court of Directors of the Sierra Leone Company, to the General Court of Proprietors, On Thursday the 27th of March 1794.*

https://babel.hathitrust.org/cgi/pt?id=nnc1.0036706159&view=1up&seq=83 [see 145.1].

London [England]: Printed by James Phillips, George Yard, Lombard Street, M.DCC.XCIV [1794].
8vo (19 cm.): 175, [1] p., folding map.
ESTC t131475.

¶ During his boyhood this man was kidnapped by the crew of an American ship near the future location of Freetown on the Sierra Leone River (ca. 1775–76?) and forcibly taken to British North America (see Maps 4 and 16). He later escaped to British forces during the American Revolutionary War and after the British defeat was evacuated to Nova Scotia, Canada. "[A]bout fifteen years" later (ca. 1792?) he returned to Freetown with other Nova Scotian blacks who had fled with the British defeat. He recognized the beach on which he had been seized in boyhood. In his nearby "native town," his elderly mother, a Temne (modern Sierra Leone) woman, identified him and they were reunited.

146.1 Unnamed woman sold to pay debts

Her story as told to a British official printed on p. 89 in *Substance of the Report Delivered by the Court of Directors of the Sierra Leone Company, to the General Court of Proprietors, On Thursday the 27th of March 1794.*

https://babel.hathitrust.org/cgi/pt?id=nnc1.0036706159&view=1up&seq=93 [see 146.1].

London [England]: Printed by James Phillips, George Yard, Lombard Street, M.DCC.XCIV [1794].
8vo (19 cm.): 175, [1] p., folding map.
ESTC t131475.

¶ As this woman told a British official connected to Sierra Leone, she had been sold by her husband on the Bullom Shore (modern Sierra Leone—see Map 4) to pay his debts, then, without her child, forced aboard a slave ship with 250 Africans at Bunce Island in the Sierra Leone River (a major slave embarkation point).

147.1 Unnamed nursing woman

Story of an African-born woman told to British official and printed on pp. 89–90 in *Substance of the Report Delivered by the Court of Directors of the Sierra Leone Company, to the General Court of Proprietors, On Thursday the 27th of March 1794.*

https://babel.hathitrust.org/cgi/pt?id=nnc1.0036706159&view=1up&seq=93 [see 147.1].

London [England]: Printed by James Phillips, George Yard, Lombard Street, M.DCC.XCIV [1794].
8vo (19 cm.): 175, [1] p., folding map.
ESTC t131475.

¶ A British official boarded a slave ship at Bunce Island in the Sierra Leone River (see Map 4) and found this woman on deck crying. After he asked why she was crying, she pointed to milk flowing from her breasts and said her baby had been torn from her arms. The captain confirmed this and said she had been taken from a nearby town. She said she had been sold "on account of her being saucy to the queen or head-woman in it."

148.1 Jean-Baptiste Belley (ca. 1746–1805)

See especially Belley's brief declaration of his African origins on p. 5 of *Le Bout d'Oreille des Colons, ou Le Systéme de l'Hôtel de Massiac, mis au jour par Gouli. Belley, Député Noir de Saint-Domingue, a ses Colleagues.*

[Colophon: **Paris, France:**] De l'Imprimerie de Pain, Passage Honore [**1794?**].
8vo (26 cm.): 8 p.

Full text: https://huskiecommons.lib.niu.edu/history-500african-voices/112/ [see 148.1].

Sole located exemplar at Howard University Library (Founders Library shelf mark 253022 Dominican Republic M972.93 I B41), Washington, DC. *The compilers thank Joellen El Bashir, Curator, Manuscript Division, Moorland-Spingarn Research Center, Founders Library, Howard University library, for her assistance in locating this rare leaflet.*

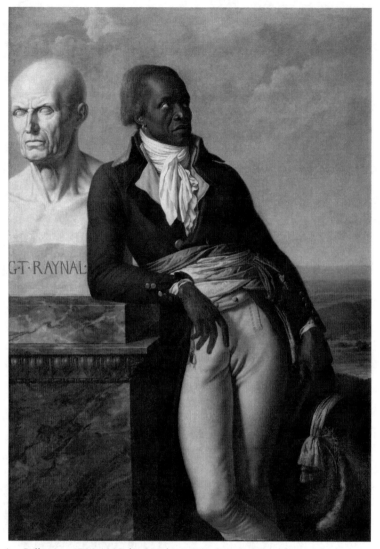

Figure 11: Portrait of Jean-Baptiste Belley (ca. 1746–1805) by Girodet (1798). Born in West Africa and taken on a slave ship to Sainte-Domingue, in the 1790s he became a military and political leader after the revolution began on that island and while in Paris fought to prevent the reestablishment of slavery on the island.

Source: Oil on canvas, by Girodet de Roucy-Trioson and Anne-Louis alias Girodet-Trioson (1797), MV 4616, Palace of Versailles, France. © RMN-Grand Palais / Art Resource, NY.

¶ Born in an unknown place in West Africa, Belley was a small child when transported enslaved to Saint-Domingue in the Caribbean (see Map 11), where he was freed in the 1760s. After the Saint-Domingue revolution began, he pursued military and political careers. From 1794 he represented Saint-Domingue in the National Convention in Paris (Map 7). In the present Convention speech (148.1) opposing France's re-institution of colonial slavery he mentions his African origins. He cooperated with the French in LeClerc's 1802 expedition against Saint-Domingue. Betrayed by LeClerc, Belley was arrested when the expedition reached Saint-Domingue, then deported to Brittany. For more on Belley see Christine Levecq, *Black Cosmopolitans: Race, Religion, and Republicanism in* *an Age of Revolution* (Charlottesville: University of Virginia Press, 2019), 75–159.

148.2 ———.

Partial English translation of 148.1 printed under heading "The True Colors of the Planters, or the System of the Hotel Massiac, Exposed by Gouli" on pp. 144–147 in *Slave Revolution in the Caribbean, 1789–1804: A Brief History with Documents,* edited by Laurent Dubois and John D. Garrigus.

Boston [Massachusetts, U.S.A.]: Bedford/St. Martin's, 2006. 8vo (22 cm.): xii, 212 p., illus., maps.

148.3 ——.

Partial English translation of 148.1 printed under heading "The True Colors of the Planters, or the System of the Hotel Massiac, Exposed by Gouli" on pp. 144–147 in *Slave Revolution in the Caribbean, 1789–1804: A Brief History with Documents,* edited by Laurent Dubois and John D. Garrigus.

New York [New York, U.S.A.]: Palgrave Macmillan, 2006. 8vo (22 cm.): xii, 212 p., illus., maps.

148.4 ——.

Partial English translation of 148.1 printed under heading "The True Colors of the Planters, or the System of the Hotel Massiac, Exposed by Gouli" on pp. 137–139 in *Slave Revolution in the Caribbean, 1789–1804: A Brief History with Documents,* edited by Laurent Dubois and John D. Garrigus. **Second edition.**

Boston [Massachusetts, U.S.A.]: Bedford/St. Martin's | Macmillan Learning, 2017. 8vo (22 cm.): xvii, 206 p., illus., maps.

Additional publications by Belley

+148-A.1 ——.

Convention Nationale. Lettre écrite de New-York par les Députés de Saint-Domingue [i.e., Duffay, Mils, and Belley]

a leurs commettans. 14 December 1793. Imprimée par ordre de la Convention Nationale ([Paris, France]: Imprimerie Nationale, [1794?]), 8vo, 20 p., including on pp. 19–20 (20 mis-paged '10') "Lettre de Belley, Député à la Convention Nationale, à ses frères. New York, 14 December 1793."

https://archive.org/details/lettrecriteden2756sain/page/n1

+148-B.1 ——.

Belley, de Saint-Domingue Représentant due Peuple, à ses collègues ([Paris, France:] Imprimerie de Pain, Passage-Honoré, [1794]), 8vo: 7 p. Signed in type on p. 7: *A Paris, le 6 fructidor l'an second de la république* [23 August 1794], *une et indivisible.* BELLEY.

https://gallica.bnf.fr/ark:/12148/bpt6k5785251f/f2.image. texteImage

+148-B.2 ——.

Extracts from +148-B.1 printed in italics within response by P. F. Page and A. J. Brulley entitled *A la Convention Nationale: Réponse de Page et Brulley, commissaires de St.-Domingue, députés près la Convention Nationale, aux calomnies qu'on a fait signer au citoyen Belley* ([Paris, France]: De l'imprimerie de Laurens ainé, rue d'Argenteuil, no. 211, [1794?]), 8vo: 34 p.

https://archive.org/details/laconventionnati2799page/page/n3

1795

149.1 Peter Panah (ca. 1770–1790)

His life story printed with shoulder-note heading "Account of a kidnapped African prince, who lately died in England" on pp. 269–270 of Part 2 (dated 1795) in Carl Bernhard Wadström, *An Essay on Colonization, particularly applied to the West Coast of Africa, with Some Free Thoughts on Cultivation and Commerce; and Brief Descriptions of the Colonies already formed, or attempted, in Africa, including those of Sierra Leona and Bulama.*

London [England]: Printed for the Author, by Darton & Harvey, Grace Church Street; and sold by G. Nicol, No. 58, Pall-Mall; W. Faden, Corner of St. Martin's Lane, Strand; J. Stockdale, No. 199, Piccadilly; J. Edwards, No. 78, Pall-Mall; E. & J. Egerton, No. 32, Charing-Cross; J. Debrett, No. 179, Piccadilly; J. Johnson, No. 72, St.-Paul's Church-yard; and C. Dilly, No. 22, Poultry, MDCCXCIV [1794–1795].

http://www.sierra-leone.org/Books/An_essay_on_colonization_particularly_ap.pdf [see 149.1].

2 parts in one vol., 4to (28 cm): [8], iv, 196, [2]; [2], 2, 363, [25] p., plates, table, maps. **Includes list of subscribers** at end of Part 2.
ESTC t96523; FN 000454.

¶ Peter Panah was the son of the Gola leader Zolu Duma (called King Peter by the English) of Mesurado (Cape Mesurado, in modern Monrovia, Liberia—see Map 3). According to Carl Wadström, Zolu Duma had—very unusually—been educated at Liverpool, England. From Mesurado Peter Panah was kidnapped and taken on an English slave ship (commanded by Captain Fraser) to Sierra Leone (Map 4), where he was sold to "a Capt. Cambeby" (perhaps a typographical error for Cambell or Campbell?), who forced him aboard a ship that sailed to Grenada in the Caribbean (Map 11). There Panah's fellow enslaved countrymen recognized him as the king of Mesurado's son (a fact "proved by the mark he bore on his breast, which is inscribed on all the king's children"). For this reason a mulatto dealer named Johnson took Panah to England (Map 8) to entice people there to redeem him for cash, supposedly so that he might be returned to Sierra Leone. Wadström learned that if Panah were thus redeemed, he would nonetheless be returned to the West Indies and again sold into slavery.

On May 6, 1788, Wadström therefore purchased Panah's freedom for £20 sterling and apparently sent him to be educated "in the first rudiments of Christianity" at James Dempster's Academy (Baron House) in Mitcham, Surrey, England. He was baptized on December 25, 1788 (perhaps a typographical error for 1789). In 1789 the artist Carl Frederick von Breda painted in oils a double portrait of Panah and Wadström and exhibited it at the Royal Academy, London, England. Panah died in Wadström's English house in October 1790, aged (Wadström thought) eighteen or twenty. A digital reproduction of von Breda's 1789 double portrait (original now in the Nordiska Museet/Nordic Museum, Stockholm, Sweden) is available here: https://digitaltmuseum.se/011023459953/tavla. In June 1792 this portrait was reproduced as an engraving published in London, England; a digital reproduction of it is available here: http://interactive.britishart.yale.edu/slavery-and-portraiture/335/the-benevolent-effects-of-abolishing-slavery-or-the-planter-instructing-his-negro

149.2 ——. [Photomechanical reprint of 149.1]

His life story printed under shoulder-note heading "Account of a kidnapped African prince, who lately died in England" on pp. 269–270 of Part 2 (dated 1795) in photomechanical reprint of C. B. Wadström, *An Essay on Colonization* (London: Printed for the Author, 1794–1795) with imprint:

Newton Abbot, Devon [England]: David & Charles Reprints, [1968].
2 parts in one, 4to (29 cm.): [8], iv, 196, [2]; [2], 2, 363, [25] p., plates, table, maps.

149.3 ——. [Photomechanical reprint of 149.1]

His life story printed under shoulder-note heading "Account of a kidnapped African prince, who lately died in England" on pp. 269–270 of Part 2 (dated 1795) in photomechanical reprint of C. B. Wadström, *An Essay on Colonization* (London: Printed for the Author, 1794–1795) with imprint:

New York [New York, U.S.A.]: Augustus M. Kelly, **1968**.
2 parts in one, 4to (28 cm.): iv, 196; 363 p. (+ plates, table, maps in pocket).

1796

150.1 Stephanus (–1796)

Account included on p. 134 within "Bambey Diarium 1796," printed on pp. 129–135 in section 3 under the date 6 June 1796 of vol. 3, Part 3.3 (published in 1917) of *Die Mission der Brüdergemeine in Suriname und Berbice im achtzehnten Jahrhundert. Eine Missionsgeschichte hauptsächlich in Auszügen aus Briefen und Originalberichten*, edited by Fritz Staehelin.

Full text: https://huskiecommons.lib.niu.edu/history-500africanvoices/113/ [see 150.1].

Herrnhut [Saxony, Germany]: Verlag C. Kersten in **Paramaribo** [Suriname] im Kommission bei der Missionsbuchhandlung in Herrnhut und für den Buchhandel bei der Unitätsbuchhandlung in **Gnadau** [Saxony, Germany], [1913–1917 (*sic*)].
3 vols., 8vo (21.5 cm.).

¶ Ca. 1746 Stephanus was taken from an unknown location in West Africa on a slave ship to the Dutch South American colony of Suriname (see Map 10) and sold. During the wars with the Saamaka Maroons, he served in the supply lines to Dutch colonial troops, until he ran off and joined the Maroons. In the treaty negotiations that ended the war, the colonial government recognized the freedom of Stephanus and all other Maroons. His wife died in the 1770s. Ca. 1780, shortly

after the Saamakas chose to welcome Moravian missionaries into their settlement at Bambey on the upper Suriname River, Stephanus joined that mostly German missionary group. He was eventually baptized, accepted for communion, and participated in their religious conferences. He told his life story to a missionary shortly before he died in Bambey in 1796.

150.2 ——.

Account printed on p. 134 within "Bambey Diarium 1796," printed on pp. 129–135 of vol. 3, Part 3.3 in photomechanical reprint of 142.1 with imprint:

Hildesheim [Saxony, Germany], **Zurich** [Switzerland]: Georg Olms Verlag, **1997**.
2 vols., 8vo (22 cm.).

151.1 Aloon Kinson (1714– ca. 1798) = Jean Jasmin Thoumazeau

Account printed in vol. 1 of Médéric Louis Elie Moreau-Saint-Méry, *Description topographique, physique, Civile, Politique et Historique de la partie française de L'isle Saint-Domingue, avec des Obser-*

https://archive.org/details/description-topog00more/page/416/mode/2up?q=Kinson [see first of 151.3].

vations générales sur sa Population, sur le Caractère, et les Mœurs de se divers Habitans; sur son Climat, sa Culture, ses Productions, son Administration, etc. etc.

Philadelphia [Pennsylvania, U.S.A.]: Imprimé chez l'Auteur, **1796.**
2 vols., 8vo (26 cm.). **Includes a list of subscribers.**
Evans 30817; ESTC w30752.

¶ Kinson was born on the Gold Coast (modern Ghana—see Map 5) in 1714 and in the 1730s was taken in the slave trade to the French colony of Saint-Domingue in the Caribbean (Map 11). There he learned masonry from his owner, was baptized in 1736 (taking the name Jasmin) and earned his freedom in 1741. He married a free woman from Ouidah in the Bight of Benin (modern Benin) and prospered as a mason in Cap Hatien, where he operated a charity hospice for poor people of color for over forty years. In 1789 Kinson was named the hospice's chief administrator for life and received a medal for his contributions. The Philadelphia Society at Cap Hatien and the Agrarian Society in Paris, France also awarded him medals.

151.2————. **[English translation of 151.1 by William Cobbett]**
Account printed in vol. 1 of Médéric Louis Elie Moreau-Saint-Méry, *A Topographical and Political Description of the Spanish Part of Saint-Domingo containing, General Observations on the Climate, Population, and Productions; on the Character and Manners of the Inhabitants; with an Account of the Several Branches of the Government: to which is prefixed, A New, Correct, and Elegant Map of the whole Island... Translated from the French by William Cobbett.*

Philadelphia [Pennsylvania, U.S.A.]: Printed and sold by the Author, Printer and Bookseller, no. 84, South Front-Street, **1796.**
2 vols., 8vo (22 cm.). **Includes a list of subscribers.**
Evans 30818; ESTC w31204.

151.3————.
Account printed on pp. 416–422 in vol. 1 of Médéric Louis Elie Moreau-Saint-Méry, *Description topographique, physique, Civile, Politique et Historique de la partie française de L'isle Saint-Domingue, avec des Observations générales sur sa Population, sur le Caractère, et les Mœurs de se divers Habitans; sur son Climat, sa Culture, ses Productions, son Administration, etc. etc.*

A Philadelphie [i.e., Philadelphia, Pennsylvania, U.S.A.]: Et s'y trouve Chez l'Auteur, au coin de Front & de Callow-Hill streets. **A Paris [France]:** chez Dupont, Libraire, rue de la Loi; et a **Hambourg [Germany]:** chez les principaux Libraires, **1797.**

2 vols., 4to. Vol. 2 (printed in 1798) includes **a list of subscribers.**
Evans 32504 (vol. 1) and 34137 (vol. 2); ESTC w30753.
https://archive.org/details/descriptiontopog00more/page/416/mode/2up?q=Kinson
https://gallica.bnf.fr/ark:/12148/bpt6k111179t/f437.item

151.4————. **[Reprinting of 151.2]**
Account printed in vol. 1 of Médéric Louis Elie Moreau-Saint-Méry, *A Topographical and Political Description of the Spanish Part of Saint-Domingo containing, General Observations on the Climate, Population, and Productions; on the Character and Manners of the Inhabitants; with an Account of the Several Branches of the Government: to which is prefixed, A New, Correct, and Elegant Map of the whole Island... Translated from the French by William Cobbett.*

Boston [Massachusetts, U.S.A.]: Printed for and sold by J. Bumstead, **1808.**
2 vols., 8vo (21 cm.).
Shaw & Shoemaker 15645.

151.5————.
Brief French-language summary account printed on pp. 124–125 in Henri Grégoire, *De la littérature des Nègres, ou, Recherches sur leurs facultés intellectuelles, leurs qualités morales et leur littérature: suivies de notices sur la vie et les ouvrages des Nègres qui se sont distingués dans les sciences, les lettres et les arts.*

Paris [France]: Chez Maradan, Libraire, Rue des Grands-Augustins, No. 9, MD.CCC.VIII [1808].
8vo (20 cm.): xvi, 287, [1].
https://gallica.bnf.fr/ark:/12148/bpt6k844925/f137.item.texteImage.zoom

151.6————. **[English translation of 151.5]**
Brief English-language summary printed on pp. 122–123 in Henri Grégoire, *An Enquiry concerning the Intellectual and Moral Faculties, and Literature of Negroes: followed with an Account of the Life and Works of fifteen Negroes & Mulattoes, distinguished in Science, Literature, and the Arts ...* translated by D. B. Warden.

Brooklyn [New York, U.S.A.]: Printed by Thomas Kirke, **1810.**
8vo (22 cm.): [4], vii (*i.e.*, viii), [1], 10–253, [3] p.
https://archive.org/details/enquiryconcernin00gr/page/122/mode/1up

151.7————.
Biographical summary printed as three numbered paragraphs on pp. 5–6 in *Biographical Sketches and Interesting Anecdotes*

of Persons of Color. To Which Is Added, a Selection of Pieces in Poetry, compiled by A[bigail] Mott.

New York [New York, U.S.A.]: Printed and Sold by Mahlon Day, No. 376, Pearl-street, **1826**.

12mo (18 cm.): iv, [5]-192 p. Preface dated on p. iv: *Hickory Grove* [NY], 11*th mo.* 1825.

http://docsouth.unc.edu/neh/mott26/mott26.html

https://babel.hathitrust.org/cgi/pt?id=hvd.hn3m6e&view=1up&seq=9

Hogg 1467.

151.8——.

Three-paragraph biographical summary printed under heading "Jasmin Thoumazeau" on p. 2 in *Biographical Sketches and Interesting Anecdotes of Persons of Colour*. Compiled by A[bigail] Mott.

York [Yorkshire, England]: Printed and Sold by W. Alexander & Son, Castlegate; sold also by Harvey & Darton, W. Phillips, E. Fry, and W. Darton, **London [England]**; R. Peart [*sic*], **Birmingham [England]**; D. F. Gardiner, **Dublin [Ireland]**, 1826.

12mo (20 cm.): xi, [2], 2–240 p.

https://babel.hathitrust.org/cgi/pt?id=nyp.33433081774204&view=1up&seq=22

151.9——.

Brief English-language summary or translated extract from 151.6 printed under heading "Moral Qualities of the Africans" in *African Repository and Colonial Journal* 1: 112–114, including on p. 114 a paragraph about Thoumazeau (= Kinson).

Washington City [D.C., U.S.A.]: Way & Gideon, Printers, **1826**.

https://babel.hathitrust.org/cgi/pt?id=hvd.hwrcg8;view=1up;seq=126

151.10——.

Three-paragraph biographical summary printed under heading on p. 2 in *Biographical Sketches and Interesting Anecdotes of Persons of Color. To Which Is Added, a Selection of Pieces in Poetry*, compiled by A[bigail] Mott. "Second Edition."

York [Yorkshire, England]: Printed and Sold by W. Alexander & Son; sold also by Harvey and Darton, W. Phillips, E. Fry, and W. Darton, **London [England]**; R. Peart, **Birmingham [England]**; D. F. Gardiner, **Dublin [Ireland]**, 1828.

8vo (19.8 cm.): xi, [1], 252 p.

151.11——.

Biographical summary printed as three numbered paragraphs under heading "Jasmin Thoumazeau" on pp. 5–6 in *Biograph-*

ical Sketches and Interesting Anecdotes of Persons of Color. To Which Is Added, a Selection of Pieces in Poetry, compiled by A[bigail] Mott. "Second Edition, much Enlarged."

New-York [New York, U.S.A.]: Mahlon Day, 374 Pearl-street, **1837**. Tpv: "Note by the publisher. By consent of the Compiler, and at the recommendation of the Trustees of the African Free Schools in New York, (who have liberally patronized the work,) ..."

8vo (19 cm.): 260 p. (of which p. [256] is blank, and pp. 257–260 are table of contents).

https://babel.hathitrust.org/cgi/pt?id=hvd.32044004358602&view=1up&seq=9

151.12——.

Biographical summary printed as two paragraphs (of which only the second is numbered) under heading "Jasmin Thoumazeau" on p. 8 in *Biographical Sketches and Interesting Anecdotes of Persons of Color. To Which Is Added, a Selection of Pieces in Poetry*, compiled by A[bigail] Mott.

New York [New York, U.S.A.]: Stereotyped for and printed by order of the Trustees of the residuary estate of Lindley Murray. M. Day, Printer, 271 Pearl St. **[1839]**. Approximate year of printing (could be slightly later) from "Advertisement," p. [ii].

12mo (19 cm.): vi, [7]-408 p.

https://archive.org/details/biographicalsket00mottrich/page/n4 (incomplete 370-page exemplar).

https://babel.hathitrust.org/cgi/pt?id=loc.ark:/13960/t2q52p-81p&view=1up&seq=3 (complete).

151.13——.

Two-paragraph biographical summary printed under heading "Jasmin Thoumazeau" on p. 460 in Wilson Armistead's compendium *A Tribute for the Negro: Being a Vindication of the Moral Intellectual, and Religious Capabilities of the Colored Portion of Mankind; with Particular Reference to the African Race*.

Manchester [England]: William Irwin; **London [England]:** Charles Gilpin; American Agent: Wm. Harned, Anti-Slavery Office, 61, John Street, **New York [New York, U.S.A.]**; and may be had of H. Longstreath and G.W. Taylor, **Philadelphia [Pennsylvania, U.S.A.]**, **1848**. Tpv: Manchester: Printed by William Irwin, 39, Oldham Street.

8vo (24 cm.): xxxv, 564 p.

https://babel.hathitrust.org/cgi/pt?id=nc01.ark:/13960/t42r4z659;view=1up;seq=13

http://docsouth.unc.edu/neh/armistead/armistead.html

151.14 ——.

Biographical summary printed as two paragraphs (of which only the second is numbered) under heading "Jasmin Thoumazeau" on p. 8 in *Biographical Sketches and Interesting Anecdotes of Persons of Color. To Which Is Added, a Selection of Pieces in Poetry*, compiled by A[bigail] Mott.

New York [New York, U.S.A.]: Stereotyped for and printed by order of the Trustees of the residuary estate of Lindley Murray, **1850.**
8vo (20 cm.): iv, [7]-408 p.

151.15———.

Biographical summary printed as two paragraphs (of which only the second is numbered) under heading "Jasmin Thoumazeau" on p. 8 in *Biographical Sketches and Interesting Anecdotes of Persons of Color. To Which Is Added, a Selection of Pieces in Poetry*, compiled by A[bigail] Mott.

New York [New York, U.S.A.]: Stereotyped for and printed by order of the Trustees of the residuary estate of Lindley Murray. D. Fanshaw, Printer, 35 Ann, corner of Nassau-street, **1854.**
12mo (19 cm.): iv, [7]-408 p.
https://digital.ncdcr.gov/digital/collection/p249901coll37/id/10206

151.16———. [New edition of 151.1]

Account printed on in vol. 1 of Médéric Louis Elie Moreau-Saint-Méry, *Description topographique, physique, civile, politique et historique de la partie française de l'Isle Saint-Domingue*. Nouvelle édition, entièrement rev. et complétée sur le manuscrit suivie d'un index des noms de personnes par Blanche Maurelet Etienne Taillemite.

Paris [France]: Société de l'Histoire des Colonies Françaises, **1958.**
2 vols., 8vo.

151.17———.

Brief French-language summary account printed on pp. 124–125 (first series) in photomechanical reprint of 1808 Paris, France, edition of Henri Grégoire, *De la littérature des Nègres* (151.5) and brief English-language summary printed on p. 122–123 (2nd series) in photomechanical reprint of 1810 Brooklyn, New York, English-language translation of the same work 151.6), the two printed together in one volume with imprint:

Nendeln, Lichtenstein: Kraus Reprint, **1971.**
8vo (22 cm.): 287, 253 p.

151.18———.

Brief French-language summary account printed on pp. 124–125 of reprint of 151.5 (Henri Grégoire, *De la littérature des Nègres* [Paris, 1808]), avec introduction et notes de Jean Lessay.

Paris [France]: Perrin, [**1991**].
8vo (20 cm.): lxxvii, 312 p.

151.19———. [Photomechanical reprint of 151.11]

Biographical summary printed as three numbered paragraphs under heading "Jasmin Thoumazeau" on pp. 5–6 in 有色人に関する伝記的資料 / *Biographical Sketches and Interesting Anecdotes of Persons of Color. To which is added, a Selection of Pieces in Poetry*, compiled by A[bigail] Mott. "Second Edition, much Enlarged."

Tokyo, Japan: 日本図書センター, Nihon Tosho Senta, **2000.**
8vo (27 cm.): 255 p.

151.20———.

Account printed in vol. 1 of Médéric Louis Elie Moreau-Saint-Méry, *Descripción Topográfica, Física, Civil, Política e Histórica de la parte Francesa de la Isla de Santo Domingo*.

Santo Domingo [Dominican Republic]: Archivo General de la Nación, **2017.**
2 vols., 4to (27 cm.). Series: Publicaciones del Archivo General de la Nacion, vols. 205–206.

152.0 Absolom (ca. 1726–1796) = Benjamin

His account included in the manuscript newsletter "Diarium von Niesky, St. Thomas," dated 16 January **1796**, written by a Moravian Brethren missionary serving in Nisky on St. Thomas, West Indies, held in the Unity Archives (Unitätsarchiv), **Herrnhut, Saxony, Germany**. Shelf number: R.15.8.b.10.d. *The editors thank Olaf Nippe of the Unity Archives in Herrnhut for locating this manuscript.*

https://collections.mun.ca/digital/collection/cns_permorv/id/32474/rec/13 [see 152.1].

¶ **Absolom was identified as Mandinka (an ethnic group residing in modern southern Mali, Guinea, and Ivory Coast—see Map 3). His father was a Muslim teacher and instructed him and his brothers. He and his wife were enslaved ca. 1746 and taken to the West Indies. There he instructed many of his countrymen in Islam for many years. Absolom was known for** his African spiritual knowledge and earned money by constructing charms and practicing herbal medicine. By 1768 he was involved with the Moravian mission in the Danish West Indies (see Map 14) but continued Islamic and other African religious practices before being baptized in 1792, when he took the name Benjamin. Thereafter, he continued to practice herbal medicine and denied ever being involved in the "black art." Late in life he took up farming a small plot. He spoke about his life while on his deathbed in 1796. His wife, also in the Moravian congregation, survived him.

152.1———.

His account provided in second person within quotation (explicitly taken "from the diary of Nisky [i.e., a manuscript newsletter written by a Moravian Brethren missionary serving in that town] in St. Thomas," West Indies) in part of a letter *perhaps* written by Christian Ignatius Latrobe printed (without naming Latrobe) under heading "Extract of a letter from

the Secretary of the Society to a Friend" on pp. 167–169 in *Periodical Accounts Relating to the Missions of the Church of the United Brethren Established Among the Heathen*, vol. 2.

London [England]: Printed [by J. Marshall] for the [Moravian] Brethren's Society for the Furtherance of the Gospel, No. 10, Nevil's Court, Fetter Lane, **[1800]**.
8vo (22 cm.): vi, [1], 4–502 p.
ESTC t6011; FN 000132.
https://collections.mun.ca/digital/collection/cns_permorv/id/32474/rec/13

1797

153.0 Ibrahim (ca. 1730–1797) = Abraham = Sambo

Manuscript *Lebenslauf* (Memoir) of Abraham written in German shortly before he died in **1797**, held in the Moravian Archives, **Winston-Salem, North Carolina, U.S.A.**

¶ Ibrahim affirmed in his memoir that he was born ca. 1730 and was a Mandinka from (upper West Africa —see Map 3). Captured in a battle against neighboring peoples and sold to European traders, he was forcibly transported to the French West Indies (Map 11). Several years later he was taken to the British North American colony of Virginia (Map 15) and sold. In 1770 he was taken to the new Moravian community in Salem, North Carolina (the colony abutting Virginia on its south) and sold again. Three years later he ran away but then returned. Thereafter, he began receiving instruction in Christianity and German and was baptized. He married in 1785.

153.1———.

"Memoir of Abraham," translated into English and edited by Erika Huber from the German-language manuscript (Moravian Archives, Winston-Salem, North Carolina), and printed on pp. 309–11 in Jon F. Sensbach, *A Separate Canaan: The Making of an Afro-Moravian World in North Carolina, 1763–1840*.

Chapel Hill [North Carolina, U.S.A.]: University of North Carolina Press, **1998**.
8vo (25 cm.): xxiii, 342 p.

154.0 Gumbu Smart

Account of his life written under the date **1797** in Zachary Macaulay's manuscript Journal, which is among the Zachary Macaulay Papers at the Huntington Library, **San Marino, California, U.S.A.**

Full text: https://huskiecommons.lib.niu.edu/history-500african-voices/282/ [see 153.1].

Note: URL and QR code for this entry unavailable. See below for a full text of the account..

¶ Smart was a native of Rokel, a town in the Loko country, on the Rokel River, a tributary of the Sierra Leone River (modern Sierra Leone—see Map 4). He was enslaved and sold to Europeans, but on the day he was to be forced aboard a slave ship on Bunce Island he escaped. Thereafter, he remained in the area and worked first as a boatman, then as a factor for his owner's trading interests. He acquired a large number of slaves but refused to transport them to Bunce Island. While participating in the slave trade, but resisting Europeans working in the *transatlantic* trade, he prospered, gained power locally, and maintained a large family (including thirty wives).

154.1———.

Account of his life printed on pp. 107–108 in the documents collection entitled *Sierra Leone Inheritance*, edited by Christopher Fyfe.

London [England]: Oxford University Press, **[1964]**.
8vo (22 cm.): 352 p., illus., maps. Series: West African History Series.
FN 00012.

Full text of Gumbo Smart's account from 154.1:
"3rd June 1797....This Smart I have formerly told you had been a slave on Bance Island. He is a native of the Loko Country which lies three days' journey or more beyond Rokelle. He had been intended for a ship bound for the West Indies, but on the day the slaves were being put on board, he [108] had concealed himself and escaped for that time. In the meantime he was employed in boats, and showing much acuteness and fidelity he was retained on the island. That is, Rokel town, up the Rokel River; Smart's own town was Rokon, higher up He grew in favour and was at length promoted to be a factor and sent to Rokelle with goods to buy slaves. As this was the key to his native country he had an opportunity of buying numbers of his own Countrymen, none of whom he sent to

the Island, but either kept them as domestics, or exchanged them with their friends for slaves of other nations. By this policy he had made himself powerful and independent. So that even Bance Island whose slave he is, stands in awe of him and

scarce ventures to press him for the Payment of 150 Slaves which owes them. His adherents amount to several Hundreds, exclusive of his own family who consists of no less than thirty wives and eighty children alive."

1798

155.1 Broteer (ca. 1729–1805) = Venture Smith

A Narrative of the Life and Adventures of Venture, a Native of Africa: but Resident above Sixty Years in the United States. Related by himself.

New-London [Connecticut, U.S.A.]: Printed by C. Holt, at the Bee-Office, **1798**. Note: Vincent Carretta (in 155.5, p. 165) locates publisher Holt's first advertisement for Smith's book in the December 26, 1798, issue of Holt's newspaper *The Bee*.

8vo (24 cm.): iv, [1], 6–32 p.

https://docsouth.unc.edu/neh/venture/venture.html
http://www.gutenberg.org/files/10075/10075-h/10075-h.htm
https://archive.org/details/TheLifeAndAdventuresOfVenture/
   010-TheLifeAndAdventuresOfVenture.m4a (audiobook).
Evans 34560; Porter 242; Hogg 1464; ESTC w13703.

¶ Broteer was born ca. 1727 in Dukandarra, an otherwise unidentified place inland from the Gold Coast (modern Ghana—see Map 5). Broteer noted that his father was a prince, but that his mother took him and placed him with a man 140 miles away, where he tended cattle. He was captured in war and sold with others onto a slave ship, which in 1739 took him via Barbados (Map 11) in the West Indies to the British North American colony of Rhode Island (Map 17). There he carded wool in the Rhode Island town of Narragansett for his owner for thirteen years. In 1751 he married an enslaved woman. He subsequently ran away with white indentured servants but was caught and reenslaved. He made money at odd jobs and in 1765 purchased his freedom. He then worked several jobs in Rhode Island and on nearby eastern Long Island (part of the colony—subsequently state—of New York), until he could purchase his wife and children. Thereafter, he prospered while living in the state of Connecticut (north across Long Island Sound from Long Island), where he died in 1805. Major critical appreciations include 155.7 and 155.9. For more on Broteer see James Brewer Stewart (ed.), *Venture Smith and the Business of Freedom* (Amherst: University of Massachusetts Press, 2010).

https://babel. hathitrust.org/ cgi/pt?id=udel.31 741113285052& view=1up&seq=1 [see 155.2].

155.2 ——.

A Narrative of the Life & Adventures of Venture, a Native of Africa; but Resident above Sixty Years in the United States of America. Related by Himself.

New London, Printed in 1798. Reprinted [at **Middletown, Connecticut, U.S.A..** by William D. Starrr ?], A.D. **1835**, and published by a descendant of Venture [perhaps his son Solomon Smith, second of that name, according to 155.7 (Saint and Krimsky, *Making Freedom*), p. 152].

8vo (20 cm.): 24 p. Text proper comprises 155.1 *minus* its concluding 7.5 lines.

https://babel.hathitrust.org/cgi/pt?id=udel.31741113285052
   &view=1up&seq=1

Porter 243.

155.3 ——.

A Narrative of the Life and Adventures of Venture A Native of Africa, But Resident Above Sixty Years in the United States of America. Related by Himself. New London: Printed in 1798. Reprinted A.D. 1835, and published by a descendant of Venture. Revised and republished with traditions by H[enry] M. Seldon, Haddam, Conn., 1896.

Middletown, Connecticut: J. S. Stewart, Printer and Bookbinder, **1897.**

8vo (24 cm.): iv, [5]–41 p. Text proper concludes with 155.1's final 7.5 lines printed within parentheses keyed to note on their omission from "later [i.e., post 1798] editions [*sic*]" etc.

http://docsouth.unc.edu/neh/venture2/venture2.html

155.4 ——.

Complete 1798 text printed on p. 1–34 in *Five Black Lives: The Autobiographies of Venture Smith, James Mars, William Grimes, The Rev. G. W. Offley [and] James L. Smith.* Introduction by Arna Bontemps.

Middletown, Connecticut [U.S.A.]: Wesleyan University Press, **1971.**

8vo (24 cm.): x, 240 p.

155.5 ——.

Complete 1798 text printed with annotations on pp. 369–387 of *Unchained Voices: An Anthology of Black Authors in the*

English-Speaking World of the Eighteenth Century, edited by Vincent Carretta.

[Lexington, Kentucky, U.S.A.]: The University Press of Kentucky, **[1996].**
8vo (24 cm.): xii, 387 p., frontispiece portrait.

155.6 ———.

Complete 1798 text printed, with new introduction and annotations, on pp. 168–185 of *The Norton Anthology of African American Literature*, edited by Henry Louis Gates Jr., Valerie Smith, and Robert G. O'Meally. **Second edition.** (Not included in this anthology's 1997 first edition.)

New York [New York, U.S.A.]: W. W. Norton & Company, **2004.**
8vo (24 cm.): xlvii, 2776 p. + audio disc.

155.7 ———.

Complete photographic facsimile of 155.1 printed on pp. 113–144 in Chandler B. Saint and George A. Krimsky, *Making Freedom: The Extraordinary Life of Venture Smith.*

Middletown, Connecticut [U.S.A.]: Wesleyan University Press, **[2009].**
8vo (24.3 cm.): xiii, [1], 186 p., illus., maps. Foreword by James O. Horton.

155.8 ———. [Photomechanical reprint of 155.1]

A Narrative of the Life and Adventures of Venture, a Native of Africa, but Resident above Sixty Years in the United States. Related by himself.

[Torrington, Connecticut, U.S.A.]: Reprinted by the Beecher House Center for the Study of Equal Rights and the Wilberforce Institute for the Study of Slavery and Emancipation, **2009.**
8vo (23 cm.): iv, [1], 6–32 p. "This publication is part of the project: Documenting Venture Smith." "Special Edition A," limited to one hundred copies.

155.9 ———.

Inexact typographic facsimile of 155.1 printed on pp. 1–32 in *Venture Smith and the Business of Slavery and Freedom*, edited by James Brewer Stewart.

Amherst and **Boston [Massachusetts, U.S.A.]:** University of Massachusetts Press, **2010.**
8vo (24.2 cm.): xvii, 279 p., illus., maps. Foreword by James O. Horton.

155.10 ———.

Excerpts from 155.1 printed on pp. 21–22 in *African Voices of the Global Past, 1500 to the Present*, edited by Trevor R. Getz.

[Boulder, Colorado, U.S.A.]: Westview Press, **[2014].**
8vo (22.7 cm.): xii, 223 p., illus., map.

155.11———.

Complete 1798 text printed with new introduction and annotations in vol. 1 of *The Norton Anthology of African American Literature*, edited by Henry Louis Gates Jr., and Valerie Smith. **Third edition.**

New York [New York, U.S.A.]: W. W. Norton & Co., **2014.**
2 vols., 8vo (24 cm.).

1799

156.0 Ashy

Her account is preserved in the Bodleian Library, Oxford University, **Oxford, England,** as MS. Eng. misc. b.4, ff. 50–51, a **1799** manuscript catalogued as "Two Narratives of slave women, written down by John Ford, Barbados."

¶ Ashy was a Fante (Akan people) from the Gold Coast (modern Ghana —see Map 5). She was taken in the slave trade to the British colony of Barbados in the West Indies (Map 11), where John Ford transcribed her brief account. For more on her and Sibell

https://ecda. northeastern. edu/item/ neu:m04150639/ [see 156.1].

(q.v. 157.0) see Jerome S. Handler, "Life Histories of Enslaved Africans in Barbados," *Slavery & Abolition*, 19:1 (April 1998): 129–141, and Stephanie E. Smallwood, *Saltwater Slavery: A Middle Passage from Africa to American Diaspora* (Cambridge: Harvard University Press, 2007), 202–207.

156.1———.

Account printed under heading "Two Narratives of slave women, written down by John Ford, Barbados" on pp. 133–134 in Jerome S. Handler, "Life Histories of Enslaved Africans in Barbados," *Slavery & Abolition* 19:1: 129–141.

Abingdon, England: Routledge, April **1998.**
https://ecda.northeastern.edu/item/neu:m04150639/

156.2——.

Account printed under heading "Two Narratives of slave women, written down by John Ford, Barbados" on pp. 43–44 in *Major Problems in African American History: Documents and Essays*, edited by Thomas C. Holt and Elsa Barkley Brown.

Boston [Massachusetts, U.S.A.]: Houghton Mifflin, 2000. 2 vols., 8vo (24 cm.).

156.3——. [Second edition of 156.2]

Account printed under heading "Two Narratives of slave women, written down by John Ford, Barbados" on pp. 43–44 in *Major Problems in African American History: Documents and Essays*, edited by Barbara Krauthamer and Chad Williams. **Second edition.**

[Boston, Massachusetts, U.S.A.]: Cengage Learning, 2018. 8vo (23 cm.): xxi, 616 p., illus.

157.0 Sibell

Her account is preserved in the Bodleian Library, Oxford University, **Oxford, England,** as MS. Eng. misc. b.4, ff. 50–51, a **1799** manuscript catalogued as "Two Narratives of slave women, written down by John Ford, Barbados."

¶ Sibell came from "Makerundy" (Makrunde), which could be either Igbo (modern southeastern Nigeria— see Map 5) or a reference not to a place but the Cameroon leader of the same name. Her father was a "great man" and her brother a warrior. She and other family members were kidnapped and carried to a barracoon on the coast, then taken on a slave ship to Barbados, a British colony in the West Indies

https://ecda. northeastern. edu/item/ neu:m04150753/ [see 157.1].

(Map 11). While telling her story of family separation and loss to John Ford, she burst into tears and could not continue. For more on her and Ashy (q.v. 156.0) see Jerome S. Handler, "Life Histories of Enslaved Africans in Barbados," *Slavery & Abolition*, 19:1 (April 1998): 129–141, and Stephanie E. Smallwood, *Saltwater Slavery: A Middle Passage from Africa to American Diaspora* (Cambridge: Harvard University Press, 2007), 202–207.

157.1——.

Account printed under heading "Two Narratives of slave women, written down by John Ford, Barbados" on pp. 132–133 in Jerome S. Handler, "Life Histories of Enslaved Africans in Barbados," *Slavery & Abolition* 19:1: 129–141.

Abingdon, England: Routledge, April 1998. https://ecda.northeastern.edu/item/neu:m04150753/

157.2——.

Account printed under heading "Two Narratives of slave women, written down by John Ford, Barbados" on pp. 43–44 in *Major Problems in African American History: Documents and Essays*, edited by Thomas C. Holt and Elsa Barkley Brown.

Boston [Massachusetts, U.S.A.]: Houghton Mifflin, 2000. 2 vols., 8vo (24 cm.).

157.3——. [Second edition of 157.2]

Account printed under heading "Two Narratives of slave women, written down by John Ford, Barbados" on pp. 43–44 in *Major Problems in African American History: Documents and Essays*, edited by Barbara Krauthamer and Chad Williams. **Second edition.**

[Boston, Massachusetts, U.S.A.]: Cengage Learning, 2018. 8vo (23 cm.): xxi, 616 p., illus.

1803

158.1 Irrouba (ca. 1720?—post 1801)

Life account (beginning "Allons [n.b.] visiter la [n.b.] Centenaire, dit quelqu'un de la compagnie") including autobiographical direct speech printed within quotation marks printed on pp. 268–271 in Pierre-Louis Berquin-Duvallon, *Vue de la Colonie Espagnole du Mississipi* [sic]*, ou des Provinces de Louisianne et Florida*

https://gallica.bnf. fr/ark:/12148/bpt-6k213553v/ f289.item [see 158.1].

occidentale en l'année 1802, par un observateur résident sur les lieux … B[erquin]-Duvallon, éditeur.

Paris [France]: a l'Imprimerie Expéditive, rue St.-Benoit, no. 21, l'an X de la République, et IV du Gouvernement Consulaire, 1803. 8vo (20 cm.): xx, 318 p., plates, folding maps.

¶ Irrouba identified (or was identified) as Senegalese (from Senegal, in West Africa—see Map 3). She was taken to Louisiana (not Jamaica, *pace* Mott, in 158.8 et seq.) on a slave ship (Map 15), probably in the first half of the 18th century, but her account does not indicate the route. There she worked enslaved in her plantation owner's house for several decades, in the process wet nursing and raising two white or mixed-race children, at least one of whom was her own son. This son subsequently inherited his father's property, including his own mother. She lived in the main plantation house until reaching old age, when her son turned her out and forced her to live alone, insufficiently clothed and malnourished, in one of the plantation's ramshackle cabins. In 1802, in extreme old age she received the visit from her son (owner) and Duvallon, an account of which Duvallon published from his contemporaneous notes in 1803.

158.2——. [Second edition of 158.1]

Life account reprinted from 158.1 on pp. 268–271 in Pierre-Louis Berquin-Duvallon, *Vue de la Colonie Espagnole du Mississipi* [sic], *ou des Provinces de Louisianne et Florida occidentale en l'année 1802, par un observateur résident sur les lieux ... B[erquin]-Duvallon, éditeur. 2e edition.*

Paris [France]: Brochot Pere et Ce., **1804**.
8vo (20 cm.): xx, 318 p., plate, folding maps.

158.3——. [Abridged German edition of 158.1]

German translation of Berquin-Duvallon's account of Irrouba (Joruba) printed on pp. 265–267 in *Schilderung von Louisiana. Aus dem Französischen des von Duvallon ... Werkes abgekürzt. Mit einer Einleitung und Zusätzen herausgegeben von Theophil Friedrich Ehrmann.*

Weimar [Thuringia, Germany]: im Verlage des F. S. pr. Landes-Industrie-Comptoirs, **1804**.
8vo (21 cm.): [2], xxviii, 344 p., folding map.

158.4——. [Another French edition of 158.1 (according to Wright Howes B-389)]

Life account reprinted from 158.1 on pp. 268–271 in Pierre-Louis Berquin-Duvallon, *Vue de la Colonie Espagnole du Mississipi* [sic], *ou des Provinces de Louisianne et Florida occidentale en l'année 1802, par un observateur résident sur les lieux ... B[erquin]-Duvallon, éditeur.*

Paris [France], **1805**.
8vo (20 cm.): xx, 318 p., plate, folding maps.

158.5——. [English translation of 158.1]

English-language translation of Berquin-Duvallon's account of Irrouba (beginning "'Let us visit the negroes,' said one of the party") printed on pp. 91–92 in *Travels in Louisiana and the Floridas, in the year, 1802, giving a correct picture of those countries. Translated from the French, with Notes, &c.* By John Davis [1774–1854].

New York [New York, U.S.A.]: Printed by and for I[saac] Riley and Co. No. 1. City Hotel, Broadway, **1806**.

8vo (18 cm.): viii, 181 p., map.
https://babel.hathitrust.org/cgi/pt?id=loc.ark:/13960/t0js9z42f&view=1up&seq=105

158.6——.

Life account (beginning "Allons [n.b.] voir la [n.b.] centenaire, dit quelqu'un de la compagnie") taken from the 1803 edition of Berquin-Duvallon, printed on pp. 111–112 in Henri Grégoire, *De la littérature des Nègres, ou, Recherches sur leurs facultés intellectuelles, leurs qualités morales et leur littérature: suivies de notices sur la vie et les ouvrages des Nègres qui se sont distingués dans les sciences, les lettres et les arts.*

Paris [France]: Chez Maradan, Libraire, Rue des Grands-Augustins, No. 9, MD.CCC.VIII [**1808**].
8vo (20 cm.): xvi, 287, [1].
https://gallica.bnf.fr/ark:/12148/bpt6k844925/f123.item

158.7——.

English-language translation (beginning "'Let us visit the old woman, [n.b.] who has seen her hundredth year,' says some one of the company") of Berquin-Duvallon's account of Irrouba as published in the first edition of Grégoire (158.6) printed on pp. 110–112 in Henri Grégoire, *An Enquiry concerning the Intellectual and Moral Faculties, and Literature of Negroes: followed with an Account of the Life and Works of fifteen Negroes & Mulattoes, distinguished in Science, Literature, and the Arts ...* translated by D. B. Warden.

Brooklyn [New York, U.S.A.]: Printed by Thomas Kirke, Main-Street, **1810**.
8vo (22 cm.): [4], vii (i.e., viii), [1], 10–253, [3] p.
https://archive.org/details/enquiryconcernin00gr/page/110/mode/1up

158.8——.

English translation (slightly altered from 158.7: here beginning "'Let us visit the old woman [n.b.] that has seen her hundredth year,' says one of the company") of Berquin-Duvallon's account of Irrouba printed as three numbered paragraphs under heading "Irrouba. | Duballon [sic] gives the following account of a woman of colour, in Jamaica, in 1802" on pp. 120–121 in *Biographical Sketches and Interesting Anecdotes of Persons of Color. To Which Is Added, a Selection of Pieces in Poetry,* compiled by A[bigail] Mott.

New York [New York, U.S.A.]: Printed and Sold by Mahlon Day, No. 376, Pearl-street, **1826**. Tpv: "Note by the publisher. By consent of the Compiler, and at the recommendation of the Trustees of the African Free Schools in New-York, (who have liberally patronized the work) the pieces in the following compilation have been divided into reading sections, with a view to have the volume introduced into

Schools, as a Class Book. It is hoped this arrangement will be equally agreeable to **Subscribers**, and to those Teachers who may use it in their schools."

12mo (18 cm.): iv, [5]–192 p. Preface dated on p. iv: *Hickory Grove* [NY], 11*th mo.* 1825. *Nota bene*: Mott's erroneous location of Irrouba on Jamaica resulted from a misreading of p. 110 of 156.7 (Warden's 1810 translation of Grégoire).

http://docsouth.unc.edu/neh/mott26/mott26.html

https://babel.hathitrust.org/cgi/pt?id=hvd.hn3m6e&view=1up&seq=124

158.9———.

158.8 (beginning "'Let us visit the old woman that has seen her [n.b.] hundredth year,' says one of the company") printed as three unnumbered paragraphs under heading "Irrouba. | Duballon [*sic*] gives the following account of a woman of colour, in Jamaica, in 1802" on pp. 171–173 in *Biographical Sketches and Interesting Anecdotes of Persons of Colour*, compiled by A[bigail] Mott.

York [Yorkshire, England]: Printed and Sold by W. Alexander & Son, Castlegate; sold also by Harvey & Darton, W. Phillips, E. Fry, and W. Darton, **London [England]**; R. Peart, **Birmingham [England]**; D. F. Gardiner, **Dublin [Ireland]**, 1826.

12mo (20 cm.): xi, [2], 2–240 p.

https://babel.hathitrust.org/cgi/pt?id=nyp.33433081774204&view=1up&seq=191

158.10———.

158.9 (beginning "'Let us visit the old woman that has seen her hundreth [*sic*] year,' says one of the company") printed as three unnumbered paragraphs under heading "Irrouba. | Duballon [*sic*] gives the following account of a woman of colour, in Jamaica, in 1802" on pp. 171–173 in *Biographical Sketches and Interesting Anecdotes of Persons of Color. To Which Is Added, a Selection of Pieces in Poetry*, compiled by A[bigail] Mott. "Second Edition."

York [Yorkshire, England]: Printed and Sold by W. Alexander & Son; sold also by Harvey and Darton, W. Phillips, E. Fry, and W. Darton, **London [England]**; R. Peart, **Birmingham [England]**; D. F. Gardiner, **Dublin [Ireland]**, [probably before September*] 1828.

8vo (19.8 cm.): xi, [1], 252 p. *Note: Judging from this account's Boston, Massachusetts, reprinting on October 10, 1828 (158.11).

158.11———.

English-language translation (beginning "'Let us visit the old woman that has seen her hundreth [*sic*] year,' says one of the company") of Berquin-Duvallon's account of Irrouba professedly reprinted from 158.5 (but actually from 158.10,

witness the repetition of "hundreth," etc.) under the heading "BENEVOLENCE" and subheading "The Poor Negro Woman. | Extract from a View of the Spanish Colony, by Duvallon" on the third page (i.e., p. 79), cols. 2–3 in the October 10, 1828 (vol. 2, no. 20) issue of the weekly magazine *The Youth's Companion*.

Boston [Massachusetts, U.S.A.]: [Nathaniel] Willis & [Asa] Rand, at the Office of the Boston Recorder, No. 22, Congress-Street, October 10, **1828.**

4to.

158.12———.

Reprinting of 158.8 (beginning "'Let us visit the old woman that has seen her hundredth year,' says one of the company") printed as three numbered paragraphs under heading "Irrouba. | Duballon [*sic*] gives the following account of a woman of colour, in Jamaica, in 1802" on pp. 168–169 in *Biographical Sketches and Interesting Anecdotes of Persons of Color. To Which Is Added, a Selection of Pieces in Poetry*, compiled by A[bigail] Mott. "Second Edition, much Enlarged."

New-York [New York, U.S.A.]: Mahlon Day, 374 Pearl-street, **1837.** Tpv: "Note by the publisher. By consent of the Compiler, and at the recommendation of the Trustees of the African Free Schools in New York, (who have liberally patronized the work,) …"

8vo (19 cm.): 260 p. (of which p. [256] is blank, and pp. 257–260 are table of contents).

https://babel.hathitrust.org/cgi/pt?id=hvd.32044004358602&view=1up&seq=172

158.13———.

Another edition 158.8 (beginning "Duballon [*sic*] gives the following account of a woman of colour, in Jamaica, in 1802:- -"'Let us visit the old woman that has seen her hundredth year,' says one of the company") printed as five paragraphs (all but the first numbered) under heading "Irrouba" on pp. 266–268 in *Biographical Sketches and Interesting Anecdotes of Persons of Color. To Which Is Added, a Selection of Pieces in Poetry*, compiled by A[bigail] Mott.

New York [New York, U.S.A.]: Stereotyped for and printed by order of the Trustees of the residuary estate of Lindley Murray. M. Day, Printer, 271 Pearl St. [**1839**]. Approximate year of printing (could have been printed slightly later) from "Advertisement," p. [ii].

12mo (19 cm.): vi, [7]-408 p.

https://archive.org/details/biographicalsket00mottrich/page/265/mode/1up

(incomplete 370-page exemplar).

https://babel.hathitrust.org/cgi/pt?id=loc.ark:/13960/t2q52p-81p&view=1up&seq=268 (complete).

158.14———.

Reprinting of 158.13 (beginning "Duballon [*sic*] gives the following account of a woman of colour, in Jamaica, in 1802: "'Let us visit the old woman that has seen her hundredth year,' says one of the company") printed as five paragraphs (all but the first numbered) under heading "Irrouba" on pp. 266–268 in *Biographical Sketches and Interesting Anecdotes of Persons of Color. To Which Is Added, a Selection of Pieces in Poetry*, compiled by A[bigail] Mott.

New York [New York, U.S.A.]: Stereotyped for and printed by order of the Trustees of the residuary estate of Lindley Murray, **1850**.
8vo (20 cm.): iv, [7]-408 p.

158.15———.

Another printing of 158.13 (beginning "Duballon [*sic*] gives the following account of a woman of colour, in Jamaica, in 1802: "'Let us visit the old woman that has seen her hundredth year,' says one of the company") printed as five paragraphs (all but the first numbered) under heading "Irrouba" on pp. 266–268 in *Biographical Sketches and Interesting Anecdotes of Persons of Color. To Which Is Added, a Selection of Pieces in Poetry*, compiled by A[bigail] Mott.

New York [New York, U.S.A.]: Stereotyped for and printed by order of the Trustees of the residuary estate of Lindley Murray. D. Fanshaw, Printer, 35 Ann, corner of Nassau-street, **1854**.
12mo (19 cm.): iv, [7]-408 p.
https://digital.ncdcr.gov/digital/collection/p249901coll37/id/10464

158.16———.

John Davis's 1806 English-language translation (beginning "'Let us visit the negroes,' said one of the party") of Berquin-Duvallon's account of Irrouba reprinted explicitly from 158.5 on pp. 173–174 within "Documents" section in *Journal of Negro History*, vol. 2, no. 2 (April 1917): 164–185.

Washington, DC [U.S.A.]: Association for the Study of Negro Life and History, **1917**.
8vo (23 cm.).
https://www.gutenberg.org/files/20752/20752-h/20752-h.htm#No2_a7

158.17———.

Life account taken from the 1803 edition of Berquin-Duvallon (beginning "Allons [n.b.] voir la [n.b.] centenaire, dit quelqu'un de la compagnie") printed on pp. 111–112 (first series) in photomechanical reprint of 1808 Paris, France, edition of Henri Grégoire, *De la littérature des Nègres* (158.6)] and D. B. Warden's English-language translation (beginning "'Let us visit the old woman, [n.b.] who has seen her hundredth year,' says some one of the company") of Berquin-Duvallon's account of Irrouba as printed in the first edition of Grégoire printed on pp. 110–11 (2nd series) in photomechanical reprint of 1810 Brooklyn, New York, English-language translation of the same work 158.7), the two printed together in one volume with imprint:

Nendeln, Lichtenstein: Kraus Reprint, **1971**.
8vo (22 cm.): 287, 253 p.

158.18———. [Photomechanical reprint of 158.12]

Reprinting of 158.12 (beginning "'Let us visit the old woman that has seen her hundredth year,' says one of the company") printed as three numbered paragraphs under heading "Irrouba. | Duballon [*sic*] gives the following account of a woman of colour, in Jamaica, in 1802" on pp. 168–169 in 有色人に関する伝記的資料 / *Biographical Sketches and Interesting Anecdotes of Persons of Color. To which is added, a Selection of Pieces in Poetry*, compiled by A[bigail] Mott. "Second Edition, much Enlarged."

Tokyo, Japan: 日本図書センター, Nihon Tosho Senta, **2000**.
8vo (27 cm.): 255 p.

1805

159.0 Cicero (ca. 1761–1805) = Carl Heinrich = Carl Heinrich Fry

Manuscript memoir (*Lebenslauf*) of Carl Heinrich Fry, dated **1805**, held in Unity Archives, **Herrnhut, Germany**, R.22. Nr. 146, 22.

¶ From unknown origins in West Africa, Carl Heinrich was taken ca. 1771, aged about ten, on a large

Full text: https://huskiecommons.lib.niu.edu/history-500africanvoices/114/ [see 159.1].

slave ship with mostly enslaved Mina people (a New World ethnic designation for Akan-speakers near Elmina Castle, modern Ghana – see Map 5), probably from the Danish fort of Christiansborg in Accra to Christiansted on St. Croix in the Danish West Indies (Map 14), where he was sold to a member of a wealthy merchant family of slave traders. At some point he was assigned the name Cicero. While living in Christiansted, he learned to read and to dress hair. In 1775 he began to embrace Moravian Christianity and when baptized took the name Carl Heinrich. His owner, who later became vice governor and held other high offices, thrice took him as his servant to Copenhagen, Denmark (Map 7). There Carl Heinrich re-acquired his freedom in 1788 and took the surname Fry. He began contributing to the Moravian mission on the plantations of St. Croix in the 1780s, witnessing to enslaved people about spiritual matters and treating black and white people medically. He married Cornelia (from one of the plantations), who also began working in the mission. They had eight children together. Carl Heinrich wrote his memoir, according to Moravian custom, a few months before he died in 1805.

159.1——.

Memoir printed on pp. 379–380 in Christian Degn, *Die Schimmelmanns im atlantischen Dreieckshandel: Gewinn und Gewissen.*

Neumünster [Schleswig-Holstein, Germany]: Karl Wachholtz Verlag, **1974.**
8vo (25 cm.): 599 p., illus.

159.2 ——. [Second printing of 159.1]

Memoir printed on pp. 379–380 in Christian Degn, *Die Schimmelmanns im atlantischen Dreieckshandel: Gewinn und Gewissen*

Neumünster [Schleswig-Holstein, Germany]: Karl Wachholtz Verlag, **1984.**
8vo (25 cm.): 599 p., illus., maps.

159.3 ——. [Third printing of 159.1]

Memoir printed on pp. 379–380 in Christian Degn, *Die Schimmelmanns im atlantischen Dreieckshandel: Gewinn und Gewissen*

Neumünster [Schleswig-Holstein, Germany]: Karl Wachholtz Verlag, **2000.**
8vo (25 cm.): 599 p., illus., maps.

1807

160.1   John Kizell (ca. 1760–after 1830) = John Kezell = John Kizzell

Life details in several letters and accounts dated 6 April 1807 to 30 January 1811 written by Kizell in Sierra Leone, and Gov. Edward H. Columbine's account of Kizell's life as told to him by Kizell dated 27 January 1811, printed within section headed "Extracts from the Correspondence of Mr. John Kizell with Governor Columbine, respecting his Negotiations with the Chiefs in the River Sherbro, and giving an Account of that River," on pp. 113–153 of *Sixth Report of the Directors of the African Institution, Read at the Annual General Meeting on the 25th of March, 1812. To which are added, An Appendix and A List of Subscribers.*

London [England]: Printed by Ellerton & Henderson, Johnson's Court, Fleet Street. Sold by J. Hatchard, Bookseller and Publisher, 190, Piccadilly, **1812.** (Price, Two Shillings.)
8vo (22 cm.): vii, [1], 183 p.

¶ Kizell was born ca. 1760 significantly inland from Sherbro Island (modern Sierra Leone—see Map 4). His father was an important chief. While visiting his uncle's village he became one of few survivors of a bloody battle, after which he was enslaved and taken to Gallinas on the coast. In 1773 he was accused of witchcraft and sold to English traders, who forcibly took him on a slave ship to Charleston, the largest port city in the British North American colony of South Carolina (Map 15). There he

https://babel. hathitrust.org/cgi/ pt?id=nyp.33433 075935142&view=1up&seq=127 [see 160.1].

was sold. Responding to the 1779 British Philipsburg Proclamation (which promised freedom to enslaved men who fought for Britain), he ran away and fought on the British side in the War of the American Revolution (1775–1783). After the British lost the war, he evacuated with other black and white Loyalists to Nova Scotia, Canada (Map 16). In 1792 he was part of the large group that migrated from Nova Scotia to Sierra Leone. He married, had three children, embraced Christianity, and became a Baptist preacher. He was a partner in a shipping business and worked as a diplomat among local chiefs for British authorities in their campaign to end the slave trade and promote so-called legitimate trade in the area. See Kevin Lowther, *The African Odyssey of John Kizell: A South Carolina Slave Returns to Fight the Slave Trade in His African Homeland* (Columbia: University of South Carolina Press, 2011).

160.2——.

160.1 reprinted on pp. 68–84 in *The Second Annual Report of the American Society for Colonizing the Free People of Colour in the United States. With an Appendix. Second Edition.*

Washington [District of Columbia, U.S.A.]: Printed by Davis and Force, Pennsylvania Avenue, **1819.**
8vo (21 cm.): 153, [1] p. Note: 160.1 is not reprinted in this *Report*'s first edition, which is the edition included in the Negro University Press's 1969 photomechanical reprint of these reports.

160.3——.

Derivative biographical sketch and related letters printed on p. 109 et seq. in *West-African Sketches: compiled from the reports of Sir G. R. Collier, Sir Charles MacCarthy, and other official sources.*

London [England]: Printed for L. B. Seeley and Son, Fleet Street ... MDCCCXXIV [**1824**]. Tpv: Printed by L. B. Seeley, Weston-Green, Thames-Ditton.

8vo (25 cm.): viii, 273 p.

https://babel.hathitrust.org/cgi/pt?id=hvd.32044074322108&view=1up&seq=137

160.4——.

Gov. Edward H. Columbine's account of Kizell's life as Kizell told it to him printed (from 158.1 or 158.2?) on pp. 102–104 of Archibald Alexander, DD, *A History of Colonization on the Western Coast of Africa.*

Philadelphia [Pennsylvania, U.S.A.]: William S. Martien [*sic*], No. 37 South Seventh Street. **New York [New York, U.S.A.]:** No. 23 Centre Street. **1846**. Tpv carries William S. Martien's 1846 copyright notice.

8vo (24 cm.): xii, 603 p., folding map.

https://archive.org/details/historyofcolonizationon00alex/page/102/mode/1up

160.5——.

Gov. Edward H. Columbine's account of Kizell's life as Kizell told it to him printed (from 160.1 or 160.2?) on pp. 102–104 of Archibald Alexander, DD, *A History of Colonization on the Western Coast of Africa. ... Second edition.*

Philadelphia [Pennsylvania, U.S.A.]: William S. Martien [*sic*], No. 142 Chestnut [*sic*] Street, **1849**. Tpv carries William S. Martien's 1849 copyright notice.

8vo (24 cm.): xii, 659 p., folding map.

https://babel.hathitrust.org/cgi/pt?id=yale.39002003651065&view=1up&seq=116

160.6——.

Derivative life sketch of Kizell with letter quotations printed on pp. 219–221 in Rev. S. R. B. Attoh Ahuma, *Memoirs of West African Celebrities Europe &c. (1700–1850). With special reference to the Gold Coast.*

Liverpool [England]: D. Marples & Co., 508 Lord Street, **1905**.

8vo (19 cm.): xx, 260 p.

160.7——. [Mimeographed reproduction of 160.3]

Derivative biographical sketch and related letters printed on p. 109 et seq. in *West-African Sketches: compiled from the reports of Sir G. R. Collier, Sir Charles MacCarthy, and other official sources.*

Legon [Ghana]: Institute of African Studies, University of Ghana, **1963**.

8vo (25 cm.): viii, 273 p.

160.8——. [Another printing of 160.7]

Derivative biographical sketch and related letters printed on p. 109 et seq. in *West-African Sketches: compiled from the reports of Sir G. R. Collier, Sir Charles MacCarthy, and other official sources.*

Legon [Ghana]: Institute of African Studies, University of Ghana, [**1967**].

8vo (25 cm.): viii, 273 p. Series: Sources and Documents, no. 6.

160.9——. [Photomechanical reprint of 160.4]

Gov. Edward H. Columbine's account of Kizell's life as told to him by Kizell printed (from 160.1 or 160.2?) on pp. 102–103 of photomechanical reprint of the 1846 edition of Archibald Alexander, DD, *A History of Colonization on the Western Coast of Africa*, with imprint:

New York [New York, U.S.A.]: Negro Universities Press. [**1969**].

8vo (23 cm.): xii, [5], 603 p., folding map.

160.10——. [Photomechanical reprint of 160.5]

Gov. Edward H. Columbine's account of Kizell's life as Kizell told it to him printed (from 160.1 or 160.2?) on pp. 102–104 Archibald Alexander, DD, *A History of Colonization on the Western Coast of Africa.*

Freeport [New York, U.S.A.]: Books for Libraries Press, **1971**.

8vo (23 cm.): xii, 659 p., folding map.

1808

161.0 Télémaque (–1808?) = Congo Rouge

Substantive attention to Télémaque's life story present within manuscript "Interrogatoire des nègres marrons au chantier de Nancibo, 5 et 6 juin **1808**," held in Archives Départementales de la Guyane, **Cayenne, French Guiana**. Note: This manuscript also includes references to two Maroons, Hercule and Catherine, but because these references do not include

sufficient evidence of African birth, we have not included them in the present catalog.

¶ Born in an unknown location in Africa, Télémaque was taken in the slave trade to French Guiana on the northern coast of South America (see Map 10). He was held enslaved there by a Madame Gaëtan when he ran away in 1806, whereupon he lived as a Maroon for two years, violently resisting the colony's attempt to reenslave all runaways. In 1808 he was arrested and convicted of killing a gendarme. For this he was probably executed.

161.1——.
161.0 printed in "Télémaque dit Congo Rouge, Hercule et Cather-

Full text: https://huskiecommons.lib.niu.edu/history-500africanvoices/115/ [see 161.1].

ine, esclaves marrons. Guyane, 1808," pp. 115–122 (especially 118–119) *Voix d'Esclaves Antilles, Guyane et Louisane Françaises, XVIIIᵉ–XIXᵉ Siècles*, edited by Dominique Rogers.

Paris [France]: Karthala; CIRESC*; **Fort-de-France [Martinique]**: SAA**, 2015.
*Centre Internationale de Recherches sur les Esclavages.
**Society of American Archivists.
8vo (22 cm.): 184 p., plates.

1810

162.1 Boyrereau Brinch (ca. 1742–1827) = Jeffrey Brace

The Blind African Slave, or, Memoirs of Boyrereau Brinch, nick-named Jeffrey Brace. Containing an account of the kingdom of Bow Woo, in the interior of Africa, with the soil, climate and natural productions, laws and customs peculiar to that place. With an account of his captivity, sufferings, sales, travels, emancipation, conversion to the Christian religion, knowledge of the scriptures, &c. Interspersed with strictures on slavery, speculative observations on the qualities of human nature, with quotations from scripture. By [i.e., as dictated to] *Benjamin F. Prentiss, Esq.*

St. Albans, V[ermon]t. [U.S.A.]: Printed by Harry Whitney, 1810.
12mo (17 cm.): 204 p., illus. Note: This is the first book printed in St. Albans, Vermont, and the first printed by Harry Whitney, q.v. John Buechler, "Brace, Bran, and St. Albans," *New-England Galaxy* 20.2 (1978): 35–41.
Shaw, *American Bibliography*, 21130.

¶ Brinch was from the interior West African kingdom of Bowwoo, which (based on linguistic clues) Kari J. Winter suggests was within present-day Mali (162.2, pp. 4–5)—see Map 3. Captured at age sixteen in 1758, he was taken on a slave ship to Barbados, the British colony in the West Indies. After brief, intensely violent enslavement on Barbados, he was sold and fought in the Caribbean as an enslaved sailor on a British ship during the Seven Years War (1757–1763). Thereafter, he was taken by his owner to the British North American colony of Connecticut (Map 17) and there resold. In 1777 he enlisted in the army of the newly formed United States of America and served as an infantryman until war's end. In 1783 he was honorably discharged and, by virtue of his military service, emancipated from slavery a year later. He then bought land in the new state of Vermont and married. He was baptized in

http://docsouth.unc.edu/neh/brinch/brinch.html [see 162.1].

1805. His wife died in 1807, and Brinch himself died in 1827. For more on him, see the editorial apparatus in 162.2 (edited by Kari J. Winter) and Kari J. Winter, "Jeffrey Brace in Barbados: Slavery, Interracial Relationships, and the Emergence of a Global Economy," in *Nineteenth-Century Contexts*, 29: 2–3 (June/Sept. 2007): 111–125.

162.2——.
The Blind African Slave: or, Memoirs of Boyrereau Brinch, nicknamed Jeffrey Brace, edited by Kari J. Winter. [Emended edition of 160.1, with introduction, annotations, related documents, bibliography, etc.]

Madison [Wisconsin, U.S.A.]: University of Wisconsin Press, 2004.
8vo (24 cm.): xvi, 244 p., illus. "For the ease of the reader, I [i.e., Kari J. Winter] have silently corrected some of the obvious printing, punctuation, subject-verb agreement and spelling errors that appear to me to have no meaning or relation to either the conscious authorial intentions or the unconscious attitudes of Prentiss or Brace" (p. 84).

162.3——. [Second printing of 162.2]
The Blind African Slave: or, Memoirs of Boyrereau Brinch, nicknamed Jeffrey Brace, edited by Kari J. Winter. [Emended edition of 162.1, with introduction, annotations, related documents, bibliography, etc.]

Madison [Wisconsin, U.S.A.]: University of Wisconsin Press, [2004?].
8vo (23 cm.): xvi, 244 p., illus.

162.4——.
Extracts from *The Blind African Slave: or, Memoirs of Boyrereau Brinch* printed in *American Antislavery Writings: Colonial Beginnings to Emancipation*, edited by James G. Basker.

New York [New York, U.S.A.]: The Library of America, [2012].
8vo (21 cm.): xli, 963 p., illus.

163.1   Unnamed woman from Bow-woo (ca. 1731–)

Account embedded (as direct speech within quotation marks) on pp. 123–129 in 162.1, Jeffrey Brace = Boyrereau Brinch, *The Blind African Slave …. By* [i.e., as dictated to] *Benjamin F. Prentiss, Esq.*

St. Albans, V[ermon]t. [U.S.A.]: Printed by Harry Whitney, 1810.
12mo (17 cm.): 204 p., illus. Note: This is the first book printed in St. Albans, Vermont, and the first printed by Harry Whitney, q.v. John Buechler, "Brace, Bran, and St. Albans," *New-England Galaxy* 20.2 (1978): 35–41. Shaw, *American Bibliography*, 21130.

http://docsouth.unc.edu/neh/brinch/brinch.html [see 163.1].

¶ This is an embedded account. Within his own account, Boyrereau Brinch (q.v. 162.1) describes a woman he met in the colonies who came from his homeland, the kingdom of Bow-woo, which (based on linguistic clues) Kari J. Winter suggests was within present-day Mali (162.2, pp. 4–5)—see Map 3. Brinch asked her to tell him her story, which he then incorporated verbatim in his own account. Judging from the dates and ages in the account, she was born ca. 1731, captured ca. 1748, and ca. 1752 married a ship captain named Lecois, who had helped her escape to Barbados, the British colony in the West Indies (Map 11), where he treated her kindly and where she met Brinch in 1759–60.

163.2———.

Account embedded on pp. 143–146 in *The Blind African Slave: or, Memoirs of Boyrereau Brinch, nicknamed Jeffrey Brace*, edited by Kari J. Winter. [Emended edition of 163.1, with introduction, annotations, related documents, bibliography, etc.]

Madison [Wisconsin, U.S.A.]: University of Wisconsin Press, 2004.
8vo (24 cm.): xvi, 244 p., illus. "For the ease of the reader, I [i.e., Kari J. Winter] have silently corrected some of the obvious printing, punctuation, subject-verb agreement and spelling errors that appear to me to have no meaning or relation to either the conscious authorial intentions or the unconscious attitudes of Prentiss or Brace" (p. 84).

163.3———. [Second printing of 163.2]

Account embedded on pp. 143–146 in *The Blind African Slave: or, Memoirs of Boyrereau Brinch, nicknamed Jeffrey Brace*, edited by Kari J. Winter. [Emended edition of 163.1, with introduction, annotations, related documents, bibliography, etc.]

Madison [Wisconsin, U.S.A.]: University of Wisconsin Press, [2004?].
8vo (23 cm.): xvi, 244 p., illus.

163.4———.

Account embedded in extracts from *The Blind African Slave: or, Memoirs of Boyrereau Brinch* printed in *American Antislavery Writings: Colonial Beginnings to Emancipation*, edited by James G. Basker.

New York [New York, U.S.A.]: The Library of America, [2012].
8vo (21 cm.): xli, 963 p., illus.

Ca. 1810

164.1   Unnamed Muslim man

Account of "the man who prayed five times a day" printed on pp. 143 and 145–160 in Charles Ball, *Slavery in the United States. A Narrative of the Life and Adventures of Charles Ball, a Black Man* [as told to Mr. Fisher]. [Third edition.]

https://babel.hathitrust.org/cgi/pt?id=loc.ark:/13960/t6ww7h067&iew=1up&seq=143 [see 164.1].

Pittsburgh [Pennsylvania, U.S.A.]: Printed and Published by J. T. Shryock, 1853. Tpv copyright notice: "Entered … … in the year [n.b.] 1836, by [n.b.] John W. Shugert." This edition does *not* include a printed edition statement.
8vo (19 cm.): [2], v–vi, 9–446 p.
https://archive.org/details/slaveryinunit00ballcha/page/143/mode/1up?view=theater

Note: This account is not printed in the first or second editions of Ball's *Narrative* (Lewistown, Penn., 1836; New York, 1837), nor in its *stated* 4th edition (1857), nor in the unauthorized reprinting of the 1836 edition entitled *Fifty Years in Chains* (New York, 1859 et seq.); it is therefore not part of the Negro History Press's 1970 edition (which copies the first edition), nor of Dover's 1970 edition (which is a photomechanical reprint of the 4th), nor of photomechanical reprints of *Fifty Years in Chains.*

¶ This man was Muslim, probably Tuareg or Maure, and came from the southern Sahara west of Timbuctu (modern Mali—see Map 3). He was captured in war, but after two years (during which he had a close encounter with a lion) he was rescued by his own countrymen. Subsequently seized in yet another war, he was taken southwestward and sold to a slave ship crew on the Gambia River. His account of his survival in the Sahara and during the Middle Passage to the port city of Charleston, South Carolina, U.S.A. (Map 15), ca. 1805 is horrifyingly detailed. This man told his story to American-born Charles Ball when they were enslaved alongside each other on a plantation in South Carolina. Ball, in turn, told this man's story to Fisher; and most of it is printed inside quotation marks in the third edition of Ball's *Narrative* (164.1).

164.2———. [Except for title page, printed from the same setting of type as 164.1.]
Account of a man "who prayed five times every day" printed on pp. 143 and 145–160 in Charles Black, *Slavery in the United States. A Narrative of the Life and Adventures of Charles Ball, a Black Man … [as told to Mr. Fisher]. Third edition.*

Pittsburgh [Pennsylvania, U.S.A.]: John T. Shryock … Western Publisher, 1854. Tpv copyright notice: "Entered … … in the year [n.b.] 1836, by [n.b.] John W. Shugert." Note: Edition statement printed on title page directly above publisher's imprint.
8vo (19 cm.): [2], v-vi, 9–446 p.
https://babel.hathitrust.org/cgi/pt?id=iau.31858027910805&view=1up&seq=145

164.3———. [German translation]
Account of "the man who prayed five times a day" translated into German and printed on pp. 144 and 146–160 in vol. 1 (Erster Band) of Charles Ball, *Leben und Abenteuer eines Negers, während seines vierzigjährigen Aufenthalts in verschiedenen Staaten Amerikas.*

Berlin [Prussia, Germany]: Verlag von Julius Springer, 1854. Colophon: Druck von Gebrüder Katz in Dessau.
2 vols., 8vo.
https://reader.digitale-sammlungen.de/de/fs1/object/display/bsb10122021_00150.html

164.4———.
Account of "the man who prayed five times a day" printed, minus a few early paragraphs but with an editorial introduction,

under the chapter heading "A Man Treed by a Lion. | *Slave Trade in Africa---Horrors of the middle passage,*" on pp. 3–27 in vol. IV of *Uncle Tom's Kindred, or the Wrongs of the Lowly; exhibited in a series of sketches and narratives. In ten volumes,* compiled for the use of Sabbath Schools by E. Smith, M.G.

Mansfield, O[hio, U.S.A.]: Published by E. Smith, for the Wesleyan Methodist Connection of America, 1855. Tpv carries E. Smith's 1853 Ohio district copyright notice.
10 vols., 12mo (15 cm.).

164.5———. [German translation]
Account of "the man who prayed five times a day" translated into German and printed on pp. 144 and 146–160 in vol. 1 of Charles Ball, *Leben und Abenteuer eines Negers, während seines vierzigjährigen Aufenthalts in verschiedenen Staaten Amerikas.*

Wittenberg [Saxony-Anhalt, Germany], 1856.
2 vols., 8vo.

164.6———. [German translation]
Account of "the man who prayed five times a day" translated into German and printed on pp. 144 and 146–160 in vol. 1 of Charles Ball, *Leben und Abenteuer eines Negers, während seines vierzigjährigen Aufenthalts in Sklavenlebens verschiedenen Staaten Amerikas.*

Wittenberg [Saxony-Anhalt, Germany]: Mohr, 1857.
2 vols., 8vo.

164.7———. [German translation]
Leben und Abenteuer eines Negers während seines vierzigjährigen Sklavenlebens in verschiedenen Staaten Amerika's.

Berlin [Prussia, Germany]: Springer, n.d. [1857?].

164.8———.
Unter der Sklavengeißel Erlebnisse des Negersklaven Charles Ball von ihm selbst erzählt.

Leipzig [Saxony, Germany]: Weise, 1931.
317 p.

164.9———.
"Narrative of the African 'Who Prayed Five Times Every Day'" printed from 164.2 on pp. 691–704 in *African Muslims in Antebellum America: A Source Book,* edited by Allan D. Austin.

New York [New York, U.S.A.]: Garland Publishing, 1984.
8vo (23 cm.): xiv, 759 p., illus.

Ca. 1812

165.1 John Jea (1773–)

The Life, History, and Unparalleled Suffering of John Jea, The African Preacher. Compiled and Written by Himself.

Printed for the author. [Colophon:] [James] Williams, Printer and Book-binder, 143, Queen Street, **Portsea [Plymouth, England]**, [ca. 1812?].

8vo (21 cm.): 96 p., portrait.

http://docsouth.unc.edu/neh/jea-john/jeajohn.html [see 165.1].

¶ Jea (pronounced "Jay") was born in Calabar (lower Cross River, southeastern Nigeria—see Map 5) in 1773. He describes his parents as poor but industrious. When Jea was between two and three years old, he and his family were kidnapped and taken in the slave trade to the British North American colony of New York (Map 17). He eventually learned to read English and Dutch, converted to Christianity, and began preaching. He lived and preached in England, especially in Liverpool, Lancashire, Yorkshire, and Sunderland (Map 8), and he traveled to Boston (United States), Buenos Aires (Argentina—Map 9) and Ireland (Limerick and Cork—Map 7) to preach. After imprisonment in Cambrai, France during wartime, he went to England, where he remained and continued to preach. For more on Jea see: John Saillant, "Traveling in Old and New Worlds with John Jea, the African Preacher, 1773–1816," *Journal of American Studies* 33 (1999): 473–490.

165.2 ——.

An Explanation of that Part of the Life and Unparalleled Sufferings of the Reverend John Jea, (African Preacher of the Gospel) respecting his learning to read: intended to convince those who disbelieve it, and requisite to be had by all who have purchased The History of his Life.

Portsea [Plymouth, England]: [James] Williams, printer, [ca. 1813?].

12mo (17 cm.): 36 pages. Only located exemplar is in Harvard University Libraries, Houghton Library call number *AC8. J3404.811e. Houghton Library cataloguers have posited year of printing as ca. 1811?, perhaps discounting that part of the title that refers to our 165.1.

165.3 ——.

Excerpts from 165.1 printed, with new introductory note, on pp. 117–126 in *Black Writers in Britain, 1760–1890: An Anthology,* edited by Paul Edwards and David Dabydeen.

Edinburgh [Scotland]: Edinburgh University Press, **1991**. 8vo (22 cm.): xv, 239 p.

165.4 ——.

165.1 reprinted on pp. 87–163 of *Black Itinerants of the Gospel: The Narratives of John Jea and George White,* edited with an introduction by Graham Russell Hodges.

Madison, Wisconsin [U.S.A.]: Madison House, **1993**. 8vo (24 cm.): viii, 200 p., illus. (including portrait), map.

165.5 ——. [Second printing of 165.3]

Excerpts from 165.1 printed, with new introductory note, on pp. 117–126 in *Black Writers in Britain, 1760–1890: An Anthology,* edited by Paul Edwards and David Dabydeen.

Edinburgh [Scotland]: Edinburgh University Press, **1995**. 8vo (22 cm.): xv, 239 p.

165.6 ——.

165.1 reprinted on pp. 367–439 of *Pioneers of the Black Atlantic: Five Slave Narratives from the Enlightenment, 1772–1815,* edited by Henry Louis Gates Jr. and William L. Andrews.

Washington, DC [U.S.A.]: Civitas Counterpoint, **1998**. 8vo (23 cm.): xiv, 439p.

165.7 ——.

165.1 reprinted on pp. 87–163 of *Black Itinerants of the Gospel: The Narratives of John Jea and George White,* edited with an introduction by Graham Russell Hodges.

New York [New York, U.S.A.]: Palgrave, **2002**. 8vo (24 cm.): viii, 200 p., illus., map.

165.8 ——. [Third printing of 165.3]

Excerpts from 165.1 printed, with new introductory note, on pp. 117–126 in *Black Writers in Britain, 1760–1890: An Anthology,* edited by Paul Edwards and David Dabydeen.

Edinburgh [Scotland]: Edinburgh University Press, **2003**. 8vo (22 cm.): xv, 239 p.

165.9 ——.

Three long block quotations and additional shorter quotations from *The Life, History, and Unparalleled Suffering of John Jea* printed within historical discussion on pp. 69–74 in David Kazanjian, *The Colonizing Trick: National Culture and Imperial Citizenship in Early America.*

Minneapolis [Minnesota, U.S.A.]: University of Minnesota Press, **2003**. 8vo (23 cm.): xii, 311 p.

165.10——.

Extracts "From The life, history, and unparalleled sufferings of John Jea, the African preacher: compiled and written by himself" printed in *Early Black British Writing: Olaudah Equiano, Mary Prince, and others: Selected texts with introduction, critical essays*, edited by Alan Richardson and Debbie Lee.

Boston [Massachusetts, U.S.A.]: Houghton Mifflin, 2004.
8vo (21 cm.): ix, 443 p.
Additional publication by John Jea

+165-A.1 ——.

A Collection of Hymns. Compiled and Selected by John Jea, African Preacher of the Gospel. (Portsea [Plymouth, England]: Printed by J. Williams, 1816.) 12mo: 251 p. Single-page Preface signed in typed: John Jea *Portsea, June* 18, 1816. Note: As-yet only located exemplar discovered in the Bodleian Library, Oxford, by David Dabydeen in 1983 (165.3, p. 119), *pace* Colin Campbell, "1816 Hymnal Identified as Work of Ex-Slave," *New York Times*, 21 February 1985, p. C-17.

http://dbooks.bodleian.ox.ac.uk/books/PDFs/600100757.pdf

+165-A.2 ——.

Extracts "From A Collection of Hymns: compiled and selected by John Jea, African Preacher of the Gospel," printed from +163-A.1 with introduction, annotations, and photographic reproduction of 1816 title page as Appendix 1 on pp. 164–177 of *Black Itinerants of the Gospel: The Narratives of John Jea and George White*, edited with an introduction by Graham Russell Hodges (Madison [Wisconsin, U.S.A.]: Madison House, 1993).

+165-A.3 ——.

Extracts "From A Collection of Hymns: compiled and selected by John Jea, African Preacher of the Gospel," printed in *Early Black British Writing: Olaudah Equiano, Mary Prince, and others: Selected texts with introduction, critical essays*, edited by Alan Richardson and Debbie Lee (Boston [Massachusetts, U.S.A.]: Houghton Mifflin, 2004).

Ca. 1815?

166.1 Chloe Russell (ca. 1745–)

Autobiographical passages found only on p. 8 et seq. of incomplete exemplar of (this as yet otherwise unknown edition of *The complete fortune teller* .... (for full title see +166-A.1).

[United States of America?: s.n., ca. 1815?]
8vo (19 cm.): [3]-19 p.
Note: Edition known from Library Company of Philadelphia (Philadelphia, Pennsylvania, U.S.A.) exemplar, which lacks title leaf and pp. 11–12 (LCP record number 000001190).

Full text: https://huskiecommons.lib.niu.edu/history-500africanvoices/116/ [see 166.2].

¶ According to Russell's autobiographical passages, as yet found *only* in the incomplete Library Company of Philadelphia exemplar of a tentatively dated edition of this work (166.1), she was born in southwest Africa, kidnapped when nine years old ca. 1754, and taken on a slave ship to the British North American colony of Virginia (see Map 15). While held enslaved on a plantation near the town of Petersburg, Virginia, she developed a reputation as a spiritual adviser and seer. For this she earned a following and enough money to emancipate herself and others. After living a few years as a free woman in Virginia, she moved to the port city of Boston, Massachusetts (U.S.A.—see Map 17), where in 1824, according to Eric Gardner (in 166.2), she owned her own house. Gardner argues persuasively that her autobiographical passages are, for the most part, fact not fiction.

166.2——.

Autobiographical passages from 166.1 followed by full text of +166-A.2b (= +166-A2a) as edited by Eric Gardner printed on pp. 269–273 of his article "The Complete Fortune Teller and Dream Book: An Antebellum Text By Chloe Russel [*sic*], a Woman of Colour [in the State of Massachusetts]," *New England Quarterly*, 78:2: 259–288.

Boston [Massachusetts, U.S.A.]: The New England Quarterly, June 2005.
8vo (21.5 cm.).
Other editions of Chloe Russell's pamphlet lacking her account

+166-A.1 ——.

The Complete Fortune Teller and Dream Book, By which every person may acquaint themselves with the most important events that shall attend them through life. To which is added Directions for Young Ladies how to obtain the Husband they most desire--and for Young Gentlemen, how to obtain the Wife they most desire. By astrology--physiognomy and palmistry; anatomy [sic]--geometry--moles, cards and dreams. By Chloe Russel, A Woman of Colour in the State of Massachusetts (Boston [Massachusetts, U.S.A.]--Printed by Tom Hazard [(jocular pseudonym), date ca. 1800 posited by Boston Athenaeum or Brown University cataloguers, perhaps from typographical appearance; paper evidence not mentioned]). 12mo (20 cm.): 24 p., illustrated with two relief-cuts, viz.: frontispiece portrait with typographic caption beginning, n.b., "Chloe Russell" on p. [2] (p. [1] blank?); man of signs (not in Reilly) on title page (i.e., p. [3]). Sectional chain/garland (not in Reilly) used as headband atop p. 5 (first page of text proper) and as ornamental box-rule (with four distinct not-in-Reilly ornaments at or near corners) enclosing "Fortune Table" on p. 19; no long esses.

Not in ESTC, Evans, Bristol (cf. B10746, 128 p.), Shipton-Mooney, or Shaw-Shoemaker.

Note: Edition known from exemplars at the Boston Athenaeum (Boston, Massachusetts, U.S.A.) and Brown University Libraries (Providence, Rhode Island, U.S.A.). https://cdm.bostonathenaeum.org/digital/collection/ p15482coll3/id/4525/rec/1

+166-A.2a ————.

The complete fortune teller, and dream book, by which every person may acquaint themselves with the most important events that shall attend them through life. To which is added, Directions for young ladies how to obtain the husband they most desire; and for young gentlemen, how to obtain the wife

they most desire. By astrology--physiognomy, and palmistry. Anatomy--geometry--moles, cards and dreams. By Chloe Russell (Exeter [New Hampshire, U.S.A.]: Published by Abel Brown, 1824). 12mo (20 cm.): 20 p., illustrated with following relief-cuts: seal of the U.S.A. on title page; sun face with motto "sol clarior astro" ([The] sun [is] brighter [than a] star) on p. 11; man with a telescope looking through a window on p. 17. Note: edition known from New Hampshire Historical Society (pp. 1–12 only), American Antiquarian Society (pp. 1–12 only), and privately held (complete, incorporated within +166-A.2) exemplars.

+166-A.2b ————.

The complete fortune teller, and dream book, by which every person may acquaint themselves with the most important events that shall attend them through life. To which is added, Directions for young ladies how to obtain the husband they most desire; and for young gentlemen, how to obtain the wife they most desire. By astrology--physiognomy, and palmistry. Anatomy--geometry--moles, cards and dreams. By Chloe Russell (Exeter [New Hampshire, U.S.A.]: Published by Abel Brown, 1824 [sheets later issued with original title leaf intact and unaltered within a larger chapbook fronted with Abel Brown's collective title *Amusing Budget* bearing printed date 1827, as recorded by Eric Gardner in 166.2 from a privately held exemplar]). 12mo (20 cm.): 20 p.

1816

167.1 Yero Mamdou (ca. 1736–1823) = Yarrow Mamout = Yaro = Old Yarrow = Old Yarrah

Account (with long concluding passage of direct speech attributed to Yaro recorded within quotation marks) printed in text proper with introductory statement "The following account of Yaro, an African, still living in Georgetown, was communicated to me [i.e., D. B. Warden, 1778–1845] by General Mason" (i.e., John Mason, 1766–1849) on pp. 48– 51 in David Bailie Warden, *A Chorographical and Statistical Description of the District of Columbia Seat of the General Government of the United States.*

Paris [France]: Printed and sold by Smith, Rue Montmorency. To be had also of T. Barrois, Foreign Bookseller, No. 11, Quai Voltaire, and Delaunay, Bookseller, in the Palais-Royal, 1816.
8vo (21 cm.): vii, 212 p., illus., map.

https://archive. org/details/ chorographicalst- 00ward/page/48/ mode/1up [see 167.1].

¶ Yero, a Muslim and probably Fulani (Fula or Fulbi or Peul people in the modern country Guinea—see Map 3), was captured with his sister, taken in 1752 on the slave ship *Elijah* to the port of Annapolis in the British North American colony of Maryland (Map 15), and sold to an affluent family with tobacco farms, mills, and a forge in Frederick County, Maryland, where Yero was his owner's body servant. He married Jane Chambers (an enslaved woman), with whom he had one child, whose freedom Yero purchased. In 1788–1789 Yero and his family moved with their owner's family to Georgetown, on the banks of the Potomac River in Maryland. At some point Yero learned brickmaking, began to handle money, and became an excellent swimmer. In 1796, after years of hard service, he was manumitted. Later he twice lost all the money he had saved while free by entrusting it to individuals who went bankrupt or absconded. Subsequently Yero earned more, purchased his own house, kept his savings in a bank, and lived as a respected octogenarian in Georgetown (which in 1791 became part of the United States of America's newly created District of Columbia). In 1819 he sat for his portrait by the painter Charles Wilson Peale; three years later he sat for another portrait, this time by the artist Alexander Simpson.

Both portraits survive (Philadelphia Museum of Art, Philadelphia, Pennsylvania, U.S.A., and District of Columbia Library, Georgetown, DC, U.S.A.). Yero remained a practicing Muslim until his dying day in 1823. For more on him see James H. Johnston, *From Slave Ship to Harvard: Yarrow Mamout and the History of an African American Family* (167.9).

167.2———.

Account printed (*without* concluding passage of direct speech included in 167.1) as long footnote headed "The following account of Yaro, an African, still living in Georgetown, was communicated to me [i.e., D. B. Warden] by General Mason" (i.e., John Mason, 1766–1849) on pp. 202–203 in vol. 3 of David Bailie Warden, *A Statistical, Political, and Historical Account of the United States of North America; from the period of their first colonization to the present day.*

Edinburgh [Scotland]: Printed for Archibald Constable and Co. Edinburgh; Longman, Hurst, Rees, Orme, and Brown, and Hurst, Robinson, and Company, **London [England], 1819.** Tpv: Printed by George Ramsay and Co. Edinburgh, 1819.
3 vols., 8vo (21 cm.).
https://babel.hathitrust.org/cgi/pt?id=hvd.hxkdde&view=1up&seq=220

167.3———.

Account printed (again *without* concluding long passage of direct speech, which is present in 167.1 but absent from 167.2) explicitly from "Warden's United States" (167.2) on pp. 328–329 of Charles Hulbert, *Museum Americanum; or, Select Antiquities, Curiosities, Beauties, and Varieties, Of Nature and Art, in America; compiled from Eminent Authorities, Methodically Arranged, interspersed with original hints, observations, &c.*

Shrewsbury [Shropshire, England]: Printed and Published by C. Hulbert; Sold by G. & W. B. Whittaker, W. Baynes and Son, and T. Blanshard [*sic*], **London [England]**; and all other Booksellers, **1823.**
16mo (17 cm.): iv, [5]-346 p., plates.

167.4———.

Account printed *with* concluding long passage (which is present in 167.1 but not in 167.2 or 167.3) of direct speech attributed to Yaro recorded within quotation marks printed in an unseen issue (1834 or earliest 1835?) of the weekly newspaper *Sabbath School Instructor.*

Portland, [Maine, U.S.A.]: Daniel C. Colesworthy, for the Board of Managers of the Sunday School Union, ca. **1834.**
Dimensions not known. Entry based on 167.5 and MARC record for this newspaper title.

167.5———.

Account reprinted explicitly from *Sabbath School Instructor* (as it was printed there *with* concluding long passage of direct speech attributed to Yaro) under headline "Persevering Industry of an African" on first page (i.e., 29), col. 6, of the antislavery newspaper *The Liberator*, vol. 5, no. 8.

Boston [Massachusetts, U.S.A.]: William Lloyd Garrison and Isaac Knapp, Publishers, February 21, **1835.**
Broadsheet bifolium (49 cm.): 4 p.
http://fair-use.org/the-liberator/1835/02/21/the-liberator-05-08.pdf

167.6———.

Additional life details about "Old Yarrow" printed at the end of Chapter X on pp. 170–171 in Grace Dunlop Ecker, *A Portrait of Old George Town.*

Richmond, Virginia [U.S.A.]: Garrett & Massie, [1933].
8vo (22 cm.): xiii, [2], 271 p., illus.
https://babel.hathitrust.org/cgi/pt?id=mdp.39015028563461&view=1up&seq=198

167.7———.

Additional life details along with Charles Willson Peale's diary entries on his meetings with Yarrow printed in Charles Coleman Sellers's article "Charles Willson Peale and Yarrow Mamout," pp. 99–102 in *The Pennsylvania Magazine of History and Biography*, vol. 71, no. 2.

Philadelphia, Pennsylvania [U.S.A.]: The Historical Society of Pennsylvania, April **1947.**
8vo (22.5 cm.).
https://journals.psu.edu/pmhb/article/view/30179/29934

167.8———.

Additional life details about "Old Yarrow" reprinted from 167.6 near the end of Chapter XII on p. 206 in Grace Dunlop Ecker, *A Portrait of Old George Town ... Second edition, revised and enlarged.*

Richmond, Virginia [U.S.A.]: The Dietz Press, Incorporated, **1951.**
8vo (22 cm.): xvi, 324 p., illus., maps.
https://www.gutenberg.org/files/27716/27716-h/27716-h.htm

167.9———.

Details of Yaro's life story as told to Charles Willson Peale and written down by him in an 1819 diary entry printed on p. 652 in vol. 3 ("The Belfield Farm Years, 1810–1820") of *The Selected Papers of Charles Willson Peale and His Family*, edited by Lillian B. Miller, Sidney Hart, David C., and Rose S. Emerich.

New Haven [Connecticut, U.S.A.]: Yale University Press, **1991**. 8vo (25 cm.): xlvii, 914 p., illus.

167.10 ———.

Portions of account and long concluding passage of direct speech attributed to Yero printed in quotation marks and

as indented block quotations explicitly from 165.9 on pp. 95–96 in James H. Johnston, *From Slave Ship to Harvard: Yarrow Mamout and the History of an African American Family.*

New York [New York, U.S.A.]: Fordham University Press, **2012**. 8vo (23.6 cm.): viii, [2], 302 p., plates.

1818

168.1 **Thomas Joiner**

His story printed on p. 22 (apparently under date 22 March **1818**) within Appendix headed (on p. 19) "Abstract of a Journal of the late Rev. Samuel John Miles, written while in Africa" in *The Second Annual Report of the American Society for Colonizing the Free People of Colour in the United States. With an Appendix. Second edition.*

https://www.loc.gov/resource/lcrbmrp.t1504/?sp=22&r=-0.668,0.081,2.336,0.886,0 [see 168.1].

Washington [District of Columbia, U.S.A.]: Printed by Davis and Force, Pennsylvania Avenue, **1819**.
8vo (21 cm.): 153, [1] p.
Note: 168.1 is not printed in this *Report*'s first edition, which is the edition included in the Negro University Press's 1969 photomechanical reprint of these reports.

¶ Joiner was the son of a distinguished prince who lived about 600 miles up the Gambia River (modern Senegal—see Map 3), which means that he was likely a Muslim and identified as Mandinka (an ethnic group residing in modern southern Mali, Guinea, and Ivory Coast). Kidnapped as a boy and sold in the West Indies, he was later redeemed by an English ship captain who knew Joiner's father. The captain took Joiner to England and ensured he received an education there. Thereafter, he was returned to his home country, where he acquired property and influence. Joiner sent two of his sons to England to be educated and when interviewed by John Mills at St. Mary's church on Banjul Island (modern Gambia—Map 3) at the mouth of the Gambia River on 16 March 1818, announced his desire to buy a brig the next year to begin importing trade goods.

168.2———.

His story printed from 168.1 within quotation marks on p. 242 (within review of the second edition of *The Second Annual Report of the American Society for Colonizing the Free People of Colour in the United States* printed on pp. 241–250)

in the monthly magazine *The Panoplist, and Missionary Herald*, vol. 15, no. 6.

Boston [Massachusetts, U.S.A.]: Published by Samuel T. Armstrong, No. 50, Cornhill, **1819**.
8vo (22 cm.).

168.3———.

His story printed on p. 163 of Gardiner Spring, DD (Pastor of the Brick Presbyterian Church, in the City of New-York), *Memoirs of the Rev. Samuel J. Miles, Late Missionary to the South Western Section of the United States, and Agent of the American Colonization Society Deputed to Explore the Coast of Africa.*

New-York [New York, U.S.A.]: New-York Evangelical Missionary Society, J. Seymour, printer, **1820**. Tpv carries copyright notice dated **March 9**, 1820.
8vo (21 cm.): 247 p. Untitled preliminary notice dated in type: New-York, **March**, 1820. Erratum at foot of table of contents page: "Page 106, tenth line from bottom, for *Bombay*, read Bambey."
https://archive.org/details/memoirsofrevsamu00spri/page/163

168.4———.

His story printed on p. 139 of Gardiner Spring, DD (Pastor of the Brick Presbyterian Church, in the City of New York), *Memoirs of the Rev. Samuel J. Miles. Late Missionary to the South Western Section of the United States, and Agent of the American Colonization Society. Deputed to Explore the Coast of Africa.*

London [England]: Printed for Francis Westley, 10, Stationers' Court, and Ave Maria Lane, **1820**. Tpv: W. Flint, Printer, Angel Court, Skinner Street.
12mo (19 cm.): [2], [v]-ix, [2], 214 p. Preface signed in type: T. James, London, **April**, 1820 (p. ix). "Bambey" correctly set on p. 88 (corresponding to p. 106 in the New York edition, which the compositors of this London edition followed, correctly heeding its erratum statement).
https://babel.hathitrust.org/cgi/pt?id=mdp.39015005766707&vi
FN 000138.

168.5————.

His story printed on pp. 162–163 of Gardiner Spring, DD, *Memoir of Samuel John Mills.* **Second edition.**

Boston [Massachusetts, U.S.A.]: Published by Perkins & Marvin; New-York [New York, U.S.A.]: J. Leavitt and J. P. Haven, **1829.**
12mo (17 cm.): viii, 259, [1] p. (final page being publishers' advertisement). Tpv carries 2nd edition copyright notice dated Sept. 26, 1829. Untitled preliminary editorial note dated in type: *Theol. Sem. Andover, Sept. 22, 1829.*
https://babel.hathitrust.org/cgi/pt?id=hvd.32044024415903&view=1up&seq=174
FN 000138.

168.6————. [Reissue of 168.5 with cancellans title leaf.]

His story printed on pp. 162–163 of Gardiner Spring, DD, *Memoir of Samuel John Mills.* **Second edition.**

New-York [New York, U.S.A.]: Saxton & Miles, Publishers and Booksellers, 205 Broadway, **1842.** (Copy-right secured.) Tpv: blank.
12mo (16 cm.): viii, 259, [1] p. (final page being same publishers' advertisement found in 165.5). Exemplar at British Library.

Ca. 1819

169.1 Unnamed woman enslaved on Antigua

"[A]ccount of the dying hours of a converted native of Africa …" recorded "by a Lady who witnessed her sufferings and comfort," printed (as recorded on title page of 167.2) in J[ohn] G[regory] Pike, *The Consolations of Gospel Truth, exhibited in various Interesting Anecdotes, respecting the Dying Hours, of Different Persons, who Gloried in the Cross of Christ. To which are added, some Affecting Narratives, describing the Horrors of Unpardoned Sin, in the prospect of Death and Eternity…. Second edition.*

?London [England]: 1819? Price: 3 shillings and 6 pence.*
12mo?: 360 p? N
*Second edition listed under "Select List of New Publications" on p. 152 of the April 1819 issue of *The Evangelical Magazine and Missionary Chronicle,* vol. 28 (London). This "Account of the dying hours of a converted native of Africa" was not printed in the Derby 1817 edition nor in the London 1817 edition of Pike's *Consolations.* Note that 169.4 (below, dated 1826) is Hogg 1467.

¶ All that is yet known of this unnamed African-born woman who was held enslaved for most of her life in the British colony of Antigua in the Caribbean (see Map 11), where she died, comes from the terse account of her deathbed words and situation *apparently* first printed in 1819. If the account was, before John Gregory Pike printed it, not simply factually based hearsay circulating in certain English social circles, we

https://babel.hathitrust.org/cgi/pt?id=uva.x030809934&view=1up&seq=299&skin=2021 [see 169.3].

may yet expect to find an earlier printing in English periodical literature (newspapers, reviews, or magazines)—unless Pike himself heard it from the "Lady who witnessed her sufferings and comfort" or a correspondent of that lady known to Pike.

169.2————.

"[A]ccount of the dying hours of [n.b.] another converted native of Africa …" recorded "by a [n.b.] lady who witnessed her sufferings and comfort," printed on pp. 270–272 in J[ohn] G[regory] Pike, *The Consolations of Gospel Truth, exhibited in various Interesting Anecdotes, respecting the Dying Hours, of Different Persons, who Gloried in the Cross of Christ. To which are added, some Affecting Narratives, describing the Horrors of Unpardoned Sin, in the prospect of Death and Eternity…. First American edition, from the Second London edition.*

New York [New York, U.S.A.]: Printed by Abraham Paul, for the benefit of John Midwinter, **1823.**
8vo (18 cm.): 360 p.

169.3————.

"[A]ccount of the dying hours of [n.b.] another converted native of Africa …" recorded "by a [n.b.] lady who witnessed her sufferings and comfort," printed on pp. 291–293 in J[ohn] G[regory] Pike, *The Consolations of Gospel Truth, exhibited in various Interesting Anecdotes, respecting the Dying Hours, of Different Persons, who Gloried in the Cross of Christ. To which are added, some Affecting Narratives, describing the Horrors of Unpardoned Sin, in the prospect of Death and Eternity…. Second edition, revised and improved.*

New York [New York, U.S.A.]: Printed by Abraham Paul, for the benefit of John Midwinter, **1824.**
8vo (18 cm.): 360 p.

https://babel.hathitrust.org/cgi/pt?id=uva.x030809934&
view=1up&seq=299&skin=2021

169.4———.

"[A]ccount of the dying hours of [n.b.] a converted native of
Africa …" recorded "by a [n.b.] Lady who witnessed her sufferings and comfort," printed as nine paragraphs numbered
1–9 on pp. 122–124 in *Biographical Sketches and Interesting
Anecdotes of Persons of Color. To Which Is Added, a Selection of Pieces in Poetry*, compiled by A[bigail] Mott.

New York [New York, U.S.A.]: Printed and Sold by Mahlon
Day, No. 376, Pearl-street, **1826**.

12mo (18 cm.): iv, [5]–192 p. Preface dated on p. iv: *Hickory
Grove* [NY], 11*th* mo. 1825.

http://docsouth.unc.edu/neh/mott26/mott26.html
https://babel.hathitrust.org/cgi/pt?id=hvd.hn3m6e&
view=1up&seq=126

Hogg 1467.

169.5———.

"[A]ccount of the dying hours of [n.b.] a converted native
of Africa …" recorded "by a [n.b.] lady who witnessed her
sufferings and comfort," printed on pp. 175–178 in *Biographical Sketches and Interesting Anecdotes of Persons of Colour*,
compiled by A[bigail] Mott.

York [Yorkshire, England]: Printed and Sold by W. Alexander & Son, Castlegate; sold also by Harvey & Darton, W.
Phillips, E. Fry, and W. Darton, **London [England]**; R. Peart
[*sic*], **Birmingham [England]**; D. F. Gardiner, **Dublin [Ire-
land]**, **1826**.

12mo (20 cm.): xi, [2], 2–240 p.

https://babel.hathitrust.org/cgi/pt?id=nyp.33433081774204
&view=1up&seq=195

169.6———.

"[A]ccount of the dying hours of [n.b.] a converted native of
Africa …" recorded "by a [n.b.] lady who witnessed her
sufferings and comfort," printed as nine un-numbered paragraphs on pp. 175–178 in *Biographical Sketches and Interesting
Anecdotes of Persons of Color. To Which Is Added, a Selection
of Pieces in Poetry*, compiled by A[bigail] Mott. "Second Edition."

York [Yorkshire, England]: Printed and Sold by W. Alexander
& Son; sold also by Harvey and Darton, W. Phillips, E. Fry,
and W. Darton, **London [England]**; R. Peart, **Birmingham
[England]**; D. F. Gardiner, **Dublin [Ireland]**, **1828**.

8vo (20 cm.): xi, [1], 252 p.

169.7———.

"[A]ccount of the dying hours of [n.b.] another converted native of Africa …" recorded "by a [n.b.] lady who witnessed
her sufferings and comfort," printed on pp. 193–195 of J[ohn]
G[regory] Pike, *True Happiness Displayed, in Narratives Representing the Excellence and Power of Early Religion, with
Anecdotes, illustrating the Guilt and Misery of Irreligion and
Infidelity … With Additions and Alterations.*

Dover [New Hampshire, U.S.A.]: David Marks, For the Free-
will Baptist Connexion, **1834**. Tpv carries David Marks's
1834 copyright notice.

24mo (11.3 cm.): 240 p. Examined exemplars at NhHi* and
ScU; others at NhD and NhU.

Note: The examined exemplars are bound in their original
leather-backed boards (variously marbled or tan), spines
horizontally ruled in gilt. *Until 27 March 2019 the NhHi
exemplar was mistakenly catalogued as having been printed
in 1831 (the final digit in its title page's final line ["1834."]
was poorly inked).

169.8———.

"[A]ccount of the dying hours of [n.b.] a converted native of
Africa …" recorded "by a [n.b.] lady who witnessed her sufferings and comfort," printed as nine paragraphs numbered
1–9 on pp. 170–172 in *Biographical Sketches and Interesting
Anecdotes of Persons of Color. To Which Is Added, a Selection of Pieces in Poetry*, compiled by A[bigail] Mott. "Second
Edition, much Enlarged."

New-York [New York, U.S.A.]: Mahlon Day, 374 Pearl-
street, **1837**.

8vo (19 cm.): 260 p.

https://babel.hathitrust.org/cgi/pt?id=hvd.32044004358602
&view=1up&seq=174

169.9———.

"[A]ccount of the dying hours of [n.b.] a converted native of
Africa …" recorded "by a [n.b.] lady [*sic*] who witnessed her
sufferings and comfort," printed as [n.b.] eight paragraphs
numbered [1] 2–8 on p. 270–273 under the heading "A Negro
Slave" in *Biographical Sketches and Interesting Anecdotes of
Persons of Color. To Which Is Added, a Selection of Pieces in
Poetry*, compiled by A[bigail] Mott.

New York [New York, U.S.A.]: Stereotyped for and printed
by order of the Trustees of the residuary estate of Lindley
Murray. M. Day, Printer, 271 Pearl St. **[1839]**. Approximate
year of printing (could have been printed slightly later) from
"Advertisement," p. [ii].

12mo (19 cm.): vi, [7]-408 p.

https://archive.org/details/biographicalsket00mottrich/
page/269/mode/1up

(incomplete 370-page exemplar).
https://babel.hathitrust.org/cgi/pt?id=loc.ark:/13960/t2q52p-
81p&view=1up&seq=272 (complete).

169.10———.

"[A]ccount of the dying hours of [n.b.] another converted native of Africa …" recorded "by a [n.b.] lady who witnessed her sufferings and comfort," printed on pp. 172–174 of J[ohn] G[regory] Pike, *True Happiness, or, The Excellence and Power of Early Religion.*

Derby [Derbyshire, England]: Thomas Richardson, [ca. **1840**]. Colophon: Printed by Thomas Richardson, Derby.
24mo (11.0 cm.): 216 p.

Title page of this edition of Pike's work (complete title no longer than is recorded above) and its frontispiece are relief-cut illustrations within Gothic architectonic frames initialled within the cuts "O. Jewitt". The binding historian Todd Pattison estimates the examined exemplar's original cloth binding to date 1837–1838 +/– 2 years (personal communication 22 January 2019). The examined exemplar's front pastedown endpaper carries a gift inscription dated 11 April 1842 (University of South Carolina, Hollings Library, Irvin Dept. of Rare Books & Special Collections). Printing year estimated on the basis of Mr. Pattison's opinion and the examined exemplar's gift inscription date, presuming that the volume was inscribed when newly purchased, but that it had lingered on a provincial bookseller's shelves before finding a buyer.

169.11———. [Translation into French]

"Le récit suivant des dernières heures d'un autre africain a été donné par une dame qui fut elle-même témoin de ses souffrances et de ses joies" printed in J[ohn] G[regory] Pike, *Le vrai Bonheur; ou, Avantages dune* [sic] *éducation Chrétienne. Traduit de l'Anglais.*

Toulouse [France]: Impr. de K.-Cadaux, **1842**.
12mo (15 cm.): vii, 186 p.

169.12———.

"[A]ccount of the dying hours of [n.b.] another converted native of Africa …" recorded "by a [n.b.] lady who witnessed her sufferings and comfort," printed on pp. 142–144 of J[ohn] G[regory] Pike, *True Happiness, or, The Excellence and Power of Early Religion.*

New York [New York, U.S.A.]: Robert Carter, 58 Canal Street, **1848**.
12mo (16 cm.): iv, 179 p.
https://babel.hathitrust.org/cgi/pt?id=hvd.hwt7ew;view=
1up;seq=5

169.13———.

"[A]ccount of the dying hours of [n.b.] a converted native of Africa …" recorded "by a [n.b.] lady who witnessed her sufferings and comfort" printed as [n.b.] eight paragraphs numbered [1] 2–8 on pp. 270–273 in *Biographical Sketches and Interesting Anecdotes of Persons of Color. To Which Is Added, a Selection of Pieces in Poetry*, compiled by A[bigail] Mott.

New York [New York, U.S.A.]: Stereotyped for and printed by order of the Trustees of the residuary estate of Lindley Murray, **1850**.
8vo (20 cm.): iv, [7]–408 p.

169.14———. [Translation into French]

"Le récit suivant des dernières heures d'un autre africain a été donné par une dame qui fut elle-même témoin de ses souffrances et de ses joies" printed in J[ohn] G[regory] Pike, *Le vrai Bonheur …. Traduit de l'Anglais.*

Toulouse [France]: Librairie Protestante, Rue de Lycée, 14, **1850**.
24mo, 210 p.

169.15———.

"[A]ccount of the dying hours of a converted native of Africa …" recorded "by a Lady who witnessed her sufferings and comfort," printed on pp. 392–394 of *Death-Bed Scenes; or, Dying with and without Religion: designed to Illustrate the Truth and Power of Christianity*, edited by Davis W. Clark, DD.

New York [New York, U.S.A.]: Published by Lane & Scott, 200 Mulberry-street. Joseph Longking, Printer, **1851**.
8vo (19 cm.): 569 p.
https://archive.org/details/cu31924031696770/page/n397

169.16———.

"[A]ccount of the dying hours of a converted native of Africa …" recorded "by a Lady who witnessed her sufferings and comfort," printed on pp. 392–394 of *Death-Bed Scenes; or, Dying with and without Religion: designed to Illustrate the Truth and Power of Christianity*, edited by Davis W. Clark, DD.

New York [New York, U.S.A.]: Published by Lane & Scott, 200 Mulberry-street. Joseph Longking, Printer, **1852**.
8vo (19 cm.): 569 p.
https://babel.hathitrust.org/cgi/pt?id=hvd.hn2efv&view=
1up&seq=398

169.17———.

"[A]ccount of the dying hours of [n.b.] a converted native of Africa …" recorded "by a [n.b.] lady who witnessed her sufferings and comfort" printed under heading "A Negro Slave" on pp. 170–171 in *Biographical Sketches and Interesting An-*

ecdotes of Persons of Color. To Which Is Added, a Selection of Pieces in Poetry, compiled by A[bigail] Mott.

New York [New York, U.S.A.]: Stereotyped for and printed by order of the Trustees of the residuary estate of Lindley Murray. D. Fanshaw, Printer, 35 Ann, corner of Nassau-street, **1854**. 12mo (19 cm.): iv, [7]–408 p.
https://digital.ncdcr.gov/digital/collection/p249901coll37/id/10468

169.18——.

"[A]ccount of the dying hours of a converted native of Africa ..." recorded "by a Lady who witnessed her sufferings and comfort," printed on pp. 392–394 of *Death-Bed Scenes; or, Dying with and without Religion: designed to Illustrate the Truth and Power of Christianity*, edited by Davis W. Clark, DD.

New York [New York, U.S.A.]: Carleton and Phillips, **1854**. 8vo (19 cm.): 569 p.

169.19——.

"[A]ccount of the dying hours of a converted native of Africa ..." recorded "by a Lady who witnessed her sufferings and comfort," printed on pp. 392–394 of *Death-Bed Scenes; or, Dying with and without Religion: designed to Illustrate the Truth and Power of Christianity*, edited by Davis W. Clark, DD.
New York [New York, U.S.A.]: Carleton and Phillips, **1855**.

8vo (19 cm.): 569 p.

169.20——.

"[A]ccount of the dying hours of a converted native of Africa ..." recorded "by a Lady who witnessed her sufferings and comfort," printed on pp. 392–394 of *Death-Bed Scenes; or, Dying with and without Religion: designed to Illustrate the Truth and Power of Christianity*, edited by Davis W. Clark, DD.

New York [New York, U.S.A.]: Carleton and Phillips, **1856**. 8vo (19 cm.): 569 p.

169.21——.

"[A]ccount of the dying hours of a converted native of Africa ..." recorded "by a Lady who witnessed her sufferings and comfort," printed on pp. 392–394 of *Death-Bed Scenes; or, Dying with and without Religion: designed to Illustrate the Truth and Power of Christianity*, edited by Davis W. Clark, DD.

New York [New York, U.S.A.]: Carleton and Porter, **1857**. 8vo (19 cm.): 569 p.

169.22——.

"[A]ccount of the dying hours of a converted native of Africa ..." recorded "by a Lady who witnessed her sufferings and comfort," printed on pp. 392–394 of *Death-Bed Scenes; or, Dying with and without Religion: designed to Illustrate the Truth and Power of Christianity*, edited by Davis W. Clark, DD.

New York [New York, U.S.A.]: Carlton & Lanahan; San Francisco: E. Thomas; Cincinnati: Hitchcock & Walden, **1872**. 8vo (19 cm.): 569, [6] p.

1820

170.1 Popo = William Carr

His spoken deposition written down at Freetown, Sierra Leone, by Thomas Gregory and Edward Fitzgerald on **18 February 1820**, printed under heading "Answers to Special Interrogatories put to Popo, otherwise Will Carr" on pp. 86–89 in *British and Foreign State Papers, 1820–1821. Compiled by the Librarian and Keeper of the Papers*, [Great Britain] *Foreign Office*. [Vol. 8.]

London [England]: Printed by J. Harrison and Son, Orchard Street, Westminster, **1830**.
Folio, xv, 1,334 p.
FN 000114.

https://babel.hathitrust.org/cgi/pt?id=hvd.hj131a&view=1up&seq=108&skin=2021 [see 170.1].

¶ Popo, who identified as Kru (possibly Ngere [or Guéré] or Dan in modern northeastern Liberia and the west central Ivory Coast—see Map 3), had been living in Sierra Leone, probably Freetown, for two years when he was enslaved for a supposed debt to Charles Gomez, a slave dealer operating with a barracoon at the mouth of the River Mano (modern Sierra Leone—Map 4). Gomez sold Popo to the master of the slave ship *St. Salvador*, which was captured by a British warship on 25 January 1820, while still at anchor the day after Popo was sold on the ship and placed in irons. Popo gave his testimony on 20 February 1820 at the hearing on the ship seizure in Freetown.

170.2——.

His deposition reprinted from 170.1 on pp. 88–89 in *British and Foreign State Papers, 1820–1821*.

London [England]: James Ridgway & Sons, Piccadilly, **1851**.

171.0 Yamsey (ca. 1800–) = Josiah

Original manuscript of his first-person account written down by William Augustin Bernard Johnson 24 March 1820 held in the Church Missionary Society (CSM) Archive, Cadbury Research Library Special Collections, University of Birmingham, **Birmingham, England**, where it is filed under CMS Sierra Leone Mission CA1/O126/121.

https://babel.hathitrust.org/cgi/pt?id=coo.31924057470738&view=1up&seq=262 [see 171.1].

¶ Yamsey was the son of a king in Bamba in the northwest interior of modern Cameroon (see Map 5). Orphaned as a small child, he was taken in by a brother, who became king. After journeying to Bandjoun he was captured and sold many times in many places to many people (described in detail), finally to a Portuguese man, who forced him aboard a large slave ship, the *Dido*, which was intercepted by a British warship in 1815. After rescue, Yamsey was taken to Sierra Leone (Map 4) in late 1815 or early 1816. After three weeks in Freetown he was moved to Regent's Town, where, when he eventually told his life story to William A. B. Johnson, he had been learning English, working as a cook, and embracing Christianity.

171.1 ——.

His first-person account printed, with introductory statements by Mr. [William Augustin Bernard] Johnson, under heading "Account of a Liberated Negro: Illustrative of the Oppressive Influence of the Slave Trade," on pp. 236–241 in *Proceedings of the Church Missionary Society for Africa and the East, Twenty-First Year, 1820–1821*.

London [England]: Printed by R. Watts, Crown Court, Temple Bar. Published for the Society, by L. B. Seeley, 169, Fleet Street; and J. Hatchard and Son, Piccadilly; sold by M. Keene, J. Parry, and T. Johnson, **Dublin [Ireland]**; and, in **Edinburgh [Scotland]**, by Oliphant, Waugh, & Innes, and by R. Guthrie, **1821**. Price, Four Shillings and Sixpence.

8vo (22 cm.): xvi, 368 p. + extensive lists of contributors of money.

https://babel.hathitrust.org/cgi/pt?id=coo.31924057470738&view=1up&seq=262

1821

172.0 Richard Pierpoint (ca. 1744–1837) = Capt. Dick = Black Dick = Richard Parepoint = Richard Pawpine

The Petition of Richard Pierpoint [to Lieutenant Governor Sir Peregrine Maitland, Upper Canada], now of the Town of Niagara, a Man of Colour, a native of Africa, and an inhabitant of this Province since the year 1780 (21 July **1821**). Civil Secretary's Correspondence, Upper Canada Sundries: C-4607, July–September 1821, RG 5, A 1, Vol. 53, p. 26441–22444, Public Archives, **Ottawa, Ontario, Canada**. Black and white photograph of contemporary manuscript secretarial copy of Pierpoint's petition and Lt. Col. Nathaniel Coffin's supporting letter published online by *Héritage* at:

http://heritage.canadiana.ca/view/oocihm.lac_reel_c4607/268?r=1&s=4.

Full text: https://huskiecommons.lib.niu.edu/history-500africanvoices/284/ [see 172.2].

¶ The man known as Richard Pierpoint was from the Muslim state of Fuuta Bondu or Bundu, which was on the Senegal River in what is now Senegal (see Map 3). After he was captured in 1760, he was taken to the coast, probably via the Gambia River, and then to British North America. During the American Revolutionary War (1775–1783), he escaped from his owner in the former British colony (now newly independent state) of Pennsylvania (Map 16) by fleeing to British forces. He subsequently fought with the British regiment Butler's Rangers and retreated to Canada at war's end. Early in the War of 1812 he organized a black military unit that fought at the Battle of Queenston Heights, Upper Canada (now Ontario), which turned back an invasion from the United States. His account survives in his unsuccessful 1821 petition to Upper Canada's lieutenant governor for his return to Fuuta Bondu and for financial relief. For more on Pierpoint see Peter Meyler and David Meyler, *A Stolen Life: Searching for Richard Pierpoint* (Toronto: Natural Heritage Books, 1999), and Robert L. Fraser, "Pierpoint, Richard" in *Dictionary of Canadian Biography*, vol. 7 (http://www.biographi.ca/en/bio/pierpoint_richard_7E.html).

172.1 ——.

His petition printed from 172.0 with ellipsis after final "Bondou" then closing "York Upper Canada | 21st July 1821" on p. 98 in Headley Tulloch, *Black Canadians: A Long Line of Fighters*.

Toronto [Ontario, Canada]: NC Press Limited [Division of New Canada Publications], 1975.
8vo (~ 18 cm. [examined exemplar rebound]): 186, [2] p., illus., + advertisements.

172.2 ——.

His petition printed from 172.0 or 172.1 with ellipsis after final "Bondou" then closing "York Upper Canada | 21st July 1821" on p. 94 in Joan Magee and others, *Loyalist Mosaic: A Multi-ethnic Heritage.*

Toronto [Ontario, Canada] and **Charlottetown [Prince Edward Island, Canada]**: Dundurn Press, **1984**.
8vo (23.6 cm.): 246 p., illus.

172.3 ——.

His petition printed from 172.1 with ellipsis after final "Bondou" but without concluding place and date clauses on pp. 103–104 in Peter Meyler and David Meyler, *A Stolen Life: Searching for Richard Pierpoint.*

Toronto [Ontario, Canada]: Natural Heritage Books, **1999**.
8vo (23 cm.): 141 p., illus. (including portraits), maps.
Another statement partly attributable to Richard Pierpoint

+172-A.1 ——.

Undated manuscript "The Petition of Free Negroes" to Canada's Lt. Gov. John Graves Simcoe, requesting that the petitioners ("Soldiers during the late war between Great Britain & America" and others) be granted "a Tract of Country to settle on," signed by 19 Canadians, including Richard Pierpoint, reproduced *in toto* as photographic illustration (from the Records of the Executive Council: Upper Canada, Land Petitions 1791–1817, RG 1 L3 Vol. 196 "F" Bundle Misc. file 68, Manuscript Division, Public Archives of Canada, Ottawa) on p. 90 of Joan Magee and others, *Loyalist Mosaic: A Multi-ethnic Heritage* (Toronto [Ontario, Canada]: Dundurn Press, 1984).

+172-A.2 ——.

Large portion of "The Petition of Free Negroes" (dated by editor June 29, 1794) to Canada's Lt. Gov. John Graves Simcoe, requesting that the petitioners ("Soldiers during the late war between Great Britain & America" and others) be granted "a Tract of Country to settle on," signed by 19 Canadians, including Richard Pierpoint, printed from the original (illustrated in +172-A.1) on pp. 73–74 of Peter Meyler and David Meyler, *A Stolen Life: Searching for Richard Pierpoint* (Toronto [Ontario, Canada]: Natural Heritage Books, 1999).

1822

173.1 Dan Kano (ca. 1788–) = Duncanoo

His account printed on pp. 6–7 as footnote to Mahomed Misrah's article "Narrative of a Journey from Egypt to the West Coast of Africa. Communicated by an Officer serving in Sierra Leone," which is printed on pp. 1–16 in *The Quarterly Journal of Science, Literature, and the Arts,* no. 27 (vol. 14).

https://babel.hathitrust.org/cgi/pt?id=hvd.hxkkzf&view=1up&seq=26&skin=2021 [see 173.1].

London [England]: John Murray,
October **1822** [full volume title page dated 1823].
8vo (22 cm.).

¶ Dan Kano was Hausa, born at Birnin Yauri on the Niger River, and his name suggests his family probably came from Kano (modern northern Nigeria—see Map 5). Ca. 1806 he was seized by Fulani (Fula, Fulbi or Peul peoples throughout West Africa) forces who were involved in the *jihād* (religious reform movement that involved warfare). He was sold to a merchant who took him southwest along the important trade route to Asante (Akan people), where he was sold on the Gold Coast (modern Ghana) and taken to Bahia, Brazil (Map 9), on a Portuguese slave ship. After three years he was put aboard a slave ship as a crew member; this ship was then captured off the African coast by a British ship, which liberated Dan Kano and the others and took them to Sierra Leone (Map 4) ca. 1810.

173.2 ——.

Dan Kano's narrative printed on pp. 521–522 as a footnote to an article by Mahomed Misrah entitled "Narrative of a Journey from Egypt to the West Coast of Africa. Communicated by an Officer serving in Sierra Leone" reprinted "From the Quarterly Journal of Science" (i.e., 173.1) in magazine *The Museum of Foreign Literature and Science* (edited by Robert Walsh Jr.), vol. 1, no. 6, p. 518–528.

Philadelphia [Pennsylvania, U.S.A.]: Published by E. Little … and in **Trenton [New Jersey, U.S.A.]** and by R. Norris Henry … **New York [New York, U.S.A.]**, December **1822**.
8vo (22 cm.).
https://babel.hathitrust.org/cgi/pt?id=nyp.33433081756425; view=1up;seq=530

173.3 ——.

Dan Kano's account translated from 173.1 into German and printed on pp. 186–188 of article by Mahomed Misrah entitled

"Mahomed Misrah's Bericht von einer Reise von Aegypten nach der westlichen Küste Afrika's" in magazine *Neue Allgemeine Geographische und Statistische Ephemeriden* 12: 174–188.

Weimar [Thuringia, Germany]: Verlage des Landes-Industrie-Comptoirs, 1823.
8vo (20 cm.).
https://babel.hathitrust.org/cgi/pt?id=nyp.33433003647751; view=1up;seq=214

173.4 ———.

Dan Kano's account printed as a footnote to reprinting of 173.1 under caption title *Narrative of a journey from Egypt to the western coast of Africa by Mahomed Misrah* as vol. 9, no. 3 in series *Tour over the Alps and in Italy* [sic]: *New Voyages and Travels*.

[London, England: Printed for Sir Richard Phillips & Co., 1823.]
8vo (24 cm.): p. 81–85.
Exemplars at Henry E. Huntington Library, San Marino, California (Rare Books call # 4472 Anal) and University of Minnesota.

174.1 Perault Strohhecker

An account of his background and testimony is printed intermittently on pp. 110–170 in *An Official Report of the Trials of sundry Negroes charged with an Attempt to Raise an Insurrection in the State of South-Carolina: preceded by an introduction and narrative and, in an appendix, a report of the trials of four white persons on indictments for attempting to excite the slaves to insurrection*, edited by Lionel Henry Kennedy and Thomas Parker.

https://www.loc.gov/resource/rbc0001.2019gen07205/?sp=110 [see 174.1].

Charleston [South Carolina, U.S.A.]: Printed by James R. Schenck, 1822.
8vo (22 cm.): [4], [iii]-xv, [17]-188, x, 4 p.

¶ Perault was born in Jumba, about a week's travel from Gorée (modern Senegal—see Map 3), and was probably Mandinka (an ethnic group residing in modern southern Mali, Guinea, and Ivory Coast). His father, a wealthy merchant, owned about sixty slaves and traded in tobacco and salt. Perault engaged in three battles with Hausa and two with "Darah," but was captured and taken to Darah, which apparently was on the Senegal River. After a ransom attempt failed, he was transported enslaved to Charleston, South Carolina, U.S.A. (Map 15). There he worked as a blacksmith and participated in the alleged conspiracy led by free Black Denmark Vesey to overthrow the slaveholder regime in Charleston and the surrounding countryside. During the Vesey trials Pearault

demonstrated that he understood French and French Creole, which his owner verified for the court. Because he gave the court useful testimony, he was sentenced not to death, but transportation outside of the United States.

174.2 ———.

174.1 reprinted on p. 208 in *The Denmark Vesey Affair: A Documentary History*, edited by Douglas Egerton and Robert Paquette.

Gainesville [Florida, U.S.A.]: University Press of Florida, 2017.
Large 8vo (27 cm.): xlii, 812 p.

175.1 Tom

His 24 January 1822 autobiographical testimony printed under heading "Deposition of a Negro named Tom, of the Schooner Rosalia" on pp. 17–18 [Class B] *Correspondence with the British Commissioners, at Sierra Leone, the Havannah, Rio de Janiero, and Surinam, relating to the Slave Trade 1822, 1823, presented to both Houses of Parliament, by Command of his Majesty, 1823.*

https://babel.hathitrust.org/cgi/pt?id=hvd.hj131c&view=1up&seq=324 [see 175.2].

London [England]: Printed by R. G. Clarke, at the London-Gazette Office, Cannon-Row, Westminster, [1823].
Folio, vii, 150, p. FN 000108

¶ Tom identified as from Vai country, near Cape Mount (modern coastal Liberia—see Map 3). He was taken prisoner during warfare in 1819 and sold to a European on York Island (modern Sierra Leone—Map 4), where he remained for four months. He was then sold to a man on Isle de Los (further north, in modern Guinea), where he stayed for eleven months. In October 1821 he was sold to a European at Rio Pongo (also in modern Guinea) and put in a barracoon until forced aboard the slave ship *Rosalia*, which was seized by a British warship while still at anchor at the mouth of the Rio Pongo. Tom testified before the inquiry on board the *Rosalia* on 24 January 1822.

175.2———.

His 24 January 1822 autobiographical testimony printed under heading "Deposition of a Negro named Tom, of the Schooner Rosalia" on p. 300 in *British and Foreign State Papers, 1822—1823. Compiled by the Librarian and Keeper of the Papers, Foreign Office. Vol. 10.*

London [England]: Printed by J. Harrison and Son, Lancaster Court, Strand, 1828. Tpv: London: Printed by Harrison and

Son, St. Martin's Lane. Tpv: blank. [Colophon:] London: Printed by Harrison and Son, Lancaster Court, Strand. Folio, xvi, 11140 p.

https://babel.hathitrust.org/cgi/pt?id=hvd.hj131c&view=1up&seq=324

175.3————. [Reissue of 175.2 with cancellans title leaf and other resetting at front and back]

His 24 January **1822** autobiographical testimony printed under heading "Deposition of a Negro named Tom, of the Schooner Rosalia" on p. 300 in *British and Foreign State Papers, 1822–1823. Compiled by the Librarian and Keeper of the Papers, Foreign Office. Vol. 10.*

London [England]: James Ridgway and Sons, Piccadilly, **1850.** Tpv: London: Printed by Harrison and Son, St. Martin's Lane. [Colophon:] London: Printed by Harrison and Son, St. Martin's Lane.

Folio, xvi, 11140 p.

https://babel.hathitrust.org/cgi/pt?id=mdp.39015035798522&view=1up&seq=320

175.4————. [Facsimile reprint of 175.1 with other British Parliamentary Papers]

His 24 January **1822** autobiographical testimony printed under the heading "Deposition of a Negro named Tom, of the Schooner Rosalia" on pp. 17–18 (2nd pagination series) [Class B] *Correspondence with the British Commissioners, at Sierra Leone, the Havannah, Rio de Janiero, and Surinam, relating to the Slave Trade 1822, 1823,* in *British Parliamentary Papers: Correspondence with Foreign Powers and with British Commissioners Relative to the Slave Trade* [Class A and Class B], Slave Trade, vol. 9.

Shannon [County Clare, Ireland]: Irish University Press, **1969.** Folio (35 cm): viii, 165; vii, 150; vi, 82; vi, 206.

1823

176.0   Abubakar (ca. 1779+7yrs–1833) = Abou Bouker = William Pascoe/Pasco

His life recorded in second person within a fifteen-page manuscript headed "A short Account of Houssa, a Kingdom in the interior of Africa, situated on the Banks of the Niger, obtained from Abou Bouker [= William Pasco], a native of that Country and a Seaman now belonging to H.M.S. Owen Glendower Commander Sir Robert Mends Capn, Coast of Africa **April 1823,** drawn up by John Evans Admiralty Clerk," in [UK] National Archives (formerly the Public Records Office) ADM/1/1815 (box file "Letters from Captains F 1823" / Captain Filmore), **Kew, London, England.**

¶ Abubakar was born in Katsina but was seized in Gobir (Hausa states, modern northern Nigeria—see Map 5) during the *jihād* (religious reform movement that involved warfare), sold to a trader traveling to Asante (Akan people, modern Ghana), then to a Portuguese slave ship in Ouidah (modern Benin) bound for Bahia, Brazil (Map 9). This ship was captured at sea by a British warship, which liberated the enslaved cargo. Abubakar stayed with the British Navy and served as an interpreter on several colonial expeditions up the Niger River in the 1820s and 30s.

https://babel.hathitrust.org/cgi/pt?id=hvd.32044058302977&view=1up&seq=607 [see 176.1].

176.1————.

His life recounted (from 176.0) within article entitled "Note. In Continuation of Intelligence respecting the Interior of Africa" in *The Quarterly Review* 29: 597–598.

London [England]: John Murray, Albemarle Street, [April & July] **1823.** Tpv: London: Printed by C. Roworth, Bell Yard, Temple Bar.

https://babel.hathitrust.org/cgi/pt?id=hvd.32044058302977&view=1up&seq=607

176.2————.

His life recounted in vol. 1, pp. 203–217 of Richard Lander, *Records of Captain Clapperton's Last Expedition to Africa, by Richard Lander, his faithful Attendant and only surviving Member of the* [1825–1827] *Expedition* [along Africa's West Coast and into Kano and Sokoto].

London [England]: Henry Colburn and Richard Bentley, New Burlington Street, **1830.** Colophon: J. B. Nichols and Son, 25, Parliament Street.

2 vols., 8vo (19 cm.).

https://archive.org/details/recordscaptainc01landgoog/page/n231

176.3————.

Photomechanical reprint of 176.2 in series Cass Library of African Studies: Travels and Narratives no. 21 with imprint:

London [England]: Frank Cass and Co., **1967.** 2 vols., 8vo (22 cm.).

176.4———.

176.0 printed (as transcribed by Kenneth Lupton) on pp. 306–321 as an appendix to Kenneth Lupton's historical novel *Pascoe, Prince of Gobir*.

[Milton Keyne, Buckinghamshire, England]: AuthorHouse [*sic*], [2009]. Tpv: Printed in the United States of America | Bloomington, Indiana. Colophon: Breinigsville, PA, U.S.A. 11 January 2010 [...].

8vo (23 cm.): xxxii, [2], 327 p., illus., map.

1824

177.1   Primus (c. 1744–after 1824)

His account provided directly to Lydia Huntley Sigourney (1791–1865), who published it on pp. 81–90 (especially 84–90) in her book *Sketch of Connecticut, Forty Years Since.*

Hartford [Connecticut, U.S.A.]: Oliver D. Cooke & Sons, 1824.
(20 cm.) [4], 278, [2] p.

https://archive.org/details/sketchconn00sigorich/page/80/mode/2up [see 177.1].

¶ Primus came from a small kingdom between the Gambia and Senegal Rivers, about fifty miles from the coast. He grew up in a home on a branch of the Senegal River (in modern Senegal—see Map 3). When about ten years old (ca. 1754) he and his father were captured during a war with a neighboring nation. After a day's travel with many other chained and gagged prisoners, Primus and his father were taken on an English slave ship with hundreds of others to the British North American colony of New York (Map 17)—a horrifying journey he describes in detail, including the death of his father and many others. Upon arrival, Primus and others were taken across Long Island Sound to the colony of Connecticut and sold. There he lived the rest of his life. Primus learned to read, especially the Bible (taught by his owner) and became Christian. He married and had one child. His owner freed Primus in his will and allowed him to live in a large house that was part of the estate. After his wife's death, Primus lived there with his daughter and looked after his neighbors' gardens in his old age. He was at least 80 years old when interviewed by Lydia Sigourney (1791–1865), the prolific poet and writer.

177.2———.

His account provided on pp. 81–90 (especially 84–90) in reprint of Lydia Huntley Sigourney, *Sketch of Connecticut, Forty Years Since.*

London [England]: Forgotten Books (Classic Reprint Series), 2015.
(23.5 cm), 286 p.

177.3———.

His account provided on pp. 81–90 (especially 84–90) in reprint of Lydia Huntley Sigourney, *Sketch of Connecticut, Forty Years Since.*

Boston [Massachusetts, U.S.A.]: Northeastern University Women Writers Project, 2016.

Ca. 1825?

178.0   Akeiso (ca. 1786–) = Florence Hall

Account known from an incomplete manuscript written sometime during the period 1818–1833 in the Papers of Robert Johnston (1789–1839) at the Historical Society of Pennsylvania, Philadelphia, Pennsylvania, U.S.A.

Full text: https://huskiecommons.lib.niu.edu/history-500african-voices/117/ [see 178.1].

¶ Akeiso was Igbo (modern southeastern Nigeria—see Map 5) from a village on a large river in the interior. Enemies of her country captured her and others when she was a small child, took her to the coast, and sold her to a slave ship, which took her to Jamaica in the Caribbean ca. 1790 (Map 13). There she was sold to Robert Johnston, a planter, who wrote down her account sometime between 1818 and 1833.

178.1———.

Account printed on p. 216 in Randy M. Browne and John Wood Sweet's article "Florence Hall's 'Memoirs': Finding African Women in the Transatlantic Slave Trade," in *Slavery & Abolition: A Journal of Slave and Post-Slave Studies*, 37: 206–221.

Abingdon, England: Routledge, 2016.
8vo.

1825

179.1 Belinda Lucas (ca. 1726–)

Her account printed (much of it as direct speech within quotation marks) in twelve numbered paragraphs on pp. 52–55 in *Biographical Sketches and Interesting Anecdotes of Persons of Color. To Which Is Added, a Selection of Pieces in Poetry*, compiled by A[bigail] Mott.

https://babel.hathitrust.org/cgi/pt?id=hvd.hn-3m6e&view=1up&seq=56

New-York [New York, U.S.A.]: Printed and sold by Mahlon Day, no. 376, Pearl-Street, 1826.
12mo (18 cm.): 192 p.
http://docsouth.unc.edu/neh/mott26/mott26.html
Hogg 1467.

¶ Lucas was captured as a small child in an unknown place in Africa, taken to the coast, sold to a slave ship, and carried to the British colony of Antigua in the West Indies (see Map 11). Soon thereafter a ship captain purchased her and took her to New York (Map 17), the largest port city in the British North American colony of New York, where she was sold several times and married twice. At about age forty she underwent baptism, purchased her freedom, and shortly thereafter married her last husband. After purchasing *his* freedom they went together to the port city of Charleston in the British North American colony of South Carolina (Map 15). After her husband died ca. 1773/74, Lucas returned to New York City, where she owned a house and rented out the upstairs rooms. She lived into extreme old age (by repute to about one hundred) and spoke her account when interviewed in the spring of 1825, shortly before her death.

179.2——.

Her account printed (much of it as direct speech within quotation marks) under heading "Belinda Lucas" on pp. 74–80 in *Biographical Sketches and Interesting Anecdotes of Persons of Color. To Which Is Added, a Selection of Pieces in Poetry*, compiled by A[bigail] Mott.

York [Yorkshire, England]: Printed and sold by W. Alexander & Son; Sold also by Harvey and Darton, W. Phillips, E. Fry, and W. Darton, **London [England]**; R. Peart [*sic*], **Birmingham [England]**; D. F. Gardiner, **Dublin [Ireland]**, 1826.
12mo (20 cm.): xi, [2], 2–240 p.
https://babel.hathitrust.org/cgi/pt?id=nyp.33433081774204&view=1up&seq=94

179.3——.

Account printed (much of it as direct speech within quotation marks) on pp. 74–80 in *Biographical Sketches and Interesting Anecdotes of Persons of Color. To Which Is Added, a Selection of Pieces in Poetry*, compiled by A[bigail] Mott. "Second Edition."

York [Yorkshire, England]: Printed and Sold by W. Alexander & Son; sold also by Harvey and Darton, W. Phillips, E. Fry, and W. Darton, **London [England]**; R. Peart, **Birmingham [England]**; D. F. Gardiner, **Dublin [Ireland]**, 1828.
8vo (19.8 cm.): xi, [1], 252 p.

179.4——.

Account printed (much of it as direct speech within quotation marks) in twelve numbered paragraphs on pp. 70–74 in *Biographical Sketches and Interesting Anecdotes of Persons of Color. To which is added, a Selection of Pieces in Poetry*, compiled by A[bigail] Mott. "Second Edition, much Enlarged."

New-York [New York, U.S.A.]: Mahlon Day, 374 Pearl-street, 1837. Tpv: "Note by the publisher. By consent of the Compiler, and at the recommendation of the Trustees of the African Free Schools in New York, (who have liberally patronized the work,) …"
8vo (19 cm.): 260 p. (of which p. [256] is blank, and pp. 257–260 are **table of contents**).
https://babel.hathitrust.org/cgi/pt?id=hvd.32044004358602&view=1up&seq=74

179.5——.

Account printed (mostly as direct speech within quotation marks) as twelve paragraphs (all but the first numbered) on pp. 114–119 in *Biographical Sketches and Interesting Anecdotes of Persons of Color. To which is added, a Selection of Pieces in Poetry*, compiled by A[bigail] Mott.

New York [New York, U.S.A.]: Stereotyped for and printed by order of the Trustees of the residuary estate of Lindley Murray, M. Day, Printer, 374 Pearl St., **1838**.
8vo (18.7 cm.): iv, 408 p.

179.6——.

Account printed (mostly as direct speech within quotation marks) as twelve paragraphs (all but the first numbered) on pp. 114–119 in *Biographical Sketches and Interesting Anecdotes of Persons of Color. To which is added, a Selection of Pieces in Poetry*, compiled by A[bigail] Mott.

New York [New York, U.S.A.]: Stereotyped for and printed by order of the Trustees of the residuary estate of Lindley

Murray. M. Day, Printer, 271 Pearl St. [1839]. Approximate year of printing (could have been printed slightly later) from "Advertisement," p. [ii].
12mo (19 cm.): vi, [7]–408 p.
https://archive.org/details/biographicalsket00mottrich/page/114/mode/1up (incomplete).
https://babel.hathitrust.org/cgi/pt?id=loc.ark:/13960/t2q52p-81p&view=1up&seq=116 (complete).

179.7——.
Account printed (mostly as direct speech within quotation marks) as twelve paragraphs (all but the first numbered) on pp. 114–119 in *Biographical Sketches and Interesting Anecdotes of Persons of Color. To which is added, a Selection of Pieces in Poetry*, compiled by A[bigail] Mott.

New York [New York, U.S.A.]: Stereotyped for and printed by order of the Trustees of the residuary estate of Lindley Murray, 1850.
12mo (20 cm.): iv, [7]–408 p.

179.8——.
Account printed (mostly as direct speech within quotation marks) as twelve paragraphs (all but the first numbered) on pp. 114–119 in *Biographical Sketches and Interesting Anecdotes of Persons of Color. To which is added, a Selection of Pieces in Poetry*. Compiled by A[bigail] Mott.

New York [New York, U.S.A.]: Stereotyped for and printed by order of the Trustees of the residuary estate of Lindley Murray. D. Fanshaw, Printer, 35 Ann, corner of Nassau-street, 1854.
12mo (19 cm.): iv, [7]–408 p.
https://digital.ncdcr.gov/digital/collection/p249901coll37/id/10312

179.9——. [Photomechanical reprint of 179.4]
Account printed (much of it as direct speech within quotation marks) in 12 numbered paragraphs on pp. 70–74 in 有色人に関する伝記的資料 / *Biographical Sketches and Interesting Anecdotes of Persons of Color. To which is added, a Selection of Pieces in Poetry*, compiled by A[bigail] Mott. "Second Edition, much Enlarged."

Tokyo, Japan: 日本図書センター, Nihon Tosho Senta, 2000.
8vo (27 cm.): 255 p.

180.0   Tomás Mandinga = Tom

Confession recorded in June **1825** in Macurijes, Cuba, preserved in Archivo Nacional de la República de Cuba (ANC), **La Habana, Cuba,** Comisión Militar, 1/3, 4, 5.

¶ Tomás identified as Mandinka (an ethnic group residing in modern southern Mali, Guinea, and Ivory Coast). After

transport to Cuba on a slave ship and sale, by 1825 he was more than 25 years old and worked enslaved on *La Yaba* coffee plantation in the Mantanzas area. In that year he became involved in a violent insurrection on the plantation, for which he later provided a detailed description at a hearing of the *Comisión Militar.* Tomás described the leadership, planning, use of amulets for protection, and the sequence of events from beginning to end of the insurrection and its aftermath. His testimony included his own role in these events, as well as those of other men included here who also participated (see below). During the insurrection described by Tomás two of the main rebel leaders were killed. In the aftermath eight more were executed, and many others were sentenced to flogging and were shackled or tethered for several years (see 180.2, p. 183n142 or 180.3, p. 202n10).

Full text: https://huskiecommons.lib.niu.edu/history-500africanvoices/118/ [see 180.3].

180.1——.
Confession printed on pp. 199–202 in *La esclavitud desde la esclavitud: La visión de los siervos* by Gloria García Rodríguez.

México [Distrito Federal, Estados Unidos Mexicanos]: Centro de Investigación Científica "Ing. Jorge L Tamayo," **1996.**
8vo (21 cm.): 251 p.

180.2——.
Confession printed on pp. 178–181 *La esclavitud desde la esclavitud*, by Gloria García.

La Habana [Cuba]: Editorial de Ciencias Sociales, **2003.**
8vo (21 cm.): xx, 222 p.

180.3——.
English translation of confession printed on pp. 171–174 in *Voices of the Enslaved in Nineteenth-Century Cuba: A Documentary History*, edited by Gloria García Rodríguez. Translated [from 178.1] by Nancy L. Westrate; foreword by Ada Ferrer.

Chapel Hill [North Carolina, U.S.A.]: University of North Carolina Press, **2011.**
8vo (23.5 cm.): xviii, 220 p.

181.0   Clemente Gangá (1803–)

Statement recorded in June **1825** in Macurijes, Cuba, preserved in Archivo Nacional de la República de Cuba (ANC), **La Habana, Cuba,** Comisión Militar, 1/3, 4, 5.

¶ Clemente identified as Gangá (modern Banta region in southern Sierra Leone). After transport to Cuba on a slave ship and sale, by 1825 he worked enslaved on a coffee plantation called *Arcadia* in the Matanzas area. Although not admitting to his own participation in the insurrection described by Tomás Mandinga (q.v. 180.0), at the later hearing he described in detail the prior planning at his own plantation, making clear that the insurrection was coordinated across more than one plantation.

181.1——.

Statement printed on pp. 202–203 in *La esclavitud desde la esclavitud: La visión de los siervos* by Gloria García Rodríguez.

México [Distrito Federal, Estados Unidos Mexicanos]: Centro de Investigación Científica "Ing. Jorge L Tamayo," **1996.**
8vo (21 cm.): 251 p.

181.2——.

Statement printed on p. 181 *La esclavitud desde la esclavitud*, by Gloria García.

La Habana [Cuba]: Editorial de Ciencias Sociales, **2003.**
8vo (21 cm.): xx, 222 p.

181.3——.

English translation of statement printed on p. 174 in *Voices of the Enslaved in Nineteenth-Century Cuba: A Documentary History*, edited by Gloria García Rodríguez. Translated [from 181.1] by Nancy L. Westrate; foreword by Ada Ferrer.

Chapel Hill [North Carolina, U.S.A.]: University of North Carolina Press, **2011.**
8vo (23.5 cm.): xviii, 220 p.

Full text: https://huskiecommons.lib.niu.edu/history-500africanvoices/119/ [see 181.3].

182.0 Sandi Quisi (c. 1800–)

Statement recorded in June **1825** in Macurijes, Cuba, preserved in Archivo Nacional de la República de Cuba (ANC), **La Habana, Cuba,** Comisión Militar, 1/3, 4, 5.

¶ Sandi identified as Quisi (a subgroup of either Mandinka from the upper Guinea coast or Gangá modern Banta region in southern Sierra Leone). He was transported on a slave ship to Cuba and sold there. By 1825 he was working enslaved as a contramayoral (lower supervisor) on the *Arcadia* coffee plantation in the Matanzas area. That year he participated in the insurrection

Full text: https://huskiecommons.lib.niu.edu/history-500africanvoices/120/ [see 182.3].

described by Tomás Mandinga (q.v. 180.0). At a subsequent hearing he testified that he had heard rumors that a ship from his homeland was coming loaded with people intending to fight on behalf of the enslaved people against the *criollos* and whites. His posttrial fate is unknown. For identification of the Quisi ethnic subgroup see Henry B. Lovejoy, "The Registers of Liberated Africans of the Havana Slave Trade Commission: Transcription Methodology and Statistical Analysis," *African Economic History*, 38 (2010):107–135, esp. 132–133.

182.1——.

Statement printed on p. 203 in *La esclavitud desde la esclavitud: La visión de los siervos* by Gloria García Rodríguez.

México [Distrito Federal, Estados Unidos Mexicanos]: Centro de Investigación Científica "Ing. Jorge L Tamayo," **1996.**
8vo (21 cm.): 251 p.

182.2——.

Statement printed on p. 182 *La esclavitud desde la esclavitud: La visión de los siervos*, by Gloria García.

La Habana [Cuba]: Editorial de Ciencias Sociales, **2003.**
8vo (21 cm.): xx, 222 p.

182.3——.

English translation of statement printed on p. 175 in *Voices of the Enslaved in Nineteenth-Century Cuba: A Documentary History*, edited by Gloria García Rodríguez. Translated [from 179.1] by Nancy L. Westrate; foreword by Ada Ferrer.

Chapel Hill [North Carolina, U.S.A.]: University of North Carolina Press, **2011.**
8vo (23.5 cm.): xviii, 220 p.

183.0 Ramon Mandinga

Statement recorded in June **1825** in Macurijes, Cuba, preserved in Archivo Nacional de la República de Cuba (ANC), **La Habana, Cuba,** Comisión Militar, 1/3, 4, 5.

¶ Ramon identified as Mandinka (an ethnic group residing in modern southern Mali, Guinea, and Ivory Coast). After transport to Cuba on a slave ship and sale, by 1825 he worked enslaved on a coffee plantation called *Santa Ana* in the Matanzas area that was owned by a US citizen American. The morning after the insurrection described by Tomás Mandinga (q.v. 180.0), in which a fellow enslaved man (and probably friend of Ramon's) was killed, Ramon spoke with a Lucumí man, a New World ethnic

Full text: https://huskiecommons.lib.niu.edu/history-500africanvoices/121/ [see 183.3].

identity attributed to and named for people from the Yorùbá (modern day Nigeria, Benin, and Togo) on another plantation, who planned to kill his owner and discouraged him to do so, in part because Ramon had a high opinion of that owner. (The Lucumí man was among the rebels later executed.)

183.1————.

Statement printed on p. 204 in *La esclavitud desde la esclavitud: La visión de los siervos* by Gloria García Rodríguez.

México [Distrito Federal, Estados Unidos Mexicanos]: Centro de Investigación Científica "Ing. Jorge L Tamayo," **1996**. 8vo (21 cm.): 251 p.

183.2————.

Statement printed on p. 183 *La esclavitud desde la esclavitud*, by Gloria García.

La Habana [Cuba]: Editorial de Ciencias Sociales, **2003**. 8vo (21 cm.): xx, 222 p.

183.3————.

English translation of statement printed on p. 176 in *Voices of the Enslaved in Nineteenth-Century Cuba: A Documentary History*, edited by Gloria García Rodríguez. Translated [from 182.1] by Nancy L. Westrate; foreword by Ada Ferrer.

Chapel Hill [North Carolina, U.S.A.]: University of North Carolina Press, **2011**. 8vo (23.5 cm.): xviii, 220 p.

1826

¶ Note for 184.1 to 188.1, five Hausa men's accounts. These accounts were originally recorded in Portuguese by J. B. de Andrada e Silva in 1819 and then translated into French for publication. All five men spoke of the physical and cultural-geographic details of the Hausa homeland, in response to the interviewer's queries on the course of the Niger River for a scientific journal. Additionally, each describes his capture and provides details of transportation to the slave ship on the coast, but no further. Silva does not note his location in Brazil when interviewing the Hausa men.

184.1 Mathieu of Birnin Daura

Account printed on pp. 306–308 (mispaged 206–208) in António de Menèzes Vasconcellos Drummond, "Lettres sur l'Afrique Ancienne et Moderne ...," *Journal des Voyages, Découvertes et Navigations Modernes, ou, Archives Géographiques du XIXe siècle* 32: 290–324.

Paris [France]: MM. Verneur et Frieville, **1826**.

https://opacplus. bsb-muenchen.de/ Vta2/bsb10465505/ bsb:10784637?page=5 [see 184.1].

¶ A native of Birnin Daura, north of Kano (modern Nigeria), Mathieu was taken prisoner in the *jihād* (religious reform movement that involved warfare) of the Muslims under Fulani leadership. He was taken south through Kano, Zaria (Hausa States, northern Nigeria), and Nupe to Katunga, the capital of Oyo (Middle Belt, central Nigeria), before being sent to the coast and put on a slave ship that took him to Brazil, where he conversed with Silva in 1819.

185.1 Bernard of Gobir

Account printed on pp. 306–308 (mispaged 206–208) in António de Menèzes Vasconcellos Drummond, "Lettres sur l'Afrique Ancienne et Moderne ...," *Journal des Voyages, Découvertes et Navigations Modernes, ou, Archives Géographiques du XIXe siècle* 32: 290–324.

Paris [France]: MM. Verneur et Frieville, **1826**.

https://opacplus. bsb-muenchen.de/ Vta2/bsb10465505/ bsb:10784637?page=5 [see 185.1].

¶ Bernard was from Gobir (in the Hausa States, modern northern Nigeria). His town (Alkalawa) contained a large fort with many soldiers (cavalry and infantry) with striking uniforms and equipped with swords, lances, bows, and arrows. Bernard was taken prisoner in the desert called Dallol Fogha, sold for locally produced salt, and taken to the seaport of Porto Novo (Agaey), where he was placed on a slave ship bound for Brazil. There he conversed with Silva in 1819.

186.1 Benoit of Gaya

Account printed on p. 309 (mispaged 209) in António de Menèzes Vasconcellos Drummond, "Lettres sur l'Afrique Ancienne et Moderne ...," *Journal des Voyages, Découvertes et Navigations Modernes, ou, Archives Géographiques du XIXe siècle* 32: 290–324.

Paris [France]: MM. Verneur et Frieville, **1826**.

¶ Benoit came from Gaya, a significant town in the kingdom of Zazzau (Tzotazoh) which was a vassal of Birnin Katsina (Hausa States, northern Nigeria). He was captured in the area where iron was mined, near Nupe (central Nigeria), and taken to Lagos (Akuh, southwest Nigeria). After a journey of fifty days they reached the seaport of Porto Novo (Aigaaschei, modern Benin), where Benoit was put on a slave ship and sent to Brazil. There he conversed with Silva in 1819.

https://opacplus.bsb-muenchen.de/Vta2/bsb10465505/bsb:10784637?page=5 [see 186.1].

187.1 Boniface of Kebbi

Account printed on pp. 309–312 (mispaged 209–212) in António de Menèzes Vasconcellos Drummond, "Lettres sur l'Afrique Ancienne et Moderne ...," *Journal des Voyages, Découvertes et Navigations Modernes, ou, Archives Géographiques du XIXe siècle* 32: 290–324.

Paris [France]: MM. Verneur et Frieville, 1826.

https://opacplus.bsb-muenchen.de/Vta2/bsb10465505/bsb:10784637?page=5 [see 187.1].

¶ Boniface was from Kebbi (Hausa states, modern northwestern Nigeria), which he describes in detail in 187.1 (but which was not—despite his reported contrary claim—in the kingdom of Zamfara). He was taken as a slave along the trade route to Asante (Akan people). After a journey of six months he arrived at the fort at Elmina (Accra, modern Ghana), where he was sold and sent on a slave ship to Brazil. There he conversed with Silva in 1819.

https://opacplus.bsb-muenchen.de/Vta2/bsb10465505/bsb:10784637?page=5 [see 188.1].

188.1 François of Kano

Account printed on pp. 312–316 (mispaged 212–216) in António de Menèzes Vasconcellos Drummond, "Lettres sur l'Afrique Ancienne et Moderne ...," *Journal des Voyages, Découvertes et Navigations Modernes, ou, Archives Géographiques du XIXe siècle* 32: 290–324.

Paris [France]: MM. Verneur et Frieville, 1826.

¶ François was a Qur'anic schoolteacher from Kano (modern northern Nigeria), which he describes at length. He was captured and taken by caravan (the trek took five months) to Timbuktu (modern Mali), where he was sold. He endured a three-month journey to Porto Novo (Aghey, modern Benin), where he was put on a slave ship and taken to Brazil. There he conversed with Silva in 1819.

1827

189.1 Uncle Jack (ca. 1750-1843)

Brief memoir based on conversations Uncle Jack had with the Rev. Dr. John H. Rice during the summer of 1826 published in [*The Virginia*] *Evangelical and Literary Magazine*, vol. 10, no. 1,* edited by the Rev. Dr. John H. Rice.

Richmond, Virginia [U.S.A.]: Printed by [Nathan] Pollard & [Amasa] Converse, 1827. 8vo (23 cm.).

*Reference to this article in this volume and issue printed on pp. 14–15 in 189.3, in which part of this article was reprinted on pp. 15–19.

¶ Uncle Jack was kidnapped in Africa aged seven and forcibly taken to the British North American colony of Virginia, perhaps

https://babel.hathitrust.org/cgi/pt?id=uc1.31175035250763&view=1up&seq=9 [see 189.3].

about 1758. He remembered participating with his parents in his homeland in what he called idolatrous rites and ceremonies. After being sold on the James River to a man named Stewert, he was taken to Nottoway County, Virginia, where he lived the rest of his life. Influenced by the preaching of Hampden-Sidney College President John Blair Smith (in office 1779–1789) and others, Uncle Jack embraced Christianity, enticed his owner's children to teach him to read the Bible, and became a popular licensed Baptist preacher. After his owner's death a collection was taken to purchase his freedom for him, so he could remain in the area. With this assistance he acquired land and, while living in a log cabin, continued to preach with little compensation until the commonwealth of Virginia outlawed Black preaching. His command of English diction was considered especially notable by white auditors in his time and place (see, for instance, 189.3, pp. 7–8). He married a widow with a large family, lost his sight, hearing, and some of his powers of speech ca. 1839, and died in 1843. Note that this account has sometimes been irresponsibly cataloged as fiction (despite its many verifiable internal references). Lyle H. Wright properly excluded it from his catalog *American Fiction 1774–1850*, 2nd revised edition (San Marino, California: The Huntington Library, 1969).

189.2——.

"The African Preacher" printed on p. 69, 73, 77, 81, 85, and 91* in vol. 2 (Sept. 1838 to Aug. 1839) of the Presbyterian Church weekly newspaper *The Watchman of the South*, edited by William Swan Plumer.

Richmond, Virginia [U.S.A.]: [Printed by B. R. Wren?], 1838–1839.
Folio or quarto, 208 p. Exemplar: Huntington Library, San Marino, CA, U.S.A.
Reference to this article printed on p. 24 in 189.3.
*Cited page numbers are printed in volume 2's Index (under "African Preacher") on the volume's final page, i.e., the fourth page [208] of vol. 2, no. 52 (August 22, 1839).

189.3——.

His life story told from conversations with him and first-hand accounts quoted from printed articles (e.g., partial reprinting of 187.1 on p. 15–19) and manuscript letters (some by named correspondents, e.g., Dr. James Jones [1772–1848], on pp. 20–22) in William S[potswood] White (1800–1873), *The African Preacher. An Authentic Narrative.*

Philadelphia [Pennsylvania, U.S.A.]: Presbyterian Board of Publication. [n.d.]. Tpv: Entered according to the act of Congress in the year **1849**, by Alexander W. Mitchell, M.D…. [no stereotype notice].
12mo (16 cm.): 139 p., illus. Plates. Dedication signed in type and dated by the author: William S. White. The Manse, Lexington, Va. March 10, 1849 (p. 3). *Nota bene*: sometimes inaccurately cataloged as fiction (see our lead note, above).
https://babel.hathitrust.org/cgi/pt?id=uc1.31175035250763 &view=1up&seq=9

189.4——.

His life story told from conversations with him and first-hand accounts quoted from printed articles (e.g., partial reprinting of 189.1 on pp. 15–19) and manuscript letters (some by named correspondents, e.g., Dr. James Jones [1772–1848], on pp. 20–22) in William S[potswood] White (1800–1873), *The African Preacher. An Authentic Narrative.*

Philadelphia [Pennsylvania, U.S.A.]: Presbyterian Board of Publication, No. 265 Chestnut Street, [n.d., but perhaps ca. 1850?]. Tpv: [copyright notice reprinted from 187.3, and below that (between horizontal rules, the bottom one of which is slightly bent but uninterrupted near left end): Stereotyped by Wm. S. Sloat, No. 19 St. James Street, Philadelphia.

12mo (16 cm.): 139 p., illus. Plates. Dedication signed in type and dated by the author: William S. White. The Manse, Lexington, Va. March 10, 1849 (p. 3).
https://babel.hathitrust.org/cgi/pt?id=mdp.39015030858032 &view=1up&seq=9 (facsimile = 189.8)

189.5——.

His life story told from conversations with him and first-hand accounts quoted from printed articles (e.g., partial reprinting of 187.1 on pp. 15–19) and manuscript letters (some by named correspondents, e.g., Dr. James Jones [1772–1848], on pp. 20–22) in William S[potswood] White (1800–1873), *The African Preacher. An Authentic Narrative.*

Philadelphia [Pennsylvania, U.S.A.]: Presbyterian Board of Publication, No. 265 Chestnut Street, [n.d., but perhaps ca. 1852]. Tpv: [copyright notice reprinted from 189.4, and below that (between horizontal rules, the bottom one of which is badly bent and interrupted near left end): Stereotyped by Wm. S. Sloat, No. 19 St. James Street, Philadelphia.
12mo (16 cm.): 139 p., illus. Plates. Dedication signed in type and dated by the author: William S. White. The Manse, Lexington, Va. March 10, 1849 (p. 3).
https://babel.hathitrust.org/cgi/pt?id=hvd.32044019675958 &view=1up&seq=11

189.6——.

His life recounted, with quotations from 189.1 as printed in 189.3 on pp. 96–98 in Joseph B. Earnest Jr., *The Religious Development of the Negro in Virginia.*

Charlottesville, Virginia [U.S.A.]: The Michie Company, Printers, **1914.**
8vo (23 cm.): 233 p. University of Virginia Ph.D. dissertation.

189.7——.

Substantial quotations from 189.1 as printed in 189.3 printed on pp. 31–32 in W[illiam] H[enry] Brown, *The Education and Economic Development of the Negro in Virginia.*

[Charlottesville, Virginia, U.S.A.]: [Printed by Suber-Aurundale Company], [**1923**].
8vo (23 cm.): 150 p., maps. Series: Publications of the University of Virginia, Phelps-Stokes Fellowship Papers, Number Six.

189.8——.

Photomechanical reprint of 189.4 with imprint:

Freeport, New York [U.S.A.]: Books for Libraries Press, **1972.**
8vo (22 cm.): 139 p., illus. *Nota bene*: sometimes inaccurately cataloged as fiction (see our lead note, above).
https://babel.hathitrust.org/cgi/pt?id=mdp.39015030858032 &view=1up&seq=7

190.0 Buenaventura (Ventura) Congo

Statement provided in Güira de Melena, Cuba on 23 October **1827**, preserved in Archivo Nacional de la República de Cuba (ANC), **La Habana, Cuba,** Miscelánea de Expedientes, 223/F.

Full text: https://huskiecommons.lib.niu.edu/history-500africanvoices/122/ [see 190.3].

¶ Ventura identified as Congolese. Transported to Cuba on a slave ship, he was there sold to the owner of an estate in or near Güira de Melena, where he was married before 1827. That year he participated in collective action by enslaved people against their higher supervisor (mayoral) as follows: One day the mayoral was unfairly flogging a young man, who in desperation broke away and jumped into a nearby well. Enslaved onlookers tried to rescue the young man but failed. Ventura then demanded that the mayoral go down into the well and rescue him. After the mayoral refused, the crowd began threatening him. Ventura prevented someone from sounding the alarm. He then joined the crowd, which chased the mayoral into the big house, where the mayoral, now armed with a machete, locked himself into a room. At a subsequent hearing Ventura claimed that they were trying to scare, not kill, the mayoral and that the latter had habitually abused them with unfair punishments. The hearing's outcome is not recorded.

190.1———.

Statement printed on p. 152 in *La esclavitud desde la esclavitud: La visión de los siervos* by Gloria García Rodríguez.

México [Distrito Federal, Estados Unidos Mexicanos]: Centro de Investigación Científica "Ing. Jorge L Tamayo," **1996.** 8vo (21 cm.): 251 p.

190.2———.

Statement printed on p. 136 in *La esclavitud desde la esclavitud,* by Gloria García.

La Habana [Cuba]: Editorial de Ciencias Sociales, 2003. 8vo (21 cm.): xx, 222 p.

190.3———.

English translation of statement printed on p. 129 in *Voices of the Enslaved in Nineteenth-Century Cuba: A Documentary History,* edited by Gloria García Rodríguez. Translated [from 190.1] by Nancy L. Westrate; foreword by Ada Ferrer.

Chapel Hill [North Carolina, U.S.A.]: University of North Carolina Press, **2011.** 8vo (23.5 cm.): xviii, 220 p.

191.0 Pomuceno = Juan Nepomuceno (1807–)

Statement provided in Güira de Melena, Cuba on 23 October **1827** preserved in Archivo Nacional de la República de Cuba (ANC), **La Habana, Cuba,** Miscelánea de Expedientes, 223/F.

Full text: https://huskiecommons.lib.niu.edu/history-500africanvoices/123/ [see 191.3].

¶ Pomuceno identified as Congolese. He was taken to Cuba on a slave ship and sold to an estate in or near Güira de Melena. Working as a cook and still single in 1827 (and referred to by others a "youth," although he was twenty years old), one day Pomuceno refused to comply with his abusive mayoral's order and was severely flogged in front of other enslaved people. After one man in the crowd intervened and forced the mayoral to stop, Pomuceno threw himself into the nearby well to end his life. The events that transpired against the mayoral while Pomuceno was in the well are described in 188.0 (above). Following his rescue there was a hearing, in which Pomuceno explained that he was not drunk, as the mayoral had claimed, and that he was fed up with the mayoral's abuse and his designs on black women of the estate.

191.1———.

Statement printed on pp. 152–153 in *La esclavitud desde la esclavitud: La visión de los siervos* by Gloria García Rodríguez.

México [Distrito Federal, Estados Unidos Mexicanos]: Centro de Investigación Científica "Ing. Jorge L Tamayo," **1996.** 8vo (21 cm.): 251 p.

191.2———.

Statement printed on pp. 136–137 *La esclavitud desde la esclavitud,* by Gloria García.

La Habana [Cuba]: Editorial de Ciencias Sociales, 2003. 8vo (21 cm.): xx, 222 p.

191.3———.

English translation of statement printed on pp. 129–130 in *Voices of the Enslaved in Nineteenth-Century Cuba: A Documentary History,* edited by Gloria García Rodríguez. Translated [from 188.1] by Nancy L. Westrate; foreword by Ada Ferrer.

Chapel Hill [North Carolina, U.S.A.]: University of North Carolina Press, **2011.** 8vo (23.5 cm.): xviii, 220 p.

1828

192.1 Ibrahim Abdul al-Rahman (1762–1829) = Abduhl Rahhahman = Abd ar-Rahman = Prince

Ibrahim Abduhl al-Rahman's life story told in detail by an unnamed acquaintance* (who knows Abduhl Rahhahman "familiarly" as Prince) in a letter to *The African Repository's* editor dated Natchez, Mississippi, Dec. 13, 1827, printed under heading "The unfortunate Moor" on pp. 364–367 in the February 1828 issue (vol. 3, no. 12) of *The African Repository and Colonial Journal*, edited by Ralph Randolph Gurley.

Washington, [DC, U.S.A.]: Published by order of the Managers of the American Colonization Society, James C. Dunn, Printer and Publisher, Georgetown, D.C., [February] 1828.
8vo (24 cm.).
*Note: Perhaps John Rousseau Cox, son of Dr. John Coates Cox (q.v. 189.2)?

¶ Abdul al-Rahman came from the Muslim state of Fuuta Jalon (modern Guinea). His father was Ibrahim Sori, ruler of Fuuta Jalon from 1751 to 1784. Abdul al-Rahman studied at Timbuktu but was later captured in warfare between Fuuta Jalon and Kabu and sold down the Gambia River. He was forcibly sent to Dominica in the Caribbean and subsequently to Natchez, Mississippi, U.S.A., where he was sold to Thomas Foster ca. 1789. Freed in 1828, he began touring the United States to raise money to free his family and take them to his home in Fuuta Jalon via Liberia. He died shortly after reaching Liberia with his wife. For more on him see: "Abduhl Rahaman," in Edward Everett, *Orations and Speeches on Various Occasions* (Boston: Little, Brown & Co., 1870), 3: 186–194 (which reprints Everett's August 1851 letter to the editor of the *Albany Journal and Telegraph*); and Terry Alford, *Prince among Slaves* (New York: Harcourt Brace Jovanovich, 1977), which served as the basis for the historical documentary film, "Prince among Slaves" (directed by Andrea Kalin, Unity Productions Foundation/PBS, 2006).

192.2——.

"Abduhl Rahahman's History" and "His Interview with Dr. Cox,"* printed within article headlined "Abduhl Rahahaman: The Unfortunate Moorish Prince" on pp. 77–81 in the May 1828 issue (vol. 4, no.3) of *The African Repository and Colonial Journal*, edited by Ralph Randolph Gurley.

https://babel.hathitrust.org/cgi/pt?id=hvd.hwrc-ga&view=1up&seq [see 192.1].

Washington, [DC, U.S.A.]: Published by order of the Managers of the American Colonization Society, James C. Dunn, Printer and Publisher, Georgetown, D.C., [May] 1828.
8vo (24 cm.).
*Note: Dr. John Coates Cox (b. Ireland? d. Natchez, Miss., U.S.A., 1816).
https://babel.hathitrust.org/cgi/pt?id=hvd.hwrcgb&view=1up&seq=89
Hogg 1469.

192.3——.

"Abduhl Rahahman's History" and "His Interview with Dr. Cox," in "Abduhl Rahahaman: The Unfortunate Moorish Prince," explicitly reprinted from 192.1 on the seventh page (of eight, i.e., p. 287) of vol. 1, no. 36 of the Quaker (Society of Friends) weekly magazine *The Friend: A Religious and Literary Journal*.

Philadelphia [Pennsylvania, U.S.A.]: John Richardson, corner of Carpenter and Seventh Street, [21 June] 1828.
4to.
https://babel.hathitrust.org/cgi/pt?id=hvd.ah6fel&view=1up&seq=311

192.4——.

His life related in Rev. T[homas] H[opkins] Gallaudet, *A Statement with Regard to the Moorish Prince, Abduhl Rahhahman.*

New York [New York, U.S.A.]: Daniel Fanshaw, 1828.
8vo (22 cm.): [1–3] 4–8 p. Note: Gallaudet recounts al-Rahman's life by digesting the accounts included in 192.1 and the statements of other people who had recorded al-Rahman's story or knew him well.
https://babel.hathitrust.org/cgi/pt?id=uc1.31175035250789
Hogg 1470.

192.5——.

Summary of Abdul al-Rahman's story printed on pp. 14–17 in *The Twelfth Annual Report on the American Society for Colonizing the Free People of Colour of the United States.*

[Washington, DC, U.S.A.: s.n., 1829]. Note: Publication place posited from imprint of 192.2.
8vo (19 cm.): 80, [1] p.
https://babel.hathitrust.org/cgi/pt?id=uiug.30112004192677

192.6——.

Letter by Abdul al-Rahman dated Monrovia, Liberia, 5 May 1829, to editor Ralph Randolph Gurley in the magazine *The African Repository and Colonial Journal* 5: 158.

192.1 Ibrahim Abdul al-Rahman

Washington, D.C. [U.S.A.]: James C. Dunn, Printer and Publisher, Georgetown, July **1829**.
8vo (24 cm.) https://babel.hathitrust.org/cgi/pt?id=hvd.hwrc-gc;view=1up;seq=170

192.7———.
Brief summary of Abdul al-Rahman's story (explicitly derived from 192.5) printed in the *Bulletin de la Société de Géographie* 12:79: 33–34.
Paris [France]: Arthus-Bertrand, July **1829**.
https://gallica.bnf.fr/ark:/12148/bpt6k376091/f32.image

192.8———.
Account of his life headed "Abduhl Rahahman" drawing on 192.4 etc. printed in the antislavery periodical *Colonizationist and Journal of Freedom* 1: 29–31.
Boston [Massachusetts, U.S.A.]: Published by Geo. W. Light, Lyceum Depository, **1834**.
8vo (23.5 cm.): 383 p.
https://babel.hathitrust.org/cgi/pt?id=chi.39510459;view=1up;seq=35
Hogg 1476.

192.9———.
Abdul al-Rahman's 5 May 1829 letter to *The African Repository and Colonial Journal* printed from 192.6 on p. 18 and "Abduhl Rahahman's History" and "His Interview with Dr. Cox" reprinted from 192.2 on pp. 682–86 in *Slave Testimony: Two Centuries of Letters, Speeches, Interviews, and Autobiographies*, edited by John W. Blassingame.
Baton Rouge [Louisiana, U.S.A.]: Louisiana State University Press, **1977**.
8vo (24 cm.): lxv, 777 p., illus., portraits.

192.10———. **[Second printing of 192.9]**
Abdul al-Rahman's 5 May 1829 letter to *The African Repository and Colonial Journal* printed from 192.6 on p. 18 and "Abduhl Rahahman's History" and "His Interview with Dr. Cox" reprinted from 192.2 on pp. 682–86 in *Slave Testimony: Two Centuries of Letters, Speeches, and Autobiographies*, edited by John W. Blassingame.
Baton Rouge [Louisiana, U.S.A.]: Louisiana State University Press, **1977**. Second printing.
8vo (23 cm.): lxv, 777 p., illus., portraits.

192.11———. **[Another printing of 192.9]**
Abdul al-Rahman's 5 May 1829 letter to *The African Repository and Colonial Journal* printed from 192.6 on p. 18 and "Abduhl Rahahman's History" and "His Interview

with Dr. Cox" reprinted from 192.2 on pp. 682–86 in *Slave Testimony: Two Centuries of Letters, Speeches, and Autobiographies*, edited by John W. Blassingame.
Baton Rouge [Louisiana, U.S.A.]: Louisiana State University Press, **1979**. 1979 printing.
8vo (23 cm.): lxv, 777 p., illus., portraits.

192.12———. **[Another printing of 192.9]**
Abdul al-Rahman's 5 May 1829 letter to *The African Repository and Colonial Journal* printed from 192.6 on p. 18 and "Abduhl Rahahman's History" and "His Interview with Dr. Cox" reprinted from 192.2 on pp. 682–86 in *Slave Testimony: Two Centuries of Letters, Speeches, and Autobiographies*, edited by John W. Blassingame.
Baton Rouge [Louisiana, U.S.A.]: Louisiana State University Press, **1980**. 1980 printing.
8vo (23 cm.): lxv, 777 p., illus., portraits.

192.13———.
"Abduhl Rahahman's History" and "His Interview with Dr. Cox," reprinted from 192.2 on pp. 146–148, along with numerous contemporary biographical sketches and commentaries about Ibrahim Abduhl al-Rahman, letters by him, and an extensive editorial apparatus in (pp. 121–263) in *African Muslims in Antebellum America: A Sourcebook*, edited by Allan D. Austin.
New York [New York, U.S.A.]: Garland Publishing, **1984**.
8vo (23 cm.): xiv, 759 [*sic*] p., maps.

192.14———. **[Another printing of 192.9]**
Abdul al-Rahman's 5 May 1829 letter to *The African Repository and Colonial Journal* printed from 192.6 on p. 18 and "Abduhl Rahahman's History" and "His Interview with Dr. Cox" reprinted from 190.2 on pp. 682–86 in *Slave Testimony: Two Centuries of Letters, Speeches, and Autobiographies*, edited by John W. Blassingame.
Baton Rouge [Louisiana, U.S.A.]: Louisiana State University Press, **1989**. 1989 printing.
8vo (23 cm.): lxv, 777 p., illus., portraits.

192.15———. **["Radical condensation" of 192.13 with additional material]**
"Abduhl Rahahman's History" and "His Interview with Dr. Cox," reprinted from 192.2 on pp. 80–82 in Allan D. Austin, *African Muslims in Antebellum American: Transatlantic Stories and Spiritual Troubles*.
New York [New York, U.S.A.] and **London [England]:** Routledge, **1997**.
8vo (22.7 cm.): xiii, 198 p., maps, portraits.

192.16———. [Another printing of 192.9]

Abdul al-Rahman's 5 May 1829 letter to *The African Repository and Colonial Journal* printed from 192.6 on p. 18 and "Abduhl Rahahman's History" and "His Interview with Dr. Cox" reprinted from 192.2 on pp. 682–86 in *Slave Testimony: Two Centuries of Letters, Speeches, and Autobiographies*, edited by John W. Blassingame.

Baton Rouge [Louisiana, U.S.A.]: Louisiana State University Press, **1998**. 1998 printing.

8vo (23 cm.): lxv, 777 p., illus., portraits.

192.17———.

Long passage reprinted from 192.13 under heading "Abd Ar--Rahman | From *African Muslims in Antebellum America* | Africa, 1828" on pp. 68–69 in *Autobiography of a People: Three Centuries of African American History Told by Those who Lived It*, edited by Herb Boyd.

New York [New York, U.S.A.]: Doubleday, [2000].

8vo (24.2 cm.): xviii, [2], 459, [3] p.

192.18———. [Another printing of 192.9]

Abdul al-Rahman's 5 May 1829 letter to *The African Repository and Colonial Journal* printed from 192.6 on p. 18 and "Abduhl Rahahman's History" and "His Interview with Dr. Cox" reprinted from 192.2 on pp. 682–86 in *Slave Testimony: Two Centuries of Letters, Speeches, and Autobiographies*, edited by John W. Blassingame.

Baton Rouge [Louisiana, U.S.A.]: Louisiana State University Press, **2002**. 2002 printing.

8vo (23 cm.): lxv, 777 p., illus., portraits.

192.19———. [Another printing of 192.9]

Abdul al-Rahman's 5 May 1829 letter to *The African Repository and Colonial Journal* printed from 192.6 on p. 18 and "Abduhl Rahahman's History" and "His Interview with Dr. Cox" reprinted from 192.2 on pp. 682–86 in *Slave Testimony: Two Centuries of Letters, Speeches, and Autobiographies*, edited by John W. Blassingame.

Baton Rouge [Louisiana, U.S.A.]: Louisiana State University Press, **2009**.

8vo (24 cm.): lxv, 777 p., illus., portraits.

192.20———. [Another printing of 192.15]

"Abduhl Rahahman's History" and "His Interview with Dr. Cox," reprinted from 192.2 on pp. 80–82 in *African Muslims in Antebellum America: Transatlantic Stories and Spiritual Troubles*, edited by Allan D. Austin.

New York [New York, U.S.A.]; Routledge, **2011**.

8vo (22.7 cm.): xiii, 198 p., maps, portraits.

Additional publications by Abduhl Rahhahman

+192.A.1 ———.

al-Rahman's own English translation of a letter he first wrote in Arabic at Washington, DC, on 7 June 1828, to Rev. T. H. Gallaudet at New York, printed in the June 1828 issue (vol. 4) of the Hartford, Connecticut, newspaper *Connecticut Observer*.

+192.A.2 ———.

Reprinting of +192.A.1 "[f]rom the Connecticut Observer" on the fifth of eight pages (p. 109), cols. 1–2, of the 27 June 1828 issue (vol. 2, no. 14) of the New York, NY, newspaper *Freedom's Journal* (published by Samuel E. Cornish and John Brown Russwurm). https://archive.org/details/FreedomsJournalVol.2/page/n99/mode/2up

193.1   Flora Gardner (ca. 1713?–1828)

Her obituary notice printed (with her full name and reference to her purchaser "Capt. Lee of Marblehead") in an issue of the *Massachusetts Journal* (edited by David Lee Child) published at least several days before October 10, 1828, as recorded in 193.2

Boston [Massachusetts, U.S.A.]: Published by H. J. Pickering, *before* October 10, **1828**.

Large 4to. Entry posited from 190.2.

https://archive.org/details/FreedomsJournal-Vol.2/page/n222 [see 193.2].

¶ Gardner was born at an unknown location in Africa reportedly ca. 1713, the daughter of an important man. She had two husbands and five children when she was captured with her mother in a raid on their village and forcibly transported to the West Indies. She had worked there several years when a Captain Lee (perhaps Capt. Jeremiah Lee [1721–1775]) of Marblehead, Essex County, Massachusetts (at that time a British province), purchased her, took her to Marblehead (in 1748 according to 193.4, p. 231; several years after 1754 according to 193.2), and sold her. There she had three more husbands. If not already freed by 1780, Massachusetts law would have freed her then. One source notes that her corpse was interred in the "eastern Methodist meeting house" in Lynn, Essex County, Massachusetts, U.S.A.

193.2———.

Her obituary notice reprinted (with her full name and reference to her purchaser "Capt. Lee of Marblehead") from the "*M. Jour.*" (i.e., *Massachusetts Journal*) on the seventh of eight pages (p. 231, col. 2) of the weekly newspaper *Freedom's*

Journal ("devoted to the improvement of the coloured population"), vol. 2, no. 31.

New-York, [New York, U.S.A.]: Jno. B. Russwurm[*], 10 October **1828.** *John Brown Russwurm (1799–1851).
Large 4to, pp. 226–232. FN 000103.
https://archive.org/details/FreedomsJournalVol.2/page/n222

193.3——.

Her obituary notice reprinted (with her full name and reference to her purchaser "Capt. Lee of Marblehead") on the sixth of eight pages (p. 46, col. 2) of the weekly newspaper *The Atlas or Literary, Historical and Commercial Reporter,* vol. 1, no. 6.

New-York, [New York, U.S.A.]: Published weekly for T. D. Porter & E. Prescott, at 21 Jones' Court, 50 Wall-Street, 25 October **1828.**
Large 4 to, pp. 41–48.

193.4——.

Her life story printed in greater detail than in 193.1 through 193.3 (but without her surname; and without reference to Capt. Lee; recording her age at death to be 115) on pp. 230–231 in Alonzo Lewis, *The History of Lynn.*

Boston [Massachusetts, U.S.A.]: Press of J. H. Eastburn, 60, Congress St., **1829.**
8vo (22 cm.): 260 p., illus., plates.
https://babel.hathitrust.org/cgi/pt?id=loc.ark:/13960/t8w95b-49b&view=1up&seq=244

193.5——.

Her detailed life story reprinted (again without her surname or reference to Capt. Lee; recording her age at death to be 115), probably from 193.4, under the heading "Obituary" on the back page (i.e., p. 28), col. 2, of the February 12, 1831 issue (vol. 1, no. 7) of the antislavery newspaper *The Liberator.*

Boston [Massachusetts, U.S.A.]: William Lloyd Garrison and Isaac Knapp, Publishers, February 12, **1831.**
Broadsheet bifolium (49 cm.): 4 p.
http://fair-use.org/the-liberator/1831/02/12/the-liberator-01-07.pdf

193.6——.

Shorter version of her life story printed abridged from 193.4 (again without her surname or reference to Capt. Lee; recording her age at death to be 113 [*sic*]) on pp. 391–392 in Alonzo Lewis and James R. Newhall, *History of Lynn, Essex County, Massachusetts, including: Lynnfield, Saugus, Swampscot and Nahant.*

Boston [Massachusetts, U.S.A.]: John L. Shorey, Publisher, 13 Washington Street, **1865.**

8vo (24 cm.): viii, 9–620 p., illus., plates.
https://babel.hathitrust.org/cgi/pt?id=yale.39002000006149&view=1up&seq=413

194.0 Feliciano Carabalí (ca. 1783–)

Statement by Carabalí recorded in Guanajay, Cuba, 12 July **1828,** preserved in Archivo Nacional de la República de Cuba (ANC), **La Habana, Cuba,** Gobierno Superior Civil, 936/33025.

Full text: https://huskiecommons.lib.niu.edu/history-500african-voices/124/ [see 194.3].

¶ Feliciano Carabalí's second name, Carabali, suggests he might have been from Calabar in the Cross River Region of Nigeria and northwest Cameroon. He was taken on a slave ship to Cuba and sold there. By 1828 he was married and worked enslaved weaving baskets in the infirmary in Guanajay. In July of that year he and Casimiro (q.v. 195.0) escaped from an abusive mayoral by fleeing into the "scrub," where they lived in a small Maroon community. Although Feliciano himself denied it, Casimiro and others in the community claimed Felicano was their leader. They later turned themselves in to their owner, but fearing the mayoral ran off again. Feliciano received twenty-five lashes as punishment and was shackled for six months.

194.1——.

Statement printed on pp. 126–127 in *La esclavitud desde la esclavitud: La visión de los siervos* by Gloria García Rodríguez.

México [Distrito Federal, Estados Unidos Mexicanos]: Centro de Investigación Científica "Ing. Jorge L Tamayo," **1996.**
8vo (21 cm.): 251 p.

194.2——.

Statement printed on pp. 112–114 *La esclavitud desde la esclavitud,* by Gloria García.
La Habana [Cuba]: Editorial de Ciencias Sociales, **2003.**
8vo (21 cm.): xx, 222 p.

194.3——.

English translation of statement printed on pp. 105–107 and 199n2 in *Voices of the Enslaved in Nineteenth-Century Cuba: A Documentary History,* edited by Gloria García Rodríguez. Translated [from 194.1] by Nancy L. Westrate; foreword by Ada Ferrer.

Chapel Hill [North Carolina, U.S.A.]: University of North Carolina Press, **2011.**
8vo (23.5 cm.): xviii, 220 p.

195.0 Casimiro (ca. 1798–)

Statement of Casimiro recorded in Guanajay, Cuba, 12 July **1828**, preserved in Archivo Nacional de la República de Cuba (ANC), **La Habana, Cuba,** Gobierno Superior Civil, 936/33025.

¶ Casimiro identified as Mina (a New World ethnic designation for Akan speakers near Elmina Castle, modern Ghana). He was forcibly transported on a slave ship to Cuba, where he was sold. By 1828 he had married. While living in or near Guanajay, he and Feliciano Carabalí (q.v. 194.0) fled abuse (including wrist shackling) by their mayoral and escaped into the scrub. After returning to plead their case to the owner and receiving assurances of safety, Casimiro and many others were attacked in their quarters by white men and placed in stocks. With the owner's assistance they were released but were then attacked again by white men with dogs. Casimiro received twenty-five lashes as punishment and was shackled for three months.

Full text: https://huskiecommons.lib.niu.edu/history-500africanvoices/125/ [see 195.3].

195.1——.

Statement printed on pp. 127–129 in *La esclavitud desde la esclavitud: La visión de los siervos* by Gloria García Rodríguez.

México [Distrito Federal, Estados Unidos Mexicanos]: Centro de Investigación Científica "Ing. Jorge L Tamayo," **1996.** 8vo (21 cm.): 251 p.

195.2——.

Statement printed on pp. 114–115 *La esclavitud desde la esclavitud*, by Gloria García.

La Habana [Cuba]: Editorial de Ciencias Sociales, **2003.** 8vo (21 cm.): xx, 222 p.

195.3——.

English translation of statement printed on pp. 107–108 and 199n2 in *Voices of the Enslaved in Nineteenth-Century Cuba: A Documentary History*, edited by Gloria García Rodríguez. Translated [from 195.1] by Nancy L. Westrate; foreword by Ada Ferrer.

Chapel Hill [North Carolina, U.S.A.]: University of North Carolina Press, **2011.** 8vo (23.5 cm.): xviii, 220 p.

196.0 Pedro Lucumí (ca. 1783–)

His statement was recorded in Guanajay, Cuba on 12 July **1828,** preserved in Archivo Nacional de la República de Cuba (ANC), **La Habana, Cuba,** Gobierno Superior Civil, 936/33025.

¶ Pedro identified as Lucumí, a New World ethnic identity attributed to Yorùbá people (modern day Nigeria, Benin and Togo), suggesting he was probably Yorùbá (possibly from Oyo, modern Nigeria). He was forcibly transported on a slave ship to Cuba and sold there. By 1828 he was married and worked enslaved in or near Guanajay weeding fields and doing chores. After severe treatment and punishment by a new mayoral, he and others ran away into the scrub and joined a small Maroon community led by Feliciano Carabalí (*q.v.* 194.0). Pedro told his story at a court hearing following their capture. He received twenty-five lashes as punishment and was shackled for three months.

Full text: https://huskiecommons.lib.niu.edu/history-500africanvoices/126/ [see 196.3].

196.1——.

His statement printed on p. 129-130 in *La esclavitud desde la esclavitud: La visión de los siervos* by Gloria García Rodríguez.

México [Distrito Federal, Estados Unidos Mexicanos]: Centro de Investigación Científica "Ing. Jorge L Tamayo," **1996.** 8vo (21 cm.): 251 p.

196.2——.

His statement printed on p. 116 *La esclavitud desde la esclavitud*, by Gloria García.

La Habana [Cuba]: Editorial de Ciencias Sociales, **2003.** 8vo (21 cm.): xx, 222 p.

196.3——.

English translation of statement printed on pp. 108–109 and 199n2 in *Voices of the Enslaved in Nineteenth-Century Cuba: A Documentary History*, edited by Gloria García Rodríguez. Translated [from 196.1] by Nancy L. Westrate; foreword by Ada Ferrer.

Chapel Hill [North Carolina, U.S.A.]: University of North Carolina Press, **2011.** 8vo (23.5 cm.): xviii, 220 p.

197.0 Cristóbal Carabalí (ca. 1783–)

His statement was recorded in Guanajay, Cuba on 12 July **1828** preserved in Archivo Nacional de la República de Cuba (ANC), **La Habana, Cuba,** Gobierno Superior Civil, 936/33025.

¶ Cristóbal identified as Carabalí, meaning he was probably from Calabar in the Cross River region (modern Nigeria and northwest Cameroon). He was forcibly transported on a slave ship to Cuba and there sold. By 1828 he worked (still unmarried) enslaved on a plantation in or near Guanajay. In that year, fed up with illness and the severe work regime, he began slacking off and then ran away and joined a small Maroon community led by Feliciano (q.v. 192.0) in the scrub. After capture he received twenty-five lashes as punishment and was shackled for three months.

Full text: https://huskiecommons.lib.niu.edu/history-500african-voices/127/ [see 197.3].

197.1———.

Printed on p. 130 in *La esclavitud desde la esclavitud: La visión de los siervos* by Gloria García Rodríguez.

México [Distrito Federal, Estados Unidos Mexicanos]: Centro de Investigación Científica "Ing. Jorge L Tamayo," **1996.** 8vo (21 cm.): 251 p.

197.2———.

Printed on p. 116 *La esclavitud desde la esclavitud*, by Gloria García.

La Habana [Cuba]: Editorial de Ciencias Sociales, 2003. 8vo (21 cm.): xx, 222 p.

197.3———.

English translation of statement printed on p. 109 and 199n2 in *Voices of the Enslaved in Nineteenth-Century Cuba: A Documentary History*, edited by Gloria García Rodríguez. Translated [from 197.1] by Nancy L. Westrate; foreword by Ada Ferrer.

Chapel Hill [North Carolina, U.S.A.]: University of North Carolina Press, **2011.** 8vo (23.5 cm.): xviii, 220 p.

1829

198.1 Unnamed Mina woman

Her account was taken down in writing in **1829** and printed on pp. 346–348 of volume 2 of Robert Walsh, *Notices of Brazil in 1828 and 1829.*

London [England]: Frederick Westley and A. H. Davis, Stationers' Hall Court, **1830.** Tpv: London: Printed by R. Clay, Bread-Street-Hill, Cheapside. 2 vols., 8vo (23 cm.), folding map.

https://babel.hathitrust.org/cgi/pt?id=hvd.32044011445871&view=1up&seq=378&skin=2021 [see 198.1].

¶ This woman identified as Mina (a New World ethnic designation for Akan speakers near Elmina Castle, modern Ghana) and probably came from Popo (Hula, modern Benin). After being seized at night from her home, she was forced aboard a slave ship that took her to Rio de Janeiro, Brazil, where she was sold at the Valongo Wharf. She was baptized in the church of Candelária and purchased by a Capt. Phillipe, who took her to his *chacara* near Botafogo. There she worked as a laundress until cruel treatment caused her to run away. While being returned after recapture, she threw herself into the sea. Robert Walsh witnessed this, intervened, and was able to prevent further punishment, but could not prevent her reenslavement to the same owner.

198.2———.

Her account was reprinted on pp. 397–398 within extract from Robert Walsh's *Notices of Brazil* (198.1) printed under title "Dr. Walsh's Views of Slavery in Brazil," on pp. 396–403 of *The Anti-Slavery Monthly Reporter*, vol. 3, no. 1.

London [England]: Printed for the London Society for the Abolition of Slavery throughout the British Dominions … September 20, **1830.** https://babel.hathitrust.org/cgi/pt?id=hvd.32044014161046&view=1up&seq=465

198.3———.

Her account was reprinted on pp. 191–192 of volume 2 of Robert Walsh, *Notices of Brazil in 1828 and 1829.*

Boston [Massachusetts, U.S.A.]: Richardson, Lord & Holbrook, William Hyde, Crocker & Brewster, and Carter, Hendee & Babcock; **New York [New York, U.S.A.]:** G. & C. & H. Carvill, and H. C. Sleight; **Philadelphia [Pennsylvania, U.S.A.]** Carey & Hart, **1831.** 2 vols., 8vo (21 cm.).

https://babel.hathitrust.org/cgi/pt?id=gri.ark:/13960/t7fr-
4w02k&view=1up&seq=200

198.4———.

Her account was reprinted on second page (i.e., 102), cols.
2–3, within extract from 198.3 under headline *"From Walsh's
Notes on Brazil"* in the antislavery newspaper *The Liberator*,
vol. 1, no. 26.

Boston [Massachusetts, U.S.A.]: William Lloyd Garrison and
Isaac Knapp, Publishers, June 25, **1831**.
Broadsheet bifolium (49 cm.): 4 p.
http://fair-use.org/the-liberator/1831/06/25/the-libera-
tor-01-26.pdf

199.0   Maria Guadalupe Mandinga (1794–)

Her statement recorded in Aguacate
on 11 November **1829**, preserved in
Archivo Nacional de la República de
Cuba (ANC), **La Habana, Cuba**, Miscelánea de Expedientes, 1246/C.

¶ Maria Guadalupe identified as
Mandinka (an ethnic group residing
in southern Mali, Guinea, and Ivory
Coast). After transport to Cuba on a
slave ship and sale, by 1829 she lived
and worked on an estate called San Matias near Aguacate.

https://hus-
kiecommons.lib.
niu.edu/histo-
ry-500african-
voices/128/ [see
199.3].

She married a Cuban-born man, who was also enslaved and
worked as a lower supervisor (contramayoral). In 1829 she
intervened in a dispute in which her husband attempted to
discipline an enslaved man under his supervision. During the
fray the man stabbed her in the thigh and killed her husband.
For this the stabber was executed.

199.1———.

Her statement printed on p. 144 in *La esclavitud desde la esclavitud: La visión de los siervos* by Gloria García Rodríguez.

México [Distrito Federal, Estados Unidos Mexicanos]: Centro de Investigación Científica "Ing. Jorge L Tamayo," **1996**.
8vo (21 cm.): 251 p.

199.2———.

Her statement printed on p. 129 *La esclavitud desde la esclavitud*, by Gloria García.

La Habana [Cuba]: Editorial de Ciencias Sociales, **2003**.
8vo (21 cm.): xx, 222 p.

199.3———.

English translation of her statement printed on p. 122 in *Voices
of the Enslaved in Nineteenth-Century Cuba: A Documentary
History*, edited by Gloria García Rodríguez. Translated [from
199.1] by Nancy L. Westrate; foreword by Ada Ferrer.

Chapel Hill [North Carolina, U.S.A.]: University of North
Carolina Press, **2011**.
8vo (23.5 cm.): xviii, 220 p.

1830

200.0   Rafael Mina (1800–)

Statement recorded in Tapaste, Cuba
on 28 July **1830**, preserved in Archivo Nacional de la República de Cuba
(ANC), **La Habana, Cuba**, Miscelánea de Expedientes 936/33031.

¶ Rafael identified as Mina (a New
World ethnic designation for Akan-
speakers near Elmina Castle, modern
Ghana). After forcible transport
to Cuba on a slave ship and sale,
eventually to a coffee plantation in
or near Tapaste, he became involved ten years later in a deadly incident there in 1830. Still single at the time, the mayoral
ordered him to be placed in the stocks for eating fruit in the
mango grove on a Sunday. After Rafael resisted, the mayoral
hit him on the head three times with the flat of his sword and

Full text: https://
huskiecommons.
lib.niu.edu/histo-
ry-500africanvoic-
es/129/ [see 200.3].

set the dogs on him. Rafael defended himself with his work machete and was helped by three others (one of whom later died
of his wounds), after which they all fled to the owner to plead
their case. Although the owner promised to investigate, the next
day eleven men appeared with dogs to apprehend Rafael and
the others. They used their machetes to defend themselves but
were eventually apprehended. At the hearing Rafael described
his frustration at a long history of abuse by the mayoral, including denial of privileges typically given to enslaved people and
that he wanted to be free of this oppression.

200.1———.

Statement printed on p. 154 in *La esclavitud desde la esclavitud: La visión de los siervos* by Gloria García Rodríguez.

México [Distrito Federal, Estados Unidos Mexicanos]: Centro de Investigación Científica "Ing. Jorge L Tamayo," **1996**.
8vo (21 cm.): 251 p.

200.2——.

Statement printed on p. 138 *La esclavitud desde la esclavitud,,* by Gloria García.

La Habana [Cuba]: Editorial de Ciencias Sociales, **2003.** 8vo (21 cm.): xx, 222 p.

200.3——.

English translation of his statement printed on pp. 130–131 in *Voices of the Enslaved in Nineteenth-Century Cuba: A Documentary History*, edited by Gloria García Rodríguez. Translated [from 200.1] by Nancy L. Westrate; foreword by Ada Ferrer.

Chapel Hill [North Carolina, U.S.A.]: University of North Carolina Press, **2011.** 8vo (23.5 cm.): xviii, 220 p.

201.0 Ceferino Mina (1805–)

Statement recorded in Tapaste, Cuba on 28 July **1830**, preserved in Archivo Nacional de la República de Cuba (ANC), **La Habana, Cuba,** Miscelánea de Expedientes 936/33031.

Full text: https:// huskiecommons. lib.niu.edu/history-500africanvoices/130/ [see 201.3].

¶ Ceferino identified as Mina (a New World ethnic designation for Akanspeakers near Elmina Castle, modern Ghana). After transport on a slave ship to Cuba and sale to a coffee plantation owner near Tapaste, in 1830 he became involved in violent resistance against an abusive mayoral, in part to support his fellow Mina compatriot Rafael (q.v. 200.0). Ceferino was still single at the time and had been enslaved on the plantation for ten years. Provoked by the sight of the mayoral putting Rafael in shackles for a minor offense, he fled with him and two others (including Felipe, q.v. 202.0). At the hearing following the incident, which left one of their number dead, Ceferino explained that he was fed up with the abusive treatment by the mayoral and wanted privileges present on other plantations, allowing him to improve his lot by working toward freedom.

201.1——.

Printed on p. 155 in *La esclavitud desde la esclavitud: La visión de los siervos* by Gloria García Rodríguez.

México [Distrito Federal, Estados Unidos Mexicanos]: Centro de Investigación Científica "Ing. Jorge L Tamayo," **1996.** 8vo (21 cm.): 251 p.

201.2——.

Printed on p. 139 *La esclavitud desde la esclavitud*, by Gloria García.

La Habana [Cuba]: Editorial de Ciencias Sociales, **2003.** 8vo (21 cm.): xx, 222 p.

201.3——.

English translation of his statement printed on pp. 131–132 in *Voices of the Enslaved in Nineteenth-Century Cuba: A Documentary History*, edited by Gloria García Rodríguez. Translated [from 201.1] by Nancy L. Westrate; foreword by Ada Ferrer.

Chapel Hill [North Carolina, U.S.A.]: University of North Carolina Press, **2011.** 8vo (23.5 cm.): xviii, 220 p.

202.0 Felipe Mina (1810–)

Statement recorded in Tapaste, Cuba on 28 July **1830**, preserved in Archivo Nacional de la República de Cuba (ANC), **La Habana, Cuba,** Miscelánea de Expedientes 936/33031.

Full text: https:// huskiecommons. lib.niu.edu/history-500africanvoices/131/ [see 202.3].

¶ Felipe identified as Mina (a New World ethnic designation for Akanspeakers near Elmina Castle, modern Ghana). After transport as a child to Cuba on a slave ship he was sold, eventually to a coffee plantation near Tapaste. In 1830, after having worked there for ten years on the same plantation and still single, he became involved in a violent incident

with Rafael Mina (q.v. 200.0), Ceferino Mina (q.v. 201.0), and another to help Rafael resist abusive treatment by their supervisor (mayoral) for a minor offense. At the hearing Felipe described their harsh treatment, including the mayoral's refusal to allow them to maintain a garden plot, livestock, or any means to raise money, so that they might improve their lot (i.e., work toward their freedom).

202.1——.

Printed on p. 155 in *La esclavitud desde la esclavitud: La visión de los siervos* by Gloria García Rodríguez.

México [Distrito Federal, Estados Unidos Mexicanos]: Centro de Investigación Científica "Ing. Jorge L Tamayo," **1996.** 8vo (21 cm.): 251 p.

202.2——.

Printed on p. 139 *La esclavitud desde la esclavitud*, by Gloria García.

La Habana [Cuba]: Editorial de Ciencias Sociales, **2003.** 8vo (21 cm.): xx, 222 p.

202.3——.

English translation of his statement printed on p. 132 in *Voices of the Enslaved in Nineteenth-Century Cuba: A Documentary History*, edited by Gloria García Rodríguez. Translated [from 202.1] by Nancy L. Westrate; foreword by Ada Ferrer.

Chapel Hill [North Carolina, U.S.A.]: University of North Carolina Press, **2011.**

8vo (23.5 cm.): xviii, 220 p.

203.1 John Davis

His autobiographical deposition sworn 17 December **1830** printed on pp. 156–157 [Class B] *Correspondence with Foreign Powers relative to Slave Trade 1831, Presented to both Houses of Parliament, by Command of His Majesty, 1832.*

London [England]: Printed by R. G. Clarke, at the London Gazette Office, Cannon Row, Westminster, **[1832].**

Folio (35 cm): viii, 193 p.

FN 000425 (FN number shared with our 204.1).

Full text: https://huskiecommons.lib.niu.edu/history-500african-voices/132/ [see 203.1].

¶ John Davis was a "King's boy" from Sierra Leone. He grew up with a man, perhaps his father, who was sent to "prison." Davis was then apprenticed for six years to a man living on the Kissy Town road, after which his master sold him to a Mandinka man (an ethnic group residing in southern Mali, Guinea, and Ivory Coast), who took him to that country for a month, then sold him to John Ormond, a merchant on the Rio Pongo (in modern Guinea). Ormond employed Davis as a household worker until he sold him to the captain of a French slave ship sailing for the West Indies, *La Carolina*, with fifty other enslaved Africans on board. After three days at sea, HMS *Conflict* freed them and took them to Sierra Leone, where Davis gave his deposition to the colony's chief justice aboard the *Conflict* on 17 December 1830.

203.2——. [Facsimile reprint of 203.1 and other British Parliamentary Papers.]

His autobiographical deposition sworn 17 December **1830** printed on pp. 156–157 (2nd pagination series) [Class B] *Correspondence with Foreign Powers relative to Slave Trade 1831, Presented to both Houses of Parliament, by Command of His Majesty, 1832*, in *British Parliamentary Papers: Correspondence with British Commissioners and with Foreign Powers Relative to the Slave Trade* [Class A and B], Slave Trade, vol. 13.

Shannon [County Clare, Ireland]: Irish University Press, **1968.**
Folio (35 cm): viii, 139; viii, 193; viii, 96; viii, 79; vi, 130.

204.1 George

His autobiographical deposition sworn 17 December **1830** printed on p. 157 [Class B] *Correspondence with Foreign Powers relative to Slave Trade 1831, Presented to both Houses of Parliament, by Command of His Majesty, 1832.*

London [England]: Printed by R. G. Clarke, at the London Gazette Office, Cannon Row, Westminster, **[1832].**

Folio (35 cm): viii, 193 p.
FN 000425 (FN number shared with our 203.1).

Full text: https://huskiecommons.lib.niu.edu/history-500african-voices/133/ [see 204.1].

¶ George was a "King's boy" who lived with a Mandinka man (an ethnic group residing in southern Mali, Guinea, and Ivory Coast), in Freetown, Sierra Leone. He sold blue baft until he was taken to the Rio Pongo (modern Guinea) and sold to the man running the barracoon (possibly John Ormond; see previous entry). George describes in detail the brutal treatment there, his escape, recapture, and consequent flogging. After three months he was sold to the captain of the French slave ship sailing for the West Indies, *La Caroline*, which HMS *Conflict* intercepted at sea. Freed by the British and taken to Sierra Leone, George testified to British authorities there, still aboard the *Conflict*, on 17 December 1830.

204.2——. [Facsimile reprint of 204.1 and other British Parliamentary Papers.]

His autobiographical deposition sworn 17 December **1830** printed on p. 157 (2nd pagination series) [Class B] *Correspondence with Foreign Powers relative to Slave Trade 1831, Presented to both Houses of Parliament, by command of his Majesty, 1832*, in *British Parliamentary Papers: Correspondence with British Commissioners and with Foreign Powers Relative to the Slave Trade* [Class A and B], Slave Trade, vol. 13.

Shannon [County Clare, Ireland]: Irish University Press, **1968.**
Folio (35 cm): viii, 139; viii, 193; viii, 96; viii, 79; vi, 130.

205.1 Cotty

His autobiographical deposition sworn 22 December **1830** printed on p. 158 of [Class B] *Correspondence with Foreign Powers relative to Slave Trade 1831, Presented to both Houses of Parliament, by Command of His Majesty, 1832.*

Full text: https://huskiecommons.lib.niu.edu/history-500africanvoices/134/ [see 205.1].

London [England]: Printed by R. G. Clarke, at the London Gazette Office, Cannon Row, Westminster, [1832].
Folio (35 cm): viii, 193 p.

¶ Born in Panna, near Sommbia and Kru Bay in Freetown, Sierra Leone, and captured as a young man during warfare, Cotty escaped and was recaptured twice before being sold to John Ormond (see 203.1) on Rio Pongo (modern Guinea), who sold him to the captain of the French slave ship sailing for the West Indies, *La Caroline*, in 1828. After a few days at sea HMS *Conflict* intercepted *La Caroline*, freed Cotty and the others, and took them to Sierra Leone, where Cotty provided a statement to British authorities.

205.2——. [Facsimile reprint of 205.1 and other British Parliamentary Papers.]

His autobiographical deposition sworn 22 December **1830** printed on p. 158 (2nd pagination series) [Class B] *Correspondence with Foreign Powers relative to Slave Trade 1831, Presented to both Houses of Parliament, by Command of His Majesty, 1832*, in *British Parliamentary Papers: Correspondence with British Commissioners and with Foreign Powers Relative to the Slave Trade* [Class A and B], Slave Trade, vol. 13.

Shannon [County Clare, Ireland]: Irish University Press, **1968**. Folio (35 cm): viii, 139; viii, 193; viii, 96; viii, 79; vi, 130.

1831

206.0   Umar ibn Sayyid (1770– 1864) = Omora = Uncle Moreau = Meroh = Morro = Prince Omeroh = Omar Ibn Said = Umar ibn Said

https://www.loc. gov/resource/ amedsaid1831. dw042/?sp=1 [see 206.1].

Holograph Arabic manuscript autobiography "on some fifteen pages of quarto paper" (206.7, p. 789), bearing the added English title (in another hand) "The life of Omar ben Saeed, called Morro, a Fullah Slave, in Fayetteville, N.C. [North Carolina, U.S.A.], owned by Governor [John] Owen, Written by Himself in **1831** & sent to Old Paul, or Lamine Kabā [q.v. 226.1], in New York, in 1836, Presented to Theodore Dwight by Paul in 1836, Translated by Hon. [Alexander I.] Cotheal, Esq. 1848." (Regarding Cotheal's linguistic interests and collection of Arabic manuscripts, see James Wynne, *Private Libraries of New York* [New York: E. French, 1860, pp. 169–172, as suggested by J. Franklin Jameson in 206.7.) In 1925 this manuscript was held by its editor Jameson's friend Mr. Howland Wood (see 206.7), curator of the American Numismatic Society, New York, New York, U.S.A. Seventy years later, in 1995, this manuscript turned up with related papers in northern Virginia, U.S.A., and was acquired by the African Americana collector Derreck Joshua Beard (1958–2018). Courtesy of Mr. Beard, Allan D. Austin published photographic illustrations of the manuscript's opening pages in *African Muslims in Antebellum America: Transatlantic Spiritual Narratives* (New York: Routledge, 1997), pp. 154–155. The **Library of Congress, Washington, DC, U.S.A.**, acquired the manuscript from Mr. Beard in 2017 (through private sale by Sotheby's, London, England), and has digitally published it at:

¶ Umar ibn Sayyid was born in Fuuta Toro (modern Senegal) and became a pious Muslim scholar. Ca. 1807 he was captured in war, taken to sea, and sold to a slave dealer who transported him to Charleston, South Carolina, U.S.A. He escaped to North Carolina, where his Arabic writings interested a new owner. He was held enslaved in Bladen County, North Carolina, for over fifty years and at least nominally embraced Presbyterian Christianity in 1821. Ca. 1836 (at least) he corresponded with Lamine Kabā (q.v. 226.1). He remained enslaved until his death in 1864. For more on him see: George H. Callcott, "Omar Ibn Seid, a Slave who Wrote an Autobiography in Arabic," *The Journal of Negro History* 39:1 (January 1954): 58–63; and Allan D. Austin, *African Muslims in Antebellum America: Transatlantic Spiritual Narratives* (New York: Routledge, 1997), pp. 128–156.

206.1——.

Biographical article printed on pp. 306–307 in the magazine *The Christian Advocate* (conducted by Ashbell Green, DD), vol. 3, issue for July.

Philadelphia [Pennsylvania, U.S.A.]: Published by A. Finley, N.E. corner of Chesnut [sic] and Fourth Streets. Clark & Raser, Printers, 33 Carter's Alley, **July 1825**. 8vo (23 cm.). https://babel.hathitrust.org/cgi/pt?id=iau.31858051932584& view=1up&seq=312

206.2——.

Biographical article reprinted explicitly from 206.1 but with textual alterations, and with added concluding editorial note, under heading "Prince Moro" on pp. 152–154 in the magazine *The African Repository, and Colonial Journal*, vol. 1, no. 5.

Washington City [District of Columbia, U.S.A.]: [Published by order of the Managers of the American Colonization Society] Way & Gideon, Printers, **July 1825.**
8vo (23 cm.).
https://babel.hathitrust.org/cgi/pt?id=mdp.39015011061036&view=1up&seq=130

206.3——.
Account of Umar ibn Sayyid's life and ideas derived from an interview with him (here named "Moro") and including quotations from several of his letters included on pp. 203–205 within R[alph] R[andolph] Gurley, "Secretary's Report … May 21st, 1837" printed on pp. 201–206 in the monthly periodical *The African Repository, and Colonial Journal*, vol. 13, no. 7.

Washington [District of Columbia, U.S.A.]: Published [by order of the Managers of the American Colonization Society] by James C. Dunn, **July 1837.**
8vo (23 cm.).
https://babel.hathitrust.org/cgi/pt?id=mdp.39015027751000&view=1up&seq=223

206.4——.
Additional facts about Sayyid's life derived from conversation with him, but not in his autobiography, are printed under the headline "Meroh, a Native African" over type-set attribution to "A Wayfaring Man" (i.e., the Rev. Mr. William S. Plumer) on the first page of the January 8, 1863 issue (vol. 12, no. 2?) of the newspaper *The New-York Observer*.

New York [New York, U.S.A.], January 8, **1863.**
Broadsheet bifolium: 4 p.

206.5——.
Long extract from 206.0 as translated by Alexander I. Cotheal printed on pp. 88–89 within Theodore Dwight's article "Condition and Character of Negroes in Africa," which is printed on pp. 77–90 in *Methodist Quarterly Review* (D. D. Whedon, editor), vol. 46 (4th Series, vol. 16), "January Number."

New York [New York, U.S.A.]: Published by Carlton & Porter, 200 Mulberry Street, January, **1864.**
8vo (23 cm.).
https://babel.hathitrust.org/cgi/pt?id=coo.31924057403440&view=1up&seq=96

206.6——.
Second-person account written up by the Rev. Dr. Matthew B. Grier (1820–1899) from his conversations with Sayyid (and James Owen) printed under title "Uncle Moreau" on pp. 172–176 of the American Colonization Society's monthly magazine *African Repository*, vol. 45.

Washington [District of Columbia, U.S.A.]: Colonization Building, Corner Pennsylvania Avenue and Four-and-a-Half Street, [June] **1869.**
8vo.
https://babel.hathitrust.org/cgi/pt?id=hvd.hwrcck&view=1up&seq=184

206.7——.
Autobiography (206.0) translated into English by the Rev. Mr. Isaac Bird (1793–1876), "slightly" revised by Dr. F. M. Moussa of the Egytian Legation to Washington, DC, and edited by John Franklin Jameson under title "Autobiography of Omar Ibn Said, Slave in North Carolina, 1831" in *The American Historical Review* 30 (4:) 787–795.

New York, New York [U.S.A.]: American Historical Association, July **1925.**
8vo.
https://www.loc.gov/resource/amedsaid1831.dw024/?sp=1&r=-0.27,0.285,1.296,0.492,0
http://docsouth.unc.edu/nc/omarsaid/omarsaid.html   [This digitized transcription *appears* to originate the error "D o r m a n" for "D o n n a n" in its fourth paragraph (second paragraph of the original article).]
Hogg 1554.

206.8——. [Photomechanical reprint of 206.3]
Account of Umar ibn Sayyid's life and ideas derived from an interview with him (here named "Moro") and including quotations from several of his letters included on pp. 203–205 within R[alph] R[andolph] Gurley, "Secretary's Report … May 21st, 1837" printed on pp. 201–206 in photomechanical reprint of the monthly periodical *The African Repository, and Colonial Journal*, vol. 13, no. 7 (July 1837), with new imprint:

New York [New York, U.S.A.]: Kraus Reprint Corporation, **1967.** Tpv: Printed in the United States of America.
8vo (24 cm.).
https://babel.hathitrust.org/cgi/pt?id=uc1.$b541061&view=1up&seq=219

206.9——.
Second-person account reprinted from 206.6 under heading "Uncle Moreau (Omar Ibn Said)" on pp. 470–474 in *Slave Testimony: Two Centuries of Letters, Speeches, and Autobiographies*, edited by John W. Blassingame.

Baton Rouge [Louisiana, U.S.A.]: Louisiana State University Press, **1977.**
8vo (24 cm.): lxv, 777 p., illus., portraits.

206.10———. [Second printing of 206.9]
Second-person account reprinted from 206.6 under heading "Uncle Moreau (Omar Ibn Said)" on pp. 470–474 in *Slave Testimony: Two Centuries of Letters, Speeches, and Autobiographies*, edited by John W. Blassingame.

Baton Rouge [Louisiana, U.S.A.]: Louisiana State University Press, **1977.** Second printing.
8vo (23 cm.): lxv, 777 p., illus., portraits.

206.11———. [Another printing of 206.9]
Second-person account reprinted from 206.6 under heading "Uncle Moreau (Omar Ibn Said)" on pp. 470–474 in *Slave Testimony: Two Centuries of Letters, Speeches, and Autobiographies*, edited by John W. Blassingame.

Baton Rouge [Louisiana, U.S.A.]: Louisiana State University Press, **1979.** 1979 printing.
8vo (23 cm.): lxv, 777 p., illus., portraits.

206.12———. [Another printing of 206.9]
Second-person account reprinted from 206.6 under heading "Uncle Moreau (Omar Ibn Said)" on pp. 470–474 in *Slave Testimony: Two Centuries of Letters, Speeches, and Autobiographies*, edited by John W. Blassingame.

Baton Rouge [Louisiana, U.S.A.]: Louisiana State University Press, **1980.** 1980 printing.
8vo (23 cm.): lxv, 777 p., illus., portraits.

206.13———.
Reprinting of 206.7 on pp. 464–468 within larger section on Umar ibn Sayyid printed on pp. 445–523, as well as a reprinting of 206.5 on pp. 432–433 in *African Muslims in Antebellum American: A Source Book*, edited by Allan D. Austin.

New York [New York, U.S.A.]: Garland Publishing, **1984.**
8vo (23 cm.): xiv, 759 [*sic*] p., maps.

206.14———. [Another printing of 206.9]
Second-person account reprinted from 206.6 under heading "Uncle Moreau (Omar Ibn Said)" on pp. 470–474 in *Slave Testimony: Two Centuries of Letters, Speeches, and Autobiographies*, edited by John W. Blassingame.

Baton Rouge [Louisiana, U.S.A.]: Louisiana State University Press, **1989.** 1989 printing.
8vo (23 cm.): lxv, 777 p., illus., portraits.

206.15———. [Another printing of 206.9]
Second-person account reprinted from 206.6 under heading "Uncle Moreau (Omar Ibn Said)" on pp. 470–474 in *Slave Testimony: Two Centuries of Letters, Speeches, and Autobiographies*, edited by John W. Blassingame.

Baton Rouge [Louisiana, U.S.A.]: Louisiana State University Press, **1998.** 1998 printing.
8vo (23 cm.): lxv, 777 p., illus., portraits.

206.16———.
"The Life of Omar Ibn-Said, Written by Himself" facsimile of 206.0 with introduction and translation into English by Ala A. Alryyes on pp. 58–93 in *The Multilingual Anthology of American Literature: A Reader of Original Texts with English Translations*, edited by Marc Shell and Werner Sollors.

New York [New York, U.S.A.]: New York University Press, **2000.**
8vo (23 cm.): xiii, 750 p.

206.17———. [Another printing of 206.9]
Second-person account reprinted from 206.6 under heading "Uncle Moreau (Omar Ibn Said)" on pp. 470–474 in *Slave Testimony: Two Centuries of Letters, Speeches, and Autobiographies*, edited by John W. Blassingame.

Baton Rouge [Louisiana, U.S.A.]: Louisiana State University Press, **2002.** 2002 printing.
8vo (23 cm.): lxv, 777 p., illus., portraits.

206.18———.
Paraphrases and quotations from Ala A. Alryyes's English translation (206.16) of Omar Ibn-Said's manuscript autobiography in Ghada Osman and Camille F. Forbes's article "Representing the West in the Arabic Language: The Slave Narrative of Omar Ibn Said" in *Journal of Islamic Studies* 15:3: 331–343.

Oxford [England]: Oxford Centre for Islamic Studies, **2004.**
http://www.artsrn.ualberta.ca/amcdouga/Hist446/reading_assignments_2010/slave_narratives/narrative_omar_ibn_said.pdf

206.19———.
"Autobiography Of [*sic*] Omar Ibn Said, Slave in North Carolina, 1831" professedly reprinted from 206.7 (as stated on p. 20), but (because it prints "Dorman" instead of "Donnan" in its *third* paragraph) perhaps actually reprinted from Documenting the American South's transcription of it, on pp. 187–200 in *Five Classic Muslim Slave Narratives: Selim Aga, Job Ben Sulaiman, Nicholas Said, Omar ibn Said, [and] Abu Bakr Sadiq*, edited by Muhammad A. Al-Ahari.

[Chicago, Illinois, U.S.A.]: Magribine Press, **[2006].** "First edition." Examined exemplar's colophon: Made in U.S.A. | Columbia, SC | 30 June 2018.
8vo (23 cm.): 210 p., illus. (portraits). Al-Ahari's introductory essay "Rescuing Arabic and English Islamic Slave Narratives from the Shifting Sands of Time: The Historicity of Muslim

Narratives in the Americas," pp. 7–36, asserts of J. Franklin Jameson's 1925 edition (206.7), "Like many 'scholars' Jameson used Cotheal work [*sic*] and called it his own" (p. 22). In fact, on pp. 191–192 of Al-Ahari's reprint of Jameson's work (i.e., the present item), Jameson states that the translation he presents to readers in 1925 is "a better version [i.e., than Cotheal's] from [i.e., by] the Rev. Isaac Bird (1793–1876) of Hartford [Connecticut] … slightly revised through the kindness of Dr. F. M. Moussa, secretary of the Egyptian Legation in Washington [DC]".

206.20———. [Another printing of 206.9]

Second-person account reprinted from 206.6 under heading "Uncle Moreau (Omar Ibn Said)" on pp. 470–474 in *Slave Testimony: Two Centuries of Letters, Speeches, and Autobiographies*, edited by John W. Blassingame.

Baton Rouge [Louisiana, U.S.A.]: Louisiana State University Press, 2009.

8vo (24 cm.): lxv, 777 p., illus., portraits.

206.21———.

A Muslim American Slave: The Life of Omar Ibn Said, translated into Englsih and edited by Ala A. Alryyes.

Madison, Wisconsin [U.S.A.]: University of Wisconsin Press, 2011.

8vo (23 cm.): xii, 222 p.

Additional published letter by Sayyid

+206-A.1———.

John O. Hunwick, "I Wish to be Seen in Our Land Called Afrika: Umar b. Sayyid's Appeal to be Released from Slavery (1819)," *Journal of Arabic and Islamic Studies* 5:3 (2003–2004): 62–77. Hunwick translates an Arabic letter of Sayyid written in 1819 with extended commentary and numerous devotional Qur'anic quotations of praise and blame, good and evil, accusation, etc., amidst which Sayyid expressed his desire to return to his African homeland.

207.1 Asa-Asa = Louis

"Narrative of Louis Asa-Asa, a Captured African … The Negro Boy's Narrative" printed on pp. 41-44 (signed in type and dated at end "Louis Asa-Asa, London, **January 31, 1831**") in Mary Prince, *The History of Mary Prince, A West Indian Slave, Related by Herself, with a Supplement by the Editor*

http://www.gutenberg.org/files/17851/17851-h/17851-h.htm [see 207.1].

[Thomas Pringle]. *To which is added the Narrative of Asa-Asa, a Captured African.*

London [England]: Published by F. Westley and A. H. Davis, Stationers' Hall Court; And by Waugh & Innes, **Edinburgh [Scotland]**, 1831. Colophon: London: S. Bagster, Jun., Printer, Bartholomew Close.

8vo (20 cm.): iv, 44 p. Preface dated (on p. iv) January 25, 1831.

Hogg 1473.

¶ Asa-Asa was born near a large town called Egie in a country called Bycla (an as yet unknown location). His father was a Clashoquin from Byola (also an unknown location). As a youth, Asa-Asa was captured with many others during warfare in 1826, taken to the coast, and sold to French slavers. He provides a detailed description of the Middle Passage. The French slave ship he was on was intercepted by the British at sea, and Asa-Asa and others were taken to London, England.

207.2———.

"Narrative of Louis Asa-Asa, a Captured African … The Negro Boy's Narrative" printed on pp. 41-44 (signed in type and dated at end "Louis Asa-Asa, London, January 31, 1831") in Mary Prince, *The History of Mary Prince, A West Indian Slave, Related by Herself, with a Supplement by the Editor* [Thomas Pringle]. *To which is added the Narrative of Asa-Asa, a Captured African.* **2nd edition.**

London [England]: [F. Westley and A. H. Davis*], 1831. *Principal publishers suggested by 207.1 and 207.3. Entry posited from 207.3.

8vo (20 cm?): iv, 44 p? Postscript—Second edition dated March 22, 1831, according to 207.3 p. ii.

207.3———.

"Narrative of Louis Asa-Asa, a Captured African … The Negro Boy's Narrative" printed on pp. 41-44 (signed in type and dated at end "Louis Asa-Asa, London, January 31, 1831") in Mary Prince, *The History of Mary Prince, A West Indian Slave, Related by Herself, with a Supplement by the Editor* [Thomas Pringle]. *To which is added the Narrative of Asa-Asa, a Captured African.* **3rd edition.**

London [England]: Published by F. Westley and A. H. Davis, Stationer's Hall Court; and by Waugh & Innes, **Edinburgh [Scotland]**: And supplied at trade price to Anti-Slavery Associations, by Joseph Phillips, 18, Aldermanbury, **1831.**

8vo (20 cm.): iv, 44 p. Preface dated (on p. ii) January 25, 1831. Postscript--Second edition dated (on p. ii) March 22, 1831. Appendix includes a letter dated (on p. 41) March 28, 1831.

207.4———.

"Narrative of Louis Asa-Asa, a Captured African ... The Negro Boy's Narrative" printed in Mary Prince, *The History of Mary Prince, A West Indian Slave, related by herself.* Edited with an introduction by Moira Ferguson; with a preface by Zigi Alexander.

London [England]: Pandora, **1987.**
8vo (20 cm.): xvi, 124 p.

207.5———.

Photomechanical reprint of 207.1 as first of six complete books reproduced in *Six Women's Slave Narratives*, with an Introduction by William L. Andrews. (A volume in the series: The Schomburg Library of Nineteenth-Century Black Women Writers, general editor Henry Louis Gates Jr.)

New York [New York, U.S.A.]: Oxford University Press, **1988.**
12mo (17 cm.) xli, [1], iv, 44, [2], 19, [1], 42, [64], 62, [2], 97 p.

207.6———.

"Narrative of Louis Asa-Asa, a Captured African ... The Negro Boy's Narrative" printed (without concluding typeset signature and dateline) on pp. 121–124 in Mary Prince, *The History of Mary Prince, A West Indian Slave, related by herself,* edited with an introduction by Moira Ferguson.

Ann Arbor [Michigan, U.S.A.]: University of Michigan Press, **[1993].**
8vo (21 cm.): xvi, 124 p.

207.7———. [Revised edition of 207.6]

"Narrative of Louis Asa-Asa, a Captured African ... The Negro Boy's Narrative" printed (without concluding typeset signature and dateline) on p. 132-135 in Mary Prince, *The History of Mary Prince, A West Indian Slave, related by herself,* edited with an introduction by Moira Ferguson. Revised edition.

Ann Arbor [Michigan, U.S.A.]: University of Michigan Press, **[1997].**
8vo (20.3 cm.): vii, [3], 173 p., map.

207.8———. [French translation]

Printed in Mary Prince, *La Véritable Histoire de Mary Prince, Esclave Antillaise, racontée par elle-même,* translated by Monique Baile.

Paris [France]: Albin Michel, **2000.**
8vo (20 cm.): 133 p.

207.9———.

Account printed from 207.3 (London, 1831) in *The History of Mary Prince, A West Indian Slave Narrative.*

Mineola, New York [U.S.A.]: Dover Publications, **2004.**
8vo (22 cm.): iii, 69 p.

207.10———.

Account printed in *The History of Mary Prince, A West Indian Slave, Related by Herself, with a Supplement by the Editor* [Thomas Pringle]. *To which is added the Narrative of Asa-Asa, a Captured African.*

Calumet, Michigan: Published by Richard Buchko, **2014.**
8vo (20 cm.): 88 p.

207.11———.

Account printed in *Mary Prince and Ashton Warner: Two Slave Narratives transcribed by Susannah Moodie. A Critical Edition.* Edited by Molly Blyth and Michael Peterman.

Ottawa [Ontario] Canada: The Tecumseh Press, **2018.**
8vo (22 cm.): 327 p.

208.1 Unnamed father and husband

Account printed under the heading "Juvenile Department" within "A short history of the poor slaves who are employed in cultivating Sugar, cotton, coffee, &c; intended to make little children pity them, and use their endeavours to relieve them from bondage. No II," on second page [i.e., 190], col. 4, of the antislavery newspaper *The Liberator*, vol. 1, no. 48.

http://fair-use.org/the-liberator/1831/11/26/the-liberator-01-48.pdf [see 208.1].

Boston [Massachusetts, U.S.A.]: William Lloyd Garrison and Isaac Knapp, Publishers, November 26, **1831.**
Broadsheet bifolium (49 cm.): 4 p.

¶ **This husband and father of several children from an unknown place in Africa was violently kidnapped when getting water from a spring, taken some distance, and sold to men who took him to a slave ship, which transported him to the United States of America.**

209.0 Savad Carabalí Bibí

His statement was recorded on 1 July **1831** in Puerta de la Güira, Cuba, in a manuscript preserved in Archivo Nacional de la República de Cuba (ANC), **La Habana, Cuba,** Miscelánea de Expedientes, 207/F.

¶ Savad identified as Carabalí and Bibí (Ibibio), likely referring to Calabar in the Cross River region (modern Nigeria and northwestern Cameroon) and may have been baptized while young. He was transported on a slave ship to Cuba and sold. In 1831 he lived alone in the infirmary of a plantation in or near Puerta de la Güira and did not get along well with other enslaved people because no one knew his language and they believed he was pursuing their wives. Charged with assaulting his white supervisor, a carter, with a machete, Savad replied in court through an interpreter that the carter had been abusing him, then attacked him with a whip, so Savad defended himself with his machete. He denied trying to seduce the carter's wife, who was white. After the attack Savad ran away, but the mayoral led a group to catch him, which they did, hitting him on the head and severely injuring him in the process. A record of Savad's fate is lacking, but he was likely executed for assaulting a white man with his machete.

Full text: https://huskiecommons.lib.niu.edu/history-500africanvoices/135/ [see 209.3].

209.1——.

Statement printed on p. 132 in *La esclavitud desde la esclavitud: La visión de los siervos* by Gloria García Rodríguez.

México [Distrito Federal, Estados Unidos Mexicanos]: Centro de Investigación Científica "Ing. Jorge L Tamayo," **1996.** 8vo (21 cm.): 251 p.

209.2——.

Statement printed on p. 118 *La esclavitud desde la esclavitud,* by Gloria García.

La Habana [Cuba]: Editorial de Ciencias Sociales, **2003.** 8vo (21 cm.): xx, 222 p.

209.3——.

English translation of statement printed on pp. 109–110 in *Voices of the Enslaved in Nineteenth-Century Cuba: A Documentary History,* edited by Gloria García Rodríguez. Translated [from 209.1] by Nancy L. Westrate; foreword by Ada Ferrer.

Chapel Hill [North Carolina, U.S.A.]: University of North Carolina Press, **2011.** 8vo (23.5 cm.): xviii, 220 p.

210.0 Boticario = Francisco de Paulo Congo (1801–1831)

Statement recorded in Bauta, Cuba on 4 March **1831,** in a manuscript preserved in Archivo Nacional de la República de Cuba (ANC), **La Habana, Cuba,** Miscelánea de Expedientes, 2027/D.

¶ Boticario identified as Congolese. He was forcibly transported on a slave ship to Cuba and sold there. By 1831 he was single and worked enslaved on an estate in or near Bauta as a carter. He ran away at least twice, each time placed in leg irons after capture. In the last case, after eight days in hiding he broke into an enslaved man's hut to find liquor and tobacco, but was surprised by its occupant and the contramayoral, who lay in waiting. In the ensuing scuffle Boticario killed the occupant. After his hearing in 1831, Boticario was executed by hanging.

Full text: https://huskiecommons.lib.niu.edu/history-500africanvoices/136/ [see 210.3].

210.1——.

Printed on p. 146 in *La esclavitud desde la esclavitud: La visión de los siervos* by Gloria García Rodríguez.

México [Distrito Federal, Estados Unidos Mexicanos]: Centro de Investigación Científica "Ing. Jorge L Tamayo," **1996.** 8vo (21 cm.): 251 p.

210.2——.

Printed on p. 131 *La esclavitud desde la esclavitud,* by Gloria García.

La Habana [Cuba]: Editorial de Ciencias Sociales, **2003.** 8vo (21 cm.): xx, 222 p.

210.3——.

English translation of statement printed on p. 124 in *Voices of the Enslaved in Nineteenth-Century Cuba: A Documentary History,* edited by Gloria García Rodríguez. Translated [from 210.1] by Nancy L. Westrate; foreword by Ada Ferrer.

Chapel Hill [North Carolina, U.S.A.]: University of North Carolina Press, **2011.** 8vo (23.5 cm.): xviii, 220 p.

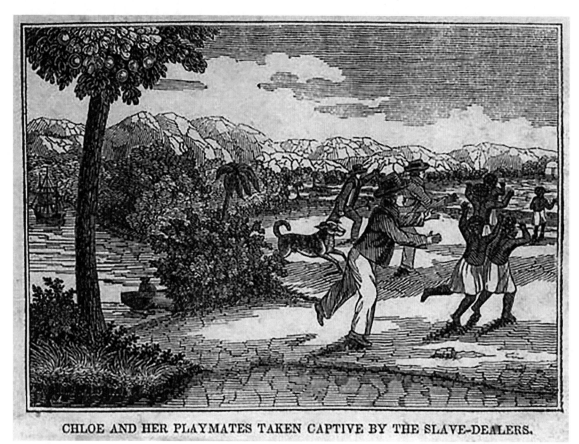

CHLOE AND HER PLAYMATES TAKEN CAPTIVE BY THE SLAVE-DEALERS.

Figure 12: Engraving opposite title page of Chloe Spear, *Memoir of Mrs. Chloe Spear, A Native of Africa, who was Enslaved in Childhood, and died in Boston, January 3, 1815 … Aged 65 Years*, edited by *A Lady of Boston* (Boston: James Loring, 1832).

1832

211.1 Chloe Spear (ca. 1750–1815)

Memoir of Mrs. Chloe Spear, A Native of Africa, who was Enslaved in Childhood, and died in Boston, January 3, 1815 … Aged 65 Years, edited by A Lady of Boston [i.e., Rebecca Warren Brown].

Boston [Massachusetts, U.S.A.]: James Loring, 132 Washington Street, **1832**. [See report of publication in Garrison and Lloyd's newspaper *The Liberator*, vol. 2, no. 19 (May 12, 1832).]
12mo (15 cm.): [4], iii, [2], 10–108 p.
http://docsouth.unc.edu/neh/brownrw/brownrw.html
Hogg 1474.

¶ Ca. 1762 Spear, aged twelve, was transported with other enslaved children from Africa (unknown location) to the city of Philadelphia in the British North American colony of Pennsylvania, then sold there and taken north to the city of

https://archive.org/stream/memoirofmrschloe-00lady#page/n7 [see 211.1].

Boston in the province of Massachusetts. In 1780 newly independent Commonwealth of Massachusetts law emancipated all enslaved individuals, including her. She converted to Christianity and lived the rest of her life in Massachusetts. Spear's manuscript last will and testament survives, as does the probate inventory of her estate, for both of which see http://www.royallhouse.org/chloe-spear-by-margot-minardi/.

211.2——.

Excerpt from 211.1 printed under two-column relief-cut illustration captioned "Chloe and her playmates taken captive by the slave-dealer" and headline "Memoir of Chloe Spear" on second page (i.e., 82), cols. 2–3, of antislavery newspaper *The Liberator*, vol. 2, no. 21.

Boston [Massachusetts, U.S.A.]: William Lloyd Garrison and Isaac Knapp, Publishers, May 26, **1832**.
Broadsheet bifolium (49 cm.): 4 p.
http://fair-use.org/the-liberator/1832/05/26/the-liberator-02-21.pdf

1833

212.0 Ayuso = Guillermo

Statement recorded in Banes, Cuba, on 13 August **1833** in a manuscript preserved in Archivo Nacional de la República de Cuba (ANC), **La Habana, Cuba,** Miscelánea de Expedientes, 540/B.

¶ From an unknown location in Africa, Ayuso was forcibly transported to Cuba on a slave ship and sold. By 1833 he worked enslaved on a plantation in the Mariel area when an insurrection erupted. He witnessed planning for it at a distance but was rebuffed by the conspirators when he approached because they did not trust him. Speaking through an interpreter at a hearing later, Ayuso described how the leaders intimated others into following them. During the rebellion they burned many houses and killed a number of white people until troops fired and dispersed them. The rebels, some also with firearms, unsuccessfully returned their fire from within houses.

Full text: https://huskiecommons.lib.niu.edu/history-500africanvoices/137/ [see 212.3].

212.1——.

Statement printed on p. 206 in *La esclavitud desde la esclavitud: La visión de los siervos* by Gloria García Rodríguez.

México [Distrito Federal, Estados Unidos Mexicanos]: Centro de Investigación Científica "Ing. Jorge L Tamayo," **1996.** 8vo (21 cm.): 251 p.

212.2——.

Statement printed on p. 184 *La esclavitud desde la esclavitud,* by Gloria García.

La Habana [Cuba]: Editorial de Ciencias Sociales, 2003. 8vo (21 cm.): xx, 222 p.

212.3——.

English translation of statement printed on p. 177 in *Voices of the Enslaved in Nineteenth-Century Cuba: A Documentary History,* edited by Gloria García Rodríguez. Translated [from 212.1] by Nancy L. Westrate; foreword by Ada Ferrer.

Chapel Hill [North Carolina, U.S.A.]: University of North Carolina Press, **2011.** 8vo (23.5 cm.): xviii, 220 p.

213.0 Eguiyove = Matías (ca. 1819–)

Statement recorded in Banes, Cuba, on 13 August **1833** in a manuscript preserved in Archivo Nacional de la República de Cuba (ANC), **La Habana, Cuba,** Miscelánea de Expedientes, 540/B.

¶ From an unknown location in Africa, Eguiyove was transported as a child on a slave ship to Cuba. By 1833 he worked enslaved as a contramayoral on the coffee plantation *El Salvador* in the Mariel area. At a later hearing, he explained how two leaders of an insurrection (also described in our 212.0) forced all enslaved people to join them and arm themselves with sticks, stones, and machetes for an assault on the big house. One of the leaders threatened to kill anyone who fled or hid. Like all other males, Eguiyove was forced to march on the town of Banes. They returned at daybreak and then marched on the nearby estate to the beat of two drums and the tune of a flute. Eguiyove described the destruction there in detail.

Full text: https://huskiecommons.lib.niu.edu/history-500africanvoices/138/ [see 213.3].

213.1——.

Statement printed on pp. 206–207 in *La esclavitud desde la esclavitud: La visión de los siervos* by Gloria García Rodríguez.

México [Distrito Federal, Estados Unidos Mexicanos]: Centro de Investigación Científica "Ing. Jorge L Tamayo," **1996.** 8vo (21 cm.): 251 p.

213.2——.

Statement printed on pp. 184–185 *La esclavitud desde la esclavitud,* by Gloria García.

La Habana [Cuba]: Editorial de Ciencias Sociales, 2003. 8vo (21 cm.): xx, 222 p.

213.3——.

English translation of statement printed on pp. 177–178 in *Voices of the Enslaved in Nineteenth-Century Cuba: A Documentary History,* edited by Gloria García Rodríguez. Translated [from 213.1] by Nancy L. Westrate; foreword by Ada Ferrer.

Chapel Hill [North Carolina, U.S.A.]: University of North Carolina Press, **2011.** 8vo (23.5 cm.): xviii, 220 p.

214.0 Margarita Lucumí

Her statement recorded in Banes, Cuba, on 13 August **1833** in a manuscript preserved in Archivo Nacional de la República de Cuba (ANC), **La Habana, Cuba,** Miscelánea de Expedientes, 540/B.

¶ Margarita identified as Lucumí, a New World ethnic identity attributed to Yorùbá people (modern-day Nigeria, Benin and Togo) meaning that she was probably Yorùbá. After transport to Cuba on a slave ship and sale, by 1833 she was more than 25 years old, married with two small children, and worked as a servant in the big house of a plantation in the Mariel area. At a later hearing she described how she heard the rebels in an insurrection (also described in our 214.0) plan their actions in their own language. When she asked against whom they plotted and why, they responded they would make war against the whites because of their harsh treatment of enslaved people and that with the war they would be free. When she tried to dissuade them, they threw stones at her. When her Lucumí husband, also a rebel, arrived, he scolded her, gave her a violent blow, and took one of the children. She refused, however, to follow him and the other rebels. Later in the day she saw smoke billowing in the distance over Banes, to where the rebels had marched.

Full text: https://huskiecommons.lib.niu.edu/history-500african-voices/139/ [see 214.3].

214.1——.

Her statement printed on pp. 207–208 in *La esclavitud desde la esclavitud: La visión de los siervos* by Gloria García Rodríguez.

México [Distrito Federal, Estados Unidos Mexicanos]: Centro de Investigación Científica "Ing. Jorge L Tamayo," **1996.**
8vo (21 cm.): 251 p.

214.2——.

Her statement printed on pp. 185–186 *La esclavitud desde la esclavitud*, by Gloria García.

La Habana [Cuba]: Editorial de Ciencias Sociales, **2003.**
8vo (21 cm.): xx, 222 p.

214.3——.

English translation of her statement printed on pp. 178–179 in *Voices of the Enslaved in Nineteenth-Century Cuba: A Documentary History*, edited by Gloria García Rodríguez. Translated [from 214.1] by Nancy L. Westrate; foreword by Ada Ferrer.

Chapel Hill [North Carolina, U.S.A.]: University of North Carolina Press, **2011.**
8vo (23.5 cm.): xviii, 220 p.

215.0 Ayai = Pascual

Statement recorded in Banes, Cuba, on 13 August **1833** in a manuscript preserved in Archivo Nacional de la República de Cuba (ANC), **La Habana, Cuba,** Miscelánea de Expedientes, 540/B.

¶ From an unknown location in Africa, Ayai was transported to Cuba on a slave ship and sold. By 1822 he worked enslaved on the coffee plantation *El Salvador* in the Mariel area. He was involved in an insurrection (also described in 215.0 et seq.) and at the later hearing, when questioned whether he did not know that to rob, kill, commit arson, and resist arrest were punishable offenses, he responded that in Guinea they execute people for such crimes, but that the problem here lay with the enslaved Christians (*ladinos*), not the Africans (*bozales*), who were harmless.

Full text: https://huskiecommons.lib.niu.edu/history-500african-voices/140/ [see 215.3].

215.1——.

Printed on p. 208 in *La esclavitud desde la esclavitud: La visión de los siervos* by Gloria García Rodríguez.

México [Distrito Federal, Estados Unidos Mexicanos]: Centro de Investigación Científica "Ing. Jorge L Tamayo," **1996.**
8vo (21 cm.): 251 p.

215.2——.

Printed on p. 186 *La esclavitud desde la esclavitud*, by Gloria García.

La Habana [Cuba]: Editorial de Ciencias Sociales, **2003.**
8vo (21 cm.): xx, 222 p.

215.3——.

English translation of statement printed on p. 179 in *Voices of the Enslaved in Nineteenth-Century Cuba: A Documentary History*, edited by Gloria García Rodríguez. Translated [from 215.1] by Nancy L. Westrate; foreword by Ada Ferrer.

Chapel Hill [North Carolina, U.S.A.]: University of North Carolina Press, **2011.**
8vo (23.5 cm.): xviii, 220 p.

216.0 Fanguá = Prudencio (ca. 1813–)

Statement recorded in Banes, Cuba, on 13 August **1833** in a manuscript preserved in Archivo Nacional de la República de Cuba (ANC), **La Habana, Cuba,** Miscelánea de Expedientes, 540/B.

¶ From an unknown location in Africa, Fanguá was transported to Cuba on a slave ship and sold. By 1833 he worked enslaved on the coffee plantation *El Salvador* in the Mariel area. He was involved in the insurrection described above and at the later hearing explained that the reason why so many people followed the leaders was that one had said he would lead them back to the land of the Blacks. He and others had also promised that they could eat all of the sweet corn on the farm they wanted, of which there was plenty.

Full text: https://huskiecommons.lib.niu.edu/history-500african-voices/141/ [see 216.3].

216.1——.

Statement printed on p. 208 in *La esclavitud desde la esclavitud: La visión de los siervos* by Gloria García Rodríguez.

México [Distrito Federal, Estados Unidos Mexicanos]: Centro de Investigación Científica "Ing. Jorge L Tamayo," **1996.** 8vo (21 cm.): 251 p.

216.2——.

Statement printed on p. 186 *La esclavitud desde la esclavitud,* by Gloria García.

La Habana [Cuba]: Editorial de Ciencias Sociales, **2003.** 8vo (21 cm.): xx, 222 p.

216.3——.

English translation of statement printed on p. 179 in *Voices of the Enslaved in Nineteenth-Century Cuba: A Documentary History,* edited by Gloria García Rodríguez. Translated [from 213.1] by Nancy L. Westrate; foreword by Ada Ferrer.

Chapel Hill [North Carolina, U.S.A.]: University of North Carolina Press, **2011.** 8vo (23.5 cm.): xviii, 220 p.

217.0 Gonzalo Mandinga

Statement recorded in Banes, Cuba, on 13 August **1833** in a manuscript preserved in Archivo Nacional de la República de Cuba (ANC), **La Habana, Cuba,** Miscelánea de Expedientes, 540/B.

Full text: https://huskiecommons.lib.niu.edu/history-500african-voices/142/ [see 217.3].

¶ Gonzalo identified as Mandinka (an ethnic group residing in modern southern Mali, Guinea, and Ivory Coast). After forcible transport to Cuba on a slave ship and sale, by

1833 he was over 30 years old and worked enslaved on the *El Salvador* coffee plantation in the Mariel area. He joined the insurrection described above and declared at the later hearing that they wanted to go to the scrubland to be free.

217.1——.

Statement printed on p. 208 in *La esclavitud desde la esclavitud: La visión de los siervos* by Gloria García Rodríguez.

México [Distrito Federal, Estados Unidos Mexicanos]: Centro de Investigación Científica "Ing. Jorge L Tamayo," **1996.** 8vo (21 cm.): 251 p.

217.2——.

Statement printed on p. 187 *La esclavitud desde la esclavitud,* by Gloria García.

La Habana [Cuba]: Editorial de Ciencias Sociales, **2003.** 8vo (21 cm.): xx, 222 p.

217.3——.

English translation of statement printed on p. 179 in *Voices of the Enslaved in Nineteenth-Century Cuba: A Documentary History,* edited by Gloria García Rodríguez. Translated [from 217.1] by Nancy L. Westrate; foreword by Ada Ferrer.

Chapel Hill [North Carolina, U.S.A.]: University of North Carolina Press, **2011.** 8vo (23.5 cm.): xviii, 220 p.

218.0 Churipe = Romualdo (ca. 1793–)

Statement recorded in Banes, Cuba, on 13 August **1833** in a manuscript preserved in Archivo Nacional de la República de Cuba (ANC), La Habana, Cuba, Miscelánea de Expedientes, 540/B.

Full text: https://huskiecommons.lib.niu.edu/history-500african-voices/143/ [see 218.3].

¶ From an unknown location in Africa, Churipe was transported to Cuba on a slave ship and sold. By 1833 he worked enslaved on the *El Salvador* coffee plantation in the Mariel area, where an insurrection broke out that he joined. When asked later at a hearing why he joined the rebels, he responded through an interpreter that for a long time he had wanted to return to the land of the Blacks to be free, but it was not until this point that they had enough people to try it. He believed their leaders, who assured them that nothing would happen to them—even if they were killed, they would be in a place where no one could harm them.

218.1——.

Statement printed on p. 209 in *La esclavitud desde la esclavitud: La visión de los siervos* by Gloria García Rodríguez.

México [Distrito Federal, Estados Unidos Mexicanos]: Centro de Investigación Científica "Ing. Jorge L Tamayo," **1996.** 8vo (21 cm.): 251 p.

218.2——.

Statement printed on p. 187 *La esclavitud desde la esclavitud,* by Gloria García.

La Habana [Cuba]: Editorial de Ciencias Sociales, 2003. 8vo (21 cm.): xx, 222 p.

218.3——.

English translation of statement printed on p. 180 in *Voices of the Enslaved in Nineteenth-Century Cuba: A Documentary History*, edited by Gloria García Rodríguez. Translated [from 218.1] by Nancy L. Westrate; foreword by Ada Ferrer.

Chapel Hill [North Carolina, U.S.A.]: University of North Carolina Press, **2011.** 8vo (23.5 cm.): xviii, 220 p.

219.0 Chobó = Agustín (ca. 1815–)

Statement recorded in Banes, Cuba, on 13 August **1833** in a manuscript preserved in Archivo Nacional de la República de Cuba (ANC), **La Habana, Cuba,** Miscelánea de Expedientes, 540/B.

¶ From an unknown location in Africa, Chobó was taken to Cuba on a slave ship and sold. By 1833 he worked enslaved on the *El Salvador* coffee plantation in the Mariel area. He joined the insurrection described in the entries above and de-

scribed through an interpreter at the later hearing how the leaders planned to lead the enslaved people on his and surrounding farms to rise up, kill the white people, and establish a free state ruled by themselves in the town of Banes.

219.1——.

Statement printed on p. 209 in *La esclavitud desde la esclavitud: La visión de los siervos* by Gloria García Rodríguez.

México [Distrito Federal, Estados Unidos Mexicanos]: Centro de Investigación Científica "Ing. Jorge L Tamayo," **1996.** 8vo (21 cm.): 251 p.

219.2——.

Statement printed on p. 187 *La esclavitud desde la esclavitud,* by Gloria García.

La Habana [Cuba]: Editorial de Ciencias Sociales, 2003. 8vo (21 cm.): xx, 222 p.

219.3——.

English translation of statement printed on p. 180 in *Voices of the Enslaved in Nineteenth-Century Cuba: A Documentary History*, edited by Gloria García Rodríguez. Translated [from 216.1] by Nancy L. Westrate; foreword by Ada Ferrer.

Chapel Hill [North Carolina, U.S.A.]: University of North Carolina Press, **2011.** 8vo (23.5 cm.): xviii, 220 p.

Full text: https://huskiecommons.lib.niu.edu/history-500african-voices/144/ [see 219.3].

1834

220.1 James Bradley

Account printed under heading "Brief Account of an Emancipated Slave written by Himself, at the request of the Editor," signed and dated in type "JAMES BRADLEY, Lane Seminary, June 1834" on pp. 106–112 in the avowedly abolitionist gift book (or annual) *The Oasis*, edited by Mrs. [Lydia Maria] Child.

https://babel.hathitrust.org/cgi/pt?id=osu.32435004550596&view=1up&seq=138 [see 220.1].

Boston [Massachusetts, U.S.A.]: Allen and Ticknor, **1834.** Tpv: Entered according to act of Congress, in the year 1834, by Allen & Ticknor … Boston: Tuttle and Weeks, Printers, No. 8, School Street. 12mo (16 cm.): xvi, 276 p., plates.

¶ Bradley was taken at age two or three on a slave ship from an unknown African location to Charleston, South Carolina, U.S.A. A subsequent owner took him to the state of Arkansas, U.S.A., where he purchased his own freedom. He converted to Christianity in 1828, taught himself to read and write using the Bible, then matriculated at Lane Theological Seminary (Cincinnati, Ohio, U.S.A.), where he told his story at antislavery meetings.

220.2 ——. [Distinct issue of 220.1 with variant title-page]

Account printed under heading "Brief Account of an Emancipated Slave written by Himself, at the request of the Editor," signed and dated in type "JAMES BRADLEY, Lane Seminary, June 1834" on pp. 106–112 in the avowedly abolitionist gift book (or annual) *The Oasis*, edited by Mrs. [Lydia Maria] Child.

Boston [Massachusetts, U.S.A.]: Benjamin C. Bacon, **1834.** Tpv: Entered according to act of Congress, in the year 1834, by Allen & Ticknor ... Boston: Tuttle and Weeks, Printers, No. 8, School Street.

12mo (16 cm.): xiv, 276 p., plates.

https://archive.org/stream/oasis00chilgoog#page/n138/mode/1up

220.3 ——.

Account reprinted "From the Oasis" (220.1) under headline "Brief Account of an Emancipated Slave" and over typeset signature and date "JAMES BRADLEY, Lane Seminary, June 1834" on the first page, cols. 3–4, of the newspaper *The Ohio Observer* no. 38.

Hudson, Ohio [U.S.A.]: James B. Walker, **November 20, 1834.**

220.4 ——.

Account reprinted "From the Oasis" (220.1) under headline "Brief Account of an Emancipated Slave" and over typeset signature and date "JAMES BRADLEY, *Lane Seminary, June* 1834 [sic]" on p. 4, cols. 2–3 of the abolitionist newspaper *Herald of Freedom* (edited by Joseph Horace Kimball), vol. 1, no.1.

Concord, New Hampshire [U.S.A.]: Published by an Association of Gentlemen, Joseph Horace Kimball, editor, Elbridge G. Chase, Printer, **March 7, 1835.**

Broadsheet bifolium: 4 p.

220.5 ——.

Account "Written, 1835" (*sic*) printed explicitly from 220.5 on pp. 686–690 in *Slave Testimony: Two Centuries of Letters, Speeches, Interviews, and Autobiographies*, edited by John W. Blassingame.

Baton Rouge [Louisiana, U.S.A.]: Louisiana State University Press, **1977.**

8vo (23 cm.): lxv, 777 p., illus., portraits. Year in phrase "Written, 1835" is an error for 1834.

220.6 ——. [Second printing of 220.6]

Account "Written, 1835" (*sic*) printed from 220.5 on pp. 686–690 in *Slave Testimony: Two Centuries of Letters, Speeches, and Autobiographies*, edited by John W. Blassingame.

Baton Rouge [Louisiana, U.S.A.]: Louisiana State University Press, **1977.** Second printing.

8vo (23 cm.): lxv, 777 p., illus., portraits. Year in phrase "Written, 1835" is an error for 1834.

220.7 ——. [Another printing of 220.6]

Account "Written, 1835" (*sic*) printed explicitly from 220.5 on pp. 686–690 in *Slave Testimony: Two Centuries of Letters, Speeches, and Autobiographies*, edited by John W. Blassingame.

Baton Rouge [Louisiana, U.S.A.]: Louisiana State University Press, **1979.** 1979 printing.

8vo (23 cm.): lxv, 777 p., illus., portraits. Year in phrase "Written, 1835" is an error for 1834.

220.8 ——. [Another printing of 220.6]

Account "Written, 1835" (*sic*) printed explicitly from 220.5 on pp. 686–690 in *Slave Testimony: Two Centuries of Letters, Speeches, and Autobiographies*, edited by John W. Blassingame.

Baton Rouge [Louisiana, U.S.A.]: Louisiana State University Press, **1980.** 1980 printing.

8vo (23 cm.): lxv, 777 p., illus., portraits. Year in phrase "Written, 1835" is an error for 1834.

220.9 ——. [Another printing of 220.6]

Account "Written, 1835" (*sic*) printed explicitly from 220.5 on pp. 686–690 in *Slave Testimony: Two Centuries of Letters, Speeches, and Autobiographies*, edited by John W. Blassingame.

Baton Rouge [Louisiana, U.S.A.]: Louisiana State University Press, **1989.** 1989 printing.

8vo (23 cm.): lxv, 777 p., illus., portraits. Year in phrase "Written, 1835" is an error for 1834.

220.10 ——. [Another printing of 220.6]

Account "Written, 1835" (*sic*) printed explicitly from 220.5 on pp. 686–690 in *Slave Testimony: Two Centuries of Letters, Speeches, and Autobiographies*, edited by John W. Blassingame.

Baton Rouge [Louisiana, U.S.A.]: Louisiana State University Press, **1998.** 1998 printing.

8vo (23 cm.): lxv, 777 p., illus., portraits. Year in phrase "Written, 1835" is an error for 1834.

220.11 ——. [Another printing of 220.6]

Account "Written, 1835" (*sic*) printed explicitly from 220.5 on pp. 686–690 in *Slave Testimony: Two Centuries of Letters, Speeches, and Autobiographies*, edited by John W. Blassingame.

Baton Rouge [Louisiana, U.S.A.]: Louisiana State University Press, **2002.** 2002 printing.

8vo (23 cm.): lxv, 777 p., illus., portraits. Year in phrase "Written, 1835" is an error for 1834.

220.12——.

"An Account of the Life of James Bradley, Black Abolitionist" printed from 220.1 on pp. 15–17 in popular history magazine *Kentucky Explorer,* unnumbered issue for November 2003.

Jackson, Kentucky [U.S.A.]: Charles Hayes, Publisher, **November 2003.** Price $2.50.
Cf. digitized transcription:
http://www.kykinfolk.com/pendleton/history/bradley.html

220.13——. [Another printing of 220.6]

Account "Written, 1835" (*sic*) printed explicitly from 220.5 on pp. 686–690 in *Slave Testimony: Two Centuries of Letters, Speeches, and Autobiographies,* edited by John W. Blassingame.

Baton Rouge [Louisiana, U.S.A.]: Louisiana State University Press, **2009.**
8vo (24 cm.): lxv, 777 p., illus., portraits. Year in phrase "Written, 1835" is an error for 1834.

221.0 Claudio Carabalí (–1834)

Statement recorded in Guanabaoca, Cuba on **13 August 1834**, preserved in Archivo Nacional de la República de Cuba (ANC), **La Habana, Cuba,** Miscelánea de Expedientes, 256/Q.

Full text: https://huskiecommons.lib.niu.edu/history-500african-voices/145/ [see 221.3].

¶ Claudio identified as Carabalí, likely referring to Calabar in the Cross River region (modern Nigeria and northwestern Cameroon). He was taken on a slave ship to Cuba and sold to work enslaved, eventually on the estate *Jesus María* (near Guanabaoca) owned by a widowed countess. His job was to guard the banana groves at night to prevent theft. One night in 1834 he stopped three black men making away with three large sacks of plantains. During the ensuing scuffle they wounded him badly with a machete and made off. A few days after providing his testimony, Claudio died of tetanus contracted from the machete wounds.

221.1——.

Printed on pp. 146–147 in *La esclavitud desde la esclavitud: La visión de los siervos* by Gloria García Rodríguez.

México [Distrito Federal, Estados Unidos Mexicanos]: Centro de Investigación Científica "Ing. Jorge L Tamayo," **1996.**
8vo (21 cm.): 251 p.

221.2——.

Printed on pp. 131–132 *La esclavitud desde la esclavitud*, by Gloria García.

La Habana [Cuba]: Editorial de Ciencias Sociales, **2003.**
8vo (21 cm.): xx, 222 p.

221.3——.

English translation of his statement printed on pp. 124–125 in *Voices of the Enslaved in Nineteenth-Century Cuba: A Documentary History,* edited by Gloria García Rodríguez. Translated [from 222.1] by Nancy L. Westrate; foreword by Ada Ferrer.

Chapel Hill [North Carolina, U.S.A.]: University of North Carolina Press, **2011.**
8vo (24 cm.): xviii, 220 p.

222.1 Abū Bakr al-Siddiq (1790–) = Abou Bekir Sadiki = Abon [sic] Becr Sadiki = Abú Bekr es Siddīk = Abou Beehn Saduky Shirreiff = Edward Donellan = Edward Doulan

2 vols., 8vo (19 cm.). https://babel.hathitrust.org/cgi/pt?id=hvd.32044011327756&view=1up&seq=122 [see 222.2].

Several versions or parts of his life story based on an autobiographical essay written by Abū Bakr al-Siddiq on Jamaica in 1834, an English translation thereof by Abū Bakr al-Siddiq and Dr. Richard R. Madden (dated at 20 September 1834), and an autobiographical letter written by Abū Bakr al-Siddiq (as Edward Doulan) at Kingston, Jamaica on 18 October 1834 to Muhammed Kaba (Robert Tuffit) were the basis for the following publications: (Vol. 1) Richard R. Madden to J. F. Savoy, St. Andrews, Jamaica, 30 March 1835 (1: 126–131); Al-Siddiq [Doulan] to Madden, Kingston, 1 November 1834 (1: 131–132) and (Vol. 2) Richard R. Madden to J. Buckingham, Kingston, 15 September 1834 et seq. (2: 157–182); "The History of Abon Becr [sic] Sadiki [sic], Known in Jamaica by the Name of Edward Donlan [sic]" (2: 183–189); Al-Siddiq [Doulan] to Muhammed Kaba [Robert Tuffit], Kingston, Jamaica, 18 October 1834, etc. (2: 200–201); William Rainsford, Benjamin Cochran, Benjamin Larten, Edward Doulan to Madden, Kingston, 2 October 1834 (2: 203–207); all printed in vol. 1 and 2 of Richard R. Madden, *A Twelvemonth's Residence in the West Indies, During the Transition from Slavery to Apprenticeship, with Incidental Notices of the State of Society, Prospects, and Natural Resources of Jamaica and other Islands.*

London [England]: James Cochrane and Co., Waterloo Place, **1835.** Tpv: Printed by A. J. Valpy, Red Lion Court, Fleet Street.

2 vols., 8vo (20 cm.).

Hogg 1477.

Vol. 1: https://babel.hathitrust.org/cgi/pt?id=mdp.3901501470
7494&view=1up&seq=7

Vol. 2: https://babel.hathitrust.org/cgi/pt?id=mdp.390150147
07395&view=1up&seq=195

¶ Abū Bakr al-Siddiq was born in Timbuktu (modern Mali) ca. 1790 and raised by a wealthy learned Muslim family in Djenne, where he learned to read the Qu'ran. In 1805 he was at Bouna, where his uncle was an important merchant, when an Asante (Akan people, modern Ghana) army invaded to resume its control over the town. Along with many other residents, Abū Bakr was enslaved and marched to the coast, where he was sold to a slave ship bound for the British colony of Jamaica in the Caribbean. In 1834 he was freed and the following year left Jamaica for England via New York under the protection of his benefactor Capt. William Oldrey, RN, on HMS *Hyacinth*. On 29 August 1835 Abū Bakr left London with the British traveler John Davidson, and on 3 September 1835 they sailed for Gibraltar. (Before Abū Bakr left England he had interviews with King George IV and the Duke of Sussex, as noted in +222-A.1.) On 12 November 1835 (222.4, p. 7) Abū Bakr crossed from Gibraltar to Morocco with Davidson's exploring party and went into the desert. This party was attacked and its leader killed on 17 or 18 December 1836, but Abū Bakr may have survived and lived at Jenne in 1841 (222.10, p. 156). For more on Abū Bakr al-Siddiq, see Ivor Wilks' introduction in 222.10.

222.2——.

Account reprinted from 222.1 on pp. 108–125, 126–130, 136–141, and 200–201 in vol. 2 of Richard R. Madden, *A Twelvemonth's Residence in the West Indies, During the Transition from Slavery to Apprenticeship, with Incidental Notices of the State of Society, Prospects, and Natural Resources of Jamaica and other Islands.*

Philadelphia [Pennsylvania, U.S.A.]: Carey, Lea and Blanchard, **1835.**

2 vols., 8vo (19 cm.). https://babel.hathitrust.org/cgi/pt?id=hvd.32044011327756&view=1up&seq=122

222.3——.

English translation of variant account written in Arabic by Abū Bakr al-Siddiq while near London England in 1835 printed with annotations on pp. 102–107 in the Rev. Mr. George Cecil Renouard's article "Routes in North Africa, by Abú Bekr es Siddīk … Read 25th April, 1836," which is printed on pp. 100–113 in vol. 6 of *Journal of the Royal Geographical Society.*

London, England: John Murray, Albemarle-Street, MDCCCXXXVI [**1836**]. Tpv: London: Printed by William Clowes and Sons | Stamford Street.

8vo.

https://archive.org/details/in.ernet.dli.2015.70673/page/n141/mode/1up

222.4——.

English translation of variant account written in Arabic by Abū Bakr al-Siddiq reprinted with annotations explicitly from 222.3 on pp. 208–212 of *Notes taken during Travels in Africa, by the late John Davidson, F.R.S. F.S.A., &c.* [Edited by T. Davidson.] *Printed for Private Circulation only.*

London [England]: Printed by J. L. Cox and Sons, 75, Great Queen Street, Lincoln's-Inn Fields, **1839.**

4ot (27 cm.): [vi], 218 p., plates.

https://archive.org/details/notestakenduring00davi/page/208/mode/1up

222.5——.

Variant account reprinted explicitly from 222.3 under heading "Narrative of a Native of Tomboktu [*sic*]" on pp. 151–153 of the August 1841 issue (vol. 1, no. 10) of the periodical *The Friend of Africa; by the Society for the Extinction of the Slave Trade, and for the Civilization of Africa* (edited by George Cecil Renouard).

London [England]: Published by John W. Parker, 445, West Strand; and sold by all booksellers, August **1841.**

8vo (23 cm.).

222.6——.

Long derivative summary of Abou Bekr's life and "superior intelligence" printed on p. 240 in John Frost, *The Book of Travels in Africa, from the Earliest Ages to the Present Time, compiled from the best authorities.*

New-York [New York, U.S.A.]: D. Appleton & Company, 200 Broadway; **Philadelphia [Pennsylvania, U.S.A.]:** Geo. S. Appleton, 148 Chestnut Street, **1847.**

8vo (20 cm.): xii, 252 p., illus., folding map.

222.7——.

Account printed from 222.1 (Madden) under heading "Sadiki; A Learned Slave" on pp. 241–249 of Wilson Armistead's compendium *A Tribute for the Negro: Being a Vindication of the Moral Intellectual, and Religious Capabilities of the Colored Portion of Mankind; with Particular Reference to the African Race.*

Manchester [England]: William Irwin; **London [England]:** Charles Gilpin; American Agent: Wm. Harned, Anti-Slavery Office, 61, John Street, **New York [New York, U.S.A.]**; and may be had of H. Longstreath and G.W. Taylor, **Philadelphia [Pennsylvania, U.S.A.], 1848.** Tpv: Manchester: Printed by William Irwin, 39, Oldham Street.

8vo (24 cm.): xxxv, 564 p.

222.1 Abū Bakr al-Siddiq

https://babel.hathitrust.org/cgi/pt?id=nc01.ark:/13960/
t42r4z659&view=1up&seq=295
http://docsouth.unc.edu/neh/armistead/armistead.html

222.8——.

Account reprinted from 222.7 (Armistead, following 222.1)
as lead story under heading "Sadiki, a Learned Slave" on first
through fourth pages (i.e., pp. 121–124) in the June 2, 1856,
issue of *The Anti-Slavery Reporter and Aborigines' Friend*
[edited by Louis Alexis Chamerovzow], new series vol. 4, no. 6.

London [England]: The British and Foreign Anti-Slavery Society, June 2, **1856.** Price Fourpence Stamped, Threepence
Unstamped.
8vo.
https://babel.hathitrust.org/cgi/pt?id=mdp.39015020435940;
view=1up;seq=133

222.9——.

English-language manuscript translation (different than that
used by Madden in 222.1) of al-Siddiq's Arabic autobiographical sketch found ca. 1935 by C. H. Wesley "at the office of
the Anti-Slavery Society, Dennison [i.e., Denison] House,
London, England" printed with minor alterations by Charles
H. Wesley in "Abou Bekir Sadiki, Alias Edward Doulan" on
pp. 52–55 in *Journal of Negro History*, vol. 21, no. 1.

New York and Washington, DC [U.S.A.]: United Publishing
Corporation, January, **1936.**
8vo.
Hogg 1568.

222.10——.

Account and travel routes printed mostly from 222.3 (Renouard) with variants from 222.1 (Madden) on pp. 157–163
and letter with autobiographical content *to* Muhammad
Kaba Saghanughu dated Kingston, Jamaica, October 18,
1834, reprinted, with added annotations, from 222.1
(Madden, identified on p. 157 and 164, as *Twelve Months*
[sic] *Residence in the West Indies* ... London, 1837 [*sic*]")
on pp. 165–166 within chapter entitled "Abū Bakr Al-Siddiq
of Timbuktu," edited with introduction by Ivor Wilks on pp.
152–169 in *Africa Remembered: Narratives by West Africans
from the Era of the Slave Trade,* edited by Philip D. Curtin.

Madison [Wisconsin, U.S.A.]: University of Wisconsin Press,
1967.
8vo (24 cm.): x, 363 p., illus., maps.

222.11——. [Second printing of 222.10]

Account (autobiographical sketch identical to 222.10) and
travel routes printed mostly from 222.3 (Renouard) with vari-

ants from 222.1 (Madden) on pp. 157–163 and letter with
autobiographical content *to* Muhammad Kaba Saghanughu
dated Kingston, Jamaica, October 18, 1834, reprinted, with
added annotations, from 222.1 (Madden, identified on
p. 157 and 164, as *Twelve Months* [sic] *Residence in the
West Indies* ... London, 1837 [*sic*]") on pp. 165–166 within
chapter entitled "Abū Bakr Al-Siddiq of Timbuktu," edited
with introduction by Ivor Wilks on pp. 152–169 in *Africa
Remembered: Narratives by West Africans from the Era of
the Slave Trade,* edited by Philip D. Curtin.

Madison [Wisconsin, U.S.A.]: University of Wisconsin Press,
1968.
8vo (22 cm.): x, 363 p., illus., maps.

222.12——. [Photomechanical reprint of 222.8]

Account reprinted from 222.7 (Armistead, following 222.1)
as lead story under heading "Sadiki, a Learned Slave" in
photomechanical reprint of 222.8, being *The Anti-Slavery
Reporter and Aborigines' Friend* [edited by Louis Alexis Cha-
merovzow], new series vol. 4, no. 6: 121–124, with imprint:

Nendeln, Liechtenstein: Kraus Reprint, **1969.**
8vo.
https://babel.hathitrust.org/cgi/pt?id=mdp.39015020435940;
view=1up;seq=133

222.13——. [Reprinting of 222.10]

Account (autobiographical sketch identical to 222.10) and
travel routes printed mostly from 222.3 (Renouard) with
variants from 222.1 (Madden) on pp. 157–163 and letter with
autobiographical content *to* Muhammad Kaba Saghanughu
dated Kingston, Jamaica, October 18, 1834, reprinted, with
added annotations, from 222.1 (Madden, identified on p. 157
and 164, as *Twelve Months* [sic] *Residence in the West Indies*
... London, 1837 [*sic*]") on pp. 165–166 within chapter entitled
"Abū Bakr Al-Siddiq of Timbuktu," edited with introduction by
Ivor Wilks on pp. 152–169 in *Africa Remembered: Narratives
by West Africans from the Era of the Slave Trade,* edited by
Philip D. Curtin.

Prospect Heights, Illinois [U.S.A.]: Waveland Press, **1997.**
8vo (23 cm.): x, 363 p., illus., maps.

222.14——.

Biographical summary and analysis, with long block quotation as published by Renouard in 1836 (222.3) printed on
pp. 41–42 in Allan D. Austin, *African Muslims in Antebellum
America: Transatlantic Stories and Spiritual Struggles.*

New York [New York, U.S.A.] and London [England]:
Routledge, **[1997].**
8vo (24 cm.): xiii, 194 pp.

222.15——.

"'Abu Bekr Sheriff of Timbuktoo—Written in Jamaica 1834"*
printed on pp. 201–207 in *Five Classic Muslim Slave Narratives: Selim Aga, Job Ben Sulaiman, Nicholas Said, Omar ibn Said,* [and] *Abu Bakr Sadiq,* edited by Muhammad A. Al-Ahari.

[Chicago, Illinois, U.S.A.]: Magribine Press, **[2006].** "First edition." Examined exemplar colophon: Made in U.S.A. | Columbia, SC | 30 June 2018. Series: American Islamic Heritage Series.

8vo (23 cm.): 210 p., illus. (portraits).

*Text explicitly reported to be "[b]ased on the translation by Richard Madden dated September 20, 1835 [*sic*], found in "Documents" *the Journal of Negro History* (July [*sic*] 1936): 52–55 [see 219.9]; his *Twelve Months in the West Indies* [*sic*] II, pp. 108–109 [see 219.1] and G. C. Renouard, "Routes in North Africa by 'Abu Bekr es-Siddik," *Journal of the Royal Geographical Society,* VI (1836): 99–113 [see 219.3]" (p. 203, n. 27).

222.16——.

Biographical summary and analysis, with long block quotation from as published by Renouard in 1836 (222.3) printed on pp. 41–42 in Allan D. Austin, *African Muslims in Antebellum America: Transatlantic Stories and Spiritual Struggles.*

New-York [New York, U.S.A.] and London [England]: Routledge, **[2011].**

8vo (23 cm.): xiii, 198 p.

Additional publication by Abū Bakr al-Siddiq

+222-A.1——.

Letter* written by Abū Bakr al-Siddiq (here recorded as Abou Beehn Saduky Shirreiff) from Morocco to RN Capt. William Oldrey, printed with editorial introduction on p. 180, cols. 2–3 of the March 5, 1836, issue (no. 436) of the weekly magazine *The Athenaeum* (London, England).

*Editorial introduction includes: "The original was written in beautifully penned Arabic, a translation of which was made by Abou himself, in the best English of which he was capable, and [n.b.] written down (*verb. et lit.*) by Mr. Davidson [i.e., the British traveller John Davidson (1797–Dec. 18, 1836)]."

+222-A.2——.

Reprinting of +222-A.1 on the final page (i.e., p. 256), col. 2, of the 17 April 1836 issue of *The London and Paris Observer; or, Chronicle of Literature, Science, and the Fine Arts* (Paris, France, 1836).

223.1   William Rainsford

Account included in a letter written by Rainsford and co-signed by Gorah Condran [= Benjamin Cochrane], Benjemin [*sic*] Larten, and Abū Bakr Al-Siddiq [= Edward Doulan], Kingston, Jamaica, 2 October 1834, printed in vol. 2, pp. 203–207 of Richard R. Madden, *A Twelvemonth's Residence in the West Indies, During the Transition from Slavery to Apprenticeship, with Incidental Notices of the State of Society, Prospects, and Natural Resources of Jamaica and other Islands.*

London [England]: James Cochrane and Co., Waterloo Place, 1835. Tpv: Printed by A. J. Valpy, Red Lion Court, Fleet Street.

2 vols., 8vo (19 cm.).

¶ Within the 2 October 1834 letter published in Madden's *A Twelvemonth's Residence* (223.1), Rainsford identifies himself as its author, with the others co signing, and presents his own life story of birth in Sancran in Mandinka country (modern southern Mali, Guinea, and Ivory Coast), upbringing as a learned warrior, and enslavement. His slave ship appears to have been intercepted by the British and its passengers (including Rainsford) taken to Jamaica in the Caribbean.

223.2——.

Account reprinted in vol. 2, pp. 138–141 of Richard R. Madden, *A Twelvemonth's Residence in the West Indies, During the Transition from Slavery to Apprenticeship, with Incidental Notices of the State of Society, Prospects, and Natural Resources of Jamaica and other Islands.*

Philadelphia [Pennsylvania, U.S.A.]: Carey, Lea, and Blanchard, **1835.**

2 vols., 8vo (19 cm.).

https://babel.hathitrust.org/cgi/pt?id=hvd.32044011327756; view=1up;seq=9

https://babel.hathitrust.org/cgi/pt?id=mdp.39015014707395&view=1up&seq=215&skin=2021 [see 223.1].

224.0   Muhammed Kabā Saghanughu (1748–1845) = Kabā Saghanughu = Robert Peart = Tuffit = Dick = Mahomed Cover

224.0a: (I) Robert Tuffit's (Kabā Saghanughu's) account in his letter to Edward Doulan (q.v. 224.0), enclosed within **(II)** manuscript letter written by B. Angell at Manchester, Jamaica, West Indies, on **7 October 1834** to Richard R. Madden. Both first printed in 1835 (224.1). **MSS. not yet located.**

224.0b: (I) Manuscript address expressing gratitude for emancipation (including thanks to Jamaican governor Sir Lionel Smith) comprising English words phonetically approximated with Arabic letters written and signed (also in Arabic) by Kabā Saghanughu (as Robert Peart) in **1838**; (II) contemporary manuscript incomplete (i.e., bowdlerized) translation of 224.0(I). Both MSS. preserved among Sir Lionel Smith's papers in the Public Record Office of Northern Ireland (PRONI), **Belfast, Northern Ireland.** 224.0b(I) first published in 2019 (224.8), when a photograph of it was printed on p. 290 as fig. 1. 224.0b(II) first published in 1838 (224.3 and 224.4).

https://babel. hathitrust.org/cgi/ pt?id=mdp.39015 014707395&vie w=1up&seq=208 [see 224.1].

¶ Kabā Saghanughu came from Bouka, in Mandinka country (an ethnic group residing in southern Mali, Guinea and Ivory Coast), on the eastern frontier of Fuuta Jalon, on one of the tributaries of the Niger River (modern Guinea). His family was Muslim, with the name Saghanughu indicating both a Soninke origin and an association with the Qadiriyya Islamic brotherhood and well-known for Islamic education. His father owned a plantation with 140 enslaved people and much livestock. His father and uncle (a lawyer) educated Kabā. In 1777 he was kidnapped while traveling to Timbuktu to study law. He was taken to the coast and put on a slave ship bound for the British colony of Jamaica in the Caribbean. There he lived and worked enslaved on *Spice Grove* plantation in Manchester Parish for the rest of his long life. He embraced Moravian Christianity in 1813. He was implicated in the 1831 uprising, as was one of his sons, who was executed. In 1834 he met Richard R. Madden, who wrote down his story. In 1838, aged 90, he composed an address to the British governor of Jamaica for a formal Emancipation Day ceremony (q.v. 224.0b(I), 224.4, and 224.8). For more biographical information, see: "Muhammad Kabā Saghanughu and the Muslim Community of Jamaica," in *Slavery on the Frontiers of Islam*, edited by Paul E. Lovejoy (Princeton: Markus Wiener Publisher, 2004), pp. **199–218.**

224.1———.

Robert Tuffit's account in his letter to Edward Doulan (224.0a(I)) printed immediately after the letter enclosing it (and carrying a supporting statement), viz. B. Angell's letter to Richard R. Madden, 7 October 1834 (224.0a(II)), on pp. 196–199 in vol. 2 of Richard R. Madden, *A Twelvemonth's Residence in the West Indies, During the Transition from Slavery to Apprenticeship, with Incidental Notices of the State of Society, Prospects, and Natural Resources of Jamaica and other Islands.*

London [England]: James Cochrane and Co., Waterloo Place, **1835.** Tpv: Printed by A. J. Valpy, Red Lion Court, Fleet Street.
2 vols., 8vo (21 cm.).
https://babel.hathitrust.org/cgi/pt?id=mdp.39015014707395 &view=1up&seq=208

224.2———.

224.1 reprinted on pp. 134–136 in vol. 2 of Richard R. Madden, *A Twelvemonth's Residence in the West Indies, During the Transition from Slavery to Apprenticeship, with Incidental Notices of the State of Society, Prospects, and Natural Resources of Jamaica and other Islands.*

Philadelphia [Pennsylvania, U.S.A.]: Carey, Lea and Blanchard, **1835.**
2 vols., 8vo (19 cm.).
https://babel.hathitrust.org/cgi/pt?id=hvd.32044011327756 &view=1up&seq=150

224.3———.

Incomplete English translation (224.0b(II)) of his concise 1838 Emancipation day address (signed in type at end "Robert Peart, Manchester … 1st day of August, 1838") printed in an as-yet unidentified Jamaican newspaper. Three Jamaican newspapers are named in 224.4 (immediately below) as its sources: *Jamaica Morning Journal, Kingston Journal, Royal Gazette.*

[Kingston or **Manchester? Jamaica]:** [not yet known], August 2, 1838.

224.4———.

Incomplete English translation (224.0b(II)) of his concise 1838 Emancipation address reprinted from 224.3, here within long news article (composed from articles published in Jamaican newspapers dated Aug. 2 to Aug. 13 recently received at Boston via New York City, which these papers had reached on Aug. 31 aboard the ship *John W. Cater* from Kingston, Jamaica*) by Oliver Johnson (editor pro tem) headlined "Glorious News from the West Indies!" printed on the second and third pages (i.e., pp. 142–143) of the antislavery newspaper *The Liberator*, vol. 8, no. 36.

Boston [Massachusetts, U.S.A.]: William Lloyd Garrison and Isaac Knapp, Publishers, September 7, **1838.**
Broadsheet bifolium.
Note: This printed English version of Kabā Saghanughu's address is signed in type at the end "Robert Peart, Manchester … 1st day of August, 1838."
http://fair-use.org/the-liberator/1838/09/07/the-liberator-08-36.pdf

224.5———.

Letter written by Kabā to Abū Bakr Al-Siddiq (q.v. 224.1) printed from 224.1 (not, as stated on p. 164, from "*Twelve Months* [sic] *Residence in the West Indies* ... London, 1837 [*sic*]") on pp. 164–165 within chapter entitled "Abū Bakr Al-Siddiq of Timbuktu," edited with introduction by Ivor Wilks on pp. 152–169 of *Africa Remembered: Narratives by West Africans from the Era of the Slave Trade*, edited by Philip D. Curtin.

Madison [Wisconsin, U.S.A.]: University of Wisconsin Press, **1967.**
8vo (24 cm.): x, 363 p., illus., maps.

224.6———. [Another printing of 224.5]

Letter written by Kabā to Abū Bakr Al-Siddiq (q.v. 224.1) printed from 224.1 (not, as stated on p. 164, from "*Twelve Months* [sic] *Residence in the West Indies* ... London, 1837 [*sic*]") on pp. 164–165 within chapter entitled Abū Bakr Al-Siddiq of Timbuktu," edited with introduction by Ivor Wilks on pp. 152–169 of *Africa Remembered: Narratives by West Africans from the Era of the Slave Trade*, edited by Philip D. Curtin.

Madison [Wisconsin, U.S.A.]: University of Wisconsin Press, **1968.**
8vo (22 cm.): x, 363 p., illus., maps.

224.7———. [Another printing of 224.5]

Letter written by Kabā to Abū Bakr Al-Siddiq (q.v. 224.1) printed from 224.1 (not, as stated on p. 164, from "*Twelve Months* [sic] *Residence in the West Indies* ... London, 1837 [*sic*]") on pp. 164–165 within chapter entitled "Abū Bakr Al-Siddiq of Timbuktu," edited with introduction by Ivor Wilks on pp. 152–169 of *Africa Remembered: Narratives by West Africans from the Era of the Slave Trade*, edited by Philip D. Curtin.

Prospect Heights [Illinois, U.S.A.]: Waveland Press, **1997.**
8vo (23 cm.): x, 363 p., illus., maps.

224.8———.

224.0b(I) printed for the first time (and reproduced photographically), with transliteration, and 224.4 reprinted, both with extensive commentary and contextualization, in Elizabeth A. Dolan and Ahmed Idrissi Alami, "Muhammad Kabā Saghanughu's Arabic Address on the Occasion of Emancipation in Jamaica," *The William and Mary Quarterly*, 3rd series, 76:2: 289–312.

Williamsburg, Virginia [U.S.A.]: Omohundro Institute, April **2019.**
8vo (23.5 cm.).

Another composition by Muhammed Kabā Saghanughu

+224-A.1 ———.

His *Kitāb al-Salāt* (= Book of Praying) printed in Yacine Daddi Addoun and Paul E. Lovejoy, "The Arabic Manuscript of Muhammad Kabā Saghanughu of Jamaica, c. 1820," in *Caribbean Culture: Soundings on Kamau Brathwaite*, edited by Annie Paul (Kingston [Jamaica]: University of West Indies Press, 2007), pp. 313–341.

225.1 Gorah Condran = Anna Moosa [Moses] = Benjamin Cochrane

Account written within Richard R. Madden's letter to J. F. Savory, 30 March 1835, and Condran's letter to Madden, Kingston, **1 November 1834**, printed together in that order at vol. 1, pp. 126–132 in Richard R. Madden, *A Twelvemonth's Residence in the West Indies, During the Transition from Slavery to Apprenticeship, with Incidental Notices of the State of Society, Prospects, and Natural Resources of Jamaica and other Islands.*

https://babel. hathitrust.org/cgi/ pt?id=mdp.39015 014707494&vie w=1up&seq=146 [see 225.1].

London [England]: James Cochrane and Co., Waterloo Place, **1835.** Tpv: Printed by A. J. Valpy, Red Lion Court, Fleet Street.
2 vols., 8vo (21 cm.).

¶ Condran, a Mandinka (an ethnic group residing in southern Mali, Guinea and Ivory Coast) from Kasson on the upper Senegal River (modern Mali), was a self-educated doctor and a warrior who could read and write Arabic. His father was a Mandinka chief. Condran and others were captured in battle, taken to the coast, and forced aboard a slave ship that was intercepted near the Caribbean island of Tortola by a British warship. The British forced Condran and his 360 cargo mates to work seven years gratis for the king. This Condran did at least partly on the British Caribbean colony of Antigua, where he took the name Anna Moosa, or Moses, which equates with the Muslim name Musa. He was then freed and taken to Jamaica in the Caribbean, but authorities there thought Condran had run away and therefore reenslaved him. The governor intervened and returned him to Antigua, where he was freed again. But when Condran returned to Jamaica, he was reenslaved yet again, this time for three years. Only after the governor intervened again was Condran freed. Condran served under British Admiral Alexander Cochrane on Barbados (also a British island colony) during the Napoleonic

Wars and took his surname. He converted to Christianity and became an accomplished free doctor in British service in the Atlantic. By 1834 he was working among Blacks in Kingston, Jamaica, where he met Madden, who took down his story "pretty much in his own words" (225.1, p. 128) and agreed to help him become a member of the Royal College of Physicians (London, England).

225.2———.

Account reprinted in vol. 1 of Richard R. Madden, *A Twelve-month's Residence in the West Indies, During the Transition from Slavery to Apprenticeship, with Incidental Notices of the State of Society, Prospects, and Natural Resources of Jamaica and other Islands.*

Philadelphia [Pennsylvania, U.S.A.]: Carey, Lea and Blanchard, 1835.
2 vols., 8vo (19 cm.).

225.3———.[Photomechanical reprint of 225.2]

Account reprinted in vol. 1 of photomechanical reprint of the 1835 Philadelphia edition of Richard R. Madden, *A Twelve-month's Residence in the West Indies, During the Transition from Slavery to Apprenticeship, with Incidental Notices of the State of Society, Prospects, and Natural Resources of Jamaica and other Islands.*

Westport, Connecticut [U.S.A.]: Negro Universities Press, 1970.
8vo (23 cm.): volume 1 only (all published).

225.4———.

Account printed on pp. 547–550 and 576 in *African Muslims in Antebellum America: A Source Book*, edited by Allan D. Austin.

New York [New York, U.S.A.]: Garland Publishing, 1984.
8vo (23 cm.): xiv, 759 p., illus., maps.

226.1 Lamine Kabā (ca. 1760–) = Lamin Kibby = Lamen Kebe = Lamine Kebe = Paul = Paul the aged = Old Paul

Basic facts of Lamine Kabā's life story as he told them to a New York City reporter printed under headline "Interesting Case" of the newspaper *The New York Journal of Commerce.*

http://fair-use.org/the-liberator/1835/01/03/the-liberator-05-01.pdf [see 226.3].

New York [New York, U.S.A.]:
David Hale and Gerard Hallock, [before 11 December, witness 224.2], 1834.
Broadsheet bifolium (71 cm.): 4 p.?

First phrases of article proper: "In the ship Alabama, which arrived a few days since from New Orleans, came passenger [*sic*], a native African, about 75 years of age, who was stolen from the land of his birth about 38 years ago …"

¶ Lamine Kabā, a Muslim, came from Fuuta Jalon (where, according to 226.7, he "spent thirty or more of the first years of his life"), the state founded in *jihād* (religious reform movement that involved warfare) in what is now Guinea. He spoke Sarakole (Soninke), and his father was identified with the Jahanke merchant class; his mother was Mandinka (an ethnic group residing in southern Mali, Guinea, and Ivory Coast). After studying in the city of Bunder (Bundu, eastern Senegal), and teaching school in the city of Kaba (possibly Mali), he was kidnapped, taken away from his wife and two children to the sea, and ca. 1797 (226.1) sold to a slaver who took him to Charleston, South Carolina, U.S.A. There he was sold to Gen. Charles Cotesworth Pinckney, for whom he worked enslaved "about six years." Then he was sold to "a Mr. Pratt, of Edgefield District … and so on, till at length he passed into the hands of Pressly Halsey, of Sumner County, Tennessee … and subsequently of James Hoard [i.e. Howard?], Esq. of Vicksburg, Miss[issippi]" (226.1). In all, he lived enslaved "about 38 years" before Hoard (?) freed him in 1834 and paid his passage to New York City (226.1). There he lived for "several months" (226.7) or "about a year" (226.8), supported by the American Colonization Society, awaiting passage to Liberia. During that time he spoke at a public meeting at least once (226.4) and met with Theodore Dwight Jr. several times (226.6, etc.).

The date of Lamine Kabā's departure for Liberia is not yet known. An inscription on Umar ibn Sayyid's Arabic manuscript autobiography (q.v. 206.0) suggests that Lamine Kabā was still in New York in 1836; and this seems to be supported (and perhaps narrowed to the year's earlier months?) by Ralph R. Gurley's assertion of May 21, 1837, that "more than a year ago … [Lamine Kabā] was preparing to embark at New York for Liberia" (204.3 [*sic*], p. 204). *Cf.* "Departure of Emigrants [on brig *Luna*]," *New-York Spectator*, July 7, 1836, p. 3, col. 2. On the other hand, Allan D. Austin, *African Muslims in Antebellum America: Transatlantic Stories* (New York: Routledge, 1997), 118, identifies Lamine Kabā with "Paul A. Mandingo" from "North Georgia" who aged ca. 60 reached Liberia aboard the *Indiana* on August 19, 1835. *Cf. The African Repository, and Colonial Journal* 11 (1835): 285.

226.2———.

Article 226.1 reprinted with credit line "*From the New York Journal of Commerce*" under headline "Interesting Case" on the third page (of four), col. 2, of the newspaper *The Maryland Gazette*, vol. 89, no. 50.

Baltimore [Maryland, U.S.A.]: Printed and published by Jonas Green, at the Brick Building on the Public Circle, **December 11, 1834.**
Broadsheet bifolium: 4 p.

226.3———.
Article 226.1 reprinted **without** credit line under headline "Interesting Case" on last page (i.e., p. 4), col. 2, of the antislavery newspaper *The Liberator*, vol. 5, no. 1.

Boston [Massachusetts, U.S.A.]: Garrison and Knapp, Publishers, **January 3, 1835.**
Broadsheet bifolium: 4 p.
http://fair-use.org/the-liberator/1835/01/03/the-liberator-05-01.pdf

226.4———.
Account of brief remarks by "Paul, the aged" spoken (after introduction by the Rev. Mr. John Breckinridge) to a "meeting of ladies and gentlemen friendly to the cause of African Colonization … held [on January 9] at Masonic Hall in" New York City included in col. 2 within article headlined "Colonization Meeting" printed on p. 1, cols. 1–3 in the biweekly newspaper *New-York Spectator*.

New York [New York, U.S.A.]: Published by Francis Hall & Co., **January 15, 1835.**
Broadsheet bifolium: 4 p.

226.5———.
Account of brief remarks by "Paul, the aged" spoken (after introduction by the Rev. Mr. John Breckinridge) to a "meeting of ladies and gentlemen friendly to the cause of African Colonization … held at Masonic Hall in" New York City included on p. 18 within article 223.4 reprinted on pp. 14–20 in the monthly magazine *The African Repository, and Colonial Journal*, vol. 11 (eleven), no. 1.

Washington [District of Columbia, U.S.A.]: [Published by order of the Managers of the American Colonization Society] Published by James C. Dunn, **January 1835.**
8vo.
https://babel.hathitrust.org/cgi/pt?id=mdp.39015019348963&view=1up&seq=28

226.6———.
Theodore Dwight Jr.'s summary account of parts of Lamine Kabā's life, including quotations of Lamine Kabā's autobiographical statements, printed within Dwight's article "On the Sereculeh Nation in Nigritia: Remarks on the Sereculehs, an African nation, accompanied by a Vocabulary of their Language. Presented to the American Lyceum [May 8 or 9, 1835]" in the professional journal *American Annals of Education and Instruction* (edited by William Channing Woodbridge), Series 3, vol. 5, no. 10, pp. 451–456.

Boston [Massachusetts, U.S.A.]: Published by William D. Ticknor. Press of Light & Horton, **October, 1835.**
8vo.
https://babel.hathitrust.org/cgi/pt?id=hvd.32044096992508&view=1up&seq=517
First phrases of article proper: "The following Vocabulary, which has been obtained from a native African of education, and for some years a teacher of a school in Nigritia…"
Hogg 1478.

226.7———.
Part of his life story included in an unsigned article by Theodore Dwight Jr., printed under headline "An Interesting African" on pp. 6–8 in double-column weekly magazine *American Penny Magazine and Family Newspaper*, edited by Theodore Dwight Jr., vol. 1, no. 1.

New York [New York, U.S.A.]: [Theodore Dwight Jr., Express Office, 112 Broadway], **February 8, 1845.** [Note: price, 3 cents per 16-page large 8vo issue.]
8vo (26 cm.). General title-page for all 1845 issues bound together carries title: *Dwight's American Magazine and Family Newspaper*.
https://babel.hathitrust.org/cgi/pt?id=wu.89066347238&view=1up&seq=14
First phrases of article proper: "In the years 1833 and 1834 an aged African spent several months in the city of New York, under the charge of the Colonization Society, who had received him from his late master in one of the Western States, to be sent back to his native country."

226.8———.
Account as written by Theodore Dwight derived from "numerous prolonged interviews" with "Old Paul" *or* Lamine Kabā, much of it "from the voluminous notes which he took from the lips of the old man, (some of them in stenography,)" on pp. 80–84 of Dwight's article, "Condition and Character of Negroes in Africa," which is printed on pp. 77–90 in *Methodist Quarterly Review*, edited by Daniel Denison Whedon, D.D., vol. 46 (4th series vol. 16), "January Number."

New York [New York, U.S.A.]: Published by Carlton & Porter, 200 Mulberry-Street, **1864.**
8vo.
https://babel.hathitrust.org/cgi/pt?id=umn.31951d003190229;view=1up;seq=90
First phrases of article proper: "The erroneous impressions which prevail in the civilized world respecting the of the Negro race in Africa are discreditable to the intelligence of the age."
Hogg 1509.

226.9——.

Account included as the principal content in an as-yet un-located (and perhaps never published) *book* (planned to include at least "Preface," "Narrative," and "Appendix," as noted below), for the preface to which an undated (but see below) printer's galley slip survives at the Library of Congress, Washington, DC, U.S.A. The text of this galley slip begins: "PREFACE. | The contents of the following account were communicated to me, in 1834 and '35, by the aged and venerable African, Lahmen Kibby, called "Old Paul," in whose name I now present them." Its eighth paragraph reads in full: "The editor wishes, in this book, to pay a small part of the debt which Americans owe to Africans, for their long, severe, and unrequited labor and sufferings, by vindicating the character and capacities of the race, gratifying their friends, and casting merited disgrace upon their inhuman, conceited, and malignant traducers." We tentatively date this galley slip **March? 1864**, positing that Daniel Bliss referred to it in his March 29, 1864, letter to Theodore Dwight Jr., in which he wrote "I came into the city this evening & have seen for the first time the proof sheets of the Narrative of our old friend Kibby" (Omar ibn Said Collection, Library of Congress).

https://www.loc.gov/resource/amedsaid1831.dw016/?sp=1

226.10——.

226.8 printed on pp. 48–53 within Theodore Dwight's article "Condition and Character of Negroes in Africa," which is reprinted as chapter 3 (pp. 43–61) in *The People of Africa: A Series of Papers on Their Character, Condition, and Future Prospects by E. W. Blyden, D.D. Tayler Lewis, Theodore Dwight, Esq., etc., etc.* [edited by Henry Maunsell Schieffelin].

New York [New York, U.S.A.]: A. D. F. Randolph & Co., **1871.** Tpv: St. Johnland Stereotype Foundry, Suffolk County, N.Y.
8vo (19 cm): [vi], 157 p.., plates, illus.
https://archive.org/details/peopleofafricase00schi/page/43/mode/1up
First phrases of article proper: "The erroneous impressions which prevail in the civilized world respecting the of the Negro race in Africa are discreditable to the intelligence of the age."

226.11——.

226.8 printed on pp. 323–326 within Theodore Dwight's article "The Natives of Western Africa" "[f]rom The Methodist Quarterly Review," which is printed on pp. 321–330 of the monthly periodical *The African Repository*, vol. 48, no. 11.

Washington [District of Columbia, U.S.A.]: [American Colonization Society], November **1872.** General title page for

entire volume (that is, all twelve 1872 issues) carries the imprint: Washington City: Colonization Building, 450 Pennsylvania Avenue, 1872.
8vo (24 cm.).
https://babel.hathitrust.org/cgi/pt?id=hvd.hwrccn&view=1up&seq=333
First phrases of article proper: "The erroneous impressions which prevail in the civilized world respecting the of the Negro race in Africa are discreditable to the intelligence of the age."

226.12——. [Photomechanical reprint of 226.5]

Account of brief remarks by "Paul, the aged" spoken (after introduction by the Rev. Mr. John Breckinridge) to a "meeting of ladies and gentlemen friendly to the cause of African Colonization ... held at Masonic Hall in" New York City included on p. 18 within article 226.4 reprinted on pp. 14–20 in photomechanical reprint of the monthly magazine *The African Repository, and Colonial Journal*, vol. 11 (eleven), no. 1 (January 1835), with new imprint:

New York [New York, U.S.A.]: Kraus Reprint Corporation, **1967.** Tpv: Printed in the United States of America.
8vo.
https://babel.hathitrust.org/cgi/pt?id=uc1.$b541060&view=1up&seq=24

226.13————. [Photomechanical reprint of 226.10]

226.8 printed within Theodore Dwight's article "Condition and Character of Negroes in Africa," which is reprinted as chapter 3 in *The People of Africa: A Series of Papers on Their Character, Condition, and Future Prospects*, edited by Henry Maunsell Schieffelin. **Second edition**, with a new index and introduction by K. Mahmud.

Ibadan, Nigeria: Ibadan University Press, **1974.**
8vo (20 cm.): xxiii, 164 p., plates, illus.

226.14 ——. [Annotated printings of 226.5, 226.6, and 226.8]

Accounts as written by John Breckinridge and Theodore Dwight, the latter derived from "numerous prolonged interviews" with "Old Paul" or, much of it "from the voluminous notes which he took from the lips of the old man, (some of them in stenography,)" within Dwight's article, "Condition and Character of Negroes in Africa" as printed from 226.8, pp. 409–444 (especially pp. 410, 414–420, and 421–433) of *African Muslims in Antebellum American: A Source Book*, edited by Allan D. Austin.

New York [New York, U.S.A.]: Garland Publishing, **1984.**
8vo (23 cm.): xiv, 759 [*sic*] p., maps.

226.15 ————.

Excerpts from account printed within article by Jonathan Curial headlined "The Life of Omar Ibn Said," printed on pp. 34–39 of the March/April 2020 (vol. 61, no. 2) of the corporate magazine *Saudi Aramco World*.

Houston, Texas [U.S.A.]: Aramco Services Company, March 2020.
https://archive.aramcoworld.com/issue/201002/the.life. of.omar.ibn.said.htm

1835

227.1 Antonio Ferrer (ca. 1815–1850?)

Account "For the Liberator" printed under headline "Antonio Ferrer" on first page (i.e., 17), cols. 2–4, of the antislavery newspaper *The Liberator*, vol. 5, no. 5.

Boston [Massachusetts, U.S.A.]: William Lloyd Garrison and Isaac Knapp, Publishers, January 31, 1835. Broadsheet bifolium (49 cm.): 4 p.

http://fair-use. org/the-liberator/1835/01/31/ the-liberator-05-05.pdf [see 227.1].

¶ Ferrer lived in an inland African village (evidence in Hillard *A Full and Accurate Report…* suggests he may have come from Cape Lopez, modern Gabon). Kidnapped at about age seven, he was shipped to Barcelona, Spain, where the law freed him. Years later an employer took him to Havana, Cuba, where he was reenslaved. After years of hard labor, Ferrer purchased his freedom, then worked as a paid servant for the schooner *Panda*'s captain. While later working as the *Panda*'s cook, Ferrer was captured (along with the rest of the crew) by a British warship, whose captain falsely accused them of brigandage, attempted to extort money and confessions of slave running, and forced them to Boston, Massachusetts, U.S.A., where Ferrer and his crew mates remained jailed throughout a long trial that ended in their acquittal.

227.2 ————.

Portions of his life story incorporated in the address to the jury by his defense counsel George S. Hillard (1808–1879) in vol. 10, p. 744 of *American State Trials: A Collection of the Important and Interesting Criminal Trials which have taken place in the United States, from the beginning or our Government to the Present Day, with notes and annotations, John D. Lawson, LL.D., editor.*

St. Louis [Missouri, U.S.A.]: F. H. Thomas Law Book Co., 1918.
8vo (25 cm.): xxviii, 902 p.
https://babel.hathitrust.org/cgi/pt?id=hvd.hl54yj&view= 1up&seq=776

228.0 Rosa Maria de Conceição (–1843)

Manuscript will and inventory of Rosa Maria da Conceição written in **1835**, held in the Arquivo Público do Estado da Bahia (**Salvador, Bahia, Brazil**), Seção Judiciária, Inventários e Testamentos, 05/2956/2428/O6, fols. 3r-5v, 8r.

¶ An account from an unknown location of coastal Africa, Conceição was transported enslaved to Brazil. Having achieved her freedom, she wrote her will in the province of Bahia in 1835 and died a widow in 1843.

Full text: https:// huskiecommons. lib.niu.edu/history-500african-voices/146/ [see 228.1].

228.1————.

Will and inventory printed with annotations by Hendrik Kraay on pp. 290–293 in *Colonial Lives: Documents on Latin American History, 1550–1850*, edited by Richard Boyer and Geoffrey Spurling.

New York [New York, U.S.A.]: Oxford University Press, 2000. 8vo (25 cm.): xviii, 350 p.

229.1 William Andrew de Graftenreid

His account recorded within quotations as direct speech to the writer of a letter to the editor entitled "Is Slaveholding Right?—Judge Ye!" signed "B. F. R."* printed on third page (i.e., 39), cols. 1–2 of the antislavery newspaper *The Liberator*, vol. 5, no. 10.

Boston [Massachusetts, U.S.A.]: William Lloyd Garrison and Isaac Knapp, Publishers, March 7, **1835**. Broadsheet bifolium (49 cm.): 4 p.

*Note: B. F. R. was probably the freeborn Massachusetts African American activist and (for a while) printer-publisher

http://fair-use. org/the-liberator/1835/03/07/ the-liberator-05-10.pdf [see 229.1].

Benjamin Franklin Roberts (1814–1887), son of Robert Roberts (1770–1860), African American author of *The House Servant's Directory* (Boston: Munroe and Francis, 1827).

¶ According to his perhaps contrived or embellished account, de Graftenreid was born in Bedagua (an as-yet-unidentified location). At age six, while fishing on the borders of the Red Sea with his mother, he and she were kidnapped by twenty-four men, who took them in two boats to their slave ship, then to St. Thomas in the Caribbean, where they were sold. After six years of difficult servitude de Graftenreid was separated from his mother and sold in Buenos Aires, Argentina. Nine months later he was taken to the Danish colony of St. Croix in the Caribbean, where he worked in a plantation house. Sold again, he was taken to Gibraltar, the British colony at the southern tip of the Iberian peninsula in Europe, then back to St. Croix, then New York City in the United States of America, where he worked as a restaurant waiter. After his owner threatened his life, de Graftenreid escaped and found help from friends. He subsequently told his story to the person who quoted it to the editor of *The Liberator*, the US abolitionist newspaper. The veracity of de Graftenreid's account was questioned in a follow-up letter to the editor by "J. S.—*Providence* [Rhode Island]" (who asserted that he knew de Graftenreid when de Graftenreid lived in Providence) printed in *The Liberator*, vol. 5, no. 15 (April 11, 1835), second page (i.e., 58), cols. 3–4, which is available on-line at:

http://fair-use.org/the-liberator/1835/04/11/the-liberator-05-15.pdf

230.1 English-speaking girl from Sierra Leone

Several of her life facts in an article in the *anti*-emancipation semiweekly newspaper *The Bahama Argus*, vol. 5.

Nassau [Bahamas]: George Biggs, before July, **1835**.

¶ After capture "in the vicinity of Sierra Leone," this "girl who [spoke] English" was taken on the Portuguese slave ship *Creole*, which (after it had been at sea twenty-five days and dysentery had broken out among them) was captured off Santo Domingo in the Caribbean by the British eighteen-gun brig-sloop HMS *Gannet*. The *Gannet*'s

http://fair-use.org/the-liberator/1836/07/02/the-liberator-06-27.pdf [see 230.2].

captain and crew freed the 307 captives, chiefly children, and took them aboard the *Creole* to the British colonial town of Nassau in the Bahamas. The slave deck on the *Creole* did not exceed two feet in height.

230.2———.

230.1 reprinted under headline "The Slave Trade" on last page (i.e., 108), col. 5, of the antislavery newspaper *The Liberator*, vol. 6, no. 27.

Boston [Massachusetts, U.S.A.]: William Lloyd Garrison and Isaac Knapp, Publishers, July 2, **1835**.
Broadsheet bifolium (49 cm.): 4 p.
http://fair-use.org/the-liberator/1836/07/02/the-liberator-06-27.pdf

231.1 Unnamed father from the Cape of Good Hope

Several of his life facts are printed in an article in the *anti*-emancipation semiweekly newspaper *The Bahama Argus*, vol. 5, no.

Nassau [Bahamas]: George Biggs, before July, **1835**.

¶ This man came from the Cape of Good Hope (modern South Africa). While journeying with his son beyond a disputed frontier, both were captured and sold to the Portuguese slave ship *Creole*, which (after it had been sea twenty-five days and dysentery had broken out among them) was captured off Santo Domingo in the Caribbean by the British eighteen-gun brig-sloop HMS *Gannet*. The *Gannet*'s captain and crew freed the 307 captives, chiefly children, and took them aboard the *Creole* to the British colonial town of Nassau in the Bahamas. The slave deck on the *Creole* did not exceed two feet in height.

http://fair-use.org/the-liberator/1836/07/02/the-liberator-06-27.pdf [see 231.2].

231.2———.

231.1 reprinted under the headline "The Slave Trade" on last page (i.e., 108), col. 5, of the antislavery newspaper *The Liberator*, vol. 6, no. 27.

Boston [Massachusetts, U.S.A.]: William Lloyd Garrison and Isaac Knapp, Publishers, July 2, **1836**.
Broadsheet bifolium (49 cm.): 4 p.
http://fair-use.org/the-liberator/1836/07/02/the-liberator-06-27.pdf

232.0 José Francisco (ca. 1807–)

Statement recorded in Macurijes, Cuba on 14 August **1835**, preserved in Archivo Nacional de la República de Cuba (ANC), **La Habana, Cuba**, Miscelánea de Expendientes, 614/A.

¶ After transport from an unknown location in Africa on a slave ship to Cuba, José Francisco identified with an African nation, the description of which in the manuscript is illegible. He was single and living enslaved in or near Macurijes when called on to testify in the hearing of another who violently attacked their supervisor. José Francisco described the incident and the abusive treatment that he, the accused, and others suffered from their supervisor.

232.1——.

Statement printed on p. 136 in *La esclavitud desde la esclavitud: La visión de los siervos* by Gloria García Rodríguez.

México [Distrito Federal, Estados Unidos Mexicanos]: Centro de Investigación Científica "Ing. Jorge L Tamayo," **1996**.
8vo (21 cm.): 251 p.

232.2——.

Statement printed on p. 122 in *La esclavitud desde la esclavitud*, by Gloria García.

La Habana [Cuba]: Editorial de Ciencias Sociales, 2003.
8vo (21 cm.): xx, 222 p.

232.3——.

English translation of statement printed on p. 115 in *Voices of the Enslaved in Nineteenth-Century Cuba: A Documentary History*, edited by Gloria García Rodríguez. Translated [from 229.1] by Nancy L. Westrate; foreword by Ada Ferrer.

Chapel Hill [North Carolina, U.S.A.]: University of North Carolina Press, **2011**.
8vo (23.5 cm.): xviii, 220 p.

Full text: https://huskiecommons.lib.niu.edu/history-500african-voices/147/ [see 232.3].

233.0 Francisco Mina = Pancho

Statement recorded on 31 August **1835** in Cayajabos, Cuba, preserved in Archivo Nacional de la República de Cuba (ANC), **La Habana, Cuba,** Gobierno Superior Civil, 616/19688.

¶ Francisco identified as Mina (a New World ethnic designation for Akan-speakers near Elmina Castle, modern Ghana). After transport to Cuba on a slave ship and sale before 1815, he worked as a cart driver on a coffee plantation. Still single when his owner sold him to a coffee plantation, where his mayoral punished him severely because he was unaccustomed to such work, he ran away and joined small Maroon communities in places called Vuelta de Abajo and Guanes. He was never the leader of these palenques. In one he lived with about ten mostly African Maroons, who survived by eating rats and snakes. The Maroons in his group went to trade with friendly enslaved people on a coffee plantation called *Santa Teresa* (or Landlot), where Francisco was eventually caught. He was sentenced to four to six years in prison, followed by transfer to a place far from the hills of Cuzco, where he had been living.

233.1——.

Statement printed on pp. 191–193 in *La esclavitud desde la esclavitud: La visión de los siervos* by Gloria García Rodríguez.

México [Distrito Federal, Estados Unidos Mexicanos]: Centro de Investigación Científica "Ing. Jorge L Tamayo," **1996**.
8vo (21 cm.): 251 p.

233.2——.

Statement printed on pp. 171–172 *La esclavitud desde la esclavitud*, by Gloria García.

La Habana [Cuba]: Editorial de Ciencias Sociales, 2003.
8vo (21 cm.): xx, 222 p.

233.3——.

English translation of her statement printed on pp. 164–165 and 202n7 in *Voices of the Enslaved in Nineteenth-Century Cuba: A Documentary History*, edited by Gloria García Rodríguez. Translated [from 230.1] by Nancy L. Westrate; foreword by Ada Ferrer.

Chapel Hill [North Carolina, U.S.A.]: University of North Carolina Press, **2011**.
8vo (23.5 cm.): xviii, 220 p.

Full text: https://huskiecommons.lib.niu.edu/history-500african-voices/148/ [see 233.3].

1837

234.0   Ajayi (1806?-1891) = Samuel Ajayi Crowther = Adjai = Samuel Adjai Crowther

234.0a Manuscript letter written by Crowther to the Church Missionary Society while he was a student at Fourah Bay College, Sierra Leone, in **1837**, in which "he gives a vivid account of his childhood capture into slavery and the months up to his release" (Cadbury Research Library, *Black History Guide*, updated to 8 March 2019, p. 5) held in the University of Birmingham's Cadbury Research Library (**Birmingham, England**), Special Collections, Church Missionary Society Archive, CMS/B/OMS/C A1 O79 (item 2).

https://archive. org/details/ journalsofrev- jam00scho/page/ n407/mode/1up [see 234.2].

234.0b Manuscript of a letter Crowther wrote in **1841** (at the request of his Niger Expedition ship's captain) which, like 232.0a, also describes his capture and liberation. First printed as 234.19 in 1965.

¶ Ajayi came from Osogun in Oyo (modern Nigeria). In 1821 he was captured and enslaved during the war waged by Oyo Muslims (from Ilorin) and their Fulani (Fula, Fulbi or Peul peoples throughout West Africa) allies involved in *jihād* (religious reform movement that involved warfare). Spanish and Portuguese traders in Lagos sold him to a slave ship bound for Brazil, but British warships captured their ship during their first evening at sea, took them to Sierra Leone, and freed them. Crowther converted to Christianity and went to England, where he went to school in Islington (London). Later became the first African bishop in the Anglican church. He participated in the Niger Expedition in 1841 and remained in the region as a missionary until forced to resign in 1890, the year before he died. Early biographies include C. F. Childe, *Good out of Evil; or, The History of Adjai, the African Slave Boy: An Authentic Biography of the Rev. S. Crowther,* London, 1850 (Hogg 1497) and (composed for less experienced readers) *The African Slave Boy: A Memoir of the Rev. Samuel Crowther,* London, 1852 (Hogg 1498). For more on him see Femi J. Kolapo, *Christian Missionary Engagement in Central Nigeria, 1857–1891: The Church Missionary Society's All-African Mission on the Upper Niger* (London: Palgrave Macmillan, 2019).

234.1————.

"The Narrative of Samuel Ajayi Crowther," being Crowther's 22 February 1837 letter to Rev. William Jowett (232.0a), printed on pp. 217–223 in vol. 8, no. 10 of the monthly periodical *Church Missionary Record.*

London [England]: Seeleys, Hatchard, Nisbet, Simpkin, Marshall [etc.], October, 1837. Colophon: London: Printed by Richard Watts, Crown Court, Temple Bar.
8vo (22 cm.).

234.2————.

"Letter [234.1] from Mr. Samuel Crowther to the Rev. William Jowett, in 1837, then secretary of the Church Missionary Society, detailing the circumstances connected with his being sold as a slave," printed as Appendix III on pp. 371–385 in *Journals of the Rev. James Frederick Schön and Mr. Samuel Crowther, who… accompanied the Expedition up the Niger, in 1841.*

London [England]: Hatchard and Son, Piccadilly; Nisbet and Co., Berners St.; Seeleys, Fleet St., **1842.** Tpv: London: Richard Watts [Printer], Crown Court, Temple Bar.
8vo (21 cm.): [8], xxii, [2], 393 p., folding map.
https://archive.org/details/journalsofrevjam00scho/page/ n407/mode/1up
Hogg 1484.

234.3————.

Adjaï, ou le Jeune Esclave Africain. Récit authentique destiné à la jeunesse.

Toulouse [France]: Société des Livres Religieux, **1867.**
24mo: 88 p., illus. Exemplar at Bibliothèque Cantonale et Universitaire, Lausanne, site Cèdres.
Hogg 1511.

234.4————. [Second edition or printing of 234.3]

Adjaï, ou le Jeune Esclave Africain. Récit authentique destiné à la jeunesse. 2e édition.

Toulouse et Paris [France]: Société des Livres Religieux, **1869.**
24mo: 88 p., illus. Note: Edition statement and publication year from Jean Gay, *Bibliographie des ouvrages relatif a l'Afrique et a l'Arabie* (San Remo [Italy]: J. Gay et fils, 1875), p. 63.

234.5————.

Adjai; or, the true story of a little African slave boy. Published under the Direction of the Tract Committee.

London [England]: Society for the Promotion of Christian Knowledge [reported to carry four addresses for publisher], [1882?]. BL exemplar.
12mo (15 cm.): 16 p. Advertised for price One Penny in 1888.

Figure 13: 1864 photograph of Ajayi, also known as Samuel Ajayi Crowther (1806?–1891). He came from Osogun in Oyo (modern Nigeria) and was taken on a slave ship bound for Brazil in 1821. A British warship intercepted them, however, liberated the enslaved passengers, and took them to Sierra Leone, where Ajayi converted and became a missionary and eventually the first African bishop in the Church of England.

Source: Photograph by Ernest Edwards, albumen carte-de-visite, 1864, NPG x132392, National Portrait Gallery, London.

234.6———. [Third edition or printing of 234.3]

Adjaï, ou le Jeune Esclave Africain. Récit authentique destiné à la jeunesse. 3e édition.

Toulouse [France]: Imprimerie Chauvin et fils, Librairie Lagard; **Paris** [France]: Les Librairies Protestantes, [1886?] 24mo: 87 [*sic*?] p. Published by the Société des Livres Religieux de Toulouse. Publication details from *Journal Général de l'Imprimerie et de la Librairie* (Paris [France]: au Cercle de la Librairie), 75e année (2e Série), no. 46 (13 Nov. 1886), p. 693.

234.7———.

Paragraph from 234.1 printed within quotation marks on p. 36 of Jesse Page, *Samuel Crowther, The Slave Boy who became Bishop of the Niger.*

London [England]: S. W. Partridge & Company, [1888]. Colophon (from 234.8): London [England]: Knight, Printer, Middle Street, Aldersgate, E. C. [Some catalogs supply publication year 1889, but see below.]

8vo (19 cm.): xii, [13]-160 p., portrait, illus., map. Note: "Author's forward" to 234.13 (1908) begins (on its p. ix), "It is a reminder of the flight of time that twenty years have passed since I saw Bishop Crowther and wrote a short sketch of his life in my series of missionary biographies published by Messrs. Partridge." Year of publication and publisher apparently confirmed by announcement in *The Literary World* (London, England), vol. 38 (New Series), no. 1,000 (Dec. 28, 1888), p. 561, col. 1, where copies of 232.7 are priced 1 shilling 6 pence each.

234.8——. [Sheets of 234.7 with cancellans title leaf]
Paragraph from 234.1 printed within quotation marks on p. 36 of Jesse Page, *Samuel Crowther, The Slave Boy who became Bishop of the Niger.*

New York [New York, U.S.A.] and Chicago [Illinois, U.S.A.]: Fleming H. Revell Company, Publishers of Evangelical Literature, **[1889?]**. Colophon: London [England]: Knight, Printer, Middle Street, Aldersgate, E. C.
8vo (19 cm.): xii, [13]-160 p., portrait, illus., map.
https://babel.hathitrust.org/cgi/pt?id=mdp.39015063163516
&view=1up&seq=7

234.9——.
Paragraph from 234.1 printed within quotation marks on p. 36 of Jesse Page, *Samuel Crowther, The Slave Boy who became Bishop of the Niger.* **Second** edition, ------- thousand.

Fleming H. Revell Company, New York [New York, U.S.A.], Chicago [Illinois, U.S.A.], Toronto [Ontario, Canada], Publishers of Evangelical Literature, **[ca. 1893?]**. Colophon: London [England]: Knight, Printer, Middle Street, Aldersgate, E. C.
8vo (19 cm.): xii, [13]-160 p., portrait, illus., map. *Nota bene*: not found; entry posited from 231.10's edition statement.

234 10——.
Paragraph from 234.1 printed within quotation marks on p. 36 of Jesse Page, *Samuel Crowther, The Slave Boy who became Bishop of the Niger.* **Third** edition, Thirteenth thousand.

Fleming H. Revell Company, New York [New York, U.S.A.], Chicago [Illinois, U.S.A.], Toronto [Ontario, Canada], Publishers of Evangelical Literature, **[1896?]**. Colophon: London [England]: Knight, Printer, Middle Street, Aldersgate, E. C.
8vo (19 cm.): xii, [13]-160 p., portrait, illus., map.
https://babel.hathitrust.org/cgi/pt?id=umn.31951001867566
0&view=1up&seq=7

234.11——.
Paragraph from 234.1 printed within quotation marks on p. 36 of Jesse Page, *Samuel Crowther, The Slave Boy who became Bishop of the Niger.* **Fourth** edition, Eighteenth thousand.

Fleming H. Revell Company, New York [New York, U.S.A.], **Chicago [Illinois, U.S.A.], Toronto [Ontario, Canada]**, Publishers of Evangelical Literature, **[1899?]**. Colophon: London [England]: Knight, Printer, Middle Street, Aldersgate, E. C.
8vo (19 cm.): xii, [13]-160 p., portrait, illus., map.
https://babel.hathitrust.org/cgi/pt?id=osu.32435008995086
&view=1up&seq=7

234.12——. [Fourth edition or printing of 234.3]
Adjaï, ou le Jeune Esclave Africain. Récit authentique destiné à la jeunesse. **4e édition.**

Toulouse [France]: Imprimerie Chauvin et fils, Société des Livres Religieux, 7, rue Romiguieres, **1900**.
24mo: 88 p., illus. Exemplar at Bibliothèque Nationale de France. Title-page imprint may be differently phrased.

234.13——.
Condensed version (first clause on p. 9, "I suppose some time about the commencement of the year 1821"; final clause on p. 17, "and unkind in its nature") of 234.1 or 234.2 printed on pp. 9–17 in Jesse Page, *The Black Bishop: Samuel Adjai* [sic] *Crowther.*

London [England]: Hodder and Stoughton, MCMVIII [1908]. Colophon: Wm. Brendon and Son, Ltd., Printers, Plymouth [England].
8vo (22 cm.): xv, [1], 440 p., illus., plates, map. Preface by Eugene Stock.
https://archive.org/details/blackbishopsamu00pagegoog/page/
n7

234.14——. [From the sheets of 234.13 with variant title leaf]
Condensed version (first clause on p. 9, "I suppose some time about the commencement of the year 1821"; final clause on p. 17, "and unkind in its nature") of 234.1 or 234.2 printed on pp. 9–17 in Jesse Page, *The Black Bishop: Samuel Adjai* [sic] *Crowther.*

New York [New York, U.S.A.]: Chicago [Illinois, U.S.A.]: Fleming H. Revell Company, **[1909?]**. Tpv: Wm. Brendon and Son, Ltd. Printers Plymouth, England. Colophon: Wm. Brendon and Son, Ltd., Printers, Plymouth [England].
8vo (22 cm.): xv, [1], 440 p., illus., plates, map. Preface by Eugene Stock.
https://babel.hathitrust.org/cgi/pt?id=uc2.ark:/13960/t6n-
017n1m&view=1up&seq=31

234.15——. ["Second and cheaper edition" of 234.13]
Condensed version (first clause on p. 7, "I suppose some time about the commencement of the year 1821"; final clause on

p. 17, "and unkind in its nature") of 234.1 or 234.2 printed on pp. 9–17 in Jesse Page, *The Black Bishop: Samuel Adjai* [sic] *Crowther.*

London [England]: Simpkin, Marshall & Co., **1910.**
8vo: xv, [1], 440 p., illus., plates, map. Preface by Eugene Stock.

234.16————.
The Slave Boy who became a Bishop. Or, The Story of Samuel Adjai Crowther.

London [England]: Church Missionary Society, **1913.**
8vo: 32 p. Exemplar at British Library, cataloged with Crowther as author.

234.17————.
Paragraph from 234.1 printed within quotation marks in Jesse Page, *Samuel Crowther, The Slave Boy who became Bishop of the Niger.*

London [England]: Pickering & Inglisa, [1931].
8vo (19 cm.): 190 p., plates, illus. In series: *Bright Biographies, Stirring Life Stories of Christian Men and Women,* 11.

234.18————.
Condensed version (first clause on p. 7, "I suppose some time about the commencement of the year 1821"; final clause on p. 17, "and unkind in its nature") of 234.1 or 234.2 printed on pp. 9–17 in Jesse Page, *The Black Bishop: Samuel Adjai* [sic] *Crowther.*

New York [New York, U.S.A.]: Fleming H. Revell, [1932?].
8vo (22 cm.): xv, [1], 440 p., illus., plates, map. Preface by Eugene Stock.

234.19————.
"A Second Narrative of Samuel Ajayi Crowther's Early Life [1841]," edited by Andrew F. Walls, printed on pp. 5–14 in *Bulletin of the Society for African Church History* vol. 2, no. 1.

Aberdeen, Scotland: Society for African Church History, **1965** (*sic*).
8vo (22 cm.). Note: This is the first publication of 232.0b, a letter Crowther wrote in 1841, which, like his 1837 letter, describes his capture and liberation.
Hogg 1590.

234.20————.
234.1 printed with annotations under heading "The Narrative of Samuel Ajayi Crowther" on pp. 298–316 within chapter entitled "Samuel Ajayi Crowther of Oyo" by J. F. Ade Ajayi on

pp. 289–316 in *Africa Remembered: Narratives by West Africans from the Era of the Slave Trade,* edited by Philip D. Curtin.

Madison [Wisconsin, U.S.A.]: University of Wisconsin Press, **1967.**
8vo (24 cm.): x, 363 p., illus., maps.

234.21————. [Second printing of 234.20]
234.1 printed with annotations under heading "The Narrative of Samuel Ajayi Crowther" on pp. 298–316 within chapter entitled "Samuel Ajayi Crowther of Oyo" by J. F. Ade Ajayi on pp. 289–316 in *Africa Remembered: Narratives by West Africans from the Era of the Slave Trade,* edited by Philip D. Curtin.

Madison [Wisconsin, U.S.A.]: University of Wisconsin Press, **1968.**
8vo (22 cm.): x, 363 p., illus., maps.

234.22————. [Photomechanical reprint of 234.2, with new intro. by J. F. Ade Ajayi]
"Letter [234.1] from Mr. Samuel Crowther to the Rev. William Jowett, in 1837, then secretary of the Church Missionary Society, detailing the circumstances connected with his being sold as a slave," printed from 232.2 as Appendix III on pp. 371–385 in *Journals of the Rev. James Frederick Schön and Mr. Samuel Crowther, who… accompanied the Expedition up the Niger, in 1841.*

London [England]: Frank Cass, **1970.**
8vo (22 cm.): xviii, [7], xxiii, 393 p. In series: *Cass Library of African Studies,* no. 18.

234.23————. [Photomechanical reprint of 234.13]
Condensed version (first clause on p. 7, "I suppose some time about the commencement of the year 1821"; final clause on p. 17, "and unkind in its nature") of 234.1 or 234.2 printed on pp. 9–17 in photomechanical reprint of 234.13, i.e., Jesse Page, *The Black Bishop: Samuel Adjai* [sic] *Crowther,* with new imprint:

Westport [Connecticut, U.S.A.]: Greenwood Press, **1979.**
8vo (23 cm.): xv, [1], 440 p., plates.

234.24————.
234.1 printed with annotations under heading "The Narrative of Samuel Ajayi Crowther" on pp. 298–316 within chapter entitled "Samuel Ajayi Crowther of Oyo" by J. F. Ade Ajayi on pp. 289–316 in *Africa Remembered: Narratives by West Africans from the Era of the Slave Trade,* edited by Philip D. Curtin.

Prospect Heights, Illinois [U.S.A.]: Waveland Press, **1997.**
8vo (23 cm.): x, 363 p., illus., maps.

Other publications by Crowther

+234-A.1——. and James F. Schön.

Journals of the Rev. James Frederick Schön and Mr. Samuel Crowther: Who, with the Sanction of Her Majesty's Government, Accompanied the Expedition Up the Niger, in 1841, in Behalf of the Church Missionary Society. With Appendices and Map (London [England]: Hatchard and Son, 1842). https://babel.hathitrust.org/cgi/pt?id=uc1.$b303658&view=1up&seq=7

+234-B.1——.

Vocabulary of the Yoruba Language (London [England]: Printed for the Church Missionary Society. Sold by Hatchard and Son, Piccadilly; Nisbet & Co., Berners Street; and Seeley, Burnside, & Seeley, Fleet Street, MDCCCXLIII [1843]). 8vo (20 cm.): [4], vii, 48, 195, [1] p.

+234-B.2——.

A Vocabulary of the Yoruba Language (London [England]: Seeleys, Fleet Street, and Hanover Street, Hanover Square, 1852). 8vo: v, [2], 38, [2], 291 p.

https://babel.hathitrust.org/cgi/pt?id=uc2.ark:/13960/t4nk3d-46f&view=1up&seq=5

+234-C.1——.

"Letters from the Rev. Samuel Crowther, a Native of the Yoruba Country, and a Clergyman of the Church of England at Abbeokuta, and the Rev. Henry Townsend, of the Church Missionary Society at Abbeokuta" in *The Colonial Magazine and East Indian Review*, vol. 20, no. 6 (London [England]: John Mortimer, Publisher, 141, Strand, December 1850): 508–517.

https://www.nla.gov.au/ferguson/1460602X/18501200/e0200006/31-40.pdf

https://www.nla.gov.au/ferguson/1460602X/18501200/e0200006/41-50.pdf

+234-C.2——.

Letters from the Rev. Samuel Crowther, a Native of the Yoruba Country, and a Clergyman of the Church of England at Abbeokuta, and the Rev. Henry Townsend, of the Church Missionary Society at Abbeokuta. Extracted from "The Colonial Magazine" for December 1850. [Above title:] *Slave Trade.—African Squadron.* (London [England]: John Mortimer, Publisher, 141, Strand, December, MDCCCL [1850]). 8vo (21 cm.): 15 p. (offprint of +232-C.1).

+234-D.1——.

Journal of an Expedition up the Niger and Tschadda Rivers, undertaken by Macgregor Laird, Esq., in connection with

the British Government, *in 1854* (London [England]: Church Missionary House, Salisbury Square; Seeley, Jackson, and Halliday, Fleet Street, MDCCCLV [1855]).

8vo: xxiii, [1], 234 p., folding map. https://archive.org/details/journalofexpedit00crow/page/n4

+234-E.1——. and John C. Taylor.

The Gospel on the Banks of the Niger: Journals and Notices of the Native Missionaries Accompanying the Niger Expedition of 1857–1859 (London [England]: Church Missionary House, 1859).

https://archive.org/details/gospelonbanksofn00crow/page/n4

+234-F.1——.

A Grammar and Vocabulary of the Nupe Language (London [England]: Church Missionary House, Salisbury Square, 1864). 8vo (22 cm.); 208 p.

https://babel.hathitrust.org/cgi/pt?id=hvd.32044004554689&view=1up&seq=7

+234-G.1——.

A Charge Delivered on the Banks of the River Niger in West Africa (London [England]: Seeley, Jackson & Halliday, 1866). 8vo (21 cm.): 42 p., map.

https://babel.hathitrust.org/cgi/pt?id=uiuo.ark:/13960/t76t0vq32&view=1up&seq=5

+234-H.1——.

Bishop Crowther's Report of the Overland Journey from Lokoja to Bida on the River Niger, and thence to Lagos on the Sea Coast, from November 10th, 1871, to February 8th, 1872 (London [England]: Church Missionary House, 1872). 8vo, 36 p.

http://anglicanhistory.org/africa/crowther/niger1872.html

235.1 Robert Johnson (ca. 1788–1861)

His account, as delivered aloud (and written down by a stenographer whose account attempts to reproduce Johnson's accent*) at the Massachusetts Anti-Slavery Society's Fifth Annual Meeting in Boston, Thursday, January 26, 1837, printed on second page (i.e., 22), cols. 2–3 of the antislavery newspaper *The Liberator*, vol. 7, no. 6.

http://fair-use.org/the-liberator/1837/02/04/the-liberator-07-06.pdf [see 235.1].

Nota bene: *This reporter did not attempt to reproduce any white speakers' accents, at least one variety of which (Yankee), and perhaps two (Yankee and Brahmin) would have struck any unbiased reporter as equally worthy of reproduction. Cf. 235.3, Joshua Coffin's account of this delivery of Mr. Johnson's speech or, perhaps, another of his deliveries of the same or a similar speech.

Boston [Massachusetts, U.S.A.]: W. L. Garrison and Isaac Knapp, Publishers, **February 4, 1837**. Note: Within this version of Johnson's account, the murder victim's head is cut off, Christopher Olney of Providence, RI, is *not* named as a witness, etc. Garrison and Knapp printed 3,000 extra copies of this issue of their paper because of the anticipated popularity of their account of the Massachusetts Anti-Slavery Society's Fifth Annual Meeting (p. 23, col. 5).

¶ Johnson came from "several hundred miles up the Gambia River" (modern Guinea) and identified as Kisse. He was kidnapped by Vai people when nine years old and taken to Mesurado or Cape Mount (modern coastal Liberia), where he first saw white people. After being sold twice, he was taken in the 1790s on the Rhode Island–based slave ship *Hunter* to Savannah, Georgia (U.S.A.), and then sold to Commodore Oliver Bowen (1742–1800), a former Rhode Islander who had served in the Revolution and subsequently settled in Georgia. The commodore's will reportedly promised Johnson freedom, but after the commodore died in 1800, his nephew Jabez Bowen Jr. (1774–1816, son of the commodore's heir) violated the will and kept Johnson enslaved. After several moves within Georgia (during which Johnson witnessed the murder of an enslaved maid serving at table in 1802, differently recorded in 235.1 and 235.3), Johnson accompanied his new owner to Providence, Rhode Island, U.S.A., when Bowen himself was taken there to recover from mental illness following a courthouse contretemps. Bowen was subsequently taken—for treatments during bouts of insanity—to Uxbridge, Massachusetts, and Philadelphia, Pennsylvania, where he died in 1816. At some point during these later years, Johnson fled from Providence to Boston, Massachusetts. There he was jailed, then forcibly returned to Providence. One or two years later he was manumitted. By 1835 he was practicing medicine in the West End section of Providence, Rhode Island, and by 1839 he was an officer in the African Baptist Church on Belknap Street, Boston, involved in school reform and the antislavery cause. He died in Roxbury, Massachusetts, 15 April 1861. For more on him see Randy J. Sparks, *Africans in the Old South: Mapping Exceptional Lives across the Atlantic World* (Cambridge, MA: Harvard University Press, 2016), pp. 81–102.

235.2———.

235.1 printed (with very slight alterations, none material as to the factual details of Johnson's speech) on p. xxvi–xviii of *Proceedings of the Massachusetts Anti-Slavery Society, at its Fifth Annual Meeting, held at Boston, Jan. 25, 1837*, which are printed as p. i–xlviii at the end of *Fifth Annual Report of the Board of Managers of the Massachusetts Anti-Slavery Society, with some account of the Annual Meeting, January 25, 1837.*

Boston [Massachusetts, U.S.A.]: Printed by Isaac Knapp, 25, Cornhill, [*post* February 3 (internal evidence)] **1837**.
8vo (22 cm.): 72, xlviii (sic) p.
https://babel.hathitrust.org/cgi/pt?id=iau.31858045551227&view=1up&seq=300

235.3———. [Variant account]

His account, perhaps as delivered aloud at the Massachusetts Anti-Slavery Society's Fifth Annual Meeting in Boston, Thursday, January 26, 1837, but if so, **with added details, shortened, and heard differently or altered** (with "standard English" instead of stenographer's attempts to reproduce Mr. Johnson's accent, *cf.* 235.1), and enclosed in quotation marks within a letter written and sent **by Joshua Coffin** to the Corresponding Secretary of the Massachusetts Anti-Slavery Society printed on p. 72 of *Fifth Annual Report of the Board of Managers of the Massachusetts Anti-Slavery Society, with some account of the Annual Meeting, January 25, 1837.*

Boston [Massachusetts, U.S.A.]: Printed by Isaac Knapp, 25, Cornhill, [*post* February 3 (internal evidence)] **1837**.
8vo (22 cm.): 72, xlviii (sic) p. Note: Within this version of Mr. Johnson's account, the murder victim's throat is cut, Christopher Olney of Providence, RI, is named as a witness and his reaction to the crime is described, etc.
https://babel.hathitrust.org/cgi/pt?id=iau.31858045551227&view=1up&seq=274 (facsimile).

235.4———.

Reprintings of 235.2 and 235.3 within photomechanical reprint of *First [-Tenth] Annual Report[s] of the Board of Managers of the Massachusetts Anti-Slavery Society … with new imprint:*

Westport, Connecticut [U.S.A.]: Negro Universities Press, **[1970]**.
8vo (22 cm.): various paginations.
https://babel.hathitrust.org/cgi/pt?id=iau.31858045551227&view=1up&seq=274

235.5———.

235.1 printed under heading "The Slave's Story" on pp. 124–128 in *Slave Testimony: Two Centuries of Letters, Speeches, Interviews, and Autobiographies*, edited by John W. Blassingame.

Baton Rouge [Louisiana, U.S.A.]: Louisiana State University Press, **1977**.
8vo (23 cm.): lxv, 777 p., illus., portraits.

235.6——. [Second printing of 235.5]

235.1 printed under heading "The Slave's Story" on pp. 124–128 in *Slave Testimony: Two Centuries of Letters, Speeches, and Autobiographies*, edited by John W. Blassingame.

Baton Rouge [Louisiana, U.S.A.]; Louisiana State University Press, **1977.** Second printing.
8vo (23 cm.): lxv, 777 p., illus., portraits.

235.7——. [Another printing of 235.5]

233.1 printed under heading "The Slave's Story" on pp. 124–128 in *Slave Testimony: Two Centuries of Letters, Speeches, and Autobiographies*, edited by John W. Blassingame.

Baton Rouge [Louisiana, U.S.A.]; Louisiana State University Press, **1979.** 1979 printing.
8vo (23 cm.): lxv, 777 p., illus., portraits.

235.8——. [Another printing of 235.5]

235.1 printed under heading "The Slave's Story" on pp. 124–128 in *Slave Testimony: Two Centuries of Letters, Speeches, and Autobiographies*, edited by John W. Blassingame.

Baton Rouge [Louisiana, U.S.A.]; Louisiana State University Press, **1980.** 1980 printing.
8vo (23 cm.): lxv, 777 p., illus., portraits.

235.9——. [Another printing of 235.5]

235.1 printed under heading "The Slave's Story" on pp. 124–128 in *Slave Testimony: Two Centuries of Letters, Speeches, and Autobiographies*, edited by John W. Blassingame.

Baton Rouge [Louisiana, U.S.A.]; Louisiana State University Press, **1989.** 1989 printing.
8vo (23 cm.): lxv, 777 p., illus., portraits.

235.10——. [Another printing of 235.5]

235.1 printed under heading "The Slave's Story" on pp. 124–128 in *Slave Testimony: Two Centuries of Letters, Speeches, and Autobiographies*, edited by John W. Blassingame.

Baton Rouge [Louisiana, U.S.A.]; Louisiana State University Press, **1998.** 1998 printing.
8vo (23 cm.): lxv, 777 p., illus., portraits.

235.11——. [Another printing of 235.5]

235.1 printed under heading "The Slave's Story" on pp. 124–128 in *Slave Testimony: Two Centuries of Letters, Speeches, and Autobiographies*, edited by John W. Blassingame.

Baton Rouge [Louisiana, U.S.A.]; Louisiana State University Press, **2002.** 2002 printing.
8vo (23 cm.): lxv, 777 p., illus., portraits.

235.12——. [Another printing of 235.5]

235.1 printed under heading "The Slave's Story" on pp. 124–128 in *Slave Testimony: Two Centuries of Letters, Speeches, and Autobiographies*, edited by John W. Blassingame.

Baton Rouge [Louisiana, U.S.A.]; Louisiana State University Press, 2009.
8vo (24 cm.): lxv, 777 p., illus., portraits.

235.13——.

Substantial parts of Johnson's account printed explicitly from 235.1 and 235.2 on pp. 81–87 in Randy J. Sparks, *Africans in the Old South: Mapping Exceptional Lives Across the Atlantic World.*

Cambridge, Massachusetts [U.S.A.]: Harvard University Press, **2016.**
8vo (25 cm.): 204 p.

236.0 María de los Dolores Frías

Petition Filed by María de los Dolores Frías, Havana, Cuba, **11 September 1837,** preserved in Archivo Nacional de la República de Cuba (ANC), **La Habana, Cuba,** Gobierno Superior Civil, 938/33099.

¶ María de los Dolores Frías said she was born in Africa but did not say where. She was taken on a slave ship to Cuba and sold. She lived in Barrio de Guadalupe in 1837 and had a daughter owned by another man when María petitioned the court in Havana for assistance in getting her daughter a new master because of his abuse. At first denied, she petitioned twice further until her daughter was finally allowed to seek a new owner in March 1838.

Full text: https://huskiecommons.lib.niu.edu/history-500african-voices/149/ [see 236.3].

236.1——.

Her statement printed on pp. 107–108 in *La esclavitud desde la esclavitud: La visión de los siervos* by Gloria García Rodríguez.

México [Distrito Federal, Estados Unidos Mexicanos]: Centro de Investigación Científica "Ing. Jorge L Tamayo," **1996.**
8vo (21 cm.): 251 p.

236.2——.

Her statement printed on pp. 95–96 *La esclavitud desde la esclavitud*, by Gloria García.

La Habana [Cuba]: Editorial de Ciencias Sociales, 2003.
8vo (21 cm.): xx, 222 p.

236.3———.

English translation of her statement printed on p. 90 in *Voices of the Enslaved in Nineteenth-Century Cuba: A Documentary History*, edited by Gloria García Rodríguez. Translated [from 233.1] by Nancy L. Westrate; foreword by Ada Ferrer.

Chapel Hill [North Carolina, U.S.A.]: University of North Carolina Press, **2011**.
8vo (23.5 cm.): xviii, 220 p.

237.0   José Antonio Avilés Congo (ca. 1805–)

Statement in Havana, Cuba on 5 October **1837**, preserved in Archivo Nacional de la República de Cuba (ANC), **La Habana, Cuba**, Gobierno Superior Civil, 938/33095.

Full text: https://huskiecommons.lib.niu.edu/history-500african-voices/150/ [see 237.3].

¶ José Antonio Avilés identified as Congolese. After transport on a slave ship to Cuba and sale, by 1837 he was an enslaved shoemaker, still single, and resided in the *La Salud* neighborhood of Havana. At a hearing in that year he complained that he was struggling to present his owner with his wages earned in shoemaking because a customer from an English ship in the harbor had refused to pay him. He went to the English captain, who was unable to help him.

237.1———.

Statement printed on p. 159 in *La esclavitud desde la esclavitud: La visión de los siervos* by Gloria García Rodríguez.

México [Distrito Federal, Estados Unidos Mexicanos]: Centro de Investigación Científica "Ing. Jorge L Tamayo," **1996**.
8vo (21 cm.): 251 p.

237.2———.

Statement printed on p. 143 *La esclavitud desde la esclavitud*, by Gloria García.

La Habana [Cuba]: Editorial de Ciencias Sociales, **2003**.
8vo (21 cm.): xx, 222 p.

237.3———.

English translation of statement printed on p. 136 in *Voices of the Enslaved in Nineteenth-Century Cuba: A Documentary History*, edited by Gloria García Rodríguez. Translated [from 237.1] by Nancy L. Westrate; foreword by Ada Ferrer.

Chapel Hill [North Carolina, U.S.A.]: University of North Carolina Press, **2011**.
8vo (23.5 cm.): xviii, 220 p.

238.0   Agustín Carabalí (1777–)

Statement recorded in Guanajay, Cuba in August **1837**, preserved in Archivo Nacional de la República de Cuba (ANC), **La Habana, Cuba**, Miscelánea de Expedientes, 604/M.

Full text: https://huskiecommons.lib.niu.edu/history-500african-voices/151/ [see 238.3].

¶ **Agustín identified as Carabalí (likely from Calabar in the Cross River region of modern Nigeria and northwestern Cameroon). After transport to Cuba on a slave ship and sale, by 1837 he worked enslaved on a sugar** plantation called *El Muriel* near Guanajay. He escaped that spring after abusive treatment by his supervisor. He ran to the coffee plantation of a previous owner and hid in the nearby scrub for about a month, when he met a woman and two men, all runaways from *El Muriel*, after which they turned themselves in. His punishment was not recorded.

238.1———.

Statement printed on p. 193 in *La esclavitud desde la esclavitud: La visión de los siervos* by Gloria García Rodríguez.

México [Distrito Federal, Estados Unidos Mexicanos]: Centro de Investigación Científica "Ing. Jorge L Tamayo," **1996**.
8vo (21 cm.): 251 p.

238.2———.

Statement printed on p. 173 *La esclavitud desde la esclavitud*, by Gloria García.

La Habana [Cuba]: Editorial de Ciencias Sociales, **2003**.
8vo (21 cm.): xx, 222 p.

238.3———.

English translation of statement printed on p. 166 in *Voices of the Enslaved in Nineteenth-Century Cuba: A Documentary History*, edited by Gloria García Rodríguez. Translated [from 238.1] by Nancy L. Westrate; foreword by Ada Ferrer.

Chapel Hill [North Carolina, U.S.A.]: University of North Carolina Press, **2011**.
8vo (23.5 cm.): xviii, 220 p.

239.0   Antonio Mina (1777–)

Statement recorded in Guanajay, Cuba in August **1837**, preserved in Archivo Nacional de la República de Cuba (ANC), **La Habana, Cuba**, Miscelánea de Expedientes, 604/M.

¶ **Antonio identified as Mina (a New World ethnic designation for Akan-speakers near Elmina Castle, modern Ghana). After** transport to Cuba on a slave ship and sale, he was single in 1837 and worked enslaved on the *El Muriel* sugar plantation near Guanajay, guarding prisoners as one of his assignments. At his hearing he stated briefly that he ran away after the prisoners escaped because he feared punishment. While in hiding he joined Agustín Carabalí (q.v. 238.0), Vicente Bibí (q.v. 240.0), and Hilario Congo (q.v. 241.0). Unable to bear Maroon life further, Antonio and Agustin followed Vincente, who turned himself in to his mistress, who said they would not be punished.

239.1———.

Statement printed on p. 194 in *La esclavitud desde la esclavitud: La visión de los siervos* by Gloria García Rodríguez.

México [Distrito Federal, Estados Unidos Mexicanos]: Centro de Investigación Científica "Ing. Jorge L Tamayo," **1996.**
8vo (21 cm.): 251 p.

239.2———.

Statement printed on p. 173 *La esclavitud desde la esclavitud,* by Gloria García.

La Habana [Cuba]: Editorial de Ciencias Sociales, **2003.**
8vo (21 cm.): xx, 222 p.

239.3———.

English translation of statement printed on p. 166 in *Voices of the Enslaved in Nineteenth-Century Cuba: A Documentary History,* edited by Gloria García Rodríguez. Translated [from 239.1] by Nancy L. Westrate; foreword by Ada Ferrer.

Chapel Hill [North Carolina, U.S.A.]: University of North Carolina Press, **2011.**
8vo (23.5 cm.): xviii, 220 p.

240.0 Vicente Bibí (1805–)

Statement recorded in Guanajay, Cuba, on August **1837,** preserved in Archivo Nacional de la República de Cuba (ANC), **La Habana, Cuba,** Miscelánea de Expedientes, 604/M.

¶ Vicente identified as Bibí (Ibibia people of the Cross River region, modern southern Nigeria, northwest Cameroon). After transport to Cuba on a slave ship and sale, by 1837 he

Full text: https://huskiecommons.lib.niu.edu/history-500african-voices/152/ [see 239.3].

Full text: https://huskiecommons.lib.niu.edu/history-500african-voices/153/ [see 240.3].

was enslaved on the *Zacanini* coffee plantation near Guanajay. Still single, he ran away by himself during milling season because he had no clothing. He managed to survive for about four months and at some point met Agustin Carabalí (q.v. 238.0) and Antonio Mina (q.v. 239.0), and probably Hilario Congo (q.v. 241.0). No longer able to bear the conditions of Maroon life, he turned himself in to his mistress, who agreed to look the other way concerning their infractions. Augustin and Antonio joined him.

240.1———.

Statement printed on p. 194 in *La esclavitud desde la esclavitud: La visión de los siervos* by Gloria García Rodríguez.

México [Distrito Federal, Estados Unidos Mexicanos]: Centro de Investigación Científica "Ing. Jorge L Tamayo," **1996.**
8vo (21 cm.): 251 p.

240.2———.

Statement printed on p. 173 *La esclavitud desde la esclavitud,* by Gloria García.

La Habana [Cuba]: Editorial de Ciencias Sociales, **2003.**
8vo (21 cm.): xx, 222 p.

240.3———.

English translation of statement printed on pp. 166–167 in *Voices of the Enslaved in Nineteenth-Century Cuba: A Documentary History,* edited by Gloria García Rodríguez. Translated [from 240.1] by Nancy L. Westrate; foreword by Ada Ferrer.

Chapel Hill [North Carolina, U.S.A.]: University of North Carolina Press, **2011.**
8vo (23.5 cm.): xviii, 220 p.

241.0 Hilario Congo (1787–)

Statement recorded in Guanajay, Cuba, in August **1837,** preserved in Archivo Nacional de la República de Cuba (ANC), **La Habana, Cuba,** Miscelánea de Expedientes, 604/M.

¶ Hilario identified as Congolese. After transport to Cuba on a slave ship and sale, he was single and worked enslaved on a coffee plantation near Guanajay in 1837, when he ran away during the milling season to the *Santo Tomás* coffee plantation. After twenty days in the bush he returned to the plantation, apparently in ill health, and was sent to the infirmary for recovery. A month after returning to work he ran off again and was caught twelve days later. While in hiding he met Vicente Bibí (q.v. 240.0).

Full text: https://huskiecommons.lib.niu.edu/history-500african-voices/154/ [see 241.3].

241.1———.

Statement printed on pp. 194–195 in *La esclavitud desde la esclavitud: La visión de los siervos* by Gloria García Rodríguez.

México [Distrito Federal, Estados Unidos Mexicanos]: Centro de Investigación Científica "Ing. Jorge L Tamayo," **1996**. 8vo (21 cm.): 251 p.

241.2———.

Statement printed on p. 174 *La esclavitud desde la esclavitud*, by Gloria García.

La Habana [Cuba]: Editorial de Ciencias Sociales, 2003. 8vo (21 cm.): xx, 222 p.

241.3———.

English translation of statement printed on p. 167 in *Voices of the Enslaved in Nineteenth-Century Cuba: A Documentary History*, edited by Gloria García Rodríguez. Translated [from 241.1] by Nancy L. Westrate; foreword by Ada Ferrer.

Chapel Hill [North Carolina, U.S.A.]: University of North Carolina Press, **2011**. 8vo (23.5 cm.): xviii, 220 p.

1838

242.1 Slamank (1750–) = Adam

"The Petition of Slamank, otherwise Adam" "To the Right Honourable Sir G. Hill, Bart. Colonel of the Londonderry Militia, Lieutenant-Governor, &c, &c" printed on p. 358 (with related sentences on pp. 151–152) of Capt. Studholme Hodgson, *Truths from the West Indies. Including a Sketch of Madeira in 1833.*

London [England]: William Ball, Paternoster Row, 1838. Tpv: R. Clay, Printer, Bread-Street-Hill.
8vo (20 cm.): xv, 372 p., frontis.
FN 000199.

https://archive.org/details/in.ernet.dli.2015.43187/page/n370 [see 242.1].

¶ Slamank was a Muslim cleric who identified as Mandinka (a group living in modern southern Mali, Guinea, Ivory Coast). Enslaved and forcibly taken to the British Caribbean colony of Trinidad and Tobago in 1785, he worked in the sugar fields there for fifty years, until emancipated under British law after 1833. In his petition to Sir G. Hill (242.1) he expressed his resentment at the five-year "apprentice" system that followed emancipation, which mandated that he "learn" a trade he had practiced without remuneration for fifty years. He did not expect to live long enough to experience full emancipation, which would have occurred in 1838.

243.1 Mohammedu Siseï (1788–)

His life detailed from information he shared with John Washington printed in Washington's article "Some Account of Mohammedu-Siseï, a Mandingo, of Nyáni-Marú on the Gambia" on pp. 448–454 in vol. 8 of the *Journal of the Royal Geographical Society of London.*

London, England: John Muray, 1838.
https://archive.org/details/jstor-1797825
Hogg 1480.

https://babel.hathitrust.org/cgi/pt?id=hvd.320441 05225916&view=1up&seq=552 [see 243.1].

¶ Mohammedu Siseï was born in a Mandinka village (an ethnic group residing in modern southern Mali, Guinea, and Ivory Coast) called Nyáni-Marú on the northern bank of the Gambia River (modern Gambia). He was learned, read the Qur'an, and wrote in Arabic. He married, taught Qur'anic school, and traveled widely, including to Gorée Island (modern Senegal) in 1805, having been captured in war. After several months he was forced aboard a French slave ship on the Gambia River. The British intercepted this ship at sea and took its human cargo, including Siseï, to Antigua, their Caribbean island colony. There Siseï was freed and placed in the 3rd West Indian Regiment, in which he served as a grenadier in the West Indies, 1811–1825. Discharged on the British island colony of Trinidad in 1825, he received some land as a pension, and helped establish a society of Muslims that purchased the freedom of fellow Muslims enslaved in the Caribbean. For more on Siseï and the context of his enslavement in West Africa see Sean Kelley, "Enslavement in Upper Guinea during the Era of the Transatlantic Slave Trade: Biographical Perspectives," *African Economic History*, 48:1 (2020), 46–73.

¶ Note for entries 244 through 255. On 14 November 1838 *The British Emancipator* published a long story about twelve "Kangas" abducted from the Guinea coast and transported on a Portuguese slave ship that the British Navy intercepted at sea. The editors of Oldendorp's Danish West Indies accounts (q.v. 30.0 to 110.0) posited that the Kanga people spoke a Kru language and probably came from modern southern Liberia (see Oldendorp, *Historie der caribishcen Inseln Sanct Thomas, Sanct Crux, and Sanct Jan*, vol. 1, p. 378n57). Taken on the British ship to Jamaica in the Caribbean, they became apprentices in the year emancipation was fully realized in the British West Indies. Examined in a custom house on 18, 23, and 30 July 1838, they all told their stories separately through an interpreter. Of particular interest to British officials and *The British Emancipator* reporter was their testimony that the slave ship's Portuguese crew (called "Spanish" by those providing these accounts) murdered one of the enslaved passengers, butchered his body, and tried to feed it to the other enslaved passengers. A Mr. Evelyn, to whom Manu (q.v. 244.1) was apprenticed, reported the evidence to the colonial secretary. Margaret Lambert (age 40) and George Robinson (age 46) served as the interpreters. Both identified as Kanga and had been enslaved: Lambert to Dr. Butler's estate, Robinson to the Haughton Court estate.

244.1 Manu (ca. 1824–) = Mary

Her testimony as translated by Margaret Lambert (a "Portuguese-Kanga") printed within news story headlined "Unexampled Horrors of the Slave Trade in 1838" on the first page (i.e., 177), col. 1, in the newspaper *The British Emancipator*, no. 31.

London [England]: [Published] Under the sanction of the Central Negro Emancipation Committee, November 14, **1838**. Colophon: Printed by John Haddon, Castle Street, Finsbury. Broadsheet bifolium (50 cm.).

Full text: https://huskiecommons.lib.niu.edu/history-500african-voices/155/ [see 244.1].

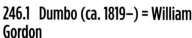

¶ Manu, aged fourteen, was from the Kanga country (a New World term referring to people from modern southern Liberia whose language was Kru). She was captured, forced aboard a slave ship bound for Brazil, intercepted by a British warship, liberated, and taken to Jamaica in the Caribbean, where she was apprenticed. There she described her Middle Passage experience.

245.1 Saru (ca. 1825–) = Jane

Her testimony as translated by Margaret Lambert (a "Portuguese-Kanga") printed within news story headlined "Unexampled Horrors of the Slave Trade in 1838" on the first page (i.e., p. 177), col. 1, in the newspaper *The British Emancipator*, no. 31.

London [England]: [Published] Under the sanction of the Central Negro Emancipation Committee, November 14, **1838**.

Colophon: Printed by John Haddon, Castle Street, Finsbury. Broadsheet bifolium (50 cm.).

¶ Saru was from the Kanga country (a New World term referring to people from modern southern Liberia whose language was Kru). She was captured, forced aboard a slave ship bound for Brazil, intercepted by a British warship, liberated, and taken to Jamaica in the Caribbean, where she was apprenticed. There she described her Middle Passage experience.

246.1 Dumbo (ca. 1819–) = William Gordon

His testimony as translated by George Robinson (a "Portuguese-Kanga") printed within news story headlined "Unexampled Horrors of the Slave Trade in 1838" on the first page (i.e., p. 177), cols. 1–2, in the newspaper *The British Emancipator*, no. 31.

London [England]: [Published] Under the sanction of the Central Negro Emancipation Committee, November 14, 1838. Colophon: Printed by John Haddon, Castle Street, Finsbury. Broadsheet bifolium (50 cm.).

Full text: https://huskiecommons.lib.niu.edu/history-500african-voices/156/ [see 245.1].

¶ Dumbo was from the Kanga country (a New World term referring to people from modern southern Liberia whose language was Kru). He was captured, forced aboard a slave ship bound for Brazil, intercepted by a British warship, liberated, and taken to Jamaica in the Caribbean, where he was apprenticed in the Kew estate. There he described his Middle Passage experience.

247.1 Fahbrona (ca. 1826–) = Fabron = Robert

His testimony as translated by George Robinson (a "Portuguese-Kanga") printed within news story headlined "Unexampled Horrors of the Slave Trade in 1838" on the first page (i.e., p. 177), col. 2, in the newspaper *The British Emancipator*, no. 31.

Full text: https://huskiecommons.lib.niu.edu/history-500african-voices/157/ [see 246.1].

Full text: https://huskiecommons.lib.niu.edu/history-500african-voices/158/ [see 247.1].

London [England]: [Published] Under the sanction of the Central Negro Emancipation Committee, November 14, 1838. Colophon: Printed by John Haddon, Castle Street, Finsbury. Broadsheet bifolium (50 cm.).

¶ Fahbrona was from the Kanga country (a New World term referring to people from modern southern Liberia whose language was Kru). He was captured, forced aboard a slave ship bound for Brazil, intercepted by a British warship, liberated, and taken to Jamaica in the Caribbean, where he was apprenticed to M. Da Costas. There he described his Middle Passage experience, which included his direct observation of the killing and dismemberment of one of the enslaved men on the ship.

248.1 Foolah (ca. 1826–) = Thomas

His testimony as translated by Margaret Lambert and George Robinson ("both Portuguese-Kangas") printed within news story headlined "Unexampled Horrors of the Slave Trade in 1838" on the first page (i.e., p. 177), col. 2, and the second page (i.e., p. 178), col. 1 in the newspaper *The British Emancipator*, no. 31.

London [England]: [Published] Under the sanction of the Central Negro Emancipation Committee, November 14, 1838. Colophon: Printed by John Haddon, Castle Street, Finsbury. Broadsheet bifolium (50 cm.).

Full text: https:// huskiecommons. lib.niu.edu/history-500african-voices/159/ [see 248.1].

¶ Foolah was from the Kanga country (a New World term referring to people from modern southern Liberia whose language was Kru). He was captured, forced aboard a slave ship bound for Brazil, intercepted by a British warship, liberated, and taken to Jamaica in the Caribbean, where he was apprenticed on the Kew estate. There he described his Middle Passage experience.

249.1 Bussrah (ca. 1806–) = Richard Willicks

His testimony as translated by George Robinson (a "Portuguese-Kanga") printed within news story headlined "Unexampled Horrors of the Slave Trade in 1838" on the first page (i.e., p. 177), col. 2, in the newspaper *The British Emancipator*, no. 31.

Full text: https:// huskiecommons. lib.niu.edu/history-500african-voices/160/ [see 249.1].

London [England]:[Published] Under the sanction of the Central Negro Emancipation Committee, November 14, 1838. Broadsheet bifolium (50 cm.).

¶ Bussrah was from the Kanga country (a New World term referring to people from modern southern Liberia whose language was Kru). He was captured, forced aboard a slave ship bound for Brazil, intercepted by a British warship, liberated, and taken to Jamaica in the Caribbean, where he was apprenticed on the Kew estate. There he described his Middle Passage experience.

250.1 Gema (ca. 1828–) = Thomas Wilson

His testimony as translated by George Robinson (a "Portuguese-Kanga") printed within news story headlined "Unexampled Horrors of the Slave Trade in 1838" on the first page (i.e., p. 177), cols. 2–3, in the newspaper *The British Emancipator*, no. 31.

London [England]: [Published] Under the sanction of the Central Negro Emancipation Committee, November 14, 1838. Colophon: Printed by John Haddon, Castle Street, Finsbury. Broadsheet bifolium (50 cm.).

Full text: https:// huskiecommons. lib.niu.edu/history-500african-voices/161/ [see 250.1].

¶ Gewa was from the Kanga country (a New World term referring to people from modern southern Liberia whose language was Kru). He was captured, forced aboard a slave ship bound for Brazil, intercepted by a British warship, liberated, and taken to Jamaica in the Caribbean, where he was apprenticed in the Kew estate. There he described his Middle Passage experience.

251.1 Samoo (ca. 1823–) = Jane

Her testimony as translated by Margaret Lambert (a "Portuguese-Kanga") printed within news story headlined "Unexampled Horrors of the Slave Trade in 1838" on the first page (i.e., p. 177), col. 3, in the newspaper *The British Emancipator*, no. 31.

London [England]: [Published] Under the sanction of the Central Negro Emancipation Committee, November 14, 1838. Colophon: Printed by John Haddon, Castle Street, Finsbury. Broadsheet bifolium (50 cm.).

Full text: https:// huskiecommons. lib.niu.edu/history-500african-voices/162/ [see 251.1].

¶ Samoo was from the Kanga country (a New World term referring to people from modern southern Liberia whose language was Kru). She was captured, forced aboard a slave ship bound for Brazil, intercepted by a British warship, liberated, and taken to Jamaica in the Caribbean, where she was apprenticed to the Rev. Mr. John Straiesky. There she described her Middle Passage experience.

252.1 Kenga (ca. 1819–) = Sophia

Her testimony as translated by Margaret Lambert (a "Portuguese-Kanga") printed within news story headlined "Unexampled Horrors of the Slave Trade in 1838" on the first page (i.e., p. 177), col. 3, in the newspaper *The British Emancipator*, no. 31.

London [England]: [Published] Under the sanction of the Central Negro Emancipation Committee, November 14, **1838**. Colophon: Printed by John Haddon, Castle Street, Finsbury. Broadsheet bifolium (50 cm.).

Full text: https:// huskiecommons. lib.niu.edu/history-500african-voices/163/ [see 252.1].

¶ Kenga was from the Kanga country (a New World term referring to people from modern southern Liberia whose language was Kru). She was captured, forced aboard a slave ship bound for Brazil, intercepted by a British warship, liberated, and taken to Jamaica in the Caribbean, where she was apprenticed. There she described her Middle Passage experience.

253.1 Sydea (ca. 1818–) = Sarah

Her testimony as translated by Margaret Lambert (a "Portuguese-Kanga") printed within news story headlined "Unexampled Horrors of the Slave Trade in 1838" on the first page (i.e., p. 177), col. 3, in the newspaper *The British Emancipator*, no. 31.

London [England]: [Published] Under the sanction of the Central Negro Emancipation Committee, November 14, **1838**. Colophon: Printed by John Haddon, Castle Street, Finsbury. Broadsheet bifolium (50 cm.).

Full text: https:// huskiecommons. lib.niu.edu/history-500african-voices/164/ [see 253.1].

¶ Sydea was from the Kanga country (a New World term referring to people from modern southern Liberia whose language was Kru). She had at least one half-brother and two brothers (q.v. 254.1). She and the two brothers were captured, forced aboard a slave ship bound for Brazil, intercepted by

a British warship, liberated, and taken to Jamaica in the Caribbean, where she was apprenticed to a Mr. Allenwood. There she described her Middle Passage experience, which included the slave ship crews' murder and butchering of one of her brothers.

254.1 Cawley (ca. 1819–) = Thomas Barker

His testimony as translated by George Robinson (a "Portuguese-Kanga") printed within news story headlined "Unexampled Horrors of the Slave Trade in 1838" on the first page (i.e., p. 177), col. 3, in the newspaper *The British Emancipator*, no. 31.

London [England]: [Published] Under the sanction of the Central Negro Emancipation Committee, November 14, **1838**. Colophon: Printed by John Haddon, Castle Street, Finsbury.
Broadsheet bifolium (50 cm.).

Full text: https:// huskiecommons. lib.niu.edu/history-500african-voices/165/ [see 254.1].

¶ Cawley was from the Kanga country (a New World term referring to people from modern southern Liberia whose language was Kru). He, his sister Sydea (q.v. 253.1), and a brother were captured, forced aboard a slave ship bound for Brazil, intercepted by a British warship, liberated, and taken to Jamaica in the Caribbean, where he was apprenticed to T. Allenwood, Esq. There he described his Middle Passage experience. He worked as a cook on the slave ship. The slave ship crew murdered and butchered his brother. An eyewitness to the atrocity, he provided a detailed description of how it was done. Cawley spoke English fairly well and gave part of his testimony in that language.

255.1 Nangoo (ca. 1818–) = Morgianna

Her testimony as translated by Margaret Lambert and George Robinson ("both Portuguese-Kangas") printed within news story headlined "Unexampled Horrors of the Slave Trade in 1838" on the first page (i.e., p. 177), cols. 3–4, in the newspaper *The British Emancipator*, no. 31.

London [England]: [Published] Under the sanction of the Central Negro Emancipation Committee, November 14, **1838**. Colophon: Printed by John Haddon, Castle Street, Finsbury.

Full text: https:// huskiecommons. lib.niu.edu/history-500african-voices/166/ [see 255.1].

Broadsheet bifolium (50 cm.).

¶ Nangoo was from the Kanga country (a New World term referring to people from modern southern Liberia whose language was Kru). She was captured, forced aboard a slave ship bound for Brazil, intercepted by a British warship, liberated, and taken to Jamaica in the Caribbean, where she was apprenticed to Mrs. Dally. There she described her Middle Passage experience, which included her direct observation of the murder of one of her fellow passengers.

256.0   Josefa Rita Bibí (ca. 1812–)

Statement recorded in August 1838 in Santiago de Cuba, preserved in Archivo Nacional de la República de Cuba (ANC), **La Habana, Cuba,** Miscelánea de Expedientes, 1107/F.

Full text: https://huskiecommons.lib.niu.edu/history-500african-voices/167/ [see 256.3].

¶ Josefa Rita identified as Bibí (Ibibia people of the Cross River region, modern southern Nigeria, northwest Cameroon—see Map 5). After forced transport to the Spanish colony of Cuba in the Caribbean (Map 12) on a slave ship and sale she worked enslaved as a laundress and presser

in the hamlet of Bayamo, near Santiago de Cuba. At some point she ran away and joined a Maroon community with more than thirty shanties called El Cedro. Each shanty housed a husband and wife. A captain, deputy, and council led the community. Leadership conferences excluded women. They survived by planting gardens and eating rats and wild boar. The record does not state whether she was captured, turned herself in, or anything else about her ultimate fate. For accounts by other members of her community, see 241.0, 257.0, 258.0, 259.0, and 260.0.

256.1——.

Her statement printed on p. 195 in *La esclavitud desde la esclavitud: La visión de los siervos* by Gloria García Rodríguez.

México [Distrito Federal, Estados Unidos Mexicanos]: Centro de Investigación Científica "Ing. Jorge L Tamayo," **1996.**
8vo (21 cm.): 251 p.

256.2——.

Her statement printed on pp. 174–175 *La esclavitud desde la esclavitud*, by Gloria García.

La Habana [Cuba]: Editorial de Ciencias Sociales, **2003.**
8vo (21 cm.): xx, 222 p.

256.3——.

English translation of her statement printed on p. 168 in *Voices of the Enslaved in Nineteenth-Century Cuba: A Documentary History*, edited by Gloria García Rodríguez. Translated [from 256.1] by Nancy L. Westrate; foreword by Ada Ferrer.

Chapel Hill [North Carolina, U.S.A.]: University of North Carolina Press, **2011.**
8vo (23.5 cm.): xviii, 220 p.

257.0   Dionisia Calas Gangá (ca. 1799–)

Statement recorded in August 1838 in Santiago de Cuba, preserved in Archivo Nacional de la República de Cuba (ANC), **La Habana, Cuba,** Miscelánea de Expedientes, 1107/F.

Full text: https://huskiecommons.lib.niu.edu/history-500african-voices/168/ [see 257.3].

¶ Dionisia Calas identified as Gangá (modern Banta region southern Sierra Leone—see Map 4). After transport to the Spanish colony of Cuba in the Caribbean (Map 12) on a slave ship and sale, she lived enslaved in a hamlet called Bayamo in the area around Santiago de Cuba, working as a day laborer, when she ran away and joined a Maroon community called El Cedro that included Josefa Rita Bibí (q.v. 256.0) and Manuela Cálas Gangá, Federico Bibí, and Bartolomé Portuondo Congo (qq.v. 258.0, 259.0, and 260.0). In her statement she described discipline and punishment within their palenque (Maroon community).

257.1——.

Her statement printed on p. 196 in *La esclavitud desde la esclavitud: La visión de los siervos* by Gloria García Rodríguez.

México [Distrito Federal, Estados Unidos Mexicanos]: Centro de Investigación Científica "Ing. Jorge L Tamayo," **1996.**
8vo (21 cm.): 251 p.

257.2——.

Her statement printed on p. 175 *La esclavitud desde la esclavitud*, by Gloria García.

La Habana [Cuba]: Editorial de Ciencias Sociales, **2003.**
8vo (21 cm.): xx, 222 p.

257.3——.

English translation of her statement printed on p. 168 in *Voices of the Enslaved in Nineteenth-Century Cuba: A Documentary History*, edited by Gloria García Rodríguez. Translated [from 254.1] by Nancy L. Westrate; foreword by Ada Ferrer.

Chapel Hill [North Carolina, U.S.A.]: University of North Carolina Press, **2011**.
8vo (23.5 cm.): xviii, 220 p.

258.0 Manuela Calás Gangá (ca. 1808–)

Statement recorded in August 1838 in Santiago de Cuba, preserved in Archivo Nacional de la República de Cuba (ANC), **La Habana, Cuba**, Miscelánea de Expedientes, 1107/F.

Full text: https://huskiecommons.lib.niu.edu/history-500african-voices/169/ [see 258.3].

¶ Manuela Calás identified as Gangá (modern Banta region southern Sierra Leone—see Map 4). After transport to the Spanish colony of Cuba in the Caribbean (Map 12) on a slave ship and sale, she worked enslaved in or near Bayamo as a grazier, turning her daily wages over to her owner. She ran away because of his harsh treatment and joined the palenque called El Cedro that included several members in this catalog. At her hearing she described leadership, raiding parties, and music of the palenque.

258.1——.

Her statement printed on p. 196 in *La esclavitud desde la esclavitud: La visión de los siervos* by Gloria García Rodríguez.

México [Distrito Federal, Estados Unidos Mexicanos]: Centro de Investigación Científica "Ing. Jorge L Tamayo," **1996**.
8vo (21 cm.): 251 p.

258.2——.

Her statement printed on p. 175 *La esclavitud desde la esclavitud*, by Gloria García.

La Habana [Cuba]: Editorial de Ciencias Sociales, **2003**.
8vo (21 cm.): xx, 222 p.

258.3——.

English translation of her statement printed on pp. 168–169 in *Voices of the Enslaved in Nineteenth-Century Cuba: A Documentary History*, edited by Gloria García Rodríguez. Translated [from 258.1] by Nancy L. Westrate; foreword by Ada Ferrer.

Chapel Hill [North Carolina, U.S.A.]: University of North Carolina Press, **2011**.
8vo (23.5 cm.): xviii, 220 p.

259.0 Federico Bibí (ca. 1798–)

Statement recorded in August 1838 in Santiago de Cuba, preserved in Archivo Nacional de la República de Cuba (ANC), **La Habana, Cuba**, Miscelánea de Expedientes, 1107/F.

¶ Federico identified as Bibí (Ibibia people of the Cross River region, modern southern Nigeria northwest Cameroon—see Map 5). After transport to the Spanish colony of Cuba in the Caribbean (Map 12) on a slave ship and sale, he worked enslaved as a tiller in the hamlet of Bayamo. After running away he joined a palenque called El Cedro that included several members whose accounts are included here (qq.v. 256.0, 257.0, 258.0, and 260.0). At his hearing he described the community's tobacco cultivation and their clothing made from tree bark.

Full text: https://huskiecommons.lib.niu.edu/history-500african-voices/170/ [see 259.3].

259.1——.

Statement printed on p. 196 in *La esclavitud desde la esclavitud: La visión de los siervos* by Gloria García Rodríguez.

México [Distrito Federal, Estados Unidos Mexicanos]: Centro de Investigación Científica "Ing. Jorge L Tamayo," **1996**.
8vo (21 cm.): 251 p.

259.2——.

Statement printed on p. 176 *La esclavitud desde la esclavitud*, by Gloria García.

La Habana [Cuba]: Editorial de Ciencias Sociales, **2003**.
8vo (21 cm.): xx, 222 p.

259.3——.

English translation of statement printed on p. 169 in *Voices of the Enslaved in Nineteenth-Century Cuba: A Documentary History*, edited by Gloria García Rodríguez. Translated [from 259.1] by Nancy L. Westrate; foreword by Ada Ferrer.

Chapel Hill [North Carolina, U.S.A.]: University of North Carolina Press, **2011**.
8vo (23.5 cm.): xviii, 220 p.

260.0 Bartolomé Portuondo Congo (ca. 1798–)

Statement recorded in August 1838 in Santiago de Cuba, preserved in Archivo Nacional de la República de Cuba (ANC), **La Habana, Cuba**, Miscelánea de Expedientes, 1107/F.

¶ Bartolomé Portuondo identified as Congolese. After transport to the Spanish colony of Cuba in the Caribbean (see Map 12) in a slave ship and sale,

Full text: https://huskiecommons.lib.niu.edu/history-500african-voices/171/ [see 260.3].

he lived and worked enslaved on an estate called *Jicotea*, in the area of Santiago de Cuba. He ran away alone because of abusive treatment and encountered several other runaways in the scrubland. Together they marched deeper into the scrub and built a shanty town settlement at Demajagual, where wild yams grew that could sustain them. After the yams ran out they pushed farther on, where there were more. After about a year they met Vicente Bibí (q.v. 240.0) and two other men, who invited them to join their palenque of El Cedro, where there was plenty to eat.

260.1——.

Statement printed on pp. 196–197 in *La esclavitud desde la esclavitud: La visión de los siervos* by Gloria García Rodríguez.

México [Distrito Federal, Estados Unidos Mexicanos]: Centro de Investigación Científica "Ing. Jorge L Tamayo," **1996.**
8vo (21 cm.): 251 p.

260.2——.

Statement printed on p. 176 *La esclavitud desde la esclavitud*, by Gloria García.

La Habana [Cuba]: Editorial de Ciencias Sociales, **2003.**
8vo (21 cm.): xx, 222 p.

260.3——.

English translation of statement printed on p. 169 in *Voices of the Enslaved in Nineteenth-Century Cuba: A Documentary History*, edited by Gloria García Rodríguez. Translated [from 257.1] by Nancy L. Westrate; foreword by Ada Ferrer.

Chapel Hill [North Carolina, U.S.A.]: University of North Carolina Press, **2011.**
8vo (23.5 cm.): xviii, 220 p.

1839

261.0 Joseph Wright (ca. 1810-1850s)

Manuscript entitled "The Life of Joseph Wright: A Native of Ackoo" dated June **1839**, in the box labeled "Sierra Leone, 1835–1840" held in the Archives of the Methodist Missionary Society, 25 Marylebone Road, **London [England].** Located by Philip D. Curtin through the kindness of Christopher Fyfe (261.2, p. 322).

¶ Wright was Egba from the Yorùbá hinterland that was part of the Oyo Empire (modern Nigeria—see Map 5). His father was not rich but served on his town's council. Wright was captured in the Owu War sometime during the years 1819–1825 and enslaved. He was subsequently sold to Portuguese in Lagos, forced aboard a slave ship, captured the next day at sea by British warships, and taken to Freetown, Sierra Leone (Map 4). He subsequently became a Methodist, traveled to England for missionary training in 1842–44, and returned to Sierra Leone. For more on him see editorial commentary in 261.2.

261.1——.

261.0 printed under title "Description of a Slave War" on pp. 349–358 in John Beecham, *Ashantee and the Gold Coast; being a Sketch of the History, Social State, and Superstitions of the Inhabitants of those Countries: with a Notice of the State and Prospects of Christianity among them.*

London [England]: Sold by J. Mason, **1841.**

https://babel.hathitrust.org/cgi/pt?id=njp.32101063289282;view=1up;seq=377 [see 261.1].

8vo (23 cm.): xix, 376 p., folding map.
https://babel.hathitrust.org/cgi/pt?id=njp.32101063289282;view=1up;seq=377
Hogg 1483.

261.2——.

261.0 printed from the original manuscript, with added annotations, under heading "The Narrative of Joseph Wright" on pp. 322–333 within chapter entitled "Joseph Wright of the Egba" by Philip D. Curtin on pp. 317–333 in *Africa Remembered: Narratives by West Africans from the Era of the Slave Trade*, edited by Philip D. Curtin.

Madison [Wisconsin, U.S.A.]: University of Wisconsin Press, **1967.**
8vo (24 cm.): x, 363 p., illus., maps.

261.3——. [Second printing of 261.2]

261.0 printed from the original manuscript, with added annotations, under heading "The Narrative of Joseph Wright" on pp. 322–333 within chapter entitled "Joseph Wright of the Egba" by Philip D. Curtin on pp. 317–333 in *Africa Remembered: Narratives by West Africans from the Era of the Slave Trade*, edited by Philip D. Curtin.

Madison [Wisconsin, U.S.A.]: University of Wisconsin Press, **1968.**
8vo (22 cm.): x, 363 p., illus., maps.

261.4——.

Photomechanical reprint of 261.1, with added introduction and notes by G. E. Metcalf, and imprint:

262.1 Osifekunde

London [England]: Dawsons, **1968.**
8vo (19 cm.): [4], xxxi, xix, 376 p., folding map.

261.5——.
Photomechanical reprint of 261.1 with imprint:

New York [New York, U.S.A.]: Johnson Reprint Corp., [1970].
8vo (23 cm.): xix, 376 p., folding map.

261.6——.[Another printing of 261.2]
261.0 printed from the original manuscript, with added annotations, under heading "The Narrative of Joseph Wright" on pp. 322–333 within chapter entitled "Joseph Wright of the Egba" by Philip D. Curtin on pp. 317–333 in *Africa Remembered: Narratives by West Africans from the Era of the Slave Trade*, edited by Philip D. Curtin.

Prospect Heights, Illinois [U.S.A.]: Waveland Press, **1997.**
8vo (23 cm.): x, 363 p., illus., maps.

262.1 Osifekunde (ca. 1798–) = Joachim

His account (written in **1839**–1840) printed in French on pp. 18–31, 34, 37, 42–44, 56–59, 67–73, 81–94, 101-102, and 105 within "Notice sur le pays et le peuple des Yébous, en Afrique," edited by Marie Armand Pascal d'Avezac-Macaya, in *Memoires de la Société Ethnologique*, vol. 2, part 2, pp. 1–105.

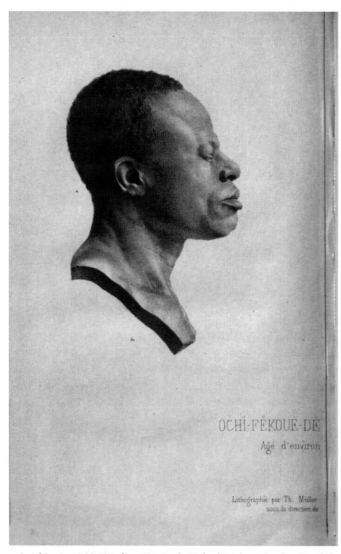

Figure 14: Osifkunde, also known as Joachim (c. 1798– ?), from Epe in the Ijebu kingdom (modern southwestern Nigeria). He was taken on a slave ship to Brazil and freed when his owner took him to France, where slavery by then was illegal.

Source: Lithograph from a life mask made in Paris ca. 1838 printed in D'Avezac, "Notice sur le pays et le people des Yébous, en Afrique," edited by Marie Armand Pascal d'Avezac-Macaya, in *Memoires de la Société Ethnologique* (Paris: Librarie Orientale de Mme Ve Dondey-Dupré, 1845), vol. 2, part 2, between p. 44 and 46.

Paris [France]: Librairie Orientale de Mme Ve Dondey-Dupré, rue des Pyramides, 8, 1845.

Hogg 1486. Half title verso: Imprimerie de Mme Ve Dondey-Dupré, rue Saint-Louis, 46, au Marais.

https://babel.hathitrust.org/cgi/pt?id=pst.000070827897&view=1up&seq=418 [see 262.1].

¶ Osifekunde was born in Epe, in the Ijebu kingdom (modern southwest Nigeria—see Map 5) on the Guinea Coast. Like his father, he became a merchant. While carrying trade goods in 1820 he was ambushed by Ijo pirates near Lagos, taken to Warri, and

sold to slavers who sailed to Brazil (Map 9). There he lived in Rio de Janeiro enslaved by a French man who took him ca. 1836/37 to Paris, France (Map 7), where Osifekunde was freed by law upon arrival. Thereafter, Osifekunde worked as a house servant. Avezac interviewed him in Paris in 1839, struggling to understand Osifekunde's Portuguese Creole, and completed his article in 1840. Osifekunde later returned to Brazil. For more on him see: Olatunji Ojo, "Osifekunde of Ijebu (Yorubaland)," in vol. 10 of *UNESCO General History of Africa: Global Africa*, vol. 10 (Paris [France]: UNESCO, 2020); and Aderivaldo Ramos de Santana, "A extraordinária odisseia do comerciante Ijebu que foi escravo no Brasil e homem livre na França (1820–1842)," *Afro-Ásia* 57 (2018), 9–53; of which the latter is available here:

https://portalseer.ufba.br/index.php/afroasia/article/view/26068/15747

262.2———.

"Osifekunde of Ijebu," translated from 262.1 into English and edited with commentary by P. C. Lloyd on pp. 217–288 in *Africa Remembered: Narratives by West Africans from the Era of the Slave Trade*, edited by Philip D. Curtin.

Madison [Wisconsin, U.S.A.]: University of Wisconsin Press, **1967.**

8vo (24 cm.): x, 363 p., illus., maps.

262.3———. [Second printing of 262.2]

"Osifekunde of Ijebu," translated from 262.1 into English and edited with commentary by P. C. Lloyd on pp. 217–288 in *Africa Remembered: Narratives by West Africans from the Era of the Slave Trade*, edited by Philip D. Curtin.

Madison [Wisconsin, U.S.A.]: University of Wisconsin Press, **1968.**

8vo (22 cm.): x, 363 p., illus., maps.

262.4———. [Another printing of 262.2]

"Osifekunde of Ijebu," translated from 262.1 into English and edited with commentary by P. C. Lloyd on pp. 217–288 in *Africa Remembered: Narratives by West Africans from the Era of the Slave Trade*, edited by Philip D. Curtin.

Prospect Heights, Illinois [U.S.A.]: Waveland Press, **1997.**

8vo (23 cm.): x, 363 p., illus., maps.

263.1 Pharaoh Sack N'Jaie (ca. 1771–) = Pharaoh Moses

His full account contained in a letter Pharaoh dictated and signed with his mark (sideways X) to British Colonial Secretary Thomas Cole at Freetown, Sierra Leone, 7 January 1839, printed in *Class D, Correspondence with Foreign Powers, Not Parties to Conventions Giving Mutual Right of Search of Vessels Suspected of Slave Trade, 1839–40*, fifth of six enclosures, United States, No. 142, Viscount Palmerston to H. S. Fox, 14 August 1839, pp. 142–143.

Full text: https://huskiecommons.lib.niu.edu/history-500african-voices/172/ [see 263.1].

London [England]: Printed by William Clowes and Sons, Stamford-Street, for Her Majesty's Stationery Office, **1840.**

Folio, xi, 213 p.

Note: On 6 December 1831, eight years prior to providing the above account, Pharaoh Sack N'Jaie delivered a speech at a meeting of the "free people of color" of Charleston, South Carolina that included a brief autobiographical account that was published twice:

On p. 76 in an article entitled "Emigration to Liberia" in the May 1832 issue (vol. 8, no. 3) of *The African Repository, and Colonial Journal*, edited by Ralph Randolph Gurney.

Washington, [DC, U.S.A.]: James F. Dunn, Printer and Publisher, Georgetown, DC [May 1832]. 8vo (24 cm.).

https://babel.hathitrust.org/cgi/pt?id=hvd.hwrc-ge&view=1up&seq=86

On p. 2, col. 5 in the June 22, 1832, issue (vol. 7, no. 25, whole no. 323) of the newspaper *Vermont Chronicle*, edited by Joseph Richards and John Tracy.

Windsor, Vermont [U.S.A.]: Richards & Tracy, Publishers, June 22, **1832.**

Broadsheet bifolium: 4 p.

Because this account is so brief and precedes spectacular events in his life included in his lengthy account in 260.1, this entry is placed under the year 1839 instead of 1831.

¶ Pharaoh Sack N'Jaie was born on Gorée Island (modern Senegal—see Map 3) in 1771. His name suggests he was probably Mandinka (an ethnic group residing in southern Mali, Guinea and Ivory Coast) and Muslim. Though still young, he was married with two children when forcibly taken, probably ca. 1804–1808, on a slave ship to the United States seaport of Charleston, South Carolina (Map 15). There the merchant Miah Moses purchased him. Pharaoh subsequently worked as a stone cutter and married an African American woman, with whom he had two children. He purchased his own freedom and in late 1832 sailed with his second family on the *Hercules* to Liberia in West Africa. He reached Liberia in early 1833 and reunited there with children from his first marriage (son Sack N'Jaie and daughter Mary Sack N'Jaie). Difficult living conditions in Liberia caused them to move to Freetown, Sierra Leone, in 1836. In 1837 his son Sack N'Jaie was lost at sea. In 1838 Pharaoh learned that his son had been rescued, taken illegally to Alabama (U.S.A.), and enslaved there (Map 15). Pharoah therefore obtained assistance to write to the local British Colonial Secretary to secure his son's release. For more on him see Randy J. Sparks, *Africans in the Old South: Mapping Exceptional Lives Across the Atlantic World* (Cambridge, MA: Harvard University Press, 2016), pp. 134–156.

264.1 Charles Smith

His sworn deposition, including details on the life of Pharaoh Sack N'Jaie (q.v. 263.1), recorded by British Colonial Secretary Thomas Cole (or a staff amanuensis) at Freetown, Sierra Leone, 31 January 1839, printed in *Class D, Correspondence with Foreign Powers, Not Parties to Conventions Giving Mutual Right of Search of Vessels Suspected of Slave Trade, 1839–40*, sixth of six enclosures, United States, No. 142, Viscount Palmerston to H. S. Fox, 14 August 1839, pp. 143–145.

Full text: https://huskiecommons.lib.niu.edu/history-500african-voices/173/ [see 264.1].

London [England]: Printed by William Clowes and Sons, Stamford-Street, for Her Majesty's Stationery Office, 1840. Folio, xi, 213 p.

¶ Smith stated he came from Old Calabar, i.e., the Calabar ward of Old Town (located on a tributary of the Cross River in the Bight of Biafra—see Map 5). Old Calabar (Ákwá Ákpá) or the four major settlements of the Efik people of the Cross River region of modern southeast Nigeria. Ca. 1827 he was enslaved with many others and forcibly taken with them on a slave ship. Intercepted at sea by a British warship, all captives were taken to Sierra Leone (Map 4) and

there liberated. Shortly thereafter Smith traveled some five hundred miles to a British base on an island at the mouth of the Gambia River (modern Banjul, St. Mary's Island in the Gambia—Map 3), where he worked as a seaman until 1838. That year he sailed on the *William and Robert* to New York City (U.S.A.) [Map 17], where he obtained his freedom papers and was discharged after a dispute with the captain over the terms of his service. Two months later he sailed as a steward on an American barque to Mobile, Alabama, U.S.A. (Map 15). There he was arrested, taken illegally in chains to a cotton plantation, and forced to work enslaved. On this plantation he met others from Sierra Leone who had been illegally transported to Alabama (including Sack N'Jaie, son of Pharaoh Sack N'Jaie, q.v. 263.1). Smith, fearful that someone might destroy his freedom papers, delayed showing them until the right moment. He chose his moment well, and was released and told to leave the United States at once. He did so as a steward aboard the *Sarah Nicholson*, which sailed from Mobile to Liverpool, England (Map 8). From Liverpool Smith walked across the country to London, where he booked passage on the barque *Lord Wellington* for Freetown, Sierra Leone, which he reached in December 1838. For more on him see Randy J. Sparks, *Africans in the Old South: Mapping Exceptional Lives Across the Atlantic World* (Cambridge: Harvard University Press, 2016), pp. 134–156.

¶ Note for 265.1 to 301.1, accounts of three women and thirty-four men who survived the *Amistad* slave ship rebellion. All these men and women came from what is now southern and eastern Sierra Leone (see Map 4). Twenty-five whose ethnicity could be identified were Mende, while four were Gbandi, three were Kono, two were Temne, and one each were Loma, Gola, and Bullom. All but the Bullom man were from interior areas. After capture, in the port of Lomboko they were forced aboard the slave ship *Teçora*, which sailed for Havana, Cuba in April 1839 (Map 12). After a few days in Havana they were forcibly transferred to the *Amistad*, which then sailed for Puerto Principe, Cuba. While at sea the captives rebelled, took over the ship, and attempted to sail back to West Africa. But in August 1839, after seven weeks at sea during which ten rebels died, they were intercepted by a US Revenue Service ship off the eastern end of Long Island, New York, U.S.A., whence authorities took them across Long Island Sound to New Haven, Connecticut, and then to Hartford, Connecticut (Map 17). (They were imprisoned in both places.) A series of trials for murder and conspiracy in New Haven and Hartford culminated in their acquittal on 11 January 1841. On 9 March 1841, the United States Supreme Court confirmed the acquittal and freed them for good.

During the Africans' imprisonment John Warner Barber interviewed them, aided by the interpreter Kawweli (q.v. 301.1). Barber noted in his 1840 *History of the Amistad Captives* that six men died in prison before he could interview them. He published short biographical sketches of every survivor. Phrenologists visited the Africans in prison and drew their portraits, which Barber reproduced in his volume. Upon release from prison, many of the survivors toured the northeastern United States to raise money for their own transportation back to Africa. In New York City on 27 November 1841 they boarded the *Gentleman*, which reached Freetown, Sierra Leone, with them on 13 January 1842. The US nationals who accompanied them to Freetown wanted them to work in Sierra Leone at a Christian mission; but most of the *Amistad* survivors disregarded these wishes and instead returned to their homes.

Recent scholarship on the *Amistad* rebellion and its aftermath is extensive. See, for example, Marcus Rediker, *The Amistad Rebellion: An Atlantic Odyssey of Slavery and Freedom* (New York: Viking Penguin, 2012).

265.1 Gilabaru = Grabeau = Grabaung

Summary of court proceedings including Gilabaru's detailed testimony on the Middle Passage printed under headline "Narrative of the Africans" with cover letter from George E. Day dated New Haven, Oct. 8, 1839, on p. 2 of the *New York Journal of Commerce*.

https://docsouth. unc.edu/neh/ barber/support1. html [see 265.4].

New York [New York, U.S.A.], October 10, 1839.

¶ Gilabaru was Mende, born in Fulu (Sierra Leone—see Map 4). He was a married rice farmer when his uncle sold him to a Spaniard in Lomboko (modern Sierra Leone) to pay a debt. In 1839 he and other Mende were taken on a slave ship to the Spanish colonial city of Havana, Cuba in the Caribbean (Map 12). In addition to his native Mende, he spoke Vai, Kono, and Kissi. In Havana his new owners placed him and fifty-two other Africans (mostly Mende) on the *Amistad* for shipment to plantations elsewhere in the Caribbean. The Africans took over the ship, and Gilabaru was second in command (after Sengbe, q.v. 266.1) of the rebellion.

265.2———.

Gilabaru's relatively long responses to questions asked of him and two other *Amistad* mutineers (for the others, see 266.4 and 267.2) in a Connecticut prison on 7 October 1839 constitute the largest part of the interview as printed in the Connecticut newspaper the *Record* (edited by Samuel Porter).

New Haven, Connecticut [U.S.A.]: Printed by William Storer Jr., October 12, 1839.
Broadsheet bifolium: 4 p.

265.3———. [Reprint of 265.1]

Summary of court proceedings including Grabaung's (Gilabaru's) description of the voyage reprinted (here under headline "Narrative of the Africans") from the October 10, 1839, issue of the [New York] *Journal of Commerce* with cover letter to that paper from George E. Day dated New Haven, Oct. 8, 1839, on second page (i.e., 166), col. 1, of the antislavery newspaper *The Liberator*, vol. 9, no. 42.

Boston [Massachusetts, U.S.A.]: William Lloyd Garrison and Isaac Knapp, Publishers, October 18, 1839.
Broadsheet bifolium (49 cm.): 4 p.
http://fair-use.org/the-liberator/1839/10/18/the-liberator-09-42.pdf.

265.4———.

His account translated into English by Kawweli (q.v. 301.1) printed on pp. 9–10 in *A History of the Amistad Captives Being a Circumstantial Account of the Capture of the Spanish Schooner Amistad, by the Africans on Board*, edited by John Warner Barber (1798–1885).

New Haven, Connecticut [U.S.A.]: Published by E. L. & J. W. Barber, Hitchcock and Stafford Printers, 1840.
8vo (23 cm.): 32 p., folding plate, map, portraits.
https://archive.org/details/historyofamistad00barb/page/8/mode/2up

265.5———.

A shortened version of his account appears on p. 12 within the issue-long article "Documents relating to the Africans taken in the Amistad" in *The American and Foreign A. S.* [i.e., *Anti-Slavery*] *Reporter*, EXTRA, December 1840, which includes an image of him.

New York [New York, U.S.A.]: American and Foreign Anti-Slavery Society, December 1840.
4to: 16 p. *The compilers thank Dr. Joseph Yannielli for calling this item to their attention.*
https://digitalcommons.law.yale.edu/cgi/viewcontent.cgi?article=1016&context=amtrials

265.6———.

Quotations of Gilabaru's speech at a meeting printed in a Philadelphia newspaper article entitled "The Amistad Africans," *Pennsylvania Inquirer and Daily Courier*, 29 May 1841 (p. 2, 4th and 5th cols.). Vol. 24, nr. 126

Philadelphia, Pennsylvania [U.S.A.]: Published by Jesper Harding, May 29, 1841.
(66 cm.): 4 p.

265.7——.

His account and testimony used to construct the factual but partially dramatized account of William A. Owens's *Slave Mutiny: The Revolt on the Schooner Amistad*.

New York [New York, U.S.A.]: The John Day Company, [**1953**].
8vo (21.3 cm.): viii, 312 p., plates (including portraits).

265.8——.

His account and testimony used to construct the factual but partially dramatized account of William A. Owens's *Black Mutiny: The Revolt on the Schooner Amistad*.

Philadelphia [Pennsylvania, U.S.A.]: Pilgrim Press, [**1968**].
8vo (21.3 cm.): xiv, 322 p., plates (including portraits).

265.9——.

His account included in photomechanical reprint of 265.5, *A History of the Amistad Captives Being a Circumstantial Account of the Capture of the Spanish Schooner Amistad, by the Africans on Board; Their Voyage, and Capture Near Long Island, New York; with Biographical Sketches of Each of the Surviving Africans*, edited by John Warner Barber, with imprint:

New York [New York, U.S.A.]: Arno Press, **1969**.
8vo (24 cm.): 32 p., folding plate, map, portraits.

265.10——.

His account included in photomechanical reprint of a portion of 265.5 as Appendix I "From *A History of the Amistad Captives* by John W. Barber (1840)" on pp. 159–167 in Mary Cable, *Black Odyssey: The Case of the Slave Ship Amistad*.

New York [New York, U.S.A.]: The Viking Press, [**1971**].
8vo (22 cm.): [8], 183 p., map, portraits.

265.11——.

265.3 reprinted on pp. 198–200 in *Slave Testimony: Two Centuries of Letters, Speeches, Interviews, and Autobiographies*, edited by John W. Blassingame.

Baton Rouge [Louisiana, U.S.A.]: Louisiana State University Press, **1977**.
8vo (23 cm.): lxv, 777 p.

265.12——. [Second printing of 265.10]

265.4 reprinted on pp. 198–200 in *Slave Testimony: Two Centuries of Letters, Speeches, and Autobiographies*, edited by John W. Blassingame.

Baton Rouge [Louisiana, U.S.A.]: Louisiana State University Press, **1977**. Second printing.
8vo (23 cm.): lxv, 777 p., illus., portraits.

265.13——. [Another printing of 265.10]

265.3 reprinted on pp. 198–200 in *Slave Testimony: Two Centuries of Letters, Speeches, and Autobiographies*, edited by John W. Blassingame.

Baton Rouge [Louisiana, U.S.A.]: Louisiana State University Press, **1979**. 1979 printing.
8vo (23 cm.): lxv, 777 p., illus., portraits.

265.14——. [Another printing of 265.10]

265.3 reprinted on pp. 198–200 in *Slave Testimony: Two Centuries of Letters, Speeches, and Autobiographies*, edited by John W. Blassingame.

Baton Rouge [Louisiana, U.S.A.]: Louisiana State University Press, **1980**. 1980 printing.
8vo (23 cm.): lxv, 777 p., illus., portraits.

265.15——. [Another printing of 265.10]

265.3 reprinted on pp. 198–200 in *Slave Testimony: Two Centuries of Letters, Speeches, and Autobiographies*, edited by John W. Blassingame.

Baton Rouge [Louisiana, U.S.A.]: Louisiana State University Press, **1989**. 1989 printing.
8vo (23 cm.): lxv, 777 p., illus., portraits.

265.16——. [Another printing of 265.10]

265.3 reprinted on pp. 198–200 in *Slave Testimony: Two Centuries of Letters, Speeches, and Autobiographies*, edited by John W. Blassingame.

Baton Rouge [Louisiana, U.S.A.]: Louisiana State University Press, **1998**. 1998 printing.
8vo (23 cm.): lxv, 777 p., illus., portraits.

265.17——. [Another printing of 265.10]

265.3 reprinted on pp. 198–200 in *Slave Testimony: Two Centuries of Letters, Speeches, and Autobiographies*, edited by John W. Blassingame.

Baton Rouge [Louisiana, U.S.A.]: Louisiana State University Press, **2002**. 2002 printing.
8vo (23 cm.): lxv, 777 p., illus., portraits.

265.18——. [Another printing of 265.10]

265.3 reprinted on pp. 198–200 in *Slave Testimony: Two Centuries of Letters, Speeches, and Autobiographies*, edited by John W. Blassingame.

Baton Rouge [Louisiana, U.S.A.]: Louisiana State University Press, **2009**.
8vo (24 cm.): lxv, 777 p., illus., portraits.

266.1 Sengbe Pieh = Singgbe = Cinque = Joseph

Summary of court proceedings including some of Sengbe's description of the voyage printed under headline "Narrative of the Africans" with cover letter from George E. Day dated New Haven, Oct. 8, 1839, on p. 2 of the *New York Journal of Commerce*.

New York [New York, U.S.A.], October 10, 1839.
Broadsheet bifolium: 4 p.
https://glc.yale.edu/narrative-africans
https://docsouth.unc.edu/neh/barber/support1.html

https://archive.org/details/historyofamistad-00barb/page/20/mode/2up
[see 266.5].

¶ Sengbe Pieh was Mende, born in Mani, in Dzhopoa (possibly Gbarpolu in the Cape Mount region of modern coastal Liberia—see Map 3). He lived with his father, wife, and three children. and was a rice planter and a warrior. He was kidnapped and taken to Gendema (or Geduma, southern Sierra Leone) in Gallinas country (Map 4), then taken by a Manu man to Lomboko (Sierra Leone), where he was sold to a Spaniard and placed on the slave ship *Teçora* bound for the Spanish colonial city of Havana, Cuba in the Caribbean (Map 12). He was one of thirty-five *Amistad* mutineers who survived the mutiny and subsequent court proceedings in New Haven, Connecticut (U.S.A.) [Map 17] and returned to Sierra Leone. Having learned English during the long ordeal, Sengbe wrote English-language letters (some of which were published, q.v. +266-A.1 et seq.) until he reached Sierra Leone in 1842. For a silhouette image of Sengbe done by an artist during his incarceration see 266.7, p. 9. For further information see note preceding entry 265.1.

266.2———.

Sengbe's verbal confirmation of Gilabaru's account (265.2) of their story and brief additions in response to questions asked of him and two other *Amistad* mutineers (qq.v. 265.3 and 267.2) interviewed in a Connecticut prison on 7 October 1839 constitute a small part of the interview as printed in the New Haven, Connecticut, newspaper the *Record* (edited by Samuel Porter).

New Haven, Connecticut [U.S.A.]: Printed by William Storer Jr., October 12, 1839.
Broadsheet bifolium: 4 p.

266.3———.

266.1 reprinted (here under headline "Narrative of the Africans") from the October 10, 1839, issue of the [*New York*] *Journal of Commerce* with cover letter to that paper from George E. Day dated New Haven, Oct. 8, 1839, on second

page (i.e., p. 166), col. 1, of the antislavery newspaper *The Liberator*, vol. 9, no. 42.

Boston [Massachusetts, U.S.A.]: William Lloyd Garrison and Isaac Knapp, Publishers, October 18, 1839.
Broadsheet bifolium: 4 p.
http://fair-use.org/the-liberator/1839/10/18/the-liberator-09-42.pdf.

266.4———.

Additional commentary from Sengbe printed in a letter to the editor, signed in type by John Scoble and dated from Hounslow [London, Enland], October 14, 1839, under headline "Case of the Amistad, Spanish Slaver" in the antislavery journal *The British Emancipator*.

London [England], October 26, 1839.

266.5———.

His account translated into English by Kawweli (q.v. 301.1) printed on pp. 20–21 in *A History of the Amistad Captives Being a Circumstantial Account of the Capture of the Spanish Schooner Amistad, by the Africans on Board; Their Voyage, and Capture Near Long Island, New York; with Biographical Sketches of Each of the Surviving Africans; also, an Account of the Trials had on Their case, Before the District and Circuit Courts of the United States, for the District of Connecticut,* edited by John Warner Barber (1798-1885).

New Haven, Connecticut [U.S.A.]: Published by E. L. & J. W. Barber, Hitchcock and Stafford Printers, 1840.
8vo (23 cm.): 32 p., folding plate, map, portraits.
http://docsouth.unc.edu/neh/barber/barber.html
https://archive.org/details/historyofamistad00barb/page/20/mode/2up
Hogg 1481.

266.6———.

A slightly expanded version on 266.5 appears on p. 12 within the issue-long article "Documenting relating to the Africans taken in the Amistad" in *The American and Foreign A. S. [i.e., Anti-Slavery] Reporter*, Extra, December 1840.

New York [New York, U.S.A.]: American and Foreign Anti-Slavery Society, December 1840.
4to: 16 p., illus. (portrait). *The compilers thank Dr. Joseph Yannielli for calling this item to their attention.*
https://digitalcommons.law.yale.edu/cgi/viewcontent.cgi?article=1016&context=amtrials

266.7———.

His first and second speeches to fellow Africans aboard the *Amistad* reprinted on pp. 335–336 of Simeon E. Baldwin,

"The Captives of the Amistad (Read May 17, 1886)," in *Papers of the New Haven Colony Historical Society* 4: 331–370.

New Haven [Connecticut, U.S.A.]: Printed for the [New Haven Colony Historical] Society, **1888.** Tpv: Tuttle, Morehouse & Taylor, Printers, 371 State Street, New Haven, Conn.
8vo (23.5 cm.): viii, 456 p.

266.8——.

His account included in photomechanical reprint of 266.5, *A History of the Amistad Captives Being a Circumstantial Account of the Capture of the Spanish Schooner Amistad, by the Africans on Board; Their Voyage, and Capture Near Long Island, New York; with Biographical Sketches of Each of the Surviving Africans*, edited by John Warner Barber.

New York [New York, U.S.A.]: Arno Press, **1969.**
8vo (24 cm.): 32 p., folding plate, map, portraits.

266.9——.

His account included in photomechanical reprint of most of 266.5 as Appendix I "From *A History of the Amistad Captives* by John W. Barber (1840)" on pp. 159–167 in Mary Cable, *Black Odyssey: The Case of the Slave Ship Amistad*.

New York [New York, U.S.A.]: The Viking Press, **[1971].**
8vo (22 cm.): [8], 183 p., map, portraits.

266.10——.

266.4 reprinted on pp. 199–200 in *Slave Testimony: Two Centuries of Letters, Speeches, Interviews, and Autobiographies*, edited by John W. Blassingame.

Baton Rouge [Louisiana, U.S.A.]: Louisiana State University Press, **1977.**
8vo (23 cm.): lxv, 777 p.

266.11——. **[Second printing of 266.11]**

266.1 reprinted on pp. 199–200 in *Slave Testimony: Two Centuries of Letters, Speeches, and Autobiographies*, edited by John W. Blassingame.

Baton Rouge [Louisiana, U.S.A.]: Louisiana State University Press, **1977.** Second printing.
8vo (23 cm.): lxv, 777 p., illus., portraits.

266.12——. **[Another printing of 266.11]**

266.1 reprinted on pp. 199–200 in *Slave Testimony: Two Centuries of Letters, Speeches, and Autobiographies*, edited by John W. Blassingame.

Baton Rouge [Louisiana, U.S.A.]: Louisiana State University Press, **1979.** 1979 printing.
8vo (23 cm.): lxv, 777 p., illus., portraits.

266.13——. **[Another printing of 266.11]**

266.1 reprinted on pp. 199–200 in *Slave Testimony: Two Centuries of Letters, Speeches, and Autobiographies*, edited by John W. Blassingame.

Baton Rouge [Louisiana, U.S.A.]: Louisiana State University Press, **1980.** 1980 printing.
8vo (23 cm.): lxv, 777 p., illus., portraits.

266.14——. **[Another printing of 266.11]**

266.1 reprinted on pp. 199–200 in *Slave Testimony: Two Centuries of Letters, Speeches, and Autobiographies*, edited by John W. Blassingame.

Baton Rouge [Louisiana, U.S.A.]: Louisiana State University Press, **1989.** 1989 printing.
8vo (23 cm.): lxv, 777 p., illus., portraits.

266.15——. **[Another printing of 266.11]**

266.1 reprinted on pp. 199–200 in *Slave Testimony: Two Centuries of Letters, Speeches, and Autobiographies*, edited by John W. Blassingame.

Baton Rouge [Louisiana, U.S.A.]: Louisiana State University Press, **1998.** 1998 printing.
8vo (23 cm.): lxv, 777 p., illus., portraits.

266.16——. **[Another printing of 266.11]**

266.1 reprinted on pp. 199–200 in *Slave Testimony: Two Centuries of Letters, Speeches, and Autobiographies*, edited by John W. Blassingame.

Baton Rouge [Louisiana, U.S.A.]: Louisiana State University Press, **2002.** 2002 printing.
8vo (23 cm.): lxv, 777 p., illus., portraits.

266.17——. **[Another printing of 266.1]**

266.1 reprinted on pp. 199–200 in *Slave Testimony: Two Centuries of Letters, Speeches, and Autobiographies*, edited by John W. Blassingame.

Baton Rouge [Louisiana, U.S.A.]: Louisiana State University Press, **2009.**
8vo (24 cm.): lxv, 777 p., illus., portraits.

Other writings by Sengbe

+266-A.1–8 ——.

Letter dated Westville, Connecticut, U.S.A., 20 December 1840, to Lewis Tappan at New York City, printed on p. 33 of *Slave Testimony: Two Centuries of Letters, Speeches, Interviews, and Autobiographies*, edited by John W. Blassingame (Baton Rouge: Louisiana State University Press, eight printings 1977–2009). Photographic reproduction of manuscript with transcription at: https://digitallibrary.tulane.edu/islandora/object/tulane%3A54191

+266-B.1–8 ———.

Letter dated Westville, Connecticut, U.S.A., 9 February 1841 to Roger S. Baldwin at New Haven, Conn., printed on pp. 34–36 in *Slave Testimony: Two Centuries of Letters, Speeches, Interviews, and Autobiographies,* edited by John W. Blassingame (Baton Rouge: Louisiana State University Press, eight printings 1977–2009). Photographic reproduction of manuscript with transcription at: https://digitallibrary.tulane.edu/islandora/object/tulane%3A54184

+266-C.1 ———.

Letter dated Farmington, Connecticut, U.S.A., 5 October 1841 to President John Tyler at Washington, DC, printed in the periodical *African Repository* 17 (December 1841): 361–62.

+266-C.2–9 ———.

Letter dated Farmington, Connecticut, U.S.A., 5 October 1841 to President John Tyler at Washington, DC, printed on p. 42 in *Slave Testimony: Two Centuries of Letters, Speeches, Interviews, and Autobiographies,* edited by John W. Blassingame (Baton Rouge: Louisiana State University Press, eight printings 1977–2009).

+266-D.1 ———.

Letter dated Boston, Massachusetts, U.S.A., 6 November 1841 to John Quincy Adams printed in the periodical *The Philanthropist* (8 December 1841).

+266-D.2–9 ———.

Letter dated Boston, Massachusetts, U.S.A., 6 November 1841 to John Quincy Adams printed on pp. 42–43 in *Slave Testimony: Two Centuries of Letters, Speeches, Interviews, and Autobiographies,* edited by John W. Blassingame (Baton Rouge: Louisiana State University Press, eight printings 1977–2009).

+266-E.1 ———.

Letter dated at sea near Sierra Leone 13 January 1842 to Lewis Tappan at New York, New York, U.S.A., printed in the *American and Foreign Anti-Slavery Reporter* 2 (June 1842): 63.

+266-E.2–9 ———.

Letter dated at sea near Sierra Leone 13 January 1842 to Lewis Tappan at New York, New York, U.S.A., printed on pp. 43–44 in *Slave Testimony: Two Centuries of Letters, Speeches, Interviews, and Autobiographies,* edited by John W. Blassingame (Baton Rouge: Louisiana State University Press, eight printings 1977–2009).

267.1 Kimbo

Summary of court proceedings includes Kimbo's support for Grabaung's (Gilabaru's) testimony about the voyage printed under headline "Narrative of the Africans" with cover letter from George E. Day dated New Haven, Oct. 8, 1839, on p. 2 of the *New York Journal of Commerce.*

New York [New York, U.S.A.], October 10, 1839.
https://docsouth.unc.edu/neh/barber/support1.html

https://archive.org/details/historyofamistad-00barb/page/10/mode/2up [see 267.6].

¶ **Kimbo (cricket) identified as Mende, born in Mawkoba (or Mankobsch, a town of Sevenuwah in Mende country, modern Sierra Leone—see Map 4). When Kimbo's father (a "gentleman") died, the king enslaved Kimbo and later sold him to a Bullom man, who subsequently sold him to a Spaniard in Lomboko (Sierra Leone). From there Kimbo was taken to the slave ship *Teçora,* which took him to the Spanish colonial town of Havana, Cuba in the Caribbean (Map 12). While on the *Amistad* he was severely flogged for exceeding his allotment of drinking water. He was one of the successful *Amistad* mutineers. For a silhouette image of Kimbo done by an artist during his incarceration see 267.6, p. 10. For further information see note preceding entry 265.1.**

267.2 ———.

His verbal confirmation of Gilabaru's account (265.2) of their story and brief additions in response to questions asked of him and another *Amistad* mutineer (q.v. 266.4) interviewed in a Connecticut prison on 7 October 1839 constituted a small part of the interview as printed in the New Haven, Connecticut, newspaper the *Record* (edited by Samuel Porter).

New Haven, Connecticut [U.S.A.]: Printed by William Storer Jr., **October 12, 1839.**
Broadsheet bifolium.

267.3 ———.

Summary of court proceedings including Kimbo's support for Grabaung's (Gilabaru's) testimony about the voyage reprinted from 267.1 (here under headline "Narrative of the Africans) from the October 10, 1839, issue of the [New York] *Journal of Commerce* with cover letter to that paper from George E. Day dated New Haven, Oct. 8, 1839, on second page (i.e., 166), col. 1, of the antislavery newspaper *The Liberator,* vol. 9, no. 42.

Boston [Massachusetts, U.S.A.]: William Lloyd Garrison and Isaac Knapp, Publishers, **October 18, 1839.**

Broadsheet bifolium (49 cm.): 4 p.
http://fair-use.org/the-liberator/1839/10/18/the-libera-tor-09-42.pdf.

267.4——.

Additional commentary from Kimbo not included in earlier items printed in the antislavery newspaper *The New York Emancipator*.

New York [New York, U.S.A.], late Oct early Nov., 1839.

267.5——.

267.4 reprinted from *The New York Emancipator* on p. 1 of the antislavery newspaper *The British Emancipator*, no. 58.

London [England]: [Published] Under the sanction of the Central Negro Emancipation Committee, **November 27, 1839.** Colophon: Printed by John Haddon, Castle Street, Finsbury. Broadsheet bifolium (50 cm.).

267.6——.

His account translated into English by Kawweli (q.v. 301.1) printed on p. 10 in *A History of the Amistad Captives Being a Circumstantial Account of the Capture of the Spanish Schooner Amistad, by the Africans on Board*, edited by John Warner Barber (1798–1885).

New Haven, Connecticut [U.S.A.]: Published by E. L. & J. W. Barber, Hitchcock and Stafford Printers, **1840.**
8vo (23 cm.): 32 p., folding plate, map, portraits.
https://archive.org/details/historyofamistad00barb/page/10/mode/2up

267.7——.

His account included in photomechanical reprint of 267.6 *A History of the Amistad Captives Being a Circumstantial Account of the Capture of the Spanish Schooner Amistad, by the Africans on Board; Their Voyage, and Capture Near Long Island, New York; with Biographical Sketches of Each of the Surviving Africans*, edited by John Warner Barber.

New York [New York, U.S.A.]: Arno Press, **1969.**
8vo (24 cm.): 32 p., folding plate, map, portraits.

267.8——.

His account included in photomechanical reprint of portion of 267.6 as Appendix I "From *A History of the Amistad Captives* by John W. Barber (1840)" on pp. 159–167 in Mary Cable, *Black Odyssey: The Case of the Slave Ship Amistad*.

New York [New York, U.S.A.]: The Viking Press, **[1971].**
8vo (22 cm.): [8], 183 p., map, portraits.

267.9——.

267.2 reprinted on pp. 199–200 in *Slave Testimony: Two Centuries of Letters, Speeches, Interviews, and Autobiographies*, edited by John W. Blassingame.

Baton Rouge [Louisiana, U.S.A.]: Louisiana State University Press, **1977.**
8vo: lxv, 777 p.

267.10——. [Second printing of 267.9]

267.2 reprinted on pp. 199–200 in *Slave Testimony: Two Centuries of Letters, Speeches, and Autobiographies*, edited by John W. Blassingame.

Baton Rouge [Louisiana, U.S.A.]: Louisiana State University Press, **1977.** Second printing.
8vo (23 cm.): lxv, 777 p., illus., portraits.

267.11 ——. [Another printing of 267.9]

267.2 reprinted on pp. 199–200 in *Slave Testimony: Two Centuries of Letters, Speeches, and Autobiographies*, edited by John W. Blassingame.

Baton Rouge [Louisiana, U.S.A.]: Louisiana State University Press, **1979.** 1979 printing.
8vo (23 cm.): lxv, 777 p., illus., portraits.

267.12 ——. [Another printing of 267.9]

267.2 reprinted on pp. 199–200 in *Slave Testimony: Two Centuries of Letters, Speeches, and Autobiographies*, edited by John W. Blassingame.

Baton Rouge [Louisiana, U.S.A.]: Louisiana State University Press, **1980.** 1980 printing.
8vo (23 cm.): lxv, 777 p., illus., portraits.

267.13——. [Another printing of 267.9]

267.2 reprinted on pp. 199–200 in *Slave Testimony: Two Centuries of Letters, Speeches, and Autobiographies*, edited by John W. Blassingame.

Baton Rouge [Louisiana, U.S.A.]: Louisiana State University Press, **1989.** 1989 printing.
8vo (23 cm.): lxv, 777 p., illus., portraits.

267.14——. [Another printing of 267.9]

267.2 reprinted on pp. 199–200 in *Slave Testimony: Two Centuries of Letters, Speeches, and Autobiographies*, edited by John W. Blassingame.

Baton Rouge [Louisiana, U.S.A.]: Louisiana State University Press, **1998.** 1998 printing.
8vo (23 cm.): lxv, 777 p., illus., portraits.

267.15——. [Another printing of 267.9]

267.2 reprinted on pp. 199–200 in *Slave Testimony: Two Centuries of Letters, Speeches, and Autobiographies*, edited by John W. Blassingame.

Baton Rouge [Louisiana, U.S.A.]: Louisiana State University Press, 2002. 2002 printing.

8vo (23 cm.): lxv, 777 p., illus., portraits.

267.16——. [Another printing of 267.9]

267.2 reprinted on pp. 199–200 in *Slave Testimony: Two Centuries of Letters, Speeches, and Autobiographies*, edited by John W. Blassingame.

Baton Rouge [Louisiana, U.S.A.]: Louisiana State University Press, 2009.

8vo (24 cm.): lxv, 777 p., illus., portraits.

1840

268.1 Nazhaulu = Konnoma

His account translated into English by Kawweli (q.v. 301.1) printed on p. 10 in *A History of the Amistad Captives Being a Circumstantial Account of the Capture of the Spanish Schooner Amistad, by the Africans on Board*, edited by John Warner Barber (1798–1885).

New Haven, Connecticut [U.S.A.]: Published by E. L. & J. W. Barber, Hitchcock and Stafford Printers, 1840.

8vo (23 cm.): 32 p., folding plate, map, portraits.

https://babel.hathitrust.org/cgi/pt?id=njp.32101037454285&view=1up&seq=18&skin=2021 [see 268.1].

¶ Nazhaulu, aka Konnoma (a water stick), a Kono (modern eastern Sierra Leone—see Map 4), was one of the surviving *Amistad* mutineers. For further information see note preceding entry 265.1. For a silhouette image of Nazhaulu done by an artist during his incarceration see 268.1, p. 10.

268.2——.

His account included in photomechanical reprint of portion of 268.1 as Appendix I "From *A History of the Amistad Captives* by John W. Barber (1840)" on pp. 159–167 in Mary Cable, *Black Odyssey: The Case of the Slave Ship Amistad*.

New York [New York, U.S.A.]: The Viking Press, [1971]. 8vo (22 cm.): [8], 183 p., map, portraits.

268.3——.

His account included in photomechanical reprint of 268.1, *A History of the Amistad Captives Being a Circumstantial Account of the Capture of the Spanish Schooner Amistad, by the Africans on Board; Their Voyage, and Capture Near Long Island, New York; with Biographical Sketches of Each of the Surviving Africans*, edited by John Warner Barber.

New York [New York, U.S.A.]: Arno Press, 1969. 8vo (24 cm.): 32 p., folding plate, map, portraits.

269.1 Burna (younger)

His account translated into English by Kawweli (q.v. 301.1) printed on p. 10 in *A History of the Amistad Captives Being a Circumstantial Account of the Capture of the Spanish Schooner Amistad, by the Africans on Board*, edited by John Warner Barber (1798–1885).

New Haven, Connecticut [U.S.A.]: Published by E. L. & J. W. Barber, Hitchcock and Stafford Printers, 1840.

8vo (23 cm.): 32 p., folding plate, map, portraits.

https://babel.hathitrust.org/cgi/pt?id=njp.32101037454285&view=1up&seq=18 [see 269.1].

¶ Burna, a Mende (modern Sierra Leone—see Map 4), was a blacksmith in his native village and also grew rice. He spoke Mende, Bullom, and Temne. He had a wife, one child, and three siblings when kidnapped and sold to a Spaniard at Lomboko. Burna was one of the surviving *Amistad* mutineers. For a silhouette image of Burna done by an artist during his incarceration see 269.1, p. 10. See Rediker, *The Amistad Rebellion*, especially pp. 27, 30, 41, 42–43, and 200. For further information see note preceding entry 265.1.

269.2——.

His account included in photomechanical reprint of 269.1, *A History of the Amistad Captives Being a Circumstantial Account of the Capture of the Spanish Schooner Amistad, by the Africans on Board; Their Voyage, and Capture Near Long Island, New York; with Biographical Sketches of Each of the Surviving Africans*, edited by John Warner Barber.

New York [New York, U.S.A.]: Arno Press, 1969. 8vo (24 cm.): 32 p., folding plate, map, portraits.

269.3——.

His account included in photomechanical reprint of portion of 269.1 as Appendix I "From *A History of the Amistad Captives* by John W. Barber (1840)" on pp. 159–167 in Mary Cable, *Black Odyssey: The Case of the Slave Ship Amistad.*

New York [New York, U.S.A.]: The Viking Press, [**1971**]. 8vo (22 cm.): [8], 183 p., map, portraits.

270.1 Gbatu = Bartu

His account translated into English by Kawweli (q.v. 301.1) printed on pp. 10–11 in *A History of the Amistad Captives Being a Circumstantial Account of the Capture of the Spanish Schooner Amistad, by the Africans on Board*, edited by John Warner Barber (1798–1885).

https://archive.org/details/historyofamistad00barb/page/10/mode/2up [see 270.1].

New Haven, Connecticut [U.S.A.]: Published by E. L. & J. W. Barber, Hitchcock and Stafford Printers, **1840**. 8vo (23 cm.): 32 p., folding plate, map, portraits.

¶ Gbatu or Bartu (a club or sword) was born in Tuma (where the king resided) near a large lake called Mawua (possibly Rokel River, Sierra Leone—see Map 4). He was sent by his father (a "gentleman") to a village to buy clothes, and while returning was kidnapped and taken to Lomboko (Sierra Leone), then to a slave ship. Gbatu was one of the surviving *Amistad* mutineers. For a silhouette image of Gbatu done by an artist during his incarceration see 270.1, p. 10. For further information see note preceding entry 265.1.

270.2——.

His account included in photomechanical reprint of 270.1, *A History of the Amistad Captives Being a Circumstantial Account of the Capture of the Spanish Schooner Amistad, by the Africans on Board; Their Voyage, and Capture Near Long Island, New York; with Biographical Sketches of Each of the Surviving Africans*, edited by John Warner Barber.

New York [New York, U.S.A.]: Arno Press, **1969**. 8vo (24 cm.): 32 p., folding plate, map, portraits.

270.3——.

His account included in photomechanical reprint of portion of 270.1 as Appendix I "From *A History of the Amistad Captives* by John W. Barber (1840)" on pp. 159–167 in Mary Cable, *Black Odyssey: The Case of the Slave Ship Amistad.*

New York [New York, U.S.A.]: The Viking Press, [**1971**]. 8vo (22 cm.): [8], 183 p., map, portraits.

271.1 Gnakwoi

His account translated into English by Kawweli (q.v. 301.1) printed on p. 11 in *A History of the Amistad Captives Being a Circumstantial Account of the Capture of the Spanish Schooner Amistad, by the Africans on Board*, edited by John Warner Barber (1798–1885).

New Haven, Connecticut [U.S.A.]: Published by E. L. & J. W. Barber, Hitchcock and Stafford Printers, 1840. 8vo (23 cm.): 32 p., folding plate, map, portraits.

https://archive.org/details/historyofamistad-00barb/page/10/mode/2up [see 271.1].

¶ Gnakwoi (in Balu dialect, second-born), was born at Konggolahung in the Balu country, on the Zalibu or Kalwara River (modern Sierra Leone—see Map 4). When going to the gold country to buy clothes, he was taken and sold to a Vai man who sold him to a Spaniard. Gnakwoi had a wife and one child. During his enslavement he learned the Mende language. He was one of the surviving *Amistad* mutineers. He learned the Mende language and called himself a Balu man when interviewed. For a silhouette image of Gbatu done by an artist during his incarceration see 271.1, p. 10. For further information see note preceding entry 265.1.

271.2——.

His account included in photomechanical reprint of 271.1, *A History of the Amistad Captives Being a Circumstantial Account of the Capture of the Spanish Schooner Amistad, by the Africans on Board; Their Voyage, and Capture Near Long Island, New York; with Biographical Sketches of Each of the Surviving Africans*, edited by John Warner Barber.

New York [New York, U.S.A.]: Arno Press, **1969**. 8vo (24 cm.): 32 p., folding plate, map, portraits.

271.3——.

His account included in photomechanical reprint of portion of 271.1 as Appendix I "From *A History of the Amistad Captives* by John W. Barber (1840)" on pp. 159–167 in Mary Cable, *Black Odyssey: The Case of the Slave Ship Amistad.*

New York [New York, U.S.A.]: The Viking Press, [**1971**]. 8vo (22 cm.): [8], 183 p., map, portraits.

272.1 Kwong = Kagnwawni

Account translated into English by Kawweli (q.v. 301.1) printed on p. 11 in *A History of the Amistad Captives Being a Circumstantial Account of the Capture of the Spanish*

Schooner Amistad, by the Africans on Board, edited by John Warner Barber (1798–1885).

New Haven, Connecticut [U.S.A.]: Published by E. L. & J. W. Barber, Hitchcock and Stafford Printers, 1840.
8vo (23 cm.): 32 p., folding plate, map, portraits.

¶ Kwong was born at Mambui, a town in the Mende country (modern Sierra Leone—see Map 4). When a boy he was called Kagnwawni; Kwong is a Bullom name. He was sold by a Temne man in the Dubu country to a Spaniard at Lomboko (Sierra Leone) and then taken to a slave ship. Kwong was one of the successful *Amistad* mutineers. For a silhouette image of Kwong done by an artist during his incarceration see 272.1, p. 10. For further information see note preceding entry 263.1.

272.2——.

His account included in photomechanical reprint of 272.1, *A History of the Amistad Captives Being a Circumstantial Account of the Capture of the Spanish Schooner Amistad, by the Africans on Board; Their Voyage, and Capture Near Long Island, New York; with Biographical Sketches of Each of the Surviving Africans*, edited by John Warner Barber.

New York [New York, U.S.A.]: Arno Press, 1969.
8vo (24 cm.): 32 p., folding plate, map, portraits.

272.3——.

His account included in photomechanical reprint of portion of 272.1 as Appendix I "From *A History of the Amistad Captives* by John W. Barber (1840)" on pp. 159–167 in Mary Cable, *Black Odyssey: The Case of the Slave Ship Amistad*.

New York [New York, U.S.A.]: The Viking Press, [1971].
8vo (22 cm.): [8], 183 p., map, portraits.

273.1 Fuliwa = Fuli = George Brown

His account translated into English by Kawweli (q.v. 301.1) printed on p. 11 in *A History of the Amistad Captives Being a Circumstantial Account of the Capture of the Spanish Schooner Amistad, by the Africans on Board*, edited by John Warner Barber (1798–1885).

https://archive.org/details/historyofamistad-00barb/page/10/mode/2up [see 271.1].

https://archive.org/details/historyofamistad-00barb/page/10/mode/2up [see 273.1].

New Haven, Connecticut [U.S.A.]: Published by E. L. & J. W. Barber, Hitchcock and Stafford Printers, 1840.
8vo (23 cm.): 32 p., folding plate, map, portraits.

¶ Fuliwa or Fuli (meaning sun in Mende) was born in the Mende town of Mano (where his king, Tikba, resided) and lived with his parents and five brothers (in modern Sierra Leone—see Map 4). He was captured in war, taken to Lomboko, sold to Europeans, and put on a slave ship. Fuliwa was one of the surviving *Amistad* mutineers. He was middle-aged when reaching New Haven, Connecticut, U.S.A. (Map 17). There he wrote English-language letters (several of which have survived; see +273-A.1 et seq.) before he reached Sierra Leone in 1842, after which he journeyed with some of the others to Bullom country. For a silhouette image of Fuliwa done by an artist during his incarceration see 273.1, p. 11. For further information see note preceding entry 265.1.

273.2——.

Quotations of Fuliwa's speech at a meeting printed in a Philadelphia newspaper article entitled "The Amistad Africans," *Pennsylvania Inquirer and Daily Courier*, 29 May 1841 (p. 2, 4th and 5th cols.). Vol. 24, nr. 126

Philadelphia, Pennsylvania [U.S.A.]: Published by Jesper Harding, May 29, 1841.
(66 cm.): 4 p.

273.3——.

His account included in photomechanical reprint of 273.1, *A History of the Amistad Captives Being a Circumstantial Account of the Capture of the Spanish Schooner Amistad, by the Africans on Board; Their Voyage, and Capture Near Long Island, New York; with Biographical Sketches of Each of the Surviving Africans*, edited by John Warner Barber.

New York [New York, U.S.A.]: Arno Press, 1969.
8vo (24 cm.): 32 p., folding plate, map, portraits.

273.4——.

His account included in photomechanical reprint of portion of 273.1 as Appendix I "From *A History of the Amistad Captives* by John W. Barber (1840)" on pp. 159–167 in Mary Cable, *Black Odyssey: The Case of the Slave Ship Amistad*.

New York [New York, U.S.A.]: The Viking Press, [1971].
8vo (22 cm.): [8], 183 p., map, portraits.

Other writings by Fuliwa

+273-A.1–8 ——.

Letter dated Westville, Connecticut, U.S.A., March 1841, to Lewis Tappan at New York City, printed on p. 37 in *Slave Testimony: Two Centuries of Letters, Speeches, Interviews, and Autobiogra-*

phies, edited by John W. Blassingame (Baton Rouge: Louisiana State University Press, eight printings 1977–2009). Photographic reproduction of manuscript and transcription at: https://digitallibrary.tulane.edu/islandora/object/tulane%3A54193.

+273-B.1–8 ——.
Letter dated Farmington, Connecticut, U.S.A., 15 April 1841, to Lewis Tappan at New York City, printed on pp. 40–41 in *Slave Testimony: Two Centuries of Letters, Speeches, Interviews, and Autobiographies,* edited by John W. Blassingame (Baton Rouge: Louisiana State University Press, eight printings 1977–2009). Photographic reproduction of manuscript and transcription at:

https://digitallibrary.tulane.edu/islandora/object/tulane%3A53589

+273-C.0 ——.
Manuscript letter dated Farmington, Connecticut, U.S.A., 5 May 1841, to John Quincy Adams, reproduced photographically and transcribed at:

https://digitallibrary.tulane.edu/islandora/object/tulane%3A53601.

+273-D.1 ——.
Letter by George Brown = Fuliwa dated Sierra Leone 15 April 1842 to Lewis Tappan at New York City printed in *American and Foreign Anti-Slavery Reporter* 2 (June 1842): 72.

+273-D.2–9 ——.
Letter by George Brown = Fuliwa dated Sierra Leone 15 April 1842 to Lewis Tappan at New York City printed on p. 44 in *Slave Testimony: Two Centuries of Letters, Speeches, Interviews, and Autobiographies,* edited by John W. Blassingame (Baton Rouge: Louisiana State University Press, eight printings 1977–2009).

274.1 Pie = Bia

His account translated into English by Kawweli (q.v. 301.1) printed on p. 11 in *A History of the Amistad Captives Being a Circumstantial Account of the Capture of the Spanish Schooner Amistad, by the Africans on Board,* edited by John Warner Barber (1798–1885).

New Haven, Connecticut [U.S.A.]: Published by E. L. & J. W. Barber, Hitchcock and Stafford Printers, **1840.** 8vo (23 cm.): 32 p., folding plate, map, portraits.

https://archive.org/details/historyofamistad-00barb/page/10/mode/2up [see 274.1].

¶ Pie, or Bia, a Temne (modern Sierra Leone—see Map 4), was a big game hunter. He had a wife and four children, one of whom was Fuliwulu (q.v. 279.1). Pie, like his son Fuliwulu, was one of the surviving *Amistad* mutineers. For a silhouette image of Pie done by an artist during his incarceration see 274.1, p. 11. For further information see note 271.1 preceding entry 265.1.

274.2——.
His account included in photomechanical reprint of 274.1, *A History of the Amistad Captives Being a Circumstantial Account of the Capture of the Spanish Schooner Amistad, by the Africans on Board; Their Voyage, and Capture Near Long Island, New York; with Biographical Sketches of Each of the Surviving Africans,* edited by John Warner Barber.

New York [New York, U.S.A.]: Arno Press, **1969.** 8vo (24 cm.): 32 p., folding plate, map, portraits.

274.3——.
His account included in photomechanical reprint of portion of 274.1 as Appendix I "From *A History of the Amistad Captives* by John W. Barber (1840)" on pp. 159–167 in Mary Cable, *Black Odyssey: The Case of the Slave Ship Amistad.*

New York [New York, U.S.A.]: The Viking Press, **[1971].** 8vo (22 cm.): [8], 183 p., map, portraits.

275.1 Pugnwawni = Pungwuni

His account translated into English by Kawweli (q.v. 301.1) printed on pp. 11–12 in *A History of the Amistad Captives Being a Circumstantial Account of the Capture of the Spanish Schooner Amistad, by the Africans on Board,* edited by John Warner Barber (1798–1885).

New Haven, Connecticut [U.S.A.]: Published by E. L. & J. W. Barber, Hitchcock and Stafford Printers, **1840.** 8vo (23 cm.): 32 p., folding plate, map, portraits.

https://archive.org/details/historyofamistad-00barb/page/10/mode/2up [see 275.1].

¶ Pugnwawni (duck) was born at Febaw in Sando, between Mende and Kono (modern eastern Sierra Leone—see Map 4). Sold by his mother's brother for a coat, he was kidnapped and taken to a home six days away and forced to cultivate rice for two years. Thereafter he was sold again and taken to a slave ship. Pungwuni was one of the surviving *Amistad* mutineers. For a silhouette image of Pungnwawni done by an artist during his incarceration see 275.1, p. 11. For further information see note preceding entry 265.1.

275.2——.

His account included in photomechanical reprint of 275.1, *A History of the Amistad Captives Being a Circumstantial Account of the Capture of the Spanish Schooner Amistad, by the Africans on Board; Their Voyage, and Capture Near Long Island, New York; with Biographical Sketches of Each of the Surviving Africans*, edited by John Warner Barber.

New York [New York, U.S.A.]: Arno Press, **1969.**
8vo (24 cm.): 32 p., folding plate, map, portraits.

275.3——.

His account included in photomechanical reprint of portion of 275.1 as Appendix I "From *A History of the Amistad Captives* by John W. Barber (1840)" on pp. 159–167 in Mary Cable, *Black Odyssey: The Case of the Slave Ship Amistad*.

New York [New York, U.S.A.]: The Viking Press, [**1971**].
8vo (22 cm.): [8], 183 p., map, portraits.

276.1 Sessi

His account translated into English by Kawweli (q.v. 301.1) printed on p. 12 in *A History of the Amistad Captives Being a Circumstantial Account of the Capture of the Spanish Schooner Amistad, by the Africans on Board*, edited by John Warner Barber (1798–1885).

New Haven, Connecticut [U.S.A.]: Published by E. L. & J. W. Barber, Hitchcock and Stafford Printers, **1840.**
8vo (23 cm.): 32 p., folding plate, map, portraits.

https://archive.org/details/historyofamistad-00barb/page/12/mode/2up [see 276.1].

¶ Sessi, a Bandi who spoke Mende, was one of the surviving *Amistad* mutineers. He was born in Massakum (modern Sierra Leone—see Map 4) and had three brothers (one of whom taught him to be a blacksmith), two sisters, a wife, and three children. He was wounded and taken captive by soldiers, then sold twice before being taken to Lomboko, where he was forced aboard a slave ship. During the ordeal in New Haven, Connecticut, U.S.A. (Map 17), he wrote a letter that expressed Christian sentiments (see +276-A.1 below). For a silhouette image of Sessi done by an artist during his incarceration see 276.1, p. 11. For further information see note preceding entry 265.1.

276.2——.

His account included in photomechanical reprint of 276.1, *A History of the Amistad Captives Being a Circumstantial*

Account of the Capture of the Spanish Schooner Amistad, by the Africans on Board; Their Voyage, and Capture Near Long Island, New York; with Biographical Sketches of Each of the Surviving Africans, edited by John Warner Barber.

New York [New York, U.S.A.]: Arno Press, **1969.**
8vo (24 cm.): 32 p., folding plate, map, portraits.

276.3——.

His account included in photomechanical reprint of portion of 276.1 as Appendix I "From *A History of the Amistad Captives* by John W. Barber (1840)" on pp. 159–167 in Mary Cable, *Black Odyssey: The Case of the Slave Ship Amistad*.

New York [New York, U.S.A.]: The Viking Press, [**1971**].
8vo (22 cm.): [8], 183 p., map, portraits.

Additional writing by Sessi

+276-A.1–8 ——.

Letter dated Westville, Connecticut, U.S.A., 7 December 1840 to Lewis Tappan at New York City, printed on pp. 31–32 in *Slave Testimony: Two Centuries of Letters, Speeches, Interviews, and Autobiographies*, edited by John W. Blassingame (Baton Rouge: Louisiana State University Press, eight printings 1977–2009).

277.1 Moru

His account translated into English by Kawweli (q.v. 301.1) printed on p. 12 in *A History of the Amistad Captives Being a Circumstantial Account of the Capture of the Spanish Schooner Amistad, by the Africans on Board*, edited by John Warner Barber (1798–1885).

New Haven, Connecticut [U.S.A.]: Published by E. L. & J. W. Barber, Hitchcock and Stafford Printers, 1840.
8vo (23 cm.): 32 p., folding plate, map, portraits.

https://archive.org/details/historyofamistad-00barb/page/12/mode/2up [see 277.1].

¶ Moru was born at Sanka, in the Bandi (Gbandi) country (modern eastern Sierra Leone—see Map 4). His parents died during his childhood. His master sold him, after which he was taken to Lomboko, where he was resold to a Spaniard and forced aboard a slave ship. Moru was one of the surviving *Amistad* mutineers who stood trial in New Haven, Connecticut, U.S.A. (Map 17). For a silhouette image of Moru done by an artist during his incarceration see 277.1, p. 11. For further information see note preceding entry 265.1.

277.2———.

His account included in photomechanical reprint of 277.1, *A History of the Amistad Captives Being a Circumstantial Account of the Capture of the Spanish Schooner Amistad, by the Africans on Board; Their Voyage, and Capture Near Long Island, New York; with Biographical Sketches of Each of the Surviving Africans*, edited by John Warner Barber.

New York [New York, U.S.A.]: Arno Press, **1969**.
8vo (24 cm.): 32 p., folding plate, map, portraits.

277.3———.

His account included in photomechanical reprint of portion of 277.1 as Appendix I "From *A History of the Amistad Captives* by John W. Barber (1840)" on pp. 159–167 in Mary Cable, *Black Odyssey: The Case of the Slave Ship Amistad*.

New York [New York, U.S.A.]: The Viking Press, [**1971**].
8vo (22 cm.): [8], 183 p., map, portraits.

278.1 Ndamma

His account translated into English by Kawweli (q.v. 301.1) printed on p. 12 in *A History of the Amistad Captives Being a Circumstantial Account of the Capture of the Spanish Schooner Amistad, by the Africans on Board*, edited by John Warner Barber (1798–1885).

New Haven, Connecticut [U.S.A.]: Published by E. L. & J. W. Barber, Hitchcock and Stafford Printers, 1840.
8vo (23 cm.): 32 p., folding plate, map, portraits.

https://archive.org/details/historyofamistad-00barb/page/12/mode/2up [see 278.1].

¶ Ndamma ("put on," or "up") was born in the Mende country on the river Male (modern Sierra Leone—see Map 4). His father was dead, and he lived with his mother and siblings when captured on the road by twenty men, who took him to Lomboko (Sierra Leone), twenty days away. Thereafter, he was taken to a slave ship. Ndamma was one of the surviving *Amistad* mutineers who stood trial in New Haven, Connecticut, U.S.A. (Map 17). For a silhouette image of Ndamma done by an artist during his incarceration see 278.1, p. 11. For further information see note preceding entry 265.1.

278.2———.

His account included in photomechanical reprint of 278.1, *A History of the Amistad Captives Being a Circumstantial Account of the Capture of the Spanish Schooner Amistad, by the Africans on Board; Their Voyage, and Capture Near Long Island, New York; with Biographical Sketches of Each of the Surviving Africans*, edited by John Warner Barber.

New York [New York, U.S.A.]: Arno Press, **1969**.
8vo (24 cm.): 32 p., folding plate, map, portraits.

278.3———.

His account included in photomechanical reprint of portion of 278.1 as Appendix I "From *A History of the Amistad Captives* by John W. Barber (1840)" on pp. 159–167 in Mary Cable, *Black Odyssey: The Case of the Slave Ship Amistad*.

New York [New York, U.S.A.]: The Viking Press, [**1971**].
8vo (22 cm.): [8], 183 p., map, portraits.

279.1 Fuliwulu = Fuli

Account translated into English by Kawweli (q.v. 301.1) printed on p. 12 in *A History of the Amistad Captives Being a Circumstantial Account of the Capture of the Spanish Schooner Amistad, by the Africans on Board*, edited by John Warner Barber (1798–1885).

New Haven, Connecticut [U.S.A.]: Published by E. L. & J. W. Barber, Hitchcock and Stafford Printers, 1840.
8vo (23 cm.): 32 p., folding plate, map, portraits.

https://archive.org/details/historyofamistad-00barb/page/12/mode/2up [see 279.1].

¶ Fuliwulu or Fuli (sun) lived with his Temne parents near the Mende country (modern Sierra Leone—see Map 4). He was the son of another of the *Amistad* rebels, Pie (q.v. 274.1). He and his father were kidnapped by an African, who sold him to a Bullom man, who then resold him to a Spaniard at Lomboko (Sierra Leone), after which he was taken to a slave ship. Fuliwulu was one of the surviving *Amistad* mutineers who stood trial in New Haven, Connecticut, U.S.A. (Map 17). For a silhouette image of Fuliwulu done by an artist during his incarceration see 279.1, p. 12. For further information see note preceding entry 265.1.

279.2———.

His account included in photomechanical reprint of 279.1, *A History of the Amistad Captives Being a Circumstantial Account of the Capture of the Spanish Schooner Amistad, by the Africans on Board; Their Voyage, and Capture Near Long Island, New York; with Biographical Sketches of Each of the Surviving Africans*, edited by John Warner Barber.

New York [New York, U.S.A.]: Arno Press, **1969**.
8vo (24 cm.): 32 p., folding plate, map, portraits.

279.3——.

His account included in photomechanical reprint of portion of 279.1 as Appendix I "From *A History of the Amistad Captives* by John W. Barber (1840)" on pp. 159–167 in Mary Cable, *Black Odyssey: The Case of the Slave Ship Amistad.*

New York [New York, U.S.A.]: The Viking Press, **[1971].**
8vo (22 cm.): [8], 183 p., map, portraits.

280.1 Bau

Account translated into English by Kawweli (q.v. 301.1) printed on p. 12 in *A History of the Amistad Captives Being a Circumstantial Account of the Capture of the Spanish Schooner Amistad, by the Africans on Board*, edited by John Warner Barber (1798–1885).

New Haven, Connecticut [U.S.A.]: Published by E. L. & J. W. Barber, Hitchcock and Stafford Printers, 1840.
8vo (23 cm.): 32 p., folding plate, map, portraits.

https://archive.org/details/historyofamistad-00barb/page/12/mode/2up
[see 280.1].

¶ Bau (broke), who had lived near the Wowa River (likely Moa River, Sierra Leone—see Map 4), had a wife and three children. He was caught in the bush by four men while going to plant rice and taken to Lomboko, ten days away (modern Sierra Leone). Bau was one of the surviving *Amistad* mutineers who stood trial in New Haven, Connecticut, U.S.A. (Map 17). For a silhouette image of Bau done by an artist during his incarceration see 280.1, p. 12. For further information see note preceding entry 265.1.

280.2——.

His account included in photomechanical reprint of 280.1, *A History of the Amistad Captives Being a Circumstantial Account of the Capture of the Spanish Schooner Amistad, by the Africans on Board; Their Voyage, and Capture Near Long Island, New York; with Biographical Sketches of Each of the Surviving Africans*, edited by John Warner Barber.

New York [New York, U.S.A.]: Arno Press, **1969.**
8vo (24 cm.): 32 p., folding plate, map, portraits.

280.3——.

His account included in photomechanical reprint of portion of 280.1 as Appendix I "From *A History of the Amistad Captives* by John W. Barber (1840)" on pp. 159–167 in Mary Cable, *Black Odyssey: The Case of the Slave Ship Amistad.*

New York [New York, U.S.A.]: The Viking Press, **[1971].**
8vo (22 cm.): [8], 183 p., map, portraits.

281.1 Ba = David Brown

Account translated into English by Kawweli (q.v. 301.1) printed on p. 12 in *A History of the Amistad Captives Being a Circumstantial Account of the Capture of the Spanish Schooner Amistad, by the Africans on Board*, edited by John Warner Barber (1798–1885).

New Haven, Connecticut [U.S.A.]: Published by E. L. & J. W. Barber, Hitchcock and Stafford Printers, 1840.
8vo (23 cm.): 32 p., folding plate, map, portraits.

¶ Ba ("have none"), whose homeland has not been identified, was a middle-aged rice farmer with a wife and one child when he was seized by two men in the road and sold to a Gallinas Vai man, who then sold him to a Spaniard, who took him to a slave ship. Ba was one of the surviving *Amistad* mutineers who stood trial in New Haven, Connecticut, U.S.A.. After returning to Sierra Leone (see Map 4) in 1842, he was a member of the Christian mission there until his excommunication for adultery two years later. For a silhouette image of Ba done by an artist during his incarceration see 281.1, p. 12. For further information see note preceding entry 265.1.

281.2——.

His account included in photomechanical reprint of 281.1, *A History of the Amistad Captives Being a Circumstantial Account of the Capture of the Spanish Schooner Amistad, by the Africans on Board; Their Voyage, and Capture Near Long Island, New York; with Biographical Sketches of Each of the Surviving Africans*, edited by John Warner Barber.

New York [New York, U.S.A.]: Arno Press, **1969.**
8vo (24 cm.): 32 p., folding plate, map, portraits.

281.3——.

His account included in photomechanical reprint of portion of 281.1 as Appendix I "From *A History of the Amistad Captives* by John W. Barber (1840)" on pp. 159–167 in Mary Cable, *Black Odyssey: The Case of the Slave Ship Amistad.*

New York [New York, U.S.A.]: The Viking Press, **[1971].**
8vo (22 cm.): [8], 183 p., map, portraits.

https://archive.org/details/historyofamistad-00barb/page/12/mode/2up
[see 281.1].

282.1 Shule

Account translated into English by Kawweli (q.v. 301.1) printed on p. 13 in *A History of the Amistad Captives Being a Circumstantial Account of the Capture of the Spanish*

Schooner Amistad, by the Africans on Board, edited by John Warner Barber (1798–1885).

New Haven, Connecticut [U.S.A.]: Published by E. L. & J. W. Barber, Hitchcock and Stafford Printers, 1840. 8vo (23 cm.): 32 p., folding plate, map, portraits.

¶ Shule ("waterfall") was the oldest of the *Amistad* captives, and the fourth in command when the mutineers controlled the schooner. He was born at Konabu, in the open land of the Mende country, near a large river called Wuwa (likely Moa River, Sierra Leone—see Map 4), which runs south into Kono country (modern eastern Sierra Leone). He and his wife were kidnapped. Later Shule and his master were captured and enslaved, then sold twice, eventually to Spaniards at Lomboko (Sierra Leone). For a silhouette image of Shule done by an artist during his incarceration see 282.1, p. 12. From there he was taken to a slave ship. For further information see note preceding entry 265.1.

282.2——.

His account included in photomechanical reprint of 282.1, *A History of the Amistad Captives Being a Circumstantial Account of the Capture of the Spanish Schooner Amistad, by the Africans on Board; Their Voyage, and Capture Near Long Island, New York; with Biographical Sketches of Each of the Surviving Africans*, edited by John Warner Barber.

New York [New York, U.S.A.]: Arno Press, **1969**. 8vo (24 cm.): 32 p., folding plate, map, portraits.

282.3——.

His account included in photomechanical reprint of portion of 282.1 as Appendix I "From *A History of the Amistad Captives* by John W. Barber (1840)" on pp. 159–167 in Mary Cable, *Black Odyssey: The Case of the Slave Ship Amistad*.

New York [New York, U.S.A.]: The Viking Press, **[1971]**. 8vo (22 cm.): [8], 183 p., map, portraits.

283.1 Kale = George Lewis

His account translated into English by Kawweli (**q.v. 301.1**) printed on p. 13 in *A History of the Amistad Captives Being a Circumstantial Account of the Capture of the Spanish Schooner Amistad, by the Africans on Board*, edited by John Warner Barber (1798–1885).

New Haven, Connecticut [U.S.A.]: Published by E. L. & J. W. Barber, Hitchcock and Stafford Printers, **1840**.

https://archive.org/details/historyofamistad-00barb/page/12/mode/2up [see 282.1].

8vo (23 cm.): 32 p., folding plate, map, portraits.

¶ Kale ("bone"), whose homeland has not been identified, was taken while going to a town to buy rice. He was two months in traveling to Lomboko (Sierra Leone—see Map 4) and was thereafter taken to a slave ship. Kale was one of the successful *Amistad* mutineers who stood trial in New Haven, Connecticut, U.S.A. (Map 17). After his return to Sierra Leone in 1842 he joined the Christian mission there. For a silhouette image of Kale done by an artist during his incarceration see 283.1, p. 12. For further information see note preceding entry 265.1.

https://archive.org/details/historyofamistad-00barb/page/12/mode/2up [see 283.1].

283.2——.

His account included in photomechanical reprint of 283.1, *A History of the Amistad Captives Being a Circumstantial Account of the Capture of the Spanish Schooner Amistad, by the Africans on Board; Their Voyage, and Capture Near Long Island, New York; with Biographical Sketches of Each of the Surviving Africans*, edited by John Warner Barber.

New York [New York, U.S.A.]: Arno Press, **1969**. 8vo (24 cm.): 32 p., folding plate, map, portraits.

283.3——.

His account included in photomechanical reprint of portion of 283.1 as Appendix I "From *A History of the Amistad Captives* by John W. Barber (1840)" on pp. 159–167 in Mary Cable, *Black Odyssey: The Case of the Slave Ship Amistad*.

New York [New York, U.S.A.]: The Viking Press, **[1971]**. 8vo (22 cm.): [8], 183 p., map, portraits.

Additional writing by Kale

+283-A.1 ——.

Letter dated New Haven, Connecticut, U.S.A., Jan[uary] 4, 1841, to John Quincy Adams, printed on pp. 354–355 within Simeon E. Baldwin's article "The Captives of the Amistad," in *Papers of the New Haven Colony Historical Society*, vol. IV, pp. 331–370 (New Haven [Connecticut]: Printed for the Society, 1888).

https://glc.yale.edu/kale-john-quincy-adams-141841

+283-A.2 ——.

Letter dated New Haven, Connecticut, U.S.A., Jan[uary] 4, 1841, to John Quincy Adams, printed on p. 85 within Ellen Strong Barlett's article "The Amistad Captives: An Old Conflict between Spain and America," in the illustrated popular *New England Magazine*, n.s. vol. 22, pp. 72–89 (Boston, Massachusetts: Warren F. Kellogg, Publisher, 5 Park Square, March 1900).

284.1 Bagna

His account translated into English by Kawweli (q.v. 301.1) printed on p. 13 in *A History of the Amistad Captives Being a Circumstantial Account of the Capture of the Spanish Schooner Amistad, by the Africans on Board*, edited by John Warner Barber (1798–1885).

New Haven, Connecticut [U.S.A.]: Published by E. L. & J. W. Barber, Hitchcock and Stafford Printers, 1840.

8vo (23 cm.): 32 p., folding plate, map, portraits.

¶ Bagna ("sand" or "gravel") was born at Dugauna, in the Kono country (modern eastern Sierra Leone—see Map 4), where his king, Daga, lived. His parents having already died, he lived with his brother (a rice farmer) until he was enslaved and, subsequently, taken to a slave ship. He was one of the surviving *Amistad* mutineers who stood trial in New Haven, Connecticut, U.S.A. (Map 17). For a silhouette image of Bagna done by an artist during his incarceration see 284.1, p. 12. For further information see note preceding entry 265.1.

284.2———.

His account included in photomechanical reprint of 284.1, *A History of the Amistad Captives Being a Circumstantial Account of the Capture of the Spanish Schooner Amistad, by the Africans on Board; Their Voyage, and Capture Near Long Island, New York; with Biographical Sketches of Each of the Surviving Africans*, edited by John Warner Barber.

New York [New York, U.S.A.]: Arno Press, 1969.
8vo (24 cm.): 32 p., folding plate, map, portraits.

284.3———.

His account included in photomechanical reprint of portion of 284.1 as Appendix I "From *A History of the Amistad Captives* by John W. Barber (1840)" on pp. 159–167 in Mary Cable, *Black Odyssey: The Case of the Slave Ship Amistad*.

New York [New York, U.S.A.]: The Viking Press, [1971].
8vo (22 cm.): [8], 183 p., map, portraits.

https://archive.org/details/historyofamistad-00barb/page/12/mode/2up [see 284.1].

285.1 Sa

His account translated into English by Kawweli (q.v. 301.1) printed on p. 13 in *A History of the Amistad Captives Being a Circumstantial Account of the Capture of the Spanish Schooner Amistad, by the Africans on Board*, edited by John Warner Barber (1798–1885).

New Haven, Connecticut [U.S.A.]: Published by E. L. & J. W. Barber, Hitchcock and Stafford Printers, 1840.

8vo (23 cm.): 32 p., folding plate, map, portraits.

¶ Sa, whom Marcus Rediker determined was Kono (modern eastern Sierra Leone—see Map 4), was a youth and only child when, while out walking on a road, he was kidnapped by two men. He was two months in traveling to Lomboko (Sierra Leone), after which he was taken to a slave ship. Sa was one of the surviving *Amistad* mutineers who stood trial in New Haven, Connecticut, U.S.A. (Map 17). For a silhouette image of Sa done by an artist during his incarceration see 285.1, p. 10. For further information see note preceding entry 265.1.

285.2———.

His account included in photomechanical reprint of 285.1, *A History of the Amistad Captives Being a Circumstantial Account of the Capture of the Spanish Schooner Amistad, by the Africans on Board; Their Voyage, and Capture Near Long Island, New York; with Biographical Sketches of Each of the Surviving Africans*, edited by John Warner Barber.

New York [New York, U.S.A.]: Arno Press, 1969.
8vo (24 cm.): 32 p., folding plate, map, portraits.

285.3———.

His account included in photomechanical reprint of portion of 285.1 as Appendix I "From *A History of the Amistad Captives* by John W. Barber (1840)" on pp. 159–167 in Mary Cable, *Black Odyssey: The Case of the Slave Ship Amistad*.

New York [New York, U.S.A.]: The Viking Press, [1971].
8vo (22 cm.): [8], 183 p., map, portraits.

286.1 Kinna (ca. 1820–)

His account translated into English by Kawweli (*q.v.* 301.1) printed on p. 13 in *A History of the Amistad Captives Being a Circumstantial Account of the Capture of the Spanish*

https://archive.org/details/historyofamistad-00barb/page/12/mode/2up [see 285.1].

Schooner Amistad, by the Africans on Board, edited by John Warner Barber (1798–1885).

New Haven, Connecticut [U.S.A.]: Published by E. L. & J. W. Barber, Hitchcock and Stafford Printers, **1840.**
8vo (23 cm.): 32 p., folding plate, map, portraits.

¶ Kinna ("man" or "big man"), a Mende, was one of the surviving *Amistad* mutineers. He was born near Simabu, in the Mende country, where the king resided (modern Sierra Leone—see Map 4). When about eighteen years old and unmarried (Blassingame, *Slave Testimony*, 32n26), he was kidnapped (while going to Kongoli) by a Bullom man and taken to Lomboko, and then onto a slave ship to Havana in the Spanish colony of Cuba in the Caribbean (Map 12) . He expressed Christian sentiments in his letters (see +286-A.1 et seq.), which he wrote until returning to Sierra Leone in 1842. For a silhouette image of Gbatu done by an artist during his incarceration see 286.1, p. 13. Thereafter, he was loosely connected to the Christian mission there. For further information see note preceding entry 265.1.

286.2——.
Quotations of Kinna's speech at a meeting printed in a Philadelphia newspaper article entitled "The Amistad Africans," *Pennsylvania Inquirer and Daily Courier*, 29 May 1841 (p. 2, 4th and 5th cols.). Vol. 24, nr. 126

Philadelphia, Pennsylvania [U.S.A.]: Published by Jesper Harding, May 29, **1841.**
(66 cm.): 4 p.

286.3——.
Extended quotations of Kinna (not appearing in 286.1) printed in an article headlined "The Amistad Africans | Farewell Meetings and Embarkation" on abolitionists' meetings held 5–17 November 1841 in the newspaper *The New York Tribune*.

New York [New York, U.S.A.], 1841.
Folio.

286.4——.
Extended quotations of Kinna (not appearing in 286.1) reprinted in an article "From the New York Tribune" (i.e., 286.2) on abolitionists' meetings held 5–17 November 1841, here under headline "The Amistad Africans | Farewell Meet-

https://archive.org/details/historyofamistad-00barb/page/12/mode/2up [see 286.1].

ings and Embarkation" on the second page, cols. 3-6 of the antislavery newspaper *The Philanthropist*, vol. 6, no. 26.

Cincinnati [Ohio, U.S.A.]: Published by the Executive Committee of the Ohio State Anti-Slavery Society, Samuel A. Alley, Printer, 29 December **1841.**
Folio.
https://archive.org/details/184043/page/n285

286.5——.
His account included in photomechanical reprint of 286.1, *A History of the Amistad Captives Being a Circumstantial Account of the Capture of the Spanish Schooner Amistad, by the Africans on Board; Their Voyage, and Capture Near Long Island, New York; with Biographical Sketches of Each of the Surviving Africans*, edited by John Warner Barber.

New York [New York, U.S.A.]: Arno Press, **1969.**
8vo (24 cm.): 32 p., folding plate, map, portraits.

286.6——.
His account included in photomechanical reprint of portion of 286.1 as Appendix I "From *A History of the Amistad Captives* by John W. Barber (1840)" on pp. 159–167 in Mary Cable, *Black Odyssey: The Case of the Slave Ship Amistad*.

New York [New York, U.S.A.]: The Viking Press, [].
8vo (22 cm.): [8], 183 p., map, portraits.

286.7——.
Quotations of Kinna noted above in 286.4 included on pp. 203–204 of longer printing of the article mentioned therein on pp. 200–208 in *Slave Testimony: Two Centuries of Letters, Speeches, Interviews, and Autobiographies*, edited by John W. Blassingame.

Baton Rouge [Louisiana, U.S.A.]: Louisiana State University Press, **1977.**
8vo: lxv, 777 p.

286.8——. [Second printing of 286.7]
Quotations of Kinna noted above in 284.4 included on pp. 203–204 of longer printing of the article mentioned therein on pp. 200–208 in *Slave Testimony: Two Centuries of Letters, Speeches, and Autobiographies*, edited by John W. Blassingame.

Baton Rouge [Louisiana, U.S.A.]: Louisiana State University Press, **1977.** Second printing.
8vo (23 cm.): lxv, 777 p., illus., portraits.

286.9——. [Another printing of 286.7]

Quotations of Kinna noted above in 286.4 included on pp. 203–204 of longer printing of the article mentioned therein on pp. 200–208 in *Slave Testimony: Two Centuries of Letters, Speeches, and Autobiographies*, edited by John W. Blassingame.

Baton Rouge [Louisiana, U.S.A.]: Louisiana State University Press, **1979.** 1979 printing.
8vo (23 cm.): lxv, 777 p., illus., portraits.

286.10——. [Another printing of 286.7]

Quotations of Kinna noted above in 286.4 included on pp. 203–204 of longer printing of the article mentioned therein on pp. 200–208 in *Slave Testimony: Two Centuries of Letters, Speeches, and Autobiographies*, edited by John W. Blassingame.

Baton Rouge [Louisiana, U.S.A.]: Louisiana State University Press, **1980.** 1980 printing.
8vo (23 cm.): lxv, 777 p., illus., portraits.

286.11——. [Another printing of 286.7]

Quotations of Kinna noted above in 286.4 included on pp. 203–204 of longer printing of the article mentioned therein on pp. 200–208 in *Slave Testimony: Two Centuries of Letters, Speeches, and Autobiographies*, edited by John W. Blassingame.

Baton Rouge [Louisiana, U.S.A.]: Louisiana State University Press, **1989.** 1989 printing.
8vo (23 cm.): lxv, 777 p., illus., portraits.

286.12——. [Another printing of 286.7]

Quotations of Kinna noted above in 286.4 included on pp. 203–204 of longer printing of the article mentioned therein on pp. 200–208 in *Slave Testimony: Two Centuries of Letters, Speeches, and Autobiographies*, edited by John W. Blassingame.

Baton Rouge [Louisiana, U.S.A.]: Louisiana State University Press, **1998.** 1998 printing.
8vo (23 cm.): lxv, 777 p., illus., portraits.

286.13——. [Another printing of 286.7]

Quotations of Kinna noted above in 286.4 included on pp. 203–204 of longer printing of the article mentioned therein on pp. 200–208 in *Slave Testimony: Two Centuries of Letters, Speeches, and Autobiographies*, edited by John W. Blassingame.

Baton Rouge [Louisiana, U.S.A.]: Louisiana State University Press, **2002.** 2002 printing.
8vo (23 cm.): lxv, 777 p., illus., portraits.

286.14——. [Another printing of 286.7]

Quotations of Kinna noted above in 286.4 included on pp. 203–204 of longer printing of the article mentioned therein on pp. 200–208 in *Slave Testimony: Two Centuries of Letters, Speeches, and Autobiographies*, edited by John W. Blassingame.

Baton Rouge [Louisiana, U.S.A.]: Louisiana State University Press, **2009.**
8vo (24 cm.): lxv, 777 p., illus., portraits.

Additional writings by Kinna

+286-A.1–8 ——.

Letter dated Westville, Connecticut, U.S.A., 13 December 1840 to Lewis Tappan at New York City printed on p. 32 in *Slave Testimony: Two Centuries of Letters, Speeches, Interviews, and Autobiographies*, edited by John W. Blassingame (Baton Rouge: Louisiana State University Press, eight printings 1977–2009).

+286-B.1–8 ——.

Letter dated Westville, Connecticut, U.S.A., 12 March 1841 to Lewis Tappan at New York City printed on p. 37 in *Slave Testimony: Two Centuries of Letters, Speeches, Interviews, and Autobiographies*, edited by John W. Blassingame (Baton Rouge: Louisiana State University Press, eight printings 1977–2009).

+286-C.1–8 ——.

Letter dated New Haven, Connecticut, U.S.A., 15 March 1841 to Roger S. Baldwin at New Haven printed on pp. 38–39 in *Slave Testimony: Two Centuries of Letters, Speeches, Interviews, and Autobiographies*, edited by John W. Blassingame (Baton Rouge: Louisiana State University Press, eight printings 1977–2009).

+286-D.1–8 ——.

Letter dated Farmington, Connecticut, U.S.A., 20 March 1841 to Lewis Tappan at New York City printed on p. 39 in *Slave Testimony: Two Centuries of Letters, Speeches, Interviews, and Autobiographies*, edited by John W. Blassingame (Baton Rouge: Louisiana State University Press, eight printings 1977–2009).

+286-E.1–8 ——.

Letter dated Farmington, Connecticut, U.S.A., 28 March 1841 to Lewis Tappan at New York City printed on pp. 39–40 in *Slave Testimony: Two Centuries of Letters, Speeches, Interviews, and Autobiographies*, edited by John W. Blassingame (Baton Rouge: Louisiana State University Press, eight printings 1977–2009).

+286-F.1–8 ———.

Letter dated Farmington, Connecticut, U.S.A., 28 April 1841 to Lewis Tappan at New York City printed on p. 41 in *Slave Testimony: Two Centuries of Letters, Speeches, Interviews, and Autobiographies,* edited by John W. Blassingame (Baton Rouge: Louisiana State University Press, *eight printings* 1977–2009).

+286-G.1 ———.

Letter signed Fuliwa, Kali, and Kinna dated Connecticut 5 May 1841 to John Quincy Adams reproduced photographically with transcription at: https://digitallibrary.tulane.edu/islandora/object/tulane%3A53601.

+286-H.1 ———.

Letter dated Sierra Leone 13 January 1842 to Lewis Tappan at New York City printed in periodical *American and Foreign Anti-Slavery Reporter* 2: (June 1842), 63.

+286-H.2–9 ———.

+286-H.1 reprinted on p. 44 in *Slave Testimony: Two Centuries of Letters, Speeches, Interviews, and Autobiographies,* edited by John W. Blassingame (Baton Rouge: Louisiana State University Press, eight printings 1977–2009).

287.1 Ndzhagnwawni = Ngahoni

His account translated into English by Kawweli (q.v. 301.1) printed on p. 13 in *A History of the Amistad Captives Being a Circumstantial Account of the Capture of the Spanish Schooner Amistad, by the Africans on Board,* edited by John Warner Barber (1798–1885).

New Haven, Connecticut [U.S.A.]: Published by E. L. & J. W. Barber, Hitchcock and Stafford Printers, 1840. 8vo (23 cm.): 32 p., folding plate, map, portraits.

https://archive.org/details/historyofamistad-00barb/page/12/mode/2up [see 287.1].

¶ Ndzhagnwawni or Ngahoni (water bird), whose homeland is unknown, was middle-aged, with a wife and one child, when he was seized in a rice field by four men and taken on a two-week journey to Lomboko in Sierra Leone (see Map 4). Ndzhagnwawni was one of the surviving *Amistad* mutineers who stood trial in New Haven, Connecticut, U.S.A. (Map 17). For a silhouette image of Gbatu (Ngahoni) done by an artist during his incarceration see 287.1, p. 13. For further information see note preceding entry 265.1.

287.2 ———.

His account included in photomechanical reprint of 287.1, *A History of the Amistad Captives Being a Circumstantial Account of the Capture of the Spanish Schooner Amistad, by the Africans on Board; Their Voyage, and Capture Near Long Island, New York; with Biographical Sketches of Each of the Surviving Africans,* edited by John Warner Barber.

New York [New York, U.S.A.]: Arno Press, **1969.** 8vo (24 cm.): 32 p., folding plate, map, portraits.

287.3 ———.

His account included in photomechanical reprint of portion of 287.1 as Appendix I "From *A History of the Amistad Captives* by John W. Barber (1840)" on pp. 159–167 in Mary Cable, *Black Odyssey: The Case of the Slave Ship Amistad.*

New York [New York, U.S.A.]: The Viking Press, **[1971].** 8vo (22 cm.): [8], 183 p., map, portraits.

288.1 Fang = Fakinna

His account translated into English by Kawweli (q.v. 301.1) printed on p. 13 in *A History of the Amistad Captives Being a Circumstantial Account of the Capture of the Spanish Schooner Amistad, by the Africans on Board,* edited by John Warner Barber (1798–1885).

New Haven, Connecticut [U.S.A.]: Published by E. L. & J. W. Barber, Hitchcock and Stafford Printers, 1840. 8vo (23 cm.): 32 p., folding plate, map, portraits.

https://archive.org/details/historyofamistad-00barb/page/12/mode/2up [see 288.1].

¶ Fang or Fakinna, was born at Dzhopoahu, in the Mende country, at which place his father, Bawnge, was chief or king (modern Sierra Leone—see Map 4). Fang was middle-aged, with a wife and two children, when he was kidnapped by a Mende man, who held him less than a month and then took him to Lomboko (Sierra Leone). Thereafter, he was taken to a slave ship. Fang was one of the surviving *Amistad* mutineers who stood trial in New Haven, Connecticut, U.S.A. (Map 17). For a silhouette image of Fang done by an artist during his incarceration see 288.1, p. 13. For further information see note preceding entry 265.1.

288.2 ———.

His account included in photomechanical reprint of 288.1, *A History of the Amistad Captives Being a Circumstantial Account of the Capture of the Spanish Schooner Amistad, by the*

Africans on Board; Their Voyage, and Capture Near Long Island, New York; with Biographical Sketches of Each of the Surviving Africans, edited by John Warner Barber.

New York [New York, U.S.A.]: Arno Press, 1969.
8vo (24 cm.): 32 p., folding plate, map, portraits.

288.3——.

His account included in photomechanical reprint of portion of 288.1 as Appendix I "From *A History of the Amistad Captives* by John W. Barber (1840)" on pp. 159–167 in Mary Cable, *Black Odyssey: The Case of the Slave Ship Amistad*.

New York [New York, U.S.A.]: The Viking Press, [1971].
8vo (22 cm.): [8], 183 p., map, portraits.

289.1 Fahidzhinna = Faginna

Account translated into English by Kawweli (q.v. 301.1) printed on pp. 13–14 in *A History of the Amistad Captives Being a Circumstantial Account of the Capture of the Spanish Schooner Amistad, by the Africans on Board*, edited by John Warner Barber (1798-1885).

New Haven, Connecticut [U.S.A.]: Published by E. L. & J. W. Barber, Hitchcock and Stafford Printers, 1840.
8vo (23 cm.): 32 p., folding plate, map, portraits.

https://archive.org/details/historyofamistad-00barb/page/12/mode/2up [see 289.1].

¶ Fahidzhinna = Faginna ("twin") was born at Tom-bo-lu, a town in Bombali, in Mende country (modern Sierra Leone—see Map 4). His face bore smallpox scars. He and his wife were enslaved by a man named Tamu and sold to a Mende man, who resold him to the same Spaniard who purchased Gilabaru (q.v. 265.1). Fahidzhinna was one of the surviving *Amistad* mutineers who stood trial in New Haven, Connecticut, U.S.A. (Map 17). For a silhouette image of Fahidzhinna done by an artist during his incarceration see 288.1, p. 13. For further information see note preceding entry 265.1.

289.2——.

His account included in photomechanical reprint of 289.1, *A History of the Amistad Captives Being a Circumstantial Account of the Capture of the Spanish Schooner Amistad, by the Africans on Board; Their Voyage, and Capture Near Long Island, New York; with Biographical Sketches of Each of the Surviving Africans*, edited by John Warner Barber.

New York [New York, U.S.A.]: Arno Press, 1969.
8vo (24 cm.): 32 p., folding plate, map, portraits.

289.3——.

His account included in photomechanical reprint of portion of 289.1 as Appendix I "From *A History of the Amistad Captives* by John W. Barber (1840)" on pp. 159–167 in Mary Cable, *Black Odyssey: The Case of the Slave Ship Amistad*.

New York [New York, U.S.A.]: The Viking Press, [1971].
8vo (22 cm.): [8], 183 p., map, portraits.

290.1 Yaboi

His account translated into English by Kawweli (q.v. 301.1) printed on p. 14 in *A History of the Amistad Captives Being a Circumstantial Account of the Capture of the Spanish Schooner Amistad, by the Africans on Board*, edited by John Warner Barber (1798–1885).

New Haven, Connecticut [U.S.A.]: Published by E. L. & J. W. Barber, Hitchcock and Stafford Printers, 1840.
8vo (23 cm.): 32 p., folding plate, map, portraits.

https://archive.org/details/historyofamistad-00barb/page/14/mode/2up [see 290.1].

¶ Yaboi, a middle-aged man with a wife and one child, was born in Kondowalu, where his king, Kakbeni, resided (modern Sierra Leone—see Map 4). He was captured in warfare and held enslaved for ten years by a Mende man, who then sold him to a Spaniard. Thereafter, he was taken to a slave ship. Yaboi was one of the surviving *Amistad* mutineers who stood trial in New Haven, Connecticut, U.S.A. (Map 17). For a silhouette image of Yaboi done by an artist during his incarceration see 290.1, p. 13. For further information see note preceding entry 265.1.

290.2——.

His account included in photomechanical reprint of 290.1, *A History of the Amistad Captives Being a Circumstantial Account of the Capture of the Spanish Schooner Amistad, by the Africans on Board; Their Voyage, and Capture Near Long Island, New York; with Biographical Sketches of Each of the Surviving Africans*, edited by John Warner Barber.

New York [New York, U.S.A.]: Arno Press, 1969.
8vo (24 cm.): 32 p., folding plate, map, portraits.

290.3——.

His account included in photomechanical reprint of portion of 290.1 as Appendix I "From *A History of the Amistad Cap-*

tives by John W. Barber (1840)" on pp. 159–167 in Mary Cable, *Black Odyssey: The Case of the Slave Ship Amistad.*

New York [New York, U.S.A.]: The Viking Press, [1971].
8vo (22 cm.): [8], 183 p., map, portraits.

291.1 Fabanna

His account translated into English by Kawweli (*q.v.* 301.1) printed on p. 14 in *A History of the Amistad Captives Being a Circumstantial Account of the Capture of the Spanish Schooner Amistad, by the Africans on Board*, edited by John Warner Barber (1798–1885).

New Haven, Connecticut [U.S.A.]: Published by E. L. & J. W. Barber, Hitchcock and Stafford Printers, 1840.

8vo (23 cm.): 32 p., folding plate, map, portraits.

https://archive.org/details/historyofamistad-00barb/page/14/mode/2up [see 291.1].

¶ Fabanna (remember), a Mende, was from the same country as Gilabaru (*q.v.* 265.1) in modern Sierra Leone (see Map 4). He had two wives and one child when his village was surrounded by soldiers and he was captured. He was then sold twice, ultimately to a Spaniard in Lomboko, who had him forced aboard a slave ship. Fabanna was one of the surviving *Amistad* mutineers who stood trial in New Haven, Connecticut, U.S.A. (Map 17). For a silhouette image of Fabanna done by an artist during his incarceration see 291.1, p. 14. For further information see note preceding entry 265.1.

291.2 ——.

His account included in photomechanical reprint of 291.1, *A History of the Amistad Captives Being a Circumstantial Account of the Capture of the Spanish Schooner Amistad, by the Africans on Board; Their Voyage, and Capture Near Long Island, New York; with Biographical Sketches of Each of the Surviving Africans*, edited by John Warner Barber.

New York [New York, U.S.A.]: Arno Press, 1969.
8vo (24 cm.): 32 p., folding plate, map, portraits.

291.3 ——.

His account included in photomechanical reprint of portion of 291.1 as Appendix I "From *A History of the Amistad Captives* by John W. Barber (1840)" on pp. 159–167 in Mary Cable, *Black Odyssey: The Case of the Slave Ship Amistad.*

New York [New York, U.S.A.]: The Viking Press, [1971].
8vo (22 cm.): [8], 183 p., map, portraits.

Additional writing by Fabanna

291-A.1–8 ——.

Letter dated Westville, Connecticut, U.S.A., 12 March 1841 to Lewis Tappan at New York City printed on p. 38 in *Slave Testimony: Two Centuries of Letters, Speeches, Interviews, and Autobiographies*, edited by John W. Blassingame (Baton Rouge: Louisiana State University Press, eight printings 1977–2009).

292.1 Tsukama

Account translated into English by Kawweli (*q.v.* 301.1) printed on p. 14 in *A History of the Amistad Captives Being a Circumstantial Account of the Capture of the Spanish Schooner Amistad, by the Africans on Board*, edited by John Warner Barber (1798–1885).

New Haven, Connecticut [U.S.A.]: Published by E. L. & J. W. Barber, Hitchcock and Stafford Printers, 1840.

8vo (23 cm.): 32 p., folding plate, map, portraits.

https://archive.org/details/historyofamistad-00barb/page/14/mode/2up [see 292.1].

¶ Tsukama (a learner) was born at Sungaru in Mende country (modern Sierra Leone—see Map 4), where his king, Gnambe, resided. He was kidnapped and sold into the Bullom country, where he lived for a time with his master, who then sold him to a Spaniard at Lomboko. Thereafter he was taken to a slave ship. Tsuukama was one of the surviving *Amistad* mutineers who stood trial in New Haven, Connecticut, U.S.A. (Map 17). For a silhouette image of Tsukama done by an artist during his incarceration see 292.1, p. 14. For further information see note preceding entry 265.1.

292.2 ——.

Account included in photomechanical reprint of 292.1, *A History of the Amistad Captives Being a Circumstantial Account of the Capture of the Spanish Schooner Amistad, by the Africans on Board; Their Voyage, and Capture Near Long Island, New York; with Biographical Sketches of Each of the Surviving Africans*, edited by John Warner Barber.

New York [New York, U.S.A.]: Arno Press, 1969.
8vo (24 cm.): 32 p., folding plate, map, portraits.

292.3 ——.

His account included in photomechanical reprint of portion of 292.1 as Appendix I "From *A History of the Amistad Cap-*

tives by John W. Barber (1840)" on pp. 159–167 in Mary Cable, *Black Odyssey: The Case of the Slave Ship Amistad.*

New York [New York, U.S.A.]: The Viking Press, [1971].
8vo (22 cm.): [8], 183 p., map, portraits.

293.1 Bere = Berri

Account translated into English by Kawweli (q.v. 301.1) printed on p. 14 in *A History of the Amistad Captives Being a Circumstantial Account of the Capture of the Spanish Schooner Amistad, by the Africans on Board,* edited by John Warner Barber (1798–1885).

https://archive.org/details/historyofamistad-00barb/page/14/mode/2up [see 293.1].

New Haven, Connecticut [U.S.A.]: Published by E. L. & J. W. Barber, Hitchcock and Stafford Printers, 1840.
8vo (23 cm.): 32 p., folding plate, map, portraits.

¶ Bere = Berri (stick) was born at Fangte, in Gula, a large fenced town where his king, Gelewa, resided (northwestern Liberia and Sierra Leone—see Map 4). When middle-aged, he was taken by soldiers and sold to Shaka, king of Genduma (in the Vai or Gallinas country), who then resold him to a Spaniard on the Boba River. From there he was taken to a slave ship. Bere was one of the surviving *Amistad* mutineers who stood trial in New Haven, Connecticut, U.S.A. (Map 17). For a silhouette image of Bere done by an artist during his incarceration see 293.1, p. 14. For further information see note preceding entry 265.1.

293.2———.

Account included in photomechanical reprint of 293.1, *A History of the Amistad Captives Being a Circumstantial Account of the Capture of the Spanish Schooner Amistad, by the Africans on Board; Their Voyage, and Capture Near Long Island, New York; with Biographical Sketches of Each of the Surviving Africans,* edited by John Warner Barber.

New York [New York, U.S.A.]: Arno Press, 1969.
8vo (24 cm.): 32 p., folding plate, map, portraits.

293.3———.

His account included in photomechanical reprint of portion of 293.1 as Appendix I "From *A History of the Amistad Captives* by John W. Barber (1840)" on pp. 159–167 in Mary Cable, *Black Odyssey: The Case of the Slave Ship Amistad.*

New York [New York, U.S.A.]: The Viking Press, [1971].
8vo (22 cm.): [8], 183 p., map, portraits.

294.1 Fawni = Foni = Fenni = Foone (-1841)

Trial statements about the *Amistad* mutiny printed in the antislavery newspaper *The New York Emancipator,* vol.

New York [New York, U.S.A.], late Oct. early Nov., 1839.

¶ One of the surviving *Amistad* mutineers who stood trial in New Haven and Hartford, Connecticut, U.S.A. (see Map 17), Fawni was born in Yilunah, in the town of Bumbe (or Bumbeli), a large town in Mende country (modern Sierra Leone—Map 4). Married, Fawni had living parents, brothers, and sisters when, while on his way to plant rice, he was seized by two men. His captors carried him to Bembelaw in Vai country and sold him to a Spaniard, who kept him there for two months, then took him to Lomboko (Sierra Leone). Thereafter he was taken to the Spanish colonial city of Havana, Cuba in the Caribbean (Map 12). After placement on the *Amistad* and before the revolt, he was severely flogged for taking more than the meager allotment of water. After the revolt he served as cook during the long voyage to Connecticut. Following their release from jail after the favorable Supreme Court decision and while waiting to be returned home, Fawni drowned in Framington, Connecticut while swimming in a river. For a silhouette image of Fawni done by an artist during his incarceration see 294.1, p. 14. See also the note preceding entry 265.1.

294.2———.

Article 294.1 reprinted from *The New York Emancipator* on p. 1 of the antislavery journal *The British Emancipator,* no. 58.

London [England]: [Published] Under the sanction of the Central Negro Emancipation Committee, November 27, 1839. Colophon: Printed by John Haddon, Castle Street, Finsbury.

Broadsheet bifolium (50 cm.).

294.3———.

His account translated into English by Kawweli (q.v. 301.1) printed on p. 14 in *A History of the Amistad Captives Being a Circumstantial Account of the Capture of the Spanish Schooner Amistad, by the Africans on Board,* edited by John Warner Barber (1798–1885).

New Haven, Connecticut, U.S.A.: Published by E. L. & J. W. Barber, Hitchcock and Stafford Printers, 1840.
8vo (23 cm.): 32 p., folding plate, map, portraits.
https://archive.org/details/historyofamistad00barb/page/14/mode/2up

https://archive.org/details/historyofamistad-00barb/page/14/mode/2up [see 294.3].

294.4——.

Account included in photomechanical reprint of 294.3, *A History of the Amistad Captives Being a Circumstantial Account of the Capture of the Spanish Schooner Amistad, by the Africans on Board; Their Voyage, and Capture Near Long Island, New York; with Biographical Sketches of Each of the Surviving Africans*, edited by John Warner Barber.

New York [New York, U.S.A.]: Arno Press, **1969**.
8vo (24 cm.): 32 p., folding plate, map, portraits.

294.5——.

His account included in photomechanical reprint of portion of 294.3 as Appendix I "From *A History of the Amistad Captives* by John W. Barber (1840)" on pp. 159–167 in Mary Cable, *Black Odyssey: The Case of the Slave Ship Amistad.*

New York [New York, U.S.A.]: The Viking Press, [**1971**].
8vo (22 cm.): [8], 183 p., map, portraits.

295.1 Burna (elder)

Account translated into English by Kawweli (q.v. 301.1) printed on p. 14 in *A History of the Amistad Captives Being a Circumstantial Account of the Capture of the Spanish Schooner Amistad, by the Africans on Board*, edited by John Warner Barber (1798–1885).

New Haven, Connecticut [U.S.A.]: Published by E. L. & J. W. Barber, Hitchcock and Stafford Printers, 1840.
8vo (23 cm.): 32 p., folding plate, map, portraits.

https://archive.org/details/historyofamistad-00barb/page/14/mode/2up [see 295.1].

¶ His father having died, Burna (twin) lived with his mother (identified as Gbandi by evidence uncovered by Marcus Rediker), four sisters, and two brothers. While walking to the next town he was captured by three men. It took his captors six weeks to take him to Lomboko (Sierra Leone—see Map 4), where he was kept three and a half "moons," then sent on the slave ship *Teçora* to the Spanish colonial city of Havana, Cuba in the Caribbean (Map 12). Burna was one of the surviving *Amistad* mutineers who stood trial in New Haven, Connecticut, U.S.A. (Map 17). After release from jail and a fund-raising tour with the other *Amistad* rebels, Burna sailed to Freetown, Sierra Leone, on the *Gentleman*, arriving 13 January 1842. In February he found his home village and met his mother in an emotional reunion. For a silhouette image of Burna done by an artist during his incarceration see 295.1, p. 14. See also the note preceding entry 265.1.

295.2——.

Account included in photomechanical reprint of 295.1, *A History of the Amistad Captives Being a Circumstantial Account of the Capture of the Spanish Schooner Amistad, by the Africans on Board; Their Voyage, and Capture Near Long Island, New York; with Biographical Sketches of Each of the Surviving Africans*, edited by John Warner Barber.

New York [New York, U.S.A.]: Arno Press, **1969**.
8vo (24 cm.): 32 p., folding plate, map, portraits.

295.3——.

His account included in photomechanical reprint of portion of 295.1 as Appendix I "From *A History of the Amistad Captives* by John W. Barber (1840)" on pp. 159–167 in Mary Cable, *Black Odyssey: The Case of the Slave Ship Amistad.*

New York [New York, U.S.A.]: The Viking Press, [**1971**].
8vo (22 cm.): [8], 183 p., map, portraits.

296.1 Shuma

Account translated into English by Kawweli (q.v. 301.1) printed on pp. 14–15 in *A History of the Amistad Captives Being a Circumstantial Account of the Capture of the Spanish Schooner Amistad, by the Africans on Board*, edited by John Warner Barber (1798–1885).

New Haven, Connecticut [U.S.A.]: Published by E. L. & J. W. Barber, Hitchcock and Stafford Printers, 1840.
8vo (23 cm.): 32 p., folding plate, map, portraits.

https://archive.org/details/historyofamistad-00barb/page/14/mode/2up [see 296.1].

¶ Shuma (falling water), whose homeland has not been identified, was a middle-aged married father of one child when he was captured in war. It took his captors four "moons" to transport him to Lomboko (Sierra Leone—see Map 4). Thereafter he was taken to a slave ship. Shuma was one of the surviving *Amistad* mutineers who stood trial in New Haven, Connecticut, U.S.A. (Map 17). For a silhouette image of Shuma done by an artist during his incarceration see 296.1, p. 14. He could count in Mende, Temne, and Bullom. For further information see note preceding entry 265.1.

296.2——.

Account included in photomechanical reprint of 296.1, *A History of the Amistad Captives Being a Circumstantial Account of the Capture of the Spanish Schooner Amistad, by the Africans on Board; Their Voyage, and Capture Near Long*

Island, New York; with Biographical Sketches of Each of the Surviving Africans, edited by John Warner Barber.

New York [New York, U.S.A.]: Arno Press, **1969.**
8vo (24 cm.): 32 p., folding plate, map, portraits.

296.3———.

His account included in photomechanical reprint of portion of 296.1 as Appendix I "From *A History of the Amistad Captives* by John W. Barber (1840)" on pp. 159–167 in Mary Cable, *Black Odyssey: The Case of the Slave Ship Amistad.*

New York [New York, U.S.A.]: The Viking Press, **[1971].**
8vo (22 cm.): [8], 183 p., map, portraits.

297.1 Kali

Account translated into English by Kawweli (q.v. 301.1) printed on p. 15 in *A History of the Amistad Captives Being a Circumstantial Account of the Capture of the Spanish Schooner Amistad, by the Africans on Board,* edited by John Warner Barber (1798–1885).

https://archive.org/details/historyofamistad-00barb/page/14/mode/2up [see 297.1].

New Haven, Connecticut [U.S.A.]: Published by E. L. & J. W. Barber, Hitchcock and Stafford Printers, **1840.**
8vo (23 cm.): 32 p., folding plate, map, portraits.

¶ Kali (bone) was a small boy whose homeland has not been identified. His parents and siblings were still living when he was stolen from a street and taken to Lomboko, Sierra Leone (see Map 4), then in a slave ship to the Spanish colony of Cuba in the Caribbean (Map 12). He was on the *Amistad* during the mutiny and taken to New Haven, Connecticut, U.S.A. (Map 17), where he was imprisoned. During this ordeal he learned English and wrote letters in which he expressed Christian sentiments. For a silhouette image of Kali done by an artist during his incarceration see 297.1, p. 15. For further information see note preceding entry 265.1.

297.2———.

Quotations of Kali's speech at a meeting printed in a Philadelphia newspaper article entitled "The Amistad Africans," *Pennsylvania Inquirer and Daily Courier*, 29 May 1841 (p. 2, 4th and 5th cols.). Vol. 24, nr. 126

Philadelphia, Pennsylvania [U.S.A.]: Published by Jesper Harding, May 29, **1841.**
(66 cm.): 4 p.

297.3———.

Account included in photomechanical reprint of 297.1, *A History of the Amistad Captives Being a Circumstantial Account of the Capture of the Spanish Schooner Amistad, by the Africans on Board; Their Voyage, and Capture Near Long Island, New York; with Biographical Sketches of Each of the Surviving Africans*, edited by John Warner Barber.

New York [New York, U.S.A.]: Arno Press, **1969.**
8vo (24 cm.): 32 p., folding plate, map, portraits.

297.4———.

His account included in photomechanical reprint of portion of 297.1 as Appendix I "From *A History of the Amistad Captives* by John W. Barber (1840)" on pp. 159–167 in Mary Cable, *Black Odyssey: The Case of the Slave Ship Amistad.*

New York [New York, U.S.A.]: The Viking Press, **[1971].**
8vo (22 cm.): [8], 183 p., map, portraits.

Additional writings by Kali

+297-A.1 ———.

Letter dated Westville, Connecticut, U.S.A., Sept[ember 1840] to Lewis Tappan at New York City printed *in complete facsimile of Kali's handwritten original* on p. 13 of *The American and Foreign A. S.* [i.e., *Anti-Slavery*] *Reporter*, Extra, December 1840, with editorial additions on p. 12, including description of Kali as a "little boy" (p. 12). *The editors thank Dr. Joseph Yannielli for calling this item to their attention.* https://digitalcommons.law.yale.edu/cgi/viewcontent.cgi?article=1016&context=amtrials

+297-A.2–9 ———.

Letter dated Westville, Connecticut, U.S.A., September 1840 to Lewis Tappan at New York City printed on p. 30 in *Slave Testimony: Two Centuries of Letters, Speeches, Interviews, and Autobiographies,* edited by John W. Blassingame (Baton Rouge: Louisiana State University Press, eight printings 1977–2009).

+297-B.1–8 ———.

Letter dated Westville, Connecticut, U.S.A., 30 October 1840 to Lewis Tappan at New York City printed on p. 33 in *Slave Testimony: Two Centuries of Letters, Speeches, Interviews, and Autobiographies,* edited by John W. Blassingame (Baton Rouge: Louisiana State University Press, eight printings 1977–2009).

+297-C.1 ———.

Letter dated New Haven, Connecticut, U.S.A., 4 January 1841 to John Quincy Adams printed in periodical *American and Foreign Anti-Slavery Reporter*, extra no. (15 March 1841), 9.

+297-C.2 ——.

Letter dated New Haven, Connecticut, U.S.A., 4 January 1841 to John Quincy Adams printed on pp. 354–355 of Simeon E. Baldwin, "The Captives of the Amistad (Read May 17, 1886)" in *Papers of the New Haven Colony Historical Society* 4 (1888): 331–370.

+297-C.3 ——.

Letter dated New Haven, Connecticut, U.S.A., 4 January 1841 to John Quincy Adams printed in magazine *American Heritage* 22:1 (1970): 111. Hogg 1597.

+297-C.4–11 ——.

Letter dated New Haven, Connecticut, U.S.A., 4 January 1841 to John Quincy Adams printed on pp. 33–34 in *Slave Testimony: Two Centuries of Letters, Speeches, Interviews, and Autobiographies,* edited by John W. Blassingame (Baton Rouge: Louisiana State University Press, eight printings 1977–2009). Another letter from Fuliwa, Kali, Kinna to John Quincy Adams dated 5 May 1841 is reproduced photographically with a transcription at:

https://digitallibrary.tulane.edu/islandora/object/tulane%3A53601.

298.1 Teme = Maria

Account translated into English by Kawweli (q.v. 301.1) printed on p. 15 in *A History of the Amistad Captives Being a Circumstantial Account of the Capture of the Spanish Schooner Amistad, by the Africans on Board,* edited by John Warner Barber (1798–1885).

https://archive.org/details/historyofamistad-00barb/page/14/mode/2up [see 298.1].

New Haven, Connecticut [U.S.A.]: Published by E. L. & J. W. Barber, Hitchcock and Stafford Printers, 1840.
8vo (23 cm.): 32 p., folding plate, map, portraits.

¶ Teme (frog), whose homeland has not been identified, was a young girl who lived with her mother, elder brother, and sister. Her father was deceased. One night a group of men broke into her mother's house and seized them all. They were then separated, and Teme never saw her mother or siblings again. After a long journey to Lomboko (Sierra Leone—see Map 4) she was placed on a slave ship. Teme was one of four children from the *Amistad* who were freed by a judge in Connecticut, U.S.A. (Map 17) on 19 March 1841. After returning to Sierra Leone in 1842, she joined the Christian mission there. For a silhouette image of Teme done by an artist during his incarceration see 298.1, p. 15. For further information see note preceding entry 265.1.

298.2——.

Account reprinted in photomechanical reprint of 298.1, *A History of the Amistad Captives Being a Circumstantial Account of the Capture of the Spanish Schooner Amistad, by the Africans on Board; Their Voyage, and Capture Near Long Island, New York; with Biographical Sketches of Each of the Surviving Africans,* edited by John Warner Barber.

New York [New York, U.S.A.]: Arno Press, **1969.**
8vo (24 cm.): 32 p., folding plate, map, portraits.

298.3——.

Her account included in photomechanical reprint of portion of 298.1 as Appendix I "From *A History of the Amistad Captives* by John W. Barber (1840)" on pp. 159–167 in Mary Cable, *Black Odyssey: The Case of the Slave Ship Amistad.*

New York [New York, U.S.A.]: The Viking Press, **[1971].**
8vo (22 cm.): [8], 183 p., map, portraits.

299.1 Kagne = Charlotte

Account translated into English by Kawweli (q.v. 301.1) printed on p. 15 in *A History of the Amistad Captives Being a Circumstantial Account of the Capture of the Spanish Schooner Amistad, by the Africans on Board,* edited by John Warner Barber (1798–1885).

https://archive.org/details/historyofamistad00barb/page/14/mode/2up [see 299.1].

New Haven, Connecticut [U.S.A.]: Published by E. L. & J. W. Barber, Hitchcock and Stafford Printers, 1840.
8vo (23 cm.): 32 p., folding plate, map, portraits.

¶ Kagne (country) was a young girl, probably Mende (modern Sierra Leone—see Map 4). Her parents, four brothers, and four sisters were living when she was pawned by her father for a debt and sold when he could not repay it. After a long journey to Lomboko (Sierra Leone) she was taken to a slave ship. Kagne was one of four children from the *Amistad* who were freed by a judge in Connecticut, U.S.A. (Map 17) on 19 March 1841. She could count in Mende and (imperfectly) in Vai or Gallinas. After returning to Sierra Leone in 1842 she joined the Christian mission there. For a silhouette image of Kagne done by an artist during his incarceration see 299.1, p. 15. For further information see note preceding entry 265.1.

299.2——.

Account reprinted in photomechanical reprint of 299.1, *A History of the Amistad Captives Being a Circumstantial Account of the Capture of the Spanish Schooner Amistad, by the Africans on Board; Their Voyage, and Capture Near Long*

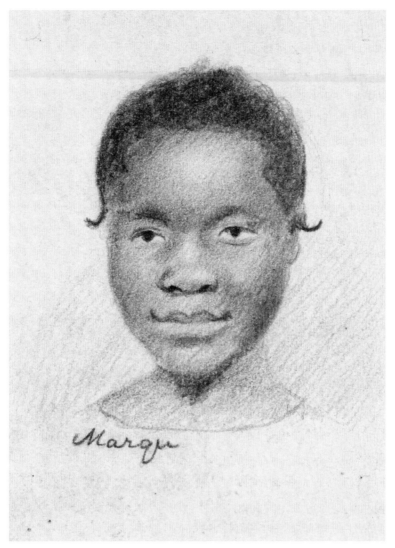

Figure 15: *Amistad* rebellion survivor Margru, also known as Sarah Kinson and Sarah Kinson Green (c. 1832– ?) in 1840. She was a child when enduring captivity and imprisonment during the trials of the *Amistad* survivors. After returning to Sierra Leone, she joined a Christian mission, whose sponsors later sent her back to the United States to complete schooling. Thereafter she resumed missionary work in Sierra Leone.

Source: Pencil drawing by William H. Townsend, Sketches of the *Amistad* Captives, GEN MSS 335, General Collection, Beinecke Rare Book and Manuscript Library, Yale University, New Haven, Connecticut.

Island, New York; with Biographical Sketches of Each of the Surviving Africans, edited by John Warner Barber.

New York [New York, U.S.A.]: Arno Press, 1969.
8vo (24 cm.): 32 p., folding plate, map, portraits.

299.3——.
Her account included in photomechanical reprint of portion of 299.1 as Appendix I "From *A History of the Amistad Captives* by John W. Barber (1840)" on pp. 159–167 in Mary Cable, *Black Odyssey: The Case of the Slave Ship Amistad.*

New York [New York, U.S.A.]: The Viking Press, [1971].
8vo (22 cm.): [8], 183 p., map, portraits.

300.1 Margru = Sarah Kinson = Sarah Kinson Green (c. 1832– ?)

Account translated into English by Kawweli (q.v. 301.1) printed on p. 15 in *A History of the Amistad Captives Being a Circumstantial Account of the Capture of the Spanish Schooner Amistad, by the Africans on Board,* edited by John Warner Barber (1798– 1885).

https://archive.
org/details/his-
toryofamistad-
00barb/page/14/
mode/2up
[see 300.1].

New Haven, Connecticut [U.S.A.]: Published by E. L. & J. W. Barber, Hitchcock and Stafford Printers, 1840.
8vo (23 cm.): 32 p., folding plate, map, portraits.

¶ Margru was born ca. 1832 in Pendemu, Mandinka country (see Map 3). Her own account reveals that her parents, four sisters, and two brothers were still living when she was taken as a young girl. Her father pawned her for a debt, and after he could not pay it, she was sold and placed on a slave ship. Margru was one of four children from the *Amistad* who were freed by a judge in Connecticut, U.S.A. (Map 17) on 19 March 1841. After returning to Sierra Leone (Map 4) in 1842 she joined the Komende Christian mission 120 miles south of Sherbro Island, where she became Christian, led prayer meetings, taught school, and assisted in household direction. From 1846 to 1849 she returned to the United States to study at the Oberlin Institute in the state of Ohio (Map 16), sponsored by the American Mission Association, after which she went briefly to New York City (Map 17) and then returned to Sierra Leone to work as a school mistress in the Komende Mission school. In 1852 she married an African man who also taught at the school and was Christian. By 1855 her husband was dismissed from the school for flagrant misconduct toward the girls, so the couple planned to move into the interior to start their own mission, but Margru's subsequent history is unknown. For more on her see Ellen NicKenzie Lawson with Marlene D. Merrill (eds.), *The Three Sarahs: Documents of Antebellum Black College Women* (New York: Edwin Mellen Press, 1984), pp. 3–45, which includes nine letters written by Margru while at Oberlin and at the Komende Mission station (see below). For a silhouette image of Margu done by an artist during her incarceration see 300.1, p. 15. For further information regarding the *Amistad* rebellion see note preceding entry 265.1.

300.2——.

Account reprinted in photomechanical reprint of 300.1, *A History of the Amistad Captives Being a Circumstantial Account of the Capture of the Spanish Schooner Amistad, by the Africans on Board; Their Voyage, and Capture Near Long Island, New York; with Biographical Sketches of Each of the Surviving Africans*, edited by John Warner Barber.

New York [New York, U.S.A.]: Arno Press, 1969.
8vo (24 cm.): 32 p., folding plate, map, portraits.

300.3——.

Her account included in photomechanical reprint of portion of 300.1 as Appendix I "From *A History of the Amistad Captives* by John W. Barber (1840)" on pp. 159–167 in Mary Cable, *Black Odyssey: The Case of the Slave Ship Amistad.*

New York [New York, U.S.A.]: The Viking Press, [1971].
8vo (22 cm.): [8], 183 p., map, portraits.

Also by Margru = Sarah Kinson = Sarah Kinson Green

+300-A.1 ——.

Nine letters from Margru while studying in Oberlin, Ohio [U.S.A.] and working at Komende Mission in Sierra Leone dated 1847–1855 printed on pp. 26–40 in Ellen N. Lawson with Marlene D. Merrill (eds.), *The Three Sarahs: Documents of Antebellum Black College Women* (New York: E. Mellen Press, 1984). Her third letter therein to Charles Avery dated 28 January 1854 was reportedly printed in the *Pittsburgh Gazette* and reprinted in the *American Missionary* magazine (December 1854).

301.1 Kawweli (ca. 1820–) = James Covey

Account related in English by Kawweli himself printed on p. 15 in *A History of the Amistad Captives Being a Circumstantial Account of the Capture of the Spanish Schooner Amistad, by the Africans on Board*, edited by John Warner Barber (1798–1885).

https://archive.org/details/historyofamistad-00barb/page/14/mode/2up [see 301.1].

New Haven, Connecticut [U.S.A.]: Published by E. L. & J. W. Barber, Hitchcock and Stafford Printers, 1840.
8vo (23 cm.): 32 p., folding plate, map, portraits.

¶ Kawweli (born ca. 1820), a Mende (modern Sierra Leone—see Map 4), was not an *Amistad* mutineer but rather a paid interpreter to whom John Warner Barber turned to enable him to interview the successful mutineers during their imprisonment. Kawweli's father was of Kono (modern eastern Sierra Leone) descent, and his mother Gissi. Kawweli was taken by three men from his parents' house at Golahung, carried to Bullom country, and sold as a slave to Bayimi, the king of the Bullom, who resided at Mani. There Kawweli lived for three years, employed to plant rice. He was sold to a Portuguese man who lived near Mani. This man carried him, with two or three hundred other enslaved men and women, to Lomboko. They were forced aboard a Portuguese slave ship that was intercepted at sea and taken to Sierra Leone, where Kawweli and the others were liberated. Kawweli lived there five or six years and learned to read and write English in the Church Missionary Society schools. In 1838 he enlisted as a sailor on a British warship, and a year later while the ship was docked in New York City (Map 17), his services as an interpreter for the *Amistad* rebels were procured. He expressed Christian sentiments in his letters. Kawweli went to Sierra Leone in 1842 with the rebels after they had been freed. He and others then went to Bullom country, where he had been previously enslaved. For a silhouette image of Kawweli cut by an artist during the trial of the *Amistad* rebels in Connecticut see 301.1, p. 15. For further information see note preceding entry 265.1. In addition to item +301-A.1 below, five letters Kawweli wrote to Lewis Tappan (not elsewhere published in print, to our knowledge) have been digitized and are available online at:

https://digitallibrary.tulane.edu/islandora/object/tulane%3A53404

https://digitallibrary.tulane.edu/islandora/object/tulane%3A53444

https://digitallibrary.tulane.edu/islandora/object/tulane%3A54190

https://digitallibrary.tulane.edu/islandora/object/tulane%3A54182

https://digitallibrary.tulane.edu/islandora/object/tulane%3A53598

301.2——.

A slightly shorter version of 301.1 appears on p. 12 within the issue-long article "Documents relating to the Africans taken in the Amistad" in *The American and Foreign A. S. [i.e., Anti-Slavery] Reporter*, Extra, December 1840, which includes an image of him.

New York [New York, U.S.A.]: American and Foreign Anti-Slavery Society, December **1840.**

4to: 16 p. *The editors thank Dr. Joseph Yannielli for calling this item to their attention.*

https://digitalcommons.law.yale.edu/cgi/viewcontent.cgi?article=1016&context=amtrials

301.3——.

Account included in photomechanical reprint of 301.1, *A History of the Amistad Captives Being a Circumstantial Account of the Capture of the Spanish Schooner Amistad, by the Africans on Board; Their Voyage, and Capture Near Long Island, New York; with Biographical Sketches of Each of the Surviving Africans*, edited by John Warner Barber.

New York [New York, U.S.A.]: Arno Press, **1969.**

8vo (24 cm.): 32 p., folding plate, map, portraits.

301.4——.

His account included in photomechanical reprint of portion of 301.1 as Appendix I "From *A History of the Amistad Cap-*

tives by John W. Barber (1840)" on pp. 159–167 in Mary Cable, *Black Odyssey: The Case of the Slave Ship Amistad.*

New York [New York, U.S.A.]: The Viking Press, [**1971**].

8vo (22 cm.): [8], 183 p., map, portraits.

Also by Kawweli = James Covey

+301-A.1——.

Letter dated 5 November 1840 to Lewis Tappan at New York City printed on p. 12 within the issue-long article "Documents relating to the Africans taken in the Amistad" in *The American and Foreign A. S. [i.e., Anti-Slavery] Reporter*, Extra, December 1840. *The compilers thank Dr. Joseph Yannielli for calling this item to their attention.*

https://digitalcommons.law.yale.edu/cgi/viewcontent.cgi?article=1016&context=amtrials

302.1   Unnamed Asante man

"The Lives of Two Ashantee, Coast of Guinea, Slaves, Who Were Sold in Rio Grand."

[Portsmouth? England: unnamed printer for the unnamed Two Asantee, 1840?]

Small broadside, [1] p., illustrated with three relief cuts, verso blank. Wide headlines followed by text in three columns separated by wiggly rules, all within ornamental border; full-width final single-line statement immediately inside bottom border: "Please to purchase a paper of a poor Ashantee. —— Price One Penny."

Note: Printing place and year posited by the British Library, which holds the only reported exemplar (General Reference Collection shelfmark HS.74/1251.(8.)).

Hogg 1482.

Full text: https://huskiecommons.lib.niu.edu/history-500african-voices/174/

¶ This Asante man (from modern Ghana—see Map 5) speaks for himself and a second man. The speaker was taken as a boy from the Rio Grande (probably the Volta, in modern southeastern Ghana) on a slave ship probably to Charleston, South Carolina, U.S.A. (Map 15). After suffering severe treatment there, he escaped to a German ship that took him to Hamburg, Germany (Map 7), from which port he was taken aboard a United States ship to the Spanish colonial city of Havana, Cuba in the Caribbean (Map 12), probably to be sold as a slave, but a British ship entered the harbor, freed him, and took him to Portsmouth, England (Map 8). His broadside comprises prose and poetry reflecting his reverence for Christianity and includes calls to end slavery and Christianize Africa.

303.0 Francisco Carabalí (ca. 1802–)

Statement made in Guaminao, Santiago de Cuba, 23 June **1840**, preserved in Archivo Nacional de la República de Cuba (ANC), **La Habana, Cuba,** Miscelánea de Expedientes, 235/H.

¶ Francisco identified as Carabalí (probably Calabar in the Cross River region of modern Nigeria and northwestern Cameroon—see Map 5). After transport on a slave ship to the Spanish colony of Cuba in the Caribbean (Map 12) he was sold in or near Guaminao, Santiago de Cuba. He was single, enslaved, and a contramayoral on a coffee plantation when he became involved in a violent attack against a mayoral. Francisco claimed at the later hearing that he was trying to help the mayoral, but other witnesses testified that he, Nicolás Gangá (below), and a Cuban-born man were the lead figures in the attack. As punishment Francisco and the other two men received two hundred lashes and ten years imprisonment in Africa, followed by exile.

303.1——.

Statement printed on p. 138 in *La esclavitud desde la esclavitud: La visión de los siervos* by Gloria García Rodríguez.

México [Distrito Federal, Estados Unidos Mexicanos]: Centro de Investigación Científica "Ing. Jorge L Tamayo," **1996.**

8vo (21 cm.): 251 p.

303.2——.

Statement printed on p. 124 *La esclavitud desde la esclavitud,* by Gloria García.

La Habana [Cuba]: Editorial de Ciencias Sociales, 2003.
8vo (21 cm.): xx, 222 p.

303.3——.

English translation of statement printed on p. 116 in *Voices of the Enslaved in Nineteenth-Century Cuba: A Documentary History,* edited by Gloria García Rodríguez. Translated [from 300.1] by Nancy L. Westrate; foreword by Ada Ferrer.

Chapel Hill [North Carolina, U.S.A.]: University of North Carolina Press, **2011.**
8vo (23.5 cm.): xviii, 220 p.

304.0 Nicolás Gangá (ca. 1795–)

Statement made in Guaminao, Santiago de Cuba, 23 June **1840**, preserved in Archivo Nacional de la República de Cuba (ANC), **La Habana, Cuba,** Miscelánea de Expedientes, 235/H.

Full text: https://huskiecommons.lib.niu.edu/history-500african-voices/175/

¶ Nicolás identified as Gangá (modern Banta region southern Sierra Leone—see Map 4). After transport to the Spanish colony of Cuba in the Caribbean (Map 12) on a slave ship he was sold and worked on a coffee plantation near Guaminao. Still single in 1840, he and several others (including Francisco Carabali, q.v. 303.0) attacked, tied up, and whipped their mayoral, who had habitually bludgeoned Nicolás and recently knocked out some of his teeth. At the hearing Nicolás admitted that he was the first to attack the mayoral, but only after the latter had begun beating him with a stick again. As punishment he and two others (including Francisco Carabalí) received two hundred lashes and ten years imprisonment in Africa, followed by exile.

Full text: https://huskiecommons.lib.niu.edu/history-500african-voices/176/

304.1——.

Statement printed on p. 138 in *La esclavitud desde la esclavitud: La visión de los siervos* by Gloria García Rodríguez.

México [Distrito Federal, Estados Unidos Mexicanos]: Centro de Investigación Científica "Ing. Jorge L Tamayo," **1996.**
8vo (21 cm.): 251 p.

304.2——.

Statement printed on p. 124 *La esclavitud desde la esclavitud,* by Gloria García.

La Habana [Cuba]: Editorial de Ciencias Sociales, 2003.
8vo (21 cm.): xx, 222 p.

304.3——.

English translation of statement printed on pp. 116–117 in *Voices of the Enslaved in Nineteenth-Century Cuba: A Documentary History,* edited by Gloria García Rodríguez. Translated [from 304.1] by Nancy L. Westrate; foreword by Ada Ferrer.

Chapel Hill [North Carolina, U.S.A.]: University of North Carolina Press, **2011.**
8vo (23.5 cm.): xviii, 220 p.

305.0 Victor Gangá

Statement recorded in Rancho Veloz, Cuba on 31 July **1840**, preserved in Archivo Nacional de la República de Cuba (ANC), **La Habana, Cuba,** Miscelánea de Expedientes, 235/E.

¶ Victor identified as Gangá (modern Banta region southern Sierra Leone—see Map 4) and was transported to the Spanishi colony of Cuba in the Caribbean (Map 12) on a slave ship and sold. Still enslaved, he was a contramayoral on a plantation in or near Rancho Veloz in 1840, still single, when caught in the middle of a violent attack on his mayoral led by Malade (q.v. 308.0) and several other Lucumí. Victor witnessed most of what happened but claimed that it was wholly a Lucumí affair in which he was not involved.

305.1——.

Statement printed on pp. 139–140 in *La esclavitud desde la esclavitud: La visión de los siervos* by Gloria García Rodríguez.

México [Distrito Federal, Estados Unidos Mexicanos]: Centro de Investigación Científica "Ing. Jorge L Tamayo," 1996. 8vo (21 cm.): 251 p.

305.2——.

Statement printed on p. 125 *La esclavitud desde la esclavitud,* by Gloria García.

La Habana [Cuba]: Editorial de Ciencias Sociales, 2003. 8vo (21 cm.): xx, 222 p.

305.3——.

English translation of statement printed on p. 118 in *Voices of the Enslaved in Nineteenth-Century Cuba: A Documentary History*, edited by Gloria García Rodríguez. Translated [from 305.1] by Nancy L. Westrate; foreword by Ada Ferrer.

Chapel Hill [North Carolina, U.S.A.]: University of North Carolina Press, 2011. 8vo (23.5 cm.): xviii, 220 p.

Full text: https://huskiecommons.lib.niu.edu/history-500african-voices/177/

306.0 Nicolás Lucumí

Statement recorded in Rancho Veloz, Cuba on 31 July 1840, preserved in Archivo Nacional de la República de Cuba (ANC), La Habana, Cuba, Miscelánea de Expedientes, 235/E.

¶ Nicolás identified as Lucumí, a New World designation for people who were primarily Yorùbá (modern day Nigeria, Benin and Togo—see Map 5). After transport to the Spanish colony of Cuba in the Caribbean (Map 12) on a slave ship and sale he worked enslaved on a plantation in or near Rancho Veolz. In 1840 he and other fellow Lucumí supported Malade (q.v. 308.0), who had murdered an abusive mayoral. Nicolás told authorities that, even though he knew it was a crime, he and the others followed

Full text: https://huskiecommons.lib.niu.edu/history-500african-voices/178/

Malade because they had loved and respected him as a leader back in their native country.

306.1——.

Statement printed on pp. 140–141 in *La esclavitud desde la esclavitud: La visión de los siervos* by Gloria García Rodríguez.

México [Distrito Federal, Estados Unidos Mexicanos]: Centro de Investigación Científica "Ing. Jorge L Tamayo," 1996. 8vo (21 cm.): 251 p.

306.2——.

Statement printed on p. 126 *La esclavitud desde la esclavitud,* by Gloria García.

La Habana [Cuba]: Editorial de Ciencias Sociales, 2003. 8vo (21 cm.): xx, 222 p.

306.3——.

English translation of statement printed on pp. 118–119 in *Voices of the Enslaved in Nineteenth-Century Cuba: A Documentary History*, edited by Gloria García Rodríguez. Translated [from 306.1] by Nancy L. Westrate; foreword by Ada Ferrer.

Chapel Hill [North Carolina, U.S.A.]: University of North Carolina Press, 2011. 8vo (23.5 cm.): xviii, 220 p.

307.0 Pedro Lucumí

Statement recorded in Rancho Veloz, Cuba on 31 July 1840, preserved in Archivo Nacional de la República de Cuba (ANC), La Habana, Cuba, Miscelánea de Expedientes, 235/E.

¶ Pedro identified as Lucumí, a New World designation for people who were primarily Yorùbá (modern day Nigeria, Benin and Togo—see Map 5). After transport to the Spanish colony of Cuba in the Caribbean (Map 12) on a slave ship not long before 1840, he was sold and worked enslaved in or near Rancho Veloz. In 1840 he became involved in the incident in which Malade (q.v. 308.0) murdered an abusive mayoral. At the later hearing, Pedro, by then an elderly man, spoke through an interpreter and explained that killing was not necessarily a crime in his home country.

Full text: https://huskiecommons.lib.niu.edu/history-500african-voices/179/

307.1——.

Statement printed on p. 141 in *La esclavitud desde la esclavitud: La visión de los siervos* by Gloria García Rodríguez.

México [Distrito Federal, Estados Unidos Mexicanos]: Centro de Investigación Científica "Ing. Jorge L Tamayo," **1996**. 8vo (21 cm.): 251 p.

307.2———.

Statement printed on p. 126 *La esclavitud desde la esclavitud*, by Gloria García.

La Habana [Cuba]: Editorial de Ciencias Sociales, **2003**. 8vo (21 cm.): xx, 222 p.

307.3———.

English translation of statement printed on p. 119 in *Voices of the Enslaved in Nineteenth-Century Cuba: A Documentary History*, edited by Gloria García Rodríguez. Translated [from 307.1] by Nancy L. Westrate; foreword by Ada Ferrer.

Chapel Hill [North Carolina, U.S.A.]: University of North Carolina Press, **2011**. 8vo (23.5 cm.): xviii, 220 p.

308.0 Malade = Fermin Lucumí (–1840?)

Statement recorded in Rancho Veloz, Cuba on 31 July **1840**, preserved in Archivo Nacional de la República de Cuba (ANC), **La Habana, Cuba,** Miscelánea de Expedientes, 235/E.

¶ Malade identified as Lucumí, a New World designation for people who were primarily Yorùbá (modern day Nigeria, Benin and Togo—see Map 5). After transport to the Spanish col-

Full text: https:// huskiecommons. lib.niu.edu/history-500african-voices/180/

ony of Cuba in the Caribbean (Map 12) on a slave ship he was sold and worked enslaved on a plantation in or near Rancho Veloz. In 1840 he retaliated against an abusive mayoral by decapitating him with a work machete. While fleeing, several fellow Lucumí on the plantation noticed his distress and followed him into the scrubland, where they were later captured. Speaking through an interpreter at his hearing, Malade said he only killed because he had been attacked. Although a resolution to his case is not in the file, he was probably executed for his actions.

308.1———.

Statement printed on p. 141 in *La esclavitud desde la esclavitud: La visión de los siervos*, by Gloria García Rodríguez.

México [Distrito Federal, Estados Unidos Mexicanos]: Centro de Investigación Científica "Ing. Jorge L Tamayo," **1996**. 8vo (21 cm.): 251 p.

308.2———.

Statement printed on p. 126 in *La esclavitud desde la esclavitud*, by Gloria García.

La Habana [Cuba]: Editorial de Ciencias Sociales, **2003**. 8vo (21 cm.): xx, 222 p.

308.3———.

English translation of statement printed on p. 119 in *Voices of the Enslaved in Nineteenth-Century Cuba: A Documentary History*, edited by Gloria García Rodríguez. Translated [from 308.1] by Nancy L. Westrate; foreword by Ada Ferrer.

Chapel Hill [North Carolina, U.S.A.]: University of North Carolina Press, **2011**. 8vo (23.5 cm.): xviii, 220 p.

1841

309.1 Gavino Pinedo = Gabino Mamé (ca. 1802–)

"Declaration of Gavino" spoken to Great Britain's abolitionist Consul David Turnbull at Havana, Cuba, on 18 September **1841** [*sic*], printed on pp. 82–83 of *Class B. Correspondence with Spain, Portugal, Brazil, the Netherlands, Sweden, Monte Video, the Argentine Federation, and Bolivia. Relative to the Slave Trade. From January 1 to December 31, 1842* [*sic*], *inclusive. Presented to both Houses of Parliament by command of her Majesty.*

https://babel.hathitrust.org/cgi/pt?id=coo.31924078180035&view=1up&seq=442

London [England]: Printed by William Clowes and Sons, Stamford Street, for Her Majesty's Stationery Office, **1843**. Folio (33 cm.): xviii, 498 p. Within: Great Britain, Parliamentary Papers, *General Report of the Emigration Commissioners*, vol. 2.

¶ While in the Spanish colony of Cuba in the Caribbean (see Map 12), Gavino identified as Lucumí, a New World designation for people who were primarily Yorùbá (modern day Nigeria, Benin and Togo). In 1824, while still in Africa, he and companions were searching for food on a river he called the Ossa (probably the Osse or Osun, southwest Nigeria—Map 5) when they encountered two warring parties and were captured. After several months imprisoned in a nearby Spanish barracoon, they were forced aboard the Spanish brigantine *Orestes*, which sailed for Cuba with 285 closely packed enslaved people, almost all Lucumí. After many of these people had died, the *Orestes* reached the Bahamas (Map 11), whereupon two British schooners pursued it until it ran aground on one of the keys. Gavino was among the survivors taken by the HMS *Speedwell* to Cuba, where they remained imprisoned in another barracoon many weeks until a court freed them on 15 March 1826. Gavino was then forced into a five-year apprenticeship under the widow Doña Maria Luisa de la Paz. As an *emancipado*, Gavino worked as an *aquadore* (door-to-door water deliverer), ceding all profits to the widow. The widow succeeded in bribing officials to extend Gavino's five-year apprenticeship four times. In 1828 he was baptized without Christian instruction. Years later, when Gavino wanted to marry an enslaved woman with whom he had long enjoyed a relationship (Candalaria), he secured Christian instruction from a priest. Permission to marry was nonetheless denied. In 1840 David Turnbull, British Consul and Superintendent of Liberated Africans in Havana, directed an interpreter to interview Gavino during Turnbull's investigation of Spanish abuses of Cuban *emancipados*. After British diplomats pressured the Spanish government, Gavino and many other mistreated Cuban *emancipados* were fully emancipated on 1 April 1842. For more on Gavino see Randy J. Sparks, "Gavino of the Lucumí Nation: David Turnbull and the Liberated Africans of Havana," pp. 198–211 in *Liberated Africans and the Abolition of the Slave Trade, 1807–1896*, edited by Richard Anderson and Henry B. Lovejoy (Rochester, NY: University of Rochester Press, 2020).

309.2——.

His account, digested from 309.1 or from the original manuscript underlying it or from David Turnbull's personal knowledge or from all or some of these, printed on pp. 135–136 in *The Jamaica Movement for Promoting the enforcement of Slave-Trade Treaties; with statements of Fact, Convention, and Law: prepared by the request of the Kingston Committee* [by David Turnbull].

London [England]: Charles Gilpin, 5, Bishopsgate Without. Printed for gratuitous distribution, 1850. Tpv: London: Jacob Unwin, Gresham Steam Press, Bucklersbury.
8vo (22 cm.): [iv], 430 p. Editor David Turnbull's Dedication dated on p. [iii]: Jamaica, 22nd October, 1849.

309.3——.

His digested account reprinted explicitly from 309.2 on p. 272 in "The Emancipados and Their Fatherland," *Church Missionary Intelligencer*, 6: 267–279.

London [England]: Seeley, Jackson, Halliday, Fleet Street; and Hanover Street, Hanover Square; T. Hatchard, Piccadilly;

and J. Nisbet and Co., Berners Street, [December] 1855. Tpv: W. M. Watts, Crown Court, Temple Bar.
8vo (21 cm.).
https://archive.org/details/1855TheChurchMissionaryIntelligencer/page/n287/mode/1up

309.4——. [Photomechanical reprint of 309.2]

His account digested from 309.2 or from the original manuscript underlying it or from David Turnbull's personal knowledge printed on pp. 135–136 in *The Jamaica Movement for Promoting the enforcement of Slave-trade Treaties, with statements of fact, convention, and law.*

New York [New York, U.S.A.] Negro Universities Press, 1969.
8vo (22 cm.): [iv], 430 p.

310.1 James Macaulay

Account printed on pp. 204 and 210–211 (and reference to Macaulay on p. 171) in *Journals of the Rev. James Frederick Schön and Mr. Samuel Crowther: Who, with the Sanction of Her Majesty's Government, Accompanied the Expedition Up the Niger, in 1841, in Behalf of the Church Missionary Society.*

https://archive.org/details/journalsofrevjam-00scho/page/206/mode/1up

London [England]: Hatchard and Son, Piccadilly; Nisbet and Co., Berners Street; Seeleys, Fleet Street 1842. Tpv: London: Richard Watts, Crown Court, Temple Bar.
8vo (21 cm.): xxii, 393 p., map.

¶ Macaulay was born at Mamagia in Nupe on the Niger River near its confluence with the Benue River (modern Nigeria—see Map 5). When just a boy he was enslaved by Fulani (Fula, Fulbi or Peul peoples throughout West Africa) and ca. 1821 taken to Egba (modern western Nigeria), where he was sold to a Kakanda Muslim cleric, who sold him to a Budda woman. She in turn sold him to King Obi, who sold him with others to a Spanish slave ship captain. A British warship intercepted them at sea and took Macaulay to Sierra Leone (Map 4). He worked there as an interpreter, then in 1841 joined the Niger Expedition, with which he traveled to his old homeland. There he met his sister (whom he had not seen in twenty years) and a woman who had sold him decades earlier.

310.2——.

Variant account printed on pp. 109 and 117–118 in vol. 2 of Capt. William Allen and T. R. H. Thomson, *A Narrative of the Expedition Sent by Her Majesty's Government to the River Niger in 1841. Under the Command of Capt. H. D.*

Trotter, R.N.... Published with the Sanction of the Colonial Office and the Admiralty.

London [England]: Richard Bentley, New Burlington Street, Publisher in Ordinary to Her Majesty, **1848.** Tpv: London: Printed by Schultz and Co., 13, Poland Street.

2 vols., 8vo (22 cm.).

https://babel.hathitrust.org/cgi/pt?id=uc1.b3114049&view=1up&seq=129

310.3———.

Variant account 310.2 reprinted on pp. 109 and 117–118 in vol. 2 of photomechanical reprint of Capt. William Allen and T. R. H. Thomson, *A Narrative of the Expedition Sent by Her Majesty's Government to the River Niger in 1841* (London, 1848) with imprint:

New York [New York, U.S.A.]: Johnson Reprint Corp., **1967.**
2 vols., 8vo (23 cm.). Series: Landmarks in Anthropology.

310.4———.

Variant account 310.2 reprinted on pp. 109 and 117–118 in vol. 2 of photomechanical reprint of Capt. William Allen and T. R. H. Thomson, *A Narrative of the Expedition Sent by Her Majesty's Government to the River Niger in 1841* (London, 1848) with imprint:

London [England]: Frank Cass, **1968.**
2 vols., 8vo (22 cm.). Series: Cass Library of African Studies, Travels and Narratives, 35.

310.5———.

Account 310.1 reprinted on pp. 171, 204, and 210–211 in photomechanical reprint of *Journals of the Rev. James Frederick Schön and Mr. Samuel Crowther: Who, with the Sanction of Her Majesty's Government, Accompanied the Expedition Up the Niger, in 1841, in Behalf of the Church Missionary Society.*

London [England]: Frank Cass, **1970.**

8vo (22 cm.): xviii, [7], xxiii, 393 p., including new introduction by J. F. Ade Ajayi. Series: Cass Library of African Studies, 18.

311.1 Samba Makumba (1776–) = Simon Boissere

Account printed on pp. 108–112 in George Truman, John Jackson, and Thomas B. Longstreth, *Narrative of a Visit to the West Indies, in 1840 and 1841.*

Philadelphia [Pennsylvania, U.S.A.]: Merrihew and Thompson, Printers. No. 7 Carter's Alley, **1844.**
12mo (17 cm.): 130 p. "The following narrative has been extracted from notes taken during a visit to the West Indies in 1840 and 1841" (p. [3]).

https://babel.hathitrust.org/cgi/pt?id=hvd.32044080401201&view=1up&seq=124

¶ Samba Makumba, by descent a chief and Muslim cleric among the Mandinka, was from Fuuta Toro (modern Senegal—see Map 3). Ca. 1797 he was captured in war, forcibly sent on a slave ship to the British Caribbean colony of Trinidad (Map 11), and there sold to a French planter. He spoke several languages in addition to Mandinka, including Arabic and French. Eventually he became a plantation supervisor and earned enough money to purchase his freedom. As a Muslim cleric, he had a large following among Mandinka who practiced Islam in a community and pooled their resources to purchase and free Mandinka from slave ships in Trinidad and surrounding islands. In 1841 he told his life story to Quakers passing through Trinidad.

311.2———.

Account printed on pp. 108–112 in photomechanical reprint of 311.1 with imprint:

Freeport, New York [U.S.A.]: Books for Libraries Press, **1972.**
8vo (23 cm.): 130 p. Series: Black Heritage Library Collection.

1842

312.1 George Coffee

His autobiographical answers to questions, printed under heading "Questions addressed to a Native of Grand Sesters, called by Europeans George Coffee, and Answers taken down on the spot as delivered, respecting Religion, etc." on

https://babel.hathitrust.org/cgi/pt?id=umn.31951002323758q&view=1up&seq=290

pp. 280–281 of Nr. 15—Report of Commissioner of Inquiry on the West Coast of Africa, Sierra Leone, in Part II Appendix and Index of Great Britain, House of Commons, *Report from the Select Committee on the West Coast of Africa; Together with the Minutes of Evidence, Index, and Appendix. Ordered, by the House of Commons, to be Printed, 5 August 1842.*

[**London, England:** House of Commons, **1842.**]
2 vols., folio (34 cm.).
FN 000117.

¶ Coffee identified himself as Kru, a native of Grand Sesters, now Grand Cess, on the Liberian coast (see Map 3). He was not married, and his people were neither Christian nor Muslim. (They had previously rejected visiting Christian missionaries.) Presumably liberated from a slave ship at sea by the British ship *May* and taken to Sierra Leone (Map 4). While on board the *May* he answered questions about his natal country's religion, customs, wildlife, *etc.*

313.1 W. Henry Graham

"Letter from a Native African," dated York, Sierra Leone, 6 October 1842, Graham to Lewis Tappan at New York City printed in the newspaper *American and Foreign Anti-Slavery Reporter* 2: 108–09.

Full text: https://huskiecommons.lib.niu.edu/history-500african-voices/181/

New York [New York, U.S.A.]: American and Foreign Antislavery Society, 1 January 1843.
4to (32 cm.).
https://go-gale-com.auth.lib.niu.edu/ps/navigateToIssue?volume=&loadFormat=page&issueNumber=&userGroupName=deka36484&inPS=true&mCode=057E&prodId=AAHP&issueDate=118430101

¶ A native of Akuh (modern southwestern Nigeria—see Map 5), Graham (as he later called himself) was stolen from his parents, sold to a Spanish trader, and in 1829 forced aboard a slave ship. A British warship intercepted this ship at sea and took Graham and the others to Sierra Leone (Map 4). Graham attended school in the village of York, Sierra Leone, but did not have the opportunity for public worship until 1837, after which he embraced Christianity. He met the successful *Amistad* rebels (qq.v. 265.1 to 301.1) after they had returned to Sierra Leone in 1842.

313.2——.

Graham's 6 October 1842 letter to Tappan printed from 313.1 on pp. 45–46 in *Slave Testimony: Two Centuries of Letters, Speeches, Interviews, and Autobiographies*, edited by John W. Blassingame.

Baton Rouge [Louisiana, U.S.A.]: Louisiana State University Press, **1977**.
8vo (23 cm.): lxv, 777 p.

313.3——. [Second printing of 313.2]

Graham's 6 October 1842 letter to Tappan printed from 313.1 on pp. 45–46 in *Slave Testimony: Two Centuries of Letters, Speeches, and Autobiographies*, edited by John W. Blassingame.

Baton Rouge [Louisiana, U.S.A.]: Louisiana State University Press, **1977**. Second printing.
8vo (23 cm.): lxv, 777 p., illus., portraits.

313.4——. [Another printing of 313.2]

Graham's 6 October 1842 letter to Tappan printed from 313.1 on pp. 45–46 in *Slave Testimony: Two Centuries of Letters, Speeches, and Autobiographies*, edited by John W. Blassingame.

Baton Rouge [Louisiana, U.S.A.]: Louisiana State University Press, **1979**. 1979 printing.
8vo (23 cm.): lxv, 777 p., illus., portraits.

313.5——. [Another printing of 313.2]

Graham's 6 October 1842 letter to Tappan printed from 313.1 on pp. 45–46 in *Slave Testimony: Two Centuries of Letters, Speeches, and Autobiographies*, edited by John W. Blassingame.

Baton Rouge [Louisiana, U.S.A.]: Louisiana State University Press **1980**. 1980 printing.
8vo (23 cm.): lxv, 777 p., illus., portraits.

313.6——. [Another printing of 313.2]

Graham's 6 October 1842 letter to Tappan printed from 313.1 on n pp. 45–46 in *Slave Testimony: Two Centuries of Letters, Speeches, and Autobiographies*, edited by John W. Blassingame.

Baton Rouge [Louisiana, U.S.A.]: Louisiana State University Press, **1989**. 1989 printing.
8vo (23 cm.): lxv, 777 p., illus., portraits.

313.7——. [Another printing of 313.2]

Graham's 6 October 1842 letter to Tappan printed from 313.1 on pp. 45–46 in *Slave Testimony: Two Centuries of Letters, Speeches, and Autobiographies*, edited by John W. Blassingame.

Baton Rouge [Louisiana, U.S.A.]: Louisiana State University Press, **1998**. 1998 printing.
8vo (23 cm.): lxv, 777 p., illus., portraits.

313.8——. [Another printing of 313.2]

Graham's 6 October 1842 letter to Tappan printed from 313.1 on pp. 45–46 in *Slave Testimony: Two Centuries of Letters, Speeches, and Autobiographies*, edited by John W. Blassingame.

Baton Rouge [Louisiana, U.S.A.]: Louisiana State University Press, **2002**. 2002 printing.
8vo (23 cm.): lxv, 777 p., illus., portraits.

313.9——. [Another printing of 313.2]

Graham's 6 October 1842 letter to Tappan printed from 313.1 on pp. 45–46 in *Slave Testimony: Two Centuries of Letters, Speeches, and Autobiographies*, edited by John W. Blassingame.

Baton Rouge [Louisiana, U.S.A.]: Louisiana State University Press, **2009**.
8vo (24 cm.): lxv, 777 p., illus., portraits.

314.1   J. B.

Account included in a letter to the editor signed in type V. D. M. (i.e., Verbi Dei Minister = minister of the word of God, probably a dissenting English minister) printed under heading "Some Account of J. B., a Native of Africa, and Once a West Indian Slave" on pp. 84–85 of vol. 2, no. 20 (June 1842) in the monthly periodical *The Friend of Africa. By the Committee of the Society for the Extinction of the Slave Trade and for the Civilization of Africa.*

[Colophon] **London [England]:** Printed by Thomas Richard Harrison, of No. 45, St. Martin's Lane, in the Parish of St. Martin in the Fields; and Published by John William Parker, No. 445, West Strand **[June 1842]**. Price 2 d. Stamped 3 p.
8vo (23 cm.).
FN 000100.

https://archive.org/details/friendafrica00afrigoog/page/n321/mode/1up

¶ J. B. was born in Africa and taken in the slave trade to the West Indies before 1808. Enslaved there, he worked on a coffee plantation, became Christian, worshipped in the church "some years ago in the island of Jamaica" (see Map 13), learned to read, and taught himself writing and arithmetic. When his enslaved plantation community was threatened with sale and separation, J. B. led a successful armed uprising against the local constables, who at least temporarily did not enforce their separation and departure.

315.0   Limbano Carabalí

Statement recorded on 22 July **1842** in Macurijes, Cuba, preserved in Archivo Nacional de la República de Cuba (ANC), **La Habana, Cuba,** Comisión Militar, 28/I.

¶ Limbano identified as Carabalí (probably Calabar in the Cross River region of modern Nigeria and northwestern Cameroon—see Map 5). Af-

Full text: https://huskiecommons.lib.niu.edu/history-500african-voices/182/

ter transport to the Spanish colony of Cuba in the Caribbean (Map 12) on a slave ship, he was eventually sold to a sugar plantation, where he had become a contramayoral by 1842 and was single. In that year he was peripherally involved in a violent incident involving Jorge (q.v. 317.0) and other Lucumí people on the plantation. At the hearing later Limbano explained that he had been in the cane field with forty-nine others that day when he heard the commotion in the distance and saw the Lucuo halt and leave him alone in the cane field, umís in the field with him begin running toward where Jorge was. They ignored Limbano's plea until a white man found him and took him to the plantation houses.

315.1——.

Statement printed on p. 157 in *La esclavitud desde la esclavitud: La visión de los siervos* by Gloria García Rodríguez.

México [Distrito Federal, Estados Unidos Mexicanos]: Centro de Investigación Científica "Ing. Jorge L Tamayo," **1996**.
8vo (21 cm.): 251 p.

315.2 ——.

Printed on p. 141 in *La esclavitud desde la esclavitud*, by Gloria García.

La Habana [Cuba]: Editorial de Ciencias Sociales, **2003**.
8vo (21 cm.): xx, 222 p.

315.3 ——.

English translation of statement printed on pp. 133–134 in *Voices of the Enslaved in Nineteenth-Century Cuba: A Documentary History*, edited by Gloria García Rodríguez. Translated [from 315.1] by Nancy L. Westrate; foreword by Ada Ferrer.

Chapel Hill [North Carolina, U.S.A.]: University of North Carolina Press, **2011**.
8vo (23.5 cm.): xviii, 220 p.

316.0   Anselmo Carabalí

Statement recorded on 22 July **1842** in Macurijes, Cuba, preserved in Archivo Nacional de la República de Cuba (ANC), **La Habana, Cuba,** Comisión Militar, 28/I.

¶ Anselmo identified as Carabalí (probably Calabar in the Cross River region of modern Nigeria and northwestern Cameroon—see Map 5). After transport to the Spanish colony of Cuba in the Caribbean (Map 12) on a slave ship and eventual enslavement on a sugar plantation near Macurijes,

Full text: https://huskiecommons.lib.niu.edu/history-500african-voices/183/

in 1842 he became peripherally involved in a violent incident involving Jorge (q.v. 317.0) and other Lucumí people on the plantation. At the hearing Anselmo explained that while supervising his multiethnic crew in the cane fields, an enslaved man told them that soldiers and had tied up and wounded a Lucumí, after which all the Lucumí in Anselmo's crew ran to the site to assist their compatriot.

316.1——.

Statement printed on p. 157 in *La esclavitud desde la esclavitud: La visión de los siervos* by Gloria García Rodríguez.

México [Distrito Federal, Estados Unidos Mexicanos]: Centro de Investigación Científica "Ing. Jorge L Tamayo," **1996.** 8vo (21 cm.): 251 p.

316.2 ——.

Printed on p. 141 in *La esclavitud desde la esclavitud*, by Gloria García.

La Habana [Cuba]: Editorial de Ciencias Sociales, 2003. 8vo (21 cm.): xx, 222 p.

316.3 ——.

English translation of statement printed on p. 134 in *Voices of the Enslaved in Nineteenth-Century Cuba: A Documentary History*, edited by Gloria García Rodríguez. Translated [from 316.1] by Nancy L. Westrate; foreword by Ada Ferrer.

Chapel Hill [North Carolina, U.S.A.]: University of North Carolina Press, **2011.** 8vo (23.5 cm.): xviii, 220 p.

317.0 Jorge Lucumí (1820–)

Statement recorded on 22 July **1842** in Macurijes, Cuba, preserved in Archivo Nacional de la República de Cuba (ANC), **La Habana, Cuba,** Comisión Militar, 28/I.

Full text: https://huskiecommons.lib.niu.edu/history-500african-voices/184/

¶ Jorge identified as Lucumí, a New World designation for people who were primarily Yorùbá (modern day Nigeria, Benin and Togo—see Map 5). After transport to the Spanish colony of Cuba in the Caribbean (Map 12) on a slave ship, he was eventually sold to a sugar plantation near Macurijes. He was single in 1842, when he became the center of a violent incident on the estate. He testified later that while visiting a friend in the infirmary, his higher mayoral ordered him to restrain another enslaved man for punishment. Jorge refused because his hand was injured. Later many whites and soldiers rushed into the infirmary,

bludgeoned Jorge and his friend on the heads, and took them to the stocks. Later in the day the Lucumís on the plantation forced the mayoral to release Jorge and his friend. Jorge explained that he knew nothing of their threats because he had been locked up in the boiler room. The Lucumís set fire to the estate's tile work before soldiers chased them into the fields. Jorge was sentenced to eight years imprisonment in Cueta for his role in the affair.

317.1 ——.

Statement printed on pp. 157–158 in *La esclavitud desde la esclavitud: La visión de los siervos* by Gloria García Rodríguez.

México [Distrito Federal, Estados Unidos Mexicanos]: Centro de Investigación Científica "Ing. Jorge L Tamayo," **1996.** 8vo (21 cm.): 251 p.

317.2 ——.

Printed on pp. 141–142 in *La esclavitud desde la esclavitud*, by Gloria García.

La Habana [Cuba]: Editorial de Ciencias Sociales, 2003. 8vo (21 cm.): xx, 222 p.

317.3 ——.

English translation of statement printed on p. 134 in *Voices of the Enslaved in Nineteenth-Century Cuba: A Documentary History*, edited by Gloria García Rodríguez. Translated [from 317.1] by Nancy L. Westrate; foreword by Ada Ferrer.

Chapel Hill [North Carolina, U.S.A.]: University of North Carolina Press, **2011.** 8vo (23.5 cm.): xviii, 220 p.

318.0 Gregorio Lucumí

Statement recorded on 22 July **1842** in Macurijes, Cuba, preserved in Archivo Nacional de la República de Cuba (ANC), **La Habana, Cuba,** Comisión Militar, 28/I.

Full text: https://huskiecommons.lib.niu.edu/history-500african-voices/185/

¶ Gregorio identified as Lucumí, a New World designation for people who were primarily Yorùbá (modern day Nigeria, Benin and Togo—see Map 5). After transport to the Spanish colony of Cuba in the Caribbean (Map 12) on a slave ship, he was eventually sold to a sugar plantation near Macurijes. In 1842 he was single and claimed at the hearing that he was working in the fields with others, supervised by Limbano (q.v. 315.0), when others forced the mayoral to remove Jorge Lucumí's (q.v. 317.0) leg irons. Gregorio claimed that he was not involved in any of the dis-

turbances and ran into the scrub when soldiers came riding toward them. The military commission concluded otherwise and sentenced him to suffer a hundred lashes and ten years imprisonment in Ceute, followed by exile.

318.1 ——.

Statement printed on p. 158 in *La esclavitud desde la esclavitud: La visión de los siervos* by Gloria García Rodríguez.

México [Distrito Federal, Estados Unidos Mexicanos]: Centro de Investigación Científica "Ing. Jorge L Tamayo," **1996.**
8vo (21 cm.): 251 p.

318.2 ——.

Printed on p. 142 in *La esclavitud desde la esclavitud*, by Gloria García.

La Habana [Cuba]: Editorial de Ciencias Sociales, **2003.**
8vo (21 cm.): xx, 222 p.

318.3 ——.

English translation of statement printed on p. 135 and 200n20 in *Voices of the Enslaved in Nineteenth-Century Cuba: A Documentary History*, edited by Gloria García Rodríguez. Translated [from 318.1] by Nancy L. Westrate; foreword by Ada Ferrer.

Chapel Hill [North Carolina, U.S.A.]: University of North Carolina Press, **2011.**
8vo (23.5 cm.): xviii, 220 p.

1843

319.1 William Thomas (1808–)

"Narrative of William Thomas, A Native of Africa, Twice Rescued from Slavery" printed on the sixth and seventh pages (of eight, i.e., p. 22–23) of the February 8, 1843, is-

https://babel.hathitrust.org/cgi/pt?id=uc1.d0004516092&view=1up&seq=34

sue (vol. 4, no. 3) of *The British and Foreign Anti-Slavery Reporter, Under the Sanction of the British and Foreign Anti-Slavery Society*, [whole no.] LXXXII. [Price 4*d*.] (*sic*)

[Colophon] Printed by William Tyler and Charles Reed, of No. 5, Bolt-Court, in the Parish of St. Dunstan, and City of **London** [England]; and Published by Lancelot Wilde, of 13, Catherine-street, Strand, in the Parish of St. Mary-le-Strand, and City of Westminster, at 13, Catherine-street, Strand, as aforesaid [*sic*]. Sold by W. Everett, 16, Finch-lane, Cornhill. **February 8th, 1843.**
4to (34 cm.): p. 17–24.

¶ Thomas was from Cameroon (see Map 5). He was captured and placed on a slave ship twice. The first time he was kidnapped during a war and then forced aboard a Spanish slave ship. That ship was intercepted at sea by a British warship, which took Thomas and the others to Sierra Leone (Map 4). Seven years later, while on a trading expedition in Vai country, he was captured again and forced aboard a Spanish slave ship that took him to the Spanish Caribbean colony of Cuba (Map 12). After working enslaved on a sugar plantation, he escaped to Great Britain's consul in Havana and was taken to

London (England—Map 8), where British officials planned to return Thomas to Sierra Leone.

319.2——.

Account reprinted from 319.1 on p. 8 of the 12 August 1843 issue of the *Sierra Leone Watchman*.

Freetown, Sierra Leone: Wesleyan Methodist Missionary Society, 12 August **1843.**

319.3——.

Account printed from 319.1 under heading "William Thomas" on pp. 225–29 in *Slave Testimony: Two Centuries of Letters, Speeches, Interviews, and Autobiographies*, edited by John W. Blassingame.

Baton Rouge [Louisiana, U.S.A.]: Louisiana State University Press, **1977.**
8vo (23 cm.): lxv, 777 p.

319.4——. [Second printing of 319.3]

Account printed from 319.1 under heading "William Thomas" on pp. 225–29 in *Slave Testimony: Two Centuries of Letters, Speeches, and Autobiographies*, edited by John W. Blassingame.

Baton Rouge [Louisiana, U.S.A.]: Louisiana State University Press, **1977.** Second printing.
8vo (23 cm.): lxv, 777 p., illus., portraits.

319.5——. [Another printing of 319.3]

Account printed from 319.1 under heading "William Thomas" on pp. 225–29 in *Slave Testimony: Two Centuries of Letters, Speeches, and Autobiographies*, edited by John W. Blassingame.

Baton Rouge [Louisiana, U.S.A.]: Louisiana State University Press, **1979**. 1979 printing.
8vo (23 cm.): lxv, 777 p., illus., portraits.

319.6———. **[Another printing of 319.3]**

Account printed from 319.1 under heading "William Thomas" on pp. 225–29 in *Slave Testimony: Two Centuries of Letters, Speeches, and Autobiographies*, edited by John W. Blassingame.

Baton Rouge [Louisiana, U.S.A.]: Louisiana State University Press, **1980**. 1980 printing.
8vo (23 cm.): lxv, 777 p., illus., portraits.

319.7———. **[Another printing of 319.3]**

Account printed from 319.1 under heading "William Thomas" on p. 225–29 in *Slave Testimony: Two Centuries of Letters, Speeches, and Autobiographies*, edited by John W. Blassingame.

Baton Rouge [Louisiana, U.S.A.]: Louisiana State University Press, **1989**. 1989 printing.
8vo (23 cm.): lxv, 777 p., illus., portraits.

319.8———. **[Another printing of 319.3]**

Account printed from 319.1 under heading "William Thomas" on pp. 225–29 in *Slave Testimony: Two Centuries of Letters, Speeches, and Autobiographies*, edited by John W. Blassingame.

Baton Rouge [Louisiana, U.S.A.]: Louisiana State University Press **1998**. 1998 printing.
8vo (23 cm.): lxv, 777 p., illus., portraits.

319.9———. **[Another printing of 319.3]**

Account printed from 319.1 under heading "William Thomas" on pp. 225–29 in *Slave Testimony: Two Centuries of Letters, Speeches, and Autobiographies*, edited by John W. Blassingame.

Baton Rouge [Louisiana, U.S.A.]: Louisiana State University Press, **2002**. 2002 printing.
8vo (23 cm.): lxv, 777 p., illus., portraits.

319.10———. **[Another printing of 319.3]**

Account printed from 319.1 under heading "William Thomas" on pp. 225–29 in *Slave Testimony: Two Centuries of Letters, Speeches, and Autobiographies*, edited by John W. Blassingame.

Baton Rouge [Louisiana, U.S.A.]: Louisiana State University Press, **2009**.
8vo (24 cm.): lxv, 777 p., illus., portraits.

320.0   Román Lucumí (ca. 1823–)

Statement recorded in Santa Ana Mantanzas, Cuba on 5 November **1843**, preserved in Archivo Nacional de la República de Cuba (ANC), **La Habana, Cuba,** Comisión Militar, 30/3.

Full text: https://huskiecommons.lib.niu.edu/history-500african-voices/186/

¶ Román identified as Lucumí, a New World designation for people who were primarily Yorùbá (modern day Nigeria, Benin and Togo—see Map 5). After forced transport to the Spanish colony of Cuba in the Caribbean (Map 12) on a slave ship and sale, by 1843 he worked enslaved as an oxherd on the *El Triunvirato* sugar plantation near Santa Ana in the Mantanzas area. He had been working after hours as a night sentry at the sugar mill (*trapiche*) for several weeks when an insurrection broke out (qq.v. 321.0 through 326.0). At a subsequent hearing, Román testified that one night before the rebellion he encountered several rebels and stopped them. When the rebellion came, all 240 enslaved people joined, presumably including Román.

320.1 ———.

Statement printed on p. 212 in *La esclavitud desde la esclavitud: La visión de los siervos* by Gloria García Rodríguez.

México [Distrito Federal, Estados Unidos Mexicanos]: Centro de Investigación Científica "Ing. Jorge L Tamayo," **1996**.
8vo (21 cm.): 251 p.

320.2 ———.

Printed on pp. 189–190 in *La esclavitud desde la esclavitud*, by Gloria García.

La Habana [Cuba]: Editorial de Ciencias Sociales, **2003**.
8vo (21 cm.): xx, 222 p.

320.3 ———.

English translation of statement printed on p. 182 in *Voices of the Enslaved in Nineteenth-Century Cuba: A Documentary History*, edited by Gloria García Rodríguez. Translated [from 320.1] by Nancy L. Westrate; foreword by Ada Ferrer.

Chapel Hill [North Carolina, U.S.A.]: University of North Carolina Press, **2011**.
8vo (23.5 cm.): xviii, 220 p.

321.0 Nicolas Gangá (c. 1818–)

Statement recorded in Santa Ana Mantanzas, Cuba on 5 November 1843, preserved in Archivo Nacional de la República de Cuba (ANC), **La Habana, Cuba,** Comisión Militar, 30/3.

¶ Nicolas identified as Gangá (modern Banta region in southern Sierra Leone—see Map 4). After forced transport to the Spanish colony of Cuba in the Caribbean (Map 12) on a slave ship and sale, by 1843 he was older than twenty-five and working enslaved as a carter on the *El Triunvirato* sugar plantation near Santa Ana in the Mantanzas area when a large rebellion broke out (qq.v. 320.0 through 326.0). At the subsequent hearing Nicolas explained that planning for the rebellion had begun two months earlier, when leaders began meeting in huts, the cane fields, and the sugar mill. They had plotted to gather the greatest possible number of enslaved inhabitants from all the farms in the area, wage war against their owners, secure their own freedom, and escape the onerous work they had been doing. When the rebellion began, all 240 enslaved people on the *El Triunvirato* estate joined, including Nicolas.

Full text: https:// huskiecommons. lib.niu.edu/his- tory-500african- voices/187/

321.1 ——.

Statement printed on p. 212 in *La esclavitud desde la esclavitud: La visión de los siervos* by Gloria García Rodríguez.

México [Distrito Federal, Estados Unidos Mexicanos]: Centro de Investigación Científica "Ing. Jorge L Tamayo," **1996.** 8vo (21 cm.): 251 p.

321.2 ——.

Printed on p. 190 in *La esclavitud desde la esclavitud*, by Gloria García.

La Habana [Cuba]: Editorial de Ciencias Sociales, **2003.** 8vo (21 cm.): xx, 222 p.

321.3 ——.

English translation of statement printed on pp. 182–183 and 203n12 in *Voices of the Enslaved in Nineteenth-Century Cuba: A Documentary History*, edited by Gloria García Rodríguez. Translated [from 321.1] by Nancy L. Westrate; foreword by Ada Ferrer.

Chapel Hill [North Carolina, U.S.A.]: University of North Carolina Press, **2011.** 8vo (23.5 cm.): xviii, 220 p.

322.0 Manuel Gangá (before 1818–1843)

Statement recorded in Santa Ana Mantanzas, Cuba on 5 November 1843, preserved in Archivo Nacional de la República de Cuba (ANC), **La Habana, Cuba,** Comisión Militar, 30/3.

¶ Manuel identified as Gangá (modern Banta region in southern Sierra Leone—see Map 4). After forced transport to the Spanish colony of Cuba in the Caribbean (Map 12) on a slave ship and sale, by 1843 he was older than twenty-five and working enslaved as a cartwright and field hand on the *El Triunvirato* sugar plantation near Santa Ana in the Mantanzas area. He became a leader of the large insurrection that broke out there in 1843 (qq.v. 320.0 through 326.0). At a subsequent hearing Manuel detailed his role with others in planning, recruiting, and leading hundreds of rebels, facing down their owners and threatening them, breaking into a big house and killing the occupants, burning factories, setting fire to the huts of enslaved people who refused to join, marching to other plantations to carry out more of the same, and the rebels' use of war drums and leather hides as shields. For his leading role in the rebellion, Manuel was sentenced to execution.

Full text: https:// huskiecommons. lib.niu.edu/his- tory-500african- voices/188/

322.1 ——.

Statement printed on pp. 212–215 in *La esclavitud desde la esclavitud: La visión de los siervos* by Gloria García Rodríguez.

México [Distrito Federal, Estados Unidos Mexicanos]: Centro de Investigación Científica "Ing. Jorge L Tamayo," **1996.** 8vo (21 cm.): 251 p.

322.2 ——.

Printed on pp. 190–192 in *La esclavitud desde la esclavitud*, by Gloria García.

Habana [Cuba]: Editorial de Ciencias Sociales, **2003.** 8vo (21 cm.): xx, 222 p.

322.3 ——.

English translation of statement printed on pp. 183–185 and 203n12 in *Voices of the Enslaved in Nineteenth-Century Cuba: A Documentary History*, edited by Gloria García Rodríguez. Translated [from 322.1] by Nancy L. Westrate; foreword by Ada Ferrer.

Chapel Hill [North Carolina, U.S.A.]: University of North Carolina Press, **2011.** 8vo (23.5 cm.): xviii, 220 p.

323.0 Gonzalo Lucumí (before 1818–)

Statement recorded in Santa Ana Mantanzas, Cuba on 5 November 1843, preserved in Archivo Nacional de la República de Cuba (ANC), **La Habana, Cuba,** Comisión Militar, 30/3.

¶ Gonzalo identified as Lucumí, a New World designation for people who were primarily Yorùbá (modern day Nigeria, Benin and Togo—see Map 5). After forced transport to the Spanish colony of Cuba in the Caribbean (Map 12) on a slave ship and sale, by 1843 he was older than twenty-five and working enslaved as a mason on the *El Triunvirato* sugar plantation near Santa Ana in the Mantanzas area when a large insurrection broke out (qq.v. 320.0 through 326.0). Gonzalo testified at the subsequent hearing that as he went to alert his mayoral that rebels were approaching, he encountered several of them, whom he followed into houses where their owners lived. While there several rebels accused him of snitching on them and threatened to kill him. At the hearing he identified a freedom fighter who beat a drum during the attack.

Full text: https://huskiecommons.lib.niu.edu/history-500africanvoices/189/

323.1 ——.

Statement printed on p. 215 in *La esclavitud desde la esclavitud: La visión de los siervos* by Gloria García Rodríguez.

México [Distrito Federal, Estados Unidos Mexicanos]: Centro de Investigación Científica "Ing. Jorge L Tamayo," **1996.** 8vo (21 cm.): 251 p.

323.2 ——.

Printed on pp. 192–193 in *La esclavitud desde la esclavitud,* by Gloria García.

La Habana [Cuba]: Editorial de Ciencias Sociales, **2003.** 8vo (21 cm.): xx, 222 p.

323.3 ——.

English translation of statement printed on p. 185 in *Voices of the Enslaved in Nineteenth-Century Cuba: A Documentary History,* edited by Gloria García Rodríguez. Translated [from 323.1] by Nancy L. Westrate; foreword by Ada Ferrer.

Chapel Hill [North Carolina, U.S.A.]: University of North Carolina Press, **2011.** 8vo (23.5 cm.): xviii, 220 p.

324.0 Adriano Gangá (before 1818–)

Statement recorded in Santa Ana Mantanzas, Cuba on 5 November 1843, preserved in Archivo Nacional de la República de Cuba (ANC), **La Habana, Cuba,** Comisión Militar, 30/3.

¶ Adriano identified as Gangá (modern Banta region in southern Sierra Leone—see Map 4). After forced transport to the Spanish colony of Cuba in the Caribbean (Map 12) on a slave ship and sale, by 1843 he was working enslaved as a coppersmith and field hand on the *El Acana* plantation in the Mantanzas area when a large insurrection broke out (qq.v. 320.0 through 326.0). At a subsequent hearing Adriano testified that when rebels from the *El Trinuvirato* plantation reached *El Ancana* they burst into the enslaved workers' quarters and ordered everyone to get up and join them. Adriano and others refused and ran into the cane fields but noticed that the rebels released seventeen people on the estate who had been locked up for punishment. He also described the killing of the mayoral, his family, and others.

Full text: https://huskiecommons.lib.niu.edu/history-500africanvoices/190/

324.1 ——.

Statement printed on pp. 215–216 in *La esclavitud desde la esclavitud: La visión de los siervos* by Gloria García Rodríguez.

México [Distrito Federal, Estados Unidos Mexicanos]: Centro de Investigación Científica "Ing. Jorge L Tamayo," **1996.** 8vo (21 cm.): 251 p.

324.2 ——.

Printed on p. 193 in *La esclavitud desde la esclavitud,* by Gloria García.

La Habana [Cuba]: Editorial de Ciencias Sociales, **2003.** 8vo (21 cm.): xx, 222 p.

324.3——.

English translation of statement printed on pp. 185–186 in *Voices of the Enslaved in Nineteenth-Century Cuba: A Documentary History,* edited by Gloria García Rodríguez. Translated [from 324.1] by Nancy L. Westrate; foreword by Ada Ferrer.

Chapel Hill [North Carolina, U.S.A.]: University of North Carolina Press, **2011.** 8vo (23.5 cm.): xviii, 220 p.

325.0   Anastasio Mina (before 1818–)

Statement recorded in Santa Ana Mantanzas, Cuba on 5 November 1843, preserved in Archivo Nacional de la República de Cuba (ANC), **La Habana, Cuba,** Comisión Militar, 30/3.

Full text: https://huskiecommons.lib.niu.edu/history-500african-voices/191/

¶ Anastasio identified as Mina (a New World ethnic designation for Akan speakers near Elmina Castle, modern Ghana—see Map 5). After forced transport to the Spanish colony of Cuba in the Caribbean (Map 12) on a slave ship and sale, by 1843 he was more than twenty-five and working enslaved as a field hand on the *San Lorenzo* estate in the Mantanzas area when a large rebellion broke out (qq.v. 320.0 through 326.0). At a subsequent hearing, Anastasio explained how the rebels approached *San Lorenzo* and appealed to them to join their undertaking. Anastasio testified that he and others refused to rebel because they believed they were being treated well.

325.1 ——.

Statement printed on pp. 216–217 in *La esclavitud desde la esclavitud: La visión de los siervos* by Gloria García Rodríguez.

México [Distrito Federal, Estados Unidos Mexicanos]: Centro de Investigación Científica "Ing. Jorge L Tamayo," **1996.** 8vo (21 cm.): 251 p.

325.2 ——.

Printed on p. 194 in *La esclavitud desde la esclavitud*, by Gloria García.

La Habana [Cuba]: Editorial de Ciencias Sociales, **2003.** 8vo (21 cm.): xx, 222 p.

325.3 ——.

English translation of statement printed on pp. 186–187 in *Voices of the Enslaved in Nineteenth-Century Cuba: A Documentary History*, edited by Gloria García Rodríguez. Translated [from 325.1] by Nancy L. Westrate; foreword by Ada Ferrer.

Chapel Hill [North Carolina, U.S.A.]: University of North Carolina Press, **2011.** 8vo (23.5 cm.): xviii, 220 p.

326.0   Mariano Gangá (before 1818–)

Statement recorded in Santa Ana Mantanzas, Cuba on 5 November 1843, preserved in Archivo Nacional de la República de Cuba (ANC), **La Habana, Cuba,** Comisión Militar, 30/3.

Full text: https://huskiecommons.lib.niu.edu/history-500african-voices/192/

¶ Mariano identified as Gangá (modern Banta region in southern Sierra Leone—see Map 4). After forced transport to the Spanish colony of Cuba in the Caribbean (Map 12) on a slave ship and sale, by 1843 he was an enslaved field hand working on the *San Rafael* estate in the Mantanzas area when a significant rebellion broke out (qq.v. 320.0 through 325.0). At a subsequent hearing he testified that when the rebels approached San Rafael, the men and women enslaved there agreed to support their owner and defend his estate. However, when they realized that the rebels greatly outnumbered them, they scattered and hid in the factories. From there they observed the destruction, and some of them agreed to join the rebels to persuade them to stop. Later, Mariano said, a troop of cavalry arrived, engaged the rebels, and inflicted many casualties.

326.1 ——.

Statement printed on p. 217 in *La esclavitud desde la esclavitud: La visión de los siervos* by Gloria García Rodríguez.

México [Distrito Federal, Estados Unidos Mexicanos]: Centro de Investigación Científica "Ing. Jorge L Tamayo," **1996.** 8vo (21 cm.): 251 p.

326.2 ——.

Printed on pp. 194–195 in *La esclavitud desde la esclavitud*, by Gloria García.

La Habana [Cuba]: Editorial de Ciencias Sociales, **2003.** 8vo (21 cm.): xx, 222 p.

326.3 ——.

English translation of statement printed on p. 187 in *Voices of the Enslaved in Nineteenth-Century Cuba: A Documentary History*, edited by Gloria García Rodríguez. Translated [from 326.1] by Nancy L. Westrate; foreword by Ada Ferrer.

Chapel Hill [North Carolina, U.S.A.]: University of North Carolina Press, **2011.** 8vo (23.5 cm.): xviii, 220 p.

1844

327.1 Sāhil Bilāli (ca. 1770–) = Sali-bul-Ali = Tom

His account recounted within a letter from James Hamilton Couper printed on pp. 68–75 in William Brown Hodgson, *Notes on Northern Africa, the Sahara, and the Soudan, in relation to the Ethnography, Languages, History, Political and Social Condition, of the Nations of those Countries.*

https://babel.hathitrust.org/cgi/pt?id=nyp.33433074372313&view=1up&seq=90

New-York [New York, U.S.A.]: Wiley and Putnam, 1844.
  Tpv: New-York: William Osborn, Printer, 88 William-street.
8vo (25 cm.): [1–9] 10–107, [4] p.
https://archive.org/details/b29349230/page/68
Hogg 1485.

¶ Sāhil Bilāli was born ca. 1770 in Kiniah, in Massina, on the Niger River upstream from Timbuctu (modern Mali—see Map 3). Ca. 1782 he was captured by people from Bambara (a non-Muslim state in the middle Niger valley), probably from Segu or Kaarta, then sold south through Asante (Akan people) until delivered to Anomabu on the Gold Coast (modern Ghana—Map 5). From there he was sent to the Bahamas, the British Caribbean colony (Map 11). Ca. 1800 he was sold in the state of Georgia, U.S.A. (Map 15), where he worked enslaved on the *Hopeton* plantation (Glynn County, Georgia), becoming a driver (field supervisor of other enslaved workers) in 1816. He told his life story to William Brown Hodgson, who published it. In 327.2 et seq. Ivor Wilks reprints Bilāli's entire account, which, except for the final paragraph (on his own capture), is about his homeland.

327.2——.

"Sāhil Bilāli Recollections of Massina," edited and annotated by Ivor Wilks on pp. 145–151 of *Africa Remembered: Narratives by West Africans from the Era of the Slave Trade*, edited by Philip D. Curtin.

Madison [Wisconsin, U.S.A.]: University of Wisconsin Press, 1967.
8vo (24 cm.): x, 363 p., illus., maps.

327.3——. [Second printing of 327.2]

"Sāhil Bilāli Recollections of Massina," edited and annotated by Ivor Wilks on pp. 145–151 of *Africa Remembered: Narratives by West Africans from the Era of the Slave Trade*, edited by Philip D. Curtin.

Madison [Wisconsin, U.S.A.]: University of Wisconsin Press, 1968.
8vo (22 cm.): x, 363 p., illus., maps.

327.4——. [Reprinting of 327.2]

"Sāhil Bilāli Recollections of MMariano Gangáassina," edited and annotated by Ivor Wilks on pp. 145–151 of *Africa Remembered: Narratives by West Africans from the Era of the Slave Trade*, edited by Philip D. Curtin.

Prospect Heights, Illinois [U.S.A.]: Waveland Press, 1997.
8vo (23 cm.): x, 363 p., illus., maps.

328.0 Alejandro Congo

Statement recorded in Candelaria, Cuba on 21 August 1844, preserved in Archivo Nacional de la República de Cuba (ANC), La Habana, Cuba, Gobierno Superior Civil, 943/33261.

Full text: https://huskiecommons.lib.niu.edu/history-500african-voices/193/

¶ Alejandro identified as Congolese. He was brought to the Spanish colony of Cuba in the Caribbean (Map 12) on a slave ship as a child, long before 1844. Eventually he worked enslaved on the *Desierto* coffee plantation near Candelaria. He fled abusive treatment (severe whippings, confinement in leg irons for minor infractions) at least twice. After his last escape he spent a month with several other Maroons in the Songuito backcountry, where they slept in palm bark- and leaf-covered shanties and subsisted on rats, wild yucca, and honey. They used their work machetes as weapons and traded beeswax with a black man from a nearby plantation. Their leader kept the money and took it to a larger Maroon community at some location unknown to Alejandro. Alejandro was captured while gathering mangoes at another plantation, eight months after he had run away.

328.1 ——.

Statement printed on pp. 197–199 in *La esclavitud desde la esclavitud: La visión de los siervos* by Gloria García Rodríguez.

México [Distrito Federal, Estados Unidos Mexicanos]: Centro de Investigación Científica "Ing. Jorge L Tamayo," 1996.
8vo (21 cm.): 251 p.

328.2 ——.

Printed on pp. 176–178 in *La esclavitud desde la esclavitud*, by Gloria García.

La Habana [Cuba]: Editorial de Ciencias Sociales, 2003. 8vo (21 cm.): xx, 222 p.

328.3 ——.

English translation of statement printed on pp. 169–171 in *Voices of the Enslaved in Nineteenth-Century Cuba: A*

Documentary History, edited by Gloria García Rodríguez. Translated [from 328.1] by Nancy L. Westrate; foreword by Ada Ferrer.

Chapel Hill [North Carolina, U.S.A.]: University of North Carolina Press, 2011. 8vo (24 cm.): xviii, 220 p.

1846

329.1 Unnamed African man

His account contained in a letter he wrote to the Church Missionary Society's Honorary General Secretary, printed under the heading "A Liberated African's Account of his Slavery, and Subsequent Course" printed on pp. 16–18 if the February issue (vol. 6, no. 3) and pp. 27–30 in the March issue (vol. 6, no. 3) of *Church Missionary Gleaner*.

https://archive.org/details/1846Church-MissionaryGlean-erVol6/page/n23

London [England]: Sold at the Church Missionary House, Salisbury Square; by Seeley, Burnside, & Seeley, Fleet Street; Hatchard & Son, Piccadilly; & J. Nisbet & Co., Berners Street, [February-March] 1846. Hogg 1489.

¶ This man lost his parents while young, was sold by a relative, then resold several times somewhere (in upper West Africa), eventually to someone on an island with many Africans whose language he did not understand. Here, ca. 1820, he was forced aboard a Portuguese slave ship. This ship was intercepted at sea by a British warship that took them to Freetown, Sierra Leone (see Map 4). There this man worked as a tailor, embraced Christianity, and married in 1823. He became a school master in 1825 and moved to Charlotte, Sierra Leone, the next year. In 1828 he began to teach in Bathurst, Sierra Leone. He worked in several other stations for the Society at Sierra Leone and still did so when he included his account in a letter he wrote to the society's Honorary Clerical Secretary.

330.1 John Joseph = Jack Sambo

The Life and Sufferings of John Joseph [a Native of Ashantee, in Western Africa: Who was Stolen from His Parents at Age of 3 Years, and Sold to Mr. Johnstone, a Cotton Planter, in New Orleans, South America].

Edinburgh [Scotland]: Printed for John Joseph by Andrew Jack, MDCCCXLVI [1846].
8vo: 8 p. British Library Shelfmark: General Reference Collection DRT Digital Store 8157.b.6.(4.)
Hogg 1490.

¶ Joseph, son of a local official, was from Asante (Akan people) inland from the Gold Coast (modern Ghana—see Map 5). Captured at age three with his sister and many others, he was taken to the coast and put on a large slave ship bound for New Orleans, Louisiana, U.S.A. (Map 15). A cotton planter purchased him and his sister at auction there and placed him in a "calaboosh" (barracoon) until he was old enough to do field work. Harsh treatment on the plantation motivated him to escape, but he was recaptured and sold to a rice planter in South Carolina, U.S.A. (Map 15), where, again working under severe conditions, he converted to Christianity. Resold to a tobacco planter in Virginia, U.S.A., he endured further cruelties there. On his third escape attempt in 1843, he reached the coast and was picked up by a British ship that took him to safety in England, where he underwent Christian baptism. He published 330.1 and 330.2 himself and sold exemplars of both on the streets and door-to-door.

http://docsouth.unc.edu/neh/jjoseph/jjoseph.html

330.2 ——.

The Life and Sufferings of John Joseph, a Native of Ashantee, in Western Africa: Who was Stolen from His Parents at Age of 3 Years, and Sold to Mr. Johnstone, a Cotton Planter, in New Orleans, South America.

Wellington [Somerset, England*]: Printed for John Joseph by J[ohn] Greedy, MDCCCXLVIII [1848]. *N.b.*, not Wellington, New Zealand.
8vo (18 cm.): 8 p., illus.
Note: The University of Missouri, Kansas City, Nichols Library, LaBudde Special Collections, holds the only reported exemplar (call number E441.J64.1848).
http://docsouth.unc.edu/neh/jjoseph/jjoseph.html

330.3 ——.

Excerpts from 330.2 printed on pp. 24–25 in *African Voices of the Global Past, 1500 to the Present*, edited by Trevor R. Getz.

[Boulder, Colorado, U.S.A.]: Westview Press, [2014]. 8vo (22.7 cm.): xii, 223 p., illus., map.

1847

331.1 John Homrn (1823–)

Nota bene: surname is H-o-m-r-n / H-O-M-R-N.

"Narrative John Homrn" printed in periodical *The British and Foreign Anti-Slavery Reporter*, New Series vol. 2, no. 16, p. 61-62 and no. 17, p. 74.

London [England]: British and Foreign Anti-Slavery Society, 1 April and 1 May **1847**.
Large 8vo (34 cm.).

https://babel.hathitrust.org/cgi/pt?id=uiug.30112067876166&view=1up&seq=287 (reprint).

¶ Homrn was born in Sierra Leone in 1823 (see Map 4). In 1845 his father allowed him to work for a United States merchant as a valet in order to further his education through travel. The U.S.A. citizen took him to Rio Pongo (Sierra Leone) for two years, then the Spanish Caribbean colonial city of Havana, Cuba (Map 12), where he treated him as a slave and sold him to a planter. More than four years later Homrn escaped on a British ship to England, where the British & Foreign Anti-Slavery Society housed him at the Sailors' Home in London (Map 8) and then helped him return to Sierra Leone.

331.2———.

"Narrative John Homrn" printed in photomechanical reprint of 331.1 with imprint:

Nendeln, Lichtenstein: Kraus Reprint, **1969**.
https://babel.hathitrust.org/cgi/pt?id=uiug.30112067876166&view=1up&seq=287

331.3———.

Account reprinted from 331.1 on pp. 254–261 in *Slave Testimony: Two Centuries of Letters, Speeches, Interviews, and Autobiographies*, edited by John W. Blassingame.

Baton Rouge [Louisiana, U.S.A.]: Louisiana State University Press, **1977**.
8vo (23 cm.): lxv, 777 p.

331.4———. [Second printing of 331.3]

Account reprinted from 331.1 on pp. 254–261 in *Slave Testimony: Two Centuries of Letters, Speeches, and Autobiographies*, edited by John W. Blassingame.

Baton Rouge [Louisiana, U.S.A.]: Louisiana State University Press, **1977**. Second printing.
8vo (23 cm.): lxv, 777 p., illus., portraits.

331.5———. [Another printing of 331.3]

Account reprinted from 331.1 on pp. 254–261 in *Slave Testimony: Two Centuries of Letters, Speeches, and Autobiographies*, edited by John W. Blassingame.

Baton Rouge [Louisiana, U.S.A.]: Louisiana State University Press, **1979**. 1979 printing.
8vo (23 cm.): lxv, 777 p., illus., portraits.

331.6———. [Another printing of 331.3]

Account reprinted from 331.1 on pp. 254–261 in *Slave Testimony: Two Centuries of Letters, Speeches, and Autobiographies*, edited by John W. Blassingame.

Baton Rouge [Louisiana, U.S.A.]: Louisiana State University Press, **1980**. 1980 printing.
8vo (23 cm.): lxv, 777 p., illus., portraits.

331.7———. [Another printing of 331.3]

Account reprinted from 331.1 on pp. 254–261 in *Slave Testimony: Two Centuries of Letters, Speeches, and Autobiographies*, edited by John W. Blassingame.

Baton Rouge [Louisiana, U.S.A.]: Louisiana State University Press, **1989**. 1989 printing.
8vo (23 cm.): lxv, 777 p., illus., portraits.

331.8———. [Another printing of 331.3]

Account reprinted from 331.1 on pp. 254–261 in *Slave Testimony: Two Centuries of Letters, Speeches, and Autobiographies*, edited by John W. Blassingame.

Baton Rouge [Louisiana, U.S.A.]: Louisiana State University Press, **1998**. 1998 printing.
8vo (23 cm.): lxv, 777 p., illus., portraits.

331.9———. [Another printing of 331.3]

Account reprinted from 331.1 on pp. 254–261 in *Slave Testimony: Two Centuries of Letters, Speeches, and Autobiographies*, edited by John W. Blassingame.

Baton Rouge [Louisiana, U.S.A.]: Louisiana State University Press, **2002**. 2002 printing.
8vo (23 cm.): lxv, 777 p., illus., portraits.

331.10———. [Another printing of 331.3]

Account reprinted from 331.1 on pp. 254–261 in *Slave Testimony: Two Centuries of Letters, Speeches, and Autobiographies*, edited by John W. Blassingame.

Baton Rouge [Louisiana, U.S.A.]: Louisiana State University Press, **2009**.
8vo (24 cm.): lxv, 777 p., illus., portraits.

1848

332.1 Benomê (ca. 1817–)

Account of her life printed under the title "Little Benome, A Liberated African Girl. A Tale of Slavery" (over typeset signature and dateline: Rev. W. Moister | On Board the "Bangalore" at Sea, August, 1847) on pp. 16–20 in the monthly periodical *Wesleyan Juvenile Offering: A Miscellany of Missionary Information for Young Persons*, vol. 5, no. 2.

https://babel.ha-thitrust.org/cgi/pt?id=inu.30000011565631&view=1up&seq=348

London [England]: Sold at the Wesleyan Mission-House, Bishopsgate-Street-Within: also by John Mason, 66, Paternoster-Row, [February] 1848. Tpv: London: Printed by James Nichols, Hoxton-Square.

8vo (17 cm.). *The compilers owe the discovery of this printing to Mr. Fabio Silva (see further note at 330.2.).*

¶ Benomê was born ca. 1817 in Radda (probably Rabba), in the interior of what is now Nigeria (see Map 5). Kidnapped at age seven during a raid on her village, she was separated from her family and taken to a barracoon at Abeokuta, Badagry, then forced aboard a slave ship ca. 1825. The ship had been at sea three weeks when a British warship intercepted it, liberated the Africans, and took them to the British colony of Trinidad in the Caribbean (Map 11). Benomê was made to work as an indentured child servant in William Moister's house. While living for nine years with the Moister family she learned to sew, read, and write, and underwent Christian baptism. When the Moisters left Trinidad, she remained behind, but later went alone to the Caribbean island of Grenada, where she reunited with the Moisters and lived with them until they left for England. Thirteen years later (ca. 1849) she wrote to Moister, noting that she was now married and had three children. Her husband came from her country in Africa and was a precentor in the local Christian church.

332.2———.

Account of her life explicitly reprinted from 332.1 (but *without* typeset signature or dateline) under title "Little Benome, A Liberated African Girl. A Tale of Slavery" on pp. 82–84 in the periodical *The Children's Monthly Missionary Newspaper. Designed to communicate interesting intelligence respecting the Missionary Efforts of All Evangelical Denominations, in language adapted to the capacity of children*, vol. 5, no. 11 (eleven).

Edinburgh [Scotland]: Gail and Inglis. Glasgow [Scotland]: G. Gallie. London [England]: Houlston and Stoneman. Liv-

erpool [England]: G. Philip. Hull [Yorkshire, England]: G. Philip. Dublin [Ireland]: J. Robertson. Belfast [Ireland]: W. M'Comb, [November 1848].

12mo (16 cm). *The compilers thank Fabio Silva for sharing with them his discovery of this edition and 332.1, the original printing of which antedates 332.3 (below) by at least 23 months.*

332.3———.

Account of her life closely related to 332.1 printed on pp. 342–345 of William Moister, *Memorials of Missionary Labours in Western Africa and the West Indies; with historical and descriptive observations.*

London [England]: Sold by John Mason, 66, Paternoster Row; and by all booksellers, 1850. Tpv: Isle of Wight: Printed by H. Kingswell, Quay Street, Newport.

8vo (19 cm.) 368 p. FN 000457.

https://babel.hathitrust.org/cgi/pt?id=inu.30000011565631&view=1up&seq=348

332.4———.

Account of her life printed on pp. 324–326 of William Moister, *Memorials of Missionary Labours in Western Africa and the West Indies; with historical and descriptive observations. Revised and enlarged from the English edition.*

New-York [New York, U.S.A.]: Published by Lane & Scott, 200 Mulberry street. Joseph Longking, printer. 1851.

8vo (19 cm.) 348 p. (*sic*).

https://babel.hathitrust.org/cgi/pt?id=osu.32435001570993&view=1up&seq=330

332.5———.

Account of her life **with additional letter from her** printed on pp. 67–70 of William Moister, *Memorials of Missionary Labours in Western Africa, the West Indies, and at the Cape of Good Hope: with historical and descriptive observations, illustrative of natural scenery, the progress of civilization, and the general results of the missionary enterprise. Third edition, revised and enlarged.*

London [England]: Sold at 66, Paternoster Row; and by all booksellers, 1866. Tpv: London: Printed by William Nicols, 46, Hoxton Square.

8vo (19 cm.) viii, 592 p., frontis.

https://babel.hathitrust.org/cgi/pt?id=mdp.39015047691921&view=1up&seq=81

333.1 First of two unnamed Nyungwe refugees

Account printed in Eugène de Froberville, "Notes sur les Va-Niungue et les Mabsiti, peuples de l'Afrique orientale." *Bulletin de la Société de Géographie*, ser. 3, vol. 10: 65–81, August **1848**, in bound volume with general title page carrying imprint:

Paris [France]: Chez Arthus-Bertrand, Librarie de la Société de Géographie, **1849**.
8vo (23 cm.).
Hogg 1492.

https://archive.org/details/bulletindelasoci-10pari/page/64/mode/2up

¶ This Nyungwe man, along with many other previously enslaved Nyungwe and Mabsiti refugees on the island of Mauritius (the British colony in the Indian Ocean, east of Madagascar—see Map 2), was interviewed by Froberville. Having survived a massacre, they had been sold to the Portuguese and shipped to Brazil (Map 9) on a slave ship, which was intercepted off the coast by a British corvette. Froberville wrote out the description of the Mabsiti (possibly located in modern Mozambique) homeland on the right bank of the Zambezi ("under Portuguese domination") provided by the informants he presumed to be deem the "two most intelligent" of the group.

334.1 Second of two unnamed Nyungwe refugees

Account printed in Eugène de Froberville, "Notes sur les Va-Niungue et les Mabsiti, peuples de l'Afrique orientale." *Bulletin de la Société de Géographie*, ser. 3, vol. 10, 65–81.

August **1848**, in bound volume with general title-page carrying imprint:
Paris [France]: Chez Arthus-Bertrand, Librarie de la Société de Géographie, **1849**.
8vo (23 cm.).
Hogg 1492.

https://archive.org/details/bulletindelasoci-10pari/page/64/mode/2up

¶ This Nyungwe man, along with many other previously enslaved Nyungwe and Mabsiti refugees on the island of Mauritius (the British colony in the Indian Ocean, east of Madagascar—see Map 2), was interviewed by Froberville. Having survived a massacre, they had been sold to the Portuguese and shipped to Brazil (Map 9) on a slave ship, which was intercepted off the coast by a British corvette. Froberville took

down the description of the Mabsiti homeland on the right bank of the Zambezi ("under Portuguese domination"—possibly in modern Mozambique) provided by the informants he presumed to deem the "two most intelligent" of the group.

335.1 William Henry Pratt

Autobiographical testimony given 4 July **1848** printed on pp. 181–185, Third Report, in vol. 4 of British Parliamentary Papers, *First Second Third and Fourth Reports from the Select Committee on The Slave Trade with Minutes of Evidence Appendix and Index. Slave Trade.*

London [England]: Her Majesty's Printing Office, **1849**.
Folio (35 cm.): iv, 278; iv, 233; 27; vii, 111 p.

Full text: https://huskiecommons.lib.niu.edu/history-500african-voices/194/

¶ From unknown origins in Africa, Pratt was enslaved and forced aboard a slave ship bound for Brazil in 1822. Liberated at sea by a British warship, he was taken to Sierra Leone (see Map 4). There he attended a Church Missionary Society school for seven years, then worked for merchants (learning their ways in the process) until 1837, when he went into business for himself. He converted to Christianity in 1835 and began assisting Wesleyan missionaries in Sierra Leone. In 1838 he began developing business connections in England and was there in 1848 to pursue business interests and investigate schools for his children, when he testified in London (Map 8) about the slave trade (335.1). Coordinating with British authorities, he hired liberated Africans as indentured apprentices for his business in Sierra Leone.

335.2——. [Facsimile reprint of 335.1 and other British Parliamentary Papers.]

Autobiographical testimony given 4 July 1848 printed on pp. 181–185 (3rd pagination series), Third Report in *First Second Third and Fourth Reports from the Select Committee on The Slave Trade with Minutes of Evidence Appendix and Index. Slave Trade*, in British Parliamentary Papers: Correspondence with British Commissioners and with Foreign Powers Relative to the Slave Trade [Class A and B], Slave Trade, vol. 13.

Shannon [County Clare, Ireland]: Irish University Press, **1968**.
Folio (35 cm.): iv, 278; iv, 179; iv, 233; 27; xii, 111 p.

336.1 James Will

Autobiographical testimony given 4 July **1848** printed on pp. 184–185, Third Report in vol. 4 of *British Parliamentary Papers (Slave Trade), First Second Third and Fourth Reports* *from the Select Committee on The Slave Trade with Minutes of Evidence Appendix and Index. Slave Trade.*

London [England]: Her Majesty's Printing Office, **1849**.
Folio (35 cm.): iv, 278; iv, 233; 27; vii, 111 p.

¶ Will came from the hinterland of the Bight of Benin (modern coastal Benin, Togo, Nigeria—see Map 5) and was kidnapped and enslaved when very young. Forced aboard a slave ship bound for Brazil in 1822, he was liberated by a British warship after three nights at sea and taken to Sierra Leone (Map 4). There he eventually became a business partner of William Henry Pratt (q.v. 335.1), provisioning British ships. He cultivated and sold large quantities of fine white arrow-root and ginger.

336.2——. [Reprint of 336.1 and other Parliamentary Papers.]

Autobiographical testimony given 4 July 1848 printed on pp. 184–185, Third Report in vol. 4 (originally published 1849) of Irish University Press Series: *British Parliamentary Papers (Slave Trade), First Second Third and Fourth Reports from the Select Committee on The Slave Trade with Minutes of Evidence Appendix and Index. Slave Trade.*

Shannon [County Clare, Ireland]: Irish University Press, **1968**.
Folio (35 cm.): iv, 278; iv, 233; 27; vii, 111 p.

337.1 James Campbell

Partially autobiographical testimony recorded 28 March **1848** and printed on pp. 78–80, First Report, in vol. 4 of *British Parliamentary Papers (Slave Trade), First Second Third and Fourth Reports from the Select Committee on The Slave Trade with Minutes of Evidence Appendix and Index. Slave Trade.*

London [England]: Her Majesty's Printing Office, **1849**.
Folio (35 cm.): iv, 278; iv, 233; 27; vii, 111 p. FN 000102.

Full text: https://huskiecommons.lib.niu.edu/history-500african-voices/196/

¶ Campbell came from Kossoh (a British town for liberated Africans in Sierra Leone, possibly Mende—see Map 4), where his father was a farmer. When he was a small boy his village was attacked, and he was taken prisoner and kept in a Spanish barracoon on the Gallinas River for a month, until liberated by a British warship that sent a shore party to the barracoon. Ca.

Full text: https://huskiecommons.lib.niu.edu/history-500african-voices/195/

1842 he was taken by this British party to Sierra Leone, where he worked as a mason. In 1848 he was taken to London, England (Map 8), to testify before members of Parliament about conditions in his homeland, the slave trade, and Sierra Leone; and was there asked whether he might wish to migrate to the British West Indies as a free laborer. He said he preferred to live in the free country of Sierra Leone, at least until he might live free in the West Indies and earn higher wages.

337.2——. [Reprint of 337.1 and other Parliamentary Papers.]

Partially autobiographical testimony recorded 28 March 1848 and printed on pp. 78–80, First Report in vol. 4 (originally published 1849) of Irish University Press Series: *British Parliamentary Papers (Slave Trade), First Second Third and Fourth Reports from the Select Committee on The Slave Trade with Minutes of Evidence Appendix and Index. Slave Trade.*

Shannon [County Clare, Ireland]: Irish University Press, **1968**.
Folio (35 cm.): iv, 278; iv, 233; 27; vii, 111 p. FN 000102.

338.1 Joseph Will

Autobiographical speech delivered 25 October **1848** at the Jewin Street Wesleyan Chapel, London, England, printed on pp. 594–595 of William Fox, *A Brief History of the Wesleyan Missions on the Coast of Africa: including Biographical Sketches of all the Missionaries who have died in that important field of labour. With some account of the European settlements, and of the Slave-Trade.*

https://babel.hathitrust.org/cgi/pt?id=hvd.32044020524088&view=1up&seq=640

London [England]: Printed for the Author. Published by Aylott and Jones 8, Paternoster-Row; Sold also by John Mason, 66, Paternoster-Row, MDCCCLI [1851]. Tpv: London: Printed by James Nichol, Hoxton-Square.
8vo (23 cm.) xx, 624 p., plates, illus., folding map.
FN 000123.

¶ Will was born in the African interior, a hundred miles (by his own estimation) from the sea. Kidnapped when young and separated from his parents, he was sold ca. 1829 to a slave ship bound for the Spanish Caribbean colonial city of Havana, Cuba. A British warship intercepted this ship at sea, took Will and the others to Sierra Leone (see Map 4), and freed them. Deemed "heathen" upon arrival, Will embraced Christianity ca. 1835 and successfully preached locally. In 1848 he accompanied white missionaries to London, England (Map 8), on a promotional tour. While there he gave his testimony and conducted a chapel service.

1849

339.1 Augustino (ca. 1818–)

Autobiographical answers to questions put to him on 24 May 1849 printed on pp. 162–163 in *Report from the Select Committee of the House of Lords, Appointed to Consider the Best Means which Great Britain Can Adopt for the Final Extinction of the African Slave Trade. Session 1849.* [At head of title:] *Brought from the Lords, 12 February 1850.*

[London, England: Her Majesty's Printing Office, 1850.] Folio (33 cm.): iv, 574 p.

https://babel.hathitrust.org/cgi/pt?id=umn.31951t00257009e&view=1up&seq=218

¶ Augustino came from Sofala, a part of the Mutapa in Southeast Africa (see Map 2). In 1830 he was seized by a merchant to cover a debt, taken to the coast (about two weeks travel time), forced aboard a slave ship, and taken to Brazil (Map 9). Freed in a manner not described, he provided a horrifyingly detailed description of the Middle Passage when he testified before a British House of Lords committee in London, England (Map 8), on 24 May 1849.

339.2 ——.

339.1 reprinted on pp. 37–39 in *Children of God's Fire: A Documentary History of Black Slavery in Brazil*, edited by Robert Edgar Conrad.

Princeton [New Jersey, U.S.A.]: Princeton University Press, **1983**. 8vo (25 cm.): xxviii, 515 p.

339.3 ——.

339.2 reprinted on pp. 37–39 in *Children of God's Fire: A Documentary History of Black Slavery in Brazil*, edited by Robert Edgar Conrad.

University Park, Pennsylvania [U.S.A.]: Pennsylvania State University Press, **1994**. 8vo (24 cm.): xxviii, 515 p.

339.4 ——.

339.2 reprinted on pp. 37–39 in *Children of God's Fire: A Documentary History of Black Slavery in Brazil*, edited by Robert Edgar Conrad.

University Park, Pennsylvania [U.S.A.]: Pennsylvania State University Press, **1997**. 8vo (23 cm.): xxviii, 515 p.

1850

340.1 Thomas Hadden

Account taken down in writing by British Consul R. Hesketh at Rio de Janiero, Brazil, on **29 November 1850**, printed under heading "Declaration of Thomas Hadden" on pp. 379–381 (especially 380) of Great Britain, House of Commons, [*Accounts and Papers*, vol. 56, Part II, Session 4, 4 February to 8 August 1851] *Class B. Correspondence with British Ministers and Agents in Foreign Countries, and with Foreign Ministers in England, relating to the Slave Trade, from April 1, 1850, to March 31, 1851.*

London [England]: Printed by Harrison and Son, [1851]. Folio (33 cm.): 886 p. FN 000127.

Full text: https://huskiecommons.lib.niu.edu/history-500african-voices/197/

¶ Hadden grew up in Sierra Leone (see Map 4) with parents and siblings firmly part of the colonial British antislavery project there. He was therefore already fluent in English when in 1847 he was working as a cook on a ship trading between Sierra Leone and Gallinas. On that voyage that year the ship's Sierra Leonian owner suddenly sold Hadden to a Brazilian

ship captain, who, evading pursuit by a British warship, took him to the Brazilian province of Bahia (Map 9), where he was sold. In Bahia he worked enslaved as a cook for two years, until he was sold again to a man in Rio de Janeiro, Brazil. After working there for nine months confined indoors, he absconded to the British consulate, where he testified to a consular officer, who, believing his story, sent him to London, England (Map 8), with his written declaration of what had happened to him.

341.1 Ali Eisami Gazirmabe (ca. 1786–) = William Harding

Account printed in the original Kanuri on pp. 115–121 and in English translation on pp. 248–256 of Sigismund Wilhelm Koelle, *African Native Literature, or Proverbs, Tales, Fables, & Historical Fragments in the Kanuri or Bornu Language, to Which Are Added a Translation of the Above and a Kanuri-English Vocabulary.*

https://babel.hathitrust.org/cgi/pt?id=coo1.ark:/13960/t7jq1jj7g&view=1up&seq=137&q1=115

341.1   Ali Eisami Gazirmabe

ALI EISAMI GAZIRMA.

Figure 16: Ali Eisami Gazirmabe, also known as William Harding (c. 1786– ?) in Freetown, Sierra Leone ca. 1850. He was a well-educated man from Gazir in Borno (modern northeastern Nigeria) who after capture was placed on a slave ship at Porto Novo (modern Benin). A British warship intercepted them at sea, liberated the enslaved passengers, and took them to Sierra Leone, where Gazirmabe later became an informant about West African languages to the German linguist Sigismund Wilhelm Koelle.

Source: Engraving by J. Johnston opposite title page of S.W. Koelle, *Grammar of the Bornu or Kanuri Language* (London: Church Missionary House, 1854).

London [England]: Church Missionary House, Salisbury Square, 1854. Tpv: Printed by C. & F. Unger in **Berlin** [**Prussia, Germany**], 51, Markgrafen Str.

4to (23 cm.): xiv, 434 p.

Hogg 1499.

¶ Ali Eisami Gazirmabe came from the metropolitan district of Gazir in Borno (modern northeast Nigeria—see Map 5). Born ca. 1786, Eisami had been educated for at least five years in Qur'anic school before he was enslaved in 1812 after Fulani forces of the Sokoto *ihad* (religious reform movement that involved warfare) reoccupied central Borno and destroyed the capital and many towns and villages. Taken through the Sokoto Caliphate, he was held enslaved in Katunga, the capital of the Oyo Empire, for five years. In 1817 he was sold to the coast during the Muslim uprising at the military outpost of Ilorin. At Porto Novo (modern Benin) he was sold to a slave ship that the British anti-slave-trade squadron intercepted at sea and took to Sierra Leone (Map 4). In 1849 Eisami became a principal informant of German linguist and missionary Sigismund Koelle, to whom he dictated his autobiography and numerous historical and fictional accounts in Kanuri. For more on him see his portrait published by Koelle in *Grammar of the Bornu or Kanuri Language* and reproduced in Curtin, 341.2 et seq., p. 213; and Paul E. Lovejoy, "Ali Eisami's Enslavement and Emancipation: The Trajectory of a Liberated African," in *Liberated Africans and the Abolition of the Slave Trade, 1807–1896*, edited by Richard Anderson and Henry B. Lovejoy (Rochester [New York]: University of Rochester Press, 2020).

341.2———.

"Ali Eisami Gazirmabe of Bornu," edited by H. F. C. Smith, D. M. Last, and Gambo Gubio on pp. 199–216 in *Africa Remembered: Narratives by West Africans from the Era of the Slave Trade*, edited by Philip D. Curtin.

Madison [Wisconsin, U.S.A.]: University of Wisconsin Press, 1967.

8vo (24 cm.): x, 363 p., illus., maps

341.3———. [Second printing of 341.2]

"Ali Eisami Gazirmabe of Bornu," edited by H. F. C. Smith, D. M. Last, and Gambo Gubio on pp. 199–216 in *Africa Remembered: Narratives by West Africans from the Era of the Slave Trade*, edited by Philip D. Curtin.

Madison [Wisconsin, U.S.A.]: University of Wisconsin Press, 1968.

8vo (22 cm.): x, 363 p., illus., maps.

341.4———.

Photomechanical reprint of 341.1.

Freeport, New York [U.S.A.]: Books for Libraries Press, 1970.

8vo (23 cm.): xiv, 434 p.

341.5———. [Reprinting of 341.2]

"Ali Eisami Gazirmabe of Bornu," edited by H. F. C. Smith, D. M. Last, and Gambo Gubio on pp. 199–216 in *Africa Remembered: Narratives by West Africans from the Era of the Slave Trade*, edited by Philip D. Curtin.

Prospect Heights, Illinois [U.S.A.]: Waveland Press, 1997.

8vo (23 cm.): x, 363 p., illus., maps.

342.1 James Gerber

Account headed "The Sufferings and Deliverance of James Gerber, a Twice-Liberated African" in *Christian Missionary Gleaner*, New Series vol. 1, no. 2 (May 1850): 20–23.

https://babel.hathitrust.org/cgi/pt?id=hvd.ah-6j43;view=1up;seq=30

London [England]: Seeleys, Fleet Street, and Hanover Street, Hanover Square, 1850. Tpv: William M. Watts, Printer, Crown Court, Temple Bar.

8vo (21 cm.).

Hogg 1404.

¶ Gerber was from Ijaye, near Lagos (modern Nigeria—see Map 5). He was captured *ca.* 1828, sold into the European slave trade, liberated by the British, and taken to Sierra Leone (Map 4), where he lived for fifteen years, was a communicant at the Christian church in Hastings, married, and had one child. In 1843 he moved with his wife and child to Badagry near his homeland and worked at various occupations. Near the end of August 1848 he went to Ijaye, where his brother, a slave trader, lived. There he and other family members were kidnapped and enslaved again, now in Ibadan, and sold to a Portuguese merchant. Before Gerber could be forced aboard another slave ship, he was ransomed. He then returned to Abbeokuta (now Abeokuta, Nigeria), where he lived when providing his account.

1851

343.1 Betsey Johnson

Account of her life and piety printed on pp. 33–34 of Mary W. Thompson, *Sketches of the History, Character, and Dying Testimony of Beneficiaries of the Colored Home, in the City of New-York.*

New York [New York, U.S.A.]: John F. Trow, Printer, 49, 51 & 53 Ann-St., 1851.
8vo (19 cm.) [8], [3]-78 p. Bind-

https://babel.hathitrust. org/cgi/pt?id=nnc1. cu55569994& view=1up&seq=45 [see 343.1].

ing cover title and internal half title: *Broken Gloom.* Note that this work also includes, on pp. 20–22, very brief prose sketches of African-born and formerly enslaved Tommy Warner and "blind Sopha"; neither sketch includes sufficient material to qualify for inclusion in the present catalog. https://docsouth.unc.edu/neh/thompson1/thompson.html FN 000942.

¶ Enslaved and taken from Africa to the West Indies early in her life, the young girl later named Betsey Johnson was taken to the British North American colony of Virginia (see Map 15) during the "Old War" (perhaps the French and Indian War, 1754–1763). She lived during the American Revolutionary War (1775–1783) with several different owners in Virginia and elsewhere in the newly organized United States of America. Johnson also married during this period and subsequently bore several children. Ca. 1841 she embraced Christianity and joined New York City's Spring Street Presbyterian Church (Map 17). In her final years she led an exemplary spiritual life in a New York City home for (mostly aged) Blacks in need of support, where she told Thompson her life story. She died before Thompson published 343.1.

¶ Note for entries 344 through 366, interviews with twenty-three named West Africans enslaved in Bahia, Brazil. The following accounts are based on responses Francis de Castelnau (1812–1880) gathered during interviews with Africans enslaved in Bahia, Brazil, in order to better understand the geography of Africa.

344.1 Mahammah = Manuel

Interview (one of twenty-three with West African men enslaved in Bahia, Brazil) with this Hausa man incorporated on pp. 10–25 of Francis de Castelnau, *Renseignements sur l'Afrique Centrale et sur une Nation d'Hommes a Queue qui s'y Trouverait, d'après le Rapport de Nègres du Soudan, Esclaves a Bahia.*

Paris [France]: P. Bertrand, Libraire-Éditeur, rue Saint-André-des-Arcs, 53, 1851. Half title verso: Paris: Imprimerie de L. Martinet, rue Mignon, 2.
8vo (22.5 cm.) 63 p., 4 plates (including map) + advertisements. Examined exemplar issued in original printed boards with publisher's advertisements dated 15 Septembre 1851.

https://babel. hathitrust.org/cgi/ pt?id=mdp.3901506 3860988&view=1u p&seq=14 [see 344.1].

¶ Mahammah was Hausa, born in Kano, the largest city under the Sokoto Caliphate (modern northern Nigeria—see Map 5). He was enslaved in Borgu after capture during a military expedition across the Niger River. He and other prisoners were taken through Yorùbá country to Lagos (western Nigeria). He was enslaved in Bahia, Brazil (Map 9), when interviewed in 1851.

345.1 Braz = Adam

Interview (one of twenty-three with West African men enslaved in Bahia, Brazil) with this Hausa man incorporated on pp. 26–28 of Francis de Castelnau, *Renseignements sur l'Afrique Centrale et sur une Nation d'Hommes a Queue qui s'y Trouverait, d'après le Rapport de Nègres du Soudan, Esclaves a Bahia.*

Paris [France]: P. Bertrand, Libraire-Éditeur, rue Saint-André-des-Arcs, 53, 1851. Half title verso: Paris: Imprimerie de L. Martinet, rue Mignon, 2.
8vo (22.5 cm.) 63 p., 4 plates (including map) + advertisements. Examined exemplar issued in original printed boards with publisher's advertisements dated 15 Septembre 1851.

https://babel. hathitrust.org/cgi/ pt?id=mdp.39015 063860988&view =1up&seq=30 [see 345.1].

¶ Braz was Hausa, from Baban Zaure village in Zaria (Zazzau, modern northern Nigeria—see Map 5). He was taken prisoner during a military expedition against Toto, located north of the confluence of the Niger and Benue rivers. He was taken to Lagos (western Nigeria) and was enslaved in Bahia, Brazil (Map 9), when interviewed in 1851.

346.1 Karo = Manuel

Interview (one of twenty-three with West African men enslaved in Bahia, Brazil) with this Bernou man incorporated on p. 29 of Francis de Castelnau, *Renseignements sur l'Afrique*

Centrale et sur une Nation d'Hommes a Queue qui s'y Trouverait, d'après le Rapport de Nègres du Soudan, Esclaves a Bahia.

Paris [France]: P. Bertrand, Libraire-Éditeur, rue Saint-André-des-Arcs, 53, **1851**. Half title verso: Paris: Imprimerie de L. Martinet, rue Mignon, 2.

8vo (22.5 cm.) 63 p., 4 plates (including map) + advertisements. Examined exemplar issued in original printed boards with publisher's advertisements dated 15 Septembre 1851.

https://babel.hathitrust.org/cgi/pt?id=mdp.39015063860988&view=1up&seq=33 [see 346.1].

¶ Karo was from Borno, not far from the Logone River and Mandara (modern northeastern Nigeria—see Map 5). He was captured in warfare near Damaturu and taken to Kano and then sold south to Lagos (western Nigeria). He was enslaved in Bahia, Brazil (Map 9), when interviewed in 1851.

347.1 Damoutourou

Interview (one of twenty-three with West African men enslaved in Bahia, Brazil) with this Borno man incorporated on p. 30 of Francis de Castelnau, *Renseignements sur l'Afrique Centrale et sur une Nation d'Hommes a Queue qui s'y Trouverait, d'après le Rapport de Nègres du Soudan, Esclaves a Bahia.*

Paris [France]: P. Bertrand, Libraire-Éditeur, rue Saint-André-des-Arcs, 53, **1851**. Half title verso: Paris: Imprimerie de L. Martinet, rue Mignon, 2.

8vo (22.5 cm.) 63 p., 4 plates (including map) + advertisements. Examined exemplar issued in original printed boards with publisher's advertisements dated 15 Septembre 1851.

https://babel.hathitrust.org/cgi/pt?id=mdp.39015063860988&view=1up&seq=34 [see 347.1].

¶ Damoutourou, whose name suggests that he was from Damaturu, was a farmer in Borno (modern Chad and Nigeria—see Map 5). Captured in the *jihād* ca. 1820, then transported on a slave ship to Brazil, he had been enslaved in Bahia, Brazil (Map 9) for thirty years when interviewed and still resented the Hausa for attacking his homeland.

348.1 Aba-Hama

Interview (one of twenty-three with West African men enslaved in Bahia, Brazil) with this Borno man incorporated on pp. 30–31 of Francis de Castelnau, *Renseignements sur l'Afrique Centrale et sur une Nation d'Hommes a Queue qui s'y Trouverait, d'après le Rapport de Nègres du Soudan, Esclaves a Bahia.*

Paris [France]: P. Bertrand, Libraire-Éditeur, rue Saint-André-des-Arcs, 53, **1851**. Half title verso: Paris: Imprimerie de L. Martinet, rue Mignon, 2.

8vo (22.5 cm.) 63 p., 4 plates (including map) + advertisements. Examined exemplar issued in original printed boards with publisher's advertisements dated 15 Septembre 1851.

https://babel.hathitrust.org/cgi/pt?id=mdp.39015063860988&view=1up&seq=34 [see 348.1].

¶ Aba-Hama was from Borno (modern Chad and Nigeria—see Map 5), where he was a citizen (*"shepherd"*) when captured and enslaved during the *jihād* (religious reform movement that involved warfare). He and others were taken through the interior to Lagos (western Nigeria). He had not been in Bahia, Brazil (Map 9), long when interviewed in 1851.

349.1 Sulaiman

Interview (one of twenty-three with West African men enslaved in Bahia, Brazil) with this Borno man incorporated on pp. 30–31 of Francis de Castelnau, *Renseignements sur l'Afrique Centrale et sur une Nation d'Hommes a Queue qui s'y Trouverait, d'après le Rapport de Nègres du Soudan, Esclaves a Bahia.*

Paris [France]: P. Bertrand, Libraire-Éditeur, rue Saint-André-des-Arcs, 53, **1851**. Half title verso: Paris: Imprimerie de L. Martinet, rue Mignon, 2.

8vo (22.5 cm.) 63 p., 4 plates (including map) + advertisements. Examined exemplar issued in original printed boards with publisher's advertisements dated 15 Septembre 1851.

https://babel.hathitrust.org/cgi/pt?id=mdp.39015063860988&view=1up&seq=34 [see 349.1].

¶ Sulaiman was from Borno (modern Chad and Nigeria—see Map 5), where he was a citizen (*shepherd*) when captured and enslaved during warfare with the Hausa, that is, during the *jihād* (religious reform movement that involved warfare) of the Sokoto Caliphate. He and others were taken through the interior to Lagos (western Nigeria). He had not been in Bahia, Brazil (Map 9) long when interviewed in 1851.

350.1 Ali

Interview (one of twenty-three with West African men enslaved in Bahia, Brazil) with this Borno man incorporated on pp. 30–31 of Francis de Castelnau, *Renseignements sur l'Afrique Centrale et sur une Nation d'Hommes a Queue qui s'y Trouverait, d'après le Rapport de Nègres du Soudan, Esclaves a Bahia.*

Paris [France]: P. Bertrand, Libraire-Éditeur, rue Saint-André-des-Arcs, 53, **1851**. Half title verso: Paris: Imprimerie de L. Martinet, rue Mignon, 2.

8vo (22.5 cm.) 63 p., 4 plates (including map) + advertisements. Examined exemplar issued in original printed boards with publisher's advertisements dated 15 Septembre 1851.

https://babel.hathitrust.org/cgi/pt?id=mdp.39015063860988&view=1up&seq=34 [see 350.1].

¶ Ali was from Borno (modern Chad and Nigeria—see Map 5), where he was a citizen (*shepher*d) when captured and enslaved during the *jihād* (religious reform movement that involved warfare). He and others were taken through the interior to Lagos (western Nigeria). He had not been in Bahia, Brazil (Map 9) long when interviewed in 1851.

351.1 Abubakar

Interview (one of twenty-three with West African men enslaved in Bahia, Brazil) with this Bagirmi man incorporated on pp. 31–32 of Francis de Castelnau, *Renseignements sur l'Afrique Centrale et sur une Nation d'Hommes a Queue qui s'y Trouverait, d'après le Rapport de Nègres du Soudan, Esclaves a Bahia.*

Paris [France]: P. Bertrand, Libraire-Éditeur, rue Saint-André-des-Arcs, 53, **1851**. Half title verso: Paris: Imprimerie de L. Martinet, rue Mignon, 2.

8vo (22.5 cm.) 63 p., 4 plates (including map) + advertisements. Examined exemplar issued in original printed boards with publisher's advertisements dated 15 Septembre 1851.

https://babel.hathitrust.org/cgi/pt?id=mdp.39015063860988&view=1up&seq=35 [see 351.].

¶ Abubakar was from Bagirmi, a tributary of Borno, from a large town called Massaigné on the Shari River (modern Chad and Nigeria—see Map 5). He traveled widely and was taken as a prisoner to Kukawa, the Borno capital, and from there to Kano. He was then taken to Lagos (western Nigeria). He was enslaved in Bahia, Brazil (Map 9) when interviewed in 1851.

352.1 Umaru [Mammarou]

Interview (one of twenty-three with West African men enslaved in Bahia, Brazil) with this Borno man incorporated on pp. 33–34 of Francis de Castelnau, *Renseignements sur l'Afrique Centrale et sur une Nation d'Hommes a Queue qui s'y Trouverait, d'après le Rapport de Nègres du Soudan, Esclaves a Bahia.*

Paris [France]: P. Bertrand, Libraire-Éditeur, rue Saint-André-des-Arcs, 53, **1851**. Half title verso: Paris: Imprimerie de L. Martinet, rue Mignon, 2.

8vo (22.5 cm.) 63 p., 4 plates (including map) + advertisements. Examined exemplar issued in original printed boards with publisher's advertisements dated 15 Septembre 1851.

https://babel.hathitrust.org/cgi/pt?id=mdp.39015063860988&view=1up&seq=37 [see 352.1].

¶ Umaru was from the mountainous region near Mandara and south of Borno (modern Chad and Nigeria—see Map 5). He was taken prisoner during warfare, almost certainly the *jihād* (religious reform movement that involved warfare), and taken west to Kano and then south to Lagos (western Nigeria). He was enslaved in Bahia, Brazil (Map 9) when interviewed in 1851.

353.1 So-Allah = David

Interview (one of twenty-three with West African men enslaved in Bahia, Brazil) with this man from Adamawa incorporated on pp. 35–36 of Francis de Castelnau, *Renseignements sur l'Afrique Centrale et sur une Nation d'Hommes a Queue qui s'y Trouverait, d'après le Rapport de Nègres du Soudan, Esclaves a Bahia.*

Paris [France]: P. Bertrand, Libraire-Éditeur, rue Saint-André-des-Arcs, 53, **1851**. Half title verso: Paris: Imprimerie de L. Martinet, rue Mignon, 2.

8vo (22.5 cm.) 63 p., 4 plates (including map) + advertisements. Examined exemplar issued in original printed boards with publisher's advertisements dated 15 Septembre 1851.

https://babel.hathitrust.org/cgi/pt?id=mdp.39015063860988&view=1up&seq=39 [see 353.1].

¶ So-Allah was from Adamawa (modern western Nigeria—see Map 5), his name suggesting that he was already enslaved. He was a cowherd, aged ten, when captured by Hausa and taken to Bauchi (modern central Nigeria). A year later he was sold, moved from place to place, then resold to a merchant from

Zaria (Zaazua, northern Nigeria), who took him to Lagos (western Nigeria). He arrived in Bahia, Brazil (Map 9) in 1851, just eight days prior to the interview. Because So-Allah did not know Portuguese, Muhammad (q.v. 357.1) interpreted for him.

354.1 Muhammad

Interview (one of twenty-three with West African men enslaved in Bahia, Brazil) with this Hausa man incorporated on p. 36 of Francis de Castelnau, *Renseignements sur l'Afrique Centrale et sur une Nation d'Hommes a Queue qui s'y Trouverait, d'après le Rapport de Nègres du Soudan, Esclaves a Bahia.*

https://babel.hathitrust.org/cgi/pt?id=mdp.39015063860988&view=1up&seq=40 [see 354.1].

Paris [France]: P. Bertrand, Libraire-Éditeur, rue Saint-André-des-Arcs, 53, **1851**. Half title verso: Paris: Imprimerie de L. Martinet, rue Mignon, 2.
8vo (22.5 cm.) 63 p., 4 plates (including map) + advertisements. Examined exemplar issued in original printed boards with publisher's advertisements dated 15 Septembre 1851.

¶ Muhammad was Hausa from Kano (modern northern Nigeria—see Map 5). About eighty years old when interviewed, he remembered little of his homeland. He had been in Bahia, Brazil (Map 9) for approximately sixty years when interviewed in 1851.

355.1 Usman = Francisco

Interview (one of twenty-three with West African men enslaved in Bahia, Brazil) with this Hausa man incorporated on pp. 37–38 of Francis de Castelnau, *Renseignements sur l'Afrique Centrale et sur une Nation d'Hommes a Queue qui s'y Trouverait, d'après le Rapport de Nègres du Soudan, Esclaves a Bahia.*

https://babel.hathitrust.org/cgi/pt?id=mdp.39015063860988&view=1up&seq=41 [see 355.1].

Paris [France]: P. Bertrand, Libraire-Éditeur, rue Saint-André-des-Arcs, 53, **1851**. Half title verso: Paris: Imprimerie de L. Martinet, rue Mignon, 2.
8vo (22.5 cm.) 63 p., 4 plates (including map) + advertisements. Examined exemplar issued in original printed boards with publisher's advertisements dated 15 Septembre 1851.

¶ Usman was Hausa, from Shira, east of Katsina (modern northwestern Nigeria—see Map 5). He was captured during a military expedition against Java (possibly Jigawa, in mod-

ern northwestern Nigeria) in which his master was killed. He was then sold and taken to Agadez to the north of Hausa country. He was then taken south into Zamfara and sold at Talata Mafara. Thereafter, he was taken to Ilorin and then Lagos (western Nigeria), where he was sold to European slave merchants and forced aboard a slave ship bound for Brazil ca. 1849/50. He had been enslaved in Bahia, Brazil (Map 9) less than a year when interviewed.

356.1 Idrisa [Grusa] = Augusto

Interview (one of twenty-three with West African men enslaved in Bahia, Brazil) with this Hausa-speaking man incorporated on pp. 38–39 of Francis de Castelnau, *Renseignements sur l'Afrique Centrale et sur une Nation d'Hommes a Queue qui s'y Trouverait, d'après le Rapport de Nègres du Soudan, Esclaves a Bahia.*

https://babel.hathitrust.org/cgi/pt?id=mdp.39015063860988&view=1up&seq=42 [see 356.1].

Paris [France]: P. Bertrand, Libraire-Éditeur, rue Saint-André-des-Arcs, 53, **1851**. Half title verso: Paris: Imprimerie de L. Martinet, rue Mignon, 2.
8vo (22.5 cm.) 63 p., 4 plates (including map) + advertisements. Examined exemplar issued in original printed boards with publisher's advertisements dated 15 Septembre 1851.

¶ Idrisa, an enslaved man from Zaria (Zaazua, modern Nigeria—see Map 5), spoke Hausa. He had never traveled but was sold to a merchant who took him to Lagos via Ilorin (western Nigeria), where he arrived after a journey lasting thirty-five days. He was enslaved in Bahia, Brazil (Map 9), when interviewed in 1851.

357.1 Muhammad = Manuel (ca. 1770–)

Interview (one of twenty-three with West African men enslaved in Bahia, Brazil) with this Hausa man incorporated on p. 39 of Francis de Castelnau, *Renseignements sur l'Afrique Centrale et sur une Nation d'Hommes a Queue qui s'y Trouverait, d'après le Rapport de Nègres du Soudan, Esclaves a Bahia.*

https://babel.hathitrust.org/cgi/pt?id=mdp.39015063860988&view=1up&seq=43 [see 357.1].

Paris [France]: P. Bertrand, Libraire-Éditeur, rue Saint-André-des-Arcs, 53, **1851**. Half title verso: Paris: Imprimerie de L. Martinet, rue Mignon, 2.

8vo (22.5 cm.) 63 p., 4 plates (including map) + advertisements. Examined exemplar issued in original printed boards with publisher's advertisements dated 15 Septembre 1851.

¶ Muhammad was Hausa (possibly modern northern Nigeria—see Map 5). He was taken prisoner by Fulani (Fula, Fulbi or Peul peoples throughout West Africa) in the *ihad* (religious reform movement that involved warfare) and sold about fifty years before he was interviewed in 1851. When interviewed in Bahia, Brazil (Map 9), he was more than eighty years old and could read and write. He knew of Timbuctu and recalled that his father wore a green turban.

358.1 Bawa = Boué = Antonio

Interview (one of twenty-three with West African men enslaved in Bahia, Brazil) with this Hausa man incorporated on p. 40 of Francis de Castelnau, *Renseignements sur l'Afrique Centrale et sur une Nation d'Hommes a Queue qui s'y Trouverait, d'après le Rapport de Nègres du Soudan, Esclaves a Bahia.*

https://babel.hathitrust.org/cgi/pt?id=mdp.39015063860988&view=1up&seq=44 [see 358.1].

Paris [France]: P. Bertrand, Libraire-Éditeur, rue Saint-André-des-Arcs, 53, **1851**. Half title verso: Paris: Imprimerie de L. Martinet, rue Mignon, 2.
8vo (22.5 cm.) 63 p., 4 plates (including map) + advertisements. Examined exemplar issued in original printed boards with publisher's advertisements dated 15 Septembre 1851.

¶ Bawa was Hausa from Zaria (Zaazua, modern northern Nigeria—see Map 5) who saw many countries during warfare. Taken as a prisoner in Nada, south of Bauchi, he was sold on the coast via Nupe and Asante. He saw a white person for the first time at Kumasi, the Asante capital (modern Ghana). He probably boarded a slave ship bound for Brazil at Petit Popo (Aneho, modern Togo). He was still in Bahia, Brazil (Map 9) when interviewed in 1851. For more on Bawa see Paul E. Lovejoy, *Jihād in West Africa during the Age of Revolutions* (Athens: Ohio University Press, 2016), 153 and 306n56, and João José Reis, *Slave Rebellion in Brazil: The Muslim Uprising of 1835 in Bahia*, translated by Arthur Brakel (Baltimore: Johns Hopkins University, 1993), 102–03.

359.1 Idris = Gross = Quacho

Interview (one of twenty-three with West African men enslaved in Bahia, Brazil) with this Hausa man incorporated on pp. 40–41 of Francis de Castelnau, *Renseignements sur l'Afrique Centrale et sur une Nation d'Hommes a Queue qui s'y Trouverait, d'après le Rapport de Nègres du Soudan, Esclaves a Bahia.*

Paris [France]: P. Bertrand, Libraire-Éditeur, rue Saint-André-des-Arcs, 53, **1851**. Half title verso: Paris: Imprimerie de L. Martinet, rue Mignon, 2.
8vo (22.5 cm.) 63 p., 4 plates (including map) + advertisements. Examined exemplar issued in original printed boards with publisher's advertisements dated 15 Septembre 1851.

https://babel.hathitrust.org/cgi/pt?id=mdp.39015063860988&view=1up&seq=44 [see 359.1].

¶ Idris was Hausa, a native of Lafia, to the west of Bauchi (modern Nigeria—see Map 5), who spoke Bada. He was a soldier, who after being captured was taken to a slave ship bound for Brazil. He was enslaved in Bahia, Brazil (Map 9) when interviewed in 1851.

360.1 Meidassara

Interview (one of twenty-three with West African men enslaved in Bahia, Brazil) with this Hausa man incorporated on pp. 41–42 of Francis de Castelnau, *Renseignements sur l'Afrique Centrale et sur une Nation d'Hommes a Queue qui s'y Trouverait, d'après le Rapport de Nègres du Soudan, Esclaves a Bahia.*

https://babel.hathitrust.org/cgi/pt?id=mdp.39015063860988&view=1up&seq=45 [see 360.1].

Paris [France]: P. Bertrand, Libraire-Éditeur, rue Saint-André-des-Arcs, 53, **1851**. Half title verso: Paris: Imprimerie de L. Martinet, rue Mignon, 2.
8vo (22.5 cm.) 63 p., 4 plates (including map) + advertisements. Examined exemplar issued in original printed boards with publisher's advertisements dated 15 Septembre 1851.

¶ Meidassara, probably Mai Nassara, was Hausa, a native of Kano (modern northern Nigeria—see Map 5), where he herded cattle and was a soldier. He was part of a military expedition against the Gwari when taken prisoner. As a captive, he was taken through Ilorin to Lagos (western Nigeria), where he was sold to Europeans and forced aboard a slave ship bound for Brazil. He was enslaved in Bahia, Brazil (Map 9) when interviewed in 1851.

361.1 Kiwa

Interview (one of twenty-three with West African men enslaved in Bahia, Brazil) with this Hausa man incorporated on p. 42 of Francis de Castelnau, *Renseignements sur l'Afrique Centrale et sur une Nation d'Hommes a Queue qui s'y Trouverait, d'après le Rapport de Nègres du Soudan, Esclaves a Bahia.*

Paris [France]: P. Bertrand, Libraire-Éditeur, rue Saint-André-des-Arcs, 53, **1851**. Half title verso: Paris: Imprimerie de L. Martinet, rue Mignon, 2.

8vo (22.5 cm.) 63 p., 4 plates (including map) + advertisements. Examined exemplar issued in original printed boards with publisher's advertisements dated 15 Septembre 1851.

https://babel.hathitrust.org/cgi/pt?id=mdp.39015063860988&view=1up&seq=46 [see 361.1].

¶ Kiwa was Hausa, from Zamfara (modern northwestern Nigeria—see Map 5), where he was a laborer. He was captured in war, mostly likely the *jihād* (religious reform movement that involved warfare), and taken to Lagos (western Nigeria), thereafter on a slave ship to Brazil. He was enslaved in Bahia, Brazil (Map 9) when interviewed in 1851.

362.1 Ibrahim

Interview (one of twenty-three with West African men enslaved in Bahia, Brazil) with this Borno man incorporated on p. 43 of Francis de Castelnau, *Renseignements sur l'Afrique Centrale et sur une Nation d'Hommes a Queue qui s'y Trouverait, d'après le Rapport de Nègres du Soudan, Esclaves a Bahia.*

Paris [France]: P. Bertrand, Libraire-Éditeur, rue Saint-André-des-Arcs, 53, **1851**. Half title verso: Paris: Imprimerie de L. Martinet, rue Mignon, 2.

8vo (22.5 cm.) 63 p., 4 plates (including map) + advertisements. Examined exemplar issued in original printed boards with publisher's advertisements dated 15 Septembre 1851.

https://babel.hathitrust.org/cgi/pt?id=mdp.39015063860988&view=1up&seq=47 [see 362.1].

¶ Ibrahim was from Borno (modern Chad and Nigeria—see Map 5). His father was also from Borno, and his mother was Hausa. His father, a pious Muslim, took him to Mecca (Map 2). He was taken on a slave ship to Brazil and was enslaved in Bahia (Map 9) when interviewed in 1851. Castelnau describes him as a young man.

363.1 Abu = Élias

Interview (one of twenty-three with West African men enslaved in Bahia, Brazil) with this Hausa man incorporated on p. 43 of Francis de Castelnau, *Renseignements sur l'Afrique Centrale et sur une Nation d'Hommes a Queue qui s'y Trouverait, d'après le Rapport de Nègres du Soudan, Esclaves a Bahia.*

Paris [France]: P. Bertrand, Libraire-Éditeur, rue Saint-André-des-Arcs, 53, **1851**. Half title verso: Paris: Imprimerie de L. Martinet, rue Mignon, 2.

8vo (22.5 cm.) 63 p., 4 plates (including map) + advertisements. Examined exemplar issued in original printed boards with publisher's advertisements dated 15 Septembre 1851.

https://babel.hathitrust.org/cgi/pt?id=mdp.39015063860988&view=1up&seq=47 [see 363.1].

¶ Abu was Hausa, a native of Katsina (modern northwestern Nigeria—see Map 5). After capture, he was taken prisoner at "Curucu" (perhaps Kuduru; the location has not yet been identified) and passed through various other places before being transported on a slave ship to Brazil. He was enslaved when interviewed in Bahia, Brazil (Map 9) in 1851.

364.1 Rescou

Interview (one of twenty-three with West African men enslaved in Bahia, Brazil) with this Upea man incorporated on p. 44 of Francis de Castelnau, *Renseignements sur l'Afrique Centrale et sur une Nation d'Hommes a Queue qui s'y Trouverait, d'après le Rapport de Nègres du Soudan, Esclaves a Bahia.*

Paris [France]: P. Bertrand, Libraire-Éditeur, rue Saint-André-des-Arcs, 53, **1851**. Half title verso: Paris: Imprimerie de L. Martinet, rue Mignon, 2.

8vo (22.5 cm.) 63 p., 4 plates (including map) + advertisements. Examined exemplar issued in original printed boards with publisher's advertisements dated 15 Septembre 1851.

https://babel.hathitrust.org/cgi/pt?id=mdp.39015063860988&view=1up&seq=48 [see 364.1].

¶ Rescou was from Upea, a native of Moïga, a large town eight days from Rabba in Nupe (that is, Miga in Jigawa, modern northwestern Nigeria—see Map 5), where he was a farmer and raised yams. Castelnau's account states that his people were "idolaters." He was taken on a slave ship to Brazil and was enslaved in Bahia (Map 9) when interviewed in 1851.

365.1 Bagué

Interview (one of twenty-three with West African men enslaved in Bahia, Brazil) with this Tapa man incorporated on pp. 45–46 of Francis de Castelnau, *Renseignements sur l'Afrique Centrale et sur une Nation d'Hommes a Queue qui s'y Trouverait, d'après le Rapport de Nègres du Soudan, Esclaves a Bahia.*

Paris [France]: P. Bertrand, Libraire-Éditeur, rue Saint-André-des-Arcs, 53, **1851**. Half title verso: Paris: Imprimerie de L. Martinet, rue Mignon, 2.

8vo (22.5 cm.) 63 p., 4 plates (including map) + advertisements. Examined exemplar issued in original printed boards with publisher's advertisements dated 15 Septembre 1851.

¶ Bagué was from Rabba, the capital of Nupe and a large town on the Niger River (modern northwestern Nigeria—see Map 5). He was taken on a slave ship to Brazil and was enslaved in Bahia (Map 9) when interviewed in 1851.

https://babel.hathitrust.org/cgi/pt?id=mdp.39015063860988&view=1up&seq=49 [see 365.1].

366.1 Muhammad Abdullah (ca. 1780 –)

Interview (one of twenty-three with West African men enslaved in Bahia, Brazil) with this Fulani man incorporated on pp. 46–48 of Francis de Castelnau, *Renseignements sur l'Afrique Centrale et sur une Nation d'Hommes a Queue qui s'y Trouverait, d'après le Rapport de Nègres du Soudan, Esclaves a Bahia.*

Paris [France]: P. Bertrand, Libraire-Éditeur, rue Saint-André-des-Arcs, 53, **1851**. Half title verso: Paris: Imprimerie de L. Martinet, rue Mignon, 2.

8vo (22.5 cm.) 63 p., 4 plates (including map) + advertisements. Examined exemplar issued in original printed boards with publisher's advertisements dated 15 Septembre 1851.

¶ Muhammad Abdullah was Fulani (Fula, Fulbi or Peul peoples throughout West Africa), a native of Kano (modern northern Nigeria—see Map 5), who had been in Bahia, Brazil (Map 9), for thirty years. A pious Muslim, he had traveled to Mecca (Map 2) before he was captured in the *jihād* (religious reform movement that involved warfare) and taken to Katsina and then Lagos (western Ghana), where he was forced aboard a slave ship bound for Brazil. He eventually purchased his

https://babel.hathitrust.org/cgi/pt?id=mdp.39015063860988&view=1up&seq=50 [see 366.1].

freedom and worked as a carpenter. Aged 70, he was learning to read and write Portuguese when interviewed in 1851 and did not readily cooperate with Castelnau. For more on him, see Paul E. Lovejoy, *Jihād in West Africa*, 153–54.

367.1 Dasalu = Ogan = John Baptist Dasalu

Account of his life (including premature report of his death) printed under heading "John, one of the killed at Abbeokuta" on pp. 220–223 in October 1851 issue (New Series vol. 1, no. 19) of *The Church Missionary Gleaner.*

https://babel.hathitrust.org/cgi/pt?id=uc1.a0007600034&view=1up&seq=257 [see 367.2].

London [England]: Seeleys, Fleet Street, and Hanover Street, Hanover Square, **October 1851**. General volume tpv: William M. Watts, Printer, Crown Court, Temple Bar, London. 8vo (21 cm.). Note: Hogg 1503 is 367.10 below.

¶ Dasalu was Yorùbá, son of the ruler, from Abeokuta (modern southwest Nigeria—see Map 5). As a young man he was a warrior and slave trader and had two wives. After hearing Christian preaching, he created a sensation by publicly converting and giving up his non-Christian wife. Thereafter, he preached against slavery, practiced Christianity secretly at night, and after his father's death declined to accept a high position that he viewed as corrupt. On Christmas Day 1849 Dasalu and others began worshiping openly in church, which prompted a persecution that singled out Dasalu. In 1851 he fought in a war against King Gezo of Dahomey (modern Benin) and helped repel an attack on Abeokuta, in part by uniting Christian and non-Christian forces. In the follow-up campaign Dasalu was captured and held in Abomey (modern Benin) until late 1853 or early 1854. After redemption failed, he was taken to Ouidah (modern Benin) for some time, then forcibly transported on a slave ship to the Spanish colony of Cuba in the Caribbean (Map 12). At sea a Spanish cruiser intercepted this ship, took Dasalu and the other enslaved Africans to Havana, Cuba, and liberated them. As an *Emancipado* his freedom was restricted until Church Missionary Society officials heard his story, successfully convinced the British Consul in Havana to intervene on Dasalu's behalf, and paid his passage to Lagos via England. He reached England in August 1856, then continued on to Lagos.

367.2——.

Account of his life printed within Chapter XVI (entitled "John Baptist Dasalu," drawing on 367.1 and other articles, and written after Dasalu was discovered to be alive) on pp. 220–225 in Sarah Tucker, *Abbeokuta; or Sunrise within the Tropics: An Outline of the Origin and Progress of the Yoruba Mission.*

London [England]: James Nisbet and Co., Berners Street, 1853. Tpv: London: C. Richards, 11 St. Martin's Lane.

8vo (18 cm.): vi, 278 p., plates, folding map. Preface dated in type (p. iv): West Hendred [Berkshire, England], *April,* 1853.

https://babel.hathitrust.org/cgi/pt?id=uc1.a0007600034& view=1up&seq=257

367.3———.

Account of his life printed within Chapter XVI (entitled "John Baptist Dasalu") on pp. 220–225 in Sarah Tucker, *Abbeokuta; or Sunrise within the Tropics: An Outline of the Origin and Progress of the Yoruba Mission. Second edition.*

London [England]: James Nisbet and Co., Berners Street, 1853.

8vo (18 cm.): vi, 278 p., plates, folding map.

367.4———.

Account of his life printed within Chapter XVI (entitled "John Baptist Dasalu") on pp. 220–225 in Sarah Tucker, *Abbeokuta; or Sunrise within the Tropics: An Outline of the Origin and Progress of the Yoruba Mission.*

New York [New York, U.S.A.]: Robert Carter and Brothers, No. 285 Broadway, 1853. Tpv blank. [Noticed by *The New York Daily Times*, October 25, 1853.]

8vo (18 cm.): vi, 278 p., plates, folding map. This and subsequent New York editions appear to have been printed from stereotype plates obtained from the publishers of 367.2 and .3.

https://babel.hathitrust.org/cgi/pt?id=hvd.32044088678420 &view=1up&seq=252

367.5———.

Account of his life printed within Chapter XVI (entitled "John Baptist Dasalu") on pp. 220–225 in Sarah Tucker, *Abbeokuta; or Sunrise within the Tropics: An Outline of the Origin and Progress of the Yoruba Mission. Third edition.*

London [England]: James Nisbet and Co., Berners Street, 1854.

8vo (18 cm.): vi, 278 p., plates, folding map.

367.6———.

Account of his life printed within Chapter XVI (entitled "John Baptist Dasalu") on pp. 220–225 in Sarah Tucker, *Abbeokuta; or Sunrise within the Tropics: An Outline of the Origin and Progress of the Yoruba Mission. Fourth edition.*

London [England]: James Nisbet and Co., Berners Street, 1854. Tpv blank.

8vo (18 cm.): vi, 278 p., plates, folding map.

https://babel.hathitrust.org/cgi/pt?id=ucbk.ark:/28722/ h2pr7mv26&view=1up&seq=248

367.7———.

Account of his life printed within Chapter XVI (entitled "John Baptist Dasalu") on pp. 220–225 in Sarah Tucker, *Abbeokuta; or Sunrise within the Tropics: An Outline of the Origin and Progress of the Yoruba Mission.*

New York [New York, U.S.A.]: Robert Carter and Brothers, 1854.

8vo (18 cm.): vi, 278 p., plates, folding map.

367.8———.

French translation of account of his life (explicitly from 367.5) printed within Chapter XVI on pp. 237–246 in Sarah Tucker, *Le Christianisme sous les Tropiques: Abbeokuta: origine et développement du Christianisme et de la Civilisation dans l'Afrique Centrale.* Traduit de l'anglais, sur la 3me edition, par J. G., pasteur.

Paris [France]: Grassart, Libraire-Editeur, 11, rue de la Paix; Genève [Switzerland]: E. Béroud, Libraire; Lausanne [Switzerland]: Delafontaine et Cie; 1854. Half title verso: Abbeville: Imp. Jennet, rue Saint-Gilles, 108.

8vo (19 cm.): 298 p.

https://gallica.bnf.fr/ark:/12148/bpt6k5723294x/f246.item

367.9———.

Account of his life printed within Chapter XVI (entitled "John Baptist Dasalu") on pp. 220–225 in Sarah Tucker, *Abbeokuta; or Sunrise within the Tropics: An Outline of the Origin and Progress of the Yoruba Mission.*

New York [New York, U.S.A.]: Robert Carter and Brothers, No. 285 Broadway, 1855. Tpv blank.

8vo (18 cm.): vi, 278 p., plates, folding map.

https://archive.org/details/sunrisetropics00tuckuoft/page/ n237/mode/1up

367.10 ———.

Account of his life to date ("John Dasalu is [now] in Cuba, an Emancipado") printed on pp. 275–276 within the long double-column article "The Emancipados and Their Fatherland," which is printed on pp. 267–279 in *The Church Missionary Intelligencer, A Monthly Journal of Missionary Information,* vol. 6, December issue.

London [England]: Seeley, Jackson, and Halliday, Fleet Street, and Hanover Street, Hanover Square; T. Hatchard, Piccadilly;

and J. Nisbet and Co., Berners Street, [December] **1855**. Colophon: [Printed by] W. M. Watts, Crown Court, Temple Bar. Hogg 1503.
https://archive.org/details/1855TheChurchMissionaryIntelligencer/page/n290/mode/1up

367.11 ———.

Brief account of his life up to the time he was on Cuba awaiting the Church Missionary Society's application for assistance to the British government to convince the Spanish government to allow Dasalu to leave for England printed on pp. 11–13 in *The Yoruba Mission*, No. II [i.e. 2].

London [England]: Seeleys, Fleet Street, and Hanover Street, Hanover Square; and Wertheim and Macintosh, 24, Paternoster Row, [**1855** or early **1856**]. One Penny, or 5 s. per 100. Colophon: T. C. Johns, Printer, Wine Office Court, Fleet Street.
8vo (18 cm.): 15 p., illustrated wrapper (neither Dasalu nor his torture depicted, *qq.v* 367.13 and 365.14). Series: Church Missionary Tracts, No. 16.

367.12 ———.

Account of his life printed within Chapter XVI (entitled "John Baptist Dasalu") on pp. 220–225 in Sarah Tucker, *Abbeokuta; or Sunrise within the Tropics: An Outline of the Origin and Progress of the Yoruba Mission. Fifth edition.*

London [England]: James Nisbet and Co., Berners Street, **1856**. Tpv: London: Printed by Sercombe and Jack, 16 Great Windmill Street.
8vo (18 cm.): vi, 278 p., illus.
https://babel.hathitrust.org/cgi/pt?id=hvd.32044088678438&view=1up&seq=250

367.13 ———.

Account of his life (including his voyage from Cuba to England in August 1856 and subsequent return to Lagos) printed on pp. 241–244 (with illustration of **Dasalu enduring torture** on p. 242) within the article "Slave Trade Operations," which is printed on pp. 241–255 in *The Church Missionary Intelligencer, A Monthly Journal of Missionary Information*, vol. 7, October issue.

London [England]: Seeley, Jackson, and Halliday, Fleet Street, and Hanover Street, Hanover Square; T. Hatchard, Piccadilly; and J. Nisbet and Co., Berners Street, [October] **1856**. Tpv: [Printed by] W. M. Watts, Crown Court, Temple Bar.
https://archive.org/details/1856TheChurchMissionaryIntelligencer/page/n264/mode/1up

367.14 ———.

German-language account of his life printed within wide-ranging article under title "John Baptist Dasalu" on pp. 49–79 of the February 1857 issue and pp. 125–141 of the March 1857 issue

of *Evangelisches Missions-Magazin*, Neue folge, vol. 1, herausgegeben im Auftrag der Evangelischen Missionsgesellschaft [= Lutheran Mission Society] von Dr. Albert Ostertag.

Basel [Switzerland]: Im Verlag des Missions-Comptoirs, In Commission bei J. F. Steinkopf in **Stuttgart [Württemberg, Germany]**, [February-March] **1857**.
8vo (23 cm.). Illus. (**bust-length portrait of Dasalu** on p. 49; Dasalu enduring torture on p. 129). Note: this text is the basis of 367.16.
https://babel.hathitrust.org/cgi/pt?id=hvd.ah6elw&view=1up&seq=63

367.15 ———.

Account of his life printed within Chapter XVI (entitled "John Baptist Dasalu") on pp. 220–225 in Sarah Tucker, *Abbeokuta; or Sunrise within the Tropics: An Outline of the Origin and Progress of the Yoruba Mission.*

New York [New York, U.S.A.]: Robert Carter and Brothers, No. 530 Broadway, **1857**. Tpv blank.
12mo (16 cm.): vi, 278, plates, folding map.
https://babel.hathitrust.org/cgi/pt?id=nyp.33433000854335&view=1up&seq=242

367.16 ———.

French-language account of his life within wide-ranging article entitled "Missions Evangeliques" printed as No. 32 (Supplement du no. 31), 8 Novembre 1857, of *Feuille Religieuse du Canton de Vaud*.

Lausanne [Switzerland]: Au Bureau de la Feuille Religieuse, rue de Grand St-Jean, no. 41, **1857**. Colophon: Lausanne [Switzerland]: Imprimerie Genton, Voruz et Vinet.
8vo (xx cm.): pp. 497–512.
https://babel.hathitrust.org/cgi/pt?id=hvd.ah6ez2&view=1up&seq=507

367.17 ———.

German-language account of his life within wide-ranging work editorially altered or authorially revised from 367.14 separately printed with title *John Baptist Dasalu: ein Lebensbild aus West-Afrika.*

Basel [Switzerland]: Verlag des Missionshauses, **1858**.
Small 8vo (17 cm.): 63 p., illus. (relief-cut illustration of Dasalu enduring torture on p. 47). Examined exemplar lacks printed wrapper (hence imprint). Text adapted from 365.14 and here printed in nine numbered sections, viz.: 1. Die vorlaufende Gnade. 2. Die Glaubensproben. 3. Das rätselhafte Verschwinden. 4. Die Emancipados auf der Insel Cuba. 5. Die wiedergefundene Spur Dasalu's. 6. Leandro Llopar. 7. Dasalu's Gefangennehmung. 8. Dasalu in die Sklaverei verkauft. 9. Die Heimkehr.

367.18 ——.

Norwegian translation of 367.14 printed in three parts under heading "John Baptist Dasalu. (Meddeelt efter *Baseler Missions-Magazin* af perf. Cavell. P. Winsnes)" on pp. 28–33 in the February 1858 issue (vol. 13, no. 2), pp. 37–48 in the March 1858 issue (vol. 13, no. 3), and pp. 73–81 in the May 1858 issue (vol. 13, no. 5) of *Norsk Missions-Tidende, utgiven af Det Norske Missionsselstab*, edited by P. Blessing.

Colophon: **Stavanger** [**Norway**]: Utgiven paa det Norske Missionsselstabs Forlag af P. Blessing, Trykt hos L. C. Keilland [February-May] **1858.**

8vo (21 cm.).

https://babel.hathitrust.org/cgi/pt?id=hvd.ah669w&view=1up&seq=36

367.19——. [German translation of Sarah Tucker's *Abbeokuta*]

Account of his life printed within Chapter XVI (entitled "John Baptist Dasalu") on p. 204 in *Abbeokuta; oder, Sonnenaufgang zwischen den Wendekreisen: eine Schilderung der Mission im Lande Yoruba; aus dem Englischen, bis auf die Gegenwart fortgeseszt und wesentlich erweitert durch die Einleitung: Die Morgenröthe des tropischen Afrika von W. Hoffmann.*

Berlin [**Prussia, Germany**]: Verlag von Wiegandt und Grieben, **1859.** Colophon: Berlin, druck von Gustav Schade, Marienstrasse Nr. 10.

8vo (xx cm.): vi, [2], 318, folding map. Note: Hoffman's foreword dated in type (p. iv): Berlin, den 25. Januar 1859.

https://babel.hathitrust.org/cgi/pt?id=uc1.a0000018564&view=1up&seq=218

367.20——.

Account of his life printed within Chapter XVI (entitled "John Baptist Dasalu") on pp. 220–225 in Sarah Tucker, *Abbeokuta; or Sunrise within the Tropics: An Outline of the Origin and Progress of the Yoruba Mission.*

New York [**New York, U.S.A.**]: Robert Carter and Brothers, No. 530 Broadway, **1859.** Tpv blank.

12mo (16 cm.): vi, 278, plates, folding map.

https://babel.hathitrust.org/cgi/pt?id=hvd.32044004616272&view=1up&seq=271

367.21 ——.

Account of his life printed within Chapter XVI (entitled "John Baptist Dasalu") on pp. 220–225 in Sarah Tucker, *Abbeokuta; or Sunrise within the Tropics: An Outline of the Origin and Progress of the Yoruba Mission.*

New York [**New York, U.S.A.**]: General Protestant Episcopal Sunday School Union and Church Book Society, **1859.**

12mo (16 cm.): vi, 278, plates, folding map.

367.22 ——.

French-language account of his life printed as Chapter XII (entitled "Dasalu. Vie et aventures d'un chef nègre devenu chrétien, transporté comme esclave en Amérique et ramené plus tard dans son pays") on pp. 179–205 in Adam Vuillet, *Scènes et Aventures de Voyages: Histoires et Récits destinés à intéresser à l'étude de la géographie. 4e partie: Récits sur l'Afrique.*

Paris [**France**]: Librairie de Ch. Meyrueis et Ce, Editeurs, rue de Rivoli, 174, **1859.** Half title verso: Paris: Typographie de Ch. Meyrueis et Ce, rue de Grès, 11.

12mo (19 cm.): 252 p.

367.23——.

Norwegian translation (distinct from 367.18) of 367.14 printed in three parts under heading "John Baptist Dasalu. (Meddeelt efter *Baseler Missions-Magazin* af perf. Cavell. P. Winsnes)" on pp. 171–175 in the November 1859 issue (vol. 4, no. 11), pp. 25–29 in the January 1860 issue (vol. 5, no. 1), and pp. 46–50 in the February 1860 issue (vol. 5, no. 2) of *Kirkelig Maanedstidende for den norsk-evangelisk-Lutherske kirke i Amerika*, edited by H. A. Preus.

Vol. 4 imprint: **Madison, Wisconsin** [**U.S.A.**]: Udgivet af Den Skandinavische Presse-Forening, "Emigrantens" Tryk i Offizen, [November] **1859.** Note: Imprint from title page for this year of issues.

8vo (22 cm.).

Vol. 5 imprint: **Madison, Wisconsin** [**U.S.A.**]: Udgivet af C. Fr. Solberg, "Emigrantens" Offizen, [January-February] **1860.** Note: Imprint from title page for bound annual volume.

8vo (22 cm.).

https://babel.hathitrust.org/cgi/pt?id=iau.31858045162033&view=1up&seq=403

https://babel.hathitrust.org/cgi/pt?id=hvd.ah6eg9&view=1up&seq=33

367.24 ——.

Account of his life printed within Chapter XVI (entitled "John Baptist Dasalu") on pp. 220–225 in Sarah Tucker, *Abbeokuta; or Sunrise within the Tropics: An Outline of the Origin and Progress of the Yoruba Mission.*

New York [**New York, U.S.A.**]: General Protestant Episcopal Sunday School Union and Church Book Society, **1861.**

12mo (16 cm.): vi, 278, plates, folding map.

367.25 ——.

Malayalam-language account of his life separately printed with title *John Baptist Dasalu.*

Tellicherry [i.e., **Thalassery, Kerala, India**]: [Tellicherry Mission Press], **1862.**

8vo?: 33 p. Report of the printing of eight hundred copies on a lithographic press at Tellicherry in *Report of the Basel Evangelical Missionary Society, Forty-Seventh Year, 1862; Twenty-Third Report of the Basel Evangelical Mission in South Western India* (Mangalore: Printed by J. Hunziker: Basel Mission Press, 1863), pp. 45–46.

367.26 ——.

Account of his life printed within Chapter XVI (entitled "John Baptist Dasalu") on pp. 220–225 in Sarah Tucker, *Abbeokuta; or Sunrise within the Tropics: An Outline of the Origin and Progress of the Yoruba Mission.*

London [England]: James Nisbet and Co., Berners Street, 1863.
8vo (18 cm.): vi, 278 p., plates, folding map.

367.27 ——.

Bishop John Payne's account of John Gottlieb Auer's oral retelling of Dasalu's life story at a Missionary Society meeting held on 17 June 1868 at Cavalla Mission, Cape Palmas, Liberia, printed under heading "Dasalu" on p. 767 in the October issue (vol. 33, no. 10) of *The Spirit of Missions;* edited for the Board of Missions of the Protestant Episcopal Church in the United States of America, by the Secretaries and General Agents of the two committees of the Freedman's Commission.

New York [New York, U.S.A.]: Published for the Board of Missions at Nos. 17 & 19 Bible House. Sanford, Cushing & Co., 644 & 646 Broadway, October **1868.** [Imprint from monthly issues' printed paper covers.]
8vo (24 cm.). Note comment by Auer or Payne: "Why do we need *fictitious* stories when we have many *so much more interesting* in the real history of the kingdom of Providence and grace."
https://babel.hathitrust.org/cgi/pt?id=wu.89064896947&view=1up&seq=783

367.28 ——.

Dutch-language account of his life (a translation from a German-language account) printed on pp. 28–52 in W[ilhelm] Ziethe, *De Gelukkige Schipbreuk, en John Baptist Dasalu: twee verhalen.* Uit het Hoogduitsch vertaald onder toezicht van T[theodorus] M[atthijs] Looman.

Utrecht [The Netherlands]: J. H. Van Peursem, **1868.** Tpv: Snelpersdruk: Kemink en Zoon, te Utrecht.
8vo: 52 p.
https://www.delpher.nl/nl/boeken1/gview?coll=boeken1&identifier=fKpZAAAAcAAJ

367.29 ——.

German-language account of his life written by Pastor [Georg Eduard Wilhelm] Licht of Wulkow (in office 1854–1883) printed under title *Dasalu, eine Missionsgeschichte aus Westafrika: für die lieben Kinder erzählt.*

Neu-Ruppin [Brandenburg, Germany]: Druck von G. Buchbinder, [s.a., perhaps 1872+/-8 years?]. Note: imprint combined from colophon and outer front wrapper.
8vo (19 cm.): 16 p., including 2 illus. (including Dasalu withstanding torture on p. 13) + relief-cut portrait of Dasalu printed on front wrapper.
https://digital.library.temple.edu/digital/collection/p16002coll5/id/10504

367.30 ——.

German-language account of his life separately printed with title *John Baptist Dasalu.*

Cleveland, Ohio [U.S.A.]: [Verlag von] W. F. Schneider* [214–220 Woodland Avenue], [s.a., perhaps 1875+/-4 years?].
24mo (13 cm.): 32 p., illus. Exemplar reported at Drew University, Madison, New Jersey, U.S.A..
*Note: the Rev. Mr. W. F. Schneider (1834–1879) was a Cleveland publisher and book agent connected with religious publications during at least his final decade.

367.31 ——.

Account of his life printed within Chapter XVI (entitled "John Baptist Dasalu") on pp. 220–225 in Sarah Tucker, *Abbeokuta; or Sunrise within the Tropics: An Outline of the Origin and Progress of the Yoruba Mission.*

New York [New York, U.S.A.]: Robert Carter and Brothers, **1875.**
12mo (16 cm.): vi, 278, plates, folding map.

367.32 ——.

German-language account of his life separately printed with title *John Baptist Dasalu : ein Lebensbild aus West-Afrika.*

Basel [Switzerland]: Verlag des Missionsbuchhandlung, **1877.**
8vo (18 cm.): 62 p.

367.33 ——.

Abridged account of his life printed on p. 32, with relief-cut illustration of Dasalu enduring torture printed on p. 30, in the March 1885 issue (vol. 12, no. 135) of *The Church Missionary Gleaner.*

London [England]: Church Missionary House, Salisbury Square. Seeley, Jackson, & Halliday, 46, 47, 48, Essex Street, Strand., **1885.**
4to.

367.34 ———.

Account of his life printed on pp. 118–119 in vol. 2 of *The History of the Church Missionary Society, Its Environment, Its Men, and Its Work,* edited by Eugene Stock.

London [England]: Church Missionary Society, Salisbury Square, E.C, **1899.** Tpv: London: Printed by Gilbert and Rivington, LD. [*sic*], St. John's House, Clerkenwell, E.C. 3 vols., 8vo (23 cm.).

https://archive.org/details/historychurchmis02stoc/page/118/mode/1up

1852

368.1 Adéolà (ca. 1802–) = Diola = Triumfo Souchay

Account taken down in writing in Cuba by Franz Hugo Hesse, Prussian General Consul to Central America, and sent to the university geography professor in Berlin, Carl Ritter, who published it in German on pp. 12–

https://www.digizeitschriften.de/dms/img/?PID=P-PN391365584_1853_0010llog12&physid=phys30#navi [see 368.1].

14 of his article "Mittheilungen über einige westafricanische Stämme in Cuba, gesammelt von Hesse," *Monatsberichte über die Verhandlungen der Gesellschaft für Erdkunde zu Berlin,* New Series vol. 10: 12–16.

Berlin [Germany]: bei Simon Schropp und Comp., **1853.** Colophon: Druck von Trowitzsche und Sohn in Berlin. 8vo: xvi, 228 p.

¶ Adéolà identified as Lucumí, a New World designation for people who were primarily Yorùbá (Carl Ritter identifies him in 368.1 as Igbo), from the lower Niger River area (see Map 5). He was captured by the Afanga people in war, sold to Europeans, and taken to the West Indies when aged fifteen, ca. 1817. He lived and worked with 320 enslaved people (one third of whom were African) on the *Angerena* plantation near Artemisa in the Western Department of the Spanish Caribbean colony of Cuba (Map 12). Adéolà bought his own freedom with lottery winnings and remained on the plantation, working as a smith. In 1852 he told Hesse his story, which included many details about life in his homeland.

368.2 ———.

English translation of a significant portion of Adéolà's account printed on p. 97 in Henry B. Lovejoy, *Prieto: Yorùbá Kingship in Colonial Cuba during the Age of Revolutions.*

Chapel Hill [North Carolina, U.S.A.]: University of North Carolina Press, **2018.** 8vo (24 cm.): xviii, 219 p.

368.3 ———.

English translation of a significant portion of Adéolà's account printed on p. 97 in Henry B. Lovejoy, *Prieto: Yorùbá Kingship in Colonial Cuba during the Age of Revolutions.*

Chapel Hill [North Carolina, U.S.A.]: University of North Carolina Press, **2019.** 8vo (24 cm.): xviii, 220 p.

369.1 Bokary (ca. 1777–) = Banco

Account taken down in writing in Cuba by Franz Hugo Hesse, Prussian General Consul to Central America, and sent to the university geography professor in Berlin, Carl Ritter, who published it in German on p. 14 of his article "Mittheilun-

https://www.digizeitschriften.de/dms/img/?PID=P-PN391365584_1853_0010llog12&physid=phys30#navi [see 369.1].

gen über einige westafricanische Stämme in Cuba, gesammelt von Hesse," *Monatsberichte über die Verhandlungen der Gesellschaft für Erdkunde zu Berlin,* New Series vol. 10: 12–16.

Berlin [Germany]: bei Simon Schropp und Comp., **1853.** Colophon: Druck von Trowitzsche und Sohn in Berlin. 8vo: xvi, 228 p. FN000954.

¶ Bokary identified as Mandinka (an ethnic group residing in modern southern Mali, Guinea, and Ivory Coast—see Map 3), where his father was a priest (neither Muslim nor Christian). Ca. 1806 he was taken from Africa to the West Indies on a slave ship, where he lived and worked for forty-six years with 320 other enslaved people (one third of whom were African) on the *Angerena* plantation near Artemisa in the Western Department of the Spanish Caribbean colony of Cuba (Map 12). In 1852 he told Hesse his story, which included some details about religious life in his homeland.

370.1 Bela = Rafael

Account taken down in writing in Cuba by Franz Hugo Hesse, Prussian General Consul to Central America, and sent to the university geography professor in Berlin, Carl Ritter, who published it in German on p. 14 of his article "Mittheilungen über einige westafricanische Stämme in Cuba, gesammelt von Hesse," *Monatsberichte über die Verhandlungen der Gesellschaft für Erdkunde zu Berlin*, New Series vol. 10: 12–16.

https://www.digi-zeitschriften.de/dms/img/?PID=PPN391365584_1853_0010llog12&physid=phys30#navi [see 370.1].

Berlin [Germany]: bei Simon Schropp und Comp., 1853. Colophon: Druck von Trowitszche und Sohn in Berlin.
8vo: xvi, 228 p.

¶ Bela identified as Gangomanie, a people not yet identified. After being taken prisoner during war, he was sold at age fourteen to another people and subsequently to Europeans who took him to the West Indies on a slave ship. In the Western Department of the Spanish Caribbean colony of Cuba (see Map 12) he lived and worked with 320 other enslaved people (one third of whom were African) on the *Angerena* plantation near Artemisa. In 1852 he told Hesse his story, which included details about religious life, weaponry, and trade in his homeland.

371.1 Sidice = Julio

Account taken down in writing in Cuba by Franz Hugo Hesse, Prussian General Consul to Central America, and sent to the university geography professor in Berlin, Carl Ritter, who published it in German on pp. 14–16 of his article "Mittheilungen über einige westafricanische Stämme in Cuba, gesammelt von Hesse," *Monatsberichte über die Verhandlungen der Gesellschaft für Erdkunde zu Berlin*, New Series vol. 10: 12–16.

https://www.digizeitschriften.de/dms/img/?PID=PPN391365584_1853_0010llog12&physid=phys32#navi [see 371.1].

Berlin [Germany]: bei Simon Schropp und Comp., 1853. Colophon: Druck von Trowitszche und Sohn in Berlin.
8vo: xvi, 228 p.

¶ Sidice, a Muslim, identified as Mandinka (an ethnic group residing in modern southern Mali, Guinea, and Ivory Coast—

see Map 3), from an interior country whose capital was Vudi. In 371.1 Carl Ritter identified Sidice's homeland (which Sidice said bordered the land of the Susu) as on the upper Niger River, based on his king's name (Kankan). Sidice was taken in the slave trade to the West Indies. He lived in the Spanish Caribbean colony of Cuba's Western Department (Map 12) and worked for thirty years as a carpenter with 320 other enslaved people (one third of whom were African) on the *Angerena* plantation near Artemisa. In 1852 he told Hesse his story and included extensive details on agriculture, wildlife, fishing and hunting, slavery, and other subjects about his homeland.

372.0 Ngeve (ca. 1820–1891) = Catherine Mulgrave = Catherine Zimmermann = Kitty

Her account incorporated in a letter written by her husband Johann Zimmermann to Basel Mission Headquarters, from Usu (i.e., Accra) 18 November 1852, preserved in the Basel Mission Archives (Archives of the Basel Mission), Basel, Switzerland.

https://doczz.fr/doc/1369155/the-provenance-of-catherine-mulgrave-zimmermann [see 372.1].

¶ Ngeve was a young girl when in 1833 she was enslaved on a Luanda beach (modern Angola—see Map 6) and forced aboard a slave ship bound for the Spanish Caribbean colony of Cuba (Map 12). When the ship wrecked in the Caribbean off Jamaica's coast, Ngeve survived and was freed. Governor Mulgrave and his wife, after whom Ngeve was renamed, took her and others into his household in Jamaica (Map 13). After the Mulgraves left Jamaica, she was placed in the Moravian Mission in Fairfield, Manchester Parish, Jamaica, where she became a teacher. In 1841, she married George Thompson (who was originally from Liberia and a representative of the Basel Mission in Switzerland) and they moved to the Basel Mission on the Gold Coast in what became Accra (modern Ghana—Map 5). After Thompson died, she married the Basel Mission's head, Johann Zimmermann, and to him dictated her life story, which he incorporated in 372.0. For more on Ngeve see Maureen Warner-Lewis, "Catherine Mulgrave's Unusual Transatlantic Odyssey," *Jamaica Journal* 31 (2008): 32–43.

372.1———.

372.0 transcribed by Dr. Peter Haenger and printed in the original German on pp. 259–261 followed by her obituary notice on p. 262 in Paul E. Lovejoy, "Les origines de Catherine Mulgrave Zimmermann: considérations méthodologiques," translated by Carole Masseaut, *Cahiers des Anneaux de la Mémoire: Une Revue Historique sur la Traite de l'Esclavage* , no. 14 ("L'Afrique centrale atlantique"), pp. 247–263.

Figure 17: Ngeve, also known as Catherine Mulgrave, Catherine Zimmermann, and Kitty (ca. 1820–1891), sitting third from left, with husband and five children. After experiencing capture as a child in Luanda (modern Angola), enslavement, a shipwreck, freedom, and life on Jamaica, she married a man from the Basel Mission in Accra (modern Ghana) and was living there when this photograph was made.

Source: Unknown studio, 1872–1873, Reference Number QS-30.002.0237.02, Basel Mission Archives/Basel Mission Holdings, Basel, Switzerland.

See https://www.bmarchives.org/items/browse#q=QS-30.002.0237.02.

Paris [France]: Karthala, **2011.**
8vo (24 cm.): 383 p.
Note: For the above article in the original English, along with the transcriptions in German of the letter an obituary see Paul E. Lovejoy, "The Provenance of Catherine Mulgrave

Zimmermann: Methodological Considerations," Harriet Tubman Seminar, York University, Toronto [Canada], 12 October 2010.

https://doczz.fr/doc/1369155/the-provenance-of-catherine-mulgrave-zimmermann

1853

373.0   Abuncare (– ca. 1853) = Abubakar = José Maria Rufino

"Auto de perguntas feitas ao preto forro Rufino José Maria," in Arquivo Nacional, **Rio de Janeiro, Brazil,** IJ1 326 (1853–1854), Pernambuco, Offícios do Presidente da Província ao Ministro da Justiça.

¶ José Maria Rufino was born in Oyo, an ancient empire encompassing modern Benin and western Nigeria (see Map 5).

A Muslim, he was taken on a slave ship to Bahia, Brazil, in 1822 or 1823 and bought by a druggist in Salvador, Bahia (Map 9). Ca. 1830 he was taken with his owner's son south to Rio Grande do Sul province and there sold to a merchant, who absconded in bankruptcy two years later. Rufino was then purchased at auction by a judge. He bought his own freedom in 1835, went to Rio de Janeiro, Brazil, and later worked as a cook on slave ships running between Angola (Map 6) and Pernambuco, Brazil. In 1841 his ship was captured by a British antislavery patrol, which took everyone, including Rufino, to Sierra Leone (Map 4). Not wanting to stay there, Rufino returned to Pernambuco, where he sold textiles for a few months, then returned to Sierra Leone to study Islam and Arabic at Fourah Bay College in Freetown. Proficient in Arabic, he returned to Brazil. He settled with his son in Recife in 1845, but soon moved to Rio de Janeiro and then Bahia. In 1853 he was arrested with others and held for two weeks in Recife for possessing Arabic manuscripts, which the police believed promoted a conspiracy among the enslaved. For more on him, see João José Reis, Flávio dos Santos Gomes, and Marcus Caravalho, *O Alufá Rufino: Tráfico, escravidão e liberdade no Atlantico Negro c. 1822–c. 1853* (São Paulo: Companhia das Letras, 2010) or Sabrina H. Gledhill's translation of this work, published under the title *The Story of Rufino Slavery, Freedom, and Islam in the Black Atlantic* (Oxford: Oxford University Press, 2020), and Habeeb Akande, *Illuminating the Blackness: Blacks and African Muslims in Brazil* (London: Rabaah Publishers, 2016), 239–243.

373.1——.

Account within article by a Recife (Pernambuco, Brazil) journalist printed under dateline 16 de setembro de 1853 on p. [1], col. 5, of the 25 September 1853 issue (anno XXVIII, n. 266) of the Rio de Janeiro newspaper *Jornal do Commercio*.

Rio de Janeiro, Brazil: em casa de Junius Villeneuve e C., rua do Ovidor n. 65; de F. Duprat, na **Bahia** [Brazil], e de L. Lecomte Feron e C., em **Pernambuco** [Brazil], 1853.
Broadsheet quadrifolium.
http://memoria.bn.br/DocReader/DocReader.aspx?bib=364568_04&pagfis=5964

374.0 Aneaso (ca. 1790–1864) / Aniaso = Toby = Archibald Monteith / Monteath / Archy

The lengthy print history of Aneaso's autobiography is based on several texts produced from 1843 to ca. 1872 and recorded by Moravian missionaries who spoke at length with Aneaso in their community at New Carmel, Jamaica:

(1) Correspondence of John Elliot from 1843, first published in:

Description of Archey [*sic*] Monteith's (Aneaso's) mission work at New Carmel, Jamaica, including extended quotations of his direct speech, in missionary correspondence from Brother John Elliot, dated New Carmel, 26 June 1843, printed in German on pp. 1055–1056 in sechstes Heft [sixth issue]

http://memoria.bn.br/DocReader/DocReader.aspx?bib=364568_04&pagfis=5964 [see 373.1].

of vol. 25 (for 1843) of the Moravian journal *Nachrichten aus der Brüder-Gemeine.*

Gnadau [Saxony, Germany]: im Verlag der Buchhandlung der evangelischen Brüder-Unität bei Hans Franz Burkhard, so wie in allen Brüder-Gemeinen; bei E. Kummer in **Leipzig [Saxony, Germany]** und bei Felix Schneider in **Basel [Switzerland]**, [mid-1843].
8vo (20 cm.).
https://collections.mun.ca/digital/collection/nachrichten/id/40394/rec/148
https://babel.hathitrust.org/cgi/pt?id=hvd.ah3mxl&view=1up&seq=577

(2) A manuscript produced by Moravian missionary John H. Buchner in 1844 based on conversation(s) with Aneaso, first published in:

Description and characterization of Archibald Monteith (Aneaso) recorded by Moravian missionary John H. Buchner, based on conversation(s) with Aneaso in 1844, including quotations of Aneaso's direct speech, printed in German in "Bericht von Bruder Buchner von Bethanien auf Jamaika vom Jahr 1844," pp. 207–237 (especially 229–233) in Zweites Heft [second issue] of vol. 29 (for 1847) of the Moravian journal *Nachrichten aus der Brüder-Gemeine.*

Gnadau [Saxony, Germany]: im Verlag der Buchhandlung der evangelischen Brüder-Unität bei H. L. Menz, so wie in allen Brüder-Gemeinen; bei Eduard Kummer in **Leipzig [Saxony, Germany]** und bei Felix Schneider in **Basel [Switzerland]**, [1847].
8vo (20 cm.).
https://collections.mun.ca/digital/collection/nachrichten/id/41209/rec/168
https://babel.hathitrust.org/cgi/pt?id=hvd.ah3mx-4&view=1up&seq=241

[Part 1]:
https://babel.hathitrust.org/cgi/pt?id=hvd.ah3sec&view=1up&seq=463
[Part 2]:
https://babel.hathitrust.org/cgi/pt?id=hvd.ah3sec&view=1up&seq=511
[see 374.5].

(3) An English manuscript recorded by Moravian missionary Joseph Horsfield Kummer in 1853 and copied by Kummer ca. 1872 (first published in 1966—see 374.17). The original manuscript has not yet been located, but Kummer's own copy is held in the Moravian Archives, **Bethlehem, Pennsylvania, U.S.A.**, which has digitized it here:

https://www.moravianchurcharchives.findbuch.net/php/main. php#4d6973734a6d63x56.

(4) An English manuscript recorded by Moravian missionary Hermine Geissler in 1864 (first published in 1867—see 374.10).

(5) Geissler's 1864 German translation of her own English recording (first published in 1864—see 374.3).

Note: Because the 1853 (3) version is a much more substantial and complete autobiographical account than the two that preceded it, the compilers have placed this entry under 1853 instead of 1843. For a comparative assessment of the 1853 and 1864 texts see Angelo Costanzo, "The Narrative of Archibald Monteith, a Jamaican Slave," in *Callaloo: A Journal of African Diaspora Arts and Letters,* 13:1 (Winter 1990): 115–130, and Vernon H. Nelson (see 372.14), which contains the complete text with an explanatory apparatus.

¶ Probably born about 1789 (as per Thomas Harvey in 374.8) or 1792 (Maureen Warner-Lewis in 374.16, p. 41), Aneaso was Igbo (modern southeast Nigeria—see Map 5), the son of a field worker. Sometime before adolescence Aneaso was kidnapped, put on a slave ship, and taken to Kingston, Jamaica, the British Caribbean colony (Map 13). His detailed account includes his description of the Middle Passage aboard a large slave ship. Upon reaching Jamaica he was sold to John Monteath, a Moravian planter who renamed Aneaso "Toby," and took him to New Carmel plantation, where he began work as a house slave. He received some schooling and became a supervisor in 1815 after his owner's death. Ca. 1820 he began living first with one woman and then four. He converted and embraced Moravian Christianity, and in 1826 married Rebecca Hart, also a Moravian. Thereafter, Aneaso helped build the church at New Carmel and became an official and teacher in the church community of enslaved people. He purchased his freedom in 1837, the year before general Jamaican emancipation. In 1853 he provided his autobiography in English to the missionary pastor J. H. Kummer. In 1864 he provided it again to Moravian missionary Hermine Geissler during his final illness. For more on Aneaso and the people among whom he lived in Africa and Jamaica, see Maureen Warner-Lewis, *Archibald Monteath, Igbo, Jamaican, Moravian* (Kingston: University of the West Indies Press, 2007). On 11 March 2007 a documentary film showing Aneaso's/Archibald Monteith's British descendant David Monteith trace his great-great-great-great-grand-father's journey from Nigeria to Jamaica, entitled "The Last Slaves," aired on British television's Channel 4 (BBC 4).

374.1———.

Memoir (*Lebenslauf*) dictated in 1864 in English to Moravian missionary Hermine Geissler at New Carmel, Jamaica and translated into German by Geissler, printed in German under heading "Erlebnisse eines ehemaligen Sclaven in Jamaica," in two parts, i.e., on pp. 87–102 in issue no. 5 (May), and on pp. 105–115 in issue no. 6 (June) of *Missions-Blatt aus der Brüdergemeine,* vol. 28 (1864).

Herrnhut [Saxony, Germany]: Verlag der Missionsverwaltung, **[May-June] 1864.**
8vo (22 cm.).

374.2———.

German translation by Geissler (374.1) printed as "Erlebnisse eines ehemaligen Sclaven in Jamaika" in issue no. 18 of *Das Missions-Blatt,* edited by Pastor [Ernst Hermann?] Thümmel.

Barmen [Prussian territory, Germany]: Missions-Gesellschaft; **Leipzig [Saxony, Germany]:** Wagner, **1864.**

374.3———.

Elements of the German translation by Geissler (374.1) printed in six sections prefixed with Roman numerals I–VI under heading "Aneaso" (within a longer multipart article headed "Jamaika einst und jetzt" [= "Jamaica then and now"]) on pp. 529–568 in the December 1864 issue (new series vol. 8, no. 12) of the *Evangelisches Missions-Magazin,* edited by Albert Ostertag.

Basel [Switzerland]: im Verlag des Missions-Comptoirs. In commission bei J. F. Steinkopf in **Stuttgart [Württemberg, Germany]** und Bahnmaier's Buchhandlung (...) in Basel, **[December, 1864].**
8vo (23 cm.).
http://idb.ub.uni-tuebingen.de/opendigi/GkII73-1864_HG-Jamaika-4#p=5

374.4———.

His life story retold in *Aneaso, der Neger aus dem Ibo-Lande.*

Basel [Switzerland]: Verlag des Missionshaus, **1865.**
8vo (18 cm.): 55 p. Note: Sometimes attributed to Dr. Hermann Gundert (1814–1893).

374.5———.

English-language original of memoir (*Lebenslauf*) dictated in 1864 [374.0(4)] or loose English retranslation of its German-language publication 374.0(1) above printed in two parts (with an added introductory paragraph before the first, and quotation of several paragraphs written by Br. [Abraham] Lichtenthaeler of New Carmel recounting Aneaso's final months, death, and burial, at end of the second) under heading "Memoir of Br. Archibald Monteith, who departed this life at Carmel, Jamaica, July 5th, 1864" as the lead articles in the September (pp. 433–441) and December (pp. 481–485) 1865 issues of the Moravian journal *Periodical Accounts Relating to the Missions of the Church of the United Brethren, Established Among the Heathen,* vol. 25.

London [England]: Printed by W. M'Dowell, 7, Church Passage, Chancery Lane. For the Brethren's Society for the Furtherance of the Gospel among the Heathen. Sold at 97 Hatton Garden and by all Booksellers, 1863 [1865]. Note: Vol. 25's general title page (covering issues published from December 1863 to March 1866, as listed on p. 600) is misleadingly dated only 1863.

8vo (22 cm.).

[Part 1]: https://babel.hathitrust.org/cgi/pt?id=hvd.ah3sec& view=1up&seq=463

[Part 2]: https://babel.hathitrust.org/cgi/pt?id=hvd.ah3sec& view=1up&seq=511

374.6 ———.

His life story retold in *Aneaso, der Neger aus dem Ibo-Lande.*

Basel [Switzerland], 1866.

8vo: 55 p. Note: Sometimes attributed to Dr. Hermann Gundert (1814–1893).

374.7 ———.

His life story retold in *Aneaso, der Neger aus dem Ibo-Lande.*

Berlin [Prussia, Germany]: E. Beck, 1866.

8vo: 55 p. Note: Sometimes attributed to Dr. Hermann Gundert (1814–1893).

374.8 ———.

1864 Memoir (*Lebenslauf*) reprinted from *Periodical Accounts* (374.5), with the added introductory paragraph and concluding quotation of several paragraphs written by Br. [Abraham] Lichtenthaeler recounting Aneaso's final months, death, and burial printed there, as Appendix C on pp. 88–100 in Thomas Harvey and William Brewin, *Jamaica in 1866: A Narrative of a Tour Through the Island, with Remarks on its Social, Educational, and Industrial Condition.*

London [England]: A. W. Bennett, 5, Bishopsgate Street Without, **1867.** Tpv: Printed by Edward Newman, 9, Devonshire Street, Bishopsgate.

8vo (22 cm.): viii, 126, folding map.

374.9 ———. [Second edition of 374.6]

His life story retold in *Aneaso, oder Durch Sklaverei Zur Freiheit.*

Basel [Switzerland]: Verlag der Missionsbuchhandlung, **1883.**

8vo: 48 p. Note: Attributed variously to Dr. Hermann Gundert (1814–1893) and Albert Ostertag (1810–1871).

374.10 ———.

His life story retold and printed under caption title "Archibald Monteith" as no. 21 in the tract series *Missionsstunden aus der Brüdergemeine.*

Herrnhut [Saxony, Germany]: Missionsbuchhandlung der Missionsanstalt der Evang. Brüder-Unität, **1898.**

8vo, 15 p.

Note: First page reproduced as full-page illustration in Warner-Lewis, 2007, p. 10. According to Warner-Lewis's list of sources (p. 357), Mary Kuck translated this tract into English in 1997.

374.11a ———. [Discrete issue of 374.11b or vice versa; priority not established]

Concise synopsis of Aneaso's memoir written by Bishop Augustus Westphal printed on p. 165 in Walter Hark and Augustus Westphal, *The Breaking of the Dawn; or, Moravian Work in Jamaica, 1754–1904.*

London [England]: The Moravian Mission Agency, 32, Fetter Lane, **[1904].** Price, 2 shillings, 6 pence.

8vo (22 cm.): 188 p., plates. Reference for this imprint/issue: *"The Harmony": The Missionary Ship of the Society for the Furtherance of the Gospel*, vol. 6, no. 61 (March 1905), p. 56; and Warner-Lewis, 2007, p. 355.

374.11b ———. [Discrete issue of 374.11a or vice versa; priority not established]

Concise synopsis of Aneaso's memoir written by Bishop Augustus Westphal printed on p. 165 in Walter Hark and Augustus Westphal, *The Breaking of the Dawn; or, Moravian Work in Jamaica, 1754–1904.*

Belfast [County Antrim, Ireland]: [Printed by Wm.] Strain [& Sons, Gt. Victoria Street], **[1904].**

8vo (22 cm.): 188 p., plates. Reference for this imprint/issue: 374.15, p. 129, note 3.

374.11c ———. [Another issue of previous two items; priority not established]

Concise synopsis of Aneaso's memoir written by Bishop Augustus Westphal printed on p. 165 in Walter Hark and Augustus Westphal, *The Breaking of the Dawn; or, Moravian Work in Jamaica, 1754–1904.*

[*Sine loco*]: Jamaican Moravian Church, **[1904?].**

8vo (22 cm.): 188 p., plates. Reference for this imprint/issue: MARC record.

374.12 ———.

Aneaso's 1853 autobiography [374.0(3)] as recorded by Moravian missionary Joseph Horsfield Kummer, printed with annotations by Vernon H. Nelson under title "Archibald John Monteith: Native Helper and Assistant in the Jamaica Mission at New Carmel [1853]" on pp. 29–52 in *Transactions of the Moravian Historical Society*, vol. 21, no. 1.

Nazareth, Pennsylvania [U.S.A.]: Moravian Historical Society, **1966**.
8vo (23 cm.).
Hogg 1591.

374.13 ——.

His life story retold in John Aaon's article "The Story of Aneaso, the Son of Durl and Dirinejah" printed on pp. 53–58 in vol. 7, nos. 3–4, of *Jamaican Historical Society Bulletin.*

[**Kingston, Jamaica**]: Jamaica Historical Society, **1977**.
4to (28 cm.).

374.14 ——.

His life story retold in John Aaon's article "The Story of Archibald Monteith" printed on pp. 73–77 in vol. 7, nos. 5, of *Jamaican Historical Society Bulletin.*

[**Kingston, Jamaica**]: Jamaica [sic] Historical Society, **1977**.
4to (28 cm.).

374.15 ——.

Aneaso's 1853 autobiography as recorded by Moravian missionary Joseph Horsfield Kummer, printed with annotations by Vernon H. Nelson (see 317.12) under title "Archibald John Monteith: Native Helper and Assistant in the Jamaica Mission at New Carmel [1853]" on pp. 102–114 in *Callaloo: A Journal of African Diaspora Arts and Letters,* vol. 13, no. 1.

Baltimore [**Maryland, U.S.A.**]: Johns Hopkins University Press, Winter **1990**.
8vo (26 cm.).

374.16 ——.

Memoir (*Lebenslauf*) dictated in 1864 and printed in German in 372.1 translated into English in 2002 by Mary Kuck and printed with annotations as Appendix 1 on pp. 267–285 in Maureen Warner-Lewis, *Archibald Monteath* [sic]: *Igbo, Jamaican, Moravian.*

Kingston [**Jamaica**]: University of the West Indies Press, **2007**.
8vo (26 cm.): xv, 367 p., maps, illus.

374.17 ——.

Aneaso's 1853 autobiography as recorded by Moravian missionary Joseph Horsfield Kummer reprinted with annotations by Vernon H. Nelson from 374.12 as Appendix 2 on pp. 286–304 in Maureen Warner-Lewis, *Archibald Monteath* [sic]: *Igbo, Jamaican, Moravian.*

Kingston [**Jamaica**]: University of the West Indies Press, **2007**.
8vo (26 cm.): xv, 367 p., maps, illus.

Another published work by John Archibald Monteith

+374-A.1 ——.

Letter professing his faith and devotion to the New Carmel community written by John Archibald Monteith at New Carmel, Jamaica, on 29 November 1855 to John Jacob Kummer (father of New Carmel's Moravian minister Joseph Horsfield Kummer) printed in 1966 on pp. 51–52n18 of 317.12.

+374-A.2 ——.

Letter professing his faith and devotion to the New Carmel community written by John Archibald Monteith at New Carmel, Jamaica, on 29 November 1855 to John Jacob Kummer reproduced in reduced facsimile in 2007 as fig. 10.2 on p. 239 of 374.16.

1854

¶ Note for entries 375 through 434, sixty named individuals from Sierra Leone. As noted under Hogg 1611 (Sigismund Wilhelm Koelle, *Polyglotta Africana; or a Comparative Vocabulary of Nearly three hundred words and phrases, in more than one Hundred distinct African Languages* [London, Church Missionary House, 1854]), the Rev. Mr. S. W. Koelle interviewed approximately 180 men, most of whom had been enslaved but had become Liberated Africans after being taken off slave ships by the British Royal Navy in Freetown, Sierra Leone (see Map 4). These included people from a large number of language groups covering much of West and West Central Africa, as well as a few outlying districts in East Africa. The sixty men whose accounts are listed below were taken from slave ships or coastal barracoons and transported by British warships directly or indirectly to Freetown. For more on Koelle's work with these men, see: P. E. H. Hair, "The Enslavement of Koelle's Informants," *Journal of African History,* 6 (1965): 193–203; and Franz Pruner-Bey, "'Rapport sur la 'Polyglotta Africana'... de Sigismund Wilhelm Koelle," in *Bulletin de la Société de Géographie,* 5e série, 6 (July 1863): 333–346.

375.1 Isambakon (ca. 1808–) = George File

Account of this man from Fúlup (Senegal) printed on p. 1 of S. W. Koelle, *Polyglotta Africana.*

London [**England**]: Church Missionary House, Salisbury Square, Fleet Street, MDCCCLIV [1854].
Folio (50 cm.): vi, 24 (2 columns each), 188 (8 columns each) p., folding map, errata slip.
Hogg 1611.

¶ Isambakon was born in a village called Bátēndu (probably in Senegal's Casamance region [see Map 3], since he spoke Fúlup Jola-Felupe). Kidnapped by Esin people ca. 1830, he was then sold in Elálāp. After five years there he was taken to Gádsou, or Kadsiou, where he spent three years in the hands of a Portuguese man, then five years in Bissau (modern Guinea Bissau). After thirteen years of enslavement in Africa, he was put on a slave ship bound for Brazil or Cuba in 1843. This ship was intercepted at sea by a British warship and taken to Sierra Leone (Map 4). Isambakon lived in the village of Kissy near Freetown when Koelle interviewed him.

Full text: https://huskiecommons.lib.niu.edu/history-500africanvoices/198/ [see 375.1].

375.2——.

Photomechanical reprint of 375.1 with addition of historical introduction by P. E. H. Hair. Limited to two hundred copies "distributed free of charge to scholars of African languages throughout the world."

Freetown [Sierra Leone]: University College of Sierra Leone, Fourah Bay College, **1963.** Tpv: This numbered edition of two hundred copies is not available for distribution through the book-trade.
Folio (38 cm.): 19, vi, 24, 188 p., folding map.

375.3——.

Photomechanical reprint of 375.1, with additions, viz. *Polyglotta Africana / Vermehrt durch eine historische Einführung von P. E. H. Hair und einen Wortindex von David Dalby.* Published in association with *The African Language Review.*

Graz [Austria]: Akademische Druck- u. Verlagsanstalt [**1963**].
Folio (38 cm.): 19, vi, 24, 188 p., folding map.

376.1 Kayawon = Abraham Belford

Account of this man from Filham or Filhal printed on p. 1 of S. W. Koelle, *Polyglotta Africana.*

London [England]: Church Missionary House, Salisbury Square, Fleet Street, MDCCCLIV [**1854**].
Folio (50 cm.): vi, 24 (2 columns each), 188 (8 columns each) p., folding map, errata slip.
Hogg 1611.

Full text: https://huskiecommons.lib.niu.edu/history-500africanvoices/199/ [see 376.1].

¶ Kayawon was born in Búntun (modern Senegal—see Map 3), the Filham capital, and spoke that language or Filhal (Dyola). In his sixth year his family moved to Tónari, where he grew up, married, and had four children. His oldest child was eight when Kayawon was captured during warfare with Báyūn. He was forcibly taken on a slave ship into the Atlantic and arrived ca. 1840 in Demerara, the British colony on the northern coast of South America (Map 10 – in northeastern Suriname at the time the borders of the map represented), where slavery ended by 1838. It is unclear whether his slave ship was intercepted at sea by the British, who liberated the passengers and took them to Demerara, or whether the slave ship took Kayawon to another colony, from which he escaped to Demerara. How he traveled from there to Sierra Leone (Map 4) is also unclear. He lived in Kissy near Freetown when Koelle interviewed him.

376.2——.

Photomechanical reprint of 376.1 with addition of historical introduction by P. E. H. Hair. Limited to two hundred copies "distributed free of charge to scholars of African languages throughout the world."

Freetown [Sierra Leone]: University College of Sierra Leone, Fourah Bay College, **1963.** Tpv: This numbered edition of two hundred copies is not available for distribution through the book-trade.
Folio (38 cm.): 19, vi, 24, 188 p., folding map.

376.3——.

Photomechanical reprint of 376.1, with additions, viz. *Polyglotta Africana / Vermehrt durch eine historische Einführung von P. E. H. Hair und einen Wortindex von David Dalby.* Published in association with *The African Language Review.*

Graz [Austria]: Akademische Druck- u. Verlagsanstalt [**1963**].
Folio (38 cm.): 19, vi, 24, 188 p., folding map.

377.1 Bukar (ca. 1811–) = John Campbell

Account of this man from Biafada printed on p. 1 of S. W. Koelle, *Polyglotta Africana.* **London [England]:** Church Missionary House, Salisbury Square, Fleet Street, MDCCCLIV [**1854**].

Folio (50 cm.): vi, 24 (2 columns each), 188 (8 columns each) p., folding map, errata slip.
Hogg 1611.

Full text: https://huskiecommons.lib.niu.edu/history-500africanvoices/200/ [see 377.1].

¶ Bukar was born in a village called Taba and spoke Biafada, a language spoken near Bissau and Cacheu (modern Guinea Bissau—see Map 3). When aged sixteen, he moved with his family to Wakora, where they lived together for six years. Bukar was then captured during a civil war, sold, and forced aboard a slave ship ca. 1833. A British cruiser intercepted the ship and took it to Sierra Leone Map 4), where Bukar met Koelle some twenty years later.

377.2——.

Photomechanical reprint of 377.1 with addition of historical introduction by P. E. H. Hair. Limited to two hundred copies "distributed free of charge to scholars of African languages throughout the world."

Freetown [Sierra Leone]: University College of Sierra Leone, Fourah Bay College, **1963.** Tpv: This numbered edition of two hundred copies is not available for distribution through the book-trade.
Folio (38 cm.): 19, vi, 24, 188 p., folding map.

377.3——.

Photomechanical reprint of 377.1, with additions, viz. *Polyglotta Africana / Vermehrt durch eine historische Einführung von P. E. H. Hair und einen Wortindex von David Dalby.* Published in association with *The African Language Review.*

Graz [Austria]: Akademische Druck- u. Verlagsanstalt [**1963**].
Folio (38 cm.): 19, vi, 24, 188 p., folding map.

378.1 Téte = Frederick Gibbon

Account of this man from Gbótūe printed on p. 4 of S. W. Koelle, *Polyglotta Africana.* London [England]: Church Missionary House, Salisbury Square, Fleet Street, MDCCCLIV [**1854**].

Folio (50 cm.): vi, 24 (2 columns each), 188 (8 columns each) p., folding map, errata slip.
Hogg 1611.

Full text: https://huskiecommons.lib.niu.edu/history-500african-voices/201/ [see 378.1].

¶ Téte was born in Gbótūe (a Ewe or Adangebe area in modern Ghana, Togo, or Benin—see Map 5) and spoke Adámpe. He married there and had a child aged five when seized by Gádsa people because of a debt owed by another (otherwise unconnected) Gbótūe man. After five months imprisonment Téte was carried to Gírefē, a Dahomean slave port (probably Ouidah in modern Benin). There he was forced aboard a slave ship that the British subsequently intercepted at sea and took to Sierra Leone (Map 4) ca. 1827. Immediately after arrival in Sierra Leone, Téte enlisted as a soldier and served under the British

flag for twenty-one years in Sierra Leone and Gambia. He was discharged five years before Koelle interviewed him in Freetown (where he resided).

378.2——.

Photomechanical reprint of 378.1 with addition of historical introduction by P. E. H. Hair. Limited to two hundred copies "distributed free of charge to scholars of African languages throughout the world."

Freetown [Sierra Leone]: University College of Sierra Leone, Fourah Bay College, **1963.** Tpv: This numbered edition of two hundred copies is not available for distribution through the book-trade.
Folio (38 cm.): 19, vi, 24, 188 p., folding map.

378.3——.

Photomechanical reprint of 378.1, with additions, viz. *Polyglotta Africana / Vermehrt durch eine historische Einführung von P. E. H. Hair und einen Wortindex von David Dalby.* Published in association with *The African Language Review.*

Graz [Austria]: Akademische Druck- u. Verlagsanstalt [**1963**].
Folio (38 cm.): 19, vi, 24, 188 p., folding map.

379.1 Atigózi = James Richard

Account of this man from Ouidah printed on p. 4 of S. W. Koelle, *Polyglotta Africana.*

London [England]: Church Missionary House, Salisbury Square, Fleet Street, MDCCCLIV [**1854**].
Folio (50 cm.): vi, 24 (2 columns each), 188 (8 columns each) p., folding map, errata slip.
Hogg 1611.

Full text: https://huskiecommons.lib.niu.edu/history-500african-voices/202/ [see 379.1].

¶ Atigózi was born in Agwe (Agūe, in modern Togo—see Map 5) and spoke Hweda. He grew up there and was married for three years when captured during a war with the Dahomeans, sold to Portuguese at Ouidah (modern Benin), and forced aboard a slave ship ca. 1838. The British intercepted this ship at sea and took it to Sierra Leone (Map 4), where the ship's captain was tried before a Court of Mixed Commission and the freed captives apprenticed as Liberated Africans. Atigózi lived in Freetown when Koelle interviewed him.

379.2——.

Photomechanical reprint of 379.1 with addition of historical introduction by P. E. H. Hair. Limited to two hundred copies "distributed free of charge to scholars of African languages throughout the world."

Freetown [Sierra Leone]: University College of Sierra Leone, Fourah Bay College, **1963**. Tpv: This numbered edition of two hundred copies is not available for distribution through the book-trade.
Folio (38 cm.): 19, vi, 24, 188 p., folding map.

379.3———.

Photomechanical reprint of 379.1, with additions, viz. *Polyglotta Africana / Vermehrt durch eine historische Einführung von P. E. H. Hair und einen Wortindex von David Dalby*. Published in association with *The African Language Review*.

Graz [Austria]: Akademische Druck- u. Verlagsanstalt [**1963**]. Folio (38 cm.): 19, vi, 24, 188 p., folding map.

380.1 Odíēmi = James Wilhelm

Account of this man from Dsumu, or Idsumu, printed on p. 6 of S. W. Koelle, *Polyglotta Africana*.

London [England]: Church Missionary House, Salisbury Square, Fleet Street, MDCCCLIV [**1854**].
Folio (50 cm.): vi, 24 (2 columns each), 188 (8 columns each) p., folding map, errata slip.
Hogg 1611.

Full text: https:// huskiecommons. lib.niu.edu/history-500african-voices/203/ [see 380.1].

¶ Odíēmi was born in Gori in (modern western Nigeria—see Map 5) the Niger River valley and spoke Dsumu, or Idsumu. Aged eighteen, he moved to Okuro, another Idsumu town, where he lived for ten years until Nupes and Agoi invaded and conquered Dsumu, destroying all its towns. Odíēmi was captured, sold to Yorùbá people (modern Nigeria, Benin and Togo), and carried to the coast, where he was forced aboard a slave ship that was intercepted at sea by the British. After freeing its enslaved passengers, the British ship took them to Sierra Leone (Map 4). Odíēmi lived in Freetown when Koelle interviewed him.

380.2———.

Photomechanical reprint of 380.1 with addition of historical introduction by P. E. H. Hair. Limited to two hundred copies "distributed free of charge to scholars of African languages throughout the world."

Freetown [Sierra Leone]: University College of Sierra Leone, Fourah Bay College, **1963**. Tpv: This numbered edition of two hundred copies is not available for distribution through the book-trade.
Folio (38 cm.): 19, vi, 24, 188 p., folding map.

380.3———.

Photomechanical reprint of 380.1, with additions, viz. *Polyglotta Africana / Vermehrt durch eine historische Einführung von P. E. H. Hair und einen Wortindex von David Dalby*. Published in association with *The African Language Review*.

Graz [Austria]: Akademische Druck- u. Verlagsanstalt [**1963**]. Folio (38 cm.): 19, vi, 24, 188 p., folding map.

381.1 'Elīfo (ca. 1798–) = Peter Mamma

Account of this man from Oworo, or Eyagi, printed on p. 6 of S. W. Koelle, *Polyglotta Africana. Africana.*

Full text: https:// huskiecommons. lib.niu.edu/history-500african-voices/204/ [see 381.1].

London [England]: Church Missionary House, Salisbury Square, Fleet Street, MDCCCLIV [**1854**].
Folio (50 cm.): vi, 24 (2 columns each), 188 (8 columns each) p., folding map, errata slip.
Hogg 1611.

¶ 'Elīfo was born and grew up in a village called 'Eka (in modern western Nigeria—see Map 5) and spoke Oworo, or Eyagi. His people were subject to the Nupes, near the Niger Valley. Ca. 1823, when aged 28, he was betrayed by a supposed friend, sold, taken to the coast, and forced aboard a slave ship. A British warship intercepted this ship, freed the enslaved passengers, and took them to Sierra Leone (Map 4). 'Elīfo lived in Gloucester when Koelle interviewed him.

381.2———.

Photomechanical reprint of 381.1 with addition of historical introduction by P. E. H. Hair. Limited to two hundred copies "distributed free of charge to scholars of African languages throughout the world."

Freetown [Sierra Leone]: University College of Sierra Leone, Fourah Bay College, **1963**. Tpv: This numbered edition of two hundred copies is not available for distribution through the book-trade.
Folio (38 cm.): 19, vi, 24, 188 p., folding map.

381.3———.

Photomechanical reprint of 381.1, with additions, viz. *Polyglotta Africana / Vermehrt durch eine historische Einführung von P. E. H. Hair und einen Wortindex von David Dalby*. Published in association with *The African Language Review*.

Graz [Austria]: Akademische Druck- u. Verlagsanstalt [**1963**]. Folio (38 cm.): 19, vi, 24, 188 p., folding map.

2

382.1 Lagēgu (ca. 1812) = William Isaak

Account of this man, an 'Ife, printed on p. 6 of S. W. Koelle, *Polyglotta Africana*. **London [England]:** Church Missionary House, Salisbury Square, Fleet Street, MDCCCLIV [**1854**].

Folio (50 cm.): vi, 24 (2 columns each), 188 (8 columns each) p., folding map, errata slip.
Hogg 1611.

Full text: https://huskiecommons.lib.niu.edu/history-500african-voices/205/ [see 382.1].

¶ Lagēgu was born in the Yorùbá city of Ife, a large town three-days journey from Lagos (modern Nigeria—see Map 5). He was about seventeen when kidnapped, sold to Portuguese ca. 1829, and forced aboard a slave ship. The British intercepted this ship at sea and took it with all aboard to Sierra Leone (Map 4), where the ship's captain was tried before a Court of Mixed Commission and the freed captives apprenticed as Liberated Africans. Lagēgu was interviewed by Koelle twenty-four years later.

382.2———.

Photomechanical reprint of 382.1 with addition of historical introduction by P. E. H. Hair. Limited to two hundred copies "distributed free of charge to scholars of African languages throughout the world."

Freetown [Sierra Leone]: University College of Sierra Leone, Fourah Bay College, **1963**. Tpv: This numbered edition of two hundred copies is not available for distribution through the book-trade.
Folio (38 cm.): 19, vi, 24, 188 p., folding map.

382.3———.

Photomechanical reprint of 382.1, with additions, viz. *Polyglotta Africana / Vermehrt durch eine historische Einführung von P. E. H. Hair und einen Wortindex von David Dalby*. Published in association with *The African Language Review*.

Graz [Austria]: Akademische Druck- u. Verlagsanstalt [**1963**].
Folio (38 cm.): 19, vi, 24, 188 p., folding map.

383.1 Māku (ca. 1826–) = William Harding

Account of this man, an 'Ondō, printed on p. 6 of S. W. Koelle, *Polyglotta Africana*.

London [England]: Church Missionary House, Salisbury Square, Fleet Street, MDCCCLIV [**1854**].
Folio (50 cm.): vi, 24 (2 columns each), 188 (8 columns each) p., folding map, errata slip.
Hogg 1611.

¶ Māku was born in the Yorùbá city of Ondō (modern southwestern Nigeria—see Map 5) where he lived until about nineteen years old. At that age ca. 1845 he was on a trading journey when kidnapped by Dsesas, sold to Portuguese, and forced aboard a slave ship. The British intercepted this ship at sea and took it with all aboard to Sierra Leone (Map 4), where the ship's captain was tried before a Court of Mixed Commission and the freed captives apprenticed as Liberated Africans. Koelle interviewed Māku a few years later.

Full text: https://huskiecommons.lib.niu.edu/history-500african-voices/206/ [see 383.1].

383.2———.

Photomechanical reprint of 383.1 with addition of historical introduction by P. E. H. Hair. Limited to two hundred copies "distributed free of charge to scholars of African languages throughout the world."

Freetown [Sierra Leone]: University College of Sierra Leone, Fourah Bay College, **1963**. Tpv: This numbered edition of two hundred copies is not available for distribution through the book-trade.
Folio (38 cm.): 19, vi, 24, 188 p., folding map.

383.3———.

Photomechanical reprint of 383.1, with additions, viz. *Polyglotta Africana / Vermehrt durch eine historische Einführung von P. E. H. Hair und einen Wortindex von David Dalby*. Published in association with *The African Language Review*.

Graz [Austria]: Akademische Druck- u. Verlagsanstalt [**1963**].
Folio (38 cm.): 19, vi, 24, 188 p., folding map.

384.1 Adsíma (ca. 1820–) = John Wilhelm

Account of this man from Gúrma printed on p. 7 of S. W. Koelle, *Polyglotta Africana*.

London [England]: Church Missionary House, Salisbury Square, Fleet Street, MDCCCLIV [**1854**].
Folio (50 cm.): vi, 24 (2 columns each), 188 (8 columns each) p., folding map, errata slip.
Hogg 1611.

Full text: https://huskiecommons.lib.niu.edu/history-500african-voices/207/ [see 384.1].

¶ Adsíma was born in Búngu and raised in Dátánu, where he spoke Gúrma (the language of a people residing in modern

Togo, northern Benin, and southwestern Niger—see Map 5). Ca. 1844 he was kidnapped and three years later sold to Spaniards in Asánte (Akan people, modern Ghana), then forced aboard a slave ship. In 1847 a British warship intercepted this ship at sea and took it with all aboard to Sierra Leone (Map 4), where the ship's captain was tried before a Court of Mixed Commission and the freed captives apprenticed as Liberated Africans. Adsíma lived in the Liberated African community in Freetown when Koelle interviewed him.

384.2———.

Photomechanical reprint of 384.1 with addition of historical introduction by P. E. H. Hair. Limited to two hundred copies "distributed free of charge to scholars of African languages throughout the world."

Freetown [Sierra Leone]: University College of Sierra Leone, Fourah Bay College, **1963.** Tpv: This numbered edition of two hundred copies is not available for distribution through the book-trade.
Folio (38 cm.): 19, vi, 24, 188 p., folding map.

384.3———.

Photomechanical reprint of 384.1, with additions, viz. *Polyglotta Africana / Vermehrt durch eine historische Einführung von P. E. H. Hair und einen Wortindex von David Dalby.* Published in association with *The African Language Review.*

Graz [Austria]: Akademische Druck- u. Verlagsanstalt [1963].
Folio (38 cm.): 19, vi, 24, 188 p., folding map.

385.1   Sem (ca. 1790–) = Peter Kondo

Account of this man from Káure printed on p. 7 of S. W. Koelle, *Polyglotta Africana.*

London [England]: Church Missionary House, Salisbury Square, Fleet Street, MDCCCLIV [1854].
Folio (50 cm.): vi, 24 (2 columns each), 188 (8 columns each) p., folding map, errata slip.
Hogg 1611.

Full text: https://huskiecommons.lib.niu.edu/history-500african-voices/208/ [see 385.1].

¶ Sem was born and raised in a village called Wúram and spoke Káure (possibly Kazaure in northern Nigeria—see Map 5). When aged about 30 ca. 1820 he went to the Basare country (modern southeastern Senegal—Map 3) to buy Guinea corn and was kidnapped, carried to the sea, and forced aboard a slave ship. The British intercepted this ship at sea and took it with all aboard to Sierra Leone (Map 4), where the ship's

captain was tried before a Court of Mixed Commission and the freed captives apprenticed as Liberated Africans. Sem had lived in Sierra Leone for about thirty years when Koelle interviewed him.

385.2———.

Photomechanical reprint of 385.1 with addition of historical introduction by P. E. H. Hair. Limited to two hundred copies "distributed free of charge to scholars of African languages throughout the world."

Freetown [Sierra Leone]: University College of Sierra Leone, Fourah Bay College, **1963.** Tpv: This numbered edition of two hundred copies is not available for distribution through the book-trade.
Folio (38 cm.): 19, vi, 24, 188 p., folding map.

385.3———.

Photomechanical reprint of 385.1, with additions, viz. *Polyglotta Africana / Vermehrt durch eine historische Einführung von P. E. H. Hair und einen Wortindex von David Dalby.* Published in association with *The African Language Review.*

Graz [Austria]: Akademische Druck- u. Verlagsanstalt [1963].
Folio (38 cm.): 19, vi, 24, 188 p., folding map.

386.1   Bādsóróso = Richard Laudman

Account of this man from Gúngōníma printed on p. 7 of S. W. Koelle, *Polyglotta Africana.*

London [England]: Church Missionary House, Salisbury Square, Fleet Street, MDCCCLIV [1854].
Folio (50 cm.): vi, 24 (2 columns each), 188 (8 columns each) p., folding map, errata slip.
Hogg 1611.

Full text: https://huskiecommons.lib.niu.edu/history-500african-voices/209/ [see 386.1].

¶ Bādsóróso was born in Gúngōníma and spoke Bágbālan in a country called Bāgbáleuze (possibly Sisaala Tumulung in northern Ghana, on the modern Burkina Faso border—see Map 5). There he grew up and had three wives and a child aged five years when kidnapped at the instigation of his brother-in-law. After being sold several times over two years, he was taken to the sea and forced aboard a slave ship in 1851. This ship was intercepted at sea by the British, who took Bādsóróso and the others to Sierra Leone (Map 4), where the ship's captain was tried before a Court of Mixed Commission and the freed captives apprenticed as Liberated Africans. Bādsóróso had lived two years and eight months in Sierra Leone and resided in a barracks in Freetown when interviewed by Koelle, who wrote that Bādsóróso was the only person who spoke Bágbālan in the colony.

386.2——.

Photomechanical reprint of 386.1 with addition of historical introduction by P. E. H. Hair. Limited to two hundred copies "distributed free of charge to scholars of African languages throughout the world."

Freetown [Sierra Leone]: University College of Sierra Leone, Fourah Bay College, **1963.** Tpv: This numbered edition of two hundred copies is not available for distribution through the book-trade.
Folio (38 cm.): 19, vi, 24, 188 p., folding map.

386.3——.

Photomechanical reprint of 386.1, with additions, viz. *Polyglotta Africana / Vermehrt durch eine historische Einführung von P. E. H. Hair und einen Wortindex von David Dalby.* Published in association with *The African Language Review.*

Graz [Austria]: Akademische Druck- u. Verlagsanstalt [**1963**].
Folio (38 cm.): 19, vi, 24, 188 p., folding map.

387.1 Bagólōmo (ca. 1827–) = James Thomas

Account of this man from Kápu printed on p. 7 of S. W. Koelle, *Polyglotta Africana.* **London [England]:** Church Missionary House, Salisbury Square, Fleet Street, MDCCCLIV [**1854**].

Folio (50 cm.): vi, 24 (2 columns each), 188 (8 columns each) p., folding map, crrata slip.
Hogg 1611.

Full text: https://huskiecommons.lib.niu.edu/history-500african-voices/210/ [see 387.1].

¶ Bagólōmo was born in Kápu (modern Burkina Faso, northern Ghana border—see Map 5) and spoke Kásm (the language of an area east of Kúndsoro and west of Gúrēsa, two months' travel to the sea). The circumstances of his enslavement are unclear. The British intercepted the slave ship on which he was being transported across the Atlantic and took it with all aboard to Sierra Leone (Map 4), where the ship's captain was tried before a Court of Mixed Commission and the freed captives apprenticed as Liberated Africans. He lived in York, was aged 22, and had been in Sierra Leone about two and a half years when interviewed by Koelle, who noted that Bagólōmo was the only one in the colony who spoke his language.

387.2——.

Photomechanical reprint of 387.1 with addition of historical introduction by P. E. H. Hair. Limited to two hundred copies "distributed free of charge to scholars of African languages throughout the world."

Freetown [Sierra Leone]: University College of Sierra Leone, Fourah Bay College, **1963.** Tpv: This numbered edition of two hundred copies is not available for distribution through the book-trade.
Folio (38 cm.): 19, vi, 24, 188 p., folding map.

387.3——.

Photomechanical reprint of 387.1, with additions, viz. *Polyglotta Africana / Vermehrt durch eine historische Einführung von P. E. H. Hair und einen Wortindex von David Dalby.* Published in association with *The African Language Review.*

Graz [Austria]: Akademische Druck- u. Verlagsanstalt [**1963**].
Folio (38 cm.): 19, vi, 24, 188 p., folding map.

388.1 Bánena = Andrew George

Account of this man from Kiamba, or Dsamba, printed on p. 7 of S. W. Koelle, *Polyglotta Africana.*

London [England]: Church Missionary House, Salisbury Square, Fleet Street, MDCCCLIV [**1854**].
Folio (50 cm.): vi, 24 (2 columns each), 188 (8 columns each) p., folding map, errata slip.
Hogg 1611.

Full text: https://huskiecommons.lib.niu.edu/history-500african-voices/211/ [see 388.1].

¶ Bánena was born and raised in a town called Kiafado (possibly Tado, in eastern Benin—Map 5) and spoke Kiamba, or Dsamba. He married and had a child aged about fourteen when he was seized after a relative's death and sold to Gbési people, who carried him via Dahomey to the seacoast. There ca. 1830 he was forced aboard a slave ship. A British warship intercepted this ship at sea and took it with all aboard to Sierra Leone (Map 4), where the ship's captain was tried before a Court of Mixed Commission and the freed captives apprenticed as Liberated Africans. Bánena lived there when Koelle interviewed him.

388.2——.

Photomechanical reprint of 388.1 with addition of historical introduction by P. E. H. Hair. Limited to two hundred copies "distributed free of charge to scholars of African languages throughout the world."

Freetown [Sierra Leone]: University College of Sierra Leone, Fourah Bay College, **1963**. Tpv: This numbered edition of two hundred copies is not available for distribution through the book-trade.
Folio (38 cm.): 19, vi, 24, 188 p., folding map.

388.3———.

Photomechanical reprint of 388.1, with additions, viz. *Polyglotta Africana / Vermehrt durch eine historische Einführung von P. E. H. Hair und einen Wortindex von David Dalby*. Published in association with *The African Language Review*.

Graz [Austria]: Akademische Druck- u. Verlagsanstalt [**1963**].
Folio (38 cm.): 19, vi, 24, 188 p., folding map.

389.1 Esikānyi = Jacob Egypt

Account of this man from Isiele or Isiel printed on p. 8 of S. W. Koelle, *Polyglotta Africana*.

London [England]: Church Missionary House, Salisbury Square, Fleet Street, MDCCCLIV [**1854**].
Folio (50 cm.): vi, 24 (2 columns each), 188 (8 columns each) p., folding map, errata slip.
Hogg 1611.

Full text: https://
huskiecommons.
lib.niu.edu/his-
tory-500african-
voices/212/
[see 389.1].

¶ Esikānyi was born in Ake (possibly Aku, which is Yorùbá) and spoke Isele, or Isiel. He had a three-year-old child when kidnapped and sold to Igala people (modern Nigeria—see Map 5), who took him to the coast and sold him to a slave ship ca. 1842. A British warship intercepted this ship at sea and took it with all aboard to Sierra Leone (Map 4), where the ship's captain was tried before a Court of Mixed Commission and the freed captives apprenticed as Liberated Africans. Esikānyi lived in Wilberforce when Koelle interviewed him.

389.2———.

Photomechanical reprint of 389.1 with addition of historical introduction by P. E. H. Hair. Limited to two hundred copies "distributed free of charge to scholars of African languages throughout the world."

Freetown [Sierra Leone]: University College of Sierra Leone, Fourah Bay College, **1963**. Tpv: This numbered edition of two hundred copies is not available for distribution through the book-trade.
Folio (38 cm.): 19, vi, 24, 188 p., folding map.

389.3———.

Photomechanical reprint of 389.1, with additions, viz. *Polyglotta Africana / Vermehrt durch eine historische Einführung von P. E. H. Hair und einen Wortindex von David Dalby*. Published in association with *The African Language Review*.

Graz [Austria]: Akademische Druck- u. Verlagsanstalt [**1963**].
Folio (38 cm.): 19, vi, 24, 188 p., folding map.

390.1 Adíbe (ca. 1801) = George Rose

Account of this man, an Aro, printed on p. 8 of S. W. Koelle, *Polyglotta Africana*.

London [England]: Church Missionary House, Salisbury Square, Fleet Street, MDCCCLIV [**1854**].
Folio (50 cm.): vi, 24 (2 columns each), 188 (8 columns each) p., folding map, errata slip.
Hogg 1611.

Full text: https://
huskiecommons.
lib.niu.edu/his-
tory-500african-
voices/213/
[see 390.1].

¶ Adíbe was born in Isoama country, probably Bonny (modern coastal Nigeria—see Map 5), and spoke Aro. He was stolen as a little boy and raised in Aro country in a village called Asage, where he lived for twenty-four years, until about 1829, when he was sold to Portuguese in Obane and forced aboard a slave ship. A British warship intercepted this ship at sea and took it with all aboard to Sierra Leone (Map 4). Adíbe lived in Wilberforce when Koelle interviewed him.

390.2———.

Photomechanical reprint of 390.1 with addition of historical introduction by P. E. H. Hair. Limited to two hundred copies "distributed free of charge to scholars of African languages throughout the world."

Freetown [Sierra Leone]: University College of Sierra Leone, Fourah Bay College, **1963**. Tpv: This numbered edition of two hundred copies is not available for distribution through the book-trade.
Folio (38 cm.): 19, vi, 24, 188 p., folding map.

390.3———.

Photomechanical reprint of 390.1, with additions, viz. *Polyglotta Africana / Vermehrt durch eine historische Einführung von P. E. H. Hair und einen Wortindex von David Dalby*. Published in association with *The African Language Review*.

Graz [Austria]: Akademische Druck- u. Verlagsanstalt [**1963**].
Folio (38 cm.): 19, vi, 24, 188 p., folding map.

391.1 Adsōro (ca. 1809–)

Account of this man from the Dsháda islands printed on p. 9 of S. W. Koelle, *Polyglotta Africana*.

London [England]: Church Missionary House, Salisbury Square, Fleet Street, MDCCCLIV [1854].
Folio (50 cm.): vi, 24 (2 columns each), 188 (8 columns each) p., folding map, errata slip.
Hogg 1611.

Full text: https://huskiecommons.lib.niu.edu/history-500african-voices/214/ [see 391.1].

¶ Adsōro was born in a village called Libo, two miles from Ebokei (whose capital was Egbīra or Egba, modern western Nigeria—see Map 5). When aged 22 he was kidnapped by Básas people and sold to Igala. After eighteen months with them, he was taken to the coast and forced aboard a slave ship. A British warship intercepted this ship at sea and took it with all aboard to Sierra Leone (Map 4) ca. 1833. Adsōro lived in Hastings when interviewed by Koelle, who remarked that he had a "loathsome" disease.

391.2——.

Photomechanical reprint of 391.1 with addition of historical introduction by P. E. H. Hair. Limited to two hundred copies "distributed free of charge to scholars of African languages throughout the world."

Freetown [Sierra Leone]: University College of Sierra Leone, Fourah Bay College, 1963. Tpv: This numbered edition of two hundred copies is not available for distribution through the book-trade.
Folio (38 cm.): 19, vi, 24, 188 p., folding map.

391.3——.

Photomechanical reprint of 391.1, with additions, viz. *Polyglotta Africana / Vermehrt durch eine historische Einführung von P. E. H. Hair und einen Wortindex von David Dalby.* Published in association with *The African Language Review.*

Graz [Austria]: Akademische Druck- u. Verlagsanstalt [1963].
Folio (38 cm.): 19, vi, 24, 188 p., folding map.

392.1 Abāli (ca. 1826–)

Account of this man from the Dsháda islands printed on p. 10 of S. W. Koelle, *Polyglotta Africana*.

London [England]: Church Missionary House, Salisbury Square, Fleet Street, MDCCCLIV [1854].
Folio (50 cm.): vi, 24 (2 columns each), 188 (8 columns each) p., folding map, errata slip.
Hogg 1611.

¶ Abāli spoke Kanèm and was born in the town of Boso on one of the islands off the northeastern shore of Lake Chad (modern Chad—see Map 5) and was probably Buduma. There he lived until aged 22, when he became a warrior and joined an expedition against Dambarára, part of Oúsa or 'Abūno, who were Hausa. After being taken prisoner he was carried to Lagos (modern Nigeria) on the coast and forced aboard a slave ship, which was in turn intercepted at sea by a British warship and taken with all aboard to Sierra Leone (Map 4). There the ship's captain was tried before a Court of Mixed Commission and the freed captives apprenticed as Liberated Africans. Abāli had been in Sierra Leone four years and lived in Freetown when Koelle interviewed him.

Full text: https://huskiecommons.lib.niu.edu/history-500african-voices/215/ [see 392.1].

392.2——.

Photomechanical reprint of 392.1 with addition of historical introduction by P. E. H. Hair. Limited to two hundred copies "distributed free of charge to scholars of African languages throughout the world."

Freetown [Sierra Leone]: University College of Sierra Leone, Fourah Bay College, 1963. Tpv: This numbered edition of two hundred copies is not available for distribution through the book-trade.
Folio (38 cm.): 19, vi, 24, 188 p., folding map.

392.3——.

Photomechanical reprint of 392.1, with additions, viz. *Polyglotta Africana / Vermehrt durch eine historische Einführung von P. E. H. Hair und einen Wortindex von David Dalby.* Published in association with *The African Language Review.*

Graz [Austria]: Akademische Druck- u. Verlagsanstalt [1963].
Folio (38 cm.): 19, vi, 24, 188 p., folding map.

393.1 Yon (ca. 1808–) = William Macfoi

Account of this man born in Páti printed on pp. 11–12 of S. W. Koelle, *Polyglotta Africana*.

London [England]: Church Missionary House, Salisbury Square, Fleet Street, MDCCCLIV [1854].
Folio (50 cm.): vi, 24 (2 columns each), 188 (8 columns each) p., folding map, errata slip.
Hogg 1611.

Full text: https://huskiecommons.lib.niu.edu/history-500african-voices/216/ [see 393.1].

¶ Yon was born in Páti (modern Cameroon, Gabon—see Map 5) and lived there until aged eighteen, when Tébāle came and set fire to his town. Yon and others fled to Pázā country, where he was captured and enslaved ca. 1826. During forcible transport to the sea he was held enslaved for three years in Kónwan and an additional three and one-half years in Efek or Kálabā (Calabar, Cross River region, in modern Nigeria and northwestern Cameroon). There he was forced aboard a slave ship, which was in turn intercepted at sea by a British warship. The British freed the enslaved passengers and took them to Sierra Leone (Map 4), where Yon arrived ca. 1833. He lived in Hastings when Koelle interviewed him.

393.2———.

Photomechanical reprint of 393.1 with addition of historical introduction by P. E. H. Hair. Limited to two hundred copies "distributed free of charge to scholars of African languages throughout the world."

Freetown [Sierra Leone]: University College of Sierra Leone, Fourah Bay College, 1963. Tpv: This numbered edition of two hundred copies is not available for distribution through the book-trade.
Folio (38 cm.): 19, vi, 24, 188 p., folding map.)

393.3———.

Photomechanical reprint of 393.1, with additions, viz. *Polyglotta Africana / Vermehrt durch eine historische Einführung von P. E. H. Hair und einen Wortindex von David Dalby.* Published in association with *The African Language Review.*

Graz [Austria]: Akademische Druck- u. Verlagsanstalt [1963].
Folio (38 cm.): 19, vi, 24, 188 p., folding map.

394.1 Mbowe (ca. 1817–) = James Harris

Account of this man, a Diwala, printed on p. 11 of S. W. Koelle, *Polyglotta Africana.*

London [England]: Church Missionary House, Salisbury Square, Fleet Street, MDCCCLIV [1854].
Folio (50 cm.): vi, 24 (2 columns each), 188 (8 columns each) p., folding map, errata slip.
Hogg 1611.

Full text: https:// huskiecommons. lib.niu.edu/history-500african-voices/217/ [see 394.1].

¶ Mbowe was born in a village called Bākóko, a two-day journey from the Atlantic, and spoke Diwala (or Duala, a city in modern Cameroon—see Map 5). He lived there until his sixteenth year, when (both of his parents being dead)

his guardian sold him to a Portuguese. He was forced aboard a slave ship, which a British warship subsequently intercepted at sea. After freeing the enslaved passengers, the British took them to Sierra Leone (Map 4) ca. 1833. Mbowe lived in Gloucester when Koelle interviewed him.

394.2———.

Photomechanical reprint of 394.1 with addition of historical introduction by P. E. H. Hair. Limited to two hundred copies "distributed free of charge to scholars of African languages throughout the world."

Freetown [Sierra Leone]: University College of Sierra Leone, Fourah Bay College, 1963. Tpv: This numbered edition of two hundred copies is not available for distribution through the book-trade.
Folio (38 cm.): 19, vi, 24, 188 p., folding map.

394.3———.

Photomechanical reprint of 394.1, with additions, viz. *Polyglotta Africana / Vermehrt durch eine historische Einführung von P. E. H. Hair und einen Wortindex von David Dalby.* Published in association with *The African Language Review.*

Graz [Austria]: Akademische Druck- u. Verlagsanstalt [1963].
Folio (38 cm.): 19, vi, 24, 188 p., folding map.

395.1 Síse (ca. 1807–) = John Cole

Account of this man born in Bándsāre printed on p. 12 of S. W. Koelle, *Polyglotta Africana.*

London [England]: Church Missionary House, Salisbury Square, Fleet Street, MDCCCLIV [1854].
Folio (50 cm.): vi, 24 (2 columns each), 188 (8 columns each) p., folding map, errata slip.
Hogg 1611.

Full text: https:// huskiecommons. lib.niu.edu/history-500african-voices/218/ [see 395.1].

¶ Síse was born in a hamlet called Bánon, a day's journey from Ntar, the Bagba capital (modern Burkina Faso, northeast Ghana—see Map 5). Aged thirty, he was taken in a war against the Tebale, who came from afar on horses, conquered many countries, and spread terror with poisoned weapons. Síse was taken through many places during his long journey to Kálabā (Calabar, Cross River region in modern Nigeria and northwestern Cameroon), where ca. 1838 he was forced onto a slave ship that was later intercepted at sea by the British, who liberated all enslaved passengers and took them to Sierra Leone (Map 4). There Sise had lived fifteen years and resided in Gloucester when interviewed by Koelle.

395.2——.

Photomechanical reprint of 395.1 with addition of historical introduction by P. E. H. Hair. Limited to two hundred copies "distributed free of charge to scholars of African languages throughout the world."

Freetown [Sierra Leone]: University College of Sierra Leone, Fourah Bay College, **1963**. Tpv: This numbered edition of two hundred copies is not available for distribution through the book-trade.
Folio (38 cm.): 19, vi, 24, 188 p., folding map.

395.3——.

Photomechanical reprint of 395.1, with additions, viz. *Polyglotta Africana / Vermehrt durch eine historische Einführung von P. E. H. Hair und einen Wortindex von David Dalby*. Published in association with *The African Language Review*.

Graz [Austria]: Akademische Druck- u. Verlagsanstalt [**1963**].
Folio (38 cm.): 19, vi, 24, 188 p., folding map.

396.1 Kámsi (1816–) = John Thomas

Account of this man born in Bándsāre printed on p. 12 of S. W. Koelle, *Polyglotta Africana*.

Full text: https://huskiecommons.lib.niu.edu/history-500african-voices/219/ [see 396.1].

London [England]: Church Missionary House, Salisbury Square, Fleet Street, MDCCCLIV [**1854**].
Folio (50 cm.): vi, 24 (2 columns each), 188 (8 columns each) p., folding map, errata slip.
Hogg 1611.

¶ Kámsi was born in Bándsāre (spoke Balu = modern Cameroon—see Map 5). At age twenty he was taken by Tíbār, whom Koelle believed were the Fúla (Fulani, Fulbi or Peul peoples throughout West Africa). After capture in 1836 he was forced aboard a slave ship that a British warship intercepted at sea. After freeing the enslaved passengers, the British took them to Sierra Leone (Map 4), where Kámsi had lived for eighteen years. He resided in Wellington when Koelle interviewed him and was the only one of his people that Koelle knew.

396.2——.

Photomechanical reprint of 396.1 with addition of historical introduction by P. E. H. Hair. Limited to two hundred copies "distributed free of charge to scholars of African languages throughout the world."

Freetown [Sierra Leone]: University College of Sierra Leone, Fourah Bay College, **1963**. Tpv: This numbered edition of

two hundred copies is not available for distribution through the book-trade.
Folio (38 cm.): 19, vi, 24, 188 p., folding map.

396.3——.

Photomechanical reprint of 396.1, with additions, viz. *Polyglotta Africana / Vermehrt durch eine historische Einführung von P. E. H. Hair und einen Wortindex von David Dalby*. Published in association with *The African Language Review*.

Graz [Austria]: Akademische Druck- u. Verlagsanstalt [**1963**].
Folio (38 cm.): 19, vi, 24, 188 p., folding map.

397.1 Nyámse (ca. 1803–) = James Harding

Account of this man born in the Bálumfa country printed on p. 12 of S. W. Koelle, *Polyglotta Africana*.

Full text: https://huskiecommons.lib.niu.edu/history-500african-voices/220/ [see 397.1].

London [England]: Church Missionary House, Salisbury Square, Fleet Street, MDCCCLIV [**1854**].
Folio (50 cm.): vi, 24 (2 columns each), 188 (8 columns each) p., folding map, errata slip.
Hogg 1611.

¶ Nyámse was born in the Bálumfa country (modern Cameroon—see Map 5), but was brought as a child to Tiapōn, five days journey from Fómbān (the Bámom capital) and two hours from the Mepōan River, where he grew up and lived until age 22, speaking Mom or Bámom. During a trading tour to Bákōan country, he was seized to pay a debt of another Tiapōn man, then sold and resold for four years, passing through Bárīwa, Ntóntu, Mbírēkam, Bárnīa, Kórrgūan, and Kálaba (normally a two-month journey over this distance). On the coast he was forced aboard a slave ship, which a British warship subsequently intercepted at sea. After freeing the enslaved passengers, the British took them to Sierra Leone (Map 4) in 1831, where Nyámse lived in Freetown when interviewed by Koelle twenty-three years later. By then he had lost his native language.

397.2——.

Photomechanical reprint of 397.1 with addition of historical introduction by P. E. H. Hair. Limited to two hundred copies "distributed free of charge to scholars of African languages throughout the world."

Freetown [Sierra Leone]: University College of Sierra Leone, Fourah Bay College, **1963**. Tpv: This numbered edition of two hundred copies is not available for distribution through the book-trade.
Folio (38 cm.): 19, vi, 24, 188 p., folding map.

397.3——.

Photomechanical reprint of 397.1, with additions, viz. *Polyglotta Africana / Vermehrt durch eine historische Einführung von P. E. H. Hair und einen Wortindex von David Dalby.* Published in association with *The African Language Review.*

Graz [Austria]: Akademische Druck- u. Verlagsanstalt [1963]. Folio (38 cm.): 19, vi, 24, 188 p., folding map.

398.1 Mbépe (ca. 1812–) = James John

Account of this man born in the village of Ndób printed on p. 12 of S. W. Koelle, *Polyglotta Africana.*

London [England]: Church Missionary House, Salisbury Square, Fleet Street, MDCCCLIV [1854]. Folio (50 cm.): vi, 24 (2 columns each), 188 (8 columns each) p., folding map, errata slip. Hogg 1611.

Full text: https:// huskiecommons. lib.niu.edu/his- tory-500african- voices/221/ [see 398.1].

¶ Mbépe was born in the village of Ndób (not to be confused with the country of same name) or Pándób, where he lived until eighteen years, old and spoke Ngóāla (northwest Cameroon—see Map 5). Ca. 1830 the Típāla burned all of the towns in the area, forcing Mbépe to flee to 'Mbara, where he was seized and enslaved. When the Típāla attacked 'Mbara, he fled with his master to Pram and was again seized and taken ca. 1831 to the coast (after one month of constant walking) at Kálabā (Calabar, Cross River region in modern Nigeria and northwestern Cameroon). Three years later he was forced aboard a slave ship, which a British warship subsequently intercepted at sea. After freeing the enslaved passengers, the British took them to Sierra Leone (Map 4), where Mbépe lived in Waterloo when Koelle interviewed him twenty years later.

398.2——.

Photomechanical reprint of 398.1 with addition of historical introduction by P. E. H. Hair. Limited to two hundred copies "distributed free of charge to scholars of African languages throughout the world."

Freetown [Sierra Leone]: University College of Sierra Leone, Fourah Bay College, 1963. Tpv: This numbered edition of two hundred copies is not available for distribution through the book-trade. Folio (38 cm.): 19, vi, 24, 188 p., folding map.

398.3——.

Photomechanical reprint of 398.1, with additions, viz. *Polyglotta Africana / Vermehrt durch eine historische Einführung*

von P. E. H. Hair und einen Wortindex von David Dalby. Published in association with *The African Language Review.*

Graz [Austria]: Akademische Druck- u. Verlagsanstalt [1963]. Folio (38 cm.): 19, vi, 24, 188 p., folding map.

399.1 Nyámasi = Thomas John

Account of this man from N'halemoe printed on p. 12 of S. W. Koelle, *Polyglotta Africana.*

London [England]: Church Missionary House, Salisbury Square, Fleet Street, MDCCCLIV [1854]. Folio (50 cm.): vi, 24 (2 columns each), 188 (8 columns each) p., folding map, errata slip. Hogg 1611.

Full text: https:// huskiecommons. lib.niu.edu/his- tory-500african- voices/222/ [see 399.1].

¶ Nyámasi was born in Momanka, a two-day journey from a deep river called Rība that flowed from Mómēya to Bórēso (Bamum state, near Foumban city, northwestern Cameroon—see Map 5). His people were called Mōménya or Bāméya. He lived there until his oldest child was six, at which time Bámbum people destroyed his town, forcing Nyámasi to flee to Monste or Bantse, where he did not understand the language. There he was seized, enslaved, and sold a year later to Múfōlan people, who took him to the coast via Músōlan, Bágan, Mbe or Bámbe, Mómbēonkua, Mōnkúngban, and Niwára, i.e., Cameroons. There ca. 1835 he was forced onto a slave ship that was intercepted by the British at sea. Nyámasi and others were liberated and taken to Sierra Leone (Map 4), where he lived in Allentown when interviewed by Koelle eighteen years later.

399.2——.

Photomechanical reprint of 399.1 with addition of historical introduction by P. E. H. Hair. Limited to two hundred copies "distributed free of charge to scholars of African languages throughout the world."

Freetown [Sierra Leone]: University College of Sierra Leone, Fourah Bay College, 1963. Tpv: This numbered edition of two hundred copies is not available for distribution through the book-trade. Folio (38 cm.): 19, vi, 24, 188 p., folding map.

399.3——.

Photomechanical reprint of 399.1, with additions, viz. *Polyglotta Africana / Vermehrt durch eine historische Einführung von P. E. H. Hair und einen Wortindex von David Dalby.* Published in association with *The African Language Review.*

Graz [Austria]: Akademische Druck- u. Verlagsanstalt [1963]. Folio (38 cm.): 19, vi, 24, 188 p., folding map.

400.1 Edía = Thomas Renner

Account of this man from N'halemoe printed on p. 13 of S. W. Koelle, *Polyglotta Africana*.

London [England]: Church Missionary House, Salisbury Square, Fleet Street, MDCCCLIV [1854].
Folio (50 cm.): vi, 24 (2 columns each), 188 (8 columns each) p., folding map, errata slip.
Hogg 1611.

Full text: https://huskiecommons.lib.niu.edu/history-500african-voices/223/ [see 400].

¶ Edia was born and grew up in a village called Báningar (southwest Cameroon near Lonako-Manengouba mountains—see Map 5) and spoke N'halemoe. He had seven wives and a child aged ten when jealous countrymen sold him. He was taken to the coast via Cameroon and forced aboard a slave ship ca. 1818. A British warship intercepted this ship at sea, freed the enslaved passengers, and took them to Sierra Leone (Map 4). Edia lived in Bathurst when Koelle interviewed him.

400.2——.

Photomechanical reprint of 400.1 with addition of historical introduction by P. E. H. Hair. Limited to two hundred copies "distributed free of charge to scholars of African languages throughout the world."

Freetown [Sierra Leone]: University College of Sierra Leone, Fourah Bay College, **1963.** Tpv: This numbered edition of two hundred copies is not available for distribution through the book-trade.
Folio (38 cm.): 19, vi, 24, 188 p., folding map.

400.3——.

Photomechanical reprint of 400.1, with additions, viz. *Polyglotta Africana / Vermehrt durch eine historische Einführung von P. E. H. Hair und einen Wortindex von David Dalby.* Published in association with *The African Language Review.*

Graz [Austria]: Akademische Druck- u. Verlagsanstalt [1963].
Folio (38 cm.): 19, vi, 24, 188 p., folding map.

401.1 Kindsímbi or Dsindsímbi (ca. 1809–) = John Baptist

Account of this man from Kabénda or Bákabénda printed on p. 13 of S. W. Koelle, *Polyglotta Africana.*

London [England]: Church Missionary House, Salisbury Square, Fleet Street, MDCCCLIV [1854].
Folio (50 cm.): vi, 24 (2 columns each), 188 (8 columns each) p., folding map, errata slip.
Hogg 1611.

¶ Kindsímbi was born in a town called Káyi on the coast (near modern borders of Angola, Democratic Republic of Congo and Republic of Congo—see Map 6) and spoke Kabénda or Bákabénda. Ca. 1823, aged fourteen, he was sold, forced aboard a slave ship, and taken to Brazil (Map 9). Disguised as a sailor ca. 1838, he escaped on a merchant vessel that took him to Sierra Leone (Map 4). He lived in Freetown when Koelle interviewed him.

401.2——.

Photomechanical reprint of 401.1 with addition of historical introduction by P. E. H. Hair. Limited to two hundred copies "distributed free of charge to scholars of African languages throughout the world."

Freetown [Sierra Leone]: University College of Sierra Leone, Fourah Bay College, **1963.** Tpv: This numbered edition of two hundred copies is not available for distribution through the book-trade.
Folio (38 cm.): 19, vi, 24, 188 p., folding map.

401.3——.

Photomechanical reprint of 401.1, with additions, viz. *Polyglotta Africana / Vermehrt durch eine historische Einführung von P. E. H. Hair und einen Wortindex von David Dalby.* Published in association with *The African Language Review.*

Graz [Austria]: Akademische Druck- u. Verlagsanstalt [1963].
Folio (38 cm.): 19, vi, 24, 188 p., folding map.

Full text: https://huskiecommons.lib.niu.edu/history-500african-voices/224/ [see 401.1].

402.1 Sángars = William Parker

Account of this man born in the village of Pamínka printed on p. 13 of S. W. Koelle, *Polyglotta Africana.*

London [England]: Church Missionary House, Salisbury Square, Fleet Street, MDCCCLIV [1854].
Folio (50 cm.): vi, 24 (2 columns each), 188 (8 columns each) p., folding map, errata slip.
Hogg 1611.

Full text: https://huskiecommons.lib.niu.edu/history-500african-voices/225/ [see 402.1].

¶ Sángars spoke Papīsh and was born in the village of Pamínka at the foot of a mountain called Mpenko (possibly Mt. Oku near Ndop plain, northwest Cameroon—see Map 5). He lived here until aged sixteen, when Pamom attacked and destroyed his village, sending Sángars and others into hiding in the forests. After running out of food, they were captured, taken to Ntóntu country, and sold. Thereafter Sángars was taken to sea via the Cameroons and was forced aboard a slave ship that a British warship intercepted at sea. After freeing the enslaved passengers, the British took them to Sierra Leone (Map 4). Sángars lived in Allentown when Koelle interviewed him.

402.2———.

Photomechanical reprint of 402.1 with addition of historical introduction by P. E. H. Hair. Limited to two hundred copies "distributed free of charge to scholars of African languages throughout the world."

Freetown [Sierra Leone]: University College of Sierra Leone, Fourah Bay College, 1963. Tpv: This numbered edition of two hundred copies is not available for distribution through the book-trade.
Folio (38 cm.): 19, vi, 24, 188 p., folding map.

402.3———.

Photomechanical reprint of 402.1, with additions, viz. *Polyglotta Africana / Vermehrt durch eine historische Einführung von P. E. H. Hair und einen Wortindex von David Dalby*. Published in association with *The African Language Review*.

Graz [Austria]: Akademische Druck- u. Verlagsanstalt [1963].
Folio (38 cm.): 19, vi, 24, 188 p., folding map.

403.1 Nyámasi (ca. 1811–) = Andrew Wilhelm

Account of this man born in the village of Bépot or Mbépot printed on p. 13 of S. W. Koelle, *Polyglotta Africana*.

London [England]: Church Missionary House, Salisbury Square, Fleet Street, MDCCCLIV [1854].
Folio (50 cm.): vi, 24 (2 columns each), 188 (8 columns each) p., folding map, errata slip.
Hogg 1611.

Full text: https://huskiecommons.lib.niu.edu/history-500african-voices/226/ [see 403.1].

¶ Nyámasi was from the town of Bépot or Mbépo (or Mbe, modern northern Cameroon—see Map 5) where he lived until aged nineteen. He was then kidnapped by Papīak people and sold to Peti and Kálabā (Calabar, Cross River region in modern Nigeria and northwestern Cameroon), where ca. 1831 Nyámasi was forced aboard a slave ship that a British warship intercepted at sea. The British freed the enslaved passengers

and took them to Sierra Leone (Map 4), where Nyámasi had lived for twenty-two years when Koelle interviewed him. He resided in Freetown when interviewed.

403.2———.

Photomechanical reprint of 403.1 with addition of historical introduction by P. E. H. Hair. Limited to two hundred copies "distributed free of charge to scholars of African languages throughout the world."

Freetown [Sierra Leone]: University College of Sierra Leone, Fourah Bay College, 1963. Tpv: This numbered edition of two hundred copies is not available for distribution through the book-trade.
Folio (38 cm.): 19, vi, 24, 188 p., folding map.

403.3———.

Photomechanical reprint of 403.1, with additions, viz. *Polyglotta Africana / Vermehrt durch eine historische Einführung von P. E. H. Hair und einen Wortindex von David Dalby*. Published in association with *The African Language Review*.

Graz [Austria]: Akademische Druck- u. Verlagsanstalt [1963].
Folio (38 cm.): 19, vi, 24, 188 p., folding map.

404.1 Būnsála = Thomas Pratt

Account of this man from Mbamba or Babamba printed on p. 14 of S. W. Koelle, *Polyglotta Africana*.

London [England]: Church Missionary House, Salisbury Square, Fleet Street, MDCCCLIV [1854].
Folio (50 cm.): vi, 24 (2 columns each), 188 (8 columns each) p., folding map, errata slip.
Hogg 1611.

Full text: https://huskiecommons.lib.niu.edu/history-500african-voices/227/ [see 404.1].

¶ Būnsála was born and grew up in a town called Mukongo-mongue (Mbamba Congo, modern Brazzaville in West Central Africa—see Map 6) and spoke Mbamba or Babamba. He had been married four years when sold as punishment for adultery. He was carried to the coast, a journey that took five months, then forced aboard a slave ship ca. 1838. A British warship intercepted this ship at sea, freed its enslaved passengers, and took them to Sierra Leone (Map 4). Būnsála lived in Lomley when Koelle interviewed him.

404.2———.

Photomechanical reprint of 404.1 with addition of historical introduction by P. E. H. Hair. Limited to two hundred copies

"distributed free of charge to scholars of African languages throughout the world."

Freetown [Sierra Leone]: University College of Sierra Leone, Fourah Bay College, 1963. Tpv: This numbered edition of two hundred copies is not available for distribution through the book-trade.

Folio (38 cm.): 19, vi, 24, 188 p., folding map.

404.3———.

Photomechanical reprint of 404.1, with additions, viz. *Polyglotta Africana / Vermehrt durch eine historische Einführung von P. E. H. Hair und einen Wortindex von David Dalby.* Published in association with *The African Language Review.*

Graz [Austria]: Akademische Druck- u. Verlagsanstalt [1963]. Folio (38 cm.): 19, vi, 24, 188 p., folding map.

405.1 Mútōmp = William Francis

Account of this man from Kanyíka printed on p. 14 of S. W. Koelle, *Polyglotta Africana.*

London [England]: Church Missionary House, Salisbury Square, Fleet Street, MDCCCLIV [1854].
Folio (50 cm.): vi, 24 (2 columns each), 188 (8 columns each) p., folding map, errata slip.
Hogg 1611.

Full text: https://huskiecommons.lib.niu.edu/history-500african-voices/228/ [see 405.1].

¶ Mútōmp was born and raised in a town called Mámunyikáyīnt and spoke Kanyíka, or Kanyika-Luba, a language from Congo near the modern city of Kinshasa (see Map 6). Mútōmp had one child who could not walk when he was sold ca. 1839 to Kambúnda slave dealers as punishment for bad conduct. He was sold again into the Kasands country, yet again to Baga, and ultimately to Portuguese, who forced him aboard a slave ship ca. 1841. This ship was intercepted at sea by a British warship and taken to Sierra Leone (Map 4). Mútōmp lived in Freetown when Koelle interviewed him.

405.2———.

Photomechanical reprint of 405.1 with addition of historical introduction by P. E. H. Hair. Limited to two hundred copies "distributed free of charge to scholars of African languages throughout the world."

Freetown [Sierra Leone]: University College of Sierra Leone, Fourah Bay College, 1963. Tpv: This numbered edition of two hundred copies is not available for distribution through the book-trade.

Folio (38 cm.): 19, vi, 24, 188 p., folding map.

405.3———.

Photomechanical reprint of 405.1, with additions, viz. *Polyglotta Africana / Vermehrt durch eine historische Einführung von P. E. H. Hair und einen Wortindex von David Dalby.* Published in association with *The African Language Review.*

Graz [Austria]: Akademische Druck- u. Verlagsanstalt [1963]. Folio (38 cm.): 19, vi, 24, 188 p., folding map.

406.1 Tūt (ca. 1816–) = Charles Wilhelm

Account of this man from Mutsáya or Batsáya printed on p. 14 of S. W. Koelle, *Polyglotta Africana.*

London [England]: Church Missionary House, Salisbury Square, Fleet Street, MDCCCLIV [1854].
Folio (50 cm.): vi, 24 (2 columns each), 188 (8 columns each) p., folding map, errata slip.
Hogg 1611.

Full text: https://huskiecommons.lib.niu.edu/history-500african-voices/229/ [see 406.1].

¶ Tūt was born in a town called Mólēp (Democratic Republic of Congo west of Teke Kingdom—see Map 6) and spoke Mutsáya or Batsáya. He was kidnapped ca. 1836, taken to the coast, and forced aboard a slave ship. A British warship intercepted this ship at sea, freed the enslaved Africans, and took them to Sierra Leone (Map 4). Tūt lived in Lomley when Koelle interviewed him.

406.2———.

Photomechanical reprint of 406.1 with addition of historical introduction by P. E. H. Hair. Limited to two hundred copies "distributed free of charge to scholars of African languages throughout the world."

Freetown [Sierra Leone]: University College of Sierra Leone, Fourah Bay College, 1963. Tpv: This numbered edition of two hundred copies is not available for distribution through the book-trade.

Folio (38 cm.): 19, vi, 24, 188 p., folding map.

406.3———.

Photomechanical reprint of 406.1, with additions, viz. *Polyglotta Africana / Vermehrt durch eine historische Einführung von P. E. H. Hair und einen Wortindex von David Dalby.* Published in association with *The African Language Review.*

Graz [Austria]: Akademische Druck- u. Verlagsanstalt [1963]. Folio (38 cm.): 19, vi, 24, 188 p., folding map.

407.1 N'Gónga (ca. 1810–) = John Wilhelm

Account of this man from Kasands printed on p. 14 of S. W. Koelle, *Polyglotta Africana*.

Full text: https://huskiecommons.lib.niu.edu/history-500african-voices/230/ [see 407.1].

London [England]: Church Missionary House, Salisbury Square, Fleet Street, MDCCCLIV [1854].
Folio (50 cm.): vi, 24 (2 columns each), 188 (8 columns each) p., folding map, errata slip.
Hogg 1611.

¶ N'Gónga was born in Yōnk (modern Angola—see Map 6) and spoke Kasands (Imbangala). Aged about 28, he was kidnapped. Two years later he was sold to Portuguese, who put him on a slave ship ca. 1840. A British warship intercepted this ship at sea, freed the enslaved passengers, and took them to Sierra Leone (Map 4). N'Gónga lived in Freetown when Koelle interviewed him.

407.2 ——.

Photomechanical reprint of 407.1 with addition of historical introduction by P. E. H. Hair. Limited to two hundred copies "distributed free of charge to scholars of African languages throughout the world."

Freetown [Sierra Leone]: University College of Sierra Leone, Fourah Bay College, 1963. Tpv: This numbered edition of two hundred copies is not available for distribution through the book-trade.
Folio (38 cm.): 19, vi, 24, 188 p., folding map.

407.3 ——.

Photomechanical reprint of 407.1, with additions, viz. *Polyglotta Africana / Vermehrt durch eine historische Einführung von P. E. H. Hair und einen Wortindex von David Dalby.* Published in association with *The African Language Review.*

Graz [Austria]: Akademische Druck- u. Verlagsanstalt [1963].
Folio (38 cm.): 19, vi, 24, 188 p., folding map.

408.1 Dsíngo = James Job

Account of this man born Gílībe printed on p. 14 of S. W. Koelle, *Polyglotta Africana.*

London [England]: Church Missionary House, Salisbury Square, Fleet Street, MDCCCLIV [1854].
Folio (50 cm.): vi, 24 (2 columns each), 188 (8 columns each) p., folding map, errata slip.
Hogg 1611.

¶ Dsíngo was born in a town called Gílībe (modern Democratic Republic of Congo and Republic of Congo—see Map 6) and spoke Babúma or Mobúma (Bantu/Teke). There he lived until his eldest child was ten years old, when he was seized and sold to pay a debt. He was put on a slave ship that a British warship intercepted at sea. The British freed the enslaved Africans and took them to Sierra Leone (Map 4). Dsíngo lived in Freetown when Koelle interviewed him.

Full text: https://huskiecommons.lib.niu.edu/history-500african-voices/231/ [see 408.1].

408.2 ——.

Photomechanical reprint of 408.1 with addition of historical introduction by P. E. H. Hair. Limited to two hundred copies "distributed free of charge to scholars of African languages throughout the world."

Freetown [Sierra Leone]: University College of Sierra Leone, Fourah Bay College, 1963. Tpv: This numbered edition of two hundred copies is not available for distribution through the book-trade.
Folio (38 cm.): 19, vi, 24, 188 p., folding map.

408.3 ——.

Photomechanical reprint of 408.1, with additions, viz. *Polyglotta Africana / Vermehrt durch eine historische Einführung von P. E. H. Hair und einen Wortindex von David Dalby.* Published in association with *The African Language Review.*

Graz [Austria]: Akademische Druck- u. Verlagsanstalt [1963].
Folio (38 cm.): 19, vi, 24, 188 p., folding map.

409.1 'Okiri (ca. 1810–) = Andrew Parker

Account of this man born Ákūára printed on p. 14 of S. W. Koelle, *Polyglotta Africana.*

Full text: https://huskiecommons.lib.niu.edu/history-500african-voices/232/ [see 409.1].

London [England]: Church Missionary House, Salisbury Square, Fleet Street, MDCCCLIV [1854].
Folio (50 cm.): vi, 24 (2 columns each), 188 (8 columns each) p., folding map, errata slip.
Hogg 1611.

¶ 'Okiri was born in the town of Ákūára (modern Gabon, Republic of Congo—see Map 6) ca. 1810, where he lived until aged sixteen, at which time he was sold because his mother ran away from his father, taking 'Okiri with her. He lived enslaved for seven years in many places before arriving at Lōárrgo on the coast. There he was forced aboard a slave ship, which a British warship intercepted at sea. After freeing the ship's enslaved Africans, the British took them to Sierra Leone (Map 4) ca. 1833. 'Okiri lived in Lomley when Koelle interviewed him.

409.2——.

Photomechanical reprint of 409.1 with addition of historical introduction by P. E. H. Hair. Limited to two hundred copies "distributed free of charge to scholars of African languages throughout the world."

Freetown [Sierra Leone]: University College of Sierra Leone, Fourah Bay College, 1963. Tpv: This numbered edition of two hundred copies is not available for distribution through the book-trade.
Folio (38 cm.): 19, vi, 24, 188 p., folding map.

409.3——.

Photomechanical reprint of 409.1, with additions, viz. *Polyglotta Africana / Vermehrt durch eine historische Einführung von P. E. H. Hair und einen Wortindex von David Dalby.* Published in association with *The African Language Review.*

Graz [Austria]: Akademische Druck- u. Verlagsanstalt [1963].
Folio (38 cm.): 19, vi, 24, 188 p., folding map.

410.1 Bémbi (ca. 1808–) = William Davis

Account of this man from Pangela printed on p. 15 of S. W. Koelle, *Polyglotta Africana.*

London [England]: Church Missionary House, Salisbury Square, Fleet Street, MDCCCLIV [1854].
Folio (50 cm.): vi, 24 (2 columns each), 188 (8 columns each) p., folding map, errata slip.
Hogg 1611.

Full text: https://huskiecommons.lib.niu.edu/history-500african-voices/233/ [see 410.1].

¶ Bémbi was born in a town called Wódsimbúmba and spoke Pangela, which suggests he was Umbundu (modern west central Angola—see Map 6). When he was 28, his family was accused of witchcraft, sold, and taken on a slave ship onto the Atlantic. By ca. 1836 he was in Demerara (by then a part of the British colony of Guyana on the northern coast of South America—see Map 10), but it is not clear how he got there: either his slave ship was intercepted at sea by the British, who took him and the others there, or perhaps the slave ship took him to another colony and he escaped to Demerara. How he

reached Sierra Leone (Map 4) ca. 1842 is also unclear. He was living in Freetown when Koelle interviewed him.

410.2——.

Photomechanical reprint of 410.1 with addition of historical introduction by P. E. H. Hair. Limited to two hundred copies "distributed free of charge to scholars of African languages throughout the world."

Freetown [Sierra Leone]: University College of Sierra Leone, Fourah Bay College, 1963. Tpv: This numbered edition of two hundred copies is not available for distribution through the book-trade.
Folio (38 cm.): 19, vi, 24, 188 p., folding map.

410.3——.

Photomechanical reprint of 410.1, with additions, viz. *Polyglotta Africana / Vermehrt durch eine historische Einführung von P. E. H. Hair und einen Wortindex von David Dalby.* Published in association with *The African Language Review.*

Graz [Austria]: Akademische Druck- u. Verlagsanstalt [1963].
Folio (38 cm.): 19, vi, 24, 188 p., folding map.

411.1 Nánga (ca. 1832–) = John Smart

Account of this man from Lubálo or Mulubálo or Nalubálo printed on p. 15 of S. W. Koelle, *Polyglotta Africana.*

London [England]: Church Missionary House, Salisbury Square, Fleet Street, MDCCCLIV [1854].
Folio (50 cm.): vi, 24 (2 columns each), 188 (8 columns each) p., folding map, crrata slip.
Hogg 1611.

Full text: https://huskiecommons.lib.niu.edu/history-500african-voices/234/ [see 411.1].

¶ Nánga was born in a town called Mulukála and spoke Lubálo (or Kimbundu, in modern Angola—see Map 6)) or Mulubálo or Nalubálo. When he was 24 his mother pawned him to free her brother, and he ended up in the hands of Portuguese in Loando (Luanda), who forced him aboard a slave ship ca. 1846. A British warship intercepted this ship at sea, freed its enslaved Africans, and took them to Sierra Leone (Map 4). Nánga lived in Freetown when Koelle interviewed him.

411.2——.

Photomechanical reprint of 411.1 with addition of historical introduction by P. E. H. Hair. Limited to two hundred copies

"distributed free of charge to scholars of African languages throughout the world."

Freetown [Sierra Leone]: University College of Sierra Leone, Fourah Bay College, **1963**. Tpv: This numbered edition of two hundred copies is not available for distribution through the book-trade.
Folio (38 cm.): 19, vi, 24, 188 p., folding map.

411.3——.

Photomechanical reprint of 411.1, with additions, viz. *Polyglotta Africana / Vermehrt durch eine historische Einführung von P. E. H. Hair und einen Wortindex von David Dalby.* Published in association with *The African Language Review.*

Graz [Austria]: Akademische Druck- u. Verlagsanstalt [**1963**].
Folio (38 cm.): 19, vi, 24, 188 p., folding map.

412.1 Muséwo (ca. 1773–) = Toki Petro

Account of this man, a Songo, printed on p. 15 of S. W. Koelle, *Polyglotta Africana.*

London [England]: Church Missionary House, Salisbury Square, Fleet Street, MDCCCLIV [**1854**].
Folio (50 cm.): vi, 24 (2 columns each), 188 (8 columns each) p., folding map, errata slip.
Hogg 1611.

Full text: https://huskiecommons.lib.niu.edu/history-500african-voices/235/ [see 412.1].

¶ Muséwo was born in a town called Bópūnt (in modern Angola—see Map 6) and spoke Songo. He was kidnapped about age fifteen and carried to Loanda (Luanda), where he remained enslaved for twenty-one years by a Portuguese man who employed him to buy enslaved Songo people and transport them on slave ships to Brazil (Map 9). Upon being freed after his employer's death, Muséwo moved to Brazil, but continued to work on slave ships for another six years, until his ship was captured at sea by British warships ca. 1825. The British took Muséwo and the newly freed involuntary passengers to Sierra Leone. Muséwo was living in Freetown when Koelle interviewed him.

412.2——.

Photomechanical reprint of 412.1 with addition of historical introduction by P. E. H. Hair. Limited to two hundred copies "distributed free of charge to scholars of African languages throughout the world."

Freetown [Sierra Leone]: University College of Sierra Leone, Fourah Bay College, **1963**. Tpv: This numbered edition of

two hundred copies is not available for distribution through the book-trade.
Folio (38 cm.): 19, vi, 24, 188 p., folding map.

412.3——.

Photomechanical reprint of 412.1, with additions, viz. *Polyglotta Africana / Vermehrt durch eine historische Einführung von P. E. H. Hair und einen Wortindex von David Dalby.* Published in association with *The African Language Review.*

Graz [Austria]: Akademische Druck- u. Verlagsanstalt [**1963**].
Folio (38 cm.): 19, vi, 24, 188 p., folding map.

413.1 Frígu = Mulatto Campbell

Account of this man, a Kriman, printed on p. 15 of S. W. Koelle, *Polyglotta Africana.*

London [England]: Church Missionary House, Salisbury Square, Fleet Street, MDCCCLIV [**1854**].
Folio (50 cm.): vi, 24 (2 columns each), 188 (8 columns each) p., folding map, errata slip.
Hogg 1611.

Full text: https://huskiecommons.lib.niu.edu/history-500african-voices/236/ [see 413.1].

¶ Frígu was born in Mosádeménku (modern Mozambique—see Map 2) and spoke Kriman (Chuwabo). He had been married for ten years when a false friend enticed him to board a Portuguese ship, on which he was immediately enslaved. A British warship intercepted the ship at sea ca. 1833, freed its enslaved Africans, and took them to Sierra Leone (Map 4). Frígu was living in MacDonald when Koelle interviewed him.

413.2——.

Photomechanical reprint of 413.1 with addition of historical introduction by P. E. H. Hair. Limited to two hundred "distributed free of charge to scholars of African languages throughout the world."

Freetown [Sierra Leone]: University College of Sierra Leone, Fourah Bay College, **1963**. Tpv: This numbered edition of two hundred copies is not available for distribution through the book-trade.
Folio (38 cm.): 19, vi, 24, 188 p., folding map.

413.3——.

Photomechanical reprint of 413.1, with additions, viz. *Polyglotta Africana / Vermehrt durch eine historische Einführung von P. E. H. Hair und einen Wortindex von David Dalby.* Published in association with *The African Language Review.*

Graz [Austria]: Akademische Druck- u. Verlagsanstalt [1963]. Folio (38 cm.): 19, vi, 24, 188 p., folding map.

414.1 Tsántamélo Owágigóhi (ca. 1817–)

Account of this man from Nyámbān printed on p. 16 of S. W. Koelle, *Polyglotta Africana*.

Full text: https://huskiecommons.lib.niu.edu/history-500african-voices/237/ [see 414.1].

London [England]: Church Missionary House, Salisbury Square, Fleet Street, MDCCCLIV [1854].
Folio (50 cm.): vi, 24 (2 columns each), 188 (8 columns each) p., folding map, errata slip.
Hogg 1611.

¶ Tsántamélo (son of Kigóhi) was born in Nyámaviléni (modern Kongo—see Map 6) and spoke Nyámbān. Ca. 1835, aged sixteen, he was kidnapped by Māngúnu and a month later put on a Portuguese slave ship. A British warship intercepted this ship at sea, freed the enslaved Africans, and took them to Sierra Leone (Map 4). Tsántamélo married a countrywoman there and was living in Freetown when Koelle interviewed him.

414.2——.

Photomechanical reprint of 414.1 with addition of historical introduction by P. E. H. Hair. Limited to two hundred copies "distributed free of charge to scholars of African languages throughout the world."

Freetown [Sierra Leone]: University College of Sierra Leone, Fourah Bay College, 1963. Tpv: This numbered edition of two hundred copies is not available for distribution through the book-trade.
Folio (38 cm.): 19, vi, 24, 188 p., folding map.

414.3——.

Photomechanical reprint of 414.1, with additions, viz. *Polyglotta Africana / Vermehrt durch eine historische Einführung von P. E. H. Hair und einen Wortindex von David Dalby*. Published in association with *The African Language Review*.

Graz [Austria]: Akademische Druck- u. Verlagsanstalt [1963].
Folio (38 cm.): 19, vi, 24, 188 p., folding map.

415.1 Rúnāgo = Thomas Nicol

Account of this man from Bidsógo or Bidsóro printed on p. 16 of S. W. Koelle, *Polyglotta Africana*.

London [England]: Church Missionary House, Salisbury Square, Fleet Street, MDCCCLIV [1854].

Folio (50 cm.): vi, 24 (2 columns each), 188 (8 columns each) p., folding map, errata slip.
Hogg 1611.

Full text: https://huskiecommons.lib.niu.edu/history-500african-voices/238/ [see 415.1].

¶ Rúnāgo was born in Nágo (in modern Nigeria—see Map 5), on Ankaras island, opposite the Rio Grande, and spoke Bidsógo or Bidsóro. When very young, he moved with his family to Kére, where he grew up. Rúnāgo had a young child when he (Rúnāgo) was sold by his elder brother to Portuguese "because they could not agree." Ca. 1838 he was forced aboard a slave ship that was intercepted at sea by a British warship. The British freed the enslaved Africans and took them to Sierra Leone (Map 4). Rúnāgo was living in Kissy (near Freetown) when Koelle interviewed him.

415.2——.

Photomechanical reprint of 415.1 with addition of historical introduction by P. E. H. Hair. Limited to two hundred copies "distributed free of charge to scholars of African languages throughout the world."

Freetown [Sierra Leone]: University College of Sierra Leone, Fourah Bay College, 1963. Tpv: This numbered edition of two hundred copies is not available for distribution through the book-trade.
Folio (38 cm.): 19, vi, 24, 188 p., folding map.

415.3——.

Photomechanical reprint of 415.1, with additions, viz. *Polyglotta Africana / Vermehrt durch eine historische Einführung von P. E. H. Hair und einen Wortindex von David Dalby*. Published in association with *The African Language Review*.

Graz [Austria]: Akademische Druck- u. Verlagsanstalt [1963].
Folio (38 cm.): 19, vi, 24, 188 p., folding map.

416.1 Yéri = Sáyo

Account of this man printed on p. 16 of S. W. Koelle, *Polyglotta Africana*.

London [England]: Church Missionary House, Salisbury Square, Fleet Street, MDCCCLIV [1854].
Folio (50 cm.): vi, 24 (2 columns each), 188 (8 columns each) p., folding map, errata slip.
Hogg 1611.

Full text: https://huskiecommons.lib.niu.edu/history-500african-voices/239/ [see 416.1].

¶ Yéri was born in the town of Wakarīa (modern Guinea—see Map 3) and spoke Lándōma (Landoma). At age 30 he was sold because of adultery. He was transported to an unknown place on the coast and placed on a slave ship. He lived ca. 1847–1852 in the British South American colony of Demerara (modern Guyana—see Map 10), where slavery had been abolished in 1838. Whether the slave ship took him to another colony from which he escaped to free British territory or whether his slave ship was intercepted at sea and the liberated passengers taken to Demerara is unclear. He arrived in Sierra Leone (Map 4) eleven months before his interview with Koelle in an unnamed location.

416.2———.

Photomechanical reprint of 416.1 with addition of historical introduction by P. E. H. Hair. Limited to two hundred copies "distributed free of charge to scholars of African languages throughout the world."

Freetown [Sierra Leone]: University College of Sierra Leone, Fourah Bay College, 1963. Tpv: This numbered edition of two hundred copies is not available for distribution through the book-trade.
Folio (38 cm.): 19, vi, 24, 188 p., folding map.

416.3———.

Photomechanical reprint of 416.1, with additions, viz. *Polyglotta Africana / Vermehrt durch eine historische Einführung von P. E. H. Hair und einen Wortindex von David Dalby*. Published in association with *The African Language Review*.

Graz [Austria]: Akademische Druck- u. Verlagsanstalt [1963].
Folio (38 cm.): 19, vi, 24, 188 p., folding map.

417.1 Wúene (ca. 1820–) = William Cole

Account of this man, a Bóko, printed on p. 17 of S. W. Koelle, *Polyglotta Africana*.

Full text: https://huskiecommons.lib.niu.edu/history-500african-voices/240/ [see 417.1].

London [England]: Church Missionary House, Salisbury Square, Fleet Street, MDCCCLIV [1854].
Folio (50 cm.): vi, 24 (2 columns each), 188 (8 columns each) p., folding map, errata slip.
Hogg 1611.

¶ Wúene was born in Káiōma, in the upper Volta River region (modern Ghana—see Map 5) and spoke Bóko. A warrior, he joined an expedition against the Iloni when aged about 25. He was captured by Phula (Fulani, Fula, Fulbi or Peul peoples throughout West Africa), who immediately sold him to Yorùbá (modern day Nigeria, Benin, and Togo), who then delivered him to the Portuguese, who forced him aboard a slave ship ca. 1845. A British warship intercepted this ship at sea, freed the enslaved Afrcians, and took them to Sierra Leone (Map 4). Wúene lived in Freetown when Koelle interviewed him.

417.2———.

Photomechanical reprint of 417.1 with addition of historical introduction by P. E. H. Hair. Limited to two hundred copies "distributed free of charge to scholars of African languages throughout the world."

Freetown [Sierra Leone]: University College of Sierra Leone, Fourah Bay College, 1963. Tpv: This numbered edition of two hundred copies is not available for distribution through the book-trade.
Folio (38 cm.): 19, vi, 24, 188 p., folding map.

417.3———.

Photomechanical reprint of 417.1, with additions, viz. *Polyglotta Africana / Vermehrt durch eine historische Einführung von P. E. H. Hair und einen Wortindex von David Dalby*. Published in association with *The African Language Review*.

Graz [Austria]: Akademische Druck- u. Verlagsanstalt [1963].
Folio (38 cm.): 19, vi, 24, 188 p., folding map.

418.1 Hábu (ca. 1830–) = Sam Jackson

Account of this man, a Hausa, printed on p. 17 of S. W. Koelle, *Polyglotta Africana*.

Full text: https://huskiecommons.lib.niu.edu/history-500african-voices/241/ [see 418.1].

London [England]: Church Missionary House, Salisbury Square, Fleet Street, MDCCCLIV [1854].
Folio (50 cm.): vi, 24 (2 columns each), 188 (8 columns each) p., folding map, errata slip.
Hogg 1611.

¶ Hábu was from Kano (northern modern Nigeria—see Map 5) and spoke Hausa. He was a twenty-year-old warrior when captured during a military expedition against Gobir (Hausa state, northern Nigeria). He was immediately sold to slave dealers, taken to the sea at Lagos (western Nigeria), and forced aboard a slave ship ca. 1849. A British vessel intercepted this ship and took it to Sierra Leone (Map 4). Hábu lived in Kissy (near Freetown) when Koelle interviewed him.

418.2———.

Photomechanical reprint of 418.1 with addition of historical introduction by P. E. H. Hair. Limited to two hundred copies

"distributed free of charge to scholars of African languages throughout the world."

Freetown [Sierra Leone]: University College of Sierra Leone, Fourah Bay College, **1963.** Tpv: This numbered edition of two hundred copies is not available for distribution through the book-trade.

Folio (38 cm.): 19, vi, 24, 188 p., folding map.

418.3———.

Photomechanical reprint of 418.1, with additions, viz. *Polyglotta Africana / Vermehrt durch eine historische Einführung von P. E. H. Hair und einen Wortindex von David Dalby.* Published in association with *The African Language Review.*

Graz [Austria]: Akademische Druck- u. Verlagsanstalt [**1963**]. Folio (38 cm.): 19, vi, 24, 188 p., folding map.

419.1 Mōhámmadu = Jacob Brown

Account of this man from Hausa Berni printed on p. 17 of S. W. Koelle, *Polyglotta Africana.*

London [England]: Church Missionary House, Salisbury Square, Fleet Street, MDCCCLIV [**1854**]. Folio (50 cm.): vi, 24 (2 columns each), 188 (8 columns each) p., folding map, errata slip. Hogg 1611.

Full text: https://huskiecommons.lib.niu.edu/history-500african-voices/242/ [see 419.1].

¶ Mōhámmadu was born in Bérni Ndáda, a small walled city (likely referring to a section of Zinder in modern Niger—see Map 5), and spoke Hausa Berni. In his sixth year his parents took him to the capital, Kadzina, where he grew up. Having been married two years, he was working on his farm near Phulas when he was kidnapped, then sold to Gobur (Gobir), where he remained for three years. He was then taken to Dámagaram in Bornu country (modern southwest Niger), where he lived for eight years before being carried to the sea and forced aboard a slave ship ca. 1849. A British warship intercepted this ship at sea, freed the enslaved Africans, and took them to Sierra Leone (Map 4). Mōhámmadu lived in Freetown when Koelle interviewed him.

419.2———.

Photomechanical reprint of 419.1 with addition of historical introduction by P. E. H. Hair. Limited to two hundred copies "distributed free of charge to scholars of African languages throughout the world."

Freetown [Sierra Leone]: University College of Sierra Leone, Fourah Bay College, **1963.** Tpv: This numbered edition of

two hundred copies is not available for distribution through the book-trade.

Folio (38 cm.): 19, vi, 24, 188 p., folding map.

419.3———.

Photomechanical reprint of 419.1, with additions, viz. *Polyglotta Africana / Vermehrt durch eine historische Einführung von P. E. H. Hair und einen Wortindex von David Dalby.* Published in association with *The African Language Review.*

Graz [Austria]: Akademische Druck- u. Verlagsanstalt [**1963**]. Folio (38 cm.): 19, vi, 24, 188 p., folding map.

420.1 Muhámmadu (ca. 1790–)

Account of this man from Púlō printed on pp. 17–18 of S. W. Koelle, *Polyglotta Africana.*

London [England]: Church Missionary House, Salisbury Square, Fleet Street, MDCCCLIV [**1854**]. Folio (50 cm.): vi, 24 (2 columns each), 188 (8 columns each) p., folding map, errata slip. Hogg 1611.

Full text: https://huskiecommons.lib.niu.edu/history-500african-voices/243/ [see 420.1].

¶ Muhámmadu, a Fulbe, was born in Wúrōkáre (Gobir city state, modern northern Nigeria—see Map 5) and spoke Púlō (Fulani, Fula, Fulbi or Peul peoples throughout West Africa). Before 1808, aged seventeen, he was kidnapped by Hausas, immediately carried to the sea, and forced aboard a slave ship that sailed to the Caribbean. He lived enslaved in Jamaica (Map 13) for nine years, then was freed and taken to Sierra Leone (Map 4). At some point he became a soldier in British service and was discharged in Sierra Leone in 1833. Muhámmadu lived alone in Sierra Leone and spoke English well when Koelle interviewed him.

420.2———.

Photomechanical reprint of 420.1 with addition of historical introduction by P. E. H. Hair. Limited to two hundred copies "distributed free of charge to scholars of African languages throughout the world."

Freetown [Sierra Leone]: University College of Sierra Leone, Fourah Bay College, **1963.** Tpv: This numbered edition of two hundred copies is not available for distribution through the book-trade.

Folio (38 cm.): 19, vi, 24, 188 p., folding map.

420.3———.

Photomechanical reprint of 420.1, with additions, viz. *Polyglotta Africana / Vermehrt durch eine historische Einführung von P. E. H. Hair und einen Wortindex von David Dalby.* Published in association with *The African Language Review.*

Graz [Austria]: Akademische Druck- u. Verlagsanstalt [1963]. Folio (38 cm.): 19, vi, 24, 188 p., folding map.

421.1   Egbéno = W. Johnson

Account of this man from ʻAnān printed on p. 18 of S. W. Koelle, *Polyglotta Africana.*

London [England]: Church Missionary House, Salisbury Square, Fleet Street, MDCCCLIV [1854]. Folio (50 cm.): vi, 24 (2 columns each), 188 (8 columns each) p., folding map, errata slip. Hogg 1611.

Full text: https:// huskiecommons. lib.niu.edu/history-500african-voices/244/ [see 421.1].

¶ Egbéno was born and raised in Ngúod (likely Nugu in modern southeastern Nigeria—see Map 5) and spoke ʻAnān. He had two wives when kidnapped. Thereafter, he was carried to Obane (anglicé Bonny, southern Nigeria), sold to Portuguese, and forced aboard a slave ship ca. 1835. A British warship intercepted this ship at sea, freed the enslaved Africans, and took them to Sierra Leone (Map 4). Egbéno lived in Waterloo when Koelle interviewed him.

421.2———.

Photomechanical reprint of 421.1 with addition of historical introduction by P. E. H. Hair. Limited to two hundred copies "distributed free of charge to scholars of African languages throughout the world."

Freetown [Sierra Leone]: University College of Sierra Leone, Fourah Bay College, 1963. Tpv: This numbered edition of two hundred copies is not available for distribution through the book-trade. Folio (38 cm.): 19, vi, 24, 188 p., folding map.

421.3———.

Photomechanical reprint of 421.1, with additions, viz. *Polyglotta Africana / Vermehrt durch eine historische Einführung von P. E. H. Hair und einen Wortindex von David Dalby.* Published in association with *The African Language Review.*

Graz [Austria]: Akademische Druck- u. Verlagsanstalt [1963]. Folio (38 cm.): 19, vi, 24, 188 p., folding map.

422.1   ʻAdamu (ca. 1817–) = Edward Klein

Account of this man from Kóro printed on p. 18 of S. W. Koelle, *Polyglotta Africana.*

London [England]: Church Missionary House, Salisbury Square, Fleet Street, MDCCCLIV [1854]. Folio (50 cm.): vi, 24 (2 columns each), 188 (8 columns each) p., folding map, errata slip. Hogg 1611.

Full text: https:// huskiecommons. lib.niu.edu/history-500african-voices/245/ [see 422.1].

¶ ʻAdamu was born and raised in the city of Káno (modern northern Nigeria—see Map 5), but spoke Púlo (Fulani, Fula, Fulbi or Peul peoples throughout West Africa), because his parents were from there. He had been married five years and had two wives when forced to join a military expedition against the Málādis (an independent Hausa group east of Gebur). ʻAdamu had to flee in battle but was caught at night and secretly carried by Málādis to another country for sale, because by law they were required to execute all Fúlbe prisoners of war. His journey to the sea took less than a year. Upon arrival at the coast he was forced onto a slave ship that was intercepted at sea by the British, who liberated the enslaved passengers and took them to Sierra Leone (Map 4) ca. 1850. He was 36 years old, lived in Freetown, and spoke English well when interviewed by Koelle three years later.

422.2———.

Photomechanical reprint of 422.1 with addition of historical introduction by P. E. H. Hair. Limited to two hundred copies "distributed free of charge to scholars of African languages throughout the world."

Freetown [Sierra Leone]: University College of Sierra Leone, Fourah Bay College, 1963. Tpv: This numbered edition of two hundred copies is not available for distribution through the book-trade. Folio (38 cm.): 19, vi, 24, 188 p., folding map.

422.3———.

Photomechanical reprint of 422.1, with additions, viz. *Polyglotta Africana / Vermehrt durch eine historische Einführung von P. E. H. Hair und einen Wortindex von David Dalby.* Published in association with *The African Language Review.*

Graz [Austria]: Akademische Druck- u. Verlagsanstalt [1963]. Folio (38 cm.): 19, vi, 24, 188 p., folding map.

423.1 Gbála = Sam John

Account of this man from Kóro printed on p. 19 of S. W. Koelle, *Polyglotta Africana.*

London [England]: Church Missionary House, Salisbury Square, Fleet Street, MDCCCLIV [1854].
Folio (50 cm.): vi, 24 (2 columns each), 188 (8 columns each) p., folding map, errata slip.
Hogg 1611.

¶ Gbála was born in the village 'Etera (modern northern Nigeria—see Map 5) and spoke Kóro. When aged about nineteen, he was captured during the war with Lapias and sold to Abebere (Hausa) for a horse. His forced journey to the sea lasted a year, after which he was forced aboard a slave ship ca. 1849. A British warship intercepted this ship at sea, freed its enslaved Africans, and took them to Sierra Leone (Map 4). Gbála lived in Allenstown when Koelle interviewed him.

423.2——.

Photomechanical reprint of 423.1 with addition of historical introduction by P. E. H. Hair. Limited to two hundred copies "distributed free of charge to scholars of African languages throughout the world."

Freetown [Sierra Leone]: University College of Sierra Leone, Fourah Bay College, 1963. Tpv: This numbered edition of two hundred copies is not available for distribution through the book-trade.
Folio (38 cm.): 19, vi, 24, 188 p., folding map.

423.3——.

Photomechanical reprint of 423.1, with additions, viz. *Polyglotta Africana / Vermehrt durch eine historische Einführung von P. E. H. Hair und einen Wortindex von David Dalby.* Published in association with *The African Language Review.*

Graz [Austria]: Akademische Druck- u. Verlagsanstalt [1963].
Folio (38 cm.): 19, vi, 24, 188 p., folding map.

424.1 'Otu = John Macauly

Account of this man from Akurakkura printed on p. 19 of S. W. Koelle, *Polyglotta Africana.*

London [England]: Church Missionary House, Salisbury Square, Fleet Street, MDCCCLIV [1854].
Folio (50 cm.): vi, 24 (2 columns each), 188 (8 columns each) p., folding map, errata slip.
Hogg 1611.

Full text: https://huskiecommons.lib.niu.edu/history-500african-voices/246/ [see 423.1].

¶ 'Otu was born in 'Atām-Nómūnu (near Cross River [Oyono] modern Nigeria and Cameroon—see Map 5) and spoke Akurakkura (possibly Agwagune language). Aged about fifteen, he was sold to Akatura in the town of Aguragor (on the Calabar River, Nigeria). There he married and had a child who was about eight years old when 'Otu was sold to Spaniards and forced aboard a slave ship ca. 1833. A British warship intercepted the ship at sea and took its enslaved men and women to Sierra Leone (Map 4), where 'Otu lived when Koelle interviewed him.

Full text: https://huskiecommons.lib.niu.edu/history-500african-voices/247/ [see 423.1].

424.2——.

Photomechanical reprint of 424.1 with addition of historical introduction by P. E. H. Hair. Limited to two hundred copies "distributed free of charge to scholars of African languages throughout the world."

Freetown [Sierra Leone]: University College of Sierra Leone, Fourah Bay College, 1963. Tpv: This numbered edition of two hundred copies is not available for distribution through the book-trade.
Folio (38 cm.): 19, vi, 24, 188 p., folding map.

424.3——.

Photomechanical reprint of 424.1, with additions, viz. *Polyglotta Africana / Vermehrt durch eine historische Einführung von P. E. H. Hair und einen Wortindex von David Dalby.* Published in association with *The African Language Review.*

Graz [Austria]: Akademische Druck- u. Verlagsanstalt [1963].
Folio (38 cm.): 19, vi, 24, 188 p., folding map.

425.1 Otsétse (ca. 1802–) = John Davis

Account of this man, an Okām, printed on p. 19 of S. W. Koelle, *Polyglotta Africana.*

London [England]: Church Missionary House, Salisbury Square, Fleet Street, MDCCCLIV [1854].
Folio (50 cm.): vi, 24 (2 columns each), 188 (8 columns each) p., folding map, errata slip.
Hogg 1611.

Full text: https://huskiecommons.lib.niu.edu/history-500african-voices/248/ [see 425.1].

¶ Otsétse was born in Ofésēm (near Cross River [Oyono] modern Nigeria and northwest Cameroon—see Map 5) and spoke Okām (Mbembe). Aged about twenty-two, he was kidnapped and sold a year later to Portuguese, who put him on a slave ship ca. 1823. A British warship intercepted this ship at sea, freed the enslaved Africans, and took them to Sierra Leone (Map 4). Otsétse lived in Freetown when Koelle interviewed him.

425.2——.

Photomechanical reprint of 425.1 with addition of historical introduction by P. E. H. Hair. Limited to two hundred copies "distributed free of charge to scholars of African languages throughout the world."

Freetown [Sierra Leone]: University College of Sierra Leone, Fourah Bay College, 1963. Tpv: This numbered edition of two hundred copies is not available for distribution through the book-trade.
Folio (38 cm.): 19, vi, 24, 188 p., folding map.

425.3——.

Photomechanical reprint of 425.1, with additions, viz. *Polyglotta Africana / Vermehrt durch eine historische Einführung von P. E. H. Hair und einen Wortindex von David Dalby.* Published in association with *The African Language Review.*

Graz [Austria]: Akademische Druck- u. Verlagsanstalt [1963].
Folio (38 cm.): 19, vi, 24, 188 p., folding map.

426.1   Otén (ca. 1817) = Sam Pratt

Account of this man from Yágūa printed on p. 19 of S. W. Koelle, *Polyglotta Africana.*

London [England]: Church Missionary House, Salisbury Square, Fleet Street, MDCCCLIV [1854].
Folio (50 cm.): vi, 24 (2 columns each), 188 (8 columns each) p., folding map, errata slip.
Hogg 1611.

Full text: https://huskiecommons.lib.niu.edu/history-500african-voices/249/
[see 426.1].

¶ Otén was born in Ndúro (modern central Nigeria—see Map 5) and spoke Yásgūa (Nyankpa). When aged twenty-two ca. 1849, he was sold by his chief, taken to the sea via Asante (Akan people, modern Ghana), and forced aboard a slave ship. A British warship intercepted the ship at sea, freed the enslaved Africans, and took them to Sierra Leone (Map 4). Otén lived in Freetown when Koelle interviewed him.

426.2——.

Photomechanical reprint of 426.1 with addition of historical introduction by P. E. H. Hair. Limited to two hundred copies "distributed free of charge to scholars of African languages throughout the world."

Freetown [Sierra Leone]: University College of Sierra Leone, Fourah Bay College, 1963. Tpv: This numbered edition of two hundred copies is not available for distribution through the book-trade.
Folio (38 cm.): 19, vi, 24, 188 p., folding map.

426.3——.

Photomechanical reprint of 426.1, with additions, viz. *Polyglotta Africana / Vermehrt durch eine historische Einführung von P. E. H. Hair und einen Wortindex von David Dalby.* Published in association with *The African Language Review.*

Graz [Austria]: Akademische Druck- u. Verlagsanstalt [1963].
Folio (38 cm.): 19, vi, 24, 188 p., folding map.

427.1   Gōl (ca. 1831–) = Thomas Klein

Account of this man, a Búte, printed on p. 19 of S. W. Koelle, *Polyglotta Africana.*

London [England]: Church Missionary House, Salisbury Square, Fleet Street, MDCCCLIV [1854].
Folio (50 cm.): vi, 24 (2 columns each), 188 (8 columns each) p., folding map, errata slip.
Hogg 1611.

Full text: https://huskiecommons.lib.niu.edu/history-500african-voices/250/
[see 427.1].

¶ Gōl was born in Kúe (modern Cameroon—see Map 5) and spoke Búte. He was captured by Phula in war when aged about nineteen. The Phula (Fulani, Fula, Fulbi, or Peul peoples throughout West Africa) sold him to Hausas, who brought him to the Yorùbá (ethnicity, modern-day Nigeria, Benin, and Togo). The Yorùbá sold him to the Portuguese, who forced him aboard a slave ship ca. 1850. A British warship intercepted the ship at sea, freed the enslaved Africans, and took them to Sierra Leone (Map 4), where Gōl lived when Koelle interviewed him.

427.2——.

Photomechanical reprint of 427.1 with addition of historical introduction by P. E. H. Hair. Limited to two hundred copies "distributed free of charge to scholars of African languages throughout the world."

Freetown [Sierra Leone]: University College of Sierra Leone, Fourah Bay College, 1963. Tpv: This numbered edition of

two hundred copies is not available for distribution through the book-trade.
Folio (38 cm.): 19, vi, 24, 188 p., folding map.

427.3——.

Photomechanical reprint of 427.1, with additions, viz. *Polyglotta Africana / Vermehrt durch eine historische Einführung von P. E. H. Hair und einen Wortindex von David Dalby.* Published in association with *The African Language Review.*

Graz [Austria]: Akademische Druck- u. Verlagsanstalt [1963].
Folio (38 cm.): 19, vi, 24, 188 p., folding map.

428.1 Bíra (ca. 1812–) = George Bailey

Account of this man from Múrūndo or Bárūndo printed on p. 19 of S. W. Koelle, *Polyglotta Africana.*

London [England]: Church Missionary House, Salisbury Square, Fleet Street, MDCCCLIV [1854].
Folio (50 cm.): vi, 24 (2 columns each), 188 (8 columns each) p., folding map, errata slip.
Hogg 1611.

Full text: https:// huskiecommons. lib.niu.edu/history-500african-voices/251/ [see 428.1].

¶ Bíra was born in Okúmu (modern Cameroon—see Map 5), one day's journey from the sea, and spoke Múrūndo or Bárūndo (Bakundu). He was nineteen when kidnapped, sold, and forced aboard a slave ship ca. 1831. The ship was probably intercepted by a British warship, which freed the enslaved Africans and took them to the Island of Ascension (St. Helena), almost midway between the coasts of Africa and Brazil in the South Atlantic Ocean. In 1835 Bira went to Sierra Leone. He lived in Freetown when Koelle interviewed him.

428.2——.

Photomechanical reprint of 428.1 with addition of historical introduction by P. E. H. Hair. Limited to two hundred copies "distributed free of charge to scholars of African languages throughout the world."

Freetown [Sierra Leone]: University College of Sierra Leone, Fourah Bay College, 1963. Tpv: This numbered edition of two hundred copies is not available for distribution through the book-trade.
Folio (38 cm.): 19, vi, 24, 188 p., folding map.

428.3——.

Photomechanical reprint of 428.1, with additions, viz. *Polyglotta Africana / Vermehrt durch eine historische Einführung*

von P. E. H. Hair und einen Wortindex von David Dalby. Published in association with *The African Language Review.*

Graz [Austria]: Akademische Druck- u. Verlagsanstalt [1963].
Folio (38 cm.): 19, vi, 24, 188 p., folding map.

429.1 Disile = John Cocker

Account of this man from Tíwi printed on p. 20 of S. W. Koelle, *Polyglotta Africana.*

London [England]: Church Missionary House, Salisbury Square, Fleet Street, MDCCCLIV [1854].
Folio (50 cm.): vi, 24 (2 columns each), 188 (8 columns each) p., folding map, errata slip.
Hogg 1611.

Full text: https:// huskiecommons. lib.niu.edu/history-500african-voices/252/ [see 429.1].

¶ Disile was born and raised in Mukúwa, where he spoke Tíwi, likely referring to Tiv in modern northern Nigeria (see Map 5). He had four wives and a nine-year-old child when captured in war with the distant Gényi, who sold him to Hausa in Mbágba (modern northwestern Nigeria), who then took him to the coast via Igala (a kingdom in modern central Nigeria). A year later (ca. 1833) he was forced aboard a slave ship that was subsequently intercepted at sea by a British warship. The British freed the enslaved Africans and took them to Sierra Leone (Map 4). Disile lived in Waterloo when Koelle interviewed him.

429.2——.

Photomechanical reprint of 429.1 with addition of historical introduction by P. E. H. Hair. Limited to two hundred copies "distributed free of charge to scholars of African languages throughout the world."

Freetown [Sierra Leone]: University College of Sierra Leone, Fourah Bay College, 1963. Tpv: This numbered edition of two hundred copies is not available for distribution through the book-trade.
Folio (38 cm.): 19, vi, 24, 188 p., folding map.

429.3——.

Photomechanical reprint of 429.1, with additions, viz. *Polyglotta Africana / Vermehrt durch eine historische Einführung von P. E. H. Hair und einen Wortindex von David Dalby.* Published in association with *The African Language Review.*

Graz [Austria]: Akademische Druck- u. Verlagsanstalt [1963].
Folio (38 cm.): 19, vi, 24, 188 p., folding map.

430.0 Sórāga (ca. 1809–) = Thomas Crocker

Account of this man from Mfút or Báfut printed on p. 20 of S. W. Koelle, *Polyglotta Africana.*

London [England]: Church Missionary House, Salisbury Square, Fleet Street, MDCCCLIV [1854].
Folio (50 cm.): vi, 24 (2 columns each), 188 (8 columns each) p., folding map, errata slip.
Hogg 1611.

Full text: https://huskiecommons.lib.niu.edu/history-500african-voices/253/ [see 430.1].

¶ Sórāga was born in the town of Bálīa in Bóritsu (also known by other names—see Koelle's extended geographic description—probably in northern Nigeria—see Map 5). At age twenty-three he was kidnapped by Adínyi people "runaway slaves of the Phula" (Fulani, Fula, Fulbi, or Peul peoples throughout West Africa) and sold to Gbāgban, who hurried him to Igala (a kingdom in modern central Nigeria) and Kálabā (Calabar, Cross River region (modern Nigeria and northwestern Cameroon) on the coast. There he was forced onto a slave ship that was intercepted at sea by the British, who liberated the passengers and transported them to Sierra Leone (Map 4) ca. 1833. Twenty years after his arrival in the colony, Sórāga lived in Waterloo when Koelle interviewed him.

430.2———.

Photomechanical reprint of 430.1 with addition of historical introduction by P. E. H. Hair. Limited to two hundred copies "distributed free of charge to scholars of African languages throughout the world."

Freetown [Sierra Leone]: University College of Sierra Leone, Fourah Bay College, 1963. Tpv: This numbered edition of two hundred copies is not available for distribution through the book-trade.
Folio (38 cm.): 19, vi, 24, 188 p., folding map.

430.3———.

Photomechanical reprint of 430.1, with additions, viz. *Polyglotta Africana / Vermehrt durch eine historische Einführung von P. E. H. Hair und einen Wortindex von David Dalby.* Published in association with *The African Language Review.*

Graz [Austria]: Akademische Druck- u. Verlagsanstalt [1963].
Folio (38 cm.): 19, vi, 24, 188 p., folding map.

431.1 Yóno (ca. 1800–) = William Macauly

Account of this man from Mfút or Báfut printed on p. 20 of S. W. Koelle, *Polyglotta Africana.*

London [England]: Church Missionary House, Salisbury Square, Fleet Street, MDCCCLIV [1854].
Folio (50 cm.): vi, 24 (2 columns each), 188 (8 columns each) p., folding map, errata slip.
Hogg 1611.

Full text: https://huskiecommons.lib.niu.edu/history-500african-voices/254/ [see 431.1].

¶ Yóno was born in Bákon, where his father was king, and spoke Mfút or Báfut, a language spoken in Cameroon (see Map 5). He lived there until eighteen years old (ca. 1818), when Bále (Phula) (Fulani, Fula, Fulbi, or Peul peoples throughout West Africa) conquered the town and sold him to the Bāfólan, among whom he lived for ten years. He was then taken to the sea and forced aboard a slave ship ca. 1828. A British warship intercepted this ship at sea, freed the enslaved Africans, and took them to Sierra Leone (Map 4). Yóno lived in Freetown when Koelle interviewed him.

431.2———.

Photomechanical reprint of 431.1 with addition of historical introduction by P. E. H. Hair. Limited to two hundred copies "distributed free of charge to scholars of African languages throughout the world."

Freetown [Sierra Leone]: University College of Sierra Leone, Fourah Bay College, 1963. Tpv: This numbered edition of two hundred copies is not available for distribution through the book-trade.
Folio (38 cm.): 19, vi, 24, 188 p., folding map.

431.3———.

Photomechanical reprint of 431.1, with additions, viz. *Polyglotta Africana / Vermehrt durch eine historische Einführung von P. E. H. Hair und einen Wortindex von David Dalby.* Published in association with *The African Language Review.*

Graz [Austria]: Akademische Druck- u. Verlagsanstalt [1963].
Folio (38 cm.): 19, vi, 24, 188 p., folding map.

432.0 Tándo (ca. 1823–) = John James

Account of this man from Dsúku printed on pp. 20–21 of S. W. Koelle, *Polyglotta Africana.*

London [England]: Church Missionary House, Salisbury Square, Fleet Street, MDCCCLIV [1854].
Folio (50 cm.): vi, 24 (2 columns each), 188 (8 columns each) p., folding map, errata slip.
Hogg 1611.

¶ Tándo was born in a village called Mándsin, among the Mbe people (modern Cameroon—see Map 5). At age eighteen he was kidnapped by Tebana, who burned all towns in the area and forced their inhabitants into the woods. Tándo had been in their hands for several months when the Tebana themselves were driven out by unnamed rivals. Tándo was taken to a different land, where he did not know the language. From there it took a year to transport him to Kálabā (Calabar, Cross River region in modern Nigeria and northwestern Cameroon) on the coast, where he was forced onto a slave ship that was intercepted at sea by the British, who freed its enslaved passengers and took them to Sierra Leone (Map 4) ca. 1843. Tándo lived in Gloucester when interviewed by Koelle.

Full text: https:// huskiecommons. lib.niu.edu/history-500african-voices/255/ [see 432.1].

432.2———.

Photomechanical reprint of 432.1 with addition of historical introduction by P. E. H. Hair. Limited to two hundred copies "distributed free of charge to scholars of African languages throughout the world."

Freetown [Sierra Leone]: University College of Sierra Leone, Fourah Bay College, **1963.** Tpv: This numbered edition of two hundred copies is not available for distribution through the book-trade.
Folio (38 cm.): 19, vi, 24, 188 p., folding map.

432.3———.

Photomechanical reprint of 432.1, with additions, viz. *Polyglotta Africana / Vermehrt durch eine historische Einführung von P. E. H. Hair und einen Wortindex von David Dalby.* Published in association with *The African Language Review.*

Graz [Austria]: Akademische Druck- u. Verlagsanstalt [**1963**]. Folio (38 cm.): 19, vi, 24, 188 p., folding map.

433.0 Bungo (ca. 1816–) = Robert Shilling

Account of this man from Dsúku printed on p. 21 of S. W. Koelle, *Polyglotta Africana.*

London [England]: Church Missionary House, Salisbury Square, Fleet Street, MDCCCLIV [**1854**].
Folio (50 cm.): vi, 24 (2 columns each), 188 (8 columns each) p., folding map, errata slip.
Hogg 1611.

Full text: https:// huskiecommons. lib.niu.edu/history-500african-voices/256/ [see 433.1].

¶ Bungo was born in a town called Túntu, three days from Kémbo, the Nso or Banso capital (modern northwest Cameroon—see Map 5). At age thirteen he went to Bámom to collect a debt, but the debtor and others seized Bungo and sold him. Two years later he was taken to Kálabā (Calabar, Cross River region in modern Nigeria and northwestern Cameroon) country, normally a two-month journey. There he was forced onto a slave ship that was intercepted at sea by the British, who liberated the enslaved passengers and took them to Sierra Leone (Map 4) ca. 1831. Bungo lived in Aberdeen when Koelle interviewed him twenty-two years later.

433.2———.

Photomechanical reprint of 433.1 with addition of historical introduction by P. E. H. Hair. Limited to two hundred copies "distributed free of charge to scholars of African languages throughout the world."

Freetown [Sierra Leone]: University College of Sierra Leone, Fourah Bay College, **1963.** Tpv: This numbered edition of two hundred copies is not available for distribution through the book-trade.
Folio (38 cm.): 19, vi, 24, 188 p., folding map.

433.3———.

Photomechanical reprint of 433.1, with additions, viz. *Polyglotta Africana / Vermehrt durch eine historische Einführung von P. E. H. Hair und einen Wortindex von David Dalby.* Published in association with *The African Language Review.*

Graz [Austria]: Akademische Druck- u. Verlagsanstalt [**1963**]. Folio (38 cm.): 19, vi, 24, 188 p., folding map.

434.1 'Ndsu (ca. 1803–) = John Macauly

Account of this man from Dsúku printed on p. 21 of S. W. Koelle, *Polyglotta Africana.*

London [England]: Church Missionary House, Salisbury Square, Fleet Street, MDCCCLIV [**1854**].
Folio (50 cm.): vi, 24 (2 columns each), 188 (8 columns each) p., folding map, errata slip.
Hogg 1611.

Full text: https:// huskiecommons. lib.niu.edu/history-500african-voices/257/ [see 434.1].

¶ 'Ndsu was born in Bíōka and spoke Dsúku (a language in the Benue area of modern southeastern Nigeria—see Map 5). At age seventeen he was captured in war and carried to the town of Báke. After two years there he was moved elsewhere for another two years, then taken to the coast and forced aboard a slave ship ca. 1824. A British warship intercepted this ship at sea, freed the enslaved Africans, and took them to Sierra Leone (Map 4). 'Ndsu lived in Freetown when Koelle interviewed him.

434.2——.

Photomechanical reprint of 434.1 with addition of historical introduction by P. E. H. Hair. Limited to two hundred copies "distributed free of charge to scholars of African languages throughout the world."

Freetown [Sierra Leone]: University College of Sierra Leone, Fourah Bay College, 1963. Tpv: This numbered edition of two hundred copies is not available for distribution through the book-trade.
Folio (38 cm.): 19, vi, 24, 188 p., folding map.

434.3——.

Photomechanical reprint of 434.1, with additions, viz. *Polyglotta Africana / Vermehrt durch eine historische Einführung von P. E. H. Hair und einen Wortindex von David Dalby.* Published in association with *The African Language Review.*

Graz [Austria]: Akademische Druck- u. Verlagsanstalt [1963]. Folio (38 cm.): 19, vi, 24, 188 p., folding map.

435.1 Mahommah Gardo Baquaqua (ca. 1824– after 1863)

http://docsouth.unc.edu/neh/baquaqua/baquaqua.html [see 435.1].

Biography of Mahommah G. Baquaqua, a native Zoogoo, in the interior of Africa. (A convert to Christianity.) With a description of that part of the world: including the Manners and Customs of the Inhabitants, Their Religious Notions, Form of Government, Laws, Appearance of the Country, Buildings, Agriculture, Manufactures, Shepherds and Herdsmen, Domestic Animals, Marriage Ceremonials, Funeral Services, Styles of Dress, Trade and Commerce, Modes of Warfare, System of Slavery, &c. &c. Mahommah's early life, his education, his capture and slavery in Western Africa and Brazil, his escape to the United States, from thence to Hayti (the city of Port Au Prince,) His reception by the Baptist missionary there, The Rev. W. L. Judd; His Conversion to Christianity, Baptism, and Return to this Country, His Views, Objects and Aim. Written and Revised from His Own Words, by Samuel Moore, Esq.

Detroit [Michigan, U.S.A.]: Printed for the Author, Mahommah Gardo Baquaqua, by Geo. E. Pomeroy & Co., Tribune Office, 1854.

8vo (22 cm.): 65, [1] p. Relief-cut portrait of Baquaqua (reportedly from a daguerreotype by Moses Sutton) on front wrapper.
Hogg 1500.

¶ Baquaqua was born ca. 1824 in the city of Djougou (modern Bénin—see Map 5) on the important trade route between the Sokoto caliphate and Asante (Akan people, modern Ghana). His mother was from the Hausa city of Katsina; his father from Nikki in Borgu. Fluent in Hausa and Dendi, Baquaqua also had some schooling in Arabic. He was captured in war, but his brother obtained his freedom. He was subsequently kidnapped by associates he had thought friendly, then sent to Dahomey, then Ouidah (modern Benin) before leaving Little Popo (modern Togo) for Brazil on a slave ship in 1845. Enslaved in the Brazilian province of Pernambuco (Map 9), he was next sold in Rio de Janeiro to a sea captain, who in 1847 took him on a ship laden with consigned coffee to New York City in the United States (Map 17). There abolitionists collaborated to free him, and in 1847 he was sent to Haiti and freedom in the Caribbean (Map 11). He returned to New York in 1849 to attend Central College near Cortland in upstate New York. Associated with Baptist abolitionists, he published his autobiography (435.1) in Detroit in 1854, then went to Liverpool, England (Map 8), in his attempt to return to Africa. Helped by the American Colonization Society, he appears to have reached Liberia in 1862 or 1863 (Map 3). For more on Baquaqua, see 435.7 and the website "Project Baquaqua."

435.2——. [Excerpt of account 435.1]

Pages 34–45 of Baquaqua's memoir are reprinted on pp. 23–28 in *Children of God's Fire: A Documentary History of Black Slavery in Brazil,* edited by Robert Edgar Conrad.

Princeton [New Jersey, U.S.A.]: Princeton University Press, 1983. 8vo (25 cm.): xxviii, 515 p., illus., map.

435.3——. [Excerpt of account 435.1]

Pages 34–45 of Baquaqua's memoir are reprinted on pp. 23–28 in *Children of God's Fire: A Documentary History of Black Slavery in Brazil,* edited by Robert Edgar Conrad.

University Park [Pennsylvania, U.S.A.]: Pennsylvania State University Press, 1994. 8vo (24 cm.): xxviii, 515 p., illus., map.

435.4——. [Annotated edition of 435.1]

The Biography of Mahommah Gardo Baquaqua: His Passage from Slavery to Freedom in Africa and America, edited by Robin Law and Paul E. Lovejoy.

Princeton, New Jersey [U.S.A.]: Markus Wiener Publishers, 2001. 8vo (24 cm.): xv, [1], 272 p., illus., maps.

Figure 18: Relief-cut portrait of Mahommah G. Baquaqua (ca. 1824– after 1863), reportedly from a daguerreotype by Moses Sutton. Baquaqua was from the city of Djougou (modern Bénin). After schooling in Arabic he was captured in war, freed, kidnapped, and sent via Dahomey, Ouidah, and Little Popo to Brazil on a slave ship in 1845. His peripatetic life in slavery and freedom continued in the Americas from the Brazilian province of Pernambuco to Rio de Janeiro, then New York City, Haiti, and back to New York in 1849 to attend college. After publishing his autobiography in Detroit in 1854, he went to Liverpool, England, in his attempt to return to Africa and appears to have reached Liberia in 1862 or 1863.

Source: Title page of *Biography of Mahommah G. Baquaqua, a Native Zoogoo, in the Interior of Africa ....* Detroit: Geo. E. Pomeroy & Co., Tribune Office, 1854.

435.5——. [Another printing of 435.4]

The Biography of Mahommah Gardo Baquaqua: His Passage from Slavery to Freedom in Africa and America, edited by Robin Law and Paul E. Lovejoy.

Princeton, New Jersey [U.S.A.]: Markus Wiener Publishers, [2003].
8vo (24 cm.): xv, [1], 272 p., illus., maps.

435.6——. [Stated second printing of 435.4]

The Biography of Mahommah Gardo Baquaqua: His Passage from Slavery to Freedom in Africa and America, edited by Robin Law and Paul E. Lovejoy.

Princeton, New Jersey [U.S.A.]: Markus Wiener Publishers, [2006].
8vo (24 cm.) xv, 278 p., illus., maps.

435.7———. [Revised edition of 435.4]

The Biography of Mahommah Gardo Baquaqua: His Passage from Slavery to Freedom in Africa and America, edited by Robin Law and Paul E. Lovejoy. Revised and expanded second edition.

Princeton, New Jersey [U.S.A.]: Markus Wiener Publishers, 2007.

8vo (24 cm.): xix, [1], 278 p., illus., maps. "Preface to the Second Edition," pp. xvii–xix.

435.8———. [Second printing of 435.7]

The Biography of Mahommah Gardo Baquaqua: His Passage from Slavery to Freedom in Africa and America, edited by Robin Law and Paul E. Lovejoy. Revised and expanded second edition. [Second printing.]

Princeton, New Jersey [U.S.A.]: Markus Wiener Publishers, 2009.

8vo (24 cm.): xix, [1], 278 p., illus., maps. "Preface to the Second Edition," p. xvii–xix.

Additional contemporary publications of Baquaqua's writings (with later reprintings)

+435-A.1 ———.

"Two Letters from Mahommah, the Fugitive from Brazilian Slavery" printed in the *Christian Contributor and Free Missionary* (Utica, New York [U.S.A.]: Cyrus P. Grosvenor, December 13, 1848).

+435-A.2-6 ———.

+435-A.1 printed with annotations on pp. 233–235 of 435.4 and 435.5 and 435.6?, and pp. 236–238 of 435.7 and 435.8, *The Biography of Mahommah Gardo Baquaqua: His Passage from Slavery to Freedom in Africa and America*, edited by Robin Law and Paul E. Lovejoy (Princeton, New Jersey [U.S.A.]: Marcus Wiener Publishers, *five printings of two editions* 2001–2009).

+435-B.1 ———.

Letter dated at Freetown, 28 September 1850, printed under headline "Mahommeh" in *The American Baptist*, Utica, New York, U.S.A.: Board of the American Baptist Free Mission Society, October 11, 1850.

+435-B.2-6 ———.

+435-B.1 printed with annotations on on pp. 235–236 of 432.4 and 435.5 and 435.6?, and pp. 238–239 of 435.7 and 435.8, *The Biography of Mahommah Gardo Baquaqua: His Passage from Slavery to Freedom in Africa and America*, edited by Robin Law and Paul E. Lovejoy (Princeton, New Jersey [U.S.A.]: Marcus Wiener Publishers, *five printings of two editions* 2001–2009).

+435-C.1 ———.

Letter dated at Freetown Corners, 21 February 1851, printed under headline "Letter from Mahommah" in *The American Baptist* (Utica, New York, U.S.A.: Board of the American Baptist Free Mission Society, March 6, 1851).

+435-C.2-6 ———.

+435-C.1 printed with annotations on pp. 236–237 of 435.4 and 435.5 and 435.6?, and pp. 239–240 of 435.7 and 435.8, *The Biography of Mahommah Gardo Baquaqua: His Passage from Slavery to Freedom in Africa and America*, edited by Robin Law and Paul E. Lovejoy (Princeton, NJ: Marcus Wiener Publishers, *five printings of two editions* 2001–2009).

¶ Note for entries 436 through 452, seventeen named women and men from Lagos enslaved in Cuba, returning home. In 1854 the London, England, newspaper *The Anti-Slavery Reporter* printed an article on twenty-three African-born men, women, and children who had been forcibly enslaved and taken to the Spanish Caribbean colony of Cuba (Map 12), where they purchased their own freedom and then traveled to England, after stopping first on the Danish West Indies colony of St. Thomas (Map 14). Most of them were "Lucumí," a label that slave traders generally used for people from the Bight of Benin hinterland who spoke Yorùbá. After purchasing their freedom, they chartered a ship to return to Africa. The ship miscarried, and these Africans reached Southampton, England (Map 8) on the *Avon* in a "mostly pitiable" state—scantily attired, suffering from hunger, cold, and dampness after being compelled to lie on the deck through their voyage, even though they had paid for steerage and rations. In England they spoke at length to *The Anti-Slavery Reporter*'s journalist. None of them could read or write, but all were fluent in Spanish, not English. They asked to be taken to Lagos (Map 5), not Liberia or Sierra Leone, and on 1 July 1854, three weeks after their arrival, they sailed from Southampton on the *Candice* for that destination. For more on this group see Henry B. Lovejoy, "The Commodification of Freedom in Cuba during Second Slavery," in the essay collection *The Atlantic and Africa: The Second Slavery and Beyond,* edited by Dale W. Tomich and Paul E. Lovejoy (Albany: SUNY Press, 2021).

436.1 Òkúsono (ca. 1818–) = Ocusona = Lorenzo Clarke

Account (one of seventeen) of this man from Lagos printed in unsigned article "Cuban Slaves in England" in the 2 October 1854 issue of the British and Foreign Anti-Slavery Society's monthly magazine *The An-*

https://babel.hathitrust.org/cgi/pt?id=uiug.30112037763411&view=1up&seq=542 [see 436.1].

ti-Slavery Reporter [edited by Louis Alexis Chamerovzow], ser. 3, vol. 2: 234–239.

London [**England**]: [Printed for the British and Foreign Anti-Slavery Society], **1854**. Price, Fourpence Stamped, Threepence Unstamped.
Hogg 1501.

¶ Clarke came from Lagos (modern Nigeria—see Map 5). Captured during warfare, ca. 1832 he was forced aboard a large slave ship bound for the Spanish colonial Caribbean city of Havana, Cuba (Map 12). A British warship intercepted this ship not far from Cuba and after defeating the slave ship in battle took the enslaved passengers to government barracoons in or near Havana. With the knowledge and support of the British consulate, Clarke and hundreds of others were put to work on public roads and told they would be freed in ten years. Clarke worked for twelve years on a railroad as a servant for a United States engineer (whose last name he took). After earning some money and winning a lottery, he attempted to buy his freedom, but his owner stole the money. Clarke reported him and won back his money and freedom. Thereafter, he worked as a porter on wharves and quays. He was married to Maria Rosalia Garcia (q.v. 437.1); and they had three children who accompanied him to Southampton, England (Map 8) in 1854 on the *Avon*.

436.2——.
Photomechanical reprint of 436.1 in unsigned article "Cuban Slaves in England" in *British and Foreign Anti-Slavery Reporter*, ser. 3, vol. 2: 234–239, with imprint:

Nendeln, Lichtenstein: Kraus Reprint, **1969**. Tpv: Printed in **Germany**, Lessing-Druckerei, **Wiesbaden** [**Hesse**].
4to (33 cm.).

436.3——.
Account printed (on pp. 308–309) within section headed "Eighteen Cuban Slaves," which comprises pp. 306–320 in *Slave Testimony: Two Centuries of Letters, Speeches, and Autobiographies*, edited by John W. Blassingame.

Baton Rouge [**Louisiana, U.S.A.**]: Louisiana State University Press, **1977**. Second printing.
8vo (23 cm.): lxv, 777 p., illus., portraits.

436.4——. [**Second printing of 436.3**]
Account printed (on pp. 308–309) within section headed "Eighteen Cuban Slaves," which comprises pp. 306–320 in *Slave Testimony: Two Centuries of Letters, Speeches, and Autobiographies*, edited by John W. Blassingame.

Baton Rouge [**Louisiana, U.S.A.**]: Louisiana State University Press, **1979**. 1979 printing.
8vo (23 cm.): lxv, 777 p., illus., portraits.

436.5——. [**Another printing of 436.3**]
Account printed (on pp. 308–309) within section headed "Eighteen Cuban Slaves," which comprises pp. 306–320 in *Slave Testimony: Two Centuries of Letters, Speeches, and Autobiographies*, edited by John W. Blassingame.

Baton Rouge [**Louisiana, U.S.A.**]: Louisiana State University Press, **1980**. 1980 printing.
8vo (23 cm.): lxv, 777 p., illus., portraits.

436.6——. [**Another printing of 436.3**]
Account printed (on pp. 308–309) within section headed "Eighteen Cuban Slaves," which comprises pp. 306–320 in *Slave Testimony: Two Centuries of Letters, Speeches, and Autobiographies*, edited by John W. Blassingame.

Baton Rouge [**Louisiana, U.S.A.**]: Louisiana State University Press, **1989**. 1989 printing.
8vo (23 cm.): lxv, 777 p., illus., portraits.

436.7——. [**Another printing of 436.3**]
Account printed on pp. 308–309 within section headed "Eighteen Cuban Slaves," which comprises pp. 306–320 in *Slave Testimony: Two Centuries of Letters, Speeches, and Autobiographies*, edited by John W. Blassingame.

Baton Rouge [**Louisiana, U.S.A.**]: Louisiana State University Press, **1998**. 1998 printing.
8vo (23 cm.): lxv, 777 p., illus., portraits.

436.8——. [**Another printing of 436.3**]
Account printed on pp. 308–309 within section headed "Eighteen Cuban Slaves," which comprises pp. 306–320 in *Slave Testimony: Two Centuries of Letters, Speeches, and Autobiographies*, edited by John W. Blassingame.

Baton Rouge [**Louisiana, U.S.A.**]: Louisiana State University Press, **2002**. 2002 printing.
8vo (23 cm.): lxv, 777 p., illus., portraits.

436.9——. [**Another printing of 436.3**]
Account printed on pp. 308–309 within section headed "Eighteen Cuban Slaves," which comprises pp. 306–320 in *Slave Testimony: Two Centuries of Letters, Speeches, and Autobiographies*, edited by John W. Blassingame.

Baton Rouge [**Louisiana, U.S.A.**]: Louisiana State University Press, **2009**.
8vo (24 cm.): lxv, 777 p., illus., portraits.

437.1 Maria Rosalia Garcia (1824–)

Account (one of seventeen) of this woman from Lagos printed in unsigned article "Cuban Slaves in England" in the 2 October 1854 issue of the British and Foreign Anti-Slavery Society's monthly magazine *The Anti-Slavery Reporter* [edited by Louis Alexis Chamerovzow], ser. 3, vol. 2: 234–239.

https://babel.hathi-trust.org/cgi/pt?id=ui-ug.30112037763411 &view=1up&seq=542 [see 437.1].

London [England]: [Printed for the British and Foreign Anti-Slavery Society], **1854**. Price, Fourpence Stamped, Threepence Unstamped.
Hogg 1501.

¶ Garcia came from Lagos (modern Nigeria—see Map 5) and was taken at age eight, ca. 1832, on the same slave ship as her informal husband (q.v. 436.1) to the Spanish Caribbean colonial city of Havana, Cuba (Map 12). After intervention of a British warship and placement in the government barracoon at Havana, she was sold to Dolorez Garcia, whose name she took. While enslaved, she worked as an embroideress. The government demanded her back and placed her in a charity institute (*Beneficienza*) for a few days, after which she was taken to a shoemaker, who paid her a wage. She also worked as a laundress. After four years, she purchased her liberty ca. 1843. Thereafter, she sailed with her husband Lorenzo Clarke and others to Southampton, England (Map 8) in 1854 on the *Avon*, then to Lagos on the *Candace*.

437.2——.

Photomechanical reprint of 437.1 in unsigned article "Cuban Slaves in England" in *British and Foreign Anti-Slavery Reporter*, ser. 3, vol. 2: 234–239, with imprint:

Nendeln, Lichtenstein: Kraus Reprint, **1969**. Tpv: Printed in **Germany**, Lessing-Druckerei, **Wiesbaden [Hesse].**
4to (33 cm.).
https://babel.hathitrust.org/cgi/pt?id=uiug.30112037763411 &view=1up&seq=542.

437.3——.

Account printed on pp. 309–310 within section headed "Eighteen[*] Cuban Slaves," which comprises pp. 306–320 in *Slave Testimony: Two Centuries of Letters, Speeches, Interviews, and Autobiographies*, edited by John W. Blassingame. [*Blassingame includes in this total a child born in Cuba who falls outside the present catalog's scope.]

Baton Rouge [Louisiana, U.S.A.]: Louisiana State University Press, **1977**.
8vo: lxv, 777 p.

437.4——. [Second printing of 437.3]

Account printed on pp. 309–310 within section headed "Eighteen Cuban Slaves," which comprises pp. 306–320 in *Slave Testimony: Two Centuries of Letters, Speeches, and Autobiographies*, edited by John W. Blassingame.

Baton Rouge [Louisiana, U.S.A.]: Louisiana State University Press, **1977**. Second printing.
8vo (23 cm.): lxv, 777 p., illus., portraits.

437.5——. [Another printing of 437.3]

Account printed on pp. 309–310 within section headed "Eighteen Cuban Slaves," which comprises pp. 306–320 in *Slave Testimony: Two Centuries of Letters, Speeches, and Autobiographies*, edited by John W. Blassingame.

Baton Rouge [Louisiana, U.S.A.]: Louisiana State University Press, **1979**. 1979 printing.
8vo (23 cm.): lxv, 777 p., illus., portraits.

437.6——. [Another printing of 437.3]

Account printed on pp. 309–310 within section headed "Eighteen Cuban Slaves," which comprises pp. 306–320 in *Slave Testimony: Two Centuries of Letters, Speeches, and Autobiographies*, edited by John W. Blassingame.

Baton Rouge [Louisiana, U.S.A.]: Louisiana State University Press, **1980**. 1980 printing.
8vo (23 cm.): lxv, 777 p., illus., portraits.

437.7——. [Another printing of 437.3]

Account printed on pp. 309–310 within section headed "Eighteen Cuban Slaves," which comprises pp. 306–320 in *Slave Testimony: Two Centuries of Letters, Speeches, and Autobiographies*, edited by John W. Blassingame.

Baton Rouge [Louisiana, U.S.A.]: Louisiana State University Press, **1989**. 1989 printing.
8vo (23 cm.): lxv, 777 p., illus., portraits.

437.8——. [Another printing of 437.3]

Account printed on pp. 309–310 within section headed "Eighteen Cuban Slaves," which comprises pp. 306–320 in *Slave Testimony: Two Centuries of Letters, Speeches, and Autobiographies*, edited by John W. Blassingame.

Baton Rouge [Louisiana, U.S.A.]: Louisiana State University Press, **1998**. 1998 printing.
8vo (23 cm.): lxv, 777 p., illus., portraits.

437.9———.[Another printing of 437.3]

Account printed on pp. 309–310 within section headed "Eighteen Cuban Slaves," which comprises pp. 306–320 in *Slave Testimony: Two Centuries of Letters, Speeches, and Autobiographies*, edited by John W. Blassingame.

Baton Rouge [Louisiana, U.S.A.]: Louisiana State University Press, 2002. 2002 printing.
8vo (23 cm.): lxv, 777 p., illus., portraits.

437.10———.[Another printing of 437.3]

Account printed on pp. 309–310 within section headed "Eighteen Cuban Slaves," which comprises pp. 306–320 in *Slave Testimony: Two Centuries of Letters, Speeches, and Autobiographies*, edited by John W. Blassingame.

Baton Rouge [Louisiana, U.S.A.]: Louisiana State University Press, 2009.
8vo (24 cm.): lxv, 777 p., illus., portraits.

438.1 Miguel Marino (ca. 1794–)

Account (one of seventeen) of this man from Lagos printed in unsigned article "Cuban Slaves in England" in the 2 October 1854 issue of the British and Foreign Anti-Slavery Society's monthly magazine *The Anti-Slavery Reporter* [edited by Louis Alexis Chamerovzow], ser. 3, vol. 2: 234–239.

https://babel.hathi-trust.org/cgi/pt?id=ui-ug.30112037763411&view=1up&seq=542 [see 438.1].

London [England]: [Printed for the British and Foreign Anti-Slavery Society], 1854. Price, Fourpence Stamped, Threepence Unstamped.
Hogg 1501.

¶ Marino was a native of Lagos (modern Nigeria—see Map 5). From there he was taken ca. 1830 on a large Spanish slave ship to the Spanish Caribbean colonial city of Havana, Cuba (Map 12). There he was purchased from a barracoon by a baker, who had him undergo Christian baptism. After resale to another baker, he worked for eighteen months, saved money, and won $1,000 in a lottery, which he used to purchase the freedom of himself and his wife (q.v. 439.1). Thereafter, he became a porter. He had a daughter by another woman. Marino sailed with others to Southampton, England (Map 8) in 1854 on the *Avon*, then to Lagos on the *Candace*.

438.2———.

Photomechanical reprint of 438.1 in unsigned article "Cuban Slaves in England" in *British and Foreign Anti-Slavery Reporter*, ser. 3, vol. 2: 234–239, with imprint:

Nendeln, Lichtenstein: Kraus Reprint, 1969. Tpv: Printed in Germany, Lessing-Druckerei, Wiesbaden [Hesse].
4to (33 cm.).
https://babel.hathitrust.org/cgi/pt?id=uiug.30112037763411&view=1up&seq=542.

438.3———.

Account printed (on p. 310) within section headed "Eighteen[*] Cuban Slaves," which comprises pp. 306–320 in *Slave Testimony: Two Centuries of Letters, Speeches, Interviews, and Autobiographies*, edited by John W. Blassingame. [*Blassingame includes in this total a child born in Cuba who falls outside the present catalog's scope.]

Baton Rouge [Louisiana, U.S.A.]: Louisiana State University Press, 1977.
8vo (23 cm.): lxv, 777 p.

438.4———.[Second printing of 438.3]

Account printed (on p. 310) within section headed "Eighteen Cuban Slaves," which comprises pp. 306–320 in *Slave Testimony: Two Centuries of Letters, Speeches, and Autobiographies*, edited by John W. Blassingame.

Baton Rouge [Louisiana, U.S.A.]: Louisiana State University Press, 1977. Second printing.
8vo (23 cm.): lxv, 777 p., illus., portraits.

438.5———. [Another printing of 438.3]

Account printed (on p. 310) within section headed "Eighteen Cuban Slaves," which comprises pp. 306–320 in *Slave Testimony: Two Centuries of Letters, Speeches, and Autobiographies*, edited by John W. Blassingame.

Baton Rouge [Louisiana, U.S.A.]: Louisiana State University Press, 1979. 1979 printing.
8vo (23 cm.): lxv, 777 p., illus., portraits.

438.6———.[Another printing of 438.3]

Account printed (on p. 310) within section headed "Eighteen Cuban Slaves," which comprises pp. 306–320 in *Slave Testimony: Two Centuries of Letters, Speeches, and Autobiographies*, edited by John W. Blassingame.

Baton Rouge [Louisiana, U.S.A.]: Louisiana State University Press, 1980. 1980 printing.
8vo (23 cm.): lxv, 777 p., illus., portraits.

438.7———.[Another printing of 438.3]

Account printed (on p. 310) within section headed "Eighteen Cuban Slaves," which comprises pp. 306–320 in *Slave Testimony: Two Centuries of Letters, Speeches, and Autobiographies*, edited by John W. Blassingame.

Baton Rouge [Louisiana, U.S.A.]: Louisiana State University Press, **1989**. 1989 printing.
8vo (23 cm.): lxv, 777 p., illus., portraits.

438.8———. [Another printing of 438.3]
Account printed (on p. 310) within section headed "Eighteen Cuban Slaves," which comprises pp. 306–320 in *Slave Testimony: Two Centuries of Letters, Speeches, and Autobiographies*, edited by John W. Blassingame.

Baton Rouge [Louisiana, U.S.A.]: Louisiana State University Press, **1998**. 1998 printing.
8vo (23 cm.): lxv, 777 p., illus., portraits.

438.9———. [Another printing of 438.3]
Account printed (on p. 310) within section headed "Eighteen Cuban Slaves," which comprises pp. 306–320 in *Slave Testimony: Two Centuries of Letters, Speeches, and Autobiographies*, edited by John W. Blassingame.

Baton Rouge [Louisiana, U.S.A.]: Louisiana State University Press, **2002**. 2002 printing.
8vo (23 cm.): lxv, 777 p., illus., portraits.

438.10———. [Another printing of 438.3]
Account printed (on p. 310) within section headed "Eighteen Cuban Slaves," which comprises pp. 306–320 in *Slave Testimony: Two Centuries of Letters, Speeches, and Autobiographies*, edited by John W. Blassingame.

Baton Rouge [Louisiana, U.S.A.]: Louisiana State University Press, **2009**.
8vo (24 cm.): lxv, 777 p., illus., portraits.

439.1 Margarita Cabrera (ca. 1794–)

Account (one of seventeen) of this man from Lagos printed in unsigned article "Cuban Slaves in England" in the 2 October 1854 issue of the British and Foreign Anti-Slavery Society's monthly magazine *The Anti-Slavery Reporter* [edited by Louis Alexis Chamerovzow], ser. 3, vol. 2: 234–239.

https://babel.hathi-trust.org/cgi/pt?id=uiug.30112037763411&view=1up&seq=542 [see 439.1].

London [England]: [Printed for the British and Foreign Anti-Slavery Society], **1854**. Price, Fourpence Stamped, Threepence Unstamped.
Hogg 1501.

¶ Cabrera identified as Caravali, from the west of Africa (possibly interior Cross River region of modern Nigeria and northwestern Cameroon—see Map 5). She was kidnapped when aged about twenty-three and taken ca. 1818 on a large slave ship to the Spanish Caribbean colonial city of Havana, Cuba (Map 12), where a merchant purchased her. For fifteen years she remained enslaved to him, working on his sugar and coffee plantations under harsh conditions. Then she was sold ca. 1833 to a saddle and harness maker, for whom she did washing. Ca. 1842 she was purchased and employed as a laundress by a free Caravali woman who had been brought to Cuba enslaved. At this time Cabrera renamed herself. She married Miguel Marino (q.v. 438.1), who purchased her freedom and his own after winning the lottery. Thereafter, she sailed to Southampton, England (Map 8) in 1854 on the *Avon*, then to Lagos on the *Candace* with her husband.

439.2———.
Photomechanical reprint of 439.1 in unsigned article "Cuban Slaves in England" in *British and Foreign Anti-Slavery Reporter*, ser. 3, vol. 2: 234–239, with imprint:

Nendeln, Lichtenstein: Kraus Reprint, **1969**. Tpv: Printed in **Germany**, Lessing-Druckerei, **Wiesbaden** [Hesse].
4to (33 cm.).
https://babel.hathitrust.org/cgi/pt?id=uiug.30112037763411&view=1up&seq=542.

439.3———.
Account printed (on pp. 310–311) within section headed "Eighteen[*] Cuban Slaves," which comprises pp. 306–320 in *Slave Testimony: Two Centuries of Letters, Speeches, Interviews, and Autobiographies*, edited by John W. Blassingame. [Blassingame includes in this total a child born in Cuba who falls outside the present catalog's scope.]

Baton Rouge [Louisiana, U.S.A.]: Louisiana State University Press, **1977**.
8vo (23 cm.): lxv, 777 p.

439.4———. [Second printing of 439.3]
Account printed (on pp. 310–311) within section headed "Eighteen Cuban Slaves," which comprises pp. 306–320 in *Slave Testimony: Two Centuries of Letters, Speeches, and Autobiographies*, edited by John W. Blassingame.

Baton Rouge [Louisiana, U.S.A.]: Louisiana State University Press, **1977**. Second printing.
8vo (23 cm.): lxv, 777 p., illus., portraits.

439.5———. [Another printing of 439.3]
Account printed (on pp. 310–311) within section headed "Eighteen Cuban Slaves," which comprises pp. 306–320 in

Slave Testimony: Two Centuries of Letters, Speeches, and Autobiographies, edited by John W. Blassingame.

Baton Rouge [Louisiana, U.S.A.]: Louisiana State University Press, **1979.** 1979 printing.
8vo (23 cm.): lxv, 777 p., illus., portraits.

439.6———. [Another printing of 439.3]

Account printed (on pp. 310–311) within section headed "Eighteen Cuban Slaves," which comprises pp. 306–320 in *Slave Testimony: Two Centuries of Letters, Speeches, and Autobiographies*, edited by John W. Blassingame.

Baton Rouge [Louisiana, U.S.A.]: Louisiana State University Press, **1980.** 1980 printing.
8vo (23 cm.): lxv, 777 p., illus., portraits.

439.7———. [Another printing of 439.3]

Account printed (on pp. 310–311) within section headed "Eighteen Cuban Slaves," which comprises pp. 306–320 in *Slave Testimony: Two Centuries of Letters, Speeches, and Autobiographies*, edited by John W. Blassingame.

Baton Rouge [Louisiana, U.S.A.]: Louisiana State University Press, **1989.** 1989 printing.
8vo (23 cm.): lxv, 777 p., illus., portraits.

439.8———. [Another printing of 439.3]

Account printed (on pp. 310–311) within section headed "Eighteen Cuban Slaves," which comprises pp. 306–320 in *Slave Testimony: Two Centuries of Letters, Speeches, and Autobiographies*, edited by John W. Blassingame.

Baton Rouge [Louisiana, U.S.A.]: Louisiana State University Press, **1998.** 1998 printing.
8vo (23 cm.): lxv, 777 p., illus., portraits.

439.9———. [Another printing of 439.3]

Account printed (on pp. 310–311) within section headed "Eighteen Cuban Slaves," which comprises pp. 306–320 in *Slave Testimony: Two Centuries of Letters, Speeches, and Autobiographies*, edited by John W. Blassingame.

Baton Rouge [Louisiana, U.S.A.]: Louisiana State University Press, **2002.** 2002 printing.
8vo (23 cm.): lxv, 777 p., illus., portraits.

439.10———. [Another printing of 439.3]

Account printed (on pp. 310–311) within section headed "Eighteen Cuban Slaves," which comprises pp. 306–320 in *Slave Testimony: Two Centuries of Letters, Speeches, and Autobiographies*, edited by John W. Blassingame.

Baton Rouge [Louisiana, U.S.A.]: Louisiana State University Press, **2009.**
8vo (24 cm.): lxv, 777 p., illus., portraits.

440.1 Ignatio Moni (ca. 1813–)

Account (one of seventeen) of this man from Lagos printed in unsigned article "Cuban Slaves in England" in the 2 October 1854 issue of the British and Foreign Anti-Slavery Society's monthly magazine *The Anti-Slavery Reporter* [edited by Louis Alexis Chamerovzow], ser. 3, vol. 2: 234–239.

https://babel.hathitrust.org/cgi/pt?id=uiug.30112037763411&view=1up&seq=542 [see 440.1].

London [England]: [Printed for the British and Foreign Anti-Slavery Society], 1854. Price, Fourpence Stamped, Threepence Unstamped.
Hogg 1501.

¶ Moni was from Lagos (modern Nigeria—see Map 5) and ca. 184 was forcibly taken on a large slave ship to the Spanish Caribbean colonial city of Havana, Cuba (Map 12). There he was purchased from a barracoon by a builder, who then resold him to Don Pedro Moni (a farrier), whose surname he took. During his nine years enslaved to the farrier he married Catarina Bosc (q.v. 441.1), who was also enslaved, then with her worked to purchase their freedom. After gaining freedom he worked as a porter on wharves and quays until he sailed with Catarina for Southampton, England (Map 8) in 1854 on the *Avon*, then to Lagos on the *Candace*. He hoped to find his birth family upon returning to Lagos.

440.2———.

Photomechanical reprint of 440.1 in unsigned article "Cuban Slaves in England" in *British and Foreign Anti-Slavery Reporter*, ser. 3, vol. 2: 234–239, with imprint:

Nendeln, Lichtenstein: Kraus Reprint, **1969.** Tpv: Printed in **Germany**, Lessing-Druckerei, **Wiesbaden [Hesse].**
4to (33 cm.).
https://babel.hathitrust.org/cgi/pt?id=uiug.30112037763411&view=1up&seq=542.

440.3———.

Account printed (on p. 311) within section headed "Eighteen[*] Cuban Slaves," which comprises pp. 306–320 in *Slave Testimony: Two Centuries of Letters, Speeches, Interviews, and Autobiographies*, edited by John W. Blassingame. [*Blassingame includes in this total a child born in Cuba who falls outside the present catalog's scope.]

Baton Rouge [Louisiana, U.S.A.]: Louisiana State University Press, **1977**.
8vo (23 cm.): lxv, 777 p.

440.4———. **[Second printing of 440.3]**
Account printed (on p. 311) within section headed "Eighteen Cuban Slaves," which comprises pp. 306–320 in *Slave Testimony: Two Centuries of Letters, Speeches, and Autobiographies*, edited by John W. Blassingame.

Baton Rouge [Louisiana, U.S.A.]: Louisiana State University Press **1977**. Second printing.
8vo (23 cm.): lxv, 777 p., illus., portraits.

440.5———. **[Another printing of 440.3]**
Account printed (on p. 311) within section headed "Eighteen Cuban Slaves," which comprises pp. 306–320 in *Slave Testimony: Two Centuries of Letters, Speeches, and Autobiographies*, edited by John W. Blassingame.

Baton Rouge [Louisiana, U.S.A.]: Louisiana State University Press, **1979**. 1979 printing.
8vo (23 cm.): lxv, 777 p., illus., portraits.

440.6———. **[Another printing of 440.3]**
Account printed (on p. 311) within section headed "Eighteen Cuban Slaves," which comprises pp. 306–320 in *Slave Testimony: Two Centuries of Letters, Speeches, and Autobiographies*, edited by John W. Blassingame.

Baton Rouge [Louisiana, U.S.A.]: Louisiana State University Press, **1980**. 1980 printing.
8vo (23 cm.): lxv, 777 p., illus., portraits.

440.7———. **[Another printing of 440.3]**
Account printed (on p. 311) within section headed "Eighteen Cuban Slaves," which comprises pp. 306–320 in *Slave Testimony: Two Centuries of Letters, Speeches, and Autobiographies*, edited by John W. Blassingame.

Baton Rouge [Louisiana, U.S.A.]: Louisiana State University Press, **1989**. 1989 printing.
8vo (23 cm.): lxv, 777 p., illus., portraits.

440.8———. **[Another printing of 440.3]**
Account printed (on p. 311) within section headed "Eighteen Cuban Slaves," which comprises pp. 306–320 in *Slave Testimony: Two Centuries of Letters, Speeches, and Autobiographies*, edited by John W. Blassingame.

Baton Rouge [Louisiana, U.S.A.]: Louisiana State University Press, **1998**. 1998 printing.
8vo (23 cm.): lxv, 777 p., illus., portraits.

440.9———. **[Another printing of 440.3]**
Account printed (on p. 311) within section headed "Eighteen Cuban Slaves," which comprises pp. 306–320 in *Slave Testimony: Two Centuries of Letters, Speeches, and Autobiographies*, edited by John W. Blassingame.

Baton Rouge [Louisiana, U.S.A.]: Louisiana State University Press, **2002**. 2002 printing.
8vo (23 cm.): lxv, 777 p., illus., portraits.

440.10———. **[Another printing of 440.3]**
Account printed (on p. 311) within section headed "Eighteen Cuban Slaves," which comprises pp. 306–320 in *Slave Testimony: Two Centuries of Letters, Speeches, and Autobiographies*, edited by John W. Blassingame.

Baton Rouge [Louisiana, U.S.A.]: Louisiana State University Press, **2009**.
8vo (24 cm.): lxv, 777 p., illus., portraits.

441.1 Catarina Bosc (ca. 1814–)

Account (one of seventeen) of this woman from Lagos printed in unsigned article "Cuban Slaves in England" in the 2 October 1854 issue of the British and Foreign Anti-Slavery Society's monthly magazine *The Anti-Slavery Reporter* [edited by Louis Alexis Chamerovzow], ser. 3, vol. 2: 234–239.

https://babel.hathi-trust.org/cgi/pt?id=ui-ug.30112037763411&view=1up&seq=542 [see 441.1].

London [England]: [Printed for the British and Foreign Anti-Slavery Society], **1854**. Price, Fourpence Stamped, Threepence Unstamped.
Hogg 1501.

¶ **Bosc came from Lagos (modern Nigeria—see Map 5) and was married to Ignatio Moni (q.v. 440.1). Ca. 1834 she was taken on a large Spanish slave ship to the Spanish Caribbean colony of Cuba (Map 12) and sold to one Bosc (a merchant), whose surname she took. She worked for him as a cook and laundress for four and one-half years before he sold her to a free African (Caravali) woman who sold provisions in the streets and kept an "eating house." Catarina Bosc's husband purchased her freedom for $500, the largest sum legally allowed for purchasing one's own freedom. Thereafter, she sailed with him to Southampton, England (Map 8) in 1854 on the *Avon*, then to Lagos on the *Candace*.**

441.2———.
Photomechanical reprint of 441.1 in unsigned article "Cuban Slaves in England" in *British and Foreign Anti-Slavery Reporter*, ser. 3, vol. 2: 234–239, with imprint:

Nendeln, Lichtenstein: Kraus Reprint, **1969**. Tpv: Printed in **Germany**, Lessing-Druckerei, **Wiesbaden [Hesse]**.

4to (33 cm.).

https://babel.hathitrust.org/cgi/pt?id=uiug.30112037763411 &view=1up&seq=542.

441.3——.

Account printed (on pp. 311–312) within section headed "Eighteen[*] Cuban Slaves," which comprises pp. 306–320 in *Slave Testimony: Two Centuries of Letters, Speeches, Interviews, and Autobiographies*, edited by John W. Blassingame. [*Blassingame includes in this total a child born in Cuba who falls outside the present catalog's scope.]

Baton Rouge [Louisiana, U.S.A.]: Louisiana State University Press, **1977**.

8vo (23 cm.): lxv, 777 p.

441.4——. [Second printing of 441.3]

Account printed (on pp. 311–312) within section headed "Eighteen Cuban Slaves," which comprises pp. 306–320 in *Slave Testimony: Two Centuries of Letters, Speeches, and Autobiographies*, edited by John W. Blassingame.

Baton Rouge [Louisiana, U.S.A.]: Louisiana State University Press, **1977**. Second printing.

8vo (23 cm.): lxv, 777 p., illus., portraits.

441.5——. [Another printing of 441.3]

Account printed (on pp. 311–312) within section headed "Eighteen Cuban Slaves," which comprises pp. 306–320 in *Slave Testimony: Two Centuries of Letters, Speeches, and Autobiographies*, edited by John W. Blassingame.

Baton Rouge [Louisiana, U.S.A.]: Louisiana State University Press, **1979**. 1979 printing.

8vo (23 cm.): lxv, 777 p., illus., portraits.

441.6——. [Another printing of 441.3]

Account printed (on pp. 311–312) within section headed "Eighteen Cuban Slaves," which comprises pp. 306–320 in *Slave Testimony: Two Centuries of Letters, Speeches, and Autobiographies*, edited by John W. Blassingame.

Baton Rouge [Louisiana, U.S.A.]: Louisiana State University Press, **1980**. 1980 printing.

8vo (23 cm.): lxv, 777 p., illus., portraits.

441.7——. [Another printing of 441.3]

Account printed (on pp. 311–312) within section headed "Eighteen Cuban Slaves," which comprises pp. 306–320 in *Slave Testimony: Two Centuries of Letters, Speeches, and Autobiographies*, edited by John W. Blassingame.

Baton Rouge [Louisiana, U.S.A.]: Louisiana State University Press **1989**. 1989 printing.

8vo (23 cm.): lxv, 777 p., illus., portraits.

441.8——. [Another printing of 441.3]

Account printed (on pp. 311–312) within section headed "Eighteen Cuban Slaves," which comprises pp. 306–320 in *Slave Testimony: Two Centuries of Letters, Speeches, and Autobiographies*, edited by John W. Blassingame.

Baton Rouge [Louisiana, U.S.A.]: Louisiana State University Press, **1998**. 1998 printing.

8vo (23 cm.): lxv, 777 p., illus., portraits.

441.9——. [Another printing of 441.3]

Account printed (on pp. 311–312) within section headed "Eighteen Cuban Slaves," which comprises pp. 306–320 in *Slave Testimony: Two Centuries of Letters, Speeches, and Autobiographies*, edited by John W. Blassingame.

Baton Rouge [Louisiana, U.S.A.]: Louisiana State University Press, **2002**. 2002 printing.

8vo (23 cm.): lxv, 777 p., illus., portraits.

441.10——. [Another printing of 441.3]

Account printed (on pp. 311–312) within section headed "Eighteen Cuban Slaves," which comprises pp. 306–320 in *Slave Testimony: Two Centuries of Letters, Speeches, and Autobiographies*, edited by John W. Blassingame.

Baton Rouge [Louisiana, U.S.A.]: Louisiana State University Press, **2009**.

8vo (24 cm.): lxv, 777 p., illus., portraits.

442.1 Gabriel Crusati (ca. 1814–)

Account (one of seventeen) of this man from Lagos printed in unsigned article "Cuban Slaves in England" in the 2 October 1854 issue of the British and Foreign Anti-Slavery Society's monthly magazine *The Anti-Slavery Reporter* [edited by Louis Alexis Chamerovzow], ser. 3, vol. 2: 234–239.

https://babel.hathitrust.org/cgi/pt?id=uiug.30112037763411 &view=1up&seq=542 [see 442.1].

London [England]: [Printed for the British and Foreign Anti-Slavery Society], **1854**. Price, Fourpence Stamped, Threepence Unstamped.

Hogg 1501.

¶ **Crusati was a native of Lagos (modern Nigeria—see Map 5). Ca. 1842 he was taken on a large slave ship to the Spanish**

Caribbean colony of Cuba (Map 12). There he was purchased from a barracoon by a merchant, who put him to work on a wharf in the capital city of Havana. After seven months he was sold to another merchant, who employed him similarly. After six years he was sold again, and several years thereafter Crusati purchased his freedom. He married Maria Luisa Macorra (q.v. 443.1) and worked as a free man on wharves and quays until he sailed with her for Southampton, England (Map 8) in 1854 aboard the *Avon*, then to Lagos on the *Candace*.

442.2———.

Photomechanical reprint of 442.1 in unsigned article "Cuban Slaves in England" in *British and Foreign Anti-Slavery Reporter*, ser. 3, vol. 2: 234–239, with imprint:

Nendeln, Lichtenstein: Kraus Reprint, **1969.** Tpv: Printed in **Germany**, Lessing-Druckerei, **Wiesbaden [Hesse].**
4to (33 cm.).
https://babel.hathitrust.org/cgi/pt?id=uiug.30112037763411 &view=1up&seq=542.

442.3———.

Account printed on p. 312 within section headed "Eighteen[*] Cuban Slaves," which comprises pp. 306–320 in *Slave Testimony: Two Centuries of Letters, Speeches, Interviews, and Autobiographies*, edited by John W. Blassingame. [*Blassingame includes in this total a child born in Cuba who falls outside the present catalog's scope.]

Baton Rouge [Louisiana, U.S.A.]: Louisiana State University Press, **1977.**
8vo (23 cm.): lxv, 777 p.

442.4———. [**Second printing of 442.3**]

Account printed on p. 312 within section headed "Eighteen Cuban Slaves," which comprises pp. 306–320 in *Slave Testimony: Two Centuries of Letters, Speeches, and Autobiographies*, edited by John W. Blassingame.

Baton Rouge [Louisiana, U.S.A.]: Louisiana State University Press, **1977.** Second printing.
8vo (23 cm.): lxv, 777 p., illus., portraits.

442.5———. [**Another printing of 442.3**]

Account printed on p. 312 within section headed "Eighteen Cuban Slaves," which comprises pp. 306–320 in *Slave Testimony: Two Centuries of Letters, Speeches, and Autobiographies*, edited by John W. Blassingame.

Baton Rouge [Louisiana, U.S.A.]: Louisiana State University Press, **1979.** 1979 printing.
8vo (23 cm.): lxv, 777 p., illus., portraits.

442.6———. [**Another printing of 442.3**]

Account printed on p. 312 within section headed "Eighteen Cuban Slaves," which comprises pp. 306–320 in *Slave Testimony: Two Centuries of Letters, Speeches, and Autobiographies*, edited by John W. Blassingame.

Baton Rouge [Louisiana, U.S.A.]: Louisiana State University Press, **1980.** 1980 printing.
8vo (23 cm.): lxv, 777 p., illus., portraits.

442.7———. [**Another printing of 442.3**]

Account printed on p. 312 within section headed "Eighteen Cuban Slaves," which comprises pp. 306–320 in *Slave Testimony: Two Centuries of Letters, Speeches, and Autobiographies*, edited by John W. Blassingame.

Baton Rouge [Louisiana, U.S.A.]: Louisiana State University Press, **1989.** 1989 printing.
8vo (23 cm.): lxv, 777 p., illus., portraits.

442.8———. [**Another printing of 442.3**]

Account printed on p. 312 within section headed "Eighteen Cuban Slaves," which comprises pp. 306–320 in *Slave Testimony: Two Centuries of Letters, Speeches, and Autobiographies*, edited by John W. Blassingame.

Baton Rouge [Louisiana, U.S.A.]: Louisiana State University Press, **1998.** 1998 printing.
8vo (23 cm.): lxv, 777 p., illus., portraits.

442.9———. [**Another printing of 442.3**]

Account printed on p. 312 within section headed "Eighteen Cuban Slaves," which comprises pp. 306–320 in *Slave Testimony: Two Centuries of Letters, Speeches, and Autobiographies*, edited by John W. Blassingame.

Baton Rouge [Louisiana, U.S.A.]: Louisiana State University Press, **2002.** 2002 printing.
8vo (23 cm.): lxv, 777 p., illus., portraits.

442.10———. [**Another printing of 442.3**]

Account printed on p. 312 within section headed "Eighteen Cuban Slaves," which comprises pp. 306–320 in *Slave Testimony: Two Centuries of Letters, Speeches, and Autobiographies*, edited by John W. Blassingame.

Baton Rouge [Louisiana, U.S.A.]: Louisiana State University Press, **2009.**
8vo (24 cm.): lxv, 777 p., illus., portraits.

443.1 Maria Luisa Macorra (ca. 1826–)

Account (one of seventeen) of this woman from Lagos printed in unsigned article "Cuban Slaves in England" in the 2

October 1854 issue of the British and Foreign Anti-Slavery Society's monthly magazine *The Anti-Slavery Reporter* [edited by Louis Alexis Chamerovzow], ser. 3, vol. 2: 234–239.

London [England]: [Printed for the British and Foreign Anti-Slavery Society], **1854.** Price, Fourpence Stamped, Threepence Unstamped.
Hogg 1501.

https://babel.hathitrust.org/cgi/pt?id=uiug.30112037763411&view=1up&seq=542 [see 443.1].

¶ Macorra was a Lucumí, a New World ethnic identity attributed to and named for people from the Yorùbá (modern-day Nigeria, Benin, and Togo—see Map 5) from Lagos (modern Nigeria). In 1837 she was forcibly taken on a large slave ship to the Spanish Caribbean colonial city of Havana, Cuba (Map 12), and there put in the fortress *Castilio Principe*. A man named Macorra purchased her, and she worked for him as a house servant under severe conditions for seven years. After being resold several more times, she purchased status as a *curatada* (an enslaved person who works off an agreed sum to achieve freedom). Macorra acquired her freedom in 1849, married Gabriel Crusati (q.v. 442.1) and worked as a laundress until she sailed with her husband for Southampton, England (Map 8) in 1854 aboard the *Avon*, then to Lagos on the *Candace*.

443.2——.

Photomechanical reprint of 443.1 in unsigned article "Cuban Slaves in England" in *British and Foreign Anti-Slavery Reporter*, ser. 3, vol. 2: 234–239, with imprint:

Nendeln, Lichtenstein: Kraus Reprint, **1969.** Tpv: Printed in **Germany**, Lessing-Druckerei, **Wiesbaden [Hesse].**
4to (33 cm.).
https://babel.hathitrust.org/cgi/pt?id=uiug.30112037763411&view=1up&seq=542.

443.3——.

Account printed (on pp. 312–313) within section headed "Eighteen[*] Cuban Slaves," which comprises pp. 306–320 in *Slave Testimony: Two Centuries of Letters, Speeches, Interviews, and Autobiographies*, edited by John W. Blassingame. [*Blassingame includes in this total a child born in Cuba who falls outside the present catalog's scope.]

Baton Rouge [Louisiana, U.S.A.]: Louisiana State University Press, **1977.**
8vo (23 cm.): lxv, 777 p.

443.4——. [Second printing of 443.3]

Account printed (on pp. 312–313) within section headed "Eighteen Cuban Slaves," which comprises pp. 306–320 in *Slave Testimony: Two Centuries of Letters, Speeches, and Autobiographies*, edited by John W. Blassingame.

Baton Rouge [Louisiana, U.S.A.]: Louisiana State University Press, **1977.** Second printing.
8vo (23 cm.): lxv, 777 p., illus., portraits.

443.5——. [Another printing of 443.3]

Account printed (on pp. 312–313) within section headed "Eighteen Cuban Slaves," which comprises pp. 306–320 in *Slave Testimony: Two Centuries of Letters, Speeches, and Autobiographies*, edited by John W. Blassingame.

Baton Rouge [Louisiana, U.S.A.]: Louisiana State University Press, **1979.** 1979 printing.
8vo (23 cm.): lxv, 777 p., illus., portraits.

443.6——. [Another printing of 443.3]

Account printed (on pp. 312–313) within section headed "Eighteen Cuban Slaves," which comprises pp. 306–320 in *Slave Testimony: Two Centuries of Letters, Speeches, and Autobiographies*, edited by John W. Blassingame.

Baton Rouge [Louisiana, U.S.A.]: Louisiana State University Press, **1980.** 1980 printing.
8vo (23 cm.): lxv, 777 p., illus., portraits.

443.7——. [Another printing of 443.3]

Account printed (on pp. 312–313) within section headed "Eighteen Cuban Slaves," which comprises pp. 306–320 in *Slave Testimony: Two Centuries of Letters, Speeches, and Autobiographies*, edited by John W. Blassingame.

Baton Rouge [Louisiana, U.S.A.]: Louisiana State University Press, **1989.** 1989 printing.
8vo (23 cm.): lxv, 777 p., illus., portraits.

443.8——. [Another printing of 443.3]

Account printed (on pp. 312–313) within section headed "Eighteen Cuban Slaves," which comprises pp. 306–320 in *Slave Testimony: Two Centuries of Letters, Speeches, and Autobiographies*, edited by John W. Blassingame.

Baton Rouge [Louisiana, U.S.A.]: Louisiana State University Press, **1998.** 1998 printing.
8vo (23 cm.): lxv, 777 p., illus., portraits.

443.9——. [Another printing of 443.3]

Account printed (on pp. 312–313) within section headed "Eighteen Cuban Slaves," which comprises pp. 306–320 in

Slave Testimony: Two Centuries of Letters, Speeches, and Autobiographies, edited by John W. Blassingame.

Baton Rouge [Louisiana, U.S.A.]: Louisiana State University Press, **2002.** 2002 printing.
8vo (23 cm.): lxv, 777 p., illus., portraits.

443.10——. [Another printing of 443.3]

Account printed (on pp. 312–313) within section headed "Eighteen Cuban Slaves," which comprises pp. 306–320 in *Slave Testimony: Two Centuries of Letters, Speeches, and Autobiographies*, edited by John W. Blassingame.

Baton Rouge [Louisiana, U.S.A.]: Louisiana State University Press, **2009.**
8vo (24 cm.): lxv, 777 p., illus., portraits.

444.1 Deloré Réal (ca. 1814–)

Account (one of seventeen) of this woman from Lagos printed in unsigned article "Cuban Slaves in England" in the 2 October 1854 issue of the British and Foreign Anti-Slavery Society's monthly magazine *The Anti-Slavery Reporter* [edited by Louis Alexis Chamerovzow], ser. 3, vol. 2: 234–239.

https://babel.hathi-trust.org/cgi/pt?id=uiug.30112037763411&view=1up&seq=542 [see 444.1].

London [England]: [Printed for the British and Foreign Anti-Slavery Society], **1854.** Price, Fourpence Stamped, Threepence Unstamped.
Hogg 1501.

¶ Deloré Réal was a native of Lagos (modern Nigeria—see Map 5) and identified as Lucumí, a New World ethnic identity attributed to and named for people from the Yorùbá (in modern day Nigeria, Benin and Togo). In 1834 she was forcibly taken on a large Spanish slave ship to the Spanish Caribbean colony of Cuba (Map 12). After landing near Cardenas and being taken to a barracoon in the capital city of Havana, she and eight or nine other women were sold to Carmen Réal, a free laundress from Lagos. This laundress held Deloré Réal enslaved for six years, then sold her to a priest. Seven years later Deloré Réal purchased her own freedom. Thereafter, she resumed work as a laundress, until she sailed for Southampton, England (Map 8) in 1854 on the *Avon*. She hoped to return to her family in Lagos and sailed with the others on the *Candace*.

444.2——.

Photomechanical reprint of 444.1 in unsigned article "Cuban Slaves in England" in *British and Foreign Anti-Slavery Reporter*, ser. 3, vol. 2: 234–239, with imprint:

Nendeln, Lichtenstein: Kraus Reprint, **1969.** Tpv: Printed in **Germany**, Lessing-Druckerei, **Wiesbaden [Hesse].**
4to (33 cm.).
https://babel.hathitrust.org/cgi/pt?id=uiug.30112037763411&view=1up&seq=542.

444.3——.

Account printed (on pp. 313–314) within section headed "Eighteen[*] Cuban Slaves," which comprises pp. 306–320 in *Slave Testimony: Two Centuries of Letters, Speeches, Interviews, and Autobiographies*, edited by John W. Blassingame. [*Blassingame includes in this total a child born in Cuba who falls outside the present catalog's scope.]

Baton Rouge [Louisiana, U.S.A.]: Louisiana State University Press, **1977.**
8vo (23 cm.): lxv, 777 p.

444.4——. [Second printing of 444.3]

Account printed (on pp. 313–314) within section headed "Eighteen Cuban Slaves," which comprises pp. 306–320 in *Slave Testimony: Two Centuries of Letters, Speeches, and Autobiographies*, edited by John W. Blassingame.

Baton Rouge [Louisiana, U.S.A.]: Louisiana State University Press, **1977.** Second printing.
8vo (23 cm.): lxv, 777 p., illus., portraits.

444.5——. [Another printing of 444.3]

Account printed (on pp. 313–314) within section headed "Eighteen Cuban Slaves," which comprises pp. 306–320 in *Slave Testimony: Two Centuries of Letters, Speeches, and Autobiographies*, edited by John W. Blassingame.

Baton Rouge [Louisiana, U.S.A.]: Louisiana State University Press, **1979.** 1979 printing.
8vo (23 cm.): lxv, 777 p., illus., portraits.

444.6——. [Another printing of 444.3]

Account printed (on pp. 313–314) within section headed "Eighteen Cuban Slaves," which comprises pp. 306–320 in *Slave Testimony: Two Centuries of Letters, Speeches, and Autobiographies*, edited by John W. Blassingame.

Baton Rouge [Louisiana, U.S.A.]: Louisiana State University Press, **1980.** 1980 printing.
8vo (23 cm.): lxv, 777 p., illus., portraits.

444.7——. [Another printing of 444.3]

Account printed (on pp. 313–314) within section headed "Eighteen Cuban Slaves," which comprises pp. 306–320 in *Slave Testimony: Two Centuries of Letters, Speeches, and Autobiographies*, edited by John W. Blassingame.

Baton Rouge [Louisiana, U.S.A.]: Louisiana State University Press, **1989**. 1989 printing.
8vo (23 cm.): lxv, 777 p., illus., portraits.

444.8——. [Another printing of 444.3]

Account printed (on pp. 313–314) within section headed "Eighteen Cuban Slaves," which comprises pp. 306–320 in *Slave Testimony: Two Centuries of Letters, Speeches, and Autobiographies*, edited by John W. Blassingame.

Baton Rouge [Louisiana, U.S.A.]: Louisiana State University Press, **1998**. 1998 printing.
8vo (23 cm.): lxv, 777 p., illus., portraits.

444.9——. [Another printing of 444.3]

Account printed (on pp. 313–314) within section headed "Eighteen Cuban Slaves," which comprises pp. 306–320 in *Slave Testimony: Two Centuries of Letters, Speeches, and Autobiographies*, edited by John W. Blassingame.

Baton Rouge [Louisiana, U.S.A.]: Louisiana State University Press, **2002**. 2002 printing.
8vo (23 cm.): lxv, 777 p., illus., portraits.

444.10——. [Another printing of 444.3]

Account printed (on pp. 313–314) within section headed "Eighteen Cuban Slaves," which comprises pp. 306–320 in *Slave Testimony: Two Centuries of Letters, Speeches, and Autobiographies*, edited by John W. Blassingame.

Baton Rouge [Louisiana, U.S.A.]: Louisiana State University Press, **2009**.
8vo (24 cm.): lxv, 777 p., illus., portraits.

445.1 Mariana Mercedes Piloto (ca. 1819–)

Account (one of seventeen) of this woman from Lagos printed in unsigned article "Cuban Slaves in England" in the 2 October 1854 issue of the British and Foreign Anti-Slavery Society's monthly magazine *The Anti-Slavery Reporter* [edited by Louis Alexis Chamerovzow], ser. 3, vol. 2: 234–239.

https://babel.hathitrust.org/cgi/pt?id=uiug.30112037763411&view=1up&seq=542 [see 445.1].

London [England]: [Printed for the British and Foreign Anti-Slavery Society], **1854**. Price, Fourpence Stamped, Threepence Unstamped.
Hogg 1501.

¶ Piloto came from Lagos (modern Nigeria—see Map 5) and was called Lucumí, a New World ethnic identity attributed to and named for people from the Yorùbá (in modern day Nigeria, Benin and Togo) in the Spanish Caribbean colony of Cuba (Map 12). Ca. 1832 she was forcibly taken to Cuba on a large Spanish slave ship, which landed near the capital city of Havana. There her owner, a grocer, hired her out as a laundress. Despite being bought and sold several times, Piloto earned and saved enough money to buy her own freedom in 1850. In 1854 she sailed to Southampton, England (Map 8) on the *Avon*. After three weeks there she sailed with the others to Lagos on the *Candace*.

445.2——.

Photomechanical reprint of 445.1 in unsigned article "Cuban Slaves in England" in *British and Foreign Anti-Slavery Reporter*, ser. 3, vol. 2: 234–239, with imprint:

Nendeln, Lichtenstein: Kraus Reprint, **1969**. Tpv: Printed in **Germany**, Lessing-Druckerei, **Wiesbaden** [Hesse].
4to (33 cm.).
https://babel.hathitrust.org/cgi/pt?id=uiug.30112037763411&view=1up&seq=542.

445.3——.

Account printed (on pp. 314–315) within section headed "Eighteen[*] Cuban Slaves," which comprises pp. 306–320 in *Slave Testimony: Two Centuries of Letters, Speeches, Interviews, and Autobiographies*, edited by John W. Blassingame. [*Blassingame includes in this total a child born in Cuba who falls outside the present catalog's scope.]

Baton Rouge [Louisiana, U.S.A.]: Louisiana State University Press, **1977**.
8vo (23 cm.): lxv, 777 p.

445.4——. [Second printing of 445.3]

Account printed (on pp. 314–315) within section headed "Eighteen Cuban Slaves," which comprises pp. 306–320 in *Slave Testimony: Two Centuries of Letters, Speeches, and Autobiographies*, edited by John W. Blassingame.

Baton Rouge [Louisiana, U.S.A.]: Louisiana State University Press, **1977**. Second printing.
8vo (23 cm.): lxv, 777 p., illus., portraits.

445.5——. [Another printing of 445.3]

Account printed (on pp. 314–315) within section headed "Eighteen Cuban Slaves," which comprises pp. 306–320 in *Slave Testimony: Two Centuries of Letters, Speeches, and Autobiographies*, edited by John W. Blassingame.

Baton Rouge [Louisiana, U.S.A.]: Louisiana State University Press, **1979**. 1979 printing.
8vo (23 cm.): lxv, 777 p., illus., portraits.

445.6———. [Another printing of 445.3]

Account printed (on pp. 314–315) within section headed "Eighteen Cuban Slaves," which comprises pp. 306–320 in *Slave Testimony: Two Centuries of Letters, Speeches, and Autobiographies*, edited by John W. Blassingame.

Baton Rouge [Louisiana, U.S.A.]: Louisiana State University Press, **1980**. 1980 printing.
8vo (23 cm.): lxv, 777 p., illus., portraits.

445.7———. [Another printing of 445.3]

Account printed (on pp. 314–315) within section headed "Eighteen Cuban Slaves," which comprises pp. 306–320 in *Slave Testimony: Two Centuries of Letters, Speeches, and Autobiographies*, edited by John W. Blassingame.

Baton Rouge [Louisiana, U.S.A.]: Louisiana State University Press, **1989**. 1989 printing.
8vo (23 cm.): lxv, 777 p., illus., portraits.

445.8———. [Another printing of 445.3]

Account printed (on pp. 314–315) within section headed "Eighteen Cuban Slaves," which comprises pp. 306–320 in *Slave Testimony: Two Centuries of Letters, Speeches, and Autobiographies*, edited by John W. Blassingame.

Baton Rouge [Louisiana, U.S.A.]: Louisiana State University Press, **1998**. 1998 printing.
8vo (23 cm.): lxv, 777 p., illus., portraits.

445.9———. [Another printing of 445.3]

Account printed (on pp. 314–315) within section headed "Eighteen Cuban Slaves," which comprises pp. 306–320 in *Slave Testimony: Two Centuries of Letters, Speeches, and Autobiographies*, edited by John W. Blassingame.

Baton Rouge [Louisiana, U.S.A.]: Louisiana State University Press, **2002**. 2002 printing.
8vo (23 cm.): lxv, 777 p., illus., portraits.

445.10———. [Another printing of 445.3]

Account printed (on pp. 314–315) within section headed "Eighteen Cuban Slaves," which comprises pp. 306–320 in *Slave Testimony: Two Centuries of Letters, Speeches, and Autobiographies*, edited by John W. Blassingame.

Baton Rouge [Louisiana, U.S.A.]: Louisiana State University Press, **2009**.
8vo (24 cm.): lxv, 777 p., illus., portraits.

446.1 Luca Martino (ca. 1809–)

Account (one of seventeen) of this man from Lagos printed in unsigned article "Cuban Slaves in England" in the 2 October 1854 issue of the British and Foreign Anti-Slavery Society's monthly magazine *The Anti-Slavery Reporter* [edited by Louis Alexis Chamerovzow], ser. 3, vol. 2: 234–239.

https://babel.hathitrust.org/cgi/pt?id=uiug.30112037763411&view=1up&seq=542 [see 446.1].

London [England]: [Printed for the British and Foreign Anti-Slavery Society], **1854**. Price, Fourpence Stamped, Threepence Unstamped.
Hogg 1501.

¶ Martino was from Lagos (modern Nigeria—see Map 5). Ca. 1823 he was taken on a large Spanish slave ship headed for the Spanish Caribbean colony of Cuba (Map 12), but a British warship intercepted this ship at sea and took its enslaved passengers to government barracoons in Casa Blanca, a town across the harbor from the capital city of Havana, Cuba. After three months Martino was hired out to carry water for weekly wages but was treated like a slave. Despite this he earned and saved enough money to purchase his own freedom in 1840. He was married to a free-born Creole, had five children with her, and was living in Havana when he sailed for Southampton, England (Map 8) aboard the *Avon*. He intended to return to Africa and work, then send money back to his family so they could join him. After three weeks in Southampton he sailed with the others to Lagos on the *Candace*.

446.2———.

Photomechanical reprint of 446.1 in unsigned article "Cuban Slaves in England" in *British and Foreign Anti-Slavery Reporter*, ser. 3, vol. 2: 234–239, with imprint:

Nendeln, Lichtenstein: Kraus Reprint, **1969**. Tpv: Printed in **Germany**, Lessing-Druckerei, **Wiesbaden [Hesse]**.
4to (33 cm.).
https://babel.hathitrust.org/cgi/pt?id=uiug.30112037763411&view=1up&seq=542.

446.3———.

Account printed (on pp. 315–316) within section headed "Eighteen[*] Cuban Slaves," which comprises pp. 306–320 in *Slave Testimony: Two Centuries of Letters, Speeches, Interviews, and Autobiographies*, edited by John W. Blassingame. [*Blassingame includes in this total a child born in Cuba who falls outside the present catalog's scope.]

Baton Rouge [Louisiana, U.S.A.]: Louisiana State University Press, **1977.**
8vo (23 cm.): lxv, 777 p.

446.4———. [Second printing of 446.3]

Account printed (on pp. 315–316) within section headed "Eighteen Cuban Slaves," which comprises pp. 306–320 in *Slave Testimony: Two Centuries of Letters, Speeches, and Autobiographies*, edited by John W. Blassingame.

Baton Rouge [Louisiana, U.S.A.]: Louisiana State University Press, **1977.** Second printing.
8vo (23 cm.): lxv, 777 p., illus., portraits.

446.5———. [Another printing of 446.3]

Account printed (on pp. 315–316) within section headed "Eighteen Cuban Slaves," which comprises pp. 306–320 in *Slave Testimony: Two Centuries of Letters, Speeches, and Autobiographies*, edited by John W. Blassingame.

Baton Rouge [Louisiana, U.S.A.]: Louisiana State University Press, **1979.** 1979 printing.
8vo (23 cm.): lxv, 777 p., illus., portraits.

446.6———. [Another printing of 446.3]

Account printed (on pp. 315–316) within section headed "Eighteen Cuban Slaves," which comprises pp. 306–320 in *Slave Testimony: Two Centuries of Letters, Speeches, and Autobiographies*, edited by John W. Blassingame.

Baton Rouge [Louisiana, U.S.A.]: Louisiana State University Press, **1980.** 1980 printing.
8vo (23 cm.): lxv, 777 p., illus., portraits.

446.7———. [Another printing of 446.3]

Account printed (on pp. 315–316) within section headed "Eighteen Cuban Slaves," which comprises pp. 306–320 in *Slave Testimony: Two Centuries of Letters, Speeches, and Autobiographies*, edited by John W. Blassingame.

Baton Rouge [Louisiana, U.S.A.]: Louisiana State University Press, **1989.** 1989 printing.
8vo (23 cm.): lxv, 777 p., illus., portraits.

446.8———. [Another printing of 446.3]

Account printed (on pp. 315–316) within section headed "Eighteen Cuban Slaves," which comprises pp. 306–320 in *Slave Testimony: Two Centuries of Letters, Speeches, and Autobiographies*, edited by John W. Blassingame.

Baton Rouge [Louisiana, U.S.A.]: Louisiana State University Press, **1998.** 1998 printing.
8vo (23 cm.): lxv, 777 p., illus., portraits.

446.9———. [Another printing of 446.3]

Account printed (on pp. 315–316) within section headed "Eighteen Cuban Slaves," which comprises pp. 306–320 in *Slave Testimony: Two Centuries of Letters, Speeches, and Autobiographies*, edited by John W. Blassingame.

Baton Rouge [Louisiana, U.S.A.]: Louisiana State University Press, **2002.** 2002 printing.
8vo (23 cm.): lxv, 777 p., illus., portraits.

446.10———. [Another printing of 446.3]

Account printed (on pp. 315–316) within section headed "Eighteen Cuban Slaves," which comprises pp. 306–320 in *Slave Testimony: Two Centuries of Letters, Speeches, and Autobiographies*, edited by John W. Blassingame.

Baton Rouge [Louisiana, U.S.A.]: Louisiana State University Press, **2009.**
8vo (24 cm.): lxv, 777 p., illus., portraits.

447.1 Telaforo Savedra (ca. 1806–)

Account (one of seventeen) of this man from Lagos printed in unsigned article "Cuban Slaves in England" in the 2 October 1854 issue of the British and Foreign Anti-Slavery Society's monthly magazine *The Anti-Slavery Reporter* [edited by Louis Alexis Chamerovzow], ser. 3, vol. 2: 234–239.

https://babel.hathi-trust.org/cgi/pt?id=ui-ug.30112037763411&view=1up&seq=542 [see 447.1].

London [England]: [Printed for the British and Foreign Anti-Slavery Society], **1854.** Price, Fourpence Stamped, Threepence Unstamped.
Hogg 1501.

¶ Ca. 1825 Savedra, a Lagos native (modern Nigeria—see Map 5), was forcibly taken aboard a large Spanish slave ship bound for the Spanish Caribbean colony of Cuba (Map 12). A British warship intercepted this ship not far from the Cuban coast and took the enslaved passengers to barracoons. With the knowledge, if not support, of the British consulate, Savedra was hired out under government surveillance for ten days to a chocolate manufacturer and confectioner, who flogged him several times. He was then hired out to another man in the same trade, who had paid the government for his labor. By 1847, after twelve years working under these conditions, Savedra had saved enough money to pay back the British consulate and get his freedom papers (and pay a transaction fee in the process). Thereafter, he worked at a trade and earned enough money to book passage on the *Avon*, which sailed for

Southampton, England (Map 8) in 1854. After three weeks there, he sailed with the others on the Candace to Lagos.

447.2———.

Photomechanical reprint of 447.1 in unsigned article "Cuban Slaves in England" in *British and Foreign Anti-Slavery Reporter*, ser. 3, vol. 2: 234–239, with imprint:

Nendeln, Lichtenstein: Kraus Reprint, **1969**. Tpv: Printed in **Germany**, Lessing-Druckerei, **Wiesbaden** [Hesse].
4to (33 cm.).
https://babel.hathitrust.org/cgi/pt?id=uiug.30112037763411
&view=1up&seq=542.

447.3———.

Account printed (on p. 316) within section headed "Eighteen[*] Cuban Slaves," which comprises pp. 306–320 in *Slave Testimony: Two Centuries of Letters, Speeches, Interviews, and Autobiographies*, edited by John W. Blassingame. [*Blassingame includes in this total a child born in Cuba who falls outside the present catalog's scope.]

Baton Rouge [Louisiana, U.S.A.]: Louisiana State University Press, **1977**.
8vo (23 cm.): lxv, 777 p.

447.4———. [Second printing of 447.3]

Account printed (on p. 316) within section headed "Eighteen Cuban Slaves," which comprises pp. 306–320 in *Slave Testimony: Two Centuries of Letters, Speeches, and Autobiographies*, edited by John W. Blassingame.

Baton Rouge [Louisiana, U.S.A.]: Louisiana State University Press, **1977**. Second printing.
8vo (23 cm.): lxv, 777 p., illus., portraits.

447.5———. [Another printing of 447.3]

Account printed (on p. 316) within section headed "Eighteen Cuban Slaves," which comprises pp. 306–320 in *Slave Testimony: Two Centuries of Letters, Speeches, and Autobiographies*, edited by John W. Blassingame.

Baton Rouge [Louisiana, U.S.A.]: Louisiana State University Press, **1979**. 1979 printing.
8vo (23 cm.): lxv, 777 p., illus., portraits.

447.6———. [Another printing of 447.3]

Account printed (on p. 316) within section headed "Eighteen Cuban Slaves," which comprises pp. 306–320 in *Slave Testimony: Two Centuries of Letters, Speeches, and Autobiographies*, edited by John W. Blassingame.

Baton Rouge [Louisiana, U.S.A.]: Louisiana State University Press, **1980**. 1980 printing.
8vo (23 cm.): lxv, 777 p., illus., portraits.

447.7———. [Another printing of 447.3]

Account printed (on p. 316) within section headed "Eighteen Cuban Slaves," which comprises pp. 306–320 in *Slave Testimony: Two Centuries of Letters, Speeches, and Autobiographies*, edited by John W. Blassingame.

Baton Rouge [Louisiana, U.S.A.]: Louisiana State University Press, **1989**. 1989 printing.
8vo (23 cm.): lxv, 777 p., illus., portraits.

447.8———. [Another printing of 447.3]

Account printed (on p. 316) within section headed "Eighteen Cuban Slaves," which comprises pp. 306–320 in *Slave Testimony: Two Centuries of Letters, Speeches, and Autobiographies*, edited by John W. Blassingame.

Baton Rouge [Louisiana, U.S.A.]: Louisiana State University Press, **1998**. 1998 printing.
8vo (23 cm.): lxv, 777 p., illus., portraits.

447.9———. [Another printing of 447.3]

Account printed (on p. 316) within section headed "Eighteen Cuban Slaves," which comprises pp. 306–320 in *Slave Testimony: Two Centuries of Letters, Speeches, and Autobiographies*, edited by John W. Blassingame.

Baton Rouge [Louisiana, U.S.A.]: Louisiana State University Press, **2002**. 2002 printing.
8vo (23 cm.): lxv, 777 p., illus., portraits.

447.10———. [Another printing of 447.3]

Account printed (on p. 316) within section headed "Eighteen Cuban Slaves," which comprises pp. 306–320 in *Slave Testimony: Two Centuries of Letters, Speeches, and Autobiographies*, edited by John W. Blassingame.

Baton Rouge [Louisiana, U.S.A.]: Louisiana State University Press, **2009**.
8vo (24 cm.): lxv, 777 p., illus., portraits.

448.1 Augustin Acosta (ca. 1814–)

Account (one of seventeen) of this man from Lagos printed in unsigned article "Cuban Slaves in England" in the 2 October 1854 issue of the British and Foreign Anti-Slavery Society's monthly magazine *The Anti-Slavery Reporter* [edited by Louis Alexis Chamerovzow], ser. 3, vol. 2: 234–239.

https://babel.hathitrust.org/cgi/pt?id=uiug.30112037763411&view=1up&seq=542 [see 448.1].

London [England]: [Printed for the British and Foreign Anti-Slavery Society], **1854**. Price, Fourpence Stamped, Threepence Unstamped.
Hogg 1501.

¶ Acosta, a Lagos native (modern Nigeria—see Map 5), was forcibly taken on a large Spanish slave ship to the Spanish Caribbean colony of Cuba (Map 12) ca. 1830. After landing near the capital city of Havana, he and the other enslaved Africans were taken to a barracoon. Acosta and forty others were then sold to a dealer, who hired him out as a sugar plantation laborer. Acosta worked under brutal conditions in a sugar house for twelve years. He was then resold and worked as a house servant for two years before being sold again, this time to a coffee and sugar planter. After nine more years he was able to purchase his own freedom. Thereafter, he sailed to Southampton, England (Map 8) in 1854 on the *Avon*, then three weeks later on the *Candace* to Lagos.

448.2———.
Photomechanical reprint of 448.1 in unsigned article "Cuban Slaves in England" in *British and Foreign Anti-Slavery Reporter*, ser. 3, vol. 2: 234–239, with imprint:

Nendeln, Lichtenstein: Kraus Reprint, **1969**. Tpv: Printed in **Germany**, Lessing-Druckerei, **Wiesbaden [Hesse]**.
4to (33 cm.).
https://babel.hathitrust.org/cgi/pt?id=uiug.30112037763411&view=1up&seq=542.

448.3———.
Account printed (on pp. 316–317) within section headed "Eighteen[*] Cuban Slaves," which comprises pp. 306–320 in *Slave Testimony: Two Centuries of Letters, Speeches, Interviews, and Autobiographies*, edited by John W. Blassingame. [*Blassingame includes in this total a child born in Cuba who falls outside the present catalog's scope.]

Baton Rouge [Louisiana, U.S.A.]: Louisiana State University Press, **1977**.
8vo (23 cm.): lxv, 777 p

448.4———. [Second printing of 448.3]
Account printed (on pp. 316–317) within section headed "Eighteen Cuban Slaves," which comprises pp. 306–320 in *Slave Testimony: Two Centuries of Letters, Speeches, and Autobiographies*, edited by John W. Blassingame.

Baton Rouge [Louisiana, U.S.A.]: Louisiana State University Press, **1977**. Second printing.
8vo (23 cm.): lxv, 777 p., illus., portraits.

448.5———. [Another printing of 448.3]
Account printed (on pp. 316–317) within section headed "Eighteen Cuban Slaves," which comprises pp. 306–320 in *Slave Testimony: Two Centuries of Letters, Speeches, and Autobiographies*, edited by John W. Blassingame.

Baton Rouge [Louisiana, U.S.A.]: Louisiana State University Press, **1979**. 1979 printing.
8vo (23 cm.): lxv, 777 p., illus., portraits.

448.6———. [Another printing of 448.3]
Account printed (on pp. 316–317) within section headed "Eighteen Cuban Slaves," which comprises pp. 306–320 in *Slave Testimony: Two Centuries of Letters, Speeches, and Autobiographies*, edited by John W. Blassingame.

Baton Rouge [Louisiana, U.S.A.]: Louisiana State University Press, **1980**. 1980 printing.
8vo (23 cm.): lxv, 777 p., illus., portraits.

448.7———. [Another printing of 448.3]
Account printed (on pp. 316–317) within section headed "Eighteen Cuban Slaves," which comprises pp. 306–320 in *Slave Testimony: Two Centuries of Letters, Speeches, and Autobiographies*, edited by John W. Blassingame.

Baton Rouge [Louisiana, U.S.A.]: Louisiana State University Press, **1989**. 1989 printing.
8vo (23 cm.): lxv, 777 p., illus., portraits.

448.8———. [Another printing of 448.3]
Account printed (on pp. 316–317) within section headed "Eighteen Cuban Slaves," which comprises pp. 306–320 in *Slave Testimony: Two Centuries of Letters, Speeches, and Autobiographies*, edited by John W. Blassingame.

Baton Rouge [Louisiana, U.S.A.]: Louisiana State University Press, **1998**. 1998 printing.
8vo (23 cm.): lxv, 777 p., illus., portraits.

448.9———. [Another printing of 448.3]
Account printed (on pp. 316–317) within section headed "Eighteen Cuban Slaves," which comprises pp. 306–320 in *Slave Testimony: Two Centuries of Letters, Speeches, and Autobiographies*, edited by John W. Blassingame.

Baton Rouge [Louisiana, U.S.A.]: Louisiana State University Press, **2002**. 2002 printing.
8vo (23 cm.): lxv, 777 p., illus., portraits.

448.10———. [Another printing of 448.3]
Account printed (on pp. 316–317) within section headed "Eighteen Cuban Slaves," which comprises pp. 306–320 in

Slave Testimony: Two Centuries of Letters, Speeches, and Autobiographies, edited by John W. Blassingame.

Baton Rouge [Louisiana, U.S.A.]: Louisiana State University Press, 2009.
8vo (24 cm.): lxv, 777 p., illus., portraits.

449.1 Joaquim Perez (ca. 1799–)

Account (one of seventeen) of this man from Lagos printed in unsigned article "Cuban Slaves in England" in the 2 October 1854 issue of the British and Foreign Anti-Slavery Society's monthly magazine *The Anti-Slavery Reporter* [edited by Louis Alexis Chamerovzow], ser. 3, vol. 2: 234–239.

https://babel.hathitrust.org/cgi/pt?id=uiug.30112037763411&view=1up&seq=542 [see 449.1].

London [England]: [Printed for the British and Foreign Anti-Slavery Society], 1854. Price, Fourpence Stamped, Threepence Unstamped.
Hogg 1501.

¶ A native of Lagos (modern Nigeria—see Map 5), Joaquim Perez was forcibly taken to the Spanish Caribbean colony of Cuba (Map 12) on a large slave ship ca. 1824. Upon landing in the capital city of Havana, he was taken with the rest of the ship's human cargo to the barracoon at the fortress *Castilio Principe*. He became the property of one Pere (a merchant), one of the venture's shareholders. Joaquim Perez worked enslaved by this merchant for twelve years on a quay with a gang of other enslaved workers until sold to Joachim Lupcio, who kept him for another fifteen years. Joaquim Perez then bought his own freedom. He married Martina Segui (q.v. 448.1). By the time the couple embarked for Southampton, England (Map 8) in 1854 on the *Avon*, they had an eighteen-year-old son who sailed with them. Three weeks later they sailed on the *Candace* for Lagos.

449.2——.

Photomechanical reprint of 449.1 in unsigned article "Cuban Slaves in England" in *British and Foreign Anti-Slavery Reporter*, ser. 3, vol. 2: 234–239, with imprint:

Nendeln, Lichtenstein: Kraus Reprint, 1969. Tpv: Printed in **Germany**, Lessing-Druckerei, **Wiesbaden** [Hesse].
4to (33 cm.).
https://babel.hathitrust.org/cgi/pt?id=uiug.30112037763411&view=1up&seq=542.

449.3——.

Account printed (on p. 317) within section headed "Eighteen[*] Cuban Slaves," which comprises pp. 306–320 in *Slave Testimony: Two Centuries of Letters, Speeches, Interviews, and Autobiographies*, edited by John W. Blassingame. [*Blassingame includes in this total a child born in Cuba who falls outside the present catalog's scope.]

Baton Rouge [Louisiana, U.S.A.]: Louisiana State University Press, 1977.
8vo (23 cm.): lxv, 777 p.

449.4——. [Second printing of 449.3]

Account printed (on p. 317) within section headed "Eighteen Cuban Slaves," which comprises pp. 306–320 in *Slave Testimony: Two Centuries of Letters, Speeches, and Autobiographies*, edited by John W. Blassingame.

Baton Rouge [Louisiana, U.S.A.]: Louisiana State University Press, 1977. Second printing.
8vo (23 cm.): lxv, 777 p., illus., portraits.

449.5——. [Another printing of 449.3]

Account printed (on p. 317) within section headed "Eighteen Cuban Slaves," which comprises pp. 306–320 in *Slave Testimony: Two Centuries of Letters, Speeches, and Autobiographies*, edited by John W. Blassingame.

Baton Rouge [Louisiana, U.S.A.]: Louisiana State University Press, 1979. 1979 printing.
8vo (23 cm.): lxv, 777 p., illus., portraits.

449.6——. [Another printing of 449.3]

Account printed (on p. 317) within section headed "Eighteen Cuban Slaves," which comprises pp. 306–320 in *Slave Testimony: Two Centuries of Letters, Speeches, and Autobiographies*, edited by John W. Blassingame.

Baton Rouge [Louisiana, U.S.A.]: Louisiana State University Press, 1980. 1980 printing.
8vo (23 cm.): lxv, 777 p., illus., portraits.

449.7——. [Another printing of 449.3]

Account printed (on p. 317) within section headed "Eighteen Cuban Slaves," which comprises pp. 306–320 in *Slave Testimony: Two Centuries of Letters, Speeches, and Autobiographies*, edited by John W. Blassingame.

Baton Rouge [Louisiana, U.S.A.]: Louisiana State University Press, 1989. 1989 printing.
8vo (23 cm.): lxv, 777 p., illus., portraits.

449.8——.[Another printing of 449.3]

Account printed (on p. 317) within section headed "Eighteen Cuban Slaves," which comprises pp. 306–320 in *Slave Testimony: Two Centuries of Letters, Speeches, and Autobiographies*, edited by John W. Blassingame.

Baton Rouge [Louisiana, U.S.A.]: Louisiana State University Press, **1998**. 1998 printing.
8vo (23 cm.): lxv, 777 p., illus., portraits.

449.9——.[Another printing of 449.3]

Account printed (on p. 317) within section headed "Eighteen Cuban Slaves," which comprises pp. 306–320 in *Slave Testimony: Two Centuries of Letters, Speeches, and Autobiographies*, edited by John W. Blassingame.

Baton Rouge [Louisiana, U.S.A.]: Louisiana State University Press, **2002**. 2002 printing.
8vo (23 cm.): lxv, 777 p., illus., portraits.

449.10——.[Another printing of 449.3]

Account printed (on p. 317) within section headed "Eighteen Cuban Slaves," which comprises pp. 306–320 in *Slave Testimony: Two Centuries of Letters, Speeches, and Autobiographies*, edited by John W. Blassingame.

Baton Rouge [Louisiana, U.S.A.]: Louisiana State University Press, **2009**.
8vo (24 cm.): lxv, 777 p., illus., portraits.

450.1 Martina Segui (ca. 1800–)

Account (one of seventeen) of this woman from Lagos printed in unsigned article "Cuban Slaves in England" in the 2 October 1854 issue of the British and Foreign Anti-Slavery Society's monthly magazine *The Anti-Slavery Reporter* [edited by Louis Alexis Chamerovzow], ser. 3, vol. 2: 234–239.

https://babel.hathitrust.org/cgi/pt?id=uiug.30112037763411&view=1up&seq=542 [see 450.1].

London [England]: [Printed for the British and Foreign Anti-Slavery Society], 1854. Price, Fourpence Stamped, Threepence Unstamped.
Hogg 1501.

¶ Segui, a native of Lagos (modern Nigeria—see Map 5), was married to Joachim Perez (q.v. 449.1). Ca. 1822 she was forcibly taken on a large slave ship to the Spanish Caribbean colonial city of Havana, Cuba (Map 12) and there sold to a planter, who sent her out to sell provisions. A year later he sold her to a free Mandinka man, who was a foreman on a quay. She sold provisions for him and became a *curatada* (an enslaved person who works off an agreed sum to achieve freedom). After ten years she still owed money and was sold. Three years later, in 1847, she was able to free herself and her son, who was eighteen and worked making cigars. Thereafter, she sailed to Southampton, England (Map 8) in 1854 on the *Avon*. Three weeks later she sailed on the *Candace* for Lagos.

450.2——.

Photomechanical reprint of 450.1 in unsigned article "Cuban Slaves in England" in *British and Foreign Anti-Slavery Reporter*, ser. 3, vol. 2: 234–239, with imprint:

Nendeln, Lichtenstein: Kraus Reprint, **1969**. Tpv: Printed in **Germany**, Lessing-Druckerei, **Wiesbaden [Hesse]**.
4to (33 cm.).
https://babel.hathitrust.org/cgi/pt?id=uiug.30112037763411&view=1up&seq=542.

450.3——.

Account printed (on pp. 317–318) within section headed "Eighteen[*] Cuban Slaves," which comprises pp. 306–320 in *Slave Testimony: Two Centuries of Letters, Speeches, Interviews, and Autobiographies*, edited by John W. Blassingame. [*Blassingame includes in this total a child born in Cuba who falls outside the present catalog's scope.]

Baton Rouge [Louisiana, U.S.A.]: Louisiana State University Press, **1977**.
8vo (23 cm.): lxv, 777 p.

450.4——.[Second printing of 450.3]

Account printed (on pp. 317–318) within section headed "Eighteen Cuban Slaves," which comprises pp. 306–320 in *Slave Testimony: Two Centuries of Letters, Speeches, and Autobiographies*, edited by John W. Blassingame.

Baton Rouge [Louisiana, U.S.A.]: Louisiana State University Press, **1977**. Second printing.
8vo (23 cm.): lxv, 777 p., illus., portraits.

450.5——. [Another printing of 450.3]

Account printed (on pp. 317–318) within section headed "Eighteen Cuban Slaves," which comprises pp. 306–320 in *Slave Testimony: Two Centuries of Letters, Speeches, and Autobiographies*, edited by John W. Blassingame.

Baton Rouge [Louisiana, U.S.A.]: Louisiana State University Press, **1979**. 1979 printing.
8vo (23 cm.): lxv, 777 p., illus., portraits.

450.6———. [Another printing of 450.3]

Account printed (on pp. 317–318) within section headed "Eighteen Cuban Slaves," which comprises pp. 306–320 in *Slave Testimony: Two Centuries of Letters, Speeches, and Autobiographies*, edited by John W. Blassingame.

Baton Rouge [Louisiana, U.S.A.]: Louisiana State University Press, **1980**. 1980 printing.
8vo (23 cm.): lxv, 777 p., illus., portraits.

450.7———. [Another printing of 450.3]

Account printed (on pp. 317–318) within section headed "Eighteen Cuban Slaves," which comprises pp. 306–320 in *Slave Testimony: Two Centuries of Letters, Speeches, and Autobiographies*, edited by John W. Blassingame.

Baton Rouge [Louisiana, U.S.A.]: Louisiana State University Press, **1989**. 1989 printing.
8vo (23 cm.): lxv, 777 p., illus., portraits.

450.8———. [Another printing of 450.3]

Account printed (on pp. 317–318) within section headed "Eighteen Cuban Slaves," which comprises pp. 306–320 in *Slave Testimony: Two Centuries of Letters, Speeches, and Autobiographies*, edited by John W. Blassingame.

Baton Rouge [Louisiana, U.S.A.]: Louisiana State University Press, **1998**. 1998 printing.
8vo (23 cm.): lxv, 777 p., illus., portraits.

450.9———. [Another printing of 450.3]

Account printed (on pp. 317–318) within section headed "Eighteen Cuban Slaves," which comprises pp. 306–320 in *Slave Testimony: Two Centuries of Letters, Speeches, and Autobiographies*, edited by John W. Blassingame.

Baton Rouge [Louisiana, U.S.A.]: Louisiana State University Press, **2002**. 2002 printing.
8vo (23 cm.): lxv, 777 p., illus., portraits.

450.10———. [Another printing of 450.3]

Account printed (on pp. 317–318) within section headed "Eighteen Cuban Slaves," which comprises pp. 306–320 in *Slave Testimony: Two Centuries of Letters, Speeches, and Autobiographies*, edited by John W. Blassingame.

Baton Rouge [Louisiana, U.S.A.]: Louisiana State University Press, **2009**.
8vo (24 cm.): lxv, 777 p., illus., portraits.

451.1 Manuel Vidau (ca. 1812–)

Account (one of seventeen) of this man from Lagos printed in unsigned article "Cuban Slaves in England" in the 2 Oc-

tober 1854 issue of the British and Foreign Anti-Slavery Society's monthly magazine *The Anti-Slavery Reporter* [edited by Louis Alexis Chamerovzow], ser. 3, vol. 2: 234–239.

London [England]: [Printed for the British and Foreign Anti-Slavery Society], **1854**. Price, Fourpence Stamped, Threepence Unstamped.
Hogg 1501.

https://babel.hathitrust.org/cgi/pt?id=uiug.30112037763411&view=1up&seq=542 [see 451.1].

¶ Vidau, a native of Lagos (modern Nigeria—see Map 5), was taken prisoner of war and ca. 1834 forcibly sent on a large slave ship to the Spanish Caribbean colonial city of Havana, Cuba (Map 12). There he was sold from a barracoon to a general shop owner and cigar maker. He worked making about four hundred cigars daily for eleven years and was brutally treated whenever he did not make enough. He was then sold to a coffee and sugar broker, who licensed Vidau to hire himself out making cigars. Vidau saved his money and joined thirty-nine others in purchasing a lottery ticket that netted them $16,000, or $400 each; this enabled him to purchase his freedom ca. 1846. Thereafter, he did well making cigars to support himself, his wife Marie Luisa Picard (q.v. 452.1), and their adopted child. Desiring to return to Lagos, he booked passage on the *Avon*, which sailed in 1854 for Southampton, England (Map 8). Three weeks later he sailed on the *Candace* for Lagos.

451.2———.

Photomechanical reprint of 451.1 in unsigned article "Cuban Slaves in England" in *British and Foreign Anti-Slavery Reporter*, ser. 3, vol. 2: 234–239, with imprint:

Nendeln, Lichtenstein: Kraus Reprint, **1969**. Tpv: Printed in **Germany**, Lessing-Druckerei, **Wiesbaden** [Hesse].
4to (33 cm.).
https://babel.hathitrust.org/cgi/pt?id=uiug.30112037763411&view=1up&seq=542.

451.3———.

Account printed (on pp. 318–319) within section headed "Eighteen[*] Cuban Slaves," which comprises pp. 306–320 in *Slave Testimony: Two Centuries of Letters, Speeches, Interviews, and Autobiographies*, edited by John W. Blassingame.

[*Blassingame includes in this total a child born in Cuba who falls outside the present catalog's scope.]

Baton Rouge [Louisiana, U.S.A.]: Louisiana State University Press, **1977**.
8vo (23 cm.): lxv, 777 p.

451.4———. [Second printing of 451.3]

Account printed (on pp. 318–319) within section headed "Eighteen Cuban Slaves," which comprises pp. 306–320 in *Slave Testimony: Two Centuries of Letters, Speeches, and Autobiographies*, edited by John W. Blassingame.

Baton Rouge [Louisiana, U.S.A.]: Louisiana State University Press, **1977**. Second printing.
8vo (23 cm.): lxv, 777 p., illus., portraits.

451.5———. [Another printing of 451.3]

Account printed (on pp. 318–319) within section headed "Eighteen Cuban Slaves," which comprises pp. 306–320 in *Slave Testimony: Two Centuries of Letters, Speeches, and Autobiographies*, edited by John W. Blassingame.

Baton Rouge [Louisiana, U.S.A.]: Louisiana State University Press, **1979**. 1979 printing.
8vo (23 cm.): lxv, 777 p., illus., portraits.

451.6———. [Another printing of 451.3]

Account printed (on pp. 318–319) within section headed "Eighteen Cuban Slaves," which comprises pp. 306–320 in *Slave Testimony: Two Centuries of Letters, Speeches, and Autobiographies*, edited by John W. Blassingame.

Baton Rouge [Louisiana, U.S.A.]: Louisiana State University Press, **1980**. 1980 printing.
8vo (23 cm.): lxv, 777 p., illus., portraits.

451.7———. [Another printing of 451.3]

Account printed (on pp. 318–319) within section headed "Eighteen Cuban Slaves," which comprises pp. 306–320 in *Slave Testimony: Two Centuries of Letters, Speeches, and Autobiographies*, edited by John W. Blassingame.

Baton Rouge [Louisiana, U.S.A.]: Louisiana State University Press, **1989**. 1989 printing.
8vo (23 cm.): lxv, 777 p., illus., portraits.

451.8———. [Another printing of 451.3]

Account printed (on pp. 318–319) within section headed "Eighteen Cuban Slaves," which comprises pp. 306–320 in *Slave Testimony: Two Centuries of Letters, Speeches, and Autobiographies*, edited by John W. Blassingame.

Baton Rouge [Louisiana, U.S.A.]: Louisiana State University Press, **1998**. 1998 printing.
8vo (23 cm.): lxv, 777 p., illus., portraits.

451.9———. [Another printing of 451.3]

Account printed (on pp. 318–319) within section headed "Eighteen Cuban Slaves," which comprises pp. 306–320 in

Slave Testimony: Two Centuries of Letters, Speeches, and Autobiographies, edited by John W. Blassingame.

Baton Rouge [Louisiana, U.S.A.]: Louisiana State University Press, **2002**. 2002 printing.
8vo (23 cm.): lxv, 777 p., illus., portraits.

451.10———. [Another printing of 451.3]

Account printed (on pp. 318–319) within section headed "Eighteen Cuban Slaves," which comprises pp. 306–320 in *Slave Testimony: Two Centuries of Letters, Speeches, and Autobiographies*, edited by John W. Blassingame.

Baton Rouge [Louisiana, U.S.A.]: Louisiana State University Press, **2009**.
8vo (24 cm.): lxv, 777 p., illus., portraits.

452.1 Maria Luisa Picard (ca. 1822–)

Account (one of seventeen of this woman from Lagos printed in unsigned article "Cuban Slaves in England" in the 2 October 1854 issue of the British and Foreign Anti-Slavery Society's monthly magazine *The Anti-Slavery Reporter* [edited by Louis Alexis Chamerovzow], ser. 3, vol. 2: 234–239.

https://babel.hathitrust.org/cgi/pt?id=uiug.30112037763411&view=1up&seq=542 [see 452.1].

London [England]: [Printed for the British and Foreign Anti-Slavery Society], 1854. Price, Fourpence Stamped, Threepence Unstamped.
Hogg 1501.

¶ Picard was a native of Lagos (modern Nigeria—see Map 5). Ca. 1833 she was forcibly taken on a large Spanish slave ship to the Spanish Caribbean colony of Cuba (Map 12). This ship landed near the capital city of Havana, and Picard was promptly taken to a barracoon. A "gentleman" purchased her to be his house servant. After two years she became a *curatada* (an enslaved person who works off an agreed sum to achieve freedom), and eight years later, ca. 1847, she bought her own freedom. About that time she married Manuel Vidau (q.v. 451.1). They had no offspring of their own but adopted a small child. Picard sailed with her family to Southampton, England (Map 8) on the *Avon* in 1854. Three weeks later they sailed on the *Candace* for Lagos.

452.2———.

Photomechanical reprint of 452.1 in unsigned article "Cuban Slaves in England" in *British and Foreign Anti-Slavery Reporter*, ser. 3, vol. 2: 234–239, with imprint:

Nendeln, Lichtenstein: Kraus Reprint, 1969. Tpv: Printed in Germany, Lessing-Druckerei, Wiesbaden [Hesse].

4to (33 cm.).

https://babel.hathitrust.org/cgi/pt?id=uiug.30112037763411&view=1up&seq=542.

452.3——.

Account printed (on pp. 319–320) within section headed "Eighteen[*] Cuban Slaves," which comprises pp. 306–320 in *Slave Testimony: Two Centuries of Letters, Speeches, Interviews, and Autobiographies*, edited by John W. Blassingame. [*Blassingame includes in this total a child born in Cuba who falls outside the present catalog's scope.]

Baton Rouge [Louisiana, U.S.A.]: Louisiana State University Press, **1977.**

8vo (23 cm.): lxv, 777 p.

452.4——. [Second printing of 452.3]

Account printed (on pp. 319–320) within section headed "Eighteen Cuban Slaves," which comprises pp. 306–320 in *Slave Testimony: Two Centuries of Letters, Speeches, and Autobiographies*, edited by John W. Blassingame.

Baton Rouge [Louisiana, U.S.A.]: Louisiana State University Press, **1977.** Second printing.

8vo (23 cm.): lxv, 777 p., illus., portraits.

452.5——. [Another printing of 452.3]

Account printed (on pp. 319–320) within section headed "Eighteen Cuban Slaves," which comprises pp. 306–320 in *Slave Testimony: Two Centuries of Letters, Speeches, and Autobiographies*, edited by John W. Blassingame.

Baton Rouge [Louisiana, U.S.A.]: Louisiana State University Press, **1979.** 1979 printing.

8vo (23 cm.): lxv, 777 p., illus., portraits.

452.6——. [Another printing of 452.3]

Account printed (on pp. 319–320) within section headed "Eighteen Cuban Slaves," which comprises pp. 306–320 in *Slave Testimony: Two Centuries of Letters, Speeches, and Autobiographies*, edited by John W. Blassingame.

Baton Rouge [Louisiana, U.S.A.]: Louisiana State University Press, **1980.** 1980 printing.

8vo (23 cm.): lxv, 777 p., illus., portraits.

452.7——. [Another printing of 452.3]

Account printed (on pp. 319–320) within section headed "Eighteen Cuban Slaves," which comprises pp. 306–320 in *Slave Testimony: Two Centuries of Letters, Speeches, and Autobiographies*, edited by John W. Blassingame.

Baton Rouge [Louisiana, U.S.A.]: Louisiana State University Press, **1989.** 1989 printing.

8vo (23 cm.): lxv, 777 p., illus., portraits.

452.8——. [Another printing of 452.3]

Account printed (on pp. 319–320) within section headed "Eighteen Cuban Slaves," which comprises pp. 306–320 in *Slave Testimony: Two Centuries of Letters, Speeches, and Autobiographies*, edited by John W. Blassingame.

Baton Rouge [Louisiana, U.S.A.]: Louisiana State University Press, **1998.** 1998 printing.

8vo (23 cm.): lxv, 777 p., illus., portraits.

452.9——. [Another printing of 452.3]

Account printed (on pp. 319–320) within section headed "Eighteen Cuban Slaves," which comprises pp. 306–320 in *Slave Testimony: Two Centuries of Letters, Speeches, and Autobiographies*, edited by John W. Blassingame.

Baton Rouge [Louisiana, U.S.A.]: Louisiana State University Press, **2002.** 2002 printing.

8vo (23 cm.): lxv, 777 p., illus., portraits.

452.10——. [Another printing of 452.3]

Account printed (on pp. 319–320) within section headed "Eighteen Cuban Slaves," which comprises pp. 306–320 in *Slave Testimony: Two Centuries of Letters, Speeches, and Autobiographies*, edited by John W. Blassingame.

Baton Rouge [Louisiana, U.S.A.]: Louisiana State University Press, **2009.**

8vo (24 cm.): lxv, 777 p., illus., portraits.

453.0 Canuto Houssin

Autobiographical statement included in manuscript dated Havana, Cuba, 14 February 1854, preserved in Archivo Nacional de la República de Cuba (ANC), **La Habana, Cuba**, Gobierno Superior Civil, 949/33588.

Full text: https://huskiecommons.lib.niu.edu/history-500african-voices/258/ [see 453.3].

¶ **Canuto Houssin identified as native African but did not say from where. After forced transport on a slave ship to the Spanish colony of Cuba in the Caribbean (see Map 12) and** sale there, he reacquired his freedom and lived in the town of El Carro. He earned enough cash to purchase an enslaved woman (Juliana), whom he wished to marry, according to an agreement with her owner, but a bureaucratic problem caused a court to order that Canuto Houssin petition authorities in the town of Cárdenas. He responded that he was ill and had no means to do this.

453.1——.

Statement printed on pp. 113–114 in *La esclavitud desde la esclavitud: La visión de los siervos* by Gloria García Rodríguez.

México [Distrito Federal, Estados Unidos Mexicanos]: Centro de Investigación Científica "Ing. Jorge L Tamayo," **1996.**
8vo (21 cm.): 251 p.

453.2——.

Printed on pp. 100–101 in *La esclavitud desde la esclavitud*, by Gloria García.

La Habana [Cuba]: Editorial de Ciencias Sociales, **2003.**
8vo (21 cm.): xx, 222 p.

453.3——.

English translation of statement printed on pp. 94–95 in *Voices of the Enslaved in Nineteenth-Century Cuba: A Documentary History*, edited by Gloria García Rodríguez. Translated [from 450.1] by Nancy L. Westrate; foreword by Ada Ferrer.

Chapel Hill [North Carolina, U.S.A.]: University of North Carolina Press, **2011.**
8vo (24 cm.): xviii, 220 p.

454.0 Pedro Real Congo

Statement recorded in Havana on 21 April 1854, preserved in Archivo Nacional de la República de Cuba (ANC), **La Habana, Cuba,** Gobierno Superior Civil, 948/33540.

¶ **Pedro Real identified as Congolese.** After forced transport to the Spanish colony of Cuba in the Caribbean (see Map 12) on a slave ship and sale there, by 1854 he had reacquired his freedom. He was a widower, a tobacconist, a resident on Gloria Street in the Chávez neighborhood of Havana, and the chief (*capataz*) of an association of fellow Congolese in the city. In 1854, acting in his role as association *capataz*, he spoke to authorities on behalf of an enslaved Congolese woman. She was struggling to find a new owner, as was her right, in order to finish a contract to work toward her freedom.

454.1——.

Statement printed on p. 163 in *La esclavitud desde la esclavitud: La visión de los siervos* by Gloria García Rodríguez.

México [Distrito Federal, Estados Unidos Mexicanos]: Centro de Investigación Científica "Ing. Jorge L Tamayo," **1996.**
8vo (21 cm.): 251 p.

454.2——.

Printed on p. 146 in *La esclavitud desde la esclavitud*, by Gloria García.

La Habana [Cuba]: Editorial de Ciencias Sociales, **2003.**
8vo (21 cm.): xx, 222 p.

454.3——.

English translation of statement printed on pp. 139–140 in *Voices of the Enslaved in Nineteenth-Century Cuba: A Documentary History*, edited by Gloria García Rodríguez. Translated [from 454.1] by Nancy L. Westrate; foreword by Ada Ferrer.

Chapel Hill [North Carolina, U.S.A.]: University of North Carolina Press, **2011.**
8vo (24 cm.): xviii, 220 p.

Full text: https://huskiecommons.lib.niu.edu/history-500africanvoices/259/ [see 454.3].

1857

455.1 Odusinna

His story printed on pp. 46–54 in Mary Ann Serrett Barber, *Oshielle: or, Village Life in the Yoruba Country; from the Journals and Letters of a Catechist there; describing the Rise of a Christian Church in an African Village.*

https://babel.hathitrust.org/cgi/pt?id=wu.89003910411&view=1up&seq=74 [see 455.1].

London [England]: James Nisbet and Co. Berners Street. MDCCCLVII [1857]. Tpv: T. C. Johns, Printer, Wine-office-court, Fleet-street.
12mo (15 cm): xxiv, [9]–222 p.

¶ **Odusinna was Egba** (Yorùbá hinterland, formerly part of the Oyo Empire, modern Nigeria—see Map 5) and came from a village near Awoyade, under the control of Abeokuta (modern southwestern Nigeria). When he was a young child, ca. 1821, his village was attacked, and Odussina was separated from his family, taken to the coast, and forced aboard a slave ship. A British warship intercepted this ship at sea, liberated

Odusinna and the others, and took them to Sierra Leone (Map 4). There Odusinna went to a mission school and embraced Christianity. Later he worked as a catechist, married, and had children. In 1851 he took his family by land to his homeland (reuniting with his sister) to begin work in the Christian mission at Abeokuta. After the war with Dahomey subsided, he began work in the new chapel at Oshielle and lived with his family there.

456.1   Tallen (ca. 1800–) = John Bull = Demock Charlton = Dimmock Charlton

His life history to date printed under layered headlines "Enslavement of a British Subject. Forty-Five Years in Bondage. Remarkable and Interesting Narrative. Persevering Struggle for Freedom. Singular Appropriation of a U.S. Prisoner of War" on first page (of eight), cols. 1–2, of *The New York Daily Times*, vol. 6, no. 1812.

https://babel.hathi-trust.org/cgi/pt?id=ui-ug.30112117735883&view=1up&seq=654 [see 456.9].

New York [New York, U.S.A.]: [Raymond, Jones & Co.], July 10, 1857. Price 2 cents.

¶ Tallen was a native of Kissee, a village on a large river in Sierra Leone (see Map 4). At age twelve, ca. 1812, he was captured with others during warfare between Mandinka (an ethnic group residing in modern southern Mali, Guinea, and Ivory Coast—Map 3) and Kuree, taken on a four-week journey to the coast, there forced aboard a large Spanish slave ship, likely from the Rio Pongo (modern Guinea), and taken to sea. A British warship subsequently intercepted this ship; and while most of the Liberated Africans were taken to England, Tallen was taken aboard the HMS *Peacock,* renamed John Bull, and employed as a free cabin boy. In 1813 the *Peacock* was sunk by the USS *Hornet,* whose captain took Tallen to Savannah, Georgia, U.S.A. (Map 15), and there pretended he was still enslaved. Tallen took legal action to reacquire his freedom. Failing in that action, he tried, but failed, to purchase himself. Ultimately, during more than forty years of enslavement in Savannah, he was bought and sold several times before he finally purchased his freedom in 1856. He then sailed as a passenger to New York City (Map 17), though his wife and children remained enslaved in Georgia. While in the Northeast he secured the freedom of one of his grandchildren, with whom he sailed to Liverpool, England (Map 8), to secure further help from abolitionists. Tallen subsequently crossed the country to London, where he expressed a desire to go to Canada to work there, yet he was still in London in

1866. For more on him see Randy J. Sparks, *Africans in the Old South: Mapping Exceptional Lives Across the Atlantic World* (Cambridge Massachusetts: Harvard University Press, 2016), 103–122.

456.2———.

His life history to date partially reprinted from 456.1 without headline on the second page (of four), i.e., p. 12, col. 3, of *The Westerly Echo, and Pawtucket Advertiser,* vol. 7, no. 4 (whole no. 315).

Westerly, Rhode Island [U.S.A.]: Published by James H. Hoyt, July 15, 1857.
Broadsheet bifolium.
https://chroniclingamerica.loc.gov/lccn/sn83021534/1857-07-16/ed-1/seq-2/#date1

456.3———.

His life history to date reprinted explicitly from 456.1 under headline "Enslavement of a British Subject" on the first page (of four), cols. 2–4, of the July 23, 1857, issue (vol. 25, no. 30, whole no. 1278) of *The Carroll Free Press,* edited by John H. Tripp and William McCoy.

Carrollton, Ohio [U.S.A.]: Tripp & M'Coy, Editors & Publishers, July 23, 1857.
Broadsheet bifolium.
https://chroniclingamerica.loc.gov/lccn/sn83035366/1857-07-23/ed-1/seq-1/#date1

456.4———.

His life history to date reprinted explicitly from 456.1 under headline "Enslavement of a British Subject" on the first page (of four), cols. 2–4, of the July 25, 1857, issue (vol. 12, no. 49, whole no. 615) of *The Anti-Slavery Bugle,* edited by Marius R. Robinson.

Salem, Ohio [U.S.A.]: Ann Pearson, Publishing Agent, July 25, 1857.
Broadsheet bifolium.
https://chroniclingamerica.loc.gov/lccn/sn83035487/1857-07-25/ed-1/seq-1/

456.5———.

Detailed summary of 456.1 printed under headline "Enslavement of a British Subject—Forty-Five Years in Bondage" in the July 25, 1857, issue (vol. 14, no. 19, p. 297, col. 1) of the Quaker weekly *Friends' Intelligencer,* edited by an Association of Friends.

Philadelphia [Pennsylvania, U.S.A.]: Published by William W. Moore, No. 324 South Fifth Street, [July 25, 1857].

456.6——.

His life history to date condensed within article headlined "A Curious History" printed on p. 1, col. 1 in the daily newspaper *Evening Bulletin* (edited by Thomas S. King), vol. 4, no.121.

San Francisco [California, U.S.A.]: Printed and published by C. O. Gerberding & Co., **August 27, 1857.**

Broadsheet bifolium: 4 p. First phrases of article proper: "Our [i.e., the San Francisco *Evening Bulletin*'s] Washington correspondent, in his last regular letter, relates the following curious tale".

456.7——.

"Dimmock Charlton and His Grandchild" printed in the weekly anti-slavery newspaper *National Anti-Slavery Standard*.

New York, New York [U.S.A.]: American Anti-Slavery Society; **Philadelphia, Pennsylvania [U.S.A.]:** Pennsylvania Anti-Slavery Society, **August 29, 1857.**

456.8——.

His life history printed in the weekly anti-slavery newspaper *National Anti-Slavery Standard*.

New York, New York [U.S.A.]: American Anti-Slavery Society; **Philadelphia, Pennsylvania [U.S.A.]:** Pennsylvania Anti-Slavery Society, **December, 1857.**

Multipage broadsheet (63 cm.).

456.9——. [Augmented reprinting of 456.8]

His updated life history "extracted from the columns of the *National Anti-Slavery Standard*" (i.e., reprinted from 456.8), with added related text (including information on the legal actions Tallen took to free his family in Savannah, Georgia), under headline "Dimmock Charlton and His Grandchild" on pp. 4–9 in the (double-column, small type) magazine *The Anti-Slavery Reporter* [edited by Louis Alexis Chamerovzow], New series, vol. 6, no. 1.

[London, England]: The British and Foreign Anti-Slavery Society, **January 1, 1858.**

https://babel.hathitrust.org/cgi/pt?id=uiug.30112117735883 &view=1up&seq=654 (facsimile = 456.13).

456.10 ——.

"Dimmock Charlton—His Story Confirmed" on first page (of four), cols. 5–6 of the February 13, 1858, issue (vol. 13, no. 26, whole no. 644) of *The Anti-Slavery Bugle*, edited by Marius R. Robinson.

Salem, Ohio [U.S.A.]: Ann Pearson, Publishing Agent, **February 13, 1858.**

Broadsheet bifolium. **First sentence of news story:** "Our readers will remember the romantic and touching story of "Dimmock Charlton and His Grandchild," which appeared in the Standard of August 29th [i.e., our 456.7]."

https://chroniclingamerica.loc.gov/lccn/sn83035487/1857-07-25/ed-1/seq-1/

456.11 ——.

456.1 reprinted on pp. 3–7 and 456.8 reprinted (minus concluding paragraph) on pp. 7–14, with added introductory text printed on pp. 1–3 (signed in type on p. 3 by Mary L. Cox and Susan H. Cox of Philadelphia, Pennsylvania) and three added testimonial letters printed on p. 15, in (front wrapper title) *Narrative of Dimmock Charlton, A British Subject Taken from the Brig "Peacock" by the U. S. Sloop "Hornet," Enslaved while a Prisoner of War, and Retained Forty-Five Years in Bondage.*

[Philadelphia, Pennsylvania, U.S.A.: Printed for Mary L. & Susan H. Cox, **ca. May–June 1859**]. Note: Some exemplars of *this edition* have been catalogued with supplied date "1860?", even though the added introductory text is dated on p. 3: *"Phila., 5 mo. 7th 1859."*

8vo (18 cm.): 15 p. Caption title on p. [1]: Dimmock Charlton. | A Defence.

https://archive.org/details/narrativeofdimmo00incoxm http://docsouth.unc.edu/neh/cox/cox.html Hogg 1506.

456.12 ——.

Another telling of his life history as he told it directly to Frederick Douglass printed on p. 117, cols. 2–3, in the monthly antislavery periodical *Douglass' [sic] Monthly*, vol. 2, no. 3.

Rochester, [New York U.S.A.]: [Frederick Douglass], **August 1859.** Price—Five shillings per An'm [i.e., annum].

Folio: p. [113]–128. Includes a **list of subscription agents** living in England, Ireland, and Scotland.

https://babel.hathitrust.org/cgi/pt?id=inu.30000007703154& view=1up&seq=129&size=125

456.13 ——.

Photomechanical reprint of 456.9 printed under headline "Dimmock Charlton and His Grandchild" on pp. 4–9 in *The Anti-Slavery Reporter* [edited by Louis Alexis Chamerovzow], New series, vol. 6, no. 1, with imprint:

Nendeln, Lichtenstein: Kraus Reprint, **1969.** Tpv: Printed in **Germany**, Lessing-Druckerei, **Wiesbaden.**

https://babel.hathitrust.org/cgi/pt?id=uiug.30112117735883 &view=1up&seq=654

456.14 ——.

Article 456.12 printed on p. 117 in vol. 1 within two-volume photomechanical reprinting of *Douglass' [sic] Monthly*, of which vol. 1 comprises the original volumes 1–3 (1859–1861).

New York [New York U.S.A.]: Negro Universities Press, **1969.** 2 vols., folio (31 cm.). Vol. 1 includes historical note (correcting earlier bibliographical notes) by the 1969 publisher on Frederick Douglass's publication of this periodical. https://babel.hathitrust.org/cgi/pt?id=inu.30000007703154& view=1up&seq=129&size=125

456.15 ——.

Article 456.9 printed with annotations on pp. 325–338 in *Slave Testimony: Two Centuries of Letters, Speeches, Interviews, and Autobiographies*, edited by John W. Blassingame.

Baton Rouge [Louisiana, U.S.A.]: Louisiana State University Press, **1977.**
8vo: lxv, 777 p.

456.16——. **[Second printing of 456.15]**

Article 456.9 printed with annotations on pp. 325–338 in *Slave Testimony: Two Centuries of Letters, Speeches, and Autobiographies*, edited by John W. Blassingame.

Baton Rouge [Louisiana, U.S.A.]: Louisiana State University Press, **1977.** Second printing.
8vo (23 cm.): lxv, 777 p., illus., portraits.

456.17——. **[Another printing of 456.15]**

Article 456.9 printed with annotations on pp. 325–338 in *Slave Testimony: Two Centuries of Letters, Speeches, and Autobiographies*, edited by John W. Blassingame.

Baton Rouge [Louisiana, U.S.A.]: Louisiana State University Press, **1979.** 1979 printing.
8vo (23 cm.): lxv, 777 p., illus., portraits.

456.18——. **[Another printing of 456.15]**

Article 456.9 printed with annotations on pp. 325–338 in *Slave Testimony: Two Centuries of Letters, Speeches, and Autobiographies*, edited by John W. Blassingame.

Baton Rouge [Louisiana, U.S.A.]: Louisiana State University Press, **1980.** 1980 printing.
8vo (23 cm.): lxv, 777 p., illus., portraits.

456.19 ——. **[Another printing of 456.15]**

Article 456.9 printed with annotations on pp. 325–338 in *Slave Testimony: Two Centuries of Letters, Speeches, and Autobiographies*, edited by John W. Blassingame.

Baton Rouge [Louisiana, U.S.A.]: Louisiana State University Press, **1989.** 1989 printing.
8vo (23 cm.): lxv, 777 p., illus., portraits.

456.20——. **[Another printing of 456.15]**

Article 456.9 printed with annotations on pp. 325–338 in *Slave Testimony: Two Centuries of Letters, Speeches, and Autobiographies*, edited by John W. Blassingame.

Baton Rouge [Louisiana, U.S.A.]: Louisiana State University Press, **1998.** 1998 printing.
8vo (23 cm.): lxv, 777 p., illus., portraits.

456.21——. **[Another printing of 456.15]**

Article 456.9 printed with annotations on pp. 325–338 in *Slave Testimony: Two Centuries of Letters, Speeches, and Autobiographies*, edited by John W. Blassingame.

Baton Rouge [Louisiana, U.S.A.]: Louisiana State University Press, **2002.** 2002 printing.
8vo (23 cm.): lxv, 777 p., illus., portraits.

456.22——. **[Another printing of 456.15]**

Article 456.9 printed with annotations on pp. 325–338 in *Slave Testimony: Two Centuries of Letters, Speeches, and Autobiographies*, edited by John W. Blassingame.

Baton Rouge [Louisiana, U.S.A.]: Louisiana State University Press, **2009.**
8vo (24 cm.): lxv, 777 p., illus., portraits.

457.0 Carolina Conga

Account of her life recorded by Rio de Janeiro police on 24 November **1857,** within the manuscript entitled "Amália Guilhermina de Oliveria Coutinho, Pedido de emancipação para a Africana livre Carolina Congo," 2 December 1857, Arquivo Nacional, GIFI 6D-136, **Rio de Janeiro, Brazil.**

Full text: https:// huskiecommons. lib.niu.edu/history-500african-voices/260/ [see 457.1].

¶ Carolina identified as Congolese and in 1834 was forcibly taken thence to Brazil (see Map 9) on the slave ship *Duquesa de Bragança* with nearly three hundred enslaved passengers. The ship was captured at sea and condemned for illegal slaving. The enslaved African men and women were freed and placed under care of the Brazilian government for a forced apprenticeship to last fourteen years. Carolina ultimately served over twenty years, effectively enslaved the entire time, on a tea plantation near Rio de Janeiro called "Paquequer," owned by the man in charge of administering the apprenticeship program. During this time she married Domingos, who was also enslaved on the same plantation. Together they had four children. After Carolina and one of their daughters escaped to Rio de Janeiro (abetted by her owner's daughter), she began (in 1857) the long process for full manumission by applying to the Ministry of Justice, which resulted in the interrogation that, written down at the time, preserves her life story.

457.1————.

Her account printed on p. 235 in Beatriz Gallotti Mamigonian, "Conflicts over the Meanings of Freedom: The Liberated Africans' Struggle for Emancipation in Brazil, 1840s–1860s," pp. 235–264, in *Paths to Freedom: Manumission in the Atlantic World*, edited by Rosemary Brana-Shute and Randy J. Sparks.

Columbia [South Carolina, U.S.A.]: University of South Carolina Press, 2009.

8vo (24 cm.): viii, 397 p., illus.

1858

458.0 Ikubaje (ca. 1804–) = James Thomas

Manuscript journals and letters written by him are held in the Church Missionary Society Archives, Cadbury Research Library Special Collections, University of Birmingham (Birmingham, England) in the collection labelled: James Thomas, Letters and Journals, Niger Mission, CA3\038, 1858–1879.

Full text: https://huskiecommons.lib.niu.edu/history-500africanvoices/261/ [see 458.1].

¶ Ikubaje came from Eki-Bunu, near the confluence of the Niger and Benue Rivers (modern Nigeria—see Map 5). Aged about twenty, Ikubaje was kidnapped during a period of regional tension and warfare and taken to Aboh for about a year in 1834. Then he was sold to Bonny (southern Nigeria) and forced aboard a slave ship. After a British warship intercepted this ship at sea, Ikubaje and the others were taken to Sierra Leone (Map 4), where he remained for about twen-

ty-three years. While living in Sierra Leone, Ikubaje converted to Christianity, married, and had three children. In 1858 he began work as a missionary and British citizen in the Niger Mission in Gbebe/Lokoja, his homeland at the confluence of the Niger and Benue rivers. He knew the Nupe, Bassa, Eki, and English languages. He remained in the mission, keeping a journal and writing letters until 1879.

458.1 ————.

Extracts from journals published in Femi J. Kolapo, "The 1858–1859 Gbebe Journal of CMS Missionary James Thomas," *History in Africa*, 27: 159–192.

New York: Cambridge University Press, 2000.

458.2 ————.

Journals, letters, and reports 1858–1879 published as *The Journals of Church Missionary Society Agent, James Thomas, in Mid-Nineteenth-Century Nigeria*, edited by Femi J. Kolapo.

Lewiston, [New York, U.S.A.]: Edwin Mellen Press, 2013.

8vo (24 cm.): vii, 292 p., map.

1860

459.1 Laiguandai (ca. 1811-1859) = Peter Wilson

His account told in Eliza Wilson, *A Brief Memoir of the late Peter Wilson, Member of Kissy Road Church. By His Wife Eliza.*

[Freetown, Sierra Leone]: [*sine nomine*], 1860. Title page bordered by printed ornamental box-rule.
12mo: 6 p. Exemplar: Church Missionary Society (CMS) Archive (Cadbury Research Library Special

Full text: https://huskiecommons.lib.niu.edu/history-500africanvoices/262/ [see 459.1].

Collections, University of Birmingham, Birmingham, England), CMS Sierra Leone Mission CA1/O6/53.

¶ Laiguandai was a native Aku, that is Yorùbá (modern-day Nigeria, Benin and Togo—see Map 5), born in the town of Owu, near Lagos (modern Nigeria). He lost his father as an infant and was sold while young to Portuguese, who in 1824 took him on the slave ship *Anizo*, bound for Brazil with 465 enslaved people. Intercepted at sea by HMS *Maidstone*, they were taken to Sierra Leone (Map 4), a forty-three-day voyage, and liberated. Thereafter Laiguandai, aged thirteen, was apprenticed under the care of another liberated Aku. He subsequently worked eleven years as a domestic servant for a British official and became a sergeant in the Sierra Leone militia corps. He married in 1833 and had one child. In 1839 he was baptized and became a member of the church in Kissy, where he lived. His wife died in 1845, and he remarried the same year in Kissy. After brief employment in the Cape Lighthouse, he and his second wife moved to Freetown. Ca.

1854 he began a small trading business, which in 1859 took him for a few months to Lagos, where he revisited his early childhood home. After returning to Kissy his health declined. While Laiguandai lay on his deathbed, his wife wrote up this memoir from his notes.

1862

460.0 Manuela de la Guardia

Statement recorded on 26 November 1861 in Havana, Cuba, preserved in Archivo Nacional de la República de Cuba (ANC), **La Habana, Cuba,** Gobierno Superior Civil, 954/33678.

Full text: https://huskiecommons.lib.niu.edu/history-500african-voices/263/ [see 460.3].

¶ Manuela de la Guardia identified as Gangá (modern Banta region in southern Sierra Leone—see Map 4). After forced transport to the Spanish colony of Cuba in the Caribbean (Map 12) on a slave ship and sale, in 1859 her owner took her and José Ruiz (who was also enslaved) to the north of the United States (Map 16). While there he told them they were free because slavery was forbidden there. Thinking she would be free in Cuba as well, she and the other man returned with Ruiz to Cuba; but there her former owner reenslaved them at this home on Amargura Street in Havana. She therefore spoke with a government official, who ordered an investigation, which prompted her owner to have them both bound, taken home, and put in stocks, with a threat to send Manuela to the country for harsher work. Authorities then forced her owner to agree to *coartación*—a contract that would allow her to work toward freedom.

460.1———.

Statement printed on pp. 188–189 in *La esclavitud desde la esclavitud: La visión de los siervos* by Gloria García Rodríguez.

México [Distrito Federal, Estados Unidos Mexicanos]: Centro de Investigación Científica "Ing. Jorge L Tamayo," **1996.** 8vo (21 cm.): 251 p.

460.2———.

Statement printed on p. 169 in *La esclavitud desde la esclavitud*, by Gloria García.

La Habana [Cuba]: Editorial de Ciencias Sociales, 2003. 8vo (21 cm.): xx, 222 p.

460.3———.

English translation of statement printed on p. 162 and 202n2 in *Voices of the Enslaved in Nineteenth-Century Cuba: A*

Documentary History, edited by Gloria García Rodríguez. Translated [from 460.1] by Nancy L. Westrate; foreword by Ada Ferrer.

Chapel Hill [North Carolina, U.S.A.]: University of North Carolina Press, **2011.** 8vo (24 cm.): xviii, 220 p.

461.0 Manuel Congo

Statement recorded on 13 February 1862 in Havana, Cuba, preserved in Archivo Nacional de la República de Cuba (ANC), **La Habana, Cuba,** Gobierno Superior Civil, 954/33745.

Full text: https://huskiecommons.lib.niu.edu/history-500african-voices/264/ [see 461.3].

¶ Manuel identified as Congolese. After forced transport to the Spanish colony of Cuba in the Caribbean (see Map 12) on a slave ship and sale, by 1862 he lived in the city of Bejucal with his owner. In that he year he complained to authorities that while following the formal agreement (*coartacion*) to work off his appraised value and thus achieve his freedom, the syndic in charge of such matters for the government colluded with Manuel's owner to unfairly raise the price he had to pay and then did not properly handle the money he had already paid toward his freedom.

461.1———.

Statement printed on p. 165 in *La esclavitud desde la esclavitud: La visión de los siervos* by Gloria García Rodríguez.

México [Distrito Federal, Estados Unidos Mexicanos]: Centro de Investigación Científica "Ing. Jorge L Tamayo," **1996.** 8vo (21 cm.): 251 p.

461.2———.

Statement printed on p. 148 in *La esclavitud desde la esclavitud*, by Gloria García.

La Habana [Cuba]: Editorial de Ciencias Sociales, 2003. 8vo (21 cm.): xx, 222 p.

461.3————.

English translation of statement printed on p. 141 in *Voices of the Enslaved in Nineteenth-Century Cuba: A Documentary History*, edited by Gloria García Rodríguez. Translated [from 461.1] by Nancy L. Westrate; foreword by Ada Ferrer.

Chapel Hill [North Carolina, U.S.A.]: University of North Carolina Press, **2011.**
8vo (24 cm.): xviii, 220 p.

462.0 José Mina (ca. 1780–)

Statement recorded in Havana on 4 April 1862, preserved in Archivo Nacional de la República de Cuba (ANC), **La Habana, Cuba,** Gobierno Superior Civil, 943/33734.

¶ José identified as Mina (a New World ethnic designation for Akanspeakers near Elmina Castle, modern Ghana—see Map 5). After forced transport to the Spanish colony of Cuba in the Caribbean (Map 12) on a slave ship and sale, he still lived enslaved in Havana in 1862, more than fifty years after his arrival. During these decades he had saved five ounces in gold to purchase his freedom, yet although he was over 80, had asthma, a broken bone, and erysipelas on his legs (all which scarcely allowed him to work), they raised his appraised value, so that he must pay even more to acquire his freedom. The captain general was sympathetic and promised to have the situation rectified, if it proved to be true.

Full text: https://huskiecommons.lib.niu.edu/history-500africanvoices/265/ [see 462.3].

462.1————.

Statement printed on pp. 165–166 in *La esclavitud desde la esclavitud: La visión de los siervos* by Gloria García Rodríguez.

México [Distrito Federal, Estados Unidos Mexicanos]: Centro de Investigación Científica "Ing. Jorge L Tamayo," **1996.**
8vo (21 cm.): 251 p.

462.2————.

Statement printed on pp. 148–149 in *La esclavitud desde la esclavitud*, by Gloria García.

La Habana [Cuba]: Editorial de Ciencias Sociales, **2003.**
8vo (21 cm.): xx, 222 p.

462.3————.

English translation of statement printed on p. 141 and 201n10 in *Voices of the Enslaved in Nineteenth-Century Cuba: A Documentary History*, edited by Gloria García Rodríguez. Translated [from 462.1] by Nancy L. Westrate; foreword by Ada Ferrer.

Chapel Hill [North Carolina, U.S.A.]: University of North Carolina Press, **2011.**
8vo (24 cm.): xviii, 220 p.

1864

463.0 Manuel Valero

See manuscript recorded in Havana, Cuba, 13 June 1864, preserved in Archivo Nacional de la República de Cuba (ANC), **La Habana, Cuba,** Gobierno Superior Civil, 1056/37611.

¶ Manuel Valero identified as Congolese. He was forcibly taken on a slave ship to the Spanish colony of Cuba in the Caribbean (see Map 12) and in 1864 lived enslaved in the city of Santa María del Rosario. He was sold that year on the condition that he receive a pass monthly to visit his children and that he had the right to seek a new owner if dissatisfied with his situation. After his owner denied him both rights, he petitioned the court for help, either by forcing his owner to comply or allowing him to seek a new owner. His petition was rejected when his owner denied everything and claimed Valero had gone missing by early September.

Full text: https://huskiecommons.lib.niu.edu/history-500africanvoices/266/ [see 463.3].

463.1————.

Statement printed on p. 119 in *La esclavitud desde la esclavitud: La visión de los siervos* by Gloria García Rodríguez.

México [Distrito Federal, Estados Unidos Mexicanos]: Centro de Investigación Científica "Ing. Jorge L Tamayo," **1996.**
8vo (21 cm.): 251 p.

463.2————.

Statement printed on pp. 105–106 in *La esclavitud desde la esclavitud*, by Gloria García.

La Habana [Cuba]: Editorial de Ciencias Sociales, **2003.**
8vo (21 cm.): xx, 222 p.

463.3——.

English translation of statement printed on pp. 99–100 and 198n23 in *Voices of the Enslaved in Nineteenth-Century Cuba: A Documentary History*, edited by Gloria García Rodríguez. Translated [from 463.1] by Nancy L. Westrate; foreword by Ada Ferrer.

Chapel Hill [North Carolina, U.S.A.]: University of North Carolina Press, **2011**.
8vo (24 cm.): xviii, 220 p.

464.0 Emilio Piñeiro

See manuscript recorded in Havana, Cuba in December 1864, preserved in Archivo Nacional de la República de Cuba (ANC), **La Habana, Cuba,** Gobierno Superior Civil, 961/34046.

Full text: https://huskiecommons.lib.niu.edu/history-500african-voices/267/ [see 464.3].

¶ Emilio Piñeiro identified as Congolese. After forced transport to the Spanish colony of Cuba in the Caribbean (see Map 12) on a slave ship, he was sold at some point to Manuel Piñeiro, who owned a canteen on the Plaza del Cristo in Havana. After Emilio's lover won the lottery and gave him fifteen ounces of gold to begin the process toward self-purchase of his freedom, his owner refused to honor the agreement and had Emilio seized and taken to another district in Havana, where he was badly beaten several times. During the ordeal the gold in his waistband went missing. Emilio knew who took it and petitioned the court to help him get his gold back.

464.1——.

Statement printed on p. 119 in *La esclavitud desde la esclavitud: La visión de los siervos* by Gloria García Rodríguez.

México [Distrito Federal, Estados Unidos Mexicanos]: Centro de Investigación Científica "Ing. Jorge L Tamayo," **1996**.
8vo (21 cm.): 251 p.

464.2——.

Statement printed on pp. 106–107 in *La esclavitud desde la esclavitud*, by Gloria García.

La Habana [Cuba]: Editorial de Ciencias Sociales, **2003**.
8vo (21 cm.): xx, 222 p.

464.3——.

English translation of statement printed on pp. 100–101 in *Voices of the Enslaved in Nineteenth-Century Cuba: A Documentary History*, edited by Gloria García Rodríguez. Translated [from 464.1] by Nancy L. Westrate; foreword by Ada Ferrer.

Chapel Hill [North Carolina, U.S.A.]: University of North Carolina Press, **2011**.
8vo (24 cm.): xviii, 220 p.

465.0 Román Lucumí (ca. 1829–)

Confession recorded on 16 February 1864 in Cimirrones, Cuba, preserved in Archivo Nacional de la República de Cuba (ANC), **La Habana, Cuba,** Comisión Militar, 33/1.

Full text: https://huskiecommons.lib.niu.edu/history-500african-voices/268/ [see 465.3].

¶ Román identified as Lucumí, a New World ethnic identity attributed to Yorùbá people in modern day Nigeria, Benin, and Togo (see Map 5). After forced transport to the Spanish colony of Cuba in the Caribbean (Map 12) on a slave ship and sale, by 1864 he was single, worked enslaved on the *San José* estate near Cimirrones, and practiced herbal medicine. When interviewed by the authorities, Román confessed that two of the leaders of a rebellion had asked him to find plants in the scrub and prepare concoctions that would help the rebels succeed. Román did as they asked and sold the concoctions to other enslaved people (cf. similar work by Telésforo Lucumí, q.v. 466.0).

465.1——.

Statement printed on pp. 220–221 in *La esclavitud desde la esclavitud: La visión de los siervos* by Gloria García Rodríguez.

México [Distrito Federal, Estados Unidos Mexicanos]: Centro de Investigación Científica "Ing. Jorge L Tamayo," **1996**.
8vo (21 cm.): 251 p.

465.2——.

Statement printed on p. 197 in *La esclavitud desde la esclavitud*, by Gloria García.

La Habana [Cuba]: Editorial de Ciencias Sociales, **2003**.
8vo (21 cm.): xx, 222 p.

465.3——.

English translation of statement printed on p. 189 in *Voices of the Enslaved in Nineteenth-Century Cuba: A Documentary History*, edited by Gloria García Rodríguez. Translated [from 465.1] by Nancy L. Westrate; foreword by Ada Ferrer.

Chapel Hill [North Carolina, U.S.A.]: University of North Carolina Press, **2011**.
8vo (24 cm.): xviii, 220 p.

466.0 Telésforo Lucumí (ca. 1809–)

Confession recorded on 16 February 1864 in Cimirrones, Cuba, preserved in Archivo Nacional de la República de Cuba (ANC), **La Habana, Cuba,** Comisión Militar, 33/1.

¶ Telésforo identified as Lucumí, a New World ethnic identity attributed to Yorùbá people in modern-day Nigeria, Benin, and Togo (see Map 5). After forced transport to the Spanish colony of Cuba in the Caribbean (Map 12) on

Full text: https://huskiecommons.lib.niu.edu/history-500africanvoices/269/ [see 466.3].

a slave ship and sale, by 1864 he worked enslaved on the *San José* estate near Cimirrones. During the planning of a enslaved people's insurrection, he made talismans from roots, trees, cow horns, and leather, which he sold on credit to enslaved people from a neighboring plantation so they could fight more effectively in battle (cf. similar work by Román Lucumí, q.v. 465.0).

466.1———.

Statement printed on p. 220 in *La esclavitud desde la esclavitud: La visión de los siervos* by Gloria García Rodríguez.

México [Distrito Federal, Estados Unidos Mexicanos]: Centro de Investigación Científica "Ing. Jorge L Tamayo," 1996. 8vo (21 cm.): 251 p.

466.2———.

Statement printed on p. 197 in *La esclavitud desde la esclavitud*, by Gloria García.

La Habana [Cuba]: Editorial de Ciencias Sociales, 2003. 8vo (21 cm.): xx, 222 p.

466.3———.

English translation of statement printed on pp. 189–190 in *Voices of the Enslaved in Nineteenth-Century Cuba: A Documentary History*, edited by Gloria García Rodríguez. Translated [from 466.1] by Nancy L. Westrate; foreword by Ada Ferrer.

Chapel Hill [North Carolina, U.S.A.]: University of North Carolina Press, 2011. 8vo (24 cm.): xviii, 220 p.

467.0 Cristóbal Gangá (ca. 1824–)

Confession recorded on 16 February 1864 in Cimirrones, Cuba, preserved in Archivo Nacional de la República de Cuba (ANC), **La Habana, Cuba,** Comisión Militar, 33/1.

¶ Cristóbal identified as Gangá (modern Banta region in southern Sierra Leone—see Map 4). After forced transport

to the Spanish colony of Cuba in the Caribbean (Map 12) on a slave ship and sale, he worked enslaved on the *San José* estate near Cimirrones. Still single in 1864, he was one of the leaders of a planned rebellion of the area's enslaved people. At a subsequent hearing he confessed that he and others had planned a large-scale uprising, in which people from numerous estates (including those transported with them to Cuba who now worked in the warehouses near Camino de Hierro) would join forces. The rebels were almost ready to act when the authorities discovered the plot and arrested its leaders, including Cristóbal and Francisco Mina (q.v. 468.0).

Full text: https://huskiecommons.lib.niu.edu/history-500africanvoices/270/ [see 467.3].

467.1———.

Statement printed on pp. 220–221 in *La esclavitud desde la esclavitud: La visión de los siervos* by Gloria García Rodríguez.

México [Distrito Federal, Estados Unidos Mexicanos]: Centro de Investigación Científica "Ing. Jorge L Tamayo," 1996. 8vo (21 cm.): 251 p.

467.2———.

Statement printed on p. 198 in *La esclavitud desde la esclavitud*, by Gloria García.

La Habana [Cuba]: Editorial de Ciencias Sociales, 2003. 8vo (21 cm.): xx, 222 p.

467.3———.

English translation of statement printed on p. 190 in *Voices of the Enslaved in Nineteenth-Century Cuba: A Documentary History*, edited by Gloria García Rodríguez. Translated [from 467.1] by Nancy L. Westrate; foreword by Ada Ferrer.

Chapel Hill [North Carolina, U.S.A.]: University of North Carolina Press, 2011. 8vo (24 cm.): xviii, 220 p.

468.0 Francisco Mina (ca. 1832-1864)

Confession recorded on 16 February 1864 in Cimirrones, Cuba, preserved in Archivo Nacional de la República de Cuba (ANC), **La Habana, Cuba,** Comisión Militar, 33/1.

¶ Francisco identified as Mina (a New World ethnic designation for Akanspeakers near Elmina Castle, modern Ghana—see Map 5). After forced transport to the Spanish colony of Cuba in the Caribbean (Map 12) on a slave ship and sale, he worked enslaved as a field hand on the *Asuncion* sugar plantation near Cimirrones. In 1864 he became involved in the planning of a large-scale uprising by his region's enslaved people. At a subsequent hearing he explained that Pancho Gangá was their "king," and he himself was the chief captain. He was going to a night meeting to finish planning the uprising when authorities seized them. Their plan was to kill all their owners on their farm, set fire to the sugar cane and factories, and then travel the *Camino de Hierro* that cut through the farm, in order to join other rebels and continue fighting against local owners. During the lengthy legal proceedings, Francisco was one of the seven conspirators who died while in custody.

468.1———.

Statement printed on p. 221 in *La esclavitud desde la esclavitud: La visión de los siervos* by Gloria García Rodríguez.

Full text: https://huskiecommons.lib.niu.edu/history-500african-voices/271/ [see 468.3].

México [Distrito Federal, Estados Unidos Mexicanos]: Centro de Investigación Científica "Ing. Jorge L Tamayo," **1996.** 8vo (21 cm.): 251 p.

468.2———.

Statement printed on pp. 198–199 in *La esclavitud desde la esclavitud,* by Gloria García.

La Habana [Cuba]: Editorial de Ciencias Sociales, **2003.** 8vo (21 cm.): xx, 222 p.

468.3———.

English translation of statement printed on p. 191 in *Voices of the Enslaved in Nineteenth-Century Cuba: A Documentary History,* edited by Gloria García Rodríguez. Translated [from 468.1] by Nancy L. Westrate; foreword by Ada Ferrer.

Chapel Hill [North Carolina, U.S.A.]: University of North Carolina Press, **2011.** 8vo (24 cm.): xviii, 220 p.

1866

469.0 Dolores Roca

Manuscript recorded in Havana, Cuba, 30 August 1866, preserved in Archivo Nacional de la República de Cuba (ANC), **La Habana, Cuba,** Gobierno Superior Civil, 967/34139.

¶ Dolores Roco was African but did not say from where. After forced transport to the Spanish colony of Cuba in the Caribbean (see Map 12) on a slave ship, she reacquired her freedom and lived as a free *morena* (person of color) in Havana. In 1866 she petitioned the court for aid to help her enslaved daughter be appraised for resale to another owner, as per the daughter's right, because of the abuse she was then suffering. After journeying to Corral Falso, the distant district of the city where her daughter was enslaved, and paying a large court fee and living expenses, her case was continually delayed rather than resolved. According to one account she worked as a laundress during the ordeal.

469.1———.

Statement printed on pp. 120–121 in *La esclavitud desde la esclavitud: La visión de los siervos* by Gloria García Rodríguez.

México [Distrito Federal, Estados Unidos Mexicanos]: Centro de Investigación Científica "Ing. Jorge L Tamayo," **1996.** 8vo (21 cm.): 251 p.

Full text: https://huskiecommons.lib.niu.edu/history-500african-voices/272/ [see 469.3].

469.2———.

Statement printed on pp. 107–108 in *La esclavitud desde la esclavitud: La visión de los siervos,* by Gloria García Rodríguez.

La Habana [Cuba]: Editorial de Ciencias Sociales, **2003.** 8vo (21 cm.): xx, 222 p.

469.3———.

English translation of statement printed on pp. 101–102 in *Voices of the Enslaved in Nineteenth-Century Cuba: A Documentary History,* edited by Gloria García Rodríguez. Translated [from 469.1] by Nancy L. Westrate; foreword by Ada Ferrer.

Chapel Hill [North Carolina, U.S.A.]: University of North Carolina Press, **2011.** 8vo (24 cm.): xviii, 220 p.

470.0 Antonio Quesada (ca. 1799–)

Statement recorded in Havana on 21 November 1866, preserved in Archivo Nacional de la República de Cuba (ANC), **La Habana, Cuba,** Gobierno Superior Civil, 968/34190.

¶ Antonio Quesada identified as Congolese. After forced transport on a slave ship to the Spanish colony of Cuba in the Caribbean (see Map 12), he was sold and resold, eventually in 1856 with a *coartado* contract for 300 pesos to Don Carlos Marazo. Antonio always paid the amount due on time until he developed dropsy and a vision problem in

1864. Seeing it would be a long illness, his owner stopped paying his medical bills and would not send him to hospital. Apparently to win sympathy, in 1866 Antonio told authorities that he wished to sell himself as a field hand, although he had no experience. He then asked other Congolese for help, and the *capataz* of the Congo nation in Havana agreed to contribute 100 pesos toward his freedom and to help Antonio during his convalescence.

Full text: https://huskiecommons.lib.niu.edu/history-500african-voices/273/ [see 470.3].

470.1———.

Statement printed on p. 168 in *La esclavitud desde la esclavitud: La visión de los siervos* by Gloria García Rodríguez.

México [Distrito Federal, Estados Unidos Mexicanos]: Centro de Investigación Científica "Ing. Jorge L Tamayo," 1996.

8vo (21 cm.): 251 p.

470.2———.

Statement printed on pp. 150–151 in *La esclavitud desde la esclavitud*, by Gloria García.

La Habana [Cuba]: Editorial de Ciencias Sociales, 2003. 8vo (21 cm.): xx, 222 p.

470.3———.

English translation of statement printed on pp. 143–144 in *Voices of the Enslaved in Nineteenth-Century Cuba: A Documentary History*, edited by Gloria García Rodríguez. Translated [from 470.1] by Nancy L. Westrate; foreword by Ada Ferrer.

Chapel Hill [North Carolina, U.S.A.]: University of North Carolina Press, 2011. 8vo (24 cm.): xviii, 220 p.

1870-71

471.1 Sitiki (ca. 1795-1882) = Jack Smith = Uncle Jack

Account Sitiki dictated to Buckingham Smith in 1870-71, first published as *The Odyssey of an African Slave, by Sitiki*, edited by Patricia C. Griffin.

Gainesville [Florida, U.S.A.]: University Press of Florida, 2009.
8vo (24 cm.): xii, 211 p., illus.
Note: Since the first publication of this work is recent and the entire book is Sitiki's account, a link to the full text of this work cannot be made available as part of this project. Readers are encouraged to obtain either edition of the book to read Sitiki's account.

¶ Sitiki, son of a male cotton weaver, was born in an interior western African country, possibly in a walled town called Mora or Moria (near Fuuta Jallon in modern Guinea – see Map 3). He learned Arabic and remembered many details, although only four or five years old when he and his family were captured in a raid (in which his father was probably killed). He was then taken to Seko or Sulko, where he remained enslaved and tended sheep. He never saw his family again. Eventually he was taken to the coast, passing through a Fulah (Fula, Fulbi or Peul peoples throughout West Africa) camp and Kissi to an "English slave factory," where he labored as a house servant near Jolof and the Gambia River (modern Senegal) from 1801 to 1807. Ca. 1807 he was put on a British slave ship bound for Charleston, South Carolina (U.S.A.) – see Map 15, sold to its master, and served as a cabin boy. The captain took him to Savannah, Georgia, and sold him to a merchant

there in 1808. Sitiki assisted in the merchant's store and accompanied him to Connecticut (Map 17), where he learned to read, before returning to St. Mary's, Georgia, and then Cumberland Island (part of Camden County, on the Georgia coast) in 1810. During a British attack in 1814, Sitiki's owner fled to Spanish Florida, leaving Sitiki behind. In 1817, Sitiki moved with his owner to St. Augustine, Florida. Later he embraced Christianity and began preaching. After emancipation at the end of the Civil War, he continued to live in St. Augustine until his death in 1882. A depiction of Sitiki and his cabin without any presence of Sitiki's voice is printed on p. 170 in Constance Fenimore Woolson, "The Ancient City, In Two Parts, Part II," *Harper's New Monthly Magazine* 50 (January 1875): 165-185, which is available here:

http://www.unz.com/print/Harpers-1875jan-00165/

471.2———.

Account Sitiki dictated to Buckingham Smith in 1870-71, reprinted from 471.1 as *The Odyssey of an African Slave, by Sitiki*, edited by Patricia C. Griffin.

Gainesville [Florida, U.S.A.]: University Press of Florida, 2015. 8vo (23 cm.): xii, 211 p., illus.

472.1 Poli (ca. 1795-1880) = Judie Smith

Account embedded within Sitiki's account (q.v. 471.1) dictated to Buckingham Smith in 1870–71 first printed on pp. 17–18 in *The Odyssey of an African Slave, by Sitiki*, edited by Patricia C. Griffin.

Gainesville [Florida, U.S.A.]: University Press of Florida, 2009.
8vo (24 cm.): xii, 211 p., illus.

¶ In this embedded account Poli explained that she was from a town called Mayon in West Africa (exactly where is unknown) and was captured with her brother in wartime by a neighboring enemy. Several years later she was taken to the coast and forced aboard a slave ship bound for Charleston, South Carolina (U.S.A.)—see Map 15, where she was separated from her brother forever, then transported to Savannah, Georgia,

Full text: https://huskiecommons.lib.niu.edu/history-500african-voices/281/ [see 472.1].

and sold there. In 1808, aged thirteen and enslaved to the same merchant as Sitiki (q.v. 471.1 above), she tended this merchant's children. After the War of 1812, she moved to St. Augustine, Florida, and may have married Sitiki. She became a Methodist, was emancipated during the Civil War, and lived the rest of her life in St. Augustine.

472.2———.

Account embedded within Sitiki's account (q.v. 471.1) dictated to Buckingham Smith in 1870–71 reprinted from 472.1 on pp. 17–18 in *The Odyssey of an African Slave, by Sitiki*, edited by Patricia C. Griffin.

Gainesville [Florida, U.S.A.]: University Press of Florida, 2015.
8vo (23 cm.): xii, 211 p., illus.

1897

¶ Note for entries 473 through 476. These brief accounts are responses to Henry Romeyn's questions to survivors of the *Clotilda*, the last slave ship that entered the United States (illegally, in 1860, near Mobile, Alabama, U.S.A.—see Map 15). Romeyn interviewed these survivors in June 1896 and noted they most regularly spoke their native language but also spoke English well enough to communicate with him. See Sylviane A. Diouf, *Dreams of Africa in Alabama: The Slave Ship Clotilda and the Story of the Last Africans Brought to America* (New York: Oxford University Press, 2009).

473.1   Zuma

Brief responses to questions asked by Henry Romeyn, incorporated in Romeyn's article "'Little Africa': The Last Slave Cargo Landed in the United States," *The Southern Workman and Hampton School Record*, 26:1: 14–17, especially 16.

Hampton, Virginia [U.S.A.]: The Hampton Institute, January 1897.

Full text: https://huskiecommons.lib.niu.edu/history-500african-voices/274/ [see 473.1].

¶ Zuma came from Loandi (likely Louzani Borgu in modern northern Benin—see Map 5). She was captured and sold twice before being taken to Ouidah (Benin) and put on the slave ship *Clotilda*, which illegally took her to its home port in Mobile Bay, Alabama (U.S.A.)—Map 15, in 1860. She was emancipated in 1865, after the Civil War, and lived in Africatown, near Mobile, when interviewed in 1897.

474.1   Maum Pólee (1840–)

Brief responses to questions asked by Henry Romeyn, incorporated in Romeyn's article "'Little Africa': The Last Slave Cargo Landed in the United States," *The Southern Workman and Hampton School Record*, 26:1: 14–17, especially 16.

Hampton, Virginia [U.S.A.]: The Hampton Institute, January 1897.

Full text: https://huskiecommons.lib.niu.edu/history-500african-voices/275/ [see 474.1].

¶ Maum Pólee came from a "long way from Dahomey," according to Romeyn, probably from around Lake Chad (modern Chad, Nigeria, and Cameroon border—see Map 5). She was nineteen years old when captured, transported to Ouidah (modern coastal Benin), and forced aboard the slave ship *Clotilda*, which illegally took her to its home port in Mobile Bay, Alabama (U.S.A.)—Map 15, in 1860. She was emancipated in 1865, after the Civil War, and lived in Africatown, near Mobile, when interviewed in 1897.

475.1   Peter Goolth

Brief responses to questions asked by Henry Romeyn, incorporated in Romeyn's article "'Little Africa': The Last Slave Cargo Landed in the United States," *The Southern Workman and Hampton School Record*, 26:1: 14–17, especially 16.

Hampton, Virginia [U.S.A.]: The Hampton Institute, January 1897.

¶ Goolth came from Dahomey (modern Benin—see Map 5) and was regarded as a headman, in the middle of his life, when "stolen by his king" and sold at Ouidah (modern coastal Benin) to the captain of the slave ship *Clotilda*, which illegally took him to its home port Mobile Bay, Alabama (U.S.A.) in 1860 (Map 15). He was emancipated in 1865, after the Civil War, and lived in Africatown, near Mobile, when interviewed in 1897.

Full text: https://huskiecommons.lib.niu.edu/history-500african-voices/276/ [see 475.1].

476.1 Unnamed woman from Dahomey

Brief responses to questions asked by Henry Romeyn, incorporated in Romeyn's article "'Little Africa': The Last Slave Cargo Landed in the United States," *The Southern Workman and Hampton School Record*, 26:1: 14–17, especially 16.

Hampton, Virginia [U.S.A.]: The Hampton Institute, January 1897.

¶ This woman also came from Dahomey (modern Benin—see Map 5) and was captured in a raid, taken to Ouidah (modern coastal Benin) and sold to the captain of the slave ship *Clotilda*, which illegally took her to its home port in Mobile Bay, Alabama (U.S.A.) in 1860 (Map 15). She was emancipated in 1865, after the Civil War, and lived in Africatown, near Mobile, when interviewed in 1897.

Full text: https://huskiecommons.lib.niu.edu/history-500african-voices/277/ [see 476.1].

1904

477.1 Cilucǎngy (1845?–1914?) = Ward Lee

His account printed as one-paragraph mendicant circular (plus date-line, salutation, and closing) headed "Trenton, S. C., Sept. 14, 1904 | *To the Public*:" and closing "Yours truly, Ward Lee."

[Trenton?, South Carolina, U.S.A.]: [Unnamed job printer for Ward Lee], 1904.
Small handbill: [1] p., verso blank.
  Nota bene: Entry posited from 477.2; no exemplar located.
  *Life dates tentatively posited from the gravestone for Ward Lee in the Mount Canaan Baptist Church Cemetery, Trenton, Edgefield County, South Carolina, U.S.A.

¶ Cilucǎngy came from a village called Cowǎny in a mountainous region, probably the Madimba district on the Mbidizi River, near the Kongo capital city at the time of São Salvador (today Mbanga Kongo) deep in the interior of West Central Africa (see Map 6). The king was named Mfǒtila. Cilucǎngy's mother lived in Colombǎndy. Cilucǎngy was enslaved as a child, probably during the civil war then raging, and in 1858 transported illegally on the United States–based slave ship *Wanderer* from the mouth of the Congo River to Jekyll Island, Georgia (U.S.A.)—Map 15. Along with about

https://digitalcollections.nypl.org/items/510d47e4-5fc2-a3d9-e040-e00a18064a99 [see 477.1].

170 other enslaved passengers he was then sent by steamboat up the Savannah River to a plantation on the South Carolina side of the river two miles below Augusta, Georgia. There he was sold. After emancipation in 1865, he remained in the area. According to Charles J. Montgomery (in 477.2), Cilucǎngy converted to Christianity in 1904, having been known for some time as Ward Lee, and published a circular (477.1) soliciting money to finance his return to Africa. John K. Thornton notes, however, that his home region in the Kongo had converted to Christianity long before this period (unpublished paper noted below). In 1908, when interviewed by Charles J. Montgomery (see 477.2), Cilucǎngy was still in Edgefield County, South Carolina, remembered much about his homeland, and spoke its language fluently. For the larger context of his forced transportation to the United States see Erik Calonius, *The Wanderer: The Last American Slave Ship and the Conspiracy That Set Its Sails* (New York: St. Martin's Press, 2006). See also The Wanderer Project at https://thewandererproject.wordpress.com/. *The compilers thank John K. Thornton for sharing an unpublished manuscript that supplements and corrects Montgomery's work on the origins of Cilucǎngy and other enslaved* Wanderer *passengers.*

Note: John Thornton (unpublished manuscript received by present compilers 30 April 2020) thinks that the men Montgomery interviewed contributed to the Edgefield Pottery Works in South Carolina, which produced a peculiar genre of ceramic called "Jug Face." Their language, with one exception, was Kikongo, and the villages to which Cilucängy referred were along the Bēzy River (or Mbidizi River, sometimes called M'bridge on old maps of Angola). Their region was the Madimba district, which at the time included the Kongo capital of São Salvador (today Mbanga Kongo). This district was just south of the capital, on the southern border of the Mbidizi River. A civil war raged there in 1857–58, when the *Wanderer* captives were taken, and they were probably victims.

477.2——.

His account reprinted in full from an exemplar of 477.1 on p. 621, with added details of his life on p. 614 (and photographic portrait of him between p. 612 and 613) in Charles J. Montgomery, "Survivors from the Cargo of the Negro Slave Yacht *Wanderer*," *American Anthropologist*. n.s. 10:4: pp. 611–623.

Lancaster, Pennsylvania [U.S.A.]: American Anthropological Association, 1908. Tpv: Press of the New Era Printing Company, Lancaster, Pa.

https://digitalcollections.nypl.org/items/510d47e4-5fc2-a3d9-e040-e00a18064a99

477.3——.

477.1 reprinted from 477.2 with one ellipsis and without date-line, salutation, or closing on p. 253 in Erik Calonius, *The Wanderer: The Last American Slave Ship and the Conspiracy That Set Its Sails.*

New York, [New York, U.S.A.]: St. Martin's Press, [2006]. 8vo (24.3 cm.): xiv, [4], 298 p., map, plates.

477.4——. [Second printing of 477.3]

477.1 reprinted from 477.2 with one ellipsis and without dateline, salutation, or closing on p. 253 in Erik Calonius, *The Wanderer: The Last American Slave Ship and the Conspiracy That Set Its Sails.*

New York, [New York, U.S.A.]: St. Martin's Press; **Godalming [Surrey, England]:** Melia [distributors], 2008. 8vo (21 cm.): xiv, [4], 298 p., map, plates.

1906

¶ Note for entries 478 and 479. These brief accounts were included by Samuel H. M. Byers in "The Last Slave-Ship" after he interviewed Gossalow, his wife (whose answers were either negligible or insufficiently recorded by Byers), and Abacky, all survivors of the *Clotilda*, the last ship to (illegally) import enslaved African-born women and men into the United States of America in 1860 (in this case, 116 enslaved women and men from West Africa to Mobile Bay, Alabama—see Map 15).

478.1 Abacky

One of three brief life stories (the third of which we have not accorded a discrete catalogue entry for reasons stated in the lead note above) in Samuel Hawkins Marshall Byers, "The Last Slave-Ship," *Harper's Monthly Magazine* 113: 742–746, especially 742–43.

https://www.unz.com/print/Harpers-1906oct-00742/ [see 478.1].

New York [New York, U.S.A.]: Harper & Brothers, Publishers, October 1906.

¶ Abacky came from a village called Ataka (possibly Atakora in modern northwestern Benin—see Map 5) and farmed until captured with others in a raid by Dahomean soldiers, who burned down their village and transported them to Ouidah (modern coastal Benin) for sale. Abacky was sold to men on the United States–based slave ship *Clotilda* and taken illegally to Mobile Bay, Alabama (U.S.A.) in 1860 (Map 15). She was emancipated in 1865, after the Civil War, and lived in Africatown, near Mobile, Alabama, when interviewed by Byers in 1906.

479.1 Gossalow (ca. 1836–)

One of three brief life stories (the third of which, for Gossalow's wife by her own account, we have not accorded a discrete catalogue entry for reasons stated in the lead note above) in Samuel Hawkins Marshall Byers, "The Last Slave Ship," *Harper's Monthly Magazine* 113: 742–746, especially 742–43.

https://www.unz.com/print/Harpers-1906oct-00742/ [see 479.1].

New York [New York, U.S.A.]: Harper & Brothers, Publishers, October 1906.

¶ Gossalow and his wife (for whom there is no discrete catalog entry) came from Whinney (modern southern Benin—see Map 5). They were enslaved, taken to Ouidah (modern coastal Benin), and sold to men on the United States–based slave ship *Clotilda*, which transported them illegally to Mobile Bay, Alabama (U.S.A.) in 1860 (Map 15). Gossalow and his wife were emancipated in 1865, after the Civil War, and lived in Africatown, near Mobile, Alabama when interviewed by Byers in 1906.

1908

¶ Note for entries 480 to 485. These accounts are from survivors of the United States–based slave ship *Wanderer*, which in 1858 illegally transported enslaved people from the mouth of the Congo River to Jekyll Island, Georgia (U.S.A.)— see Map 15. Along with about 170 other enslaved passengers, they were then taken by steamboat up the Savannah River and sold. Emancipated at the end of the US Civil War in 1865, they remained in the area. In 1908 the anthropologist Charles J. Montgomery interviewed and photographed them. For the larger context of this forced transportation to the United States, see Erik Calonius, *The Wanderer: The Last American Slave Ship and the Conspiracy That Set Its Sails* (New York: St. Martin's Press, 2006). See also The Wanderer Project at https://thewandererproject.wordpress.com/.

480.1 Zow Uncola = Tom Johnson

Autobiographical paragraph printed on p. 613 (with photographic portrait of him between p. 612 and 613) in Charles J. Montgomery, "Survivors from the Cargo of the Negro Slave Yacht *Wanderer*," *American Anthropologist*, n.s. 10:4: 611–623.

Lancaster, Pennsylvania [U.S.A.]: American Anthropological Association, 1908. Tpv: Press of the New Era Printing Company, Lancaster, Pa.

https://digitalcollections.nypl.org/items/510d47e4-5fc2-a3d9-e040-e00a18064a99 [see 480.1].

¶ Zow Uncola came from a coastal area, probably the Soyo province south of the Congo River in modern Angola (according to John Thornton's correction of Charles J. Montgomery's speculation; see 480.1 note following biographical paragraph)—see Map 6. After transport in 1858 on the slave ship *Wanderer* from the mouth of the Congo River to Jekyll Island, Georgia (U.S.A.) and then by steamboat with others to a plantation on the South Carolina side of the river two miles below Augusta, Georgia (see lead note), he was sold (Map 15). After emancipation in 1865, Uncola remained in the area. When interviewed by Charles J. Montgomery in 1908 he lived in Aiken County, SC.

481.1 Manchuella = Katie Noble

Autobiographical paragraph printed on p. 613 (with photographic portrait of her between p. 612 and 613) in Charles J. Montgomery, "Survivors from the Cargo of the Negro Slave Yacht *Wanderer*," *American Anthropologist* n.s. 10:4: 611–623.

Lancaster, Pennsylvania [U.S.A.]: American Anthropological Association, 1908. Tpv: Press of the New Era Printing Company, Lancaster, Pa.

¶ Manchuella came from a mountainous region, probably the Madimba district on the Mbidizi River, near the Kongo capital city at the time of São Salvador (today Mbanga Kongo) deep in the interior of West Central Africa (see Map 6). She was "practically grown" when enslaved and in 1858 transported on the *Wanderer* from the mouth of the Congo River to Jekyll Island, Georgia (U.S.A.)— Map 15. She and her child, along with about 170 other enslaved passengers, were then sent by steamboat up the Savannah River to a plantation on the South Carolina side of the river two miles below Augusta, Georgia, where she was sold (see collective lead note before item 480.1). After emancipation in 1865, Manchuella remained in the area. When interviewed by Charles Montgomery in 1908 she lived in Edgefield County, SC.

https://digitalcollections.nypl.org/items/510d47c4-5fc2-a3d9-e040-e00a18064a99 [see 481.1].

482.1 Mabiala = Uster Williams

Autobiographical paragraph printed on p. 614 (with photographic portrait of him between p. 612 and 613) in Charles J. Montgomery, "Survivors from the Cargo of the Negro Slave Yacht *Wanderer*," *American Anthropologist*, n.s. 10:4: pp. 611–623.

Lancaster, Pennsylvania [U.S.A.]: American Anthropological Association, 1908. Tpv: Press of the New Era Printing Company, Lancaster, Pa.

https://digitalcollections.nypl.org/items/510d47e4-5fc2-a3d9-e040-e00a18064a99 [see 482.1].

¶ Mabiala came from a mountainous region, probably the Madimba district on the Mbidizi River, near the Kongo capital city at the time of São Salvador (modern Mbanga Kongo) deep in the interior of West Central Africa (see Map 6). He was enslaved and in 1858 taken on the slave ship *Wanderer* from the mouth of the Congo River to Jekyll Island, Georgia (U.S.A.), then by steamboat with others up the Savannah River to a plantation on the South Carolina side of the river two miles below Augusta, Georgia (see collective lead note before item 480.1), where he was sold (Map 15). After emancipation in 1865, Mabiala remained in the area. When interviewed by Montgomery in 1908, he was blind and lived in a Richmond County, Georgia home for sick and elderly, near Augusta. His memory of Africa, including language and customs, was remarkable, Montgomery wrote.

483.1 Lucy Lanham (1854?–1914?)

Autobiographical paragraph printed on p. 614 (with photographic portrait of her between p. 612 and 613) in Charles J. Montgomery, "Survivors from the Cargo of the Negro Slave Yacht *Wanderer*," *American Anthropologist*, n.s. 10:4: pp. 611–623.

Lancaster, Pennsylvania [U.S.A.]: American Anthropological Association, 1908. Tpv: Press of the New Era Printing Company, Lancaster, Pa.

*Life dates tentatively posited from Lucy Lanham's gravestone in Science Hill Missionary Baptist Church Cemetery, Trenton, Edgefield County, South Carolina, U.S.A.

https://digitalcollections.nypl.org/items/510d47e4-5fc2-a3d9-e040-e00a18064a99 [see 483.1].

¶ Lanham came from a mountainous region, probably the Madimba district on the Mbidizi River, near the Kongo capital city at the time of São Salvador (modern Mbanga Kongo) deep in the interior of West Central Africa (see Map 6). She was enslaved as a small child and in 1858 transported on the slave ship *Wanderer* from the mouth of the Congo River to Jekyll Island, Georgia (U.S.A.), then by steamboat with others up the Savannah River to a plantation on the South Carolina side of the river two miles below Augusta, Georgia (see collective lead note before item 480.1), where she was sold (Map 15). After emancipation in 1865, Lanham remained in the area. When interviewed by Charles Montgomery in 1908 she lived in Edgefield County, SC, on the plantation of US Senator Benjamin "Pitchfork" Tillman.

484.1 Pucka Geata = Tucker Henderson

Life details printed on p. 614 and 615 (with photographic portrait of him with two others between p. 614 and 615) in Charles J. Montgomery, "Survivors from the Cargo of the Negro Slave Yacht *Wanderer*," *American Anthropologist* n.s. 10:4: 611–623.

Lancaster, Pennsylvania [U.S.A.]: American Anthropological Association, 1908. Tpv: Press of the New Era Printing Company, Lancaster, Pa.

https://digitalcollections.nypl.org/items/510d47e4-5fc2-a3d9-e040-e00a18064a99 [see 484.1].

¶ Pucka Geata came from a mountainous region, probably the Madimba district on the Mbidizi River, near the Kongo capital city at the time of São Salvador (modern Mbanga Kongo) deep in the interior of West Central Africa (see Map 6). He was enslaved and in 1858 transported on the slave ship *Wanderer* from the mouth of the Congo River to Jekyll Island, Georgia (U.S.A.), then by steamboat with others up the Savannah River to a plantation in Aiken County, South Carolina, two miles below Augusta, Georgia (see collective lead note before item 480.1), where he was sold (Map 15). After emancipation in 1865, Geata remained in the area. When interviewed by Charles Montgomery in 1908 he lived in Augusta.

485.1 Tahro = Romeo

Life details printed on p. 614 (with photographic portrait of him with two others between p. 614 and 615, as well as photographs of the house he built between p. 616 and 617 and between p. 618 and 619) in Charles J. Montgomery, "Survivors from the Cargo of the Negro Slave Yacht *Wanderer*," *American Anthropologist* n.s. 10:4: pp. 611–623.

Lancaster, Pennsylvania [U.S.A.]: American Anthropological Association, 1908. Tpv: Press of the New Era Printing Company, Lancaster, Pa.

https://digitalcollections.nypl.org/items/510d47e4-5fc2-a3d9-e040-e00a18064a99

¶ Tahro came from a mountainous region, probably the Madimba district on the Mbidizi River, near the Kongo capital city at the time of São Salvador (modern Mbanga Kongo) deep in the interior of West Central Africa, where his home was in Kuluwäka (see Map 6). As a grown man, he was enslaved and in 1858 transported on the slave ship *Wanderer* from the mouth of the Congo River to Jekyll Island, Georgia (U.S.A.), then by steamboat with others up the Savannah River to a plantation in Aiken County, South Carolina, two miles below Augusta, Georgia (see collective lead note before item 480.1), where he was sold (Map 15). After emancipation, he remained in the area and in Edgefield County, SC, where he built a house that Charles Montgomery photographed when interviewing him in 1908. When interviewed, Romeo (as he had been known for some time) remembered much about his homeland and was fluent in the language.

Figure 19: Photograph of house built by Tahro, also known as Romeo, in Edgefield County, South Carolina. In 1858 he was transported illegally on the *Wanderer* to Georgia (USA) from his home on the Mbidizi River, near São Salvador (modern Mbanga Kongo), then the Kongo capital city. He lived in the house when interviewed and photographed in 1908.

Source: Charles J. Montgomery, "Survivors from the Negro Slave Yacht *Wanderer*," *American Anthropologist* n.s. 10:4 (Oct-Dec 1908): 611–623, here following p. 616.

1910

486.1 André do Amaral (1782–)

Account printed under headline "Um Ancestral" on p. 1, column 7, of the 8 July 1910 issue of the newspaper *A Província do Pará*, anno 35, no. 10, 648.

Belém do Pará, Brazil, July 8, 1910.
Broadsheet newspaper. FN00447.

Full text: https://hus-kiecommons.lib.niu.edu/history-500afri-canvoices/278/ [see 486.1].

¶ By his own account Amaral was born in Africa in 1782, but he does not specify where. In 1822 he was taken prisoner, sold as a slave, and taken on a slave ship to Brazil (see Map 9). There he lived and worked on José do Amaral's farm from 1822 to 1860, when he was sold to Francisco Balduino, for whom he labored while enslaved until general emancipation in Brazil in 1888. Our source described him living in excellent physical and spiritual condition in Capivary, São Paulo, at the unlikely age of 128.

1914

487.1 Kossola (1841-1935) = Cudjo Lewis

Reminiscences of Kossola incorporated within pp. 76–126 of Emma Langdon Roche, *Historic Sketches of the South*.

New York [New York, U.S.A.]: Knickerbocker Press, **1914**.
8vo (21 cm.): iii, [2], 148 p., plates, including portrait.
Note: Kossola's is the only African voice given a substantial enough hearing (and ink) by Roche to warrant inclusion in this catalog.

https://archive.org/details/historicsketche00rochgoog [see 487.1].

¶ Kossola was Yorùbá (ethnic group, modern-day Nigeria, Benin, and Togo—see Map 5). His father had three wives, and he was the third of nine children by the first wife. He learned to hunt and trained to be a warrior. Captured at age nineteen with others by Dahomean (modern Benin) warriors, he was marched through Eko (Lagos, modern Nigeria), Budigree (Badagry, modern Nigeria), and Adaché (Porto Novo, Benin) to a barracoon at Ouidah (modern coastal Benin). After three weeks there he was sold to the captain of the slave ship *Clotilda* (the last slave ship to enter the U.S.A.), which illegally transported Kossola and 115 others to its home port in Mobile Bay, Alabama, U.S.A., in 1860 (Map 15). He was liberated by Union soldiers at the end of the US Civil War on 12 April 1865. With other *Clotilda* survivors, Kossola helped found the settlement of Africatown, which still exists near Mobile. He married an African woman and converted to Christianity. In 1902 he was badly injured when a train hit the buggy he was driving. No longer capable of heavy labor, he worked as sexton in Africatown's church. Two of his sons were killed before his wife left him in 1908. In short order another son died. Kossola lived on, alone. Many still and motion picture photographs of Kossola are extant; for the latter see "Zora Neale Hurston's Fieldwork Footage (1928)" and National Film Preservation Foundation, *More Treasures from American Film Archives, 1894–1931*. For more on enslaved Africans transported aboard the *Clotilda*, see Sylviane A. Diouf, *Dreams of Africa in Alabama: The Slave Ship Clotilda and the Story of the Last Africans Brought to America* (New York: Oxford University Press, 2009).

Note: In addition to the publications listed here, many periodical articles about Kossola were published containing factual errors or, in the case of an 1887 *Harper's Weekly* article, only a short quotation or two from Kossola. As shown throughout the present catalog, more often than not many variant editions of *one* account by a given African achieved publication; but in the case of Kossola's story, several writers working over the course of many years *interviewed* one African, Kossola, and from his words composed several variant accounts more or less attributable to him. Two writers who produced significant accounts capturing what may well be Kossola's voice are Emma Langdon Roche (487.1) and Zora Neale Hurston (487.2 et seq.), with Hurston herself publishing several differing accounts (some distorted, according to Sylviane Diouf).

487.2——.

Kossola's reminiscences retold in Zora Neale Hurston's article "Cudjo's Own Story of the Last African Slaver" in the *Journal of Negro History*, vol. 12, no. 4: 647–663.

New York and Washington, DC [U.S.A.]: United Publishing Corporation, October **1927**.
Hogg 1559.

487.3——.

Excerpts from interviews with Kossola included on pp. 144–149 in Zora Neale Hurston, *Dust Tracks on a Road: an Autobiography*.

Philadelphia [Pennsylvania, U.S.A.]: J. B. Lippincott, [**1942**].
8vo (21 cm.): 294 p.

487.4——.

Excerpts from interviews with Kossola included in Zora Neale Hurston, *Dust Tracks on a Road: an Autobiography*.

London [England]: Hutchinson, **1944**.
8vo (22 cm.): 148 p.

487.5——.

Zora Neale Hurston's elaborations (some involving artistic license; cf. 487.2, 487.3, and 487.4) of the life story she heard directly from Kossola included in her article "The Last Slave Ship," printed on pp. 351–358 in the magazine *The American Mercury*, vol. 58.

New York [New York, U.S.A.]: Mercury Publications [Lawrence E. Spivak], March **1944**.
8vo.

487.6——.

Excerpts from interviews with Kossola included on pp. 144–149 in photomechanical reprint of the 1942 New York edition (487.3) of Zora Neale Hurston, *Dust Tracks on a Road*.

New York [New York, U.S.A.]: Arno Press, **1969**.
8vo (23 cm.): v, 294 p.

487.7———.

Excerpts from interviews with Kossola included in Zora Neale Hurston, *Dust Tracks on a Road: An autobiography,* edited with an introduction by Robert Hemenway.

Urbana [Illinois, U.S.A.]: University of Illinois Press, **1970.**
8vo (21 cm.): xxxix, 348 p.

487.8———.

Excerpts from interviews with Kossola included in Zora Neale Hurston, *Dust Tracks on a Road: an Autobiography,* with an introduction by Larry Neale.

New York [New York, U.S.A.]: Lippincott, **1971.**
8vo (23 cm.): xxv, 286 p.

487.9———.

Excerpts from interviews with Kossola included on pp. 198–204 in Zora Neale Hurston, *Dust Tracks on a Road: an Autobiography,* edited with an introduction by Robert Hemenway.

Urbana [Illinois, U.S.A.]: University of Illinois Press, **1984.**
8vo (21 cm.): xxxix, 348 p.

487.10———.

Excerpts from interviews with Kossola included in Zora Neale Hurston, *Dust Tracks on a Road: an Autobiography,* With a new introduction by Dellita L. Martin.

London [England]: Virago, **1986.**
8vo (20 cm.): xviii, 348 p.

487.11———.

Excerpts from interviews with Kossola included in Zora Neale Hurston, *Dust Tracks on a Road: an Autobiography,* With a new introduction by Dellita L. Martin.

London [England]: Virago, **1989.**
8vo (20 cm.): xviii, 348 p.

487.12———.

Excerpts from interviews with Kossola included in Zora Neale Hurston, *Dust Tracks on a Road: an Autobiography.* With a new foreword by Maya Angelou.

New York [New York, U.S.A.]: HarperPerennial, **1991.**
8vo (21 cm.): xii, 278 p.

487.13———.

Excerpts from interviews with Kossola included in Zora Neale Hurston, *Dust Tracks on a Road* in Zora Neale Hurston, *Folklore, Memoirs, and other Writing.*

New York [New York , U.S.A.]: Library of America, **1995.**
8vo (21 cm.): 1001 p., illus.

487.14———.

Excerpts from interviews with Kossola included in Zora Neale Hurston, *Dust Tracks on a Road* reprinted from 487.3 in *The Norton Anthology of African American Literature,* edited by Henry Louis Gates Jr. and Nellie Y. McKay.

New York [New York, U.S.A.]: W. W. Norton, **1997.**

487.15———.

Excerpts from interviews with Kossola included in Zora Neale Hurston, *Dust Tracks on a Road: an Autobiography.* With a new foreword by Maya Angelou.

New York [New York, U.S.A.]: HarperPerennial, **2002.**
8vo (21 cm.): xii, 308 p. The restored text, established by the Library of America (487.13).

487.16———.

Excerpts from interviews with Kossola included in Zora Neale Hurston, *Dust Tracks on a Road: an Autobiography,* with a foreword by Maya Angelou.

New York [New York, U.S.A.]: Harper Perennial Modern Classics, **2006.**
8vo (21 cm.): xii, 308, 16 p., illus. The restored text, established by the Library of America (our 487.13).

487.17———.

Kossola's account as retold by Zora Neale Hurston from her 1927 interviews with him, in her previously unpublished 1931 manuscript account, here entitled *Barracoon: The Last "Black Cargo"* and edited with an introduction by Debora G. Plant. Foreword by Alice Walker.

New York [New York, U.S.A.]: Amistad, an imprint of HarperCollins Publishers, **2018.**
8vo (22 cm.): xxviii, 171 p.

Note: For comparison of 485.17's account vis-a-vis 485.3 see Sylviane A. Diouf, *Dreams of Africa in Alabama: The Slave Ship Clotilda and the Story of the Last Africans Brought to America* (New York: Oxford University Press, 2009).

487.18———.

Kossola's account as retold by Zora Neale Hurston from her 1927 interviews with him, in her previously unpublished 1931 manuscript account, here entitled *Barracoon: The Last "Black Cargo"* and edited by Debora G. Plant. Foreword by Alice Walker. **Large print edition.**

New York [New York, U.S.A.]: Amistad, an imprint of HarperCollins Publishers, **2018.**
8vo (23 cm.): xxviii, 209 p., portrait.

487.19———.

Kossola's account as retold by Zora Neale Hurston from her 1927 interviews with him, in her previously unpublished 1931 manuscript account, here entitled *Barracoon: The Last* "*Black Cargo*" and edited by Debora G. Plant. [New York, New York, U.S.A.]: Amistad, 2019.

8vo (22 cm.): xxviii, 171 p.

1931

488.1 Matilda [Tildy] McCrear (1857/8–1940)

Account in interview with Octavia S. Wynn printed under headline "Woman Survivor of Last Slave Ship, Erect and Vigorous at Advanced Age, Walks Fifteen Miles for Gov't Help" on p. 11 in the 20 Dec. 1931 issue (vol. 12, no. 295) of daily newspaper *The Selma Times-Journal*.

Selma, Alabama [U.S.A.]: The Selma Times-Journal Co., December 20, 1931.

Full text: https://huskiecommons.lib.niu.edu/history-500african-voices/279/ [see 488.1].

¶ McCrear was Yorùbá (modern-day Nigeria, Benin and Togo—see Map 5) and came from the same village as Kossola (q.v. 487.1), Redoshi (q.v. 489.1), and other survivors of the *Clotilda*, the last slave ship to enter the United States. She was about two years old when her village was attacked by Dahomey (modern Benin) warriors, who killed most of the aged residents and enslaved those who were younger, including McCrear, three older sisters, and her mother. After being taken to Ouidah (modern coastal Benin) and sold to the captain of the *Clotilda*, they were all transported illegally to Mobile Bay, Alabama (U.S.A.) in 1860 (Map 15). There she, her mother, and one sister were sold to a wealthy planter near Selma, in northern Alabama. She never saw her other two sisters again. After emancipation at the conclusion of the Civil War in 1865, McCrear grew up in a sharecropper family, then lived in a common-law marriage with a German Jewish immigrant (with whom she had fourteen children). Widowed late in life, she lived with a child when interviewed by Octavia Wynn in 1931. Later she lived with another child in Selma, where she died in 1940. For more on McCrear see: Hannah Durkin, "Uncovering the Hidden Lives of Last *Clotilda* Survivor Matilda McCrear and Her Family," *Slavery & Abolition* 41:3 (September 2020): 431–457. Note that Durkin's research on Matilda McCrear and her descendants was recorded in articles appearing in the magazines *National Geographic, Smithsonian*, and others, beginning in March 2020.

1932

489.1 Redoshi (ca. 1848–1937) = Sally Smith

Her reminiscences published in S. L. Flock, "Survivor of Last Slave Cargo Lives on Plantation near Selma," on p. 13 of the 31 January 1932 issue (vol. 104, no. 31) of the progressive daily newspaper *The Montgomery Advertiser*, edited by Grover Cleveland Hall.

Montgomery, Alabama [U.S.A.]: Published by Franklin P. Glass, January 31, 1932.

Full text: https://huskiecommons.lib.niu.edu/history-500african-voices/280/ [see 489.1].

¶ Redoshi was Yorùbá (modern-day Nigeria, Benin, and Togo—see Map 5) and came from Tarkaw (an as yet unidentified place in West Africa). When she was ca. twelve years old, her husband was killed in a raid by Dahomeans (modern Benin) on the same place where Kossola (q.v. 487.1) was captured, and she and others were marched to Ouidah (modern coastal Benin). Redoshi, Kossola, and others were taken on the *Clotilda* to Mobile Bay, Alabama (U.S.A.) in 1860 (Map 15). After being sold to Mr. Washington Smith, Redoshi married another *Clotilda* survivor, Yawith (later named Billy Smith), and was taken with him to Quarles Plantation near a community that she called Bogue Chitto and later scholars identify as Selma, Alabama. She lived in that area the rest of her life—after emancipation in 1865 as a sharecropper with her husband and later as landowners. She died in 1937, two years after Kossola. The 1938 US Department of Agriculture documentary motion picture film *The Negro Farmer: Extension Work for Better Farming and Better Living* includes eighteen seconds of footage of Redoshi. For an extensive study of her life and publication of relevant documents, see Hannah Durkin, "Finding Last Middle Passage Survivor Sally 'Redoshi' Smith on the Page and Screen," *Slavery and Abolition* 40:4 (December 2019): 631–658.

Figure 20: Photograph of *Clotilda* survivor Matilda McCrear, also known as Tildy (1857/8–1940), living near Selma, Alabama when interviewed in 1931. She was the longest-lived African-born slave ship survivor in North America, having died in 1940.

Source: Photograph ca. 1930, courtesy of the McCrear family.

489.2———.

Extensive quotations noted during an interview with Redoshi by Amelia Platts Boynton (later Robinson) included (most especially on pp. 29–35) in Boynton Robinson's memoir *Bridge Across Jordan: The Story of the Struggle for Civil Rights in Selma, Alabama*. There are discrepancies between the accounts in 489.2 and 489.1.

New York [New York, U.S.A.]: Carlton Press, **1979**.
8vo (21 cm.): 190 p.

489.3———. [Revised edition of 489.2]

Extensive quotations noted during an interview with Redoshi by Amelia Boynton Robinson included (most especially on pp. 64–68) in Amelia Boynton Robinson's memoir *Bridge Across Jordan: The Story of the Struggle for Civil Rights in Selma, Alabama*. Revised edition.

Washington, DC [U.S.A.]: Schiller Institute, **1991**.
8vo (22 cm.): xxxi, 414 p., illus., including portraits.   **489.4**———. [German translation of 489.2]

Extensive quotations noted during an interview with Redoshi by Amelia Platts Boynton (sometimes Robinson) included in the German edition of her memoir published as *Brücke über den Jordan*.

Wiesbaden [Hesse, Germany]: Böttiger, **2000**.
8vo (21 cm.): 304 p.

489.5———. [Reset printing of 489.3?]

Extensive quotations noted during an interview with Redoshi by Amelia Platt Boynton (sometimes Robinson) included in Amelia Platt Boynton's memoir *Bridge Across Jordan: The Story of the Struggle for Civil Rights in Selma, Alabama*.

Washington, DC [U.S.A.].: Schiller Institute, **2003**. 8vo (21 cm.): xxxi, 409 p., illus., including portraits.

1936

490.1 Silvia King (ca. 1840–1937)

Transcribed interview printed on pp. 290–295 of vol. 16 (*Texas Narratives*, Part 2) of *Slave Narratives: A Folk History of Slavery in the United States*.

Washington, DC [U.S.A.]: Federal Writers Project, Works Progress Administration, **1941**. 17 volumes in 33, 4to (29 cm.).

https://www.loc. gov/resource/ mesn.162/?sp=295 [see 490.1].

¶ Silvia King was born in Morocco (see Map 2) and stolen from her husband and three children. A slave ship took her first to Bordeaux, France (Map 7), then to New Orleans, Louisiana (U.S.A.)—Map 15. After being sold at auction and marched in chains to a plantation near LaGrange in Fayette County, Texas, King cooked, gardened, and did other work in and around the plantation owner's large house. She remarried and had one child. She and others began attending a racially integrated church but also met in the creek bottoms at night with Black preachers for singing, shouting, and dancing. She said nothing about life after the Civil War and emancipation. She was estimated to be nearly one hundred years old when interviewed in Marlin, Texas, shortly before she died in 1937.

490.2———.

Interview with Silvia King included in vol. 4, pp. 290–295 of photomechanical reprint of 490.1 retitled *The American Slave: A Composite Autobiography*, edited by George P. Rawick, **together with additional account** by Silvia King, not in 490.1, first printed on pp. 2224–2239 in Supplement, Series 2, *Texas Narratives*, Part 6, vol. 5, added to this reprint.

Westport, Connecticut [U.S.A.]: Greenwood Press, **1972**. 12 vols., 4to.

490.3———.

Transcribed interview printed on pp. 290–295 of vol. 4 (*Texas Narratives*, Part 2) of photomechanical reprint of 490.1, *Slave Narratives: A Folk History of Slavery in the United States*, with imprint:

St. Clair Shores, Michigan [U.S.A.]: Scholarly Press, **1976**. 17 vols., 4to. Digitized in Project Gutenberg: 420272.

490.4———.

Transcribed interview printed on pp. 290–295 of vol. 4 of photomechanical reprint of the Texas narratives (only) in 490.1, retitled *Texas Slave Narratives: A Folk History of Slavery in the United States from Interviews with Former Texas Slaves*.

Hamburg, Michigan [U.S.A.]: Native American Books, [2003?]. 4 parts in 2 vols, 4to (28 cm.).

Bibliography

Primary Sources

Al-Ahari, Muhammad A., ed. *Five Classic Muslim Slave Narratives: Selim Aga, Job Ben Sulaiman, Nicholas Said, Omar ibn Said, Abu Bakr Sadiq.* Chicago: Magribine Press, 2006.

Austin, Allan D., ed. *African Muslims in Antebellum America: A Source Book.* New York: Garland Publishing, 1984.

Armistead, Wilson. *A Tribute for the Negro: Being a Vindication of the Moral, Intellectual, and Religious Capabilities of the Coloured Portion of Mankind; with Particular Reference to the African Race.* Manchester: W. Irwin, 1848.

Ball, Charles. *Slavery in the United States: A Narrative of the Life and Adventures of Charles Ball, a Black Man,* 3rd edition. Pittsburgh: J. T. Shryock, 1853.

Barber, John Warner, ed. *History of the Amistad Captives Being a Circumstantial Account of the Capture of the Spanish Schooner Amistad, by the Africans on Board.* New Haven, CT: Hitchcock and Stafford Printers, 1840.

Belley, Jean-Baptist. *Le Bout d'Oreille des Colons ou Le Système de l'Hôtel de Massiac, mis au jour par Gouli. Belley, Député noir de Saint-Domingue, à ses collegues.* Paris, n.d.

Blassingame, John W., ed. *Slave Testimony: Two Centuries of Letters, Speeches, Interviews, and Autobiographies.* Baton Rouge: Louisiana State University, 1977.

Bluett, Thomas, ed. *Some Memoirs of the Life of Job, the Son of Solomon the High Priest of Boonda in Africa; Who was a Slave about two Years in Maryland; and afterwards being brought to England, was set free, and sent to his native Land in the Year 1734.* London: Richard Ford, 1734.

Brinch, Boyrereau. *The Blind African Slave, Or Memoirs of Boyrereau Brinch, Nicknamed Jeffrey Brace,* edited by Kari J. Winter. Madison: University of Wisconsin Press, 2004.

Capitein, Jacobus Elisa Johannes. *Dissertatio politico-theologica de servitute libertati Christianæ non contraria.* Leiden: Samuelem Luchtmans & filium, 1742.

Carretta, Vincent, ed. *Quobna Ottobah Cugoano: Thoughts and Sentiments on the Evil of Slavery and Other Writings.* New York: Penguin Books, 1999.

Carretta, Vincent, ed. *Unchained Voices: An Anthology of Black Authors in the English-Speaking World of the 18th Century.* Lexington: University Press of Kentucky, 1996.

Carretta, Vincent, and Ty M. Reese, eds. *The Life and Letters of Philip Quaque, the First African Anglican Missionary.* Athens: University of Georgia Press, 2010.

Castelnau, Francis de. *Renseignements sur l'Afrique Centrale et sur une Nation d'Hommes a Queue qui s'y Trouverait, d'après le Rapport de Nègres du Soudan, Esclaves a Bahia.* Paris: P. Bertrand, 1851.

Curtin, Philip D., ed. *Africa Remembered: Narratives by West Africans from the Era of the Slave Trade.* Madison: University of Wisconsin Press, 1967.

Donnan, Elizabeth, ed. *Documents Illustrative of the Slave Trade to America,* 4 vols. Washington: Carnegie Institution, 1930–35.

Bibliography

Drummond, Antônio de Menezes Vasconcellos. "Lettres sur l'Afrique ancienne et moderne," *Journal des Voyages découvertes et navigations modernes, ou, Archives géographiques du XIXe siècle*, 32 (1826): 290–24.

Dubois, Laurent, and John D. Garrigus, eds. *Slave Revolution in the Caribbean, 1789–1804: A Brief History with Documents*. Boston: Bedford/ St. Martin's, 2006.

Federal Writers Project, Works Progress Administration. *Slave Narratives: A Folk History of Slavery in the United States from Interviews with Former Slaves*, 17 vols. St. Clair Shores, Michigan: Scholarly Press, 1976.

García Rodríguez, Gloria, ed. *Voices of the Enslaved in Nineteenth-Century Cuba: A Documentary History*. Chapel Hill: University of North Carolina Press, 2011.

Gates, Henry Louis, Jr., ed. *The Classic Slave Narratives: The Life of Olaudah Equiano, The History of Mary Prince, Narrative of the Life of Frederick Douglass, Incidents in the Life of a Slave Girl*. New York: Mentor, 1987.

Gates, Henry Louis, Jr., and William L. Andrews, eds. *Pioneers of the Black Atlantic: Five Slave Narratives from the Enlightenment, 1772–1815*. Washington, DC: Civitas Counterpoint, 1998.

Griffin, Patricia C., ed. *The Odyssey of an African Slave, By Sitiki*. Gainesville: University Press of Florida, 2009.

Horton, James Africanus B. "Geographical Constitution of Ahanta, Gold Coast," published in "Geographical Treatise by a Native African." *African Repository*, 47 (January 1871): 18–22.

Horton, James Africanus B. *The Political Economy of British West Africa: with the Requirements of Several Colonies and Settlements*. London, 1865.

Horton, James Africanus B. *West African Countries and Peoples, British and Native ... and a Vindication of the African Race*. London: W. J. Johnson, 1868.

Jameson, John Franklin, ed. "Autobiography of Omar Ibn Said, Slave in North Carolina, 1831." *American Historical Review* 30(4) (July 1925): 787–95.

McKnight, Kathryn Joy, and Leo J. Garofalo, eds. *Afro-Latino Voices: Narratives from the Early Modern Ibero-Atlantic World, 1550–1812*. Indianapolis: Hackett Publishing Co., 2009.

Montgomery, Charles J. "Survivors from the Cargo of the Negro Slave Yacht Wanderer." *American Anthropologist* n.s. 10(4) (1908): 611–23.

Moreau-Saint-Méry, Médéric Louis Elie. *Description topographique, physique, Civile, Politique et Historique de la partie française de L'isle Saint-Domingue ...*, 2 vols. Philadelphia: Imprimé chez l'Auteur, 1797.

Mott, Abigail, ed. *Biographical Sketches and Interesting Anecdotes of a Person of Colour. To Which Is Added, a Selection of Pieces in Poetry*. New York: Mahlon Day, 1826.

Oldendorp, Christian Georg Andreas. *Geschichte der Mission der evangelischen Brueder auf den caraibischen Inseln S. Thomas, S. Croix, und S. Jan*, edited by Johann Jakob Bossart. Barby, Saxony-Anhalt: Christian Friedrich Laur; Leipzig: Weidmanns Erben and Reich, 1777.

Oldendorp, C. G. A. [Christian Georg Andreas]. *A Caribbean Mission: History of the Mission of the Evangelical Brethren on the Caribbean Islands of St. Thomas, St. Croix, and St. John*, edited by Johann Jakob Bossard and translated by Arnold R. Highfield and Vladimir Barac. Ann Arbor, Michigan: Karoma Publishers, 1987.

Oldendorp, C. G. A. [Christian Georg Andreas]. *Historie der caribischen Inseln Sanct Thomas, Sanct Crux und Sanct Jan, insbesondere der dasigen Neger und der Mission der evangelischen Brüder unter denselben: kommentierte Ausgabe des vollständigen Manuskriptes aus dem Archiv der Evangelischen Brüder-Unität Herrnhut*, edited by Gudrun Meier et al., two volumes in four. Berlin: Verlag für Wissenschaft und Bildung, 2000–2002.

Paniagua, Juan Carlos Miguel de, ed. *Compendio de la vida exemplar de la venerable madre Sor Teresa Juliana de Santo Domingo*. Salamanca, Spain: Eugenio García de Honorato and J.S. Miguel, 1752.

Prince, Mary. *The History of Mary Prince, A West Indian Slave, Related by Herself, with a Supplement by the Editor, to Which Is Added the Narrative of Asa-Asa, a Captured African*. London: F. Westley and A.H. Davis, 1831.

Rawick, George P., et al., eds. *The American Slave: A Composite Autobiography*, 41 vols. Westport, Connecticut: Greenwood Press, 1972–79.

Rogers, Dominique, ed. *Voix d'Esclaves: Antilles, Guyane et Louisiane Françaises, XVIIIe–XIXe Siècles*. Paris: Karthala, 2015.

The Royal African: or, Memoirs of the Young Prince of Annamaboe … London: Printed for W. Reeves, 1749.

Said, Nicholas. *The Autobiography of Nicholas Said; A Native of Bornou, Eastern Soudan, Central Africa*. Memphis, Tennessee: Shotwell & Co., 1873.

Smith, Venture. *A Narrative of the Life and Adventures of Venture, a Native of Africa: but Resident above Sixty Years in the United States. Related*. New-London, Connecticut: C. Holt, 1798.

Staehelin, Fritz, ed. *Die Mission der Brüdergemeine in Suriname und Berbice im achtzehnten Jahrhundert: Eine Missionsgeschichte hauptsächlich in Auszügen aus Briefen und Originalberichten*. Paramaribo: Verlag C. Kersten, 1913–17.

Stedman, John Gabriel. *Narrative, of a Five Years' Expedition, against the Revolted Negroes of Surinam, in Guiana, on the Wild Coast of South America; from the year 1772, to 1777*. Edited Richard Price and Sally Price. Baltimore: The Johns Hopkins University Press, 1988.

Wheatley, Phillis. *Poems on Various Subjects, Religious and Moral, by Phillis Wheatley, Negro Servant to Mr. John Wheatley, of Boston, in New England*. London: A. Bell, 1773.

Secondary Sources

Aljoe, Nicole N. "'Going to Law': Legal Discourse and Testimony in Early West Indian Slave Narratives." *Early American Literature* XLVI (2011): 351–81.

Austin, Allen. *African Muslims in Antebellum America: Transatlantic Stories and Spiritual Struggles*. New York: Routledge, 1997.

Bailey, Anne C. *African Voices of the Atlantic Slave Trade: Beyond the Silence and the Shame*. Boston: Beacon Press, 2005.

Bezerra, Nielson Rosa, and Moisés Peixoto. "Biographies, Slavery, and Freedom: Wills as Autobiographical Documents of Africans in Diaspora." *African Economic History* 48(1) (2020): 91–108.

Calonius, Erik. *The Wanderer: The Last American Slave Ship and the Conspiracy That Set Its Sails*. New York: St. Martin's Press, 2006.

Caretta, Vincent. "Olaudah Equiano or Gustavus Vassa? New Light on an Eighteenth-Century Question of Identity." *Slavery & Abolition* 20(3) (1999): 96–105.

Cavalcante, Berenice. *José Bonifácio: Reason and Sensibility, a History in Three Times*. Rio de Janeiro, Brazil: FGV, 2001.

Christie, Nancy, Michael Gauvreau, and Clare Haru Crowston, conveners. Symposium on "Voices in the Legal Archives in the French Atlantic." North Hatley, Quebec (28–30 May 2018).

Clendinnen, Inga. "'Fierce and Unnatural Cruelty': Cortés and the Conquest of Mexico." *Representation* 33, Special Issue: The New World (Winter, 1991): 65–100.

Conrad, Robert Edgar. *Children of God's Fire: A Documentary History of Black Slavery in Brazil*. Princeton, NJ: Princeton University Press, 1983.

Bibliography

Du Bois, W. E. Burghardt. *The Souls of Black Folk: Essays and Sketches.* Chicago: A. C. McClurg and Co., 1903.

Durkin, Hannah. "Finding Last Middle Passage Survivor Sally 'Redoshi' Smith on the Page and Screen." *Slavery and Abolition* 40(4) (December 2019): 631–58.

Durkin, Hannah. "Uncovering the Hidden Lives of Last *Clotilda* Survivor Matilda McCrear and Her Family." *Slavery & Abolition* 41(3) (September 2020): 431–57.

Egerton, Douglas R. *Thunder at the Gates: The Black Civil War Regiments That Redeemed America.* New York: Basic Books, 2016.

Fortin, Jeffrey A., and Mark Meuwese, eds. *Atlantic Biographies: Individuals and Peoples in the Atlantic World.* Leiden: Brill, 2014.

Gates, Henry Louis, Jr. *The Signifying Monkey: A Theory of African-American Literary Criticism.* Oxford: Oxford University Press, 1988.

Gilroy, Paul. *The Black Atlantic: Modernity and Double Consciousness.* Cambridge, MA: Harvard University Press, 1993.

Handler, Jerome S. "Survivors of the Middle Passage: Life Histories of Enslaved Africans in British America." *Slavery and Abolition* 23(1) (2002): 23–56.

Hogg, Peter C., ed. *The African Slave Trade and Its Suppression: A Classified and Annotated Bibliography of Books, Pamphlets and Periodical Articles.* London: Routledge, 1973.

Hurston, Zora Neale. *Barracoon: The Story of the Last "Black Cargo,"* edited by Deborah G. Plant. New York: Amistad of HarperCollins Publishers, 2018.

Kelley, Sean. "Enslavement in Upper Guinea during the Era of the Transatlantic Slave Trade: Biographical Perspectives." *African Economic History* 48(1) (2020): 46–73.

Levecq, Christine. *Slavery and Sentiment: The Politics of Feeling in Black Atlantic Antislavery Writing, 1770–1850.* Durham: University of New Hampshire Press, 2008.

Lindsay, Lindsay A., and John Wood Sweet, eds. *Biography and the Black Atlantic.* Philadelphia: University of Pennsylvania Press, 2014.

Lovejoy, Paul E. "Biography as Source Material: Towards a Biographical Archive of Enslaved Africans." Pp. 119–40 in *Source Material for Studying the Slave Trade and the African Diaspora*, edited by Robin Law. Stirling, Scotland: Centre of Commonwealth Studies, University of Stirling, 1997.

Lovejoy, Paul E. "'Freedom Narratives' of Transatlantic Slavery." *Slavery & Abolition* 32(1) (2011): 91–107.

Lovejoy, Paul E. "Olaudah Equiano or Gustavus Vassa—What's in a Name?" *Atlantic Studies* 9(2) (2012): 165–184.

Mudimbe, V.Y. *The Invention of Africa: Gnosis, Philosophy, and the Order of Knowledge.* Bloomington: Indiana University Press, 1988.

Northrup, David. *Africa's Discovery of Europe, 1450–1850.* New York: Oxford University Press, 2002.

Peabody, Sue. "Microhistory, Biography, Fiction: The Politics of Narrating the Lives of People under Slavery." *Transatlantica*: 2 (2012) n.p.

Potkay, Adam, and Sandra Burr, eds. *Black Atlantic Writers of the Eighteenth Century: Living the New Exodus in England and the Americas.* New York: St. Martin's Press, 1995.

Sensbach, Jon. "Black Pearls: Writing Black Atlantic Women's Biography." Pp. 93–107 in Lindsay A. and John Wood Sweet, eds. *Biography and the Black Atlantic.* Philadelphia: University of Pennsylvania Press, 2014.

Sidbury, James. *Becoming African in America: Race and Nation in the Early Black Atlantic.* Oxford: Oxford University Press, 2007.

Sidbury, James. "Early Slave Narratives and the Culture of the Atlantic Market." Pp. 260–74 and 363–66 in *Empire and Nation: The American Revolution in the Atlantic World*, edited by Eliga H. Gould and Peter S. Onuf. Baltimore, MD: The Johns Hopkins University Press, 2005.

Sparks, Randy L. *Two Princes of Calabar: An Eighteenth-Century Atlantic Odyssey.* Cambridge, MA: Harvard University Press, 2004.

Thornton, John. *Africa and Africans in the Making of the Atlantic World, 1400–1800*, 2nd edition. New York: Cambridge University Press, 1998.

Thorp, Daniel, ed. "Chattel with a Soul: The Autobiography of a Moravian Slave." *The Pennsylvania Magazine of History & Biography* 112(3) (July 1988): 433–51.

Vidal, Cécile. "Comba, esclave noire de Louisiane. Marronage et sociabilité, 1764." Pp. 61–66 in *Voix d'Esclaves Antilles, Guyane et Louisane Françaises, XVIIIe–XIXe Siècles*, edited by Dominique Rogers. Paris: Karthala, 2015.

Warner-Lewis, Maureen. *Archibald Monteath: Igbo, Jamaican, Moravian.* Kingston: University of the West Indies Press, 2007.

White, Luise, Stephan F. Miescher, and David William Cohen, eds. *African Words, African Voices: Critical Practices in Oral History.* Bloomington: Indiana University Press, 2001.

White, Sophie. *Voices of the Enslaved: Love, Labor, and Longing in French Louisiana.* Chapel Hill: University of North Carolina Press, 2019.

White, Sophie, and Trevor Burnard, eds. *Hearing Enslaved Voices: African and Indian Slave Testimony in British and French America, 1700–1848.* New York: Routledge, 2020.

Williams, Daryle, et al., eds. *The Enslaved Project.* East Lansing: Michigan State University Press, forthcoming.

Websites

Akyeampong, Emmanuel K., Henry Louis Gates Jr., and Steven J. Niven. Dictionary of African Biography. Hutchinson Center for African and African American Research, Harvard University. https://hutchinscenter.fas.harvard.edu/DAB.

Brock, Terry, and Mary Furlong Minkoff. Montpelier Digital Collections Project. The Montpelier (Virginia) Foundation. https://collections.montpelier.org/. In progress.

Eltis, David, et al. Slave Voyages 2.0. slavevoyages.org.

van Galen, Coen, and Maurits Hassankhan. The Slave Registers of Suriname: Day-to-Day Records of the Enslaved Population of Suriname from 1830 to 1863. National Archives of Suriname (Nationaal Archief Suriname) and National Archives of the Netherlands (Nationaal Archief in Nederland). https://www.nationaalarchief.nl/onderzoeken/index/nt00451?searchTerm=. http://www.nationaalarchief.sr/collecties/online-slavenregisters.

Gates, Henry Louis, Jr., Evelyn Brooks Higginbotham, and Steven J. Niven. African American National Biography. Hutchinson Center for African and African American Research, Harvard University. https://hutchinscenter.fas.harvard.edu/AANB.

Gates, Henry Louis, Jr., Franklin W. Knight, and Steven J. Niven. Dictionary of Caribbean and Afro-Latin American Biography. Hutchinson Center for African and African American Research, Harvard University. https://hutchinscenter.fas.harvard.edu/DCALAB.

Hall, Gwendolyn Midlo. Afro-Louisiana History and Genealogy. https://www.ibiblio.org/laslave/.

Bibliography

Hawthorne, Walter; Dean Rehberger; and Daryle Williams, Enslaved: Peoples of the Historical Slave Trade, Michigan State University, East Lansing, Michigan, Enslaved.org. Hill, Jobie. The Slave House Database.

http://www.savingslavehouses.org/saving-slave-houses-project/slave-house-database-2/. In progress.

Kelley, Sean. Documenting Africans in Trans-Atlantic Slavery (DATAS) Project. In progress.

Lady, Martha, Katrina Keefer, and Kartikay Chadha. The Language of Marks: A Web-portal for Trans-Atlantic Slave Trade Data Collection, Visualization, and Transcription.

https://www2.ocadu.ca/research/val/project/creating-a-visual-language-of-marks. In progress.

Landers, Jane. Slave Societies Digital Archive. Jean and Alexander Heard Library, Vanderbilt University, Nashville, Tennessee. https://www.slavesocieties.org.

Lovejoy, Henry B. Liberated Africans. https://liberatedafricans.dev.matrix.msu.edu/about.php.

Lovejoy, Henry B. *Slavery Images:* A Visual Record of the African Slave Trade and Slave Life in the Early African Diasporas. slaveryimages.org.

Lovejoy, Paul E. *Freedom Narratives: Testimonies of West Africans from the Era of Slavery.* http://freedomnarratives.org/.

Misevich, Philip. African Origins: Portal to Africans Liberated from Transatlantic Slave Vessels. Emory University. https://legacy.african-origins.org/.

Prochnow, Kyle. "The West India Regiments in the Digital Age: Building a Database of Enslaved and Free African Soldiers." In progress.

Robichaud, Léon. Marronnage in Saint-Domingue (Haïti): History, Memory, and Technology. http://www.marronnage.info/en/metho.php. In progress.

White, Sophie. Hearing Slaves Speak: A Database of Voices of the Voiceless in French Colonial Louisiana. In progress.

Indexes

First Printings

Note: All numbers refer to the Catalog number, not the page number.

Non-English Languages

Editors or Other Intermediaries

Places of Publication and Printing

Note: All places are listed for an entry when multiple publishers and printers were involved. For the period before 1900, places where distribution and sale of the publication took place are listed, when available. Location within modern nation state provided in parentheses.

Publishers and Printers

Note: All firms and individuals are listed for an entry when multiple publishers and printers were involved. For the period before 1900, firms and individuals involved in the distribution and sale of the book are listed, when available.

Subsequent Printings

Note: All numbers refer to the Catalog number, not the page number.

Non-English Languages

Danish 37, 42, 43, 52, 53, 81, 87, 88, 92, 93, 94, 95

Dutch 13, 18, 114, 117, 118, 119, 129, 130, 367

French 18, 114, 117, 118, 119, 126, 130, 135–144, 151, 158, 169, 192, 207, 234, 367

German 12, 37, 39, 42, 43, 44, 46, 51, 52, 53, 61, 68, 69, 73, 74, 75, 76, 81, 87, 88, 92, 93, 94, 95, 96, 99, 108, 112, 114, 117, 121, 122, 123, 129, 130, 131, 150, 158, 159, 164, 173, 367, 374, 375–434, 489

Greek 130

Hebrew 130

Italian 18, 114, 117, 118, 119, 130

Malayalam 367

Norwegian 367

Portuguese 23

Russian 130

Saamaka 18

Spanish 1, 2, 3, 4, 5, 6, 7, 9, 17, 125, 127, 128, 130, 180–183, 190, 191, 194–197, 199–202, 209, 210, 212–219, 221, 232, 233, 236–241, 256–260, 303–308, 315–318, 320–326, 328, 453, 454, 460–470

Swedish 18, 39, 42, 43, 44, 46, 51, 53, 61, 68, 69, 74, 75, 76, 81, 87, 88, 92, 93, 94, 95, 96, 99, 108, 117, 130

Welsh 112

Editors or Other Intermediaries

Aaron, John 374

Ahuma, Samuel Richard Brew Attoh 11, 13, 126, 130, 160

Al–Ahari, A. 11, 222

Al–Ahari, Muhammad A. 206

Alexander, Archibald 160

Allart, Johannes 18

Allen, William 310

Allison, Robert J. 130

Alryyes, Ala A. 206

Andrews, William L. 112, 130, 165, 207

Angelou, Maya 487

Armistead, Wilson 11, 13, 113, 126, 130, 151, 222

Auer, John Gottlieb 367

Austin, Allan D. 11, 164, 192, 206, 222, 225, 226

Baile, Monique 207

Baldwin, Simeon E. 266

Ball, Charles 164

Ball, W.W. Rouse 129

Barac, Vladimir 12, 37, 39, 42, 43, 44, 46, 51, 52, 53, 61, 68, 69, 73, 74, 75, 76, 87, 88, 92, 93, 94, 95, 96, 99, 108

Barber, James Warner 265, 301

Barkley, Elsa 156, 157

Barlow, Fred 129

Barlow, Joel 129

Barnard, J.G. 129

Basker, James G. 162, 163

Baur, William 111

Beatty–Medina, Charles 1, 2

Bednarek, Catherine 18

Berquin-Duvallon, Pierre-Louis 158

Beyreuther, Erich 37, 39, 42, 43, 44, 46, 52, 53, 61, 68, 69, 73, 74, 75, 76, 81, 87, 88, 92, 93, 94, 95, 96, 99, 108

Bird, Isaac 206

Black, Charles 164

Blaquiere, Edward 117

Blassingame, John W. 11, 192, 206, 220, 235, 265, 266, 273, 286, 297, 313, 319, 331, 436–452, 456

Blessing, P. 367

Bluett, Thomas 11

Blyden, E.W. 226

Blyth, Molly 207

Boggess, Arthur Clinton 120

Bontemps, Arna 15

Borghi, Bartolomeo 18, 114, 117, 118, 129

Bossart, Johann Jakob 12, 37, 39, 42, 43, 44, 46, 51, 52, 53, 61, 68, 69, 73, 74, 75, 76, 81, 87, 88, 92, 93, 94, 95, 96, 99, 108

Editors or Other Intermediaries

Editors or Other Intermediaries

Places of Publication and Printing

Note: All places are listed for an entry when multiple publishers and printers were involved. For the period before 1900, places where distribution and sale of the publication took place are listed, when available. Location within modern nation state provided in parentheses.

Publishers and Printers

Note: All firms and individuals are listed for an entry when multiple publishers and printers were involved. For the period before 1900, firms and individuals involved in the distribution and sale of the book are listed, when available.

Publishers and Printers

Publishers and Printers

Names of Africans

Note: All numbers refer to the Catalog number, not the page number.

Note: All known names of Africans providing accounts are listed. Multiple names are cross-listed.

Aaron 104
Aba-Hama 348
Abacky 478
Abāli 392
Abdullah, Muhammad 366
Abraham (Ibrahim, Sambo) 153
Absolom (Benjamin) 152
Abu (Élias) 363
Abubakar (Abou Bouker, William Pascoe/Pasco) 176
Abubakar 351
Abuncare (Abubakar, José Maria Rufino) 373
Acosta, Augustin 448
Adam (Braz) 345
Adam (Sarri) 136
Adam (Slamank) 242
'Adamu (Edward Klein) 422
Adéolà (Diola, Triumfo Souchay) 368
Adíbe (George Rose) 390
Adsíma (John Wilhelm) 384
Adsōro 391
Afia (Afiba) 137
African Calculator (Thomas Fuller, Tom, Negro Tom, The Virginia Calculator) 129
Agüero, Pablo 127, 128
Agustín (Chobó) 219
Ajayi (Samuel Ajayi Crowther, Adjai, Samuel Adjai Crowther) 234
Akeiso (Florence Hall) 178
Ali 350
Álvares, Domingos 14
Amaral, André do 486
Anamabu, Prince of (Ansa Sasraku, William Ansah Sessarakoo) 16
Anchico (Sebastián) 3
Anderson, Isaac 134
Andrew the Moor (Ofodobendo Wooma) 19, 108
Aneaso (Aniaso, Toby, Archibald Monteith, Monteath, Archy) 374

Angola, Francisco 3, 4
Anna Margaretha 105
Ansel (Antson Zizer) 132
Antigózi (James Richard) 379
Antonio (Bawa, Boué) 358
Apongo (Wager) 22
Archy (Aneaso, Aniaso, Archibald Monteith, Monteath, Toby) 374
Asa-Asa (Louis) 207
Ashy 156
Augustino 339
Augusto (Grusa, Idrisa) 356
Ayai (Pascual) 215
Ayuso (Guillermo) 212
Ba (David Brown) 281
Bādsóróso (Richard Laudman) 386
Bagólōmo (James Thomas) 387
Bagué 365
Bailey, George (Bíra) 428
Banco (Bokary) 369
Bánena (Andrew George) 388
Baptist, John (Dsindsímbi, Kindsímbi) 401
Baquaqua, Mahommah Gardo 435
Barbara 106
Barker, Thomas (Cawley) 254
Bartholomäus- 34
Bartu (Gbatu) 270
Bau 280
Bawa (Boué, Antonio) 358
Bela (Rafael) 370
Belford, Abraham (Kayawaon) 376
Belinda (Belinda Royall, Belinda Sutton) 124
Belley, Jean-Baptiste 148
Bémbi (William Davis) 410
Benjamin (Absolom) 152
Benoit 186
Benomê 332
Bere (Berri) 293
Bernard 185
Bia (Pie) 274
Biáfara, Francisco 5, 6

Wright, Joseph 261
Wúene (William Cole) 417
Yaboi 290
Yamousa 144
Yamsey (Josiah) 171
Yao (Yaw, Quaw) 142
Yaro (Yero Mamdou, Yarrow Mamout, Yaro, Old Yarrow, Old Yarrah) 167

Yéri (Sáyo) 416
Yon (William Macfoi) 393
Yóno (William Macauly) 431
Zimmermann, Catherine (Ngeve, Catherine Mulgrave, Kitty) 372
Zizer, Antson (Ansel) 132
Zuma 473

African Origins

Note: All numbers refer to the Catalog number, not the page number.

Note: Places of African origin or the people with whom Africans providing accounts identified are listed. The current nation in which places are located provided in parentheses.

Abeokuta, Badagry (Nigeria) 367
Accra (Ghana) 49, 159
Adamawa (western Nigeria) 353
Agūe (Togo) 380
Aja (southern Togo) 67
Ajumako/Agimaque (Ghana) 126
Akan (Ghana) 18, 137, 142, 156
Ake/Aku/Akuh (southwestern Nigeria) 313, 389
Ákūára (Gabon, Republic of Congo) 409
Akuropon (Ghana) 47
Akyem (Ghana) 46
Alkalawa, Gobir (Nigeria) 185
Allada (Benin) 61
Alo/Edo/Aro (near Egypt) 108
Amina (Ghana) 8, 23, 34, 36, 42, 43, 45, 87, 104
Anamabu/Anomabu, Fante country (Ghana) 16, 138
Angola 4, 134
Asante (Ghana) 139, 141, 330
Ataka/Atakora (northwestern Benin) 478
'Atām-Nómūnu (Nigeria, Cameroon) 424
Awoyade, Egba, Oyo (Nigeria) 455
Bagirmi/Massiagné, Borno (Chad, Nigeria) 351
Bākóko (Cameroon) 394
Bákon (Cameroon) 431
Bálīa, Bóritsu (northern Nigeria) 430
Bálumfa country (Cameroon) 397
Bamba (Cameroon) 171
Bándsāre (Cameroon) 396
Báningar (southwestern Cameroon) 400
Bánon, Bagba (Burkina Faso, Ghana) 395
Bātēndu, Casamance region (Senegal) 375
Beafada (Guinea–Bissau) 5
Bedagua (unidentified, Africa) 229
Bépot/Mbébo/Mbe (northern Cameroon) 403
Béri Ndāda, Zinder (Niger) 419
Bibí (southern Nigeria, northwestern Cameroon) 240, 256, 259

Bight of Benin, interior (Benin, Togo, Nigeria) 133, 336
Bíōka (southeastern Nigeria) 434
Birnin Duara (Nigeria) 184
Birnin Yauri (northern Nigeria) 173
Bonny, Isoama country (coastal Nigeria) 390
Bópūnt (Angola) 412
Borno/Bournou (Chad, Nigeria) 112, 346, 348, 349, 350, 362
Boso island, Lake Chad (Cameroon, Chad) 392
Bouka (southern Mali, Guinea, Ivory Coast) 224
Bournou/Borno (Chad, Nigeria) 112, 346, 348, 349, 350, 362
Bow-woo (Mali) 162, 163
Bumbe/Bumbeli, Yilunah (Sierra Leone) 294
Búngu (Togo, Benin, Niger) 384
Búntun (Senegal) 376
Calabar (Nigeria/northwestern Cameroon) 115, 116, 164, 194, 197, 209, 221, 238, 240, 303, 315, 316
Cameroon 319
Cape of Good Hope (South Africa) 231
Cape Lopez (Gabon) 227
Cape Mesurado/Mesurado (Liberia) 149
Cape Mount, Vai country (Liberia) 175
Carabali/Ijo (Nigeria/northwestern Cameroon) 93, 105, 107, 194, 197, 221, 304, 315, 316
Caravali (Nigeria, northwestern Cameroon) 439
Casmance River (Senegal) 7
Chamba/Kassenti/Tschamba/Tjamba (Togo) 144
Congo 10, 25, 75, 76, 128, 136, 190, 191, 210, 237, 241, 260, 328, 454, 457, 461, 463, 464, 470
Coromantyn (Ghana) 77
Cowăny, Madimba district, São Salvador/Mbanga Kongo (Angola) 477
Cross River region (southern Nigeria, northwestern Cameroon) 256
Dahomey (Benin) 22, 475, 476
Damaturu, Borno (Chad/Nigeria) 347
Diola/Jola (Senegal) 7
Djougou (Benin) 435

Places

Note: All numbers refer to the Catalog number, not the page number.

Note: Places on both sides of the Atlantic Ocean where Africans who provided an account were present are listed. The current nation in which the places are located are noted in parentheses.

Places

Ports of Embarkation

Note: All numbers refer to the Catalog number, not the page number.

Note: Known ports in Africa where those providing accounts were forced onto slave ships are noted. The current nation in which ports are located is in parentheses.

Abeokuta, Badagry (Nigeria) 332

Anamabu/Anomabu, Fante country (Ghana) 327

Bonny (Nigeria) 458

Bunce Island (Sierra Leone) 146, 147, 154

Calabar (southeastern Nigeria) 115, 116, 403, 430, 432, 433

Cape Coast Castle (Ghana) 22

Christiansborg, Fort (Ghana) 159

Congo River, mouth of (Democratic Republic of Congo, Angola) 477

Elmina Castle (Ghana) 58, 187

Gambia River (Senegal, Guinea) 243

Jakin, Godomey/Lake Nacoué (Benin) 14

Lagos (Nigeria) 234, 261, 344–357, 360, 361, 366, 392, 418, 437

Little Popo (Togo) 435

Lomboko (Sierra Leone) 265–301

Ouidah/Whydah (Benin) 176, 367, 378, 379, 473–477, 478, 479, 487, 488, 489

Petit Popo/Ancho (Ghana) 358

Porto Novo (Benin) 185, 188, 341

Rio Pongo, mouth of (Guinea) 175, 456

São Tomé (Bight of Benin) 17

Warri (Nigeria) 262

Whydah/Ouidah (Benin) 176, 367, 378, 379, 473–477, 478, 479, 487, 488, 489

Ports of Initial Disembarkation

Note: All numbers refer to the Catalog number, not the page number.

Note: Known ports in the Atlantic world where those providing accounts initially disembarked from slave ships are noted. If slave ships were intercepted at sea, the port to which the liberated Africans were initially taken thereafter is noted. The current nation in which ports are located are in parentheses.

Annapolis, Maryland (USA) 11, 167

Antigua (Caribbean) 108, 131, 179, 243

Bahia (Brazil) 125, 344–366

Barbados (Caribbean) 16, 112, 130, 155, 156, 157, 162

Barcelona (Spain) 227

Bordeaux (France) 490

Boston, Massachusetts (USA) 113

Bristol, Rhode Island (USA) 15

Bunce Island (Sierra Leone) 154

Cardenas (Cuba) 444

Caribbean 124

Cartegena, New Spain (Colombia) 3, 4, 5, 6, 111

Charleston, South Carolina (USA) 134, 160, 164, 174, 206, 220, 226, 263, 302, 471, 472

Danish West Indies (US Virgin Islands) 12, 30, 110

Demerara (Guyana) 376

Dominica (Caribbean) 115, 116, 192

France 133

Freetown (Sierra Leone) 170, 171, 203–205, 234, 261, 264, 310, 312, 313, 319, 329, 335–337, 338, 341, 342, 375, 377–400, 402–434, 458, 459

Grenada (Caribbean) 126, 149

Havana (Cuba) 265–301, 331, 367, 436–443, 445–452

Jamaica (Caribbean) 22, 135–144

Jekyll Island, Georgia (USA) 477, 480–485

Kingston (Jamaica) 374

London (England) 207

Long Island, New York (USA) 265–301

Mobile Bay, Alabama (USA) 473–476, 478, 479, 487, 488, 489

Nassau (Bahamas) 230, 231

New Orleans, Louisiana (USA) 10, 24, 25, 26, 27, 28, 29, 330

New York City (USA) 165, 177

Paramaribo (Suriname) 14, 117, 118, 119, 121, 122, 123, 150

Pernambuco (Brazil) 14

Philadelphia, Pennsylvania (USA) 19, 109, 211

Rio de Janeiro (Brazil) 23, 198, 457

Saint-Domingue (Haiti) 20, 21

Salvador (Brazil) 373

Savannah, Georgia (USA) 235, 456

St. Croix, Danish West Indies (US Virgin Islands) 34, 35, 61, 104, 105, 159

St. Eustachius (Caribbean) 97

St. Thomas, Danish West Indies (US Virgin Islands) 33, 36, 54, 74, 96, 229

Tortola (Caribbean) 225

Trinidad (Trinidad and Tobago) 311, 322

Trinidad and Tobago 242

Virginia (USA) 129

York, Ontario (Canada) 172

Women

Note: All numbers refer to the Catalog number, not the page number.

Note: Listed are women who provided accounts in the catalog. In many cases these individuals were quite young when taken into the transatlantic slave trade, but all were adults when providing their accounts. African names only are provided (when known), otherwise European names.

Catalog Number	Name
7	María de Huancavelica
9	Ana de la Calle
12	Damma
15	Luce Bijah
17	Chicaba
19	Magdalene Beulah Brockden
21	Vénus
23	Rosa Egipcíaca
24	Comba
25	Marguerite
30	Un-named African woman
32	Un-named African woman
33	Un-named African woman
38	Un-named woman
39	Un-named Mangree woman
40	Sanjam woman
52	Un-named Tembu (Temba) woman
54	Un-named Tchamba woman
58	First un-named Papaa (Popo) woman
59	Second un-named Papaa (Popo) woman
60	Third un-named Papaa (Popo) woman
62	First un-named Watje woman
63	Second un-named Watje woman
67	Un-named Atja woman
68	Un-named Wawu woman
72	Un-named Moko woman
82	First un-named Kanga woman
83	Second un-named Kanga woman
91	Un-named Mandinka woman
94	Un-named Carabali woman
97	Un-named Mandongo woman
105	Anna Margaretha
106	Barbara
113	Phillis Wheatley
124	Belinda
131	Molly
137	Afia
138	Clara
140	Esther
146	Un-named woman sold to pay debts
147	Un-named nursing woman
156	Ashy
157	Sibell
158	Irrouba
163	Un-named woman from Bow-woo
166	Chloe Russell
169	Un-named woman enslaved on Antigua
178	Akeiso
179	Belinda Lucas
193	Flora Gardner
198	Un-named Mina woman
199	Maria Guadalupe Mandinga
211	Chloe Spear
214	Margarita Lucumí
228	Rosa Maria de Conceiçáo
230	English-speaking girl from Sierra Leone
236	María de los Dolores Frías
244	Manu
245	Saru
251	Samoo
252	Kenga
253	Sydea
255	Nangoo
256	Josefa Rita Bibí
257	Dionisia Calas Gangá
258	Manuela Calás Gangá
298	Teme
299	Kagne
300	Margru
332	Benomê
343	Betsey Johnson
372	Ngeve
437	Maria Rosalia Garcia

Children

Note: All numbers refer to the Catalog number, not the page number.

Note: Refers to Africans providing accounts who were children at the time of enslavement in the transatlantic slave trade. The age of transition from childhood to adulthood varied over time and place and was never a specific year; however, we chose to list all individuals less than sixteen years old during their Middle Passage in order to provide some assistance in the study of younger people involved. African names only are provided (when known), otherwise European names.

Catalog Number	Name
1	Alonso de Illescas
4	Francisco Angola
13	Jacobus Elisa Johannes Capitein
17	Chicaba
23	Rosa Egipcíaca
36	Johannes
101	First un-named rebel
108	Ofodobendo Wooma
111	Ignatius Sancho
113	Phillis Wheatly
119	Gwacoo
124	Simeon
126	Quobna Ottabah Cugoano
129	Thomas Fuller
130	Olaudah Equiano
133	Tammata
135	Un-named Mandinka man
136	Sarri
148	Jean-Baptiste Belley
159	Cicero
160	John Kizell
164	Un-named Muslim man
166	Chloe Russell
168	Yero Mamdou
171	Yamsey
177	Primus
178	Akeiso
179	Belinda Lucas
189	Uncle Jack
207	Asa-Asa
211	Chloe Spear
220	James Bradley
222	Abû Bakr al-Siddiq
227	Antonio Ferrer
229	William Andrew de Graftenreid
230	English-speaking girl from Sierra Leone
234	Ajayi
235	Robert Johnson
244	Manu
297	Kali
298	Teme
299	Kagne
300	Margru
302	Un-named Asante man
310	James Macaulay
327	Sâhil Bilâli
328	Alejandro Congo
330	John Joseph
332	Benomê
336	James Will
337	James Campbell
338	Joseph Will
343	Betsey Johnson
353	So-Allah
354	Muhammad
368	Adéolà
370	Bela
372	Ngeve
374	Aneaso
376	Kayawon
400	Edía
401	Kindsímbi
437	Maria Rosalia Garcia
455	Odusinna
456	Tallen
459	Laiguandai
471	Sitiki
477	Cilucängy
488	Matilda McCrear
489	Redoshi

Maroons

Note: All numbers refer to the Catalog number, not the page number.

Note: Below are listed individuals in the catalog who provided accounts in which they reported that they had lived in a Maroon community in the Americas during their lifetimes. African names only are provided (when known), otherwise European names.

Catalog Number	Name
1	Alonso de Illescas
3	Anchico
4	Francisco Angola
18	Kwasimukámba
27	Louis
117	Un-named heroic man
150	Stephanus
161	Télémaque
197	Cristóbal Carabalí
233	Francisco Mina
239	Antonio Mina
240	Vincente Bibí
256	Josefa Rita Bibí
257	Dionisia Calas Gangá
258	Manuela Calás Gangá
259	Federico Bibí
260	Bartolomé Portuondo
328	Alejandro Congo

Middle Passage Accounts

Note: All numbers refer to the Catalog number, not the page number.

Note: The eighty-eight accounts listed below contain substantive descriptions of the Middle Passage (i.e., slave-ship experience only). Some accounts are quite brief, but if they contain significant information about the slave-ship experience, they are included. Accounts that only reference passage on a slave ship without any description are excluded. African names only are provided (when known), otherwise European names.

Catalog
Number   *Name*

Catalog Number	Name
11	Ayuba Sulayman Diallo
16	Chicaba
41	Gien man man
45	Amina man
64-66	Three Watje men (one described the Middle Passage)
73	Un-named Loango man
86	Un-named Amina merchant
90	Third un-named Mandinka man
101	First un-named rebel
100	Un-named man
102	Second un-named rebel
115	Little Ephraim Robin John
116	Ancona Robin Robin John
121	Un-named man transported to Paramaribo in 1779
124	Belinda Royall
126	Quobna Ottabah Cugoano
130	Olaudah Equiano
145	Un-named man from the Sierra Leone River
146	Un-named woman sold to pay debts
147	Un-named nursing woman
155	Broteer
159	Cicero
160	John Kizell
162	Boyrereau Brinch
166	Chloe Russell
169	Yamsey

Catalog Number	Name
173	Dan Kano
177	Primus
178	Akeiso
185	Bernard
203	John Davis
206	Umar ibn Sayyid
207	Asa-Asa
217	Gorah Condran
220	James Bradley
222	Abū Bakr Al-Ṣiddiq
231	Father from the Cape of Good Hope
234	Ajayi
244	Manu
245	Saru
246	Dumbo
247	Fahbrona
248	Foolah
250	Gema
251	Samoo
252	Kenga
253	Sydea
254	Cawley
255	Nangoo
261	Joseph Wright
262	Osifekunde
265	Gilabaru
267	Kimbo
294	Fawni
309	Gavino
319	William Thomas
327	Sāhil Bilāli 332 Benomê
338	Joseph Will
339	Augustino
340	Thomas Hadden
341	Ali Eisami Gazirmabe
372	Ngeve
374	Aneaso
435	Mahommah Gardo Baquaqua
436	Òkúsono
438	Miguel Marino
439	Margarita Cabrera

About the Authors

Aaron Spencer Fogleman is a Distinguished Research Professor in the History Department at Northern Illinois University. He has written a number of books and articles about forced and free transatlantic migrations, revolution, slavery, religion, and gender in the Atlantic World and Early America. He previously taught at the University of South Alabama and has been a Guggenheim Fellow, Distinguished Fulbright Chair at the Goethe University in Frankfurt, and an Alexander von Humboldt Fellow at the Max Planck Institute for History in Göttingen. He received the PhD from the University of Michigan in 1991, the *Magister Artium* from Albert Ludwigs University in Freiburg, Germany, and the bachelor of arts degree from Oklahoma State University. In addition to *Five Hundred African Voices*, he is also completing a monograph about four centuries of forced and free transatlantic migrations, tentatively entitled *Immigrant Voices*. Aaron is from Burlington, North Carolina, and lives with his family in Batavia, Illinois.

Robert Hanserd is Associate Professor of History at Columbia College Chicago. West African culture and history and its circulation throughout the Atlantic World (West Africa, America and Western Europe) are his central academic focus. Research interests include West African Gold Coast and Bight of Benin cosmologies, cultures, and histories; AfroAtlantic inspirations to maroons', freeblacks', and slaves' struggles for freedom and identity in the Caribbean and North America; and a range of topics related to African, Caribbean, and African American history and life. Recent publications include *Identity, Spirit and Freedom in the Atlantic World: The Gold Coast and the African Diaspora* (Routledge, 2019) and *African Indigenous Systems* (SubSaharan Publishers, forthcoming in 2023). He is also working on a manuscript entitled *American African*. Hanserd is a member of the African Studies Association and the Ghana Studies Association, and he has presented his research on numerous panels and symposia. His other interests include the study of African diasporas from a range of interdisciplinary, historical, and cultural settings, as well as study abroad programming, multimedia research and production, and public history.